WESTERN NEVADA COMMUNITY COLLEGE

3 1439 00053 437

P9-ECW-524

JUN 2 3 1999

DATE DUE

WITHDRAWN

Library & Media Services
Western Nevada Community College
2201 West College Parkway
Carson City, NV 89703

The *Cambridge History of Seventeenth-Century Philosophy* is without close precedent in its field. Like other recent Cambridge histories of philosophy, it consists of a series of chapters on topics or themes – rather than on individuals – by authors chosen for their special interests and achievements. Together these contributions add up to a comprehensive, expert, and innovative overview, from a wide variety of vantage points, of a period which supplied the philosophical seed-bed of the modern (and 'post-modern') world. The story that emerges lays less emphasis than usual on supposed innovations in epistemology, more on the replacement (or transformation) of Aristotelian scholastic science, dominant though under attack at the beginning of the century, by 'corpuscularian' mechanism. This direct ancestor of present-day physics drew largely, for its philosophical credentials, either on Platonism or on the atomism of Epicurus. With its uneasy relation to religious and political disputes and its internecine divisions, it generated much of the energy, hardly parallelled before or since, powering philosophical debates. Like the debates themselves, the present volumes overspill a narrow conception of 'seventeenth-century philosophy' in both subject-matter and temporal scope. Their structure in part represents a seventeenth-century perspective, reflecting a time when the 'philosopher' was as likely to be peering through a microscope or preaching on divine justice as discussing scepticism, consciousness, or the concepts of good and evil. The contributors have often looked back to the ancient, mediaeval, and Renaissance ideas which informed the arguments examined. A guiding assumption is that context illuminates meaning, a principle with surprising consequences for the interpretation of classic, still influential, but often seriously misunderstood texts. The same principle facilitates reassessment of works formerly consigned to obscurity. The volumes include an extensive bibliography of both primary and secondary materials, as well as an appendix containing brief biographies and bibliographies for a wide range of philosophers. They are expected to serve not only as an important reference source for students and teachers but also as a valuable tool for research into the history both of philosophy and of ideas in general.

THE CAMBRIDGE HISTORY OF
SEVENTEENTH-CENTURY PHILOSOPHY
I

WNC
B
801
.C35
1998
v.1

The Cambridge History of Seventeenth-Century Philosophy

Volume I

EDITED BY

DANIEL GARBER   MICHAEL AYERS

University of Chicago   *Wadham College, University of Oxford*

with the assistance of Roger Ariew and Alan Gabbey

CAMBRIDGE
UNIVERSITY PRESS

PUBLISHED BY THE PRESS SYNDICATE OF THE UNIVERSITY OF CAMBRIDGE
The Pitt Building, Trumpington Street, Cambridge CB2 1RP, United Kingdom

CAMBRIDGE UNIVERSITY PRESS
The Edinburgh Building, Cambridge CB2 2RU, United Kingdom
40 West 20th Street, New York, NY 10011-4211, USA
10 Stamford Road, Oakleigh, Melbourne 3166, Australia

© Cambridge University Press 1998

This book is in copyright. Subject to statutory exception
and to the provisions of relevant collective licensing agreements,
no reproduction of any part may take place without
the written permission of Cambridge University Press.

First published 1998

Printed in the United States of America

Typeset in Bembo

A catalog record for this book is available from the British Library.

Library of Congress Cataloging-in-Publication Data
The Cambridge history of seventeenth-century philosophy / edited by
Daniel Garber, Michael Ayers, with the assistance of Roger Ariew and
Alan Gabbey.
p.   cm.
Includes bibliographical references and indexes.
ISBN 0-521-58864-2
1. Philosophy, Modern – 17th century. I. Garber, Daniel, 1949–
II. Ayers, Michael, 1935–
B801.C35   1997   96-25475
190'.9'032 – dc20   CIP

Volume I ISBN 0-521-30763-5 hardback
Available only as a set: ISBN 0-521-58864-2

CONTENTS

VOLUME I

VOLUME II

VII Will, action, and moral philosophy

CONTRIBUTORS

ROGER ARIEW
Department of Philosophy
Virginia Polytechnic Institute and State
  University

JEAN-ROBERT ARMOGATHE
Section des Sciences Religieuses
  (Sorbonne)
Ecole Pratique des Hautes Etudes,
  Paris

MICHAEL AYERS
Wadham College
University of Oxford

MARTHA BOLTON
Department of Philosophy
Rutgers University

VERE CHAPPELL
Department of Philosophy
University of Massachusetts at Amherst

BRIAN COPENHAVER
Departments of History and
  Philosophy
University of California, Los Angeles

LORRAINE DASTON
Max-Planck-Institut für
  Wissenschaftsgeschichte (Berlin)

PETER DEAR
Department of History
Cornell University

MICHAEL DELLA ROCCA
Department of Philosophy
Yale University

ALAN GABBEY
Department of Philosophy
Barnard College

DANIEL GARBER
Department of Philosophy
University of Chicago

KNUD HAAKONSSEN
Department of Philosophy
Boston University

GARY HATFIELD
Department of Philosophy
University of Pennsylvania

JOHN HENRY
Science Studies Unit
University of Edinburgh

SUSAN JAMES
Girton College
University of Cambridge

NICHOLAS JOLLEY
Department of Philosophy
University of California, San Diego

LYNN JOY
Department of Philosophy
Duke University

JILL KRAYE
The Warburg Institute
University of London

CHARLES LARMORE
Department of Philosophy
University of Chicago

THOMAS M. LENNON
Department of Philosophy
University of Western Ontario

MICHAEL MAHONEY
Department of History
Princeton University

JEAN-LUC MARION
UER de Philosophie
Université de Paris IV (Sorbonne)

CHARLES MCCRACKEN
Department of Philosophy
Michigan State University

STEPHEN MENN
Department of Philosophy
McGill University

J. R. MILTON
Department of History and Philosophy
  of Science
King's College London

D. E. MUNGELLO
Department of History
Baylor University

STEVEN NADLER
Department of Philosophy
University of Wisconsin–Madison

GABRIEL NUCHELMANS
Faculty of Philosophy
University of Leiden

RICHARD POPKIN
Department of Philosophy
Washington University (St. Louis)

ROBERT SLEIGH, JR.
Department of Philosophy
University of Massachusetts at Amherst

UDO THIEL
Department of Philosophy
Australian National University

RICHARD TUCK
Jesus College
University of Cambridge

MARGARET WILSON
Department of Philosophy
Princeton University

PREFACE

This Cambridge history had its origin in an outline that Michael Ayers made, at the request of Jeremy Mynott of Cambridge University Press, early in 1982, which was circulated for comment to a number of scholars in the field. In the summer of that year, Ayers was invited to be an editor of the book, and a search began for another editor. There had been many helpful responses to the original plan, but Daniel Garber's seemed to indicate particular interest in the project. In December 1982, Ayers visited Princeton University, gave a paper to Garber's seminar, and stayed a day or two to discuss the project. These lively discussions continued by mail, and in the fall of 1983 Mynott invited Garber and Ayers to be the coeditors of the book. Serious work began in September 1984 when Garber visited Ayers in Oxford and they began making concrete plans for the project. At this stage, consultations with editors of the immediately previous volumes were enormously useful. Garber would like to thank Norman Kretzmann for an informative and illuminating afternoon in a coffee shop at O'Hare Airport, discussing the practical details of *The Cambridge History of Later Medieval Philosophy*. Both of the present editors deeply appreciate the time spent with the late Charles Schmitt, then at work editing *The Cambridge History of Renaissance Philosophy*, during Garber's 1984 visit to Oxford. We have tried to live up to the sage advice of these superb scholars and editors during our own travail. Garber would also like to acknowledge advice given at the start of this project by Arnaldo Momigliano, a contributor to two generations of Cambridge histories, who graciously overlooked Garber's monumental ignorance of the history of Western thought and sought to advise him (and educate him) with great kindness.

Plan followed plan until we finally settled on desiderata. It took even longer to find people able and willing to carry out our somewhat utopian scheme, which was, indeed, yet further modified in this task. Then, since we had decided on an interventionist editorial rôle, the real work began. We wrote as detailed comments on the drafts as we could manage, or called on appropriate experts to do so, and rather often this led to further exchanges. Some contributors were prompt with initial drafts and rewriting; others were less prompt, and both the editors had to

spend time fulfilling other commitments. While we would like to thank all
contributors for bearing with us during this long and difficult gestation, we are
particularly grateful to those who turned their material in on time. But because of
their promptness, their chapters may suffer by not including some of the most
recent literature. We apologize for this and want the reader to know that such
apparent deficiencies (the blame for which we take upon ourselves) are really a
sign of deeper virtue. Gabriel Nuchelmans passed away during the last stages of
editing; Michael Ayers is responsible for the final corrections in his chapters. This
Cambridge history took far longer to produce than we had intended. But then it
turned out to be far larger and more complex a task than we had ever expected.
Partly for logistical reasons, the brunt of the final preparation of the typescript,
including the work of checking the notes for completeness, the imposition of
uniformity, of method of reference, the standardizing, as far as possible, of editions
referred to, and the like, was borne by Daniel Garber. Otherwise, the two editors
shared the work at each stage, but the order of their names on the title page
reflects the relative weights of the total burdens borne.

Much of the work for this book was produced with the aid of the National
Endowment for the Humanities (grant #RO-21434-87), whose support we gratefully acknowledge. We had optimistically hoped that we would be able to finish
these volumes by the time the grant ended in June 1993. Although we missed our
deadline, the grant did enable us to have some time off for research connected
with the writing and editing of the volumes and to purchase the first generation
of computers used in the production of the book. The National Endowment for
the Humanities (NEH) also helped by funding a Summer Institute in the History
of Early Modern Philosophy, held in the summer of 1988 at Brown University
(grant #EH-20738-87). There, many of the contributors were able to gather and
discuss their work in progress. We would like to thank Jules Coleman and the
Council for Philosophical Studies for their help in applying for the grant, Brown
University for its hospitality, and Dolores Iorizzo for her invaluable aid with day-
to-day organization. Many others helped us while this work was in progress. A
number of the contributors were consulted about issues outside their own chapters, and we gratefully acknowledge their advice. Alan Gabbey was virtually
another coeditor during the discussions surrounding Part IV of the history, 'Body
and the Physical World'. He helped divide up the chapters and choose contributors, and then read and commented on drafts when they arrived. Roger Ariew
took charge of the Biobibliographical Appendix. He played a major rôle in
deciding which figures were to be treated, in soliciting the entries (writing a large

number of them himself), and in the initial editing of the text. Heather Blair was Garber's assistant during the period of the NEH grant. She set up the structures for editing on computer and taught him how to use the rather daunting machinery carted into his office one December day in 1987. She also began the Bibliography and returned to help with bibliographical problems from time to time during the production of the volumes. Daniel Smith prepared the final indexes with admirable speed and accuracy as we sprinted toward the final deadline. Ben Martinez and Jacqueline Block helped realize the handsome device that appears on the cover of this book. D. Linda Asher, resident magician in the office of the provost at the University of Chicago, devoted too many hours to helping Garber in the final stages of the preparation of this book; without her invaluable aid, the project would have been delayed even longer. Others too numerous to mention responded to our requests for help and advice with dispatch and good cheer. But one deserves special mention, Terence Moore, the editor at Cambridge University Press who inherited our project. He is a very patient man.

DANIEL GARBER

MICHAEL AYERS

LIST OF ABBREVIATIONS

The abbreviation is given in the left column; the full title, in the right.

ARISTOTLE
Post. an.   *Posterior analytics*
Pr. an.   *Prior analytics*
De gen. et cor.   *De generatione et corruptione*
Etc.

BACON
Nov. org.   *Novum organum*

BERKELEY
Pr. Hum. Kn.   *Principles of Human Knowledge*
3 Dial.   *Three Dialogues between Hyals and Philonous*
Phil. Com.   *Philosophical Commentaries*
New Th. Vis.   *New Theory of Vision*
Th. Vis. Vind.   *New Theory of Vision Vindicated*

CHARRON
Sag.   *De la sagesse*

DESCARTES
AT   *Oeuvres de Descartes,* Adam and Tannery (Descartes
                            1964–74)
CSM   Cottingham et al., *The Philosophical Writings of
                            Descartes* (Descartes 1984–91)
CB   Cottingham, *Conversation with Berman*
Disc.   *Discours de la méthode*
Med. IV   Meditatio IV
Meds.   *Meditationes*

Obj. II	Second set of objections to *Meditationes*
Pass. âme	*Passions de l'âme*
Princ.	*Principia philosophiae*
Resp. II	Replies to second set of objections to *Meditationes*

HOBBES
Eng. Works	*The English Works of Thomas Hobbes of Malmesbury,* ed. Molesworth (Hobbes 1839–45b)
Lat. Works	*Opera philosophica quae Latine scripsit omnia,* ed. Molesworth (Hobbes 1839–45a)
Lev.	*Leviathan*

LEIBNIZ
Disc. mét.	*Discours de métaphysique*
Ger.	*Die philosophischen Schriften,* ed. Gerhardt (Leibniz 1875–90)
Ger. Math.	*Mathematische Schriften,* ed. Gerhardt (Leibniz 1849–63)
LAkad	Akademie Edition (Leibniz 1923–).
Mon.	*Monadologie*
Nouv. ess.	*Nouveaux essais*
PNG	*Principes de la nature et de la grace*
Spec. dyn.	*Specimen dynamicum*
Syst. nouv.	*Système nouveau . . .*
Théod.	*Théodicée*

LOCKE
| *Ess.* | *Essay concerning Human Understanding* |

MALEBRANCHE
Rech.	*Recherche de la vérité*
TNG	*Traité de la nature et de la grace*
Ent. mét.	*Entretiens sur la métaphysique*
Mal. *OC*	*Oeuvres complètes,* ed. Robinet (Malebranche 1958–84)

PASCAL
| *Pens.* | Pascal *Pensées* [Lafuma numbering as in Pascal 1963] |

PUFENDORF
De officio — *De officio hominis et civis* . . . (Pufendorf 1927)
Elem. juris. — *Elementorum jurisprudentiae universalis* . . . (Pufendorf 1931)

SPINOZA
De int. emen. — *De intellectus emendatione*
Korte ver. — *Korte Verhandeling*
Tract. th.-pol xiv — *Tractatus theologico-politicus*
Princ. phil. cart. — *Renati Des Cartes principiorum philosophiae* . . .
Eth. — *Ethica*
Geb. — *Opera,* ed. Gebhardt (Spinoza 1925)

SUÁREZ
Disp. met. — *Disputationes metaphysicae*
Su., *Op. omn.* — *Opera omnia* (Suárez 1856–78)

THOMAS AQUINAS
Summa th. — *Summa theologiae*

Miscellaneous abbreviations
BHPC — Bouillier, *Histoire de la philosophie cartésienne* (Bouillier 1868)
DSB — *Dictionary of Scientific Biography* (Gillispie 1970–80)
EP — *Encyclopedia of Philosophy* (Edwards 1967)

INTRODUCTION

MICHAEL AYERS AND DANIEL GARBER

The *Cambridge History of Seventeenth-Century Philosophy* was planned to provide a comprehensive overview of European philosophy in the seventeenth century in a series of contributions, each written by an appropriate specialist or group of specialists. As in the immediately previous volumes in the series, and in deliberate contrast to most histories of philosophy, the subject is treated by topic or theme, rather than chronologically or by individual. Since history does not come in neat bundles, our response to the boundary problems engendered by such a project has been deliberately flexible. First, we have allowed our subject-matter to overflow, with the oeuvres of individuals and with particular debates, into the adjacent scenturies. Contributors have also been encouraged to explicate the meaning and wider significance of seventeenth-century argument by reference to antecedent or, if it seemed appropriate, consequent theory. The former has often meant reference both to mediaeval and Renaissance ideas and to the antiquity directly studied and avidly plundered even by some of the reputedly most 'modern' philosophers. The geographical scope of the volume is admittedly more restricted, although we are pleased to be able to include one chapter on the intense interest of some European philosophers in Chinese culture and thought.

Second, we have allowed some compromise between what the term 'philosophy' meant then and what it means now. In the seventeenth century it was unremarkable if the same 'philosophers' who wrote on metaphysics, logic, ethics, and political theory, on the existence of God, or on the varieties of human knowledge and belief also made contributions to mathematics, offered an account of the laws of motion, peered through microscopes or telescopes, recorded the weather, conducted chemical experiments, practised medicine, invented machines, debated the nature of madness, or argued about church government, religious toleration, and the identity and interpretation of divine revelation. The present 'history of philosophy' includes neither a history of natural science nor a history of religious doctrine and practice, but much is said in it about the sometimes surprising connections between theory and argument in such areas and what is more recognizably in ancestral relation to the 'philosophy' (or philosophies) of today. One fundamental shift is reflected in the change in the sense of the word 'science'. For (as the reader should beware) this word was still employed technically in the seventeenth century for all systematic, indeed philosophical, knowledge, a usage which looked back to ancient theories of knowledge at the same time as some philosophers were beginning to foresee something less like Aristotelian demonstration and more like the institutionalized, essentially speculative onslaught on the secrets of nature nowadays given the name of 'science'. The relationship between philosophy and theology has undergone, and was then undergoing, a similarly significant change. Yet, whatever philosophy has become, it still bears the marks of its history.

Third, the division of our story into topics or strands has necessarily been somewhat arbitrary. Our original plan underwent alteration and expansion in some directions in order to accommodate the interests and preferences of those invited to contribute; other editorial proposals fell on stony ground. Moreover, some authors tried to make their contribution as comprehensive as possible, whereas others offered a more partial, suggestive view of their topic. Some overlap has also proved unavoidable, and it is perhaps no bad thing in so far as different approaches to the same material can be complementary. Despite such changes, one central feature of our original plan still stands: the structure of the collection corresponds to one way, at any rate, in which an educated European of the seventeenth century might have organized the domain of philosophy, while emphasizing some of the issues likely to be of particular interest to students of philosophy in our own time. Thus, Part II deals with what would have fallen under the heading of 'Logic', typically the first serious philosophical topic that students were expected to study. Parts III–V treat successively the three types of beings generally, although not universally, recognized by seventeenth-century thinkers: God, bodies (or matter), and souls (including minds). Parts VI and VII, in Volume II, explore doctrines relating to the two sides of the soul or mind, its cognitive faculties and its faculties of will and appetition. Consequently, although epistemology was certainly important, it is not until Part VI that there is systematic discussion of the epistemological issues that philosophers today are likely to look back on, whether rightly or wrongly, as the most important concerns of early modern philosophy. There is a single theme which, despite the variety of their subject-matter, runs through many of the contributions, but it is a different one. At the beginning of the century, the intellectual world was dominated by a synthesis of Aristotelian and scholastic philosophy which dated back to the rediscovery of the main corpus of Aristotelian texts in the late twelfth and early thirteenth centuries. This synthesis had had its critics since it first appeared, and some of those critics had competing programs to offer. But in the seventeenth century one competitor came to rival and, eventually, to eclipse the philosophy of the schools: the mechanistic, or 'corpuscularian', philosophy, a descendant of ancient atomism and the ancestor of present-day physics. A main theme of the present volumes is the emergence and establishment of the different versions of this 'new philosophy', together with its variously worked out, often somewhat ambivalent relationships to traditional metaphysics, ethics, theology, logic, method, theory of knowledge, and other areas of thought.

As well as overlap, there are some regretted gaps. Our efforts to achieve a systematic treatment of seventeenth-century linguistic theory, for example, proved abortive. But one omission from Part I which the editors particularly regret is that of any extended discussion either of the rôle of women in philosophical debate or of seventeenth-century arguments, advanced by philosophers of both sexes, about the place of women in society and specifically in intellectual life. It was perhaps difficult to get such a chapter written partly because other work on this question was already under way. The reader must here be referred, for example, to the collection on women in early modern philosophy edited by Eileen O'Neill and forthcoming from Oxford University Press. Brief accounts of some of the more important female thinkers are included in our Biobibliographical Appendix.

References are in the first instance to editions in the original language of the text in question, with translations cited when available.[1] Furthermore, all works mentioned or cited are referred to by their original titles. It may seem awkward and pedantic to call Descartes's familiar book *Meditationes* rather than *Meditations,* or Spinoza's main work *Ethica* and not the *Ethics,* but titles can be translated in different ways, and our general rule requiring original-language titles may make it easier for those who are not familiar with standard translations into English to identify some of the works in question.

When the book was originally planned, the editors shared the view that some movement was badly needed, with respect to the teaching of 'history of philosophy' in philosophy departments, towards a more historical approach to early modern philosophy. Indeed, an important purpose of this Cambridge history is to provide material for a reassessment of the canonical seventeenth-century texts which have long been familiar, if not second nature, to students of philosophy at every level. Such works as Descartes's *Meditationes,* Spinoza's *Ethica,* and Locke's *Essay concerning Human Understanding* appear again and again in the curriculum from introductory courses to graduate seminars, while other writers of the period, even those, such as Kenelm Digby, Pierre Gassendi, or Nicolas Malebranche, who were giants to their contemporaries, are generally ignored. Whatever philosophical or practical reasons there may be for this verdict of history, one consequence of such partial knowledge of the debate is that our view of philosophy as a discipline has largely been shaped by a standard account and critique, in many respects tendentious and over-simplified, of the opposed positions of which the canonical few are the supposed spokesmen. Commentators in the analytic tradition in particular, writing very much out of their own philosophical interests and preconceptions, have often lost sight of the complex context in which philosophy was written. In doing so, they not only have distorted its achievements but also have often denied themselves the tools necessary for the interpretation of the very words and sentences they continue to expound.

Contributors to the present volume do not in general avoid analytic discussion of the canonical texts, but they engage in it always with an eye on the wider intellectual context. This bias towards a more strictly historical approach ought not by any means to make the volumes irrelevant to present-day philosophical interests. Such is the continuing influence on philosophy of a certain largely dismissive estimate of seventeenth-century conceptions (e.g., of the notions of an idea, of matter, and of a substance) that a better grasp of their historical meaning could hardly fail to have a beneficial effect. We must certainly understand past philosophies before we can learn either from their insights or from their mistakes. One thing the editors wished this Cambridge history to demonstrate by example was that the historical and the philosophical understanding of a text are not as separable as philosophers have often seemed, from both their practice and their methodological pronouncements, to have supposed. To a significant extent, however, the situation has been remedied in the last few years at the level of publication and research. Several considerable books, for example, have been published in English on Gassendi and on Malebranche – if not yet (in 1997) on Digby.[2] The general level of published work on the relations between philosophers, and on their philosophical motivations, has also become more sophisticated. There have been new editions and translations of strangely neglected texts (Arnauld's philosophically fascinating *Des vrayes et des fausse idées* comes to mind, also the subject of both a recent translation and a recent monograph),[3] new journals and societies for the history of philosophy have sprung up, and there is, we feel, more interaction and a greater sense of community among an increasing number of those who teach history and do historical research in philosophy departments in the English-speaking world. We can hope that the present volume will further this tendency, and will aid such research, for the sake both of history and of philosophy.

NOTES

1 The practice is somewhat different for references to Descartes. Since the now standard English translations in Descartes 1984–91 give the volume and page numbers for the original-language text in Descartes 1964–74, no special reference to the translation of Descartes's writings will normally be given. The situation is similar for Leibniz's *Nouveaux Essais,* where the translations in Leibniz 1981 give the pagination for the French edition in LAkad VI.VI.

2 See, e.g., Brundell 1987, Joy 1987, and Osler 1994 on Gassendi; and Jolley 1990, McCracken 1983 and Nadler 1992 on Malebranche.

3 See Arnauld 1990 and Nadler 1989.

I

THE CONTEXT OF
SEVENTEENTH-CENTURY PHILOSOPHY

THE INSTITUTIONAL SETTING

RICHARD TUCK

I

In 1600 the population of Western Europe (that is, Europe West of the Elbe) was about 60 million; by 1750 it had become somewhat more than 75 million. So the continent which the philosophers of the seventeenth century inhabited had a population approximately the same as that of the islands of Britain and Ireland today; England, to pursue this parallel, had a population the same as that of the modern Republic of Ireland, about 4 million. The most populous country was France, with about 19 million inhabitants, though the states of Italy contained between them scarcely fewer people. The states of Germany held about 12 million; Spain, about 7 million; and the Netherlands (modern Holland and Belgium), about 3 million.[1] The densest population was in the two great urbanised areas at each side of the continent, Italy and the Netherlands. They were also still the economic centres of Europe, though by the end of the century the growth of extra-European commerce had tilted the balance more towards the Atlantic and left Italy relatively worse off. The wealth of these two areas was matched by their cultural predominance: the history of the fine arts in early modern Europe could be told almost entirely in terms of the artists who worked in Italy and the Netherlands. This is less true of philosophy, but one is constantly made aware of the extent to which philosophers working outside these historic centres of European culture (other than in Paris) thought of themselves as somewhat provincial.

The 60 million people at the start of the century spoke more than a dozen languages (with the dialects of German and Italian often amounting to separate languages). Yet they formed a remarkably cohesive cultural unit, largely because to be educated anywhere on the continent was to have been taught an international language, Latin. Latin was still taught as a living language, with most schools forcing pupils to speak nothing else during school hours; the texts from which it was learned often included many works by modern Latin authors such as Erasmus. Moreover, very little else was studied at school; the school curriculum which had stabilised after the Renaissance put what would be to our eyes a quite astonishing

emphasis upon linguistic skills. But this was necessary if the pupils were subsequently to have access to any of the high culture of their societies – Latin was still
the language not only of a great deal of imaginative literature but also of such
things as technical works on mining engineering. In theory, educated Europeans
could read not only one another's writings in Latin but could also speak to one
another in it; there were, however, problems about this, particularly for the English
with their eccentric phonology. It is said that an Englishman once called on
Scaliger at Leiden and addressed him in Latin for several minutes; Scaliger courte-
ously explained his lack of response by apologising for his inability to understand
English.[2]

But Latin was gradually displaced as the language of intellectual life for some
countries in the course of the seventeenth century. Italians (e.g., Galileo) had for
many years been ready to tackle the most important issues in their vernacular, but
this readiness came in large part from their awareness that Italian was the closest
living language to Latin (indeed, most people who could read Latin could read
Renaissance Italian, or at least the *lingua toscana,* reasonably easily). Montaigne
wrote his *Essais* in French, but they had little technical vocabulary; Descartes's
essays on scientific subjects with the *Discours de la méthode* as their preface probably
deserve their reputation as the first technical philosophy written in a vernacular
other than Italian. But Descartes still felt obliged to have all his important work
published in Latin also, as did his English rival Hobbes. Hobbes, in fact, seems to
have written his major philosophical works in both English and Latin versions,
sometimes with successive drafts of the same work being in different languages.
John Locke's *An Essay Concerning Human Understanding* was also translated into
Latin quite quickly (the edition appearing in 1701),[3] while the most technical of
all works of seventeenth-century philosophy, Newton's *Principia,* was written in
Latin. Even Kant felt it necessary to have the *Kritik der reinen Vernunft* translated
into Latin.

Because to be educated at all in early modern Europe was thus to be taught the
language of high culture, and because so little (relatively) was available in most
vernaculars, the rôle of education in the society was quite different from anything
we are used to. We are accustomed to assuming that a high proportion of our
populations will be literate and capable of mastering (in principle) anything in our
culture; but we also assume that only a small proportion of the literate population
will have had a higher education. The opposite of both these assumptions was the
case in early modern Europe: most of its populations remained illiterate, but once
basic literacy was acquired there was a high probability of the person concerned
receiving a very full and high-level education. It is this fact which makes the

surviving literatures of political debate, and even the imaginative literatures of the various societies, seem so remarkably sophisticated. Probably about 60 or 70 per cent of the male population of Europe was illiterate in 1600, and 90 per cent or more of the female population;[4] but this was balanced by the surprisingly high proportion of the population going to university. In England, for example, which probably (as now) had an unusually mean provision of university places, about 1 in 50 of the male year-group entered the two universities during the 1630s (the most popular period for university entrance), and the figures were never below 1 in 70 until the catastrophic collapse of the English university system in the 1680s.[5] In Spain, which had a more generous provision of places, about 1 in 30 of the male year-group went to university in the last quarter of the sixteenth century.[6] It is worth observing that this figure was not reached in England until the 1950s; the level in the 1920s was still 1 in 40. (It has since changed to about 1 in 10.)[7] So, literate men in early modern Europe had a much higher chance of receiving a university education than literate men in England did until very recently.

As I said, illiteracy remained high among females, partly no doubt because the institutions of higher education remained closed to women, and petty literacy was much less worth acquiring if higher learning was unavailable. But there were a few famous exceptions to this, and as salon culture developed in the late seventeenth century there did come to be a distinctive and prestigious rôle for the educated woman, separate from the traditional professional disciplines. This culture even gave rise to a minor genre of works devoted to the history of woman's rôle in the arts and philosophy.[8] As will become clear presently, a similar alternative career developed for heterodox male thinkers, who were often correspondingly unusually sensitive to the possible social rôle of women (Selden, Hobbes, and Locke being obvious English examples). But the special and mysterious gift of linguistic genius might help girls to acquire a good education in the interstices of the formal institutions, helped by schoolteachers in their spare time or by male relatives (or, of course, in wealthy households by a private tutor). The daughters of scholars or intellectuals were always more likely to be educated than other girls, and the letters of the young Locke give a vivid picture of the lively and well-educated girls to be found in Oxford clerical households of the 1650s and 1660s.[9]

But educated boys of this period might come from a much lower social class than the educated girls. It was rare for them to be from the poor bulk of the population, day-labourers in England or their continental equivalents, largely employed in agricultural labour. But artisans in towns, peasant farmers, and clerks could all see the utility of having their sons educated and could often contrive to pay for it. Pierre Gassendi's parents were peasants, as were Marin Mersenne's;[10]

Selden's father was a poor farmer in the uplands of Sussex, earning (according to Aubrey) no more than £40 per year. Aubrey records the remarkably Hardy-esque story of Selden as an undergraduate spending Christmas in the manor house of an Oxford friend and finding his father at the bottom end of the hall playing the fiddle for the farmers of the estate – a graphic illustration of how education could take a boy out of his former social class.[11] There were even more extraordinary rises: Tommaso Campanella was the son of a Calabrian cobbler and got his early education by listening at the window of the local school. Hobbes and Locke also came from relatively poor backgrounds (the former the son of an alcoholic and non-graduate clergyman, the latter the son of the clerk to the Somerset justices and educated at Westminster through the help of his father's old army commander). Because of the distinctive character of public life in Germany (see below), German philosophers were rather different in their social origins from those of England, France, or Italy; far more of them were the sons of educated clergymen or university teachers. Johannes Andreae and Samuel Pufendorf were the sons of Lutheran ministers, while Leibniz was the son of a professor at the university of Leipzig. But in all the throng of philosophers which the century produced, only two came from unimpeachably upper-class backgrounds, namely Descartes and (highest of all) Robert Boyle. The presence of a nobleman such as Boyle among the philosophers was, indeed, a constant source of self-congratulation to his companions (and sardonic humour to his opponents such as Hobbes), much as Francis Bacon's peerage had been to an earlier generation.

Such rises in the social scale would, of course, have been impossible without suitable jobs available for poor but educated boys. The availability of such jobs was in fact a constant source of concern to rulers and commentators across the continent, who were worried that a class of unemployed intellectuals was being produced. A Spanish writer observed in 1608:

Nowadays every farmer, trader, cobbler, blacksmith and plasterer, each of whom love their sons with indiscreet affection, wish to remove them from work and seek for them a more glamorous career. Toward this end, they put them to study. And being students, they learn little but they become delicate and presumptuous. Consequently, they remain without a trade or are made into sacristans or scribes.[12]

Hobbes even attributed the outbreak of the English Civil War in part to the creation of this unemployed intelligentsia. Underlying this concern was the assumption that the main employers of boys skilled in Latin would be the three traditional professions – the church, the law, and medicine – and that the professions could not expand indefinitely, as, indeed, proved to be the case. Towards the end of the century, the constraints on employment led to the dramatic collapse of the old system of education in many European countries – in both Spain and England the proportion of the population learning Latin, and the proportion going to university, fell markedly. As far as one can tell, there was not such a marked fall in France, and this may have helped to produce the distinctively French intelligentsia of the late ancien régime.

Though the education system as a whole was geared to the professions, and though the initial reason for a father putting his son to school must usually have been the hope that the young man would enter a profession, a talent specifically for philosophy was not necessarily best adapted to life in a profession. The study of philosophy was traditionally the heart of the arts course in a university – the lower-level preliminary to the technical study of the professional course – and in a sense the philosopher wanted to continue playing with what sober contemporaries might regard as childish things. The primary task of the professions was to provide specific services to the community, of which philosophical reflection was not one; and though the church, in particular, could offer posts devoted to contemplation or teaching, it required a degree of philosophical orthodoxy which most seventeenth-century thinkers found irksome. On the continent the church was nevertheless the main vehicle for philosophers from impoverished backgrounds – Gassendi and Mersenne both relied on it for their livelihoods, and Campanella hoped to make his career in it (though his extraordinary life history of struggle against its authorities illustrates the problems involved). In England, the only figure of comparable importance who was able to cope with the demands of the church was Berkeley, and it may be significant that he found preferment in the peculiar circumstances of the Church of Ireland rather than the Church of England.

Teaching in a university was in most cases a job closely connected with the church, and one which presented some of the same difficulties. It is notable how few major seventeenth-century philosophers managed to exist comfortably within the environment of a university. Gassendi succeeded in doing so, but Locke effectively cut short his career at Oxford rather than submit to the discipline of a life in the church. Germany, again, was rather different: Pufendorf found it possible to spend much of his working life teaching in universities, first at Heidelberg and then at Lund (in Sweden, but a university of the German type). It may also be significant that the principal English seventeenth-century philosophers who managed to survive within a university were the Cambridge Platonists – Cambridge was the English university which most resembled the universities of Germany.

Given these pressures, many of the more interesting thinkers found the most appealing way to live was in the manner of their Renaissance forebears – as secretaries, tutors, librarians, or advisers to great lay aristocrats. This was, after all, the way of life for which the arts course of the universities had always prepared people best, for it required linguistic skills and theoretical acumen, but no commitment to a professional discipline. Hobbes spent virtually his entire life in this fashion, in the household of the Earls of Devonshire; Locke moved into the household of the Earl of Shaftesbury, and Selden into that of the Earl of Kent. The same way of life was possible in France, where Gabriel Naudé was librarian to Richelieu and Mazarin, and La Mothe le Vayer acted as tutor to the Duc d'Anjou; and even in Germany, where Leibniz worked first for the Elector of Mainz and then for the Elector of Hanover.

If none of these jobs was available, then in most cases it was impossible for anyone to pursue philosophical enquiry. The one great exception to this (as to many other generalisations) was Spinoza. His heterodoxy led to his falling foul of his church, just as heterodox Christians had fallen foul of theirs; but he could not find the supportive aristocratic household to protect him which both Hobbes and Locke were able to rely on (though the De Witts, the great Dutch politicians, were able to provide some help for him). But the special character of the Dutch economy and society meant that he could survive as what later would have been a kind of artisan – a lens-grinder – albeit of a superior and scientifically important kind.

Spinoza lived in lodgings most of his life, without a wife or family, and this was very often the pattern of existence for a seventeenth-century philosopher. If he lived in an aristocratic household he could not maintain an ordinary household of his own, and if he depended on the church the same would be true, at least in Catholic countries (and to an extent in Protestant ones also – Oxford and Cambridge, after all, required celibacy of their college fellows). Again, in a sense he was required to prolong an irresponsible or child-like existence, and not settle down in the powerful and ancient institutions within which most adults lived, both at home and at work. The circumstances of their employment meant that most of the great seventeenth-century philosophers lived in what was (compared with the bulk of the population) an intersticial fashion.

II

As was said, a commitment to philosophical enquiry represented a short-circuiting of the conventional career pattern of an educated man; but in its earlier stages, the educational experience of the philosopher was, of course, identical to that of his contemporaries destined for the professions. The universities of Europe provided (to modern eyes) a remarkably similar education for their students; but there were significant national differences, most strikingly between the universities of Italy (and, to a lesser extent, Spain) and those of the rest of Europe.

The mediaeval universities of northern Europe, modelling themselves generally upon the University of Paris, had offered a course of study divided into two broad sections. The first was in the arts, the general subjects (including philosophy) which played a propaedeutic rôle. The second was in one of the three higher and professional subjects: law, medicine, or theology. The arts course in origin, and always thereafter in theory, was a seven-year course culminating in the award of a master's degree. But by the late Middle Ages all important northern universities required a candidate for the M.A. to pass a test known as the 'determination' after three and a half years of the course. The existence of this test divided the M.A. course into two parts, and the first part came to be seen as a separate course leading to the award of a bachelor's degree.[13] Often, it was possible to take a B.A. after three years without 'determining' if one did not intend to proceed to the M.A., and the requirements for the degree were correspondingly slightly simpler than those for the determination; but the decision whether to proceed or not must often have been taken quite late in the student's B.A. course, and no doubt much of the student's work would in fact be governed by the syllabus specified for the determination.

The division between B.A. and M.A. was a division between the texts studied by the students: for the B.A. and determination, they studied higher grammar (elementary grammar having been mastered at an earlier school), rhetoric, some elementary mathematics, the logical works of Aristotle (*Prior* and *Posterior Analytics, Sophistici Elenchi, Topica, Categories, De Interpretatione*) and his *De Anima*. This set of texts was sometimes described as those pertaining to the 'seven liberal arts'. For the M.A., the student would study the other works of Aristotle, on natural philosophy, moral philosophy, and metaphysics.[14] With a few minor variations, this was the arts curriculum common to the northern universities of the late Middle Ages, and it formed essentially a tightly structured course on the works of Aristotle, with the more substantial and intellectually rewarding works being left until the master's course.

In Italy, on the other hand, the universities (modelling themselves usually on the University of Bologna) offered a very flexible and loosely defined course. Essentially, these universities were schools of either law or medicine; furthermore, theology played at first very little part in their activities. But they also offered a course in the 'arts', that is, the general study of philosophy and the humanities, leading to the degree of doctor or master – the terms were interchangeable. As at Paris, this course could be either free-standing or preliminary to a course in law or medicine. Indeed, very often the artists were simply members of the medical faculty, as was true of Bologna, Pisa, and Padua, the three greatest Italian universities of the late Middle Ages. The standard structure of the course in the late Middle Ages, a structure which persisted in most cases through the sixteenth and seventeenth centuries, was a five-year course in any selection or combination of a variety of subjects. Thus at Padua in 1607 the subjects offered were logic (based on Porphyry and Aristotle's *Posterior Analytics*), philosophy (Aristotle's *Physics, De caelo, De anima, De generatione, Meteorologia,* and *Parva naturalia*), metaphysics (Aristotle's *Metaphysics*), theology (the Master of the Sentences), and grammar and Greek (no specified texts).[15] This was broadly similar in character to a late mediaeval Italian course – at Bologna in the fifteenth century, for example, artists could choose from logic (*Prior* and *Posterior analytics*), philosophy (the *Physics*), astrology (a Bolognese speciality, based on the *Sphaera* and *Algorismi*), rhetoric (Cicero's *Ad Herennium* and *De inventione*), and grammar (Priscian's *De constructione* and *De partibus*).[16] What is striking about all these Italian courses, in addition to their flexibility, is their readiness to specify quite advanced philosophical literature for relatively junior students, and their lack of interest in moral philosophy. Philosophy in an Italian university was largely a propaedeutic for medicine, and ethics played little part in it.[17]

The other great universities of southern Europe, those of Spain, were characteristically intermediate between the northern and the southern pattern. On the one hand, they imposed a tighter structure on the arts course than the Italians and took the degree of bachelor very seriously; they also gave instruction in theology as much as in law and medicine. On the other hand, the arts courses they offered took students to a high level extremely quickly, since (in general) students did not bother to take a master's or doctor's degree in the arts. For example, at the premier Spanish university of Salamanca, whose curriculum was in essence governed throughout the sixteenth and seventeenth centuries by the statutes of Pope Martin V issued in 1422, the statutes of the B.A. course prescribed a first year studying logic (*Vetera* and *Nova*), a second year studying logic and natural philosophy, and a third studying natural philosophy and moral philosophy.[18]

The slow and elaborate character of the arts courses in the northern universities came under general attack in the sixteenth century, largely because there was an alliance in effect (if not always in intention) between humanist theorists with a particular idea about how men should be educated and both Protestants and

Catholics anxious to speed up the production of trained ministers and priests, and to give theological students somewhat more time to master the huge modern literature of theological controversy. The humanists' contribution came from their central commitment that philosophy could not be understood nor taught in isolation from rhetoric, and from an understanding of the imaginative and historical literature of antiquity. This had two implications. The first was that a proper study of Aristotle's ethics (for example) could not be treated as a technical discipline divorced from thinking about the ethical views of 'rhetoricians' such as (above all) Cicero. To this end, humanists of the fifteenth century produced new translations of Aristotle into the Latin of Cicero and Seneca and thereby made him a participant in a philosophical conversation initiated by the Romans (the theoretical significance of these new translations was instantly seen by opponents of humanism).[19] But the second implication was that there was no point in studying the rules of rhetoric or logic in isolation from the important substantive theories contained in Aristotle's more advanced works.

The consequence of both these implications was that the ancient division between the B.A. and the M.A. was undermined, and the advanced works of Aristotle were opened up to the younger men who were equipped simply with a good knowledge of classical or Ciceronian Latin and had not yet learned the complicated technical vocabulary needed to understand the mediaeval Aristotelian texts. Once again, one can see that after the Renaissance philosophy became more of a young man's activity than had hitherto been the case. The controversial theologians welcomed this development, since in most cases it radically shortened the old arts course and allowed students to begin their theology much earlier than had previously been possible. The practical result, oddly enough, was that across northern Europe the mediaeval Spanish system in effect became the model, though whether this was fully appreciated by the reformers at the time is not clear. It is, however, very likely that it was the new appropriateness of Spanish methods of teaching in the rest of Europe which helped the 'School of Salamanca' to achieve the intellectual predominance in theological and philosophical matters which it enjoyed in the middle of the sixteenth century.

The other general development which affected the universities, and which may have had a considerable indirect effect on the kind of philosophy written in Europe, was the marked increase in the power over them of their national governments. The southern universities had traditionally been governed by elected representatives of the students, whose fees after all had funded the institutions; but the sixteenth and seventeenth centuries saw the general growth of princely control over them. At Perugia, for example, the reforms of Urban VIII in 1625 removed all vestiges of control either by the students or by the old commune of the city and substituted control by a vescovo and the professors, who the Pope believed would respond to his own wishes more readily and would manage the university more efficiently.[20] But the same was true in the North, where the universities had been governed by the regent masters; there, too, local rulers forced revisions of statutes whereby an elite among the masters (in England the heads of the Oxford and Cambridge colleges) could assume an increased managerial rôle.[21] So civil governments exercised a much tighter control on the universities and what was taught within them than had been the case in the Middle Ages. Nevertheless, the universities remained (from the princes' point of view) in many ways intractable bodies, and many princes helped to foster alternative centres of intellectual life such as the academies and societies of philosophers which began to appear from the late sixteenth century onwards in most European countries.

As far as the study of philosophy was concerned, the institutional form into which was put this new, younger study of the advanced works of Aristotle varied from country to country and university to university, as did the success which the new arts courses enjoyed. In France, for example, the new course came to be based in institutions modelled on a peculiarly Parisian prototype, the *collège de plein exercise*. The *collège de plein exercise* was a fifteenth-century development in Paris, in which some of the residential colleges of the university had started to teach philosophy courses independent of the university faculty of arts – perhaps to provide instruction in nominalist philosophy at a time when the faculty had abandoned it. The independent character of these colleges suited the humanists, who were able to bring their courses more in line with the humanist ideals (the links between nominalism and humanism which this implies would be worth further investigation, particularly with regard to the hostility to universals found among both nominalist and humanist logicians).[22]

So during the first half of the sixteenth century the colleges developed into institutions teaching both Latin and Greek grammar and literature, and philosophy; so successful were they that by the seventeenth century all the professors of philosophy and the humanities in Paris were in these colleges, and the old faculty structure existed merely to give the degree of M.A. to applicants from the colleges. The Collège Royal (in which Gassendi held his chair of mathematics from 1645 to 1649) was slightly different from the other colleges, in that it gave specialised courses to students who had usually already been to another college. The example of Paris was followed in the rest of France, and most importantly also by the founders of the Jesuit order from the 1560s onwards. The Jesuits saw the advantages for their own programme of colleges of this type and persuaded many municipalities to set them up; by 1610 there were forty such Jesuit colleges in France (including La Flèche, the school for both Descartes and Mersenne). In 1789 there were 348 *collèges de plein exercise* altogether, of which 171 gave instruction to the end of the philosophy course.

The colleges illustrate very well the effect of humanist ideas, for they put into one institution a six-year course in the 'humanities' (elementary Latin and Greek grammar and rhetoric) and a two-year course in philosophy (natural, moral, and metaphysical). Boys would enter the college at the age of ten or so (the age at which Descartes went to La Flèche) and would finish their study of philosophy and perhaps take an M.A. (if their college was associated with a university) at the age of eighteen – in marked contrast to the mediaeval pattern, which would not have allowed them to take their M.A. until their late twenties. The study of philosophy thus not only became an extension of childhood pursuits, rather than something institutionally quite separate from them, but was also very securely integrated into the general study of the humanities. This helps to emphasise the fact that seventeenth-century philosophy was very largely one element in a broadly humanist view of the world and that the great philosophers of the period would have seen themselves as closer kin to the classical scholars such as Lipsius or Scaliger than to the scholastic philosophers of the Middle Ages.

It must be emphasised, however, that despite the lowering of the age at which advanced philosophy was studied, and despite its closer association with the other humanities, it remained in these institutions (and, indeed, in the whole European university system) throughout the sixteenth and most of the seventeenth centuries essentially a study of the works of Aristotle. Aristotle was, as was mentioned earlier, studied in a humanist guise and what that implied could be the subject of strenuous debate (as between the 'Ramists' and 'Aristotelians' in Paris in the mid sixteenth century); but there was no question of replacing his works as the defining texts of philosophy at the colleges and universities.

In other countries, different solutions were found to the problem of how to change the mediaeval arts curriculum. In Germany, particularly in the Protestant universities, the combination of the need to re-organise the theology faculties and a humanist desire to restructure the arts course led universities themselves (rather than ancillary colleges, as in Paris) to alter their curricula. At Leipzig in electoral Saxony, which was the biggest and most important German university (900 students in 1600), under the statutes drawn up by Joachim Camerarius the B.A. course was transformed into a preliminary course lasting only three semesters and devoted to grammar, rhetoric, dialectic, poetry, and some elementary physics and mathematics. The M.A. course then lasted two years and dealt with Aristotle's

Organon, his Physics, and his Ethics.[23] Effectively, therefore, the old B.A. course had been made to cover the most advanced philosophy formerly taught only to men doing the M.A. course, and graduates received an M.A. rather than a B.A. They could then proceed straight to their technical theological training, which was, in Germany even more than in France, one of the chief points of the reform: the production of trained ministers would be speeded up and (as a corollary) made much cheaper.

As was usual in late sixteenth-century Protestant universities, the Leipzig statutes allowed no rôle for metaphysics; too much should not be read into this, as from 1600 almost all Protestant universities began to introduce courses in metaphysics into their arts courses. Leiden, for example, which was essentially a university of the German type, did so in 1604.[24] This normally happened without much discontent among the Protestant theologians of the universities; indeed, at Leiden (where the discussion is well documented) the theologians were the people who pressed for the official recognition of metaphysics. Earlier reluctance on the part of Protestants to preserve metaphysics in their arts courses seems to have been due primarily to the absence of suitable secondary works to use as teaching aids in the exposition of Aristotle, as existing ones were (in their eyes) far too contaminated by Catholic theological assumptions. The emergence of a new kind of metaphysics in the works of Suárez, in which metaphysical issues were discussed in more theologically neutral terms (despite, or perhaps because of, the Jesuit training of their author), meant that Protestants had available to them a suitable literature, and they began to expound metaphysics first from Suárez and then from various authentically Protestant metaphysicians such as Christoph Scheibler of the Lutheran university of Giessen in Hesse-Darmstadt.[25] It is worth pointing out that Salamanca never prescribed the study of metaphysics for either its arts or its theology students, and some of the freshness and freedom displayed by the metaphysics of Suárez and his followers may be the result of this.

In the universities of the other principal Protestant nation, England, yet another solution was found. Here, the formal structure of the mediaeval seven-year M.A., followed by a technical training in theology, law, or medicine, persisted, but the level at which everything was studied was effectively moved down one notch. Thus the B.A. course came to include philosophy of the kind formerly studied only on the M.A., and the M.A. course came to be in practice the basic technical training for theologians; only men who were expected to have a very distinguished career in the church would proceed to the old theological qualifications of B.D. and D.D. The attack on law in the English universities which the Reformation induced no doubt helped the M.A. to become largely a preserve of theologians (ecclesiastical bodies had always been the chief employers of university-trained lawyers in England – practising common lawyers were, of course, trained in the Inns of Court). The 1570 statutes of Cambridge are honest about the new arrangements: for the B.A. they specify a first year spent on rhetoric, second and third years on dialectic, and the fourth on 'philosophy' (including ethics, which had always been left to the M.A. in the mediaeval university).[26] Determination survived, but as a necessary preliminary to taking the B.A. rather than the first stage of an M.A. (this is in fact the origin of the modern Tripos). Candidates for the M.A., on the other hand, were now required to study theology. Cambridge had perhaps always been readier to thrust advanced work upon its students than most universities – the late mediaeval statutes, unusually, specified metaphysics as well as natural philosophy for the determination, though they reserved ethics for the M.A.[27]

At Oxford, the sixteenth-century statutes are more evasive, and this has led some writers to contrast the greater 'modernity' of Cambridge with Oxford's more traditional approach;[28] but Oxford's 1576 statutes allow a place for 'Morall' (i.e., ethics) in the determination, in sharp contrast to its mediaeval practice (e.g., the 1409 statutes).[29] This was repeated in the great Laudian Code of 1636, under which Oxford was governed for the next two centuries, which made determination an examination in logic, grammar, rhetoric, ethics, and politics. The main difference between the two universities was that Oxford preserved the determination as a post-B.A. test for the M.A. candidate; but the actual work of undergraduates at both Oxford and Cambridge must have been very similar.

The southern universities needed reform much less than the northern ones for, as was already pointed out, the kind of arts course they offered was more appropriate to the circumstances of the Renaissance and Reformation. Because the arts courses in Italian universities were so loosely defined, it was always possible for humanist methods of exposition to be applied to the Aristotelian texts, and many humanists flourished in the arts and medical faculties of Italian universities.[30] But it was also the case that the relatively quick and superficial treatment of philosophy, and particularly of moral philosophy, in the Italian arts courses left a large gap to be filled both by private schools run by humanists and by the houses of religious orders near university cities (of which the most notable example was the Jesuits' Collegio Romano). It was also the case that in the late Middle Ages theology faculties had been founded or developed in the leading Italian universities, and that the teachers of theology began to encroach upon the traditional preserves of the arts professors – at Perugia, for example, the arts philosophers engaged in a long struggle with the theologians about who could award degrees in philosophy, beginning with a protest in 1610 and not ending until a compromise was reached in 1786.[31]

Nevertheless, students continued to go to the Italian universities throughout the seventeenth century in order to study philosophy, particularly of the non-ethical kind; the career of Galileo exemplifies the rôle which Italian universities still played, for though he studied the arts course first in a convent at Vallambrossa, he studied mathematics and physics in much more detail at the university of Pisa and was, of course, employed at Pisa and Padua until 1610. But Galileo's career also illustrates the limitations on pursuing philosophy at an early seventeenth-century Italian university (and, it should be said, at a university in more or less any European country), since as his work became more controversial he (like Hobbes and Locke in England) found it much easier to rely on the private patronage of a great nobleman – in Galileo's case, the Grand Duke of Tuscany himself.

Although the Spanish pattern of studies in the late Middle Ages became in some ways the model for the rest of Europe after the Renaissance, ironically, Spanish students themselves began to repudiate it. Increasingly, they turned for their arts education to institutions more like the French *collèges de plein exercise* – municipal schools and colleges, particularly (once again) those organised by the Jesuit order expressly on the model of the Parisian colleges. By the seventeenth century, the study of philosophy in Spain was almost entirely conducted within these institutions. The reason for this development is fairly clear: the Spanish government and the church offered graduates in law an extensive range of secure and well-paid jobs, and there was a great incentive for students to acquire these lucrative qualifications as quickly as possible. So they matriculated into one of the law faculties (usually the faculty of canon law – the predominance of canonists over civilians is a striking feature of Spanish intellectual life), having obtained a minimal knowledge of philosophy while at school.[32] As the pattern of education in Spain shifted towards that in France, philosophy came to be studied extensively outside the universities.

It has been suggested that the relatively poor quality of Spanish intellectual life in the seventeenth century (striking in comparison with the major philosophical contributions of Iberian writers in the sixteenth century) was in part due to this predominance of legal studies and the complete divorce between universities and the study of the liberal arts.[33] But no one could accuse seventeenth-century France of having an impoverished intellectual life, and yet the same kind of divorce can be found there. Much more important was the absence in Spain of the alternative sources of employment and patronage for philosophers and other literary figures available in France; great figures such as Richelieu fostered a wide range of intellectual activities, whereas in Spain the court tended to rely much more heavily on technically trained and bureaucratically minded lawyers (though there are, of course, some exceptions to this – Count Olivares, the minister of Philip IV, had a wider outlook and was a patron to such men as the Italian Tacitist Virgilio Malvezzi).

III

The inability or unwillingness of contemporary universities to sustain more than a small proportion of the important philosophical work carried out in seventeenth-century Europe, and the reliance of many major figures on private patronage, put a particular emphasis on informal associations of philosophers and on their participation in the unstructured and international *respublica litterarum*. There were two ways in which the ideas of a philosopher could come to be known in this invisible republic; one was, of course, through the appearance in print of his ideas, but the other was through the remarkable network of letters which writers across the continent exchanged with one another. European scholars had always been busy letter-writers; Erasmus complained that he had to write more than ten a day, and his surviving correspondence bears witness to his labours. The posts across the continent were surprisingly efficient; it is very rare to find any seventeenth-century scholar complaining that a letter had been lost in the post, and the post between major cities was fairly quick (Paris to The Hague in a week or ten days, and Paris to London the same).[34] On the other hand, it could take a long time for a letter to reach a country address; letters between Hobbes in Orléans and his patrons in Derbyshire in 1630 took just over a month.[35] But in general, it was perfectly possible to carry on an extensive and speedy correspondence. Writing letters had become part of the humanist culture, and schoolboys were brought up on Cicero's letters to his friends; moreover, there was much less sense of privacy in a correspondence than there would be today. Lipsius regularly published his own letters in volumes of a hundred at a time, cutting out only a few passages which would be particularly embarrassing to the correspondents concerned,[36] and most letters addressed to Mersenne by his extraordinary circle of correspondents were available for inspection in his chambers.[37] Lack of privacy had other aspects, however: letters were frequently opened by government agents, and Locke's concern about this during his period of exile in the United Provinces led him to write elaborately coded references to political matters (though it seems no scholar actually wrote in numerical codes, as many contemporary politicians did).

The result of this semi-public character of scholarly correspondence was that reputations could be made almost entirely on the basis of manuscripts and letters. This was the case with Hobbes: he came to enjoy considerable intellectual prestige in Paris long before he had published anything, largely on the basis of the letters and papers which he exchanged with Mersenne and (through him) with Descartes. His first philosophical work, the *Elements of Law,* made him a comparable reputation in England but was never published with his approval; instead, it circulated very widely in manuscript copies (over ten of which still survive). The same was true of Gassendi, who had a great reputation long before anything substantial appeared in print, and Descartes himself, whose ideas were well known from letters and early manuscripts long before the *Discours de la méthode* and its accompanying essays were published. Only a few seventeenth-century scholars went into print at all readily; John Selden seems to have printed most of what he wrote very quickly, but he did so sometimes through cheap and unreliable printers and had to disown what had been done to his text.[38]

The development in the late seventeenth century of formal, state-recognised or sponsored societies of philosophers in many ways systematised these informal contacts, as well as providing them with certain resources and privileges which they could not otherwise have enjoyed. A number of traditions converged in such societies. One was the custom which had grown up in sixteenth-century Italy of literary and philosophical figures banding together in an *accadèmia* to discuss questions put to the group much in the manner of an ancient rhetoric school. The usual practice was for a question on more or less any topic to be published to the academy, and for the answers to be given at a subsequent meeting, with the principal aim being to display rhetorical accomplishment. This kind of academy persisted into the seventeenth century, both in Italy and in those places elsewhere in Europe under Italian influence; for example, at the house of the Venetian resident in Paris in the 1650s an academy of this kind met to discuss such questions as (allegedly) 'whether tickling to death or dying for love be the greatest pain'.[39] The Académie Française was a particularly famous and government-sponsored instance. The form these academic discussions took influenced those of more specialised assemblies, including the philosophical academies. The Society of Antiquaries which met in the late sixteenth and early seventeenth centuries in England[40] also conducted its meetings along similar lines. The close association between the practice of rhetoric and the study both of history and of philosophy meant that the framework for formal discussion in the latter cases was likely to be drawn from the well-established customs of the former.

The second main tradition which gave rise to the distinctive character of the seventeenth-century philosophical societies was, as just mentioned, the organised exchange of correspondence between scholars. The need for an efficient means of disseminating information of all kinds was widely felt in the early seventeenth century and gave rise inter alia to some of the Utopian schemes of men like Comenius; it also influenced Théophraste Renaudot in his foundation of the curious institution, the Bureau d'Adresse, in Paris in the 1630s.[41] The Bureau provided a wide variety of informational services, ranging from sale advertisements to medical advice; Renaudot also organised discussions at the Bureau like those of a rhetorical academy, illustrating the connexion which was thought to exist at many levels between the exchange of information and the practice of debate.

The third element in the origins of the seventeenth-century societies would, however, have been less familiar to a Renaissance humanist: it was the need to provide funds collectively in some way for the purchase and manufacture of scientific equipment, which most individuals could no longer afford to buy for themselves. This need was one of the strongest reasons for seeking state support of some kind for the societies; as Samuel Sorbière said in 1663, proposing the formal reorganisation of a loose-knit group of French philosophers which had first met in Mersenne's rooms, and subsequently at the house of Henri-Louis Habert de Montmor, a *maître des requêtes* to Louis XIV,

> To imagine that we might erect in this house a Shop, a Forge, and a Laboratory, or to put it in a word, build an Arsenal of machines to perform all sorts of experiments, is not possible at all, and is not the proper undertaking of a few private persons.... Truly, Messieurs, only Kings and wealthy Sovereigns, or a few wise and prosperous Republics, can undertake to set up a physical academy, where everything would pass in continual experiments. Places must be built to order; there must be numerous hired craftsmen; there must be a considerable fund for expenses.[42]

The combination of semi-formal discussions, the centralised provision of equipment, and the management of a clearing-house for relevant correspondence mark out all the major philosophical and scientific societies, including the three greatest, the Accadèmia del Cimento of Tuscany, the Royal Society of England, and the Académie des Sciences of France. All three began from unofficial groups of philosophers meeting in an organised way to pursue discussions and read letters. The Tuscan Accadèmia began with groups of philosophers meeting in a laboratory furnished by Grand Duke Ferdinand II and his brother Leopold from 1651 onwards and was formally organised by the Grand Duke as an academy in 1657. The Royal Society grew out of the interests of a group of natural philosophers, first at Oxford and then at Oxford and London, who at first were chiefly interested in medical problems and their physical implications (such as the nature of the air we breathe). The society received a royal charter in 1662. The Académie des Sciences was, indeed, the refounding of the Montmor academy which Sorbiere requested, and it began to meet under royal sponsorship in rooms of the Royal Library in 1666; members of the *académie* received royal pensions.

What is striking about these societies and needs more explanation than is usually provided is the fact that all three were under state patronage.[43] Both the state and the philosophers benefitted from incorporating scholarship of this kind into the structure of privileged institutions characteristic of ancien régime Europe. The state benefitted because it thereby gained the kind of purchase on intellectual activity which had been denied it (to some extent) by the mediaeval constitutions of the universities, but the benefits to the philosophers were more straightforward and tangible. In part they were funds, though the Royal Society, despite early expectations characteristically raised and then disappointed by Charles II, never received government money. It was extremely fortunate that Robert Boyle was a leading member of the early society, for he was the son of the richest peer in the United Kingdom and could provide it with such eye-catching equipment as the famous air-pump. But there were other benefits which only a state could provide and which the Royal Society did enjoy along with its continental counterparts: in particular, the charter of the society expressly exempted the foreign correspondence of the society from government intervention.[44] As was indicated, the secret surveillance of letters was a constant problem for seventeenth-century intellectuals, and only a privileged body like the Royal Society could win exemption from it; even so, Henry Oldenburg, the first secretary of the society, spent some months in the Tower of London in 1667, accused of conducting treasonable correspondence with foreigners.[45] The other privilege for which both the Royal Society and the Académie des Sciences needed royal permission was the right to dissect dead bodies – a highly controversial matter in early modern Europe, but one to which the particular scientific interests of these philosophers gave a very high priority. It was worth incurring the disciplines of formal incorporation in order to secure these rights. From the point of view of a philosopher like Hobbes, however, who deeply detested all privileged associations such as guilds or corporations, the willingness of the English natural philosophers to become incorporated in this manner made them the object of fierce criticism.

IV

Though a philosopher might find that private or semi-private groups such as the Mersenne circle or the formal societies could be the centre of his intellectual activity, sooner or later he would be likely to put his ideas into print and address a wider audience. In the course of the seventeenth century, publishing became a multi-national and highly entrepreneurial business, in which new markets for books were explored (particularly by the Dutch) as quickly as other companies were discovering new international markets for such things as textiles or coffee. By the end of the century, books, including many works of philosophy, had become part of an international culture intent on new and sophisticated forms of consumption.

At the beginning of the century, printing and publishing were still conducted in broadly the way in which they had been established in the middle of the sixteenth century. Paris probably contained more printing-houses and bookshops than anywhere else, but Venice and Frankfurt also contributed many volumes to the international market. The technology of printing was also still the same and, indeed, remained essentially the same down to the end of the eighteenth century: a printing-house would need at least one hand press, three or four workmen to compose type and work the press, and a fount of type (about 1,000 kilograms was usual). The capital costs of the business were very high, particularly for the type – the 1,000 kilograms would cost the same as the annual wages of the workmen and would, of course, need constant renewing as the type wore down (a press, by contrast, would cost only one-tenth of the price of the type and would last much longer). Most printing-houses were thus rather small affairs, with only a couple of presses and without many resources to expend on marketing or other means of developing their businesses. Correspondingly, they tended to produce books in editions of no more than two thousand copies, and often fewer.[46] Authors were not paid directly for their work (unless they were, for example, commissioned to translate something); instead, they received free copies which they could dispose of on the market if they chose. Twenty-five copies was reasonable to expect in the late sixteenth century,[47] so that in modern terms even the most successful philosophical author might receive no more than a 2 per cent royalty, and some of that would have to be used up in presentation copies to friends and patrons.

The principal method of marketing in the early years of the century, for all European publishers, was the traditional trip to the Frankfurt book fair in March, where deals would be struck between publishers of different countries to sell one another's books through their retail outlets. Grotius's *De iure belli ac pacis* of 1625, for example, was rushed through the presses of its French publisher in order to be on sale at the fair. It should be remembered that all early modern printers were also, usually, booksellers, retailing both their own products and those of other printers; their shops usually developed a particular intellectual character and could come to resemble clubs or coffee-houses. Thus, it was well known that the London printer Richard Royston not only published royalist political tracts during the Civil War but also acted as a host for meetings of royalists to discuss politics or to conspire against the new regime after 1649. Furthermore, a printer could become associated with a particular author and offer people who dropped into his shop the opportunity to look at unpublished work – thus, the firm of Crooke, who published Hobbes's English works, allowed visitors in the 1670s to read some of his manuscripts which the government would not permit them to print.[48]

The only printer in the late sixteenth century who managed to break away significantly from these constraints was the famous Christopher Plantin of Antwerp, who was central to the international scholarly world. At the height of his firm's success in the 1570s it was running sixteen presses; it also began to establish itself directly in other countries, with a Parisian bookshop tied to its products from 1567 onwards.[49] Its sophistication and scale of operation mirrored the comparable features of other Flemish businesses, but like those other businesses it was eclipsed in the next century by the activities of Dutch firms. During the middle years of the seventeenth century, they developed a new kind of publishing business, very closely analogous to the new businesses in other fields with which the Dutch startled and dazzled their contemporaries, and marked out particularly by a constant search for new commercial opportunities.

The firm of Elzevier in Amsterdam, for example, employed full-time travelling salesmen to tour Europe negotiating the sale of its books; it also ran a depot in Venice for the Italian market and several unofficial bookshops in Paris (where a formal foreign presence would have been illegal).[50] Elzevier's technique was sometimes to lend a struggling bookseller enough money to set up in business again and thus to bind him to the firm – a technique remarkably comparable to that used by the Dutch on a vast scale to acquire influence over princes and governments around the world. What made this kind of activity possible was, of course, the ease with which any Dutch firm could acquire large amounts of capital from investors at home and could therefore embark on strategies which would have been beyond the means even of Plantin, let alone the struggling printers of seventeenth-century Paris (where in 1644 about half the presses in the city's printing-houses were idle).[51] Dutch printers also modified the technology of the presses in various ways to make their operations more efficient. Their print runs expanded accordingly: mid-seventeenth-century Dutch publishers effectively took over the English market for Bibles by printing them in runs of six thousand or more at a time when English printers were forbidden by guild regulations to print books in editions of more than three thousand.[52]

Dutch investors required a decent return on their money, however, and this obliged the printers to look for new kinds of product and new customers, or, very often, for a product which had been invented but insufficiently developed by some less well-endowed enterprise. For example, the Elzeviers and their Amsterdam competitors the Blaeus made a lot of money out of mass-producing pocket editions both of the classics and of contemporary political analyses which could be used in circumstances where conventional books would have been inappropriate (Hobbes used to read them in the ante-rooms of English aristocrats), an idea which a number of publishers had had in the sixteenth century but which had never taken off until the Amsterdam publishers perfected the techniques involved. But the Amsterdam firms also perceived the existence of a new market for a new kind of philosophy and played a major part in developing it.

The publishing history of Grotius's *De iure belli ac pacis* illustrates this very neatly. It was published first in 1625 by a French printer, Nicholas Buon, whose primary marketing strategy was to sell it via the Frankfurt fair (although, Grotius commented, 'he prefers to sell books in France rather than anywhere else').[53] In a development also redolent of an earlier period, it was promptly pirated on a small scale by a Frankfurt printer. The immediate success of the book prompted both Buon and Grotius to project a second edition, but Buon persistently failed to organise his affairs effectively enough to produce it.[54] Grotius began to look for other publishers, despite the legal problems (which were partly resolved by Buon's death in 1629). Willem Blaeu of Amsterdam then moved in and offered Grotius the prospect of a sumptuous new edition in folio with all the author's emendations and additions, and a cheap popular edition in octavo;[55] these duly appeared in 1631 and 1632, and Grotius remained with Blaeu as his publisher (with two more editions in 1642 and 1646). Interestingly, the Elzeviers also bid for the book, one of them making a personal visit to Grotius in Paris;[56] while another Amsterdam firm, Johann Janssen, which specialised in cheap and illicit editions of other people's products, got an octavo edition of the 1631 text out earlier in 1632 than the Blaeus could manage – a graphic illustration of the fiercely competitive character of the Amsterdam publishers.[57] In the late 1630s Grotius was expecting a hundred free copies of his books to be sent by the Dutch printers,[58] which suggests that the Dutch were also able to pay the equivalent of five times as much to their authors as older publishers had managed; Grotius also commented in 1637 that even 'Marquises and other great men' were now seeking money for their books, though he would stand aside from such vulgar behaviour.[59] This suggests that the effects of the Dutch innovations included the growth of a market in authorship as well as in printing.

The same story could be told about Hobbes: his *De Cive* was first published in Paris in 1642, in what amounted to a private edition (there was no bookseller's name on the title page, and Grotius was told that it was not for sale). Again, the book was a success, and the Elzeviers picked it up in 1646, producing an expanded second edition the following year in much larger numbers (indeed, printing two editions of the work in 1647). Later, in 1668, the Blaeus agreed to publish Hobbes's complete Latin works, including a translation of *Leviathan,* in what must again have been a very large print run; an unknown Dutch printer was also responsible for printing an edition of *Leviathan* in English at a time when Hobbes was not allowed to publish it in England. Descartes, too, benefitted from the entrepreneurial skills of the Dutch publishers: though the essays prefixed by a *Discours de la méthode* had been published at Leiden in 1637, it was a Parisian printer called Michel Soly who undertook to publish his major philosophical work, the *Meditationes de prima philosophia* in 1641. This was the work which fully established Descartes's reputation; but, just as in the case of Grotius's *De iure belli ac pacis,* Descartes was dissatisfied with what his French publisher offered and switched to the Elzeviers for a second and more accurate edition in the following year. Thereafter, all his major works were published by the Elzeviers.

The same thing happened when in the 1660s a new publishing idea appeared in France: the learned journal which would appear frequently and regularly, and which would convey philosophical and other ideas to a wider audience than the small groups of the scholars themselves. At this point, in a sense, the world of the intellectuals became something which could easily be consumed as a spectacle by a fashionable public. The first such periodical was the *Journal des savants,* which appeared in January 1665 and was published every week; the assumption at first seems to have been that a Dutch publisher would take it up and reprint it, and, indeed, the Elzeviers expressed an interest in doing so,[60] though in the end only a counterfeit edition appeared in Holland.[61] The *Journal des savants* had a somewhat erratic career in its first years, but it proved the existence of a new market; the political turmoil in Holland during the 1670s delayed a Dutch take-over, but from 1684 onwards they began to dominate this market also with Bayle's *Nouvelles de la république des lettres* and Le Clerc's *Bibliothèque universelle et historique.*

By the end of the century, therefore, the institutional and commercial frame-work was in place for a new kind of philosopher, working completely outside the universities and selling his works to a fairly large lay public. Writing in the vernacular developed at the same time, as philosophy became part of the nascent salon society across the parts of Europe under French or Dutch influence: it was in this society that the very word 'philosopher' came to acquire a distinctive meaning as the culture of the *philosophes* developed. In the late eighteenth century the universities struck back, in the persons of (for example) Adam Smith and Immanuel Kant; but the transformation of both philosophy and its practitioners in the seventeenth century had altered the character of the subject for ever.

NOTES

1 These figures are derived from the figures for England, Holland, Spain, Germany, France, Italy, and Spain (all modern boundaries) in Livi-Bacci 1992, p. 69. I have added about five million for the population of the smaller West European populations not included in this list.

2 Sandys 1906–8, vol. 2, p. 234. The same kind of joke is found about a Frenchman in Erasmus's *De recta pronuntiatione,* ed. J. K. Sowards, in Erasmus 1974– , vol. 26, p. 472.

3 For the translation of the *Essay,* see the edition by Peter Nidditch, Locke 1975, p. xxxvii.

4 This is, of course, an extremely rough estimate; for more precise discussions see Graff 1987, pp. 137–63; and Houston 1988, pp. 130–54.

5 These are my calculations, based on Wrigley and Schofield 1981, p. 528; and Stone 1964, p. 51. They correspond to the estimates in Houston 1988, pp. 84–5.

6 Kagan 1974, pp. 360–2.

7 My calculations, from *Returns from Universities and University Colleges in Receipt of Treasury Grant 1922–3* (1924); Office of Population, Censuses and Surveys (Great Britain) (1982), *Census 1981: Historical Tables, 1801–1981: England and Wales;* and *Annual Abstract of Statistics* (1992).

8 The genre was effectively founded by Gilles Ménage with his *Historia mulierum philosopharum* (1690). For his followers and imitators, see Santinello 1981, vol. 2, p. 87; and Ballard 1752.

9 See, e.g., Locke 1976–92, vol. 1, letters nos. 71, 83, 86, 121, 185, 193, 214, 222, 225, 232.

10 Mersenne 1932–88, vol. 1, p. xix.

11 Wood 1813–20, vol. 3, col. 377. Selden's father would have counted as a 'yeoman', and (in England) a majority of yeomen and urban tradesmen were literate. See Graff 1987, pp. 154–5; and Houston, 1988, pp. 140–1.

12 Kagan 1974, pp. 43–4.

13 Rashdall 1936, vol. 1, pp. 452 ff.

14 Rashdall 1936, vol. 1, pp. 442–3; vol. 3, pp. 153–6.

15 *Statuta Almae Universitatis D.D. Philosophorum, & Medicorum* (1607), pp. 80, 161–3.

16 Malagola 1888, pp. 487 ff.

17 Rashdall 1936, vol. 1, p. 235.

18 Gonzalez de la Calle, Urbano, and Huarte y Echenique 1925–6, p. 366.

19 For a brief discussion of this, see Tuck 1993, pp. 12–15.

20 Ermini 1947, pp. 183–5.

21 See, e.g., the remarks in P. Williams 1986, pp. 402–3.

22 For the *collèges,* Brockliss 1987, pp. 19–22, 55–6.

23 Evans 1981, p. 189. The second largest university, Wittenberg, also in electoral Saxony, had 850 students, and the third, Frankfurt on the Oder (Brandenburg), had 600; the average size of the remaining nineteen universities of the Empire was only 260.
24 Dibon 1954, p. 67.
25 Dibon 1954, pp. 70–1; Kearney 1970, p. 78.
26 See, e.g., Costello 1958, pp. 41–2.
27 *Documents Relating to the University and Colleges of Cambridge* (1852), vol. 1, pp. 385, 459.
28 E.g., Fletcher 1981, pp. 9–13.
29 Gibson 1931, pp. 406, 202; Fletcher 1986, p. 183.
30 See Denley 1981.
31 Ermini 1947, p. 196.
32 Kagan 1974, pp. 52–6; Rodriguez-San Pedro Bezares 1986, vol. 2, pp. 739–43.
33 Kagan 1974, pp. 212–17.
34 For Paris to The Hague, see the correspondence between Grotius and Uytenbogaert in 1630. Uytenbogaert (in The Hague) kept notes on when he received each letter from Grotius (in Paris). Grotius 1928– , vol. 4. pp. 139, 168, 214, etc.
35 See De Beer 1950, pp. 203–4.
36 Lipsius 1586, 1591, 1601, 1604c, 1605a, 1605b, 1607. For his editing, see, e.g., letter 418 in Lipsius 1978– , vol. 2, p. 206.
37 Mersenne 1932–88, p. xlvi.
38 See his remarks in Selden 1726, vol. 2, p. 210.
39 Brown 1934, p. 78.
40 For its proceedings, clearly modelled on a rhetoric chamber, see Hearne 1720.
41 Solomon 1972.
42 Brown 1934, p. 127.
43 See Hunter 1989, pp. 3–15, for a discussion of this (including some interesting speculations about the connexion with Harrington's Rota Club).
44 Sprat 1667, p. 142.
45 See *Calendar of State Papers* . . . (1860–1939), vol. 7, pp. 214, 297, 261, 311, 509. Oldenburg pleaded in defence that he had arranged for his letters from France and Holland to be delivered at the office of Secretary of State Arlington, 'to be opened at his pleasure' (p. 297; he did the same while in the Tower, p. 509).
46 See Gaskell 1972, pp. 162–4, 176–7.
47 Clair 1960, p. 214.
48 See Locke 1976–92, vol. 1, no. 268.
49 Voet 1969–72, vol. 2, p. 398.
50 Willems 1880, pp. lxx–lxxi; Martin 1969, vol. 2, p. 592.
51 Martin 1969, vol. 1, pp. 372–3. This can be calculated on the basis of the number of employees, assuming three to four men per press.
52 Davies 1954, p. 128; Gaskell 1972 p. 162.
53 Grotius 1928– , vol. 2, p. 453.
54 Grotius 1928– , vol. 3, pp. 169, 187, 188, 446.
55 Grotius 1928– , vol. 4, p. 135.
56 Grotius 1928– , vol. 4, p. 169.
57 For all these editions, see ter Meulen and Diermanse 1950, pp. 228–30.
58 Grotius 1928– , vol. 8, pp. 375, 716.
59 Grotius 1928– , vol. 9, p. 334.
60 Brown 1934, p. 190.
61 Reesink 1931, p. 68.

2

THE INTELLECTUAL SETTING

STEPHEN MENN

The seventeenth century saw the emergence of the corpuscularian, or 'mechanical', philosophy, which succeeded far beyond any previous science or philosophy in explaining particular phenomena of nature, and which, as a general framework for thought about the physical world, has continued to guide philosophical and scientific investigation down to the present day. Modern scholars have often sought to understand the emergence of this new philosophy by placing it within the context of some previous tradition of thought. In the words of J. H. Randall:

We are confronted by many scholars, each of whom has been exploring some one of these traditions, and each of whom has not unnaturally come to be a vigorous partisan of the basic importance of the particular body of ideas he has investigated. It is well to have each of these intellectual currents carefully explored by men vitally interested in it. For if one thing at least has now grown clear, it is that 'the emergence of modern science' was a very complicated affair, and involved a great variety of factors. The central problem, however, is that of the judicious appraisal of the relative importance of a number of 'necessary conditions'; and for such a wise balancing and weighing we seem hardly ready yet. Each of us may have his own suspicions, but they have certainly not as yet produced agreement.[1]

Two generations later, there is still no agreement. In what follows I will not attempt to assess the relative importance of the different intellectual traditions leading up to the seventeenth century (in any case, the relative importance of these different traditions as background will vary widely, depending on which seventeenth-century figure we wish to study), but I will try to indicate the broad range of intellectual traditions in terms of which the various seventeenth-century figures defined their attempts to establish a new philosophy. I will also suggest a partial explanation for the actual successes of the science which emerged, not by

I have received helpful comments on various drafts and sections of this essay from Heather Blair, Alan Gabbey, Dan Garber, Lynn Joy, Alison Laywine, Christia Mercer, Ann Moyer, Richard Popkin, and two anonymous commentators. Gabbey and Garber encouraged me to write the piece, and they and Mercer discussed the original outline with me and suggested improvements. Blair shared with me her work on Renaissance and early modern theories of the soul, on which her dissertation, Blair 1995, is an important reference. Gabbey and Moyer gave particularly helpful overall comments. I am grateful to all of these and to any others I have failed to mention by name.

pointing to some one earlier tradition which could be expected to yield progressive results but by indicating the conditions which led to an explosion of many new varieties of philosophy, any of which *might* have brought the promised wisdom. Some of these succeeded, through luck or merit, in establishing themselves as strands within 'the new philosophy', whereas many others perished in the end.

Traditions deriving from three earlier periods are relevant for understanding seventeenth-century philosophy: the contending schools (Platonist, Peripatetic, Stoic, Epicurean, and sceptic) of antiquity, the scholastic Aristotelianism of the mediaeval universities, and the 'new philosophies' of the Renaissance (which may be put for philosophical purposes at 1450–1600). Seventeenth-century scholasticism is, of course, directly continuous with mediaeval scholasticism; but the main concern in this chapter is to understand the emergence of *new* philosophies, whose exponents were conscious of themselves as innovators. This is a phenomenon which begins in the Renaissance and extends throughout the seventeenth century. These philosophies, even when they claimed to be continuing ancient traditions, defined themselves as 'new' in contrast to the 'old' Aristotelian philosophy of the schools:[2] the new philosophies initially developed outside the universities, or at least outside the philosophy faculties,[3] and if they won a place in the curriculum it was through protracted struggle. People produced such new philosophies because there was a demand for a new philosophy, that is, a current expectation of what a philosophy should do, and a sentiment that the old philosophy was not doing it properly. Indeed, one may say that the chief philosophical legacy which the sixteenth century bequeathed to the seventeenth was not any particular new philosophy but just this *expectation* of a new philosophy.

The philosophers of the Renaissance turned their attention to texts from previously neglected ancient schools, and they laboured to extract from their favoured sources a discipline comprehensive enough to compete with the old philosophy; in this way they produced a whole range of 'new philosophies'. The philosophers of the seventeenth century took over their predecessors' criticisms of scholasticism, and they happily made use of the ancient materials which Renaissance scholarship had published and translated and digested; but they were not satisfied that any of the proposed 'new philosophies' had filled the intellectual vacuum, and they looked in other directions for the new philosophy their predecessors had taught them to expect. Thus in setting seventeenth-century philosophy in the context of the Renaissance critique of scholasticism and the Renaissance revivals of ancient philosophies, our primary concern is to trace the phenomenon of the expectation of a new philosophy from its beginnings in mere distrust of Aristotle to its end, when the 'new philosophy' became a synonym for 'the mechanical philosophy'.

I. RELIGIOUS BACKGROUND:
THE CHURCH REFORM MOVEMENT

We can best understand what a new philosophy was supposed to do by seeing how scholastic Aristotelianism failed to do it. Although the new philosophies of the seventeenth century were most innovative in their physics, and although they ensured their survival chiefly by explaining phenomena of nature, the search for a new philosophy was originally motivated by Christian complaints about the moral and religious effects of scholasticism. Since the view persists that the Middle Ages were the great age of faith and that scholasticism was a happy marriage of Aristotelian philosophy to Christian theology, it will help to recall some ecclesiastical history in order to explain the divorce.

Aristotelian philosophy owed its prestige, and its place in the universities, to its service in supporting the higher disciplines, especially Christian theology. Some Aristotelian philosophy professors in the thirteenth century, following Averroes, had interpreted Aristotle as denying God's creation of the world, God's knowledge and guidance of sublunar events, and the immortality of the individual human soul; these philosophers had thus come into conflict with the teaching of the theology faculty and with church authority. But when Averroism was condemned by bishops and universities, the works of Aristotle, as reinterpreted by Thomas Aquinas and other theologians, were saved from condemnation. The Dominicans (who chose Thomas as the official doctor of their order) and the Franciscans (who followed John Duns Scotus) wished to use Aristotelian concepts and arguments in developing the doctrines of scripture and the Church Fathers into a systematic theology. Thus, Thomas asserts in the *Summa contra gentiles* that natural human reason, as interpreted by Aristotelian philosophy, can demonstrate some Christian doctrines, including the existence of God and the immortality of the soul, and show at least the *possibility* of the other Christian teachings, which must be affirmed by faith. While the scholastic theology of the Dominicans and Franciscans retained its prestige in the church, Aristotelian scholastic philosophy was also preserved, and an attack on this philosophy might be taken as an attack on the foundations of theology. But when the established structures of the church, including the teaching orders and their theology, no longer satisfy moral and religious aspirations, then quite naturally the philosophy on which their theology is based also comes under challenge.

Reform movements seeking a return to the purity of the early church are as old as the church itself; the Dominican and Franciscan orders are themselves the product of an earlier reform movement, and the Franciscans continued to be torn between compromisers and more radical reformers. But by the late fourteenth century, many regarded the whole structure of the church, the teaching orders included, as radically corrupt. This growing discontent may be ascribed as much to an increase in expectations as to a worsening of conditions. But certainly one did not have to look very hard, at the end of the fourteenth century, to find something gravely wrong with the condition of the church. Communion between Rome and Constantinople had been broken, and the Latin occupation of Constantinople (1204–61) had destroyed all trust between East and West. Though several Byzantine emperors had tried to reunite the churches in order to gain Western military support against the Turkish threat, their work had been destroyed by the hostility of the Byzantine church and people, which preferred Muslim to Catholic rule. In part because of this Christian disunity, the Ottoman Turks were steadily swallowing up the Byzantine empire, and a vast territory of formerly Christian Europe was passing to Muslim rule. In the West, the church had become entangled in a web of conflicts and alliances, first with the German empire and then with the French and other national monarchies, leading first to the 'Babylonian captivity' of the papacy at Avignon (1309–77) under the patronage of the French monarchy, and then to the Great Western Schism (1378–1417), in which the French church remained loyal to a pope at Avignon, whereas the German empire and most other nations supported a rival pope at Rome. Even after the healing of the schism, the papacy continued to be involved with the other European powers in a shifting pattern of political and military alliances. Offices within the church were commonly treated as 'benefices', as sources of income and power, with a consequent degradation in service to the Christian community; simony, the sale of ecclesiastical offices, was widespread and became the most frequently denounced sin of the age. Multiple benefices, and thus clerical absenteeism, were common. And even if a cleric resided in his parish, it did not follow that he performed his duties properly: illiteracy among the lower clergy, and sexual offenses at all levels, were frequent complaints.

Aristotelian philosophy was not responsible for these corruptions; but it had done little to stop them, and it was largely by-passed by the reforming movement. The reforming movement took many forms in a long and complex history which is not yet fully understood;[4] only the most general lines which the reforming movement took are indicated here, inasmuch as they served to encourage or discourage different varieties of philosophical activity.

It was broadly agreed that the age required a 'reformation of the church in head and members'; it was not agreed how this reformation would come about, or what changes it would make. Some expected a reformation from above, in which a good pope would restore Christian discipline to the whole church; others sought a general council which would correct the abuses of the papal court, as well as reunite the Latins with the Greeks and the quarrelling Latins with each other. Some reformers desired merely that the existing theology should be more widely taught and the existing discipline more strictly enforced; these reformers had no effect on the scholastic synthesis except to institutionalise it further.

But more radical reformers saw roots of the abuses in the scholastic theology and therefore demanded a new theology. It was easy enough to find objections against 'the more recent Christian theologians, who write in the Parisian style by little questions':[5] in place of the scriptures they studied merely human traditions, Aristotle and Peter Lombard and their commentators, and they used these men's authority to dispute questions not touched on in scripture. It was common to contrast the simplicity of the apostles with the subtlety of the Scotists, and to ridicule scholastic questions 'whether God could have taken on the nature of a woman, of the devil, of an ass, of a cucumber, of a piece of flint; and then how the cucumber would have preached, performed miracles, and been nailed to the cross'.[6] Needless disputation on such issues distracted one from the essentials of the faith and from the life which they command; and it could only weaken the Christian virtues of humility and charity.

Beyond this, some reformers saw in the scholastic theology substantive errors of doctrine which excused the corruptions of the church and hindered the work of reformation. Erasmus thought that the mistake was to justify external 'ceremonies' as means of grace, leading the faithful to seek salvation through the magical powers of the priests and not through pure and blameless lives. Luther, too, rejected the doctrine of the means of grace, while simultaneously rejecting Erasmus's programme for a *moral* reformation: both Erasmus and the scholastics seemed to place salvation in some type of good works and not in faith in God's forgiveness of sin. But for all their disagreements, reformers of Erasmian, Lutheran, and many other persuasions agreed in rejecting the theology of the mediaeval church along with its institutions; and they called instead for a theology after the model of the scriptures and the Fathers of the Church. The goal might be a simple non-doctrinal faith, or a correct doctrine of grace free from pagan corruptions; it might be a rule of practical morality, or a discipline of spiritual contemplation. All of these could be found in the Fathers of the Church: Augustine especially supplied models for many different strands of the reform movement, which regularly appealed to him over the heads of the scholastics.

One wing of the reforming movement produced the Protestant Reformation and thus divided Western Christendom into two opposing camps; but the reform agitation also continued in countries which remained Catholic, and the hierarchy gave it institutional form at the Council of Trent, as it had to if Catholicism was to compete effectively with Protestantism for the loyalties of Europe. Both Protestant and Catholic Reformations attempted to fulfil the demands of earlier reforming movements, rebuilding the structures of the church to make them more effective means of Christianising a society only superficially converted in the past. Both were concerned to broaden and deepen the extent of religious education among clergy and laity, and both were ready to discard any philosophy or theology which failed to advance this religious education.

Philosophy was at best an incidental concern of the reform movement. Some strands of the movement supported the old Aristotelian philosophy, especially in those Catholic countries where the reforms were in the hands of the teaching orders, but in some Protestant countries as well.[7] Many reformers attacked all philosophy. But it was the church reform movement, and its dissatisfaction with the mediaeval order, which encouraged scholars to discover Aristotle's faults, and which provided a receptive audience, first for the criticisms of Aristotle, and later for the proposed alternatives to his philosophy.

We must now examine the varieties of anti-Aristotelianism and the alternative new philosophies. As we shall see, it was not the case that Aristotle worked well at supporting Christianity, and that the new philosophies disrupted this alliance. On the contrary, it was widely recognised that Aristotle worked badly, and he was retained only because there was no clear alternative. A Christian impulse opened the door to philosophical criticisms and philosophical replacements of Aristotle; it does not follow that everything that walked in the door and made itself at home did so from Christian motivations.

II. VARIETIES OF ANTI-ARISTOTELIANISM

'The long history of anti-Aristotelianism has yet to be written.'[8] The Middle Platonists of the second century A.D. were already compiling arsenals of objections against Aristotle, and the arguments which they and their successors discovered were used and re-used by anti-Aristotelian polemicists of widely varying place, time, and ideology: identical criticisms of technical points of Aristotelian logic can be found in the French Epicurean Gassendi and in the Persian illuminationist mystic Suhrawardi. For the purposes of this discussion it is not necessary to catalogue all the inherited criticisms of Aristotle but merely to indicate the forms which anti-Aristotelianism took in the Renaissance, in so far as they helped to shape the expectation of a new philosophy.

1. Platonist and Christian anti-Aristotelianisms

All the religious objections to the introduction of Aristotelian philosophy in the thirteenth century continued to be put forward up through the seventeenth century. They can be distinguished into two types by their origin: they derive either from the Platonist tradition of philosophical religion or from the Jewish, Christian, and Muslim tradition of revealed religion.

The Platonists generally object to what they see as the Peripatetics' superficiality and dependence on the senses; and they couch some of their objections in religious terms, as protests against impiety. The Peripatetics are accused of denying the immortality of the human soul and of holding such insufficient opinions of God's causality as that he is only a final and not an efficient cause, that he causes only motion and not existence, and that he governs only the celestial and not the sublunar realm. Sometimes the Platonists accuse Aristotle of holding these opinions himself; but at least equally often they try to 'defend' Aristotle against Peripatetics like Alexander of Aphrodisias, who had interpreted Aristotle (correctly) as holding those opinions. Where Aristotle criticises Plato for metaphorical language and mythological conceptions, the Platonist may reply by explaining Plato's true philosophical insight which Aristotle could not perceive behind its metaphoric expression. But, equally well, a Platonist may say that Aristotle knows and agrees with Plato's true opinion, and that he is really criticising only the vulgar Platonists who took Plato's metaphors as literal descriptions of truth: he can then defend *both* Plato and Aristotle against vulgar Platonist anti-Aristotelians (like Plutarch and later John Philoponus) and against extreme Aristotelians like Alexander, who take Aristotle to be criticising Plato. By debating this whole spectrum of solutions, the pagan Platonists passed on to their Muslim and Jewish and Christian successors a version of anti-Aristotelianism, and a version of Aristotelianism as well.

Philosophy as it was passed on first to the Muslim and then to the Christian world was fundamentally Aristotelian philosophy; but because of its religious context it often took on a Platonist coloring. The Christian and Muslim religions, which give a special value to a religious *knowledge* going beyond mere faith, are naturally open to philosophies which promise an understanding of God, man, and the world and which may serve in interpreting and systematising the teachings of the scriptures. But they are also highly suspicious of philosophies of pagan origin which may undermine the scriptures, perhaps even in claiming to reveal the scriptures' true meaning. Thus when Aristotelianism appeared in Islam and Christendom, a theological anti-Aristotelianism appeared alongside it.[9] The most serious charges against the philosophers are that they subvert God's creation by teaching the eternity of the world, that they deny God's knowledge and providence over sublunar individuals, and that they deny the immortality of the soul and the eventual resurrection of the dead; and, more generally, that they deny God's ability to affect created things by an act of his will. The philosophers attempted to meet these charges, both because other members of their society had these religious concerns and because they themselves did. The charges were similar to the Platonist accusations against Aristotelianism, and the philosophers often used the Platonist defense of Aristotelianism in reply: they say that whereas some interpreters have taken Aristotle in an irreligious sense, Aristotle himself believed in creation and providence and immortality and intended to criticise only low, mythological conceptions of these doctrines. It was impossible to maintain that Aristotle had believed in miraculous temporal acts of God's will, such as creation in time or the resurrection of the dead; here the Muslim philosophers assert that the Aristotelian doctrines are the true inner meaning of the scriptural expressions, whereas Christian thinkers like Thomas and Scotus say that Aristotle *leaves open the possibility* of extraordinary divine acts beyond what natural reason can know. For the Christian scholastics, reconciling Aristotle with scripture meant reconciling him with Augustine, the most authoritative patristic interpreter of scripture; and Augustine already had used Platonic philosophy to elucidate the scriptural doctrines of God and the soul. The scholastics are thus able to present Aristotelian philosophy (in Avicenna's Platonising interpretation) as human reason's partial discovery of the truths which only the scriptures (in Augustine's Platonising interpretation) would fully reveal.

The Thomist and Scotist compromise, which Platonised Aristotle's philosophy to some extent, and to some extent admitted the possibility of divine action outside the Aristotelian framework, was not stable. Bishop Tempier's condemnation of the Averroists in 1277 had already stressed the contradictions between Aristotelian philosophy and the possibility of miraculous divine action; and the *via moderna* of the fourteenth century pushed this assertion of divine omnipotence to its logical conclusions in undermining the Aristotelian philosophy of nature.[10]

Typical of this new approach is the *Livre du ciel et du monde* which Nicole Oresme composed in French in 1377 at the request of the King of France, who,

Oresme tells us, had made him bishop of Lisieux.[11] The treatise is, in form, a translation and commentary on Aristotle's *De caelo*; but the commentary is often curiously hostile. Oresme has no systematic alternative to Aristotelian physics, and he remains within the terms of the scholastic Aristotelian synthesis in criticising particular Aristotelian propositions. But within this framework he exercises remarkable ingenuity in envisaging possible ways in which Aristotle's doctrines might fail to hold. Sometimes Oresme explicitly bases these '*ymaginacions*' or thought-experiments on God's absolute power to create things outside the natural order, as when he discusses the possibility that there are other worlds outside our own.[12] But even where this is not explicit, Oresme's imagination has clearly been freed by a habitual consideration of divine omnipotence; and although his refutations of Aristotle are sometimes just ingeniously playful (like the proof that an infinite heavy body can have a finite weight),[13] often they are motivated by a defense of Christian doctrine. Oresme uses Ptolemaic eccentrics and epicycles to 'explain by philosophy and astronomy a truth consonant with our faith and contrary to the opinion of Aristotle and Averroes', that no intelligences other than God are absolutely unmoved;[14] and he explains how God might have tampered with the Aristotelian world order to stop the sun in the time of Joshua, or to flood the earth in the time of Noah. Aristotle was an excellent philosopher, but his attacks on Plato are unreasonable; on the authority of Augustine, Oresme reminds us that Plato's philosophy (of which he knows little or nothing) is more suited to the Catholic faith than Aristotle's.[15]

2. Humanist anti-Aristotelianism

The origins of the humanist movement in the fourteenth century are continuous with this current of Christian and Augustinian anti-Aristotelianism. Francesco Petrarca (1304–74), whom the humanists saw as their forerunner or founder, shares with the scholastic Augustinians the same Christian suspicions of pagan Aristotelian philosophy.[16] Petrarca takes offence at the modern theologians and philosophers of the teaching orders, who follow Aristotle and Averroes in their theology, scorning the authority of Augustine and of the apostles, and implicitly of Christ himself. He objects in particular to their doctrine of the eternity of the world; and he angrily rejects their pretence to believe as Christians that the world was created in time, while their reason tells them the contrary.

Petrarca is no doubt exaggerating in his portrayal of these modern theologians: it is unlikely that a member of a religious order in the fourteenth century would defend Averroes against Augustine, let alone against St. Paul, as Petrarca claims.[17] For Petrarca, as for a great many thinkers from the thirteenth through the seventeenth century, anti-Averroism is both a motivation and an excuse for a broader anti-Aristotelianism. Petrarca, like some Franciscan scholastics, had a personal religious devotion to St. Augustine, and he promotes Augustine as a model in opposition to Aristotle: Augustine is a true philosopher, and Aristotle and Plato are not.[18] But Petrarca is not content merely to secure a specifically Christian and Augustinian modification of the Aristotelian philosophical framework: he wishes to reassess what philosophy is supposed to do for Christianity, and to find someone who will do it better than Aristotle. Petrarca's judgement on Aristotle stems from his concern with the moral reform of Christianity; in this he contrasts with Oresme, who accepted a bishopric through royal patronage just in time to take the French side in the Great Schism.

Petrarca condemns the arrogance of the philosophers in their claims of knowledge: their doctrines are largely false, being derived not from reason but from the dubious authority of Aristotle, and they express themselves so obscurely that they themselves cannot understand what they mean; but 'even if [their doctrines] were true, they would not contribute anything whatsoever to the blessed life.'[19] Petrarca complains, as if equivalently, that they prefer this useless learning to scripture, or that they prefer it to virtue. What the pagan philosophers might genuinely contribute is an incitement to virtue, the path which leads to true happiness in God, even though they themselves were unable to follow up this path. But Aristotle does not do this: if we attend a university lecture on Aristotle's *Ethics,* we may emerge more learned but not morally better, more able to define virtue but not more inclined to love it.[20]

Petrarca and later humanists therefore reject Aristotelian philosophy as a suitable ally for Christianity and replace it with Ciceronian rhetoric. It is Cicero and Seneca, and the better poets, but not Aristotle, who possess in their eloquence those 'goads and firebrands of words, by which the mind is spurred and inflamed toward love of virtue and hatred of vice'.[21] In turning towards Cicero, Petrarca is following his admired Augustine and many other Latin Fathers who had been Ciceronians before they became Christians. Though troubled by Cicero's paganism, they could not help trying to correlate their Christian faith with Ciceronian rhetoric. When Petrarca speaks of Cicero's ability to inflame the mind with a love of virtue which only Christianity can satisfy, he recalls Augustine's description of his reading of Cicero's (lost) *Hortensius,* which had turned Augustine from a mere orator into a true philosopher, a lover of wisdom, and thus set him on the path to Christianity: 'suddenly every vain hope seemed worthless to me, and I desired the immortality of wisdom with an incredible burning in my heart, and I began to rise up to return to [God].'[22] The mature Augustine takes Cicero's ideal of the perfect philosopher-orator for granted; he is concerned to defend Christianity, not Ciceronianism. The humanists, however, finding a Christianity universally professed but scarcely felt, are moved to revive Ciceronianism as a means to reawakening Christianity.

Ciceronian humanism, like Aristotelian philosophy, rapidly took on a life of its own. Many humanists in the fifteenth and sixteenth centuries were chiefly in love with the force of Cicero's eloquence, the breadth of his learning, and the purity of his Latinity, whereas others viewed him as a mere auxiliary to Christianity. It is perfectly possible to be concerned with rhetoric but not morality, with morality but not religion, or with religion but not Christianity, and the Renaissance saw all these intellectual possibilities actualised. Our interest here, however, is not with these varieties of Ciceronianism as such but with Ciceronianism as a standpoint for criticism of Aristotle, yielding criticisms compatible with, but distinct from, the Platonist and Christian criticisms discussed above.

Cicero offers few direct criticisms of Aristotle, towards whom he is generally well disposed; what he offers are criticisms, from an oratorical standpoint, of dogmatic philosophy. Cicero's philosophical ambition was to 'imitate' Greek philosophy into Latin, as the Latin poets had imitated Greek poetry, and so to make philosophical materials available to the Roman orator. The orator who has acquired the ability to argue philosophically will indeed be the perfect philosopher, able 'to join practical wisdom [*prudentia*] with eloquence', and 'to speak about the greatest questions with fullness and adornment'.[23] To attain this goal, Cicero practises the method of the sceptical New Academy, which he traces back to Socrates and Plato, 'this method in philosophy of arguing against everything and passing clear judgment on nothing', by reciting the arguments which the different dogmatic schools have produced on both sides of every question. From the orator's point of view, this is the best kind of philosophy, since having both sides of a question is twice as good as having only one: 'If it is a great thing to know the disciplines one at a time, how much greater will it be to know them all at once? But this is what they must do who propose, for the sake of discovering the truth, to speak both against all the philosophers and also for them all.'[24] But Cicero's scepticism is restrained by his concern, as a political orator, with the maintenance of virtue: he rejects as irresponsible Carneades' willingness to extend his scepticism to moral questions, and to speak against justice as well as for it. Cicero attempts to adapt the Stoic moral ideal to the situation of a Roman statesman: although he is troubled by the Stoic paradoxes that external goods are nothing to the sage and tempted to moderate the Stoic harshness, the pure ideal still appears in his oratory, and it seems to exercise a personal attraction for him, as it certainly did for such readers as Augustine and Petrarca.

Cicero provides much material for attacking the dogmatic schools, of which the humanists made use both in incidental swipes and in sustained polemics against the Aristotelians.[25] In the first place, the dogmatic philosophers seem to despise eloquence. Cicero speaks of Aristotle's 'golden stream of eloquence',[26] but as this is not evident in Latin translations of Aristotle, still less in disputations conducted in the barbarous 'Parisian' language, the scholastics may be accused of falling short of their master; the scholastic logic is particularly attacked and contrasted with the true art of discourse which the orators possess. Related to their neglect of eloquence is the scholastics' lack of concern for virtue, and for the welfare of the public: they prefer instead to cultivate esoteric speculations and disputes about words. These charges become much stronger if the Aristotelian speculations are not just useless but false or uncertain; and there is again Ciceronian material to buttress these charges against dogmatic philosophy. There is no question which the different philosophers do not argue on opposite sides; there is no position so absurd that some philosopher has not maintained it.[27] Cicero and Seneca opened the door for the humanists to the non-Aristotelian dogmatists, the Stoics and Epicureans, and to the sceptical philosophers (including Plato on Cicero's account) who used the arguments of the different dogmatists against each other. Whether these other philosophers were ultimately any better than Aristotle or not, they provided new perspectives from which Aristotle could be attacked.

Perhaps the best humanist attack on Aristotelianism, and on dogmatic philosophy in general, is Gianfrancesco Pico della Mirandola's *Examen vanitatis doctrinae gentium et veritatis christianae disciplinae.*[28] Unlike many such attacks, it engages the philosophers on a wide range of issues and does not simply reject the philosophical mode of discourse. But Pico's goals and methods are essentially no more philosophical than those of Vives or Nizolio. Pico's goal in each of his six books is to contrast Christianity with philosophy, revealing the errors and confusions of the philosophers and showing that Christianity alone is sound and true. And his methods in criticising the philosophers are typically humanist: he uncovers ancient sources who disagree with Aristotle and with each other, and he takes over their arguments almost without change. Pico sets out a general 'history of variations' of the pagan philosophers, showing that they disagreed on even the most fundamental bases of their teaching. He recalls the sceptical criticisms of the criteria of truth, and of each specific art and science: here Sextus Empiricus serves Pico both as an example of a philosopher who disagreed with the other philosophers and as a witness to the disagreements of earlier philosophers among themselves.

After this general refutation of the philosophers, Pico devotes a final three books to a special criticism of Aristotle, since it is he who has the most defenders in modern times. Pico begins by citing the many philosophers who have criticised Aristotle, and by giving a series of humanist criticisms (mostly ill-founded) of the integrity and intelligibility of the Aristotelian corpus. But Pico goes on to a more interesting kind of criticism of Aristotle, drawn from the dogmatic Platonist sources which had become available. The Platonists had criticised Aristotelian philosophy as relying on the senses and remaining contented with the superficial appearances of things; and Pico, without adopting the Platonists' alternative of an intellectual vision of the incorporeals, is happy to take up their criticisms of Aristotle. In Book Six, Pico extracts, from John Philoponus and from the Jewish philosopher Hasdai Crescas, particular criticisms of Aristotle's doctrines of place, time, void, the quintessence and the eternity of the world; but of more fundamental importance is the sustained argument of Book Five 'against the art of knowing and of demonstrating transmitted in the *Posterior Analytics*'.

Pico gives a great many criticisms of the uncertainty of sensation and of definition, sources of knowledge according to Aristotle: but his basic criticism is that if we begin where Aristotle says we must begin, with the accidental properties of things that fall under our senses, we will never be able to reach the intuitions of universal essences, which are for Aristotle the necessary foundations of the sciences. Aristotle holds that the mind can begin with sensible phenomena and trace them up by a process of analysis to the intelligible first principles from which they arise; once we have grasped these principles by an intellectual intuition, we can reverse the analysis, working downwards until we have deduced the sensible phenomena with which we began. Pico charges that if we begin by assuming sensible phenomena, our postulations of principles will remain contingent on these phenomena, and the deduction of the phenomena will be a circle. Although this criticism often comes from Platonist quarters, it can equally be taken up by an extreme nominalist like Nizolio, who (unlike scholastic nominalists) rejects all universal affirmations. Pico himself revives the old Augustinian illuminationism to mediate between the Platonist and extreme nominalist positions: he agrees that we can know something beyond sensible particulars, but only through the divine grace of illumination, which no philosophical method can procure.

Through Pico's critique of Aristotelian science, the humanist complaints about logomachies and barbarous terminology acquire a more serious philosophical content: it is charged that when the scholastics invoke essences, qualities, and other non-evident entities, they are using abstract nouns as labels for causes of which they have no real conception. A favourite example is the abstract noun '*gravitas*', heaviness: as Hobbes, Descartes, and many others note, to say that heavy bodies fall because of heaviness does not indicate a true cause, but 'is as much as to say, that bodies descend . . . because they do'.[29] Ockham had already accused his scholastic brethren of misconstruing abstract nouns as names for abstract entities: but a more radical nominalism charges that this is not merely a grammatical mistake but a disguise for scientific ignorance. The scholastics base their claim to scientific knowledge on their claim to discern the universal essences from which the activities of natural things arise; but, it is said, their discoveries are merely verbal and do not reveal any such essences. Perhaps, as the extreme nominalists say, there are no such essences to be known; and this view can be supported by the Christian charge that such essences as the scholastics posit would be eternal and independent of God. On the other hand, perhaps there are such essences (dependent somehow on God), and perhaps a true philosopher who exercises intellectual intuition or is favoured with divine illumination could come to grasp them.

Pico's attack on the Aristotelian claims to knowledge was not necessarily unanswerable, and such scholastics as Jacopo Zabarella devoted themselves to restating the Aristotelian method of analysis and defending it from the charge of circularity.[30] But for many opponents of Aristotle, this kind of criticism seemed to get at the heart of what made Aristotelian science useless as a means to wisdom. Perhaps all science is tautologous, and wisdom must be sought elsewhere; but perhaps a new and more substantive science could lead us on to practical wisdom. If the Aristotelian method does not lead to the sources of true knowledge, then perhaps a new method will discover everything we really are capable of knowing, collecting the true sources of knowledge – sensations, or pure rational intuitions, or scriptural revelation, or all three together – and systematising them into a new *pansophia*.[31] From the cumulative Platonist, Christian, and humanist criticisms of Aristotle there arose, side by side, both a general hostility to philosophy and an expectation of a new philosophy. In the end, 'the new philosophy' came to mean an actually existing movement, the mechanical philosophy, which could be contrasted with the old philosophy; and when the old philosophy vanished, and the mechanical philosophy developed its own internal divisions and crises, the phrase 'new philosophy' gradually vanished too. But it is important to recollect, beneath the neutral historical use of the phrase 'new philosophy', the original rather apocalyptic expectation of a new discipline which would reunite theoretical science and practical morality, Christian faith and natural reason, ancient wisdom and modern discoveries, and so on. No doubt much of the excitement was premature. Comenius in *Labyrint světa a ráj srdce (The labyrinth of the world and the paradise of the heart)* describes the 'new philosophy' of the Rosicrucians, which promised to extend human life for several centuries and to restore human wisdom to the perfection it possessed in the Garden of Eden, as a collection of boxes, painted with exotic titles, but proving to be empty when opened; and the Rosicrucians' 'new philosophy' was not so different from many other varieties.[32] Aristotelianism had not been nearly as bad as its opponents represented it, and their expectations of what they could accomplish through philosophical tyrannicide were unreasonably high. But though their first steps towards a new philosophy were stumbling and may be compared unfavourably with the accomplishments of late scholasticism, we may see with hindsight that their bold experiments prepared the way for the emergence of mechanical philosophy and science.

III. A MAP OF RENAISSANCE PHILOSOPHY

What alternatives did Renaissance thinkers find to replace Aristotelian philosophy? It is impossible to survey here all the philosophies which were proclaimed in the fifteenth and sixteenth centuries. But we may try to isolate some of the basic intellectual strategies which philosophers of different persuasions adopted to meet the criticisms of the old philosophy: for it is the range of strategies for replacing Aristotle, and not the details of the new philosophical systems, which were fruitful for the philosophers of the seventeenth century.

Three main regions may be distinguished on the intellectual map of Renaissance philosophy. First, there is the Aristotelian scholasticism whose different schools, characterised above all by the great conflict between Thomism and Averroism, remained the official philosophy of the universities. Second, there are the revived Hellenistic philosophies, with a moral emphasis, which arose out of the humanist movement: scepticism, Stoicism, and (more marginally at first) Epicureanism. Third, there is the revived Platonic school, mediated through the late ancient and Byzantine traditions. After sketching these varieties of philosophy, I will also discuss the category of 'naturalism' which has been applied to Renaissance philosophy and suggest some cautions which should attach to this concept.

1. Scholasticism: The Averroist controversy and its outcome

Aristotelian scholasticism was not annihilated by its Renaissance critics; at least in the Catholic countries, the traditional schools were intellectually vigorous throughout the sixteenth century, recovering and developing in new directions after the grim period of European decline and of the Great Schism. The new developments of the traditional schools and the controversies between them are mentioned here only as they relate to the Renaissance criticisms of Aristotle and the search for a new philosophy.

The two countries in which sixteenth-century scholasticism was strongest, Italy and Spain (together with Portugal), present two very different pictures. Spanish scholasticism, although of great intrinsic merit, was little influenced by, and in turn influenced little, the search for a new philosophy. The stimulus for Spanish philosophy came externally from Spain's emergence as a world power after the discovery of America, and internally from the Spanish Counter-Reformation. Both the old teaching orders and the new Society of Jesus were responsible for the theological education not only of the clergy at home but of missionaries everywhere from Mexico to Japan; so they taught theology according to the doctors of their orders, and they taught the philosophy on which this theology was based. The old battles of *via antiqua* against *via moderna,* and within the *via antiqua* of Thomism against Scotism, were pursued with vigour, both on theological and on philosophical questions. Within the Thomist camp, the strict Thomism of the Dominicans clashed on a number of questions with the more eclectic and innovative theology and philosophy of the Jesuits. All parties to these controversies remain within the broadly Thomist consensus (shared also by Scotus and others) reconciling Aristotelianism with Christianity; they are not trying to establish a new philosophy. But they too share the general wish to do philosophy more piously than Aristotle. The Jesuit Francisco Suárez writes his *Disputationes metaphysicae* for the utilitarian reason that one must 'lay firm foundations in metaphysics' before proceeding to theology; he therefore 'philosophizes in this work, but always so as to have before my eyes that our philosophy ought to be Christian, and the servant of divine Theology'. Thus, instead of writing the usual commentary on Aristotle, Suárez rearranges the topics of Aristotle's *Metaphysics* in a rationalised order which the student of theology will find easier to learn and remember and apply; and on each question he 'selects the opinions which seem to serve better piety and revealed doctrine', saving Aristotle for these opinions if possible but abandoning him if necessary.[33] The Dominicans are suspicious of the Jesuits' tendency to find neat new labour-saving solutions to old difficulties; they adhere firmly to Thomas and so remain more Aristotelian than the Jesuits. But the Dominicans, too, hope to make their philosophy Christian; and at least in Italy, some Dominicans try to follow Thomas against Aristotle.

Outside the scholastic world the effects of the Spanish Golden Age were limited. The continuing commitments to Aristotelian principles in physics and other disciplines make Spanish scholasticism, however Christian, unsalvageable for the anti-Aristotelians; although the Spanish scholastics certainly helped to define a vocabulary for later philosophers, their main influence came on topics Aristotle had not treated: the *theological* doctrines of God's predestination and foreknowledge of human actions, and the *political* doctrines of natural law developed in defense of the Catholic order.[34]

Italian scholasticism presents a very different appearance. The reason is *not,* as might be thought, that Italian humanist scholarship had corrected mediaeval misunderstandings of Aristotle. Humanist editions and translations were available in Spain as in Italy, and they made no essential difference to the content of scholastic philosophy: only uncritical acceptance of humanist propaganda could make us think that scholasticism was what it was because of incompetence or ignorance, so that it would be forced to radical change by the mere availability of new Greek texts or new translations of Aristotle. The mediaeval translations of Aristotle, and of later Aristotelians such as Averroes, were certainly imperfect, and they presented only a part of the fruits of Greek and Arabic philosophy; but they are accurate enough, and copious enough, to afford a sound knowledge of Aristotelian philosophy.[35] Given this basis, the scholastics could and did learn to quote Aristotle in new translations, or to cite the views of Plato and Plotinus on disputed questions, without altering their traditional commitments. Humanist scholarship helped open the door for those who wished to abandon these commitments, but it did not expel those who wished to remain with them.

Unlike Spain and Portugal, the states of northern Italy afforded wide freedom both for Christian (and not-so-Christian) anti-Aristotelianisms, and for varieties of Aristotelianism outside the broadly Thomist consensus. The Averroists, who would have been killed in Spain, had chairs in the Italian universities alongside the Thomists and Scotists; and the Averroists were in constant and public conflict with the other schools over philosophical questions and over the interpretation of Aristotle. By reopening the question whether Aristotelianism was really compatible with Christianity, these controversies played a major rôle in shaping both scholasticism and the anti-Aristotelian philosophies in Italy.

Whereas in the fourteenth century Oresme and the other followers of the *via moderna* had used a wide conception of divine omnipotence to attack Aristotle's natural philosophy, in the late fifteenth and sixteenth centuries, amidst the general wave of moral and religious criticism of scholasticism, the chief concern was with more directly religious issues, creation and providence and especially immortality. Thomas and his contemporaries had interpreted Aristotle as holding these doctrines, or at worst as leaving the questions open; but the Averroists denied that this could be Aristotle's view, and they convinced many of their hearers. Already Petrarca had said that Aristotle was ignorant of immortality, and this remained part of the stereotype of the 'Peripatetic' throughout the Renaissance and into the seventeenth century: thus, when Cornelius Agrippa describes the revenge which the different sects and professions will take for his *De incertitudine et vanitate omnium scientiarum et artium* (1526), he fears that 'the wicked Peripatetickes will make my soule mortall and exclude it out of Paradise.'[36] But if, as Petrarca and later humanists thought, a philosopher's proper contribution to his Christian readers is to inflame them toward a life of virtue leading to immortality in God, then a philosopher who denies or omits the doctrine of immortality will be of little use; and Aristotle seemed to many scholastics as well as to humanists to be such a philosopher.

The questions of creation, providence, and immortality are all linked by the interpreters of Aristotle. Creation is the production of something out of nothing; but Aristotle does not seem to admit any production besides the generation of sublunar substances from preexisting matter, governed by the cyclical motion of the heavens. But if there is only such generation and not also creation, then sublunar things are governed not by providence but by the heavenly bodies, which care only about their Movers and produce sublunar things as unintended by-products. Again, if the human soul is not created by God at birth, but is educed from the potency of matter (like other sublunar forms) as part of this natural cycle, then it will be resolved back into matter when its body is destroyed, having no independent subsistence. Thomas had saved immortality by invoking creation. The human soul is immortal because it subsists independently of the body: it is not a 'material form' educed from matter but an immaterial substance specially created by God, which for a limited time takes on the rôle of a form informing matter. Thomas effectively established this doctrine as orthodoxy, and by the fourteenth century all Christian scholastics accepted the doctrine as true; but the Franciscans and other non-Thomists doubted whether it was known to Aristotle or to natural reason, and the revival of Averroism intensified these doubts.[37] It was common to deny that Aristotle could conceive of creation, or of a form informing matter that was not a material form. Further, although Aristotle asserts the immortality at least of the 'agent intellect' and perhaps of the rational soul, it seems that several Aristotelian principles will be violated if individual human souls produced at birth continue to exist after death: most painfully, a plurality (and, if the world has existed from eternity, an *infinite* plurality) of separate souls will now exist, somehow maintaining their non-identity without being distinguished either by species or by individuating matter. These difficulties lead the Averroists to conclude that the intellect is not the form of the body but a single separate substance doing the thinking of the whole human race, a doctrine which all its opponents describe as 'monstrous', but which an Aristotelian cannot easily avoid.[38]

Unlike the Spaniards, the Italian Thomists generally become convinced, as a result of their controversy with the Averroists, that Aristotle did not hold the Thomist doctrine of the special creation and consequent separability of the human soul; at the same time, they refuse to believe that he could have held the Averroist doctrine. This is a difficult position for a Thomist to be in: the Thomists reacted in several ways, which can be illustrated with some representative figures.

The Dominican Girolamo Savonarola (1452–98) thinks that Aristotle was forced by the light of reason to assert both that the human soul is the form of its body and that it is an immaterial substance; but Aristotle was unable to reconcile these two doctrines. Savonarola uses this antinomy to show that the 'wisdom' of the philosophers is defective and cannot lead to salvation. Almost all the philosophers, says Savonarola, were forced to deny one or the other of these principles about the soul, thus falling short of the demands of natural reason itself. Only Aristotle, 'a man of the most acute intellect', avoided both these errors; and he could do so only because 'considering that the light of human reason is too dim for a perfect knowledge of the intellective soul, therefore, in order not to be refuted, he treated it cautiously and obscurely',[39] so obscurely as to leave room for the 'monstrous' Averroist doctrine. Savonarola thinks that only Thomism, modifying Aristotle's philosophy by the Christian doctrine of creation, is able to solve the antinomy. Savonarola thus makes common cause with the humanists to discover a Thomist anti-Aristotelianism. Savonarola's humanist admirer Gianfrancesco Pico will claim in his *Examen vanitatis doctrinae gentium et veritatis christianae disciplinae* that he is continuing the example of the *Summa contra gentiles:* whereas Thomas had refuted only those doctrines of the philosophers which contradicted Christianity, politely accepting their other doctrines for the purposes of the argument, Pico will refute *all* their doctrines, whether contrary to Christianity or not.[40]

Pietro Pomponazzi (1462–1525) also began his career as a Thomist, and he retains his respect for Thomas throughout; but, having been worsted in debate by the Averroists, he feels constrained by their criticisms to admit that Thomism cannot stand as an interpretation of Aristotle.[41] In his mature works, Pomponazzi takes an Averroist position on most questions, though he professes, unconvincingly, to accept the Thomist position on faith even while his reason agrees with Aristotle and Averroes.[42] On the crucial question of immortality, however, Pomponazzi believes that the Thomists and the Averroists have rationally refuted each other's positions without establishing their own. Pomponazzi begins his treatise *Tractatus de immortalitate animae*[43] by noting the same apparent antinomy Savonarola had used to refute the philosophers: the human soul must be both somehow mortal, a material form like the souls of beasts, and somehow immortal, an immaterial form like the intelligences governing the heavenly bodies. Pomponazzi then reviews the different solutions which the philosophers had proposed. Pomponazzi, like Savonarola, thinks that Thomas has decisively refuted, on purely rational grounds, the monstrous Averroist view that the immortal intellect is one thing and the mortal soul informing the body is another. But Pomponazzi finds Thomas's own positive position, that the same human soul is essentially an immortal intellect but temporarily acts as a mortal soul informing the body, to be impossible for Aristotle and unintelligible to natural reason: we cannot understand how a separate substance could inform a body, or whence it could be created at birth.

Pomponazzi offers his own alternative, which he thinks is genuinely Aristotelian, and which he hopes will reconcile the insights that the human soul is somehow mortal and that it is somehow immortal. But in effect Pomponazzi denies that the human soul is immortal. It is immortal only in the sense that it exercises the act of intellection, an incorporeal act performed by the soul alone and not by the composite; thus, it shares in the intellectual nature, intrinsically immaterial and immortal, which is manifested in the intelligences of the spheres. But the individual human intellect which participates in this intellectual nature is not itself immortal: it is the form of a material sublunar body, and like all such forms it perishes with its body.

Many Renaissance philosophers reacted in horror to Pomponazzi's denial, on Aristotelian grounds, of human immortality. To understand what they were reacting against, one must recognise Pomponazzi for what he was. Pomponazzi has been described as a humanist influenced by a rediscovery of the original un-Christianised Aristotle; as a naturalist uninterested in separate substances; and as a 'humanist' in the twentieth-century sense, a believer in the dignity of man. Pomponazzi was none of these things. He was not a humanist but a conservative scholastic, who preserved the Averroist line wherever it did not seem 'monstrous'; his gestures of respect towards the rediscovered Alexander of Aphrodisias are merely gestures, and he supports Averroes against Alexander on every disputed question except the separation of the human intellect.[44] And he is far, indeed, from rejecting separate substances or proclaiming the dignity of man; he rejects the Thomist doctrine of immortality precisely because it would elevate humanity to the dignity of the heavenly spheres, which are the absolute rulers of men and all other sublunar things, the only mediators of God's action, the only possessors of separate intelligences. Man's dignity consists only in the fact that 'the philosophers, who alone are terrestrial gods, and as different from [all] others . . . as real men are from painted ones', can by exercising their intellect acquire some of the properties of the heavenly spheres; as for the *prophanum vulgus,* 'whoever does not participate in philosophy is a beast.'[45]

Thomists who decided that Aristotle did not agree with Thomas on creation, providence and immortality, might react like Savonarola and Gianfrancesco Pico, by making Thomas an anti-philosophical theologian; or they might, like Pomponazzi, prefer the philosophers to the theologians. But they might also, like the Dominican Cardinal Cajetan, declare that Thomas too was a philosopher, and a better philosopher than Aristotle: creation and immortality are not revealed doctrines which the philosophers did not understand but philosophical doctrines which 'this Greek' did not understand.[46] As Savonarola points out, reason perceives both that the human soul is separable and that it informs the body, doctrines which cannot be reconciled without the doctrine of creation; thus, natural reason, in the person of Thomas, can put these two doctrines together and derive on its own terms the doctrine of creation *ex nihilo.* In this way, Italian Thomism joins the consensus against the impious Peripatetics and attempts to make itself pass as a new philosophy.

2. Philosophies emerging from humanism: Scepticism, Stoicism, Epicureanism

The Renaissance expectation of a new philosophy, and many of the new philosophies themselves, first arose out of the Christian humanist critique of Aristotle. Yet the humanist attitude towards philosophy was ambivalent at best. The humanists believed, with varying emphases, in the supremacy of eloquence, of morality, and of Christianity; in attacking Aristotle, they were at the same time attacking philosophy itself. *Philosophia* is a Greek word, borrowed into Latin to signify a Greek institution; and it continued to bear the primary meaning, not of 'philosophy' according to some abstract definition, but of the particular disciplines taught by the followers of the Greek philosophical schools. This is what the humanists were criticising: Aristotle was merely the nearest target, most dangerous not because his doctrines were the worst but because they were the most widely taught.[47]

But when Aristotelian philosophy is described as an evil which is corroding Christianity, this may be explained either by saying that philosophy is an evil, or that Aristotelianism is just bad philosophy. The thinkers of the Renaissance slipped easily from the first to the second. In the first place, they had uncovered alternate ancient philosophies in searching Cicero and other classical authors for moral lessons, anticipations of Christianity, and refutations of Aristotle; and certainly Cicero had given high praise to philosophy in the service of eloquence. But beyond this, it is difficult to find anything to say against the love of wisdom as such; so it is natural to charge instead that those who are commonly called philosophers are not lovers of wisdom and thus not philosophers, that what is commonly called philosophy is 'not philosophy but Aristotelity'.[48] Those who speak thus will claim that what they are doing is the true philosophy (whether it is a revival of some Greek school or not), and they will reinterpret the commonplaces against philosophy as being against bad philosophy; so Augustine had explained the New Testament condemnation of 'the philosophers of this world' as applying only to the materialists and not to the Platonists, philosophers of *another* world.[49]

This new philosophy may be Christianity: thus, Erasmus speaks of 'the philosophy of Christ', and Gianfranceso Pico contrasts human with divine philosophy. The new philosophy may be Ciceronian rhetoric: thus, Mario Nizolio contrasts his 'truly philosophical and oratorical' teaching with the 'barbarous and pseudo-philosophical' Aristotelianism.[50] But the new philosophy might also be scepticism, Stoicism, or even Epicureanism, as parts of a broader humanistic program; or it might be Platonism, or something altogether new.

Scepticism was the first of these philosophies to emerge from the humanist movement; Petrarca already had declared himself a 'proselyte of the Academy',[51] meaning the sceptical Academy Cicero had praised. The humanists used sceptical materials from Cicero and Sextus Empiricus in criticising Aristotle; and they easily moved from using scepticism as a witness against the philosophers to adopting scepticism as their own philosophy. The modern sceptics, like their forebears, used the conflicts between the ancient schools to cast doubt on the dogmatists' claims to knowledge, and to induce suspension of judgement. But whereas ancient scepticism was the natural result of previous conflicts among the dogmatic schools, the Renaissance order is the reverse: the humanists begin with their Christian, moral, or rhetorical hostilities towards Aristotelianism and are therefore motivated to exhume the old philosophical controversies. And their scepticism remains subordinated to their original Christian, moral, or rhetorical motives. One might suppose that sceptical attacks on the sciences would devote themselves primarily to refuting claims of knowledge, either by general critiques of the sources of knowledge, or by raising controversies about the particular sciences under attack;

but in fact these theoretical criticisms are often eclipsed by more practical concerns.[52]

Typical is Cornelius Agrippa's *De incertitudine et vanitate omnium scientiarum et artium:* finding the sciences too much praised, Agrippa will argue the other side, that 'there can chaunce to the life and saluation of our Soules, nothing more hurtfull and pestilente, than these Artes and Sciences.' Agrippa does this in detail, adducing all the considerations he can think of against each science in turn: and although he certainly does point out, inter alia, that 'al Sciences are nothinge els, but the ordinaunces and opinions of men', and therefore 'doubtful and full of errour and contention', his main point is that none of the arts and sciences, from arithmetic and metaphysics to gambling and 'the whoorish Artes', can make us happier or morally better. Agrippa recommends instead the divine wisdom of the scriptures, to be received in faith and not subjected to dialectical disputations.[53]

Many other writers, although they avoid Agrippa's rhetorical excesses, yet share his suspicion of the sciences and take up scepticism in the service of faith or morals. Pierre Charron's frontispiece to his *De la sagesse* contains an allegorical depiction of Wisdom, her device reading *je ne sçay*; but the book is primarily devoted to teaching practical wisdom, first through self-knowledge and then through the rules of conduct which follow from it. Charron's scepticism appears in his low assessment of the capacities of human nature, and then in his treatment of education: parents wrong their children by teaching them the sciences, mere compilations of lore which exercise only the memory, when they should teach them to develop the practice of judgement, in which alone true wisdom consists.[54] The sceptical thesis of Charron and of his friend Michel de Montaigne is not really that nothing can be known (although they sometimes say or suggest this) but that nothing practically or morally important can be known, that the claim of science to produce wisdom is a fraud.

Humanist scepticism coexisted easily with humanist Stoicism. Both had their sources in Cicero, and both could be developed from rhetorical commonplaces into more seriously elaborated philosophies. The same writer might (like Charron) develop both sides of Ciceronian philosophy; but different varieties of anti-Aristotelianism might motivate the development of sceptical or Stoic alternatives. Petrarca had said equally that a true philosophy should lead us to virtue, or that it should lead us to Christianity; but these are not necessarily the same criterion. If our chief concern is to protect a simple Christianity from divisive and corrupting philosophical elaborations, scepticism will be the best philosophy: this was Gianfrancesco Pico's inclination in 1520, and subsequent sectarian conflicts made it all the more plausible. But if we want a philosophy to lead ourselves and others to the virtuous life, then Stoicism might well be superior. And for humanists beset by the tumults of a divided Europe and discontented with professional controversies, struggles for patronage, and the striving for pure Ciceronian Latin, Stoicism was an attractive source of consolation and edification.

The principal reviver of Stoicism as a systematic philosophy was Justus Lipsius (1547–1606). Lipsius's training was humanistic, and he was a professor of history when he wrote his chief philosophical works; but though he never rejects rhetoric or the other humanistic disciplines, he wishes to subordinate them to philosophy, and he protests against the Ciceronian subversion of this order. As counter-models to Cicero, Lipsius proposes Epictetus and above all Seneca, philosophers who leave their reader 'aroused and inflamed with love of virtue'.[55] In his *Manuductio ad Stoicam philosophiam* and his *Physiologia Stoicorum,* written 'to illuminate Seneca and other writers', Lipsius undertakes to defend and systematically present the Stoic philosophy. Against Christian criticisms, Lipsius replies that only bad philosophy is dangerous, or a philosophy which dominates over Christianity: a Christian may appropriate what is true in Stoic philosophy, while rejecting what contradicts Christian doctrine; the scholastics had exercised the same liberty with Aristotle. Against Cicero, 'an Academic and therefore an *ex professo* enemy of the Stoics', Lipsius defends the technical discipline of Stoic philosophy.[56] A philosopher must make subtle distinctions and pose paradoxes to his readers; he may not simply accept common opinions, as an orator does before a crowd. Cicero says that the Stoics do not move the souls of their hearers, even when they compel assent; Lipsius replies that true philosophical eloquence, which moves the soul of a solitary and meditative reader, disdains to appeal to the emotions of the crowd. Both Academics and Christians accuse the Stoics of imposing impossible demands on human nature and making arrogant claims for their sage; Lipsius admits that the Stoic sage cannot exist, but he defends the ideal of the sage as a means to awaken us from our moral complacency.

The ideal sage must be omniscient: we will therefore study not only ethics, but also physics.[57] Here Lipsius, in pursuit of philosophical seriousness, goes far beyond the earlier humanist Stoicism, which found value only in the moral philosophy. The Stoics tell us to follow nature, by which (says Lipsius) they mean God; but to know how to do this we must understand God and nature, and this is the domain of physics. Where the *Manuductio* had led us *to* Stoic philosophy, only the *Physiologia* will take us *inside* it, to begin the work of philosophy proper. Physics first treats the two principles, God and matter, then the elements of the world proceeding from the principles; Lipsius, true to his moral purpose, concentrates on God and His providence, and on man as the microcosm and image of

God. But he also lays out the whole Stoic cosmology, and he is eager to show that its emphasis on providence and the omnipresence of God make it a more pious alternative to Aristotle's. Unfortunately, the Stoics call God a fiery body and sometimes identify Him with the world. Although Lipsius cannot entirely defend this, he shows that they use 'body' loosely to mean any existent thing, and that when they speak 'more cautiously and closer to the truth', they make God a spirit or soul or reason present within the world, and not a literal fiery body. Lipsius cites precedents for a Christian corporealism, and he offers a mixture of criticism and reinterpretation not unlike the scholastic treatment of Aristotle.

Pierre Gassendi belongs in the body of this volume, not in its introduction; but we may note some parallels between him and Lipsius.[58] Epicureanism had a reputation as immoral and irreligious, and it had been little known; but when the humanists discovered Lucretius's *De rerum natura* and Diogenes Laertius's *Life of Epicurus,* they found not a gross hedonism but a practical moral ideal with some similarities to Stoicism. Thus, in such writers as Lorenzo Valla we find a humanist Epicureanism, like a shadow-image of humanist Stoicism. So, in Gassendi's early humanist work, the *Exercitationes paradoxicae adversus Aristoteleos,* he had set out to establish not only the Pyrrhonist doctrine 'that nothing is known' but also 'the opinion of Epicurus about pleasure, showing how the supreme good consists in pleasure, and in what way the praise of the virtues and of human actions depends upon this principle'.[59] But the mature Gassendi, like the mature Lipsius, rejects this cavalier treatment of philosophy and applies his humanist scholarship to presenting and defending a complete Epicurean philosophy. Epicurean physics, like Stoic physics, is corporealist, and unlike Stoic physics it denies divine providence. But Gassendi argues, sincerely and forcefully, that Epicurus is no worse than Aristotle; and he presents a Christian modification of corporealism that closely parallels Thomas's modification of hylemorphism. Epicurus's corporeal gods have no care for the world and contemplate only themselves, but so do Aristotle's incorporeal intelligences: Thomas adds a creator God on top of the system, and so does Gassendi. Epicurus makes the soul a body, and so mortal, but Aristotle makes it the form of a body, and so mortal: Thomas makes the rational soul a special case, an incorporeal substance united to a body, and Gassendi does the same.[60]

Humanist moral philosophy transcends itself in such writers as Lipsius and Gassendi, who worked to recover from the ancient sources a full philosophical system of logic and physics and ethics. To compete effectively with scholasticism, such a philosophy had to be at least as coherent and comprehensive as Aristotle's, and it also had to be at least as compatible with scripture. Thus, although we may say the 'Mosaic philosophy' which attempted to draw a systematic physics from the book of Genesis was itself one of the humanistic new philosophies, we may also say that *all* new philosophers were necessarily Mosaic philosophers, that 'Mosaic philosophy' was a condition presupposed by all of the new philosophies: thus, Lipsius cites 'Mosaic philosophy' as presenting God under the guise of fire, and Cudworth will prove that *atomism* was the 'Mosaical philosophy'.[61] A Renaissance thinker could pass easily and continuously from arguing defensively that his chosen philosophy was compatible with scripture, to arguing offensively that his philosophy was *more* compatible with scripture than others were, to proving that his chosen philosophy was implicitly *contained* in scripture, to constructing a whole new philosophy out of hints in the sacred books.

3. *The revival of dogmatic Platonism*

Christian and humanist critics of Aristotle, following Augustine and Cicero, praised Plato above all other pagan philosophers. But they had little direct knowledge of Plato's writings and no acquaintance with Platonism as a living philosophical tradition. Augustine cites Platonist sources in explicating Christian doctrines of God and the soul, but he does not pass on a systematic philosophy; Cicero, and the humanists who follow him, contrast Plato the sceptic with the later dogmatic schools. But Platonism had been a living tradition in Byzantium since the eleventh century; and when the political and religious upheavals of the fifteenth century brought Byzantine Platonism into contact with the West, the West was for the first time exposed to a systematic philosophy as serious as Aristotelianism in its scientific aspirations but sharing the religious concerns of the Christian critics of Aristotle.[62]

Here it is important to recall the distinction indicated above between the general religious criticisms of Aristotle, initiated by the Platonists, and the specific criticisms arising from Jewish, Christian, and Muslim revealed religion. The first man who brought the texts, and the living tradition, of Plato to the West was in fact the one certifiable pagan of the fifteenth century, George Gemistus Plethon (1355?–1452); but Plethon's criticisms of Aristotle in his essay on the differences of Aristotle and Plato, *De differentiis,* come from strong and basic religious beliefs which were shared equally by Christians and by pagan Platonists.[63] Plethon had come to Italy as philosophical adviser to the Greek Orthodox delegation at the reunion Council of Florence (1439–40) and had become a local celebrity through his knowledge of Greek literature and Platonic philosophy: the *De differentiis* and other writings emerge from his lectures to the Florentine humanists. Plethon was used to a philosophy which claimed its origin in Plato, accommodating Aristotle only in so far as he could be harmonised with his master; but in the West, Plethon discovered, the philosophers followed Averroes in preferring Aristotle to Plato. Plethon endeavours to correct this judgement by a short summary of all the usual Platonist criticisms of Aristotle, emphasising the ways in which Aristotle imperils the dignity of God and of the human soul. Plethon wobbles between accusing Aristotle of holding impious doctrines, or merely of speaking in such a way as to give Alexander and Averroes grounds for their impious interpretations.

The philosophy which Plethon and other Byzantine Platonists had introduced to Italy occupied an ambiguous position both in relation to Aristotelianism and in relation to Christianity. As was already noted, Platonism had the capacity to slide between Aristotelianism and anti-Aristotelianism, and the Platonists of the Italian Renaissance exercised this capacity to the full, taking up the whole range of possible positions. It was also possible to slide, within the spectrum of religious philosophy, from an active Christian apologetics to indifference or even outright hostility to Christianity. Platonism was not, of course, the first philosophy to have such an ambiguous relation to Christianity: even for Thomas, Aristotelian philosophy could establish only natural and not revealed religious truths, and other Aristotelians had inclined both to narrow the scope of natural theology and to ignore or deny the claims of revealed doctrine. But Platonism differed from Aristotelianism, not merely by giving a richer content to natural religion, but also by undermining the distinction between natural and revealed religion. The pagan Platonists, far from denying revelation, claimed that many ancient prophets and wonder-workers had received revelations which clothed Platonic doctrines in a mystical language; and they discovered, or wrote themselves, documents ascribed to Orpheus, Zoroaster, Pythagoras, Hermes Trismegistus, and other *prisci theologi.* Platonism in a Christian context had to decide the relation of Moses and Jesus Christ to these other bearers of revelation. Were the *prisci theologi* pagan pseudo-prophets, were they pagan anticipators of Christ, did they learn their teachings from Moses; or were they rather Moses' teachers, were they equals of Moses, perhaps even of Christ; or were they the real prophets, and Jesus the impostor? All of these positions were taken, so that the Platonists filled a spectrum, not only from Aristotelianism to anti-Aristotelianism, but also from Christianity to universal-prophetic religion.

Italian Platonism began with Plethon's *De differentiis,* and it remained for a long time a controversy among Byzantine expatriates. The West assimilated it slowly. When Cosimo de' Medici found scholars for his 'Platonic Academy' who could translate the new Greek texts and take up the philosophical tradition which they transmitted, these men did not take from Platonism anything radically contradict-

ing the previously reigning philosophy or theology. The Florentine Platonists
wished to refute both 'the perverse minds of many, who yield unwillingly only to
the authority of the divine law' and the Christian opponents of philosophy 'who
very impiously wish to separate the study of philosophy from holy religion . . . as
if someone would remove the love of wisdom from the honor due to wisdom
itself, or true understanding from a right will'[64] by showing that sound, Platonic
philosophy leads to knowledge of soul and God and confirms the Christian faith.
In this they were natural allies of the Thomists and Scotists against their enemies
from both Averroist and humanist quarters. Giovanni Pico della Mirandola makes
this alliance explicit in a famous letter to the humanist Ermolao Barbaro, who had
ridiculed the barbarisms of the scholastics: Pico defends the 'Parisians' in pleading
the cause of philosophy against rhetoric, and he concludes by comparing Lucretius
with Duns Scotus, a common butt of humanist ridicule. If Scotus were to write a
poem on the nature of things, he would break all the rules of the grammarians
and the poets; but Scotus would obey the more important laws of God and nature
if he made God a separate mind who knows and provides for his creatures, where
Lucretius had made him a body and unaware of our concerns.[65]

Pico had proposed, in the spirit of late ancient Platonism, to write a philosophical encyclopaedia harmonising Plato and Aristotle on all questions; but as this was
broken off after a promising beginning, the major systematic statement of Florentine Platonism remains the *Theologia platonica* completed in 1474 by Marsilio
Ficino, the translator of Plato, Plotinus, and 'Hermes Trismegistus'.[66]

Ficino borrows his title from Proclus, and his whole argument takes place
within the scholastic framework which Proclus had constructed to systematise the
Platonist doctrines of the different levels of reality. Ficino wishes to turn his
readers away from sensible bodies to recognise their own incorporeal nature as
rational souls; and since the soul is itself 'divine' and bears the image of God, we
will be able to ascend further from knowing ourselves to knowing God. Ficino
subtitles his work 'On the immortality of souls', and he devotes many chapters to
proofs that every rational soul (and only rational souls are souls in the strict sense)
is immortal: the real issue is not so much immortality as the soul's ontological
status as a substance existing independently of matter. Following Platonist method,
Ficino leads us up the chain of realities, from moved bodies through moving
powers (immanent in bodies) to self-moved movers and to unmoved movers,
from divisible bodies through forms divided in bodies to undivided forms, from
multiplicities to simple unities. Once he has traced a given object, such as the
human soul, back to its proper place in the hierarchy, he will then be able to
derive its particular attributes from its ontological status.

Ficino generally operates with a five-fold classification of realities into body, quality, soul, angel, and God. We may present this as a guide to Platonist ontology, but the particular enumeration should not be taken too seriously: all school-Platonists agree on the fundamental divisions of being, but they rename them freely or subdivide more or less finely to get the desired number of levels on a given occasion.

Since Ficino does not count matter as a separate level, he puts body in the lowest rank: bodies are merely extended matter, infinitely divisible by their very essence, and purely passive. Above bodies are 'qualities', powers, natures, or material forms: these are not divided in their essence, but as they cannot exist apart from the matter in which they operate, they are accidentally divided in matter; unlike bodies, they can transmit motion when they are moved, but they cannot initiate it of themselves. Above qualities are souls, defined as self-moved movers, self-subsisting forms which do not become divided when they give life to bodies: following Proclus, Ficino insists that the only true self-motion is the mind's thinking of itself, and that the only true souls are the rational souls of human beings, of the heavenly bodies, and of the world as a whole. The rational soul, for all Platonists, is the middle link in the chain of realities, eternal in its substance but changeable in its activity, superior to purely temporal things which are moved from without, but inferior to purely eternal things which are unmoved movers. Since Ficino has distinguished two levels below the soul, he also distinguishes two above it, where other writers may find one or three. Immediately above the rational soul is the Reason in which souls participate, the *nous* of the Greek Platonists; Latin writers use different terms for this entity, and Ficino chooses 'angel' instead of the more common '(agent) intellect'. Even though souls are self-moved, they cannot be the highest causes, since the souls' essence by itself is not sufficient to guarantee that their thinking will be perfectly rational, or that they will move themselves with the perfect motion, the uniform and rational rotation of the souls of the heavens. Instead, the souls must be guided by some higher being which remains eternally constant and contains within its essence the Ideas, the standards of rational thought; souls will think rationally and will govern the physical world according to rational laws only to the extent, greater or lesser, to which they participate in this divine Reason. Some Christian writers identify this being with their God, but Ficino and many other Platonists argue that since this being contains a plurality of intelligible exemplars, it is 'angelic' and inferior to the highest God, who is pure unity and above the intelligibles.[67] God may even be said to be above being, since it is the intelligibles which are most properly beings, but this manner of talking is hazardous both on Christian and on ordinary rational grounds; Giovanni Pico solves the problem by saying that God is above the beings (*entia*) but identical with Being (*esse*), but later writers like Patrizi are less hesitant in exalting God above being.[68]

Ficino and his associates were experimenting at introducing the Byzantine Platonic theology to solve the Western controversies. And they had grounds for hope that they could break the deadlock between an un-Christian Aristotelianism and an anti-philosophical theology, if they could explain and justify creation, providence, and immortality from a purely philosophical standpoint. Especially in accounting for the special status of the human soul Platonism seemed more promising than Aristotelianism: indeed, Avicenna and Thomas had preserved immortality for Aristotle only by importing the Platonist intellect not very harmoniously into the world of material forms. But Ficino had not yet fully established a Platonic philosophy in the West: he had written only a Platonic theology, with a heavy concentration on the soul, and not a complete Platonic philosophy treating both corporeal and incorporeal things. Later Platonists, following out Ficino's program, construct a distinctively Platonist physics, so as to present a systematic alternative to Aristotelianism. These philosophers are developing traditional Platonist religious concerns, and like other philosophers of the sixteenth century they present their work as a contribution to the reformation of the church. But also, as they develop their religious thought, the possibility increases for tension between universally religious and specifically Christian concerns.

An exemplary figure of sixteenth-century Platonism is Francesco Patrizi.[69] Patrizi was a participant in humanist controversies and very fond of contention; and he takes up with enthusiasm the old Platonist polemics against Aristotle. Besides its other faults, Aristotelianism is impious in its denial of providence; Patrizi therefore urges, in letters to cardinals and popes, that Aristotle's works should be banned and Aristotelian professors replaced by Platonists in the universities. Patrizi succeeded to a surprising degree and was named professor of Platonic philosophy, alongside Aristotelian colleagues, first at Ferrara (1578), and then under papal patronage at Rome (1592). Patrizi won the pope's favour by a work entitled *Nova de universis philosophia,* a new philosophy of everything (1591): Patrizi assures the pope in his letter of dedication that if his new philosophy replaces Aristotle, it will do more to win back the Protestants than either military force or moral example.

Everywhere Patrizi is concerned to exhibit the full glory of the Platonist system, and to do better than Aristotle. It is not enough to hypothesise God as a source of motion: Patrizi begins with light (*lumen*), which is the most evident thing of all, and ascends to a vision of God as an incorporeal light (*lux*). Patrizi then discusses the system of principles, and instead of Ficino's five, he distinguishes nine levels of being, plus a God who is beyond being and a matter which is beneath being. Then, after discussing the nature of soul in a manner similar to Ficino's, he goes on to produce a full anti-Aristotelian natural philosophy, supplementing the Platonists from the *Chaldean Oracles* and similar texts. The first principle of bodies is the space in which God may create the physical world; then God, who is an intellectual light (*lux*) and an intellectual fire, pours forth light (*lumen*) and heat into the space of the world. God also produces in space a fluid principle (*fluor*), in which and on which the heat exercises its activity: this fluid, in rarer or denser forms, is the substrate of bodies and is the source of their passivity and resistance. Each of these principles exists in a causal and exemplary form at each level of being, so that a purely incorporeal fire produces a supercelestial fire, which produces the fire of the stars, which produces ordinary sublunar fire. Thus, Patrizi finally constructs the elements of the sensible universe, and he shows how their action is governed by the incorporeal principles.

Patrizi failed to establish his version of Platonism as the philosophy of the Catholic Reformation. Patrizi's professorship at Rome, and the personal protection of the pope, could not keep the *Nova philosophia* from suffering the fate its author had wished on the works of Aristotle, of being placed on the index of forbidden books. Although the exact reason for the condemnation is not clear, the result is hardly surprising. But because the failure of Platonism to become 'the new philosophy' was of such great importance, and because this failure is often described in a potentially misleading way, it will help to have a short separate discussion of this topic.

4. *The question of 'naturalism'*

Patrizi and the other Platonists of the Renaissance, as well as such non-Platonic philosophers as Pomponazzi, are commonly described as 'naturalists' or 'philosophers of nature', where the latter phrase suggests not merely that they studied nature but that they took nature as the governing principle of their whole philosophy. But there is in reality no philosophical movement, and probably no single philosopher, whom these terms would accurately describe. This does not mean that the category of 'naturalism' has been applied purely arbitrarily: there is a real phenomenon which it has been used to designate. But one must be careful to delineate the phenomenon precisely, and 'naturalism' and its synonyms have tended instead to blur it.

Modern scholars most often describe as 'naturalists' philosophers whom their own contemporaries described, with hostile intent, as 'atheists'. To be sure, this term had an extremely broad polemical use, and there were probably no philoso-phers in the sixteenth or seventeenth centuries who were atheists in the modern sense, that is, who subscribed to the proposition 'there is no God.' But although some philosophers were accused of atheism for no objective reason at all, it seems that there was a real tendency of thought which understood God's nature and relation to the world in a way incompatible with orthodox Christianity. Instead of calling this tendency 'atheism', we call it 'naturalism'; but this remains a blank symbol waiting to be given a meaning.

The most obvious meaning of 'naturalist' is a philosopher who denies that there are incorporeal substances but admits only bodies and immanent principles inseparable from bodies. Such a philosopher, like Spinoza in the seventeenth century, could believe in God, but not in a God separate from the world. But no Renaissance Platonist or Aristotelian, perhaps no Renaissance philosopher of any school, was a naturalist in this sense. The two philosophers who come closest to such a 'naturalism' are Justus Lipsius and Bernardino Telesio (1509–88). Lipsius, as was explained earlier, finds corporealism an embarrassing feature of pagan Stoicism and attempts to remove it in the process of Christianisation. Telesio constructs a new physics of vaguely Stoic and pre-Socratic inspiration, which resembles the lowest two layers of the Platonist system, body and 'nature' or 'quality', and so he seems led to the conclusion that nothing can exist in separation from body; but Telesio, like Lipsius, Gassendi, and St. Thomas, makes exceptions for God and for rational souls.[70] While Lipsius or Telesio or some of their followers *may* have been insincere, there is no clear reason to suppose that they were.

The Platonists, especially, are very far from 'naturalism' in the indicated sense. The Platonists, like the Stoics, are concerned to maintain divine providence in their physics; unlike the Stoics, they are equally concerned to maintain God's independence and separation from the world. They reconcile the two concerns by positing a series of intermediary beings through whose movements God maintains order in the world, while remaining himself unmoved: thus, the eternal divine pattern governs the movements of the world-soul, which in turn direct the natural powers operating within bodies. The Platonists satisfy their general religious concerns with this theory, but they do not necessarily satisfy Christian concerns, and therefore the possibility of conflict arises. There is nothing to prevent an orthodox Christian from believing in a world-soul; but the theory of the world-soul justifies a universal providence, and if presented by itself it tends to undermine the special status of the biblical chosen people and of biblical miracles.[71]

This subversion of biblical miracle is the real phenomenon which has been labeled 'naturalism'. It was, apparently, unusual in the sixteenth century to deny that the biblical miracles had occurred: more common was to explain them in such a way as to deny that they were strictly miraculous. Two types of explanation were particularly favoured: if the miracles of (say) Moses did not result from a special divine intervention, then either they were predetermined by rare astrological configurations or else Moses himself produced them through the magical arts which he had learned from the wise men of Egypt. The Aristotelians tend naturally towards the astrological explanation, the Platonists towards the magical.

Pomponazzi in his *De naturalium effectuum causis sive de incantationibus* sets out the Aristotelian explanation of miracles, which he takes over from Averroes and passes on to Cardano and Vanini. Revealed religion is genuine: the successive religions or 'laws' are all founded by inspired prophets, who demonstrate their claims with genuine miracles; but this is a natural phenomenon, governed by great periods of the heavenly configurations. The spirits which inspire the prophets are the intelligences: they work by continuing the constant motion of their spheres, which through physical causality govern all sublunar things and which in particular produce the appropriate images in the prophets' imaginations; these celestial influences also produce, through natural means, the marvelous signs which are necessary, once in a great period, to induce people to leave the old decaying law and submit to the new. The Christian religion, like its predecessors, is 'true' in that it is a divinely sanctioned mode of conduct (and of belief for the non-philosophical masses); but it, too, is now decaying, and it cannot escape what the stars decree. Faith is weak, there are no true miracles now, only frauds; the end of our religion is near, and we cannot yet tell what new religion will replace it.[72]

The Platonists reject the Aristotelian astrological explanation of religion, of miracles, and of sublunar things generally: astral influences are real, and the heavenly bodies are certainly among the intermediaries God uses in governing the world, but cosmic soul and the human soul itself are also incorporeal powers in direct contact with divine principles. Platonists, like Christians, reject astrological determinism as reducing divine providence to a mechanical fatality, and denying human reason its power over bodily conditions. Thus, such Platonists as Giovanni Pico della Mirandola take the lead in the polemic against divinatory astrology.[73] But the alternate accounts of providence which Platonism offers can be equally subversive of the Christian doctrine of miracles: Platonism allows all too many ways in which, through different intermediary agents, divine principles can produce effects on visible things. This danger becomes especially clear where the *prisci theologi* are invoked: such sages as Hermes and Zoroaster are supposed to possess a divine wisdom enabling them to perform marvellous works, and some of the writings ascribed to them seem to provide a foundation for magical practices.

The Platonists are very careful to distinguish the magic of these ancient sages, which is 'the practical part of natural science', a legitimate and indeed the most noble part of physics, from 'all that magic which is in use among the moderns, and which the Church rightly exterminates'.[74] The actual magical practices are not always so different, but the Platonists' magic is supported by a cosmology which is supposed to make it both scientifically and religiously sound.

This cosmology is found in the *Chaldean Oracles* (perhaps the most popular source of ancient revelation among the Platonists, ascribed to Zoroaster by the arbitrary whim of Plethon), and in the *Corpus Hermeticum*.[75] These texts speak of three worlds: the supercelestial world of the divine intellect, the celestial world of the stars and the seven planets, and the sublunar or material world of generable and corruptible bodies. The supercelestial world governs the celestial world; since the supercelestial world is reason itself, the celestial world is rationally ordered. The heavenly bodies in turn govern the sublunar world, and subject it to an irrational fatality. But the human intellect, unlike anything else beneath the moon, can by-pass the heavens to participate immediately in the supercelestial intellect, and so escape the dominion of fate.

This cosmology is innocent enough, and simply expresses in more colorful terms conceptions common to all Platonists. But the mind may be tempted to escape the dominion of fate, not by mere philosophical contemplation, but by magical practices; and the traditions ascribing marvellous powers to the *prisci theologi* made it impossible for Platonism to shake off this temptation. Systems of correspondences are worked out to connect the three worlds, and the mind uses its freedom to manipulate sublunar things so as to bring out their hidden powers and draw down the appropriate celestial and supercelestial influences. Thus, despite the best efforts of such Platonists as Pico, there was always continuity between Platonist magic and popular European superstition.[76]

The Platonism of the Renaissance failed to establish itself in large part because of this recurring temptation towards magic, and especially because of the temptation to use magic to explain the manifestations of divine power described in the Bible. Giovanni Pico made perhaps the most serious attempt to keep magic in its proper place, both by subordinating magic to kabbalah and by denying that either magic or kabbalah could accomplish the works of Christ.[77] Kabbalah, as Pico presents it, is not so very different from the *prisca theologia* of Hermes and Zoroaster and Orpheus. But it is derived from the Hebrew learning of which Pico was so proud, and it thus has several religious advantages over the *prisca theologia*. Kabbalah claims to be the work not of some dubious old pagan but of Moses himself, and the key to the inner meaning of the Mosaic law: thus, not only is kabbalah itself religiously unimpeachable, but it allows Pico to legitimate other philosophical traditions as reflections, more or less distorted, of the original Mosaic wisdom. Further, since Christianity is the inner meaning of the Mosaic law, sound kabbalah should be able to discover this; and indeed Pico finds he can prove the divinity of Christ by this most Jewish of means, and so perhaps accomplish the last and highest task of Christian piety, the conversion of the Jews.[78]

For all Pico's ingenuity and religious sincerity, his solution did not stick. His proposed disputation on nine hundred theses drawn from all the sources of wisdom was banned by church authority, and he spent much of the rest of his short life in defending himself; and his successors fared no better. Magic and kabbalah were too bizarre and too dangerous, and there was no way of keeping them under control: if kabbalah proved the divinity of Christ today, it could be proving something quite else tomorrow. Platonism was the best candidate the Renaissance had for the new philosophy, but it was not good enough. The expectation of a new philosophy remained, but it could be satisfied only by something more Christian, more scientific, and altogether more sober and reliable.

IV. THE SEVENTEENTH-CENTURY REACTION

The new philosophers of the seventeenth century, including those who proposed some version of the 'mechanical philosophy', both continued the work of their Renaissance predecessors and at the same time reacted against it. Aristotelian philosophy had been the target, both of religious and moral objections, and of challenges to its scientific and practical value. While Renaissance philosophers had not succeeded in constructing a new philosophy immune to these objections, the philosophers of the seventeenth century continued to repeat the same criticisms of Aristotle and continued to be moved by the same religious and scientific concerns in working out their 'new philosophies'. In addition, the mere fact of the existence and failure of so many 'new philosophies' led the philosophers of the seventeenth century to seek in different directions for their new philosophy. In order to understand the 'new philosophies' of the seventeenth century, it will help both to sketch the religious and the scientific conditions of the seventeenth-century reaction to Renaissance philosophy, and also to discuss two transitional figures, Francis Bacon and Marin Mersenne – not because they created new philosophies, but because they captured the philosophical concerns of their time, and helped to reshape the conditions for a new philosophy which their contemporaries and successors tried to satisfy. Finally, we note the consummation and disappearance of the expectation of a new philosophy in the emergence of the mechanical philosophy. How precisely the mechanical philosophy attempted to satisfy this expectation in the different fields of philosophy, and what transformations and new controversies it brought about in these fields, will be major themes of this volume.

In the history of Christianity, the early to mid seventeenth century was an age of continual crisis, and of searching for a formula for stability. The fragile balance between Catholic and Protestant Europe had been destroyed by the ambitions of the Spanish crown to unite Europe under Habsburg and Catholic hegemony. The revolt of the Protestant Netherlands against Spanish rule and the overthrow by Bohemian Protestants of their Habsburg ruler combined to precipitate the Thirty Years' War (1618–48), the culmination of all earlier wars of religion, which involved, and threatened to destroy, every European state.

Philosophy was affected by the theological controversies, but also more generally by the search for a formula of peace. In England, suspicions of a royal conspiracy to restore Catholicism helped spur the parliamentary revolution, and thus the civil wars. The turmoil provided the environment for all varieties of religious sectarianism, and for hot debates on the Christian duty of obedience to authority, and on the interpretation of scripture generally. Many of the sectaries rejected the use of philosophy in the interpretation of scripture and questioned doctrines which had been accepted for centuries as the philosophical content of Christianity: many denied the existence of moral standards apart from God's particular will, and many took up the 'mortalist' thesis denying the soul's separate existence between death and resurrection.[79] Hobbes, Digby, Charleton, and the Cambridge Platonists all attempt to resolve these religious battles through their new philosophies. Many of these thinkers use Platonist or Cartesian philosophy to defend immortality and other traditional Christian theses against the sectaries; Hobbes does the reverse, defending Christian mortalism. But Hobbes, too, is concerned to argue against a false philosophy undermining Christianity and morality: in a strange twist, Hobbes attacks the doctrine of incorporeal substances as a pagan Aristotelian corruption, introduced by the scholastics to shore up priestly power, which has undermined the authority of the sovereign and led to civil war.[80]

As many of the English philosophers had royalist sympathies and some spent time in exile in France, the new philosophies that emerged in England were often influenced by French models. The French state had been safely Catholic since the conversion of Henri IV, and it offered only an unstable toleration to its Protestant minority. But the French crown, and its chief minister Cardinal Richelieu, were more interested in preserving their independence from Spain than they were in a pan-Catholic alliance: when France finally entered the Thirty Years' War, it did so on the Protestant side. Since the crown retained the right to make ecclesiastical appointments, the hierarchy could not implement the Tridentine reforms in France as it did in Spain; and the Jesuits, though they were eventually admitted into the kingdom, were widely suspected of being Spanish agents. Thus, when the Counter-Reformation finally took root in France, its base was not in institutions but in saintly individual reformers with popular followings. Often these reformers took Augustine as their model and so depreciated scholastic theology against him; instead, like Bishop Cornelius Jansen, they praised Augustine's 'positive' theology of grace, or, like Cardinal Pierre de Berulle, his 'mystical' theology of spiritual contemplation.[81]

In the introductory book 'on reason and faith in theological matters' prefaced to the second volume of his *Augustinus,* Jansen attacks philosophy as the chief source of theological conflict within the church and praises instead the authority of the Fathers, above all of Augustine, to whom Jansen specifically reassigns the titles of honor traditionally given to Thomas, Scotus, and other scholastic doctors.[82] On the face of it, this does not seem promising for philosophy, but there is the familiar ambiguity: perhaps it is only the bad old philosophy of Aristotle which has had these unfortunate results, and a new philosophy could do better.

By the early seventeenth century, there were far too many new philosophies available: the problem was to find a single good one. Baillet's *Vie de M. Descartes* has preserved the story of a certain Sieur de Chandoux, 'one of those free spirits who appeared in great enough number in the time of Cardinal Richelieu, and who undertook to throw off the yoke of scholasticism'. In 1628 Chandoux gave a lecture at the home of his patron, the Papal Nuncio, in which he attempted to impress Berulle and other notables with his 'new philosophy'. The then unknown Descartes rose to refute Chandoux and proved that Chandoux's new philosophy was mere probability, and different only verbally from scholasticism; and although Berulle lost interest in Chandoux, he did not lose hope for a new philosophy and encouraged Descartes to complete the work instead. Descartes followed Berulle's advice and attempted to derive his new philosophy from the Augustinian discipline for contemplating the soul and God; Pascal and other Jansenists would attack Cartesianism (as they attacked all other philosophies), but both the Jansenist Antoine Arnauld and the Berullian Nicolas Malebranche hailed Descartes as fulfilling their Augustinian expectation of a new and more Christian philosophy.[83]

Also present with Descartes and Berulle at the home of the Nuncio was the Minim (reformed Franciscan) Marin Mersenne, a professional observer of new philosophies, the friend and adviser of Descartes, Gassendi, and the exiled

Hobbes.[84] Mersenne was above all an apologist for Christianity, and he undertook in such works as the *Quaestiones celeberrimae in Genesim* to defend the scriptures against the magical and astrological accounts of miracles favoured by the 'new philosophies'. Mersenne is not insensitive to the accumulated criticisms of Aristotelian philosophy, but he is not convinced that the new philosophies are better. Mersenne admits that Aristotle has erred on a number of specific points, especially where he contradicts Christian belief in creation and providence. But Aristotle's critics (and Mersenne names several, including Patrizi) are earthbound creatures who cannot mount high enough to knock Aristotle down. Their favoured disciplines (Mersenne discusses alchemy in particular) are neither more pious nor more scientific than Aristotelian philosophy. If Aristotle is not yet a Christian philosopher, the alchemists who 'put our Redeemer in parallel with their universal spirit and their center of nature' are in positive contempt of Christianity.[85] Again, if the principles of Aristotle's philosophy are not known as clearly as the criteria of science demand, at least his matter and form are intelligible, incorporeal beings: he does not, like the alchemists, remain prisoner to sense and imagination.

Mersenne regards the Aristotelian principles as a probable hypothesis, more probable than any other we have. A Christian philosopher is well advised to follow the model of St. Thomas, and to appropriate the principles of Aristotle's philosophy, except where they contradict the Christian faith. But he remains free to diverge from Aristotle: the only authority is God, who is the source of all truth, whether He sends it through Aristotle or through some other vessel. Thus, 'We do not approve Aristotle's doctrine in all its parts, and we do not embrace it because it is Aristotle's, but because we do not find any which is more true, which is better connected, or which is more general and universal.'[86] Mersenne deliberately chooses this negative form of praise: he will not say that Aristotle's is the best possible philosophy, for he acknowledges 'that God is omnipotent, and can raise up some mind which will penetrate a hundred times further into the nature of things than all the Peripatetics, all the Platonists, all the Alchemists and all the Kabbalists have done'.[87] Thus, Mersenne takes up an attitude of provisional acceptance of Aristotle's philosophy, except on particular controverted points, while keeping watch for the mind through which God might grant a new philosophy genuinely more scientific and more Christian than Aristotle's.

In many places, Mersenne considers the charges of circularity and tautology brought against the Aristotelian method of analysis and concludes they are well founded. But he finds that the charges bear equally on the Platonist alternative:

The supposition of a universal soul gives us no more light and no more facility in philosophizing. For when I ask you, for example, why amber and crystal attract fur, I know no more and am no more satisfied, if you tell me that it is the soul of the world which produces this effect through the conjunction of the various accidents by which it is limited and circumscribed, than if you tell me that it comes about through the particular property of the specific form which brings it about that amber has this power.[88]

Currently, only mathematics can demonstrate its conclusions from rationally intuited first principles; but since mathematics is restricted to quantity and cannot deal with substances or with the causes of things, it would be inferior to a science of nature, if there were one. Sometimes Mersenne argues that there cannot be a science of nature, at least not a science meeting Aristotle's criteria: for a science must be of immutable truths, and God can change the laws of physics as He will.[89] But at other times he speaks with hope of 'a single principle of physics which would be as fertile as those of mathematics'.[90] Even without principles proper to natural things, we may still apply mathematical results to physics. But if we cannot understand natural phenomena from first principles, then alternate explanations will always be possible. Mersenne continues:

I do not see that one can demand anything from the most learned except for their observations, and what they may remark about the different effects or phenomena of nature. For example, since one cannot demonstrate whether the earth is at rest or in motion, one must content oneself with knowing all the observations which the astronomers have made in the heavens, and in everything which seems to have some manner of regular motion.[91]

By accepting the negative without the positive results of Renaissance anti-Aristotelianism, Mersenne is led close to the position of Francis Bacon on the method for discovering a new philosophy. In many respects, Bacon was a typical Renaissance anti-Aristotelian.[92] His *Essays* are purely humanist productions, and he takes pleasure in presenting his views as interpretations of ancient fables or revivals of pre-Socratic wisdom. He agrees with the humanists that Aristotelian philosophy has corrupted Christianity, and that it offers only disputations and verbal solutions without practical effects. Like Erasmus and Charron, Bacon calls for a practical philosophy, which should be judged by its usefulness for human life; but he places his emphasis differently from the earlier humanists. Although Bacon agrees that philosophy should make us virtuous, he is chiefly concerned that it should make us technically able to achieve the ends of human life through the mastery of nature. When Bacon surveys the history of philosophies old and new, they seem to him productions of the imagination, which vanish and leave no solid works behind them; it is not the famous philosophers, but the anonymous inventors of gunpowder, of printing, and of the magnetic compass who have left the world transformed.

When Bacon speaks of discovering the latent powers of nature and bringing them together for the service of human life, he is echoing the language of the magicians. But he is highly critical of the esotericism and charlatanry which dominate the practice of magic, and he wishes 'the practical part of natural science' to emulate instead the mechanical arts, which progressively expand their knowledge through honest collaborative effort. Bacon agrees with many others of his time that a method is needed for systematically exploiting the sources of knowledge, be they sensations or intellections or divine revelations. In a manner familiar from humanist compilations, Bacon proposes to assemble everything which has been learned on each particular topic, whether in the mechanical arts or through incidental observations. We can then sift through this 'historical' data to induce general laws of cause and effect; from these laws we can build up a philosophy which will inform our practice, by showing us which cause we must apply in order to yield any desired effect. By gathering new observations and extracting new consequences, we will continually improve our mastery of nature, and thus the felicity of human life.

Mersenne doubts Bacon's claims for his 'method' and wishes to reserve a greater place than Bacon for the disciplines of pure intellect, metaphysics and mathematics and logic; but he approves Bacon's belief in scientific progress through the accumulation of observations. On the question whether 'one now has more knowledge of some art or science than did the ancients', Mersenne prefers the ancients: they possessed arts now lost, and their texts remain our standards for scientific knowledge. If we surpass the ancients, it is only in astronomical observations, and in the invention of clocks, printing, artillery, and optical devices. But, says Mersenne, the Greeks did not 'pull up the ladder after them', and we remain capable, through methodical and collaborative work, of augmenting and even reforming the established sciences.[93]

Philosophers of the seventeenth century take to distinguishing their new philosophies from the vain imaginings of the past by citing new observations, especially in astronomy, and new mechanical inventions.[94] The prominence of these new discoveries is not necessarily related to their direct philosophical consequences. They had chiefly a symbolic importance, as decisive refutations of the Aristotelian world-system, and tokens of the progress of knowledge. A philosopher might take some newly discovered phenomenon as a model for the other phenomena of nature and so construct a whole philosophy upon it; he may say that the new phenomenon 'proves' the new philosophy, but this means only that it tips the balance towards his new philosophy *as against* the old philosophy of Aristotle. Thus, Hobbes takes Harvey's discovery of the circulation of the blood as proving that life is motion, and that phenomena should be explained through local motion and not through immaterial causes. William Gilbert writes a book, full of his empirical discoveries, *De magnete, magnetisque corporibus, et de magno magnete tellure* (On the magnet and magnetic bodies and the great magnet, the earth); but he subtitles it 'a new physics, demonstrated with many arguments and experiments', and he uses his 'magnetic philosophy' to construct another book, *De mundo nostro sublunari nova philosophia,* subtitled 'A new physics against Aristotle'.[95] Gilbert's discovery that the earth is a magnet has destroyed (he thinks) the Aristotelian doctrine that the sublunar world is made of four corruptible elements, and the heavens of an eternal fifth body: the body we live on is made not, as Aristotle charges, of dirt but of magnet, an incorruptible, uniformly rotating, and animated substance, identical with the substance of the stars. Similarly, Tycho Brahe's parallax observations proving that comets and novae were supralunar, and then Galileo's discovery of the sunspots, were used to show that the heavens were not incorruptible and not made of solid spheres, and thus to justify physical theories which treat celestial and sublunar bodies alike. From this time on, even if a new philosophy did not wish to base itself on magnetism or on the moons of Jupiter, it would be expected to give an account of these phenomena.

The religious and scientific components of the expectation of a new philosophy combined in different ways in the programmes of the different seventeenth-century philosophers. Pre-eminent were Mersenne's three friends Descartes, Gassendi, and Hobbes, his candidates to be the new Aristotle of the modern Christian world. Their new philosophies took different attitudes towards metaphysics and gave different foundations for morality and religion, but they all attempted to establish physics on 'a single principle . . . as fertile as those of mathematics'. It is Descartes who says 'my whole physics is nothing but mechanics', but the others could have said the same. Rejecting Aristotelian substantial forms and real qualities, and equally rejecting Platonist souls and natures, sympathies and antipathies and influences, they instead describe the world 'on the likeness of a machine'.[96] Using the mathematical science of mechanics, as strengthened by the recent discovery of the natural persistence of motion, they undertake to derive even such implausible phenomena as magnetism and animal life from the geometric and kinematic properties of the parts of matter. If they can succeed in generating a practical wisdom from these self-evident principles (and, for Descartes, from a knowledge of God and the soul), then their philosophy will be at once a better science than Aristotle's and a better wisdom than the humanists', refuting the contention of Montaigne and Charron that science is useless for wisdom.

The 'mechanical philosophy' was not a single doctrine but a group of competing 'new philosophies', taking their origins from an incongruous mixture of Archimedean mechanics, chemical and medical traditions, humanist Epicurean- ism, scholastic voluntarism and nominalism, and many another philosophy new or old. But the common core of the mechanical philosophy survived, through its own successes and by the elimination of its competitors, to become identical with 'the new philosophy'. When Baillet, from 1691, surveys the conditions of the sciences at the birth of his hero Descartes, he divides philosophy into 'the old' and 'the new': 'The old philosophy, and particularly that of Aristotle, was then finding itself rudely attacked by Francesco Patrizi,' while 'Chancellor Bacon was already laying the foundations of the new philosophy.'[97] Patrizi's destructive *Discussiones peripateticae* are well remembered, but his *Nova de universis philosophia* is forgotten: it is but one of the many works destined not to become the new philosophy.

NOTES

1 Randall 1961, p. 118. Randall himself sees naturalistic Aristotelianism at the root of modern science; Duhem 1913 (or see Duhem 1985) sees the exactly opposite pole of scholasticism, namely theological voluntarist anti-Aristotelianism, as responsible. Most other scholars pick some non-scholastic tendency: Puritanism, latitudinarianism, hu- manism, mathematical Platonism (Koyré 1978), Epicurean atomism, Hermetic magic (Yates 1964), the defense of orthodoxy against Hermetic magic (Lenoble 1971), scepticism (Popkin 1979), Christian and Jewish millenarianism (Popkin 1986a) have been favourites. These are all views held by serious scholars, and there is almost certainly some truth in each of them. The *Cambridge History of Renaissance Philosophy* (Schmitt, Skinner, and Kessler 1988) gives a general survey, with full bibliography, of the period of the history of philosophy here under discussion. The articles in that volume by Cesare Vasoli (chap. 3) and Alfonso Ingegno (chap. 9) cover many of the same philosophers and themes discussed in this chapter, although I have serious differ- ences of approach and interpretation with both of these authors. Other articles in that volume also cover some of the topics discussed here, often in greater detail.

2 As long as a philosophy is not the one currently regnant, it may be called 'new'. Most of the 'new philosophers' saw value in being ancient, as well as in being new (Conway 1982, originally published in 1690 [Latin] and 1692 [English], is entitled *Principles of the Most Ancient and Modern Philosophy*), and represented their philosophies as revivals of an ancient wisdom long submerged (perhaps since the time of Adam) under corrupt traditions. This is often connected with a conception of the original purity, subsequent corruption, and recent reformation of the church. This connexion could be quoted from authors of many different stripes, but I will here quote it from Thomas Vaughan's *Anthroposophia theomagica* (1650): 'Thou wilt tell me perhaps, this is new Philosophy, and that of Aristotle is old. It is indeed, but in the same sence as Religion is at Rome. It is not the primitive Trueth of the Creation, not the Ancient, reall Theosophie of the Hebrewes and Egyptians, but a certaine preternaturall upstart, a vomit of Aristotle, which his followers with so much diligence lick up and swallow' (Vaughan 1984, p. 53). Bacon, Galileo, and Descartes are among the more consistently 'new' of new philoso-

phers, but Bacon attempts to find his ideas in ancient fables or in the pre-Socratics; Galileo reads his into Plato's *Timaeus* (Galilei 1890–1909, vol. 7, pp. 44–5 [Galilei 1967, pp. 20–1]); and Descartes declares that his method is not new, 'for nothing is more ancient than the truth' (AT VII 3); perhaps only Hobbes never falls into this way of speaking. As late as 1690, Sir William Temple could doubt whether any really new philosophies had yet been introduced: 'But what are the sciences wherein we pretend to excel? I know of no new philosophers that have made entries upon that noble stage for fifteen hundred years past, unless Des Cartes and Hobbs should pretend to it; of whom I shall make no critique here, but only say, that, by what appears of learned men's opinions in this age, they have by no means eclipsed the lustre of Plato, Aristotle, Epicurus, or others of the ancients. . . . There is nothing new in astronomy to vie with the ancients, unless it be the Copernican system; nor in physic, unless Harvey's circulation of the blood. But whether either of these be modern discoveries, or derived from old fountains, is disputed, nay it is so too whether they are true or no; for though reason may seem to favour them more than the contrary opinions, yet sense can very hardly allow them; and, to satisfy mankind, both these must concur. But if they are true, yet these two great discoveries have made no change in the conclusions of astronomy, or in the practice of physic, and so have been of little use to the world, though perhaps of much honour to the authors' (Temple 1963, pp. 56–7). Contrast the passage from Hobbes on the newness of philosophy, cited below in note 94.

3 Some 'new philosophers' held university positions as professors, but not as professors of philosophy: thus, Galileo held a professorship in mathematics, Justus Lipsius in history, Henricus Regius in medicine, while writing or teaching their 'new philosophies' on the side. Of the non-scholastic philosophers discussed by name below, only Patrizi and Gassendi held professorships in philosophy, and only Patrizi was able to teach his 'new philosophy' officially: Gassendi was compelled to teach the Aristotelian philosophy he despised, while on the side compiling his dossier of arguments against Aristotle, the *Exercitationes paradoxicae adversus Aristoteleos* (see Gassendi 1959, pp. 6–9). See Chapter 1 of this volume for a discussion of seventeenth-century academic institutions.

4 For a very interesting general survey of the reform movement (and of what the reformers thought needed reforming), see Oberman 1981, including translations of primary documents, a general introduction, and short introductions to particular clusters of documents. Readers of Protestant background should be warned not to associate the reform movement automatically with the Protestant Reformation; this is only a part of the wide range of ways in which the reform movement could and did develop. As Oberman says (p. 40), the Council of Trent is often closer to the fifteenth-century reform movement than the Protestant reformers were.

5 The phrase is from G. F. Pico 1972, vol. 1, sec. 2, p. 1053; the context there is not polemical, but the phrase is indelibly sarcastic. *'Parisiensis'* was a standard pejorative term for the scholastics, who are said to write in a barbarous language, 'Parisian', rather than in Latin; cf. G. Pico 1971, vol. 1, p. 356.

6 Erasmus 1969– , vol. IV-3, p. 148 (Erasmus 1979, pp. 88–9). See the editor's notes in Erasmus 1969– for the scholastic sources of these questions, except the devil and the cucumber.

7 I will return briefly to the Aristotelianism of the Spanish Dominicans and Jesuits later in the chapter. On some Protestant attitudes to Aristotelianism, in the Reformation period and later, see Petersen 1921.

8 Schmitt 1967, p. 55.

9 Besides Bishop Etienne Tempier's famous condemnation of 219 Aristotelian proposi-

tions at Paris in 1277 (available in Mandonnet 1908–11, vol. 2, pp. 175–91, and in English translation in Lerner and Mahdi 1972, pp. 335–54), important indictments of Aristotelian philosophy are, in Islam, Ghazālī's *Tahāfut al-Falāsifa* (Incoherence of the philosophers), in which the philosophers are charged with three counts of infidelity and seventeen of heresy (almost the whole text is available in English translation, along with Averroes's reply, in Averroes 1954), and, in Christendom, *Errores philosophorum* of Aegidius Romanus (Giles of Rome) (edited with English translation, Aegidius Romanus 1944). Ghazālī has arguments as well as religious condemnations; Aegidius and Bishop Tempier just condemn, but others in the same tradition argue. For a similar development (on the argumentative side) in Judaism, see Harry A. Wolfson, *Crescas' Critique of Aristotle* (Wolfson 1929).

10 Duhem 1913 contains (among other things) the classic study of the philosophical consequences of the condemnation of 1277, and in particular of the questioning of fundamental notions of Aristotelian physics by such *moderni* as Ockham, Buridan, and Oresme. The crucial part of Duhem's argument is available in English translation in Duhem 1985.

11 Oresme 1968. Oresme is cited by the folio numbers given at the top of each page in this edition. Oresme's remark that the king has made him bishop of Lisieux is at the very end of the book, f. 203c. Oresme was a student of John Buridan, and many of the views I will be citing from Oresme could also be cited from Buridan. But Oresme is unusually outspoken and is easy and pleasant to use as a source for scholastic criticisms of Aristotle. See Duhem 1913 or Duhem 1985 for discussion of the Buridan school, and of the relations between Oresme's position and those of Buridan and others on the criticism of Aristotle's physics.

12 Oresme 1968, f. 39b.

13 Oresme 1968, ff. 20cd.

14 Oresme 1968, f. 70d.

15 Oresme 1968, f. 63d.

16 Petrarca citations give the original-language text from Petrarca 1975, followed by the translation from Cassirer, Kristeller, and Randall 1948, when available. Cassirer, Kristeller, and Randall 1948 give a generous selection of Petrarca's writings and, in particular, the whole of the *De sui ipsius et multorum ignorantia,* the work this discussion will be most concerned with. For a good discussion of Petrarca and more generally of the origins of humanism and its relations to philosophy, see Seigel 1968. Many other works on the subject contain a glorified view of the philosophical interests of the humanists and should be treated with caution.

17 Cassirer, Kristeller, and Randall 1948, pp. 140–1.

18 For Petrarca's religious devotion to Augustine, see his dialogue between himself and Augustine, *De secreto conflictu curarum mearum,* Petrarca 1975, vol. 1, pp. 44–258, esp. p. 48. For Augustine rather than Plato or Aristotle as the true philosopher, see Petrarca 1975, vol. 2, p. 1104 (Cassirer, Kristeller, and Randall 1948, p. 101). There '*nostri philosophi*' means primarily Augustine; Cassirer, Kristeller, and Randall give an appropriate reference in Augustine, but they are mistaken in glossing '*nostri*' here as 'Latin' rather than 'Christian', although it can mean either in Petrarca.

19 Petrarca 1975, vol. 2, p. 1038 (Cassirer, Kristeller, and Randall 1948, p. 58).

20 Petrarca 1975, vol. 2, p. 1106 (Cassirer, Kristeller, and Randall 1948, p. 103).

21 Petrarca 1975, vol. 2, pp. 1106–8 (Cassirer, Kristeller, and Randall 1948, pp. 103–4).

22 *Confessiones* III,iv,7, recalled in Petrarca 1975, vol. 2, p. 1108 (Cassirer, Kristeller, and Randall 1948, p. 105).

23 *Tusculanae disputationes* I,iv,7.

24 *De natura deorum* I,v,11.

25 Perhaps the most important of the systematic anti-Aristotelian *summae* are Gianfrancesco Pico's *Examen vanitatis doctrinae gentium et veritatis christianae disciplinae* (in G. F. Pico 1972, vol. 1, sec. 2, pp. 710–1264), Juan Luis Vives's *Adversus pseudodialecticos* (reprinted with English translation in Vives 1979), Mario Nizolio's *De veris principiis et vera ratione philosophandi contra pseudophilosophos* (Nizolio 1956; the book is sometimes called *Antibarbarus philosophicus,* but this title is the invention of a later editor; see Nizolio 1956 p. lxxiii), Peter Ramus's *Aristotelicae animadversiones* (later called *Scholae dialecticae,* and supplemented by *Scholae physicae* and *Scholae metaphysicae,* all collected in Ramus 1569), Francesco Patrizi's *Discussiones peripateticae* (Patrizi 1581), and Pierre Gassendi's *Exercitationes paradoxicae adversus Aristoteleos* (edited with French translation in Gassendi 1959).

26 *Academica* II,xxxviii,119. For a discussion of some Renaissance follies built on this phrase of Cicero's, see Schmitt 1983a, chap. 3 and esp. p. 73. Cicero is of course thinking of Aristotle's 'exoteric' writings, which had been lost long before the Renaissance; but many of the humanists tried to discover this eloquence in the Greek text of the extant treatises and to reproduce it in their new (and supposedly more faithful) translations.

27 *De divinatione* II,lviii,119.

28 The Christian humanist and anti-philosopher Gianfrancesco Pico della Mirandola (1469–1533) is not to be confused with his uncle, the Platonist Giovanni Pico della Mirandola (1463–94); both will be discussed further below. In bibliographical references, I will cite Gianfrancesco Pico as 'G. F. Pico' and Giovanni Pico as 'G. Pico'. Thus, for the *Examen vanitatis,* see G. F. Pico 1972, vol. 1, sec. 2, pp. 710–1264. The now classic study of Gianfrancesco Pico is Schmitt 1967.

29 The quotation is from Hobbes's *Lev.* xlvi, Hobbes 1968, p. 695, but the idea is a commonplace; cf. Descartes, AT IXB 8.

30 See Zabarella's *De methodis* and especially his short treatise *De regressu,* devoted to defending Aristotelian analysis against the charge of circularity, both available in Zabarella 1597 (the *De regressu* is pp. 479–98); the *De regressu* gives a nice summary of the point at issue, and of the traditional Aristotelian position. Some scholars have seen Zabarella's doctrine of analytic method as an innovation preparing the way for Cartesian and other early modern methodologies. In fact, Zabarella was a traditional scholastic of the Averroist-Alexandrist branch, and his doctrine of method sticks very close to his predecessors: to discover this, it is often sufficient to look up the references Zabarella himself explicitly gives. The resemblances between Zabarella and Descartes (say) are real, but this means only that they are both drawing on an ancient and widely ramified tradition of thinking about the methods of analysis and synthesis, a tradition encompassing mathematicians, Aristotelian and Platonist philosophers, and practitioners of yet other disciplines. For more discussion of doctrines of method, including Zabarella's, see chap. 7 in this volume.

31 The word *pansophia,* universal wisdom, is that favoured by Johann Amos Comenius; but the ideal is shared by a great many other philosophers of the time. The tripartition of the sources of our knowledge into sensation, reason, and scripture is found in Comenius, but it is in fact a commonplace of the time; many philosophers propose a method of systematising the results of all three, or some one or two, of these sources of knowledge.

32 Comenius 1969– , vol. 3, pp. 314–16 (Comenius 1942, pp. 56–9). The Rosicrucians are an extreme manifestation, and in some ways a parody, of the expectation of a 'new philosophy'; but they and the other 'new philosophers' are parts of the same phenome-

non, and certainly at the time there was no clear criterion for sorting out serious from bogus philosophies. We may note that while the president of Comenius's Rosicrucians has attained the age of 562 years, Descartes has the more modest expectation of living for 'more than a century' (AT I 507) and will work out all the details if he has enough time and money for experiments. The eschatological prophecy that 'many shall run to and fro, and knowledge shall increase' (Daniel 12:4) becomes a commonplace in the seventeenth century; thinkers of all stripes are sure that this prophecy is being fulfilled in their own time, the first clause by the discovery of America and the second by the new philosophy, whatever the thinker in question takes that to be. Francis Bacon discusses this prophecy in several places (e.g., at Farrington 1964, pp. 131–2), and uses it as an epigraph to his *Instauratio magna*. On the importance of millenarian themes in seventeenth-century thought, see Popkin 1986a.

33 The quotations are from Suárez's preface to the *Disputationes,* unpaginated prefatory material to Su. *Op. omn.* 25.

34 Suárez's *Disp. met.* is the most important source for the metaphysics of the Spanish scholastics: Suárez always states the positions of all sides to a controversy within the narrow world of scholasticism, occasionally noting positions beyond. Suárez is very useful for understanding the technical terminology of the new philosophers, and for filling out what these philosophers assumed the scholastic position to be; but except on the special issue of divine foreknowledge, that is usually as far as it goes. On the influence of Spanish scholastic theories of natural law and the social contract, see Skinner 1978, and this volume, Chap. 35. For the controversy between the Dominicans and the Jesuits on grace, free will, and divine foreknowledge, and for the extremely wide-ranging effects of this controversy, a good introduction is Abercrombie 1936. The crucial document of the controversy is Molina 1953, partly translated in Molina 1988, with a valuable introduction (from a philosophical point of view) by Alfred Freddoso. For seventeenth-century developments influenced by this controversy see, in this volume, Chap. 33.

35 It is understandable that the humanists, in their anti-scholastic polemics, should accuse their opponents of being captive to systematically misleading translations; but for modern scholars to repeat such accusations without citing evidence is unacceptable. I would like to add a protest against something much worse, the habit of describing the Arabic translators and commentators of Aristotle, just because they were Arabs or Muslims, as corruptors of Aristotle's true sense. This piece of blatant racism continues to be repeated by scholars of the history of Aristotelianism, especially by those who know no Arabic.

36 Agrippa 1533, p. 8; compare Galileo's story (Galilei 1890–1909, vol. 7, pp. 137–8 [Galilei 1967, pp. 111–12]) of the Peripatetic who proved the soul's mortality out of Aristotle but thought it trivial enough (if required in order to publish) to modify the argument so as to prove immortality instead.

37 For Thomas on the problem of the status of the human soul, see *Summa th.*, I q 75–6, and his separate *Quaestio disputata de anima,* especially arts. 1 and 2; for the need to invoke a special divine creation of the human soul in order to make its individuation independent of matter, see, e.g., *Quaestio disputata de anima,* art. 1, *ad secundum.* For some doubts that Aristotle could have held the Thomist doctrine, or that he held any consistent position, see Duns Scotus 1987, pp. 147–52: 'It is probable that he [Aristotle] was always doubtful about this conclusion [the immortality of the soul], and seemed now to agree with one side, now with the other, according as he was treating a subject-matter more consonant with one side than with the other' (p. 148). Note that Scotus

considers it a *reductio ad absurdum* of ascribing a certain doctrine about the human soul to Aristotle that 'therefore he [Aristotle] would have conceded creation' (p. 151); Scotus correctly takes it for granted that Aristotle's God must act in an eternally immutable manner and so can produce something new only by a natural necessity, in so far as a recipient acquires a new passive power to be made into something. Scotus's final conclusion is that, from the standpoint of natural reason, the immortality of the soul is probable but not certain (p. 156, where immortality is the 'second proposition'); it becomes certain through revelation. All the difficulties facing the Thomist position as an interpretation of Aristotle are brought out by Pomponazzi *De immortalitate animae* (in Pomponazzi 1938; and in Cassirer, Kristeller, and Randall 1948), chaps. 8–9.

38 Aristotle speaks of the 'agent intellect', the source of intellectual illumination to the soul's 'potential intellect', in *De anima* III,5; his statements on the status of the rational soul are unclear. It is not likely that Aristotle intended the 'agent intellect' as a part of the soul: not only Averroes but also Alexander of Aphrodisias, Avicenna (usually), some Christian scholastics, and, in the Renaissance, Pomponazzi and Zabarella take the agent intellect to be a single eternal substance separate from human souls. Some but not all of them identify this substance with God, as Aristotle probably intended. Thomas, the ancient commentators Themistius, Philoponus, and Simplicius, and Avicenna (sometimes) take the agent intellect as part of the individual soul, because they think this is the only way of saving the doctrine of the immortality of the individual human soul on Aristotelian terms. The peculiar and 'monstrous' Averroist doctrine is that the *potential* intellect is also a single eternal substance separate from human souls. In what follows, when I discuss controversies about the doctrine of the intellect I will mean the *potential* intellect; only this would be called an 'intellect' in the modern sense of the term.

39 Savonarola, *De triumpho crucis,* Savonarola 1955– , vol. 7, p. 214.

40 G. F. Pico 1972, vol. 1, sec. 2, pp. 718–19.

41 See Randall's introduction to Pomponazzi's *Tractatus de immortalitate animae,* Cassirer, Kristeller, and Randall 1948, pp. 269–71, for Pomponazzi's biographical background as a Thomist and as an Averroist. Randall's judgements in this introduction about Pomponazzi's relations to humanism, Platonism, Stoicism, etc., are unreliable.

42 Religious insincerity is quite rare among Christian philosophers, and many philosophers (e.g. Montaigne, Hobbes, Gassendi, sometimes even Descartes) have been groundlessly accused. But there is ample evidence, from Pomponazzi's own words, that Pomponazzi follows a policy of insincerely disclaiming the views of Aristotle and natural reason; and this policy is what we would expect, given Pomponazzi's place in the Averroist tradition generally, and given in particular his Averroist understanding of the religions or 'laws', including Christianity; this is discussed later in this chapter under 'Philosophies emerging from humanism'. Pomponazzi 1567, pp. 200–208, attributes to the philosophers, including Aristotle, a policy of withholding their arcana from the *vulgus* and the 'priests'; this is historically nonsense as far as Aristotle is concerned but is all standard Averroism. Nardi 1965, pp. 122–48, discusses Pomponazzi's insincerity, citing new manuscript evidence: a reading of the texts printed by Nardi, pp. 134–5 (where Pomponazzi is commenting on Averroes), is likely to silence any doubts on the question. It should be noted, against tendencies to exaggerate the importance of 'esoteric' writing, that it is always obvious when Pomponazzi (or Averroes, etc.) is lying. The deceptive statements are perfunctory appendices to Pomponazzi's real views and can always be detached without harming the overall logic of Pomponazzi's argument; they are uttered out of willingness to conform to the rules of the game, and without any real hope of deceiving anybody. There is no irony or deception in anything

Pomponazzi says *philosophically,* and there is in particular no reason to doubt the sincerity of Pomponazzi's (or Averroes's) statements about the essential value of the 'laws', or about the existence and attributes of God and of the other separate substances. The whole philosophy would collapse without these doctrines.

43 Pomponazzi's treatise on immortality is reprinted in Pomponazzi 1938, with an English translation; a revised version of this same translation is printed in Cassirer, Kristeller, and Randall 1948, pp. 280–381. In the remainder of this paragraph I summarise Pomponazzi's negative conclusions about other theories of the soul, from the first eight chapters of the treatise; the next paragraph summarises Pomponazzi's positive view as he puts it forward in Chapter 9.

44 Pomponazzi in his commentary and questions on Averroes's *De substantia orbis* (Pomponazzi 1966) defends Averroist doctrines which others might well find monstrous, notably that the heavenly bodies are only equivocally called bodies, that they are simple substances, and that they do not have parts really distinct from one another. Pomponazzi's *De fato* (Pomponazzi 1957) defends an extreme astrological fatalism, generally agreeing with Averroes (though outdoing even him in its consistent extremism) and directly attacking Alexander's *De fato,* which had defended free will and indeterminism. Pomponazzi is about as far from humanism as a philosopher could hope to be; his only trait which might be called humanistic is a willingness to use examples from the Italian poets.

45 For Pomponazzi's rejection of the Thomist account, which would raise human beings to equality with the spheres, see *De immortalitate,* chap. 9; instead, he thinks, the souls of human beings should be placed midway between the souls of beasts and the separate intelligences of the spheres. The quotations are from Pomponazzi 1567, pp. 53 and 251.

46 See the text from Cajetan's commentary on the *De anima* cited by Cassirer, Kristeller, and Randall 1948, p. 271: Cajetan says that the human potential intellect is generable and corruptible according to Aristotle's opinion, but *not* according to philosophy (let alone according to the truth): 'This is shown to be false from faith; hence it cannot follow from the principles of philosophy. Whence I have not written these words [explicating Aristotle's doctrine] as true or as consistent or as probable in philosophy, but merely as setting forth the opinion of this Greek, which I shall endeavour to show to be false according to the principles of philosophy' (Cajetan 1598, p. 205). John of St. Thomas, after defending against Scotus the doctrine that natural reason can prove the immortality of the soul, comments on Cajetan's position: 'Nor was Cajetan right in saying, in his commentary on *Ecclesiastes* 3:21, that none of the philosophers has hitherto demonstrated the immortality of the soul. But perhaps he is speaking of the *ancient* [*antiqui,* i.e. pagan] philosophers; for when he speaks of this argument of St. Thomas, in his commentary on the *Summa theologiae,* First Part, Question 75, article 2, he defends this argument and responds to Scotus's objections' (John of St. Thomas 1930–7, vol. 3, p. 285). Thomas may thus be called a philosopher, but a *new* philosopher and not a *philosophus antiquus*; this is a difficult thing for a Thomist to say. Cajetan's attitude may be contrasted with earlier scholastic anti-Aristotelianisms: even a thinker as radical as Oresme, who is constantly finding fault with Aristotle, seems never to question Aristotle's standing as the authoritative exponent of the standpoint of natural reason.

47 See, for example, Petrarca 1975, vol. 2, p. 1102 (Cassirer, Kristeller, and Randall 1948, p. 101); Gianfrancesco Pico gives a similar explanation for why he will concentrate on attacking Aristotle in his *Examen vanitatis doctrinae gentium et veritatis christianae disciplinae,* G. F. Pico 1972, vol. 1, sec. 2, p. 720.

48 Hobbes, *Lev.* (Hobbes 1968, p. 688); similarly, Petrarca 1975, vol. 2, p. 1062 (Cassirer, Kristeller, and Randall 1948, p. 74): 'from being philosophers and eager [*studiosi*] lovers of wisdom, we have become Aristotelians, or rather Pythagoreans', since it was the Pythagoreans, as Cicero tells us, who solved all questions by '*ipse dixit*'. The common-place opposing philosophy or love of wisdom or truth to love or respect for one man is used by Plato against Homer (*Republic* X 595b9-c3), is turned by Aristotle against Plato (*Nicomachean Ethics* I,6), and is here being turned against Aristotle.

49 Augustine, *Contra academicos* III.19.42.

50 Erasmus writes, 'A philosopher is not he who is clever at dialectic or physics, but he who, scorning the false images of things, with chastened heart both sees and follows the things which are truly good: to be a philosopher and to be a Christian are different in name but the same thing in reality' (Erasmus 1969–   , vol. IV-1, p. 145). Gianfran-cesco Pico writes a comparison *De studio divinae et humanae philosophiae*, in G. F. Pico 1972, vol. 1, sec. 1, pp. 1–39: philosophy is the knowledge of truth, and it is good *per se*; but *human* philosophy, i.e., 'that invented by man and proceeding by means of the traces [*vestigia*] of nature' (pp. 7–8) is inferior to divine philosophy, i.e., that revealed in scripture. For Nizolio's contrast between 'truly philosophical and oratorical', on the one hand, and 'pseudophilosophical and barbarous' on the other, see, e.g., Nizolio 1956, vol. 2, p. 79.

51 Cassirer, Kristeller, and Randall 1948, p. 34.

52 For a useful general account of scepticism in the Renaissance and the seventeenth century, see Popkin 1979. Popkin emphasises the Christian motivations of Renaissance scepticism, particularly its polemical use against the Protestants; this is a very important side of Renaissance scepticism, although humanist anti-Aristotelianism is equally im-portant, at least in the earlier part of the period. If there is something misleading in Popkin's account, it is his tendency to emphasise the (from a modern perspective) intellectually respectable aspects of Renaissance scepticism. This may lead Popkin to overstress the importance of (1) philosophical arguments as opposed to humanist suspi-cion of philosophy, (2) rediscovered Pyrrhonism as opposed to Ciceronian Academic scepticism, and in particular (3) the sceptical arguments against the possibility of a criterion, from circularity or infinite regress. All of these elements were present in Renaissance scepticism, but they were not at the centre of the phenomenon.

53 Agrippa 1974; the first quotation is from p. 11, the second from pp. 17–18.

54 Charron 1986. In his preface, explaining the purely practical and moral sense of wisdom which he means to teach, Charron rejects the 'lofty and elevated sense of the theolo-gians and philosophers (who take pleasure in describing and picturing things which have never yet been seen and heightening them to a perfection of which human nature does not find itself capable except in imagination)', who take wisdom for 'a perfect knowledge of things divine and human, or even of the first and highest springs and causes of all things' (pp. 25–6). Charron will teach, as a foundation for right action, self-knowledge: the five chief moral attributes of man are vanity, weakness, inconstancy, misery, and presumption. This will undermine the hope of a scientific wisdom, founded on an overestimate of our capacities. Note also the way in which parents ought to educate their children, and the connexions between wisdom and judgement and between science and memory, Charron 1986, pp. 685–94.

55 Lipsius 1604a, p. 49.

56 Lipsius 1604a, p. 48.

57 Lipsius 1604a, p. 83.

58 For Gassendi see Joy 1987, Jones 1981. Jones also gives a survey of earlier Renaissance Epicureanism.

59 Gassendi 1959; the first quotation is from p. 13, the second from p. 15.

60 See this volume, Chapter 23.

61 Lipsius 1604b, p. 14. For Cudworth's argument, see Cudworth 1731, pp. 55–7. The most famous of the 'Mosaic philosophies' is Fludd 1659, but there is at least a bit of 'Mosaic philosophy' in almost every thinker of the time: see Descartes's flirtation with the idea, AT V 168–9.

62 For a general survey of Byzantine philosophy, see Tatakis 1949.

63 Plethon's main constructive work is the *Laws* (not fully extant; what remains is available in Plethon 1858), a program for a pagan Greek state to be carved out of the collapsing Byzantine empire, complete with model hymns to the different gods: the political inspiration is from Plato's *Laws,* supported by metaphysical foundations from Proclus's *In Theologiam Platonis.* Woodhouse 1986 gives a useful survey of Plethon's career, with summaries of Plethon's major works, and a complete translation of the *De differentiis,* pp. 192–214. The critical edition of the Greek text of the *De differentiis* is Lagarde 1973.

64 From the programmatic introduction to Ficino's *Theologiam platonica,* Ficino 1964, vol. 1, p. 36.

65 The letter to Barbaro is in G. Pico 1971, vol. 1, pp. 351–8. Pico defiantly accepts the accusation of a barbarian 'Parisian' language, p. 356; he contrasts Lucretius with Scotus, pp. 357–8.

66 The only part of Pico's encyclopedic project which was actually completed is *De ente et uno,* in G. Pico 1971, vol. 1, pp. 241–56 (followed by objections and replies through p. 310); there is an English translation (without the additional material) in G. Pico 1965, pp. 37–62. There is a modern edition of Ficino's *Theologiam platonica,* with French translation, in Ficino 1964, from which I will be summarising what follows. There is as yet no philosophically thorough study of Ficino, taking the background of ancient Platonism into account; Ficino, like other Renaissance philosophers, has become the property of the historians of ideas, who have viewed him as the creator of a 'system' or 'world-view', where they have not reduced him to an art-critic or a magician. Kristeller 1943 remains a useful survey of Ficino's 'system'; for the magical approach, see Walker 1958 and Yates 1964. For Ficino as a commentator on Plato, see Allen 1984 and 1989; and Ficino 1975 and 1981.

67 Thus far, this paragraph summarises Ficino 1964, vol. 1, pp. 40–72.

68 For Pico's solution, see his *De ente et uno,* as referred to in note 66. In the *Theologia platonica,* Ficino calls God unity, goodness, and truth (Ficino 1964, vol. 1, pp. 73–5) but apparently avoids getting into the question of whether God is a being, being-itself, or beyond being; but in more esoteric works, as in his commentary on the *Sophist,* he follows Plotinus in identifying the realm of being, and the chief genera of being discussed in the *Sophist,* with the intelligible world; God as pure unity is therefore superior to being (Allen 1989, pp. 234–43; see also pp. 35–82).

69 Patrizi's chief philosophical works are the *Discussiones peripateticae* (Patrizi 1581) and the *Nova de universis philosophia* (Patrizi 1591), which was reprinted in 1979 with a translation into Serbo-Croatian (since Patrizi was born in what is now Croatia); there is a short but useful survey of his work, Brickman 1941.

70 There is a modern edition of Telesio's *De rerum natura,* with Italian translation, Telesio 1965–76. In Book VIII, chap. 15, Telesio distinguishes within 'the substance which reasons in man' two components, 'the spirit educed from the seed' and 'the soul created by God' (vol. 3, p. 232); this is reminiscent of St. Thomas's distinction between the sensitive and vegetative souls educed from the potency of matter and the rational soul created by God; or of Gassendi's distinction between the corporeal lower soul and the

incorporeal rational soul. It is not clear to me how well Telesio's doctrine of the higher soul is integrated into his philosophy.

71 Lenoble 1971 has an extensive and interesting discussion of Mersenne's polemic against different varieties of 'naturalism', pp. 83–167. But Lenoble moves much too readily to lump many different kinds of philosophers under the catch-all label 'naturalism', and to assume that all these people share some doctrine or doctrines setting them apart from Christian orthodoxy. In particular, Lenoble presents the doctrine of the world-soul (very crudely interpreted) as constitutive of naturalism, and as being irreducibly pagan and even anthropologically 'primitive'. There is, in fact (as Mersenne himself recognised), nothing in Christianity which contradicts the doctrine of a world-soul, and as far as I know nobody in the Renaissance or the seventeenth century said there was. St. Augustine (e.g.) affirms a world-soul in the early period after his conversion; in later works he retracts this affirmation and professes agnosticism on the question, but he never condemns the doctrine as false or pagan. It is nonetheless true that Platonist or Stoic explanations of particular 'miraculous' events through the world-soul might undercut Christian explanations of those events through special divine intervention.

72 Pomponazzi 1567, summarising especially from pp. 278–97. The doctrine is standard Averroism. But Pomponazzi's picture of the current senescence of Christianity and of the approaching transformation (p. 286 and following) is really quite touching and puts him in an odd agreement with the Protestant and Catholic reformers, on the one hand, and with Plethon's hope for the revival of a pagan Greek nation out of the corruption and collapse of Byzantine Christianity, on the other.

73 Giovanni Pico, *Disputationes adversus astrologiam divinatricem,* in G. Pico 1971, vol. 1, pp. 411–731. Yates 1964 has some discussion of the Renaissance Platonists' polemic against astrological determinism, noting correctly that this polemic derives from Plotinus and other ancient Platonists and that it is compatible with a belief in non-determining astral influences. Yates is right in saying that the Platonist opposition to astrological determinism *could* be used to support a human ability to manipulate astral influences through magic; but the fundamental Platonist criticism of astrology was based simply on a defense of human freedom and did not necessarily involve any commitment to the possibility of magic. It is true, however, that astral magic and (deterministic) astrology were fundamentally opposed to each other, and that those most credulous of one were often sharply critical of the other.

74 Giovanni Pico, *Conclusiones magicae 1–4.* The *Conclusiones magicae* are a subdivision of Giovanni Pico's famous '900 theses'; they can be found in the critical edition G. Pico 1973. The theses are also printed in G. Pico 1971, pp. 62–113, followed by Pico's defence of himself, pp. 114–240.

75 The remains of the *Chaldean Oracles* may be consulted (in Greek with French translation) in *Oracles chaldaïques* 1971; there is now also a version with English translation and notes, *Chaldean Oracles* 1989. (The *Oracles* are now ascribed to a father and son, both named Julian, living in the second century A.D.; they have nothing whatever to do with Zoroaster, to whom they are often attributed in the Renaissance.) The *Hermetica* should be read in Hermes Trismegistus 1945–54 (Greek or Latin with French translation); Hermes Trismegistus 1924 (Greek or Latin with English translation) is eccentric. There is now also an English translation with notes and introduction by Brian Copenhaver, Copenhaver 1992c. Strictly speaking, the *Corpus Hermeticum* is a collection of Greek treatises (some in dialogue form) preserved together, and first published (for the most part) in Latin translation by Ficino; the *Hermetica* include also a dialogue called *Asclepius,* which is an ancient Latin translation of a lost Greek original and various excerpts

ascribed to Hermes and cited by various Greek or Latin authors. There are yet other works ascribed to Hermes Trismegistus, considered to be even more than usually spurious, which are not included in these editions. For a broad picture, not just of the *Hermetica* but of the whole intellectual climate from which they emerged, see Festugière 1983 and Fowden 1993. Yates 1964 presents an interesting picture of the Renaissance career of the *Hermetica* and of *prisca theologia* generally, but some cautions are in order. Yates puts too much emphasis on the exotic side of Renaissance Platonism, describing Ficino and Pico and the others as 'Hermetists' or 'syncretists' rather than as (neo-) Platonists, and suggesting that these thinkers were influenced as much by the magic of the *prisci theologi* as by the mainstream Platonic tradition; the truth is that reference to the *Chaldean Oracles* and similar writings had been a standard feature of Platonism since about A.D. 300, and that all such authorities were subjected to an interpretation bringing them strictly into line with the over-arching Platonic system, in Ficino and Pico as much as in Proclus. Also, within the realm of *prisca theologia,* Yates gives undue priority to the *Hermetica* as against the *Chaldean Oracles* and other writings.

76 It is a mistake to suppose either that Renaissance Platonists are just magicians and the philosophy is merely ideological justification for magic, or that there were no magical practices and 'magic' is merely a metaphor. Some people were more interested in the theory and others in the practice, but there was always continuity. Cornelius Agrippa *De occulta philosophia* (Agrippa 1533) gives a fair amount of practical advice, but his justification of the three kinds of magic comes straight from the philosophical theory described here.

77 *Conclusiones magicae* 15 and 7, in G. Pico 1973.

78 An entire section of the *Conclusiones* is entitled '71 Kabbalistic conclusions, according to his own [Pico's] opinion, best [*maxime*] confirming the Christian religion from the foundations of the Hebrew sages themselves'. The Christian truths thus confirmed include the facts that the Messiah is named 'Jesus', that he suffers for sinners, that he 'comes with the baptism of water', that Satan tempts him with the promise of the kingdoms of the earth, and so on. Pico's *Heptaplus* (G. Pico 1971, vol. 1, pp. 1–62 [G. Pico 1965, pp. 67–174]) is a tour de force of a Kabbalistic commentary, giving *seven* different interpretations of the seven days of creation (in seven books of seven chapters), fitted into the usual *prisca theologia* scheme of the three worlds (Pico adds man as a fourth world containing the three great worlds in abrégé). Although the seventh chapter of each book says something about Christ, it is especially the seventh book which is devoted to proving Christianity: 'I pray you, Christian brothers, to consider a little more attentively how true and sound the scheme of my interpretation is. Against the stony hearts of the Hebrews it will furnish you with powerful weapons drawn from their own arsenals. In the first place we shall prove from the testimony of the Jews that the works of the fourth day signify the coming of Christ. Secondly, we shall show that nothing represents the Messiah to us more fittingly than the sun, and we shall clearly deduce from the periods of time that the Christ is not still to come in the future but that Jesus of Nazareth, the son of the Virgin, was the Messiah promised to the Hebrews' (G. Pico 1965, p. 158 = G. Pico 1971 vol. 1, pp. 51–2). Johannes Reuchlin has a treatise *De arte cabalistica,* included in G. Pico 1971, vol. 2, pp. 733–899. On Renaissance Christian interest in kabbalah, see Blau 1944.

79 For a picture of the sectarian England of the revolutionary period, see the works of Christopher Hill, especially Hill 1972 and 1977. For a helpful survey of Christian mortalism, see Burns 1972. The best systematic statements of seventeenth-century mortalism, besides Hobbes's *Leviathan,* are Richard Overton's *Mans Mortallitie* (Overton

1644) and John Milton's posthumously published *Christian Doctrine* (in Milton 1931–8, vol. 15). Within what can be broadly called Christian mortalism, several positions should be distinguished: mortalism in the strict sense maintains that the soul does not exist between death and resurrection; 'soul-sleeping' or 'psychopannychia' maintains that the soul exists during this period in an unconscious state, so that subjectively no time will appear to have elapsed between 'falling asleep' at death and 'reawakening' on the last day; a marginal extremist position not really related to these other currents of thought denies any existence after death, and allegorises immortality and resurrection as events within this life. Soul-sleeping, shading into strict mortalism, has been a perennial minority Christian position and had the sympathy of Luther and of many other opponents of the 'philosophical' and thus pagan doctrine of separate immortality. It is an anti-historical prejudice to question the sincerity of seventeenth-century Christian mortalists; there might, of course, be reasons for doubt in some individual cases, but I am unaware of any such case (see, however, note 43 on Pomponazzi, who belongs to a very different [Averroist] intellectual tradition, and who professes not mortalism but the standard Thomist position on immortality).

80 For Hobbes on scholasticism as a corruption of Christianity by pagan philosophy, see especially *Lev.* xlvi, 'Of Darkness from Vain Philosophy and Fabulous Traditions'. We have no grounds for questioning Hobbes's religious sincerity, once we understand how widespread Christian mortalist and voluntarist doctrines were in the sectarian England of his time.

81 See the appendix to Gouhier 1972 for a discussion of 'mystical' and 'positive' theology, which Gouhier places within the context of a more general search for a 'simple and effective' theology to replace (what many Catholic reformers saw as) the useless subtleties of scholastic theology. For an immersion in the religious thought-world of the French Counter-Reformation, see the great *Histoire littéraire du sentiment religieux en France* of Henri Bremond (Bremond 1967).

82 Jansenius 1640, vol. 2, *Liber prooemialis:* philosophy as the source of everything that is wrong with scholastic theology, by contrast with the teaching of the Fathers, pp. 5–12; Augustine as 'Father of Fathers, doctor of doctors, the first [in authority] after the canonical [biblical] writers, among them all the one who is truly solid, subtle, irrefragable, angelic, seraphic, most excellent, and ineffably marvelous', pp. 53–4. On Jansenius see also the excellent Abercrombie 1936, containing (among many other things) a detailed summary of the *Augustinus.*

83 For the story about Chandoux and Berulle and Descartes, see Baillet 1691, vol. 1, pp. 160–5. For the range of attitudes Augustinian reformers took towards Cartesianism, see Gouhier 1978 and the appendix to Gouhier 1972; for Augustinian influences on Descartes himself, see Menn 1989.

84 The classic study of Mersenne is Lenoble 1971; see also Dear 1988.

85 Mersenne 1625, p. 117.

86 Mersenne 1625, p. 109.

87 Mersenne 1625, p. 110.

88 Mersenne 1624, vol. 2, p. 372.

89 Mersenne 1985, p. 216.

90 Mersenne 1985, p. 56.

91 Mersenne 1985, p. 224.

92 On Bacon, see Farrington 1964; Rossi 1968; Jardine 1974. All these studies, with different emphases, show Bacon's continuity with different trends of Renaissance anti-Aristotelianism.

93 Mersenne 1985, pp. 87–8.

94 The idea that real philosophy has only just begun may be illustrated from Hobbes, who, in the dedicatory letter to his *De corpore,* denies that either natural or moral philosophy had existed in antiquity. 'But what? were there no philosophers natural or civil among the ancient Greeks? There were men so called: witness Lucian, by whom they are derided; witness divers cities, from which they have been often by public edicts banished. But it follows not that there was *philosophy*' (*Eng. Works,* vol. 1, p. ix, translating *Lat. Works,* vol. 1, unpaginated prefatory material). The inventors of celestial physics, of general physics, of the science of the human body, and of moral philosophy, we are told, are, respectively, Copernicus, Galileo, Harvey ('the only man I know, that conquering envy, hath established a new doctrine in his life-time'), and Hobbes himself, the first to reason systematically from observations in their respective fields. Contrast the quotation from Sir William Temple cited in note 2.

95 *De magnete* (Gilbert 1600) and *De mundo* (Gilbert 1651) (as the works are usually called for short). There is a study of the *De mundo,* with comparisons to the *De magnete* and to Gilbert's contemporaries, including Bacon, in Kelly 1965. I am summarising from the *De magnete* in the next sentence.

96 The first Descartes quotation is from AT II 542, the second from AT VIII 315.

97 Baillet 1691, vol. 1, p. 10.

3

EUROPEAN PHILOSOPHICAL RESPONSES TO NON-EUROPEAN CULTURE: CHINA

D. E. MUNGELLO

I. INTRODUCTION

Most seventeenth-century European thinkers who showed a strong interest in non-European philosophy believed in the universal basis of knowledge. The truths that they discovered did not, in their view, end at the borders of Europe. Consequently, when these Europeans encountered other philosophies, they tried to understand the differences in terms of an absolute conception of truth and falsehood rather than regard these other philosophies as merely different or alternative paths to truth.

The European discovery voyages that began in the fifteenth century gradually served as a medium for learning about other cultures, although it took some time for Europeans to learn about the higher forms of knowledge of these regions. This was particularly true with regard to their philosophies. The explorers themselves provided little of this knowledge. Rather, it was missionaries who provided most of it. Because of the religious zeal of the explorer-nations, such as Portugal and Spain, passage was regularly provided on their ships for Catholic missionaries of diverse European nationalities.[1] These missionaries sought contact with peoples in Asia and the Americas and began to learn their languages and study their cultures.

Clearly, these missionaries did not come to this task with detached, impartial attitudes. Even missionaries who admired China, such as the Spanish Dominican D. Navarrete, were too prone to see superstition and idolatry where it did not always exist.[2] Nevertheless, some of these missionaries recognised the importance of learning about the philosophy and religion of these lands. They recognised the impracticality of introducing a completely new culture and religion, particularly where there was already a highly developed culture.[3] Instead, they sought to study the indigenous culture in order to find some intellectual basis for integrating Christianity into it.

The Society of Jesus was a relatively new religious order which had originated in the Counter-Reformation with the presentiments of modernity. No religious order devoted more effort to educating its members than the Jesuits. They were taught the most advanced mathematics, technology and philosophy, as well as theology, then available in Europe. Consequently, the Jesuits who went out into the world as missionaries had a disposition towards the intellectual sphere.

No nation challenged the Jesuits as much as China. When the Jesuits began arriving on its frontier in the late sixteenth century, they found a land still in its period of glory. By nearly any objective standard (population, size, wealth, learning), China was at that time the greatest nation in the world. The Chinese had dominated East Asia for centuries and believed that the key to this domination lay in their culture. No philosophy dominated the Chinese imperial court and the scholar-officials more than Confucianism.

The Jesuits recognised that the Confucian literati, or scholar-officials, were their closest Chinese counterparts in terms of education, social status, and moral cultivation. Consequently, in the late sixteenth century and throughout the seventeenth the Jesuits put considerable effort into cultivating the literati. In the process, they acquired a remarkably sophisticated knowledge of Confucian philosophy while slighting the other major philosophies of China, notably Daoism (Taoism) and Legalism. As a result, Europeans of the seventeenth century tended to associate Chinese philosophy with Confucianism.

Since missionaries needed considerable patronage in order to fund their activities in China, they applied their extensive knowledge and skills to soliciting support from European princes, clerics, and savants. Returned China missionaries would visit the courts of princes and fascinate them with exotica from China or even with Chinese companions.[4] Some even dedicated their scholarly works about China to royal personages: the first extensive translation of Confucian Classics, *Confucius Sinarum Philosophus* (Paris, 1687),[5] was dedicated to Louis XIV of France. Shortly afterwards, King Louis sponsored a mission of five scholarly French Jesuits to China. European savants such as Leibniz were cultivated by the Jesuits for the great prestige which they could bestow.

Indeed, such contacts – largely through correspondence – proved as important as books in conveying Chinese philosophy to Europeans. In the seventeenth century, correspondence served to communicate knowledge in the way that scholarly journals do today. Consequently, letters were often lengthy and were recopied by secretaries for further circulation. The medium also allowed writers to communicate ideas that were too controversial to obtain the official imprimatur needed for publication. The correspondence between Leibniz and Joachim Bouvet, the Jesuit missionary to China, from 1697 to 1704 provides one of the most striking transmissions of philosophic knowledge of that age.[6]

II. CONFUCIANISM IN EUROPE

Although European responses to information about Chinese philosophy were often limited by European intellectual preoccupations, Chinese philosophy nevertheless had a significant impact upon seventeenth-century Europe. The Jesuits played the primary rôle in shaping the European understanding of Chinese philosophy. Because of the Jesuits' intellectual inclinations, their tendency to cultivate the highest political echelons in China, and their missionary program of identifying with the Chinese scholar-officials, Confucianism was elevated in importance in the presentation of Chinese philosophy. By contrast, Daoism, a mystical nature philosophy closely associated with the development of natural science as well as pseudo-science in China, was deemphasised and criticised as a far less enlightened point of view.

The Jesuits were even responsible for the name by which Confucian philosophy became known in Europe. In China, it is known as the 'Literati Teaching' (*Ruxue*) rather than 'Confucianism' because Confucius himself stated that he was merely transmitting this teaching from the ancient sages rather than originating it. However, when the Jesuits first presented this teaching to Europe, practical necessity forced them to Latinise the Chinese name Kong-fu-zi into Confucius and, by phonetic extension, the teaching associated with this name became 'Confucianism'.

The first important work to introduce Confucianism to Europeans, *De Christiana expeditione apud Sinas,* appeared in 1615 and was based upon a manuscript originally written by the famous China missionary, Matteo Ricci (1552–1610), and edited by his fellow Jesuit, N. Trigault.[7] The work was an immediate sensation and soon was translated into five other European languages. This work presents Confucius as a virtuous pagan who was the equal of, if not superior to, most of the pagan philosophers, including the Greeks. Many Europeans were impressed by the positive effect that Confucian ethical and social philosophy had exerted on the nation of China.[8] The key to the good governance of this enormous land of 150 million people (France at that time had a population of 20 million) appeared to be the Confucian emphasis on education and learning, in both its literary and moral aspects. To study the Confucian Classics (Four Books and Five Classics) was to undergo a moral cultivation. This education was institutionalised in China in a system of literary degrees which one earned in order to qualify for appointment to a government office. Knowledge was rewarded, whereas birth and wealth went unrecognised, at least in theory. Indeed, to many Europeans, China seemed to have realised Plato's ideal of philosopher-kings. Many Europeans were struck by the extent to which Confucian philosophy focused on improving society.

The Jesuits' exaltation of Confucius culminated in their first major translation of Confucian texts, *Confucius Sinarum Philosophus* (Confucius, philosopher of the Chinese).[9] The long introduction to this work contains a brief biography and a striking frontal portrait of a gigantic Confucius standing before a structure that blends a Confucian temple with a library. The library is what made Confucius so acceptable to the Jesuit missionaries. They presented him to Europeans as a learned sage rather than a religious idol. A popularised version of this work in French entitled *La morale de Confucius* appeared in 1688, and it was soon translated into English.[10] Consequently, the essentials of Confucian philosophy were quickly spread to a very interested European readership.[11]

Confucius became for seventeenth-century Europeans the model of the scholar-official tradition in China. His belief in the absolute truths discovered in antiquity and his commitment to transmitting these truths of the ancient sages gave him a certain affinity to Europeans who deeply believed in the truths of both biblical and classical Greek antiquity. The Jesuits sought to bridge the differences between the European and Chinese traditions by arguing that Confucius taught the truths of natural theology.[12] These were truths discovered through reason and experience rather than through faith and divine revelation. Confucius was presented as teaching moral maxims which were in harmony with the Ten Commandments, such as honouring one's parents.

One of the most outspoken admirers of Confucius was Sir William Temple, the eminent English statesman.[13] In his essay *Heroic Virtue* and other writings, Temple noted that Confucius, much like Socrates, turned people's attention from metaphysical speculation to practical social morality.[14] Because of Confucius's emphasis on morality, Temple said, China was ruled by an intellectual elite selected on the basis of examinations and scrutinised while in office.[15]

Leibniz gave this admiration of Confucian philosophy its most influential expression in a preface to a small work called *Novissima Sinica* (The latest news from China) in 1697. Leibniz did not see European culture as superior to Chinese culture. Upon comparing the intellectual and philosophical achievements of Europe and China, he found them both strong, but in different areas. He suggested that God might have ordained that the highest levels of civilisation should be concentrated at the two extremes of Eurasia in order to facilitate their mutual interpenetration.[16] Whereas Europeans were strong in the more abstract subjects of logic, metaphysics, and mathematics, the Chinese excelled in 'practical philosophy . . . , that is, the precepts of ethics and politics' (*practica philosophia . . . , id est Ethicae & Politicae praeceptis*).[17] If this balance were to be preserved in the future, Leibniz said, the European missionaries who were going to China to teach the mathematical arts and essence of European philosophy as well as revealed religion should be matched by Chinese missionaries who would come to Europe to teach practical philosophy and the practice of natural religion.[18]

The seventeenth-century intellectual precursors of the eighteenth-century Enlightenment included a number of free-thinkers and sceptics, such as François La Mothe le Vayer, P. Bayle, F. Bernier, and Herbert of Cherbury, who found in Confucianism a support for their attack upon Christianity.[19] Confucianism appeared to be a form of natural religion in which notions of a supreme being and basic principles of good and evil had been determined through reason and experience and without divine revelation. By the eighteenth century, leading Enlightenment thinkers such as C. Wolff, Voltaire, J. H. G. Justi, and F. Quesnay would elevate this admiration of China into an enthusiastic Sinophilia.[20] However, seventeenth-century European thinkers were more objective in responding to the challenges Chinese culture posed to the authority of the Bible.

III. BIBLICAL CHRONOLOGY AND THE CHINESE

One of the first of these challenges had to do with the Europeans' claim of universal patrimony. The claim was based on the biblical account of Creation, which portrays Adam and Eve as the first man and woman, from whom all humans are descended. In 1658 the Jesuit missionary M. Martini published an account of Chinese history that dated the origin of Chinese history from the reign of Fu Xi in 2952 B.C.[21] Just a few years before the appearance of Martini's book, Archbishop James Ussher (1581–1656) of Ireland had published a chronology of the Old and New Testaments in which he claimed that the Creation had occurred in 4404 B.C. and that the Noachian flood had taken place in 2349 B.C.[22] Ussher's dates were soon inserted into the text of several editions of the King James version of the Bible, and they were widely accepted. In the seventeenth-century biblical view of human history, however, all mankind, except for Noah's descendants, had been destroyed at the time of the Flood. Consequently, Noah was regarded as the father of all mankind. If any other people had a continuous history dating from before the Flood, then Noah's universal patriarchy was destroyed. This was precisely the challenge that Martini's account of Chinese history posed. Chinese history, Martini reported, dated from 2952 B.C., whereas in the Ussher chronology the Flood did not occur until 2349 B.C. Either Noah was not the father of mankind or one of the chronologies was wrong.

There was a way out of the dilemma. Ussher had based his dates (Creation at 4404 B.C. and the Noachian flood at 2349 B.C.) on the Vulgate version of the

Bible, but the Septuagint version placed the Creation at 5200 B.C. and the Flood at 2957 B.C. The Septuagint dating placed the Flood five years before the beginning of Chinese history and so preserved Noah's universal patrimony. Consequently, most Jesuits advocated adopting the Septuagint version of the Bible as one way out of the dilemma.[23]

IV. CHINESE AND THE ADAMIC LANGUAGE

No endeavour more fully reflects the philosophical outlook of seventeenth-century Europe than its search for a universal language. The search was the result of several intellectual currents, including biblical tradition, a mediaeval idea, the sixteenth-century discovery voyages, and seventeenth-century science. The European discovery of many hitherto unknown languages in Asia had revived the idea of the biblical proliferation of tongues at Babel. Thus, many Europeans believed that God had given Adam a pure, exact, and utterly simple language, which was called the *lingua Adamica, lingua humana,* or the Primitive Language; and that originally all humans spoke this Primitive Language. However, when human pride led to the building of the Tower of Babel in competition with God (Genesis 11:1–9), God became so enraged that He scattered humans across the earth and confused their simple language by transforming it into a proliferation of languages.

In their encounter with new languages of the world, several seventeenth-century scholars became preoccupied with identifying the Primitive Language. Some believed that it was Samaritan, the language which Jesus spoke. Others believed it was Chaldean, Gothic, or even Chinese. However, most scholars believed that it was Hebrew, and some even attempted to reconstruct it using biblical sources.

Among those who believed Chinese to be the Primitive Language was John Webb, an eminent architect who in polyhistor style published a book in 1669 expounding his theory, which was based largely on published Jesuit works on China.[24] According to Webb, the descendants of Noah had migrated to India and eventually into China. From Martini's work, Webb hypothesised that Noah and the Chinese figure Yao were identical, and that the Flood had been universal in extent. Webb took the description of Noah's sons in Chapter 10 of *Genesis* to mean that Ham's descendants peopled Babylon, Palestine, the Arabias, and Africa; Japeth's descendants peopled Asia Minor and Europe; and Shem's descendants peopled eastern Persia, the Indias, and China. Consequently, Webb argued, China was settled before Babel by the descendants of Shem. At the time of the dispersion of tongues at Babel, Webb claimed, the ancestors of the Chinese had remained at home in China and so were able to preserve the Primitive Language.

In spite of Webb's creative hypothesis, by the 1670s a growing number of European scholars were arguing that it was not possible to reconstruct the Primitive Language and that they should devote their efforts instead to creating a new universal language using the criteria attributed to the Primitive Language, namely, simplicity, generality, modesty of expression, vitality, and brevity. The formulators of universal language schemes included Herman Hugo (1617), William Bedell (1633), Gerhard Vossius (1635), Marin Mersenne (ca. 1636), Jan Amos Comenius (1646), Francis Lodwick (1647), an anonymous Spaniard (1653), Thomas Urquhart (1653), Seth Ward (1654), Cave Beck (1657), Brian Walton (1657), Johann J. Becher (1661), George Dalgarno (1661), Edward Somerset (1663), John Wilkins (1668), Leibniz (ca. 1679), and Gaspar Schott (1687).[25]

The search for a universal language was based upon a widespread linguistic premise that it was possible to discover Real Characters, that is, symbols and sounds whose representation of things and ideas was natural, or 'real', rather than conventional. This meant that the representation of a word should be based upon the nature of things rather than upon human invention. Such a premise lies at the heart of the first seventeenth-century proposal for a universal language, put forth by Francis Bacon. Like Bacon, many figures involved in the search had solid intellectual credentials and were associated with the Scientific Revolution or were members of the London Royal Society. Some continental figures also took part in the search, among them Leibniz.

In his proposal for the development of a new universal language, Bacon had briefly referred to the Chinese language as a model. In *The Advancement of Learning,* Bacon wrote:

It is the use of China, and the kingdoms of the High Levant, to write in characters real, which express neither letters nor words in gross, but things or notions; insomuch as countries and provinces, which understand not one another's language, can nevertheless read one another's writings, because the characters are accepted more generally than the languages do extend.[26]

Bacon had probably derived his information from a book by the Spanish Augustinian Juan Gonzalez de Mendoza that was first printed in 1585.[27] However, this was a powerful idea in seventeenth-century Europe, and it was elaborated in a 1615 publication by Fathers Ricci and Trigault, who said that the Chinese script was understood by the Chinese, Japanese, Koreans, Cochinese (South Vietnamese), and Leuchian Islanders (Taiwanese) even though each of them spoke distinct languages.[28]

The passage of time is often unkind to figures who were more esteemed in their own age. No figure was more eminent in seventeenth-century European intellectual life than the Jesuit scholar Athanasius Kircher. Kircher was a prolific polymath who wrote large folio volumes on a dizzying array of subjects, but this style of scholarship has fallen out of favour, and today the emphasis is on narrow specialisation. Yet the fact remains that Kircher epitomises the seventeenth-century scholarship of ideas.

Kircher's works show how several diverse intellectual paths converged in the search for a universal language. In his *Ars magna sciendi, sive combinatoria* (The great art of knowing, or combinations), published in Amsterdam in 1669, Kircher drew upon the mediaeval idea of Ramon Lull (ca. 1232–1316) for a combinatory art (*Ars Combinatoria*) and art of memory for discovering truth. One could generate truths, Lull had argued, by mechanically combining basic elements.[29] Kircher applied Lull's combinatory art to the search for a universal language. Lull's thesis also proved attractive to the youthful Leibniz, who in 1660 drew on Lull's idea to compose a proposal entitled *Reductio linguarum ad unam* (The reduction of languages to one).[30]

Because Kircher believed that Egyptian culture had been disseminated to China by way of Noah's son Ham (rather than Shem), he regarded the Egyptian hieroglyphs as models that were purer, more ancient, and deeper in hidden meaning than the Chinese characters. And yet he believed that the hieroglyphs and the characters were composed in the same manner, that is, out of 'things of this world', rather than through an arbitrary assignment of meaning. Kircher did not exalt Chinese as a model for a universal language, as did Bacon; nor claim that Chinese contained Real Characters, as did both Bacon and Leibniz; nor claim that Chinese was the Primitive Language, as did Webb. But Kircher did disseminate information about the Chinese language gained through his fellow Jesuits, and from this information other European thinkers drew precisely these conclusions. Kircher claimed that the Chinese language had no letters of an alphabet, no syllables, no declinations, and no conjugations. Each character was said to be a complete word. Consequently, many European readers were struck by the apparent grammatical simplicity of Chinese and its one-to-one-relationships between a word and a real thing. As a result, Kircher's explanation reinforced the belief that the Chinese language contained Real Characters.

Several of the numerous and diverse schemes for a universal language were influenced by Chinese. In 1661 Dalgarno proposed a 'philosophical language' in which terms reflected not merely words but the nature of things which they represented.[31] Using twenty letters, Dalgarno constructed words which reflected genus, species, and specific differences. Additional letters were added to facilitate pronunciation and to designate necessary grammatical features. Dalgarno's scheme was greatly influenced by seventeenth-century explanations of the Chinese language. These claimed that the structure of a Chinese character could be analyzed in terms of the objects to which the character referred. Dalgarno believed the Real Characters preceded the use of vocal characters in both Chinese and Egyptian systems.

In 1688 John Wilkins attempted to construct a philosophical language that improved upon Dalgarno's scheme.[32] Wilkins expanded Dalgarno's twenty genera to forty, and then subdivided these into genera, species, and specific differences. Wilkins drew examples of specific Chinese characters from a work by a Jesuit missionary showing how certain elements of Chinese characters were based upon real things.[33]

The seventeenth-century polyhistor style reached its culmination in Leibniz. Although treated today primarily as a philosopher and secondarily as a mathematician, Leibniz would have regarded these classifications as narrowly demeaning for his age prized the facility to move with learned ease through as many fields as possible. Leibniz's polyhistor style is not something that can be easily detached from his achievements in philosophy because it could be argued (and probably would have been argued by seventeenth-century savants) that his philosophic insights were the result of his work in occupations as diverse as secretary to the ducal court of Hanover, historian of the House of Braunschweig, mathematician both in the pure realm of inventing the calculus and in the applied realm of producing a mechanical calculator, director of a Harz Mountain mine, librarian of the Herzog August Bibliothek in Wolfenbüttel, diplomat and irenical negotiator between Catholics and Protestants.

As a voracious reader who carried on a prolific correspondence, Leibniz was aware of the attempts of Dalgarno and Wilkins to create a philosophical language and also of Descartes's proposal for a philosophical language.[34] Leibniz was also influenced by the mnemonic tradition and by Lullist combinatory ideas.[35] Although Kircher had attempted to apply the Lullist art of combinations to the formulation of a universal language, he had not sought to create a philosophical language. Leibniz did so and may be seen as the convergence point of many intellectual currents. Leibniz believed that a philosophical language would ease communication and do away with many disputes through its greater precision, which would lead to truths in a manner akin to arithmetic and geometry.

Leibniz shared the belief of his contemporaries in the possibility of discovering Real Characters, though he developed his own ideas on the subject. For Leibniz, Real Characters were written, drawn, or engraved signs which signified not words, letters, or syllables but things and ideas.[36] Leibniz initially believed that Chinese characters, like Egyptian hieroglyphs and signs of chemistry and astronomy, were limited to representing ideas and did not extend to the process of reasoning or to the discovery of knowledge. Consequently, unlike arithmetical and algebraic notations, they were not suitable for his Universal Characteristic. However, Leibniz never lost interest in the Chinese language, and his assessment of its potential as a philosophical language later became more positive.

Leibniz's belief in Real Characters was consonant with his principles of Pre-Established Harmony and Sufficient Reason. The Pre-Established Harmony guaranteed that every thought in the metaphysical realm had a corresponding element in the physical realm. For Leibniz, this harmony between the soul, which acted freely according to the rules of final causes, and the body, which acted mechanically according to the rules of efficient causes, was the result of the way in which God had created the world.[37] Following from this correspondence between the abstract and sensate realms, Leibniz argued that thinking had a corresponding manifestation in letters and sounds.[38] It was this correspondence between the realm of thought and the realm of letters and sounds that led Leibniz to conclude both that a Primitive Language had existed and that a new universal language could be constructed.

Leibniz's correspondence with Jesuit missionaries in China not only gave him access to Chinese philosophy but enabled him to receive direct answers to his questions from the most knowledgeable Europeans of that time. The China missionary J. Bouvet provided information about the historical formation and structure of Chinese characters which caused Leibniz to revise his previous estimate. Instead of viewing the characters as essentially literal or pictographic representations of things, in the manner of the Egyptian hieroglyphs, Leibniz now saw them as more philosophical constructs. In responding to Leibniz's explanation of his binary system of mathematics, Bouvet explained that the earliest forms of Chinese writing – the diagrams of Fu Xi – were composed of broken and whole lines which could represent the two basic units ('0' and '1') in a binary progression.[39] This explanation reinforced Leibniz's belief in the possibility of fusing mathematics and language and was incorporated into his *Nouveaux essais*.[40]

What Bouvet communicated to Leibniz about the origins and structure of the Chinese characters was an exciting discovery. It not only had implications for a universal language, but it presented striking confirmation of another of Leibniz's ideas. In a New Year's letter of 1697 to his patron, Duke Rudolph Augustus of Braunschweig-Lüneberg-Wolfenbüttel, Leibniz had proposed the minting of a commemorative medallion.[41] One side of the medallion would show the image of Duke Rudolph and the other the *Imagio Creationis* (Image of Creation), which would consist of the binary (dyadic) system of mathematics. As this proposal indicates, Leibniz's polymathic thinking linked mathematics, religion, and politics; he believed that his binary system elucidated the manner in which God had created the world – namely, out of the units of zero (nothing) and one (God). It is this process that Leibniz referred to as the 'Secret of Creation'. Leibniz had passed this Secret of Creation on to the Jesuits in China.[42] Consequently, when Bouvet's letter came, Leibniz felt that his theory of Creation was being confirmed from the other side of the world. This discovery reinforced his belief in the universal basis of knowledge, and it was an intellectual high point to the seventeenth-century European interest in Chinese philosophy.

V. LEIBNIZ, MALEBRANCHE, AND CHINESE PHILOSOPHY

Leibniz's most substantive work on Chinese philosophy was the *Discours sur la théologie naturelle des Chinois* (Discourse on the natural theology of the Chinese).[43] He was stimulated to write it after reading a distorted interpretation of Chinese philosophy by another influential seventeenth-century European philosopher, N. Malebranche (1638–1715). Whereas Leibniz had devoted years to studying Chinese philosophy, Malebranche came to the subject late in life and only because of distinctly European concerns.[44] In fact, Malebranche's interest in Chinese philosophy was quite passive. It was his eminent reputation as a European philosopher that led one side in the Chinese Rites Controversy to seek him out. The aim was to enlist Malebranche's support in battling the Jesuits' interpretation, which was regarded as being too sympathetic to the atheistic and materialistic tendencies of the Chinese Confucian literati.

On the basis of inadequate sources provided by Bishop Artus de Lionne, a former missionary to China, Malebranche composed in 1707 a small work entitled *Entretien d'un philosophe chrétien et d'un philosophe chinois sur l'existence et la nature de Dieu* (Dialogue between a Christian philosopher and a Chinese philosopher on the existence and nature of God).[45] Malebranche was moved to write his dialogue mainly because he perceived Spinozism in Chinese philosophy. (Actually, a link between the thought of Spinoza and Chinese philosophy was perceived by several seventeenth-century European philosophers, the most eminent of whom were Bayle and Malebranche.)[46] Writing this dialogue gave him the opportunity not only to combat these irreligious traces but also to clearly distance his own philosophy from Spinozistic monism and to rebut critics like Arnauld, who claimed that Malebranche's philosophy contained Spinozistic elements.[47] Consequently, Malebranche attacked the Chinese for recognising only one substance, which consisted of matter that differed in degrees ranging from gross to rarefied. Malebranche argued that 'there are only two types of being, namely, *li* or supreme Reason, Order, Wisdom, Justice, and matter [*qi*].'[48] Furthermore, Malebranche claimed, these two types of being, *li* and matter (*qi*), cannot exist independently of one another; and not really being separate substances, they represent an atheistic and Spinozistic monism contrary to the separation of spirit and matter found in Christian philosophy.

Malebranche's interpretations unwittingly drew from a particular school of Confucian philosophy developed by Zhu Xi (1130–1200), which is commonly referred to in Western languages as Neo-Confucianism and which made a fundamental distinction between *li* (principle) and *qi* (material force). Leibniz's *Discours* rebutted Malebranche's interpretations of Neo-Confucianism and showed them to be the distortions of a philosophic Eurocentrism.[49] In addition, Leibniz explained these Neo-Confucian terms in a manner that made his *Discours* the most knowledgeable explanation of Chinese philosophy by a seventeenth-century European philosopher.

NOTES

1 See Lach 1965, pp. 229–45.
2 See Cummins 1993. See also Mungello 1985, pp. 48–9.
3 See Mungello 1985, pp. 13–20.
4 Mungello 1985, pp. 255, 301–2.
5 Couplet 1687.
6 Fifteen of the letters in the Leibniz–Bouvet correspondence have been published in the original French in Leibniz 1990. An additional letter from Bouvet to Leibniz has been transcribed in Bouvet 1989. A description in English of the Leibniz–Bouvet correspondence is found in Mungello 1977, pp. 39–68.
7 Ricci and Trigault 1615. An English translation has been made by Louis J. Gallagher, S.J., in Ricci and Trigault 1953. Ricci is a monumental figure in early Sino-Western relations and a considerable body of literature exists on him. An intriguing work that presents Ricci as meeting a favourable reception among Chinese literati as one of the last exponents of the European mediaeval mnemonic tradition is Spence 1984.

8 For detailed discussions of seventeenth-century Europeans who were positively impressed by Confucian moral and social philosophy, see Pinot 1932, pp. 367–419; Guy 1963, pp. 106–53; Appleton 1951, pp. 36–52.

9 The origin and contents of *Confucius Sinarum Philosophus* are described at length in Mungello 1985, pp. 247–99.

10 The anonymous author of *La morale de Confucius, philosophe de la Chine* (Amsterdam 1688) was probably Louis Cousin, although some sources favour Jean de Le Brune. The English translation, *The Morals of Confucius, a Chinese Philosopher*, first appeared in 1691 with a second edition in 1706 and a third probably in 1780. For a discussion of this work and its authorship, see Mungello 1987, pp. 67–70.

11 Apart from the Ricci-Trigault journals and *Confucius Sinarum Philosophus*, the most important works in introducing Confucian philosophy to seventeenth-century Europeans were Semedo 1642; Magaillans 1670; Martini 1658; Kircher 1667; and Le Comte 1696. The contents of these works are described in detail in Mungello 1985.

12 See Dunne 1962, pp. 17–18, 86–9, 227–8, 248–9; and Standaert 1991.

13 Appleton 1951, pp. 42–5

14 Temple 1814, vol. 3, pp. 313, 332–3, 342, 382.

15 Temple 1814, 'Of Health and Long Life', vol. 3, p. 297; and 'Ancient and Modern Learning', vol. 3, pp. 456–7.

16 Leibniz 1979b, p. 9. See also Leibniz 1957, p. 68.

17 Leibniz 1979b, pp. 10–1, and 1957, pp. 69, 88.

18 Leibniz 1979b, pp. 18–19, and 1957, p. 75.

19 See Pinot 1932, pp. 285 and *passim*; and Guy 1963, pp. 106–54.

20 See Lach 1968; Wolff 1985; Lach 1953; Menzel 1956.

21 Martini 1658.

22 Ussher 1650–4.

23 See Mungello 1985, pp. 125–8; and Pinot 1932, pp. 189–279.

24 Webb 1669.

25 Mungello 1985, pp. 188–91.

26 Bacon 1974, p. 131 (*The Advancement of Learning*, II.16.2).

27 Mendoza 1585.

28 Ricci and Trigault 1615, p. 27.

29 Mungello 1985, pp. 174–88.

30 Leibniz-Handschriften, V,I,1r-2v. This manuscript is reproduced in part in Leibniz 1903, pp. 536–7.

31 Dalgarno 1661.

32 John Wilkins 1688.

33 The Jesuit work that Wilkins drew from was Semedo 1642.

34 Descartes's proposal for a philosophical language can be found in a passage in a letter to Mersenne, 20 November 1629, AT I 76–82. The copy Leibniz made is preserved among the Leibniz-Handschriften and has been published in Leibniz 1903, pp. 27–8.

35 Yates 1966, pp. 378–88.

36 See Leibniz's 'Scientia Generalis. Characteristica' in Ger. VII 198–9, 204. See also Couturat 1901, p. 81.

37 See Leibniz's fifth letter to Samuel Clarke, response to paras. 31 and 32, in Ger. VII 412.

38 Leibniz, *Nouveaux essais*, LAkad VI.VI 77.

39 Bouvet to Leibniz, dated 4 November 1701 from Beijing, in Leibniz 1990, pp. 147–70.

40 LAkad VI.VI 274, 398. Also see Rita Widmaier 1983.

41 Leibniz, 'Das Geheimnis der Schöpfung, Neujahrsbrief an der Herzog Rudolph August von Branuschweig-Lüneburg-Wolfenbüttel' in Leibniz 1968, pp. 19–23.

42 Mungello 1977, pp. 44–5.

43 Leibniz (1716), *Discours sur la théologie naturelle des Chinois (Lettre sur la philosophie chinoise à M. de Remond)*. Hannover, Niedersächsische Landesbibliothek, MS 37, 1810, no. 1. For an English translation, see Leibniz 1977.

44 Mungello 1980.

45 Nicolas Malebranche, *Entretien d'un philosophe chrétien et d'un philosophe chinois sur l'existence et la nature de Dieu* (1708), in Mal. *OC* XV. For an English translation, see Malebranche 1980c.

46 See Lai 1985.

47 Mungello 1980, pp. 561–3; and Malebranche 1980c, pp. 17–23.

48 N. Malebranche, 'Avis au lecteur touchant l'entretien d'un philosophe chrétien avec un philosophe chinois', in Mal. *OC* XV, p. 40. The *Avis* (Note) was actually a point-by-point rebuttal of a critical view of Malebranche's *Entretien,* which appeared in the July 1708 issue of *Mémoires de Trévoux*. Malebranche published his *Avis* in August of 1708, and this note has consequently been included as an appendix in later editions of Malebranche's *Entretien.*

49 Mungello 1980, pp. 576–8.

II

LOGIC, LANGUAGE, AND ABSTRACT OBJECTS

4

LOGIC IN THE SEVENTEENTH CENTURY: PRELIMINARY REMARKS AND THE CONSTITUENTS OF THE PROPOSITION

GABRIEL NUCHELMANS

I. MAIN CURRENTS IN SEVENTEENTH-CENTURY LOGIC

Until fairly recently, the study of the development of logic in the seventeenth century suffered from a certain lack of comprehensiveness, depth, and historical sensitivity.[1] Yet, there can be little doubt that during this period some remarkable changes in the conception of that discipline took place. Indeed, it would be misleading to treat the seventeenth century as a kind of organic unit in the history of logic. In point of fact, there is a marked discontinuity between the principal features of the varieties of logic that were predominant in roughly the first half of the century and the way of viewing logic that came to the fore in the second half.

The first half of the seventeenth century may be characterised by a general tendency to continue teaching logic in one of the versions that had been handed down from the remote or near past. Among those traditional forms of logic, Aristotelianism, either of a scholastic type or more independent of mediaeval interpretations, maintained its strong position. The scholastic type of Aristotelianism, elaborated in the spirit of such influential thinkers as Thomas Aquinas and John Duns Scotus or adapted to the ideals of the Counter-Reformation by members of the Jesuit order, flourished especially in Roman Catholic countries but had considerable impact on the teaching of logic in the other parts of Europe as well.[2] Authoritative expositions of orthodox Thomistic doctrines are the treatises on logic included in the *Collegium Complutense philosophicum* of 1624 and in the *Cursus philosophicus Thomisticus* published by the Portuguese Dominican John of St. Thomas in 1634, while the part dealing with logic in Johannes Poncius's *Integer philosophiae cursus ad mentem Scoti* of 1643 is a good specimen of the Scotist approach. Among the many textbooks composed by Jesuits, mention may be made of the commentaries of the Collegium Conimbricense, *In universam dialecticam Aristotelis,* which saw the light at Coimbra in 1606. Of an elementary nature is Philippe Du Trieu's widely used *Manuductio ad logicam* (1614), whereas the *Logica* of Martinus Smiglecius (1618) contains erudite discussions of more advanced problems. A late representative of this Jesuit school is Hieronymus Saccherius, whose *Logica demonstrativa* came out in 1697. The best of these works profited by the results of the historical and philological research that had been undertaken by Renaissance humanists in the preceding century: they were based on familiarity with the original text of the logical writings of Aristotle and his Greek commentators or at least on more reliable translations. This easier access to the actual sources also gave rise to a great number of textbooks which offered a survey of Aristotle's doctrine that was relatively independent of the commentaries provided by the great mediaeval philosophers.[3] Examples are the *Institutio logicae* published by John Wallis in 1687 (but written much earlier) and the *Artis logicae compendium* (1691) of Henry Aldrich, which carried this kind of peripatetic lore into the next century. Besides Aristotelianism, the first decades of the seventeenth century show the last traces of humanist dialectic, mostly in the form given to that revolutionary movement by Petrus Ramus. Ramism, which had gradually absorbed the cognate type of dialectic that had been propagated by Philippus Melanchthon in Lutheran regions, remained popular in England (particularly at Cambridge), Sweden, and Switzerland, and positive or negative reactions to elements of it appear in many writings on logic of the period.[4] Finally, there was a group of logicians who tried to reconcile Aristotelianism and Ramism by integrating parts of those doctrines into a carefully constructed system. Adherents of such a syncretic eclecticism were especially numerous in Germany, where Bartholomeus Keckermann and Johann Heinrich Alsted had advocated a highly systematised organisation of textbooks. But they were also found in England and Holland, as is testified by Robert Sanderson's *Logicae artis compendium* (1615) and Franco Burgersdijck's *Institutiones logicae* (1626), both very much in demand. One text of this type published in Germany, Joachim Jungius's *Logica Hamburgensis* (1638), was highly praised by Leibniz.[5]

About the middle of the seventeenth century several new directions in the approach to logic become visible. Generally speaking, they are the outcome of three factors. In the first place, the philosophical scene was drastically changed by the novel systems developed by such anti-scholastic thinkers as Bacon, Gassendi, Hobbes, and Descartes. One of the features that are characteristic of these new philosophies is a shift of emphasis from problems connected with purely formal logic towards the epistemological and psychological aspects of human cognition. In the second place, the rise of various branches of empirical science made those who were interested in ways of expanding the field of knowledge stress methods of gaining fresh information rather than methods of organising and appraising the results of research, discovery and the inventive part of logic rather than critical judgement, and induction rather than syllogistic deduction. At the same time, the formal science of mathematics, both Euclidean geometry and algebra, began to exercise an increasing influence on the intellectual world, as the paradigm of strictly justified and organised knowledge.

Some of the philosophers who made substantial contributions to this change of outlook themselves wrote treatises of logic, for instance, Gassendi's *Institutio logica* of 1658 and Hobbes's *Computatio sive logica* (first part of De corpore) of 1655. Others, like Descartes and Locke, left it to their followers to apply the new insights to the field of logic. In the second half of the century, the Cartesian doctrine gave the strongest impulse to novel philosophical treatments of the old core of traditional logic, the most famous example being the *Logique* of Port-Royal, published, anonymously, by Arnauld and Nicole in 1662, under the title *La logique ou l'art de penser*. Other notable works by authors attracted by Descartes's philosophy are Johannes Clauberg's *Logica vetus et nova* (1654) and Arnold Geulincx's *Logica* (1662), followed in 1663 by the *Methodus inveniendi argumenta,* in which his system is set out *more geometrico*. Whereas in most of these cases it is the embedding general philosophy rather than the formal logic itself which undergoes striking changes, Leibniz deserves a place of honour in the history of logic because of the wealth of fertile ideas and suggestions by which he anticipated the radical reshaping of that very subject which was fully realised only much later.[6]

II. THE SO-CALLED PROEMIAL QUESTIONS

As a rule, seventeenth-century textbooks of logic have three main parts: one dealing with concepts or terms as elements of propositions; another discussing various types of mental, spoken, and written declarative sentences or propositions; and a third part in which reasonings as peculiar combinations of propositions were treated. Moreover, often a fourth part on method was added. Also, it was not uncommon to begin a treatise of logic with some preliminary considerations regarding its name, object, and proper division. As for the name, logicians of the seventeenth century usually preferred to call the whole of their subject logic, rather than dialectic. This preference can be explained partly as a reaction against Ramism and kindred currents, which had a predilection for the name 'dialectic'. At the same time, it was felt that 'dialectic' should be reserved for a specific part of logic rather than used for the whole, especially by authors who drew a distinction between general logic (as contained in Aristotle's *Categories, De interpre-*

tatione, and *Prior Analytics*) and special logic, under which head they dealt with three kinds of more specific syllogisms, namely, demonstrative or apodictic arguments (as in Aristotle's *Posterior Analytics*), dialectical or topical reasonings (as in Aristotle's *Topics*), and sophistical reasonings (as in Aristotle's *Sophistici elenchi*). 'Dialectic' in the narrower sense was then understood as referring to probable reasonings based on so-called topics or *loci,* commonplaces from which arguments can be drawn.

According to the Thomistic tradition, logic is concerned with things as they are conceived of by the human mind, that is, with certain accidents of being, not as being, but as known. Such accidents are entities of reason (*entia rationis*) and can be classified, according to their logical rôle, as genus, species, subject, predicate, proposition, syllogism, and so on. In his treatise *De natura logicae* of 1578, Jacopo Zabarella had characterised logic as an instrumental discipline, which forges concepts of second order (*secundae notiones*) with the purpose of furthering the understanding of the logical functions of concepts of first order.[7] These two views flow together in most statements of the nature of logic offered by the eclectics. Robert Sanderson, for instance, in his *Logicae artis compendium* of 1615, which was widely used in England, declares that logic aims at forming human reason and, secondarily, human speech. The subject-matter of logic is everything, whether really existing or not, that can be put before the mind or expressed in speech. The logician considers all such themes, not according to their own nature, but in so far as the logical instruments, that is, the concepts of second order, are applicable to them.

Now it is remarkable that several Jesuit authors who were active in the first decades of the century explicitly opposed the orthodox Thomistic tenet that the subject-matter of logic consists of *entia rationis.* According to them, logic is rather concerned with the really existing operations of the human understanding, classified either as the so-called ways of knowing (*modi sciendi*) – namely, defining, dividing, and reasoning – or as simple apprehension, judging, and reasoning. The logician, however, considers these operations from the specific viewpoint of the *dirigibilitas,* that is, in so far as they can be guided towards the achievement of such purposes as correctly discerning the true from the false.[8] This emphasis on the perfectibility of the actually existing operations of the human mind could then easily be extended from the original field of formal logic to the wider domain of all intellectual faculties that are involved in the process of gaining and justifying knowledge. Such normative and therapeutic treatises on the conduct of the understanding and the improvement of the intellect became serious competitors of the traditional books on formal logic in the strict sense and were not seldom called logic, in an altered and broadened sense of that word, including much that nowadays would be deemed to belong to epistemology and psychology.[9]

In addition to the divisions of logic into a general and a special branch or according to such mental operations as simple apprehension, judgement, and reasoning, or definition, division, and argument, Ramists, but also other logicians, such as Leibniz, regarded the dichotomy into invention – containing instructions and strategies for finding an appropriate subject-matter for disputations – and judgement – the critical examination of the ordered products of invention – as the most fundamental principle of arranging their subject. Moreover, Ramus had divided judgement, as opposed to invention, into a part dealing with isolated assertions and a discursive part. The latter was subdivided into the doctrine of syllogism and a discussion of method, which was defined as the proper arrange-ment of a plurality of sound arguments (*multorum et bonorum argumentorum dispo-sitio*). This feature of Ramist (and Melanchthonian) logic, to devote a chapter to the elucidation of method in general, was adopted by many non-Ramists, among them such influential writers as Jungius, Gassendi, Hobbes, and the authors of the Port-Royal *Logique*. The content of the section on method could vary consider-ably; Arnauld and Nicole, for instance, borrowed their methodology almost entirely from Descartes's *Regulae ad directionem ingenii* and Pascal's *De l'esprit géomé-trique*. It should be noted, however, that there were also logicians who protested against this widespread habit of mixing heterogeneous subjects. The purist Geu-lincx, for example, concludes his *Logica* of 1662 with an appendix in which he refuses to deal with method, on the ground that it belongs to a different branch of knowledge.[10]

III. TERMS

The first part of a textbook of logic was commonly devoted to the smallest relevant units that constitute a proposition. A categorical proposition contains a subject-term and a predicate-term. But besides these material constituents it also comprises elements that determine such formal features as quality and quantity, the affirmative or negative quality of a proposition being determined by the nature of the copula ('is', 'is not') and the universal or particular quantity by such words as 'every' and 'some'. Traditionally, the subject-term and the predicate-term were called categorematic signs, whereas the formal elements were referred to as syncategorematic or cosignifying signs. In the latter class were also placed the signs that are marks of those other mental activities whereby compound propositions are framed and propositions are combined into reasonings and complexes of arguments. This distinction between categorematic and syncategorematic signs was generally known in the seventeenth century, but it was often expressed in a somewhat different way. The Port-Royal *Grammaire générale et raisonnée,* published by Antoine Arnauld and Claude Lancelot in 1660, states (II, 1) that the most fundamental distinction that can be made with respect to that which occurs in the mind is the distinction between the objects of our thought and the forms or manners of our thinking. The objects of thought are the things that are apprehended through the conceptions associated with the subject-term and the predicate-term, whereas among the forms of thinking are the act of judging, the acts of conjoining and disjoining, and such movements of the soul as desires, commands, and interrogations. The general classification of words is based upon this distinction between objects of thought and manners of thinking. There can be little doubt that by it the authors wished to emphasise the difference between the passive side of the soul, which is prominent when it receives ideas, and the active side, which it shows in judging and performing the other mental operations which the Cartesians often called volitions in order to contrast them with the passive understanding. At the same time, the distinction is strongly reminiscent of the mediaeval distinction between actually performing an act or experiencing a feeling and putting that act or feeling before the mind as something merely conceived of. According to Geulincx, for instance, the copula is nothing but a mark of a simultaneously performed act of affirming (*nota affirmationis*), whereas the noun 'affirmation' is the name of that act when it is conceived of and talked about by the logician. A *nota* or mark is a sign of an act as performed, that is, a sign by means of which we make known some act or state of our own, not as something apprehended, as when its name is introduced, but as it is here and now performed or experienced by us.[11] Such marks of actually performed operations or experienced feelings were also frequently called particles.

As for the categorematic constituents of a proposition, the objects of thought and their designations, they were called, rather neutrally, *termini,* that is, points at which the analysis comes to an end, or *extrema,* on account of their being situated at the beginning and the end of the proposition. For the mental counterparts of nouns and verbs such old names as *conceptus, intentio, notio,* and *similitudo* remained in use; but they had two rivals which are worthy of note. In the first place, logicians of the eclectic type had a certain predilection for the word *thema,* which had been introduced into logic by Melanchthon in 1520. Johannes Clauberg, in his *Metaphysica de ente* of 1664, distinguished three meanings of the word *ens:* it may denote everything that can be thought of, or everything that exists even if nobody thinks of it, or that which exists by itself, as a substance. An entity in the first sense is called *thema* by the logicians. It is something that can be put before the mind and talked about and then possesses at least the kind of being which consists in being present to the mind as an object of thought (*esse obiectivum, esse cognitum*).[12] A theme, then, is apparently the very same thing as a *conceptus obiectivus,* namely, a thing in so far as it is conceived of by the mind and thus is the passive content of that act of conceiving or *conceptus formalis.* A *thema simplex* is the content of an act of simple apprehension, and a *thema coniunctum* or *complexum* is a conceived state of affairs. The part of logic that deals with these two kinds of themes, in the wake of Aristotle's *Categories* and *De interpretatione,* was called by Burgersdijck *logica thematica,* as opposed to *logica organica,* the part that is concerned with the logical instruments, the concepts of second order that are applicable to the themes.

In the second half of the seventeenth century, the word *thema* rapidly lost its attractiveness. No doubt this was partly due to the success of another designation of the objects of thought: the word *idea* as it had been introduced by Descartes. In the reply to Hobbes's fifth objection to his *Meditationes,* Descartes informs the reader that he had chosen that word as the name of the concepts that are peculiar to pure intellection because it was already commonly used by philosophers to indicate the forms involved in the conceptions of the divine intellect. In a marginal note added in the Latin edition of the *Discours de la méthode,* it is further explained that the word *idea* should be taken to stand for every thing thought of in so far as it has only some *esse obiectivum* in the mind.[13] In general, it is clear that for Descartes *idea* had practically the same meaning as the expressions *conceptus obiectivus* and *thema* had for other philosophers. The main difference is that the latter terms were restricted to the semantic and representative content of an act of conceiving, whereas in Descartes's usage *idea* often includes both the act of thinking, which always possesses real existence as an accident in an individual subject, and the determinate content of that act, the thing thought of, which may or may not have a correlate in the real world. This Cartesian use of the word *idea* quickly found its way into treatises of logic that were written by kindred spirits, in particular the widely read *Logique* of Port-Royal. But the word was also welcomed by such non-Cartesian logicians as Hobbes, Gassendi, and Leibniz, who understood it each in his own way. For Hobbes it is one of the names of the appearances of particular bodies-with-accidents produced by sense-perception, and of the images of memory and phantasy. Gassendi prefers the word *idea* for the generalised mental pictures which are the outcome of repeated and remembered particular sensations and constitute a kind of record of previous experience in the light of which new sensations may be interpreted, classified, and named. Leibniz, on the other hand, draws a distinction between a notion or concept, which is a thought-content in so far as it is actually conceived of, and an idea, which is a *cogitabile,* a potential pattern of thought that may be in the mind before and after the conception in which it is actualised.[14] Although such divergences of opinion concerning the meaning of the word *idea* as the designation of the mental constituents of a proposition make little difference for the more technical aspects of logic, it is obvious that its employment easily occasioned logicians to overlay their proper subject with considerations of an epistemological, psychological, or ontological nature.

Of the many subtle discussions of properties of terms and distinctions among kinds of terms that had been part and parcel of scholastic logic, at best remnants survive in the common run of seventeenth-century handbooks. Worthy of mention is Geulincx's interesting attempt to support the doctrine of supposition and uptake *(acceptio)* – of the ways in which a speaker lends a specific meaning to words in the context of a proposition and the audience grasps that meaning accordingly – by a set of four hierarchically arranged maxims of conversation. The first rule of interpretation lays down the absolute priority of the speaker's intention. The second rule requires that in general the hearer keep to the most usual and obvious sense. According to the third rule, the hearer should favour an interpretation that renders the utterance true. And, according to the fourth rule, the same word is to be understood consistently, with the same meaning, wherever it occurs within the utterance. Geulincx also invokes these maxims in exposing certain fallacies.[15] Furthermore, the important distinction between the formal and the material significate of a linguistic expression which had dominated mediaeval elucidations of meaning was revivified by the *Logique* of Port-Royal (I, 6) under the names *compréhension* and *étendue* or *extension.* Applied to an idea, the comprehension is described as consisting of those attributes which the idea includes and which cannot be removed from it without destroying the idea. The extension, on the other hand, is the set of inferiors or subjective parts to which the idea is applicable; this set comprises lower species as well as individuals.[16] Leibniz uses at least once – in the *Nouveaux essais*[17] – the word *intension* for what he elsewhere calls the *ratio formalis (raison formelle), formalitas (formalité), consideratio, modus considerandi,* or *modus concipiendi.* In several passages he points out that concepts which are coincident or extensionally identical cannot be substituted for each other in contexts where the truth of the statement depends upon the specific way of conceiving something. In the proposition 'Peter in so far as he was the apostle who denied Christ sinned', for example, the part 'the apostle who denied Christ' cannot, *salva veritate,* be replaced by 'Peter'.[18]

IV. CATEGORIES

In general, Aristotle's doctrine of the categories or predicaments – the ten classes of entities denoted by categorematic terms: substance, quantity, quality, relation, place, time, action, passion, posture, state – remained an obligatory item in the repertoire of seventeenth-century logicians.[19] As far as the doctrine was still taken seriously, it also occasionally aroused the old disputes concerning the question as to whether the categories are of things or of concepts and words, and whether accordingly they are to be studied in metaphysics or in logic. A category in the traditional sense was usually taken to be an ordered series of things that are, according to degrees of generality, arranged under the same highest genus. The category of substance, for instance, is the entire Porphyrian tree, from the highest genus down to the lowest species.

The Aristotelian doctrine, however, had already been sharply attacked by humanist dialecticians. Ramus had even gone so far as to replace the Aristotelian list by ten entirely new categories, which in his opinion were the genuine sources of inspiration for topical reasoners.[20] These previous criticisms had created an atmosphere of doubt concerning the adequacy of Aristotle's choice, so that many philosophers felt free to advance their own suggestions, which were often based chiefly on considerations that had little or nothing to do with logic in the strict sense. Typical of the sceptical attitude towards the underlying principles and the usefulness of the Aristotelian list is the pertinent passage in the Port-Royal *Logique* (I, 3), where the traditional lore is faithfully reproduced but provided with comments that leave no doubt about the authors' conviction that it should be replaced by a more up-to-date inventory of things in the world. Arnauld and Nicole mention a list which was held to be more fitting by the adherents of the new philosophy: mind, matter, measure, situation, figure, motion, and rest.[21]

The search for an adequate set of categories occupied a central place in Leibniz's logic. In the letter to Gabriel Wagner of 1696 he tells the addressee that already as a youth he took great pleasure in the categories and examined many books on logic to see where the best and most complete lists could be found. Also, he used to ask himself and his teachers whether, analogously to the way in which simple terms had been ordered through the traditional categories, one could not set up categories for complex terms or truths as well. Later he realised that geometricians, who arrange and demonstrate propositions according to their dependence upon each other, had long before pointed the way to solving this problem.[22] But prior to transferring their method to other fields it would at any rate be necessary to marshall non-propositional concepts according to suitable categories. This endeavour took for Leibniz the form of discovering the so-called alphabet of human thoughts, that is, the set of primitive concepts which, together with rules of combining them perspicuously into compound terms, were to constitute the core of the ideographic *characteristica universalis* that he strove to contrive. For a time, he believed that it would be possible to arrive at a number of unanalysable notions in the sense of absolutely given last elements of thought; later he seems to have contented himself with looking for a set of conceptual primes that would be the terminal points of analysis at least for us. To judge from the group of no less than thirty manuscripts in which Leibniz tried his hand at enumerating systematically the simple concepts by means of which other concepts could be defined, he considered this task extremely important, particularly in connexion with his ambitious plan for a demonstrative encyclopaedia.[23]

V. THE PREDICABLES

According to Geulincx,[24] logicians called an attribute that can be affirmed of the subject in a true statement *praedicabile*. In addition to this nuance of meaning, however, the word also had its Aristotelian-Porphyrian use as a covering term for a species (for instance 'man'), for the genus ('animal') and the specific difference ('rational') as the essential components of a species, for a *proprium* ('capable of laughing') as an attribute that is logically deducible from those essential constituents, and for an accident ('white') as a contingent predicate. Such predicables or types of predication were sometimes viewed as the *gradus praedicamentales,* that is, the degrees of generality according to which the categories are hierarchically arrayed.[25] Whereas the categories are concepts of first order, by means of which things in the outside world are apprehended, the predicables are concepts of second order, entities or attributes of reason (*entia, affectiones rationis*) that function as logical tools for distinguishing the ways in which primary concepts can be predicated of one another.[26]

The authors of the Port-Royal *Logique* (I, 7) offer a fair summary of what the schoolmen had taught on the predicables, adding the observation that more important than being generally aware of the existence of the five kinds is the ability to recognise each of them as it is truly applicable in a particular case. Geulincx acknowledges only four predicables, on the ground that the difference between genus and species is irrelevant from a purely logical point of view; he takes them therefore together under the name *superius* (for instance 'being' is a *superius* of 'body', which itself is a *superius* of 'metal'). A species is a *superius* of something that is not a *superius* of something else (for instance 'gold', which is a *superius* of 'this gold' and 'that gold', none of which is a *superius*).[27] More severe is the criticism uttered by Leibniz in his letter to Gabriel Wagner: the five predicables of Porphyry are totally inadequate, he states, since they contain only denominations that can be expressed in the nominative case, and not even all of these. Probably influenced by Ramus, Leibniz is of the opinion that the Porphyrian list should be extended to include such predicables as cause and effect, whole and part, which are found in the topics and whose expression requires other cases than the nominative.[28] Furthermore, Leibniz repeatedly insists on the arbitrariness of considering a definition like 'Man is a rational animal', where 'animal' indicates the genus and 'rational' the specific difference, as preferable to 'Man is an animal rational (being)', in which 'rational (being)' indicates the genus and 'animal' the difference. Every difference can be conceived of as a genus, and every genus as a difference.[29] A similar flexibility in assigning concepts to the predicables had been advocated by Mario Nizolio in his *De veris principiis et vera ratione philosophandi* of 1553, which was re-edited and furnished with an introduction by Leibniz in 1671.

VI. DIVISION

Of the three ways of knowing, or the main instruments of logic – dividing, defining, and reasoning – the first two concern simple apprehensions of things. The operation of dividing was characterised as the partition of something that is more general into several parts that are less general. Regarding the abstract rules to which a correct division should conform, there was hardly any difference of opinion. One point of disagreement was the question as to whether a division ought always to be dichotomous, that is, constructed according to the pattern of A being divided into B and not-B, so that the members are mutually exclusive and jointly exhaustive. Ramists followed their master in zealously favouring dichotomies, but the authors of the Port-Royal *Logique* (II, 15), for instance, did not object to divisions into more than two members if these were felt to be more natural.

With respect to the content of divisions, the variety was considerably greater. Within the field of philosophy proper, for example, Cartesian logicians like Michelangelo Fardella and Edmont Purchot advocated the replacement of the traditional Porphyrian tree for the category of substance by the so-called *arbor Purchotiana,* which starts with the partition of substances into thinking and extended ones, and then goes on with subdivisions of minds and bodies, two branches of which ('a living body that has the capacity of moving itself and is possessed of a mind' and 'an imperfect mind that is destined to be united with a body and is actually joined to a body') are finally brought together again in man.[30] Moreover, the skill of dividing that was taught in logic found a rich domain of application in the numerous classifications proposed in the nascent sciences, particularly by devisers of universal languages.[31]

VII. DEFINITION

Although in many logics of a more conservative stamp pride of place was still given to definitions that are of things and composed of nearest genus and specific difference, the doctrine of definition underwent some notable changes in the course of the seventeenth century. These reforms were due especially to Hobbes and Pascal, who were deeply impressed by the methods of defining employed in geometry, 'the only science that it has pleased God hitherto to bestow on mankind'. According to Hobbes, every synthetic proof sets out from primary or most universal propositions that are manifest of themselves; but all such principles are definitions of words, and so nominal. He distinguishes between words denoting things which have some conceivable cause, and words for things of which we can conceive no cause at all. The former names must have in their definition the cause or manner of their generation, as when a circle is defined to be a figure made by the circumduction of a straight line in a plane. Names of the other kind are well enough defined when, by speech as short as may be, we raise in the mind of the hearer perfect and clear ideas of the things named. Such a definition may consist of names for the genus and the difference; or, in the case of the most general names, it may take the form of a suitable circumlocution. Definitions are not only always nominal for Hobbes; they are stipulative inasmuch as it is pointless to dispute whether they are to be admitted. And he also stresses that definitions are arbitrary in that names which are defined one way in some one part of philosophy may in another part be otherwise defined.[32]

In *De l'esprit géométrique* and *De l'art de persuader*, written about 1658 and circulating widely in manuscript before they were published much later, Pascal, too, emphasises the stipulative and incontrovertible nature of nominal definitions, as opposed to alleged real definitions, which are true or false statements. At the same time, he insists on the vanity of attempts to define words that are already understood clearly enough. The Port-Royal *Logique* (I, 12–13; IV, 3–5) follows Pascal's views very closely but adds a chapter (II, 16) on real definitions and draws a distinction between nominal definitions which are stipulative and incontestable and nominal definitions which state what a certain word means according to ordinary usage or etymology and which therefore are true or false (I, 14).[33] Locke, on the other hand, in the *Essay*[34] (with Leibniz's comments in the *Nouveaux essais*), considers real definitions to be out of the question, at least in the case of substances, since we do not know the real essence of things, and accordingly characterises a definition as nothing else but showing the meaning of one word by several other not synonymous terms. Because the several terms of a definition signify several ideas, they cannot represent an idea that has no composition at all; hence, names of simple ideas cannot be defined.

Leibniz, in whose eyes definitions were extremely important, opposed in particular Hobbes's view that definitions are arbitrary, and that therefore truth, inasmuch as it depends upon definitions, is at the discretion of man. As the authors of the Port-Royal *Logique* (I, 1) had already observed, the arbitrariness of a definition can be situated either in the relation between a certain concept and the sounds signifying it or in the combination of concepts that constitutes the definiens. Even with respect to the first kind of arbitrariness, Leibniz is of the opinion that it is restricted by the use and connexion of characters when they are elements of a coherent system of signs.[35] Most explicitly and emphatically, however, he attacks the doctrine that concepts can be combined arbitrarily. In the *Discours de métaphysique* of 1686, as well as in several other places,[36] he draws his own distinction between real and nominal definitions. Through real definitions the possibility of a thing is ascertained, in the sense that its concept does not imply a contradiction. The possibility of a thing is known *a priori* when its concept can be consistently resolved into its necessary elements or into other concepts whose possibility has been established already. It is known *a posteriori* when the thing actually exists and hence is possible. Nominal definition, on the other hand, consists in an enumeration of signs that is sufficient only to distinguish the thing defined from all other things. There may be several such definitions of one and the same thing, for every reciprocal property can yield a nominal definition. But all nominal definitions have in common that they still leave open the question whether the thing defined is possible. At best they are provisional definitions, to be perfected by a demonstration that the thing defined is conceivable without contradiction.

Leibniz's theory of definition, then, is closely connected with his attempts to discover the last elements of human thought and the rules according to which these prime constituents may be combined. For him, a proof of truth is a proof of possibility; and a proof of possibility is achieved through a chain of definitions that terminates, without any incompatibility, in the simple concepts which are unanalysable and undefinable, either absolutely or at least for us. In this light, it is evident that the construction of a real definition does not depend on any free choice and that not all concepts can be combined with each other.

NOTES

1 Such general histories of logic as Bochenski 1961, Kneale and Kneale 1962, and Blanché 1970 tend to take a rather dim view of seventeenth-century logic and accordingly devote little space to it, except for Leibniz's contributions. By far the best sources of information are Risse 1964–70, with extensive quotations from the original texts; and Risse 1965, for bibliographical details. Geographically restricted are Howell 1956, Howell 1971, Thomas 1964, Trentman 1976 (for England); Ceñal 1972, Muñoz Delgado 1982 (for the Iberian peninsula); and Lounela 1978 (for Finland). Further, although Ashworth 1974, 1978, 1985, and 1988 and Jardine 1988 are principally concerned with the preceding period, they may be profitably consulted also with regard to several aspects of seventeenth-century logic.

2 Risse 1964–70, vol. 1, chap. 5; vol. 2, chap. 9; Trentman 1982, pp. 818–22.

3 See Risse 1964–70, vol. 2, chap. 10.

4 See Jardine 1988, pp. 184–6; Risse 1964–70, vol. 1, chap. 3: and, for England, Oldrini 1985.

5 See Risse 1964–70, vol. 1, chap. 6. For a similar synopsis of the main currents in logic in the first half of the seventeenth century by a contemporary author see the beginning of Franco Burgersdijck's *Institutiones logicae* (Risse 1964–70, vol. 2, pp. 516–17).

6 Since L. Couturat's important monograph *La logique de Leibniz d'après des documents inédits* (1901), several surveys of Leibniz's contributions to logic have appeared: Ishiguro 1972; Burkhardt 1980a (also 1983a); Knecht 1981; F. Schupp's notes in Leibniz 1982a, pp. 135–251; Andrews 1983; Heinekamp 1988; Lenzen 1990; Mugnai 1990.

7 Zabarella 1597, pp. 21–4.

8 See, for instance, Smiglecius 1658 (Risse 1964–70, vol. 1, p. 422); also Risse 1964–70, vol. 1, p. 403; and vol. 2, pp. 316, 352. Contrast, however, the remark made by the Jesuit Honoré Fabri in 1646: 'Logica, dum agnoscit AAA in prima figura esse modum legitimum, non attingit ullo modo operationem mentis, sed talem dispositionem terminorum abstractorum' (Risse 1964–70, vol. 2, p. 156).

9 For details concerning this development see Buickerood 1985; also Furlan 1974, pp. 61–8; De Dijn 1986; Gaukroger 1989. A shift in the meaning of the word 'logic' is already obvious in a passage that occurs right at the beginning of Bacon's *Instauratio magna, Distributio operis:* 'The art which I introduce . . . is a kind of logic; though the difference between it and the ordinary logic is great; indeed immense.' See also Spinoza, *Eth.* V, pref.: 'Quomodo autem et qua via debeat intellectus perfici, et qua deinde arte corpus sit curandum, ut possit suo officio recte fungi, huc non pertinet; hoc enim ad medicinam, illud autem ad logicam spectat' (Geb. II 277).

10 Geulincx 1891–3, vol. 1, p. 454: 'Methodum tractare non concernit logicam, sed aliam aliquam scientiam, secundam a logica, anonymam hactenus, quam circumloquendo vocare possemus scientiam de scientiis.' On method see also Ashworth 1985, pp. xlviii–li.

11 Geulincx 1891–3, vol. 1, p. 462: 'Nota est signum actus ut exerciti; i.e. signum quo significamus actum aliquem nostrum (ut affirmationem, negationem, amorem, odium

etc.) non simpliciter (qualiter etiam est cum nomen suum importatur), sed prout hic et nunc a nobis exercetur.' See also Nuchelmans 1986.

12 Clauberg 1691, vol. 1, pp. 283–5. See also Nuchelmans 1983, pp. 30–5.

13 AT VII 181; AT VI 559; see also AT VII 160.

14 For details about the vicissitudes of the word 'idea' in the seventeenth century see McRae 1965; Yolton 1975a, 1975b; Burkhardt 1980a, pp. 147–64; Nuchelmans 1983, pp. 36–41, 70–3, 121–4, 214–18; Chapter 30 of this book.

15 Geulincx 1891–3, vol. 1, pp. 221–6, 449–53, 487–8. See also Ashworth 1969.

16 According to Gassendi, even an individual is to be considered a species with respect to the nearest genus – for instance, Plato as a species with respect to the genus man. See Gassendi 1658, vol. 3, p. 161.

17 *Nouv. Ess.* IV.xvii.8.

18 Leibniz 1960, p. 475. See Mugnai 1979, pp. 82–92; Burkhardt 1980a, pp. 230–5; Nuchelmans 1983, pp. 223–31.

19 See Tonelli 1958.

20 See Risse 1964–70, vol. 1, p. 142: 'causae, facta, subiecta, adiuncta, dissentanea, comparata, nominum ratio, divisio, definitio, testimonium'.

21 See also Gassendi 1658, vol. 3, pp. 165ff.; Hobbes *Lat. Works*, vol. 1, pp. 22–5; Demé 1985; Locke, *Ess.* II.xxi.73.

22 Ger. VII 516–18 (Leibniz 1969, pp. 463–4); Leibniz 1903, pp. 345–6.

23 See Schepers 1966, 1969.

24 Geulincx 1891–3, vol. 1, p. 178; vol. 2, p. 81.

25 See Risse 1964–70, vol. 1, p. 446: 'Gradus seriei praedicamentalis sunt quibus in eadem serie res aliis superioribus et inferioribus intelliguntur. Vocantur vulgo praedicabilia' (from Keckermann, following Melanchthon).

26 See Risse 1964–70, vol. 1, p. 457; vol. 2, pp. 399–400, 407.

27 Geulincx 1891–3, vol. 1, p. 192.

28 Ger. VII 518 (Leibniz 1969, pp. 464–5).

29 Ger. VII 292 (Leibniz 1969, p. 229); *Nouv. ess.* III.iii.10.

30 See Risse 1964–70, vol. 2, pp. 124, 128.

31 See Slaughter 1982.

32 *Lat. Works*, vol. 1, p. 71–6; *Lev.* iv. For Hobbes's influence on Spinoza see De Dijn 1974, pp. 41–50.

33 See Rolf 1983.

34 Locke, *Ess.* III.ivff.

35 See especially Leibniz, Ger. VII 190–3 (Leibniz 1969, pp. 182–5). For details concerning Leibniz's theory of definition see Dascal 1980; Burkhardt 1980a, pp. 208–18, 250–3.

36 *Disc. mét.*, sec. 24; Ger. II 63; IV 422–6 (Leibniz 1969, pp. 291–4); VII 292–8 (Leibniz 1969, p. 231); *Nouv. ess.* III.iii.15, IV.ii.1; Leibniz 1903, pp. 220, 258, 328–9, 431.

5

PROPOSITION AND JUDGEMENT

GABRIEL NUCHELMANS

I. CATEGORICAL PROPOSITIONS

Seventeenth-century logicians commonly adhered to the usual distinction between two operations of the mind: on the one hand, simple conceptions, through which things are apprehended that, as categorematic terms, are capable of becoming the subject and the predicate of a categorical proposition; on the other, acts of predication, by which the contents of simple apprehensions are combined into a propositional complex that is a suitable potential object of assent or dissent. Although at the propositional level acts of predication and judgement will often coincide, authors were aware that there are good reasons to distinguish merely apprehensive propositions from judicative propositions. The former are states of affairs that are presented to the mind without any commitment to truth or falsity, whereas the latter actually have judicative or assertive force.[1] Notwithstanding the predominant tendency to stick to the traditional division into incomplex concepts and propositional complexes, there were also factors at work which made for blurring of that fundamental distinction. One of them was Descartes's use of the word *idea* for both the categorematic elements of a proposition and the proposition itself, as the object of judgement. Spinoza went even farther by explicitly declaring that at bottom a particular idea and a particular act of affirming or denying are one and the same thing. When, for example, the mind affirms that the sum of the three angles of a triangle is equal to two right angles, that affirmation cannot exist or be thought without the idea of a triangle. Conversely, the idea of a triangle cannot but include the affirmation that the sum of its angles is equal to two right angles.[2] Similarly, Leibniz held that every incomplex term may be regarded as involving something complex, inasmuch as it affirms the possibility of the thing conceived of. Moreover, according to him, such an abstract term as the 'rationality of man' is nothing but the truth of the proposition 'Man is rational.' On the other hand, propositions are capable of functioning as incomplex terms. For example, 'Man is rational' can be paraphrased as 'That man is rational is the case', in which the original proposition has become the subject-term. Leibniz expressed the hope that he would be able to reduce all propositions to terms; for such a reduction would greatly facilitate the construction of a universal language and the analysis of concepts.[3]

Nevertheless, in practice propositions were dealt with in a separate chapter of books on logic. In that connexion, the traditional division of categorical propositions into universal affirmative ('Every raven is black'), universal negative ('No ravens are black'), particular affirmative ('Some ravens are black'), and particular negative ('Some ravens are not black') gave rise to the question of what to do with such singular or individual propositions as 'This raven is black' or 'Socrates is a philosopher.'[4] In the past, some logicians had assimilated singular propositions to particular ones. Ramus, by contrast, had assigned them to a distinct class. Both views were opposed by John Wallis in a section of his *Institutio logicae* of 1687 that goes back to a disputation held nearly half a century earlier.[5] According to Wallis, the logical properties of universality and particularity belong, not to the terms as such, but rather to the formal manner in which the terms are affirmatively or negatively combined with one another. Since the subject of a singular proposition is an individual and thus has no logical parts, it is impossible that the predicate should be attributed to it only for a part; consequently, the predicate is affirmed of the subject as a whole, which means that in the context of a syllogism a singular proposition can be treated as a universal proposition. The same view was taken by the authors of the Port-Royal *Logique* (II, 3).

Leibniz's conception of singular propositions is somewhat more complicated. In the *Dissertatio de arte combinatoria* of 1666 and elsewhere, he supported the view that in syllogistic a singular proposition can be treated as a universal proposition, 'Socrates is the son of Sophroniscus' being analysed as 'Whoever is (identical with) Socrates is the son of Sophroniscus'; this kind of analysis he ascribed to Johannes Rauen.[6] In two later passages, however, Leibniz expresses the opinion that singular propositions might just as well be assimilated to particular ones. Since for him the concept of an individual is a completely saturated notion, there is no difference between the concept associated with 'Alexander the Great' and that associated with 'a certain Alexander the Great'. Moreover, considering that among propositions a universal affirmative and a particular negative are contradictorily opposed, he concludes that a singular proposition is equivalent both to a particular ('The apostle Peter is not a soldier') and to a universal proposition ('The apostle Peter is a soldier'). This view he saw confirmed by the fact that in such a valid syllogism of the third figure (in which the middle term is subject in each premise) as 'Every writer is a man; some writer is the apostle Peter; therefore, the apostle Peter is a man' the conclusion must be particular. A singular proposition, then, may be held to be equivalent to a particular as well as to a universal proposition. 'The apostle Peter', 'every apostle Peter', and 'some apostle Peter' simply coincide.[7]

Concerning the proper analysis of a categorical proposition in general, there was a dispute of long standing among logicians. In his *Logica* of 1618, Martinus Smiglecius extensively discusses the two rival views.[8] One party defended a tripartite analysis, into subject, copula, and predicate ('Socrates-is-writing'), while the other camp, which was clearly influenced by the grammarians, preferred a bipartite analysis, into subject and finite verb ('Socrates-writes'). Smiglecius himself favours the bipartite view, which, he says, was shared by many modern authors, pointing out that a finite verb signifies not a mere tie or conjunction but a conjunction by way of a performed action. Since an action as performed is always related to some subject that performs the action, the finite verb signifies both the action and the intrinsic relatedness of the action to a subject. Every finite verb has a signification in which there is a blank for the subject that performs or undergoes the action denoted by the verb. By contrast, the authors of the Port-Royal *Grammaire* (II, 13) introduced the tripartite analysis from logic into grammar, in the same austere version in which it was adopted in the fifth edition of the *Logique* (II, 2) and upheld by Geulincx throughout his *Logica* of 1662. According to those writers, there is only one genuine verb, the copula, whose sole function consists in being the mark of a performance of an act of affirming. Apparently they wanted to separate as clearly as possible the one element that is the mark of the actual performance of an operation of affirming, and thus of the manner of thinking which is the essential form of a proposition, from all the material elements, that is, from the categorematic signs of the objects of the passive understanding. This pure copula was even stripped of the denotation of time that was traditionally ascribed to the verb, no doubt under the influence of the doctrine that in eternal truths – the only truths with which those in search of scientific knowledge are concerned – the verb is tenseless and indicates nothing but a logical or conceptual connexion between predicate and subject.

II. PREDICATION

Both the supporters of a tripartite analysis, according to which the copula is a separate constituent of a categorical proposition, and the advocates of a bipartite analysis, according to which the tie between an action as performed and the required subject lies in a formal aspect of the finite verb, are faced with the question of the import of the connecting element in so far as it brings about the predication that is typical of the second operation of the mind. The general drift of the answer given to that question by most mediaeval philosophers may be illustrated by John of St. Thomas's explanation of such a predication as 'Man is white.'[9] Although the two conceptions of man and white are different inasmuch as they are distinct ways of thinking of something, they are conjoined in such a manner that the thing conceived of through these different thoughts is represented as the same. The subject and the predicate signify something that in spite of its being apprehended by conceptions whose content is different is the same in so far as it exists in reality. Affirmative predication, then, requires both diversity of conception (*secundum rationem*) and sameness of reference (*secundum rem*).

The general pattern of this view of predication is still clearly recognisable in writers whose philosophical outlook differed widely from Thomistic and kindred doctrines. Gassendi, for example, emphasises that in predication there is always separation, in the sense of keeping distinct the subject-concept and the predicate-concept; the uniting function of the copula consists not in identifying those concepts but rather in propounding them as applying to one and the same thing outside thought.[10] Hobbes defines a proposition as a sentence consisting of two names coupled together by which the speaker makes known that he conceives the latter name to be the name of the same thing whereof the former is the name, or that the former name is comprehended (*contineri*) by the latter, in the sense that the predicate or *continens* is the name of everything of which the subject or *contentum* is the name. However, the very act of predication in which the names raise in the mind the thought of one and the same thing also gives rise to the question as to why those names are imposed on the thing. Now, the causes for which names are imposed are the same as the causes of our conceptions, namely, the particular accidents of bodies that are modes according to which they appear to a sentient subject or modes of conceiving. Such causes of conceptions and names are denoted by abstract names, which Hobbes therefore considers as originating in the act of predication. In framing a proposition, then, one is aware of the difference between the subject and the predicate, as caused by different accidents, but simultaneously of their applicability to the same thing. According to Hobbes, this peculiar combination of divergence and sameness is also the essential feature of reasoning, which he regards as a form of calculation in which the same thing may enter into account for diverse accidents and under diverse conceptions and denominations.[11]

It is worthy of note that Hobbes's use of *continens* for the predicate and *contentum* for the subject, which is also found in Geulincx's theory of predication, was reversed by Leibniz. Although in his discussions of logical systems Leibniz often viewed predication from an extensional standpoint, as propounding a relationship between individuals and sets or between sets, there can be no doubt that on the whole he preferred an intensional interpretation. For him predication is first and foremost an act of registering a special relation of containment between two concepts. In thus following the way of ideas (*via idealis*) and the method through notions rather than the method through individuals, he believed himself to have the support of Aristotle, who had understood 'Man is an animal' as stating that the concept of animal is in the concept of man.[12] In the case of a singular proposition, this containment theory of predication[13] may be set out as follows. The subject-term is associated with a complete concept of the individual concerned, whereas the predicate-term signifies a general concept. In predicating the attribute of the subject, one uses the copula to indicate that the subject-concept contains, as one of its constituents, the predicate-concept, or that the latter is included in the former in such a way that to everything to which the subject-concept applies the predicate-concept is also applicable. When the predication corresponds to a state of affairs in the world outside thought, that correlate consists of the individual substance denoted and the individual property which inheres in that substance and falls under the general concept signified by the predicate-term.

With this idea of predication in mind, Leibniz criticised – rather superficially – Locke's definition of a true proposition as the joining or separating of signs as the things signified by them do agree or disagree one with another. According to Leibniz, such a combination of terms as *l'homme sage* is not a proposition, no more than pronouncing *l'homme* and then, separated by a pause, *sage* is a negation. Besides, the agreement or disagreement expressed by a proposition is of a very special kind, quite different from the way in which two eggs are alike or two enemies disagree.[14]

III. OVERTLY AND COVERTLY COMPOUND PROPOSITIONS

In the Port-Royal *Logique* (II, 5) – and in most other texts – simple propositions, which have only one subject and one predicate, are distinguished from compound propositions, which have more than one subject or more than one predicate. Such compound propositions should not be confused with complex propositions. Even though the subject, predicate, or copula of a proposition may be complex, in that, for instance, the subject or predicate includes a relative clause, such a complex proposition is nonetheless to be classified as simple. In the same vein, Geulincx draws a distinction between a loose enumeration (*enumeratio laxa*) and a compact enumeration (*enumeratio pressa*). He contrasts 'Peter and Paul are learned', which can be expanded into the compound proposition 'Peter is learned and Paul is learned', with 'Peter and Paul are two', which cannot be so expanded. Similarly, 'Peter or Paul is learned' differs from 'For racing either human beings or beasts are necessary', because the latter cannot be analysed into 'Either human beings are necessary for racing or beasts are necessary for racing', since both disjuncts would be false.[15] Evidently, this is the old distinction between conjoint ('Peter and Paul') or disjoint ('Peter or Paul') extremes taken in a divided sense and taken in a composite sense.

In comparison with simple or categorical propositions, the status of compound or hypothetical propositions, built by means of such connectives as 'and', 'or', 'if-then' was often felt to be somewhat questionable. If the essence of a proposition is viewed as lying in its predicating an attribute of a subject, a compound proposition, which can hardly be considered as predicating one proposition of another, is called a proposition only by courtesy and by a certain analogy, namely, in so far as it unites two categorical propositions.[16] Some logicians even reserved the name *propositio* for categorical statements, employing *enuntiatio,* which was commonly used as a synonym of *propositio,* as a generic term for both simple and compound statements.[17] For the connecting element that is essential to the two kinds of statement the name *copula* continued to be used, but a distinction was drawn between the *copula verbalis,* or *categorica,* and the *copula grammaticalis,* or *hypothetica.*

In the light of the difference in rank that was assigned to categorical and compound propositions, it is not surprising that attempts were made to reduce the latter to the former. Geulincx, for example, who conceded that superficially conditional statements are compound, held that at a deeper level they should be regarded as simple. The conditional 'If I am standing, I am able to stand' is equivalent to 'From the fact that I am standing it follows that I am able to stand' (*Ex sto sequitur stare possum,* that is, 'The affirmation *Stare possum* is a proposition that follows from (is included in) the affirmation *Sto*'), which is a simple proposition having a modal nature because it is an affirmation about an affirmation.[18] John Wallis, in his *Institutio logicae* of 1687 (II, 10), interpreted the conditional 'If the sun shines, it is day' as the universal categorical proposition 'Every case in which the sun shines is a case in which it is day', adding that the two statements are different only from a grammatical point of view, not logically.[19] And Leibniz extended his hope that he would be able to represent all propositions as terms to the reduction of all hypothetical propositions to categorical ones.[20] He tried to achieve the latter purpose by exploiting the ambiguity of the words *antecedens* and *consequens,* which in Ramist terminology could also denote the subject and the predicate of a categorical proposition, and by broadening his notion of containment. Just as in a true categorical proposition the predicate is contained in the subject, so a conditional statement may be understood as affirming that the consequent is contained in the antecedent. The conditional 'If A is B, then C is D', for instance, is taken as having the form 'L is M', in which 'L' stands for the antecedent conception that A is B and 'M' for the consequent conception that C is D, and the whole is read as 'M is contained in L.'

On the other hand, several logicians were inclined to follow those earlier authors who held that at least necessarily true universal categorical propositions actually have conditional import. Hobbes is quite explicit about the difference between necessary and contingent propositions in this respect. Whereas, 'Every man is an animal' is synonymous with 'If any thing be a man, it is also an animal', the sentence 'Every crow is black' does not mean the same as the sentence 'If any thing be a crow, the same is black.'[21] Leibniz, too, in his notes on Locke's view of eternal truths, regarded such truths as being at bottom conditional. According to him, in saying 'Every figure that has three sides will also have three angles', one says nothing but that, supposing that there be a figure with three sides, that same figure will have three angles. In that connexion he also touches upon the scholastic question as to how a proposition whose subject does not exist can yet be true. His answer is that such a proposition is a conditional truth to the effect that in case the subject ever exists it will be found to be such-and-such; the proposition expresses a connexion that is founded in a relationship between ideas.[22] Elsewhere Leibniz had drawn a distinction between propositions *per se* and propositions *per accidens*. An example of the former kind is 'Every man is rational', in which it is stated that there is an immediate and abstract coherence between being a man and being rational. By contrast, in 'Every man is white' there is no such unmediated coherence between being a man and being white; its proper form is therefore 'Everyone who is a man, is white.'[23] One might say that in Leibniz's view there are two kinds of existential import, one with regard to existence in the sense of conceivability in the region of ideas and one with regard to actual existence in the world outside thought. Both universal and particular categorical propositions may have either the one or the other type of existential import.[24]

Traditional books on logic used to draw a distinction between propositions whose compound nature is expressly marked by such connectives as 'and', 'or', 'if-then' and propositions whose compound nature is more hidden, so that they have to be expanded into a more explicit form that is equivalent for the purposes of logical inference. Such *exponibiles*, to which belong, for instance, exclusive sentences with 'only' and sentences containing 'except', were still treated in a separate chapter by the authors of the Port-Royal *Logique* (II, 10) and by Geulincx.

But the latter remarks that about this subject, though of some importance for logic, most writers had nothing to say.[25]

IV. JUDGEMENT

The diverse kinds of both categorical and compound proposition may either be merely entertained, in the sense of being present to the mind without any commitment to their truth or falsity, or become the object of an act or attitude of assent or dissent. An author who was most keenly aware of the need to uphold this distinction was John of St. Thomas, who even maintained that there are two forms of truth and falsity, one of the judgeable content as such and another of the actually judged proposition.[26] Just as a conceived state of affairs was practically always viewed as being prior in logico-semantic importance to its spoken or written expression, so the mental act of judging that a state of affairs really obtains was regarded as primary in comparison with the derivative assertion in spoken or written words. The ordinary term for the judgement occurring in the mind was *iudicium,* or its equivalent in the national languages. In seventeenth-century philosophy this word was used with several nuances of meaning. First, it could have the very general sense of faculty of discernment. Second, in opposition to 'invention' it designated the part of logic that dealt with the critical appraisal and proper arrangement of the results of applying the rules of the inventive part. Third, it had the meaning mentioned above, indicating the mental act of judging directed towards a conceived state of affairs as its object. From that meaning a fourth sense derived in which the word *iudicium* came to be used for the whole judicative complex, including both the conceived state of affairs and the act of judging directed at it. In that sense, it gradually supplanted the scholastic phrase *propositio mentalis* and was usually contrasted with the word *propositio,* which was then restricted to the spoken or written expression of the mental proposition. Finally, it should be mentioned that Locke gave a special sense to the word 'judgement'; opposing judgement to knowledge, he described it as the faculty which God has given man to supply the want of clear and certain knowledge in cases where that cannot be had.[27]

The mental act of judging was commonly held to assume either a positive or a negative form, being an act of assenting or dissenting, of affirming or denying. In this connexion, Aristotle's remark in *De interpretatione,* 5, 17a 8, to the effect that the first single statement-making sentence is the affirmation and that next is the negation, sometimes prompted the question as to whether affirmation is prior to negation.[28] In point of fact, several authors did give precedence to the positive act of judging. According to Geulincx, for example, affirmation is the root of logic; his entire system is built upon that principle.[29] And Hobbes acknowledges only an affirmative copula, attaching any negation to the predicate-term. A similar view had already been advocated by Smiglecius, in 1618, from the standpoint of a bipartite analysis of a categorical proposition. In his opinion, a negated verb is also a verb and as such it retains its peculiar capacity of relating its negated meaning to the subject.[30]

An issue that came to be much discussed in the second half of the century concerned the mental faculty to which the act of judging should be assigned. The controversy was kindled in particular by Descartes's contention that judgement belongs to the will. By this easily misleading expression Descartes meant that, whereas in receiving different ideas as objects of thought the soul is entirely passive, affirmation and negation, and also such attitudes as desire and aversion, are its active modes of taking a certain stance with respect to the received ideas. In calling such spontaneous activities modes of 'willing' (*volitio, voluntas*), Descartes probably had in mind the Stoic usage of *voluntas* as a translation of the Greek term *prohaíresis,* which indicates the domain of man's moral personality or true self, in the sense of the source of the absolutely free and autonomous determination of the attitude he can take towards received impressions.[31] This Cartesian conception of judgement finds its most striking corollary in the view that the highest degree of liberty consists in assenting to those propositional ideas which are so evident that it is impossible to disbelieve them. Among those who adhered to a similar doctrine were Antoine Le Grand, in his *Institutio philosophiae secundum principia D. Renati Descartes* of 1672, Malebranche, and, to a certain extent, Spinoza. Spinoza argued that the *voluntas* is identical with the understanding, since a particular act of affirming or denying and a particular idea are one and the same thing. Against the Cartesians, others upheld the common scholastic position that judgements are acts of the intellect, the disputants not seldom being at cross-purposes because of misunderstandings brought about by Descartes's peculiar use of the words *volitio* and *voluntas.* That at least some logicians considered the issue as lying outside their proper subject is made plausible by the fact that the authors of the Port-Royal *Logique* and Geulincx, who undoubtedly were perfectly familiar with Descartes's doctrine, never mention it in the context of their treatises on logic.[32]

A further problem concerned the precise characterisation of the act of judging. Geulincx declared explicitly that affirmation is too fundamental and familiar a phenomenon to admit of a proper definition; it can be clarified only by means of other kinds of elucidation, among them metaphor and analogy.[33] In practice, most authors followed tradition in availing themselves of language that is borrowed from a real dialogue in which the participants show assent or dissent by saying yes or no, or from situations in which after some deliberation one reaches a definite decision or makes a definite choice, particularly the situation in which an official judge finally delivers his judgement. Relatively new was the view that assent is an act of acquiescing in a conceived state of affairs when the mind ceases its investigation because the matter presented by the understanding is sufficiently evident to exclude the possibility of error.[34] In the same vein, Locke described knowledge as the faculty of mind whereby it certainly perceives, and is undoubtedly satisfied of the agreement or disagreement of any ideas, whereas judgement, in his sense, occurs when their agreement or disagreement is not perceived, but merely presumed.[35]

Leibniz explained judgement as a response to full questions, where one need say only 'It is so' or 'It is not so' (*Est aut non est*).[36] In general, it was held that in a spoken or written categorical proposition the point at which the judicative force of the mental correlate is brought to expression lies in the assertively used copula or in the finite verb in so far as it includes a copulative component, and that this assertive force of the finite verb can be made more explicit by adding such phrases as 'It is (really) so.' In compound propositions, however, the main connecting element is not a finite verb, while the finite verbs in the constituent propositions often have no assertive force. This difficulty was sometimes solved by assuming that all asserted compound propositions are to be understood as having the import of an equivalent subject–predicate proposition in which it is stated that the compound proposition is true.[37]

V. DEGREES OF ASSERTIVE FORCE

Some seventeenth-century logics draw attention to cases where, in comparison with standard judgement, assertive force is somehow weakened or even reduced to zero. Geulincx, for instance, often invokes the traditional distinction between *dicere formaliter* and *dicere consequenter,* indicating the difference between primary assertion in the sense of claiming the truth of what one's words explicitly mean and secondary assertion in the sense of committing oneself to all the logical consequences following from the explicit statement. For example, when someone says 'I am standing' (*Sto*), he formally and explicitly states only that he is standing; but in a derivative sense he thereby also commits himself to the truth of the logical consequence that he is capable of standing (*Stare possum*).[38]

Further, the Port-Royal *Grammaire* and *Logique* emphasise the difference between principal propositions and incidental propositions (*propositions incidentes*).[39]

According to the Port-Royal *Logique,* any complexity in the subject-term or the predicate-term of a categorical proposition may be expressed by a relative clause: for example, 'a transparent body' is tantamount to 'a body which is transparent.' Such a relative clause, however, can be either explicative or determinative. It is said to add an explication to the antecedent if it indicates either a feature that is part of the comprehension of the idea of the antecedent or some accident that belongs to everything falling under that idea. If, on the other hand, the relative clause restricts the extension of the antecedent, it is said to be determinative. What the authors have in mind, then, is the distinction between non-restrictive and restrictive relative clauses.[40] After these preliminary remarks in I, 8, Arnauld and Nicole devote two more chapters (II, 6–7) to the assertive force of relative clauses and to the impact which their falsity has on the truth-value of the principal proposition. As regards non-restrictive relative clauses, they hold that the attribute of the clause is affirmed of the antecedent of the relative pronoun only incidentally and in subordination to the whole proposition. This subordinate assertion of the relative clause is thought of as having taken place before the utterance of the whole proposition and as having shaded into a mere conception at the moment of utterance. Nevertheless, the subordinate affirmation is considered to be either true or false. If it is false, however, the falsity of the subordinate clause does not necessarily make the principal proposition false, precisely because the affirmation of the relative clause remains in the background and the speaker's chief concern is with the assertion of the principal proposition. Exceptions are propositions in which there is some necessary connexion between the attribute of the principal proposition and the attribute of the incidental proposition, as in 'Alexander, who was the son of Philip, was the grandson of Amyntas.' On the other hand, the judgement that is signified by the copula of a restrictive relative clause is regarded as pertaining, not to the actual connectedness of the attribute of the clause with the antecedent of the relative pronoun, but rather to the mere compatibility of the idea of the attribute with the idea of the antecedent. Although restrictive relative clauses are therefore propositions only in a very imperfect sense, they are nonetheless called true or false. For example, the authors consider the two incidental propositions that occur in 'Minds that are square are more solid than minds that are round' as false. But they do not explain what effect this falsity has on the truth-value of the whole proposition.

Besides being located in the subject-term or the predicate-term, incidental propositions may also produce complexity in the formal constituent of a categorical proposition, that is, in the copula as the mark of predication and assertion. The Port-Royal *Logique* (II, 8) gives such examples as 'I maintain (I deny, It is true, It is not true) that the earth is round.' Among these means of making the act of asserting more explicit are also counted the modal expressions 'It is possible that' and the like. That this kind of incidental proposition carries only a very weak assertive force is proved by the fact that the validity of arguments in which they occur is usually dependent solely upon the logical relations between the principal propositions, irrespective of the prefixed incidental propositions. For instance, the reasoning 'It is a divine command that kings be honoured; Louis XIV is the king; therefore, it is a divine command that Louis XIV be honoured' actually has the logical form 'Kings ought to be honoured; Louis XIV is the king; therefore Louis XIV ought to be honoured.' The incidental proposition 'It is a divine command that' serves only the purpose of strengthening the principal affirmation; from a strictly logical point of view it is superfluous (II, 11; III, 9). The authors are aware, though, that propositions which in most contexts will have to be interpreted as incidental may sometimes become the primary object of affirmation and thus play a decisive rôle with respect to the validity of arguments in which they occur essentially.

Finally, seventeenth-century logicians generally upheld the traditional view that in disjunctive and conditional compound propositions the disjuncts and the antecedent and consequent as such are not asserted. According to Geulincx, for instance, disjunctions and conditionals, as opposed to conjunctions, have parts whose assertive force has been destroyed, so that they no longer have the import they would have if they occurred by themselves.[41] Geulincx also shows a vivid awareness of the peculiar nature of those modes of thinking and speaking which he comprises under the name *supponere*. He distinguishes four types of this activity, which in general consists in propounding a proposition to which the speaker does not really commit himself. This act occurs when we posit an affirmation in order to deny it; or when we merely assume a proposition in order to draw logical consequences from it; or when we relate other people's opinions and statements; or when we depict fictitious states of affairs for didactic purposes. In all these cases there is no more than a semblance of assertion.[42]

NOTES

1 John of St. Thomas, for instance, carefully explains the difference between a *propositio enuntiativa* and a *propositio iudicativa,* as well as the difference between two functions of the copula: *copulatio* and *assertio.* See John of St. Thomas 1930–7, vol. 1, pp. 145, 153–5.
2 Spinoza, *Eth.* II, prop. 49.
3 Ger. I 385; II 472; Leibniz 1903, pp. 377, 381, 389, 397–8.

4 For a more comprehensive history of the logic of propositions about an individual subject see Barth 1974, pp. 141–79.

5 See Howell 1971, p. 29; Risse 1964–70, vol. 2, pp. 453, 456.

6 Ger. IV 50–1, 118–9; Leibniz 1903, p. 323; *Nouv. ess.* IV.xvii.8. For Rauen's contributions to logic see Risse 1965, pp. 133–4.

7 Leibniz 1903, p. 375 (Leibniz 1966, p. 65); Ger. VII 211 (Leibniz 1966, p. 115). See also Abraham 1975, pp. 7–8; Englebretsen 1982, pp. 122–4.

8 Smiglecius 1658, pp. 450–2. For details about this dispute see Nuchelmans 1980, pp. 34–5, 40–1; Nuchelmans 1983, pp. 89–90, 182–4.

9 Thomas Aquinas, *Summa th.,* I q13 a12; John of St. Thomas 1930–7, vol. 1, p. 357. See also Bondi 1966.

10 Gassendi 1658, vol. 3, p. 177.

11 *Lat. Works,* vol. 1, pp. 27–9, 44–5; *Lev.* iv–v.

12 Ger. VII 215; Leibniz 1903, p. 235. Similar formulations occur in the Port-Royal *Logique,* II, 17.

13 Ger. II 52, 56; VII 43–4; Leibniz 1903, pp. 51, 85, 324, 397. See also Abraham 1975; Burkhardt 1980b.

14 Leibniz, *Nouv. ess.* IV.v.2.

15 Geulincx 1891–3, vol. 1, pp. 213–17, 481–3.

16 See the survey of logic in *Collegium Complutense philosophicum* of 1624: 'quia enuntiare, in quo sita est essentia propositionis, secundum quid tantum convenit hypotheticae: non enim unam propositionem de alia praedicat, sicut categorica praedicat praedicatum de subjecto, in quo consistit propria ratio enuntiationis, sed tantum unit inter se propositiones categoricas, quod est umbra quaedam et similitudo propriae enuntiationis' (II, 3).

17 For instance, Philippe Du Trieu, in his *Manuductio ad logicam* of 1614 (Du Trieu 1826, II, 1, 2, 2), and Geulincx (Geulincx 1891–3, vol. 1, p. 237).

18 Geulincx 1891–3, vol. 1, pp. 241, 491, 493, 497. In general, although Geulincx is very careful to distinguish the logic of unanalysed statements from the logic of terms, at the same time he attempts to unify the two branches by treating each of them as a special elaboration of a common abstract scheme and invoking only formal properties of the part/whole relation and the relation of identity. For details see Nuchelmans 1988.

19 See Risse 1964–70, vol. 2, pp. 455, 457. Along the same lines, Wallis interpreted *quando* as *omni tempore quo* and *ubi* as *omni loco quo.* Such interpretations were not unknown to the young Leibniz; see Schepers 1975, p. 9.

20 Leibniz 1903, pp. 377, 389, 398 (Leibniz 1966, pp. 66, 78, 87). See also Leibniz 1903, pp. 262, 407–8, 423; Ger. II 473.

21 *Lat. Works,* vol. 1, pp. 34–5, 48.

22 *Nouv. ess.* IV.xi.13; Ger. I 370.

23 Ger. IV 118. See also Vailati 1986.

24 Ger. VII 211–17 (Leibniz 1966, pp. 115–21); Leibniz 1903, pp. 391–2 (Leibniz 1966, pp. 80–1). See also Burkhardt 1980a, pp. 37–42, 246–8.

25 Geulincx 1891–3, vol. 1, pp. 272–4.

26 John of St. Thomas 1930–7, vol. 1, p. 148: 'veritatem vel falsitatem inveniri tam in iudicio quam in enuntiatione, in illo asserta et iudicata, in ista ut significata et apprehensa.'

27 Locke, *Ess.* IV.xiv; Leibniz, *Nouv. ess.* IV.xiv.

28 See, for instance, John of St. Thomas 1930–7, vol. 1, p. 163.

29 Geulincx 1891–3, vol. 1, p. 175: 'Radix logices est affirmatio.'

30 Hobbes, *Lat. Works,* vol. 1, p. 31; Smiglecius 1658, pp. 455–6: 'De ratione enim verbi est referre ad subiectum; verbum autem negatum est etiam verbum, quare etiam tunc retinet vim propriam referendi rem significatam ad subiectum.'

31 For details see Nuchelmans 1983, pp. 44–50, 55–69.

32 Elsewhere Geulincx comments on it approvingly: Geulincx 1891–3, vol. 3, pp. 390–2.

33 Geulincx 1891–3, vol. 1, pp. 200–1, 455–9. Compare also Poncius, *Integer philosophiae cursus ad mentem Scoti, Logica parva,* chap. 10: 'iudicium ut sic . . . esse illud in quo particulariter convenit iudicium negativum et affirmativum magis inter se quam cum aliis actibus intellectus, quod sane magis quisque potest propria experientia discernere quam verbis exprimere alteri.'

34 This view is especially prominent in Malebranche's *Recherche de la vérité* of 1674 (I.2.1–2).

35 Locke, *Ess.* IV.v.5 and xiv.4.

36 Leibniz 1903, p. 495. See also Leibniz 1979a, p. 153, about adverbs of assertion.

37 See, for example, Geulincx 1891–3, vol. 1, pp. 234–5.

38 Geulincx 1891–3, vol. 1, p. 452, and *passim.* The notion of *dicere consequenter* probably had its origin in Aristotle, *Topics,* II, 5, 112a 16–21.

39 From the viewpoint of the copula, this difference was also expressed by the pairs *copula principalis/minus principalis* or *implicationis* and *copula propositionis/relationis.* For the early history of so-called *propositiones implicitae* see Giusberti 1982, pp. 21–85.

40 In mediaeval logic, the ambiguity of such a sentence as *Omnis homo qui est albus currit* was discussed under the heading *De restrictionibus* (for example, Peter of Spain, *Tractatus,* XI, 8–9; 1972, p. 202), or explained by invoking the distinction *sensus compositus/divisus* (for example, Ockham, *Summa logicae,* II, 15).

41 Geulincx 1891–3, vol. 1, pp. 240, 247, 277.

42 Geulincx 1891–3, vol. 1, p. 463; vol. 2, pp. 16–17, 276, 469–73. See also Leibniz 1903, p. 495.

6

DEDUCTIVE REASONING

GABRIEL NUCHELMANS

I. CONTRA AND PRO THE SYLLOGISM

Most seventeenth-century textbooks of logic follow the usual pattern according to which a discussion of the constituents of propositions and of propositions themselves leads up to a part dealing with those combinations of propositions which exhibit a valid form of deductive argument. From Aristotle onward the core of this part of logic had been the doctrine of the syllogism. Already during the period of the Renaissance, however, the privileged position of the syllogism had been vehemently attacked by those humanist dialecticians who wanted to restrain the influence of Aristotelianism on their subject. Their criticisms were taken over and elaborated by such modern thinkers as Francis Bacon, Descartes, and Locke.[1]

Bacon bases his disapproval of the use of syllogisms in natural science on the consideration that, if the notions which are signified by the words making up their constituent propositions are improperly and overhastily abstracted from facts, the whole edifice tumbles. Though he admits that the syllogism may be an acceptable instrument of reasoning in such fields as divinity, ethics, politics, and the law, in dealing with the nature of things he wants to use induction throughout.[2] In the same vein, Descartes contends that traditional dialectic is quite useless to those who are seeking truth and that at best it can serve to expound more easily to others things that one already knows; rather than to philosophy, it belongs to rhetoric. Moreover, it is, he says, an illusion to think that the truth about any question can be reached by the mechanical application of the formal rules of syllogistic inference. On the contrary, those intricate rules corrupt good sense by confounding the users and turning their attention away from the actual nature of things. The natural light of reason and good sense are a much safer guide than the artificial constructions of the dialecticians.[3] No less animosity against the logic of the schools is shown by Locke, especially in the lengthy chapter 'Of Reason' in *An Essay concerning Human Understanding*.[4] His arguments are very similar to those advanced by Descartes. God has given man a mind that can reason without being instructed in methods of syllogising; the understanding need not be taught to reason by these rules, having a native faculty to perceive the coherence or incoherence of its ideas. Even for the discovery of fallacies familiarity with syllogistic is of little assistance, since there are people who at first hearing can perceive the weakness and inconclusiveness of a long artificial and plausible discourse wherewith others better skilled in syllogism have been misled. The scholastic forms of discourse are not less liable to fallacies than the plainer ways of argumentation. Furthermore, Locke emphasises, syllogistic is practically useless when probabilities are concerned, and it is of no avail in finding out proofs and making new discoveries.

On the other side, especially Leibniz's impressive production in the field of logic may be regarded as a sustained effort to silence its detractors. More particularly, he defended its cause in a letter to Gabriel Wagner of 1696 and in his reaction to Locke in *Nouveaux essais*.[5] Though Leibniz had to confess that all the logics developed until his days were but a shadow of what he should wish and what he saw from afar, he also gratefully acknowledged that the logic taught him in school contained much that was good and useful and that it had been most fruitful to him. Leibniz disagreed with the opinion expressed by the authors of the Port-Royal *Logique,* in the introduction to the part on reasoning, to the effect that most errors men make are due to the fact that they argue on the basis of false principles, rather than to formal faults in their reasonings. According to Leibniz, errors are just as often paralogisms, which arise through a neglect of form. It is therefore no small matter that Aristotle reduced the forms of the syllogism to unerring laws, having been the first to write mathematically outside of mathematics. But Aristotle's work concerns only one kind of arguments in form, that is, of arguments which are conclusive by the mere strength of their form and in which no link is lacking. The domain of such arguments in form, which contain an art of infallibility, is far wider than the set of reasonings conferred by syllogistic. Accordingly, Leibniz was convinced that the art of reasoning could be carried incomparably higher and that with the help of mathematics a more sublime logic could be worked out which, as a truly universal and abstract science of forms and structures, would include syllogistic as a special case. It is this vision which gives a certain unity to the numerous and often fragmentary writings that Leibniz devoted to the enrichment and extension of the logic of the past. Unfortunately, as practically none of those pieces was published during his lifetime, his efforts to stem the contemporary stream of aversion to formal logic remained largely ineffective.

II. NOVEL APPROACHES TO SYLLOGISTIC

In spite of the manifold attempts to discredit the syllogism, several seventeenth-century writers succeeded in presenting the Aristotelian and scholastic treatment of that form of reasoning in more or less original guises. To begin with a less original point, Gassendi insisted that the canonical order of a syllogism should consist in always placing the middle term, which occurs once in each of the two premises, between the minor term, which also becomes the subject of the conclusion, and the major term, which becomes the predicate of the conclusion: S-M; M-P; therefore, S-P. In his opinion, that is the most natural order from the standpoint of invention; moreover, he supports his view by invoking the authority of Aristotle and by certain set-theoretical considerations. Of this standard form of the syllogism he further distinguishes two varieties, an affirmative and a negative figure. Characteristic of the affirmative version – for example, 'Man is an animal; animal is a living being; therefore, man is a living being' – is the rule that what is connected with something is also connected with that with which that something is connected (or: if the set of men is included in the set of animals and the set of animals in the set of living beings, the set of men is included in the set of living beings). The negative version – for example, 'Man is an animal; no animal is a stone; therefore, no man is a stone' – is defined by the rule that what is connected with something is unconnected with that with which that something is unconnected (or: if the set of men is included in the set of animals and the set of animals is excluded from the set of stones, the set of men is excluded from the set of stones). In each of these two Gassendian figures three moods are distinguished, according as the constituent propositions are all universal, all singular, or the second universal and the others singular or particular. To syllogisms of this kind, which partly coincide with the valid syllogisms of the Aristotelian first figure, Gassendi then reduces the less evidently valid syllogisms of the Aristotelian second and third figures, by means of transposition of the premises and the laws of conversion and subalternation, according to which, for instance, 'No man is a stone' is equivalent to 'No stone is a man' and 'Every man is an animal' implies 'Some man is an animal' as its subalternate. The indirect moods of the Aristotelian first figure, in which the subject and the predicate of the conclusion are converted – as in 'Man is an animal; animal is a living being; therefore, some living being is a man' – he prefers to leave out, on the ground that such reasonings, though not invalid, are quite unnatural.[6]

Hobbes, too, in *Computatio sive logica,* IV, considers the ideal form of a syllogism to consist in a first figure in which the terms are placed one after another according to increasing latitude of signification: the minor term first, the middle term next, and the major term last. But he is also of the opinion that in philosophy only universal propositions are relevant, and that all propositions have an affirmative copula. Strictly speaking, then, the first figure contains only one mood, in which all propositions are both universal and affirmative. Further, there are three figures which at first sight deviate from the standard form, but may be reduced to it. Syllogisms of the Aristotelian second figure are reduced to Hobbes's first figure by conversion of the major premise, that is, the premise in which the major term occurs. For example, 'Every man is an animal; every stone is not-an-animal (= no stone is an animal); therefore, every man is not-a-stone (= no man is a stone)' can be reduced to 'Every man is an animal; every animal is not-a-stone; therefore, every man is not-a-stone' because 'Every stone is not-an-animal' and 'Every animal is not-a-stone' are equipollent. Syllogisms of the Aristotelian third figure, which never have a universal conclusion and are therefore useless in philosophy, are derivable from Hobbes's first figure by conversion of the minor premise, that is, by converting, for instance, 'Every man is an animal' into 'Some animal is a man' and then adding 'Every animal is a body; therefore, some man is a body.' For the third case Hobbes gives the example 'Every stone is not-an-animal; whatsoever is not-an-animal, is not-a-man; therefore, every stone is not-a-man.' This valid syllogism may be reduced to 'Every man is an animal; every animal is not-a-stone; therefore every man is not-a-stone', by converting, according to Hobbes's instructions, the two premises and the conclusion and transposing the premises. Now, if the figures of syllogisms are numbered by the diverse situations of the middle term only, this third case can simply be assigned to the first figure. But if the figures are numbered according to the situation of all the terms involved, the third case must be counted as being an inverted form of a standard syllogism of the first figure. For although the originally negated middle term ('animal') remains in its proper place, the positive minor term of the syllogism to which the third case is reduced ('man') is the original negated major term, and the negated major term of that syllogism ('not-a-stone') is the original positive minor term. Hobbes concludes that the answer to the question as to how many figures there are depends upon the point of view that is chosen: if only the situation of the middle term is taken into account, there are three figures, but if the situation of all the terms involved is considered, there are four.[7]

For Gassendi, and *a fortiori* for Hobbes, a perfect syllogism always starts with an affirmative premise. This idea was radicalised by Geulincx, who also handled syllogisms in such a way that the whole issue of figures simply disappears.[8] Once a syllogism has been cast into standard form, the first premise is always an affirmative proposition, either universal or particular; as well as of logic in general, affirmation is the root of the syllogism. A complete syllogism is defined as an argument in which a third term is affirmatively or negatively related to one of the terms of the affirmative first premise and from that relation a similar relation between that third term and the other term of the first premise is inferred.[9] If the two terms of the first premise are abbreviated as A and B, and the third term as C, all the traditional valid syllogisms may be derived with the help of the laws of conversion, transposition of the premises, and the following eight axioms (1–6 for 'Every A is B' as first premise, 7–8 for 'Some A is B'):

1. If C is truly predicated of B, then C is truly predicated of A (I-*Barbara*).
2. Contraposition of 1: if C is not truly predicated of A, then C is not truly predicated of B (III-*Bocardo,* III-*Felapton*).
3. If C is truly made the subject of A, then C is truly made the subject of B (I-*Barbara*).
4. Contraposition of 3: if C is not truly made the subject of B, then C is not truly made the subject of A (II-*Baroco*).
5. If C is universally (or particularly) affirmed of A, then C can be particularly affirmed of B (III-*Darapti*).
6. Contraposition of 5: if C is universally denied of B, then C can be universally or particularly denied of A (I-*Celarent,* II-*Cesare,* II-*Camestres*).
7. If C is universally affirmed of A or B, then C can be particularly affirmed of B or A (I-*Darii,* III-*Datisi,* III-*Disamis*).
8. Contraposition of 7: if C is universally denied of B or A, then C can be particularly denied of A or B (I-*Ferio,* II-*Festino,* III-*Ferison*).

Whereas Geulincx derives only the valid syllogisms belonging to the traditional three figures, the authors of the Port-Royal *Logique* (III, 4) acknowledge the so-called fourth figure, in which the middle term is predicate in the first premise and subject in the second premise.[10] In support of this admission of a separate fourth figure they point out that the conclusion, as the thesis to be proved, has an unalterable form (S-P) and that the predicate of the conclusion should occur in the first premise. On these assumptions there are exactly four possibilities of placing the middle term: M-P/S-M, P-M/S-M, M-P/M-S, P-M/M-S.

Leibniz agreed with the Port-Royal view.[11] He was especially proud of having constructed a system of syllogistic in which there are exactly twenty-four valid syllogisms, six in each of the four figures. Assuming that *Barbara, Celarent, Darii, Ferio* of the first figure are valid, he first uses *Darii* and *Ferio* to derive the weakened forms *Barbari* and *Celaro,* with a subaltern conclusion, having 'some' instead of 'every' or 'no'. If, for instance, every A is B (the universal affirmative conclusion of *Barbara*) and some A is A (which is a necessarily true statement of identity), then according to *Darii,* also some A is B. Next, he applies to the now six valid syllogisms of the first figure a variant of the principle of non-contradiction, to the effect that, if in a valid syllogistic form the contradictory of the conclusion is added to one of the premises, these two together entail the contradictory of the other premise as a conclusion. For example, if in 'No A is B; every C is A; therefore, no C is B' (*Celarent*) the contradictory of the conclusion, namely, 'Some C is B', is added to the first premise, then the conclusion must be that some C is not A; the result is a valid syllogism in the second figure (*Festino*). In the same way, Leibniz derives the other five valid syllogisms of the second figure and six of the third figure from the six valid syllogisms of the first figure. After that step, he is able to prove the laws of conversion ('If some A is B, then some B is A', 'If no A is B, then no B is A', and 'If every A is B, then some B is A'), again making use of necessarily true statements of identity. If, for instance, every A is A and some A is B, then some B is A, because this pattern of reasoning has already been shown to be a valid syllogism of the third figure (*Datisi*). Finally, with the laws of conversion at his disposal, Leibniz can prove the validity of six syllogisms of the fourth figure. Although he does not dwell upon the proofs, it is clear how he would proceed. The syllogism 'Every A is B; every B is C; therefore, some C is A', for instance, can be reduced to *Barbari* of the first figure ('Every B is C; every A is B; therefore, some A is C') by transposing the premises and converting the conclusion.[12]

As Leibniz himself points out, this system of syllogistic has several attractive features. First, the outcome is attained from minimal assumptions and according to a synthetic method of discovery. Second, the number of figures and valid moods can be exactly determined, in the same way as geometricians are able to determine the number of regular bodies. In this connexion, it is important to note that the number of twenty-four valid syllogisms is reached only if due attention is paid to the weakened forms which depend on the laws of subalternation, to the effect that 'Every A is B' implies 'Some A is B' and 'No A is B' implies 'Some A is not B.' Third, the fourth figure obtains its proper place after the other figures on the logical ground that the derivation of its valid moods requires the laws of conversion. Finally, in the proofs of both subalternation and conversion, trivial statements of identity turn out to be of some use after all.

In developing the system outlined above, Leibniz felt that he was reducing the doctrine of the syllogism to geometrical rigour. This ideal, shared by other seventeenth-century logicians, he also tried to realise by making use of such geometrical devices as lines and circles in order to represent the logical relations between terms.[13] These experiments with the diagrammatic method are further evidence of his deep conviction that the syllogistic forms of reasoning fully deserve continuously renewed study.

III. ASYLLOGISTIC ARGUMENTS

Of the many patterns of reasoning that are not syllogisms in a strict sense, such immediate inferences as the laws of the so-called square of opposition (for instance, that the truth of 'Every man is an animal' implies the truth of its subalternate 'Some man is an animal' and the falsity of its contrary 'No man is an animal' and of its contradictory 'Some man is not an animal') and the laws of conversion were usually assumed in the process of proving the validity of syllogisms. Leibniz was exceptional in reversing that order by using syllogisms in his derivation of the laws of subalternation and conversion. With regard to the laws of propositional logic, which were often called *consequentiae* in a narrow sense, although they were not seldom applied implicitly, they were less often treated in the systematic way that had been typical of later scholastic logic.[14] Joachim Jungius, in the *Logica Hamburgensis* of 1638, is clearly aware of their importance and devotes ample space to numerous examples of truth-functional statements and the mutual relations peculiar to them. Geulincx, too, draws a fundamental distinction between arguments whose validity is determined by the formal properties of terms and arguments whose validity can be accounted for by merely invoking the formal properties of unanalysed statements. Further, it is worthy of note that Hieronymus Saccherius, in his *Logica demonstrativa* of 1697 (Chapter 11), attempted to prove the invalidity of certain kinds of syllogism by means of the so-called *consequentia mirabilis,* which guarantees the truth of p if p follows even from not-p.[15] A less marvellous consequence – to the effect that, if the conjunction of p and q implies r, then the conjunction of p and not-r implies not-q and the conjunction of q and not-r implies not-p – underlies Leibniz's derivation of the twelve syllogisms of the second and third figures from the six valid moods of the first figure. Although he shows familiarity with the logic of unanalysed propositions in several other places, especially in the disputations *De conditionibus* of 1665–7,[16] his general effort was directed at assimilating the logic of propositions to the logic of terms.

Besides the immediate inferences that from the very beginning had played a part in syllogistic, and the propositional laws that were at least incidentally acknowledged, some seventeenth-century authors showed a renewed interest in certain prima facie non-syllogistic arguments that have some relational notion as an essential component. To the 1681 edition of Jungius's *Logica Hamburgensis*

Johannes Vagetius had added a list of features by which, according to him, that book distinguished itself. That list includes such examples as 'David is the father of Solomon and Solomon is the son of David', 'A circle is a figure; therefore, whoever draws a circle, draws a figure.' These relational items had especially attracted the attention of Leibniz, who was a great admirer of Jungius and apparently thought that the latter felt compelled to introduce new modes of reasoning in order to cope with such relational arguments as he cited.[17]

Though many details of Leibniz's view of relational propositions and arguments are still obscure,[18] there can be no doubt that in his opinion the inferences that at first sight cannot be assimilated to syllogisms or other familiar logical patterns should be handled in rational grammar, rather than directly in logic proper. At a crucial point in the history of logic, Leibniz did not opt for enlarging its scope by admitting categorical propositions that have a relational predicate and more than one subject but attempted to analyse and expand the linguistic form of the troublesome propositions in such a way that no deviation from the traditional one-subject proposition was called for. His predilection for viewing predication as establishing an intensional relationship between an attribute and only one subject, together with his conviction that an accident cannot possibly be in two subjects at once, apparently prevented him from considering the novel step of allowing categorical propositions in which a relational predicate is stated to inhere in more than one subject. It should be emphasised, however, that his refraining from enlarging the stock of logical forms in that respect does not mean that he was also aiming at the reduction of one-subject propositions with a relational predicate to subject–predicate propositions from which the relational notions have been altogether eliminated.[19] Rather, he seems to have adhered to the common view that there is a difference between perfect and imperfect terms. Terms are perfect or complete if they are capable of filling the subject-place or the predicate-place of a categorical proposition without any addition. By contrast, terms are imperfect or incomplete if, as in the case of 'the same as', 'similar to', something must be added to them for a complete term, such as 'similar to Alexander', to arise.[20] But, as is also clear from other examples, Leibniz is far from repudiating such completed relational predicates as suitable components of categorical propositions. What he does hold is that propositions in which such predicates occur should first be subjected to an analysis according to the requirements of rational grammar before their logical rôle in arguments can be adequately explained.

In Leibniz's view, an ideal sentence of the universal characteristic contains only a noun for a thing, the copula, some adjective, and formal particles.[21] In particular, there are no oblique cases in rational grammar. Leibniz therefore aims at first reducing all oblique cases to the genitive, by changing for instance *Paris amat Helenam* ('Paris loves Helen') into *Paris est amator Helenae* ('Paris is a lover of Helen'). Next, he tries to get rid of the genitive by making the relation between a noun in the nominative case and the adjoined noun in the genitive case fully explicit with the help of other expressions. For example, *manus hominis* ('the hand of a man') is read as *manus quae est pars quatenus homo est totum* ('the hand which is a part in so far as a man is a whole').[22] In a treatise on the analysis of particles, Leibniz explains the import of the particle *quatenus,* which he very often uses in such expansions, as follows. *Homo est immortalis quatenus homo est mente praeditus* ('Man is immortal in so far as man is possessed of a mind') is tantamount to *Homo est immortalis respectu habito ad hoc: homo est mente praeditus* ('Man is immortal if account is taken of the fact that man is possessed of a mind').[23] So 'the hand which is a part in so far as a man is a whole' is equivalent to 'the hand which is a part if account is taken of the fact that a man is a whole'.[24] Along such lines the validity of many abbreviated forms of reasoning according to which people are wont to argue may be demonstrated, not directly from logical principles, but rather in a roundabout way, by first elucidating the meaning of oblique cases and particles in rational grammar, and thereafter applying the modes of reasoning that are taught in the schools.[25]

Unfortunately, Leibniz hardly offers any detailed illustrations of how this program is to be carried out. In 1687 he sent Vagetius a proof of the validity of the inference 'Painting is an art; therefore, he who learns painting, learns an art.'[26] One of the suppositions from which the proof proceeds concerns the grammatical meaning of cases. Elsewhere Leibniz had suggested that a complete predicate which is composed of two incomplete terms can be changed into a predicate that consists of two complete terms by introducing some general signs of things or terms.[27] The proposition 'Caesar is like Alexander' then becomes 'Caesar is like the A which is Alexander' or 'Caesar is like a thing which is Alexander.' Similarly, in the proof for Vagetius he assumes that a general oblique case taken with a particular direct case is equivalent to a particular oblique case: 'he who learns a thing which is painting' is equivalent to 'he who learns painting', and 'he who learns an art' is equivalent to 'he who learns a thing which is an art.' Therefore, these expressions can be substituted mutually for one another.[28] But it remains rather unclear how exactly this way of dealing with relational predicates connects with the solutions Leibniz outlines in other passages, not to mention the ontological and psychological considerations which probably have to be taken into account.

IV. LEIBNIZ'S CONCEPTION OF AN ABSTRACT CALCULUS

Mention has already been made of Leibniz's belief that the science of arguments in form might be carried to a much higher degree of perfection than had been attained in the past. In his view, this more sublime logic would have the form of a *calculus ratiocinator*. Compared with the ideographic universal characteristic and its genuinely rational grammar, such a calculus is still farther removed from the irrelevancies of the natural languages and their concrete uses through the introduction of variables and special symbols for the logical constants. Although Leibniz followed those predecessors who saw logic as a kind of computation in borrowing the needed artificial signs from arithmetic and algebra and initially even went so far as to experiment with calculi in which the subject-term and the predicate-term would be represented by numbers,[29] he was fully aware of the possibility of detaching the borrowed signs from the particular uses which they have in their original fields of application. According to him, a calculus is nothing but an operation on signs which has a place not only in the domain of numbers and quantities but in any other kind of reasoning as well. Of the infinitely many calculi that in his opinion can be excogitated, Leibniz has sketched only some specimens. His last and ripest achievement is a study in the calculus of real addition.[30] There he begins by giving definitions of 'the same' and 'different'. Two terms are the same of which either can be substituted for the other wherever we please without loss of truth; terms which are not the same are different. Next, he explains what he means by the formula 'B + N = L': it states that B is in L, or that L contains B, and that B and N together constitute L. Terms of which one is in the other are called subalternants, while terms of which neither is in the other are called disparate. The axioms of the system are 'B + N = N + B' and 'A + A = A', laying down that no account need be taken of the order of terms and of their repetition. After adding two more principles as postulates, Leibniz goes on to derive a number of theorems.

As the author himself notes, this calculus can be interpreted in various ways. The abstract formula 'B + N = L', for instance, might be understood as stating that the predicate-concept B of a categorical proposition is in the subject-concept L, constituting, together with other concepts N, the whole of L; as in 'Man is an animal' when that proposition is taken according to Leibniz's intensional view of predication. But the same formula may also be read as saying that the species B, together with other species, composes the genus L; on that interpretation, the subset of men is contained in the wider set of animals and constitutes, together with other subsets, the whole of that generic set. Furthermore, given Leibniz's doctrine that the fact that a proposition follows from another proposition is simply that a consequent is contained in an antecedent, as a term in a term,[31] the formula might even be interpreted as an assertion about relations of propositions. On such a reading, 'B + N = L' would state that the proposition B is among the logical consequences that are derivable from the proposition L. In sum, Leibniz had gained the extremely important insight that calculi can be elaborated at such a high level of abstract formality that they leave room for a great diversity of interpretations.

Moreover, one of the theorems that Leibniz is able to prove states that, if A is in B and B is in C, then A is in C: a content of a content is a content of the container. Obviously, this is the most evident law of syllogistic. Even though Leibniz apparently did not succeed in developing this particular calculus in such a manner that it would include the whole theory of the syllogism, there can be little doubt that in general he was aiming at devising a formalism in which syllogistic would be incorporated as a special case. His many attempts at preparing, as it were, the forms of categorical propositions for such an incorporation amply testify to this.[32]

V. APPLICATIONS AND EXTENSIONS OF ASSERTORIC LOGIC

Among seventeenth-century philosophers, Leibniz distinguished himself not only by his impressive contributions to the theoretical development of logic but also by his assiduous efforts to find useful applications for the results of his studies. This many-sided interest in the services that logic might render to various fields of human intellectual activity was particularly conspicuous in his attempts to chart and improve the standards of legal reasoning.[33] Already as a student of law, in 1665, Leibniz published two academic disputations, entitled *De conditionibus*; a few years later he re-edited them as *Specimen certitudinis seu demonstrationum in iure.*[34] In this work he is concerned with rules of interpretation applicable to legal documents that are tied to certain conditions. Starting from long lists of definitions, which are based upon texts of Roman and other authoritative jurisconsults and are used by him as a special kind of axiom, he derives a great number of theorems by principles of inference that predominantly belong to propositional logic. As Schepers, who has called attention to this neglected treatise, rightly remarks, this attempt at founding an axiomatic-deductive system of rules of legal interpretation on propositional logic deserves much closer investigation than it has hitherto received.

In *De conditionibus,* Leibniz also takes into account the modal notions that characterise possible, necessary, and impossible conditions. In general, his interest in the modalities has been widely recognised, especially in connexion with his views about possible worlds.[35] Until a few years ago, it was less well known that Leibniz may be regarded as one of the early pioneers of deontic logic.[36] In the *Elementa iuris naturalis* of 1671–2,[37] there are some passages in which he draws an interesting parallel between, on the one hand, the quantifiers ('some', 'not some', 'not some not', 'some not') and the modalities in a strict sense (possible, impossible, necessary, contingent), and, on the other hand, such a quartet as licit (*licitum, iustum*), illicit (*illicitum, iniustum*), obligatory (*debitum, aequum*), and not obligatory (*indebitum, omissibile*). This is another example of a valuable insight gained by Leibniz that had to wait a long time until it was reached again independently by others.

VI. CONCLUDING REMARKS

Even a superficial glance at the seventy-eight pages of the first volume of Risse's *Bibliographia logica* (1965), in which he lists the works on logic that appeared during the seventeenth century, suffices to show that this subject was far from being neglected in that period; its ups and downs would therefore seem to deserve more attention of historians than they have hitherto received. Some of the pertinent texts – for instance, the treatises by Robert Sanderson, John of St. Thomas, Jungius, Hobbes, Gassendi, Arnauld and Nicole, Geulincx – are available in more or less modern editions. The case of Leibniz, the most original logician of the century, is more complicated because of the fragmentary nature of his output; but a good deal of it is already accessible and, given the wide interest he enjoys, there is reason to hope that more will follow in the near future. However, to form a well-balanced estimate of the merits and demerits of the state of logic in the seventeenth century, it will be necessary to base its study on a much larger set of sources, and that presupposes, contrary to fact, that at least some of the more promising other material is within relatively easy reach of those who feel attracted to this sort of research. Until 1980, for example, it was practically impossible to get hold of a copy of such an interesting treatise as Saccherius's *Logica demonstrativa;* and that same complaint still applies to many other books. This situation is the more regrettable because, as Ashworth rightly remarks in her excellent introduction to a re-edition of Robert Sanderson's *Logicae artis compendium,* the textbook writers and schoolteachers of a period may be as important as the leading intellectuals, since it is by these minor figures that all innovations are accepted, altered, and made into the new commonplace.[38]

Even a partial fulfilment of the urgent need of readily available sources would greatly facilitate the production of articles and monographs devoted to aspects of seventeenth-century logic that have so far escaped notice. Most illuminating would be studies concerning the internal structure of logical systems put forward by individual authors and concerning the external influences that have contributed to giving such a system its specific structure. At the same time, such investigations in depth of particular treatises will pave the way for more comprehensive surveys of the manner in which certain special topics, for instance the logic of relations, were dealt with. Indeed, it is to be expected that these two kinds of approach will frequently complement each other. Though it is almost inevitable that this historical research will be partly – and often stimulatingly and suggestively – guided by the present state of systematic logic, it should be emphasised that a judicious evaluation of past results can be reached only after one has let the authors concerned speak for themselves and has gained a full understanding of the peculiar ways in which they attempted to solve problems as they saw them in the perspective of their own time.

As is especially evident from the writings of Bacon, Descartes, and Locke, the seventeenth century is also the period in which the alleged advantages of a thorough instruction in formal logic were increasingly called into question. On the one hand, this aversion from the inherited way of doing logic led to an exploration of other methods of gaining knowledge, the results of which were sometimes offered as a novel type of logic, but have little in common with the familiar discipline. On the other hand, the widespread influence of such philosophers as Descartes and Locke gave rise to a good many textbooks of logic in which a more or less traditional core was surrounded and coloured by considerations borrowed from the general philosophy of those innovators. In point of fact, one of the characteristic features of the development of logic in the second half of the seventeenth century is the appearance of treatises on logic that are somehow inspired by Cartesian philosophy. Naturally, Locke's influence began to be felt only at the very end of the century, to become rather conspicuous in several textbooks of the eighteenth century. Perhaps this impact of Locke's philosophical doctrines would have been less strong if the fresh ideas with which Leibniz experimented had been more widely known; but most of the contributions of that pioneer remained hidden in the mass of his manuscripts.

NOTES

1 See Passmore 1953; Lenders 1980; Clarke 1981; Pozzi 1981; Buickerood 1985, pp. 178–81, 188; R. Rossi 1987.

2 Francis Bacon, *Instauratio magna, Distributio operis*; *Nov. org.* I 11–14; *De augmentis scientiarum,* V, 2. See also Risse 1964–70, vol. 1, p. 491.

3 AT X 405–6, 440 (*Regulae ad directionem ingenii*, X and XIV); AT VI 17 (*Disc.* II; see also Descartes's comment on the passage in his conversation with Burman, AT V 175); AT IXB 13–14.

4 *Ess.* IV.xvii. See also III.x.6–13, IV.vii.8–20.

5 Ger. VII 514–27 (Leibniz 1969, pp. 462–71); *Nouv. ess.* IV.xvii.4–9.

6 Gassendi 1658, vol. 1, p. 107ff. In the first of the three Aristotelian figures, the middle term is once subject and once predicate (M-P; S-M; therefore S-P), in the second twice predicate (P-M; S-M; therefore S-P), in the third twice subject (M-P; M-S; therefore S-P). The vowels a, e, i, o in *Barbara, Bocardo* etc. stand for, respectively, universal affirmative, universal negative, particular affirmative, and particular negative propositions. I-*Barbara* is a syllogism in the mood a-a-a in the first figure (MaP; SaM; therefore SaP), while III-*Bocardo* is a syllogism in the mood o-a-o in the third figure (MoP; MaS; therefore SoP. For example, 'Some Athenians are not philosophers; every Athenian is a Greek; therefore, some Greeks are not philosophers'). For a survey of essentials see Prior 1967.

7 *Lat. Works,* vol. 1, pp. 39–49. Compare also Locke's remark about the naturalness of placing the middle term between the extremes (*Ess.* IV.xvii.8).

8 Geulincx 1891–3, vol. 1, p. 342: 'securus de cetero, an in prima, an in secunda, an in tertia figura; an directus, an indirectus; an in Barbara, an in Celarent, Darii, etc. Nihil horum te angat, nihil horum inquiras.' See also Geulincx 1891–3, vol. 1, pp. 309–13, 335–44; vol. 2, pp. 90–101.

9 Geulincx 1891–3, vol. 1, p. 339; vol. 2,. pp. 100–101: 'argumentum quo duobus terminis in affirmatione propositis ex habitudine tertii termini cum altero istorum (quoad affirmationem vel negationem) infertur similis habitudo eiusdem tertii cum termino restante.' It should be noted that Geulincx's syllogistic is virtually confined to apodictic reasonings with so-called eternal truths, that is, with necessarily true statements in which a conceptual tie between subject and predicate is expressed by a tenseless copula. For details see Nuchelmans 1988.

10 For the complicated history of this fourth figure see Rescher 1966. See also Ashworth 1985, pp. XLV–XLVII; 1988, pp. 170–1.

11 Ger. IV 51–3; VII 477–8, Leibniz 1903, pp. 196, 203–5.

12 Leibniz 1903, pp. 410–16 (Leibniz 1966, pp. 105–11), 206–10; *Nouv. ess.* IV.ii.1; IV.xvii.4; Ger. III 569.

13 Leibniz 1903, pp. 247–9, 292ff., 383–5 (Leibniz 1966, pp. 73–4). See also Burkhardt 1980a, pp. 61–2.

14 See Ashworth 1968.

15 For details see Kneale and Kneale 1962, pp. 345–8; Risse 1964–70, vol. 2, p. 257; Angelelli 1975; Hamblin 1975; Hoormann 1976; Nuchelmans 1992.

16 See Schepers 1975.

17 See Risse 1964–70, vol. 1, pp. 523–6; Ashworth 1967; Leibniz 1903, pp. 426–8; see also Leibniz 1903, pp. 244, 287, 330.

18 The chief relevant passages are Leibniz 1903, pp. 244–5 (Leibniz 1966, p. 13), 280, 284, 287 (Leibniz 1966, pp. 14–15; for a better text see Mugnai 1978, pp. 16–17), 357 (Leibniz 1966, pp. 47–8); Leibniz 1966, pp. 88–9; *Nouv. ess.* IV.xvii.4; Ger. II 486 (Leibniz 1969, p. 609); VII 401 (Leibniz 1969, p. 704). For recent comments on Leibniz's view see D'Agostino 1976; Mugnai 1978, 1979, 1992; Angelelli 1980; Kulstad 1980; Mates 1980; Moriconi 1980; Wong 1980; Rescher 1981.

19 See especially Kulstad 1980.

20 Leibniz 1903, p. 357 (Leibniz 1966, pp. 47–8). Compare also the more extensive treatment of this distinction in Geulincx 1891–3, vol. 2, pp. 244–51.
21 Leibniz 1903, p. 289.
22 Leibniz 1903, p. 245.
23 Leibniz 1979a, p. 153. See also Mugnai 1979. Further, it should be noted that from Aristotle's statement in *Categories* (7, 7b 15) to the effect that it is characteristic of most relatives that they are simultaneous by nature and that the destruction of one carries the other to destruction, a rule of the following kind was commonly derived: 'Posito relativo, necesse est poni correlativum, sed in alio subiecto, et e contra destructo uno, destruitur alterum' (quoted by Ashworth 1967, p. 75, from Melanchthon's *Erotemata dialectices* of 1547). In the present example, then, the necessary consequence or concomitance that is typically indicated by *quatenus* does not obtain between two attributes of one and the same subject, such as being possessed of a mind and being immortal, but rather between correlative attributes of different subjects.
24 On the relation part/whole see also Geulincx 1891–3, vol. 1, pp. 208–9; vol. 2, pp. 230–2.
25 Leibniz 1903, p. 36.
26 Leibniz 1966, pp. 88–9.
27 Leibniz 1903, p. 357 (Leibniz 1966, pp. 47–8).
28 Compare what the authors of the Port-Royal *Logique* observe about the sentence 'Brutus a tué un tyran': it contains both the proposition that Brutus killed someone and the proposition that the person killed was a tyran (II, 5; see also II, 11; III, 2, and 9–11). There is also a striking resemblance between Leibniz's argument and such examples as 'Le soleil est une chose insensible; les Perses adoraient le soleil; donc les Perses adoraient une chose insensible' (III, 9). The similarity lies in the fact that the import of the statements that painting is an art and that the sun is an insentient thing is brought to bear upon a mere part of the predicate of the other propositions. See also, for instance, Buridan 1985, pp. 280–1, with the example 'A man is seeing every horse and Brunellus is a horse; therefore a man is seeing Brunellus' ('Homo omnem equum est videns; Brunellus est equus; ergo homo Brunellum est videns').
29 For these abortive attempts to devise an arithmetical form of syllogistic see Leibniz 1903, pp. 77–84 (Leibniz 1966, pp. 25–32); also Burkhardt 1980a, pp. 336–9.
30 Ger. VII 236–47 (Leibniz 1966, pp. 131–44; Leibniz 1969, pp. 371–81). See also Kneale and Kneale 1962, pp. 340–5; Burkhardt 1980a, pp. 356–62.
31 Leibniz 1903, p. 398: 'Propositionem ex propositione sequi nihil aliud est quam consequens in antecedenti contineri ut terminum in termino.'
32 See Risse 1964–70, vol. 2, pp. 199–203.
33 For a detailed survey see Kalinowski 1977. Another example of the endeavour to relate logic to law is the predominantly Ramist *Demonstratio logicae verae iuridica,* published by Cyprianus Regnerus at Leiden in 1638 (Regnerus 1986).
34 LAkad VI.I, 99–150, 367–430. See also Schepers 1975.
35 See Poser 1969; Burkhardt 1983b.
36 See Kalinowski and Gardies 1974; Burkhardt 1980a, pp. 420–2.
37 LAkad VI.I, pp. 431–85, especially pp. 465ff., 480ff.
38 Ashworth 1985, p. LIV.

7

METHOD AND THE STUDY OF NATURE

PETER DEAR

Historical discussion of method in the seventeenth century has long focused on the supposed development of 'modern scientific method', attempting thereby to explain the Scientific Revolution.[1] However, doubt is now frequently expressed, on both philosophical and historical grounds, about the legitimacy of such an approach. Even leaving aside those arguments denying the very possibility, let alone existence, of a determinate and efficacious 'scientific method', the search for historical understanding through the location of its first appearance increasingly seems quixotic.[2] As a consequence, it can now be asserted that an examination of seventeenth-century 'method' in the investigation of nature will have historical validity only if it respects and interprets the intellectual categories of the time – that is, if it focuses on 'method', not 'methodology'. This essay, therefore, concerns 'method' as a logical and philosophical category; it does not purport to examine or reconstruct the procedures used by philosophers in producing new knowledge, except to the extent that these involved explicit appeal to 'method'.

Those who talked of a 'method' or 'methods' capable of generating and organising natural knowledge usually rendered this concept plausible in the context of essentialism. Hence the world was seen as being composed of essences, or natural kinds (rather than of individuals classifiable only on conventional grounds). The essences of things, furthermore, were discoverable by rational or empirical means, and the resultant knowledge was certain rather than probable. The discoverability of such knowledge was in turn sustained by talk of effective 'methods'. Throughout the century, therefore, debates about method formed part of broader contentions about the nature of knowledge itself.

I. THE MEANING OF 'METHOD'

Seventeenth-century philosophers inherited two more or less distinct conceptions of 'method'. The first of these had been elaborated by humanist pedagogues intent on providing guidelines to students for the proper presentation of entire disciplines, and it had culminated in the doctrines of Petrus Ramus. In the second, 'method' appeared as a set of techniques, resolutive and compositive, for dis-covering the principles necessary to generate scientific syllogisms of the kind described by Aristotle in the *Posterior Analytics,* and for accomplishing such dem-onstrations; it is represented in its most mature form in the logical writings of Jacopo Zabarella. It incorporated in part geometrical analysis and synthesis, espe-cially after the reassimilation in the sixteenth century of ancient Greek mathemati-cal ideas. The first conception of method focused on transmitting existing bodies of knowledge, while the second considered the problem of acquiring new knowl-edge, whether of causes or theorems.[3]

Each provided a structural model for seventeenth-century discussions of method. The humanist tradition established a vision of knowledge as an intercon-nected whole, which method might map out. The problem-solving techniques of logic and geometry made plausible the idea of routinely accomplishing the indi-vidual steps in such a grand scheme; alternatively, they could remain resources for more piecemeal philosophising. Talk of method therefore served an important function in creating and sustaining philosophical positions.

The principal locus in the seventeenth century for method as a philosophical genre was the logic text. After the debates and multiplicity of opinions of the previous century, method became the topic to be treated in the concluding part – often the fourth – of any textbook on logic. Its characterisation varied little and usually followed Zabarella's distinction between method as an overall ordering of a subject-matter (*ordo*) and method as a logical technique of discovery (*methodus,* properly so called).[4] Thus, at the close of the sixteenth century, Rudolph Goclen-ius opened the final part of his *Problemata logica* with the remark that '*ordo* and *methodus* are sometimes distinguished: so that *ordo* is the proper disposition of the precepts of any discipline; [while] *methodus* is indeed the process of declaring and proving those precepts, or the way by which the more unknown and obscure parts of a discipline are explicated and demonstrated through [things] more manifest and better known.'[5] These considerations justified the section's title: 'De ordine et methodo didascalica'. More than a hundred years later, an English logic text by Isaac Watts bore as the title of its fourth and final part: 'Of disposition and method'.[6] Throughout the intervening century, this basic subdivision of method, though not necessarily with the Zabarellan terminological distinction, formed the basic structure of textbook discussions of method.[7]

The second of the two understandings of method usually distinguished be-tween two complementary techniques, variously labelled the '*a posteriori*' and '*a priori*',[8] the 'resolutive' and 'compositive', or the 'analytic' and 'synthetic'. The last two pairs were the most common, with 'analysis' and 'synthesis' serving especially to emphasise a supposed similarity to geometrical techniques. The famous Port-Royal logic of 1662, with its strong Cartesian and Pascalian character, in fact played up the geometrical analogy as an identity, basing its exposition of method upon it.[9] That idiosyncracy was, however, firmly embedded in the precedents set by conventional practice.

A brief consideration of a widely used scholastic compendium of the period will make clearer what this conventional practice looked like. Eustachius a Sancto Paulo's *Summa philosophiae,* known to and well regarded by Descartes, first appeared in 1609 and went through countless editions in both Catholic and Protestant countries.[10] Its treatise on dialectic (a contemporary virtual synonym for 'logic') contains a short section, 'De methodo', at the end of the second of its three parts.[11] It is broken down into four 'questions', the first defining the subject-matter: 'The name of *method* is understood in two ways: first, indeed, as an order and series of all those things that are taught and arranged in some complete field of learning or a part of it; secondly, as an ordering, or that judgement of the mind [*animi*] by which those things in some discipline are disposed uninterruptedly.' The second, says Eustachius, is the more proper acceptation.[12]

The second 'question' considers the number of methods. There are two generic divisions: one is 'prudential', and is simply the procedure in different circumstances of a prudent man; the other, however, is directed by 'the certain precepts of dialectic'.[13] The latter is itself twofold, 'the one general, which is the keeping in continuous series of all parts of some discipline; the other particular, which ought to govern the explaining in every question or difficulty'.[14] This evidently corresponds to Zabarella's distinction between *ordo* and *methodus.* The latter kind of method breaks down into separate procedures, chiefly resolution or analysis and composition or synthesis (Eustachius employs both sets of terms as synonyms). These are complementary. Analysis breaks down into four basic, and very standard, types (all reductions of wholes to parts or principles), including that of the geometers.[15] Synthesis is presented as simply a reversal in each case of the four variants of analysis.[16] There is a third procedure besides analysis and synthesis, namely 'definitive', that is, operating by use of definitions. This is especially useful for teaching, says Eustachius, whereas the other two are best for the purpose of discovery.[17] Finally, the third and fourth questions briefly consider the functions of method (teaching and disputing), and the techniques of 'division and partition', these last because some people, says Eustachius, especially Platonists, believe them to be, like definition and demonstration (that is, analysis/synthesis), an instrument of knowledge.[18]

The place of method in the discussions of prominent seventeenth-century philosophers derived directly from the common understandings of the term provided in standard treatments of this kind. As a term designating a way of reasoning and a way of discovering things unknown from things known, method was understood to be the appropriate heading under which to validate claims to possession of efficacious approaches to knowledge. It therefore played a significant rôle in the arguments of the century's philosophical innovators, paradoxically structuring their arguments along lines well established in orthodox pedagogy.

II. RESOLUTION AND COMPOSITION

The demonstrative regress, the logical procedure of analysis and synthesis associated with the name of Zabarella, achieved quite widespread notoriety in the later sixteenth and seventeenth centuries. This was what Zabarella chose to call *methodus*, a way to the discovering of unknown things from known. It developed from a commentary tradition that focused on Aristotle's *Posterior Analytics*, and in particular on Aristotle's distinction between two forms of demonstration: *apodeixis tou dioti* and *apodeixis tou hoti,* usually latinised as *demonstratio propter quid* and *demonstratio quia.*[19] For our purposes, the deviation of Zabarella and others from what was probably Aristotle's true meaning is unimportant; the conception current at the beginning of the seventeenth century, however, was as follows.

Demonstratio propter quid was true scientific demonstration, that is, deductive syllogistic demonstration of an effect from an immediate cause.[20] *Demonstratio quia* (or, sometimes, *esse* or *quod*) was, in *regressus* theory, a kind of deductive move from effects back to causes – that is, a way of inventing the causal principles necessary for creating a *demonstratio propter quid.* The demonstrative regress itself consisted of a combination of these two procedures. Properly speaking, *demonstratio quia* only served to discover concomitants of effects; for the demonstrative regress to work, *demonstratio propter quid* required that the newly found concomitants be established as *causes,* so as then to explain the original effects.[21] This was done as follows: having, through *demonstratio quia,* come up with a concomitant of the effect which might serve as the necessary cause in a proper scientific *demonstratio propter quid,* one then established that it was indeed the sought necessary cause by a mysterious process that Zabarella called *consideratio* or *negotiatio.* This was some sort of contemplation that created conviction in the mind, and it relied on certain metaphysical assumptions that were not in any strict sense Aristotelian.[22] Once accomplished, the demonstration back from cause to effect followed easily. Zabarella referred to the two principal stages as the resolutive and compositive methods, following terminology derived from a commentary tradition drawing on Galen's use of those terms.[23] It should be noted that the entire procedure was aimed at the generation of certain and demonstrative, not hypothetical or probabilistic, knowledge of causes.

This 'method' came to be widely known in Europe and was endorsed, for example, in writings by Jesuit philosophers at the turn of the century. Galileo's knowledge of it has recently been established through examination of his early notes and seems to have derived from Jesuit sources.[24] Long-standing claims for the importance of *regressus* theory as a methodological foundation of Galileo's own science have thereby appeared to receive some vindication,[25] but Galileo's talk of method in his mature work reveals only a use of the concept in the geometrical sense. Rather than establishing explanatory causal principles by syllogistic inference from effects, as envisioned by Zabarella, Galileo advocated a resolutive, or analytical, procedure whereby one proceeds step by step from a conclusion assumed as true to principles *already known to be true* in themselves or through prior independent demonstration. The model he used was geometrical analysis, and the source for his account was probably Pappus's from the latter's *Collectiones mathematicae*, published in Latin in 1589.[26] Otherwise, Galileo seldom used the language of 'method' (an early manuscript does not classify the demonstrative regress as 'method', that term being restricted, following Galileo's probable Jesuit source, to the equivalent of Zabarella's *ordo*).[27]

The endless wrangling among scholars over the nature of Galileo's scientific procedures leaves a number of basic points fairly clear: he always subscribed to an Aristotelian ideal of a true science as productive of certain, necessary demonstrations; his view, by no means unusual for the period, of mathematical demonstration as the paradigm for such knowledge underpinned his emphasis on the value of mathematical procedures themselves; and examination of his actual work in mechanics and cosmology shows severe tensions between his scientific ideal and his practical science.[28] But the reason for the scholarly wrangles over details – especially over characterisations of his practical science itself – is that he eschewed systematic talk of method. In keeping with his avoidance of philosophical essentialism and his adherence to the model of the mathematical sciences,[29] Galileo had little to say about method as a seventeenth-century logical or philosophical category.

Such was not the case with Thomas Hobbes. Like Galileo, Hobbes adhered to a strict demonstrative ideal in philosophy which found its model in geometry. But he used talk of resolutive and compositive methods (also calling them 'analytic' and 'synthetic') as an integral part of his philosophical discourse. The Zabarellan flavour of his discussions of method has frequently been noted.[30] But unlike

Galileo in one way, and Zabarella in another, Hobbes denied its adequacy for natural philosophy.

> Geometry . . . is demonstrable, for the lines and figures from which we reason are drawn and described by ourselves; and civil philosophy is demonstrable, because we make the commonwealth ourselves. But because of natural bodies we know not the construction, but seek it from the effects, there lies no demonstration of what the causes be we seek for, but only of what they may be.[31]

An examination of Hobbes's meaning brings out the precise point at which he differs, crucially, from Zabarella on the power of resolutive and compositive methods.[32]

Even in natural philosophy, Hobbes held that the twin procedure of resolution into principles – or parts – followed by composition, or synthesis, from those principles back to effects was the best way to proceed. But, as the above quotation shows, he did not believe that the result would be demonstration from necessarily true causes. The resolutive method made it possible to invent physical causes capable, once accepted, of explaining the original effects, through composition, with the force of necessary demonstration. But unless the causes themselves were known to be the true ones, no *physical* demonstrations could be achieved – composition merely showed that the effects would follow if such causes were assumed. The difficulty lay at precisely the point where Zabarella had required *negotiatio*. Resolution of effects established necessary concomitants. To establish that a previously hidden concomitant of an effect was actually its immediate *cause* could not be achieved through further resolution, or through composition. *Negotiatio* filled the gap for Zabarella, but its possibility relied on the tenet that the mind could grasp universals (as causes necessarily were) corresponding to something metaphysically *real*. It was a matter of grasping intuitively a universal that had some kind of reality beyond its existence as an idea in the mind of the inquirer. But Hobbes was a nominalist. For him, meaningful talk of universals could *only* refer to concepts in the human mind (God's mind being inaccessible). Therefore true physical causes remained unknowable, whereas causes in geometry, or human society, were knowable precisely because these were themselves human constructions: the universal concepts in the mind of the inquirer were literally the same as those generating the effects to be explained. Although essentialist knowledge was not possible in natural philosophy, it *was* possible for those subjects, and the method of the demonstrative regress could serve to generate it.

Hobbes's position was idiosyncratic. Talk of method usually sanctioned the possibility of knowledge rather than its impossibility. Hobbes's denial of a truly demonstrative natural philosophy did not, of course, prevent him from developing his own accounts of the physical world, but these (or the principles on which they were based) held the status of the 'most rational' rather than the 'necessarily true'. Their cognitive status was rooted in the nature of human understanding, not in the nature of the world. By contrast, attempts by others to create a methodical natural philosophy aimed at establishing certainty. As Hobbes did with his civil philosophy, they wished to use method as a sanction of absolute truth.

III. FRANCIS BACON, METHOD, AND ESSENTIALIST OPERATIONALISM

Francis Bacon associated the word *methodus* with the pedagogical method (Zabarella's *ordo*) of the humanist dialecticians, and since he vehemently disliked the latter, he avoided the use of the term in describing his own ideas.[33] Instead, he made use of the handy Ciceronian translation of its Greek prototype: *via et ratio.* Bacon intended his own famous 'method' to pursue aims quite different from those of the 'methodical' pedagogy of the schools even though it still in fact connected closely with the cluster of ideas surrounding the various contemporary connotations of 'method', 'order', and 'way' (*methodus, ordo,* and *via*).[34]

The classic statement of Bacon's new *via et ratio,* his 'true directions concerning the interpretation of nature', is the *Novum organum* of 1620.[35] 'Method' in Bacon's sense retained the central notion of *ordo,* 'order', but the order that he wished to establish in the 'interpretation of nature' was not that of the dialecticians. Far from advocating a new way of setting out a subject-matter in an orderly fashion, he proposed an orderly way of discovering the subject-matter itself. His criticisms of the prevailing systems of logic, whether humanist or scholastic, centre on the claim that they are unproductive: in his famous metaphor, the 'reasoners resemble spiders, who make cobwebs out of their own substance'.[36] His own aims were quite different, being 'the invention not of arguments but of arts'.[37] Thus he condemned the syllogism as 'acting too confusedly and letting nature slip out of its hands'. Syllogisms were only as good as the notions of which they made use, and in neglecting the formation of notions – 'induction' – the logicians prepared their work with inadequate foundations, and, 'in many ways, the whole edifice tumbles'.[38] As Bacon had said, more moderately, in *The Advancement of Learning* (1605), 'logic doth not pretend to invent sciences, or the axioms of sciences, but passeth it over with a *cuique in sua arte credendum* [everyone in his own art is to be believed].'[39]

Bacon's own procedure required that 'particulars' of experience, the raw material of the enterprise, be ranged into tables. The use of a lay-out on a page as the focus for a *via et ratio* – a kind of 'method' – clearly echoes even the much-despised Ramus, but the actual procedure is more directly comparable to the commonplace book, a staple of methodical humanist education. Bacon drew the analogy directly in *The Advancement of Learning*. He admits the practical usefulness of 'general topics', that is, general headings for the comprehension of material to be used in disputation, but stresses that they only serve to recall and organise what we already know. There is, however, another kind of topic: 'I do receive particular topics, that is, places or directions of invention and inquiry in every particular knowledge, as things of great use, being mixtures of logic with the matter of the sciences.' By virtue of drawing up such headings, and recording (as he details in the *Novum organum*) 'particulars' under them, 'we do not only gain that part of the way which is passed, but we gain the better sight of that part of the way which remaineth.'[40]

Bacon's *via*, his road to discovery, commenced by formulating the questions the answers to which were to be discovered. Such questions were themselves strictly delimited, and concerned the 'forms' of particular phenomena or 'natures'. 'Natures' constituted a kind of phenomenal 'alphabet', including such things as whiteness, heat, yellowness, brittleness – that is (although Bacon of course avoided the comparison), the sorts of things designated by Aristotelians as 'qualities'. 'Forms' were the realities underlying 'natures'. His plan therefore necessarily presupposed a particular ontology, a philosophy of nature determining and defining the appropriate terms in which the 'forms' of 'natures' must be expressed.[41] It would have run directly counter to his intentions to admit such a thing, however. 'Forms' had to be elucidated by means of a correct 'induction' from particulars; such an 'induction' allowed (in principle) no room for the intrusion of presuppositions – what Bacon decried in existing philosophies as 'anticipations of nature'. Having ranged particulars, instances of the 'nature' under scrutiny known through experience, into tables (which Bacon described as teaching experience to 'read and write'),[42] his own special kind of 'induction' set to work to derive 'axioms', generalisations about the 'nature'. 'Axioms' rested on the firmest of inferential foundations because of the logical structure of Baconian 'induction'. Instead of the induction by enumeration used in rhetoric or dialectic – citation of favourable instances – 'the induction which is to be available for the discovery and demonstration of sciences and arts, must analyze nature by proper rejections and exclusions; and then, after a sufficient number of negatives, come to a conclusion on the affirmative instances.'[43] Bacon goes on to say that this logic of falsification, this 'induction', 'must be used not only to discover axioms, but also in the formation of notions'.[44]

Bacon succeeded in obscuring the ontological and natural philosophical assumptions underlying the conceptual apparatus of 'natures' and 'forms' by exploiting what he presented as the ultimate goal of his 'instauration', namely 'works'. 'For when I speak of forms, I mean nothing more than those laws and determinations of absolute actuality which govern and constitute any simple nature, as heat, light, weight, in every kind of matter and subject that is susceptible of them. Thus the form of heat or the form of light is the same thing as the law of heat or the law of light.'[45] The 'form' of a 'nature', and the rule for the production of that 'nature', differed in no significant respect. Thus, since an operational rule necessarily related directly to concrete, practical experience, knowledge of the 'form' appeared to be directly *constituted* by concrete experience.

The mechanism of the 'investigation of forms' was itself quite simple, but Bacon surrounded it with an elaborate classification of subdivisions and special cases. The initial stage was the compilation of the 'Tables of First Presentation', lists of individual instances (or 'particulars') of the 'nature' in question. There were three such tables, designated, in Bacon's example of heat, 'Instances Agreeing in the Nature of Heat', 'Instances in Proximity where the Nature of Heat is Absent', and 'Table of Degrees or Comparison in Heat'. The problem then became 'to find such a nature as is always present or absent with the given nature, and always increases and decreases with it; and which is . . . a particular case of a more general nature'. This involved the process of exclusion mentioned above, Bacon's own 'induction'. To God, he observed, knowledge of 'forms' is immediate. But to man, 'it is granted only to proceed at first by negatives, and at last to end in affirmatives after exclusion has been exhausted.'[46]

Despite the undoubted insufficiency of the 'Tables of First Presentation' in his worked example, Bacon sanctioned at this point a conjectural formulation of the 'form' of heat developed from his as yet imperfect 'induction', because 'truth will sooner come out from error than from confusion.'[47] Bacon had no fewer than three names for this kind of conjecture: 'Indulgence of the Understanding', 'Commencement of the Interpretation', and 'First Vintage'. Having achieved such a thing, the investigator could then proceed with a more focused collection and inspection of instances. Bacon helps him on his way with a lengthy categorisation and discussion of various 'prerogative instances', types of instances of especial exclusory value. Perhaps most notable of these are the 'Instances of the Fingerpost', which serve to decide which of two or more attendant 'natures' is the cause of the 'nature' in question.[48]

The detail in which Bacon elaborated and illustrated his techniques of investigation jars, as has long been noted, with the paucity of results which he could himself show. The importance of his *via et ratio,* his anti-method, however, lies not in any practical efficacy, and still less in its self-important terminologies, but in its designs: the 'forms' of 'natures', although intended as potential operational rules, also characterised the *essence* of those subjects in which they inhered: gold, for example, was *nothing more than* a concatenation of the appropriate simple natures, and could be made, authentically, simply by the superinducing of those natures onto matter. Bacon's central project, therefore, was to establish an orderly route towards the discovery of the unknown *essences* of things, which would of itself lead to operational control. Furthermore, his stress on discovery of new knowledge rather than transmission of an established body of learning had led Bacon to avoid the word *methodus* as a description of his plan because of his association of it with humanist pedagogical practice. Descartes, by contrast, embraced the word 'method' careless of any unwanted dialectical baggage.[49]

IV. DESCARTES, *METHODUS,* AND *ORDO:* THE METAPHYSICAL UNDERPINNING OF AN ESSENTIALIST METHOD

Descartes's is certainly the most famous of seventeenth-century 'methods'. His three *Essais* of 1637, *La dioptrique, Les météores,* and *La géometrie,* purportedly served to illustrate the power of the method discussed in their author's self-serving autobiographical preface, the *Discours de la méthode.* They did not, however, purport to illustrate *how* the method was to be applied so as to achieve the results that they presented.[50] Hence the reader had to rely, for explicit guidance, on the brief enunciation of the method's four rules given in Part II of the *Discours.*

The enunciation of the four rules (or 'precepts') of the method served Descartes's overall design in that they established that Descartes had indeed acquired the knowledge he displayed through the use of a universal method. The promise of more discoveries to come would then be rendered plausible. The pregnant precepts were as follows:

The first was never to accept anything as true if I did not have evident knowledge of its truth: that is, carefully to avoid precipitate conclusions and preconceptions, and to include nothing more in my judgements than what presented itself to my mind so clearly and so distinctly that I had no occasion to doubt it.

The second, to divide each of the difficulties I examined into as many parts as possible and as may be required in order to resolve them better.

The third, to direct my thoughts in an orderly manner, by beginning with the simplest and most easily known objects in order to ascend little by little, step by step, to knowledge of the most complex, and by supposing some order even among objects that have no natural order of precedence.[51]

And the last, throughout to make enumerations so complete, and reviews so comprehensive, that I could be sure of leaving nothing out.[52]

Leibniz's oft-quoted parody of Descartes's method has some justice: 'Take what is necessary, do as you ought, and you will get what you wanted.'[53]

A fuller understanding of Descartes's methodological precepts and their terminology rests on study of his unfinished and long-unpublished *Regulae ad directionem ingenii,* written intermittently between 1619 and 1628.[54] Descartes appears to have embedded and conflated in the *Regulae* two distinct but related ambitions, namely, a universal method encompassing everything knowable and an apparently more restricted 'universal mathematics' encompassing all problems of quantity and proportion.[55] The universal method itself is presented as a means of solving individual problems, and the claim for the universality of this method is rendered plausible by a metaphysical vision of the deductive interlinkage of all knowledge.

Descartes's discussion clearly takes its place within contemporary philosophical discussion of 'method'. What he himself specifies as his 'method' is a problem-solving tool that assumes the functions both of the demonstrative regress so much the centre of attention in scholastic logic, and of geometrical analytical techniques. It therefore corresponds to the sense of 'method' that Zabarella labelled 'methodus'. Descartes explains its concrete use in the *Regulae* through examples such as the problem of finding the anaclastic curve in optics (a task performed in the later *Dioptrique,* a work explicitly presented as an illustration of the power of the method).[56] The procedure he advocates involves the construction of a sequence of increasingly general objects of knowledge requisite to solving the problem, ending in one that can be grasped solely through 'mental intuition'.[57] The sequence is then reversed to accomplish a deductive demonstration of the problem from first, and indubitable, principles. The first stage can be seen as corresponding to analysis, the second to synthesis, although neither term appears in the *Regulae* (or, indeed, in the *Discours*). It is important to note, however, that Descartes does not regard the 'synthetic' stage as a mere inversion of the 'analytic' steps; it may very well involve additional 'enumerations' at each step – considerations of everything with a possible bearing on the inferential move – to cope with the increasing specificity.[58]

The statement of Rule 5 commences as follows: 'The whole method consists entirely in the ordering and arranging of the objects on which we must concentrate our mind's eye if we are to discover some truth.' He is here referring to the reduction of 'complicated and obscure propositions step by step to simpler ones, and then, starting with the intuition of the simplest ones of all, try to ascend through the same steps to a knowledge of all the rest'.[59] In the *Discours,* he comments further on this second, ascending stage: 'I had no great difficulty in deciding which things to begin with, for I knew already that it must be with the simplest and most easily known.'[60]

Descartes attempted to justify his method as a practical tool by arguing that the ultimate objects to which all problems may be reduced 'are very few', and he described them as 'pure and simple natures which we can intuit straight off and *per se* (independently of any others)'.[61] This account, in the early Rule 6, is supplemented in Rule 12 by a specification of the sorts of things that should properly count as 'simple natures'. These, 'which the intellect recognises by means of a sort of innate light', include, under the heading of the 'purely material', 'shape, extension and motion, etc.'[62] It is the use of these 'simple natures' which connects the method to the vision of the deductive interlinkage of all knowledge. 'It must be acknowledged', says Descartes, rejecting the conventional separation of knowledge into discrete disciplines, 'that all the sciences are so closely interconnected that it is much easier to learn them all together than to separate one from the other.' In fact, he continues, 'they are all interconnected and interdependent.'[63] This latticelike interconnexion guaranteed the possibility of passage between any one object of knowledge and another.[64] The method itself provided a means of traversing through the lattice-work from complex phenomena back to 'simple natures', and knowing which objects actually counted as 'simple natures' enabled the inquirer to direct his analysis of a problem towards the correct explanatory principles. In the *Regulae,* this conception served to assure the inquirer that if the method were followed diligently, a failure to solve a problem at least revealed another piece of knowledge, namely that the problem passed the limits of human understanding.[65] However, Descartes's project of metaphysical foundationalism, commenced in about 1629 after the abandonment of the *Regulae,* had, by the time of the *Discours de la méthode,* rendered such inherent limitations redundant – *all* phenomena in the world had *necessarily* to be derivable from known, restricted, ontologically basic principles, so that even if a problem proved insoluble from a practical point of view, it provided no evidence of fundamentally inscrutable physical principles.[66]

Despite his restriction of the term 'method' to its problem-solving sense, Descartes's lattice-work image of knowledge is itself clearly related to the 'methodical' ordering and presentation of disciplines conventional in contemporary logic texts – *ordo* rather than *methodus.* His model of the unity of all knowledge mimicked in large part the branching tables of Ramus and the humanist dialecticians, even paralleling Ramus's use of such schemes to structure the latter's procedures of *analysis* and *genesis.*[67] Descartes explicitly rejected the disciplinary boundaries observed by these common tabular lay-outs, however; his conception more closely resembled the trans-disciplinary, encyclopaedic versions produced by universalists like Alsted.[68]

Descartes's talk of his 'method' disappears after its first public outing in 1637. Presumably it had become peripheral to his overall project. Scholars have frequently attempted to identify in the procedures of the *Meditationes* of 1641 an application of the method, but two principal considerations argue against the historical legitimacy of their claims. The first is that the word itself is not used: if 'method' had been a significant component of Descartes's argumentative techniques this would not have been so. Only the unjustified assumption that Descartes's method was an instrumentally efficacious technique by which he arrived at his results can warrant the idea that a greater understanding of either the method or the *Meditationes* might emerge from their juxtaposition. The second is that the *Meditationes* does not represent the kind of investigation of specific problems described in the *Regulae* or the *Discours* and exemplified in the *Essais.* The step-by-step resolution of a problem into its ontologically basic constituents (the 'simple natures' of the *Regulae*) plays no part in the procedures of the first two *Meditationes;* only the re-ascent following the *cogito* could be squared with the method's prescriptions. Even that ascent, however, does not partake of the method's goal of solving a predetermined problem.[69]

Similarly, the outline in the *Discours* and exposition in the *Principia philosophiae* (1644) of the establishment of Cartesian ontology, that is, of the explanatory elements to be used in the solution of physical problems, are procedurally independent of Descartes's rhetoric of 'method'. Talk of method seems to have become redundant as Descartes developed his metaphysical foundationalism. Where, in the *Regulae,* method occupied the heart of Descartes's philosophical enterprise, in the *Discours* it had become vestigial, thereafter being wholly absent.[70] Descartes's new metaphysics had taken its place. There is thus a sense in which *methodus* gave way to *ordo.*[71]

Because the 'method' had always depended on a systematic ontological underpinning, however, Descartes's epistemological assumptions necessarily remained basically the same. Chief among them was essentialism, the doctrine that the achievable goal of natural philosophy was knowledge of the true natures of things. The reduction of phenomena to a concatenation of 'simple natures' promised in the *Regulae,* or the interpretation of phenomena as complex systems of matter/extension in motion described in the *Principia,* each presupposed the possibility of apprehending things as they really are – knowing them as God knows them.[72]

The plausibility of the universal method had always rested on the lattice-work model of the unity of knowledge, and that lattice-work derived its potency from the assumption that it mapped onto the structure of the world itself – that it was, literally, an essentialist map of the nature of all things. 'Method' and encyclopaedism, 'method' and essentialism, connected together closely in the seventeenth century. In that respect, Descartes is unremarkable and compares with Bacon, who is at first sight so different.[73]

The famous Port-Royal *Logique* of 1662[74] crystallised the (largely implicit) geometrical overtones of Descartes's 'method' by reducing the concept to 'analysis' and 'synthesis' taken paradigmatically in their mathematical connotation. The treatment appears as the conventionally located fourth part of the work, 'De la méthode'. It commences with a definition of method as 'the art of well-disposing a series [*suite*] of several thoughts, or of discovering the truth when we do not know it, or of proving it to others when we know it already'.[75] This, the authors contend, boils down to two sorts of method, 'one for discovering the truth, which is called *analysis,* or *method of resolution,* and which one can also call *method of invention*; and the other for making it understood to others when it has been found, which is called *synthesis,* or *method of composition,* and which one can also call *method of teaching* [*doctrine*]'.[76] The fifth page of Chapter One presents Descartes's four precepts from the *Discours,* as useful not just for analysis, but for the application of method in general.[77]

The appeal to Descartes's authority is fittingly unspecific, since the authors of Port-Royal adhere to a sharply defined conception of analysis and synthesis absent in Descartes's own writings on method but corresponding closely to the notions expressed by the Port-Royal fellow-traveller Blaise Pascal in his *L'esprit géometrique*.[78] The stress is always on clarity of definition of terms and avoidance of mistaking words for things themselves. Propositions employing well-defined terms should be certain and indubitable; from such propositions firm, true inferences can be made.[79] Throughout *La logique,* illustrative examples are taken plentifully from geometry.[80] In the second edition of the work, reference to Descartes becomes more explicit, and material is added from the (as yet unpublished) *Regulae*.[81] The clarity given to the notion of method in the Port-Royal *Logique* by the authors' adherence to their own precepts concerning unequivocal definition, and the lack of concern with incorporating all previous usages, ensured its considerable influence into the following century.[82]

Leibniz, too, may be located within this cluster of philosophical themes. Despite his jibe about the unhelpfulness of Descartes's methodical precepts, he attempted in the 1670s what amounted to an extension of Descartes's method, intended to alleviate its problems of lack of specificity. Employing the language of analysis and synthesis, with appeal to the mathematical senses of those terms – like Descartes and the Port-Royalists stressing synthesis as the best means of instruction, and analysis as the best means of invention – he envisioned a grounding for metaphysics analogous to the axiomatic grounding of geometry. His belief in the likely success of this project waned after 1680, being replaced by an epistemological rather than methodical examination of hypotheses and the criteria appropriate for deciding on their adequacy. The geometrical analogy remained firm, however, because he pointed out that Euclid's axioms themselves could only be assumed. Leibniz's encyclopaedism – his belief in the interconnectedness of all knowledge – allowed him to retain the idea of method even while admitting the necessity of using hypotheses. A universal structure of knowledge could still be investigated by a 'method' even if that method carried no guarantee of its own success. But in this, as in much else, Leibniz is very atypical.[83]

V. NON-ESSENTIALIST MODELS OF KNOWLEDGE AND THE IRRELEVANCE OF METHOD

The intimate connexion between the advocacy of methods and philosophical essentialism emerges more clearly from an examination of natural philosophers who eschewed essentialism. Two basic positions may be discerned here. The first is the denial that human knowledge can ever encompass the essences of things; only appearances are accessible. Marin Mersenne and Gilles Personne de Roberval are notable representatives of this position. The second is the denial only that human knowledge can encompass the essences of things *with certainty.* Probabilistic or hypothetical 'knowledge' of causes, abandoning the quest for *scientia,* remained available. In their various ways, Pierre Gassendi, Christiaan Huygens, and Jacques Rohault adhered to this position. Neither group talked of 'method', in the senses discussed hitherto, as a legitimation of their work or a guarantee of its promise.

Mersenne, resting his arguments on standard sceptical strategies, denied that knowledge of essences was an attainable goal, and he advocated instead the study of manifest appearances represented primarily by the traditional mixed mathematical sciences – optics, astronomy, mechanics, music and so on. These sciences did not claim to discuss the essential natures of their subjects, but only to characterise and manipulate the latter's quantitative properties.[84] Mersenne's abandonment of essentialist physics left him unconcerned with 'method' in the sense of systematic discovery of causes.[85] Although Robert Lenoble described several of Mersenne's small treatises of 1634 as a collective 'discourse on method',[86]

Mersenne never dealt with method. Instead, he discussed the kinds of knowledge that could and should be sought, relying on the ordinary practices of mathematicians, together with close examination of the behaviour of things themselves, to lend substance to his assertions. Mersenne advocated a particular approach to the study of nature more by example than by precept. Roberval, as a mathematician by profession, had a clear stake in endorsing precisely Mersenne's attitude – it elevated his own work by down-grading physics.[87] Once again, there was no need to speak of a general method, since the practices of mathematicians constituted their own unquestioned tradition.

The stance of the probabilists or hypotheticalists was less straightforward. They were prepared to consider the natures or underlying causes of things, but not to claim certainty for their conclusions. Gassendi based his renovated Epicurean atomism on a nominalist position that allowed him to postulate atomic or corpuscular mechanisms underlying phenomena as the best means of accounting for them, but on a conjectural, hypothetical basis. He did not use talk of method to legitimate his project or to sustain postulated mechanisms.[88] His great work *Syntagma philosophicum* (1658), however, contained as part of its comprehensive coverage a short treatise on logic, called *Institutio logica*. Following convention, the first part of the treatise covered the formation of concepts; the second, propositions; the third, syllogisms; and the fourth, method. Thus method found a place as a standard topical heading within the genre.[89] Pedagogical method constitutes the bulk of Gassendi's treatment, and the irrelevance of his discussion of method to his philosophical work is clear; he is covering standard ground, rather hastily, and the only advice relevant to natural philosophical *discovery* is to give due weight in judgement to sensory evidence.[90] Method was not important to Gassendi.

Huygens and Rohault both associated themselves with Cartesianism. The aspects of Descartes's ideas on which they drew were, however, those of the *Principia philosophiae* rather than of the *Discours* or the *Meditationes.* Descartes's picture of the physical world and its ontology provided them with a framework of explanation involving *hypothetical* mechanisms.[91] Descartes had himself discussed the necessity of using conjectural explanations for some phenomena, which experimentation could help to confirm through elimination of alternatives. The resulting explanation would have, at best, moral rather than absolute (metaphysical) certainty.[92] Huygens, however, refused to accord absolute certainty even to the mechanical terms of explanation themselves. Instead, he upheld them as the only appropriate ones on grounds of 'intelligibility'. A true and intelligible natural philosophy could only utilise matter and its mechanical interactions, because otherwise it would not provide any kind of real explanation at all.[93] Huygens did not feel bound by Descartes's *a priori* arguments for the impossibility of a void and accepted the legitimacy of explanations using particles moving in a vacuum. Whereas these terms or elements of explanation had to be accepted even though they could not be justified as being necessarily true of the world, explanations of specific phenomena making use of them took on only a hypothetical status, the reliability of which did not result from the elimination of all conceivable alternatives. Instead, they were justified on the merely pragmatic grounds of the accordance of their consequences with observation and their ability to make novel predictions.[94] Huygens stressed many times that natural philosophy could only aspire to probability in its explanations, although 'there are many degrees of Probable, some *nearer the Truth* than others, in the determining of which lies the chief exercise of our Judgement.'[95]

In one case at least, Huygens explicitly denied the applicability of the demonstrative regress, with its search for true causes, to his own work. Conventionally enough, he always distinguished sharply between truths of experience regarding particular phenomena and explanations of those truths.[96] When speaking of his rules of collision (finally presented posthumously in the 1703 *De motu corporum*), he remarked, 'I think I have done something by having demonstrated the rules for the communication of motion observed by nature, although I only showed the *tou hoti*.'[97] His use of the Greek term from the *Posterior Analytics,* corresponding to the Latin term *demonstratio quia,* indicates both his familiarity with the Aristotelian tradition and his denial that he has managed to produce a solid, definitive demonstration from causes (which would be a *demonstratio propter quid* or *tou dioti*). Instead, he claims to have based his work on the effects or phenomena alone, attempting to derive true generalisations from them. *Demonstratio quia,* it will be remembered, served only to infer from effects their constant underlying concomitants, without being able to ascribe to the latter any necessary causal status. Given his attitude towards the merely probabilistic nature of knowledge of causes or first principles, it is unsurprising that Huygens should have avoided portraying his work on collision as dependent upon physical principles. To achieve any kind of certainty, he needed to distance his knowledge-claims from talk of method, because method, as with the demonstrative regress, usually implied a search for definitive physical causes.

Huygens's probabilism left no room for talk of method in the sense of a navigational technique through an entire subject-matter. Nor did it allow use of a Zabarellan kind of logical technique as a packaging for individual problem-solutions. Unquestionably, his approach was piecemeal in respect of particular problems, although it included a general criterion of 'intelligibility' to guide assessments of explanatory adequacy. His extreme 'hypothetico-deductive' characterisation of natural philosophical explanation, however, effectively eliminated the analytical or resolutive stage of Zabarella's demonstrative regress: principles of explanation could be freely imagined (within general mechanistic constraints) because their only sanction came from their deductive consequences. A 'methodical' means of inventing them analytically was irrelevant to their cognitive status.

Rohault, despite his much more open acceptance of Cartesian principles (which he always and increasingly maintained were compatible with true Aristotelian teaching),[98] similarly eschewed discussion of a formal method for achieving explanations of particular effects. His use of the word 'method' was a very loose one; for example, in the preface to his *Traité de physique* (1671) he describes the over-reliance on authority of dogmatic Aristotelians as a 'method of philosophising', never using the term in a technical sense. Referring in the same work to the 'true method of philosophy on particular subjects', he says that 'in order to find out what the nature of any thing is, we are to search for some one particular in it that will account for all the effects which experience shows us it is capable of producing.'[99] Unlike Descartes, however, he fails to give methodical rules for discovering such a particular, saying only that an explanation developed along these lines must inevitably be conjectural and must inevitably be assessed only on its conformity with experience and experiment. Probability, although sometimes capable of attaining a very high degree, is the best to which we can aspire. Rohault's attitude clearly resembles Descartes's remarks on the rôle of experiments. But, as we have seen, that aspect of Descartes's epistemology is not part of his (i.e., Descartes's) 'method'.

John Locke shows especially clearly, this time explicitly rather than by silence, how those who disbelieved in the possibility of acquiring knowledge of essences in natural philosophy perceived talk of method as largely irrelevant to discussing progress in that subject. In the *Essay,* Locke's position on what kind of knowledge may be had of natural things is encapsulated in his suspicion that 'natural Philosophy is not capable of being made a Science.' In order to know that all gold is malleable we should have to perceive a necessary connexion between malleability and the properties included in our idea or definition of gold. Since such quasi-geometrical knowledge is impossible, 'for assurance I must apply myself to *Experience*; as far as that reaches, I may have certain Knowledge, but no further.' Yet experience reaches only to particulars and, although 'a Man accustomed to rational and regular Experiments' may 'be able to . . . guess righter at their yet unknown Properties, . . . this is but Judgment and Opinion, not Knowledge and Certainty'. Such probabilities may be enough for us to 'draw Advantages of Ease and Health, and thereby increase our stock of Conveniences for this Life', but more than that lies beyond the reach of our faculties.[100] The consequences of this attitude for method are indicated in the same chapter, derived via the following general consideration: 'We must therefore, if we will proceed, as Reason advises, *adapt our methods of Enquiry to the nature of the* Ideas *we examine,* and the Truth we search after. General and certain Truths are only founded in the Habitudes and Relations of abstract *Ideas*.'[101] Consequently, the methods of the mathematicians, although they might even be applicable to morality (where, as in mathematics, 'our abstract *Ideas* are real as well as nominal Essences'), are irrelevant to the gaining of knowledge of substances, which have 'an unknown real Essence' distinct from our nominal essence.[102] Experience, not reason, is the appropriate tool there, and the result is not knowledge but belief.

In mathematics itself, Locke continues, the employment of 'maxims' or 'axioms' does not lead to the discovery of new knowledge; mathematical truths 'have been discovered by the Thoughts otherways applied: The Mind had other Objects, other Views before it, far different from those Maxims, when it first got the Knowledge of such kind of Truths in Mathematicks'. Algebra is the only useful method of discovery that mathematicians have hit upon: 'Who knows what Methods, to enlarge our Knowledge in other parts of Science, may hereafter be invented, answering that of *Algebra* in Mathematicks?'[103] Locke's characterisation of mathematical 'methods' clearly refers to the commonplace synthetic/analytic distinction,[104] and his entire discussion therefore amounts to a flat rejection of the applicability of what usually appeared in logic texts as *methodus* to natural philosophy. Indeed, he showed little enthusiasm for it in any field, as the whole of Book IV, Chapter 12, 'Of the Improvement of our Knowledge', evidences.[105]

Locke also used the term 'method' to denote the proper way to handle hypotheses, in a way somewhat similar to Rohault's. A manuscript passage from 1694 which informed later editions of the *Essay concerning Human Understanding* makes his usage clear.[106] Headed 'Method', and making no use of that word in the text itself, Locke's discussion concerns the comparison and criticism of hypotheses and is based on the assumption that, since we lack certain demonstrations in most things, objections can always be raised about almost any explanation. The proper procedure is therefore to use the hypothesis that leads to the fewest, and least severe, difficulties. Locke's prescription may, perhaps, best be described as an injunction to analyse, not experience, but hypotheses. The provenance of those hypotheses themselves is not an issue.[107] The structural similarity to the 'resolutive method' no doubt contributed to Locke's decision to use the term 'method,' but the latter seems to carry very little weight. Locke suggests a way of assessing hypotheses but not a genuine 'method' of discovery – nor yet a pedagogical or organising 'method'.

As the examples of Huygens, Rohault, and Locke indicate, the idea of a 'hypothetical method' carries severe difficulties in the context of seventeenth-century understandings of those terms. 'Method' usually implied a way to certain knowledge of essences, whereas 'hypothesis' paraded the inaccessibility of such knowledge. Isaac Newton, however, stands as a curious and novel exception to the generalisation that method and essentialism went hand in hand in this period. He wanted to have his cake and eat it too – to have a methodical path to the most reliable knowledge possible of phenomena alone.

VI. NEWTON, METHOD, AND PHENOMENA

'Method' meant for Newton, centrally and above all, the 'method of analysis', although synthesis, procedurally much more straightforward and therefore not worth so much ink, was always concomitantly in the background. A well-known passage in the third edition (1717) of the *Opticks,* an expansion to what is known from that edition as Query 31, encapsulates his approach.

As in mathematics, so in natural philosophy, the investigation of difficult things by the method of analysis, ought ever to precede the method of composition. This analysis consists in making experiments and observations, and in drawing general conclusions from them by induction, and admitting of no objections against the conclusions, but such as are taken from experiments, or other certain truths. For hypotheses are not to be regarded in experimental philosophy. And although the arguing from experiments and observations by induction be no demonstration of general conclusions; yet it is the best way of arguing which the nature of things admits of, and may be looked upon as so much the stronger, by how much the induction is more general. And if no exception occur from phenomena, the conclusion may be pronounced generally. But if at any time afterwards any exception shall occur from experiments, it may then begin to be pronounced with such exceptions as occur. By this way of analysis we may proceed from compounds to ingredients, and from motions to the forces producing them; and in general, from effects to their causes, and from particular causes to more general ones, till the argument end in the most general. This is the method of analysis: and the synthesis consists in assuming the causes discovered, and established as principles, and by them explaining the phenomena proceeding from them, and proving the explanations.[108]

Newton was not a hypothetico-deductivist in the manner of Huygens, and he believed that claims about the world going beyond a bare record of particular appearances – explanatory principles of some kind – could be derived from phenomena, and not simply co-ordinated with them through testing of deductive consequences. In this he resembles Bacon, but, less superficially, he also resembles Galileo in the latter's exploitation of the mathematical tradition of analysis and synthesis. Newton's use of the word 'induction' bears little relation to Bacon's,[109] but it does form a characteristic step in his 'method of analysis'.

The procedure Newton advocates (and the argumentative structure within which he had operated in his optical controversies of the 1670s) may be summarised as follows: experimental and observational situations can be conceptually analysed to reveal necessary features of their behaviour and properties.[110] 'Induction' now serves to generalise those features. That is, induction for Newton means generalising from one exemplary situation to all others deemed similar, an indeterminate procedure made to look determinate in the *Principia*'s second 'Rule of Philosophising' ('Therefore to the same natural effects we must, as far as possible, assign the same causes').[111]

As the above quotation from the *Opticks* shows, Newton drew the intellectual pedigree of his 'method' from mathematics.[112] He saw his method of analysis as producing the *best possible* explanatory principles of a phenomenon or phenomena; it was not a heuristic for generating mere 'hypotheses' to be subjected to subsequent experimental test. In fact, the line between 'best possible' (not itself a Newtonian expression) and 'certain' seems to have been very ambiguous in Newton's mind. After contrasting the status of the knowledge acquired through analysis and synthesis with that based on 'hypotheses', he concluded: ''Tis much better to do a little with certainty and leave the rest for others that come after you than to explain all things by conjecture without making sure of anything.'[113] This remark may be compared with his famous claim, made in the 1672 letter to Oldenburg detailing his new conception of light and colours and expunged by the latter from the published version: 'A naturalist would scarce expect to see ye science of those [i.e., colours] become mathematicall, & yet I dare affirm that there is as much certainty in it as in any other part of Opticks.'[114] After receiving criticism from Hooke over the dogmatism this implied, Newton attempted to clarify his position in a reply to Oldenburg. 'I said indeed that the *Science of Colours was Mathematicall & as certain as any other part of Optiques*; but who knows not that Optiques & many other Mathematicall Sciences depend as well on Physicall Principles as on Mathematicall Demonstrations: And the absolute certainty of a Science cannot exceed the certainty of its Principles.'[115] Experimentally determined propositions, being physical, necessarily lacked absolute mathematical certainty; Newton appeals therefore to the classical tradition of 'mixed mathematics', sciences of the physical world such as optics and mechanics that relied on borrowing demonstrations from pure mathematics.

Newton's clarification fails to remove the ambiguity, however. The fourth of Newton's 'Rules of Philosophising', appearing originally in the third edition of the *Principia* (1726), reads as follows:

Rule IV

In experimental philosophy we are to look upon propositions inferred by general induction from phenomena as accurately or very nearly true, notwithstanding any contrary hypotheses that may be imagined, till such time as other phenomena occur, by which they may either be made more accurate, or liable to exceptions.

This rule we must follow, that the argument of induction may not be evaded by hypotheses.[116]

Newton does not say that inductive propositions may be *refuted* by new phenomena, only that they may be in some way *refined*. If a proposition is derived according to proper analytical procedures and 'induction' from a particular phenomenon, or phenomena, it cannot, ipso facto, be false. This relates to his position that just one experiment or phenomenon often suffices to establish some proposition.

During his optical controversies of the 1670s, Newton replied to Lucas that the latter's experiments, different from Newton's own, were beside the point, because they failed to refute Newton's own *experimentum crucis*.[117] In this instance, then, in claiming that a single experimental situation suffices to establish conclusively a proposition about light, Newton refused even to allow room for 'increased accuracy' or the listing of 'exceptions'. The apparent discrepancy between this position and Rule IV in the *Principia* is not an indication of a change in Newton's position between the 1670s and the formulation of that rule, however. He had tried, in the letter to Oldenburg considered above, to avoid the imputation that he asserted certainty for his conclusions about colours, apparently prompted by Hooke's drawing attention to his earlier remark. Conversely, in Cotes's preface, approved by Newton, to the second edition of the *Principia* (1713), the certainty of universal gravitation is defended against the criticisms of Leibniz and others: Newton 'was the only and the first philosopher that could demonstrate [universal gravitation] from appearances, and make it a solid foundation to the most noble speculations'.[118] Cotes summed up his master's approach as follows:

[Experimental philosophers] frame no hypotheses, nor receive them into philosophy otherwise than as questions whose truth may be disputed. They proceed therefore in a twofold method, synthetical and analytical. From some select [n.b.] phenomena they deduce by analysis the forces of nature and the more simple laws of forces; and from thence by synthesis show the constitution of the rest.[119]

Did Newton claim certainty for the conclusions of experimental philosophy or not, therefore? The situation is not in fact one of mere ambiguity. Newton utilised an additional resource to shore up his claims about method – a distinction between 'properties' and 'causes'. During the optical controversies, Newton argued that his conclusions held independently of any hypothesis about the true nature of light. In response to Pardies he pronounced that 'the best and safest way of philosophising seems to be this: first to search carefully for the properties of things, establishing them by experiments, and then more warily to assert any explanatory hypotheses.'[120] His claim throughout was that the propositions he put forward were *properties* of light experimentally established.[121] He thus avoided the epistemological difficulties associated with hypothetical causes. The original presentation published in the *Philosophical Transactions* drew the contrast explicitly: compared with his conclusions about colours and refrangibility, 'to determine more absolutely, what Light is, after what manner refracted, and by what modes or actions it produceth in our minds the Phantasms of Colours, is not so easie. *And I shall not mingle conjectures with certainties*' (emphasis added).[122] It might in this connexion be noted that Newton's use of the term 'theory' distanced it absolutely from 'hypothesis' – theories were generalised accounts about the workings of the world discovered through phenomena, whereas hypotheses were conjectural constructs intended to provide explanations for those theories, or the phenomena that they summarised.[123]

The classic statement of this position is found in Newton's 'General Scholium' to the second edition of the *Principia:*

But hitherto I have not been able to discover the cause of those properties of gravity from phenomena, and I feign no hypotheses;[124] for whatever is not deduced from the phenomena is to be called an hypothesis; and hypotheses, whether metaphysical or physical, whether of occult qualities or mechanical, have no place in experimental philosophy. In this philosophy particular propositions are inferred from the phenomena, and afterwards rendered general by induction.[125] . . . And to us it is enough that gravity does really exist, and act according to the laws which we have explained, and abundantly serves to account for all the motions of the celestial bodies, and of our sea.[126]

Newton's use of method amounted to an exploitation of the mathematical language of analysis and synthesis, or resolution and composition, to justify his inferential procedures in natural philosophy. Because mathematical demonstration was the paradigm of certain knowledge, it was the most persuasive court of appeal (as Descartes also knew).[127] The establishment in the sixteenth century of a way of talking about the *discovery* of mathematical theorems as resulting from a method allowed Newton to transfer meta-mathematical language to natural philosophical innovation, but in doing so one had to avoid talk about underlying causes of phenomena – that is, avoid a Zabarellan-style demonstrative regress. To claim certainty for his results, Newton had to portray them as demonstrative of properties only. The resulting tension between his proclaimed epistemological ideals and his well-articulated 'speculative' natural philosophy – carefully presented in the *Opticks* as 'queries' – is well known. Essentialism and method had not satisfactorily been unshackled.

NOTES

1 Prominent examples include Randall 1940, 1961; Crombie 1953; and essays in Madden 1960.
2 See the useful discussions in Rossi 1982 and Schuster 1984; the comments in Dear 1988, pp. 232–8; and, with specific reference to Descartes, Schuster 1986, 1993.
3 These over-neat generalisations will be nuanced below. The chief classical sources for discussions and formulations of method in the sixteenth century were Aristotle, especially the *Posterior Analytics* and the preface to the *Physics* (with elaborations by commentators such as Simplicius), and Galen, especially the *Ars parva,* which later formed the core of a long-standing medical commentary tradition on method. Important remarks by Pappus about analysis and synthesis in geometry also came into currency. See above all N. Gilbert 1961; also Edwards 1967 (which focuses on the medical commentary tradition concerning Galen's discussion of analysis and synthesis), 1976, and 1983. For more general treatments, see Risse 1964–70, vol. 1; Vasoli 1968, esp. pt. V, chap. 3, and Vasoli 1974, esp. chap. 5 on the humanist tradition; Ong 1958, esp. chap. 11.
4 Relevant texts are Zabarella 1985, or Zabarella 1597, 'De methodis', 'De regressu'. See N. Gilbert 1961, pp. 167–73; Vasoli's introduction to Zabarella 1985; and further references in Section III of this chapter.
5 Goclenius 1597, pt. V, p. 3: 'Ordo & Methodus interdum distinguuntur: ut ordo sit dispositio legitima praeceptorum disciplinae alicujus: Methodus vero sit processus declarandi & probandi praecepta illa: seu via, qua disciplinae partes ignotiores obscurioresque per manifestiora & notiora explicantur & demonstrantur.' He goes on to say that they are also sometimes accepted as the same thing. See also Goclenius 1613, pp. 683–6.
6 Watts 1726, p. 339.
7 For another example from the end of our period, see Chauvin 1713, s.v. 'Methodus'.
8 See, for example, Goclenius 1597, 'De methodis', p. 11; and below.
9 See Section IV of this chapter.
10 AT I 196 gives a list of editions to 1626. I have used Eustachius 1648.
11 The first part concerns the operations of the mind, including the Aristotelian categories; the second considers various kinds of propositions as well as method; the third concentrates on the syllogism. This is a fairly conventional breakdown except insofar as method is not given its own separate part at the end of the work.
12 Eustachius 1648, p. 106: '*Methodi* nomen dupliciter accipitur: primò quidem pro ordine & serie eorum omnium quae in universa aliqua doctrina vel ejus parte traduntur ac digeruntur; secundò, pro ordinatione seu eo animi judicio quo res illae in aliqua

disciplina continuè disponuntur.' Eustachius is quoted at length on method (from a different edition) in Gilson 1979, pp. 181–4.

13 Gilson 1979, pp. 181–4: 'certis Dialecticae praeceptis'.

14 Gilson 1979, pp. 181–4: Eustachius 1648, p. 106; 'altera generalis, quae servanda est in continuata serie omnium partium alicujus scientiae; altera particularis, quae in una-quaque quaestione aut difficultate enodanda servari debet.'

15 Gilson 1979, p. 107.

16 Gilson 1979, pp. 107–8.

17 Gilson 1979, p. 108.

18 Gilson 1979, pp. 108–10.

19 I base my account on N. Jardine 1988; see also N. Jardine 1976, esp. pp. 280–303. I have romanised the Greek. For other discussions, see Poppi 1972; Risse 1964–70, vol. 1, pp. 278–90, and Risse 1983; L. Jardine 1974, pp. 54–8.

20 There were, of course, various restrictions on what should count as proper principles in such a demonstration; see Wallace 1984, pp. 111–16.

21 See also on this McMullin 1978b, pp. 213–17.

22 See N. Jardine 1988, esp. pp. 686–93. Cf. Wallace 1984, pp. 125–6. A cause known 'materially' as a result of *demonstratio quia* needed to be turned into a cause known 'formally' if a *demonstratio propter quid* were to be produced (ibid., p. 125).

23 See esp. Edwards 1967.

24 Wallace 1984, pp. 123–6; on Galileo's Jesuit sources see also Carugo and Crombie 1983; and Wallace 1992.

25 Stemming above all from Randall 1940. See Wallace 1988a. More generally, on the importance of 'Paduan Aristotelianism' in the seventeenth century see Edwards 1983, and the more tempered approach of Schmitt 1983c, 1984a.

26 N. Jardine 1976 (and see the quotation later in ibid., pp. 305–6); N. Gilbert 1963.

27 Wallace 1984, p. 119, cites Galileo's source as distinguishing explicitly between 'resolu-tion' and 'method'; and see Section I.

28 See esp. McMullin 1978b; also Wisan 1978. Galileo's adherence to generally Aristotelian models of natural knowledge makes talk of his 'science' particularly appropriate.

29 On Galileo's eschewal of essentialism, see Gaukroger 1978, chap. 6. On the Italian scholastic background to Galileo's attitudes towards the mathematical sciences, see especially Galluzzi 1973, with further references and discussion in N. Jardine 1988, pp. 693–7, and Wallace 1984, p. 136.

30 Esp. Watkins 1965, pp. 47–71; Gargani 1971, esp. chap. 2; Edwards 1983; Talaska 1988.

31 Hobbes, *Eng. Works,* vol. 7, p. 184; cf. Watkins 1965, p. 69.

32 In what follows, I rely on the penetrating discussion in Malherbe 1984, pp. 29–39.

33 Pousseur 1984, 1985. See also L. Jardine 1974, pp. 171–3, and chap. 3, in which Jardine claims that Bacon's understanding of method seems to have come almost exclusively from sixteenth-century textbooks of humanist dialecticians. See Bacon's description of method in *The Advancement of Learning,* Bk. 2, XVII.2 (in Bacon 1860–4, vol. 6). Martin 1992 stresses the practical rootedness of Bacon's advocated procedures in the Common Law.

34 Pousseur 1984, p. 202, listing the cluster of words usually associated with 'method' in this period.

35 For earlier versions of Book I see Farrington 1964; some material is also duplicated in *The Advancement of Learning.*

36 Bacon, *Nov. org.* I 95.

37 Bacon, *Instauratio magna* (Bacon 1860–4, vol. 1; trans. ibid., vol.8).

38 Bacon, *Instauratio magna* (Bacon 1860–4, vol. 1; trans. ibid., vol. 8).
39 Bacon, *The Advancement of Learning*, Bk. II, XIII.2.
40 Bacon, *The Advancement of Learning*, Bk. II, XIII.10.
41 See, with further references on Bacon's speculative philosophy, Rees 1984a and 1984b, esp. pp. 308–9 on connexions with the method.
42 Bacon, *Nov. org.* I 101 (trans. Spedding). On Bacon's concept of *experientia literata*, see L. Jardine 1974, pp. 143–9, and esp. 1985, arguing for a fundamental ambiguity between Bacon's essentialist talk and his appeal to experience as the foundation of natural knowledge.
43 Bacon, *Nov. org.* I 105 (trans. Spedding).
44 Bacon, *Nov. org.* I 105 (trans. Spedding).
45 Bacon, *Nov. org.* II 17 (trans. Spedding). I neglect throughout, as irrelevant for present purposes, Bacon's discussions of 'latent process' and 'latent configuration'. However, see the remarkably similar independent accounts of the workings of Bacon's method in Pousseur 1988, chap. 8; and Pérez-Ramos 1988, pp. 254–64.
46 Bacon, *Nov. org.* II 15 (trans. Spedding).
47 Bacon, *Nov. org.* II 20 (trans. Spedding).
48 Bacon, *Nov. org.* II 36.
49 Close parallels between passages in Descartes's *Disc.* and in various of Bacon's writings are examined in Lalande 1911, including their views on the unity of the sciences.
50 See Descartes's remarks on this: Descartes to Mersenne, March? 1637, AT I 349. See also on Descartes's intention not to *teach* the method, *Disc.* pt. I: AT VI 4; also *Disc.* VI: AT VI 75. In describing to another correspondent how the *Essais* were not intended to show the actual use of the method, but only its results, Descartes suggested that the investigation of the rainbow in the *Météores* was a partial exception: to Vatier, 22 February 1638, AT I 559. His investigation of the rainbow is actually notable for its unacknowledged adherence to a mediaeval theoretical approach (using a water-filled globe as a model for analysis): see Sabra 1981, chap. 2; Wallace 1959; Crombie 1953, chaps. 9–11.
51 This is an appeal to a standard scholastic distinction between 'natural' and 'arbitrary' order: see Risse 1964–70, vol. 1, p. 476 n. 198.
52 *Disc.* II, AT VI 18–19, as translated in CSM I. The distinction in the final rule between enumerations and reviews is discussed in Beck 1952, p. 119.
53 See Beck 1952, p. 286. Leibniz introduced the quoted words in this way: 'I almost feel like saying that the Cartesian rules are rather like those of some chemist or other' (ibid., p. 286). The opacity, on Descartes's own account, of the means whereby the results of the *Dioptrique* or the *Météores* were acquired seems almost to warrant the secretist alchemical image Leibniz employs. Only the initiate can hope to achieve true understanding. On the vacuousness of the method (contrary to a long-standing tradition of Descartes scholarship), see Schuster 1986.
54 The dating is usually given as around 1626–8; I take the extended time-span from the persuasive arguments of Schuster 1980, which builds on the dating in Weber 1964. For a valuable annotated version of the *Regulae*, see Descartes 1977.
55 Discussed in *Regulae*, Rules 14–18, or 14–21, although 19–21 consist of headings only. See Schuster 1980 for datings; he takes 12–21 as covering universal mathematics even though mathematics does not become the subject until Rule 14. This relates to his views as in Schuster 1986. See also Crapulli 1969; Gaukroger 1980b; Kraus 1983, 1986.
56 *Regulae*, Rules 8, 13 (AT X 392–400, 430–8). Garber 1987b is an important discussion of the 'method' as a problem-solving tool and agrees with Schuster's understanding of

it in 'Cartesian Method'. See also the section ' "Method" and "Methods" ', in Schouls 1980, pp. 63–75.

57 AT X 394–5 (Rule 8). The idea of 'mental intuition' bears in this context a curious resemblance to Zabarella's 'negotiatio'.

58 At X 394–5. On the variant meanings of Descartes's term 'enumeration', see Schuster 1986, pp. 45–6; also Beck 1952, chap. 8, esp. p. 119. Note that 'enumeration' does not necessarily apply only to the synthetic or 'ascending' stage of the problem-solution.

The recognition that Descartes's method, apart from appealing to geometrical analysis, exploits in addition the precedent of *regressus* theory with its focus on the discovery of causes from effects, helps to clear up a problem identified by Hintikka and Remes. Holding that Descartes's 'whole philosophical and scientific method can be thought of as a kind of generalization from his analytical method in geometry', they observe that from an examination of the logical structure of geometrical analysis, especially with regard to the necessity of auxiliary constructions, it becomes clear that no determinate procedure of this kind can guarantee the finding of a sought solution. 'Even if the general laws governing [a physical] situation are known, it may still be the case that they serve to account for certain aspects of the interaction only if enough ingredients of the configuration are taken into consideration. Moreover, there need not be any way of telling whether enough factors have already been brought in. If so, a generalized analytical method will not be an effective discovery [procedure], however useful it may be heuristically.' Hintikka and Remes 1974, p. 112. See also Hintikka 1978. These remarks serve to underline the inherent imprecision of Descartes's notion of 'enumeration', but they also indicate the importance to Descartes's exposition of his method of tacitly appealing to the alternative logical system represented by *regressus* theory.

59 AT X 379, as trans. in CSM I.

60 AT VI 19, as trans. in CSM I.

61 AT X 383, as trans. in CSM I.

62 AT X 419, as trans. in CSM I.

63 AT X 361 (Rule 1), as trans. in CSM I. Note the anti-Ramist character of this stance. See also the expression of this idea in *Disc.* II, AT VI 19.

64 I borrow the 'lattice-work' metaphor from Schuster 1986 (see esp. p. 41).

65 AT X 396, deriving from the rule itself, Rule 8: 'If in the series of things to be examined we come across something which our intellect is unable to intuit sufficiently well, we must stop at that point, and refrain from the superfluous task of examining the remaining items.' AT X 392, as trans. in CSM I.

66 Compare *Princ.* II on the essence and properties of matter.

67 On the spread and prevalence of Ramist/Agricolan kinds of tables see Ong 1958, chap. 13; and Höltgen 1965. Bruyère 1984, pp. 385–94, argues for a reading of the *Regulae* as heavily indebted to humanist dialectic, although her stress on their specifically 'Ramist' flavour is, no doubt, too strong.

68 On Alsted, see Schmidt-Biggemann 1983, pt. II, chap. 3.

69 These points are cogently argued in Garber 1987b. Curley 1986, while emphasising the importance of the 'analytic method' in (and of) the *Meditationes,* characterises it in such a way as to distinguish it from the 'analysis' of the *Regulae.* It may therefore be dangerous to use an identical term. The applicability of the terms 'analysis' and 'synthesis' to Descartes's account of his method in the *Regulae* is in any event questionable, particularly in light of Descartes's own omission of them. Descartes uses the terms in his Resp. II to the *Meditationes,* but only to indicate means of teaching or communicating, referring specifically to the organisation of the *Meditationes* (AT IX

121–3); similarly, he apparently characterised the layout of the *Princ.* as being 'synthetic' in his *Conversations with Burman:* AT V 146–79, on p. 153. His understanding of 'analysis' and 'synthesis' is one of the many contested issues in Descartes scholarship, particularly in connexion with the *Regulae*. See, e.g., Curley 1986 (with further references), who also notes, on pp. 154–5, Descartes's apparently unorthodox use of the terms *a posteriori* and *a priori*.

70 This is the central argument of Garber 1987b, as well as Garber 1993b on Descartes's 'experimental' procedures. For a good treatment of Descartes's foundational project as it relates to the issue of solving scientific problems, see Garber 1986, and in general Garber 1992a, chap. 2.

71 The circumscribed, quasi-hypothetico-deductive use of experiment described in the *Disc.* and *Princ.,* which seems to us to be related to general ideas of 'scientific method', has no real connexion to Descartes's method properly so called, and he never suggested that it had. It was simply a logical addendum with no 'methodical' content. Descartes described experiments as necessary for deciding the cause of any particular phenomenon when a number of possible mechanisms, consistent with his explanatory principles of matter and motion, could be imagined. He used the metaphor of the clock to elucidate this: the observed motions of its hands could be produced by many different arrangements of cogs and wheels. Only by creating situations in which different possible mechanisms (of a clock or of a natural phenomenon) would yield different outcomes could the actual nature of the phenomenon be determined – and that only with probabilistic, moral certainty. Sabra 1981, chap. 1; Garber 1986; Clarke 1982, pp. 148–55 and *passim*; Rogers 1972, a reply to Laudan 1966; Sakellariadis 1982.

72 These issues are discussed in Osler 1983 and 1985b, both of which attempt to link nominalism and essentialism with attitudes towards voluntarism, although perhaps employing over-rigid categorisations.

73 See especially Couturat 1901, chap. 5, focusing on Leibniz; and more generally, Rossi 1960, pp. 179–200; also Yates 1966, chap. 10, 'Ramism as an Art of Memory'.

74 Arnauld and Nicole 1965–7. On the work as a whole, see Risse 1964–70, vol. 2, pp. 65–80. Arnauld and Nicole 1965 is a critical edition based on the fifth edition of 1683; there are some significant differences from the first edition which are duly noted.

75 Arnauld and Nicole 1965–7, vol. 1, p. 303. This material becomes Chapter 2 in later editions.

76 Arnauld and Nicole 1965–7, vol. 1, p. 303. Cf. Descartes's remarks, on analysis and synthesis with respect to discovery and teaching, in Resp. II, AT IX 121–3.

77 Arnauld and Nicole 1965–7, vol. 1, p. 307.

78 I have used Blaise Pascal, *De l'esprit geometrique et de l'art de persuader,* in Pascal 1963, pp. 348–59.

79 See esp. Arnauld and Nicole 1965–7, pt. IV, chap. 7.

80 This does not imply blind subservience to the practice of geometers, who come in for occasional criticism: e.g., Arnauld and Nicole 1965–7, pt. IV, chap. IV.

81 Arnauld and Nicole 1965, pp. 300–304.

82 Isaac Watts's *Logick,* for example, is very clearly indebted to it. On seventeenth- and eighteenth-century translations of *La logique* (including one into English in 1685) and its success, see Risse 1964–70, vol. 2, p. 79; comprehensive listings of editions and translations appear in Arnauld and Nicole 1965–7, vol. 2, pp. 19–23, and in Arnauld and Nicole 1965, pp. 4–9. The impact of *La logique* and of Descartes's *Disc.* on French logic texts in the late seventeenth and early eighteenth centuries is discussed in Brockliss 1987, pp. 203–5.

83 See, above all, Couturat 1901, chap. 6. S. Brown 1984, chaps. 5, 6, provides a useful overview; see also Schmidt-Biggemann 1983.

84 Lenoble 1971; Popkin 1979, chap. 7; Dear 1988.

85 He does put up a half-hearted defence of the demonstrative regress in his early, apologetic work, Mersenne 1625, pp. 194–205.

86 Lenoble 1971, pp. 337–65.

87 Auger 1962.

88 Bloch 1971; Rochot 1944; Joy 1987; Popkin 1979, chap. 7.

89 The treatise is reprinted with an English translation in Gassendi 1981.

90 Gassendi divides method into three types: 'the method of discovery, the method of judgment, and the method of instruction', discussing these in a series of 'canons' (Gassendi 1981, p. 156). The first 'consists in ingenuity in finding a middle term' with which to construct a syllogistic demonstration and involves resolution and composition, subdivided in conventional ways (ibid., Canon I, pp. 156–7). The second type of method, the 'method of judgment or assessment', is confirmatory, and uses resolution to check a discovery made by composition, and vice versa (ibid., Canon III, pp. 159–60). The rest of the discussion, Canons V–XIV, concerns the 'method of instruction', which 'starts from resolution and proceeds by way of composition' (ibid., Canon V, p. 161; Canons V–XIV cover pp. 161–6). On giving due weight to sensory evidence, see ibid., Canon IV, pp. 160–1.

91 On the career of physical Cartesianism after Descartes, and the place of hypotheses, see Mouy 1934; Clarke 1985, 1989.

92 See n. 71. On classifications of certainty, see Shapiro 1983, p. 84; and for an example of contemporary scholastic usage, defining the three categories of 'moral', 'physical', and 'metaphysical' certainty, see Arriaga 1632, p. 226, col. I.

93 See, e.g., Huygens, *Traité de la lumière* (1690), chap. 1, in Huygens 1888–1950, vol.19. Very much the same position can be ascribed to Robert Boyle. He advocated the 'corpuscular hypothesis' both on grounds of its pragmatic value and its pre-eminent 'intelligibility': Alexander 1985 chap. 3; Boas Hall 1952; Sargent 1986. For Boyle on hypotheses, their invention, use, and status, see especially Westfall 1956.

94 Huygens's clearest statement of this position is in *Traité de la lumière*, preface.

95 Quoted in Elzinga 1972 from 1722 English translation of *Cosmotheoros* (1698), *The Celestial Worlds Discover'd*, Bk. I pp. 9–10; for Latin original see Huygens 1888–1950, vol. 21, pp. 689. In general, see Elzinga 1980.

96 Cf. Huygens, *Traité de la lumière*, chap. 1: 'As happens in all the sciences in which geometry is applied to matter, the demonstrations concerning optics are founded on truths drawn from experience.' The 'certain' rules of optics – straight-line propagation, reflection, refraction laws – are accepted by all, but one can go further by looking for 'the origin and the causes' of these 'truths' themselves. Translation from Huygens 1912, p. 1.

97 Huygens to Henry Oldenburg, 20 October 1669: Oldenburg 1965–86, vol. 6, p. 290, trans. adapted from that on p. 292.

98 There is a discernible shift in this direction between the *Traité* and his later *Entretiens sur la philosophie:* see McClaughlin 1979, and compare Rohault 1723, vol. 1, and Rohault 1978.

99 Rohault 1723, vol. 1, pt. I, chap. 3, p. 13.

100 *Ess.,* IV.xii.10.

101 *Ess.,* IV.xii.7.

102 *Ess.,* IV.xii.7, 8, 9.

103 *Ess.,* IV.xii.15. For another statement of the possibility of as yet unforeseen new 'ways to the advancement of knowledge' being discovered, see *Ess.,* IV.xvii.7.

104 See *Ess.,* IV.vii.11, for similar sentiments.

105 For a discussion of the issues confronted by Locke in Book IV, see Woolhouse 1983, chap. 2; also, for a more general discussion, Yolton 1970, chaps. 2, 3.

106 *Ess.* IV.iii.6.

107 Quoted in Farr 1987, on pp. 70–1; the entire passage is printed as an appendix on pp. 70–2. Farr's article is really about methodology rather than method and presents a useful survey of historiography relating to Locke on hypotheses.

108 I quote from the most accessible modern edition, which reproduces the text of the fourth edition of 1730: Newton 1952, pp. 404–5 (throughout, when quoting Newton's English, I have modernised spelling and punctuation). Henry Guerlac indicates which parts of this passage first appeared in the 1717 edition, in Guerlac 1973, p. 379.

109 The word routinely bore a slew of meanings in the seventeenth century – Descartes, for example, used it to mean what looks like a species of deduction: see Clarke 1982, p. 70.

110 On Newton's claim that sometimes only a single suitable experiment is necessary, see Guerlac 1973, p. 387. Guerlac suggests that this position echoes Isaac Barrow's remarks in Barrow 1734, p. 116, although it is arguable that Barrow refers to individual *instances* rather than individual *kinds* of experiment. See also Feyerabend 1970, esp. p. 166.

111 Newton 1934, p. 398. Hintikka and Remes 1974, to which I owe my basic understanding of this issue, summarise 'the Newtonian method' as follows (p. 110): '(i) an analysis of a certain [experimental or observational] situation into its ingredients and factors → (ii) an examination of the interdependencies between these factors → (iii) a generalisation of the relationships so discovered to all similar situations ['induction'] → (iv) deductive applications of these general laws to explain and to predict other situations ['synthesis'].'

112 See also Newton's manuscript remarks quoted in Guerlac 1973, p. 385. Birch 1991 argues for the essentially mathematical character of Newton's analysis/synthesis in natural philosophy.

113 Guerlac 1973, p. 385.

114 Newton 1959–77, vol. 1, p. 96. Henry Oldenburg judiciously omitted this passage when Newton's letter was published in the *Philosophical Transactions.* For the rôle such claims played in the subsequent controversy over Newton's ideas, see Bechler 1974.

115 Newton 1959–77, vol. 1, p. 187.

116 Newton 1934, p. 400. On the development of the Rules in successive editions, see Koyré 1968c; and annotations in Newton 1972, vol. 2, pp. 550–5.

117 For material and discussion, see Feyerabend 1970, p. 162 n. 10.

118 Newton 1934, p. xxi.

119 Newton 1934, pp. xx–xxi.

120 Newton 1959–77, vol. 1, p. 164; trans. p. 169.

121 For a discussion of this point, see besides Bechler 1974, Sabra 1981, pp. 248–50, and chap. 11, esp. pp. 274–6.

122 Newton 1959–77, vol. 1, p. 100.

123 See Feyerabend 1970, p. 159 n. 7; the same goes for the *Principia,* with its various 'theories'. To the extent that it is possible to detect a further refinement of terminology in Newton, the term 'law' might be identified as one that he reserved for the most fundamental of his 'inductive' analytical generalisations, pre-eminently the 'laws of motion'. 'Theory', as for example in his talk of the 'theory of comets' (Newton

1934, preface to second edition), seems to derive from its long-standing astronomical (i.e., mathematical, in the sense of 'mixed mathematics') usage, although Newton by no means restricts it to astronomical matters.

124 On Newton's meaning here, see the classic discussion in Koyré 1968b.
125 Cf. the Third Rule of Reasoning in Newton 1934, pp. 398–400.
126 Newton 1934, p. 547.
127 On Newton's differences with Descartes see Larmore 1986.

8

UNIVERSALS, ESSENCES, AND
ABSTRACT ENTITIES

MARTHA BOLTON

I. BACKGROUND

The 'problem of universals', central in mediaeval philosophy, derived from commentaries on Aristotle written by Porphyry and Boethius, both of whom injected Platonist themes into their expositions. The problem concerned the nature of things predicated of many particulars as common to them. How can one entity (a unity) be common to many individuals? What foundation is there in distinct particulars for a common predicate? A more fundamental question concerned the order of metaphysical priority between concrete particulars and universals. Several notions of priority were expressed in the criteria for substances listed by Aristotle. What are the ultimate subjects of predication? What are the entities on which the existence of others depends? What is unchangeable and capable of definition, as subjects of necessary truths and scientific knowledge are supposed to be? Scholastic Aristotelians answered these questions in terms of the doctrine of categories. Individuals in the category of substance (primary substances) meet the first two criteria, and species that exist in primary substances, considered universally (secondary substances), meet the last criterion. In contrast, Neoplatonists gave priority (substantiality) on all three counts to abstract entities that have a mode of existence independent of, and apart from, particulars that resemble them more or less imperfectly. Elements from both traditions were retained in the seventeenth century. But the formulation of issues and the range of acceptable positions were radically changed by the anti-Aristotelian thrust of mechanism. This section sketches the background of this refocusing.

The scholastic 'problem of universals' took for granted the Aristotelian doctrine that a particular substance is a union of matter and substantial form. The form was said to determine the particular's species and was often identified with species-

I thank Gary Hatfield, Daniel Garber, and especially Michael Ayers for suggestions and comments on material in this chapter. I regret not having been able to convince some of them on certain points.

essence.[1] Accidents (or accidental forms) were often said to 'inhere in' individual substances but not strictly to constitute them.[2] Since essence and accidents are predicated of many particular substances, this account of the constituents of a substance imposed certain terms on the problem of universals. The problem was to account for the commonality of forms literally present in the make-up of subjects of predication.

'Moderate realism', favoured by many in the late sixteenth century, held that universals are concepts derived from individuals that in some way 'share' a common form. On the widely held Thomistic account, the form of horse, for example, is shared in that one form is individuated by union with the (quantified) matter of many individual horses. The form, in itself, is neither universal nor particular, but it can be considered either one or the other. The form of horse considered in Bucephalus is particular; the same form considered by intellect in the concept horse is universal. Thomists explained formal concepts by intentional species. The concept horse is the form of horse existing in the intellect, as a result of its reception by sense and a series of abstractions that strip the form of its sensible (individuating) accompaniments. Considered as universal, the form modifies (exists in) an intellect and functions as species-concept; considered as particular, it has formal existence in union with matter. There is, then, a foundation for the predicate horse. The species is predicated of all and only things conceived through the concept horse, that is, exactly those material things in which the form of horse exists formally.[3]

The main alternative was the Ockhamist doctrine that whatever exists is strictly particular; nothing is common to many particulars, and nothing in particulars can be conceived as universal. A universal was said to be a concept or linguistic name that signifies many particulars, but nothing common. In things, species were said to be founded on nothing but primitive relations of maximal similarity among particulars.[4] Moreover, Ockham repudiated intentional species, that is, forms with both mental and material (formal) existence, and accounted for general concepts without them. He initially said that general concepts are abstract entities that have a non-actual mind-dependent mode of being (*esse objectivum*),[5] but later identified concepts with concrete, determinate acts of a mind. On both views, the actual things represented by a concept were delineated by similarity to the concept.[6]

Early in the seventeenth century, the scholastic Francis Suárez proposed a theory that synthesised elements from these two traditions. He individuated substances by forms together with matter, rather than matter alone; so, for example, Bucephalus differed from all other horses by virtue of a form particular in its nature.[7] All horses have 'the same form' only in that their individual forms are similar, and this was held to imply that each horse has the capacity to be formal cause of the concept horse. The universal was identified with the concept, which was said to signify nothing common, but rather to signify many particulars, each of which is able to be its formal cause.[8] In his theory of concepts, Suárez agreed with the Thomists that forms exist both formally (in union with matter) and in faculties of sense and intellect. But for Suárez, an abstracted form remains particular. To have a general concept, intellect must compare a number of particular concepts and abstract from singulars.[9]

In addition to the problem of universals, scholastics debated a rather different set of issues posed by a Platonist strain in theories of creation. God's creation of the world is rational, some urged, because patterned after divine ideas. Species-essences were thought to be, or to be among, the archetypes. In this context, essences are posited to explain the origin (as opposed to make-up) of creatures to which they belong. Debate revolved around the nature of the distinction between the existence and essence of a creature and whether, considered as distinct, the essence intrinsically has being of some sort. This posed questions about the metaphysical status of objects of divine cognition that could be regarded as analogues of those that arise for objects of finite cognition. A related problem of 'eternal truths' arose from the presumption that necessary truths whose subjects are species hold whether or not they are instantiated; for example, 'Man is an animal' is true independently of the contingent fact that there are men. Scientific knowledge was thought to be exclusively concerned with this sort of necessary truth. The problem was to say what structure in reality corresponds to such propositions and makes them true.

Aquinas said roughly that God knows essences prior to creatures in knowing the ways the divine essence can be (partly) imitated and thus the possibilities of divine will.[10] It remained controversial whether separated essences in themselves have a mode of being (actual or non-actual, dependent on cognition or independent) or whether their being reduces to that of God's actual attributes of knowledge and power. Ockham took a stand on this issue, for even though he rejected archetypal theories of creation, he held that God knows finite things independently of their actual existence. At one time, he assigned objective being, regarded as a form of intrinsic non-actual being, to objects of divine knowledge, but later he denied them even such a diminished status, on the ground that God alone has eternal being of any sort.[11] Having rejected archetypes as bases of creation, Ockham had no use for the usual view that essential truths are grounded on archetypes. This suggested to some that the possibility and necessity actualised in creaturely essences is due to divine omnipotence; so, for example, man is an animal, because God wills it. Ockham's endorsement of this view is disputed; he did at least state that the law of non-contradiction is *not* subject to God's will.[12] In any case, theistic voluntarism with regard to necessary truths could be found not only among scholastics but also in an important Protestant tradition that stressed God's dominion over moral truths.[13]

On the being of essences and eternal truths, Suárez wrote an influential disputation. He argued that there is no efficient cause of creatures' essences except the cause of the existence of creatures themselves, namely, God's act of creating the world. Moreover, God is the *only* being with no efficient cause. He concluded that essences apart from creatures have no actual being (*existentia*); in this regard, they are, in themselves, absolutely nothing (*omnino nihil*). This was not to deny that separated essences have the being of things known by God, but, Suárez insisted, this is not actual being, but rather being in potency only.[14] It is not something positive existing in a diminished way, but rather the actual being of God's power, which extends to creatures with various essences.[15] However, Suárez recognised a further complication due to a difference among non-beings. Some involve impossibility, such as a chimera, whereas others are possible, such as a man (considered apart from existence). The former is a mere being of reason, but the latter, a real essence. In view of this complication, Suárez said that an essence intrinsically has an 'aptness' or 'non-repugnancy' to exist.[16] It is questionable that this solution is consistent with his claim that separated essences are absolutely nothing in themselves.[17]

Suárez agreed that eternal truths have the necessity required for scientific knowledge but still held they are not actually true unless creatures exist. The 'is' of essential predication expresses conditional necessity: 'A man is an animal' asserts that if God creates a man, then necessarily man is an animal. The truth of the consequent is contingent upon God's creative act, and the whole conditional is made true by God's creative power.[18] But again, it is doubtful that Suárez's account accommodates the difference between man and chimera. If God creates a chimera, then necessarily a chimera is part-goat; but this is trivial, not grounded in essence. Suárez accordingly tended to grant eternal truths a reality not fully explicated by his conditional analysis.[19]

Although scholasticism embraced some Neoplatonist themes, Neoplatonism flourished in more radical forms during the Renaissance, ceding priority to what is more abstract over what is less abstract. Here, also, a version of hylemorphism often held sway, although the Aristotelian account of substantiality was in conflict with the Neoplatonist assessment of metaphysical priority.[20] Marsilio Ficino, for example, maintained that natural bodies receive their natures from species-forms, but he held that species are substances. Species are prior, he said, for they are hierarchically ordered and thus contribute to the perfection of the universe; in contrast, since all particulars in a species are of the same order, their multiplicity adds nothing to the total perfection.[21] Issues concerning the origin and types of being were in the fore. Neoplatonists posited a hierarchical series of spheres of being (hypostases) in which each inferior receives its being and determinations from its superiors, the series culminating in the indeterminate, limitless One. In Ficino's philosophy, the one (God) is followed by mind, soul, quality (forms in matter), and body (material particulars). Mind was said to be the region of ideas or intelligible archetypes. The catalogue of ideas that reside in mind – for example, good, beauty, unity, mathematical entities, Aristotelian species – varied among philosophers. Opinions on the status of objects of scientific knowledge also differed. Ficino held we have knowledge of forms apprehended in material things; others, influenced by Augustine, said the objects of scientific knowledge are archetypes in the mind of God which we can hope to know only in the after-life.[22]

The Neoplatonists' approach to the problem of the unity of things in the same kind was very different from that taken by the scholastics. Ficino (following Plotinus) posited genera whose species are ordered in a hierarchy culminating in a *primum in genere*. Because it is the genus in perfect (limitless) form, the *primum* contains (*continet, complectitur*) all degrees of its many species (limited forms of the genus). On this basis, the *primum* could be regarded as predicated of all its members, not only its many species but also itself.[23] In addition, the *primum* was said to be the cause, in a generative sense, of the generic quality in inferior members.[24]

Thus Neoplatonist theories of divine ideas contrast markedly with scholastic doctrines of divine archetypes. The former ideas had multiple rôles. In virtue of their infinite, unlimited mode of being, they possessed generative powers, were eternal objects of scientific knowledge, and also explained the unity of things in the same kind. In contrast, scholastic discussion of archetypes primarily addressed the theory of creation, which was held distinct from the problem of universals. Often the former was consigned to theology, and the latter to metaphysics or logic.[25]

In the seventeenth century, discussion of universals and essences was drastically altered, because several tenets presupposed in scholastic discussions of these topics were no longer accepted. Most important were the doctrine that a substance is a union of matter and form and the theory of intentional species, that is, forms that exist both in matter and in the intellect. Many denied these doctrines because they were incompatible with mechanism, but even opponents of mechanism, such as the Cambridge Platonists, rejected them. As a result, the moderate realist position on universals collapsed; so did the view that essence can be identified with substantial and (secondarily) accidental forms. This left a choice between accounts based on human cognition and the natural realm or accounts that appeal to some aspect of God, either the objects of divine knowledge or abstract entities in the infinite being of God. The anti-Aristotelian mechanist climate was by no means inhospitable to Platonist themes. The Neoplatonists' extended hierarchical series of abstract generative causes no longer held appeal. Nevertheless, some influential mechanists held that divinely willed general laws are causally efficacious and posited a two-fold hierarchy of being (indeterminate, infinite, as opposed to determinate, finite being).[26]

Developments on a range of topics, in addition to the metaphysics of substance and the theory of perception and knowledge, also affected treatments of universals and essences. These include advances within particular sciences (e.g., physics, mathematics), in theology, in moral and political thought, and in the theory of language. One closely related issue concerns the sorts of distinctions that ought to be admitted (e.g., real, conceptual) and the sorts of things that are in some way distinguishable (e.g., substance and modification, object and aspect).

II. THEORIES OF UNIVERSALS

Because the scholastics' 'problem of universals' presupposed that a substance consists of matter, substantial form, and accidental forms, it had no place on the mechanists' agenda. Mechanists said matter is a substance in its own right. Matter, or material particles, were taken to be the ultimate subjects of attributes and modifications, which were restricted to 'ways of being' of one individual.[27] Immaterial substances were understood on a similar model. This left no room for entities in the make-up of a substance that are, in themselves, not yet particular and thus might be in some way common to many. As Arnauld and Nicole said in their treatise on logic, some philosophers' doctrines 'are of so little use . . . they are not believed even by those who teach them. No one, thank God, is interested in the Universal *a parte rei* . . . ; thus there is no cause to worry that someone will be offended if we do not speak of it.'[28]

In this new framework, the classificatory scheme applied to mediaeval positions on universals (realist, moderate realist, nominalist) is useless. Nominalism is often defined as the view that universals are nothing but general concepts or linguistic names, the point being that they have no common foundation in things. But no party denied that in the later period. It was widely agreed that universals are entities extrinsic to particulars. The main question was what sorts of entities they are.

The degree of 'reality' given to universals by different theories can be judged by several intersecting standards. One is whether universals are abstract entities that have non-actual existence or whether universals are identified with modifications or acts of (finite or infinite) minds. This produces a surprising division, with Digby and Malebranche urging views of the former sort, Hobbes and Cudworth, the latter. A second measure of 'reality' is whether universals are eternal and immutable entities directly dependent on God, as Descartes, Malebranche, Cudworth, and Leibniz maintained, or whether universals are temporally limited entities that depend upon finite minds. The latter was held by Digby, Hobbes, Gassendi, and Locke. Differences over whether universals are real abstract entities or actual mental modifications existing in a substance, and whether eternal or temporal, are not basic, however, for they reflect positions on a more general and pressing issue.

The deeper problem was to account for perception and other forms of cognition now that intentional species had been discarded. Many early moderns could agree to the formula that universals are (general) ideas, but they were much at odds over what ideas are: their metaphysical status, their origin, how they are known, their manner of representation, and rôle in the apprehension of actual things. For those disposed to explicate intentionality by positing objects of thought in a non-actual mode of being, it was natural to say that universals are abstractions that exist in a non-finite way (e.g., Malebranche, Digby). But for someone who embedded intentions in concrete acts of finite minds, it made sense to identify universals with certain sorts of human cognitive acts (as did Arnauld, despite Augustinian leanings).[29] Again, one's stand on innate ideas placed some constraints on one's view of whether general ideas depend directly on God and whether, or in what sense, they are eternal.

The simplest measure of 'reality' is based on the order of priority between universals and particulars. On some views, (1) the being of universals is independent of that of particulars under them, whereas on others, (2) universals presuppose particulars (at least in base cases). This is a convenient framework for detailed discussion of various theories.

1. Universals as independent of particular instances

Descartes's scanty remarks on universals are mainly in the *Principia Philosophiae,* where in the course of a technical account of his theory of substance, modes, and attributes, he came to consider duration, order, and number. Whereas some attributes or modes are in actual substances, he said, 'others are only in our thought.' For instance, numbers considered in the abstract, rather than in created things, are merely 'modes of thinking', and this goes as well for all other universals. Further:

Universals arise solely from the fact that we make use of one and the same idea for thinking of all individual items which resemble each other: we apply one and the same term to all the things which are represented by the idea in question, and this is the universal term. When we see two stones, for example, and direct our attention not to their nature but merely to the fact that there are two of them, we form the idea of the number which we call 'two'.[30]

Geometrical examples are given to illustrate the 'five common universals': genus, species, difference, *propria,* accidents. Descartes mentioned two actual stones to stress that we conceive the number two in abstraction from them; he did not mean to suggest that abstract conceptions are extracted from apprehension of particulars.[31] This passage places Descartes in the scholastic debate. In his mechanist metaphysics, there is nothing but similarity in things conceived through the same universal.

But Descartes went on to say something that helps to explain his view of what universal ideas are, in connexion with his doctrine of three types of distinctions: real, modal, and conceptual (distinction of reason). The weak distinction of reason holds between entities just in case neither can exist without the other; a substance and one of its attributes – for example, duration – are distinct in this way. Moreover: 'In the case of all the modes of thought which we consider as being in objects, there is merely a conceptual distinction between the modes and the object which they are thought of as applying to.'[32] The 'modes of thought' mentioned here apparently include universals, which were previously referred to in the same way. Although universals were said to be modes considered, not in things, but in the abstract, they were also said to be means to conceive actual things. An abstract mode does not exist in actual objects, but we use it to think of what does.[33] Applying the conceptual distinction to the number two, we can say that although we consider the number apart from any particular pair, the number cannot exist that way; nor can the things in a pair exist without being two.

Descartes made the same point in a letter, which says the weak distinction of reason holds between essence and existence, a thing and its attributes, actual things and universals. It reads in part:

Thus when I think of the essence of a triangle, and the existence of this same triangle, these two thoughts, in so far as they are thoughts, even taken objectively, are different modally in the strict sense [i.e., either thought, even considered with regard to its object, can be conceived without the other, but neither can be conceived apart from the mind in which both inhere].[34] But it is not the same for a triangle existing outside thought, in which it can clearly be seen that essence and existence are not in any way distinct. It is the same for all universals. When I say Peter is a man, the thought by which I think of Peter differs modally from the thought by which I think of man, but in Peter himself being a man is nothing other than being Peter, and so on.[35]

Essence, attributes, and (what we conceive by means of) universals in an actual thing are nothing other than, in no way distinct from, that thing. Although different universals (attributes or modes in the abstract) may enable us to conceive the same actual thing, they represent *no* multiplicity in the thing. Thus a Cartesian substance, in contrast to an Aristotelian one, has a primitive unity comprising nothing that might lend itself to a moderate realist theory of universals.

Within twenty years, this model of substance had been so widely accepted that, as already mentioned, Arnauld and Nicole excused themselves from even discussing 'universals *a parte rei*'. When they addressed the topic of universals, they began with the Cartesian thesis that universals are abstract ideas not extracted from sense. They focused on the properties of these ideas. Arnauld, who wrote a treatise on the nature of ideas, maintained that ideas are cognitive acts with intrinsic representative contents.[36] Accordingly, the treatise on logic says that a universal idea contains (*enferme*) certain attributes that cannot be removed without destroying the idea; it represents anything to which those attributes agree (*convient*). For instance, the idea of triangle includes extension, figure, three sides, and so on, and has in its 'extension' all species of triangles as well as particular triangles.[37] Although an idea of triangle is a particular act of mind, its built-in intention is abstract; one can restrict it by adding attributes, for example, being right-angled, to those it contains.[38]

Another broadly Cartesian philosopher, Malebranche, approached the issue of universal ideas assuming that their intentionality is due to their abstract and indeterminate mode of being. (John Norris, influenced by Malebranche, held a similar view.)[39] Malebranche maintained, rather as Neoplatonists had, that God exists in an infinite, unlimited, intelligible way, whereas particular substances have finite, limited, intrinsically unintelligible being. The unlimited being of God includes an array of forms of being that are still unlimited, including extension and its diversifications, mind (thinking) and its varieties, the good, and so on. Universals were said to be ideas that have unlimited existence in infinite mind. Malebranche described God as 'the being without individual restriction, the infinite being, being in general', which 'contains all being' but is 'no being in particular'. Accordingly, the *idea* of God is strictly unintelligible to created minds, for we understand things only by their determinations.[40] Yet because, as Malebranche said, God is intimately and necessarily present to finite minds, we continually have a sort of non-comprehending apprehension of the undetermined. This is a necessary condition of our knowing any ideas, because they have an indeterminate way of being:

> It even seems that the mind would be incapable of representing universal ideas of genus, species, and so on, to itself had it not seen all beings contained in one. For, given that every creature is a particular being, we cannot say that we see a created thing when, for example, we see a triangle in general. Finally . . . sense can be made of the way the mind knows certain abstract and general truths only through the presence of Him who can enlighten the mind in an infinity of different ways.[41]

It is essential to a universal that it contain infinitely many specific determinations. If we did not apprehend God, the being that contains all beings, we could not understand any being that *lacks* limitation and thereby *contains* mutually incompatible limitations.

Malebranche argued that extractionist theories of universals are mistaken, for particulars and universals are radically different types of being. If we consider a particular triangle, for example, and fail to attend to the size of its angles, we have just a partial conception of a determinate being. We do not apprehend something whose mode of being enables it to include, for example, all possible angle-ratios in virtue of having none in particular. To be undetermined is not to lack being, but rather to have the sort of perfect being that pertains to God.[42]

Because an idea is essentially indeterminate, argued Malebranche, it cannot be determined to the point where it becomes the idea of a particular. Rather he held that particular things as such are indefinable; their mode of being is finite, changing, contingent, and thus unintelligible. They are only indirectly known by means of direct knowledge of ideas, not only in our case but also in God's.[43] What even God can understand with regard to particulars is just that certain ideas are archetypes that are willed to have finite analogues. The unity of particulars under the same universal is thus of an overtly Platonist sort, not altogether foreign to suggestions by Descartes.[44] It is constituted by what can be known with regard to particulars, but is only analogous to them.

Ralph Cudworth, while not a Cartesian, did advocate an innatist theory of knowledge which implied that universals are prior to particulars under them. Like Malebranche, with whom he nevertheless had metaphysical differences, he stressed above all the unique intelligibility of universals. Indeed, for Cudworth, the essence

of a universal is to be an object of scientific knowledge.[45] Since he did not doubt
that there is genuine knowledge, he derived the properties of universals from his
analysis of what such knowledge requires. Universals must be abstract, he argued,
since the intelligible universal triangle, for example, is the same for all geometers
and must give the 'ratione of a triangle', or its unifying scheme.[46] Again, a
universal must be 'vitally portended by the knower', because, as he claimed, a
mind can know only what is 'contained in' and 'exerted from' the mind itself.[47]
This doctrine that a mind's knowledge is essentially self-generated activity was the
basis on which Cudworth maintained that knowledge must be innate. By similar
reasoning, universals cannot be extracted from sense impressions, because they are
passively received; what is more perfect, namely, 'activity and awakened energy',
cannot emerge from something less perfect, such as 'dull, sluggish, and drowsy
passion'.[48] Accordingly, universals (cognitive activities) exist apart from the material particulars that fall under them and are understood by their means. Because
objects of knowledge must be eternal and immutable, Cudworth reasoned, they
ultimately exist in God. Finite minds are ectypes that have a 'cognoscitive power'
with potential for knowing all forms, whereas the unchanging, ever-active knowing of God is their archetype.[49]

The Cartesian account of universals rested on the anti-Aristotelian doctrine of
the unity of a substance and the doctrine of innate ideas (with abstract objects).
Although Leibniz shared this general approach, he developed it in a distinctive
way. He agreed that at least a great many of our general ideas (concepts) are
innate.[50] On his theory, general concepts are dispositions to perform certain
cognitive acts; for example, the concept of triangle is a tendency to regard all
triangles as 'the same', to affirm the definition of triangle, to produce proofs of
certain theorems, make certain inferences, and so on. These operations do not,
however, suffice to make the objects of thought fully intelligible to us. For
although we can define some objects, for example, triangle, there are few, if any,
that we can reduce to primitive concepts. Leibniz accordingly maintained that our
concepts are more or less confused, or unarticulated, versions of wholly distinct
concepts in the understanding of God.[51]

In *Discours de métaphysique*, Leibniz explained what an individual substance is in
terms of its concept (as possessed by God) and the difference between incomplete
(abstract) and complete concepts: 'It is the nature of an individual substance or
complete being to have a concept so complete that it is sufficient to make us
understand and deduce from it all the predicates of the subject to which the
concept is attributed.'[52] The subject to which a concept is attributed is the (one
or more) things of which the concept is truly predicated. Leibniz's idea was that

an incomplete concept signifies actual things that have some determinations not specified in that concept. So, for example, 'being a king' expresses a concept that is ascribed to Alexander, Philip, and so on, but fails to specify these individuals completely. In contrast, a complete concept specifies an object so thoroughly that the subject to which it is attributed has no further determinations. The nature of individual substance is to be entirely determined, or to *have* a complete concept. According to Leibniz, then, as opposed to Malebranche, God has knowledge of individuals even as possible (their concepts), and this is no less direct than divine knowledge of abstract or incomplete entities. Thus the unity of particulars under a general concept is not a single means of being known; it is rather just that the general concept is contained in the complete concepts of all individuals that fall under it. Leibniz did not give the same sort of priority to universals as the others I have discussed. On his view, incomplete concepts (possessed by God) are prior to actual particulars, but this is because universals specify possibilities and, for Leibniz, both incomplete and complete beings considered as possible are prior to actual creatures. Possibilities in God's understanding provide the reasons for what there is in the actual world.

The radical unity of an individual substance was fundamental in Leibniz's thought. There is nothing in the world, he said, but simple substances (monads) and, in them, perception and appetition; the latter are only 'ways of being' of the very substances they modify.[53] He rarely addressed the problem of universals as such, and when he did, he thought it sufficient simply to say that 'universals are founded on similarity.'[54]

Many Cartesians shared with Cudworth the view that particulars can be strictly known only through more intelligible general ideas or abstract entities. Leibniz disagreed where divine knowledge is concerned, since God distinctly knows the infinitely complex concepts of individual substances. Finite minds have only confused sensory perception of individuals, but they innately tend towards distinct understanding of the abstract objects of scientific knowledge.[55] This asymmetry of intelligibility supported the view that universals are ideas independent of particulars under them. Neither the asymmetry nor the priority were accepted by many important seventeenth-century thinkers.

2. Universals as presupposing particular instances

Kenelm Digby, an early mechanist, said that universals are abstract cognitions of finite souls, innate inasmuch as they involve the notion of being but also produced partly by operations of sense. In *Two Treatises,* he observed that our capacity for abstract conceptions encourages the mistaken view that abstractions actually exist.

(This was not an uncommon diagnosis of philosophical error.)[56] Digby cited this as source of both extreme and moderate realism with regard to universals.[57]

In these treatises, Digby maintained that things apprehended by intellect exist in a 'spiritualised' mode; for example, if one has had sufficient experience to understand what a knife is, then a knife exists in one's soul in a spiritualised way.[58] Digby's strategy was to point out that entities that have spiritualised existence cannot exist in corporeal things, in order to argue that the soul, in which they do exist, must be *in*corporeal. Universals were just one case in point. They are presented as having several peculiarities: for example, the notion of animal admits mutually incompatible specifications, rational and irrational; gold exists in the soul without any particular shape, size, location; and the notion 'every man' conveys that there is particularity in every man but signifies no man in particular.[59]

Digby's account of universals may seem open to George Berkeley's later attack on the logical possibility of abstract ideas. Berkeley argued that the purported abstract idea of man, for example, is a man who is both short and tall, or perhaps neither short nor tall, either of which is impossible.[60] But construed as a refutation of Digby, this is inconclusive as it stands. Digby agreed that a man neither short nor tall cannot have material existence; his main point was that *spiritualised* existence is not subject to the same constraints (hence, the soul is immaterial). Digby took that to explain how we can think of a man without thinking of any man in particular, whereas Berkeley denied we can do that.

Although a number of other mechanists rejected all innate ideas and multiple modes of being, they roughly agreed with Digby's view that universals are general ideas derived from sensory perception of particulars. The primary questions for them were what makes an idea general and what determines the extension of a general idea among actual things? Scholastics often resolved such issues by the doctrine of intentional species abstracted from sense perception, the *same* form existing in mind and in many particular things; but that option was foreclosed. Ockham, who repudiated intentional species, explicated the extension of a general concept by similarity between the concept and the essences of particular things. The later opponents of innatism also used similarity-relations to determine the extensions of general ideas, but used them in quite different ways.

Pierre Gassendi addressed the issue of how universals are derived from sensory ideas in *Institutio Logica,* a part of his massive *Syntagma Philosophicum.* Since all ideas that come from sense are singular, general ideas must be made from singulars by certain operations of mind. Roughly following Epicurus,[61] Gassendi said in *Institutio* that this is done either by joining or separating.

    1. Attending to singulars that are similar, the mind *collects* them into one idea

and thereby makes a genus or universal; for example, a collection of ideas of 'Socrates, Plato, Aristotle, and all other similar' is the idea called the 'genus man'. (Man is a genus, not species, because Gassendi took particulars to be lowest species.) The extension of the genus-idea includes the things that caused the collected singular ideas and all others able to cause ideas similar to those.

2. Attending to singulars that are similar, the mind *abstracts* or separates out what they have in common, omitting the respects in which they differ. Noticing, for example, that Socrates, Plato, and Aristotle agree in being rational, two-legged, erect, and so on, the mind abstracts these features and omits the singular differences, for example, being middle-aged, looking like a monkey. The abstract idea is the genus man, for no particular man is represented in it, but rather man in general.[62] Although one might assume a genus-idea represents all and only actual things that have the features abstracted in the idea, this is not Gassendi's view. For part of his theory is that a general idea can represent the genus it does more or less perfectly.

A general idea is perfect to the extent it is 'complete' and 'represents that in which the singular ideas coincide'.[63] For example, a *collective* idea of man is incomplete if it includes an Asian, European, and African, but no American. And the *abstractive* idea that picks out being a rational animal four cubits high is imperfect, since the latter attribute does not belong to all men. Despite their differences and imperfections, both ideas count as the genus man, representing all and only men.[64] It seems then that something other than the explicit contents of our (various) ideas of man determines the respects in which all and only men are similar.

The canon on definition also suggests that genera are determined by something extrinsic to our general ideas. For although we look to our idea of a kind when we want to define the kind, the idea is not the *final* authority: 'If the idea represents the thing perfectly then the definition, that is, the statement in which we declare the nature or essence of the thing (that is, what or of what kind it is) is accurate; but if the idea is less precise then the statement is less accurate.'[65] One of Gassendi's examples of 'things' so defined is the genus man. Since the idea-based definition can inaccurately describe the genus man, which the idea represents, we can infer that the genus is determined by something other than the idea.

Gassendi seems to have had in mind that genera are distinguished by sets of 'inseparable' or 'necessary attributes' of things. In explaining what attributes are, he notes that 'every quality [or attribute] is either naturally inborn (*natura insitam*) and inseparable from the subject, like whiteness in the case of a swan, or accidental and separable, like whiteness in the case of a wall.'[66] A subject 'cannot exist

without' its inseparable attributes.[67] And Gassendi explicitly linked such attributes
with those by which genera are delineated:

> Whatever is inseparable from a subject is either its genus, proximate or remote, like 'being
> animal', 'being living', 'being a body' in the case of man, or is a quality belonging to this
> same subject by nature, whether it be proper to the subject, as 'reason' and 'risibility' with
> respect to man, or common to it and others, as the faculty of sense is common to man and
> all other animals, and 'being two-footed' is common to man and some others, such as
> birds.[68]

The inseparable accidents of man are the qualities traditionally involved in *defining*
the species (its genus and difference, higher genera and their differences) and those
that pertain to the species uniquely (strict *propria*) or universally but not uniquely
(so-called 'common' *propria*). The suggestion is that the natures of things, including higher and lower genera, are delineated in the world by collections of inseparable accidents, that is, accidents such that an individual has one attribute in the set
if and only if it has the rest. For instance, being animal and rational (genus and
difference) are inseparable from being risible, tool-using, and indefinitely many
other attributes (*propria*), and this unity defines a kind (humans); again, being a
sentient living body is inseparable from mobility, digestion, respiration, and further
attributes, so this unity delineates a higher kind (animal). Assuming attributes are
distributed among individuals in clusters with indefinitely many members that are
inseparable (universally co-instantiated), these patterns suffice to determine genera
and standards of accuracy for general ideas. Gassendi apparently thought experience confirmed this sort of distribution, but he assumed minimal metaphysical
underpinning for it. As a mechanist, he supposed the natures that ground inseparable attributes are nothing but enduring configurations of particles that compose
certain sensible bodies; and his notion of necessity may have been nothing more
than universality.

Gassendi's second type of general idea is a genuinely abstract conception. But
unlike Digby, Gassendi regarded ideas as actual modifications of souls, not entities
in a mode of spiritual existence. He expressed reservations about our ability to
form abstract *images:* 'Of course, it is difficult, not to say impossible, to imagine
man in general so exactly that he is of neither large nor small nor middling stature;
. . .but at least one ought to bear in mind that a man whom we wish to represent
man in general ought to be free from all these particular distinctions.'[69] Later on,
Berkeley and others cited our inability to form abstract images as a psychological
argument *against* abstract ideas.[70] Gassendi anticipated the objection. In a part of
Syntagma written after *Institutio,* he distinguished the corporeal faculty of sense

and imagination, which we share with beasts, from the incorporeal faculty of understanding, which belongs only to humans. The former receives sensory images but cannot apprehend insensibles (e.g., God, void, universal entities). He said that corporeal imagination makes collective general ideas, but incorporeal understanding forms abstractions, starting from collections made by imagination.[71] Understanding is said to be both aware of sensory images and able to *use* them to apprehend things that are neither sensible nor material.[72] Limitations of imagistic thought are thus overcome by cognitive operations that nevertheless depend on images.

Although Gassendi regarded himself as a 'nominalist',[73] his view was by no means as radical as that of Thomas Hobbes, who was described by Leibniz as a 'super-nominalist'.[74] For Hobbes, general *names*, which stand for 'many things taken one by one', are the only universals.[75] Hobbes denied that an *idea* can be universal: 'as if there might be in the mind an image of some man which is not that of any one man, but of man *simpliciter*; but this is impossible, for every idea is both one and of one thing.'[76] Other image-theorists who denied abstract ideas, such as Berkeley, argued that a mind can invest a particular idea with general signification by attending to some aspect of it and using it to represent all things similar in that respect.[77] Hobbes seems to have produced no argument that the entities we set up as general signs must be public marks or sounds, rather than ideas.[78] Presumably, he supposed a sensible mark facilitates acts of attending to the similarity among particulars named by the mark.

A name, according to Hobbes, is a mark or sound one has decided to use as mnemonic sign of one's past thoughts or agreed to use as sign to others of one's present thoughts.[79] Thus in Hobbes's theory of linguistic signification, communication of one's *thoughts* is the primary notion. A general name (in context of a proposition) signifies a thought of any one of a number of similar things. An English speaker who hears, for example, 'A horse is an animal', thinks of Bucephalus, or Rosenante, or another resembling thing.[80]

On this view, the extension of 'horse' is determined by something in addition to a similarity relation among bodies. It depends also on the fact that speakers of English are usually disposed to agree that certain bodies are similar in that respect for which things are called 'horse'. For the mark has a naming function *only if* it sustains its primary rôle in communicating thoughts.[81] In some passages, where discourse affecting civil order is in view, Hobbes even said that the agreement required for use of a name may sometimes need to be secured by civil authority.[82] But he by no means denied that things in the world contribute to determining the extensions of names. He said that some ways of naming are apt, others not;

and in discourse for the purpose of science, definitions (i.e., explanations of bases of naming) ought to be in terms of the (efficient) *causes* of things.[83]

Hobbes thus took a significant step in the direction of making the division of kinds partly dependent on human practice. Many others (e.g., Suárez, Gassendi) said the extensions of universals are determined by primitive similarity relations, without requiring that the relations be reflected in the conventional practice of a human community. But Hobbes said universals presuppose language, which nearly everyone agreed is in some respects conventional. Moreover, he made agreement within a linguistic community concerning the particulars designated by the name of a kind an ineliminable part of the apparatus that determines the extension of the kind.

John Locke construed the nature of general ideas and names, as well as what determines their extensions, quite differently from other opponents of innatism. He said that universals are general ideas, but unlike Gassendi, gave ideas, rather than external standards, sole authority to determine the kinds they represent. He also counted general names as universals, but retained the traditional (non-Hobbesian) view that names borrow their signification from that of ideas. As he put it, a name immediately signifies an idea in the mind of its user; it thereby comes to name what the idea represents.[84]

To acquire general ideas, Locke said, we begin by noting resemblances among particulars and then separate their points of similarity from individual differences. But it is difficult to see exactly how Locke thought this separation is effected, by abstraction or selective attention. Some passages of *An Essay concerning Human Understanding* suggest the former. When children have observed similarities among several human beings, they 'frame an *Idea* . . . [w]herein they make nothing new, but only leave out of the complex *Idea* they had of *Peter* and *James, Mary* and *Jane*, that which is peculiar to each, and retain only what is common to all'.[85] And Locke apparently construed general ideas as indeterminate conceptions in a passage exploited in Berkeley's attack on the logical possibility of abstract ideas. Aiming to show abstract ideas are difficult, Locke said the '*general Idea* of a *Triangle* . . . must be neither Oblique, nor Rectangle, neither Equilateral, Equicrural, nor Scalenon; but all and none of these at once.'[86] Some commentators conclude that Locke took the idea to be particular; it *represents* all features mentioned, but has only *one*. But the passage strongly suggests the idea is indeterminate; it *admits* all the specifications mentioned, but has *none* of them. However, other passages suggest a general idea is just a particular idea put to a certain use (as maintained by Locke's critic Berkeley).[87] General ideas are said to be 'particular in their Existence', their 'general Nature being nothing but the Capacity they are put into by the Understanding, of signifying or representing many particulars'.[88] Perhaps these passages can be reconciled, but scholars are not at present agreed on how to interpret them.[89]

For Locke, the extension of a general idea is defined by its content (whether due to abstraction or selective attention). The idea represents all and only things that 'conform' to it.[90] That is, the content of the idea is the final authority with respect to its extension:

> Should there be a Body found, having all the other Qualities of Gold, except Malleableness, 'twould, no doubt, be made a question whether it were Gold or no; i.e. whether it were of that *Species*. This could be determined only by that abstract *Idea,* to which every one annexed the name *Gold:* so that it would be true Gold to him, . . . who included not Malleableness in his nominal Essence [general idea], signified by the Sound *Gold*; and on the other side, it would not be true Gold . . . to him, who included Malleableness in his specifick *Idea*.[91]

Locke observed, realising it sounds odd, that any two general ideas (different in content) define two *different* kinds.[92] Unlike Gassendi, then, Locke thought the boundary of the kind represented by a general idea is fixed by the explicit content of that idea.

On Locke's account, a mind has a general idea only if it is disposed to regard certain things as conforming to the idea. Unlike Hobbes, Locke never suggested this disposition is governed by decision or convention, nor subject to change. As for simple ideas, they are formed by an entirely natural process. Compound general ideas, in contrast, are *formed* voluntarily; they are combinations of simple ideas that are to some extent 'made arbitrarily by us'.[93] While this introduces a conventional element in the definition of kinds, it does not affect Locke's account of how compound ideas function as universals, or signs of many things (see Locke on essence, in the next section).

Among those who regarded universals as ideas or names generated by human cognition of particulars, then, there were diverse views on the basis afforded by actual things, rôle of human activity, and the apparatus of signification. They accordingly had rather different notions of the unity of things in a kind. Gassendi apparently held that they share a collection of universally co-instantiated attributes represented by (often inadequate) ideas. Those with more fully developed accounts supposed that things in a kind are united by (some type of) human disposition to recognise many particulars as similar in various ways. These same philosophers tended to think that essences, too, are either in nature (as opposed to eternal) or to some extent products of human practice.

III. ESSENCES AND THE GROUND OF
GENERAL NECESSARY TRUTHS

Many seventeenth-century philosophers retained the fundamental notion of essence: the essence of a thing is what it is to be that thing, or what is expressed in
its definition, and the ground of necessary truths of which it is subject. Although
essences were no longer identified with substantial and accidental forms, essences
were still ascribed to substances and their modifications. The doctrine that essences
are the objects of scientific knowledge persisted. Because some thinkers retained
versions of the theory of divine archetypes, whereas others located essences
entirely in nature, there were many opinions on the sense in which essences are
'eternal' bases of 'necessary' truths.

Acceptance of mechanism, in place of Aristotelian science, changed the catalogue of propositions considered *to be* necessary truths. Taking substances, above
all, to have essence, scholastics supposed the various species of animals and plants
are paradigmatic subjects of necessary general truths. But for mechanists, matter,
or material particles, were basic substances and subjects of necessary truths, such
as theorems of geometry and principles of mechanics. In contrast, scholastics had
debated whether mathematics dealt with essences and was a genuine science.[94]
The move to regard matter as subject of necessary truths raised other issues.

One was that matter is the subject of some general truths whose basis in matter
was obscure and debatable, and whose status as necessary was uncertain: namely,
the laws of motion, collision, and mind–body interaction. This marred the linger-
ing Aristotelian picture of a thing's essence as sole basis of its regular, explicable
traits. (That picture was also challenged because a body's mechanically grounded
causal powers depend not just on its structure but also on structures of the bodies
around it.) To account for causal laws that were not thought to flow from the
essence of matter, mechanists tended to appeal to divine power, rationality, or
wisdom in creating or sustaining the world (see Chapter 21).

Another issue raised by mechanism was whether Aristotelian species are subjects of necessary truths (e.g., man is an animal). On the one hand, horse, oak,
water, gold, and the like are widely assumed to be projectible kinds and subjects
of indefinitely many general truths; the practical arts and crafts, as well as sciences
of biology, medicine, chemistry, and so on required this presumption. On the
other hand, in mechanist metaphysics, horses, gold, and the like were not paradigmatic substances. Species of animals, say, were not basic in explanation and the
capacities by which scholastics defined species were to be reduced to matter and
motion. Some mechanists argued that the neat division of species assumed by

scholastics does not obtain.[95] They could even doubt there is any natural division of kinds of sensible material things. A horse, for example, resembles other aggregates of particles more or less closely in criss-crossing ways. How are we to know whether horses have inner constitutions similar in ways sufficiently prominent and stable to effect a natural division between horses and other things? There was, then, a need to explain how horse, and other such kinds, are established as subjects of general, perhaps necessary, truths. This gave impetus to the view that some 'essences' are defined by convention. At the same time, many refused to think that mathematical and moral essences are dependent on human activity.

1. Eternal necessary truths

Since mathematical entities seem to allow no form–matter (essence–accident) distinction, scholastics often denied they were objects of scientific knowledge. Marin Mersenne utilised scholastic theses to defend the opposite view. One of his arguments exploited the doctrine that all possible objects of divine creation are modeled among archetypes and therefore have essences. Mersenne insisted on the traditional view that unity is inseparable from every individual in a species. Further, since unity is the basis of all number, he argued, it follows that the individuals in any species constitute a collection to which some number applies. Species are possible objects of creation (as scholastics agreed), so numbers of things can be created, as well. Thus, even though numbers as such are mind-dependent abstractions, they structure possibilities of creation and thus count among things that have essence.[96]

Descartes moved more directly to establish mathematical essences while addressing the traditional dispute over the distinction between essence and existence. His claim was based on the special clarity and distinctness with which, as he said, we apprehend the necessity of mathematical truths. It is evident to us that the natures of numbers and geometrical objects 'are something, not bare nothing' (*aliquid sunt, non merum nihil*) regardless of whether they exist outside our thought or even whether we think of them.[97] Yet they are not uncaused eternal entities that limit the creative power of God; rather, Descartes maintained, essences are causally dependent on divine will. God, acting incomprehensibly, is the efficient cause of essences, and also the cause of created minds with innate ideas of these essences. So, for example, it is necessary that the radii of a circle are equal although God has power to make it otherwise, a power that will not be exercised because divine will is immutable. Again, it is only because God wills that certain actions should be done that they are good.[98] This bold theistic voluntarism pre-empted a problem that plagued Suárez, the difference in metaphysical status between essences taken apart from existence (i.e., possible beings) and impossibilities (i.e., contradictions).

Although we have innate ideas of true and immutable natures, according to Descartes, we can also fabricate ideas of things that are possible but have no genuine essence, for example, a golden mountain, winged horse, necessarily existent lion. In reply to Caterus, Descartes explained how we can tell that an idea contains a true nature, rather than an invented one. He can be understood as saying that the object of an idea has a true nature if and only if the object has a non-trivial property that pertains necessarily to it and to nothing that can exist apart from it.[99] It seems a winged horse will not pass the test; although it may be said to have a non-trivial necessary property, for example, the capacity to whinny, that also belongs to horses without wings. In contrast, a triangle passes the test (e.g., no other straight-sided Euclidean plane figure has interior angles equal to two right angles). And a triangle inscribed in a square can be represented either by a conjunction of ideas of triangle and square or by the idea of a unitary figure with necessary properties unique to it. For it is an accident of a triangle that it is inscribed in a square, but a necessary property of a triangle-inscribed-in-a-square, unique to that figure, that the base of the triangle bisects two opposite angles of the square.

On the matter of eternal truths, Descartes had few followers. Some critics, for example, Gassendi and Hobbes, objected that essence cannot be conceived apart from actual things.[100] Others, content to recognise separate essences, were appalled at the radical voluntarism that makes the law of non-contradiction, essence, possibility, and moral value subject to divine will (see Chapter 12). They faced the old problem of explaining how eternal essences are related to the eternal being of God.

Spinoza contrived to make divine nature the *efficient cause* of essences and eternal truths, without embracing Descartes's voluntarism. To Spinoza, that was a great absurdity and obstacle to science.[101] In one of his ways of demonstrating that essences are caused by God, Spinoza took for granted that some definitions express more reality than others; and that the more reality in the thing defined, the greater the number of properties that 'flow necessarily from it' and can be inferred from its definition. But the reality of the divine nature is all-encompassing: 'But since the divine nature has absolutely infinite attributes . . . , each of which also ex-presses an essence infinite in its own kind, from its necessity there must follow . . . everything which can fall under an infinite intellect.'[102] The essences of things (or eternal truths) are included in those that follow from the nature of God in this way.[103] Spinoza took some pains to argue that God's capacity to will does not extend beyond what God actually wills; thus divine power could not make essences in any way different from those that obtain. But even though Descartes's view is impossible, Spinoza noted that in making eternal truths depend on God, he was closer to the truth than those who said God acts for the sake of the good. For the good then appears to be something distinct from God to which God's will is subject.[104]

Malebranche took a somewhat different view of essences in relation to God. He said that ideas existing in the infinite being of God are the immutable, eternal subjects of necessary truths. For instance, the subject of geometry is infinite extension as it exists in God. When scandalised critics charged that this doctrine made God extended and therefore material, Malebranche replied that ideas are subjects of a different mode of predication than finite things. Forms of the verb 'to be' express the relation between a material substance and its modifications (limitations), whereas 'to be intelligibly' expresses a non-limiting relation between ideas. The idea of extension is not long, wide, or deep; but it is intelligibly extended in three dimensions and intelligibly divisible.[105] The idea is intelligibly immobile but contains the possibility of motion in extended substance,[106] and it has intelligible, but not 'localised', parts;[107] thus the idea serves as subject of theorems of geometry. In addition to infinite extension, Malebranche posited other subjects of eternal truths, for example, intelligible mind; and he thought moral truths also have this sort of ground.[108]

Another opponent of Cartesian voluntarism, Leibniz could not accept Spinoza's reasoning that all things, thus eternal essences, flow necessarily from God, nor did he ally himself with Malebranche. He said that essences are abstract (incomplete) concepts, which are in the first instance possessed by God.[109] Sometimes he defined a necessary truth as a proposition whose denial is, or can be reduced to, a formal contradiction. Consider, for example, the necessary truth that a circle has equal radii; Leibniz maintained that if one analysed the subject and predicate concepts by replacing each with its definition and continued that process, one would eventually (in a finite number of steps) arrive at an identity (expressible in the form 'AB is AB' or 'AB is A').[110]

Like Descartes, Leibniz observed that when we conjoin concepts, we risk concocting definitions that specify nothing real. He, too, proposed a way of certifying that a concept expresses an essence. A definition is merely *nominal,* if it leaves us in doubt as to the possibility of what it defines, for example, the fastest possible motion; Leibniz claimed to derive a contradiction from that definition. In contrast, a *real* definition makes evident the possibility of its *definiendum,* thereby showing that it expresses an essence.[111]

On the question of the being of essences and their relation to the being of God, Leibniz has proved difficult to pin down. He said eternal truths, essences, and possibilities have their reality in the domain of God's understanding.[112] One question is whether Leibniz thought these entities known by God have intrinsic non-actual being or whether they are nothing other than God's actual, non-abstract attributes.[113] Leibniz said that *possibilia,* although dependent on divine cognition, are real, eternal, necessary, and independent of God's will.[114] But this does not decide among competing accounts of their mode of being.[115]

Cudworth, who also opposed voluntarism, held a view of the being of eternal essences close to certain scholastic theories. He urged that all essential truths are 'eternal and immutable', primarily to show that morality is grounded in the eternal natures of sorts of actions, rather than in commands of God (as Descartes supposed) or in decrees of the state (the view he ascribed to Hobbes).[116] Cudworth maintained that necessary truths are eternal relations among what he called *rationes,* that is, universals, which are entities with 'certain, determinate, and immutable natures of their own'.[117] Indeed, the immutable being (entity) of universals and eternal truths was the basis of his analysis of knowledge and certainty.[118] He used this doctrine to attack Descartes's voluntarism, and implicitly, his theory of knowledge: it is not in God's power to *create* nonentity (e.g., a contradiction) or to destroy the foundation of truth, (his own) knowledge, or the certainty of what is evident.[119] Despite this emphasis on the immutable being of essences, however, Cudworth did not assign them intrinsic being, even in a diminished mode: 'For since the rationes, intelligible essences, and verities of things . . . are nothing but . . . objective notions or knowledges [*sic*], which are things that cannot exist alone, but together with that actual knowledge in which they are comprehended, they are the modification of some mind or intellect.'[120] More exactly, they are a modification of the eternal and immutable mind of God. Cudworth supported this with an Aristotelian principle: 'What is neither substance nor modification of a substance, is a pure non entity.'[121] His position contrasts, not only with Malebranche's doctrine of infinite mind, but also with views that assign unreduced objective being to essences known by God. His reduction of essences to a modification of God is a solution akin to that of Suárez. As Cudworth explained, in knowing essences, the divine being knows nothing other than itself. But he also put this in a way that would have offended some Cartesians and others, that God comprehends the 'extent' and 'measure' of divine power.[122] It may well have seemed to the philosophers discussed in the next section that there was no way to posit eternal essences without endorsing either theistic voluntarism, extravagant metaphysics, or suspect theology.

2. *Necessary truths without eternal grounds*

In his objections to Descartes, Gassendi protested there *are* no eternal truths; for example, 'A man is an animal' is true only if there is (has been, will be) an actual man. As he put it, 'It is impossible to grasp how there can be a human nature if no human being exists, or how we can say a rose is a flower when not even one rose exists.'[123] Without actual humans, there simply is nothing to connect being human and being animal. For Gassendi admitted no eternal separated essence of man.[124] He did admit we have a universal idea of man that explicitly includes being animal. Because of that, we say that if anything is a man, it must be an animal. But this necessity is not ultimately grounded in the *idea*. On the contrary, the idea was drawn from observed similarities among particular things: 'The properties of human nature are not in Plato and Socrates in the sense that Plato and Socrates have received them from the universal nature; rather, the universal nature has the properties only because the intellect gave them to it after observing them in Plato, Socrates and others.'[125] The same goes for mathematical truths.[126] In Gassendi's view, there is nothing to make a proposition necessarily true but the collections of properties that occur together in actual things.

Indeed, it is not clear that for Gassendi a necessary truth is anything more than a generalisation true in every case. In *Institutio,* he said we demonstrate conclusions from premises that are necessary; but, again, the premises are known from general ideas drawn from an induction of particulars perceived by sense.[127] We have no *reason* to think, for example, that having interior angles equal to two right angles pertains to a triangle in virtue of essence; our evidence shows, at best, simply that every triangle *is* this way. So Gassendi's position on the knowledge of necessary truths strongly suggests he regarded them as nothing more than general truths.[128]

While Gassendi dispensed with eternal entities and based 'necessary' truths on structures in nature, Hobbes denied that there is any basis in things for necessity. In *De corpore,* he altogether rejected the doctrine of essence, or *de re* necessity. In effect, he argued that it involves a category error. As he put it, the names 'necessary', *'per se',* 'contingent', and *'per accidens'* are names of propositions, that is, sentences or 'speech'. Thus those who say, for instance, that the being of Socrates as a man is necessary (*per se*) and the being of Socrates as musical is contingent (*per accidens*) speak incoherently.[129] The same would go for any explanation of essence or what a thing is necessarily.

As this argument shows, Hobbes did not deny that there are necessarily true propositions. He defined a proposition as two names linked by 'is' (or some other word for the copula). A proposition is necessary if and only if 'nothing can be conceived or imagined at any time, of which the subject is a name while the predicate is not.'[130] This psychological account, based on Hobbes's theory of the basis of naming, was supplemented by a logical one: in a necessary proposition, the predicate is either equivalent to the subject (e.g., 'Man is a rational animal') or part of an equivalent name (e.g., 'Man is an animal'). Names are equivalent just in case one is the definition of the other. For Hobbes, science begins with (apt) definitions and proceeds to demonstrate conclusions by a sort of 'calculation'.[131]

As he suggested in his objections to Descartes, necessary truths merely record conventions for applying names. Propositions deduced from such premises tell us what is required for consistency in use of names but tell us nothing about essences. Descartes replied impatiently that we reason about things, not names; he charged that Hobbes refuted himself by acknowledging that names stand for things.[132] Arnauld and Nicole launched a similar attack on the scandalous 'doctrine of arbitrary truth'.[133] But it is not quite to the point, for Hobbes's claim was that the necessity of propositions, in which names stand for things, is due to the use of names, not due to supposed essences of the things.

Leibniz attacked Hobbes by pointing out that definitions are not arbitrary, and we cannot rely on them unless they are real.[134] Leibniz's main criterion for a real definition was, as noted earlier, that it contain no mutually contradictory terms. Since Hobbes also placed that requirement on definitions, this argument taken alone fails to establish essence as a non-Hobbesian ground of necessary truth. Leibniz meant to imply that an internally consistent definition expresses an entity within the creative power of an actual eternal being; but implanting essences in the intellect and power of God does not respond to Hobbes's charge that the notion of essence, necessity intrinsic to a thing, is incoherent. Nevertheless, Hobbes's radically conventionalist doctrine of necessary truth was widely despised in the seventeenth century.[135]

There was also a less radical conventionalism with regard to species in the natural domain, urged in the mechanist treatises of Robert Boyle. He sometimes described his program as one of 'mechanising forms', taking 'forms' still to mean the essences of species of natural bodies. But Boyle's forms are mechanical modifications inessential to the substance they modify (matter). They are essential, however, if a body is to have a certain sortal denomination, for example, metal or stone.[136] The suggestion was that species are distinguished by different inner 'mechanisms', so that general truths of which species are subject can be explained by mechanist laws. At the same time, Boyle rejected the view that we classify bodies on the basis of unknown and unobservable forms (mechanised or not). He stressed the practical purposes of classification. Observing certain groups of accidents regularly combined in bodies, men agreed to divide bodies into sorts for convenience and ease of communication. Bodies are ranked in species on the basis of qualities that 'most men by a kind of agreement (for the thing is more arbitrary than we are aware of) think necessary and sufficient to make . . . [a thing] belong to this or that determinate genus or species of natural bodies.'[137] Boyle's move was to recognise mechanical essences of kinds such as gold, ruby, mercury, while tying the distinction of those kinds to a partly conventional practice. Locke developed a technical philosophy to support this sort of semi-conventionalism.

Locke provided an apparatus for dealing with the general ideas central to all the various sciences. Two types of complex general ideas are central to his theory of essence: (1) ideas of substances, which are intended to represent things that 'subsist by themselves' and consist of ideas of various sensible qualities together with the general idea of substance; and (2) ideas of modes, which represent things that 'depend for their existence' on something else, and are either simple (e.g., distance, duration, numbers) or mixed. Modes include, for example, a triangle, obligation, proscription, and, as Locke put it, most of the ideas 'made use of in Divinity, Ethicks, Law, and Politicks, and several other Sciences'.[138]

All complex ideas were said to be combinations of simple ideas 'made arbitrarily by us'. For Locke, their claim to represent real entities could rest on neither their innateness nor simplicity. He needed to show how we construct ideas that are not mere fabrications in the Cartesian sense, but rather represent real essences, ground non-trivial necessary truths, and support scientific knowledge (where we have it). With ideas of substances, he urged, we intend to represent natural subjects of indefinitely many sensible qualities and causal powers. Based only on observation, these ideas include only some of the qualities united in their (natural) archetypes and are unavoidably inadequate. Still they are 'real' if and only if they include collections of qualities that *have* a union in actual things; thus Locke could distinguish the real idea of a horse, for example, from the fantastical idea of a chimera or a winged horse.[139]

Ideas of modes are not meant to represent natural subjects of qualities, but rather we intend these ideas to delineate subjects, for example, one action, discriminated in the flow of bodily motion, or one shape among the infinitely many traceable in space. Provided only a mode-idea combines simple ideas that are mutually compatible, it is 'real' according to Locke.[140] On this account, ideas of mathematical, moral, legal, and political entities, which Locke took to be subjects of scientific knowledge and non-trivial necessary truths, are no more 'real' than other mode-ideas that are subjects of merely trivial necessary truths, for example, a dance, wrestling (or Descartes's golden mountain). His position thus lacked the power of the Cartesian doctrine of true natures; still it had the economy of avoiding essences with non-actual being, as well as eternal archetypes.

Locke proposed to supplant the traditional notion of essence, on which essence both defines a kind and grounds the properties that pertain necessarily to it. In its place, he distinguished real and nominal essences of a kind.[141]

The nominal essence was said to be the general idea associated with the name of the kind. Since Locke held that a general idea represents exactly those things that conform to its content, a general idea fixes the basic necessary and sufficient conditions for membership in a kind. This ensured that we know the boundary of any kind for which we have an idea or name (as Boyle had insisted). Moreover, it meant that general ideas serve one of the functions of essence:

[Since] nothing can be a *Man*, or have a right to the name *Man*, but what has a conformity to the abstract *Idea* the name *Man* stands for; nor [can] any thing be a Man . . . but what has the Essence of that Species, it follows, that the abstract *Idea*, for which the name stands, and the Essence of the Species, is one and the same.[142]

Real essences were said to ground necessary truths; the real essence of a kind is 'that Foundation from which all its Properties flow, and to which they are all inseparably annexed'.[143] Because ideas of substances and modes grip reality differently, they define kinds whose properties have different sources. A substance-idea, if real, defines a kind by certain qualities that 'flow from' the constitutions of some actual things; the other qualities inseparable from the kind depend on the same source. So the real essence of a substance-kind is a function of its nominal essence; real essence consists in the common aspects of the inner constitutions of actual things that have the qualities specified by the nominal essence.[144] In contrast, if a mode-idea specifies an internally consistent definition, it establishes a real subject; so the properties that pertain necessarily to that subject are grounded in its definition. With modal kinds, real and nominal essences coincide.[145]

Locke said that necessary truths that are 'identities' are trifling; these are propositions in which the predicate-idea repeats all or part of the subject-idea (e.g., 'A man is a man', 'A man is an animal').[146] Locke also recognised non-identical, or 'instructive', necessary truths, which he said depend on 'immutable relations and habitudes' among our ideas. Subjects of these truths tend to be modes; for example, the idea of a triangle has an immutable relation to the idea of angles equal to two right angles. This is expressed in a conditional proposition whose necessary truth is not dependent on the existence of triangles. The same went for moral truths.[147] Locke said:

Such Propositions are therefore called *Eternal Truths,* not because they are Eternal Propositions actually formed, and antecedent to the Understanding, that at any time makes them; nor because they are imprinted on the Mind from any patterns, that are any where of them out of the Mind, and existed before: But because being once made, about abstract *Ideas,* so as to be true, they will, whenever they can be supposed to be made again at any time past or to come, by a Mind having those *Ideas,* always actually be true.[148]

In addition, Locke held there are necessary truths that ascribe certain qualities to species of substances, for example, opium makes a man sleep. Such necessary truths depend on the hidden real essences (mechanical structures) of substance-kinds.[149]

For Locke, classification is unavoidably conventional: 'The sorting of Things, is the Workmanship of the Understanding, since it is the Understanding that abstracts and makes those general *Ideas.*'[150] Substance-ideas are not made *as* arbitrarily as mode-ideas, yet even they are subject to human choice.[151] This is inevitable, on Locke's view, because we must choose which of the many qualities united in actual things to include in our ideas of substance-kinds. Sometimes this is all Locke seemed to mean when he said substance-kinds are 'made arbitrarily'.[152] But he may have thought definitions of substance-kinds are arbitrary for the more radical reason that there *is* no natural division of material things into kinds. He rejected the 'usual supposition' that we name species whose essences ground *propria,* that is, traits that necessarily belong to all things with the essence and only to them; monsters and changelings are said to refute that.[153] He also listed difficulties that bar us from knowing that nature divides species, let alone how.[154] Whatever he surmised regarding the existence of unknown natural divisions,[155] he insisted that we distinguish substance-kinds by semi-conventional definitions.

Those who refused to posit eternal essences were thus led in one way or another to qualified notions of 'necessary' and 'eternal' truth. Necessary truth was either reduced to general truth, restricted to *de dicto* necessity, or held to be dependent on human activity with at most partial basis in nature.

IV. CONCLUSION

Theories of universals and essences, topics long defined by reference to the theory of substance, were strongly affected by the seventeenth-century mechanist movement, in large part because it replaced the scholastic-Aristotelian analysis of substance with the view that matter (and perhaps immaterial mind) is substance in its own right. By mid-century, the mediaeval problem of universals, concerned with the metaphysical composition of individual substances, disappeared from philosophical discourse. The question of species unity was subsumed under other topics. Those who located universals among eternal beings tended to use those same beings to account for a variety of other matters, as their Neoplatonist predecessors had: creation, knowledge, truth, necessity, and possibility. In this context, the question of species unity tended to reduce to the question how particulars are known, primarily by God and secondarily by us. For those who reduced universals to cognitions or activities of human beings, the main problem was the basis on which a cognitive act or a name takes on general signification: what sort of cognition is required, what determines its extension, what defines the kind it represents?

The movement away from Aristotelian science replaced various species of material things as paradigmatic subjects of necessary truths; mathematics and, perhaps, the laws of physics became the prime examples. To ground necessary truths, one could no longer appeal to essences that exist as ingredients in actual things. Many philosophers took the view that essences (*qua* archetypes) are eternal and directly dependent on some aspect or other of God. Although this might involve controversial theology, it was not in itself a drawback for seventeenth-century thinkers; many (not all) appealed to God to account for some element in their natural or moral philosophies, if not for essence. (It was more of a disadvantage in the following century.) Others grounded necessary truths in the human activity of constructing ideas, including ideas based on actual things; but this Lockean position was linked to skepticism about our ability to discover the ultimate workings of nature. The most radical move was to reduce essential truths to generalisations true in the actual world or flatly to deny that necessary truths have ground in *de re* necessity. All of this made it easy for later philosophers to question the viability of a notion of essence as ground of necessary truth and object of scientific knowledge.

NOTES

1 On Scholastic use of the term *forma,* see the glossary in Suárez 1982.
2 On Ockham's attack on this doctrine, see Adams 1987, chap. 5.
3 Adams 1987, chaps. 1–2; Suárez 1964, translator's introduction, pp. 5–27.
4 Adams 1987, chaps. 2 and 4.
5 Although many Scholastics used *esse objectivum* for the being of an object of thought, they differed over what sort of being such objects have. Some identified entities that have *esse objectivum* with actual objects (e.g., the sun) in so far as they are intentionally represented by a cognitive act; accordingly, some thoughts lack anything with *esse objectivum*. Others

said that every thought has an intentional object that has a non-actual mode of being (*esse objectivum*) dependent on its being known; thus some thoughts have intentional objects that do not or cannot actually exist (e.g., a golden mountain, a universal). Still others said that all thoughts have intentional objects that have non-actual being (*esse objectivum*) independently of their being known. See Nuchelmans 1983, 1.1–1.3. On seventeenth-century theories of intentionality, see Chapter 30 in this book.

6 See Adams 1987, chap. 4.

7 Suárez, *Disp. met.* V.5.

8 Suárez, *Disp. met.* VI.1.12; VI.2.13, and VI.5.

9 Suárez 1964, translator's introduction, esp. pp. 14–21 and 24.

10 See Jordan 1984.

11 See Adams 1987, vol. 2, pp. 1050–61.

12 On the disputed question whether Ockham actually held this view, see Adams 1987, vol. 2, pp. 1079–83.

13 See Schneewind 1990, vol. 1, p. 8; McGuire 1972, pp. 539–41.

14 Suárez, *Disp. met.* XXXI.2.1.

15 Suárez, *Disp. met.* XXXI.2.7, XXXI.3.2–4.

16 Suárez, *Disp. met.* XXXI.2.10.

17 See Suárez 1983, translator's introduction, pp. 19–21.

18 Suárez, *Disp. met.* XXXI.2.8, XXXI.12.38–47.

19 Suárez 1983, translator's introduction, pp. 21–5.

20 On ways that Neoplatonist doctrines compromise the Aristotelian substance-accident ontology, see Kristeller 1943, p. 151; also Lloyd 1990, pp. 85–95; on the opposition of later 'nature philosophers' to the form–matter distinction and Aristotelian doctrine of species, see Copenhaver 1988a, pp. 289–93.

21 Kristeller 1943, p. 81.

22 Kristeller 1943, p. 148; Gresh 1986, vol. 1, pp. 403–13.

23 Kristeller 1943, pp. 146–70; on the impossibility of univocal predication of genus, see Lloyd 1990, pp. 78–85.

24 Kristeller 1943, chap. 9. On Plotinus, see Lloyd 1990, pp. 76–8. On adaptations of Neoplatonism in the natural philosophy of Paracelsus and others, see Copenhaver 1988a, pp. 296–300; Rees 1975.

25 See *Ideas universalium* in the glossary in Suárez 1982, p. 222. On the distinction of theology and metaphysics, see Lohr 1988, pp. 584–638.

26 E.g., Malebranche, *Rech.* VI.2.3, *OC* II 309–20 (Malebranche 1980a, pp. 446–52); cf. Leibniz, 'De Ipse Natura', Ger. IV 504–16 (Leibniz 1969, pp. 498–507).

27 See, e.g., Digby 1644a, p. 3; Hobbes *Eng. Works*, vol. 1, pp. 91–3 (*Concerning Body*, pt. II, chap. 8, secs. 2–3); LAkad VI.VI 65–6.

28 Arnauld and Nicole 1970, p. 45.

29 On the Malebranche–Arnauld debate over intentionality, see Chapter 30.

30 *Princ.* I 59, AT VIIIA 28.

31 See, e.g., *Resp.* V, AT VII 381–2.

32 *Princ.* I 62, AT VIIIA 30.

33 In *Princ.* I 57–58, Descartes stressed that the abstract attribute is only a mode of thought apparently to avoid implying that the attribute exists in an actual object (*contra* moderate realists). It is likely he meant also to indicate that an abstract attribute enables us to conceive many actual objects by a relation between abstract and determinate, not by virtue of an entity that exists both in thought and in objects (e.g., intentional species).

34 On the modal distinction, see *Princ.* I 60, AT VIIIA p. 29.

35 Letter to unknown correspondent, 1645 or 1646, AT IV 350.
36 Arnauld 1775–83, vol. 38, pp. 65–70. On Arnauld's theory of ideas, see Chapter 30.
37 This notion of 'extension' is thus not the present one, i.e., the set of particular things to which the term 'triangle' applies.
38 *Logique* I.5, Arnauld and Nicole 1970, pp. 86–8.
39 Norris 1701–4.
40 E.g., Malebranche, *Rech.*, III.2.7, secs. 1–2; III.2.8.1, *OC* I 448–9 and 456–9 (Malebranche 1980a, pp. 236–7 and 241–3); *Entretiens,* I, ix, *OC* XII–XIII 43–5 (Malebranche 1980b, p. 37).
41 Malebranche, *Rech.* III.2.6, *OC* I 441 (Malebranche 1980a, p. 232).
42 See e.g., Malebranche, *Entretiens* I.6, *OC* XII–XIII 39–40 (Malebranche 1980b, p. 33).
43 On Malebranche's doctrine that we 'see all things in God', see Chapter 30.
44 See the earlier discussion of Descartes's theory of attributes considered in the abstract.
45 Cudworth 1837–8, vol. 2, p. 461 also p. 424 (*Immutable Morality,* IV, iii, 13; also IV, i, 2).
46 Cudworth 1837–38, vol. 2, pp. 472 and 430 (*Immutable Morality* IV.iv.4 and IV.i.9). On Cudworth's theory of the unifying rôle of mind, see Muirhead 1931, pp. 39–46.
47 Cudworth 1837–38, vol. 2, pp. 423–8 and 480–4 (*Immutable Morality* IV.i.1–6 and IV.v.1–3).
48 Cudworth 1837–38, vol. 2, pp. 431–2, pp. 462–3, pp. 152–3 (*Immutable Morality,* IV.i.11; IV.iii.14; *Intellectual System,* V.i).
49 Cudworth 1837–38, vol. 2, pp. 462, 477–8, and 154–6 (*Immutable Morality* IV.i.5; IV.iv.11; *Intellectual System,* V.i).
50 LAkad VI.VI 48–53, 69–108; Leibniz, *Disc. mét.,* sec. 26, Ger. IV 451 (Leibniz 1969, p. 320). Leibniz sometimes suggested that some of our general conceptions, especially those that are obscure, are abstracted, not strictly from perception of particular individuals, but from that portion of the content of sense perception that is accessible to consciousness; see LAkad VI.VI 289–90, c.f. 74.
51 See Ger. IV 422–6 (Leibniz 1969, pp. 291–4); also LAkad VI.VI 74–108 (*passim*), 120, 128, 254–63, 447.
52 *Disc. mét.,* sec. 8, Ger. IV 433 (Leibniz 1969, p. 307).
53 E.g., Leibniz LAkad VI.VI 65–6 and 379. On modifications as particulars, see Clatterbaugh 1973.
54 Leibniz, LAkad VI.VI 275, 292.
55 E.g., Leibniz, LAkad VI.VI 57, 289–90.
56 See, e.g., Spinoza on universals, the faculty of will, etc. *De int. emen.* par. 92–4 and 99, Geb. II 34, 36 (Spinoza 1985, pp. 38–9, 41); *Eth.* II prop. 49 schol., Geb. II 133–5 (Spinoza 1985, pp. 488–90). Spinoza's most extensive remarks on universals are at *Eth.* II prop. 40 schol. 1. On errors due to the tendency to reify abstractions, also see Leibniz, LAkad VI.VI 57, 110 and Berkeley, *Pr. Hum. Kn.,* Intro., Berkeley 1948–57, vol. 2, pp. 25–40.
57 Digby 1644a, pp. 3–5 (*Of Bodies,* I.3). In this connexion, Digby mentioned Plato, Averroes, and Scotus, in particular.
58 Digby 1644a, pp. 3–4, 6–7, and 51–4 (*Of Man's Soule,* chap. 1, secs. 2, 4, 7; chap. 5, secs. 2–5). On this understanding of objective existence, see Chapter 30.
59 Digby 1644a, pp. 12–13 and 54–6 (*Of Man's Soule,* chap. 1, secs. 12–13 and chap. 5, secs. 6–7).
60 Berkeley 1948–57, vol. 2, pp. 27–32 (*Pr. Hum. Kn.,* Intro., secs. 6–13).
61 A roughly similar account is found in Gassendi's summary of Epicurus's philosophy; see Gassendi 1658, vol. 3, p. 8, English translation by Stanley 1701, p. 553.

62 Gassendi 1981, p. 6 (*Institutio*, I, cn 4).
63 Gassendi 1981, pp. 10–11 (*Institutio*, I, cn 8).
64 Gassendi 1981, pp. 10–11 (*Institutio*, I, cn 8). The passage says an idea that abstracts being an animal four cubits high with white face and straight nose is an imperfect general idea of man, but: 'Since . . . an idea is called general . . . because it has been selected to represent something that is common to all the singular ideas, if it should contain anything that is not shared by all, the less general it will be, and so the less perfect.' But although the idea is imperfect, it still is an idea of man. Also see *Institutio*, I, cns. 10 and 15; II, cn. 1.
65 Gassendi 1981, p. 15 (*Institutio*, I, cn. 15).
66 Gassendi 1981, pp. 16–18 (*Institutio*, I, cn. 16).
67 Gassendi 1981, p. 25 (*Institutio*, II, cn. 3).
68 'Quia quicquid inseparabile est a Subiect, aut ipsius est genus, idque tam proximum, quam remotum, ut respectu Hominis esse Animal, esse Vivens, esse Corpus; aut est qualitas eidem Subiecto a Natura insita, eaque sive illius propria ut Hominis Ratio, aptitudo ad risum; sive ipsi, aliisque communis, ut est Homini facultas sentiendi, quam habet communem cum omnibus aliis Animalibus; esse bipedem, quod habet commune cum aliquibus, puta Avibus' (Gassendi 1981, p. 25, *Institutio*, II, cn. 4).
69 Gassendi 1981, p. 11 (*Institutio*, I, cn. 8).
70 Berkeley, *Pr. Hum. Kn.*, Intro., Berkeley 1948–57, vol. 2, pp. 25–40; also Lee 1702, Preface, and p. 203, arguing against Locke's doctrines of abstract ideas and simple ideas. This psychological claim regarding our ability to form images is to be distinguished from the contention that an abstract idea is logically impossible; see Bolton 1987.
71 Gassendi 1658, vol. 2, pp. 410b–411a and 441a–b, 451b, 457b–458a. See also Bloch 1971, pp. 139–43.
72 Gassendi 1658, vol. 2, p. 451a.
73 Cf. Gassendi 1658, vol. 3, p. 159a, cited by Jones, Gassendi 1981, p. xx.
74 Leibniz, Ger. IV 158 (Leibniz 1969, p. 128).
75 Hobbes 1981, p. 205 (*De corpore* I.2.ix).
76 Hobbes 1981, pp. 277–9 (*De corpore*, I.5.viii).
77 Berkeley 1948–57, vol. 2, pp. 34–5 (*Pr. Hum. Kn.*, Intro., sec. 16).
78 See especially Hobbes 1981, pp. 311–12 (*De corpore* I.6.xi).
79 Hobbes 1981, pp. 193–9 (*De corpore* I.2.iv).
80 Hobbes 1981, p. 207 (*De corpore* I.2.ix).
81 On Hobbes's theory of signification, see the essay by Hungerland and Vick 1981, chaps. 3–4.
82 Hobbes 1983b, pp. 228–30 (*De cive*, 27.12).
83 Hobbes 1981, pp. 313–7 (*De corpore* I.v.12). On the degree to which conventions regarding the application of names may affect the truth of propositions, according to Hobbes, compare Peters 1967, pp. 50–60, and Sorrell 1986, pp. 45–50.
84 Locke 1975, pp. 410–11, 414, 404–6 (*Ess.* III.iii.6, 11; III.ii.1–2).
85 Locke 1975, pp. 411, 412, 414–17, 159 (*Ess.* III.iii.7, 9, 11–16; II.xi.9).
86 Locke 1975, p. 596 (*Ess.* IV.vii.9); for Berkeley's argument, see note 60.
87 E.g., Berkeley 1948–57, vol. 2, pp. 27 and 99 (*Pr. Hum. Kn.*, Intro. secs. 6 and 126); also Lee 1702, p. 203.
88 Locke 1975, p. 414; also see pp. 680–1, 529–30 (*Ess.* III.iii.11; IV.xvii.8; IV.i.9).
89 Compare Mackie 1976, pp. 124–5; Ayers 1991, vol. 1, pp. 248–53.
90 E.g., Locke 1975, pp. 410–11, also 409–20, 428–38, and 438–71 *passim* (*Ess.* III.iii.6; and III.iii.5; III.v and III.vi *passim*).

91 Locke 1975, p. 461.
92 E.g., Locke 1975, pp. 416, 453–4 (*Ess.* III.iii.14; III.vi.26).
93 E.g., Locke 1975, pp. 164, 430, 455–6 (*Ess.* II.xii.2; III.v.5; III.vi.28).
94 Wallace 1984, pp. 142–3.
95 Malebranche, *Rech.* III.2.10, *OC* I 495–8 (Malebranche 1980a, pp. 253–4); Locke, *Ess.,* III, iii, 17; III, vi, 14–18.
96 Dear 1988, pp. 62–79.
97 AT VII 65 (Med.V).
98 See, e.g., Resp. VI, AT VII 432–3, 434–6; letters from Descartes to Mersenne, 15 April 1630, 6 May 1630, 27 May 1630, AT I 143–54 (CSM III 22–6).
99 A non-trivial property is a property not explicitly mentioned in the definition of the thing.
100 AT VII 193–4, 319–20.
101 Spinoza, *Eth.* I prop. 25 and prop. 33 schol. 2, Geb. II 67–8 and 74–6.
102 Spinoza, *Eth.* I prop. 16 dem., Geb. II 60; see also *Eth.* I prop. 25, Geb. II 67–8.
103 See, e.g., Spinoza, *Eth.* I prop. 25 schol., Geb. II 68; also *Eth.* I prop. 17 schol. [I], Geb. II 61–2.
104 Spinoza, *Eth.* I prop. 33 schol. 2 and I app.
105 Rodis-Lewis 1963, pp. 109 and 117.
106 Malebranche, *Eclaircissement* X, reply to third objection, *OC* III 152–3 (Malebranche 1980a, p. 627).
107 Rodis-Lewis 1963, p. 117.
108 Malebranche, *Eclaircissement* X, reply to second objection, *OC* III 148–50 (Malebranche 1980a, p. 626); *Traité de Morale* I, chap. 1, *OC* XI 17–27.
109 E.g., Ger. II 48–9, 50 (Leibniz 1967, pp. 41, 54–6).
110 E.g., *Disc. mét.,*sec. 13, *Mon.,* sec. 33 (Leibniz 1969, pp. 310 and 646); Leibniz 1948, p. 326 (Leibniz 1989, pp. 94–8). On Leibniz's views on the distinction between necessary and contingent truths, see Chapter 12.
111 E.g., *Disc. mét.,* sec. 24, Ger. IV 422–6 (Leibniz 1969, pp. 292–3); Leibniz, LAkad VI.VI 295.
112 E.g., Leibniz, LAkad VI.VI 446; *Théod.* pt. I, secs. 20, 89, pt. II, sec. 335.
113 Leibniz's doctrine of 'striving possibles' might seem to indicate that he accorded some sort of intrinsic being to possibles (Ger. VII 302–8; Leibniz 1969, 486–91); but the point is debatable; see Blumenfeld 1973.
114 Especially *Théod.* pt. I, secs. 20, 149, 184, 189, pt. II, sec. 225, pt. 3, secs. 335, 380.
115 Current scholarship has not settled this question. That Leibniz identified concepts of possibles with actual modifications of God in the form of dispositions, roughly analogous to his account of the concepts of finite minds, is proposed by Mates 1986, pp. 174–8; but see Mondadori 1990.
116 Although Cudworth did argue that specifically moral principles cannot be established by mere fiat (e.g., Cudworth 1837–8, vol. 2, pp. 374–5; *Immutable Morality* I.i.3), most of his energy went to establishing the more general claim. See especially Cudworth 1837–8, vol. 2, pp. 421–97; also pp. 135–8 (*Immutable Morality,* IV; *Intellectual System,* V.1).
117 Cudworth 1837–8, vol. 2, p. 473 (*Immutable Morality,* IV.iv.4).
118 Cudworth 1837–8, vol. 2, pp. 480–9 and 136–7 (*Immutable Morality* IV.v; *Intellectual System,* V.1).
119 Cudworth 1837–8, vol. 2, pp. 378–81 (*Immutable Morality* I.iii.2–5).
120 Cudworth 1837–8, vol. 2, pp. 475–6 (*Immutable Morality* I.iii.7).

121 Cudworth 1837–8, vol. 2, p. 476 (*Immutable Morality* IV.iv.9).
122 Cudworth 1837–8, vol. 2, p. 160 (*Intellectual System* V.1). He dismissed Descartes's contention that uncreated eternal truths would subject God's will and power to the fates as 'a mere mormo or bugbear', Cudworth 1837–8, vol. 2, p. 382 (*Immutable Morality* I.iii.7; also IV.vi.3). Cudworth's bald exposition may have encouraged some later British moral philosophers to insist that the theory of eternal essences placed unacceptable limits on the power of God, e.g., Law 1734, vol. 1, p. 85.
123 Obj. V, AT VII 319.
124 Gassendi argued against Descartes that his alleged essences were either unwanted eternal beings independent of God or else neither eternal nor immutable; see Gassendi 1658, vol. 3, p. 480.
125 Obj. V, AT VII 321.
126 Also see Gassendi 1658, vol. 3, p. 160b (*Exercitationes paradoxicae*, II.2.5).
127 Gassendi 1981, pp. 144–6 (*Institutio* III, cn. 16); also Gassendi 1658, vol. 3, p. 185a–b (*Exercitationes paradoxicae*, II.5.3); Obj. V, AT VII 321–22.
128 See also Gassendi's rather scattered remarks on necessary and contingent truths in *Institutio,* II, especially cn. 11.
129 Hobbes 1981, p. 279 (*De corpore* I.5.ix).
130 Hobbes 1981, pp. 237–8 (*De corpore* I.3.x).
131 For detailed discussion, see Hungerland and Vick 1981, pp. 105–27.
132 AT VII 177–78.
133 Arnauld and Nicole 1970, pp. 68–9 (*Logique* I.i).
134 E.g., Ger. VII 296; Ger. IV. 424–5; *Disc. mét.,* sec. 24.
135 In addition to the critics named above, see Cudworth, who coupled this with other attacks on Hobbes's theory of universals; Cudworth 1837–8, vol. 2, p. 305 and pp. 463–5 (*Intellectual System* V.4; *Immutable Morality* IV.iii.15). For an attack on Locke's conventionalism, see LAkad VI.VI 293–6, 327, 397.
136 Boyle, *The Origin of Forms and Qualities . . . ,* 1979, p. 52.
137 Boyle, *The Origin of Forms and Qualities . . . ,* 1979, p. 38; also see Boyle 1772, vol. 3, pp. 36, 49–54, 128–9.
138 Locke 1975, p. 294 (*Ess.* II.xxii.12); also see pp. 163–6 (*Ess.* II.xxii.12; also II.xii).
139 Locke 1975, pp. 374, 376–7, 378–82 (*Ess.* II.xxx.5; II.xxxi.3, 6–10).
140 Locke 1975, pp. 372–4, 562, 564 (*Ess.* II.xxx; IV.iv.1, 5).
141 Locke 1975, p. 417 (*Ess.* III.iii.15).
142 Locke 1975, p. 415 (*Ess.* III.iii.12).
143 Locke 1975, pp. 411–12 (*Ess.* III.iii.18).
144 Locke 1975, p. 442 (*Ess.* III.vi.6).
145 Locke 1975, pp. 417–19 (*Ess.* III.iii.15–18).
146 Locke 1975, pp. 609–17 (*Ess.* VI.viii).
147 Locke 1975, pp. 548–52, 565 (*Ess.* III.iii.18–20; IV.iv.6–7).
148 Locke 1975, pp. 638–9 (*Ess.* IV.xi.14).
149 E.g., Locke 1975, pp. 555–7 (*Ess.* IV.iii.25–6).
150 Locke 1975, p. 415 (*Ess.* III.iii.12).
151 E.g., Locke 1975, pp. 416, 429, 453–6 (*Ess.* III.iii.14; III.v.3; III.vi.26–28).
152 E.g., Locke 1975, pp. 459–60, 457–8, 415–16 (*Ess.* III.vi.32; also 30; and III.iii.13).
153 Locke 1975, pp. 417–18, 569–71 (*Ess.* III.iii.17; also IV.iv.13–16).
154 Locke 1975, pp. 448–9 (*Ess.* III.vi.14–19).
155 On Locke's position regarding a natural classification of sensible material things, compare Ayers 1991, vol. 2, pp. 65–77 and Bolton 1992.

9

INDIVIDUATION

UDO THIEL

Seventeenth-century philosophers discussed several related questions under the heading 'individuation', although they did not always distinguish clearly between them.[1] Four of these questions in particular will be considered in this chapter. First, there is the metaphysical question about what it is that makes an individual the individual it is and distinguishes it from all other individuals of the same kind; this is the question of a 'principle of individuation', of an intrinsic cause of individuality in the things themselves. Second, there is the epistemological question of how we *know* individuals and their distinctness from one another; this question concerns the basis on which we pick out individuals and distinguish between them. The third question concerns identity through time, the conditions of an individual's *remaining* the same over time even though that individual may have undergone some change. The fourth question arises from the distinction between the metaphysical problem of what *constitutes* the identity of a being and the epistemological problem concerning our criteria for making a *judgement* about a being's identity at different points in time. The question of individuation (what brings about individuality at any one time) and the question of identity (what constitutes sameness at different points in time) were often discussed in connexion with each other; sometimes the emphasis was on individuation, and at other times it was on identity through time and partial change.

Problems of individuation and identity had been discussed extensively long before the seventeenth century. Hence, the search for a *principle of individuation* was a standard topic in mediaeval philosophy. And the mediaeval disputes about the principle of individuation formed a large part of the background to seventeenth-century discussions of the issue. Nevertheless, many of those philosophers (roughly from the middle of the century onwards) who are still well known today neglected the issue of individuation and focused on identity over time instead (e.g., Hobbes,

The collection of essays in Barber and Gracia 1994 was published after I had completed this chapter. I am grateful to Michael Ayers and Daniel Garber for a number of helpful comments on an earlier version of this chapter. I thank Christian Jessen (Göttingen) for help in obtaining material that was hard to come by.

Boyle, Locke). Also, as will become clear later in the chapter, there was in this context a marked shift away from a primarily ontological to a more subjective treatment of the topic: our *concepts* of those things whose identity is in question came to be regarded as crucial for dealing with problems of individuation and identity.

I. BACKGROUND

The mediaeval disputes over the principle of individuation can be traced to ancient Greek philosophy, especially to Aristotle. It was Boethius, however, who introduced the problem into metaphysical disputes, in the debate over the trinity. Although Boethius himself does not deal with the problem in a systematic way, his various remarks on issues that belong to the topic proved to be immensely influential in subsequent discussions.[2] Individuation presented itself as a problem to those philosophers who adopted a realist position on the ontological status of universals. For 'Platonic' or extreme realists, universals (essences, forms) have reality independently of individual beings; in fact, it is claimed that *only* universals have reality, strictly speaking. On this view, individuals belong to the realm of mere appearance; and their individuality is constituted by collections of accidents. Among the early mediaeval philosophers who adopted this position was John Eriugena.[3] Of more importance in the present context are the moderate or 'Aristotelian' realists. According to their version of realism, universals have no independent reality; they are real only in so far as they are in individual beings. For these realists (e.g., St. Thomas), each particular natural being partakes in a general (substantial or accidental) 'form' or essence, by which it is the *kind* of thing it is. Since this essence is something that each particular being shares with all other members of the same kind, the question arises, what constitutes or accounts for the individuality of each individual of a given kind?

The disputes about individuality were not purely philosophically motivated. Both in mediaeval and in seventeenth-century philosophy, problems of individuation and identity were rarely discussed in isolation from theological issues. Quite often, in both periods, the issue of individuation was explored in the course of an explanation of the doctrine of the trinity. Indeed, as just mentioned, early mediaeval discussions of individuation arose out of the trinitarian debate: If there is one God, how can there be three divine persons, Father, Son, and Holy Spirit? How can the unity of God be reconciled with the triad of divine persons? This question led to an examination of the distinction between the common (divine) *nature* and the individual (divine) *person*. In the seventeenth century, too, many theologians and philosophers inquired into concepts such as individuality, substance, person, and so on merely as a preliminary to their explanation of the unity of three persons in God (see the discussion in Chapter 26).

Other theological issues which gave rise to disputes over identity were the doctrines of transubstantiation in the Eucharist, the resurrection of the body, and the immortality of the soul. The idea of individuality, especially that of individual immortality, is central in Christian thinking. Here, Aristotelian realism with its insistence that forms exist only in individuals is clearly more compatible with Christian thinking than the extreme Platonic form of realism. Nevertheless, some versions of Aristotelian realism also clashed with the Christian idea of individual immortality. The doctrine of Averroes (1126–98) and his followers in the thirteenth century (e.g., Siger of Brabant) most sharply contrasts with Christianity in this respect. According to them, there is only one universal spirit in which all human souls inhere, and there is no individual immortality: after death human souls become part of the one universal and eternal spirit.[4] This doctrine was still debated in the seventeenth century. Leibniz, for example, attacked Averroes (as well as those seventeenth-century theories which he thought led in the same direction, like that of Spinoza), and he made it plain that he did so in the interest of the Christian idea of individual immortality.

The best-known and, perhaps, most influential mediaeval attempts to explain individuation within the realist framework were those of Aquinas, on the one hand, and Duns Scotus and his followers, on the other. With respect to his two intrinsic causes of being, form and matter, Aristotle had indicated that, whereas the form makes a thing a member of a certain kind, it is matter that brings about individuality and makes a being distinct from others of the same kind: 'All things which are many in number have matter; for many individuals have one and the same intelligible structure, for example, man, whereas Socrates is one.'[5] Aquinas agreed that in composite beings, such as human beings, matter individuates; but he modified Aristotle's theory in arguing that it is not matter as such, but *designated* matter ('materia signata') which individuates. And by 'designated matter' he meant 'that which is considered under determined dimensions. This kind of matter is not part of the definition of man as man, but it would enter into the definition of Socrates if Socrates could be defined.'[6] Matter as 'materia communis' is common to all material things of a kind; it is 'undesignated matter'. The essence of man, for example, which is common to all human beings, includes undesignated matter: 'The definition of man, on the contrary, does include undesignated matter. In this definition we do not put this particular bone and this particular flesh, but bone and flesh absolutely, which are the undesignated matter of man.'[7] Part of this theory of individuation is that, with respect to pure spirits (angels) whose 'definition' does not include matter at all, there is no plurality of beings within a species: each spirit constitutes a separate kind. Angels differ from one another specifically as well as numerically: there are as many kinds as there are individuals.

According to the Averroists, too, matter is the principle of individuation; and like Aquinas, they hold that spirits, since they are pure forms, are not multiplied within a kind. However, unlike Aquinas, they apply this account to the human soul as well, and they can therefore argue that after death, that is, after the separation from the body, there is no individuality of souls and, consequently, no individual immortality. Aquinas tried to defend the individuality of human souls after death without giving up the 'material' principle of individuation: the soul, he argued, retains its 'aptitude' to inform a particular body and thereby retains its individuality among other spiritual beings of the same kind. The complete human individual is restored at the resurrection of the body.

In contrast to both Aquinas and the Averroists, Duns Scotus and his followers looked for a principle of individuation that would allow a plurality of spirits within a kind. Scotus vehemently rejected Aquinas's theory of individuation. He argued that the human soul must be a complete individual being prior to, and independently of, its union with a body: 'In the order of nature the soul is an individual in virtue of its own singularity before its union with something material.'[8] For Scotus the issue of individuality has to be explained by analogy to that of the species: the species (e.g., man) is constituted by the addition of the *specific* difference to the genus (e.g., animal); and the individual (e.g., Socrates) in turn is constituted by the addition of the *individual* difference to the species. This individual difference ('thisness', 'haecceitas') is the principle of individuation: man becomes Socrates by the addition of the individual nature or character, the 'Socratity'. The individual nature constitutes the final difference of beings. In ascribing individuation to 'individual natures', the Scotists identify a positive reality or *formal* ground as the cause of individuality: in addition to the generic and specific forms there is a form of thisness which constitutes the ultimate reality of a being. And since, on this doctrine, matter is not required for individuation, there is no problem in allowing for a plurality of individual spirits within a kind.

Individuality was not a problem at all for any version of nominalism (or conceptualism). According to nominalist/conceptualist doctrine (most famously in Ockham, 1285–1349), there are no real universals, and that means there are no (accidental or substantial) forms or essences in reality, but only individuals; therefore there arises no question as to what brings about individuality within a kind: everything that exists is individual by itself and essentially. Universals are merely names or concepts to which nothing corresponds in reality. Consequently, nominalists regard the search for a *principle* of individuation as superfluous. In the context of the trinitarian debates, nominalists were often accused of 'tri-theism'; it was argued that since they denied real common natures, talk of three divine persons must have meant to them that there are three distinct gods.

The nominalist emphasis on individuality was taken up and developed in a different way by Renaissance philosophers, especially by Giordano Bruno (1548–1600). The notion of the individual was central in Bruno's pantheistic metaphysics, since every individual was considered a living microcosmos mirroring the universe as a whole. Thus, Bruno anticipated the notion of the individual substance as monad, which was developed systematically in the mature philosophy of Leibniz late in the seventeenth century (as explained later in the chapter).[9]

II. SUAREZ AND THE SEVENTEENTH-CENTURY DEBATE

The main *scholastic* theories concerning individuation were drawn together and discussed in detail towards the end of the sixteenth century in the fifth of Francisco Suárez's fifty-four *Disputationes metaphysicae* (1597). Suárez's two volumes proved to be immensely influential in seventeenth-century metaphysics, especially, but not only in the metaphysical textbooks of the scholastic university-philosophy of the time.[10] This was also true of Suárez's fifth metaphysical Disputatio, *De unitate individuali eiusque principio*. In particular, it provided a rich source of information on the various scholastic views and arguments concerning the issue.[11] Suárez was not, of course, the only scholastic influence on seventeenth-century discussions about individuation; and even where a treatment of the subject is very reminiscent of Suárez, it is not certain that he was the immediate source. Suárez is special, however, because his *Disputationes* was not *just* used as a source for traditional views; its impact spread beyond scholastic university-philosophy. Independent thinkers such as Leibniz and, to some extent, Descartes were also impressed by the Suárezian *solution* of the problems of individuation and identity.

Although Suárez gives some attention to identity over time, his main focus is the principle of individuation, and he keeps the two issues quite separate. After a careful analysis of the pros and cons of the traditional theories of individuation, Suárez offers his own solution to the problem. At the same time, he attempts to reconcile, at least in part, his theory with those other theories. Suárez occasionally points out the theological importance of his arguments, but on the whole his discussion of identity is much less theological in character than most of the better-known seventeenth-century contributions to the topic.

According to Suárez, the question about individuation 'concerns what basis or principle the individual difference has in reality'.[12] He thus distinguishes himself from the Scotists who equate the individual difference with the principle of individuation. Suárez agrees with the Scotists in so far as he concedes that substances are 'conceptually composed of the specific nature and the individual difference';[13] but, he argues, this individual difference must have a ground in reality, and that is what one should look for when inquiring into the principle of individuation. Suárez is also in agreement with the Scotists (and in disagreement with the Thomists) in that he looks for a principle of individuation which is the same 'in all created substances'.[14] Suárez wants to avoid having to postulate different principles of individuation for different kinds of beings; he searches for *one* principle that applies to spiritual as well as to material, to simple as well as to composite substances, and, indeed, to non-substances ('accidents').

For Suárez, *all* 'actual beings' are individual; and actual beings are things 'that exist or can exist immediately'. Suárez explains that he adds the qualification 'immediately' to rule out common natures which cannot exist apart from individual beings: 'I say "immediately" in order to exclude the common nature of beings, which, as such, cannot immediately exist or have actual entity, except in singular and individual entities. If these are removed, it is impossible for anything real to remain.'[15] The notion that things which *can* exist immediately have individuality precludes the theory according to which *existence* is the principle of individuation, a theory which Suárez ascribes to Henry of Ghent.[16] For Suárez, individuality does not depend on actual existence. Possible beings (i.e., beings which are conceived by God as alternatives to existent beings) must have individuality too. Yet Suárez argues that 'existence' can be interpreted to mean the 'actual entity of a thing'. And if interpreted in this way, the position which holds that existence is the principle of individuation does in fact coincide with Suárez's own view,[17] which is that in all created substances it is the very *entity* of a thing (i.e., those intrinsic principles which compose it), that make it the individual it is. A being does not require anything over and above its own entity for its individuation. That which individuates 'cannot be distinguished from the entity itself'. This is true of all substantial beings. Whatever it is that composes it is also that which brings about its individuality: 'There is no other principle of individuation in addition to its entity, or in addition to the intrinsic principles which constitute its entity.' A *simple* substance is individual 'from itself [*ex se*] and from its simple entity'.[18] *Composite* beings, such as men, horses, dogs, and so on, which consist of 'matter and form united',[19] are individuated neither by their form alone nor by their matter alone, but by 'this matter and this form united to each other'.[20] Since these component principles are simple, they are individuated by themselves. Thus, Suárez rejects any view according to which the principle of individuation is to be identified with only one of the two Aristotelian intrinsic causes of being (matter and form): he accepts neither the Thomists' position about 'designated matter' as the principle of individuation nor the theory that the substantial form alone constitutes individuality, a theory which Suárez ascribes to Averroes and Avicenna. Nevertheless, Suárez makes some concession to the latter view in holding that in composite substances the form is the *primary* principle of individuation. A particular composite being is what it is through its *form*. The form is primary, 'because this form is most proper to this individual, and because it is what completes numerically this whole substance'.[21] Suárez points out that the distinction between individual human beings, for example, is due to their distinct souls (form), rather than their distinct bodies (matter). In this context Suárez also considers the problem of identity *over time* and through partial change, and he indicates the importance of this problem to the theological issue of the resurrection. A man, for example, is rightly judged to be the same man when his body has changed, as long as his soul is still the same: 'For if to Peter's soul, for example, there should be united a body composed of matter distinct from the body which it first had, although the composite would not be in all its parts the same it was before, nevertheless, by a natural way of speaking [*simpliciter loquendo*], the individual is said to be the same by reason of the same soul.'[22]

The emphasis on form as the primary principle of individuation is, obviously, decidedly anti-Thomistic. Yet Suárez attempts to accommodate even the Thomists' view with his own theory: he does so by distinguishing carefully between the question of what the real intrinsic ground of individuation is in the things themselves and the problem of what the means or 'signs' are by which *we* distinguish things from one another.[23] According to Suárez, the former question is what is really at issue in debates over individuation. Nevertheless, *if* we ask about the '"principle of individuation" in relation to us',[24] that is, if we ask how *we know* the individuality and distinctness of things, then the Thomists' answer is correct: 'For, with respect to us, who derive our knowledge from material things, the distinction among individuals is often taken from matter or from the accidents which follow matter, such as quantity and other properties.'[25]

As indicated above, Suárez thought that his theory solved the problem of individuation concerning all types of beings; and these include not only various types of *substances,* but also *accidents,* that is, the non-essential qualities of substances. Other scholastics, too, had debated the question of what individuates non-substances; but whereas they argued that for accidental individuation there must be a principle different from that which is responsible for substantial individuation, Suárez deals with accidental individuation in the same way as he deals with substantial individuation. The theological motive behind the extensive discussions of the individuation of accidents is the doctrine of transubstantiation in the Eucharist; for this doctrine requires that qualities are real and remain the same through the change of substance. Mechanists such as Boyle later criticised the very notion of real accidents.[26] The most common position on the individuation of accidents (among realists) was that of Aquinas, who held that accidents are individuated by the subject, that is, by the substance in which they inhere.[27] Thus, according to Aquinas, there are different principles of individuation for substances, on the one hand, and for accidents, on the other. Substances are individuated by 'designated matter', accidents are individuated through the substance to which they belong.[28] Suárez discusses the Thomist theory of the individuation of accidents before presenting arguments for his own answer to the problem. According to Suárez, the main argument used to support the Thomist view is this: since 'an accident has all its being in relation to the subject . . . it should have individuation from the subject, for each thing should be individuated by the same principles by which it has being.'[29] On this view, since the accident is dependent for its being on the substance, the subject or substance must also be the individuating principle of the accident. The underlying assumption is, that which gives being is also that which individuates.

Now, Suárez argues explicitly against Aquinas's position and holds that 'the subject cannot be the principle individuating accidents.' This is his main argument: 'The subject cannot be said to be the intrinsic principle of the individuation of an accident, as intrinsically and essentially [*per se*] composing an accident, because we are not now discussing the composite of subject and accident, but the accidental form itself, which is certainly not intrinsically composed of the subject itself; nor is the subject its intrinsic principle of individuation in this way.'[30] For Suárez, only intrinsic constituents (matter and form) are candidates for the principle of individuation of any being. And since accidents, like substances, are intrinsically constituted by matter and (accidental) form, their individuation must be due to either of those or to both. The relation of the accident to a particular subject is not, as Aquinas seems to believe, part of its intrinsic nature; and, therefore, its relation to a subject cannot individuate the accident. Thus, Suárez argues, the claim that an individual accident has a 'natural coadaptability and relation to this subject alone is said without basis'. For 'the very same [accident] is apt of itself to inform any subject capable of such an accident.'[31] It may be true that the subject is responsible for the being of the accident; yet, that 'proves only that an accident has its individuation *in relation* to the subject and that it naturally depends from it, not, however, that the individuation of the subject is the intrinsic principle of individuation of the accident'.[32]

A further argument against St. Thomas's view on the individuation of accidents is derived from taking into account real *relations,* namely, those accidents which 'do not stand in the subject, but refer to it or lead to another in some way, as is [the case with] relations, acts, habits and similar [ones]'.[33] For here the following question arises: If the subject individuates the relation, which subject or which of the 'terms' of the relation is the individuating principle? Actions, for example, are relational: they concern the agent and what is acted upon. It is certainly not self-evident that the agent should be the individuating principle. As Suárez says, 'Why may not these accidents be said to be rather individuated by the final terms to which they naturally refer, especially since they take their essential or specific natures [*rationes*] from them and according to their common natures?'[34]

Suárez concludes that since the subject cannot be the individuating principle of accidents, there remains only one alternative; and this is that accidents are individuated by their own intrinsic constituents (matter and accidental form), that is, through their own entity. In contrast to St. Thomas, Suárez emphasises the similarity between the issue of individuation of substances and of accidents. As for substances, there is for accidents 'an individual difference, which is proper to each and contracts the species to the being of a particular individual'. So, as with substances, the question concerning the principle of individuation is 'what the physical foundation and principle of this difference is'.[35] And for Suárez, accidents, like substances, are individuated through their *entity:* 'Each accidental form is physically individuated by itself, [in so far] as it is a particular entity in act or in aptitude, and . . . it does not have any other intrinsic principle of individuation in addition to its entity.'[36] If we consider the principle of individuation of accidents 'with respect to being and to the proper constitution of a thing in itself', the true position is 'that accidents do not have their individuation and numerical distinction from the subject, but from their proper entities'.[37]

Towards the end of his disputation on individuation, Suárez addresses a question which was much discussed by scholastic philosophers, namely, whether accidents which differ only numerically can be present in the same subject. Can there be two numerically distinct accidents of the same kind in one substance? For example, can there be two instances of heat (of the same degree) or two instances of the same whiteness in Socrates? Suárez considers whether they can inhere in the same subject *simultaneously* and whether they can be in the same subject *successively.* St. Thomas's position clearly implies that two accidents which differ only numerically can *not* inhere in one and the same subject at the same time: since Socrates' whiteness is said to be the individual whiteness that it is through Socrates, the subject, a second, numerically distinct whiteness could not be in Socrates; for how could it be numerically distinct from the first, given that its subject (and that is, on this view, its individuating principle) is the same? If the subject individuates the accidents which inhere in it, then there cannot be two only numerically distinct accidents in the same subject. Suárez, however, in rejecting St. Thomas's view on the individuation of accidents, does not have to adopt this position. Since accidents are individuated through their own entity, and not through their subject, the possibility of two only numerically distinct whitenesses in Socrates cannot be ruled out. Suárez's position is that some accidents ('respective' accidents), such as whiteness and heat, can be multiplied within the same subject, whereas others ('absolute accidents') cannot: accidents 'can be multiplied when they are related to diverse terms or (when) they are ordered to diverse functions, owing to the dissimilarities they have to each other'.[38] These accidents are called 'respective' accidents, because they can relate to different aspects of the same subject at the same time; and that means there can be more than one instance of them in one subject. Thus, heat of a certain temperature can have two numerically different instances in (two parts of) a body. Accidents which cannot be multiplied within the same subject are, for example, 'the powers or connatural faculties which emanate from form in each thing'.[39] Natural faculties belong to the essence of the subject and, therefore, there cannot be two instances of the same faculty in one subject (e.g., I cannot have two capacities to acquire knowledge). So, at least *some,* namely 'respective', accidents can be 'multiplied in the same subject' at the same time. And since it is possible that two only numerically distinct accidents can inhere in the same subject *simultaneously,* Suárez argues that (*a fortiori*) it must also be possible for such accidents to inhere in the same subject *successively.*[40]

For Suárez, then, *all* 'actual beings' are individual by themselves, that is, by their entities. There has been some controversy about the relationship of Suárez's position to earlier scholastic doctrines. While scholars agree that Suárez's theory (in so far as it is not mainly concerned with our *knowledge* of individuality) is anti-Thomistic, there is less agreement about Suárez's relationship to Scotus and the nominalists or conceptualists. Some have claimed that Suárez rejects Scotus's theory because he misinterprets it and that, in truth, Suárez's theory is essentially the same as Scotist doctrine.[41] Inasmuch as Suárez emphasises that all individuals are individuals by themselves and require no principle for their individuation over and above those principles which constitute their respective entities, this 'Scotist' interpretation of Suárez is unconvincing. Rather, Suárez's position seems to be very close to the nominalist/conceptualist position on individuation; yet, unlike the nominalists, Suárez does not regard the search for a principle of individuation as superfluous. We saw that, with respect to composite substances, Suárez even speaks of the form as the *primary* principle of individuation. Thus, for Suárez, but not for the nominalists, 'individuation' is not a meaningless term. Nevertheless, there is some consensus in recent scholarship that Suárez's position is much closer to nominalism or conceptualism than it is to either Thomism or Scotism.[42]

Realism about universals was widespread among seventeenth-century metaphysicians, especially in Germany.[43] Consequently, the principle of individuation continued to be discussed at the universities and in the scholastic textbooks, and there are lengthy entries on the topic in the philosophical dictionaries of the time.[44] As in Suárez's *Disputationes metaphysicae,* the seventeenth-century metaphysical textbooks generally discuss the issue of individuation in their first part, which deals with the general properties of being. And here sometimes the issue is examined under the general title of 'unum', where the unity of the *individual* is distinguished from the unity of the universal; other times it is discussed in special chapters on singularity and universality.[45] There were representatives of most of the traditional answers to the problem of individuation. In his considerably successful *Scientiae metaphysicae compendiosum systema,* Bartholomaeus Keckermann, for instance, defends the view that *existence* individuates. As mentioned earlier, Suárez discusses this theory and ascribes it to Henry of Ghent. For Keckermann, to say that existence individuates is to say that space and time are the principle of individuation.[46] Other metaphysicians, such as Christoph Scheibler, Johannes Scharf, and Franco Burgersdijck, adopt Suárez's position. In his *Institutiones metaphysicae,* Burgersdijck argues against the doctrines of individuation of both Scotus and Aquinas; his own view is that the individual essence (Suárez's 'entity') is the principle of individuation.[47] Also, Leibniz's teachers Daniel Stahl and Jakob Thomasius identify the unity of 'this form and this matter' as the principle of individuation and thus adopt a Suárezian position on the issue.[48]

Nominalism (the view that everything that exists is singular) seems to have been more popular in England.[49] At least, all of the seventeenth-century English philosophers who are still well known today – Bacon, Hobbes, Locke – adopted some form of nominalism,[50] so individuation did not present itself as a problem to them. Hobbes and Locke did address the issue, but, as explained later in the chapter, they focused on identity *over time,* rather than on the problem of individuation. In France, too, major thinkers such as Pierre Gassendi and Antoine Arnauld were committed to the nominalist position and did not inquire into the problem of individuation in any detail.[51] Although, as is well known, the individual self has a central place in Descartes's metaphysics, Descartes did not enter into the debate about the principle of individuation either.

III. DESCARTES AND REACTIONS TO DESCARTES

Descartes assumes that there is a plurality of individual human *souls*. Each individual human self, he states, has an immediate awareness of its own thinking and thus its own existence. And on the basis of this self-awareness everybody is able to deduce the nature or essence of his or her own self, namely, that it is an unextended, indivisible (and complete) 'pure substance', capable of existing independently of matter: an immaterial soul. Descartes says, 'From the mere fact that each of us understands himself to be a thinking thing and is capable, in thought, of excluding from himself every other substance, whether thinking or extended, it is certain that each of us, regarded in this way, is really distinct from every other thinking substance and from every corporeal substance.'[52] This notion of the soul as an individual, independent, immaterial, and complete substance distinguishes Descartes's theory from the scholastic doctrine according to which the soul is the *form* of man.[53] However, the passage just quoted does not give an account of the individuality of the soul or mental substance itself; it merely attempts to account for the *certainty* we may achieve about our selves as independent thinking individual substances, a certainty that is derived from our self-awareness. Descartes does not say that this self-awareness *is* the individuating principle of the soul. And since he claims that the soul is an individual substance independently of any relation it may have to a body, he cannot (and does not) appeal to the body or to matter as the individuating principle of the soul. Thus, he rejects, if only implicitly, the Thomistic account of individuation in terms of 'designated matter'. Now, what *does* individuate immaterial souls, according to Descartes? Unfortunately, Descartes does not explicitly deal with this problem. He merely assumes the plurality of individual human souls; and he does not seem to think that this plurality requires any special explanation over and above the appeal to self-awareness. Descartes believes that the assurance we have of our individual existence through self-awareness makes the search for an individuating principle superfluous. Yet even if we follow Descartes in believing that we can arrive at *knowledge* of ourselves as individual thinking substances on the basis of self-awareness, we would still not have an account of what *makes* us individual thinking *substances*. In short, Descartes fails to explain how immaterial substances can be individuated and distinguished from one another.[54]

However, once we have accepted Descartes's notion that the soul is an individual, immaterial substance, it is plain that there arises no problem concerning its identity *over time:* even though its thoughts (i.e., its 'accidents') change, it always remains the self-same substance. Descartes addresses the issue of the human soul's identity over time only occasionally; when he does, it is in the context of pointing out the soul's natural immortality:

> The human mind is not made up of any accidents . . . , but is a pure substance. For even if all the accidents of the mind change, so that it has different objects of the understanding and different desires and sensations, it does not on that account become a different mind. . . . And it follows from this that . . . the mind (or the soul of man, for I make no distinction between them) is immortal by its very nature.[55]

Descartes's account of bodies and individual material substances is more complex than his account of the individuality and identity of the mind. Thus, in one strain of Descartes's thought, the material world (in contrast to the mental world) is not understood to be primarily a plurality of individual substances at all: body or matter, 'considered in general' is just *one* universal substance.[56] The essence of this one universal substance is extension; matter is one continuous *res extensa:* 'The matter existing in the entire universe is thus one and the same, and it is always recognised as matter simply in virtue of its being extended.'[57] According to this strain, then, the term 'corporeal substance' does not refer to a particular body, but to extension in general, to a universally extended substance or to the totality of matter. And unlike minds, matter is divisible, changeable, and modifiable; yet, 'taken in the general sense . . . it too never perishes'. As a whole, matter, too, is naturally 'incorruptible and cannot ever cease to exist unless [it is] reduced to nothingness by God's denying his concurrence to [it]'.[58] Following this strain, *particular* bodies are not substances in the strict sense; they are not entities capable of independent existence. Rather, they are merely determinate portions of the one universal substance understood as extension. Their individuality is simply a matter of their local extension.

Yet there is another strain in Descartes, according to which there is a plurality of finite material substances. There are passages, especially in the *Principia,* in which he suggests that individual quantities of matter are to be understood as individual material *substances.* Thus, in *Princ.* I 60, Descartes indicates that there is a 'real distinction' between individual quantities of matter; that is to say, they are distinct *substances:* 'Even though we may not yet know for certain that any extended or corporeal substance exists in reality, the mere fact that we have an idea of such a substance enables us to be certain that it is capable of existing. And we can also be certain that, if it exists, each and every part of it, as delimited by us in our thought, is really distinct from the other parts of the same substance.'[59] And for Descartes to say that every portion of matter may be a separate substance, is to say that every portion of matter may be capable of independent existence. Spinoza noted later that this notion of a real distinction between parts of matter is not consistent with Descartes's view about the plenum and his denial of empty space: since all parts of matter are so united that there can be no vacuum, it follows that there can be no real distinction between parts of matter.[60]

Now, for the purpose of his *physics* Descartes requires a different conception of an individual body. While every division of matter we may make in thought constitutes a separate substance, 'if the division into parts occurs simply in our thought, there is no resulting change'. Descartes tells us that 'any variation in matter or diversity in its many forms depends on *motion*.'[61] He argues that it is their respective *motion* and *rest* that distinguishes physical bodies from one another. An individual body is that amount of matter which moves together at a given time: 'By "one body" or "one piece of matter" I mean whatever is transferred at a given time, even though this may in fact consist of many parts which have different motions relative to each other.'[62] There are a number of problems with this third account of the individuation of physical bodies. Most important, Descartes's own *definition* of motion as 'the transfer of one piece of matter, or one body, from the vicinity of the other bodies, . . . to the vicinity of other bodies'[63] *presupposes* the individuation of bodies, so the account of the individuation of bodies in terms of motion and rest appears to be circular. Furthermore, as Leibniz pointed out, if there is a plenum and if the essence of body is extension alone and motion 'is merely the successive existence of the thing moved in different places', then motion and rest will not distinguish any body from another: 'There could be absolutely no variation in bodies and . . . everything would always remain the same.'[64]

When Descartes comes to discuss the identity of complex bodies *over time*, he gives two accounts, depending on a distinction between two kinds of complex body. If by 'body' we mean merely an individual quantity of matter, just a 'determinate part of matter, a part of the quantity of which the universe is composed',[65] then the identity of a body *over time* depends on the sameness of that quantity of matter: an individual body is no longer numerically the same individual as soon as even 'the smallest amount of that quantity' which constitutes the individual is removed.[66] Unlike both individual souls and matter in general, particular bodies, understood as individual quantities of matter, *are* perishable as the individual entities they are. In one passage Descartes also applies this notion of the individual to the *human* body; here, he even suggests that 'a human body loses its identity merely as a result of a change in the shape of some of its parts.' And he concludes that a human body 'can very easily perish'.[67]

However, Descartes argues elsewhere that there is a sense in which *human bodies* differ from other kinds of bodies in that they are something more unitary and do remain identical through change of size and shape. The context of this argument is a discussion of the Catholic doctrine of transubstantiation in the Eucharist.[68] As contemporary critics (Arnauld and Mesland) had pointed out to Descartes, his philosophy of matter appears to be inconsistent with that doctrine. One question that was raised had to do with Descartes's account of the individual body in terms of its local extension: If the individual body is the same as its local extension, how then can it be that in the Eucharist Christ's body is present within the dimension of the bread, rather than with its *own* extension which, on Descartes's theory, makes it the particular body it is? In response to this question, Descartes introduces a distinction between two types of body. He distinguishes between human and non-human bodies: the individuality of *non*-human bodies is simply their being determinate portions of universal extension; 'and if any particle of the matter were changed, we would at once think that the body was no longer quite the same, no longer *numerically the same*'.[69] However, Descartes points out that a *human* body is not just an isolated portion of general matter, but a body joined to a particular soul. And the soul is said to function as the body's principle of unity: Descartes argues that it is through its union with a soul that a human body remains the same through change. The soul is individual by itself and continues to be numerically the same 'pure substance'; therefore, even though there is not 'any particle of our bodies which remains *numerically* the same for a single moment, . . . our body, *qua* human body, remains always *numerically* the same so long as it is united with the same soul'. Descartes thinks this explains why we are justified in saying that 'we have the same bodies as we had in our infancy, although their quantity has much increased, and . . . there is no longer in them any part of the matter which then belonged to them, and even though they no longer have the same shape.'[70] No matter how much its shape and size have changed over time, it is still the same human body as long as it is united to the same individual soul. Both the individuation and the identity over time of the body *qua* human body are secured through its union to an individual soul. Considered independently of a soul, the body does not remain the same from one moment to the next. Descartes applies this theory to the Eucharist. The bread becomes Christ's body, even though it does not have the extension of Christ's body, by being unified with his soul: 'The miracle of transubstantiation which takes place in the Blessed Sacrament consists in nothing but the fact that the particles of bread and wine . . . are informed by his soul simply by the power of the words of consecration.'[71]

Even though this account seemed to him to be 'quite elegant',[72] Descartes anticipated that to orthodox theologians 'this explanation will be shocking at first.'[73] Descartes obviously realised that it practically *denies* the real presence of Christ's body in the sacrament. He tried to accommodate his own explanation to the traditional accounts by making use of the traditional scholastic terminology of form and matter, when he said, for example, that human bodies 'are numerically the same only because they are *informed* by the same soul'.[74] And, indeed, Descartes's account of the individuation of a human body reminds us very much of Suárez's account. For Suárez, too, the identity of a human body is preserved by the identity of the soul, the soul being the form and primary principle of individuation in humans. It is important to note, however, that despite the similar terminology in this context, Descartes's notion of the soul is quite different from that of the scholastics. For Descartes the soul is not the form of man, but a complete, individual, and independent substance. Also, unlike Suárez, Descartes does not search for a principle of individuation that applies to all beings. In Descartes, no account of individuation appeals to the Suárezian notion of 'entity'. To sum up, there is no unitary account of individuation in Descartes. There are several strains in his thought concerning individuality in the material world. And although the individuality and identity of the human body are explained as dependent on the identity of the human soul, Descartes fails to account for the individuality of the soul itself.

The view that the identity of the *human* body depends on its being united to the same soul was a common one throughout the seventeenth century; the vocabulary in which it was usually presented indicates that in most cases it derived from the scholastic tradition itself rather than from Descartes. Sir Kenelm Digby, for example, makes the same point as Descartes, but with a much more pronounced scholastic flavour. The context of Digby's discussion is the problem of the resurrection, which is why he concentrates on identity *over time*. According to Digby, it is true in general that 'that which giveth the numerical individuation to a *Body,* is the substantial forme. As long as that remaineth the same, though the matter bee in a continuall flux and motion, yet the thing is still the same.'[75] Consequently, in the case of human beings where the soul is the form, the body remains identical no matter how much it has changed, as long as it has 'the same distinguisher and individuator; to wit, the same forme, or *Soule*'.[76] This view was restated frequently and in various forms, depending on the concept of soul that was employed. As late as 1697 John Sergeant, who saw himself as defending the

'Peripatetick School', argued, against John Locke's theory of identity, that the soul preserves the identity of the human body.[77] This view is present in its Cartesian version in Robert Boyle. Boyle criticised scholastic talk of 'substantial forms' vehemently, and he adopted the Cartesian distinction between soul and body. As to the identity of an individual man, he argued, like Descartes, that 'the same soul being united to a portion of duly organised matter is said to constitute the same man, notwithstanding the vast differences of bigness that there may be at several times between the portions of matter whereto the human soul is united.'[78]

Philosophers who worked more closely within the Cartesian framework developed the problem of individuality and identity in a different way and in various forms. Thus, Spinoza rejected Descartes's notion of a plurality of immaterial thinking substances, and applied the Cartesian idea of matter as one single universal substance to the whole universe: instead of Descartes's three kinds of substance (God, souls, matter), there is only one substance of one nature, namely, God. The notion that there is, strictly speaking, only one substance is present in Descartes's own theory, since he says that the created substances, *res cogitans* et *res extensa,* are dependent beings: they are dependent on God. However, Descartes still speaks of mind and body as substances: they are substances in the restricted sense that they are dependent on no other being except God.[79] Spinoza follows through the idea of the oneness of substance. In the first part of his *Ethica* he attempts to show by way of *a priori* reasoning why there cannot be more than one substance.[80] Substance is defined as that which 'is in itself and is conceived through itself' and has attributes which constitute its nature.[81] Spinoza argues that there cannot be two or more *substances* of the same nature or attribute, because if there were, one could not be 'conceived to be distinguished from another'. In other words, if we assumed that there are two or more substances of the same nature, then we could not account for their individuation as distinct substances. Their modes or 'affections' cannot fulfil this function, because substance is said to be 'prior in nature to its affections';[82] and their nature is, by hypothesis, the same. Now, since substance is by definition that which 'is in itself', it cannot be produced by anything else – it must be its own cause, that is, *causa sui*;[83] and to say that it is 'the cause of itself' is to say that 'its essence necessarily involves existence, *or* it pertains to its nature to exist.'[84] From this idea that *existence* belongs to the *essence* of a substance, the argument for only one substance proceeds as follows. The definition of a being concerns only its nature or essence: 'No definition involves or expresses any certain number of individuals since it expresses nothing other than the nature of the thing defined. E.g., the definition of the triangle expresses nothing but the simple nature of the triangle, but not any certain number of triangles.' That is to say, the existence of a plurality of triangles cannot be derived from the definition of the nature of a triangle, but requires an additional, external cause: 'Whatever is of such a nature that there can be many individuals [of that nature] must, to exist, have an external cause to exist.' But this does *not* apply to substance, since it has been argued that existence is part of its essence. And so, 'since it pertains to the nature of a substance to exist . . . its definition must involve necessary existence, and consequently its existence must be inferred from its definition alone. But from its definition (as we have shown . . .) the existence of a number of substances cannot follow.'[85] Thus, there is only one substance. This substance is necessarily infinite;[86] it cannot be finite, for otherwise there would have to be other finite substances from which it is distinguished. This one substance is God, 'consisting of an infinity of attributes'.[87]

According to Spinoza, everything that exists is *in* God. This does not mean that for Spinoza there are no individuals except for God. However, individual beings ('things') are not independent substances, but merely 'modes' (i.e., limitations) of the divine attributes: 'Particular things are nothing but affections of God's attributes, *or* modes by which God's attributes are expressed in a certain and determinate way.'[88] Every individual is constituted by a limitation or negation of the divine attributes. In other words, with the exception of the divine substance, Spinoza's account of individuality concerns non-substances only. Thus, the human self is understood by Spinoza as one individual being consisting of mind and body. However, his account of this unity is very different from that of Descartes (and from that of the scholastics): thought and extension do not constitute two kinds of substance as they do in Descartes, they are just two of an infinite number of divine attributes. And so Spinoza explains the union of mind and body in terms of modes of the divine attributes of thought and extension, not as a substantial union: 'The Mind and the Body, are one and the same Individual, which is conceived now under the attribute of Thought, now under the attribute of Extension.'[89]

As to the individuation of bodies, it follows from Spinoza's metaphysics that bodies do not differ with respect to their substance: they have this in common that they 'involve the concept of one and the same attribute', namely, the divine attribute of extension.[90] Now, like Descartes, Spinoza assumes that extension essentially entails mobility. He states that all bodies are either in motion or rest. And he argues that the *individuation* of bodies can be explained in these terms, another idea he takes up from Descartes: 'Bodies are distinguished from one another by reason of motion and rest, speed and slowness, and not by reason of substance.'[91] Yet, just as Descartes does not say that extension as such individuates bodies, since extension in general is what all bodies have in common, so Spinoza does not say that motion and rest as such individuate bodies, for all bodies have this *in common* that they are essentially in a state of motion or rest. Spinoza holds that it is the particular *proportion* of motion and rest that individuates a body. In his early *Korte Verhandeling* (*Short Treatise on God, Man, and His Well Being*) Spinoza states this explicitly: 'There is no other mode in extension than motion and rest, and . . . each particular corporeal thing is nothing but a certain proportion of motion and rest, so much so that if there were nothing in extension except motion alone, or nothing except rest alone, there could not be, or be indicated, in the whole of extension, any particular thing.'[92] Now, according to Spinoza, each particular body is determined to its proportion of motion or rest by another body, and this body in turn 'has also been determined to motion or rest by another, and that again by another, and so on, to infinity'.[93] In other words, the individuality of each body is determined by its causal *relations* to other bodies. Unlike the scholastics, Spinoza does not account for individuation in terms of intrinsic constituents of a being, considered in isolation from other beings. On his theory, rather, the individuality of all 'things' is constituted by their inter-relatedness in the one divine substance.

With respect to composite bodies (e.g., the human body) there is an additional cause for their individuation. While the relation to other bodies remains relevant, the relationship between those bodies which make up the composite body itself is of special importance here: a composite body 'is distinguished from the others by this union of bodies', that is, by the particular relationship that holds between its component parts.[94] This notion enables Spinoza to explain what constitutes the identity of composite bodies *over time* and through the change of their parts. Since it is the relationship among its parts, rather than the parts themselves, which individuates a composite body, the numerical identity of the components is not required for the identity of the composite body. The nature of the composite can be retained by different parts, as long as they (fulfil the same function and) stand in the same relation to one another as did the previous ones: 'If the parts composing an Individual become greater or less, but in such a proportion that they all keep the same ratio of motion and rest to each other as before, then the Individual will likewise retain its nature, as before, without any change of form.'[95]

Spinoza realised that his views on the individuation of body require further clarification and argument. He points out that the topic is merely a digression, or rather a preliminary to what follows in the argument of the *Ethica,* and that it is not central to his main interest in that work.[96] However, Spinoza's account of the individuality of minds and human beings or persons has the same general features as does his theory of the individuation of bodies: it is an account of individuals as non-substantial entities, whose individuality depends on their relations to other individuals and on the relations between their component parts.[97]

Unlike Spinoza, Gerauld de Cordemoy pursues Descartes's idea of the plurality and individuality of mental substances, and he applies this idea to *matter* as well.[98] While Spinoza applies Descartes's notion of matter as one universal substance to the whole universe, Cordemoy *rejects* Descartes's identification of matter with extension in general. Cordemoy distinguishes between body or extended substance (*corps*) and matter as a whole (*matière*): matter consists of an 'assemblage' of individual bodies; that is, matter is not divisible indefinitely. Rather, the individual bodies or substances which make up matter as a whole are themselves absolutely indivisible and impenetrable. The postulation of indivisible, solid components or atoms makes it possible, according to Cordemoy, to account for the individuality of composite beings such as animal bodies. Composite beings are understood as *aggregates* of bodies or substances; they are not themselves substances. Thus the human body is 'un amas de plusieurs substances';[99] that is, it consists of a collection of atoms. Only the atoms are, strictly speaking, substances. Cordemoy does not give any detailed account of the individuation of composite beings. Within his atomistic version of Cartesianism a *problem* of the individuation of bodies does not arise, and like most Cartesians he assumes, rather than argues for, the plurality and individuality of mental substances. It is plain that Spinoza and Cordemoy are at opposite poles concerning the question of individuality. Accordingly, Leibniz regarded Spinoza's theory as a version of Averroism, and he classed Cordemoy with the ancient atomist Lucretius.

Philosophers who worked within the Cartesian framework rarely made the problem of individuation and identity an object of inquiry in its own right. However, some Cartesians did consider the problem in some detail; and they made an important contribution to the issue in that they turned to a more subjective treatment of it, a treatment which anticipates that of Locke and some eighteenth-century views on identity. Thus, the Dutch philosopher Johannes Clauberg, who attempted to reconcile Cartesian ideas with a scholastic metaphysics of being in general, indicated that attributes such as identity and distinctness cannot be ascribed to objects independently of the mind which apprehends those objects.[100] Since Clauberg adopts the nominalist notion that everything which exists is singular, individuation is not a problem for him.[101] Identity and distinctness are discussed by Clauberg under the general heading of relation. And because he denies the reality of relations and argues that relations are *entia rationis* – that is, they consist in operations of the intellect, such as the acts of comparing and distinguishing[102] – he explains identity and distinctness, too, as *entia rationis.* Identity is a relation of an individual to itself at different points in time. For Clauberg this means that identity is based on the intellectual operations of comparing and judging. Numerical identity consists in this: that a perceived object is *judged* to be the same as a previously perceived object, and that we attach the same name to it.[103] Whether or not we judge a thing to be the same at different points in time, that is, whether or not we attach the same 'name' to it, depends on *our* definition of the thing, on our 'naming' it. If the object is perceived to have changed only in respects which, on our definition of it, are not essential, then we rightly judge it to be identical. On the basis of our definition we are able to judge men, plants, trees, and rivers to be identical at different points of time, even though they have changed in various respects. Thus, Clauberg concludes, the whole issue of identity and diversity pertains more to modes of thought and speech than to things as they are in themselves.[104] A position similar to that of Clauberg can be found in another Dutch Cartesian, Arnold Geulincx. In his posthumously published *Metaphysica vera et ad mentem peripateticam* (1691), he argues that, like all attributes of being, those of oneness (*unum*) and identity are not attributes which belong to things as they are in themselves (*res in se*); rather, the human intellect ascribes them to things as a result of a unifying or identifying act.[105] This idea was developed in England by Richard Burthogge, who was probably influenced by Geulincx when studying at the University of Leiden. For Burthogge, entity, substance, accident, whole, part, cause, effect, and so on 'do not really exist without the mind'; rather, they are 'notions' under which we consider things as they appear to us.[106] And so, individuality and distinctness of things are to be understood in relation to their qualities as they appear to us, 'these being the Characters by, and under which alone, we do perceive and know, and by consequence, can only distinguish them'.[107] However, Burthogge does not deny that there are 'things themselves' independently of our notions; for our notions 'have in things without us certain *grounds* or Foundations'.[108] Indeed, Burthogge even argues for the existence of a world-soul and of individual spirits. The latter are essentially united to matter; for all spirits, including angels (to which Burthogge refers as 'invisible animals') and human minds, are 'individuated by matter'.[109] Burthogge states explicitly the problem which arises from the Cartesian view that souls are individual immaterial substances independently of their union with a body: 'Were Spirits absolutely pure and simple, without any Concretion of Matter, there could be no distinction among them as to *Individuals*.'[110] However, when addressing scholastic disputes over the principle of individuation directly,

Burthogge does not refer to matter at all and simply states that 'they seem to me to come nearest to the Truth, who do affirm, that a singular or individual becomes so, not by any distinct Principle of individuation, but immediately and *per se,* and in that, that it is in being.'[111] This is consistent with the earlier insistence on matter as individuating spirits, since Burthogge's view is that spirits are only 'in being' once they are united to matter. To say that individuality belongs to beings 'immediately and *per se*' is, obviously, to adopt a nominalist position on the issue. Burthogge does not believe in the real existence of universals: 'Particular singular beings . . . are the only beings that compose the Universe, as members or parts of it. . . . Universals . . . are not of Mundane existence.'[112]

Thus, Burthogge's theory oscillates between an objectivist account of individuation of 'things themselves' and a subjectivist explication of individuality as a function of our distinguishing between them on the basis of perceived qualities. The subjective treatment of identity was developed more elaborately by nominalists who worked within the framework of the atomist picture of the world, as it was revived in the context of the developing experimental sciences.

IV. ATOMISM AND IDENTITY: HOBBES, BOYLE, LOCKE, AND SOME SCHOLASTIC REACTIONS

The proponents of the new 'corpuscular philosophy' aimed to explain all phenomena of nature wholly in terms of 'matter and the accidents of matter',[113] without reference to any metaphysical entities such as substantial forms. Their denial of real universal forms meant that *individuation* at least did not present itself as a genuine problem to them. Hobbes and Locke, for example, may differ in the way they explain universality, but they share the basic nominalist (or conceptualist) assumption that everything that exists is individual by itself and that a search for a principle of individuation is superfluous. And Robert Boyle, for example, clearly implies that no 'principle' over and above the particular corpuscular constitution is required to account for the individuality of bodies. To Boyle, an individual body is simply a 'distinct portion of matter which a number of [corpuscles] make up'.[114] Nevertheless, Hobbes and Locke do at least address the issue of individuality, if only briefly. In doing so they make use of the old theory according to which *existence* individuates. For Hobbes and Locke, to say an individual is individual by itself is to say that it is individual through its existence at a particular place and time: all things (namely, individuals) exist in space and time, and they are the individuals they are and distinct from all other individuals by their very position in absolute space and time. As Hobbes says, 'it is manifest that no two bodies are the *same*; for seeing they are two, they are in two places at the same time; as that, which is the *same,* is at the same time in one and the same place.'[115]

In his *Essay concerning Human Understanding,* Locke, too, thinks it is 'easy to discover' that the principle of individuation which 'is so much enquired after' is simply 'Existence it self'; for, existence 'determines a Being of any sort to a particular time and place incommunicable to two Beings of the same kind'.[116] This means that, in contrast to Suárez's view, for example, individuality cannot be prior to existence; furthermore, it means that individuality is not something that existent things may or may not have. For, to exist is to be at a certain place and time, and by that itself any being is 'that very thing, and not another, which at the same time exists in another place, how like and undistinguishable soever it may be in all other respects'.[117] Not everybody who holds that existence is the principle of individuation would have to be an atomist; but it is easy to see why an atomist such as Locke would adopt that position. The postulated atoms themselves are, of course, to be thought of as distinct individual beings. Now it is possible that two atoms are the same with respect to all of their properties, except for their position in space and time. Only their different existence in space and time can guarantee their distinctness and individuality. As Locke points out against John Sergeant, the Aristotelian critic of his *Essay,* 'What complexion of accidents besides those of place & perhaps time can distinguish two attoms perfectly solid & round & of the same diameter?'[118] According to Locke, to hold that 'Existence it self' is the principle of individuation also has the advantage that one avoids having to postulate different individuating principles for different kinds of being; for, whatever the principle of individuation is, it must be 'the same in all the several species of creatures'.[119] And existence not only individuates atoms as well as composite bodies, but 'a Being of any sort'.[120] Hobbes naturally restricted his brief discussion of individuation to bodies. But Locke explicitly appeals to a distinction between three general kinds of substances in this context: he distinguishes, just like Descartes, between God, finite spirits, and bodies.[121] And Locke stresses that one thing excludes all other things of the *same kind* from its position in space and time. A body is individual and distinct from all other bodies through its spatio-temporal existence; it excludes all other bodies from its place and time.[122] Yet a body does not exclude a spiritual substance from its place. (Here, Locke obviously assumes that spirits are spatial.) God is everywhere and eternal, but does not exclude finite substances, be they spiritual or material. In short, 'these three sorts of Substances, as we term them, do not exclude one another out of the same place.'[123] Locke thought that if we attend to the distinction between the three general kinds of things, there arises no real problem concerning individuation. It is 'Existence it self' that individuates in each case. And this principle is said to apply to non-substances as well. Locke does not adopt the traditional view that individuation of accidents depends on that of substances: 'All other things being but Modes or Relations ultimately terminated in Substances, the Identity and Diversity of each particular Existence of them too will be by the same way determined.' That is to say, their individuation is determined, like that of substances, by their existence.[124] Locke does not elaborate any further on the issue of the individuality of modes and relations in general.

So individuation was not a genuine problem to the atomists. What *did* present itself as a serious problem to atomists was how to determine what preserves the identity of bodies *over time* and through change. Obviously, the option of resorting to substantial forms was not open to them. And there seemed to be no simple straightforward answer to what could replace the rôle of substantial forms here, since 'matter and the accidents of matter' themselves continuously change. Robert Boyle, for one, saw clearly that 'it is no such easy way as at first it seems, to determine what is absolutely necessary and but sufficient to make a portion of matter, considered at different times or places, to be fit to be reputed the same body.'[125] Since individuality was regarded as unproblematic, the attention shifted totally to the problem of identity over time. Both Boyle and Hobbes interpret what they refer to as the problem of 'individuation' as being concerned only with what constitutes identity over time. Hobbes states the problem thus: 'But the same body may at different times be compared with itself. And from hence springs a great controversy among philosophers about the principle of individuation, namely, in what sense it may be conceived that a body is at one time the same, at another time not the same it was formerly. For example, whether a man grown old be the same man he was whilst he was young, or another man; or whether a city be in different ages the same, or another city.'[126] Connected with this shift of attention to the issue of identity over time was the move away from the attempt to determine what constitutes identity in the thing itself to a more subjective treatment of the problem: as substantial forms were denied, it did not seem possible to pick out any constituent in the things themselves that could in all cases be regarded as that which is essential for securing identity over time. It was recognised that their identity must depend on what *we* regard as their essential constituents; in other words, what becomes crucial now are *our* criteria for *judging* whether or not a body has remained the same through change. Scholastics such as Suárez, too, occasionally considered what the basis is for our identifying and distinguishing things. The point is not merely that philosophers like Hobbes and

Locke put more emphasis on this issue; rather, on their view, the very problem of
the identity of things over time can be answered only by reference to our concepts
or 'naming' of those things whose identity is in question: for we have no
knowledge of their internal *real* essence, that is, of an ontological basis of their
identity. Therefore, it was regarded as crucial for any treatment of identity-
questions to be *clear* about our concepts of those things whose identity is under
discussion; otherwise there would be hopeless confusion. According to Boyle,
problems concerning identity over time arise, because

almost every man that thinks conceives in his mind this or that quality, or relation, or
aggregate of qualities, to be that which is essential to such a body and proper to give it such
a denomination; whereby it comes to pass that, as one man chiefly respects this thing, and
another that, in a body that bears such a name, so one man may easily look upon a body as
the *same,* because it retains what he chiefly considered in it, whilst another thinks it to be
changed into a new body, because it has lost that which *he* thought was the denominating
quality or attribute.[127]

Boyle does not develop any further the point that our concepts determine
what is required for the identity of objects over time. But Hobbes had already
explained it at some length. Hobbes's discussion is totally couched in the traditional scholastic terminology of 'form', 'matter', and 'accidents'; nevertheless, he
states the new view clearly. Hobbes begins by reviewing three rival theories of
individuation: the theory according to which form individuates, the theory which
takes matter to be the principle of individuation, and the view that the unity of
the 'aggregate of all the accidents together' is what individuates bodies. Hobbes
indicates that each of these three answers to the problem has absurd consequences.
If we take matter to be the principle of individuation, it follows that 'he that sins,
and he that is punished, should not be the same man, by reason of the perpetual
flux and change of man's body.' If we assume that the form individuates, then 'two
bodies existing both at once, would be one and the same numerical body.'[128]
Hobbes illustrates his point by way of discussing the ancient 'Ship of Theseus'
case.[129] If a ship had been continuously repaired, 'in taking out the old planks and
putting in new' until no single plank of the original remained, we would still
speak of the same numerical ship, since it has retained its 'form' or structure. Now,
if someone put together the old, discarded planks in the same order, then we
would have a second ship which is also the same numerical ship as the previous
one. Thus, we would have two bodies existing at the same time which are
numerically identical. If we say that the aggregate of accidents individuates, then
'nothing would be the same it was; so that a man standing would not be the same

he was sitting.'[130] Having pointed out the problems with three rival theories of individuation, Hobbes goes on to argue that what is really essential for deciding questions about identity over time is whether *we* have *named* the object whose identity is in question with respect to its form or with respect to its matter. If it is clear under which aspect *we consider* the object, then the question of identity or diversity can easily be decided. For, 'material' and 'formal' respects of naming provide different criteria of identity respectively. If we name an individual, Socrates, with respect to his form, then the question of identity relates to whether he is the same *man* at different times; if we name Socrates with respect to his matter, then the question relates to whether he is the same *body*. Our judgement about his identity differs according to the respect under which we consider him. Therefore we must always first be clear about the way we conceive of an individual before addressing the question of its identity:

But we must consider by what name anything is called, when we inquire concerning the *identity* of it. For it is one thing to ask concerning Socrates, whether he be the same man, and another to ask whether he be the same body; for his body, when he is old, cannot be the same it was when he was an infant, by reason of the difference of magnitude; for one body has always one and the same magnitude; yet, nevertheless, he may be the same man.[131]

Unlike Hobbes, Locke does not make use of the terminology of form and matter when discussing identity. According to Locke, identity over time is just as unproblematic as individuation, as long as we consider only *simple* substances such as finite spirits and atoms: just as the individuality of any being is provided by 'Existence it self', so is the identity of a simple substance over time secured by its *continued* existence, that is, by its spatio-temporal continuity:

Let us suppose an Atom, *i.e.* a continued body under one immutable Superficies, existing in a determined time and place: 'tis evident, that, considered in any instant of its Existence, it is, in that instant, the same with it self. For being, at that instant, what it is, and nothing else, it is the same, and so must continue, as long as its Existence is continued: for so long it will be the same, and no other.[132]

At the beginning of its existence (as at all other points of time) any being excludes all other individuals of the same kind from its particular position in absolute space and time: no two things of the same kind can begin to exist at the same spatio-temporal position. Neither can one thing have *two* beginnings of existence in space and time. Any simple substance's identity through time is secured all along because of its special relation to its own beginning of existence.[133] Locke also mentions the identity of *non*-substances, namely, that of *actions,* in this context. He points out that their identity and distinctness, too, can be explained in terms of the beginning of existence: it is the very nature of actions and motions that they exist only at one time and at one place: 'Only as to things whose Existence is in succession, such as are the Actions of finite Beings, *v.g. Motion* and *Thought,* both which consist in a continued train of Succession, concerning their Diversity there can be no question: Because each perishing the moment it begins, they cannot exist in different times, or in different places, as permanent Beings can at different times exist in distant places; and therefore no motion or thought considered as at different times can be the same, each part thereof having a different beginning of Existence.'[134] Thus, in respect of actions there can be no *numerical* identity at different points of time; for example, if a body moves continuously during the period t_1 to t_4, its movement at t_2 is not numerically identical with its movement at t_3 – the one exists independently of the other.

Continued existence, that is, spatio-temporal continuity, is relevant not only to the identity of simple substances, but also to that of composite beings. Locke recognises, though, that the fact that 'permanent Beings' (substances) are liable to change must be taken into account. And here, again, the question arises of how much a thing may change without losing its identity; this is the question about its *essential* constituents. Since Locke rejects substantial forms and denies that we have knowledge of *real* essences of substances, he holds that the answer to this question must be determined by 'nominal essences', that is, by our abstract ideas of those beings whose identity is under consideration. Abstract ideas, according to Locke, are formed on the basis of observed similarities between objects. They signify kinds of things, what *we take to be* the essence of any being. Only our abstract ideas can tell us about the essential features of substances; that is, only our abstract ideas can determine the requirements for the identity of these beings. And this is why Locke believes it is crucial to stick to that abstract (sortal) idea of any being whose identity we consider: 'Whatever makes the specifick *Idea,* to which the name is applied, if that *Idea* be steadily kept to, the distinction of any thing into the same, and divers will easily be conceived, and there can arise no doubt about it.'[135] The abstract, sortal or 'specifick' idea tells us what is required for any individual falling under that idea to preserve its identity over time. In order to find out what constitutes identity through time, we have to determine exactly the abstract idea or nominal essence of that thing of which identity is to be predicated: 'To conceive, and judge of it [i.e., identity] aright, we must consider what *Idea* the Word it is applied to stands for: . . . for such as is the *Idea* belonging to that Name, such must be the *Identity*.'[136] According to Locke, when asking about the identity of a body, we have first to be clear about what idea of 'body' we are applying. It makes a crucial difference whether by 'body' we mean an aggregate or collection of atoms or a living being (as a plant, an animal, or a human being): if we refer to a body as an aggregate of atoms, the preservation of the identity of that body requires that numerically the same atoms are retained. If, on the other hand, I refer to a living being, the sameness of all the particles is not required for identity. Locke says that in order to understand what makes an oak tree the same at different times, we have to 'consider wherein an Oak differs from a Mass of Matter'.[137] Since our idea of an oak tree is not that of an aggregate of atoms, different requirements of identity apply. An oak tree may lose some of its parts, change its shape and size, without losing its identity. What is required for identity here is that the changing particles partake in the same organised *life:*

> That being then one Plant, which has such an Organization of Parts in one coherent Body, partaking of one Common Life, it continues to be the same Plant, as long as it partakes of the same Life, though that Life be communicated to new Particles of Matter vitally united to the living Plant, in a like continued Organization, conformable to that sort of Plants.[138]

Similarly, if we take the idea of a human being to be that of an 'organiz'd living Body',[139] rather than that of a union of an immaterial and a material substance, then it is clear that the identity of a human being consists 'in nothing but a participation of the same continued Life, by constantly fleeting Particles of Matter, in succession vitally united to the same organised Body'.[140]

However, despite Locke's explicit pronouncement concerning the rôle of the 'specifick idea' for questions of identity, his discussion of particular cases (oak, horse, man) could be read as suggesting that the specific idea does not, after all, play a rôle in determining identity. On this reading, Locke's account of identity is merely nominalistic in tone, but not in content. For (1) Locke seems to assume that there is just *one* very general principle of identity for plants, animals, and human beings alike, that is, life. And (2), although it follows from the emphasis on the *specific* idea that people with different ideas of man will have different answers to questions about the identity of a man, Locke does not seem to suppose such a thing. Again, he seems to take it that everybody would accept the same general principle, namely, 'life'. Yet close attention to Locke's text reveals that he consistently sticks to the view that the specific idea has a crucial function to fulfil in questions about identity. Regarding (1), even though the identity of a man is secured by the same very general principle as is the identity of plants and animals, namely life, it is not the same sort of life in each case. Locke distinguishes between different sorts of life: horse-life is (obviously) not the same as oak-life, and that is, horse-identity is not the same as oak-identity: An oak is 'such a disposition of [particles of matter] as constitutes the parts of an Oak; and such an Organization of those parts, as is fit to receive, and distribute nourishment, so as to continue, and frame the Wood, Bark, and Leaves, *etc.* of an Oak, in which consists the vegetable Life'. The organisation of particles which secures the identity of an oak is one that is '*conformable to that sort of Plants*'.[141] Similarly, *if* our idea of man is that of a 'vital union of Parts in a *certain* shape' (i.e., in a human shape), then 'as long as that vital union and shape remains . . . it will be the same *Man*'.[142] Regarding (2): it is evident from sections 21 and 29 of the chapter on identity that Locke does suppose that people with different ideas of man would have different answers to questions about the *identity* of a man. He says, 'supposing a rational Spirit be the *Idea* of a *Man*', then 'the *same Spirit,* whether separate or in a Body will be the *same Man.*'[143] It is just that Locke believes that his notion of man is the most appropriate, and that it conforms to the idea of man 'in most Peoples Sense'.[144] So, there is no reason to believe that Locke disagreed with Boyle's statement, quoted above, that our concepts determine what is required for the identity of objects over time. This general point is again expressed in the final sentence of the chapter: 'For whatever be the composition whereof the complex *Idea* is made, whenever Existence makes it one particular thing under any denomination, the same Existence continued, preserves it the same individual *under the same denomination.*'[145] According to Locke, then, what constitutes the identity of a being through time is the continued fulfilment of those requirements which are specified by that abstract idea under which we consider the being: there can be no satisfactory treatment of identity over time independently of our abstract ideas of those things whose identity is in question.

This notion that our sortal concepts are crucial for dealing with questions of identity is still being discussed today. It is to be distinguished from what is now known as the 'relativity thesis' about identity, a thesis also often ascribed to Locke. There are various versions of the thesis in present-day theory, and there is a debate not only about which of the versions (if any) expresses the truth, but also about which version we may ascribe to Locke.[146] Two fundamentally different versions of the thesis have been attributed to Locke. On the reading which is favoured here, Locke is closest to the view that *identity* is relative: different 'specifick' or sortal *ideas* may be applied to the same individual *a* (at time *t*). This has the consequence that there are different possible answers to the question whether *b* (at time *t* + *n*) is identical with *a*, depending on which sortal idea or concept we apply (*F* or *G*, say). It is possible that *a* = *b* with respect to *F*, but not with respect to *G*, even though both *F* and *G* may be applied to both *a* and *b*.[147] To illustrate the point by Locke's example of the oak and the mass of matter, the same

individual can be considered a mass of matter and an oak: the answer to the
question of the identity of the individual at different points of time depends on
whether we apply the notion of an oak or that of a mass of matter. It may be the
same individual with respect to the notion of an oak, but not with respect to that
of a mass of matter: 'An Oak, growing from a Plant to a great Tree, and then
lopp'd, is still the same Oak: And a Colt grown up to a Horse, sometimes fat,
sometimes lean, is all the while the same Horse: though, in both these Cases,
there may be a manifest change of the parts: *So that truly they are not either of them
the same Masses of Matter, though they be truly one of them the same Oak, and the other
the same Horse.*'[148] An alternative reading of Locke suggests that he adopts a version
of the relativity thesis according to which *individuation,* rather than identity, is
relative. On this reading, Locke claims that the oak and the mass of matter are *two
distinct things* or entities at time *t*. That is to say, at time *t* we do not have *one*
individual to which different ideas may be applied, but *two* things occupying the
same place, and composed of the same matter. In fact, the sentence following the
passage just quoted in support of the '*identity*-is-relative' interpretation can be
cited in support of the 'two-thing' or 'double-existence' interpretation: 'In these
two cases of a Mass of Matter, and a living Body, *Identity* is not applied to the
same thing.'[149] However, although passages such as the latter can be construed as
an expression of the 'doctrine of double existence', they need not be read that
way. For, (a) 'thing' may be used by Locke to refer to an *idea* rather than to a
physical object, and (b) Locke nowhere endorses the 'doctrine of double existence'
explicitly.[150] But it is also true that Locke fails to distinguish explicitly between
relativity of individuation and relativity of identity and that he *can* be read as
endorsing both views in one section.[151] Locke was, of course, breaking fresh
ground here, and some confusion on his part should not surprise the modern
reader. In Locke the relativity thesis is the basis of a new theory of *personal* identity
(see Chapter 26). Here, Locke's distinction between *man* and *person* or *personality* is
crucial (in Locke 'person' is synonymous with 'personality'): 'man' and 'person'
are two distinct abstract ideas which may be applied to the same individual.

Like many of Locke's other doctrines, his views on individuation and identity
over time came under attack soon after their publication. In the late 1680s and
early 1690s the issue of individuation had been widely discussed in England,
independently of Locke, in the context of a renewed debate over the theological
problem of the trinity. Among the philosophically important contributions to this
debate were publications by Edward Stillingfleet, Bishop of Worcester, William
Sherlock, and Robert South. After the publication of the second edition of
Locke's *Essay* in 1694 (which contained, for the first time, the chapter on identity),

Locke's theory became a target of criticism by orthodox theologians: his theory of identity was perceived to be inconsistent with the doctrine of the trinity. Locke himself had tried to ignore the connexion of the metaphysical problem of individuation with the theological issue of the trinity. The philosophical relevance of the debate over the trinity concerns mainly the issue of *personal* identity, rather than the problem of individuation and identity in general, and so falls outside of the scope of this chapter (see Chapter 26). However, some authors, such as Edward Stillingfleet, also examined the issue of individuation in more general terms in this context, if only briefly.[152] And Stillingfleet, having read Locke's chapter on identity, went on to attack both Locke's theory of personal identity and his account of individuation in general. Stillingfleet argues against Locke's view that existence in space and time is the principle of individuation. He concedes that spatio-temporal location is a means by which we can distinguish between individuals; but he insists that this is merely an external difference between them and cannot constitute individuality itself. Individuality must have an intrinsic ground independently of spatio-temporal location, 'antecedent to such accidental Differences as are liable to our Observation by our Senses'.[153] According to Stillingfleet, we may reasonably suppose that there is no external difference, like the difference of place, between two individuals; nevertheless they are distinct individuals; it follows that there must be an *intrinsic* principle which makes them the individuals they are, two distinct beings of the same kind. Locke, in replying to Stillingfleet, argues that he cannot accept the supposition on which Stillingfleet bases this argument. He holds that the notion of numerical distinctness between individuals of a kind entails that of external differences between the individuals: 'I cannot, I find, suppose, that there is no such external difference between Peter and James, as difference of place; for I cannot suppose a contradiction; and it seems to me to imply a contradiction to say, Peter and James are not in different places.'[154] Stillingfleet's own account of individuation employs the scholastic notions of common natures or essences and particular subsistence.[155] He indicates that 'in gross and material Beings', this individuality and distinctness is brought about by a complex of 'peculiar Modes and Properties, which distinguish them from each other'.[156] In the case of human beings individuality is constituted by the particular union of soul and body: 'Since every Man hath a different Soul united to different Particles of Matter, there must be a real Distinction between them, without any respect to what is accidental to them.'[157] Locke replies that Stillingfleet's position violates the principle that whatever it is that brings about individuation must be 'the same in all the several species of creatures, men as well as others'. Furthermore, Locke argues that, on Stillingfleet's account, it is not clear how body and soul can be individuals before they are united into one human being. Locke continues: 'And upon this ground it will be very hard to tell what made the soul and the body individuals (as certainly they were) before their union.'[158]

John Sergeant's critique of Locke's theory of identity in his *Solid Philosophy Asserted* of 1697 is not part of the debate about the trinity. Rather, it belongs to a lengthy and careful examination of the whole of Locke's *Essay,* against the background of a scholastic metaphysics. Sergeant begins his discussion of Locke's theory by making the same point as Stillingfleet, namely, that Locke confuses the external marks by which we come to *know* the distinction between things with what intrinsically causes this distinction, and that Locke wrongly takes the former for the latter.[159] Existence at a certain place and time presupposes individuality and therefore cannot constitute it: "'Tis evident that the Individual Thing must, (in priority of Nature or Reason) be *first* constituted such, ere it can be *capable of Existence.* Wherefore 'tis impossible that Existence, consider it how we will, can be in any manner the *Principle* of *Individuation,* the constitution of the Individuum being presupposed to it.'[160]

According to Sergeant, Locke's account of individuation is circular, for it assumes something to be the principle of individuation which presupposes individuality. On Sergeant's view, individuation is to be explained on analogy with the constitution of kinds or species: the latter are explained in terms of substantial forms. Substantial forms or essences are, according to Sergeant, those complexes of properties which enable beings to perform operations which are typical of their skind. And individuation, too, is said to have a *formal* ground; the individual character or essence is constituted by a greater number of properties than that which constitutes the kind or species: 'for, the *Species* or *Kinds* of Things are but *few,* but the *Individuums* under those Kinds are *Innumerable*; and, therefore, *more* goes to distinguish *these* from one another, than was needful to distinguish or determine the *other.*'[161] It is a being's particular set of characteristics which makes it the individual it is. This individual character is 'the Intrinsecal or Formal *Principle of Individuation*'; that is, it 'ultimately' determines beings 'to be *This* or *That*'.[162] The individual character or essence is the lowest form or 'last Distinction' which completes the determination of a being as a particular. Sergeant emphasises that his explanation of individuation in terms of individual essences implies that no two individuals, 'however seemingly Uniform', can have all their properties in common: there must be some intrinsic characteristics with respect to which they differ; otherwise, 'they would be *One,* and not *One,* which is a Contradiction.'[163]

Our ideas or notions of individuals do not capture the complete set of individuating characteristics: 'We can never comprehend or reach all that belongs to the *Suppositum*, or *Individuum*.'[164] Nevertheless we are able to distinguish between individuals on the basis of external marks such as their existence in time and space. Sergeant adds that in this sense, 'and not in making them *intrinsecally* constitute the *Individuum*, Mr. *Locke's* Doctrin in this Point is admitted'.[165] Locke, obviously, could not accept this traditional scholastic appeal to the notion of substantial forms. We saw above that Locke argued on the basis of his atomism that the 'complex of accidents' relevant to individuation would have to be reduced to those of spatio-temporal location. Sergeant believes that that which individuates is also relevant to determining identity over time: as long as an individual retains its set of essential characteristics it remains the same; 'no Alteration or Defalcation of *Matter*, Quantity, or Figure, etc. makes it *Another Substance*, or *Another Thing*.' It loses its identity only through 'such a *New Form*, as makes it *unfit* for its *Primary Operation*, to which it is ordain'd, as it is a Distinct Part in Nature'.[166] Sergeant had no time for Locke's idea that abstract ideas are relevant to identity: 'How the holding to the *Specifical Idea*, in which all the *Individuums* under it do *agree*, and which makes them *one* in Nature, should clear the Distinction of *Individuals*, is altogether inexplicable.'[167] It is not surprising that a philosopher like Sergeant, who asserted the reality of substantial forms, could make little sense of Locke's relativity thesis of identity.

There were other philosophers in England around the turn of the century who critically discussed Locke's theory of identity. Henry Lee, for example, in his *Anti-Scepticism* of 1702, focuses on Locke's account of identity through time. Like Stillingfleet and Sergeant, Lee rejects the notion that 'bare Existence' individuates.[168] Lee's own view is that there are different causes for identity for different kinds of beings, but he sees this as quite different from Locke's thesis that our sortal concepts or abstract ideas determine what is required for the identity of objects over time. Rather, he states that 'as the *things themselves* are different, so they are said to be the same with themselves at several times, for different reasons.'[169] Lee proceeds to argue against Locke's notions of the various kinds of beings he discusses in this context (plants, animals, human beings): his main complaint is that for Locke human beings are 'only Vegetables a little more conveniently organiz'd'.[170]

Locke's general theory of identity was attacked not only by traditional thinkers such as Stillingfleet, Sergeant, and Lee. It had its most formidable contemporary critic in the German philosopher Gottfried Wilhelm Leibniz.

V. LEIBNIZ

Leibniz's philosophy as a whole is often characterised as 'individualism'. The individual substance, or 'monad', as he called it in his later writings, was certainly a main focus of his philosophical thinking. It appears that his interest in the individual originated in the scholastic disputes over the principle of individuation which Leibniz had studied in his early years. His first publication was a student dissertation on that topic. In his later writings he wrote in support of individual human immortality and against philosophers such as Spinoza and the 'Neo-Cartesians' (e.g., Malebranche) whose theories Leibniz took to be incompatible with immortality.[171] His other target was atomism, a position that he had adopted himself for a short time. Leibniz attempted to 'rehabilitate' substantial forms, but in a way that is compatible with the Christian doctrine of human immortality (see Chapter 26).

The method and terminology of his early dissertation, *Disputatio metaphysica de principio individui* (1663), written in Leipzig under the supervision of Jakob Thomasius, are still very scholastic in character. Leibniz carefully distinguishes between the *principium cognoscendi* and the *principium essendi,* and he states that his subject is the real or 'physical principle' of individuation in all created substances.[172] He reviews various traditional answers to the problem of individuation, and he lists authors who held those views. His own position is that of Suárez.[173] Like Suárez, he rejects the Scotist position, according to which an individual emerges through negation from a real universal, and also the theory which identifies existence as the principle of individuation. He argues that existence cannot be the principle of individuation, because existence and essence cannot be separated from one another.[174] However, Leibniz concedes that if existence is said to differ from essence only in thought ('solum ratione'), then that position coincides with his own view.[175] As noted earlier, Suárez, too, held that 'existence' can be interpreted in such a way that the 'existential' theory of individuation coincides with the Suárezian solution. Leibniz's main target is the Scotist position.[176] In fact, he spends more time examining and rejecting the Scotist theory than he does explaining his own view. For the Scotists there is a formal cause of individuation; individuation is explained in analogy to specification: just as the species emerges from the genus through the specific difference, so the individual emerges from the species through the individual difference, or 'haecceitas'. Leibniz's response is in the nominalist tradition: he rejects the real existence of genus and species;[177] and once natural kinds are rejected, the Scotist account no longer makes sense. Leibniz links his own position explicitly to the nominalist tradition (e.g., Petrus Aureolus,

Durandus), to Suárez, and to his university teacher Daniel Stahl.[178] Like Suárez he identifies the 'entity' as the positive ground of individuation: 'Every individual is individuated by its whole entity.'[179] As in Suárez, 'the whole entity' can be interpreted as the two intrinsic causes of being: matter and form. What brings about a being's individuality, according to Leibniz, is not just *one* of its component parts (form or matter), but all the constituents which make up its entity. Leibniz provides a syllogistic argument to support his position: he says that which constitutes a thing also makes it numerically one; and since a thing is intrinsically constituted by its entity, it follows that each thing is one by its own entity. The major premise is derived from the principle that oneness does not add any reality to being.[180] Leibniz's early adherence to nominalism is also expressed in a preface (1670) to an edition of Mario Nizolio's *De veris principiis et vera ratione philosophandi contra pseudophilosophos libri IV* (first published 1553). Here Leibniz states that according to the nominalists, 'everything in the world can be explained without any reference to universals and real forms', adding that 'nothing is truer than this opinion.'[181]

Leibniz's later theory of individual substances, which is so central to his metaphysics as a whole, developed from his early dissertation on the scholastic disputes over the *principium individuationis*. Leibniz later abandoned scholastic terminology and method, and came to regard the traditional search for an individuating *principle* as superfluous. Nevertheless, he continued to believe that the works of 'deeper Scholastics, such as Suárez . . . sometimes contain substantial discussions, for instance . . . of the principle of individuation'.[182] Leibniz's early position on individuation has several essential features in common with his later theory. First, there is the sharp distinction between what is relevant to the evidence or knowledge of individuality and what constitutes individuality in reality. Second, there is the insistence that individuality must have an *intrinsic* ground. Third, there is the nominalist emphasis on the priority of the individual to the universal. Fourth, there is the view that there are not different causes of individuality for different kinds of being. And fifth, there is Leibniz's later notion of 'complete being' or of 'complete entity' which is reminiscent of the Suárezian notion of the 'whole entity', which Leibniz used in the early dissertation; it certainly developed from the earlier concept.[183] However, although there are common features, the later theory is not simply identical with the early Suárezian doctrine.

I said that Leibniz was led to regard the whole debate over the *principium individuationis* as superfluous. This is implied by his famous *principle of the identity of indiscernibles*. Leibniz states this principle in many places. In the *Discours de métaphy-*

sique (1686), he formulates it thus: 'It is not true that two substances are completely alike, differing only numerically.'[184] In his *Fourth Paper* to Samuel Clarke (1716), he says: 'There is no such thing as two individuals indiscernible from each other.'[185] This is to say that no two substances have all their characteristics in common; there must be at least one property which they do not share. It also means that 'to suppose two things indiscernible, is to suppose the same thing under two names':[186] If I refer to two items as having all their properties in common, I am in fact referring to one and the same thing, only under different names. Leibniz offers both *a priori* and *a posteriori* arguments for his principle. The *a priori* argument is that the identity of indiscernibles follows from the principle of sufficient reason. Leibniz concedes that the 'supposition of two indiscernibles' is 'possible in abstract terms'; that is, it is *logically* possible that two substances are exactly alike, 'but it is not consistent with the order of things, nor with the divine wisdom, by which nothing is admitted without reason'; for if there were two indiscernibles, then 'God and nature would act without reason, in ordering the one otherwise than the other.'[187] There must, therefore, be an intrinsic difference between things which accounts for their numerical diversity.[188] Leibniz regarded the principle of the identity of indiscernibles as central to his philosophical system as a whole; he thought that together with the principle of sufficient reason it would 'change the state of metaphysics', making it 'real and demonstrative; whereas before, it did generally consist in empty words'.[189] The *a posteriori* argument is that, as a matter of fact, two things are never *found* to be exactly alike. This is not offered as a proof of the principle, but as an argument which shows that the principle is *confirmed* by experience; and Leibniz gives numerous examples. In his *Fourth Paper* to Clarke he writes:

> There is no such thing as two individuals indiscernible from each other. An ingenious gentleman of my acquaintance, discoursing with me, in the presence of Her Electoral Highness the Princess Sophia, in the garden of Herrenhausen, thought he could find two leaves perfectly alike. The Princess defied him to do it, and he ran all over the garden a long time to look for some; but it was to no purpose. Two drops of water, or milk, viewed with a microscope, will appear distinguishable from each other.[190]

In some passages Leibniz suggests that his principle is a more general application of Aquinas's view that angels or 'separate intelligences' do not only differ numerically, and that each angel constitutes a distinct kind, a 'lowest species'.[191] Clearly, Leibniz's position implies a rejection of Aquinas's view that 'materia signata' is the principle of individuation in material things. Yet, like Aquinas's angels, Leibniz's individual substances differ from each other essentially as well as numerically; all the attributes of an individual substance belong to it essentially. Individual substances each have their own natures or essences by which they are individuated. As just indicated , Leibniz makes use of the terms 'complete being' and 'complete entity', which replace the earlier Suárezian notion of 'whole entity'. And Leibniz uses 'individual substance' synonymously with 'complete being'. He states: 'The nature of an individual substance or complete being is to have such a complete notion as to include and entail all the predicates of the subject that notion is attributed to.'[192] That is to say, the intrinsic nature or complete notion of an individual substance contains all its properties.[193] The individual is a being which is completely determined. This is not to say that an individual may not *appear* undetermined to us; Leibniz recognises that we may not be able to grasp the intrinsic nature or complete notion of a substance.

When Leibniz says that no two things differ only *numerically,* he means that they do not 'differ from one another in respect of place and time alone'.[194] Leibniz concedes that the spatio-temporal position of things is in some cases a useful means for *us* to mark individuals off from one another; but like Stillingfleet and Sergeant, he argues against Locke that this must not be confused with the intrinsic cause of individuality and distinctness. According to Leibniz, we should distinguish carefully between what constitutes identity in the thing itself and what serves as a mark or sign by which we discover the identity and distinctness of things: 'In addition to the difference of time or of place there must always be an internal *principle of distinction.*'[195] Thus, although Leibniz himself refers to his principle as that of the identity of *indiscernibles,* which could suggest that he thinks of it as an epistemic principle,[196] he clearly keeps the metaphysical and epistemological issues separate. Locke's argument, that for atoms spatio-temporal location must be postulated as the only 'principle of distinction' which holds in all cases, would not have impressed Leibniz. For he employs the principle of the identity of indiscernibles as an argument against the atomist hypothesis itself. If atomism were true, Leibniz argues, then one would indeed have to accept that there are things which differ only numerically; but this cannot be accepted, because it would violate the principle of the identity of indiscernibles; and this principle must be valid, since it can be deduced *a priori* from the principle of sufficient reason. Leibniz points out in many places that the principle of the identity of indiscernibles 'overthrows the whole of purely corpuscularian philosophy'.[197] Against Locke he writes:

If there were atoms, i.e. perfectly hard and perfectly unalterable bodies which were incapable of internal change and could differ from one another only in size and shape, it is obvious that since they could have the same size and shape they would then be indistinguishable in themselves and discernible only by means of external denominations with no internal foundation; which is contrary to the greatest principles of reason.[198]

Leibniz argues that this mistaken assumption, that there are things which differ only numerically, brought about philosophers' 'perplexities about what they called the *principle of individuation*'.[199] For Leibniz, there is no need to *search* for such a principle, since it can be demonstrated that nature simply never makes two things exactly alike: every individual is individual by itself, that is, by its intrinsic nature. Things differ from each other by virtue of their individual essences.

So far Leibniz's theory of individuation centred on his principle of the identity of indiscernibles appears to be merely a more elaborate version of his early account of individuation centred on the Suárezian notion of 'whole entity'. It seems merely to make explicit certain implications of the early Suárezian version of the theory. One *difference* between Leibniz's later theory and both his own early account of individuation and the scholastic doctrines is the new emphasis on the essential *relatedness* of all individual substances to one another. Although each substance is 'independent of everything else apart from God',[200] Leibniz argues that every substance is related to all other substances: every substance mirrors the whole universe, 'expressing it in its own way, somewhat as the same town is variously represented according to the different positions of an observer'.[201] Each substance mirrors the whole universe from its own particular perspective. Leibniz emphasises the 'connexion or adaptation of all created things with each, and of each with all the rest'.[202] In the *Nouveaux essais* Leibniz says, 'In metaphysical strictness there is no wholly extrinsic denomination, because of the real connections amongst all things.'[203] One could say that since it belongs to the intrinsic nature of the individual substance that it is essentially connected to all other substances, Leibniz's metaphysics of individuality presupposes the interrelatedness of all things. We saw that Spinoza, too, accounted for individuality in terms of the relationship of individuals to the totality of which they are part. In Spinoza, of course, those individuals are not substances. Nevertheless, despite all the differences in their metaphysical systems, the idea of the essential interconnectedness of all individuals is one which Leibniz's and Spinoza's accounts of individuality have in common.

Another difference between Leibniz's early and later theory is the latter's focus on the issue of *identity through time,* which was not present in the 1663 account. As to the issue of identity over time, Leibniz seems to be concerned mainly with the problem of *personal* identity (see Chapter 26). The principle of the identity of indiscernibles implies that a substance is identical with itself at different points of time only if it has exactly the same properties at those points of time. Now this is such a strict notion of identity through time that it seems to rule out change altogether. And Leibniz recognises, of course, that things are subject to change. So, how can a substance, on Leibniz's principle, ever be said to remain identical through time and partial change? The answer is that within Leibniz's metaphysics, this is no real problem. Since the intrinsic nature or 'complete notion' of a substance contains *all* its actions and properties, it contains properties not only of the present, but also of the past and of the future. All the changes which a substance undergoes are necessarily part of its nature. Everything that will ever happen to any substance is contained all along in its intrinsic nature or complete notion: everything that will ever happen to a substance is predetermined. It follows that the *identity* of a substance through time is included in its complete notion: 'Everything occurs in every substance as a consequence of the first state which God bestowed upon it when he created it, and, extraordinary concourse excepted, his ordinary concourse consists only of preserving the substance itself in conformity with its preceding state and the changes that it bears.'[204]

Thus, each individual substance's identity over time is guaranteed *a priori* ; it is guaranteed *a priori,* because the substance's different states at different points of time are, by definition, nothing but states of one and the same unfolding individual nature. Leibniz emphasises again that this *a priori* ground of identity must not be confused with our *a posteriori* ways of discovering this identity; in the case of human souls inner experience provides the *a posteriori* evidence for identity.[205]

Leibniz later develops this doctrine of the 'complete notion' of a substance into his theory of *monads* (from ca. 1695 onwards): this theory constitutes a third important difference between his later and his early account of individuality. According to the theory of monads, what makes something remain numerically the same individual is 'an enduring principle of life which I call "monad" '.[206] Monads are immaterial, simple, indivisible 'atoms of substance', soul-like beings. *Human* souls are merely a special kind of monad; all things are in the last result composed of monads: 'The monad . . . is nothing but a simple substance which enters into compounds.'[207] Leibniz regards monads as the only true substances, the 'sources of action' and the principles or 'forms' of genuine unity and identity. As he writes in the *Système nouveau,*

I perceived that it is impossible to find *the principles of a true unity* in matter alone . . . since everything in it is but a collection or accumulation of parts *ad infinitum.* Now a multiplicity can be real only if it is made up of *true unities* which come from elsewhere and are altogether different from mathematical points. . . . Therefore, to find these *real unities,* I was constrained to have recourse to what might be called a *real or animated point* or to an atom of substance which must embrace some element of form or of activity in order to make a complete being. . . . I found then that their nature consists of force and that from this there follows something analogous to feeling and to appetite; and that therefore it was necessary to form a conception of them resembling our ordinary notion of *souls.* . . . I saw that . . . these souls must be indivisible like our mind.[208]

Monads constitute the real or objective identity of any being: there is only one single 'principle' which constitutes real identity in plants, animals, and human beings alike: the 'indivisible spirit . . . [that] animates them.'[209] Without being united to a true substance or soul or monad, organic bodies would only have 'apparent identity'; an organic body can be said to be genuinely identical only if we assume that they are united to a monad.[210] Leibniz distinguishes sharply between this genuine identity and what he calls 'accidental unity' or 'apparent identity'. This distinction is present also in writings of the mid-1680s, that is, prior to the theory of monads.[211] In the *Correspondence with Arnauld* (1686–88), Leibniz argues that genuine unity and identity are due to mindlike substances, whereas artifacts and other 'entities through aggregation', such as a society, are unified 'entities' only in the sense that they are 'entities of reason'.[212] For example, we conceive of a society 'as a single thing' because there are 'connexions between the constituents'. However, these unities 'are made complete only by thoughts and appearances'.[213] They are not unified by an intrinsic principle of unity. Thus,

a marble tile is not a single complete substance, no more than would be the water in a pool with all the fish included, even if all the water with all these fish were frozen; or a flock of sheep, even though these sheep should be bound together to such an extent that they could walk only at the same pace and that one could not be touched without all the others crying out. There is as much difference between a substance and such an entity as there is between a man and a community, such as a people, army, society or college, which are moral entities, where something imaginary exists, dependent on the fabrication of our minds.[214]

Leibniz emphasises that even these 'entities through aggregation' such as artefacts and a society presuppose genuine units or mindlike substances; for 'what constitutes the essence of an entity through aggregation is only a state of being of its constituent entities; for example, what constitutes the essence of an army is only a state of being of the constituent men. This state of being therefore presupposes a substance whose essence is not a state of being of another substance.' The multiplicity that is involved in an aggregate presupposes genuine units which make up the aggregate: 'The plural presupposes the singular, and where there is no entity, still less will there be many entities.'[215] Unlike his early dissertation on the principle of individuation, Leibniz's mature metaphysics holds that individuality is due to a soul-like immaterial being.

It is not surprising that Leibniz barely mentions Locke's thesis that our sortal concepts provide criteria of numerical identity through time. Within Leibniz's metaphysics of identity there is no room for a discussion of this thesis; Leibniz dismisses it as being merely about 'the signification of words', and he says what is at issue is the *real* ground of identity.[216] Leibniz's view that individuality requires complete determination and individual essence is reminiscent of the realist scholastic notion of the individual form or 'haecceitas'. However, Leibniz's mature theory, too, is much closer to a Suárezian or nominalist theory about individuation than it is to Scotist and Thomist versions of realism: the late as well as the early Leibniz rejects the view that individuals emerge from real universals (or natural kinds) through a process of specification and individuation. According to both the early and the late Leibniz, individuals are individuals by themselves. The individuality of substances is given immediately with their being. As Leibniz points out to Arnauld, 'What is not truly *one* entity is not truly one *entity* either.'[217]

VI. THE EIGHTEENTH CENTURY

In the eighteenth century the traditional scholastic problem of individuation attracted less interest than the special issue of *personal* identity (see Chapter 26). Very often, philosophers and theologians discussed individuation and identity in general merely as a preliminary to an account of personal identity (e.g., Butler, Reid). However, Leibniz's principle of the identity of indiscernibles had a considerable impact on eighteenth-century metaphysical debates. Of course, some of Leibniz's own writings in which he discusses his principle belong to the eighteenth century. The *Nouveaux essais* were completed in 1704 and published in 1765; and the relevant papers of the correspondence with Clarke are from 1716. In Germany, the leading metaphysician Christian Wolff adopted Leibniz's principle, and he was full of praise of it.[218] Apart from that, Wolff had little to say about individuation in general; like Leibniz, he accounted for individuality in terms of the notion of 'complete determination'.[219] Wolff's philosophy had a large following, and so Leibniz's principle was widely accepted by German metaphysicians in the first half of the eighteenth century. There were critics of the principle, however. Christian August Crusius, for example, insisted that the identity or diversity of substances is a matter which can only be determined *a posteriori*.[220] And later in the century, Johann Heinrich Lambert rejected the notion that numerical diversity between substances precludes qualitative identity.[221] In the English-speaking world, Leibniz's principle was known through his correspondence with Clarke, which was first published in English and French in 1717 (in London). Clarke himself rejected Leibniz's view that it is against the order of nature that there be two substances which are 'exactly alike'. He argued that 'there is no impossibility for God to make two drops of water exactly alike. And if he should make them exactly alike, yet they would never the more become one and the same drop of water, because they were alike. . . . Two things, by being exactly alike, do not cease to be two.'[222]

The subjective treatment of identity in the writings of some Cartesians and especially in Locke was taken up in a different way by David Hume. For Hume the question of the 'principle of individuation' is about identity through time: 'Thus the principle of individuation is nothing but the *invariableness* and *uninterruptedness* of any object, thro' a suppos'd variation of time.'[223] A notion of identity as 'invariableness' and 'uninterruptedness' is so strict that it does not allow for any change at all in the object to which we ascribe identity. Hume realises that we nevertheless do ascribe identity to changing objects; and he argues that our ascription of identity to such objects is based on a fiction of the imagination. His main task is to give a psychological explanation of how this fiction arises in our minds. In his *Essays on the Intellectual Powers of Man* of 1785, Thomas Reid similarly argues that 'continued uninterrupted existence is . . . necessarily implied in identity'.[224] He holds that 'perfect identity' precludes change of substance. And since bodies or the 'objects of sense' are 'subject to continual changes of their substance', it follows that the identity 'which we ascribe to bodies, whether natural or artificial, is not perfect identity'. Nevertheless, according to Reid, we are justified in ascribing 'identity' in a less than strict sense to bodies on the basis of observed similarities. Unlike Hume, Reid argues that the human *person* is a 'monad', (i.e., an active, indivisible substance) and has a 'perfect identity'. Immanuel Kant examined identity in the context of his new system of *transcendental* philosophy. According to Kant, the concepts of identity and difference are 'concepts of reflexion'.[225] Things, Kant says, 'can have a twofold relation to our faculty of knowledge, namely, to sensibility and to understanding'; and so 'whether things are identical or different . . . cannot be established at once from the concepts themselves by mere comparison (*comparatio*), but solely by means of a transcendental consideration (*reflexio*), through distinction of the cognitive faculty to which they belong.' In other words, to determine the question of identity and difference we need first to determine whether the objects in question are considered in relation to the faculty of sensibility or to that of the understanding. This transcendental reflexion 'contains the grounds of the possibility of objective comparison'. And it is the basis of Kant's evaluation of Leibniz's principle of the identity of indiscernibles: the principle is valid if objects are taken to be objects of 'pure understanding' (things-in-themselves, intelligibilia); but if they are taken as objects of sense (appearances), then their spatio-temporal location is 'an adequate ground for the *numerical difference*'. Kant's critique of Leibniz's principle is based on the charge that Leibniz did not distinguish between things-in-themselves and objects of sense. And Kant's own treatment of the issue clearly marks another turning point in the history of the debates over identity.

NOTES

1 This chapter is primarily concerned with individuation and identity in general; the special problem of *personal* identity is discussed in Chapter 26 in this book.

2 For an overview of the mediaeval disputes, see Assenmacher 1926; Gracia 1991, 1994. For a more detailed account of the debate in the early Middle Ages, see Gracia 1984. Gracia gives a detailed interpretation of Boethius's contribution to the debate, and he emphasises in particular the importance of Boethius's *De trinitate* in this respect (pp. 65–121; 255–62).

3 On Eriugena, see Assenmacher 1926, pp. 15–16; and, especially, Gracia 1984, pp. 129–35.

4 For Averroes (Ibn Rushd), see Averroes 1984, pp. 103–5; and Assenmacher 1926, pp. 29–30.

5 *Met.* XII.8 (1074 a), as translated in Aristotle 1936; see also *Met.* V.6 (1016 b 3).

6 *De ente et essentia,* chap. 2 (Thomas Aquinas 1946, 1968c).

7 *De ente et essentia,* chap. 2. See also St. Thomas's commentary on Aristotle's *Metaphysics,* Bk. V, lesson 8, commentary 876 (Thomas Aquinas 1950, 1961).

8 Scotus's *Quaestiones quodlibetales,* 2.16 (Duns Scotus 1968, 1975). Quoted from Duns Scotus 1975, p. 35.

9 Cf. Bruno's *De la causa, principio et uno* (Bruno 1973; English translation Bruno 1976). On Bruno, see Michel 1973; Yates 1964.

10 The influence of Suárez is present in the then widely used metaphysical textbooks by Timpler, Combach, Scheibler, and others. Joseph S. Freedman has counted ninety-seven citations of Suárez in Timpler's *Metaphysicae systema methodicum,* which first appeared in Steinfurt in 1604 (Freedman 1988, vol. 1, p. 142). For the impact of Suárez on seventeenth-century metaphysics in general, see Grabmann 1926–56, vol. 1, pp. 525–60; Lewalter 1967; Wundt 1939, pp. 41–7.

11 I have used the editions, translations, and commentaries by Rainer Specht (Suárez 1976) and J. J. E. Gracia (Suárez 1982). Translations are taken from Suárez 1982.

12 *Disp. met.* V.3.2.

13 *Disp. met.* V.3.2.

14 *Disp. met.* V.6.1.

15 *Disp. met.* V.1.4 (last two quotations).

16 For Henry of Ghent, see Assenmacher 1926, pp. 30–2.

17 *Disp. met.* V.5.2.

18 *Disp. met.* V.6.1 (last three quotations).

19 *Disp. met.* V.6.1.

20 *Disp. met.* V.6.15.

21 *Disp. met.* V.6.16.

22 *Disp. met.* V.4.4. In Suárez 1982 'simpliciter loquendo' is translated as 'strictly speaking'. The translation 'by a natural way of speaking' was suggested to me by Michael Ayers. See also the translation in Suárez 1976, V.4.4. For the same general point, see *Disp. met.* V.6.16.

23 See, e.g., *Disp. met.* V.3.28.

24 *Disp. met.* V.3.33.

25 *Disp. met.* V.6.17.

26 Boyle explicitly refers to Suárez when he rejects 'supernatural mysteries – such as those upon which divers of the physico-theological tenets of the schoolmen, especially about real qualities and the separableness of accidents from subjects of inhesion, are *manifestly,* if not also *avowedly,* grounded' (*The Origine of Formes and Qualities* [1666], in Boyle 1979, p. 8).

27 See, e.g., *Summa th.* I q29 a1.

28 Thomas Aquinas excepts quantity, which he says is individuated through its place. In *Disp. met.* V.7.2, Suárez cites *Quodlibet* VII a19 as evidence that this was Thomas Aquinas's view. (Specht points out that the reference is to VII a10: Suárez 1976,vol. 1, p. 350.) Thomas Aquinas had to except quantity to make his theory consistent with the doctrine of transubstantiation. The doctrine of transubstantiation requires that an individual quantity can be preserved without its subject. Thus, in the Eucharist, the individual quantities of bread and wine remain the same, even though the substances of bread and wine are no longer there. On this, see Specht in Suárez 1976, vol. 2, pp. 284–5.

29 *Disp. met.* V.7.2.

30 *Disp. met.* V.7.3 (last two quotations).

31 *Disp. met.* V.7.3 (last two quotations).

32 *Disp. met.* V.7.5. Emphasis added.

33 *Disp. met.* V.7.3. In scholastic philosophy, real relations were regarded as accidents. See Weinberg 1965, pp. 61–119; and Henninger 1989, esp. pp. 4–6 ('Relation as Accident'), and pp. 14 ff. (on Aquinas). On modern views, see Henninger 1989, pp. 184–6; Weinberg 1965, pp. 112–19.

34 *Disp. met.* V.7.3.

35 *Disp. met.* V.7.1 (last two quotations).

36 *Disp. met.* V.7.3.

37 *Disp. met.* V.7.4 (last two quotations).

38 *Disp. met.* V.8.19.

39 *Disp. met.* V.8.16.

40 See *Disp. met.* V.9.3.

41 See, e.g., Assenmacher 1926, pp. 94–6.

42 See Specht in Suárez 1976, vol. 1, pp. xxi, xxxii–xxxiii; and Gracia in Suárez 1982, p. 21.

43 See Wundt 1939, pp. 210–13. According to Wundt, Werner Capella was the only nominalist among the many university metaphysicians in seventeenth-century Germany.

44 Goclenius 1613, pp. 231–2; Micraelius 1662, cols. 613–14.

45 The latter is true of Scheibler's *Metaphysica.* Scheibler deals with the principle of individuation in Chapter 7 ('De Singulari et Universali') of the first book of the *Metaphysica* (Scheibler 1636). For the structure of seventeenth-century metaphysical textbooks, see Lewalter 1967; and Wundt 1939, pp. 187 ff. On the systematic place of the discussion of individuation, see Wundt 1939, pp. 207–13.

46 Keckermann 1614, vol. 1, cols. 2016–17.

47 Burgersdijk 1675, Bk. I, chap. 12, esp. pp. 68–71. On pp. 68–70, Burgersdijck discusses Scotus and Aquinas. He states his own view on p. 70. Cf. Scheibler 1636, p. 97; Scharf 1643, p. 199.

48 For Stahl and J. Thomasius, see Wundt 1939, pp. 143–4, 213.

49 See Milton 1981b, pp. 129, 134, 141.

50 See Bacon, *Nov. org.* II 2; Hobbes, *Lev.* iv; Locke, *Ess.* III.iii and vi.

51 Gassendi 1658, vol. 3, p. 159; Arnauld and Nicole 1965, pt. I, chap. 6.

52 *Princ.* I 60.

53 This is true, even though Descartes sometimes does call the soul the 'form of man'. Even when he does, however, the phrase does not mean the same as it does in scholasticism. Thus, Descartes says in Resp. V, 'If we are to take "soul" in its special sense, as meaning the "first actuality" or "principal form of man", then the term must be understood to apply only to the principle in virtue of which we think' (AT VII 356).

54 On this, see also Chapter 26. Cf. AT V 157 (CB 18–19) and Cottingham's commentary, CB pp. 84–5.

55 'Synopsis' of the *Meditationes* (AT VII 14).

56 *Princ.* II 4. See also the 'Synopsis' of the *Meditationes:* 'Body, taken in the general sense, is a substance' (AT VII 14).

57 *Princ.* II 23. See also *Princ.* I 63.

58 'Synopsis' of the *Meditationes* (AT VII 14).

59 *Princ.* I 60. Again, in *Princ.* II 55 Descartes speaks explicitly about parts of a body constituting distinct substances. In *Princ.* I 64, Descartes appears to equate the notion of a particular body with that of a substance. See also the letter to Gibieuf, 19 January 1642, where Descartes says, 'I consider the two halves of a part of matter, however small it may be, as two complete substances' (AT III 477).

60 *Eth.* I prop. 15 schol. Daniel Garber drew my attention to this passage in Spinoza.

61 *Princ.* II 23; emphasis added.

62 *Princ.* II 25.

63 *Princ.* II 25.

64 *De ipse natura* (1698), sec. 13: Ger. IV 513 (Leibniz 1969, p. 505). Leibniz goes on to argue: 'In a perfectly similar, undifferentiated, and filled mass there can arise no shape or limitation or distinction of different parts, except through motion itself. If therefore motion contains no distinguishing mark, it can also bestow none upon figure; and since everything which is substituted for a prior thing must be perfectly equivalent to it, no observer, not even an omniscient one, will see even the smallest indication of a change. And so everything will be the same as if no change or differentiation had taken place in the bodies, and no reason can be given for the diverse appearances which we experience by sense' (Ger. IV 513 [Leibniz 1969, p. 505]). Daniel Garber drew my attention to this passage.

65 Letter to Mesland (AT IV 166). Cf. ibid.: 'a determinate part of matter, or one that has a determinate size'. See also *Princ.* I 65.

66 Letter to Mesland (AT IV 166).

67 'Synopsis' of the *Meditationes* (AT VII 14).

68 Letter to Mesland (AT IV 162–70). For a fuller account of the Cartesian debate about transubstantiation, see (Rodis-)Lewis 1950b, pp. 5–7, 68–74; Watson 1982, pp. 127–48; Armogathe 1977; and, especially, Nadler 1988a.

69 Letter to Mesland (AT IV 166).

70 Letter to Mesland (AT IV 166–7; last two quotations).

71 Letter to Mesland (AT IV 168).
72 Letter to Mesland (AT IV 165).
73 Letter to Mesland (AT IV 169).
74 Letter to Mesland (AT IV 167; emphasis added).
75 Sir Kenelm Digby, *Observations upon Religio Medici,* 1643, p. 82. Page numbers refer to the second edition (Digby 1644b).
76 Digby 1644b, p. 84.
77 Sergeant 1697, p. 258.
78 *Some Physico-Theological Considerations about the Possibility of the Resurrection* (1675), in Boyle 1979, p. 205. See also Chapter 26 in this book.
79 *Princ.* I 51–2.
80 Translations of Spinoza are taken from Spinoza 1985. For a detailed discussion and critical evaluation of Spinoza's monism, see Charleton 1981.
81 *Eth.* I dfn. 3 and 4.
82 *Eth.* I prop. 5 dem (last two quotations).
83 *Eth.* I prop. 6.
84 *Eth.* I prop. 7 dem.
85 *Eth.* I prop. 8 schol. 2 (last three quotations).
86 *Eth.* I prop. 8 dem.
87 *Eth.* I dfn. 6.
88 *Eth.* I prop. 25 cor.
89 *Eth.* II prop. 21 schol. For Spinoza's account of the individual human self, see further Chapter 26 in this book.
90 *Eth.* II prop. 13 lem. 2 dem.
91 *Eth.* II prop. 13 lem. 1; for extension and mobility, see *Eth.* II prop. 13 ax. 1 and 2. See also *Eth.* II prop. 13 lem. 3 dem.: Bodies 'are singular things which . . . are distinguished from one another by reason of motion and rest.'
92 Geb. I 120; see also Geb. I 52: 'Each and every particular thing that comes to exist becomes such through motion and rest. . . . The differences between [one body and another] arise only from the different proportions of motion and rest, by which one is so, and not so, is this and not that.'
93 *Eth.* II prop. 13 lem. 3. Compare the demonstration to lem. 3. See also *Eth.* II prop. 31 dem: 'For each singular thing, like the human Body, must be determined by another singular thing to exist and produce effects in a certain and determinate way, and this again by another, and so to infinity.'
94 *Eth.* II prop. 13 lem. 3 dfn.
95 *Eth.* II prop. 13 lem. 5.
96 'If it had been my intention to deal expressly with body, I ought to have explained and demonstrated these things more fully. But I have already said that I intended something else, and brought these things forward only because I can easily deduce from them the things I have decided to demonstrate' (*Eth.* II prop. 13 lem. 7 schol.).
97 For further comment, see especially Rice 1975; Gilead 1983; Saw 1969; and Den Uyl and Rice 1990. See also the account in Chapter 26.
98 See, especially, the first Discourse in Cordemoy's *Six discours sur la distinction et l'union du corps et de l'âme,* Cordemoy 1968, pp. 95–105.
99 Cordemoy 1968, p. 97.
100 Clauberg's *Elementa philosophia sive ontosophia* first appeared in 1647; a completely new version, having little in common with the 1647 work, was published in 1664 under the title *Metaphysica de ente, quae rectius ontosophia.* References are to chapters and

paragraphs in this edition, which was included in Clauberg's *Opera omnia philosophica* (Clauberg 1691).

101 *Ontosophia* chap. viii, para. 141.
102 *Ontosophia* chap. xii, paras. 206–7, 216.
103 *Ontosophia* chap. xviii, para. 291.
104 *Ontosophia* chap. xviii, paras. 292–4.
105 Geulincx 1891–3, vol. 2, pp. 272–3. Cf. de Vleeschauwer 1953–4.
106 Burthogge 1694, p. 69.
107 Burthogge 1694, p. 107.
108 Burthogge 1694, p. 70, also 92.
109 Burthogge 1694, pp. 162, 168.
110 Burthogge 1694, p. 167. Cf. p. 154: 'The Great work and Business of the Body is to *Singularize* and Individuate the *General Vital Principle* of the Universe, that it may become a *Soul,* or a Particular Vital Principle of a certain Particular Body.'
111 Burthogge 1694, p. 270.
112 Burthogge 1694, p. 61.
113 Robert Boyle, *The Origine of Formes and Qualities* (1666), in Boyle 1979, p. 54.
114 Boyle 1979, p. 30.
115 *De corp.* II.xi.2. References are to Hobbes 1839–45b, vol. 1.
116 *Ess.* II.xxvii.3.
117 *Ess.* II.xxvii.1.
118 Locke's marginal note in his copy of Sergeant 1697, p. 258. Locke's marginal notes are reproduced in the 1984 Garland reprint of Sergeant 1697.
119 Locke 1823, vol. 4, p. 439.
120 *Ess.* II.xxvii.3.
121 *Ess.* II.xxvii.2.
122 This, to Locke, is a self-evident principle. See *Ess.* IV.vii.5; I.ii.18.
123 *Ess.* II.xxvii.2.
124 *Ess.* II.xxvii.2. The corresponding passage in John Wynne's 1696 *Abridgment* of the *Essay* (which was authorised by Locke) makes this point more clearly. See Locke 1731, p. 112: 'The Identity and Diversity of *Modes* and *Relations* are determined after the same Manner that Substances are.' See also Pierre Coste's translation of the *Essay:* 'Toutes les autres choses n'étant, après les Substances, que des *Modes* ou des *Rélations* qui se terminent aux Substances, on peut déterminer encore par la même voie l'*identité* & la *diversité* de chaque existence particulière qui leur convient' (Locke 1755, p. 259).
125 *Some Physico-Theological Considerations about the Possibility of the Resurrection* (1675), in Boyle 1979, p. 193.
126 *De corp.* II.xi.7. In Hobbes, 839–45b, vol. 1, *principium* is translated as 'beginning'.
127 Boyle 1979, p. 194.
128 *De corp.* II.xi.7 (last three quotations).
129 In a famous passage of his 'Life of Theseus' in which Plutarch reports that the Athenians preserved the ship on which Theseus had sailed, he says: 'They took away the old timbers from time to time, and put new and sound ones in their places, so that the vessel became a standing illustration for the philosophers in the mooted question of growth, some declaring that it remained the same, others that it was not the same vessel' (Plutarch, *Theseus,* chap. xxiii, in Plutarch 1959, p. 49). The 'Ship of Theseus' was still a 'standing illustration' in the seventeenth-century debates over identity:

Philosophers as diverse as Hobbes, Clauberg, and Leibniz made use of it when discussing the question of identity through time.

130 *De corp.* II.xi.7 (last two quotations).

131 *De corp.* II.xi.7.

132 *Ess.* II.xxvii.3.

133 For Locke (but not according to the Cartesian tradition) immaterial substances (if they exist) exist in space. This is implied by Locke's following remark on the identity of spirits: 'Finite Spirits having had each its determinate time and place of beginning to exist, the relation to that time and place will always determine to each of them its Identity as long as it exists' (*Ess.* II.xxvii.2).

134 *Ess.* II.xxvii.2.

135 *Ess.* II.xxvii.28.

136 *Ess.* II.xxvii.7.

137 *Ess.* II.xxvii.4.

138 *Ess.* II.xxvii.4.

139 *Ess.* II.xxvii.8.

140 *Ess.* II.xxvii.6.

141 *Ess.* II.xxvii.4 (last two quotations); emphasis added.

142 *Ess.* II.xxvii.29; first italics added.

143 *Ess.* II.xxvii.29; see also secs. 15 and 6.

144 *Ess.* II.xxvii.8.

145 *Ess.* II.xxvii.29; last emphasis added.

146 See Griffin 1977, pp. 17–18; Wiggins 1980, chap. 1; Chappell 1989, esp. pp. 69–71; Ayers 1991, pp. 217–19.

147 In the literature on the topic, this version of the thesis is commonly labelled 'R' (see Griffin 1977, pp. 15 ff.; Wiggins 1980, pp. 16 ff.; Chappell 1989, pp. 69, 71). Mackie and Griffin ascribe R to Locke (Mackie 1976, p. 160; Griffin 1977, p. 131). Chappell, however, argues against the attribution of R to Locke (Chappell 1989, pp. 71 ff.). See also Alston and Bennett 1988; Garrett 1990; Uzgalis 1990; Thornton 1991; and Ayers 1991, vol. 2, pp. 217–19.

148 *Ess.* II.xxvii.3; emphasis added.

149 *Ess.* II.xxvii.3. Chappell ascribes the 'doctrine of double existence' to Locke. See Chappell 1989, pp. 72–5.

150 Chappell concedes both points (a) and (b). See Chappell 1989, pp. 72, 75.

151 Griffin, for example, states that 'Locke was confused on the topic.' See Griffin 1977, p. 18.

152 Stillingfleet 1687, p. 27.

153 Stillingfleet 1698, p. 171.

154 Locke 1823, vol. 4, p. 173.

155 See, e.g., Stillingfleet 1698, pp. 157–65; 1687, p. 27.

156 Stillingfleet 1687, p. 27.

157 Stillingfleet 1698, p. 171.

158 Locke 1823, vol. 4, p. 439.

159 Sergeant says that Locke 'distinguishes not between the *Extrinsecal Marks* and *Signes* by which we may *know* the Distinction of *Individuals,* and what *Intrinsecally* and Essentially constitutes or *makes* them *different* Things' (Sergeant 1697, p. 261).

160 Sergeant 1697, p. 260. See also Sergeant 1696, pp. 427–8: 'Their Individuation must be *presuppos'd* to Existence; and, so, cannot depend on it as on its Principle.' Cf. Sergeant 1700, pp. 112–14.

161 Sergeant 1697, p. 257.
162 Sergeant 1697, p. 257.
163 Sergeant 1697, p. 278.
164 Sergeant 1697, p. 257.
165 Sergeant 1697, p. 279.
166 Sergeant 1697, p. 270.
167 Sergeant 1697, pp. 268–9.
168 Lee 1702, pp. 121–2.
169 Lee 1702, p. 119; emphasis added.
170 Lee 1702, p. 122.
171 See 'Considerations sur la doctrine d'un Esprit Universel Unique' (1702): 'Some discerning people have believed and still believe today, that there is only one single spirit, which is universal and animates the whole universe and all its parts. . . . Spinoza, who recognizes only one single substance, is not far from the doctrine of a single universal spirit, and even the Neo-Cartesians, who hold that only God acts, affirm it, seemingly unawares' (Ger. VI 529–30 [Leibniz 1969, p. 554]).
172 Ger. IV 17.
173 The Suárezian character of Leibniz's view on individuation has been emphasised by a number of scholars. See especially McCullough 1978. Cf. Robinet 1981, pp. 76–96. Robinet adopts a more sceptical view than do most scholars about Suárez's influence on Leibniz. Robinet points out that among the many authors whom Leibniz quotes extensively and in detail, Suárez is mentioned rarely. Paul Bartha links Leibniz's account of the nature of individual substance to Duns Scotus (Bartha 1993, pp. 51–4).
174 Ger. IV 22.
175 Ger. IV 21.
176 Ger. IV 22–6.
177 Ger. IV 24.
178 Ger. IV 18.
179 Ger. IV 18.
180 Ger. IV 18.
181 Ger. IV 158 (Leibniz 1969, p. 128).
182 *Nouv. ess.* IV.viii.9. Translations of passages from the *Nouv. ess.* are taken from Leibniz 1981.
183 *Disc. mét.,* sec. 8. See also *To Arnauld,* 30 April 1687 (Ger. II 101–2 [Leibniz 1967, pp. 127–8]). My translations from the *Disc. mét.* are taken from Leibniz 1988. Cf. McCullough 1978, p. 260.
184 *Disc. mét.,* sec. 9. See also *Mon.,* sec. 9. Leibniz's principle of the identity of indiscernibles is much discussed today, and the literature on the topic is vast. See, e.g., von Leyden 1968, pp. 173–82; Hacking 1975b; Wiggins 1980, pp. 18 ff., 55 ff.; Frankel 1981; Mates 1986, chaps. 7 and 8; Brown 1990, chap. 6.
185 Ger. VII 372 (Leibniz and Clarke 1956, p. 36).
186 Leibniz's *Fourth Paper* to Clarke (Ger. VII 372 [Leibniz and Clarke 1956, p. 37]).
187 Leibniz's *Fifth Paper* to Clarke (Ger. VII 394 [Leibniz and Clarke 1956, p. 61]).
188 See also *Primae veritates* (Leibniz 1903, pp. 518 ff. [Leibniz 1969, p. 268]): 'It follows also [from the principle of sufficient reason] that *there cannot be two individual things in nature which differ only numerically.* For surely it must be possible to give a reason why they are different, and this must be sought in some differences within themselves. . . . Never are two eggs, two leaves, or two blades of grass in a garden to be found exactly similar to each other.'

189 Leibniz's *Fourth Paper* to Clarke (Ger. VII 372 [Leibniz and Clarke 1956, p. 37]).

190 Leibniz's *Fourth Paper* to Clarke (Ger. VII 372 [Leibniz and Clarke 1956, p. 36]). See also *Nouv. ess.* II.xxvii.3.

191 *Disc. mét.*, sec. 9. *Primae veritates* (Leibniz 1903, p. 520 [Leibniz 1969, p. 268]). See also Leibniz's 'Remarques sur la Lettre de M. Arnaud'(Ger. II 42 [Leibniz 1967, p. 45]).

192 *Disc. mét.*, sec. 8.

193 Robert Sleigh distinguishes between what he calls 'superintrinsicalness' and 'superessentialism'. Superintrinsicalness is the thesis that 'every individual has all its properties intrinsically'; superessentialism is the doctrine 'that each individual substance has all its properties essentially' (i.e., necessarily) (Sleigh 1990a, pp. 51, 57). He argues that the former does not imply the latter and that Leibniz is committed to superintrinsicalness, but rejects superessentialism (Sleigh 1990a, pp. 58, 67–72). Thus, the superessentialist account of the connexion between the concept of Adam and the property of having posterity would be that 'necessarily, the complete individual concept of Adam includes the property of having posterity' (Sleigh 1990a, pp. 59–60). God could not have brought it about that Adam existed and yet lacked posterity. According to Sleigh, Leibniz holds that 'the complete individual concept of Adam includes the property of having posterity' is *contingent*, i.e., dependent on the will of God.

194 Leibniz 1903, p. 8 (Leibniz 1973, p. 133).

195 *Nouv. ess.* II.xxvii.1.

196 Leibniz's *Fourth Paper* to Clarke (Ger. VII 372 [Leibniz and Clarke 1956, p. 37]).

197 Leibniz 1903, p. 8 (Leibniz 1973, p. 133).

198 *Nouv. ess.* II.xxvii.3. For Leibniz's rejection of atomism, see also his letter to Arnauld of 30 April 1687 (Ger. II 96–9 [Leibniz 1967, pp. 120–4]).

199 Leibniz's *Fifth Paper* to Clarke (Ger. VII 395 [Leibniz and Clarke 1956, pp. 62–3]).

200 *Disc. mét.*, sec. 14.

201 *Disc. mét.*, sec. 9.

202 *Mon.*, sec. 56. Translations from *Mon.* are taken from Leibniz 1973.

203 *Nouv. ess.* II.xxv.5. See also *Nouv. ess.* II.xxv.10: 'There is no term which is so absolute or so detached that it does not involve relations and is not such that a complete analysis of it would lead to other things and indeed to all other things.' McCullough has argued that, according to Leibniz, only relations as universals or concepts of the mind are ideal; universals or concepts of the mind are founded in the properties of substances. And these properties are 'one and all relational' (McCullough 1977, esp. pp. 37–8).

204 Letter to Arnauld, 30 April 1687 (Ger. II 91–2 [Leibniz 1967, p. 115]).

205 See Leibniz's 'Remarques sur la Lettre de M. Arnaud' (Ger. II 43 [Leibniz 1967, pp.46–7]). For further discussion of Leibniz's notion of individual substance, see Hacking 1972; Woolhouse 1982; Mates 1986, pp. 138–44; Wilson 1989, pp. 88–98; Brown 1990, chap. 2; Bartha 1993.

206 *Nouv. ess.* II.xxvii.4.

207 *Mon.*, sec. 1.

208 Ger. IV 478–9 [Leibniz 1973, pp.116–17]).

209 *Nouv. ess.* II.xxvii.4.

210 *Nouv. ess.* II.xxvii.4–6.

211 Daniel Garber argues that in the *Discours de métaphysique* (1686) and in the *Correspondence with Arnauld* (1686–8) Leibniz's notion of the unities that constitute the real entities of the physical world differs from that of his later theory of monads (Garber 1985; see also Chapter 23 in this book). According to the latter, bodies are aggregates

of monads (i.e., incorporeal substances); but in the *Correspondence with Arnauld,* for example, Leibniz's view is that *corporeal* substances are the real entities of the physical world. And corporeal substances are to be understood 'in analogy to human beings, a mind or something mindlike (a substantial form), connected with a body' (Garber 1985, p. 35). These unities are the ultimate building blocks that ground bodies, not the incorporeal substances themselves. However, as Garber concedes, the *individuality* and *identity* of these corporeal substances are said by Leibniz to be constituted by the mindlike component. As Garber says, 'This principle of individuation seems to be an extension of what might be considered a simple-minded Cartesian principle of individuation for persons (same mind, same person) to the wider domain of corporeal substances, soul-like entities united to bodies' (Garber 1985, pp. 58–9).

212 Letter to Arnauld, 30 April 1687 (Ger. II 96–7 [Leibniz 1967, p. 121]).
213 Letter to Arnauld, 30 April 1687 (Ger. II 100–101 [Leibniz 1967, p. 126]).
214 Letter to Arnauld, 28 November/8 December 1686 (Ger. II 76 [Leibniz 1967, p. 94]). See also Letter to Arnauld, 30 April 1687 (Ger.II 101 [Leibniz 1967, p. 126]).
215 Letter to Arnauld, 30 April 1687 (Ger. II 97 [Leibniz 1967, p. 121]); last two quotations.
216 *Nouv. ess.* II.xxvii.28–9.
217 Letter to Arnauld, 30 April 1687 (Ger. II 97 [Leibniz 1967, p. 121]). For a different account of the relationship between Leibniz's early and mature theories of individuation, see the brief note by McCullough 1988.
218 Wolff 1751, paras. 586–90.
219 Wolff 1751, paras. 17, 180. See also Wolff 1736, paras. 227–9. For a discussion of Wolff's account of individuation, see Gracia 1993. However, Gracia does not take into account Wolff's German Metaphysics (Wolff 1751), and he does not discuss Leibniz in this context.
220 Crusius 1745, paras. 383–4.
221 Lambert 1771, vol. I, para. 129.
222 Clarke's *Fourth Reply* to Leibniz (Ger. VII 382 [Leibniz and Clarke 1956, p. 46]).
223 Hume 1978, p. 201.
224 Reid 1969; Essay III, chapter iv, 'Of Identity', pp. 338–44. All quotations are from this chapter.
225 *Kritik der reinen Vernunft* A262–3/B318–19. Translations are taken from Kant 1933.

III

GOD

10

THE IDEA OF GOD

JEAN-LUC MARION

I. POSING THE QUESTION

The seventeenth century marks a significant moment in thought concerning the definition of God. This is the period in which the radical position of subjectivity is replaced by the impersonal recognition of transcendence as a point of departure of philosophical reflection – God is now a term in a demonstration, and no longer the assumed goal of a journey towards Him. And philosophy, until this time explicitly constituted by metaphysics (*metaphysica, philosophia prima,* then *ontologia*), has to transpose into the new domain of rationality certain problems and concepts previously treated only by revealed theology (*theologia, sacra scientia*). This twofold transformation is nicely illustrated by the problem of the essence of God: from Descartes on, metaphysical discussions of the characteristics and attributes of God consist in transposing and translating, so to speak, into purely philosophical terms theological debates on the divine names as they arise until the Scriptures, through the intermediation of the formulations given of them by Pseudo-Dionysius the Areopagite (fifth century?) in his celebrated treatise *De divinis nominibus.*[1]

These innovations can best be understood in their context, a set of themes from Thomas Aquinas. Despite the long gap between the thirteenth century and the seventeenth, Thomas's views remained decisive for several reasons. The first was the renewal of the 'Thomistic' school: notably through the works of Capreolus, Sylvestre de Ferrare, and especially Cardinal Thomas de Vio, called Cajetan (1469–1534). These Thomists widely influenced university and ecclesiastical life, in particular the work of the Council of Trent (1545–63), whose sessions were presided over by a copy of the *Summa theologiae* placed upon the altar.[2] Thomistic views were also diffused in the widely circulated works of Jesuit theologians, both those from the Collegium Romanum, like Benedictus Pererius (1535–1610), and those from the great Hispanic universities, like Gabriel Vasquez (1551–1604) and Francisco Suárez (1548–1617). Suárez's *Disputationes metaphysicae* (1597), for

Translated by Thomas Carlson and Daniel Garber.

example, enjoyed a wide and lasting circulation throughout both Protestant and Catholic Europe.[3] As a notable example of the persistence of this Thomistic influence, Descartes, a former student at the Jesuit school of La Flèche, stated that the only books he carried along on his travels were the Bible and a *Summa* of Saint Thomas.[4]

Thomas set three conditions on the adequate construction of a denomination of God: (1) In God, but not in creatures, essence is indistinguishable from the fact of His being: 'The essence of God is his very being';[5] 'His essence is his being.'[6] God is therefore defined as a 'pure act',[7] which subsists through itself and as act.[8] (2) Therefore, we cannot become acquainted with this kind of transcendence directly from created beings, in which there is always a real distinction between essence and being. One can ascend to God only by way of five paths (*viae*), whose very multiplicity marks the gap between the creature and the Creator. These five ways reach God as He is understood under a variety of names, as first mover, as first efficient cause, as necessary cause, as the cause of every perfection, and, finally, as the end of all things.[9] But can we reduce these five ways to one? Or, at the very least, can we reconcile with one another the definitions of God at which they arrive, without any logical incompatibility? (3) In order to address these difficulties Thomas emphatically states that all our knowledge of God (including that obtained through the *viae*) remains analogical:[10] the gap always remains, even when our knowledge is certain; even if we can know what God is not, we cannot know what He is – He who remains to us 'profoundly unknown, *penitus ignotum*'.[11] Though Thomistic interpreters continue to disagree, the debate over the precise type of analogy in question here[12] matters less than Thomas's radical agnosticism: because we can become acquainted with God by several paths, each of which is certain, our knowledge of God terminates in inadequate and relative names, names which only allow God to be known as unknown.

Working within these Thomistic themes, seventeenth-century debates over the idea of God were played out within the space of certain questions which are, strictly speaking, theological: Can the divine names be reduced one to another? Can the divine essence be expressed adequately by any one of these names? But yet, something new transforms everything: as regards the divine names, everything becomes a question of ideas, concepts, or definitions of God.

II. THE ANALOGY OF BEING AND THE PROGRESSION TOWARDS UNIVOCITY

Ironically enough, even though the revival of Thomism was important to sixteenth- and seventeenth-century thought, Thomas's theses were often revived in a weakened form, or even in a form that reversed the original meaning altogether. That was the case with the *Disputationes metaphysicae*. In the *Disputationes,* Suárez filled the analogical gap between the finite and the infinite by a univocal concept of being (*conceptus univocus entis*), sufficient to represent to the human mind any being whatsoever in a confused and indeterminate way. In the dispute concerning the notion of being that inevitably arises between the univocal concept and traditional analogical conceptions of being, Suárez argued: 'If we must deny one of the two, we must deny analogy, which is uncertain, rather than the unity of the concept, which seems to be well demonstrated.'[13] Consequently, despite Suárez's apparent restoration of Thomas's analogical theology against its denial (by Duns Scotus) and its distortion (by Cajetan), in the end he recognised that 'being is very similar to univocal terms.'[14] Thus, being applies in the same sense (logically or intrinsically) to both creatures and God: the ontological gap between the finite and the infinite distinguishes God from his creatures less than the conceptual representation of them as beings joins them.

This theoretical reversal, in essence the victory of Duns Scotus over Thomas, had two consequences. (1) God (existence and essence) was said to derive from the univocal concept of being, of which He constitutes only one among other possible instantiations. Since the concept of being is defined primarily in terms of its internal possibility (non-contradiction), God can be the first being only in so far as He is the greatest possibility, the necessary being *par excellence:* 'a being altogether necessary', 'a being with absolute necessity, that is, a necessary being'.[15] He achieves all perfection allowed by the possible: 'It belongs to his essence to include in some way all the perfection that is possible within the whole dimension of being.'[16] Thus 'the most perfect of all possible beings'[17] achieves perfection within the scope permitted by the concept of possibility, a concept connected with the univocal concept of being. (2) The knowledge that God can have of finite essences likewise derives from a univocal concept, since these essences are defined within the scope of possibility and a univocal conception of being. Created essences do not *derive* from God as their exemplar (as in Bonaventure and Thomas), but are *seen* by God under some representation. Furthermore, this representation is true not in virtue of a divine exemplar or God's omnipotence, but by virtue of the intrinsic and independent possibility that pertains to a coherent statement, whether it be a question of logic, mathematics, or morality.[18] God therefore does not create the essences but only their existences. Statements concerning what is logically possible, statements which ground what we can say about essences, do not depend upon the creative power of God; indeed, they impose themselves upon his understanding: 'These statements are not true because they are known by God, but rather they are known because they are true, otherwise one couldn't give any reason why God would necessarily know that they are true.'[19] The univocity of the concept of being thus gives rise to a kind of epistemological univocity; representation governs the knowledge God has with respect to possibilities (creatures), as much as it does the knowledge which finite understandings claim with respect to the infinite. To this extent, at least, God's knowledge is like ours.

But one question then arises: Does the definition of God as *ens perfectissimum,* the most perfect being, always imply a tendency towards univocity?

III. GOD AS MATHEMATICIAN AND UNIVOCAL RATIONALITY

This progression towards ontological and epistemological univocity in theology is not an isolated phenomenon and corresponds to the demand of contemporary scientists for univocity. Indeed, in order to legitimate the mathematical treatment of physics (as opposed to the merely hypothetical status Aristotle granted mathematical statements in the natural sciences), seventeenth-century scientists persistently privileged one argument: humans can interpret the physical world in mathematical language because God first conceived the world that was to be created in accordance with mathematical rationality. Though this argument is certainly powerful, it has one controversial consequence: since mathematical statements are perfectly univocal, God understands them in precisely the same way that humans do. In principle, if not always in fact, God determines the world through calculation in exactly the way humans come to understand it through calculation; the mathematical laws that govern the world are understood univocally for God and for us. This consequence is emphasised by three authors in particular.

1. Johann Kepler wanted at first to become a theologian, but dedicated himself to astronomy because in it he found an equal opportunity to know and to praise the Creator.[20] He did not hesitate, therefore, to impose mathematical rationality on God Himself: 'Mathematical reasons were coeternal with God';[21] 'The reasons of geometry are coeternal with God.'[22] Indeed, Kepler goes so far as to identify mathematical rationality with God: 'Before the creation of the world, geometry [being] coeternal with the mind of God, being God Himself (for what is there in God that is not God Himself?) supplied God with exemplars for the creation of the world.'[23] Therefore God created the world exactly as we understand it: through calculation and the construction of figures, in short, 'by practicing an eternal geometry',[24] for 'God geometrised in creating.'[25] Kepler thus returns to a

slogan traditionally attributed to Plato, but in sincerely Christian terms and with a strictly epistemological intention: 'What more is needed in order to say with Plato that "God always geometrises"?'[26] Kepler formulates nothing less than a new definition of God, a new definition which allows him to free mathematics from any restriction in its application to the interpretation of the physical world; indeed, it goes so far as to guarantee for the human mind a knowledge that is 'of the same nature as that of God, *eodem genere cum Deo*'.[27] But already, an inadequate and relative divine name of the sort in Thomas is no longer at issue; this epistemological univocity in fact implies that we understand God's divinity to the same extent that we understand mathematical possibilities.

2. Galileo Galilei takes up the same definition of God for the same epistemological reasons. His famous statement that we must consider the book of nature as 'written in mathematical language'[28] meets the requirement that we go beyond the hypothetical status that Aristotle had imposed upon mathematics: for what we read mathematically in nature to have physical significance, the physical world must receive, from the beginning, a mathematical structure. Hence a second view, which forms the grounds of the first, but with an even greater emphasis, is that 'the knowledge [of the human understanding] equals [*agguagli*] the divine [knowledge] in objective certitude; . . . to make myself better understood, I say that the truth we know through mathematical demonstrations is the same as that truth the divine wisdom knows.'[29] Galileo does not affirm the connexions between God and mathematics as often as Kepler does, to be sure. However, it is not because of any timidity, but, on the contrary, because of a serene assurance with respect to an already established and indisputable thesis; it is no longer a question of demonstrating it, but rather of exploiting all of its consequences. Nevertheless, the boldness of such an equality between the human understanding and divine wisdom might well threaten the omnipotence of the creator; one presumes that this played some rôle in the accusations made against Galileo in his second trial.[30]

3. Marin Mersenne should not be ignored in this context. A friend of Descartes, and the translator of the *Méchaniques de Galilée* (1634), he continually invoked the identity of mathematics and the divine understanding, both in his scientific work and in his apologetic writings. Indeed, even atheists must admit mathematical certitude; 2 and 2 make 4 for both Don Juan and the Prince of Nassau. Now, as Plato held, mathematics constitutes the language and activity of God Himself. And so Mersenne argues, 'We can raise geometry as an objection [to the atheists], provided that they simply listen to Plato, who discovered God through this science, for he said that . . . God always practices geometry.'[31] Furthermore, Mersenne held that the 'eternal ideas'[32] of God are to be identified

with mathematical statements considered as 'the first exemplar and prototype of his reasoning',[33] to such an extent that eternal truths are 'not dependent on anything else and [are] God Himself'.[34] Thus Mersenne transforms the traditional theological thesis that the divine ideas in the end vanish into the divine essence (as in Augustine, Bonaventure and Thomas) by identifying God's omnipotence with respect to creation with the requirements of mathematical rationality; mathematical rationality is held to be the *only* possible and thinkable kind of rationality. In this way divine omnipotence is subordinated to mathematics.

The scientist's univocity of knowing combines with the univocity of being, as held by theologians like Suárez, to constitute an anthropomorphism all the more attractive in so far as it supports, all at the same time, the progress of science, a reasonable apologetic, and a metaphysical account of possibility. Such a view was common even to some who were unsympathetic to mathematics or scholastic theology. Francis Bacon, hardly a mathematician, held that 'after the word of God, natural philosophy is the most certain remedy against superstition and the best food for faith. And so one properly sees in it the most faithful and esteemed servant of religion, since the one reveals the will of God, and the other His power.'[35] And Pierre Gassendi, no friend of scholasticism, wrote in support of a Suárezian position on univocity: 'Is there thus a possibility for abstracting some concept which would be superior to God? And why not, since no one denies that the concept of being is superior to God.'[36]

IV. TRANSCENDENCE AND UNKNOWABILITY

Widespread as it was, not all seventeenth-century thinkers shared this tendency towards univocity with respect to the question of God. Counterbalancing the trend towards univocity is an exactly contrary orientation, strange but powerful, the insistence upon the radically unknowable transcendence of the divine essence. There were a number of convergent symptoms of this movement, including: (1) the translation of the works of Pseudo-Dionysius the Areopagite, published by Dom J. Goulu (Jean de Saint-François) in Paris in 1608, whose unquestioned success was certainly not due to the quality of the translation; (2) the circulation throughout all of Europe of the writings of John of the Cross (published in Alcalà in 1618), and translated by Father Cyprien de la Nativité;[37] (3) the installation of the Carmelite order in France (Dijon, Poitiers, etc.) by Bérulle; (4) the influence of Madame Acarie's circle; (5) the development of nihilistic [*néantiste*] mysticism under the influence of the Rhenish-Flemish masters (Ruysbroeck, Tauler, Dionysius Carthusianus [Denys le Chartreux], Harphius, etc.); (6) the appropriately named 'devout party' in France, whose growing political influence clashed with that of Richelieu, despite the fact that the famous 'gray Eminence' of the cardinal, Father Joseph du Tremblay (Joseph of Paris), had at first published several remarkable works of spirituality.[38]

There are three decisive figures in this deep, complex, and lasting movement.

1. The most powerful theoretician was no doubt Benoît de Canfeld (1562–1610), whose *Règle de perfection* would leave a strong mark on the age. In it, God is defined by the very impossibility of being defined. Indeed, before God's infinity, the creature must recognise itself not only as finite, but also as so immeasurably surpassed that its finitude amounts to a pure and simple nothingness; the absence of all proportion between the finite and the infinite reduces the finite to nothing: 'Reason tells us that we can only be nothing (compared with the independent being of God) since God is infinite: for if we were something, God would not be infinite; for in that case his being would end where ours began.'[39] In so far as a creature is nothing [*néant*] before God and acknowledges its 'annihilation' [*anéantissement*], it can only know God through the very characteristics that prevent it from conceiving Him: 'No speculation by the understanding can apprehend God; but the love that the will offers does. Speculation conceives of God, who is omnipotent, immense, infinite and incomprehensible, in proportion to its own small, weak capacity, while the will, on the contrary, proportions itself to God, enlarging itself in accordance with His immensity, infinity and omnipotence.'[40] The will alone can still reach God, since God, beyond every concept and beyond all measure, reveals Himself only as a pure Will, in which His entire essence is summed up:

> This Essential will is purely spirit and life, totally abstract, purified (of itself) and stripped of all forms and images of created things, bodily or spiritual, temporal or eternal; it is apprehended neither by man's sense nor by his judgement, nor by human reason; but it is outside all human capacity and beyond all human understanding, for it is nothing other than God Himself.[41]

This is no half-hearted voluntarism; Benoît de Canfeld has rediscovered the Dionysian and patristic 'way of eminence', which goes beyond affirmations and negations and reaches God only through the love that the will offers. On this view the names of God can and should all be successively asserted and denied of God, and, with a tension that is never suppressed, they are attributed to God, but as things that we cannot really say of him.[42] When in his treatise *Quinquaginta nomina Dei* (Brussels, 1640) the Jesuit L. Lessius chose infinity as the first name of God, he was following the same tradition.[43]

2. Though less powerful as a thinker, Cardinal Pierre de Bérulle was more accessible, and he was most responsible for popularising this standpoint, along with its aporias. In his *Discours de l'état et des grandeurs de Jésus Christ* (Paris, 1623) and in the *Opuscules* which complete it, he underscores three features of the idea of God. First, following the Thomistic doctrine, Bérulle holds that in God, 'His existence is His own essence.'[44] Second, following Denys the Areopagite, he holds that God's being is, nevertheless, subordinated to His unity:

> Unity is the first property that the philosophers attribute to created being: it is the first perfection that Christians recognize and adore in uncreated being. . . . And the Platonists . . . , the theologians among the philosophers . . . dare to say . . . that God has unity and not being; since the unity, according to their lofty intelligence, is something primary and superior to being.[45]

It follows that when He goes beyond being, God also goes beyond logical representation and the realm of possibility. Third, Bérulle is above all inclined to call God infinite: 'the infinite being of their [the persons of the Trinity] common essence', 'the infinite being of God'. And from infinity, incomprehensibility clearly follows for Bérulle.[46] A similar position can be found in the most important Oratorians, Bourgoing (1585–1662), Condren (1588–1641), and Gibieuf (1583–1650).[47]

3. François de Sales (1562–1622) certainly had reservations about this nihilistic mysticism, from which he was separated by his 'devout humanism' and Christocentrism. But nonetheless, like Bérulle, he belongs to the Dionysian movement. His fundamental work, the *Traité de l'amour de Dieu,* quite clearly denies that a single name might ever define God: 'In order to speak of God in any way at all, we are forced to make use of many names.'[48] According to de Sales, one must clearly and immediately recognise God's incomprehensibility, since it flows from an essential infinity, which over-determines and modifies His other attributes, all the more because it is added to them. Every attribute becomes infinite, and precisely because of this, it loses any claim to univocity: 'The Divinity is an incomprehensible abyss of all perfection, infinite in excellence and infinitely sovereign in goodness. . . . O infinite Divinity, o divine Infinity . . . the impotence of this desire comes from the infinite infinity of your perfection, which surpasses any wish and any thought.'[49] Infinity thus indicates the incomprehensibility – the 'incomprehensible goodness'[50] – in each of the perfections commonly attributed to God: 'infinite goodness', 'infinite charity', 'infinite good will', 'infinite good', and so on.[51] Such incomprehensible infinity remains accessible only to love; any

attempt to grasp it through other means, through conceptual knowledge in particular, will fail.

Philosophical debate in the seventeenth century would retain several elements from this spiritual movement: the claim that the divine essence is absolutely transcendent, against all claims of univocity, ontological or epistemological – God as incomprehensible; the rational justification of this incomprehensibility by the incommensurable disproportion between God and creature – God as infinite; and the abandonment of all attempts to represent or comprehend God through the understanding, hence the frequent appeal to the will, either love in us, or 'essential will' and omnipotence in God.

V. DESCARTES

1. The creation of the eternal truths

In three famous letters to Father Mersenne from 1630, Descartes responds clearly with force and originality to the dilemmas posed by the two dominant trends of his time. He first rejects the epistemological univocity of the scientists: 'The mathematical truths that you [Mersenne and those like him] call eternal were established by God and depend entirely upon Him. To say that these truths are independent of God is in effect to speak of Him as a Jupiter or a Saturn, and to subjugate Him to Styx and the fates.'[52] Henceforth, 2 plus 2 make 4 and the radii of a circle are equal only by virtue of a decision God made. Thus God does not reveal His own understanding and rationality through mathematics, which He transcends by virtue of creating it. Next Descartes denies the thesis of ontological univocity, reversing Suárez's doctrine almost word for word:

As for the eternal truths, I say once again that they are only true or possible because God conceived them as true or possible. They are not known as true by God in any way which would imply that they are true independently of Him. And if men indeed understood the meaning of their words, they could never say without blasphemy that the truth of something precedes God's knowledge of it, for in God to will and to know are but one.[53]

In this way Descartes the philosopher sets himself against the 'blasphemy' of the theologians: logical truths and essences do not pre-exist eternally in God's understanding, before entering into temporal existence through an act of His will. God's understanding is not a (passive) realm of possibilities; rather, it merges with the will in one single, global act of creation. From this follows a radical consequence: God 'is the author as much of the essence as of the existence of creatures'.[54] God creates all finite rationality, and in creating it, He stands above it; such transcendent rationality (if it can be so called) cannot be characterised in terms of representation, logical possibility, or calculation. But if that is the case, can we name God at all?

Despite the evident difficulties, Descartes puts forward a name for God in 1630: 'incomprehensible power', a formula found also in the *Meditationes* of 1641, where Descartes calls God 'immense and incomprehensible power'.[55] This phrase is to be understood quite literally. First, God is incomprehensible because He acts before any rationality determines or delimits His actions; therefore, from the point of view of our minds, finite and endowed with a limited rationality, the God who creates them remains inaccessible in a sense, even if He is known in another, weaker sense.[56] And second, God is a power, because in the absence of any common rationality and of any analogy of being between the finite and the infinite, only a relation of power remains: even if the understanding does not comprehend it, we are acquainted with that power. In short, as 'an infinite and incomprehensible being', God is known only as 'a cause whose power surpasses the limits of human understanding'.[57] This radical doctrine shapes the debate later in the century; its importance (not to mention its difficulties) cannot be overestimated.[58] This radical and original doctrine clearly reflected the spiritual current and strongly reaffirmed the transcendence and unknowability of God discussed in Section IV. But in transposing these themes into his metaphysics, Descartes, in fact, finds himself as isolated from the scholastic theologians and philosophers as he is from the scientists.

As original as this doctrine may be, others held similar views. Michel de Montaigne also recognised God 'as an incomprehensible power' and as a 'first cause'.[59] He therefore consistently held that it is 'presumptuous' to reduce the divine power to our understanding, to submit it to the Fates and to claim 'that human reason is in general control of all that is inside and outside the vault of heaven'.[60] What is often taken to be a simple scepticism or agnosticism derives primarily from a scrupulous respect for the transcendence of God. A follower of Montaigne, Pierre Charron anticipated certain Cartesian formulas almost word for word: 'belief in a God who is author of all things',[61] 'God primarily sovereign, and absolute Lord and master of the world', 'God Himself, or rather the first, original and fundamental law, which is God and the nature of the world, like the King and the law in a state'.[62] Bérulle, too, agreed with Descartes in defining God in terms of independence: 'Just as it is characteristic of and essential to divine and uncreated being to be independent, so is it characteristic of and essential to every created being to be needful of, adhering to and dependent on its God, its principle, and its origin.'[63] Among the heirs of Descartes, one of the rare defenders of the creation of eternal truths was Dom Robert Desgabets, particularly in his *Traité de l'indéfectabilité des créatures*. There he reaffirms the epistemological transcendence of God: 'It belongs to the nature of the infinite that it cannot be comprehended by a finite understanding; it is always unreasonable to refuse God certain things that should be attributed to Him, under the pretext that that surpasses our knowledge.' But Desgabets also defends God's ontological transcendence: 'God is the principle of all created things, with respect to both essence and existence.'[64]

The Cartesian conception of God as 'incomprehensible power' did find some support in 1630. But it was opposed to the dominant trends of contemporary epistemology and theology. Furthermore, the position was not without some pronounced difficulties. It is not surprising, then, that in his first publication, the *Discours de la méthode* of 1637, Descartes himself passes over in silence the 'incomprehensible power' of God; perhaps he still needed to think it through systematically.[65]

2. The three metaphysical names of God

The doctrine of 1630 gave rise to one obvious question: Does the transcendence of an 'incomprehensible power' allow one to justify, or even make use of reason? One of the major objectives of the *Meditationes de prima philosophia* (Paris, 1641; Amsterdam, 1642) was to address this problem. The *Meditationes* was intended to ground the certainty of the mathematical and empirical sciences. But this goal does not exclude consideration of the nature and existence of God; indeed, the demonstration that God exists (along with the *ego*) was to become the principal goal of what would later be called the 'special metaphysics (*metaphysica specialis*)'.

Descartes begins in Meditatio I with an idea of God, 'a certain long-standing opinion that there is an omnipotent God'.[66] This common and pre-philosophical conception of God is the point of departure for Descartes's project; it will be transposed into his metaphysics and given stricter treatment there. On this basis Descartes proposes three ways for demonstrating the existence of God: (1) the so-called *a posteriori* argument, wherein God is considered the cause of His idea in me (Meditatio III, in two formulations); (2) the so-called *a priori* argument, which deduces God's existence from the very idea of the divine essence (the so-called ontological argument, Meditatio V); and (3) the argument from the principle of (sufficient) reason, which finds the cause of God in God Himself, henceforth named *causa sui* (cause of itself) (Resp. I, IV). These three demonstrations are examined here not for their logical validity, but for the different conceptions of the essence (and therefore the idea) of God that they advance, and for their compatibility.

1. The *a posteriori* proof relies on the idea of an infinite substance. Descartes takes it to be beyond question that we all have such an idea.[67] In so far as we have such an idea, we are capable of perceiving 'the infinite', 'the actually infinite', 'the infinite nature'. Indeed, Descartes claims that our perception of the finite is a limitation of the infinite, just as a horizon renders visible that which stands out against its background, and thus, he claims, the perception of the finite presupposes that we have such an idea. The *a posteriori* proof also presupposes that the fact that we have such an idea of the infinite requires a cause, a cause that bears 'even upon ideas, in which only objective reality is considered'.[68] (This implies a perhaps questionable enlargement of the domain of causality, in so far as God is represented as the cause of His own idea in the *ego*.) But we still need one last condition for this argument, a condition which many will deny: the finite *ego* must acknowledge that it cannot cause the idea of infinity in itself.[69] For Descartes this acknowledgement is self-evident because it follows from the most characteristic property of infinity, its incomprehensibility; straightaway in the *Meditationes,* Descartes recognises God as incomprehensible and infinite, as a nature that is *immensa, incomprehensibilis, et infinita,* as he had since 1630.[70] The basis of Descartes's view here is quite clear. Infinity is excepted from all measure; but through method, understood in the sense of the *mathesis universalis,* we can only learn what can be measured. God therefore becomes unreachable through the method, that is, incomprehensible to objective science.[71] Thus in the first proof for the existence of God in the *Meditationes,* Descartes remains strictly consistent with his thesis from 1630.[72] The denomination of God by the idea of infinity, although the clearest and truest idea,[73] nevertheless escapes all finite representations (as well as all finite causes). Thus the old *via negativa* of theology repeats itself within the domain of Descartes's philosophy.

2. The *a priori* proof relies on the idea of a divine essence that encompasses all perfections, including existence. This proof, apparently borrowed from Anselm, was criticised by Kant under the name of the 'ontological argument'. But our concern here is to determine the definition of God that it implies. For the idea of a perfect being, *idea entis perfectissimi,* presupposes that God is identified as the supremely perfect being – *summe perfectum.*[74] On the one hand, God carries to perfection every quality finite beings possess imperfectly; on the other hand, He imbodies in Himself, without limit, all possible perfections, diverse as they may be. Thus Descartes does not hesitate to define God as 'the aggregation of perfections'.[75] This raises two questions. (1) If God is limited to perfecting properties

that are already achieved, though imperfectly, in finite beings, does He not remain continuous with them? Does the incommensurable gap between finite and infinite remain intact if God simply accumulates and completes what the finite already possesses? (2) The *a priori* proof claims to deduce the existence of God from His essence 'neither more' 'nor less' certainly than the sum of the angles of a triangle are deduced from its definition.[76] Does this equivalence not contradict the transcendence of the idea of God with relation to the ideas of the objects of method? Does it not also contradict the original aim of 'demonstrating the metaphysical truths in a manner that is clearer than the demonstrations of geometry'?[77] This second conception of God's essence would then be in opposition to the first in so far as it remains within the domain of method (as the geometrical analogy suggests) and denies the complete incomprehensibility of the infinite. In this way it constitutes a return to the affirmative path in theology.

3. The last proof relies on the principle, which Descartes thinks is manifest through natural light and therefore exempt from the order of reasons, that there must be at least as much being in the cause as in the effect.[78] When Descartes moves from Meditatio III to the First, Second, and Fourth Replies, this principle is made more radical and characterised as a dictate (*dictat*) of reason: 'The light of nature dictates that if anything exists we may always ask why it exists; that is, we may inquire into its efficient cause, or, if it does not have one, we may demand why it does not need one.'[79] The necessity of having a cause or reason, *causa sive ratio*, allows no exception, since it applies 'to God Himself'.[80] With God, there can be no question of an external cause (God would lose His divinity); so there must be an internal cause. Descartes's view is that God's very essence is the (quasi-) efficient cause of His existence. Far from claiming that God has no cause (the negative sense in which the mediaevals characterised God as being '*a se*'), Descartes argues that God in Himself is a genuine cause of Himself (*causa sui*); God's essence, interpreted at first as an 'overabundant power',[81] ends up playing the rôle of an efficient cause, though in a somewhat tangential sense. This conception of God as *causa sui* gives rise to two questions. First, Descartes here establishes the existence of God only by submitting his essence to a principle – soon after called the principle of sufficient reason – which precedes both God's essence and His existence; this third conception of God's essence therefore contradicts the first in so far as it imposes a precondition as to what is possible and what is not upon the supposedly transcendent God. Second, nevertheless, the conception of the divine essence as 'overabundant power' still preserves God's infinity: 'infinite power' reduces to the 'immense and incomprehensible power', which corresponds literally to the definition of the creator of eternal truths from 1630.[82] On this point,

therefore, the third conception of God is in agreement with the first (infinity), but in opposition to the second (the aggregate of perfections). In this way it is in accord with the so-called way of eminence.[83]

The three conceptions of God Descartes offers in his metaphysics do not mesh with one another; indeed, they seem contradictory for the most part. This apparent inconsistency does not amount to a failure, however. Rather, it attests to the fact that God cannot adequately be conceived within the limited discourse of metaphysics. Descartes here boldly and explicitly confronts the tension between the demand for a conception of God that is intelligible to humans and respect for His transcendence. The fact that Descartes's metaphysical theology remains indeterminate and breaks down into several theses (just as light breaks down when it passes through a prism) makes it, somewhat paradoxically, *the* radical position on the question of God at the beginning of modern thought.[84] This plurality of conceptions of God's essence made it difficult for Descartes's successors, at least up until Berkeley, to decide whether to follow Descartes or to criticise him.

VI. THE INDECISION OF THE CARTESIAN SCHOOL

Strictly speaking, it is incorrect to talk of a 'Cartesian school'. Even during Descartes's lifetime, some of his most public disciples (Regius, for example) distanced themselves from him, and there was no single set of doctrines to which one had to subscribe to be a member of the Cartesian school of thought. Nevertheless, after his death, several claimed to follow in his path and took up the defense of his doctrine. Three of these followers in particular demonstrate the tension between Descartes's three conceptions of God's essence: Louis de la Forge, Johann Clauberg, and Dom Robert Desgabets.

Claiming to be a spokesman for Descartes, Louis de La Forge annotated and published *L'homme* and then added his own *Traité de l'esprit de l'homme,* in which he employs the three Cartesian conceptions of God.[85] At times he refers to 'the infinite and sovereign spirit', which enables him to attach 'the idea that we have of an infinite spirit to this name, God'.[86] But then the idea that God is defined as the *ens summe perfectum* (one of whose consequences is God's infinitude) challenges this conception of God defined as infinite: 'As for the divine nature, all that we know of it, without the aid of Revelation, is founded upon that great and sublime notion of a very perfect being, whence it follows that it is very simple, necessary, infinite, all-knowing, the first and principal cause of all other beings.'[87] La Forge nevertheless adheres to the doctrine of 1630, the creation of the eternal truths:

[God] is the first of all beings, upon which all things depend, both for their essence and for their existence; He is their principal and in some way total cause, the cause which makes them be and be what they are. Thus they are good and true only because He willed, understood and produced them so. . . . In Him there is only a single action which is entirely simple and entirely pure . . . because in God to see and to will are but one thing.[88]

However, La Forge's meditation on the creation of eternal truths concentrates almost exclusively on causality, to the detriment of incomprehensibility, in order to prepare the reader for his argument for occasionalism; his account of Descartes's third conception of God (*causa sui*) is concerned with the externally directed causality of creation, and neglects the internal *causa sui*. As La Forge treats it, the 'infinite power of God' mainly concerns the 'total and proximate cause' at issue in the correspondence between thought and motion; his God is defined as 'the first, universal, and total cause of motion'. In short, 'infinite power' creates but is no longer exercised over divine existence.[89]

Johann Clauberg defends Descartes's metaphysical cause with fidelity and intelligence; his equivocations are thus all the more significant.[90] Clauberg begins by reviewing the three traditional theological paths to God, but only in order to dispose of them. The ways of eminence and negation concern only perfection, either the perfection of the Creator or the imperfection of His creatures. From the perspective of the affirmative way, only causality remains.[91] Thus only two of the three Cartesian conceptions remain operative here: perfection and causality. Either God is given as pure act, *actus purus,* 'the cause of created things not only with respect to their becoming (*secundum fieri*) but also with respect to their being (*secundum esse*)',[92] or else He is called *ens summe perfectum* or *ens perfectissimum*.[93] As to infinity, it is explicitly reduced to a particular case of perfection: 'The idea of an infinite substance, that is, the idea of His substance, which possesses absolutely all thinkable perfections in the most perfect way.'[94] Or rather, since 'the name "perfection" . . . is taken to include the contents . . . of all of the attributes',[95] 'infinity' would seem to become the equivalent of any attribute whatsoever. Thus there is at least one exception to Clauberg's Cartesian orthodoxy in so far as in his thought, the idea of infinity loses its priority over the other conceptions of the divine essence. This starts a trend that will soon become more general.

Dom Robert Desgabets constitutes a notable exception to this trend. Unlike La Forge and Clauberg, he maintains a strict balance between the three Cartesian conceptions, no doubt because he always privileges the doctrine of the creation of the eternal truths, as earlier noted. God is first defined as the 'cause of all existing things, in whatever manner they exist', as their 'only cause' and their 'only and immediate cause.'[96] But in this context, that causality is never reflected back on the existence of God Himself; though God is characterised as cause, He is not explicitly characterised as *causa sui*. (It should be remembered, though, when dealing with this Cartesian denomination of God, it is not only a matter of '*causa sui*' taken literally but the interpretation of the essence of God in terms of causality, of which the '*causa sui*' only represents the extreme case.) It remains to determine God in Himself. Sometimes Descartes characterises Him as 'a supremely perfect essence, in a word . . . the supreme perfection and reality'.[97] But this title remains rare, and does not prevent Desgabets from characterising God in terms of infinity: 'that infinite thing, which is God, exists'; reciprocally, 'God . . . by rights has the quality of infinity.'[98] Despite having carefully balanced his account, Desgabets is unable to reconcile the three conceptions of the divine essence any better than Descartes does; he simply reproduces Descartes's irresolution.

VII. METAPHYSICAL ATTEMPTS AT A UNIFICATION OF THE DIVINE NAMES

Can the multiplicity of conceptions of the divine essence (divine names), left problematic by Descartes, be reduced to one? In order to succeed here, one has to take a stand against Descartes, and only the greatest thinkers in the seventeenth century risked this. But can such a unification avoid impoverishing the notion of God?

Baruch Spinoza is generally credited with revolutionising the definition of God. But Spinoza's innovation is probably not as radical as it at first appears. Although Spinoza identified God with nature, his famous formula 'God or Nature', '*Deus sive Natura*', in fact appears only rarely in the *Ethica* and never in Part I, which is dedicated to God.[99] Furthermore, Spinoza nowhere elaborates on the phrase or gives it any special attention.[100] Furthermore, there is nothing novel about the formula that defines God as *causa sui*. The phrase certainly is defined ('that whose essence involves existence'), but here all that Spinoza does is equate these two quite different concepts without any justification; he in no way addresses the obvious logical contradiction in the notion of a *cause of self*.[101] Spinoza has an excellent reason not to enter into this debate: he admits that he is simply appealing to a notion widely known and elaborated previously by others: 'If something exists in itself [*in se*], or, as commonly said, is a cause of itself [*causa sui*], then it should be understood through its essence alone.'[102] From Spinoza's point of view, we are dealing here with a Cartesian concept, assumed to be established and usable without any special precautions.

Therefore, Spinoza added nothing new to the Cartesian conceptions of the divine essence.[103] Indeed, one text seems to imply that he simply juxtaposed Descartes's three conceptions without choosing among them. In proving that 'God . . . exists', in *Ethica I,* Proposition 11, Spinoza presents at least three demonstrations, along with a commentary. This profusion of proof and explanation, otherwise rare in the *Ethica,* is difficult to explain if we consider only the geometrical order of the *Ethica,* but it is easily understood if we consider Descartes. The first demonstration relies on the principle that existence is contained in God's essence. Now, this principle arises in the *a priori* demonstration of the Meditatio V. Moreover, in Proposition 11 Spinoza also evokes in the supreme perfection of God, the conception of God that underlies the same Cartesian argument.[104] The second demonstration relies on the principle of reason ('For every thing there must be assigned some cause or reason [*causa seu ratio*] for either why it exists, or why it does not') in order to verify that no *causa sive ratio* can prohibit the divine essence from existing. It is, indeed, curious that Spinoza does not mention here the *causa sui,* connected with the principle of reason in Descartes's version of the argument.[105] Nevertheless, it is clear that Spinoza is rehearsing the argument from Descartes's Replies I and IV. The third demonstration relies explicitly on the *ens absolute infinitum* and proceeds *a posteriori,* as noted in the scholium (which, strangely enough, then attempts an *a priori* reformulation of the proof from the idea of infinity). Here, then, Spinoza is repeating the Cartesian demonstration from Meditatio III. Hence he arrives at a somewhat paradoxical conclusion: Spinoza, even more so than Descartes, juxtaposes – without choosing among them – the three metaphysical conceptions of the divine essence; indeed, he goes so far as to merge them into a single statement: 'God is absolutely infinite. . . . [T]hat is, . . . the nature of God enjoys infinite perfection, accompanied . . . by the idea of Himself, i.e., . . . by the idea of his cause.'[106] It seems highly unlikely that such a juxtaposition of infinity, perfection, and cause of self could be justified theoretically. At least, Spinoza never undertook to show their consistency, hiding under the cloak of a deductive system the heterogeneity that Descartes himself did not conceal.

Nicolas Malebranche, on the other hand, did choose among the Cartesian conceptions of God, but it was an extremely difficult and laborious decision, made in several stages. Following Exodus 3:14, Malebranche calls God 'He who is'. But he immediately adds a gloss that is not very biblical: 'the unrestricted being, in a word, *Being,* is the idea of God.'[107] The shift from 'He who is' to 'Being' leads him to define God as 'the universal Being [that] contains all beings in itself in an intelligible manner', or rather, that which 'is all being'.[108] Malebranche must go to this extreme in order to explain how we might see in God not only God Himself (in the sense of the Augustinian vision in God), but also 'intelligible extension, numbers, infinity, in a word, all the immutable natures that God contains in the immensity of his divine substance'.[109] But, in defining God in this way as 'universal being, without particular restriction, being in general',[110] Malebranche opens himself to charges of Spinozism.[111] This difficulty, which Malebranche never resolves, is in fact overshadowed by two other conceptual choices he makes. 'Being without restriction', which is suggestive of Spinoza's conception of God, tends little by little to give way to a conception of God as 'the vast and immense idea of infinitely perfect Being'.[112] Here infinity is lowered to the rank of a simple adverb of perfection in act, that is, the sum of perfections. Thus the Cartesian transcendence of infinity, first reduced to being, then made indeterminate ('Being without restriction'), is finally dissolved into the *summe perfectum,* which itself has become a simple receptacle for the intelligible world (ideas, truths, essences), understood univocally. Even the priority that Malebranche sometimes grants the *a posteriori* proof from infinity should not mislead us: in the end Malebranche weakens it to a proof by intuition, a proof that derives from a vision of the perfect.[113]

In this way, Malebranche does privilege perfection over infinity in characterising God. But he does not ignore Descartes's third characterisation of God in terms of causality. Malebranche's occasionalism requires him to place all actual causality in God, and hence imposes on Him, besides the title of *ens summe perfectum,* that of the ultimate and omnipotent cause: 'It is not sufficient to consider the infinitely perfect Being without relation to us. On the contrary, one must above all realise that we depend on the power of God.'[114] This further distances Malebranche from Spinozism, in so far as his occasionalism would seem to require a transcendent God. But Malebranche's view conceals a radical opposition between wisdom (and hence the love of order) and power (love of the efficient cause). Malebranche asserts that 'there are not at all two divinities, Reason and power: that the Omnipotent is essentially Reason, and universal Reason is omnipotence'.[115] But this is only to join, without argument, radically different conceptions of God into one. In short, the heterogeneity of the Cartesian conception of God remains.

Leibniz does not attempt to mask the duality at which Malebranche arrives; indeed, he embraces it. According to Leibniz, there is a pre-established harmony 'between God considered as Architect of the Machine of the universe, and God considered as Monarch of the divine City of Spirits'.[116] But this harmony is needed precisely because these two distinct kingdoms (nature and grace), hence two different divine causalities (efficient and final), and two different rationalities (mechanical and active), are in fact irreducibly separated. That is why Leibniz recognises two distinct conceptions of the divine essence; Leibniz's God is both the *ens perfectissimum* or an 'infinitely perfect God',[117] and the 'cause of causes' or the 'ultimate reason for things'.[118] These are not distinguished as mere modalities of the divine essence, but as definitions necessarily inferred from one or the other of Leibniz's 'two great principles'. (1) Leibniz's first principle is the principle 'of contradiction, by virtue of which we judge that that which contains [a contradiction] is false, and that that which is opposed or contradictory to the false is true.' This principle presupposes a realm of possibles, whose reality must be grounded in God: 'God's understanding is the region of the eternal truths . . . and . . . without Him there would be nothing real in possibilities, not only nothing that exists, but nothing even possible.'[119] But since Suárez, this aspect of God has been identified with his perfection.[120] God's perfection thus becomes the ground of possibility, hence the foundation of the principle of non-contradiction. On Leibniz's view, the principle of non-contradiction must be applicable to God as well. He therefore rejects, following Spinoza, Malebranche, and many others, the Cartesian doctrine of the creation of the eternal truths.[121] (2) The 'great principle . . . that holds that nothing is done without sufficient reason' allows one to 'rise to Metaphysics'.[122] This principle of sufficient reason presupposes that the causal relation is primary and of universal validity. Because it demands, in the end, 'a necessary Being, bearing the reason for its existence within itself',[123] it leads to a definition of God as the ultimate *causa sive ratio.*

Leibniz thus adopts Malebranche's two conceptions of God and sets them out systematically. But despite his debt to Malebranche, Leibniz makes a decisive step: he offers a justification for this duality in terms of the irreducible duality of the principles of metaphysics; neither the exclusively metaphysical status of the divine names nor their submission to metaphysics ever appeared so clearly.

VIII. THE PRIVILEGING OF CAUSALITY

We have been following the Cartesian strain in the development of the conception of God. But at the same time, and not unconnected with that Cartesian thematic and its conflicting developments, there is a strong and constant trend towards defining the divine essence in terms of causality among certain other philosophers of the seventeenth century.

Thomas Hobbes, for one, still divides the attributes of God into three classes, but none is any longer intended to make a definite assertion about the nature of God. He writes, 'Hee that will attribute to God, nothing but what is warranted by naturall Reason, must either use such Negative Attributes as *Infinite, Eternal, Incomprehensible*; or Superlatives, as *Most High, most Great,* and the like; or Indefinite, as *Good, Just, Holy, Creator.*"[124] The substitution of such indefinite names for affirmative assertions about God destroys the conditions necessary for any analogy whatsoever, either an analogy of names or an analogy of being; the incomprehensibility of the infinity of God becomes in Hobbes a purely negative claim, unbalanced by any positive assertions about Him. Hobbes continues:

Whatsoever we imagine, is *Finite.* Therefore there is no Idea, or conception of any thing we call *Infinite.* No man can have in his mind an Image of infinite magnitude; nor conceive infinite swiftness, infinite time, or infinite force, or infinite power. When we say any thing is infinite, we signifie onely, that we are not able to conceive the ends, and bounds of the thing named; having no Conception of the thing, but of our inability. And therefore the name of *God* is used, not to make us conceive Him; (for He is *Incomprehensible*; and his greatness and power are unconceivable;) but that we may honor Him.[125]

Consequently, no attribute (name) agrees categorically with God except existence itself, a pure and simple fact without any other reason other than itself:

That we may know what worship of God is taught us by the light of Nature, I will begin with his Attributes. Where, First, it is manifest, we ought to attribute to Him *Existence:* For no man can have the will to honour that, which he thinks not to have any Beeing. . . . For there is but one Name to signifie our Conception of his Nature, and that is, I AM.[126]

Despite the appeal to Exodus 3:14, Hobbes does not have a conception of the divine *esse* like the one Thomas advanced, a conception of God as pure act, that which subsists through itself and as act; on the contrary, the biblical formula serves to avoid such a conception. Indeed, Hobbes uses only the simplest and most certain argument possible to show that God exists; God is simply posited as cause of the existence of the world. Hobbes writes:

Curiosity, or love of the knowledge of causes, draws a man from consideration of the effect, to seek the cause; and again, the cause of that cause; till of necessity he must come to this thought at last, that there is some cause, whereof there is no former cause, but is eternall: which is it men call God [the] one First Mover; that is, a First, and an Eternall cause of all things; which is that which men mean by the name of God.[127]

But Hobbes has nothing of interest to say about the conception of efficient causality on which this argument depends. Perhaps this is less a theoretical argument than a simple account of the beliefs of common people; and in fact, Hobbes often gives the impression of not choosing between a proof in the strict sense, and a sociological description of common belief. But even this indecision is a doctrinal position. It is often argued that Hobbes's talk of God is not to be taken seriously, and that Hobbes is really an atheist in disguise. But the ambiguity of Hobbes's theology, often denounced and rightly so,[128] is due less to hidden intentions, or literary ruses, than to the very concept of cause, which Hobbes gives a theological function inversely proportional to the theoretical elaboration he offers. Though he does not put it this way, Hobbes's philosophy actually poses a crucial question: Does the notion of an efficient cause allow one to reach the existence of God? And can the concept of cause be applied univocally both to finite beings and to God, any more than any other concept can? By reducing natural theology to causality and by sacrificing infinity (and even perfection), Hobbes opens a wide path that many will follow. But in this way he exposes metaphysical discourse on God to the danger of collapse, when Hume undermines causality itself.

Though John Locke was opposed to Hobbes's political philosophy, he did follow him in emphasising causality in his characterisation of God. When discussing the idea we have of God, Locke suggests that He is a being that contains all perfections to an infinite degree. But though his view of God may resemble Descartes's in this way, it is at root quite different. Unlike Descartes, Locke is clearly denying that such an idea of God or infinity is innate in us.[129] Rather, he argues, the idea of God is a complex idea, made by us from the same ideas of sensation and reflection that give us our idea of self. Locke writes:

> For if we examine the *Idea* we have of the incomprehensible supreme Being, we shall find, that . . . the complex *Ideas* we have both of God, and separate Spirits, are made up of the simple *Ideas* we receive from *Reflection*; *v.g.* having from what we experiment in our selves, got the *Ideas* of Existence and Duration; of Knowledge and Power; of Pleasure and Happiness; and of several other Qualities and Powers, which it is better to have, than to be without; when we would frame an *Idea* the most suitable we can to the supreme Being, we enlarge every one of these with our *Idea* of Infinity; and so putting them together, make our complex *Idea of God*.[130]

Because Locke's idea of God is constructed by us from simpler ideas, it is impossible to reach God through the sort of argument Descartes offers in Meditation III, where he argues that God must exist as the creator of the idea we have of Him. Though he grants that some may find such an argument convincing, he thinks it

> an ill way of establishing this Truth, and silencing Atheists, to lay the whole stress of so important a Point, as this, upon that sole Foundation: And take some Men's having that *Idea* of GOD in their Minds, (for 'tis evident, some Men have none, and some worse than none, and the most very different,) for the only proof of a Deity.[131]

Though Locke may hold that his God is infinite and perfect, it is a somewhat different conception of God that yields a proof of His existence.

Locke begins his argument for the existence of God by noting that '*Man has a clear Perception of his own Being.*' He continues:

> In the next place, Man knows by an intuitive Certainty, that bare *nothing can no more produce any real Being, than it can be equal to two right Angles*. . . . If therefore we know that there is some real Being, and that Non-entity cannot produce any real Being, it is an evident demonstration, that from Eternity there has been something.

Since, as Locke argues, an effect can only receive its properties from its cause, 'this eternal Source then of all being must also be the Source and Original of all Power; and so *this eternal Being must be also the most powerful*.' Furthermore, since I (the one created thing whose existence Locke grants in this argument) have knowledge and perception, 'we are certain now, that there is not only some Being, but some knowing intelligent Being in the World.' And so Locke concludes that 'from the Consideration of our selves, and what we infallibly find in our own Constitutions, our Reason leads us to the Knowledge of this certain and evident Truth, That *there is an eternal, most powerful, and most knowing Being.*' That is, God exists.[132]

Though Locke's argument is more complex than Hobbes's, the basic principle is the same: God is established as the ultimate cause of the world. Though Locke gives the appropriate nods to infinity and perfection, it is fair to say that like Hobbes, Locke privileges the conception of causality.

George Berkeley brings to completion this tendency to reduce all rational theology to divine causality. For Berkeley, of course, the concept of matter is contradictory and useless, and sensible things are reduced to collections of ideas perceived. In this context, God's primary rôle is as the cause of these sensible ideas in the finite spirits which He has created; it is in this way that God creates and sustains the world of sensible things. Hence Berkeley writes, 'Everything we see, hear, feel, or any wise perceive by sense, [is] a sign or effect of the Power of God.'[133]

Berkeley's conception of God's power is also manifested in his account of the continued existence of objects. An obvious problem for Berkeley's metaphysics is the continued existence of sensible objects when no (finite) mind is sensing them. To solve this problem, he often suggests that God sustains the world of sensible things by perceiving it.[134] But this raises an obvious problem; if God is to sustain objects by sensing them, then God Himself must have sensations, something that raises obvious problems for Berkeley.[135] A better account is suggested in his early *Philosophical Commentaries.* According to that account, sensible things exist in God's mind not as collections of sensible ideas, as they do in ours, but as powers, the power to produce particular sensations in finite minds on particular occasions. As Berkeley suggests there, 'Bodies etc do exist even w^n not perceiv'd they being powers in the active Being.'[136] Berkeley seems to have had some doubts about this view; in another entry in the *Philosophical Commentaries* he reminds himself 'not to mention the Combination of Powers but to say the things the effects themselves to really exist even w^n not actually perceiv'd.'[137] But the view still finds a place in the mature writings. One problem Berkeley must face is that of creation: What does it mean to say that God created the world at one specific time? Berkeley's solution is to say that God created the world by decreeing that at one particular time sensible things 'should become perceptible to intelligent creatures, in that order and manner which he then established, and we now call the Laws of Nature.'[138] In that way, to create a sensible thing is simply for God to decide to cause a sensation in finite minds under appropriate circumstances. An important class of divine ideas thus emerge not as passive objects for divine contemplation but as the potential manifestations of God's power.[139]

Berkeley does not ignore God's wisdom, which is manifested through the order in which we receive these ideas, an order that allows us to frame laws of motion and predict at least certain aspects of the future train of ideas from what has gone before. Indeed, this is what Berkeley emphasises in the *Principles* when God is first introduced as the cause of all of our ideas of sense:

The ideas of sense are more strong, lively, and distinct than those of the imagination; they have likewise a steadiness, order, and coherence, and are not excited at random, as those which are the effects of human wills often are, but in a regular train or series, the admirable connexion whereof sufficiently testifies the wisdom and benevolence of its Author.[140]

But though God is wise and benevolent, His wisdom and benevolence are manifested primarily in His rôle as the cause of the sensible world. And so Berkeley writes in his *Philosophical Commentaries,* 'One idea not the cause of another, one power not the cause of another. The cause of all natural things is onely God. Hence trifling to enquire after second Causes. This Doctrine gives a most suitable idea of the Divinity.'[141]

But there are obvious objections: if we have no more of an idea of God than we have of matter,[142] how can we know what this cause of ideas actually is? In particular, how can one legitimate the claim that the active cause (whatever it may be) coincides with the God of Christian Revelation?

When the theoretical validity of causality has been challenged (as it will be in Hume), or when the transcendental use of causality applied to the thing-in-itself has been excluded (as it will be in Kant), Berkeley's whole apologetic will become untenable, and along with it, every conception of God deriving from efficient causality.

IX. GOD AND EXTENSION

Seventeenth-century philosophers often defined God as supremely perfect. But what does such supreme perfection actually include? Is it appropriate to integrate *all* the perfections in God's essence? Descartes made at least one exception: for him, the 'idea of an uncreated and independent thinking substance, that is, God'[143] excludes extension and therefore all materiality from its definition.[144]

As early as his correspondence with Descartes, Henry More tried to show that 'God, in his own way, is extended';[145] in order to communicate motion, God must be able 'to touch matter', and if He could touch matter, He must be extended. This view was later elaborated in More's tract, *The Immortality of the Soul*. Here, the classic list of the perfections – '*God is a Spirit,* Eternal, Infinite in Essence and Goodness, Omniscient, Omnipotent and of Himself necessarily Existent' – is specified as an '*Essence absolutely Perfect*', which implies 'his *Omnipresence or Ubiquity,* which are necessarily included in the *Idea* of *absolute Perfection*'. Therefore, supreme perfection directly implies the ubiquity of God, which More can only conceive of as an extended 'Divine amplitude'.[146] But there is no confusion between God's extension and the extension of bodies: the two extensions are different. More argues that whereas extended body is divisible and impenetrable, both God (infinite mind) and finite mind are indivisible (indiscerpible) and penetrable.[147] Consequently 'God is everywhere', present by extension to all extension, without being confused with sensible materiality.

In challenging one of the most important Cartesian strictures on the definition of the divine essence, More opened a radical debate: Is God extended? A number of later British philosophers followed More in holding that God is extended though not corporeal. Most notable in this respect are Ralph Cudworth, John Locke, and Sir Isaac Newton. Extension, Cudworth argues, must have a subject; if the space is filled, the subject is body, if not, it is God.[148] Similarly, Locke writes, 'GOD, every one easily allows, fills Eternity; and 'tis hard to find a Reason, why any one should doubt, that he likewise fills Immensity: His infinite Being is certainly as boundless one way as another; and methinks it ascribes a little too much to Matter, to say, where there is no Body, there is nothing.'[149] And like More, Locke is very careful to argue that though extended, God is not therefore material.[150] Given this context, the position that Newton takes in *the Scholium Generale* of the *Principia* (1687) is not surprising. If one accepts the definition of God as *ens . . . absolute perfectum,* and if one interprets this absolute perfection as pertaining to all God's properties, then one must necessarily apply it even to space, as it is already applied to duration:

He is neither duration or space, but He endures and is present. He always endures and is everywhere present, and existing always and everywhere, He established [*constituit*] duration and space, eternal and infinite. God is one and the same God, always and everywhere. He is omnipresent not only through his power, but also through his substance: for power without substance cannot exist. In Him the very universe is contained and moves.[151]

In saying that God is *substantially* extended, Newton comes close to *identifying* God with extension. Why does Newton make God substantially extended? Without entering into the complex debate over Newtonian theology, there seems to be a simple explanation: as with Kepler, Galileo, Mersenne, and many others (as discussed above), Newton appeals to an epistemological univocity, here the univocity of space and absolute time, in order to provide a foundation for his science.

More radical was the position of Thomas Hobbes: writing at roughly the same time as More, he held that God is not only extended but also corporeal. The argument Hobbes offers consists of three stages. (1) By 'body' must be understood not that which can be sensed ('secondary qualities'), but 'that which has determinate magnitude and consequently is understood to be *totum* or *integrum aliquid*'.[152] Body is thus defined in terms of the so-called primary qualities. But, Hobbes argues, this concept of body is just the same as our concept of substance. He writes:

The Word *Body,* in the most generall acceptation, signifieth that which filleth, or occupyeth some certain room, or imagined place; and dependeth not on the imagination. . . . The same also, because Bodies are subject to change, that is to say, to variety of apparence to the sense of living creatures, is called *Substance*. . . . And according to this acceptation of the word, *Substance* and *Body* signifie the same thing.[153]

(2) It follows, therefore, almost trivially and through a stipulative redefinition of terms, that if it is to exist at all, all spirit must be 'body' and must thus be extended: 'men may put together words of contradictory signification, as *Spirit* and *Incorporeall*; yet they can never have the imagination of anything answering to them.' The phrase 'incorporeal spirit', which amounts to an admission of incomprehensibility, has only a 'pious' sense for Hobbes, not a theoretical one.[154] (3) In particular, God must then be corporeal or not exist at all: 'To say that God is an incorporeal substance, is to say in effect there is no God at all.' In face of the common dilemma – *either* infinite spirituality *or* finite corporeality – Hobbes responds with a paradox (at least an apparent one): 'I deny both, and say He is corporeal and infinite.' This presents a second paradox: 'God is a spirit, but corporeal.'[155] To the 'mortal god' (the commonwealth) corresponds an extended and corporeal God.

No doubt under the influence of *Leviathan,* Spinoza too rejects the Cartesian prohibition against attributing extension to God: 'Extended substance is one of the infinite attributes of God.'[156] For Spinoza, God, the unique substance containing all attributes, is an extended thing (*res extensa*) every bit as much as He is a thinking thing (*res cogitans*). In developing his position, Spinoza considers an obvious objection to this position: while extension is by definition divisible, God cannot be divided. But, Spinoza replies, extension appears divisible only to the extent that we conceive it abstractly and superficially, only to the extent that we imagine extension without thinking of it as a mode of the unique substance; substance, properly conceived in itself, can no more be divided than it can be quantified: 'It can be conceived only as one, and only as indivisible.'[157] Spinoza can attribute extension to God only because he has certain very strict distinctions at his disposal: real extension (an attribute of substance) is not confused with matter or *materia prima* (as in materialism),[158] nor with substance itself (as in Hobbes's conception of body), nor with the imaginable extension of the mathematicians (which is divisible by abstraction). However, in so far as it is neither corporeal, nor material, nor mathematical, in what sense is Spinoza's extension still extension?

Like Spinoza and Hobbes, Malebranche attempts to integrate extension into the *ens summe perfectum.* But Malebranche completely reverses their strategy. Rather than privileging real extension and criticising abstract (mathematical) extension, Malebranche places intelligible extension directly in God, while setting aside (in this life, at least) any direct access to the (sensible) extension in which created bodies exist. Transformed from its earlier Augustinian sense, our vision of the ideas in God no longer reveals God and His splendor to the human mind; above all, what we see is the idea of intelligible extension: 'God contains in Himself an infinite ideal or intelligible extension'; 'the idea of extension is not at all a modification of the mind and it is only found in God'; 'infinite intelligible extension is not at all a modification of my mind. . . . Therefore it can only be found in God.'[159] This mathematical conception of extension, what Spinoza considered imaginary and abstract, and therefore denied to substance, is the very thing that Malebranche situates in God, under the name of intelligible extension. Despite this tactical reversal, Malebranche is paradoxically closer to Hobbes than even Spinoza is: intelligible extension is not merely *in* God, but rather *is,* in a sense, God Himself: 'Intelligible extension is eternal, immense, necessary. It is the immensity of divine Being.'[160] But since Malebranche holds that this idea of God in terms of intelligible extension is primary, he risks saying that we can only think of the divine essence as extended, and deriving from extension.

The conception of God as extended does not necessarily attest to a new materialism, but rather defends what Descartes, following the greatest mediaeval thinkers, had attempted to deny: the univocity of knowledge of God and the identification of human and divine science. The position still constitutes theology, even if the very success of the program seems to eliminate one of the fundamental distinctions between the creator and the created and thus render problematic the relation between the God of philosophy and the God of revelation.

X. A SHIFT IN THE QUESTION OF GOD'S ESSENCE

If one grants that the whole debate over the conception of the divine essence played out in the seventeenth century derives from the (not altogether coherent) system of the three Cartesian conceptions of God, one thing stands out: although the *ens summe perfectum* and the *ens causa* (*sui*) enjoy ample development, either as an admitted duality (as in Spinoza, Malebranche, Leibniz), or under the domination of the notion of causality (as in Hobbes, Locke, Berkeley), the idea of infinity experiences a marked decline.

Although most would agree that God is infinite, the idea of infinity undoubtedly maintains only a few determined, if uninfluential, advocates as a basic characterisation of the nature of God. Gassendi still acknowledges the legitimacy of the denomination of infinity.[161] Arnauld and Nicole firmly maintain 'infinity as an attribute of God'.[162] Desgabets defends the 'knowledge of the infinite', in claiming that 'God by full right has the quality of infinity.'[163] But the most avowed proponent of the Cartesian conception of an infinite God remains Fénelon, who discerns in infinity 'the characteristic of divinity itself!'[164] Following Descartes, he specifies that 'that being who is through Himself, and through whom I am, is infinitely perfect; and this is what we call God'; more radically than Descartes, Fénelon even thinks that he can appeal to an 'infinite idea of infinity'.[165] Against Spinoza he defends the unity of God through the notion of His infinity: 'My conclusion is that everything composite can never be infinite', exclaiming, 'O infinite Unity!'[166] If he takes up, with some carelessness, Malebranche's definition of God as 'the infinite being who is simply Being, without adding anything',[167] it is only to criticise the submission of God to order.

But the fact remains that these statements appear marginal in the context of the history of these ideas; after Descartes (and Duns Scotus), infinity is not found among the central notions that make up the idea of the divine essence. This demotion can be compared to the parallel and contemporary abandonment of the doctrine of the creation of the eternal truths. One historical factor explains both:

the imposition of the principle of sufficient reason as the first metaphysical principle governing essence and existence, and hence all of divine creation. This excludes incomprehensibility from God and His creation. But as 'incomprehensibility is contained in the formal definition of infinity',[168] the requirement of comprehensibility opposes the priority of infinity in the divine nature. The ultimate fulfillment of rationalist metaphysics thus ought to make the infinite God a *persona non grata*.

There remains, however, a final witness to infinity, Blaise Pascal. Pascal acknowledges straightaway 'that sovereign being who is infinite by his own definition'; for he posits in principle that 'if there is a God, He is infinitely incomprehensible.'[169] It is obvious here that Pascal is taking up the Cartesian thesis. However, it will give rise to the most radical critique of Descartes imaginable and, in general, the most radical critique of any *metaphysical* conception of God. There are two reasons for this. First, the concept of infinity does not uniquely pick out God, since numbers, motion, speed, space, and even nature can be infinite as well. Second, above all, even if God's infinity did allow the construction of a proof for His existence, it would still be in vain; for 'the metaphysical proofs of God are so removed from the reasoning of men and so involved, that they make little impression'; indeed, 'this knowledge, without Jesus Christ, is useless and sterile.'[170] What is at stake for Pascal is not to *know* God, but to *love* Him;[171] the real obstacle to acknowledging Him does not rest in the uncertainty of the understanding, but in the arrogance of the will. Within such a perspective, even the doctrine of the creation of the eternal truths, which affirms the absolute transcendence of God, seems illusory: in demonstrating an 'author of the geometrical truths', one only satisfies the 'pagans'; for even 'a God who exercises his providence' is still only suitable for Judaism. In fact, only 'the God of Abraham, the God of Isaac, the God of Jacob and the God of the Christians is a God of love and consolation.'[172] The project of proving the existence or determining the essence of God must yield to the recognition of a God to be loved, because He Himself loves first. Pascal recorded his personal experience of this important shift in the *Mémorial*: 'God of Abraham, of Isaac, and of Jacob, not of the philosophers and scholars'.[173] He also marked its theoretical status by distinguishing three irreducible orders: bodies, minds, and finally the heart, where God – the God of Jesus Christ – becomes accessible only to the 'eyes of the heart and he who sees wisdom'.[174]

No doubt, in passing from the question of that which is evident, to the question of charity, Pascal reaches an entirely different transcendence from that which metaphysics (above all Cartesian metaphysics) can envisage. No doubt also, one might object that this new transcendence no longer concerns strictly metaphysical discourse. But was it not the bold and original claim of seventeenth-century metaphysics that we can determine the essence of God through philosophy alone? Its final failure would then become its most useful lesson to modern thought. The continual drift in the determination of the essence of God towards univocity should not be understood primarily or only as a simple failure to perceive God's transcendence, but as an indication of the demands made by the growing empire of metaphysical rationality, making use of its principles, principally that of sufficient reason; here we see quite clearly the importance of the new subjectivity that characterises philosophy in the seventeenth century, the significance of the Cartesian call to begin philosophy with the *cogito*. From this point of view, the rival projects of Kant and Hegel can well appear as two attempts to restore the rights of the absolute in the face of the limits of the demands of the understanding.

NOTES

1 On the constitution of the concept of *metaphysica* in the sixteenth century, see Vollrath 1962 and Courtine 1990.
2 On the revival of Thomas, see the discussion in Chapter 2 of this book.
3 See Petersen 1921; Lewalter 1967; Wundt 1939; and Trentman, 1982. For an overall picture of the second Scholasticism, see the summary in Andres 1976–7. Suárez was chosen by Melanchton to serve as a basis for the philosophical teaching in the Lutheran universities, and J. Revius published, for the Dutch reformed universities, a *Suarez repurgatus* (Revius 1643).
4 To Mersenne, 25 December 1639, AT II 630.
5 *Summa th.* I q12 a2 c. The formula is taken up again by Descartes: 'Deus est suum esse' in AT III, 433 [9], and AT VII, 383 [15].
6 *Summa th.* I q3 a4 ad 2 m and a5 c. Another formula which is also taken up by Descartes: 'in Deo non distinguitur essentia ab existentia' (AT VII, 243 [17–18]).
7 *Actus purus:* see *Summa th.* I q3 a2 c; q14 a2; q12 a1 c.; etc.
8 *Summa th.* Ia q4 a2 c: 'Deus est ipsum esse per se subsistens.' See the excellent commentaries in Gilson 1945. On the historical fate of these formulas, see Gilson 1941, 1947, and 1962.
9 *Summa th.* I q2 a3. See *Summa contra gentiles,* I, 13.
10 *Summa th.* I q4 a3 c; q13 a5 and 6. Montagnes 1963 discusses the consistency of this with other texts by Thomas on analogy: mainly *De veritate,* q2 a3 ad 4 m and a11; *In Sententiarum libros essentia* II and VII; etc.
11 'De Deo quid non sit cognoscimus, quid vero sit, penitus manet incognitum' (*Summa contra gentiles,* III, 49). See *Summa th.* I q2 a1 c: 'nos non scimus de Deo quid est'; *De potentia,* q7 a2 ad 1 m: 'substantia ejus [*sc.* Dei] est ignota, ita et esse.' See also Gilson 1967b, pp. 22 ff.
12 The main debate is over whether Thomas has in mind an analogy of attribution or an analogy of proportionality in four terms. See Aubenque 1978 and 1987. For the Thomistic heritage, see Marion 1981, pp. 27–139. The traditional position is defended in Dubarle 1986, chap. 3.

13 *Disp. met.* II.2.36 (Su. *Op. omn.* 25, p. 81). Or, put otherwise: 'Ens aeque univocum esse ac quodlibet genus, nam genus, licet univocum sit, physice seu metaphysice dici potest analogum' (*Disp. met.* XXVIII.3.20, Su. *Op. omn.* 25, p. 14).

14 *Disp. met.* XXVIII.3.17 (Su. *Op. omn.* 25, p. 19). Similarly, Suárez writes: 'Creatura denominatur ens absolute a suo esse et non ex proportione aliqua, quam servat ad esse Dei . . . ratio entis omnino absolute et intrinsece ac proprie concipitur in creatura' (XXVIII.3.4, Su. *Op. omn.* 25, p. 14). On the question of univocity in Suárez and his predecessors, see Hoeres 1965; Marion 1981, chap. 7, pp. 121 ff.; and Montagnes 1963.

15 *De divina,* I, s. 1, n. 1, in Su. *Op. omn.* 1, p. 1.

16 *Disp. met.* XXX.1.5. (Su. *Op. omn.* 26, p. 61). Suárez also writes: 'Priori modo dicitur perfectum, cui nihil deest, quod ei debitum sit natura sua ad suam integritatem. . . . Posteriori ergo modo dicitur perfectum, cui absolute nihil perfectionis deest; atque hoc modum illud ens dicitur absolute perfectum, cui omnis perfectio ita debita est, ac necessario inest, ut nulla ei omnino deesse est, nec privative nec negative, et in utroque sensu dicitur esse, de essentia Dei, esse simpliciter perfectum' (ibid., p. 60).

17 *Disp. met.* XXX.1.6, Su. *Op. omn.* 26, p. 62. See Courtine 1979 and 1980.

18 *Disp. met.* XXXI.12.40–6, Su. *Op. omn.* 26, pp. 294–8.

19 *Disp. met.* XXXI.12.40 (Su. *Op. omn.* 26, p. 295). One of the conclusions Suárez draws in s. 12 sufficiently shows that this is, indeed, his thesis: 'Unde, si per impossibile, nulla esset talis causa [sc. God, efficient cause], nihilominus illa enunciatio [sc. 'Homo est animal'] vera esset' (s. 12, n. 45, Su. *Op. omn.* 26, p. 297). For a contrary view on this question, see Hatfield 1993. Similar positions can be found in G. Vasquez, *Commentariorum ac disputationum in primam partem s. Thomae tomus primus, disputatio CIV,* c. 3, n. 9– 11, Vasquez 1609, pp. 783–4 or Vasquez 1620, vol. 1, p. 510. Here again divine perfection is measured against the possible: 'Cum enim sit primum ens, ita in se perfectus absolute est, et nulla re possibili indigeat. . . . Deus . . . dicitur . . . ita perfectus, ut quicquid non implicat contradictionem, ab eo fieri possit' (Vasquez 1609, p. 173). Velasquez's *Opera omnia* appeared from 1598 to 1617 in Alcalà. On the close relation between Suárez and Vasquez on this question, see Marion 1981, pp. 53–7.

20 See EP 91, To Hohenburg, 26 March 1598, Kepler 1937– , vol. 13, p. 193. See also the autobiographical remarks in EP 23, To Mästlin, 10 March 1595, Kepler 1937– , vol. 13, p. 40.

21 *Harmonice mundi,* IV, 1, Kepler 1937– , vol. 6, p. 219.

22 *Epitome,* IV, 1, 3, Kepler 1937– , vol. 7, p. 267.

23 *Harmonice mundi,* IV, 1, Kepler 1937– , vol. 6, p. 31. See also: 'Imo Ideae quantitatum sunt erantque Deo coaeternae, Deus ipse.' (*Mysterium cosmographicum,* Kepler 1937– , vol. 8, p. 30).

24 *Harmonice mundi,* V, 3, Kepler 1937– , vol. 6, p. 299.

25 EP 357, To Ph. Heydon, October 1605, Kepler 1937– , vol. 15, p. 235.

26 *Mysterium cosmographicum,* II, Kepler 1937– , vol. 1, p. 26. In fact, the phrase 'God always geometrises' is not found in the Platonic corpus; it comes from Plutarch (*Quaestiones conviviales,* VIII, 2, 1, 718c). On the importance of this theme, see Cassirer 1927, and especially Hübner 1975; concerning the univocity that ensues, see Simon 1979.

27 EP 117, To Hohenburg, 9 September 1599, Kepler 1937– , vol. 13, p. 309.

28 *Il saggiatore,* VI, Galilei 1929–39, vol. 6, p. 232. See also To Fortunato Liceti, January 1641, Galilei 1929–39, vol. 18, p. 295. And Burtt 1932; Crombie 1959; Koyré 1966; 1978; Clavelin 1974; and Shea 1972.

29 *Dialogo dei massimi sistemi,* I, Galilei 1929–39, vol. 7, pp. 128–9. See also To G.

Gallanzoni, 16 July 1611, Galilei 1929–39, vol. 11, p. 149. On possible mediaeval origins of this view, see Wallace 1984.

30 For the texts and discussion, see Santillana 1955; Morpurgo-Tagliabue 1963; and Marion 1981, pp. 218–21.

31 Mersenne 1623, col. 56. My interpretation of this work (Marion 1981, pp. 161–78) is opposed to that found in Lenoble 1971 and Dear 1988; limited exclusively to Mersenne, these studies ignore the parallel theses of Kepler and Galileo, thus misreading Mersenne as a fairly banal positivist.

32 Mersenne 1625, p. 227.

33 Mersenne, II, 4, theorem 1, p. 283.

34 Mersenne, I, 9, p. 108. The formula Mersenne uses here is similar to one in Kepler, given in note 23. There is some interesting information on Mersenne in Whitmore 1967, and, on his epistemology, in Crombie 1975.

35 Bacon, *Cogitata et Visa,* in Bacon 1857–74, vol. 3, p. 597.

36 Gassendi, *Exercitationes paradoxicae adversus Aristoteleos,* II, III, a. 9, in Gassendi 1658, vol. 3, p. 170b. See also Gregory 1961, and Bloch 1971, chaps. XIII and XIV.

37 See Saint John of the Cross 1645–7.

38 On these authors and the mystical movement, see the still authoritative Cognet 1966, vol. 1, esp. chaps. 7–10.

39 *Règle de perfection,* III, 8, Canfeld 1982, p. 377. The book was originally published in Rouen in 1608 (in English), in Rouen in 1609 (in French), and twice in Paris in 1610 (both a second French edition including for the first time the third part, and a Latin edition). My quotations are from the remarkable critical edition of J. Orcibal, Canfeld 1982. On the whole movement, see Cognet 1966.

40 *Règle de perfection, L'exercice de la volonté de Dieu,* VII, Canfeld 1982, p. 64. The attributes of incomprehensibility, omnipotence, and infinity here gathered in one definition anticipate the 'incomprehensible power' that characterises God in Descartes (see section V of this chapter).

41 *Règle de perfection* III, 1, Canfeld 1982, p. 333. See also III, 2: 'This Essential will or Essence of God', p. 339 (and III, 6, p. 369; III, 8, p. 377; III, 9, p. 386, etc.). Similarly: 'I think that to the extent one sees this essential will only in God, one sees God, and this [i.e., the will] as something not different [from God Himself], for in God there is nothing other than God' (*Lettre contenant le réponse à un doute touchant l'objet de la volonté de Dieu,* Canfeld 1982, p. 90).

42 See Marion 1977, chaps. 13–14.

43 Lessius 1640, chap. 1, pp. 5–8. See also Marion 1986a, p. 221.

44 *Discours* III, 1, Bérulle 1846, col. 189. See also: 'This is why God has among his qualities the following, which is his principal quality and like his motto: *He who is* (Exodus 3:14). It is his proper name uttered by Himself' (Bérulle 1846, cols. 251–2).

45 *Discours* III, 4, Bérulle 1846, col. 192. This thesis involves a doctrine of emanation, as much *ad intra* as *ad extra* (III, 3; VII, 6; XI, 6; *Opuscules* XXXV and CXLVV, respectively, Bérulle 1846, col. 191, 273 ff., 363 ff., 970 and 1200), and allows development towards univocity. See Orcibal 1965; and Marion 1981, pp. 140–60.

46 *Discours,* respectively, IV, 4; VII, 2 (see II, 13) and VI, 6 (Bérulle 1846, cols. 211, 264, 183, and 251).

47 Gibieuf's treatise, *De libertate Dei et creaturae,* published in Paris in 1630 and read by Descartes, deserves a new examination, according to Gilson 1982. See also Ferrier 1978.

48 *Traité de l'amour de Dieu,* Lyon, 1616, II, 1, quoted from François de Sales 1969, p. 411.

49 *Traité de l'amour de Dieu,* II, 1 and V, 6, François de Sales 1969, pp. 565 and 584. See

also III, 15: 'enjoying unreservedly and without any exception whatsoever that whole infinite abyss of the Divinity, nevertheless, they can never make their enjoyment equal to that infinity. The latter always remains infinitely infinite, beyond their capacity' (ibid., p. 523). Infinity therefore colours even the final beatitude with incomprehensibility.

50 *Traité de l'amour de Dieu,* V, 7, François de Sales 1969, p. 587.

51 *Traité de l'amour de Dieu,* respectively, XII, 11, François de Sales 1969, p. 968 (see also X, 14, p. 853); X, 17, p. 868; III, 1, p. 483; and XII, 2, p. 951.

52 To Mersenne, 15 April 1630, AT I 145 [1–13].

53 To Mersenne, 6 May 1630, AT I 149 [21–8]. In this last quotation, we have the virtual negation of passage from Suárez; cf. *Disp. met.* XXXI.12.40, Su. *Op. omn.* 26, p. 295. For further discussion see Garin 1932; Cronin 1966; Marion 1981, chap. 1; Rodis-Lewis 1985, pp. 113 ff.

54 To Mersenne, 27 May 1630, AT I 152 [3–4]. See also: 'but I know that God is the author of all things, and that these truths are something, and consequently that He is their author' (AT I 152 [3–9]).

55 Respectively, To Mersenne, 15 April and 6 May 1630, AT I 146 [4–5] and 150 [22]; then Resp. I, AT VII 110 [26–7]. This formula recalls that of Benoît de Canfeld (see note 39). Efficient causality characterises God completely (AT I 152, 2), that is, without recourse to a distinct formal cause.

56 Hence the distinction Descartes draws in the 1630 letters between what it is to know God (*connaître*) and what it is to comprehend Him (*comprendre*); see To Mersenne, 27 May 1630, AT I 152.

57 To Mersenne, 6 May 1630, AT I 150 [6–7 and 18–19].

58 On the historical and philosophical significance of Descartes's doctrine here, see Boutroux 1927; Boyce Gibson 1929–30; Alquié 1950; Frankfurt 1977; Marion 1981, chap. 13; Beyssade 1981; Wells 1982; Curley 1984; Rodis-Lewis 1985; Landucci 1986, chap. 3.

59 *Essais* (Bordeaux, 1580[1], 1582[2], 1588[3]), quoted from Montaigne 1967, II, 12, p. 213 a and b.

60 *Essais,* respectively, Montaigne 1967 II, 12, p. 219 a; II, 29, p. 290 a (to be compared with Descartes, AT I 145); then II, 12, p. 225 a. See also I, 17, p. 85 b; II, 12, p. 218 a; II, 32, p. 296 a; II, 30, p. 91 b; etc. See Popkin 1979 and 1989a; and Screech 1983.

61 *De la sagesse* (Bordeaux, 1601[1]; Paris, 1604[2], quoted from Charron 1986), II, 5, sect. 1, p. 446 (compare with Descartes, AT I 152). Subject to the same sceptical tendencies, Sanchez arrives at similar definitions: 'Deum optimum, maximum, primam omnium causam, omniumque finem ultimum . . . incidis in infinitum, immensum, incomprehensibilem, indicibile, inintelligibile' (Sanchez 1984, p. 50). Sanchez does not go so far as La Mothe le Vayer who, violently attacking the Stoics for having 'subjugated [God] to their famous Destiny', and Aristotle for having 'tied God so much to the Natural necessities', recognises 'his essence which is incomprehensible to everybody other than Himself' and calls Him 'All powerful' (*De la Divinité* in *Cinq autres dialogues,* Paris[?], 1631[?], reprinted in *Dialogues faits à l'imitation des anciens,* La Mothe le Vayer 1988, respectively, pp. 309, 320, 325, and 350).

62 *Petit traité de sagesse,* Paris, 1625, respectively, VI and VI (Charron 1986, pp. 843 and 844); compare with Descartes, AT I 145 [13–16].

63 *Discours,* VI, 6, Bérulle 1846, p. 253. Compare with Descartes: 'independence, being conceived distinctly, contains infinity within itself' (AT III, 191 [15–16]).

64 *Traité de l'indéfectibilité des créatures* (ca. 1654), Desgabets 1983, pp. 34 and 33. See Rodis-Lewis 1979 and 1981.

65 See Marion 1987.

66 AT VII 21 [1–2]; see also AT VII 36 [8–9]. On the status of this primitive conception of God, see Gouhier 1962, chap. 7; Gregory 1974 and 1982; Frankfurt 1970; and Kennington 1971.

67 AT VII 45, 11–12 and 40, 17. This is certainly a reference to the famous phrase 'quoddam pelagus infinitae substantiae', 'a certain ocean of infinite substance', which the mediaevals borrowed so often from John of Damascus (*De fide orthodoxa*, I, 9).

68 Respectively, AT VII 45 [28–9]; 47 [19]; 55 [20–1] and 41 [3]. See Lévinas 1983. An objective reality is one that exists as represented in something else, an idea, for example. On the notion of objective reality, see Cronin 1966.

69 On the denial of this claim, see Sec. VII of this chapter.

70 Respectively, AT VII 9 [16–17] and 55 [21–2]. Infinity is directly characterised in terms of incomprehensibility (AT VII 368 [2–4]).

71 For a fuller discussion, see Marion 1991a, chap. 3.

72 'Illa omnia tantum, in quibus aliquis ordo vel mensura examinatur, ad Mathesim [Universalem] referri' (Regula IV, AT X 377 [23]–368 [2]). Order and measure are the two conditions for the exercise of method: the idea of infinity eludes at least one of these.

73 AT VII 46 [5–28]. Incomprehensibility in no way excludes intelligibility; see Beyssade's discussion in Descartes 1981, pp. 171–81.

74 Respectively, AT VII 51 [3–4] and 54 [13–14] (see also pp. 66 [12–13]; 67 [9–10]).

75 'Cumulum perfectionum' (*Notae in programma*, AT VIIIB 362 [12]) and 'perfectionum complementum' (*Princ.* I 18). For references and discussion, see Marion 1986a, pp. 253–6.

76 AT VII 65 [21–2] 'non minus'; 66 [8 and 12] 'non magis'.

77 To Mersenne, 15 April 1630, AT I 144 [15–17] A (see also the letters of 25 November 1630, AT I 182 [2]; March 1630, AT I 350 [27–8]). Even the *Discours de la méthode* weakens 'in the same manner' to 'at least as certain' (AT VI 36 [24 and 29]). On the relation between the first two proofs, see Alquié 1950, pp. 225 ff.; Gueroult 1955, 1984, chap. 8; Beck 1965.

78 AT VII 40 [21–3].

79 AT VII 108 [19–22]: this 'dictate' is never justified (no more than the parallel statements in AT VII 164 [26]–165 [3] or 238 [11–18]). The *Disc.* already uses the phrase 'reason dictates to us' (AT VI 40 [6, 8, 10]).

80 'Hoc enim de ipso Deo quaeri potest' (AT VII 164 [29]–165 [1]); see also 'licentiam . . . in rerum omnium, etiam ipsius Dei, causas efficientes inquirendi' (238 [15–17]).

81 Potentia exuperans, AT VII 110 [27]; exuperentia potestatis, AT VII 112 [10]. On the inversion of the negative sense of the term '*a se*' among the mediaevals into positive causality see Gilson 1967a, chap. 5, pp. 224ff.; on analogy and the principle of reason, see Marion 1981, chap. 18, and 1986a, pp. 270 ff.

82 Descartes speaks of 'infinitam Dei potestam' at AT VII 220 [20]; see also 'immensitas potentiae' at AT VII 111 [4], 237 [8–9] and 'immensa potesas' at AT VII 119 [13] = 188 [23]. He speaks of 'immensa et incomprehensibilis potentia' at AT VII 110 [26–7]; see also 'puissance incompréhensible' at AT I 146 [4–5] and 150 [22].

83 In addition, more recent philosophical contemplation of God has raised a third question with respect to this conception of God. Aside from the unresolved logical difficulties connected with a thing being a cause of itself, the conception of God as *causa sui* seems to involve a fundamental philosophical difficulty: Are we dealing with one of the 'divine names', or are we dealing with the 'metaphysical conception of God' par

excellence, such as a Heideggerian conception of onto-theo-logy imposes? If it is the latter, then does the *causa sui* not establish the metaphysical idol par excellence, rendering possible the 'death of God'? On this, see Heidegger 1957b, p. 51; and Marion 1982 or 1991c.

84 For a fuller development of these themes, see Marion 1981 and 1986a.

85 *L'homme,* Paris, 1664, *Traité de l'esprit de l'homme,* Paris, 1666; the latter is reprinted in La Forge 1974.

86 *Traité de l'esprit de l'homme,* respectively, chaps. 10 and 21, in La Forge 1974, pp. 174 and 301. See also: 'God's greatness is infinite . . .' (chap. 11, La Forge 1974, p. 190).

87 *Traité de l'esprit de l'homme,* chap. 27, La Forge 1974, p. 335. In fact, this purely philosophical definition agrees perfectly with that of the 'theologians [speaking] of God as an infinite and very perfect spirit' (chap. 10, La Forge 1974, p. 161).

88 *Traité de l'esprit de l'homme,* chap. 11, La Forge 1974, p. 190. See 'general cause,' 'total cause', chap. 15, La Forge 1974, pp. 226 and 227; 'universal cause', chap. 16, La Forge 1974, p. 242. The passages in question are simply quotations from the 1630 letters to Mersenne discussed earlier.

89 *Traité de l'esprit de l'homme,* respectively, chaps. 11, 15, and 16, La Forge 1974, pp. 193 and 195, 227, and 241.

90 Clauberg's collected philosophical writings appeared in 1691 (Clauberg 1691). The *Defensio cartesiana* originally appeared in 1652, and the first edition of the *Ontosophia* appeared in 1647.

91 *Disputatio physica,* XVIII, n. 32 (Clauberg 1691, vol. 1, p. 100).

92 *Metaphysica de ente quae rectius ontosophia,* first VI, n. 96 ('Deus actus dicitur purissimus, ein stets wirkendes Wesen') then XIII, n. 223, Clauberg 1691, vol. 1, pp. 299 and 320. A cause *secundum fieri* is a cause that gives certain already existing materials their properties; in this sense, an architect is the cause of a house. But a cause *secundum esse* is a cause that brings something into existence and sustains it in existence; in this sense the sun was said to be the cause of light, and God was said to be the cause of all creatures. See, for example, St. Thomas, *Summa th.* I q104 a1; or Descartes's Responsio V, AT VII 369.

93 For example, *Ontosophia,* VI, n. 81: 'ens omnino perfectissimum' (Clauberg 1691, vol. 1, p. 296); *Disputatio physica,* XVIII, n. 32, 'ens perfectissimum' (Clauberg 1691, vol. 1, p. 100); *Exercitationes de cognitione Dei et nostri,* VI, n. 18: '*ens perfectissimum*'; VII, n. 20: 'ens summe perfectum'; VIII, n. 8: 'idea Dei, hoc est idea entis perfectissimi'; XX, n. 4, 6 and 11; XXXI, n. 15, 18 and 19; XXXVII, n. 6, etc. (Clauberg 1691, vol. 2, pp. 607, 609, 610, 630 ff., 649, and 656). Undoubtedly we are dealing with the essential conception of God for Clauberg.

94 *Exercitationes de cognitione Dei et nostri,* IX, n. 5 (Clauberg 1691, vol. 2, p. 611) or else nn. 6 and 10 (pp. 656 ff.).

95 *Ontosophia,* XI, n. 193 (Clauberg 1691, vol. 1, p. 315).

96 Respectively, *Traité de l'indéfectabilité des créatures,* I; then, *Le guide de la raison naturelle,* V: 'God is not only the universal cause, but . . . He is yet the only cause of all things'; finally, *Supplément à la philosophie de Monsieur Descartes:* 'God being the efficient cause of all our simple ideas or conceptions, since He alone is the cause of movements in our external and internal senses' (in Desgabets 1983, pp. 19, 123, and 259).

97 *Traité de l'indéfectabilité des créatures,* XIV (Desgabets 1983, p. 84). See *Supplément à la philosophie de Monsieur Descartes:* 'the sovereign perfection that is in God' (Desgabets 1983, p. 259).

98 Respectively, *Supplément à la philosophie de Monsieur Descartes,* II, 1; and *Le guide de la*

raison naturelle, XI (Desgabets 1983, pp. 216 and 137). See Rodis-Lewis 1985, and Beaude 1979.

99 The phrase '*Deus sive Natura*' only appears in *Eth. IV* (Preface, two times) and in Dutch ('de Natuur of God') in the *Korte Vorhandling,* Appendix II, (Geb. I, p. 117).

100 We must remember here that the distinction between '*natura naturans*' (in fact, God Himself) and '*natura naturata*' (in fact, nature in the strict sense) goes back at least to Thomas Aquinas; the provocative novelty of this formula stems less from Spinoza himself than from its later usages. On the distinction, see *Eth. I,* Prop. 29, schol.; the parallel passage from *Korte Vorhandling,* I, 8, explicitly acknowledges, among others, the Thomist origin of the theme (*Summa th.* Ia IIae, q85 a6 c, and *In Dionysii de divinis nominibus,* IV, 21, in Thomas Aquinas 1927, vol. 2, p. 452). On these later interpretations, see Vernière 1982.

101 *Eth. I,* Def. 1. Prop. 7, dem., Prop. 24, dem., and Prop. 25, schol. add further explanation of this concept.

102 *De intellectus emendatione,* sec. 92.

103 This claim may appear somewhat paradoxical. Spinoza defines God as a substance 'consisting of an infinity of attributes, of which each one expresses an eternal and infinite essence' (*Eth. I,* def. 6). This would seem to be quite different from anything that Descartes offers, particularly in so far as Spinoza holds that a single substance can have multiple attributes. But the infinity of attributes does not directly define God (substance), but every thing whatsoever, substance or mode, finite or infinite. While Spinoza's metaphysics is novel, and differs from Descartes's, the innovation is not exactly centred on the conception of God.

104 'Summa Dei perfectione', *Eth.* I, Prop. 33, schol.; 'ens summe perfectum' Prop. 11, dem. 2; 'ens absolute perfectum', Prop. 11, schol.; 'perfectissima Dei natura', Appendix (Geb.II 83). This parallel is also noted by Wolfson 1934, vol. 1, pp. 179–84. For the equivalence of the Cartesian and Spinozist definitions of God, see Curley 1988. See also Marion 1991b.

105 The parallel is also noted in Gueroult 1968–74, vol. 1, pp. 187 and 191.

106 *Eth. V,* Prop. 35 dem. Spinoza's inconsistency here is argued in Alquié 1981, pp. 93–117.

107 *Entretiens sur la métaphysique et la religion,* II, sec. 4, in Mal. *OC* XII 53 (Malebranche 1980b, p. 47). See also *Rech.* III.2.5, and III.2.9, sec. 4, Mal. *OC* I 435 and 473 (Malebranche 1980a, pp. 229, 251); *Réponses à Arnauld,* Mal. *OC* VI–VII 541; *Entretiens d'un philosophe chrétien et d'un philosophe chinois,* Mal. *OC* XV 3, 4, 43 and 44. See also Rome 1963, pp. 120–60 and Rodis-Lewis 1986.

108 *Rech., Eclaircissement* X, Mal. *OC* III, pp. 137–8 and III.2.5, vol. I, p. 435 (Malebranche 1980a, pp. 618, 229); see III.2.6: 'the place of minds . . .', Mal. *OC* I, p. 437 (Malebranche 1980a, p. 230). This shift was criticised by Arnauld (*Réponses à Arnauld,* Mal. *OC* VI–VII 248ff.) and more recently in Alquié 1974, pp. 126–8.

109 *Réponses à Arnauld,* Mal. *OC* VI–VII 51–2. For a discussion of Malebranche's doctrine that we see all things in God, see Chapter 30 in this book.

110 *Rech.,* III.2.8, sec. 1, Mal. *OC* I 456 (Malebranche 1980a, p. 241) (see also pp. 449 and 473, Mal. *OC* II, p. 95, Mal. *OC* III, p. 148, etc. [Malebranche 1980a, pp. 236–7, 251, 318, 624]). Likewise, *Entretiens sur la métaphysique et la religion,* II, sec. 4 (Mal. *OC* XII–XIII 53); VIII, 1 (p. 174); VIII, 8 (p. 185); etc. (Malebranche 1980b, pp. 47, 171, 181–3). There are also some extremely ambiguous phrases: 'The Being of beings' (*Réflexions sur la prémotion physique,* sec. 19, Mal. *OC* XVI 101 and 103); 'God is all being' (*Rech.,* III.2.6, Mal. *OC* I 439) (Malebranche 1980a, p. 231).

111 'Ens absolute indeterminatum', says Spinoza, *Epistola XXXVI*, Geb. IV 186. The accusation of Spinozism against Malebranche was explicitly formulated by Father Tournemine (*Mémoires de Trévoux*, November 1713, p. 229 ff. = Mal. *OC* XIX 849 ff.), by Dortous de Mairan (Letter from 9 November 1713, Mal. *OC* XIX 858).

112 *Traité de la nature et de la grâce* I, sec. 11, Mal. *OC* V 26 (see also Mal. *OC* V 64, 75, 116; *Eclaircissement* X, reply to the Second Objection, in Mal. *OC* III 148). See also *Entretiens sur la métaphysique et la religion* (Mal. *OC* XII 135, 137, 174, 175, 178, 180, 197, 199, 200, 208, 211, 212, 225, 257, 310, etc. [Malebranche 1980b, pp. 131, 133, 171, 173, 175, 177, 197, 199, 199–201, 207, 209–11, 211, 225, 257, 311]); and the *Entretiens d'un philosophe chrétien et d'un philosophe chinois* (Mal. *OC* XV 4, 5, 7, 15, 22, 24, 26, 28, 31, 33, 43, 44, etc.).

113 *Rech.*, III.2.6, Mal. *OC* I 437 (Malebranche 1980a, p. 230). On all of these questions see particularly Alquié 1974, pt. I, chap. 3, pp. 113–45.

114 *Traité de la morale*, II, 2, sec. 5, Mal. *OC* XI 159 ff. See also *Réponses à Arnauld*, Mal. *OC* VI–VII 80. And *Traité de la nature et de la grâce*, I, sec. 12; I, sec. 59; II, sec. 63, etc. (Mal. *OC* V 27, 64, 116).

115 *Traité de la morale*, II, 11, sec. 9, Mal. *OC* XI 247. Perhaps there are not 'two Divinities', but Malebranche nevertheless admits 'two powers' (II, 9, sec. 5, p. 222) claiming 'two loves' (II, 4, sec. 7, p. 179). This duality is all the more important to Malebranche's system as it renders intelligible the conflicting relations between the King (cause) and the bishop (wisdom, perfection).

116 *Mon.*, sec. 87; see *PNG*, sec. 15 and *Disc. mét.*, sec. 35: 'One must not only consider God as the principle and cause of all substances and all beings, but also as the leader of all persons or intelligent substance and as the absolute monarch of the most perfect city' (Ger. IV 460). See also Jalabert 1960; and May 1962.

117 Leibniz 1948, respectively, pp. 16 and 66 (see also pp. 79, 171, 325, etc.). Likewise, see *Disc. met*, sec. 1, 'absolutely perfect being'; *PNG*, sec. 10, 'the supreme Perfection'; and *Mon.*, sec. 41, 'absolutely perfect'.

118 Leibniz 1948, p. 580, and *Mon.*, sec. 38. See *Théod.*, pt. I secs. 7–8, Ger. VI 106–7.

119 *Mon.*, sec. 31, then sec. 43 (see also *Théod.*, pt. I sec. 335, Ger. VI 314 and *PNG*, sec. 10). This thesis obviously goes back to Suárez (see the discussion earlier in the chapter).

120 'Deus est primum ens . . . ; ergo est etiam summum et perfectissimum essentialiter; ergo de essentia ejus est, ut includat aliquo modo omnem perfectionem possibilium in tota latitudine entis' (*Disp. met.* XXX.1.5, Su. *Op. omn.* 26, p. 62).

121 On this quasi-unanimous rejection, see Gouhier 1978, pp. 156 ff.; Rodis-Lewis 1985, pp. 139 ff.; and Marion 1985. Even J.-B. Bossuet, though of Cartesian inspiration, held that 'these eternal truths . . . are something of God, or rather are God Himself', that 'this reason is in God, or rather, this reason is God Himself' (*De la connaissance de Dieu et de soi-même*, Paris, 1722, IV, sec. 5 and V, sec. 2, in Bossuet 1879, vol. 8, pp. 115 and 121).

122 *PNG*, sec. 7. See also *Théod.*, pt. I sec. 44: 'This great principle is found in all events; a contrary example can never be given. . . . Without this great principle, we could never prove the existence of God' (Ger. VI 127). Leibniz uses the very terms Descartes used to announce the *causa sui*; see the discussion earlier in the chapter.

123 *PNG*, sec. 8. See also *Mon.*, secs. 38–40, and *Disc. mét.*, sec. 16: 'God being the true cause of substances'.

124 *Lev.* xxxi, Hobbes 1968, p. 403; and in Latin in *Lat. Works*, vol. 3, p. 261.

125 *Lev.* iii, Hobbes 1968, p. 99; and in Latin in *Lat. Works,* vol. 3, p. 20. See also *Lev.* xxxiv, ilv, and ilvi; *Elements of Law,* I, 5, sec. 3; and *De corpore,* II, 7–8.

126 *Lev.* xxxi, Hobbes 1968, pp. 401, 403 (= Latin, *Lat. Works,* vol. 3, p. 261); see also *De cive,* XV, 14: 'Ut sciamus autem quem cultum Dei assignet ratio naturalis, incipiamus ab attributis: ubi manifestum est attribuendam ei esse existentiam; . . . Unicum enim ratio dictat *naturae* significativum Dei nomen, *exsistens,* sive simpliciter, *quod est*' (*Lat. Works,* vol. 2, pp. 340 and 342 = Hobbes 1983a, pp. 226 ff., and Hobbes 1983b, pp. 190 ff.)

127 *Lev.* xi and xii (Hobbes 1968, pp. 167, 170 = *Lat. Works,* vol. 2, pp. 84 and 86). See *Philosophical Rudiments . . . ,* III, 15, sec. 14: 'For by the word *God,* we understand the world's cause' (*Eng. Works,* vol. 2, pp. 213 ff.). The hypothesis of Hobbes's fundamental atheism (Strauss 1963; Polin 1981) is seductive but weak. Hobbes remains traditional; his theology is limited, adopting the Thomist schema, reducing multiple causality to efficient cause alone, following the Cartesian tradition. On this, see Warrender 1957 and Bernhardt's introduction in Hobbes 1988.

128 See, e.g., Strauss 1963, esp. chap. 5; and Polin 1982, chaps. 1–3.

129 See *Ess.* I.iv.8–17. Locke was not the only one to deny the innateness of the idea of God. Samuel Clarke also maintains that we have no innate idea of God, and therefore that one must proceed on the basis of causality in order to arrive at 'the Being of a supreme independent cause' (Clarke 1706b, pp. 19, 21, etc.). We find the same position in the Cartesian Pierre Sylvain Régis, *Cours entier de philosophie ou système générale selon les principes de M. Descartes concernant la logique, la métaphysique, la physique, at la morale,* Régis 1691a, vol. 1, p. 305; see Clarke 1980.

130 *Ess.* II.xxiii.33. The idea of God is discussed most explicitly in *Ess.* II.xxiii.33–6. The incomprehensibility of God is emphasised in *Ess.* IV.x.19. Here we are dealing with the very thesis which Descartes criticised at length in Gassendi (AT VII 365 [9–26]; 370 [6] – 371 [7]; AT III, 427 [21ff.]; etc.).

Though Locke is clear enough that God is infinite in the passage quoted and in others, the proof for the existence of God he offers in IV.x.2 ff. would seem to establish something somewhat weaker, that God is a '*most powerful, and most knowing Being*' (IV.x.6). The process of enlargement, whereby the idea of infinity in number or space is constructed from the finite ideas given to us in experience is discussed in II.xvii. Locke's basic idea is that the idea of infinity arises 'from the Power, we observe in our selves, of repeating without end our own *Ideas*' (II.xvii.6).

131 *Ess.* IV.x.7. Locke characterises the argument from the idea of God as a 'Darling Invention', suggesting that he has the more recent Cartesian argument in mind, rather than the older ontological argument, which also derives from the idea of God, though in a different way.

132 *Ess.* IV.x.2–6.

133 Berkeley, *Pr. Hum. Kn.,* sec. 148.

134 See, for example, Berkeley, *Pr. Hum. Kn.,* sec. 48, *3 Dial.* II, III (Berkeley 1948–57, vol. 2, pp. 214–15, 230–1).

135 Berkeley denies that God has sensations like ours in *3 Dial.* III (Berkeley 1948–57, vol. 2, pp. 240–1). It should, however, be said that he also develops the idea that, since the divine will and understanding are the same, God's causing the sensible world and His sustaining it by (non-passively) perceiving it are two sides of the same coin. In general there is no causality without both will and understanding: 'How can that which is *inactive* be a *cause*; or that which is *unthinking* be a *cause of thought?*' (*3 Dial.* II [Berkeley 1948–57, vol. 2, p. 216]).

136 Berkeley, *Phil. Com.* B, sec. 52. See also secs. 282, 293, 293a.
137 Berkeley, *Phil. Com.* A, sec. 802. Note also that all the entries in which Berkeley most clearly presents his view of objects in God's mind as powers are preceded by the mark '+'. Although there is still much controversy about the proper interpretation of this symbol, it often seems to indicate entries that Berkeley rejected either because they were wrong, adopted an inappropriate tone, or were simply not useful for the purposes of what he was writing.
138 Berkeley, *3. Dial.* III (Berkeley 1948–57, vol. 2, p. 253).
139 Cf Berkeley, *3. Dial.* II (Berkeley 1948–57, vol. 2, pp. 213–14).
140 Berkeley, *Pr. Hum. Kn.,* sec. 30.
141 Berkeley, *Phil. Com.* A., sec. 433. It should be noted here that this entry is also preceded by the mark '+'. In this case, I suspect that Berkeley felt that he had gone too far in denying causes other than God (Berkeley clearly held that finite spirits were genuine causes too), but that the conception of God as cause remained central in his later works.
142 'Absurd to argue the existence of God from his idea, we have no idea of God. It is impossible', *Phil. Com.* A, sec. 782. The polemic against 'Cartesian innatism', common among his contemporaries, is Berkeley's fatal weakness. See Brykman 1984. On the unknowability of matter, see *3 Dial.,* Berkeley 1948–57, p. 231. In fact, it is only by a 'reflex act' that I can consider God as an 'I' or a mind.
143 *Princ.* I, 54. See also To Arnauld, 4 June 1648, AT V 193 [17]: 'cogitationes divinae'.
144 Except in the sense that God may contain extension eminently. On the notion of eminent containment, see Chapter 12 of this book and O'Neill 1987.
145 To Descartes, 11 December 1648, AT V 238 [21]; see also AT V 238 [25–6]; 239 [2]). This correspondence first appeared in 1657, in the first volume of Clerselier's edition of Descartes's correspondence, Descartes 1657–67. More published himself as More 1662b, part of More 1662a.
146 More 1980, respectively, I, 4, sec. 2, p. 32; I, 4, sec. 3, p. 33; and I, 4, sec. 4, p. 33. See also Lichtenstein 1962, pp. 168 ff.
147 To Descartes, 11 December 1648, AT V 238 [30] and 240 [6ff.]; then 23 July 1649, AT V 379 [16]. In addition to the references to More cited in note 146, see also *Enchiridion metaphysicum* VIII, 8: 'divinum quiddam videbitur hoc extensum infinitum ac immobile.'
148 Cudworth 1678, pp. 769–70. Cudworth's position is actually somewhat more complicated than this argument might suggest. In general he is agnostic about whether or not spirits are extended. Cudworth's main goal is to refute a position like that of Hobbes (see Chapter 23), in accordance with which spirit is corporeal, including God. Cudworth's point is that incorporeal substance, *both* extended and unextended, are coherent notions, and *whichever* we adopt, Hobbes can be answered. And that is what is important. See Cudworth 1678, preface p. v and pp. 833–4.
149 *Ess.* II.xv.3.
150 See *Ess.* IV.x.13–19. It should be mentioned here that Locke is at least agnostic about the question as to whether God is the subject of the space or extension in which finite creatures exist and move.
151 *Principia philosophiae naturalis mathematica, Scholium generale,* Newton 1972, vol. 2, pp. 760–2. In the first version of the text, afterwards suppressed, Newton wrote: 'Non est locus, non spatium, sed est in loco et in spatio idque semper et ubique' (in Cohen 1971, p. 250). See also Newton 1962, pp. 98, 99, 103 ff.
152 *An Answer to Bishop Bramhall's Book, Called 'The Catching of Leviathan'* (1668), *Eng.*

Works, vol. 4, p. 309. Hobbes also writes 'By corporeal, I mean a substance that has magnitude' (ibid., p. 313). Likewise, 'Ego per *corpus* intelligo nunc id de quo vere dici potest, quod existit realiter in seipso, habetque etiam aliquam magnitudinem, non quod sit magnitudo ipsa' (*Lev.,* Appendix I, *Lat. Works,* vol. 3, p. 537).

153 *Lev.* xxxiv, Hobbes 1968, pp. 428–9.

154 *Lev.* xii, Hobbes 1968, p. 171.

155 *An Answer to Bishop Bramhall, Eng. Works,* vol. 4, pp. 305, 306, and 383. Hobbes also writes: 'Affirmat [author] quidem Deum esse corpus. . . . Magnus est Deus, sed magnitudinem intelligere sine corpore impossibile est' (*Lev.,* Appendix I, *Lat. Works,* vol. 3, p. 537). Hobbes's textual argument, the claim that the notion of an incorporeal substance does not appear in the Scriptures or in the authoritative writings of Tertullian and Athanasius, does not hide the imprecision of Hobbes's concept of 'body', which he treats as a synonym of 'substance.'

156 *Eth.* I Prop. 15, scol.

157 *Eth.* I Prop. 15, scol. See also *Eth.* II Prop. 2: 'Extensio attributum Dei est, sive Deus est res extensa.'

158 According to Olivier Bloch (Bloch 1978), one must attribute authorship of the term 'materialism' to More (More 1668, pp. 5–6).

159 Respectively, *Rech., Eclaircissement X,* Mal. OC III 152 (Malebranche 1980a, pp. 626– 7); *Conversations chrétiennes* III, Mal. OC IV 75; and *Entretiens sur la métaphysique et la religion,* II, sec. 1, Mal. OC XII–XIII 50 ff. (Malebranche 1980b, pp. 43 ff.). Leibniz establishes this usage in opposing the 'greatest materialists', the Epicurians, to the 'greatest idealists', the Platonists (*Réponses aux réflexions . . . de M. Bayle . . .* , 1702, Ger. IV 560).

160 *Méditations chrétiennes et métaphysiques,* IX, sec. 9, Mal. OC X 99.

161 Gassendi, *Exercitationes paradoxicae adversus Aristoteleos,* II, 3, 8, Gassendi 1959, pp. 331 ff.

162 *La logique ou l'art de penser* I, 2, Arnauld and Nicole 1965, p. 47. See also Bernard Lamy, *Entretiens sur les sciences,* IV, Lamy 1966, pp. 127 ff.

163 *Le guide de la raison naturelle,* IX, Desgabets 1983, p. 137.

164 François de Salignac de la Mothe Fénelon, *Traité de l'existence et des attributs de Dieu,* I, 2, Fénelon 1854, vol. 1, p. 62. See also II, 2: 'The idea that I have of infinity is neither confused nor negative . . . the term infinity is infinitely affirmative by its signification, negative as it may appear in its grammatical turn' (ibid., pp. 100–101); and 'a being that by itself is at the supreme degree of being, and consequently infinitely perfect in its essence' (ibid., p. 98). This last formula brings together the three Cartesian names of God.

165 *Traité de l'existence et des attributs de Dieu,* II, 2, Fénelon 1854, vol. 1, p. 99; then: 'Isn't this infinite idea of infinity in a limited mind the seal of the omnipotent worker, which He stamped upon his work?' (ibid., p. 107). It is precisely this last point that Pierre-Daniel Huet disputed: 'Certe rei infinitae et infinitionis idea finita est' (*Censura philosophiae cartesianae,* IV, 3, Huet 1689, p. 107).

166 *Traité de l'existence et des attributs de Dieu,* II, 3, Fénelon 1854, vol. 1, respectively, pp. 112, 115. Spinoza, of course, does not exactly deny the unity of God (substance). But God's unity is relative, in a sense, in so far as God has an irreducible plurality of attributes that are genuinely distinct from one another.

167 *Traité de l'existence et des attributs de Dieu,* II, 5, Fénelon 1854, vol. 1, p. 125. Despite a *Réfutation de Spinoza* and a *Lettre sur l'idée d'infini et sur la liberté de Dieu de créer ou de ne pas créer* (Fénelon 1854, vol. 1, pp. 220 ff. and 224 ff.), Fénelon shared a similar

suspicion of Spinozism with Malebranche. Indeed, the definition of God as 'Ens ut sic, Ens universalissimum, Ens abstractum, metaphysicum et illimitatum' will be attributed to him not much later by Jean Hardouin as a sign of 'quietism' and of 'Jansenism' (Letter to Gonzalez, 20 November 1697, quoted by Hillenaar 1967, pp. 357 ff.). On all these points, see also Gouhier 1977.

168 AT VII 368 [2–4]. We should not forget two defenders of the primacy of the idea of infinity (and also of the creation of the eternal truths); first, Pierre Poiret, whose *Cogitationum rationalium de Deo, anima et malo libri quattuor* (Poiret 1677) interprets infinity as 'Ens sibi sufficientissimum' (ed. 1715, p. 6); then, J. Fontialis (1630 ?– 1707), whose *De idea mirabilis matheseôs entis* (Fontialis 1740) carries on the Scotist tradition (see Duns Scotus 1988).

169 *Entretiens avec Monsieur de Sacy*, Pascal 1963, p. 294 a, and *Pens.*, sec. 418 (see sections 135, 420, 917, etc.). See Courcelle 1981.

170 Respectively, *Pens.*, sec. 190 (and 191), then sec. 449.

171 *Pens.*, sec. 377: 'It is a long way between knowing God and loving Him'; see also sec. 739.

172 *Pens.*, sec. 449. See Marion 1986a, chap. 5.

173 Pascal 1963, p. 618 b.

174 *Pens.*, sec. 308; see also secs. 424 and 903.

PROOFS OF THE EXISTENCE OF GOD

JEAN-ROBERT ARMOGATHE

The question of the existence of God is central for the seventeenth century at a time when atheism is no longer just an individual standpoint but a philosophical school and a genuine system of thought. Standing behind the new atheism of the seventeenth century was a new approach to the question of the nature of God. The scholastics of earlier years had first asked *an sit Deus,* whether God exists, and then discussed at length His nature: *quid sit.* But in the seventeenth century, the traditional order was reversed, as Descartes explicitly declared: since one cannot seek to establish the existence of that which one does not know, before knowing whether God exists, it is necessary to define His identity.[1] This change in perspective allowed the question of the existence of God to become a legitimate topic of atheist critiques concerning God's function in the new mathematical and mechanical universe of seventeenth-century philosophy. At this point, atheism ceased to be the easily dismissed rantings of the fool and became a real epistemological possibility. This break was crucial for metaphysics, and it is in this context that we must understand Descartes's preoccupation with proofs of the existence of God. The Cartesian discourse constituted a necessary reference for all later systematic examinations of the question, whether they were positively inspired by Descartes (Spinoza, Malebranche, Leibniz) or explicitly opposed him (Gassendi, Hobbes, Locke, Berkeley).

I. THE CONDITIONS OF ATHEISM

How did scholars come to speak of 'proofs' of the existence of God outside the classical problematic concerning God? In 1581, in the treatise *De la vérité de la religion chrétienne,* the Protestant Philippe Duplessis-Mornay, a great apologist of Christianity, wonders whether proofs of God are really necessary. But in the end he reconciles himself to the task: 'Let us nonetheless dedicate this chapter, with the permission of all charitable men, to the wickedness of our century.'[2]

Translated by Thomas A. Carlson and Daniel Garber.

At the beginning of the seventeenth century, there was much talk about atheists;[3] some were arrested and condemned, and it was under the charge of atheism that Vanini was burned in 1619. Guillaume du Bartas did his best to shut 'the blaspheming mouths of the Godless dog-men'.[4] Atheists, though, were known more through those who refuted them than through their own writings. If Mersenne, speaking of the thousands of atheists lurking in Paris, found his *Quaestiones Celeberrimae in Genesim* censured, this is because such publicity could only prove a comfort to isolated and suppressed thinkers. Mersenne multiplies the arguments to prove the existence of God.[5]

The new atheism of the sixteenth and seventeenth centuries arose from the rediscovery of classical authors. Lucretius and Lucian provided the classical arsenal against divinity, but the pious Cicero was equally well put to use. In 1581 Le Fèvre de la Boderie published a new translation of Cicero's *De Natura Deorum,* 'against the frivolous objections and vain arguments of miscreant and atheistic impostors who believe themselves to acquire the name of learned and clever when they impudently argue against God and his Providence'. But in the character of Diagoras, the text abounds with arguments in favour of atheism. The atheist thereby acquired the name 'Diagoras'.[6] Diagoras was sometimes backed by the *recentiores pseudopolitici,* avowed or hidden disciples of Machiavelli.[7] Atheism, however, was not always defended as such; more often it was unbelief that was at issue. The libertine might be either a moral libertine or a philosophical libertine, but he always presented himself as anti-Christian.[8]

Libertines went to great lengths in developing a conceptual atheism in a systematic way.[9] The corpus of libertine arguments were collected by the anonymous author of the *Theophrastus redivivus* (ca. 1659).[10] The influence of the ancients, Cicero and Lucretius, is quite obvious in the book. In the *Theophrastus* the character of the theological horizon is particularly noteworthy. The Thomistic Five Ways are entirely absent, and the book attacks only the *a posteriori* proofs of the classical tradition, proofs either from the *consensus gentium* or from the providence and order of the world.[11] The argument is further supported by the discovery of 'atheistic' peoples in the New World and in Africa.

But it is not only the desire to win over the atheists that makes the argument *de Dei existentia* so important; heated debates were also taking place among Christian theologians. The Calvinist refusal of natural theology and of appeals to natural proofs led Catholics to accuse Protestants of rampant unbelief. The Jesuit Garasse charged Luther of 'perfect [i.e., complete] atheism',[12] and Mersenne accused Luther and Calvin of paving the way for the rejection of God's existence.[13] The two sides did not always direct such accusations purely at one another, however. In 1660 the Catholic Samuel Cottiby traced the roots of atheism to those who refused the Catholic practice of auricular confession (where the sinner is confronted with the justice and the forgiveness of God), whereas the Huguenot theologian Louis Cappel saw atheism as grounded simply in natural vices and the depraved search for pleasure.[14]

Eventually, the classical proofs of the existence of God could no longer withstand the new atheist and libertine attacks. One response was to give up altogether on trying to prove the existence of God and to base Christian faith on different grounds. That was what Pascal and his followers did. Gilberte Périer relates, in her *Vie de M. Pascal* (included in editions of the *Pensées* starting in 1684), that her brother 'made no use whatsoever of metaphysical proofs': 'He said that these kinds of proofs can lead us only to a speculative knowledge of God, and that to know God in this way was not to know him.'[15]

For Pascal, proofs are doubly useless:[16] on the one hand, they are addressed to people who do not know their own misery, and 'knowledge of God without that of one's misery constitutes pride', and they are unable to convince the atheist;[17] at the same time, they contribute in no way to the salvation of the Christian. Pascal's apology proceeds by way of the critique of proofs: 'against the philosophers who have God without Jesus Christ'.[18]

Proofs are excluded not because they are false but because they are useless and dangerous: the God to whom they lead is in fact an idol. This critique of metaphysical proofs does not appear clearly in the 1670 edition of the *Pensées*. The editors of Port-Royal in fact profoundly reworked Chapter 20 of the 1670 edition: 'We know God in a useful way only through Jesus Christ.' The pre-edition of 1669, however, reproduced the following at the beginning of Pascal's text: 'I admire the boldness these persons [i.e., the classical apologists] take in speaking of God. In addressing their discourse to the impious, their first chapter is to prove the divinity by the works of nature.'[19] This text was judged dangerous and was suppressed through a cancel in the edition of 1670, which replaced it by a classical protestation of conformity: 'I am not attacking the validity of these proofs [i.e., the proofs from nature], which are consecrated by Holy Scripture.' This tone of conformity, which did not deflect all criticisms, is also found in the writings of Pierre Nicole: 'Some invented subtle and metaphysical arguments to prove [the existence of God and the immortality of the soul], and others offer more popular and more sensible arguments by calling men back to a consideration of the world's order as to a great book ever exposed to their sight.' Nicole continues: 'These are abstract and metaphysical ones, as I said, and I do not believe that it would be reasonable to take pleasure in decrying them. But there are also some that are more sensible, more fit to most minds, and that are such that we would have to do violence to resist them, and these are the ones that I intend to bring together in this discourse.'[20] Nicole testifies, with prudence, about the diffident approach towards 'metaphysical proofs' in Augustinian circles. But his attitude results from widespread confusion in Christian apologetics in the first half of the century.

Whereas some rejected the enterprise of proving the existence of God, others accepted the challenge with enthusiasm. The extraordinary number of such proofs found in the writings of Mersenne testify to the widespread perception that it was necessary to formulate short, compelling, strong proofs to combat the atheists. This was the background against which Descartes would propose his plan in the *Meditationes de philosophia prima*. It is not a question here of the gratuitous exercises of a philosopher; Descartes is aware of an urgent necessity to ground the existence of God and the immortality of the soul on incontestable arguments. It is not simply to please the Sorbonne, but rather due to a real need, that Descartes claims to establish, through the reasoning of *Meditationes,* some proofs – few in number, but compelling – 'to propose against those who lack faith'.[21]

II. THE SCHOLASTIC CONTEXT: SUAREZ

Descartes's reaction to this new intellectual climate is central to the debate surrounding the existence of God later in the seventeenth century. But Descartes's contribution cannot be fully understood without some idea of how the existence of God was treated in late scholastic thought.

Courses given at the Sorbonne at the beginning of the century had a number of features in common: there had been a decline in the traditional Thomistic Five Ways, especially the one which Thomas himself judged most important, the argument from motion; the Anselmian arguments continued to be heard; and a wealth of *a posteriori* arguments, from effects, were developed by Father Mersenne.

Scholastic thought about the existence of God was shaped in large part by Suárez.[22] Suárez begins by asking whether the existence of God falls within the domain of demonstrations in physics (the *a posteriori* ways of the scholastic tradition), or whether it is primarily a metaphysical question. In other words, does the existence of God fall within the domain of 'natural theology' or of philosophy? Zabarella and those in the Italian Aristotelian tradition, which several German Lutheran academics followed, exclude from *metaphysics* any discussion of the existence of God.[23] Suárez, though, opts for a different view, in which he is followed both by Catholics and by Protestants. His treatment of the question constitutes the predominant conceptual framework for all of the seventeenth century.[24]

Suárez avoids defining God as *ens perfectissimum*. Instead, God is known as 'a certain very noble being (*quoddam nobilissimum ens*), who surpasses all others':[25] if the concept of God remains indeterminate (*quoddam*), it is nonetheless correct and definitive of God. This concept is grounded in *a posteriori* proofs, but Suárez, sensitive to debates among his contemporaries concerning the argument from motion, begins by dismissing that traditional proof: 'The axiom that everything that is moved is moved by something else [*omne quod mouetur ab alio mouetur*], the axiom on which the entire demonstration rests, is not proved sufficiently for every kind of motion or action.'[26] Suárez also methodically undermines the proof drawn from the operations of the soul.[27] Having dismissed any physical way of arguing for the existence of God, Suárez concentrates his attention on metaphysical proofs, which alone can lead to the God that he has defined, an object not of physics but of metaphysics, not a first mover but an *ens nobilissimum*.

The only kind of argument that seems to him fully admissible and that works appropriately is an *a posteriori* proof from effects, derived from the necessity of a first cause.[28] As the efficient cause of all created things, the unique such cause, Suárez's God is a being of the greatest nobility who is the source of all, and on whom everything depends as its creator, to which all honour and all glory are due.[29] Nevertheless, Suárez does not eliminate the *a priori* proof altogether; that argument allows him to establish that the Supreme Being is unique.[30] In the end he also admits that physical proofs can render the existence of God *credible*.

The framework set in place by Suárez demonstrates why it was possible in the seventeenth century to approach the question of God's existence from a perspective entirely different from that of the mediaevals. Suárez firmly established God as a being rather than a mover: henceforth, the debate would unfold on a metaphysical terrain, where Suárez's doctrine of the univocity of being would weaken the transcendence of God.[31] But Suárez does not give up the doctrine of analogy altogether: 'Even though [God] agrees in some sense with certain created things insofar as he is a substance [*in ratione substantiae*], he does not do so univocally but analogically.'[32] Suárez's metaphysical discourse is full of compromises, even contradictions. In this way, Suárez seems to weaken the classical positions on the existence of God without substituting for them alternative arguments of greater strength.

III. RENE DESCARTES

Descartes puts forward several proofs. That, in itself, is nothing original. But these proofs are heterogeneous and irreducible to one and the same idea of God.[33] Of particular note are three proofs, in the *Meditationes, Responsiones,* and *Principia*

Philosophiae.[34] In Meditatio III Descartes presents two proofs, both *a posteriori* proofs from effects, and in Meditatio V he puts forth what, after Kant, will be called the 'ontological argument'. The order is changed, however, in part I of the *Principia*; there the 'ontological' proof comes to the fore, followed by the two *a posteriori* proofs. But in his conversation with Burman, four years after the publication of the Latin *Principia* in 1644, Descartes seems to return to the view that the two *a posteriori* proofs have precedence over the ontological proof.[35] Nevertheless, the ontological proof – which Descartes and both his followers and opponents consider *the* Cartesian proof par excellence – corresponds to the deepest impulses of the Cartesian position. But that is not to say that the proofs from effects are merely tactical or pedagogical concessions. They proceed differently, and this diversity of approaches, among which Descartes does not choose, contributes to the richness of Cartesianism; it can be seen in the choices that Spinoza, Malebranche, and Leibniz will be called upon to make.

Descartes's search for an appropriate proof of God's existence goes back at least to 1630. In a letter to Mersenne, Descartes, having said that it would be necessary to find 'a self-evident demonstration that would make everyone believe that God is', evokes 'one' such proof:

For my part, I dare indeed to pride myself on having found one that satisfies me entirely and that makes me know that God exists more certainly than I know the truth of any proposition of geometry; but I do not know whether I will be able to make it understandable to everyone in the same way that I understand it; I believe that it would be better not to touch the matter at all than to treat it imperfectly. The universal assent of all peoples is sufficient to maintain the Divinity against the affronts of the atheists, and a single person must never enter into dispute against them unless he is very certain that he will convince them.[36]

This modesty, unusual in Descartes, shows the gravity of what is at stake. In part IV of his *Discours de la méthode* (1637), Descartes passes from the *cogito* to the experience of 'the idea of a being more perfect than mine': this idea could only have been placed in me by a being that in itself has all the perfections – that is, God. It is an innate idea, therefore, like a number of others, but one that directly bears the mark of the one who has given it to us; it was 'placed in me,' since I could not have produced it. The argument remains weak, however, since Descartes, who at this point uses 'thought' or 'idea' indifferently, does not say anything about the 'objective reality' or content of the idea.[37] Apart from its objective reality, the idea of perfection remains indeterminate; consequently its relative character ('more perfect than mine') cannot be sustained, and the argument loses its value.

Descartes acknowledges, in a letter of February 1638, 'It is true that I was too obscure in what I wrote, in the treatise on Method, concerning the existence of God; and even though this is the most important part, I admit that it is the least elaborated in the whole work.' He first invokes the needs of a hurried writing, but he adds two other reasons: first, in a work written in French and addressed to all readers (even to women), he did not want to present the universal and methodical doubt that is the necessary condition for grounding his demonstration; next, he took certain notions that were familiar to him as self-evident for any reader, when in fact those notions would have required some explanation. He intends, he says, 'to give some clarification of them in a second printing'.[38]

He gets that opportunity in the *Meditationes* of 1641, in which he intended quite explicitly to answer some of the objections to the *Discours*. The basis of Meditatio III, '*de Deo, quod existat*' is that the idea of God is innate: it is mixed with my own consciousness, it affects me – which means that I have an idea of God. Two proofs are usually distinguished here – one starting from the idea of God that is in me, and another starting from my own existence (the proof Fischer calls 'anthropological').[39] But Descartes freely acknowledges that these two proofs boil down to a single one. All of the traditional proofs from effects are found here, recovered so to speak in this single central effect, the existence of an innate idea of God, which contains all effects. But, at bottom, he opposes all proofs that rest on the impossibility of an infinite series: for him, on the contrary, in Meditatio III, infinity becomes the proper name of God and takes predominance over being.[40] In order to preserve God's transcendence, Descartes is led to characterise God's being as *infinite,* allowing God's being to stand beyond our knowledge.

The *a posteriori* argument that we have been discussing shows that God exists. But Descartes is also interested in showing something stronger, that existence is *essential* to God. For this we must turn to the other arguments Descartes considers. Descartes explains that there are two ways of knowing that in God existence pertains to essence. On the one hand, since existence is a perfection, existence must be contained in our immediate idea of God as 'a supremely perfect Being' as part of its essence.

On the other hand, the necessity of God's existence is equally evident from the fact that He is *causa sui,* a being that is its own cause. In the face of objections raised by the first and second objectors to his *Meditationes,* Descartes is led to modify his interpretation of the ontological argument: in his *Responsiones* Descartes introduces the notion of God as *causa sui* and outlines proofs that will be taken up and developed by Spinoza and Malebranche. This expression, '*causa sui*', is not totally unknown to the scholastic tradition.[41] Nevertheless, Arnauld thought

God

it dangerous, and Descartes went to great lengths in the Fourth Replies to defend and explain it.[42] From God's being the *efficient* cause of Himself, it follows that His essence and His existence must be one and the same thing, Descartes holds.

Etienne Gilson has shown the influence of Suárez on Descartes with respect to this doctrine of the innate idea of God; in so far as he distinguishes our idea of God from anything we might have learned from our parents or our culture, Descartes is undoubtedly indebted to Suárez, who stresses the same point.[43] It is in Suárez (but also in Mersenne) that he could have read the clearest presentation of the ontological argument. In the discussion of it that he provides, it is much more from Suárez than from Thomas Aquinas that he borrows the discussion (and the refutation) of that argument. If he dismisses the conceptualist interpretation of the argument as different from his own interpretation, this is because he learned it from Mersenne, or perhaps from Silhon, who modifies the Anselmian argument and twists it in a conceptualist fashion.[44]

Despite the variants of it that he was led to sketch, Descartes takes the ontological argument to be a kind of demonstration, and not a simple intuitive given.[45] Or rather, what is involved here is *intellectual* intuition: God is *causa sui*.[46] Descartes could not have been unaware of the audacious character of the expression. In the scholastic tradition, to make God His own cause came down to making Him an effect, even if He was caused by Himself. Arnauld offered a fair criticism: Could one submit God to the principle of causality? But despite Arnauld's criticisms, Descartes maintained this expression along with all of its metaphysical consequences, namely, that God is caused.[47] Consistent with his theory of knowledge, Descartes holds that one can say of a thing whatever one clearly and distinctly perceives of its idea.[48] The ontological argument therefore amounts to an affirmation of the existence of God starting from the perception of His idea as necessary. What is in question here is the thought or idea itself, and no longer its cause. In the *Principia* I, Section 14, Descartes gives the argument its most formal expression:

> Just as when [thought] sees what is necessarily included in the idea that it has of the triangle – that its three angles are equal to two right angles – it is absolutely persuaded that the triangle has three angles equal to two right angles, likewise, only when it perceives that necessary and eternal existence is included in the idea of an all-perfect Being must it conclude that that all-perfect Being is or exists.[49]

The richness of the Cartesian argument amounts therefore to a twofold onto-theo-logical constitution, structured around the original concept of infinity: by the *causa* and by the *cogitatio*.[50] One arrives at the necessary existence of God by one or another of two paths. But, unfortunately, they are not consistent: we must choose the path we want to take. Descartes felt the duplicity of his argumentation. In a first formulation of the ontological proof, the major premise establishes that 'all things that I know clearly and distinctly are true.' The minor states that we understand clearly and distinctly that to exist belongs to the nature of God, and consequently the conclusion affirms that we can say of God that He exists.[51] In its second formulation, put forth in the responses to Caterus (*Primae Responsionaes*) and to Arnauld (*Quartae Responsiones*), God is *causa sui*; Descartes will even go so far as to speak of God as His own *efficient* cause.[52] The two formulations proceed from the same dynamic: as opposed to the triangle, God as infinite can be conceived (*intelligere*), and therefore proved, without being comprehended (*comprehendere*). The way this argument proceeds makes use of the vocabulary (and mental categories) of the scholastics, but it draws from them an original argument: the God Descartes succeeds in proving is reached as Supreme Being entirely in so far as He is the cause of Himself. This is less a contradiction than a paradox. But the paradox gives rise to an equivocation.

The difficulties presented by these distinct Cartesian lines of reasoning determined the paths taken both by objectors and by followers, both by the opponents of Descartes and by those who wanted to take his line of reasoning into account. Both sides – Gassendi, Hobbes, Locke, and Berkeley, on the one hand (the first two having written objections to the *Meditationes*), and Spinoza, Malebranche, and Leibniz, on the other – were led to make more consistent, but less rich, choices. In order to take account of Cartesianism, Spinoza came to identify *cogitatio* and *causa,* thought and cause; for Malebranche, the idea of God is located in God; for Leibniz, finally, *causa sive ratio* is identified with the principle of sufficient reason.

IV. THE CARTESIAN RESPONSE: SPINOZA, MALEBRANCHE, AND LEIBNIZ

1. Spinoza

Spinoza's arguments for the existence of God are written in a Cartesian vocabulary, but they are in constant debate with Descartes's thought. One can classify Spinoza's different demonstrations according to their relation to the three main proofs Descartes advanced:

1. Descartes's first *a posteriori* proof is treated by Spinoza in the *Principia philosophiae cartesianae,* part I, proposition 6, in Letter 40 (to Jelles), in a note from the *Tractatus de Intellectus Emendatione,* section 76 (*Opera* II, p. 29, n. a), and also at the beginning of the *Korte verhandeling* I, 1.[53]

2. Descartes's second *a posteriori* proof is taken up in the *Principia philosophiae cartesia-nae* (part I, proposition 7).[54]

3. Finally, the *a priori* proof has several formulations in Spinoza (as in Descartes). The formulation given in the *Principia Philosophiae Cartesianae* I, proposition V (and, perhaps, the first part of the proof in the *Korte verhandeling* I, 1) takes up the Cartesian version of the proof that starts from the idea of perfection.[55] But the formulation found in Letters 12 (to Meyer) and 34 (to Hudde) and in the second part of the proof from the *Korte verhandeling* I, 1 depends on the definition of the *causa sui,* as does the first proof from the *Ethica,* part I, proposition 11.[56] The main demonstration given in *Eth.* I, proposition 11, represents an original reinter-pretation of Descartes. Proposition 11 rests on the central premise that it belongs to the nature of a substance as such to exist, a theorem proved earlier as *Eth.* I, proposition 7. It is important to note here that the demonstration of proposition 7 Spinoza gives depends crucially on the notion of *causa sui*; because a substance is its own cause, 'its essence necessarily involves existence, that is, it pertains to its nature to exist.' As Ferdinand Alquié observed, 'under different forms, all the Spinozist proofs for the existence of God can be brought back to this *a priori* proof, itself deriving from the definition of the *cause of self*'.[57]

In addition to the *a priori* argument in proposition 11, Spinoza offers two 'alternative' arguments in the scholium that immediately follows. In the second demonstration from the *Ethica,* suggested by the ontological proof, Spinoza argues for the existence of God from the fact that there can be no cause for God's non-existence. This argument introduces the expression 'necessary existence', also used by Descartes in this connexion.[58] But Spinoza modifies its content, probably through borrowings from the mediaeval philosophic tradition; his discussion recalls certain debates between *possible* existence and *necessary* existence, where necessary existence is distinguished from possible existence *per se*.[59] The last demonstration from the scholium to *Eth.* I, proposition 11, is *a posteriori,* and argues for the existence of God from the fact that the existence of contingent beings requires the existence of a necessary being. This, again, refers back to one of Descartes's proofs.[60] But Spinoza immediately adds in the scholium: 'I wanted to show the existence of God *a posteriori,* so that the demonstration would be more easily seen. This does not mean that the existence of God does not follow *a priori* from this same principle.'

Spinoza differs from Descartes mainly in his more thoroughgoing rationalist project. The *a priori* proof in Descartes consisted essentially in recognising that divine infinity cannot be denied, though it surpasses our mind: though we know that He exists, the God of Descartes remains incomprehensible. Spinoza, on the other hand, establishes the concept of *causa sui* and uses it as an immutable principle of intelligibility, a principle of absolute rationalism.

2. Malebranche

Malebranche's proofs of the existence of God are closely connected with his theory of knowledge. One does not have an idea of God, through which He is known; God is known directly, without the intermediation of any idea.[61] As a consequence, Malebranche cannot maintain the argument of the *causa sui,* which is an *intellectual* intuition; from the twofold Cartesian conception of God he discards the *causa* and keeps only the *cogitatio.* His own twofold concern is to establish the power of God and to demonstrate that He exists.

In the *Entretien d'un philosophe chrétien et d'un philosophe chinois* (1708), Malebranche recalls that the instantaneous and simultaneous perception of objects, so varied in their size, form, and colour that make up the world, constitutes a proof of God; but already in the *Conversations chrétiennes* (1677) (First conversation) he argues from one such perception, the immediate knowledge of the pain caused by the prick of a thorn: 'If I were the cause of the pain which I suffer, I would never produce it myself since I hate it. I see that there is a superior cause that acts on me, and can render me happy or unhappy.'[62]

Malebranche offers many such *a posteriori* proofs; it is finite creatures that allow us to know God: 'Here indeed are several objects that surround us: which would you like me to use to prove that there is a God? This fire that delights us? This light that illumines us? The nature of words through whose means we converse? For . . . there is no creature that cannot serve to show us the Creator.'[63] But, although he multiplies the *a posteriori* demonstrations, Malebranche remains convinced that

all the usual proofs of the existence and perfection of God, those drawn from the existence and perfection of his creatures, have this fault: they do not all convince the mind by immediate intuition [*simple vûë*] alone. All these proofs are arguments that are convincing in themselves; but being arguments, they are not all convincing under the assumption of an evil genius who deceives us. They convince us sufficiently that there is a power superior to ourselves, for even this extravagant assumption establishes as much; but they do not convince us fully that there is a God or an infinitely perfect being. Thus, in these arguments the conclusion is more obvious than the principle.[64]

What is Malebranche's favoured argument for the existence of God? Historians of philosophy have disagreed. Bouillier[65] and Cuvillier[66] presume it is the first causal proof from Meditatio III. This, however, would be surprising, for if we have no idea of God, we cannot prove the existence of God as the cause of His idea. Along with Henri Gouhier,[67] we prefer to see the ontological argument in Malebranche's description of the proof that he favours: 'The most beautiful proof for the existence of God, the most exalted, the most solid, and the first, and that which presupposes the least is the [proof drawn from the] idea we have of infinity.'[68] Another important text in this connexion is an explicit 'eclaircissement' of 'la preuve de M. Descartes'.[69] The proof in question is Descartes's version of the ontological argument. In his discussion, Malebranche is not content simply to rehearse Descartes's demonstrations, and if it is possible to locate certain Cartesian influences, it is difficult to identify them with certainty. Malebranche first sets aside the doctrine of an innate idea of God, and then simplifies a long and complex argument: the proof that rests solely on the idea that we have of infinity is 'that which presupposes the least'.[70] He writes:

> It is clear, then, that the soul, its modes, or anything finite cannot represent the infinite, that we cannot see the infinite except in itself and in virtue of the efficacy of its substance, that the infinite does not and cannot have an archetype, or an idea distinct from it, that represents it, and that therefore if we think of the infinite, it must exist.[71]

Malebranche wants to take account of the distinction between possible and necessary existence. Things can be seen in God as essences, and their existence is therefore possible, but they are not necessary. However God is seen only in Himself, for nothing finite can represent the infinite. And to see God is to see that He exists. Furthermore, one cannot see God only as possible. But this does not imply that we have an *idea* of God. There is no idea of God other than that which God has of Himself: the Word. And the idea that we have of Him is the presence of the Word in our soul. The vision of God is therefore at once a demonstration of His existence and a definition of pure understanding.

Arnauld located the mistake in Malebranche's reasoning. Arnauld maintains that all of Descartes's opponents held what Malebranche puts forward, that one cannot have an idea of God. In this way they deprived the *a priori* proof of any efficacy.[72] But Malebranche claims that he wants only to make the proof deeper by reflecting on the very meaning of what it is to have an idea of God. Descartes deduces the existence of God from the idea that we have of Him; then he bases the truth of ideas on divine veracity: here we have the difficult problem of the 'circle' that Arnauld denounces. Malebranche acknowledges the reality of the problem, but he manages skilfully to skip over it, taking a short cut from the thought of God's existence to its reality: 'Thus if one thinks of it, it must be.'[73] This God is the Infinite Being. But if He is so conceived, it is difficult to grant God any attribute that would enable Him to become the God of the Christians. The equivocality of a philosophical approach to theology led to what Alquié has called Malebranche's lost children, the philosophers of the Enlightenment.[74]

3. Leibniz

In a letter from 1678 (to Princess Elisabeth?), Leibniz acknowledged that Descartes's arguments 'are a little suspect because they go too quickly and because they force themselves upon us without enlightening us'.[75] He reminds her of the two kinds of objections made against the Cartesian arguments:

1. 'Some have believed that there was no idea at all of God because he is not subject to the imagination'; the reference here is presumably to Hobbes's *Objectiones* to Descartes's *Meditationes*.[76]
2. Some others 'could not comprehend how existence follows [from the idea of God]': this is the sixth argument from the *Secundae Objectiones*.[77]

Leibniz shows that Descartes's response to Hobbes is insufficient: it does not suffice to say 'we know what "God" signifies, for there are some words or expressions that contain a contradiction (the fastest motion, the largest of all circles . . .); one must examine whether the notion of God, as the most perfect being, contains any contradiction: is the conceived object possible?'[78]

A second objection will later be taken up by Kant: one cannot go from possibility to being. But in opposition to this, Leibniz stresses here – and this will be a constant point in his doctrine – that *if God is possible, he necessarily exists*. Leibniz often stresses the extent to which this modal proposition is 'one of the best fruits of all Logic'.[79] God is the only one for whom the passage from possibility to being is legitimate: 'The necessary Being, if only it is possible, exists absolutely. This is the culmination of the theory of modality, whereby we can pass from essences to existences, from hypothetical truths to absolutes, from ideas to the world.'[80] Leibniz will therefore do his best to demonstrate the *possibility* of the necessary Being.[81]

Leibniz seems to take a similar view in his *Meditationes de cognitione, veritate et Ideis* (1684), his first public attack against the Cartesians. In his earlier writings, Leibniz thought it sufficient to establish the possibility of the concept of God by arguing for the compatibility of all of the perfections with respect to one another. He does so in an essay from 1676, which received Spinoza's approval: *Quod Ens perfectissimum existit*.[82] But in his *Meditationes,* Leibniz also takes a different approach, suggesting that we can know the possibility of a concept through *a posteriori* reasoning. The possibility of contingent beings would then serve to ground the possibility of the necessary Being.[83]

Yet even after the consistency of the perfections with one another has been established, a formidable question remains: Is existence a more perfect quality than non-existence? In his correspondence with the Cartesian Arnold Eckhard (1677–

9), Leibniz doubts it,[84] but over a number of years, his position evolves in a profound way, ending up at the *Monadologie* (1714). At the same time, his preference for *a posteriori* proofs also seems to increase. Even if in the *Monadologie* Leibniz envisages that 'that which contains no bounds, no negation and consequently no contradiction', must necessarily be possible and can therefore be known *a priori*,[85] he appeals equally to the eternal truths and, above all, to the proof from contingent beings. In the *Théodicée* (1710), God is 'the first reason of all things,' 'the cause of the world': that cause must be intelligent, infinite, and unique. Leibniz thus proves, 'in few words', the existence of God.[86]

Thus, from the contingency and hypothetical necessity of the world, Leibniz infers an extramundane principle, God. Against Spinozist immanence, he preserves the theological tradition of a creator God, free and transcendent. This proof by the contingency of the world invokes the *a priori* proof, which Leibniz supplements by specifying how the most perfect Being is possible.[87]

Spinoza, Malebranche, and Leibniz, respectively, modified, corrected, and enlarged the Cartesian discourse, but they were unable to get away from the original approach established by Descartes in the *Meditationes*. Their efforts to choose among the successive approaches proposed by Descartes only succeeded in underscoring his equivocation. But there were others who opposed themselves to the *Meditationes*. Starting from the debate opened by the *Objectiones* (and the responses given by Descartes), there was considerable opposition to Descartes's views on God and His existence, most notably in Hobbes and Gassendi, participants in that original exchange, and in Locke and Berkeley, who came later in the century.

V. THE EMPIRICIST REJECTION OF THE CARTESIAN APPROACH: HOBBES, GASSENDI, LOCKE, AND BERKELEY

1. Hobbes

Scholars of his thought commonly assume that Hobbes was an atheist or an agnostic.[88] But however the debate may stand, it must be agreed that Hobbes had a profound knowledge of Scripture; on a number of points he is close to the Reformers of the sixteenth century and also foreshadows the deist philosophers of the eighteenth century.[89] The absolute sovereignty of God and the determinism of predestination are expressed in terms of a rigid Calvinist orthodoxy. But Hobbes's scepticism held him apart from the impassioned rationalism of contemporary natural philosophers.

At first Hobbes does not deny the existence of a first mover, who is God.

Though we can deduce His existence through reason, Hobbes notes that God's nature is beyond any demonstration and any reasoning; He exists, but one cannot know any more about Him than that:

> The nature of God is incomprehensible; that is to say, we understand nothing of *what he is,* but only *that he is*; and therefore the Attributes we give him, are not to tell one another, *what he is,* nor to signifie our opinion of his Nature, but our desire to honor him with such names as we conceive most honorable amongst ourselves.[90]

In a famous passage in the *Leviathan,* Hobbes argues that our belief in God derives from a desire to know the ultimate causes of things: 'The acknowledging of one God, Eternall, Infinite and Omnipotent, may more easily be derived, from the desire men have to know the causes of naturall bodies, and their several vertues, and operations; than from the feare of what was to befall them in time to come.'[91] In this way Hobbes arrives at a first mover, 'that is, a First, and an Eternall cause of all things; which is that which men mean by the name of God'.[92]

The God who is susceptible of proof is a cause, the first cause of the Universe. This allows the philosopher to accept that the existence and sovereignty of God can be known through reason. This is a view that Hobbes holds not only in his great political writings, those preceding *De Corpore,* but also in his subsequent polemical treatises.[93] It has been said that Hobbes seems to accept more rational religion than his epistemology was ready to accommodate.[94] But that rationality does not bring about absolute certainty; scepticism ultimately prevails as a personal standpoint in the face of the various and multifarious religious opinions of contemporary England.[95] Even if we can affirm that God exists, we still remain ignorant of His nature and attributes, omnipotence aside. He is, for Hobbes, it would seem, simply a very powerful body.[96]

2. *Gassendi*

Gassendi underwent a notable evolution in his conception of the proofs for the existence of God, starting from his first work on Epicureanism.[97] The *Disquisitio metaphysica* appears in 1644, but it summarises the earlier *Objectiones Sextae* (1641) which Gassendi directed against Descartes's *Meditationes.* Gassendi there reproaches Descartes for having left the 'royal way' constituted by the contemplation of the universe;[98] he denies any value in the argument from universal assent, which nonetheless will be the main theme of his *De Deo* of 1642 and will be repeated in his *Syntagma philosophicum.*[99]

The final state of Gassendi's rational theology is found in this text from the *Syntagma,* which begins with the existence of God and ways in which it can be proved.[100] 'We should not multiply arguments,' he writes; 'one can reduce them to two',[101] the argument from general anticipation, and the argument from the spectacle of nature.

Gassendi insists on the *anticipatio*, the Epicurean *prolepsis*, a notion of God all humans have. Eager to distance himself from Descartes's innate ideas, Gassendi explains that this *anticipatio* develops only on a basis of sensible data from hearing or from sight. The data of hearing result from revelation or testimony, from acquiescence to an authority that is divine (in which case it is faith in the Pauline sense) or merely human (which corresponds to the Epicurean *anticipatio*). In addition, the data of vision introduce a privileged mode of knowledge. The contemplation of the universe permits us to pass to a second kind of argument, the 'proof from effects', a kind of argument contained in the first, though neglected in this respect by Epicurus.[102] But Gassendi discerns the danger of arriving at a God foreign to Christianity. He takes care to remind us that reason and the purpose for things are two ways to attain knowledge of God. The proof from anticipation allows us to know the existence of God, but the proof from effects teaches us that He is the creator of the world and the providential ruler of the universe and of humankind. The proof from anticipation thus has its limitations: 'Indeed, even if it can be established as indubitable that God exists from what has been said, we can only establish to the smallest extent who it is that exists, and what his form or nature is.'[103]

This God whose existence can be proved remains a hidden God, a God who eludes our grasp. At the most, He can be known through analogies or images: our understanding stretches the sensible upon which it reasons.[104]

3. Locke

Through his critique of intellectual intuition, of essence and of eternal truths, Gassendi foreshadows the central themes of the critique that Locke puts forward against Cartesian metaphysics in his *Essay concerning Human Understanding*. This is what Leibniz has so justly observed: 'He [i.e., Locke] obviously writes in the spirit of Gassendi . . . and he appears disposed to approve most of the objections Gassendi made to Descartes. He has enriched and reinforced this system with a thousand lovely reflections.'[105]

Although the theologians claimed that the refusal of innate ideas weakens any possibility of proving God and thus confines one to atheism,[106] Locke, celebrated for his refutation of innate ideas, fully acknowledges the importance of theology. He writes:

There is, indeed, one science incomparably above all the rest . . . , I mean theology, which, containing the knowledge of God and his creatures, our duty to him and our fellow creatures, and a view of our present and future state, is the comprehension of all other knowledge directed to its true end, i.e. the honour and veneration of the Creator, and the happiness of mankind. This is that noble study which is everyman's duty, and everyone that can be called a rational creature is capable of.[107]

Locke recognised that God has given us 'the *Christian* Religion' through revelation, the 'Voice of the Spirit' rather than 'the Voice of Reason'.[108] But he also asserts that 'we have the knowledge of the *existence* of God by demonstration.'[109] His clear preference is for *a posteriori* arguments for the existence of God. In a paper entitled *Deus,* written six years after the appearance of the *Essay,* Locke presents a radical critique of the ontological argument: 'Any idea, simple or complex, barely by being in our minds, is no evidence of the real existence of any thing out of our minds answering that idea. Real existence can be proved only by real existence; and therefore the real existence of God can only be proved by the real existence of things.'[110] Although he does not go quite so far in the *Essay,* Locke there grounds God's existence on an unusual and original formulation of the cosmological argument. Locke starts from his own being as the existence of something real, and he rises from this real existence to its cause, and to the cause of all thinking beings, which, he argues, must be a thinking Being itself. But arguing from the existence of anything at the present moment to the existence of something from eternity, Locke escapes many criticisms aimed at the classical cosmological argument. Furthermore, the use of *thinking beings* allows him to argue for a Christian God, a real (and eternal and omnipotent) thinking being. Although this reasoning sets Locke apart from contemporary Deists, he nevertheless foreshadows eighteenth-century apologists, both in his sentimental feeling of religion and in his preference for the *a posteriori* demonstration of God's existence.

4. Berkeley

The existence of God occupies a central place in Berkeley's philosophy.[111] Indeed, Berkeley's entire philosophical project is directed at establishing God's existence. Berkeley ends his *Principles of Human Knowledge* by declaring that 'what deserves the first place in our studies, is the consideration of *God* and our *duty*; which to promote . . . was the main drift and design of my labors.'[112]

For Berkeley, God is not simply the Creator of the Universe: what is at issue is the God of the Christians, a God who intervenes in the order and progression of things in the world: '[God is] not a Creator merely, but a provident Governor, actually and intimately present, and attentive to all our interests and motions, who watches over our conduct, and takes care of our minutest actions and designs throughout the whole course of our lives, informing, admonishing, and directing incessantly, in a most evident and sensible manner.'[113] Furthermore, Berkeley thinks, one needs a proof that is as quick and compelling for the atheist as Anselm's is for the fool; in the Fourth Dialogue of his *Alciphron,* Alciphron, the free-thinker demands of Euphrenor, Berkeley's stand-in: 'If there be such a thing as God, it is very strange that He should leave Himself without a witness; that men should still dispute His being, and that there should be no one evident, sensible, plain proof of it, without recourse to philosophy or metaphysics. A matter of fact is not to be proved by notions, but by facts.'[114] Traditional versions of the *a priori* argument do not satisfy; Alciphron rejects as 'dry and jejune' the metaphysical arguments 'drawn from the idea of an all perfect being or the absurdity of an infinite progression of causes'.[115] Perhaps the ontological argument in its Cartesian form is involved here, but what Alciphron has in mind seems rather to be the *a posteriori* argument from Descartes's Meditatio III and arguments from the impossibility of an infinite regression in the Aristotelian tradition.

In his main philosophical works, Berkeley proposes two proofs of the existence of God. In the *Principles* he adduces God as the *cause* of our percepts, only mentioning it as a possibility that He upholds sensory things when they are not being perceived by us.[116] But in *Three Dialogues* Berkeley gives special emphasis to an argument which uses the principle of immaterialism, the principle that *esse* is *percipi.* On this argument, God must exist because His perception is necessary to ground the evidently independent existence of the sensible world (independent, that is, of finite perceivers). Here Berkeley follows his metaphysical and epistemological thoughts about the world of bodies and our knowledge of it to their ultimate consequences. This original proof is first found at the beginning of *Three Dialogues* II, where Philonous declares:

To me, it is evident, for the reasons you allow of, that sensible things cannot exist otherwise than in a mind or spirit. Whence I conclude, not that they have no real existence, but that seeing they depend not on my thought, and have an existence distinct from being perceived by me, *there must be some other mind wherein they exist.* As sure therefore as the sensible world really exist, so sure is there an infinite omnipresent spirit who contains and supports it.[117]

This 'immaterialist' proof allows Berkeley to assert that he was able to prove the existence of God as 'a being whose spirituality, omnipresence, providence, omniscience, infinite power and goodness, are as conspicuous as the existence of sensible things, of which . . . there is no more reason to doubt, than of our own being'.[118]

This view is, in an obvious way, quite similar to Malebranche's view that we see all things in God, and to the arguments for the existence of God that follow out of that doctrine. But Berkeley attempts to distance his views from 'the enthusiasm of Malebranche'. In an addition to the 1734 edition of the Second Dialogue, Philonous (Berkeley's stand-in) spells out some of the differences between the two doctrines.[119] Malebranche (as a Platonist) gives primacy to 'the most abstract general ideas', which Berkeley rejects. He also casts doubt on the veracity of the senses and postulates absolute 'extended beings' whose true forms are unknowable. Furthermore, Berkeley claims, we do not see things in God's essence. As Philonous later argues, all our ideas of sense are passive, whereas the infinitely active Spirit can have nothing passive in His essence (although He 'knows or hath ideas' actively, and 'knows and understands' what it is like for us to perceive them passively).[120]

In the *Alciphron,* although Berkeley does not make explicit use of the principle of immaterialism, he gives another equally idiosyncratic version of the *a posteriori* demonstration. The version of the *a posteriori* argument Berkeley uses here makes essential appeal to the idea of a divine visual language, originally presented in his early *A New Theory of Vision*. On this view, the sequence of sensations that God causes in finite creatures and that, on the immaterialist doctrine, constitutes the world of sensible things is taken to be a kind of language by which God communicates with men.[121] Euphranor, Berkeley's spokesman in the *Alciphron,* addresses the free-thinker Alciphron:

[If] it shall appear plainly that God speaks to men by the intervention and use of arbitrary, outward, sensible signs, having no resemblance or necessary connexion with the things they stand for and suggest; if it shall appear that, by innumerable combinations of these signs, an endless variety of things is discovered and made known to us; and that we are thereby instructed or informed in their different natures; that we are taught and admonished what to shun, and what to pursue; and are directed how to regulate our motions, and how to act with respect to things distant from us, as well in time as place: will this content you?[122]

Euphranor (Berkeley) has no trouble showing that our senses constitute such a language. In just the way Descartes infers the existence of other finite minds from the ability others have to use language, Berkeley infers the existence of a divine mind, who speaks to us by way of this divine visual language.[123]

VI. EPILOGUE: FENELON AND MESLIER

'Is it only metaphysicians who can be Christians?' Father Hardouin's question, in his *Athei detecti,* is posed to the entire philosophical century that came before.[124] He develops his attack against metaphysical proofs and especially against the *a priori* proof; in his eyes, Ambrosius Victor, Quesnel, Arnauld, Nicole, Pascal, and Descartes are suspect of hidden or deferred *atheism.* Despite his excesses, Father Hardouin rightly saw the most paradoxical result of Descartes's sincere effort to ground the existence of God: Descartes set aside the classical proofs for the existence of God, without succeeding in giving a firm proof of his own.

An exemplary appraisal of the century is contained in the *Démonstration de l'existence de Dieu . . . par feu Messire François de Salignac de la Motte Fénelon,* published in 1718 by the Jesuit Tournemine.[125] This work is crucial for both centuries – as an appraisal of the seventeenth, but also as a reference for the eighteenth: Berkeley read it, as did Hume, and the curé Meslier chose to assert his atheism in his marginal notes on Fénelon's demonstrations.[126]

This posthumous work of Fénelon actually represents two stages in his apologetic. The first part was published by Fénelon in 1712, while the second part, though written in his youth, appears only in the 1718 edition (the complete version was only published in 1731 by the Marquis de Fénelon). The first part, earlier in publication though later in composition, is a demonstration of the existence of God from the contemplation of nature and the knowledge of mankind. In the chronologically earlier part two, the existence of God is proved 'on the basis of his own idea,' 'through more intellectual proofs'.[127]

These earlier, 'more intellectual' proofs show the clear imprint of the Cartesian approach. Fénelon rediscovers the path opened by Descartes, but brings to it certain significant modifications, both in the order of the arguments (he reverses the two *a posteriori* proofs developed in Meditatio III) and especially in their content.[128] Fénelon transforms his memories of the philosophy of the schools, adapting earlier, pre-Cartesian thought to the new intellectual situation created by the *cogito.* For his first proof, 'drawn from the imperfection of the human being', Fénelon returns to Thomas Aquinas's third and fourth ways. The act required for passing from nothingness to being recalls that needed to pass from the possible to the necessary (Thomas's third way). Fénelon also makes use of Thomas's fourth way (through 'degrees of being'), attentive to an ontology 'drawn from *Exodus*'. Only God exists to the highest degree, and his creatures possess being only in so far as they participate in God.

His second proof (from the same earlier treatise), drawn 'from the idea that we have of infinity', again takes up the Cartesian project. We have a clear and positive idea of the infinite and of infinite perfection; such an idea can only come from the infinitely perfect being. The strategy is Cartesian, but Fénelon's is definitely a Cartesianism reviewed and criticised by Malebranche, where the cause is in a certain way present in the effect: this infinitely perfect being is at the same time the cause and the immediate object of this idea. The idea of infinity must be in me more as a presence than as a representation.

Fénelon's adaptation of the Cartesian proofs is even more apparent in his third proof. This proof, Fénelon writes, 'reduces to two rules, the one, which we have already admitted, derived from pure metaphysics, namely, that we should consult our clear and immutable ideas, and the other derived from pure dialectic, namely, that we should draw the immediate consequence [of a given idea] and affirm of a thing precisely what its clear idea contains.'[129] For Fénelon, the ontological argument is of a piece with the other arguments, for 'all these ways of going to You, or rather of finding You in me, are tied and intertwined with one another.'[130] In place of a representation, Fénelon substitutes the interior presence of God: 'It is therefore true, O my God, that I find you at every turn.'[131]

In Chapter 4 of the same second and earlier part of the *Traité,* Fénelon announces a 'new proof for the existence of God, a proof from the nature of ideas'. The Augustinian (and Malebranchean) origin is even more noticeable here, by the union of my mind with the Word that contains the eternal truths. Ideas are seen in God; they are God himself: 'The immediate object of all my universal knowledge is God himself.'[132]

The materialist critique that the curé Meslier advanced against Fénelon is of the greatest importance; it shows us something of how apologetics were weakened by seventeenth-century developments, and allows us to understand how they led the way to atheism. Meslier is especially critical of Fénelon's 'intellectual' proofs, leading to a philosophical confrontation that transforms his marginalia on Fénelon into a metaphysical treatise on atheism.

Let us take Fénelon's central theory, his so-called metaphysics of Exodus. Fénelon writes, 'He is Being; or, to say it better by saying it more simply, he is.'[133] To this Meslier objects:

If God is not exactly any singular or limited thing, then he is nothing other than being in general and being without restriction, that is, nothing other than the matter and nature itself that is all in all and that makes all in all; this is precisely what we claim, and thus there will be no more argument about it.[134]

Fénelon's view therefore has this consequence, less surprising than it may appear: Meslier finds in Being in general, 'which is not exactly any singular or limited thing', organic matter and the physical world such as he conceives it to be.[135] Successive reformulations of the ontological argument have succeeded only in weakening its importance. The transformations that Leibniz and Malebranche imposed on it distorted the Cartesian formulation. Having first been rendered vulnerable to Meslier's naturalistic critique, the argument in the end falls prey to the Kantian critique, directed more at Leibniz than at Descartes himself.[136] Kant has no difficulty in dismissing the ontological proof: '*Being* is clearly not a real predicate, that is, it is not a concept of something which could be added to the concept of a thing.'[137] Thus, Kant thought himself to be bringing a long metaphysical tradition to an end. But in the end, he only succeeded in underscoring the importance of the *a posteriori* proofs, which the libertine critique had not shaken.

NOTES

1 See Descartes, Resp. I, AT VII 107.
2 Duplessis-Mornay 1581 p. 4. See also Viret 1564, *Epistre* f. IIv–IIIr, and Viret 1565 (summary of the third dialogue, p. 163 sv).
3 See Betts 1984.
4 Bartas 1611, 1ère sem. 1er jour, line 104, pp. 312D–313A.
5 Mersenne 1623. *Quaestio Ia* ('*fusissima*') treats *an Deum esse contra atheos probari possit.* Mersenne advances thirty-five arguments (listed in columns 25–6), including the Anselmian argument *ab optima entitate* (col. 35), and in an appendix ('colophon') he explicitly addresses the atheism of his contemporaries (cols. 669–74).
6 For the use of *De natura deorum* in the Jesuit collèges in France as late as 1692, see de Dainville 1978, pp. 222–3.
7 See Berriot 1984; Buckley 1987; Kors 1990; and De Mas 1982.
8 See Febvre 1982.
9 In many ways, the atheist is closely connected with Suárez's enterprise. As pointed out in the next section, Suárez conceives of God as being rather than mover; it is this conception of God that becomes vulnerable to attack. See Kors 1990.
10 Gregory 1986; *Theophrastus redivivus* 1981–2.
11 Gregory 1986, p. 56.
12 See Garasse 1623, pp. 39–46. Luther is charged together with the Manichaeans, Vanini, and the poets of the libertine *Parnasse satyrique.*
13 Mersenne 1624. See also *L'athéism e des prétendus réformés,* Poitiers, 1620, by the Minim father Nicolas Chichon.
14 Kors 1990, p. 31.
15 Gilberte Périer, *Vie de Pascal* (2d version) in Pascal 1964– , vol. 1, p. 619.
16 Carraud, 1987 and 1992.
17 *Pens.* 192.
18 *Pens.* 142.

19 *Pens.* 781.

20 Nicole 1679, pp. 27–48; von Leyden 1948.

21 AT VII 2.

22 See Suárez, *Disp. met.* XXIX.

23 On the *Cursus Philosophicus* of Cesare Cremonini, disciple of Zabarella and friend of Galileo, see Del Torre 1968. On Aristotelianism in Protestant Germany, see Petersen 1921.

24 See Marion 1981, 1986a; Courtine 1990; Robinet 1980.

25 *Disp. met.* XXIX.3.5.

26 *Disp. met.* XXIX.1.7; Grabmann 1917.

27 *Disp. met.* XXIX.1.18.

28 *Disp. met.* XXIX.2.

29 *Disp. met.* XXIX.2.5.

30 *Disp. met.* XXIX.3.2 and 3. Numerous seventeenth-century theologians writing after Suárez will propose 'brief' demonstrations, called *a priori logico (metaphysico)*, or even *a simultaneo sive a pari*. (See Ceñal 1970; this can be found already in Vazquez 1598, disp. XIX, chap. 4, p. 130.) Even if these 'demonstrations' were often confused, they represent the survival of an attempt to give a sort of *a priori* proof which does not collapse to the proof from effects. Thus one reads in the Dominican Pierre Godoy of Salamanca (*Disputationes Theologica,* 1668): 'If the existence of God is the first predicate that constitutes the divine essence, then nothing can be demonstrated of God *a priori*; and if there is both a rational and a virtual distinction between his existence and his essence, then one cannot demonstrate anything of God *a priori* in an absolute fashion. However, one can still proceed by way of a demonstration that is *a priori* in relation to us' (Godoy 1686, vol. 1, p. 28).

31 For an account of Suárez's doctrine of the univocity of being, see Chapter 10.

32 *Disp. met.* XXXII.1.9; see Marion 1981 p. 116.

33 Since Koyré 1922, there has been an abundant literature on this issue; for the main contributions, see Gouhier 1962, 1972; Marion 1981; and Chapter 10 in this book.

34 See AT VII 34–52; *Princ.* I 13–24.

35 AT V 157.

36 AT I 181–2.

37 AT VI 34.

38 AT I 560–1.

39 Fischer, 1889, I, 1, p. 308.

40 Gilson 1913, 1979; Gilen 1957; Cronin 1966.

41 See Casper 1968–9; Marion 1981, pp. 432–9.

42 AT VII 235–7.

43 *Disp. met.* XXIX.3.37.

44 According to Silhon 1991, p. 39, the last perfection of God's being is 'Being intelligence' [*Estre intelligence*]; his 'metaphysics of *Exodus* 3.14' makes him understand this notion in an eminent way, as the sum of all intelligent beings: 'This is why, as someone put it well, if God had wanted to fill out his nature after our fashion, he would have taken light for his body and the truth for his soul.'

45 Hannequin 1896.

46 Resp. I, AT VII 108.

47 AT VII 236 and 240.

48 See, e.g., AT VII 65.

49 The example of the triangle having to have the sum of its angles equal to two right

angles to illustrate the idea of necessity goes back to Aristotle, *Physics* II 19 (200a17 ff.).

50 On the Heideggerian notion of onto-theo-logy as applied to Descartes, see Marion 1986a.

51 Med. V, AT VII 65.

52 AT VII 242.

53 Geb. I 159–60; Geb IV 197–8; Geb. II 29 n. a; Geb. I 15.

54 Geb. I 166.

55 Geb. I 158–9; Geb. I 15.

56 Geb. I 15; Geb. IV 61–2, 179–80. Note that the proof from the *Kort. ver.* I, 1 in question is introduced by the remark: 'in other words' [*anderzins*]).

57 Alquié, 1981, p. 127. It is worth noting here that Spinoza has some difficulty accepting the idea of discursive proof in this connexion, though. He later claims that the crucial *Eth.* I, prop. 7, would be an axiom 'if men would attend to the nature of substance' (*Eth.* I, prop. 8 schol. 2).

58 See Resp. I, AT VII 116.

59 See Powell 1899; and Wolfson 1934, vol. 1, chap. 6.

60 See Med. III, AT VII 48

61 See, e.g., *Rech.* III.2.7, sec. 2 and IV.11.3, Mal. *OC* I, pp. 449–50, and *OC* II, pp. 100–101 (Malebranche 1980a, pp. 236–7, 318).

62 Mal. *OC* IV 25.

63 Mal. *OC* IV 15.

64 *Rech.* VI.2.6, Mal. *OC* II 371 (Malebranche 1980a, p. 481).

65 Bouillier 1868.

66 Malebranche 1948; and Cuvillier 1954.

67 Gouhier 1926b.

68 *Rech.* III.2.6, Mal. *OC* I 441 (Malebranche 1980a, p. 232).

69 The passage in question is *Rech.* IV.11.3, Mal. *OC* II 96–106 (Malebranche 1980a, pp. 318–25). Malebranche later refers to it in *Eclaircissement* X, added in 1700 to the fifth edition of the *Recherche de la Vérité* (and modified in the sixth edition of 1712); see Mal. *OC* III 143 (Malebranche 1980a, pp. 621–2).

70 *Rech.* III.2.6, Mal. *OC* I 441 (Malebranche 1980a, p. 232).

71 Mal. *OC* II 100–101 (Malebranche 1980a, p. 321).

72 Arnauld 1986, p. 246.

73 *Rech.* IV.ii.3, Mal. *OC* II 96 (Malebranche 1980a, p. 318).

74 Alquié 1974, p. 395.

75 Ger. IV 292 (Leibniz 1989, p. 237).

76 See AT VII 180.

77 See AT VII 127.

78 Ger. IV 292–3 (Leibniz 1989, p. 237).

79 Ger. IV 406. The work quoted is a short text published in 1701 directed against the Benedictine François Lamy.

80 *Specimen inventorum*, 1686?, Ger. VII 310; see also Ger. IV 406.

81 See Moreau 1967.

82 Ger. VII 261–2 (Leibniz 1969, pp. 166–7).

83 See Ger. IV 424–5 (Leibniz 1989, pp. 25–6). This recalls the debate over the proofs from *Meditationes* III and V: Are they independent of one another (Alquié, 1950, pp. 212, 225, 226) or, on the contrary, is the ontological proof subordinated to the *a posteriori* proof (Fischer, 1889, I, 1, pp. 309 ff.; Kemp Smith, 1902, p. 58; Gueroult, 1953, vol. 1, chap. 8, and 1955, followed by Beck, 1965, pp. 231–7)? See also Cress 1973.

84 Ger. I 207–314 *passim* (partly trans. in Leibniz 1969, pp. 177–80).
85 *Mon.* sec. 45, Ger. VI 614.
86 *Théod.*, pt. I sec. 7, Ger. VI 106.
87 Bausola, 1969; see also the short text concerning P. François Lamy (1701) (Ger. IV 405–6) and the *Mémoires de Trévoux* January–February 1701.
88 See Letwin 1976. For general studies of Hobbes's views on God, see, e.g., Brown 1962; and Glover 1965.
89 See Reventlow 1984, pp. 194–222.
90 *Lev.* xxxiv, Hobbes 1968, p. 430.
91 *Lev.* xii, Hobbes 1968, p. 170.
92 *Lev.* xii, Hobbes 1968, p. 170. Elsewhere, though, Hobbes seems to criticise this argument; see *De corp.* IV.26, *Lat. Works,* vol. I, p. 336. However, this criticism bears on those who pride themselves on having been able to conclude from the phenomena of nature that the world has a beginning. Two arguments are conflated here: the argument to a first mover, and the argument from design. Hobbes's criticism really holds against the second argument, the argument that 'by the visible things of this world, and their admirable order, a man may conceive there is a cause of them, which men call God' (*Lev.* xi, Hobbes 1968, p. 167; see also *Eng. Works,* vol. VII, p. 176 and *Lat. Works,* vol. II, pp. 6, 106–7). But the criticism leaves the first argument intact.
93 See especially the third part of the *Critique of the* De Mundo *of Thomas White,* Hobbes 1973 and 1976.
94 Glover 1965, p. 159; and Pacchi, in Napoli and Canziani 1990, pp. 101–22.
95 Of great interest is the description given in Edwards 1646.
96 Only in 1668 did Hobbes publicly admit that he held that God is corporeal; in the appendix to the Latin translation of the *Leviathan* he writes, 'affirmat quidem Deum esse corpus' (*Lat. Works,* vol. III, p. 561). On the theological and patristic plausibility of this opinion, see the references in Pacchi, in Napoli and Canziani 1990, pp. 108–9.
97 For a general account of Gassendi's views on God, see Bloch 1971.
98 Gassendi 1658, vol. 3, p. 329b; see Bloch 1971, pp. 414 ff.
99 See Gassendi 1642b and 1658, vol. 1, pp. 290a ff.
100 Gassendi 1642b, Bk. XXI, chap. 1, repeated in *Syntagma, De Principio efficiente rerum,* chap. 2 (Gassendi 1658, vol. 1, pp. 287b–295a).
101 Gassendi 1658, vol. 1, p. 290a.
102 See Gassendi 1658, vol. 1, p. 311a: 'Esse Deum Authorem, seu Causam productricem Mundi.'
103 *Syntagma* I, Gassendi 1658, vol. 1, p. 295 a–b.
104 Gassendi 1658, vol. 1, p. 303a.
105 *Nouv. ess.* I.i, Ger. V 63.
106 Edwards 1697: 'These natural impressions in all men's minds are the foundation of religion and the standard of truth as well as of morality' (p. 122); see Yolton 1956, pp. 1–71.
107 *Conduct of Understanding,* sec. 23.
108 *Ess.* IV.vii.11.
109 *Ess.* IV.ix.2.
110 King 1830, vol. 2, p. 138.
111 For general accounts of Berkeley's view on God, see Sillem 1957; Ayers 1987.
112 *Pr. Hum. Kn.* sec. 156.
113 *Alciphron,* 4, 14, Berkeley 1948–57, vol. 3, p. 160.
114 *Alciphron,* 4, 3, Berkeley 1948–57, vol. 3, p. 144.
115 *Alciphron,* 4, 2, Berkeley 1948–57, vol. 3, p. 142.

116 See Berkeley 1948–57, vol. 2, p. 53 (God as cause of the percepts), 61 and 80 (God upholder of sensory things). See the debate between Bennet 1968 and Ayers 1987 on this point. Ayers holds that, properly speaking, there is no 'continuity argument' for the existence of God in Berkeley.

117 Berkeley 1948–57, vol. 2, p. 212.

118 *3 Dial.*, III, Berkeley 1948–57, vol. 2, p. 257.

119 Berkeley 1948–57, vol. 2, p. 214.

120 *3 Dial.*, III, Berkeley 1948–57, vol. 2, pp. 240–1.

121 See, for example, *New Th. Vis.*, secs. 139–48; *Th. Vis. Vind.*, secs. 38 ff.; *Pr. Hum. Kn.* sec. 44, 108 (1st ed.).

122 *Alciphron,* dialogue 4, Berkeley 1948–57, vol. 3, p. 149.

123 Descartes's account of other minds is discussed in part V of the *Disc.*, AT VI 56–9. The connexion between Berkeley's argument for the existence of God in the *Alciphron* and Descartes's account of other minds is emphasised in Kline 1987. On the argument, see also Hooker 1982, who argues that Berkeley's argument is not simply a version of the argument from design.

124 Hardouin 1733, p. 210. Hardouin died in 1729, and the *Athei detecti* was published posthumously.

125 For the history of publication, see Gouhier 1977, pp. 127–31.

126 Meslier 1972.

127 Fénelon 1848–52, First section I,2.

128 As Henri Gouhier wrote: 'In the restoration of the Cartesian edifice that is his Chapter 2 [i.e. the 'more intellectual proofs' of the earlier text], Fénelon borrows some materials from the so-called second proof of the *Third Meditation,* but he does so in order to construct a new wing, where the idea of infinity no longer plays any rôle; in fact, the Cartesian theodicy is no longer at issue.' Gouhier 1977, p. 147.

129 Fénelon 1848–52, vol. 1, p. 58.

130 Fénelon 1848–52, vol. 1, p. 59.

131 Fénelon 1848–52, vol. 1, p. 59.

132 Fénelon 1848–52, vol. 1, p. 67.

133 Fénelon 1848–52, vol. 1, p. 82. The editors of the 1718 edition suppressed at the beginning of this citation three words from 1713 ('he is everything'), for fear of the accusation of pantheism; see p. 504 of the 1718 edition.

134 Fragment 213, in Meslier 1972, vol. 3, p. 332.

135 For Meslier, matter is divided into two principles: an inert matter and a subtle matter, the ultimate concession to atomism. Furthermore, to the extensive and qualitative infinity of Fénelon, Meslier opposes extension, the 'horizontal' infinity of space, time, and number. See Jean Deprun in Meslier 1972, vol. 3, p. 225.

136 'Thus the celebrated Leibniz is far from having succeeded in what he plumed himself on achieving – the comprehension *a priori* of the possibility of this sublime ideal being.' Kant, *Kritik der reinen Vernunft,* A602/B630.

137 Kant, *Kritik der reinen Vernunft,* A598/B626.

12

THE CARTESIAN DIALECTIC OF CREATION

THOMAS M. LENNON

I. TWO COMPETING TENDENCIES

By the seventeenth century, theology had established constraints on the develop-ment of metaphysics not unlike those it had imposed nearly a millennium earlier on church music. Like the *cantus firmus,* to which counterpoint and polyphony are conjectured to owe their existence,[1] these constraints were both a source of problems and a standard for success. In the seventeenth century, a main *cantus firmus* was the notion of God as creator *ex nihilo.* Although the dogma was not without ambiguity as late as the Council of Nicea (A.D. 325),[2] creation of the world *ex nihilo* had been defined against the dualism of the Albigensians and Cathars by the Fourth Lateran Council (1215): 'We firmly believe in God . . . the creator [*creator*] of all things visible and invisible, spiritual and corporeal, who by His almighty power established, from nothing, at the same time from the begin-ning of time, both spiritual and corporeal creatures [*simul ab initio temporis utramque de nihilo condidit creaturam spiritualem et corporalem*].'[3] In addition, and against the same opponents, the church insisted upon the providence of God that allowed evil in creation. Thus, although omnipotent, God nonetheless was believed to create with wisdom. God's wisdom was a divine attribute that in the seventeenth century gained metaphysical prominence even as final causes were being expunged from physical explanations.

The seventeenth century was not notably more successful than any previous period in making sense of the notion of creation *ex nihilo.* Greek antiquity found the notion unintelligible and rejected it. But constrained by their theology, the mediaevals were obligated to embrace the notion, not without philosophical difficulty. Aquinas, for example, adopted a position found at least as early as the fourth century in Gregory of Nyssa according to which God's creation is abso-lutely free, yet necessarily motivated solely by the communication of His good-

I am very grateful to Michael R. Ayers and Daniel Garber for their many useful comments on earlier drafts of this work.

ness.[4] Aquinas thus adumbrated not only the seventeenth century's orthodox position on creation but also anticipated its problems with the notion. On the one hand, he held that creation is a brute fact, a product of divine omnipotence and freedom born of indifference, which is as much to say that it has no explanation or that it is a matter of chance. On the other hand, he held that creation has a purpose, an end, and is constrained by God's wisdom. The same duality shapes later discussions. Those in the seventeenth century who argued on the basis of a principle of sufficient reason that nothing is in principle without explanation were thus driven in the direction of necessitarianism or the denial of creation, or both. In theological terms, they were led to emphasise divine wisdom at the expense of omnipotence. Others, who were more insistent on creation *ex nihilo,* were driven in the direction of a tychistic denial of universal sufficient reason. In theological terms, they were led to emphasise divine omnipotence at the expense of wisdom. This basic tension between wisdom and omnipotence shaped the seventeenth-century discussion of creation.

The report given here makes no claim to being a complete account of seventeenth-century discussions of God and creation; the Cambridge Platonists, for example, are not included, and, even though the emphasis is on the Cartesian epicentre of intellectual activity, some of the individuals (e.g., Bossuet) whose views figure prominently in religious thought within that context are omitted. Furthermore, the discussion is restricted rather narrowly to the relation thought to obtain between God and His creation. Although proofs for the existence of God typically reveal something of this relation, they will not be treated in any systematic way.[5] Rather, special attention will be given to the status of eternal truths in the seventeenth-century history of Cartesianism. The status of the eternal truths, namely, whether they are created or not, is a touchstone not only for the various Cartesian systems that differed on this question, but also for the period generally, including major figures like Spinoza and Leibniz.

The chapter begins with Descartes's views on divine causation, which adumbrated the later clash between divine wisdom and omnipotence. This is followed by a discussion of his doctrine of the creation of the eternal truths, a systematic focus of that clash. Not surprisingly, both of the impulses just mentioned are to be found in many later philosophers of the period. Next, emphasis will be placed on divine wisdom that results in Spinoza's necessitarianism and apparent denial of creation, as well as notable attempts by Leibniz and Malebranche to avoid Spinoza's excesses while continuing to emphasise God's wisdom. Then the issue of the creation of the eternal truths is taken up, and with it the emphasis on divine omnipotence as found in some later figures.

II. DIVINE WISDOM AND CREATION:
DESCARTES'S DILEMMA

An important text with respect to the competing tendencies of wisdom and omnipotence is Descartes's first attempt, in Meditatio III, to prove the existence of God. He writes:

> It is manifest by the natural light that there must be at least as much [reality] in the efficient and total cause as in the effect of that cause. For where, I ask, could the effect get its reality from, if not from the cause? And how could the cause give it to the effect unless the cause possessed it? It follows from this both that something cannot arise from nothing, and also that what is more perfect – that is, contains in itself more reality – cannot arise from what is less perfect.[6]

This looks very much like a denial of the possibility of creation and an assertion of the principle *ex nihilo nihil fit*. In the Second Replies Descartes in fact identifies this principle with his claim that there is nothing in the effect that was not previously in the cause.[7] His argument is that something in the effect not previously in the cause would be produced by nothing.

Descartes thus seems to deliver up a dilemma. Given the principle *ex nihilo nihil fit,* the existence of God prior to that which He creates does not *explain* that which He creates unless it already exists in Him and is said to come to be only as a feature of Him in the fashion, for example, of Spinoza's pantheistic emanationism. The *'ex nihilo'* principle seems to restrict intelligible change, change consistent with divine wisdom, to the zero-sum manipulation of a commodity that can be understood on the model of the various conservation laws – of motion for example, for which historically it was itself the model. Unless we were willing to relinquish the *'ex nihilo'* principle, making the world unintelligible to us and apparently inconsistent with divine wisdom, the only alternative to this kind of pantheism would be to hold that the world exists, uncaused and independent of God, in blatant contradiction to the revealed truth of Genesis. Neither horn of this dilemma is theologically acceptable as such. Descartes clearly rejects the second horn, so one looks for a way to avoid the pantheism of the first, if not in Descartes, then at least among his followers.

The doctrine of eminent containment to which Descartes occasionally alludes may be construed as an attempt to deal with the apparent problem of pantheism his position raises. Something exists eminently in something else when the object in question exists in something superior in perfection to it, not as a genuine part (that would be to exist formally), and not as an object represented (that would be to exist objectively), but as an object which the thing in question is capable of creating, either formally or objectively.[8] Thus, God may be said to create Z *ex nihilo,* but in a way that does not violate the principle *ex nihilo nihil fit,* because He contains Z eminently. But as Arnauld was to argue against Malebranche's version of the doctrine, it is far from clear what eminent containment of Z can mean if not either actual containment of Z or merely sheer power to create Z. If actual containment, then we have a kind of pantheism; if sheer power, then we have a violation of the *'ex nihilo'* principle.

Malebranche takes a different approach to the problem. He holds that God created the world *ex nihilo.*[9] At the same time, since matter (like quantity of motion) is naturally indefectible, he holds that natural causation, that is, the causing of things in nature by other things in nature, never involves such creation. He writes: 'It is a common notion . . . that nothing can be annihilated by the ordinary forces of nature; for just as it is impossible for something to be made from nothing, so it is impossible for a substance or a being to become nothing. The passage from being to nothingness or from nothingness to being is equally impossible.'[10] But this restriction of the *ex nihilo* principle to natural causation is of no help with respect to Descartes's dilemma. The conclusion that Descartes immediately draws from the *ex nihilo* principle is that there must be at least as much formal reality in the cause of an idea as there is objective reality in the idea itself; consequently, only God Himself could be the cause of the idea of Him. It is therefore essential to the argument of Meditatio III that the principle extend beyond the domain of natural causation.

Indeed, when Descartes himself goes beyond the domain of natural causation, he avoids the dilemma only because his argument seems to violate the *ex nihilo* principle. His second attempt to prove the existence of God begins with the premise that there is no real difference between creation and conservation in existence and goes on to establish God's existence from our own continued existence.[11] This was soon read by Cartesians such as La Forge, Cordemoy, and Malebranche to mean that only God could be a real cause.[12] On their not implausible reading, the real cause of the deflection of a thing's motion at a given moment is not its contact with another thing at the previous moment, which is only its occasional cause, that is, the occasion for the operation of the real cause, which is God's creating it first at the one place and then at the other.[13] This would seem to make genuine creation *ex nihilo* a common event, one that takes place literally at every moment. This leads directly to the second tendency in Descartes's thought, a doctrine of creation of the most radical kind that would seem to emphasise God's omnipotence over His wisdom.

III. DIVINE OMNIPOTENCE:
DESCARTES'S DOCTRINE OF CREATED TRUTH

If there is, in seventeenth-century terms, a nominally orthodox view on creation, it is that God creates the world *ex nihilo* in an utterly unconstrained way, but that having freely chosen to create He is constrained to do so in certain ways only. This difference between fact of creation and kind of creation was meant to preserve the delicate balance between omnipotence and divine wisdom. Descartes departed from this orthodoxy, however, and claimed that not only the existence of things but also their essence depended on a God who acts with freedom of sheer indifference. Whether he thus sacrificed all rationality, both divine and human, and all possibility of knowledge, is a question that a number of critics have raised over the years. For Descartes in his first statement of the doctrine explicitly claims that God has laid down the laws of nature as a king lays down laws in his kingdom. If a king can alter laws decreed in perpetuity, God can alter the truth value even of what we take to be necessary. Indeed, it appears that Descartes may have gone so far as to claim that since God's omnipotence requires all truth to be dependent on His will, there is no necessary truth, certainly no absolutely necessary truth.

The doctrine is found both early and late in Descartes, but only twice in what he published and then only in response to objections.[14] It is first set out, with great enthusiasm, in a letter to Mersenne in which he claims to have arrived at the foundations of physics via metaphysics, whose demonstrations are more evident than geometry. He refrains from putting it all in writing until he sees how his physics is received; however, employing the regal simile noted above, Descartes moves almost immediately to the claim that the eternal truths are established by God and depend entirely on Him.[15] Indeed, God is the cause of the eternal truths in a stronger sense than this, which indicates only God's freedom. God is the cause of the eternal truths in the same way that He is the cause of all things – He is their total and efficient cause.[16]

Three hypotheses might be offered as to why Descartes held the doctrine of created truths; they are not necessarily competing and are here suggested rather as complementary. The first might be called the *anti-holist hypothesis.*[17] The argument is as follows: both for Descartes and for the scholastics in whose wake he worried about the eternal truths, it is theologically unacceptable for there to be anything uncreated other than God.[18] To account for the eternal truths within the bounds of this restriction, Aquinas, for example, appealed to the Neoplatonic theme that the essence of individual things is the divine essence in so far as it is or can be participated in by individual things. The multiplicity of essences is a multiplicity only on the side of the things instantiating them; on the side of the One there is no multiplicity or diversity. God's contemplation of the eternal truths is a self-contemplation of the ways in which His simple substance can be the principle of intelligibility of a multiplicity of things He can create. One historical consequence of this solution, broadly speaking, was the view that because its essence was incomplete, knowledge of any individual thing (or proposition) was necessarily incomplete and deficient: the knowledge of anything was taken to involve the knowledge of everything else.[19] Now, the applicability of clarity and distinctness as criteria of truth, and thus of the whole Cartesian methodology, required absolutely discrete essences: what is clear and distinct is self-evident in the sense of being acceptable as true on the basis of nothing else. The only theologically acceptable way of securing this was to regard them as created.

A second interpretive hypothesis, what might be called *the anti-finalist hypothesis,* is the contention that the doctrine of the creation of the eternal truths is required in order decisively to expunge consideration of final causes from physics, something that Descartes wanted to assert both against the schoolmen and in opposition to the Italian-born naturalist blend of occultist Neoplatonism that dominates the previous century.[20] If God creates the eternal truths, then at the most basic level, there can be no *reason* for Him to create one thing rather than another; the good towards which God aims in His creation can only be a consequence of this initial act of free and unconstrained divine creation. Thus talk of divine purpose is meaningless, and the search for purposes, whether in the whole of nature or its parts taken separately, is to no avail. There are some passages in which Descartes suggests something weaker than this. For example, in the *Principia* he writes 'that we must beware of being so presumptuous as to think we understand the ends which God set before Himself in creating the world'.[21] This suggests that God may have had His reasons for making the world as He did, even if we cannot discover them. But although there may be purposes in God's creation, they are in an important sense arbitrary. As Descartes wrote in the Sixth Replies:

God did not will the creation of the world in time because he saw that it would be better in this way than if he had created it from eternity. . . . On the contrary, it is because he willed to create the world in time that it is better this way than if he had created it from eternity.[22]

A third and last hypothesis as to why Descartes held the doctrine of created truths might the called *the architectonic hypothesis.* This interpretation assumes that a primary aim of the Cartesian metaphysics is the refutation of scepticism, which, especially in the *Meditationes,* takes the form of a *reductio.* Rather than validating reason by proving the reliability of reason as a guide to *absolute truth* – an enterprise that involves the notorious Cartesian circle[23] – Descartes in fact attempts to show something weaker but just as useful to his program, that reason can lead to beliefs that it would be *unreasonable not to accept.* And so, the claim is that reason cannot be used, as the sceptics typically claim, to refute itself. On this interpretation, Descartes first makes the best case against reason and knowledge (the sceptical arguments of Meditatio I), and then shows (in a way that need not detain us here) that the premises of these sceptical arguments allow us to make a better case in favour of reason.[24] And so, the very premises the sceptic uses lead us to the conclusion that we have no good reason for distrusting reason, even if we cannot demonstrate that it leads us to absolute truth. On this hypothesis, the strongest sceptical case against clear and distinct perceptions would be that God could have failed to create what appears to be their object, that the existence of which would make them true, namely, the relevant eternal truths or simple natures. This sceptical possibility rests on the same grounds as Descartes's proposition that God is the total and efficient cause of the essences that in fact *are* the eternal truths. The assumption of God's omnipotence, His total power over truth, is thus, on this hypothesis, a premise both in the sceptical arguments and in the later rebuttal of scepticism. That is, the architectonic hypothesis is less a reason why Descartes held to the doctrine of created eternal truths than it is an indication of the central rôle it plays in his strategy for the validation of reason.

Much debated in the literature, the interpretation of Descartes's program on which the architectonic hypothesis rests construes Descartes, hitherto the arch-foundationalist, indeed the originator of this metaphor, as an anti-foundationalist. For him, since there are no absolutely incorrigible intuitions, there is no ultimate guarantee for anything. His view that not even eternal truths are necessarily true is, from increasingly many literary and philosophical perspectives, not so bizarre as it is remarkedly precocious.[25] Only his insistence that rationality is not framework-relative, or his failure to notice that it is, separates him from post-Nietzschean relativism.

But many have been appalled by such a prospect and the tendency has been to construe Descartes as saying something less than this. If all truth including all eternal truth could absolutely have been otherwise, then God could, for example, reward sinners and punish the virtuous, undo all of what has been done, make true everything that appears to us false, and conversely, put Himself out of existence, and so on. Such had been the tendency in the thought of Peter Damian (1007–72), who held that God was above even the law of non-contradiction. If

Descartes is to be read along such lines, then he may have held that, however necessary a proposition may seem to us, there are no absolutely necessary propositions, that the eternal truths are inherently as contingent as any other propositions,[26] and that the only difference between eternal propositions and all others is that their truth-value happens never to change. Thus, even after the charge of circularity had been laid against the *Meditationes,* Descartes asserted that although we cannot comprehend how God could have done so, He nonetheless could have made it false that the three angles of a triangle equal two right angles or, more generally, could have made it that contradictories should simultaneously both be true.[27]

Against Peter Damian, on the other hand, Aquinas had argued that the law of non-contradiction is based on God's nature and thus for Him to act contrary to it would be to act contrary to His nature. And previously Anselm had argued that omnipotence above the law of non-contradiction would in fact be impotence, for God could then annihilate Himself and thus, contrary to the premise of the ontological argument, would not be a necessary being.[28] Along these lines, it might be argued, Descartes, who himself advanced the ontological argument in Meditatio V and elsewhere, intended to distinguish two kinds of eternal truths, those about God (e.g., that He exists), and all others (e.g., those of mathematics). Very early, and presumably before being confronted with problems of circularity, Descartes wrote that the existence of God is 'the first and most eternal truth that can be and the only one whence all the others proceed'. In an effort to explain why divine power is sometimes underestimated, he went on to distinguish between God as 'a cause whose power surpasses the limits of human understanding and the necessity of [mathematical] truths [which] does not exceed our knowledge'; mathematical truths are therefore 'subject to that incomprehensible power'.[29]

One school of modern interpretation thus sees two classes of eternal truths. On the one hand are those following from God's absolutely necessary nature. For example, it is impossible that (1) He should not exist, (2) that He not be veracious, (3) that He not be able to do what we conceive to be possible, (4) that He might tolerate atoms, (5) that He might create a void, and so on; and on the other hand are all the rest. One version of this interpretation, which recalls Anselm's view, construes the former list as a set of constraints on God that follow from His omnipotence, which thus requires a 'superior order' of impossibilities. In God, being and power are one, the argument goes, and if God were able to annihilate Himself, He would not be God – in this sense, 'whatever involves non-being is an absolute impossibility.'[30]

A way of understanding this interpretation is to regard the two alleged sorts of eternal truths that follow from God's power as distinguished according to what the mediaevals called *potentia absoluta* and *potentia ordinata*.[31] In one sense God creates with an absolute freedom. But having done so, as it were, He acts within the constraints of what He has decided, the violation of which would normally be miraculous, while not absolutely impossible. Thus, in the first text in which he propounds the doctrine, Descartes himself raises the objection to the view of God as a royal legislator of eternal truths that since a king makes his own laws, so may he change them. To this he replies that God could change His truths only by changing His will; while His will is perfectly free, it is eternal and immutable and therefore, what He wills is eternal and immutable.[32] But, as Malebranche was, in effect, to argue, immutability in God cannot be incompatible with change in things. One can imagine, for example, an immutable God eternally willing that at a certain time the truth value of all propositions should be reversed. If what is known must be necessary, therefore, or even just eternal, then complete scepticism is the result of Descartes's view.[33] As an attempt to limit the scope of divine power, and thus of the hyperbolic doubt, the distinction between *potentia absoluta* and *potentia ordinata* seems to fail.

Alternatively, we might regard Descartes's view as best defensible – however unclear his actual thinking or primitive his expression of it – in terms of iterated modalities. A distinction might be made between necessary truths about necessary beings and necessary truths about contingent beings. The former might be necessarily necessary and the latter only contingently necessary.[34] The necessity of God's existence is secure, but the necessity of mathematics is in constant need of divine support, like the youthfulness of the gods in the *Niebelungenlied,* which depended on a daily supply of Freia's golden apples. Descartes did write in one place that 'while God might have willed that certain truths should be necessary, this is not to say that He necessarily willed them; for willing that they should be necessary is entirely different from willing them necessarily or being necessitated to will them.'[35] But aside from this text, there is little in Descartes to support this distinction, and there is much textual evidence against it. Presumably, if anything would apply to necessary beings, the law of non-contradiction would. Yet Descartes, without restricting that law to contingent beings, explicitly claims that God can falsify it.

IV. SPINOZA ON CREATION AND NECESSITY

One would have expected the most serious objection to Descartes on the topic of creation to have come from Gassendi, whose rehabilitation of Epicurus turned precisely on creation. By regarding atoms as created and finite in number and thus requiring Providence as an explanation of their order, Gassendi showed a way of overcoming traditional objections to Epicureanism. He ought therefore to have been sensitive to Descartes's temerity in dealing with creation. Instead, this issue became obscured by the more immediate concerns of Meditatio III, and if anything, creation *ex nihilo* was in the end denied by Gassendi. In his *Objectiones* to the *Meditationes* and in his *Disquisitio metaphysica,* a reply to Descartes's replies to those *Objectiones,* Gassendi indicates no conception of causation except one that involves only that which already exists; in fact, he suggests that those guided by reason alone should deny creation *ex nihilo.*[36]

Perhaps Gassendi was able to reconcile the philosophical rejection of creation *ex nihilo* with his own theological commitment to creation either by means of a double-truth theory[37] or, more likely, a fideist rejection of the claims of the natural light.[38] Some few others in the atomist tradition were, to use the technical term, more temerarious and were prepared to reject creation outright. One such philosopher was Noel Aubert de Versé,[39] whose position comes from the atomist tradition of which Gassendi was a part: although what exists does so accidentally, its coming to be is inconceivable, or at least inexplicable. Against the Cartesian version of the plenum Aubert argued along Gassendist lines that space and matter are different. According to Aubert, the former is immobile, penetrable, and without resistance, whereas the latter is a mobile, impenetrable, and solid extension; without this distinction, one cannot make sense of motion.[40] He also argued that the Cartesian doctrines of the identity of space and matter and of continual creation *ex nihilo* both lead to Spinozism – the view that 'there is no other God but nature, or the universe, or matter.'[41] Against this he holds that there are two eternal and independent substances. In addition to God, there is matter, which by contrast to God is imperfect, impotent, lifeless, and unconscious, yet capable of the perfections God can impress on it.[42] Although condemned as heretical well before the seventeenth century, this view has a certain claim to Biblical orthodoxy based on an ambiguity in the verb of Genesis 1:1, which can be read to mean that in the beginning God *hewed out* the heaven and the earth.[43] As it happens, Spinoza's plenist rejection of creation was developed partly in reaction to an earlier version of just this view.

Spinoza's position has its roots in a competitor to the atomist tradition, a plenist tradition that goes back to Parmenides: nothing *comes* to be, because what is, *must* be. Spinoza's views on the relation between God and the world were developed from his reading in the debates surrounding emanation theories of creation in Jewish mediaeval philosophy.[44] Such theories sought to account for the creation of a material world by an immaterial God while subscribing to a causal principle that Spinoza canonised in the *Ethica:* 'If things have nothing in common with one another, one cannot be the cause of the other.'[45] Maimonides rejected emanation in favour of an extreme voluntarism; Gersonides rejected it in favour of a rather Timaean theory that anticipated Aubert, according to which God imposed form on an eternal and otherwise formless matter. Spinoza co-opted Crescas's criticisms of both alternatives to emanation. Both fail to explain why, given divine immutability, creation takes place at one given time, rather than at some other time or at no time at all.[46] Both also violate the 'Aristotelian principle repeated in Jewish philosophic literature from earliest times', *ex nihilo, nihil fit.*[47] Spinoza's own program was to reject transeunt causation and volition, or freedom of indifference, in God no less than in man, in favour of a theory of strict necessary emanation.

The interpretation of Spinoza's program is so little debatable as to be of interest here only in showing how it is distinguishable from other seventeenth-century instantiations of sufficient reason. As part of a proof of the existence of God or infinite substance, Spinoza assumes that 'for each thing there must be assigned a cause, or reason, as much for its existence as for its nonexistence.'[48] By itself this does not, of course, argue that all existence and non-existence are necessitated. This follows only after Spinoza has specified the notion of cause, which he does in pointedly anti-Cartesian terms: 'The intellect of God, insofar as it is conceived to constitute God's essence, is really the cause both of the essence and of the existence of things.'[49] What follows from the nature of God does so in exactly the same way as the equality of the three angles of a triangle to a straight angle follows from the nature of a triangle. And what follows from the nature of God is all that can follow – 'God's power is His essence itself.'[50] So, 'whatever we conceive to be in God's power necessarily exists.'[51] The upshot is that whatever can exist does exist and does so with a kind of logical necessity. The essence of (the one) substance necessarily involves existence, and from it everything else necessarily follows. Spinoza writes:

The reason why a substance exists follows from its nature alone, because it involves existence. . . . But the reason why a circle or triangle exists, or why it does not exist, does not follow from the nature of these things, but from the order of the whole of corporeal nature. For from this it must follow either that a triangle necessarily exists now or that it is impossible for it to exist now [from which] it follows that a thing necessarily exists if there is no reason or cause which prevents it from existing.[52]

In short, for Spinoza everything necessarily follows from the necessary nature of God, and thus 'things could have been produced by God in no other way and no other order' than that in which they have been produced.[53]

From this perspective Spinoza offered three reasons why eternal truths could not have been otherwise: (1) God exists in eternity, in which there is no before or after; hence He does not exist before His decrees and hence has never existed without them. To this Descartes would of course agree; whatever His decrees, God would never exist without them, but, unless one is misled by the subjunctive present perfect, this is not to say that they might not have been otherwise. (2) Had God decreed otherwise, His intellect and will would have been otherwise. But if this change would not be incompatible with His essence, there would be no contradiction in His *now* changing His decrees. Spinoza's argument, to which Descartes seems not to have a reply, is that if the eternal truths could have been otherwise, there is no guarantee they will always be as they are. But again the use of tense is misleading. Descartes's view is that, at least as far as we can tell, the truths are eternally but contingently stable – unlike the decrees of a human monarch. (3) For Spinoza, as for Descartes, there is no distinction between intellect and will in God; and for Spinoza, if not for Descartes, neither is distinguishable from His essence. Had God created different eternal truths, His intellect and will, and hence essence would have been different, 'which is absurd'.[54]

The reason this last supposition is absurd for Spinoza is that it asserts what his initial assumption denies, namely, that there might be something ultimately without a sufficient reason; for if God could have been otherwise, everything else could have been otherwise too, and *nothing* would be intelligible. Even so, Descartes's view is 'at a less distance from the truth' according to Spinoza, than that which sees God as acting for the sake of the Good, that is, for the sake of a model or standard towards which He aims, but which does not depend on Him, and which, like fate, is contrary to His being absolutely free, contrary to His existing 'by the necessity of [His] own nature and . . . determined in [His] actions by [Himself] alone'.[55] It would seem that no God at all would be less absurd than a God thus determined, for 'we could hardly assert a greater absurdity than this.'

But even though Spinoza's God is not constrained by some external standard of the good, He is, in a sense, constrained by the principle that 'for each thing there must be assigned a cause, or reason',[56] in essence the old *'ex nihilo'* principle. It is because of this that the world as a whole must exist eternally, the necessary consequence of God's nature.

V. LEIBNIZ'S REJECTION OF SPINOZISM

Leibniz was, of course, unequivocal in his expressed opposition to Spinoza;[57] scarcely less was he opposed to Descartes, whose views he thought led to Spinozism. Indeed, he thought 'Spinoza [among others] published only paraphrases of their leader Descartes.'[58] One point on which Leibniz was critical of both is just this relative *rapprochement* that Spinoza allowed between his own view and Descartes's with respect to fatalism. Leibniz's view is that by *not* allowing God to act for an uncreated good, Descartes's voluntarism and Spinoza's determinism were no better than fatalism in their denial of Providence.[59] Descartes makes the very notion of the good depend on God and Spinoza makes it irrelevant.

Commenting on Descartes's view[60] that matter takes on, successively, all the forms of which it is capable, Leibniz argues that this would mean that nothing can be imagined so contrary to justice that it doesn't occur at some point.

These are precisely the opinions which Spinoza has expounded more clearly, namely, that justice, beauty, and order are things merely relative to us but that the perfection of God consists in that magnitude of His activity by virtue of which nothing is possible or conceivable which He does not actually produce. These are also the opinions of Mr. Hobbes, who asserts that everything that is possible is either past or present or future, and there will be no place for trust in Providence if God produces everything and makes no choice among possible beings.[61]

Leibniz's concern here is to secure a place for final causes, which he thinks no less necessary in physics than in ethics, and whose denial he thinks follows from Descartes's claim that God creates the very notion of the good. If God created the notion of the good, then His decree with respect to it would be 'without any reason'.[62]

Furthermore, God as an absolutely perfect being always acts in the most perfect way. But God would not act in the most perfect way, according to Leibniz, if the goodness of what He did depended on His indifferent and arbitrary will, and if what He did were good only insofar as He caused it. Divine perfection and wisdom in fact cease to have meaning when thus abandoned to omnipotence. Leibniz writes:

The skill of God must not be inferior to that of a workman; nay, it must go infinitely beyond it. The bare production of everything would indeed show the power of God, but it would not sufficiently show His wisdom. They who maintain the contrary will fall exactly into the error of the materialists and of Spinoza, from whom they profess to differ. They would, in such case, acknowledge power, but not sufficient wisdom, in the principle or cause of all things.[63]

God's praiseworthiness would thus be sacrificed. 'For why praise Him for what he has done if He would have been equally praiseworthy in doing exactly the opposite.' In fact, such arbitrary exercise of power would be an exercise in tyranny.

Thus, writing in 1686, Leibniz rhetorically asked 'where will His justice and wisdom be found if will takes the place of reason, and if, according to the definition of tyrants, that which is pleasing to the most powerful is by that very fact just?'[64]

Leibniz's differences from Descartes are extensive, systematic, and deep. But many such differences are traceable to a single fundamental charge, namely, that with his doctrine of the eternal truths Descartes has transgressed the 'uncreated logic'.[65] Very early Leibniz claimed that this transgression 'always seemed absurd' to him.

> For thus the necessity of the divine existence, and therefore of the divine will, itself depends on the divine will. Thus it will be a nature prior, yet posterior to itself. Besides, the principle of necessary truths is only this: that the contrary implies a contradiction in terms. . . . Since then the incompossibility of contradictories does not depend on the divine will, it follows that neither does truth depend on it. Who would say that A is not non-A because God has decreed it?[66]

But if neither logic nor the good towards which God's wisdom aims are dependent on God's will, then how does Leibniz differ from Spinoza?

There are two main points on which it has been argued that Leibniz's system collapses into Spinozism – the view, namely, that that which is actual is necessary in the sense that the sum of a triangle's interior angles is necessarily equal to a straight angle. One is from the perspective of each individual existent. All possible substances have an inherent claim to existence in proportion to their perfection – an 'exigency' that results in existence unless prohibited by a competing greater exigency of something else with greater perfection. Thus Leibniz says 'one can define *an existent* as that which is compatible with more than anything else which is incompatible with it.'[67] It would seem, then, that the existence or non-existence of all things follows directly from the logical relations they bear to other possible individuals. Thus, in so far as the existence of a finite thing is a consequence of its nature, there is an ontological argument of sorts for all existents.[68]

The other point of collapse is seen from a cosmological perspective. Leibniz tried to argue that the creation of this best of all possible worlds followed from God, not with blind necessity in the fashion of Spinoza, but for a moral reason. Because of His goodness God was inclined without being necessitated to create. But against this we might ask whether God's goodness is necessary.[69] If God's goodness is necessary, then that for which it is a sufficient reason is necessary as well. But if God's goodness is contingent, then we can ask of *its* sufficient reason whether it is necessary or contingent; if it is necessary then ultimately the world is necessary as well. But if it is contingent too, then we can inquire of its sufficient reason, and so on.

Leibniz offered two sorts of solution to the problem of contingency.[70] In some texts Leibniz argues that there are worlds other than the actual one that are possible in themselves, that is, non-contradictory, and thus, that the actual world is contingent. However, clarifying the notion of possibility with respect to worlds is not without difficulties. If we include in the concept of a world all its relations with other worlds or with God's attributes and choices there may be only one possible world.[71] The difficulties are highlighted by asking whether God is a member of all possible worlds and if not, why not. But Leibniz's greatest difficulty in any case is that this sense of contingency by his own account does not serve to distinguish his system from Spinoza's. 'I used the term *contingent,* as do others, for that whose essence does not involve existence. In this sense, particular things are contingent according to Spinoza himself., prop. 24 (*Ethica* Part I).'[72]

Elsewhere, though, Leibniz argued that God creates the actual world because it is best, but that the actual world is contingent either because it is contingent that it is the best, or because it is contingent that God creates what is best.[73] The former is Leibniz's preferred route; the sense in which it is contingent that the actual world is best is that it is not *demonstrable* that the denial of the actual world's being best can be shown (via a finite number of steps) to lead to a contradiction. We cannot use the law of non-contradiction alone to show that the actual world is best. Instead, an infinite analysis is required; indeed, several orders of infinities are required, involving comparison among an infinite number of predicates for infinitely many individuals in infinitely many worlds. But there are difficulties in this. The notion of analysis is itself problematic. Furthermore, *finite* analysis might show that at least some worlds are not best.[74] In addition, assuming that there is no trans-world identity, infinite analysability at best separates propositions about individuals from propositions about everything else, for some infinitely analysable propositions are necessary, namely, those about individuals that do not assert existence.[75] Finally, the indemonstrability of infinitely analysable propositions has often been taken to say something about our limitations, rather than about the propositions themselves, which remain demonstrable by God, 'who alone goes through an infinite series in one act of mind'.[76]

As to the second version of the second solution, while some texts Leibniz wrote indicate that it is contingent that God wills what is best, others indicate the opposite.[77] Arguments to show the contingency of the world based on an infinite series of reasons for God's creating, for example, should be taken seriously but nonetheless seem to fail.[78] In the end, even if Leibniz fails to show that this world is contingent, his system may nonetheless differ importantly from Spinoza's in that existential claims about it involve reference to value, purpose, and perfection.[79] But even here, on premises accepted by both Leibniz and Spinoza, there is no value, purpose, or perfection without the freedom grounded in contingency. It is precisely because of this that Spinoza denied freedom and that Leibniz asserted contingency.

VI. MALEBRANCHE ON CREATION AND NECESSITY

Leibniz was not the only seventeenth-century philosopher with structural tendencies towards Spinozism. Malebranche was another, who, in developing certain Cartesian ideas, was led to deny certain others that nominally distinguished Spinoza from Descartes.

In the tenth *Eclaircissement* of the *Recherche de la vérité,* Malebranche deals with the nature of ideas. He takes as self-evident the Cartesian principle that things are not cognisable by themselves, that they are not known directly. But he also argues for the principle on the grounds that sometimes what we know about things is universal, immutable or necessary, and infinite – characteristics that are possessed never by things, but only by their ideas. On Malebranche's Augustinian view, these ideas are exemplars in the mind of God. In fact, as on Aquinas's version of the Augustinian view, they are the divine essence in so far as it is the ground for created things. In the strict sense, differentiation among ideas is not in God but in things in so far as they participate to a greater or lesser degree in divine perfection, which itself is universal, immutable or necessary, and infinite and is thus the ground for anything we may know. This leads to Malebranche's celebrated theory of the vision of all things in God: if what we know in a thing is its essence or exemplar, what we know in knowing anything is God.

However much this may represent an orthodox strain of Cartesianism, it nonetheless involves the denial of some of Descartes's explicit views. Most notable is the doctrine of the creation of the eternal truths. Reason for Malebranche is independent, not only of people, but of God Himself in the sense that He is constrained to follow it in the creation and ordering of the material world, for example. God is not free to alter the truths of geometry by creating a non-Euclidean world, nor is He free to reverse moral relations so that a dog has more value than a man; with respect to geometry and moral relations, 'God could not have willed certain things, for a certain time, or for certain kinds of beings.'[80] From Malebranche's perspective, as from that of Suárez, Descartes's question as to the cause of the eternal truths was misguided, for in recognising the necessity of the eternal truths we see that they can have no cause. But if this is his position, Malebranche seems faced with a dilemma: either all truth is necessary, or some truths are independent of God's will. For if, as he holds, God's will is constrained by universal, necessary, and eternal Reason, it looks as if Malebranche must also be committed to the view that all truth is necessary, however unwelcome this conclusion may be. The ground of necessary truth is ultimately the same as the ground of so-called contingent truth; God's will is necessarily constrained by His wisdom. Like Descartes, Malebranche will hold that the difference between geometrical propositions and propositions about the weather is a difference in the duration of their truth value; it is not the difference between necessary and contingent truth. For Descartes all truth is, in effect, contingent even if in some cases eternal; for Malebranche it is all necessary, even those truths pertaining to specific finite times. The only way to avoid this without denying the ground for necessary truth would be to allow some truths which are independent of God's will, truths which are, for example, utterly accidental.

Malebranche is sometimes driven to tychism – as in his correspondence with Leibniz on Descartes's fourth rule of collision, which he finally allows to be 'arbitrary'.[81] Malebranche admits here that there is a dynamical property of things, namely, the direction and quantity of motion resulting from collision of bodies exactly equal in size and speed and opposite in direction, that cannot be accounted for by geometry (kinematics) alone. In theological terms, God's wisdom is insufficient to resolve this case, whose outcome is thus determined by God's will alone. But generally Malebranche is inclined towards a Spinozistic necessitarianism.

A strong indication of this Spinozism is found in Malebranche's discussion of the motivation for creation.[82] God creates, not from necessity, but from love, which can be only for Himself and which is expressed in His Glory. Now, God cannot be glorified, the argument goes, by mere material creation; material creation must be made divine. This is effected through the Incarnation, that is, by God becoming material. (Thus, the Redemption on this account is only incidental; had the Fall not occurred, Christ would have come anyway.) The material world is created in the way best fitted to this end, where the fitness of the infinite number of worlds that God could have created to achieve His ends is judged according to their simplicity. Thus, despite Malebranche's *claim* that God's act of creation is perfectly unconstrained and indifferent,[83] Malebranche falls into much the same problem that plagued Leibniz: the existence of this world seems deducible from a calculus of necessary divine attributes. Specifically, that He creates and maintains just this world follows from God's goodness, that is, the love He bears for Himself, and His wisdom, that is, the truth He cannot help but know.

Malebranche's position approaches that of Spinoza in another way as well. As Berkeley was later to argue, Malebranche's contingent matter is philosophically idle. Epistemologically, it makes no important difference in how we know; for the existence of matter is not *known* at all – it is *believed* on the basis of revelation.[84] Ontologically, Malebranche's assertion of a multiplicity of material substances seems gratuitous: (1) they are inconceivable apart from God; (2) given occasionalism, they are absolutely impotent; and (3) since every material substance contains and is contained by an infinite number of substances without which it is inconceivable, Malebranche's material substances seem more like Spinoza's modes than like traditional substances.[85] (Whether any of the Cartesians other than the atomist Cordemoy was able to avoid Spinozism in this sense is a good question. What was unique about Malebranche among them was his explicitness about the containment relations.) More generally, Malebranche's notion of material extension seems superfluous since it replicates the function of intelligible extension. And if the two are not distinct, then it seems difficult for Malebranche to hold a traditional Christian doctrine of creation. Thus Arnauld's unrelenting charge that Malebranche failed to distinguish material extension from intelligible extension was, in effect, the first allegation against him of Spinozism. It was an allegation that was to be made explicit several times thereafter,[86] most insistently by Dortous de Mairan.

Malebranche's polemic with Mairan was the last in a polemic-filled life, and it came when his powers were failing. The result was that he was no better able to defend himself than he had been against Arnauld's similar charge three decades earlier.[87] Perhaps the best defence of Malebranche had already been made by his disciple Lelevel in the debates of the 1690s, which are discussed later in the chapter. Lelevel tried to show that in fact it was those Cartesians who adhered to the doctrine of the created truths who ran the risk of Spinozism.

VII. LATER REACTIONS TO THE DOCTRINE OF THE CREATION OF THE ETERNAL TRUTHS

Thus far the chapter has been mainly concerned with some aspects of necessitarianism, and the reaction against it. Now it treats specifically the other main current that derives from Descartes's thought, and examines some reactions to the doctrine of the creation of the eternal truths that follows from the emphasis on God's omnipotence.

For the invariably nominalist British empiricists, the debate concerning the creation of the eternal truths was a non-starter. By rejecting the existence–essence distinction of Meditatio V, Hobbes argued that an eternal truth was only a matter of conjoining names by convention in a way that made it independent of the thing named, whose essence perished when it did.[88] Similarly, Locke, beginning with the premises that truth is strictly speaking a property of verbal or mental propositions (composed of verbal or mental 'signs'), and that the only things that exist are particulars, arrives at the conclusion that 'the Doctrine of the Immutability of *Essences,* proves them to be only abstract Ideas; and is founded on the Relation, established between them, and certain Sounds and Signs of them; and will always be true, as long as the same Name can have the same signification.'[89] Furthermore, British empiricists for the most part ignored the question whether there were constraints on divine power of creation beyond a vague notion of goodness; in general they assumed that there were none, or none that could be known.

Among those of the Cartesian school who followed Descartes in asserting the creation of the eternal truths, there were two, not entirely opposed tendencies.[90] If the eternal truths are uncreated, then as both Spinoza and Malebranche held, *a priori* reasoning is in principle sufficient to apprehend them. But if the eternal truths are arbitrary creations, then some *a posteriori* experience is necessary. This experience may be natural (empiricism), to which we shall return shortly, or it may be supernatural (mysticism), which was best represented in the thinking of Pierre Poiret.

Fundamental to Poiret's thinking is his concept of God as a perfect, self-sufficient and independent being.[91] On this basis he rejects what he takes to be the scholastic view, that there are ideas or essences independent of God that are eternal and necessary and that He must follow in any creation. Although it is true that in knowing created things, God knows ideas, such ideas are not even necessary and eternal in so far as they are in His essence. God knows through ideas that he *arbitrarily* created: 'If these must be called eternal it is only in that their free and arbitrary production has not been preceded by any other thing, by any idea, by any variable and temporal duration',[92] and because they will never cease. But they are not in themselves essential or necessary. God's self-knowledge is necessary and essential to Him, but His knowledge of everything else comes about through 'purely arbitrary pleasure, through an entirely free fiction. . . . He has freely invented [all things other than Himself] in this arbitrary concept, and has resolved to produce them externally with the same freedom.'[93]

Poiret thus attacks Malebranche's view. Ideas in God necessarily represent the individual things of creation, according to Malebranche, because they are the exemplars after which those things are created. The relation between ideatum and idea at issue here is essentially the Platonic relation of participation of a thing in its exemplar. But Poiret gives no evidence of any understanding, still less any appreciation of the Platonic concept of participation. He thus has no difficulty in spelling out objections to that view. He argues, for example, that Malebranche's view makes God's substance material in so far as it represents material things, and that it invests material things with the divine attributes of necessity, independence, immutability, and so on – all of which comes to idolatry. Poiret also criticises Malebranche's occasionalism. To deny that secondary causes have real causal efficacy, he argues, is to deny that they have real being. By the same act whereby God communicates being to creatures He communicates the power to act. According to Poiret, *no one* has ever said that the uniqueness, self-sufficiency, and absolute nature of God are incompatible with created being; no one therefore should say that divine omnipotence is incompatible with genuinely active creatures.[94] Both Malebranche's theory of ideas and his occasionalism fail to distinguish God from creation; Poiret does not mention Spinoza by name, but the cat is no less out of the bag.

The concept of such an independent and self-sufficient creator of essences, even if limited to essences other than His own, presses Poiret towards a mystical world-view. His proof for the existence of God is a very loose causal argument along Cartesian lines, based on the idea of God. But at this point Poiret abandons the way of clear and distinct ideas. The idea of God may normally be weak and languid, he says, but because the strength and vivacity of the impression an object makes on us influences our conviction that it exists, the idea of God can and should be made strong and lively. This is to be done by ignoring all other ideas and concentrating on the idea of God to such an extent that the perception of God 'affects, invests, penetrates and fills us' in a way livelier and more sensible than the perception we have of ourselves.[95] This perception is described by those who have had it as 'ineffable and beyond what the heart of man may think of it. They say they lost themselves in God, that they perceived Him without perceiving themselves, that they no longer lived their own life but God's [Paul Gal. 2:20], that they were one spirit with God [Cor. 6:17], united and consummated with Him in one [John 17:21, 23].'[96] Poiret understands God as pure being; only methodologically and because of our imperfect state do we apply the Cartesian 'I am' first to ourselves. 'I am' more properly applies to God, the infinite abyss of pure being, before whom everything else is not.[97] We might as well be dealing here with Theresa of Avila.

If the doctrine of the creation of the eternal truths led some followers of Descartes to mysticism, it led others to a kind of empiricism. Desgabets was perhaps the earliest Cartesian to show empiricist tendencies. He repeats a familiar refrain among Cartesians of all sorts when he claims on behalf of his own views that they are more Cartesian than some of the views expressed by Descartes himself. Like Malebranche, for example, Desgabets thought that although Descartes's fundamental principles were correct, his development of them was erroneous; but, he thought, the corrective could be found within Descartes's own philosophy.[98] A prime example of this is the doctrine of the created eternal truths. Desgabets writes, 'Having formally taught it, Descartes did not make the use of it he should have, letting himself be deceived by some contrary prejudices, with the result that he thoroughly disfigured the lovely body of his philosophy.'[99]

The central idea in Desgabets's rectified Cartesianism is his conception of God as an omnipotent, 'perfectly indifferent and free cause', who is nonetheless immutable in His volitions.[100] God is thus the cause not only of the (transitory) existence of things but of their (fixed) essences as well. Even if we can conceive of God before His creation, we cannot conceive of anything other than His will that might determine Him; for 'all essences, natures, attributes and truths', however immutable they appear to us, have been freely determined by God and could have been otherwise.[101] Nor is the immutability of these items only apparent, for the divine will on which they depend is immutable; God has 'to speak only once with respect to each thing and to pronounce an eternal and irrevocable yes or no'.[102] As a result, all substances are indefectible, since it is a contradiction that God should annihilate what He has created. The indefectibility of substance is linked with the immutability of eternal truths in the following way. Existence is substance determined temporally, that is, existing in a certain mode and thus considered extrinsically; matter, for example, exists as the essence of corporeal things which qua objects of experience are modes of it. Change is thus confined to modal beings.[103] But essences, that is, the 'subject and the object of eternal truth', is only 'substance considered in itself according to intrinsic attributes', without reference to time.[104] More needs to be said here, but the upshot is that even though an eternal truth such as 'man is a rational animal' is contingent upon the creation of the essence of man, it is no less irrevocable and immutable than the substance that grounds it.[105]

Another result of this doctrine according to Desgabets is that there are no 'pure possibilities' independent of God's will, which would be limitations on the kinds of things God is able to create. Despite Desgabets's image of the creator speaking once and for all with respect to each thing, suggesting a range of possibilities antecedent to creation, he is clear that the possibilities themselves are dependent upon free and unrestrained creation. Attributing it to the schoolmen,[106] Desgabets explicitly rejects the view that Leibniz will later hold, in accordance with which God's choice in creation is restricted by what is 'possible, true or impossible' independently of that choice; Desgabets rejects the view that God's choice is determined by a 'certain essential perfection in the world requiring God to create it such as it is, complete with all the beings already composing the perfection of its nature even before God has decreed anything regarding its creation'.[107] As a result, 'nothing that is not a mode, or a modal thing, can have any truly conceivable possibility that precedes existence at a certain time.'[108] Without clearly distinguishing them, Desgabets seems to employ three different senses of possibility. It is *ontologically* possible for substances to have been otherwise; they depend on sheer divine omnipotence. Substances depend on God even for their *logical* possibility; to put it in Desgabets's psychologistic way, we cannot conceive of any substances other than those God has created. Substances are not in time; *a fortiori* they do not involve *temporal* possibility, which may be defined as follows: that x is F is *temporally* possible at t if at some other time t', prior to t, it is possible that x is F. But modes do not involve *temporal* possibility either. *Qua* modes of substance, modes *ontologically* could have been otherwise; and unlike substances, they *logically* could have been otherwise. That is, we can conceive of non-actual modes as actual and of actual modes as non-actual. But, since time comes into existence, as it were, only with the creation of modes,[109] there can be no temporally prior possibility for them. To put it another way, the creation of the eternal verities in no way binds after the fact with respect to the creation even of modal beings. Thus Desgabets can unqualifiedly claim that 'God can act other than as He does at the very instant He gives being to His creatures.'[110]

   On the other hand, it is not clear that Desgabets properly can claim, as did Descartes, that divine immutability is the foundation of physics in so far as it guarantees the indefectibility of substance;[111] for motion is a mode, and modes are perforce defectible. Thus, despite what Desgabets might claim, the ground for inertial physics and for the computation of the laws for the communication of motion seems upset, for the quantity of motion either for the universe as a whole or for pairs of colliding parts of it need not be the same from one moment to the next.[112] In this way the doctrine of created truths points in the direction of empiricism, since the laws of collision cannot be known *a priori*.[113]

   On the other hand, Desgabets explicitly acknowledges that only actual creatures are possible: 'It is a contradiction to speak of minds and creatures other than those God has created.'[114] Indeed, possibility, actuality, and necessity seem to entail each other for Desgabets no less than for Spinoza. But he arrives at this conclusion by a route that shows how his view really differs quite radically from Spinoza's, despite his apparent necessitarianism. Like Malebranche, but also like Arnauld, Desgabets takes as epistemologically most basic a Parmenidean principle of intentionality: to think is to think of something.[115] For him things are directly perceived and an idea is the means by which, and not in which, a thing is perceived. As a consequence, all simple ideas necessarily conform with their objects. To put it another way, 'The reality of things or their essence and nature determines our mind to conceive them such as they are.'[116] The result for Desgabets is effectively an ontological argument for everything that exists, at least every substantial thing: from the existence of substance *in intellectu* we can conclude *a priori* its existence *in re*. What is conceivable exists, then, and what exists is inconceivable except as existing. He writes, 'All matter that is conceivable and possible being the same as that which actually exists according to Descartes, no matter can be thought of that does not actually possess outside the understanding everything perceived in it, it being ridiculous to say, on this view, that purely possible matter can be thought of.'[117]

Desgabets differs from Spinoza mainly in his grounds for claiming that the non-existent is inconceivable. For Spinoza the existence of what we know follows necessarily from God's nature; for Desgabets it follows only from the divine will acting with a freedom of indifference. Desgabets rejects Aquinas's distinction between the existence and essence of things; the two, in fact, are created together. Thus he writes, 'In order to know created things we must wait until God has given them their essence and existence which are equally contingent.'[118] The wait is, of course, another indication of the empiricism to which this analysis leads. It comes as no surprise, then, when this corrector of Descartes goes so far as to claim, *nihil est in intellectu quin prius fuerit in sensu*;[119] that because the understanding is passive it depends on the agency of the body to be actualised, and thus that there is no pure intellection;[120] that even our rationality depends on the body, without which there would be no motion to provide the succession of our thoughts and thus the possibility of one depending on another.[121]

VIII. THE DENOUEMENT: THE DEBATE BETWEEN REGIS AND LELEVEL

In his classic history of Cartesianism, Bouillier cites Pierre-Sylvain Régis as calling Desgabets one of the great metaphysicians of the century and supposes, plausibly enough, that Desgabets influenced Régis in his empiricist tendencies.[122] Indeed, not just Régis's empiricism but his views on a whole range of issues, including the created truths and the rejection of pure modalities, now seem clearly traceable to

Desgabets's principles in a way heretofore altogether unappreciated. Régis began his career with an attack on Malebranche in his first, longest, and most important work, the *Système de philosophie* (1690). Malebranche quickly replied, and a miniature version of his better-known controversy with Arnauld was begun, with the same mixture of personal bitterness and philosophical interest. With respect to issues of concern here, Malebranche's cause was taken up by his disciple Henri Lelevel.[123] This exchange between Régis and Lelevel that came at the very end of the century defined more clearly the two strands of Cartesianism on the issues examined in this chapter.

Régis, like Desgabets before him, held the view of God as 'one, simple, incapable of change, absolutely infinite, eternal, necessary, incomprehensible, omnipotent, [as] that on which all things depend, not only for their nature, but also for their existence, their order and their possibility'.[124] God has an understanding and a will but, not as in man, the former precedes the latter neither temporally nor by nature; given divine simplicity, the faculties are really one, acting together. Régis's argument, however, subordinates understanding to will. Not only can God do whatever He wants, He knows whatever He wants. Anything less would be a limitation on His omnipotence.

But Régis added several *excursus* to the doctrine of created truths that he thought followed from this conception of God. In the eternal truths he distinguished between matter and form. The matter of an eternal truth is its content, what it is about; its form is the mind's consideration of that content in a certain way, that is, as not conceivably otherwise. Since God determines the mind always to consider this content in the same way, and because, presumably, He does not alter this content, the eternal truths are immutable. But for the same reason, their immutability is not absolute but contingent. Furthermore, since only God is eternal, they are properly said to be not eternal but perpetual or eviternal.[125] Finally, Régis holds that even possibility depends on God's will; before His decree, there *is* nothing, either possible or impossible.[126] Thus, while Régis, like Desgabets, denies that there is any distinction between essence and existence in substances, which are thus inconceivable except as existing, he holds, again like Desgabets, that their existence depends upon God's absolutely free act of creation.[127]

According to Lelevel, it is misguided piety on Régis's part to make everything depend on God's will. It is not impotence but the opposite for God to will necessarily in accordance with a certain order, which, in fact, is His own wisdom.[128] According to Lelevel, Régis's view is worse than dangerous, for it leads (however inconsistently) to both scepticism and Spinozism. Lelevel's own argument for this charge of Spinozism is not well focused,[129] but the argument for scepticism is clear. Drawing on Malebranche's argument against Descartes in the *Eclaircissements* of the *Recherche,* Lelevel tried to show that if the eternal truths are created, then we are doomed to scepticism. If everything depends on the divine will, then since the divine will is not known to us, we can know nothing: 'Therefore everything is in confusion, there is no longer any certainty in the sciences, no rules for morality, no religion, no justice.'[130] Lelevel correctly sees that with this scheme there is no *a priori* knowledge, which for him is the only kind of knowledge. Before the fact of creation there can be no rational guarantee of what God creates; this can be determined only after the fact through experience. The distinction Régis explicitly draws between two kinds of truth, necessary (*de droit*) and contingent (*de fait*), thus seems to Lelevel no distinction at all. 'If there is no truth that does not depend on God's will, then since there is nothing freer than this will . . . there is also nothing more contingent than any truth that might be, and we should not despair that one day there will be squares whose four sides are not equal.'[131]

Régis later acknowledged the systematic importance of the primacy of divine will. Whether recognising their connexion to it or not, he also drew a number of the sceptico-empiricist consequences that follow from that premise. Among other things, he argued that the soul is not a *tabula rasa,* for it is never without ideas. But, he claimed, the soul's ideas nonetheless depend on the body, without which it has none. The soul 'is united to the body only because it is actually thinking through the agency [*par l'entremise*] of the body'. Indeed, all knowledge of particulars depends upon the body, either directly or through inference, as in the case of the knowledge of minds. According to Régis, knowledge beyond particulars is achieved in Aristotelian, or even Gassendist or Lockean fashion. He holds that the soul

regroups under a single idea several beings . . . by stripping from them through its specifications [*précisions*] all the modifications and all the circumstances that distinguish them. Now it is this . . . that is meant when it is said that there is nothing in the understanding that has not passed through the senses. For indeed the soul cannot strip its ideas of the circumstances that make them singular without having those ideas; nor can it have those ideas without receiving them from the senses.[132]

Régis argued on behalf of principles he likely acquired from Desgabets. Lelevel argued on behalf of principles he certainly got from Malebranche. Neither side had full claim to Cartesian orthodoxy (or Christian orthodoxy either, for that matter). For the contest between them represented the intrinsic opposition be-

tween the directions in which the Cartesian philosophy pointed. These players at
the end of the century were developing variations on the two themes that were
sounded more than half a century earlier by Descartes.

NOTES

1 Popper 1982, pp. 56 ff., offers this 'perhaps untenable historical conjecture'.
2 'We believe in one God the Father Almighty, maker [*factorem, poieten*] of all things
   visible and invisible.' Denzinger 1963, pp. 52–3. See also the Council of Constantinople
   (A.D. 381), Denzinger, 1963, pp. 66–7. But cf. Leo I (A.D. 447): 'Praeter hanc autem
   summae Trinitatis unam consubstantialem et sempiternam atque incommutabilem dei-
   tatem nihil omnino creaturarum est, quod non in exordio sui ex nihilo creatum sit.'
   Denzinger, 1963, p. 101.
3 Denzinger 1963, p. 259. See also Eugenius IV (1442), who proclaimed the church's
   'firmest belief' that 'both spiritual and corporeal creatures are made from nothing [*de
   nihilo factae sunt*].' Denzinger 1963, p. 338.
4 'Intendit solum communicare suam perfectionem, quae est ejus bonitas.' *Summa th.* I
   q44 a4. See also, a1.
5 For a more systematic account of these proofs, see Chapters 10 and 11.
6 Where not my own, Descartes translations are essentially those of Descartes 1984–91.
7 AT VII 135.
8 See AT VII 41; AT VII 104; 161. But when offered an occasion for elaboration by
   Gassendi, AT VII 288–9, Descartes ignored it. See AT VII 366. For a discussion of the
   notion, see O'Neill 1987, pp. 235–40.
9 Mal. *OC* I 422 (Malebranche 1980a, p. 222). This, presumably, is also true of God's re-
   creation of the world from one moment to the next. 'Being drawn from nothingness,
   the universe depends so closely on the universal cause that it would necessarily fall back
   into nothingness if God ceased to conserve it.' Mal. *OC* XII 157. Gassendi had
   previously argued a contrary view in his *Obj.* to Med. III: 'There are admittedly some
   effects that need the efficient cause which first produced them to be continuously
   present if they are to keep going and not give out at any moment. The light of the sun
   is such an effect. . . . But there are other effects which we see continuing not only
   when the acknowledged cause is no longer active, but even, if you like, when it is
   destroyed and reduced to nothing.' AT VII 300–301. This is the nominalist view
   anticipated by Durandus. See note 13.
10 Mal. *OC* II 23–4 (Malebranche 1980a, p. 273).
11 AT VII 48–9.
12 See Lennon in Malebranche 1980a, pp. 810 ff.
13 Régis, for example, appears to accept the crucial occasionalist premise: 'It is impossible
   to comprehend that God should will a thing to be produced and that it not be. Whereas
   [finite things] have nothing efficacious of themselves.' Yet the latter do act, even if in
   virtue of another, and are more than occasional causes, which contradict the idea of
   God. Régis 1690, vol. I, pp. 109–110.
      It is not clear whether Descartes was an occasionalist, or even whether he was
   committed to the position. The near-universal interpretation of the crucial text from
   Med. III is that Descartes held an atomistic theory of time from which his principle
   concerning creation and conservation follows. If so, then it is hard to see how he

avoids the further, occasionalist conclusion. (Laporte 1950 questioned the atomistic interpretation, however, as have Beyssade 1979; Garber 1987a; and Arthur 1988. Most recently, Secada 1990 has argued that in fact Descartes had no ascertainable view on the matter.) A further difficulty is to distinguish between occasionalism and the various theories of divine *concursus* held by almost everyone from Augustine to very late scholastics such as Fonseca and Suárez. At a minimum, they all assert that God concurs with both the continued existence and the actions of creatures; whether and in what sense creatures are also efficacious varied from author to author. From his perspective, a perspective typical of the later Cartesians, Malebranche saw two possibilities: either things after creation act independently of God, as he alleges Durandus to have held, or they are always fully dependent on God, as his own view, anticipated most closely by Biel and d'Ailly, would have it. Malebranche found the attempt to assert both the efficacy of secondary causes and the necessity of divine *concursus* plainly unintelligible. It is not clear whether Descartes himself saw things in this way. See Eclaircissement XV, Mal. *OC* III 214 ff., esp. pp. 239–44 (Malebranche 1980a, p. 663 ff., esp. pp. 678–80). For references to the texts of Augustine, Durandus, Biel, d'Ailly, Fonseca, Suárez, and other scholastics whose views fit into Malebranche's classification, see the notes of G. Rodis-Lewis to this text in Mal. *OC* III. For further discussions of the question of occasionalism, see Chapter 17.

14 See, e.g., to Mersenne, 15 April 1630; AT I 143; to More, 5 February AT V 272–3; Resp. V, AT VII 380; Resp. VI, AT VII 431–3.

15 AT I 151–2.

16 To Mersenne, 27 May 1630, AT I 151–2.

17 Bréhier 1967.

18 The scholastic background to Descartes's doctrine is in one sense straightforward. The work of Gilson 1982 (originally 1913), Bréhier 1967, and more recently Cronin 1960, among others, has made it clear that Descartes's immediate source is the *Disp. met.* of Suárez, which poses the issue for him and provides the very language in which he treats it. See also Rodis-Lewis 1980. However, exactly what view Suárez held is an exceedingly difficult question. See Wells 1981. It seems that in any case, the scholastic views before Descartes tended to cluster around either Aquinas or Peter Damian, discussed in the following paragraphs, and that Descartes tended towards neither, i.e., that his doctrine is, as Gilson held, genuinely novel.

19 See, e.g., Bréhier 1967.

20 This has been espoused by a number of people, perhaps most notably by Gilson who garnishes it, however, with another consideration, that Descartes held his view of omnipotence for other reasons as well, in particular because of his association with the Oratory, with Bérulle, and especially Gibieuf. See Gilson 1913, chaps. III, V. On occultist Neoplatonism see Simon 1981, pp. 133–5, and Chapters 16 and 17 in this volume.

21 *Princ.* III 2; cf. *Princ.* I 28.

22 AT VII 432.

23 For a discussion of the Cartesian circle, see Chapter 29.

24 Frankfurt 1967.

25 Wilson 1978, p. 126.

26 Frankfurt 1977, p. 42.

27 To Mesland, 2 May 1644; AT IV 118. That Descartes held this view so late suggests that he did not restrict divine power over truth in response to the problem of circularity generated by the hyperbolic doubt.

28 See Funkenstein 1980, p. 181.

29 To Mersenne, 6 May 1630; AT I 150.

30 Gueroult 1953, vol. 2, pp. 26 ff. Against this interpretation, however, it might be wondered on what the allegedly absolute impossibility rests if not the law of non-contradiction, which Descartes clearly regards as dependent on God's will. In addition, it would seem that any text one could cite on behalf of two classes of eternal truths equally supports a distinction limited to what we are able or unable to conceive. Thus, although Descartes talks of what is 'absolutely impossible', it is in the context of a discussion of the dependence our knowledge has on ideas and the consequence of this that 'we must *think* that everything contrary to these ideas is absolutely impossible and implies a contradiction. Thus, we *have no reason to assert* that there is no mountain without a valley.' To Gibieuf, 19 January 1642; AT III 476, emphasis added. See also Beyssade 1981, p. 88. In another letter that also restricts claims about modalities to conceivability, Descartes explicitly rejects the impossibility of the void as absolute. He writes: 'It seems to me that we should *never* say of *anything* that it cannot be brought about by God; for with everything true and good dependent on His omnipotence, I do not even dare to say that God cannot make a mountain without a valley . . . , but I say only that He has given me a mind with such a nature that I cannot conceive a mountain without a valley . . . And I say only that such things imply a contradiction in my thought. Likewise it seems to me to imply a contradiction in my conception to say that a space should be absolutely void' (To Arnauld, 29 July 1648, AT V 223–4. See also Frankfurt 1977, pp. 47–51). But if the void is not absolutely impossible, then presumably the other propositions listed above are not either.

31 See Osler 1985b, esp. pp. 350–1, 353–4.

32 To Mersenne, 15 April 1630; AT I 145–6. Even in this text, however, it is clear that the distinction in question is for Descartes, not in the scope of God's power, which is incomprehensible, but in how we conceive of it. Cf. Osler 1985b, 359.

33 Mal. *OC* III 132 (Malebranche 1980a, p. 615). See also Lelevel's critique of Régis, discussed in section VIII of this chapter. See also Bréhier 1967, p. 206.

34 See Curley 1984, esp. p. 594.

35 To Mesland, 2 May 1644; AT IV 118–19.

36 AT VII 288–91. Gassendi 1658, vol. III, pp. 332a, 348b–349a.

37 Bloch 1971, pp. 319–26.

38 Bloch 1971, pp. 350–5; Popkin 1979, chap. V.

39 Noel Aubert de Versé (d.1714) was raised Catholic, took a medical degree in Paris, but converted to Protestantism and moved to Holland where he practised as a minister. Even there his theological views got him into trouble and he returned to medicine as a livelihood. He was allowed to return to Paris on condition of renouncing Protestantism and writing against it.

40 Aubert de Versé 1684, pp. 106 ff.

41 Aubert de Versé 1684, p. 1.

42 Aubert de Versé 1684, unpaginated foreword.

43 The same ambiguity may be seen exploited in Descartes's fable version of the world's creation. While he insists both that the matter out of which the world would be formed is in any case created, and that in actual truth the world was created fully formed, he nonetheless shows how the laws of motion alone could bring the world out of a pre-existing material chaos. See *Le Monde,* chap. 6, AT XI, 31–6; *Disc.* part V, AT VI esp. 42–6; *Princ.* III 43–4 and IV 204–7.

44 Wolfson 1934, vol.1, esp. pp. 99 ff.

45 *Eth.* I prop. 3. See Watson, 1966, for the systematic significance of the causal likeness principle among the Cartesians.
46 See Sorabji 1983, chap. 15, for the history of this argument.
47 Wolfson 1934, p. 106.
48 *Eth.* I prop. 11.
49 *Eth.* I, prop. 17 scholium.
50 *Eth.* I prop. 34.
51 *Eth.* I, prop. 35.
52 *Eth.* I, prop. 11.
53 *Eth.* I, prop. 33 scholium II.
54 *Eth.* I, prop. 33 scholium II.
55 *Eth.* I, def.7.
56 *Eth.* I, prop. 11.
57 See, e.g., To de Volder, 10 November 1703; Ger. II 258 (Leibniz 1969, p. 532); '*De ipsa natura*' Ger. IV 508–9 (Leibniz 1969, p. 502).
58 To Jakob Thomasius 20/30 April 1669, Ger. I 16 (Leibniz 1969, p. 94).
59 For Descartes's apparent ambivalence on divine fatalism, see Curley 1984, p. 577, esp. fn. 15. Leibniz extended this criticism to Hobbes's nominalism as well.
60 *Princ.* III 47.
61 To Philipp, January 1680; Ger. IV 283 (Leibniz 1969, p. 273).
62 To Philipp, January 1680; Ger. IV 283 (Leibniz 1969, p. 273).
63 *Second letter to Clarke,* Ger. VII 357–8 (Leibniz 1969, p. 679).
64 *Disc. mét.* sec. 2. It is interesting to note that this is just a year after the Revocation of the Edict of Nantes, an edict that declared itself to be irrevocable within its text, but which was nonetheless revoked.
65 See Belaval 1960, p. 11 fn. 3; also his Conclusion. For a catalog of Leibniz's differences from Descartes, and for the Leibnizean response to the anti-holist, anti-finalist and architectonic hypotheses above, see Lennon 1983b.
66 Note to a letter from Eckhard, May 1677, Ger. I 253 (Leibniz 1969, p. 181 fn. 7).
67 Leibniz 1903, p. 360.
68 See, e.g., Lovejoy 1960, p. 179; but cf., e.g., Rescher 1967, pp. 29–30.
69 See Russell 1937, fn. p. 39.
70 Here I follow the account in R. M. Adams 1982, for the most part.
71 Adams 1982, p. 248.
72 Ger. I 148. See also To Justel, 4/14 February 1678; LAkad. II.I 393 (Leibniz 1969, p. 195).
73 Adams 1982, pp. 254 ff.
74 Adams 1982, pp. 258–9.
75 Okruhlik 1985, pp. 195–6.
76 Leibniz 1948, p. 303. To be sure, Leibniz says that not even God sees the end of the analysis, for there is none (Adams 1982, p. 260). But his fuller statement is that 'the analysis [of contingent truths] proceeds to infinity, only God being able to see, not the end of the analysis indeed, since there is no end, but the nexus of terms or the inclusion of the predicate in the subject, since He sees everything that is in the series' ('On Freedom' [1689?] Leibniz 1857, p. 181 [Leibniz 1969, p. 265]).
77 Adams 1982, pp. 266–9.
78 For the details, see Adams 1982, pp. 270–2.
79 Wilson 1976a, p. 285.
80 Mal. *OC* III 132 (Malebranche 1980a, p. 615).

81 See Lennon in Malebranche 1980a, pp. 834–5.
82 Mal. *OC* XII 197 ff.
83 See, e.g. *Ent. mét.* VII.ix, Mal. *OC* XII–XIII 159.
84 Mal. *OC* III 60–4 (Malebranche 1980a, pp. 572–4).
85 Malebranche argued against Gassendi's account of cohesion in terms of interlocking particles on the basis that the extended parts of such particles are themselves conceivable apart, hence substances, and could exist apart. (Mal *OC* II 423–5 [Malebranche 1980a, pp. 512–13]). Given the infinite, or at least indefinite extension of matter, and the infinite divisibility of matter into extended parts, every alleged extended substance thus is contained by and contains an infinite number of such substances.
86 See, e.g., R. J. Tournemine, preface to Fénelon 1713, unpaginated. See also Mal. *OC* XIX 835–51; Aubert de Versé 1684, pp. 144 ff.
87 See Radner 1978, esp. p. 113.
88 AT VII 193–4.
89 *Ess.*, II.xxvii.1; III.iii.1; III.iii.19.
90 See G. Rodis-Lewis 1981, p. 108.
91 E.g., Poiret 1687, p. 47.
92 Poiret 1687, p. 59.
93 Poiret 1687, p. 79.
94 Poiret 1687, pp. 64–72, 123.
95 Poiret 1687, pp. 9–12.
96 Poiret 1687, p. 12.
97 See Poiret 1687, p. 31.
98 To N.-J. Poisson, 9 March 1677, in Mal. *OC* XVIII–XIX 125.
99 Desgabets 1983, p. 209.
100 Desgabets 1983, pp. 8–9 and *passim.*
101 Desgabets 1983, pp. 208–9 and *passim.*
102 Desgabets 1983, pp. 19–20.
103 Desgabets 1983, pp. 237, 238, 246.
104 Desgabets 1983, p. 27.
105 Desgabets 1983, p. 250.
106 Desgabets 1983 mentions Aquinas, 'the School', and 'the metaphysicians'; see pp. 248, 250, and *passim*. An oft-neglected element in these sorts of debates is the continuing importance of Aristotelianism. As late as 1696, John Sergeant argued the view that Desgabets here repudiates: 'All the Verity [notions] have is their *Metaphysical* verity, or their *being truly what they are.* And they partake this from the *Idea's* in the Divine Understanding, from which they unerringly flow, and which are essentially Unchangeable' (Sergeant 1696, p. 5). There is no question here but that such '*Idea's*' are uncreated and restrictive of the kinds of things that can be created. Six years before Desgabets began his earliest work on the topic, Digby argued that eternal truths have a necessary connexion between their terms and thus an 'indefectibility insuperable'; see Digby 1644a, p. 407.
107 Desgabets 1983, pp. 209, 251. The modal beings that come and cease to be are not 'purely possible' but 'really, actually and effectively' possible in so far as it follows from the nature of matter that God has created that it is divisible; i.e., matter is 'actually what God has made it, . . . its divisibility is an existing thing, and . . . the possibility [of all particular things] is effectively nothing other than this divisibility' (Desgabets 1983, pp. 237–8).
108 Desgabets 1983, p. 238.

109 See Desgabets 1983, pp. 189–90, 39 ff.
110 Desgabets 1983, p. 19.
111 Desgabets 1983, pp. 210–12.
112 For a discussion of the foundation of the laws of motion in divine immutability, see Chapter 21.
113 Even so, Desgabets argues for the indefectibility of motion. Desgabets 1983, pp. 85 ff. As noted in section VI of this chapter, Malebranche sometimes takes a similar position on the laws of motion, and argues that they cannot be completely known *a priori*.
114 Desgabets 1983, p. 233.
115 'Nothingness or the false is not perceptible or intelligible. To see nothing is not to see; to think of nothing is not to think . . . nothingness is not perceptible. Properly speaking, this is the first principle of all knowledge.' Mal. *OC* II 99 (Malebranche 1980a, p. 320). 'There is as much absurdity in speaking about thought of nothing, an idea of nothing, a nothing that is known as in talking of a painting that represented nothing.' Desgabets 1983, p. 225. For Arnauld's view, see *Des vraies et des fausses idées*, Arnauld 1775–83, vol. 38, pp. 205–6.
116 Desgabets 1983, p. 225.
117 Desgabets 1983, p. 233.
118 Desgabets 1983, p. 249. Another version of this story is Gassendi's nominalist critique of Descartes's doctrine of the indivisibility of essences. Gassendi 1658, vol. 3, p. 352b. Similarly, Locke thought that the 'doctrine of the immutability of *Essences,* proves them to be only abstract ideas'; eternal truths about things involve only nominal essences, never real essences. *Ess.,* III.iii.19.
119 Desgabets 1983, p. 183. The slight discrepancy from the classic formula indicates for Desgabets that although all thought depends on the senses, it does not necessarily resemble the sensory process.
120 Desgabets 1983, p. 185.
121 Desgabets 1983, p. 190. See ibid., p. 269, for Desgabets's rejection of the Cartesian model of the pilot and his ship for the relation between mind and body.
122 Bouillier 1868, vol. 1, p. 531.
123 Not much is known about Henri Lelevel (1655– ?). He was also a member of the Oratory, who left it, however, to become tutor to the Duc de Saint Simon. Thoroughly imbued with the philosophy of Malebranche, he promulgated it in the various lessons he gave in Paris.
124 Régis 1704, p. 57.
125 Régis 1690, vol. 1, pp. 177–80; Régis 1704, pp. 170–3.
126 Régis 1690, pp. 102–3.
127 Régis 1704, pp. 123–5; Desgabets 1983, pp. 248–9.
128 Lelevel 1694, chap. 3.
129 Régis's discussion of modal beings, for example, certainly invites the charge. Mind and body considered in themselves are substantial beings, he says, but *particular* minds and bodies are modal beings, i.e., beings whose essence contains modes, which is to say substance considered not in itself but in a certain fashion. See Régis 1690, p. 101. Construing individual minds as modes makes the Cartesian argument for immortality problematic for Régis. He does argue the soul's immortality on the basis of the indefectibility of substance, but the substantial soul turns out to be just the universal soul it should be, given Régis's philosophical principles, if not his theological ones. 'As extension, which is the essential attribute of body is never corrupted, and it is only modes making it this or that body that perish, we are forced also to recognise that

thought, which is the essential attribute of mind, cannot be corrupted. And it is only the modes determining it to be this or that soul, for example to be the soul of Peter, Paul, John, etc., which are destroyed' (Régis 1690, pp. 266–7). If Régis also confuses substance with God by confusing matter with its idea, as Lelevel argues he does, then his Spinozism is patent.

Régis tried to respond to the charge of Spinozism, very probably as originating with Lelevel, by adding to a work of his some years later an appendix entitled *Réfutation de l'opinion de Spinoza touchant l'existence et la nature de Dieu* (in Régis 1704). His main goal there is to show that Spinoza falsely concluded that there is only one substance and that that substance is God. See Régis 1704, p. 481. Notably absent, however, is the venom usually directed at Spinoza and the near-hysterical urgency with which authors in the period generally tried to dissociate themselves from him. Instead, one finds a rather dispassionate discussion of the points on which Régis takes Spinoza to have been unclear, unjustified or just mistaken.

130 Lelevel 1694, p. 46.
131 Lelevel 1694, p. 131.
132 Régis 1704, p. 17; see also pp. 1–21.

13

THE RELATION BETWEEN
THEOLOGY AND PHILOSOPHY

NICHOLAS JOLLEY

In the Epistle to the Colossians, 2.8, Saint Paul warns the faithful against those who would seek to corrupt them through 'philosophy and vain deceit'. Almost all seventeenth-century philosophers accepted Paul's words as authoritative, but there was little agreement about how they should be understood. Indeed, the history of the relation between philosophy and theology in the period might be written in terms of contrasting responses to this one text. For many thinkers, the message was clear: Paul wished to warn Christians against Aristotle and his legacy, but he did not mean to impose a total ban on the use of philosophical arguments. On the contrary, when purged of scholasticism, philosophy had a major rôle to play in the service of Christian theology. Other thinkers drew a more radical moral from the same passage in favour of 'revealed' as opposed to 'natural' theology. They saw Paul's words as an indication that Christian theology must be purged of the whole taint of Greek influences; indeed, the Pauline text became a rallying-point for those who were hostile to the very pursuit of natural theology, the appeal to natural reason in support of theological conclusions.[1] Yet, at a deeper level, conservatives and radicals were often engaged in a common enterprise; they both sought to find a way in which theology and the 'New Philosophy' could co-exist.

If the overthrow of scholasticism made the project of reconciling philosophy and theology a major concern for most thinkers in the period, it is tempting to suppose that theology acted simply as a dead-weight, hampering the free development of philosophical thought. Yet that would be a mistake. It has been argued with respect to an earlier age that the Judeo-Christian tradition helped to fertilise philosophy by suggesting new problems and points of view.[2] To a large extent this is true of the seventeenth century as well. The theological controversies of the age created new problems which called for philosophical solutions, and some of these solutions are still with us. It is easy to suppose that almost all that is vital in seventeenth-century philosophy can be attributed to the scientific revolution, but several of the most interesting developments can be traced to the demands of theology.

I. THE RECONCILIATION OF THEOLOGY AND
PHILOSOPHY: DIFFERENT APPROACHES

Seventeenth-century philosophers who debated the relationship of philosophy
and theology could generally find precedents for their views. There had been
more than one conception of the relationship between the two disciplines within
the Christian tradition. On the whole, patristic and early mediaeval thinkers
tended not to make a sharp distinction between philosophy and theology. Clement
of Alexandria, Augustine, and Anselm conceived of philosophy more as an instrument for understanding Christianity than as an autonomous discipline; their ideal
was that faith should be wholly penetrated by understanding.[3] This conception of
the relationship between philosophy and theology persisted into the scholastic
period; it finds expression in the thirteenth century in the writings of Bonaventure.[4] But, in general, scholasticism is marked by an increasing emphasis on the
distinction between philosophy and theology. For Aquinas, theology, or 'sacred
doctrine', is unlike philosophy in that it assumes the existence of God and other
articles of faith as premises; philosophy, by contrast, begins with the objects of
sense-perception.[5] Yet, for Aquinas, the distinction between philosophy and theology is not absolute. For first, following Aristotle, Aquinas recognises a purely
philosophical part of theology.[6] Second, Aquinas holds that philosophy has a rôle
to play in defending the articles of the Christian faith against objections.[7] Later
scholastics went further than Aquinas in emphasising the distinction between
philosophy and theology. William of Ockham, for instance, held that philosophy
could not prove such truths of religion as the immortality of the soul or even
the existence of God.[8] The Christian tradition was thus marked by competing
conceptions of the relation between philosophy and theology, and it is against
this background that we must understand the positions of seventeenth-century
philosophers. Descartes is not the first thinker in the period to confront the
problem of reconciling traditional theology with the 'New Philosophy'; his older
contemporaries, such as Gassendi and Mersenne, had already sought to achieve
such a reconciliation before he published his major works. But Descartes is at
once more radical and more influential than they are by virtue of his insistence on
the need to provide new foundations for philosophical knowledge, and for this
reason it is best to begin with him. Descartes is heir to the tensions within the
tradition, and these tensions were to come to the fore in subsequent seventeenth-
century philosophy.

In the wake of the condemnation of Galileo, Descartes was well aware of the
need for care in writing about theological issues. It is not surprising, then, that he

often takes up a position on the relation between philosophy and theology which is reminiscent of Thomistic orthodoxy. In the *Notae in programma,* he distinguishes between those things which are to be believed through faith, such as the Trinity and the Incarnation, and those which, while having to do with faith, can also be investigated through natural reason, such as the existence of God and the distinction of the soul and body.[9] Like Aquinas, Descartes recognises that philosophy can play a rôle in relation to questions of the first sort; it can show that the mysteries 'are not incompatible with the natural light'.[10] But it is with regard to truths of the second sort that philosophy can make its most distinctive contribution; philosophers are encouraged by theologians to demonstrate them to the best of their ability by arguments which are grounded in human reason.[11] In the famous letter of dedication to the Sorbonne which prefaces the *Meditationes,* Descartes had written in a very similar vein; he had always thought that 'two topics – namely, God and the soul – are prime examples of subjects where demonstrative proofs are to be given with the aid of philosophy rather than theology.'[12] Here, as in the *Notae in programma,* he is careful to say nothing which is not consistent with Thomistic orthodoxy.

On closer inspection, however, Descartes's views reveal a degree of ambiguity. In correspondence, in particular, he seems to experiment with different ways of reconciling his philosophy with theology; the presence of rival strategies is most obvious in his dealings with the revealed articles of Catholic faith. Sometimes he distinguishes sharply between philosophy and theology and claims that theology, by which he means revelation, lies outside his province.[13] He declines a number of invitations to involve himself in controversies over revealed theology; he tells the Jesuit, Mesland, for instance, that he has no wish to enter into a discussion of human freedom in relation to divine grace.[14] Yet, on other occasions, Descartes is also capable of insisting on the tight connexion between philosophy and theology. With regard to the Catholic dogma of transubstantiation, he boldly tells Mersenne that his philosophy can accommodate it in a way that scholasticism cannot:

You will see that [in reply to Arnauld] I show that the teaching of the Councils about the Blessed Sacrament fits my philosophy so well that I claim that it cannot be explained in accordance with the common philosophy. I think that philosophy would have been rejected as clashing with faith if mine had been known first. I swear to you in all seriousness that I believe it is as I say. So I have decided to say so publicly, and to fight with their own weapons the people who confound Aristotle with the Bible and abuse the authority of the Church in order to vent their passions – I mean the people who had Galileo condemned.[15]

Descartes might have developed his criticism of those who confound Aristotle with the Bible by insisting on the need to keep philosophy and theology distinct.

But in fact he draws a different moral in this passage; he seems to propose that the marriage of Aristotle and the Bible should give way to a new marriage of Descartes and the Bible.

Descartes's pronouncements on philosophy and theology need not be convicted of outright contradiction. He could defend the consistency of his position by pointing to a difference between the doctrines of grace and the Eucharist. He could argue that he is compelled to discuss the Eucharist, since his philosophy – that is, his new philosophy of matter – has implications for the understanding of this doctrine. By contrast, his philosophy has no such implications for the controversy over grace. Nonetheless, Descartes's writings do contain hints of rival strategies. On the one hand, he defends his philosophy by stressing its relevance for theology; on the other hand, he defends it by stressing its independence and autonomy. His contemporaries and successors were to develop each of the strategies implicit in his teaching. This discussion begins with the second strategy.

II. THE SEPARATION OF PHILOSOPHY AND THEOLOGY

There is a powerful tendency among some seventeenth-century philosophers to make a sharp distinction between philosophy and theology. Thinkers who adopt this approach in no sense form a united movement; indeed, they differ markedly in their motivations and their allegiances. Some of those who insist on drawing boundaries between the two disciplines do so primarily in order to make room for the new philosophy; others are mainly concerned to defend the interests of theology. Indeed, in some cases, such as Pascal's, they appear to reject the very enterprise of philosophy. Yet they have enough in common to be discussed under the same rubric; they share a tendency, for instance, to insist that the God of Christianity is not the *ens realissimum* of Greek philosophy but a god who reveals himself in history.

Perhaps no philosopher was more concerned than Hobbes to safeguard the new philosophy from the encroachments of theology. Yet his strategy for defending the interests of philosophy is not strikingly original; it owes much to later mediaeval and Reformation precedents. Hobbes's defence of the autonomy of philosophy involves two main themes. In the first place, he follows the later scholastics in insisting on the incompetence of natural reason in theological matters.[16] Here, however, a distinction must be made. Hobbes is not hostile to attempts to prove the existence of God; indeed, he offers his own versions of the causal and teleological arguments. But if the existence of God can be known by natural reason, the nature of God lies completely outside its scope: 'For the nature of God is incomprehensible; that is to say, we understand nothing of *what he is,* but only *that he is.*[17] He similarly insists that the immortality of human beings cannot be established by philosophical arguments. Second, he adopts the biblical fideism of the Reformation theologians; we must simply accept the Scriptures on faith as the authoritative source of information about God.[18] The biblical revelation, however, must be purged of the corrupting influences of Greek philosophy. Hobbes regards Aristotle as the arch-enemy, but he does not limit his attack to him; in the last part of *Leviathan* he warns that the devil has sown spiritual error 'by mixing with the Scripture divers reliques of the Religion and much of the vain and erroneous Philosophy of the Greeks, especially of Aristotle'.[19] Elsewhere he complains that the Jews had adulterated the Mosaic law with 'the Vain Philosophy and Theology of the Grecians'.[20]

Hobbes's attempt to combine these two themes is fundamental to his approach, but it is not altogether satisfactory. It is true that the approach is successful in dealing with some issues, such as immortality. He argues quite coherently that though reason is silent on the subject, a doctrine of purely bodily immortality can be derived from Scripture, suitably purged of the corruptions of Greek philosophy.[21] But there are obvious tensions in his doctrine of God which are generated by his famous account of the divine attributes. According to Hobbes, the predicates which we apply to God do not strictly describe His nature; rather, they are simply expressions of our desire to honour Him.[22] Here Hobbes not merely looks back to the mediaeval doctrine of analogical predication; he also anticipates an emotivist theory of religious language. Propositions of the kind 'God is just' have, strictly speaking, no truth-value; they are more correctly interpreted as expressions of a pious attitude in the speaker. But on this theory Hobbes in effect deprives all claims about God of cognitive content; even the biblical claims cannot really express propositions with a truth-value. It is thus difficult to see how his fideism can ever get off the ground.[23]

Hobbes's theology may not be completely coherent, but it does have important polemical advantages. In the first place, by insisting on the incomprehensibility of the divine nature, he can side-step the issue of whether God falls within the scope of his materialism. It is often supposed that Hobbes does not shirk the consequence that God must be material in his system. But, in fact, this is harder to document than one might imagine; in the relevant passages, Hobbes prefers to take refuge in the incomprehensibility of the divine nature.[24] Moreover, his theology also harmonises with the thrust of his case for absolute sovereignty. To those who appealed to a rationally discoverable divine will, he replied that there can be no natural knowledge of divine commands; God's will is revealed only in the Scriptures, and like all legal texts, the Scriptures require an authoritative interpreter.[25]

Spinoza is no less keen than Hobbes to protect the new philosophy from the encroachments of revealed theology. In the *Tractatus Theologico-Politicus*, Spinoza insists on the need to stake out boundaries between philosophy and revelation.[26] But though they have a common goal of upholding the interests of philosophy, Spinoza and Hobbes differ markedly in other respects. Unlike Hobbes, Spinoza does not seek to deny or even play down the competence of reason in theological matters. As the *Ethica* shows, no one is more convinced than Spinoza of the possibility of attaining to a philosophical knowledge of the nature of God. Thus he seeks to protect philosophy against the claims of revelation in a way which leaves room for the enterprise of natural theology.

Spinoza clearly explains his strategy for achieving this goal in the *Tractatus Theologico-Politicus*. In this work he argues at length that there is no possibility of conflict between philosophy and revealed theology because they are really incommensurable enterprises; they differ fundamentally in their purposes and methods. As Spinoza says: 'Between faith or theology, and philosophy, there is no connection, nor affinity. . . . Philosophy has no end in view save truth; faith . . . looks for nothing but obedience and piety. Again, philosophy is based on axioms which must be sought from nature alone; faith is based on history and language, and must be sought for only in Scripture and revelation.'[27] In other words, the Bible does not seek to offer the kind of authoritative knowledge of the nature of God which would satisfy a philosopher. Spinoza does not deny that the Bible talks about God extensively; it pervasively describes Him as having human emotions and even human physical characteristics. But all such claims are adapted to the popular imagination, and they are put forward solely with the aim of exciting devotion and obedience.[28] By 'obedience' Spinoza effectively means 'love of one's neighbour', and it is thus clear that, for him, the aim of Scripture is essentially a moral one. Since in his view the Bible does not intend to advance philosophical claims, he concludes that 'faith . . . allows the greatest latitude in philosophical speculation.'[29]

Consistently with his overall strategy, Spinoza argues that neither philosophy nor theology should be subordinated to the other.[30] Philosophy should not be subordinated to theology: we must resist the temptation to say that a scriptural doctrine is true when it is repugnant to reason, for it is absurd to subject reason, 'the greatest of gifts and a light from on high', to a text which is quite possibly corrupt.[31] Theology in turn must not be subordinated to philosophy; we must resist the temptation to impose philosophical doctrines on to the writers of the

Bible. In particular, he argues that, where no alternative reading is available, we must accept the literal meaning of a scriptural passage as expressing the author's intention, no matter how absurd it may be from a philosophical point of view.[32] To cite Spinoza's own example, Scripture clearly teaches that God is jealous. Such a claim cannot withstand philosophical scrutiny, for it implies an unacceptably anthropomorphic conception of God.[33] But since it is not directly contradicted elsewhere in Scripture, there is no evidence that the claim is to be understood metaphorically. From passages like these we can see that Spinoza is developing a theory of biblical hermeneutics which was far ahead of his time.

In contrast to both Hobbes and Spinoza, Pascal is primarily a Christian apologist; despite his great contributions to mathematics, he has no real interest in protecting the new philosophy against the encroachments of religion. Indeed, at times he even seems to call in question the whole enterprise of philosophy; he writes that 'to have no time for philosophy is to be the true philosopher.'[34] In any case, in the *Pensées,* he largely rejects philosophy as an instrument of Christian apologetics. In particular, he rejects the kind of philosophical theology in which Descartes had engaged in the *Meditationes* and elsewhere.

In the *Pensées,* Pascal famously criticises Descartes's arguments for being useless and uncertain,[35] and this remark provides perhaps the best clue to his position; it suggests that he has two quite different kinds of criticism to make of his predecessor's efforts at philosophical theology. Reversing his own order, let us begin with the charge of uncertainty; in other words, he has purely philosophical reservations about Descartes's arguments for the existence of God and the real distinction of mind and body. For Pascal, as for others such as Huet, Descartes has not succeeded in overcoming the challenge of scepticism. The strength of the sceptics' case is their attack on first principles; as Pascal sees it, leaving faith and revelation aside, the sceptics are right that we can never know whether these principles are 'true, false or uncertain'.[36] Descartes's arguments for the existence of God clearly rely on first principles in this sense; the appeal in Meditatio III to a version of the causal likeness principle is surely a case in point.[37] The soundness of Descartes's arguments was to be attacked from a similar direction by Huet in his *Censura Philosophiae Cartesianae.*[38]

Philosophical theology, as practised by Descartes, is not merely uncertain; it is also 'useless and sterile'.[39] This criticism is really twofold. In the first place, Pascal argues that, even if we waive the question of their soundness, deductive philosophical arguments for the existence of God are psychologically ineffective. By virtue of their abstractness, they are remote from human reason; if they convince the reader at all, they do so only for a moment.[40] But his charge of uselessness and sterility comprehends a deeper, more important, criticism. At most metaphysical arguments can establish the existence only of the God of deism; and deism is 'almost as remote from the Christian religion as atheism, its complete opposite'.[41] But the Christian God is not the deistic God of the philosophers; He is the God of Abraham, Isaac, and Jacob, a god of love and consolation.[42] Such a god can be approached only through Jesus Christ, and He can be known only through the heart, not the reason.[43] Descartes would concede that philosophical arguments stop short of establishing that God has all the properties which are disclosed through revelation; but like Aquinas, he would insist that such arguments are valuable weapons in the church's armoury. Pascal, by contrast, believes that, to convert people to Christianity, the apologist must address the heart and the will, and that philosophical theology is largely irrelevant to this enterprise. Despite his Jansenist sympathies, he thus stands apart from the Augustinian conception of Christian philosophy.

Of all the traditional arguments for the existence of God, the one for which Pascal had most contempt was the argument from design. Indeed, Pascal writes that 'to give no other proof [of the existence of God] than the course of the moon and planets' is only likely to bring religion into contempt.[44] Another mathematician, by contrast, set great store by this argument. Newton clearly holds that his system is able to display the merits of this argument to better advantage than ever before; Newtonian physics exhibits a universe of extraordinary order and regularity. 'This most beautiful system of the sun, planets, and comets, could only proceed from the counsel and dominion of an intelligent and powerful being.'[45] In a letter to Bentley, Newton even indicated that in the composition of the *Principia* he had been guided by a desire to supply proofs of God's existence.[46]

Newton may have believed that 'natural philosophy' could serve the cause of religion, but he was generally hostile to the alliance between theology and traditional metaphysics. There is thus another side of Newton which has more in common with Pascal and, in particular, Hobbes. Like Hobbes, Newton deplored what he saw as the corruption of theology by Greek philosophy. He was specially incensed by the Platonic tradition in theology; he attacked the Platonists for giving esoteric meanings to scriptural names for Christ such as 'Lamb of God', 'Son of Man', and 'Son of God'. 'What all this has to do with Platonism or Metaphysicks I do not understand. . . . The Scriptures were given to teach man not metaphysics but morals.'[47] Newton's hostility to Greek metaphysics is intimately connected with his theological unorthodoxy. For Newton, the prime example of the corruption of religion by the Greek legacy was the doctrine of the Trinity. In his private writings Newton argued that the doctrine that Christ is consubstantial (*homousios*) with the Father has no basis in Scripture.[48] Newton's own positive conception of God emphasises above all His dominion or sovereignty. 'This Being governs all things, not as the soul of the World, but as Lord over all; and on account of his dominion he is wont to be called *Lord God pantokrator,* or Universal ruler.'[49] For Newton, this dominion is revealed in two complementary ways; the Bible reveals God's dominion over history, just as natural philosophy reveals His dominion over nature.[50] Newton's God is thus the God of Abraham, Isaac, and Jacob, not the God of Greek metaphysics. To this extent we can find in him resemblances to both Hobbes and Pascal.

III. THE AUGUSTINIAN TRADITION

Other thinkers in the period agreed with Hobbes and Newton that Christian theology had been infected by vain philosophy, but they drew a less radical moral from Saint Paul's strictures. In the eyes of Malebranche, for instance, the alliance between Aristotle and the church had been a disaster; Christian theologians, who should know better, had wholeheartedly embraced Aristotelian philosophy, and that philosophy was now totally discredited. The Preface to the *Recherche de la vérité* vividly conveys the flavour of Malebranche's views:

> I am not surprised that ordinary men or pagan philosophers consider only the soul's relation and union with the body, without recognising the relation and union it has with God; but I am surprised that Christian philosophers, who ought to prefer the mind of God to the mind of man, Moses to Aristotle, and Saint Augustine to some worthless commentator on a pagan philosopher, should regard the soul more as the *form* of the body than as being made in the image and for the image of God, i.e. according to Saint Augustine, for the Truth to which alone it is naturally joined.[51]

However, Malebranche and others were very far from seeking to sever the connexions between philosophy and theology; indeed, despite the impression conveyed in this passage, they did not really turn their back on the Greek philosophical tradition. Rather, they sought to revive the legacy of Augustine, and to that extent they were engaged in resurrecting Platonism in a Christian form. For Malebranche and others, the time seemed particularly ripe for such a project, for in Descartes himself they heard echoes of Augustinian teaching. They noticed, for instance, that as a strategy for refuting scepticism, Descartes's *Cogito* had been anticipated by Augustine's *Si fallor, sum*.[52]

The Augustinian dimension of Descartes's thought was exploited by rather different types of philosopher in the seventeenth century, and for rather different reasons. For Descartes's devoted disciples, it was primarily a propaganda weapon in the campaign against scholasticism. The Cartesians faced the tactical problem of rejecting scholasticism while upholding their religious orthodoxy; they may have been prepared to dismiss the scholastic synthesis as vain philosophy, but they were not willing to dismiss the whole Christian philosophical tradition. It was thus to their advantage to stress the Augustinian side of Descartes's teaching, for they could then challenge their conservative opponents to show how they could consistently attack Descartes without thereby rejecting the authority of the greatest of the church fathers. Augustine thus became a powerful ally in the struggle to legitimate Descartes in the eyes of the church.[53]

For Malebranche and other members of the Oratorian order, however, Augustine was no mere pawn in a propaganda war on behalf of Descartes; for them allegiance to Augustine was primary.[54] Malebranche and his fellow Oratorians were concerned to revive the distinctively Augustinian conception of the relationship between philosophy and theology which is expressed in the famous slogan: 'Believe in order that you may understand.' By this Augustine means at least that belief is a necessary condition of understanding the truths of religion. Augustine and his disciples also seem to have meant that the Christian should not be content with simply believing the articles of religion; his ultimate goal should be rational insight into the doctrines which were originally accepted on faith.[55] It is true, as we have seen, that even Aquinas envisaged some rôle for philosophy in relation to the revealed articles of faith; philosophy can defend these dogmas against the charge of logical incoherence. But for Malebranche as for Augustine, philosophy has a more positive contribution to make; it has a legitimate rôle in seeking to illuminate such distinctively Christian dogmas as the Trinity and the Incarnation through the use of analogy and metaphor.[56] For the Augustinian, there is no part of theology which is, as it were, off limits for the philosopher. Thus there can be no sharp distinction between philosophy and theology; rather, they are regarded as forming an almost seamless web.

Philosophers who pioneered the revival of this Augustinian conception of philosophy were in some degree Cartesians; Malebranche and Ambrosius Victor are prominent examples. But in fact such philosophers really departed from the Cartesian view of the relation between philosophy and theology. Insofar as philosophers revived not merely particular Augustinian doctrines but the whole Augustinian project of Christian philosophy, they disturbed the fragile equilibrium between the two disciplines which Descartes had established. To put the point another way, if they thought they were following Descartes, then their view of him was a very lop-sided one. It is true that there are Augustinian elements in Descartes's thought. But Descartes does not really resemble Augustine in his view of the relation between philosophy and theology; in his tendency to mark out boundaries in this area he is much closer to Aquinas.

IV. THE PLACE OF THEOLOGICAL ISSUES IN PHILOSOPHY

Unlike either Descartes or Hobbes, Malebranche and other Augustinian philosophers place no premium on preserving the independence of philosophy from theology. Although they take over Cartesian doctrines, they typically press them into the service of distinctively Christian themes; the defence of revealed Christian dogma is central, not peripheral as it is with Descartes. However, if philosophy serves the cause of theology, theology also serves the cause of philosophy. For Malebranche and the Augustinians, true metaphysics cannot afford to dispense with the articles of the Christian faith. The dogmas of revealed religion play an indispensable rôle in extending the teaching of the new, Cartesian philosophy; they even play a rôle in furnishing more adequate solutions to philosophical problems than those which Descartes had offered.[57]

Malebranche's treatment of the Fall offers a typical example of his use of Christian doctrine in order to extend Cartesian teaching; here, although he develops Cartesian teaching in a very un-Cartesian direction, he does not transform its philosophical content. Recall that, for Descartes, human beings have a natural bias to empiricism; in other words, we have a strong tendency to believe that our senses reveal the true nature of the physical world. In Meditatio I Descartes remarks that whatever he had accepted as most true, he had acquired either from the senses or through the senses.[58] But this reliance on the senses is a philosophical mistake: the true character of the physical world is revealed not by our senses but by our clear and distinct ideas. However, the empiricist tendency is so deeply implanted in our nature that we need the sceptical arguments of Meditatio I to cure us of it; they serve as a kind of aversion therapy. But if the senses do not reliably inform us about the nature of the physical world, then Descartes has a new problem on his hands; he has to explain what purpose they serve in a way that is consistent with the goodness of God. By the end of Meditatio VI Descartes is in a position to reveal the answer to this question. The purpose of the senses is, as it were, biological; they tell us what to pursue and what to avoid in the interests of physical survival.[59]

Malebranche is in complete agreement with Descartes about the nature and rôle of the senses; he also agrees with Descartes that we have a natural tendency to empiricism. But he now develops this theme in a radically un-Cartesian direction. Descartes may explain why we are endowed with senses in a way consistent with his philosophical theodicy, but he offers no explanation of our unreflective tendency to mistake their purpose. For Descartes, it would seem that this is simply a brute, inexplicable fact. For Malebranche, by contrast, here is a fact which not only calls for explanation but which can be explained by an appeal to revelation. For him, as for Glanvill and others, our natural tendency to mistake the rôle of the senses is one of the unfortunate consequences of the Fall.[60] Before the Fall, Adam was aware of the purpose for which his senses were intended; he did not suppose, as we unreflectively do, that they are designed to reveal the nature and properties of bodies. Unlike us, prelapsarian Adam would not have needed the sceptical arguments of Meditatio I. By appealing to the Fall, then, Malebranche gives a theological rationale for the Cartesian programme of distrusting the senses; theology thus serves the cause of philosophy. And by stressing the implications of the Fall for our intellectual life, Malebranche allows us to see the full import of the Christian dogma; philosophy thus serves the cause of theology.

In his use of the Fall, Malebranche adds an extra dimension to Cartesian teaching without seriously modifying it. At other times, however, Malebranche's use of Christian revelation involves a quite radical departure from Cartesian teaching. The famous doctrine of vision in God offers a particularly interesting example; for here he is criticising and transforming the Cartesian theory of ideas. Recall that, according to Descartes, ideas by their nature have two irreducible aspects. On the one hand, they are particular mental events which occur at particular times; in Descartes's terminology, this is their formal reality. On the other hand, they have objects or representational content; in Descartes's terminology, this is their objective reality.[61] According to Malebranche, such a theory is unable to do justice to the facts. In the first place, it cannot explain how the concept of a triangle can pre-exist and post-exist particular acts of thinking. Nor, in the second place, can it explain how different people can be said to think of the very same concept. In opposition to Descartes, Malebranche insists that ideas or concepts are ontologically distinct from the modifications of the mind; they are abstract, logical entities in God.[62] In modern terminology we could say that he criticises Descartes for failing to recognise the existence of a 'third realm' which is not reducible to mental events.

So far Malebranche's theory of vision in God offers a purely philosophical solution to a real problem in Descartes; a good case can be made for saying that Descartes is vulnerable to the charge of conflating logic and psychology. But there is also a theological dimension to Malebranche's doctrine. Not merely does he locate ideas – the abstract entities – in God, but he supports his thesis by an appeal to the prologue to Saint John's gospel. Following Augustine's theory of divine illumination, Malebranche identifies the intelligible world of ideas with the divine Logos or Word – 'the true light which lighteth every man that cometh into the world' (John 1.9);[63] the Word is the second person of the Trinity which became incarnate in Christ. Malebranche's allusion to Christ in this context might lead one to suppose that he is talking about a special kind of illumination which only the believer possesses, but this would be a serious misconception; on the contrary, it is Malebranche's contention that the Word is involved in all abstract thought and even in all sense-perception. Thus he is in a position to interpret the language of Saint John in the most literal sense; the Word is 'the light which lighteth *every* man that cometh into the world'.

Malebranche is not the only philosopher in the period who seeks to provide a philosophical gloss on the prologue to St John's gospel; he is followed in this respect by Leibniz. In the *Discours de métaphysique* Leibniz writes in a way that directly echoes Malebranche:

It can be said that God alone is our immediate external object, and that we see all things by means of him. For example, when we see the sun and the stars, it is God who has given us and conserves for us the ideas of them, and who determines us by his ordinary concourse actually to think of them at the time when our senses are disposed in a certain manner, following the laws that he has established. God is the sun and the light of souls, 'the Light which lighteth every man that cometh into the world'.[64]

But although Leibniz, like Malebranche, invokes the Word of St John's gospel, and even speaks of vision in God,[65] it is not clear that the philosophical underpinnings are quite the same. For Malebranche, as we have seen, there is a realm of ideas which are abstract entities in God. Leibniz, it is true, also speaks of God as the region of ideas,[66] and it sometimes seems as if he regards the intelligible world as irreducibly abstract. But this does not appear to be his considered position. For Leibniz is a nominalist who cannot countenance abstract objects as basic items of ontology; thus he must interpret talk of ideas in a way that does not involve a commitment to abstract objects. His solution to the problem is to reduce ideas to mental dispositions to think in certain ways.[67] But by thus reducing logical to mental entities, he has effectively transformed the philosophical content of the theory of divine illumination; he cannot mean, as Malebranche does, that we all perceive the same abstract objects in God. Indeed, when Leibniz says that God is the immediate external object of our minds, he means simply that He is the immediate external cause of our perceptions. God's causality here must be understood in such a way that it is consistent with Leibniz's doctrine that all the perceptual states of a human mind are caused by its earlier perceptual states.

Because of his reductionist tendencies, Leibniz is not really in a position to capture the theory of divine illumination. Nevertheless, his theory of ideas does have a significant theological dimension; it enables him to do justice to a different, but related, Christian doctrine. As against Malebranche, he insists that even if in a sense we saw all things in God, we should still need our own ideas; ideas, for him, may not be particular mental events, but they are genuine, though dispositional, properties of individual minds.[68] By insisting on this claim, he can bring out the truth of the Christian teaching that man is made in the image of God. Indeed, his whole technical theory of expression may be seen as an illustration of this Christian doctrine.[69]

The Augustinian conception of Christian philosophy is alien to the modern world; moreover, some readers may wonder how such an approach to philosophy can be justified. We have seen that, for Malebranche, philosophy and theology interact in two ways. Philosophy serves the cause of theology by preparing us for an informed acceptance of the truths of revelation; theology also serves the cause of philosophy inasmuch as the articles of religious faith play a rôle in the solution of philosophical problems. It is this latter aspect of the Augustinian conception of philosophy which is likely to be especially troubling to the modern reader; for it may seem that the Augustinian is simply arguing from authority. But in general, Augustinian philosophy, as practised by Malebranche, does not appear to be seriously vulnerable on this score. It is true that, for Malebranche, theological doctrines play a heuristic rôle in the discovery of philosophical truth. It is also true that he appeals to scriptural and patristic texts in support of philosophical doctrines. But it is a mistake to suppose that he lacks genuine arguments for his conclusions. For him, there are purely philosophical arguments for recognising the existence of a 'third realm'; the conflation of logic and psychology is a philosophical mistake. As a believing Christian, Malebranche naturally expects that Christian teaching will harmonise with philosophical truth, for truth must be indivisible. But this does not mean that Malebranche can argue for his theories only by appealing to the authority of the gospel.

In England the use of philosophy for theological purposes is perhaps nowhere more conspicuous than in the work of the Cambridge Platonists. The case of More is instructive. Throughout his career he was above all a Christian apologist; he revealingly described himself as 'a Fisher for Philosophers, desirous to draw them to or retain them in the Christian faith'.[70] He devoted much of his philosophical energy to attempting to prove the existence of God and the immortality of the soul, and he was prepared to use any arguments, of whatever philosophical inspiration, which in his view would effectively achieve these goals.

Significantly, he laid down a list of rules for philosophising which indicate that the choice of principles and arguments should be governed as much by their conformity with religious truths as by their intrinsic philosophical plausibility.[71]

Although More was always a Christian apologist, his theological militancy increased in later years, and this fact may help to explain his changing attitude towards Descartes. Despite some reservations, he initially welcomed Descartes's philosophy. He approved not just of Descartes's arguments for the existence of God and the immateriality of the soul, but also of his insistence on the infinity – strictly, in Descartes's formulation, the indefiniteness – of the physical universe. In More's eyes this doctrine provided support for belief in the omnipotence and infinite goodness of the Creator.[72] In later years, however, More's attitude to Descartes became much more critical; he was increasingly disturbed by the mechanist side of Descartes's philosophy. As a philosopher More believed that mechanist principles were insufficient to explain all physical phenomena; as a Christian apologist he believed that Descartes's mechanism was far too close to Epicurean philosophy to have any place in the campaign against atheism. Indeed, More came to hold that, in the words of one scholar, mechanism was 'tailor-made for the atheist's purposes'.[73] Although he never accused Descartes himself of atheism, he thought that in his philosophy he had shown a lack of commitment to the defence of the Christian religion.

V. PHILOSOPHY AND THEOLOGICAL CONFLICTS

The history of theological conflicts in the seventeenth century is marked by both continuity and innovation. The classic issues of the Reformation continued to be at the centre of theological controversy; at the same time quite radical doctrines were born from the turmoil of the civil and religious wars. The new philosophy exercised a fertilising influence on both kinds of development. On the one hand, the issues of the Reformation, such as grace and transubstantiation, had to be reformulated within a new conceptual framework; on the other hand, the rise of anti-scholastic, corpuscularian philosophy was closely intertwined with the growth of the radical Protestant sects. From a philosophical perspective, perhaps the most important of the radical movements was the Socinian sect, for their theological innovations stimulated the development of materialist thought.

1. Transubstantiation

One issue that was decisively transformed by the new philosophy was the Catholic dogma of transubstantiation. This dogma had been traditionally formulated in terms of the categories of Aristotelian metaphysics; the scholastics interpreted the doctrine as a supernatural variant on the ordinary processes of change as they understood them. According to Aquinas, for instance, natural changes involve only a thing's forms; in transubstantiation, however, the whole substance of the bread and wine, matter as well as form, is changed into the substance of the body and blood of Christ.[74] The doctrine was so closely wedded to scholasticism that seventeenth-century philosophers, such as Arnauld, questioned whether it could be formulated except in terms of the traditional categories.[75] The fact that transubstantiation was supposed to be miraculous provided some room for manoeuvre, but defenders of the dogma still had to show that the new philosophy had the conceptual resources to accommodate it.

Attitudes to transubstantiation were powerfully influenced by sectarian allegiances. Catholic philosophers, such as Descartes, Desgabets and Rohault, sought to defend the dogma within the framework of the new, anti-scholastic philosophy.[76] Protestant thinkers, such as Hobbes, Locke, Boyle, Newton and Jurieu, scathingly dismissed it as a superstitious relic of scholasticism; indeed, both Hobbes and Newton questioned Descartes's integrity in seeking to defend it.[77] Yet there are also complicating factors. Ironically, radical Protestant partisans of the new philosophy shared one major assumption with conservative Catholics such as the Jesuits; they were both convinced that the truth of scholastic principles was a necessary condition of the possibility of transubstantiation. Moreover, not all Protestant philosophers were openly hostile to the doctrine. As a Lutheran, Leibniz was under no doctrinal pressure to accept transubstantiation, but as an ecumenist, he was interested in showing how it could be accommodated within his own philosophy.

In the Fourth Objections, Arnauld warns Descartes that it is with respect to the Eucharist that he can expect most trouble from the theologians.[78] With his characteristic lucidity Arnauld explains why transubstantiation is a serious problem on Descartes's principles. Catholic doctrine seems to require that the sensible qualities of the bread remain despite a change in substance. 'We believe on faith', says Arnauld, 'that the substance of the bread is taken away and only the accidents remain. These are extension, shape, colour, smell, taste and other qualities perceived by the senses.'[79] But on Descartes's principles there are no sensible qualities which are not reducible to the primary qualities of bodies. Moreover, Descartes holds that there is only a formal or conceptual distinction between such qualities and the substance in which they inhere. Transubstantiation is a miracle, but in Descartes's system it is not clear that there is room for a miracle here; for it would seem that not even God could separate the states of a substance from the substance itself.

In the Fourth Replies, Descartes takes up each of Arnauld's two main objections. In the first place, Descartes explains how the properties of the bread may be said to survive in a way that is consistent with his philosophy of matter. To this end he provides his own gloss on the Tridentine formula that 'the form of the bread remains unaltered' in transubstantiation; according to Descartes, the 'form' can mean only 'the surface that is common to the individual particles of the bread and the bodies which surround them'.[80] Second, he insists that he had never actually denied the existence of real accidents – that is, accidents which can exist without inhering in any substance. In a veiled allusion to his extreme views concerning divine omnipotence, he remarks that he does not wish to deny that modes can be separated from their substance by the absolute power of God.[81] This is a very minimal concession, for on Descartes's principles it is consistent with the claim that such a separation is logically impossible.[82] But in fact he does not really want to take his stand on the possibility of real accidents. In a passage originally suppressed by Mersenne, Descartes proceeds to argue against them; indeed, he expresses the hope that the time will come when they are rejected by theologians as 'irrational, incomprehensible, and hazardous for the faith'.[83]

Descartes makes his most controversial suggestion regarding transubstantiation in response not to Arnauld but to the Jesuit Mesland. To the question of how the body of Christ can be enclosed within the dimensions of the bread, Descartes replies with some general reflections on the identity conditions of bodies: the child and the adult into which he grows have numerically the same body despite the change in determinate physical properties.[84] What constitutes the identity of the body in this case is the fact that the body of the child and the body of the man are informed by one and the same soul. It is this suggestion that he exploits for the purposes of explaining transubstantiation: 'The miracle of transubstantiation which takes place in the Blessed Sacrament consists in nothing but the fact that the particles of bread and wine, which in order for the soul of Jesus Christ to inform them naturally would have had to mingle with his blood and dispose themselves in certain specific ways, are informed by his soul simply by the power of the words of consecration.'[85] We can see that Descartes's suggestion provides him with a way of dealing with an issue raised by Arnauld. On Descartes's view, the accidents of the bread need not be separated from their substance at all in transubstantiation; the particles of the bread remain, but they become the body of Christ simply by virtue of being informed by his soul. Thus transubstantiation is construed as something like a union of two substances. Descartes's advocacy of this suggestion is tentative, and he is aware that it may appear shocking; indeed, he even asked Mesland not to disclose his authorship of the letters. Descartes's prudence was amply justified, for when his Benedictine disciple, Desgabets, later published a very similar account of transubstantiation, he was roundly denounced by Arnauld as heretical.[86]

Leibniz's interest in the topic of transubstantiation should be seen in the wider context of his lifelong ecumenism. For many years he worked for the reunion of Catholic and Protestant churches; in correspondence with Bossuet and others, he sought to remove the doctrinal obstacles in the way of reconciliation. In his philosophy Leibniz's ecumenical convictions find expression in a desire to accommodate Catholic dogma as far as possible. Transubstantiation was a major concern in this respect. As a young protégé of the Catholic convert Boineburg, Leibniz tried to reconcile the dogma with philosophical ideas which he was later to abandon as immature.[87] Around 1686 he discussed transubstantiation again in a work called the *Systema Theologicum*.[88] Here he argued that it was impossible for Descartes to explain the dogma in terms of his theory of matter, and he claimed that his own revival of substantial forms put him in a better position to explain it. Towards the end of his life transubstantiation became an even more serious concern. In 1709 the Jesuit Des Bosses invited him to show how transubstantiation could be explained in terms of the theory of monads, and the discussion continued, with interruptions, for the rest of Leibniz's life. Although Leibniz's interest in this project is in part political, it is a mistake to suppose that he writes about transubstantiation as a diplomatist, not as a philosopher.[89] In fact, his attempts to do justice to the doctrine are a good deal less ad hoc than Descartes's. It is true that Leibniz exploits the famous, or notorious, theory of the substantial bond (*vinculum substantiale*) in the interest of explaining the Catholic dogma, but we shall see that this theory was also developed to meet strictly philosophical problems in the theory of monads.[90]

Despite its later prominence in the correspondence with Des Bosses, the theory of substantial bonds plays no rôle in Leibniz's first attempt at explaining transubstantiation. On the contrary, when Des Bosses initially broached the issue, Leibniz suggested a way of understanding the dogma in terms of 'the hypothesis of mere monads':

If you hold that real accidents remain without a subject, it must be said that when the monads constituting the bread are removed as far as their primitive active and passive forces are concerned, and the presence of the monads constituting the body of Christ is substituted in their place, only the derivative forces which were in the bread remain, exhibiting the same phenomena which the monads of the bread would have exhibited.[91]

It has sometimes been suggested that this proposal was too phenomenalistic for Des Bosses's Catholic taste; in other words, it fails to do justice to the Catholic doctrine that the accidents of the bread and wine survive the miracle of transubstantiation in fact and not just in appearance.[92] This criticism is misguided, for given Leibniz's conception of derivative forces, it is not just the appearance of whiteness, for instance, but the physical basis of whiteness that remains. It is true that Des Bosses criticised this way of understanding transubstantiation, but not because it was too phenomenalistic. Rather, Des Bosses objected that the theory seemed internally incoherent. Since, according to Leibniz, the derivative forces are merely modifications of the primitive forces, Des Bosses could not understand how they could survive the removal of the latter.[93]

Leibniz next proposed his famous account of transubstantiation in terms of substantial bonds – substantial entities over and above monads:

> Granting these things, I should think that your theory of transubstantiation can be explained as follows: the monads would be preserved – this seems more in accordance with reason and the order of the universe – but the substantial bond of the body of Christ would be added by God in order to unify substantially the monads of the bread and wine, when the former substantial bond, together with its modifications or accidents, has been destroyed. Thus there would remain only the phenomena of the monads of the bread and wine, which would have been there if no substantial bond had been added by God to the monads [of the bread and wine].[94]

Although he does not completely endorse it, there seem to have been several reasons for his preference for this way of explaining transubstantiation. In the first place, he is able to avoid the objection of incoherence which Des Bosses had raised against his first proposal. Indeed, in the present proposal Leibniz makes no appeal whatever to the notion of real accidents – that is, accidents which can remain without inhering in any subject; this was a decided advantage in his eyes, for as he told Des Bosses, he found such an idea unintelligible.[95] Second, the explanation in terms of substantial bonds has the merit that it does not involve the destruction of monads; the substantial bonds may be destroyed, but the original monads are left intact. For Leibniz, the destruction of monads is not a logical impossibility, but it would be a miracle, and miracles are not to be unnecessarily multiplied.[96] Third, and perhaps most important, the theory of substantial bonds solved what he was increasingly coming to see as a problem in the doctrine of monads. In correspondence with Des Bosses he expresses his concern that 'the hypothesis of mere monads' cannot do justice to the unity which is possessed at least by organic bodies; thus something substantial must be postulated which unifies their monads.[97] The bread and wine are not themselves organic bodies (corporeal substances), but they are aggregates of them, and it is the monads of these organic bodies which must be unified by the substantial bonds.

Leibniz thus has philosophical reasons for preferring to explain the Catholic dogma in terms of substantial bonds. If transubstantiation is to be countenanced at all, it must be explained in a way that satisfies his philosophical conscience. Moreover, he had grounds for postulating substantial bonds which were quite independent of the demands of a Catholic dogma which he did not himself accept; the theory filled a lacuna in the doctrine of monads. Thus it is not fair to say that the theory of the substantial bonds is merely the concession of a diplomatist, not the philosopher. In fact, judged as a diplomatic manoeuvre, the theory was not really successful. Des Bosses raised theological scruples against it; it did not do justice to the Catholic dogma that in the Eucharist the whole substance of the bread and wine is destroyed.[98] Since, according to Leibniz's proposal, the monads remain intact, there is something substantial in the bread and wine which survives the miracle of transubstantiation.

2. Socinianism, mortalism, and materialism

As an ecumenist Leibniz tried to placate the Catholics over transubstantiation, but his ecumenism had its limits; it certainly did not extend to the radical Protestant sect of the Socinians. Leibniz's alarm over the growth of this sect was shared by many Protestants and Catholics in the period; for unlike Catholics and mainstream Protestants, the Socinians denied both the Trinity and the divinity of Christ. Deriving their name from the Italian Sozzini family of the sixteenth century, the Socinians had originally flourished in Poland where they issued the Racovian catechism; when they were driven out by the Jesuits, they moved westwards, finding refuge and winning disciples in Holland and England. Since few were willing to identify themselves publicly as Socinians, it is difficult to say precisely who should be counted among their number. But there is little doubt they found sympathisers among many leading philosophers, theologians, scientists, and men of letters. In varying degrees Hobbes, Locke, and Newton all came under the influence of Socinianism, and accepted some, if not all, of its most distinctive theological tenets.[99]

Traditionally, the Socinians have been seen as forerunners of the deist movement that flourished in the eighteenth century, but this is somewhat misleading. It is true that deists and Socinians, or Unitarians as they came to be known, may have converged in their views on a number of issues, but the grounds on which they held them were rather different. Unlike the deists, the Socinians were not hostile to revelation *per se*; on the contrary, they shared the common Protestant belief in the supremacy of Scripture as the rule of faith. Indeed, they carried to extremes the typically Protestant desire to restore Christianity to its original form; they wished to purge their religion of the hellenising tendencies which in their belief had perverted the simplicity of the gospel message. It was for this reason, among others, that they were led to reject the doctrines of the Trinity and the Incarnation. In their view these doctrines were lacking in an adequate scriptural foundation; they were rather the product of the corrupting influence of Greek philosophy.

For their contemporaries as a whole, the most shocking tenets of Socinian theology were undoubtedly the denial of the Trinity and the divinity of Christ. But among philosophers they were perhaps equally notorious for their commitment to the mortalist heresy; this is the doctrine which denies the existence of a naturally immortal soul.[100] It is the mortalist tenet of their theology which has the most interesting philosophical implications, for it is intimately connected with materialism.

Although he is not normally counted a Socinian, Hobbes shares their commitment to the mortalist thesis, and he presents an interesting version of the doctrine in *Leviathan*. Like other mortalists such as Milton and Overton, Hobbes accepts that personal immortality is a gift of divine grace; since human beings perish totally at death, it is no part of the natural order.[101] Like other mortalists, too, he claims that the gift of immortality is bestowed solely on the elect, but he develops this theme in a rather unpleasant way. On his version of the doctrine, the damned will be resurrected, but only to die a second death. However, he argues that this second death will not happen until they have begotten children in the state of damnation; this ensures that the damned will persist collectively, but not individually, for all eternity (i.e. infinite time).[102] Unpleasant as it may appear, Hobbes's account embodies a typical feature of mortalism: damnation consists in death rather than an eternity of torments.

Unlike Hobbes, Locke is not a materialist, but he adopts a position on immortality which has some affinities with Hobbes's mortalism. For one thing, Locke agrees with Hobbes's epistemological claim that 'there is no naturall knowledge of mans estate after death';[103] in other words, personal immortality cannot be established independently of revelation by philosophical argument. In the *Reasonableness of Christianity* Locke insists, as Hobbes had done, that the doctrine of personal immortality is an article of faith; our assurance of it is founded on the promise that

Christ has made to us in the gospel. Indeed, Locke adds that the announcement of this promise is one of the main motives for Christ's mission.[104] In the *Essay* and elsewhere Locke develops a philosophical position which is fully consistent with the views expressed in his religious writings. First, he notoriously argues that the immateriality of the soul cannot be proved; it is at least epistemically possible that the thinking principle in us is material.[105] Second, he holds that even if such a proof were available, it would not serve to establish personal immortality. Simply by virtue of being a substance, an immaterial soul would, if it existed, be indestructible, but such indestructibility is not sufficient, and perhaps not even necessary, for personal immortality. What personal immortality essentially involves is continuity of consciousness, and this must be something added by the grace of God.[106] Thus, despite his agnosticism about the immateriality of the soul, Locke can be said to have thought along mortalist lines.

Leibniz was one philosopher who was troubled by Locke's apparent sympathy for mortalism. In a private letter Leibniz charged that Locke 'inclined to the Socinians', and in support of this charge he claimed, somewhat unfairly, that 'Locke undermines the immateriality of the soul.'[107] Leibniz's campaign against the Socinian heresy did not begin with his reading of Locke. From an early date in his career Leibniz had made a serious study of Socinian teachings, and the main lines of his critique were soon fixed; he complained that the Socinians denied the natural immortality of the soul, and that they buttressed their mortalism with the help of materialist arguments.[108] Although it would be a mistake to describe it as an anti-Socinian tract, even the *Nouveaux essais,* Leibniz's philosophical critique of Locke, can be read as an attack on the heresy. For as Leibniz told a correspondent, his main aim in this work was 'to vindicate the immateriality of the soul which M. Locke leaves doubtful'.[109] In the *Nouveaux essais* Leibniz approaches this task obliquely: he defends a number of doctrines, such as innate ideas and the thesis that the soul always thinks, because as he sees it, they are logical consequences of the soul's immateriality.[110]

The doctrine of mortalism is interesting as a case study in the interaction of philosophy and theology. As the example of Hobbes reminds us, a philosopher might come to embrace mortalism by a mainly philosophical route. In the seventeenth century there were good reasons why materialism should have found favour with some philosophers; it offers the advantages of a unified conceptual framework which avoids the difficulties which result when the mind is exempted from the reign of physical causality. And if the immateriality and natural immortality of the soul are thought to stand and fall together, the materialist, such as Hobbes, will see himself as logically committed to the core thesis of mortalism –

namely, the denial of a naturally immortal soul. For a philosopher wishing to do justice to Christian faith, it then becomes attractive to argue that personal immortality is a gift of divine grace which begins at the general resurrection.

Yet it is also plausible to suppose that there were influences running in the opposite direction. For theological reasons alone, mortalism could seem an attractive option in the seventeenth century. For the Socinians the doctrine of a naturally immortal soul was unscriptural; it was an instance of the infection of Christianity by Greek philosophy, and it opened the door to such gratuitous absurdities as the Catholic doctrine of purgatory. Moreover, mortalism was a compelling position for the increasing number of those who were offended by the traditional idea of hell; it offered a way of interpreting the doctrine of damnation without recourse to the notion of eternal torments.[111] Mortalism satisfied the typically seventeenth-century craving for a theodicy. The Socinians and other radical theologians were thus led to mortalism for theological reasons, and the quest for philosophical underpinnings for this doctrine could lead them to embrace a form of materialism.

3. Miracles

Any philosopher in the Christian tradition must find some way of accommodating the biblical reports of miracles. It is fair to say, however, that even religiously orthodox philosophers in our period betray some discomfort when writing on this topic. The source of this discomfort is not difficult to identify. The whole tendency of seventeenth-century philosophy was in the direction of recognising the universe as a vast machine governed by a comprehensive system of physical laws, and philosophers were often reluctant to admit that these laws might be suspended or that there might be limits to their comprehensiveness. Even Malebranche, a devout Catholic, was so much of his age that he was prepared to say that God's glory was manifested more in his general laws than in his particular volitions.[112] Moreover, philosophers whose religious orthodoxy was not in question were tempted to suppose that at least some of the miracles of the Bible might be given a purely naturalistic interpretation; if they were miracles, it was because they were prodigies, rare events which in context could be construed as signs of divine power, not because they violated the laws of nature.[113] Such philosophers admitted that there were also genuine miracles, events which did violate the laws of nature, but their number might be smaller than one might suppose.[114]

The problem of miracles comes to the forefront of philosophical controversy in the work of Spinoza; indeed, it is not too much to say that subsequent discussion of the subject is, either explicitly or implicitly, a response to his challenge. It is he who does most to articulate the dominant assumptions of the new mechanistic philosophy, and to draw out their logical implications. For first, he argues that every event falls within a comprehensive system of causal laws; in other words, there can be no random event. Second, he holds that the causal laws which govern the physical world possess the same kind of necessity as the truths of logic and mathematics.[115] It is this second thesis, in particular, which raises the problem of miracles in an acute form. For such a necessitarian or rationalistic view of the laws of nature implies that miracles are logically impossible, if a miracle is defined in a traditional fashion as an event contrary to the laws of nature. In the *Tractatus Theologico-Politicus* he provided *a posteriori* support for his thesis by showing how the biblical miracles could be explained in naturalistic terms. As noted earlier, even orthodox philosophers believed that at least some of the biblical miracles could be interpreted in this way, but Spinoza went further in this direction than anyone else; for him, there is no biblical miracle which cannot be explained naturalistically, and he showed in some detail how this might be done.[116] Thus he issued a challenge to his contemporaries which they could hardly ignore. If philosophers were to meet this challenge, they must either deny his necessitarian view of the laws of nature or provide some alternative definition of a miracle. These two strategies could be combined, but either was sufficient to meet the Spinozistic challenge.

One philosopher who adopted the first strategy for answering Spinoza's challenge is Malebranche; he denies that the laws of nature are logically necessary. In his system this has the consequence that the laws of nature cannot be genuinely causal; for according to him, the causal relation is a logically necessary one: 'A true cause is one such that the mind perceives a necessary connection between it and its effect.'[117] He is quite happy to draw the consequence that there is no genuine causality in the created world. Indeed, according to occasionalist teaching, God alone is the true cause, and the laws of nature involve the workings only of occasional causality.

Since Malebranche holds that the laws of nature are not logically necessary, he can consistently claim that they can be broken; thus he has created the conceptual space for miracles, and has met Spinoza's challenge. In spite of this, Malebranche's treatment of miracles got him into trouble with his contemporaries. He insisted so strongly on the claim that God acts through general volitions that some critics, such as Arnauld, were misled into supposing that he left no room for miracles.[118] Unlike Spinoza, Malebranche may hold that the laws of nature can be broken, but he did seem committed to the weaker thesis that as a matter of contingent fact they never are. Malebranche replied that he had been misunderstood by Arnauld;

he did not intend to deny that God sometimes suspends the laws of nature by acting through particular volitions.[119] He in fact defines a miracle in the strict sense as an event which is brought about by God's particular volition, and he draws the somewhat surprising conclusion that a miracle need not be empirically detectable; for there is no contradiction in supposing that God might bring about a quite ordinary event through a particular volition.[120]

Essentially the same strategy for answering Spinoza was adopted by Leibniz. The issue of necessity in Leibniz's philosophy is controversial, but his official position is not in doubt: the laws of nature are physically but not logically or absolutely necessary; unlike the truths of logic, for instance, they are not invariant between possible worlds. He also makes the equivalent point that the laws of nature are only hypothetically necessary; that is, they are necessary on the assumption that God chooses the best of all possible worlds.[121] Thus, like Malebranche, he is in a position to hold that the laws of nature can be suspended without logical absurdity. Leibniz's principal conception of a miracle is that it is an event which is beyond the power of finite substances to produce. It is in terms of this conception, for instance, that he argues against occasionalism and the Newtonian theory of attraction.[122] Sometimes Leibniz seems to define a miracle in epistemological terms; he says that a miracle is an event which cannot be understood by any created spirit.[123] He may well have regarded these definitions as at least extensionally equivalent: an event cannot be understood by a created spirit if and only if it surpasses the power of finite substances.

An alternative strategy to that adopted by Leibniz and Malebranche is to redefine a miracle so that it does not imply a suspension of the laws of nature; on this approach, there is no need to give up the rationalistic conception of natural laws. Perhaps surprisingly, such a strategy was adopted by Locke. In his essay on miracles, he conspicuously avoids defining a miracle as an event contrary to the laws of nature; rather, for him, a miracle is a 'sensible operation which, being above the comprehension of the spectator, and in his opinion contrary to the established course of nature, is taken by him to be divine'.[124] His explicit reason for preferring this definition is clear. He argues that, on the traditional definition, the whole purpose of miracles is destroyed, for since most people are ignorant of the laws of nature, they could not know when a miracle has occurred.[125] But he also has a more implicit reason for adopting his definition. Like Spinoza, Locke is attracted by a rationalistic view of the laws of nature. There is a necessary connexion between the antecedent and the consequent of such laws, and according to him, not even God can break a necessary connexion.[126] Thus both Locke's agnosticism and his rationalism furnish him with motives for rejecting the

view of miracles which Malebranche and Leibniz adopted. It is a curious irony of
seventeenth-century philosophy that in this area Locke is more rationalistic than
either Leibniz or Malebranche.

At the beginning of this chapter it was suggested that theology was not simply a
negative factor, but that it had a creative influence on philosophy as well. The
truth of this claim should now be evident. Today it is easy to suppose that the
revival of materialist thought is simply a product of the scientific revolution, but
this account is obviously one-sided; on the contrary, its origins are to be found at
least in part in the heresy of mortalism. It is arguable, too, that the problem of
miracles was a stimulus to the development of empiricist views in the philosophy
of science. Christian philosophers had to find some way of meeting Spinoza's
challenge, and one way of doing so was to give up the necessitarian view of the
laws of nature. Thus philosophical doctrines which have wide currency today
arose in the context of theological controversies. Historians of philosophy have
been so impressed by the scientific revolution that they have sometimes neglected
to give theology the credit it deserves.

NOTES

1 See, e.g., *Lev.* xlvi: 'Of Darknesse from Vain Philosophy, and Fabulous Traditions',
   Hobbes 1968, pp. 682–703.
2 See Copleston 1972, p. 6. Copleston attributes this view to Gilson.
3 See Chadwick 1967; Markus 1967; Copleston 1972, chaps. 2, 3, and 6.
4 See Hyman and Walsh 1973, pp. 415–16; Copleston 1972, p. 163.
5 Copleston 1972, p. 182.
6 Thomas Aquinas, *Summa th.* I q1 a1; Aristotle, *Metaphysics* V.1 (1026a 19).
7 Thomas Aquinas, *Summa th.* I q1 a8.
8 The issue of Ockham's attitude to proofs of God's existence is controversial. See
   Copleston 1972, pp. 250–1.
9 *Notae in programma,* AT VIIIB 353. Descartes also distinguishes a third kind of question:
   'questions which have nothing whatever to do with faith, and which are the concern
   solely of human reasoning' (ibid.). I have made use of the cited translations, but I have
   sometimes made changes of my own.
10 *Notae in programma,* AT VIIIB 353.
11 *Notae in programma,* AT VIIIB 353.
12 AT VII 1. The sub-title of the first edition (1641) of the *Meditationes* read: 'In which are
   demonstrated the existence of God and the immortality of the soul.' In the second
   edition (1642) this was changed to: 'In which are demonstrated the existence of God
   and the distinctness of the human soul from the body.'
13 Descartes to Mersenne, 15 April 1630, AT I 143–4.
14 Descartes to Mesland, 2 May 1644, AT IV 117.

15 Descartes to Mersenne, 31 March 1641, AT III 349–50.
16 On Hobbes's antecedents see Glover 1965, pp. 141–68; Hepburn 1972, pp. 85–108.
17 *Lev.* xxxiv, Hobbes 1968, p. 430.
18 Hepburn 1972, p. 85. On Hobbes's relation to Reformation theology, see Damrosch 1979, pp. 339–52.
19 *Lev.* xliv, Hobbes 1968, p. 629.
20 *Lev.* xlvi, Hobbes 1968, p. 687.
21 *Lev.* xv, Hobbes 1968, p. 206; *Lev.* xxxviii, Hobbes 1968, p. 483; *Lev.* xliv, Hobbes 1968, p. 644.
22 *Lev.* xxxi, Hobbes 1968, p. 404; *Lev.* xxxiv, Hobbes 1968, p. 430.
23 Cf. Hepburn 1972, pp. 101–8, esp. p. 108.
24 See, e.g., *Lev.* xlvi, Hobbes 1968, pp. 689–90.
25 The issue of whether the laws of nature for Hobbes are known to be divine laws only because they are found in Scripture is a controversial one. However, it is supported by *De Cive.* See Gauthier 1969, p. 187.
26 See, for instance, *Tract. th.-pol.* XIV, Geb. III 173–80.
27 Geb. III 179.
28 *Tract. th.-pol.* XIII, Geb. III 172.
29 *Tract. th.-pol.* XIV, Geb. III 179–80.
30 *Tract. th.-pol.* XV, Geb. III 180–8.
31 *Tract. th.-pol.* XV, Geb. III 182.
32 See Allison 1987, p. 219.
33 *Tract. th.-pol.* XV, Geb. III 183.
34 *Pens.* 513.
35 *Pens.* 887.
36 *Pens.* 131.
37 Med. III, AT VII 40–1.
38 Huet 1689, pp. 178–9.
39 *Pens.* 449.
40 *Pens.* 190.
41 *Pens.* 449.
42 *Pens.* 449.
43 *Pens.* 424.
44 *Pens.* 781.
45 General Scholium, *Principia,* Newton 1972, vol. 2, p. 760 (Newton 1934, p. 544). Cf. *Opticks,* Query 28, Newton 1952, pp. 369–70.
46 Newton to Bentley, 10 December 1692, Newton 1978, p. 280. On Newton's view of the relation between science and religion, see Westfall 1958, chap. 8.
47 Yahuda MS. 15.7, fol. 190^r , quoted in Manuel 1974, p. 72.
48 Westfall 1980, p. 314.
49 Newton 1972, vol. 2, p. 760 (Newton 1934, p. 544).
50 Westfall 1980, p. 826.
51 *Rech.,* Preface, Mal. *OC* I 9–10 (Malebranche 1980a, p. xix).
52 See, e.g., Descartes to Colvius, 14 November 1640, AT III 247–8. For the quotation from Augustine, see *De civitate Dei* XI.26.
53 For an account of the propaganda use that was made of Descartes's Augustinian tendencies, see Gouhier 1978.
54 The Oratorian order, which was founded by Cardinal Bérulle in 1611, was dedicated to

the renewal of Augustinian studies. Apart from Malebranche, two prominent Oratorians who were sympathetic to Descartes were Ambrosius Victor (pseudonym for André Martin) and Père Poisson. See Gouhier 1978, chap. 4; McCracken 1983, pp. 54–5.

55 See Markus 1967, p. 352; Copleston 1972, pp. 30–1.

56 Markus 1967, pp. 352–3. Cf. Gueroult 1955–9, vol. 1, pp. 17–18, for a very helpful account of the relationship between philosophy and theology in Malebranche.

57 Gueroult 1955–9, vol. 1, pp. 17–18.

58 Med. I, AT VII 18.

59 Med. VI, AT VII 83.

60 See, e.g., *Rech.* I.1.5, Mal. *OC* I 69–77 (Malebranche 1980a, pp. 19–23); *Conversations Chrétiennes,* Mal. *OC* IV 40–1. Cf. McCracken 1983, p. 25; Radner 1978, p. 131. For Glanvill's use of the Fall, see *The Vanity of Dogmatizing,* chap. 1, Glanvill 1970, pp. 1–9.

61 Med. III, AT VII 40.

62 See, e.g., *Rech.* III.2.6, Mal. *OC* I 445 (Malebranche 1980a, p. 234). For Malebranche's critique of Descartes's theory of ideas, see Jolley 1990, chap. 4, pp. 55–80.

63 *Rech.* III.2.6, Mal. *OC* I 440 (Malebranche 1980a, p. 231).

64 *Disc. mét.,* sec. 28, Ger. IV 453 (Leibniz 1969, p. 321). Shortly before composing the *Disc. mét.,* Leibniz had read Malebranche's *Traité de la nature et de la grâce;* the *Disc. mét.* can indeed be seen as an answer to some of Malebranche's claims in the *Traité.* See Robinet 1955, pp. 139–40.

65 *Meditationes de cognitione, veritate et ideis,* Ger. IV 426 (Leibniz 1969, p. 294); *Entretien de Philarete et d'Ariste,* Ger. VI 593–4 (Leibniz 1969, p. 627).

66 *De rerum originatione radicali,* Ger. VII 305 (Leibniz 1969, p. 488).

67 *Quid sit idea?* Ger. VII 263 (Leibniz 1969, p. 207). Cf. Mates 1986, esp. p. 246.

68 *Meditationes de cognitione, veritate et ideis,* Ger. IV 426 (Leibniz 1969, p. 294).

69 See Brown 1984, p. 58; Craig 1987, pp. 51–64.

70 More 1664, p. 494, quoted in Gabbey 1982, p. 228.

71 More's third rule is perhaps particularly instructive: 'That himself is to make choice to such Principles or Conclusions of Philosophy as, having no real repugnancy with Scripture are also of themselves the most unexceptionably tenable and demonstrable, and the most easily accordable with the Attributes of God and the *Phaenomena* of Providence; and as well prevent or answer the greatest Objections the Atheist can excogitate against either the Existence of God or the Immortality of the Soul and a Reward in the World to come.' More 1664, pp. 483–9, quoted in Gabbey 1982, p. 227.

72 More 1646, A2r-v, quoted in Gabbey 1982, pp. 179–80. It should be remarked that More disapproved of Descartes's use of the term 'indefinite' as opposed to 'infinite'.

73 Gabbey 1982, p. 233.

74 Thomas Aquinas, *Summa th.* III q75 a4. Cf. Fitzpatrick 1987, pp. 120–43. Cf. Suárez, *Disp. met.,* XL.4.8.

75 See Obj. IV, AT VII 217–8.

76 See Armogathe 1977; Watson 1982, pp. 127–8; Nadler 1988a, pp. 229–46.

77 According to Aubrey, Hobbes 'could not pardon [Descartes] for writing in the Defence of Transubstantiation, which he knew to bee absolutely against his judgement, and donne meerly to putt a compliment on the Jesuites'. Aubrey 1972, p. 185. Newton told a friend that he was grateful that, as an Englishman, he was 'not obliged as Des Cartes was to go into a strange country and to say he proved transubstantiation by his philosophy.' Manuel 1974, p. 31. For Jurieu, see Nadler 1988a, p. 242. For Locke's views on transubstantiation, see *Ess.* IV.xx.10.

78 Obj. IV, AT VII 217.
79 AT VII 217.
80 Resp. IV, AT VII, p. 251. On transubstantiation and the Council of Trent, see Armogathe 1977, Section I; (Rodis-)Lewis 1950b, pp. 68f.
81 AT VII 249.
82 Descartes holds that the eternal truths of logic and mathematics are dependent upon the divine will and could have been other than they are. See, e.g., Descartes to Mersenne, 15 April 1630, AT I 145.
83 AT VII 255.
84 Descartes to Mesland, 9 February 1645, AT IV 166–7.
85 AT IV 168.
86 See Armogathe 1977, pp. 85–113; Nadler 1988a, p. 237.
87 *Demonstrationes catholicae,* LAkad VI.I 508–12 (Leibniz 1969, pp. 115–19).
88 *Systema Theologicum,* Leibniz 1860, pp. 127–9.
89 This criticism is made by Russell; Russell 1937, p. 152.
90 On the scholastic background to Leibniz's theory of the *vinculum substantiale,* see Boehm 1962.
91 Leibniz to Des Bosses, 8 September 1709, Ger. II 390–1.
92 See Broad 1975, p. 126.
93 Des Bosses to Leibniz, 18 January 1710, Ger. II 396.
94 Leibniz to Des Bosses, 20 September 1712, Ger. II 459 (Leibniz 1969, p. 607). I have considerably altered Loemker's translation.
95 Leibniz to Des Bosses, 20 September 1712, Ger. II 458 (Leibniz 1969, p. 606).
96 Leibniz to Des Bosses, 24 January 1713, Ger. II 474 (Leibniz 1969, p. 608). Cf. Adams 1983, p. 252. My account is considerably indebted to Adams's discussion.
97 Leibniz to Des Bosses, 5 February 1712, Ger. II 435 (Leibniz 1969, p. 600).
98 Des Bosses to Leibniz, 12 December 1712, Ger. II 463. Cf. Adams 1983, p. 252.
99 On Socinianism, see McLachlan 1951.
100 See Burns 1972 for a discussion of the different versions of mortalism current in the seventeenth century.
101 *Lev.* xxxviii, Hobbes 1968, p. 483; *Lev.* xliv, Hobbes 1968, p. 644. On Milton and Overton see Burns 1972, chap. 4.
102 *Lev.* xliv, Hobbes 1968, pp. 647–9. On this issue, see Pocock 1972.
103 *Lev.* xv, Hobbes 1968, p. 206. Locke does not draw attention to his agreement with Hobbes on this issue.
104 Locke 1823, vol. 7, p. 122.
105 *Ess.* IV.iii.6.
106 See Locke's journal entry, 20 February 1682, Locke 1936, pp. 121–3. See also *Ess.* II.27 for Locke's mature theory of personal identity.
107 Leibniz to Bierling, 19 November 1709, Ger. VII 488–9.
108 Leibniz also complained that the Socinians denied divine foreknowledge. See the essay entitled *Ad Christophori Stegmanni Metaphysicam Unitariorum,* Jolley 1975, pp. 176–89, esp. pp. 176–8. Cf. Leibniz to Ernst von Hessen-Rheinfels, 10? January 1691, LAkad I.VI 159–60.
109 Leibniz to Jaquelot, 28 April 1704, Ger. III 473.
110 On this issue, see Jolley 1984.
111 See Walker 1964.
112 *Méditations Chrétiennes,* VII.22, Mal. *OC* X 79; *TNG,* Discourse I, Mal. *OC* V 11–64.

113 See, e.g., *Théod.*, Ger. VI 265. For the case of Malebranche, see Gouhier 1948, p. 65.

114 E.g., *Méditations Chrétiennes*, VIII.26, Mal. *OC* X 92; *TNG*, Eclaircissement IV, Mal. *OC* V 198.

115 *Tract. th.-pol.* VI, Geb. III 86. See J. Bennett 1984, p. 112.

116 See, e.g., *Tract. th.-pol.* VI, Geb. III 89–91.

117 *Rech.* VI.2.3, Mal. *OC* II 316 (Malebranche 1980a, p. 450).

118 See Gouhier 1948, p. 56.

119 *Reponse à la dissertation*, III.l, Mal. *OC* VII 485.

120 *Reponse au livre des réflexions*, I, Mal. *OC* VIII 696.

121 See, e.g., Leibniz 1903, pp. 19–20.

122 See Leibniz to Arnauld, 30 April 1687, Ger. II 93; Leibniz to Clarke, Third Paper, Ger. VII 366–7 (Leibniz 1969, p. 684). For a discussion of Leibniz's views on miracles, see McRae 1985.

123 *Disc. mét.*, sec. 16, Ger. IV 441 (Leibniz 1969, p. 313); Leibniz to Lady Masham, 30 June 1704, Ger. III 353.

124 *Discourse on Miracles*, Locke 1823, vol. 9, p. 256.

125 *Discourse on Miracles*, Locke 1823, vol. 9, p. 264.

126 Cf. Ayers 1981b, pp. 220–1.

14

THE RELIGIOUS BACKGROUND OF SEVENTEENTH-CENTURY PHILOSOPHY

RICHARD POPKIN

I. INTRODUCTION

The philosophy of the seventeenth century has often been seen as connected with a gradual march from religious orthodoxy and oppression towards pre-Enlightenment deism, agnosticism, atheism, and toleration. In reality, though, the world of seventeenth-century religious thought is much more complicated than this simple schema would suggest. To be sure, there is a strain of religious thought that appears to lead directly to the Enlightenment. However, there is a great deal more: widespread religious movements that are quite different in character, an undercurrent of interconnected religious ideas and developments which may now look strange and distant from philosophy but were familiar to, and were taken seriously by, all the major philosophers of the period. These philosophers lived in societies dominated by religious institutions and lived through tremendous upheavals that were fundamentally generated out of religious concerns – the Reformation, the Counter-Reformation, the Thirty Years' War, the Puritan Revolution, the pogroms in Poland, the revocation of the Edict of Nantes. The point is not simply that religious ideas and events had an important influence on the philosophical thought of the period. Rather, these religious issues were deeply intertwined with philosophical conceptions of knowledge, revelation, the importance of scientific inquiry, human nature, and what it is to be reasonable. This meant, among other things, that philosophical positions had serious consequences that went far beyond the classroom, academy, or salon, as the cases of Galileo, Bruno, and Vanini show in different ways.

It is impossible to give an adequate survey of the entire religious background to seventeenth-century thought in a single short essay, and I shall not attempt to do so here. Rather, I shall discuss a few aspects of the religious background that are relatively little known, but important for understanding the philosophy of the period. The reader should be warned that this is one scholar's selection, and that it makes no pretence of completeness.

We shall begin by looking at some aspects of the religious background that appear to parallel or support similar developments in the philosophy of the period. These include certain sceptical and probabilistic strains in seventeenth-century religious thought, the millenarian movement, and some strains of mystical thought. Then we shall turn to some very different features of seventeenth-century religious thought, features that led more and more to the rejection of orthodoxy. These include the increasing interest in Judaism and in other non-Christian religions, as well as direct challenges to the authority of the Bible, developments that made possible the growth of the secular philosophy of the Enlightenment.

II. A GREAT INSTAURATION

A striking feature of the new philosophy of the seventeenth century is its claim to a complete rejection of the corrupt old philosophy of the schools; figures like Bacon, Descartes, and Glanvill, to name only a few, claim to offer philosophy a brand new start. These new messiahs of the philosophical world are connected with important currents of thought in the religious world as well. Studies of the prophets led many to believe that a new religious messiah was immediately at hand; many saw the new philosophies that emerged in the seventeenth century as an integral part of the events to come.

The interpretation of prophecy was most important in seventeenth-century interpretations of what was going on in the natural and human world.[1] The fact that Hobbes began Book III of *Leviathan* and Spinoza began his *Tractatus Theologico-Politicus* with a discussion of prophets and prophetic knowledge reflects this.[2] Although prophecy had been part of biblical religion and continued to be of significance in the Middle Ages, it took on new importance as a result of the Reformation and Counter-Reformation, and as a result of major developments in Jewish history, especially the Expulsion of the Jews from Spain in 1492. Some thinkers saw in the development of new religious institutions in Christendom, and in the emergence of strong religio-political states involved with these institutions, that the fulfilment of crucial biblical prophecies was at hand. The Reformation was not just a bureaucratic rearrangement of an institution, but the *Reform,* and the *Restitution* of religion that would soon be followed by Jesus' return, by the establishment of the Messianic Kingdom, the Millennium, the Thousand Year Reign of Christ on Earth. The monumental transformation that was in the offing was that prophesied in the books of *Daniel* and *Revelation*.

Startling facts of natural and human history reinforced this reading of the 'signs of the times' – earthquakes, floods, plus the overthrow of Catholicism in some countries; the saving of others from Protestant activities; the 'miraculous defeat' of the Spanish Armada; the 'supernatural' victory of the Dutch over the Spanish armies and the watery forces of nature; the expansion of the European world through the Voyages of Discovery; the establishment of *New* England, *Nova* Scotia, *Nieuw* Amsterdam, *New* Sweden; the threat to Christendom from the Turkish invasions from the east. The emerging new political powers saw themselves as the New Israel (a view propounded in Scotland, then England, then The Netherlands, about themselves).[3]

In the minds of many, religious and philosophical Messianism were closely connected. Chief interpreters stressed the passage in *Daniel* that as we approached the end of pre-Millennial history, 'many shall run to and fro, and knowledge shall be increased' (Daniel 12:4). Knowledge would grow and the wise would understand. The wise will understand but the wicked will not. The rapid progress in knowledge in the Renaissance and the early seventeenth century certainly seemed to indicate to the adepts that the climax of human history was near at hand.[4]

Messianism and the idea of a new philosophy were also combined in the views of the group that Charles Webster has called the 'spiritual brotherhood', an international group of religiously oriented intellectuals, who saw themselves at the beginning of the Great Instauration. Their theoretician was Jan Amos Comenius, the exiled leader of the Moravian Brethren, and leader in a movement to modernise education. Comenius spelled out how knowledge is based first on sensory information, then on reason, and finally on understanding Scripture. The aim of educational reform was to achieve pansophia, universal knowledge, the state of knowledge forecast by Daniel at the transformation of human history.[5]

Comenius, John Dury, and their associate, Samuel Hartlib, tried to make the Puritan Revolution the laboratory for their spiritual reforms. They gathered in London in 1641 and issued a stream of pamphlets on 'reforming' (in the spiritual as well as practical sense) the dissemination of knowledge. They proposed a new school system, new universities, new scientific societies, a reorganised royal library.[6] When these plans failed to materialise in England, Comenius was offered the presidency of the newly founded college in the New World, Harvard, as a place for training colonists and Indians in universal knowledge. For better or worse he turned down the opportunity and devoted himself to writing the textbooks which changed European education.[7] In 1642 Comenius and Descartes met in a castle in The Netherlands to discuss the differences in their views.

Descartes left the meeting complaining that the great Comenius did not know enough mathematics, and Comenius complained that Descartes's knowledge of Scripture was too deficient for him to have true understanding.[8]

After all these preparations for the Messianic Age to come, a messiah did finally appear. But the consequences were far different from the expectations of those who had awaited his coming. In 1666 Sabbatai Zevi announced he was the long-awaited Messiah, a claim eventually accepted by vast numbers of Jews in Europe, Asia, and Africa. He soon started acting the part by changing Jewish law, Jewish prayers, holidays, replacing the kings of the earth, and so on. The Sultan had him arrested, and in jail Sabbatai held court for Jews from all over the world. But when the Sultan threatened to kill him, Sabbatai announced he always wanted to be a Moslem, put on a fez, and became a minor official of the Ottoman Empire. He lived ten years after his apostasy. Most Jews were heart-broken, and dismayed. His followers claimed that only his body had become Moslem, but his spirit would come back; he had to commit the greatest sin, they claimed, in order to save mankind. (These followers are still awaiting his second coming.)[9] Christian cynics pounced upon the sad episode to contend that Jews lacked a criterion of messiahship and could not tell a true from a false messiah. Hence they should become Christians.[10] In an immensely popular book called *Letters Writ by a Turkish Spy Living in Paris for 45 years* (also known as *L'Espion turc*), it was argued that they should give up rabbinical Judaism and adopt the religion of reason (which for the spy seems to have been a combination of Spinozism, pacificism, and vegetarianism.)[11] Further consideration of the Sabbatai Zevi case raised the question of whether Jesus was just the same sort of historical personality. If Sabbatai Zevi had been killed by the Sultan, the Jews might still accept him. But had Jesus any better credentials? The debacle of Jewish Messianism in the seventeenth century raised critical doubts about all Messianism.

III. SCEPTICAL CURRENTS

The importance of scepticism for understanding seventeenth-century philosophy is well established. But the sceptical currents in philosophy are also connected to certain trends in religious thought.

1. Sceptical arguments and sceptical religion

Leading religious thinkers of the early Reformation period, such as Erasmus and Luther, saw as one of the fundamental issues in dispute the establishment of a 'rule of faith', the criterion by which one distinguishes true religious knowledge from false views. Luther and Calvin insisted that the criterion in question was not the pronouncements of the institutional church, but rather one's conscience guided by the Holy Spirit and Scripture. The Catholics insisted that it was the church, and its teaching as set forth by the church fathers, popes, and church councils. This basic dispute was seen as a new version of the problem of the criterion set forth in Sextus Empiricus's ancient sceptical writings.[12] Catholic arguers tried to show how unreliable the Reformers' standards were, since they depended on subjective factors like conscience, and personal, perhaps, idiosyncratic, readings of Scripture. Using arguments from Sextus, Catholic arguers, like Father François Veron, S.J., a teacher at La Flèche when Mersenne and Descartes studied there, tried to undermine any and all attempts to ground faith on Scripture and conscience. Veron developed a powerful epistemological case that the Reformers could find no justification for identifying any book as the Bible, for identifying its contents, and for determining what religious beliefs to hold.[13] Protestants reversed the argument, contending Catholics had no way of determining with certainty who is the pope, what church fathers have said, and what councils have decreed.[14] The sceptical exchange about the basis of religious knowledge continued throughout the seventeenth century and into the eighteenth.[15] Pierre Bayle was apparently persuaded to give up Calvinism for Catholicism by sceptical criticisms that he learned of at the Jesuit college at Toulouse. He then gave up Catholicism and reverted to Calvinism because of the sceptical critique of the Catholic rule of faith.[16] Late in the century two Protestant works appeared, *De insanabili romanae Ecclesiae scepticismo* and *Pyrrhonismus pontificus,* while Catholics like John Sergeant tried to reduce the Protestant case to nothing by sceptical argumentation.[17] (A Jewish version, undermining Christianity by scepticism with regard to its possible rules of faith, was penned in Amsterdam in the late seventeenth century.)[18]

I have argued elsewhere that this debate over the rule of faith, a basic debate within European Christianity, played an important rôle in the development of modern philosophy by creating a sceptical crisis with respect to religious knowledge, quickly extended to all human knowledge by Michel de Montaigne in his 'Apologie de Raimond Sebond'.[19] The extreme scepticism that Bacon said at the outset that he was rejecting, and that Descartes and others were attempting to overcome, grew out of the doubts created by the debate over the rule of faith, and the sceptical possibilities that were introduced therein. The solution or resolution offered by Montaigne, and taken up by leading French Counter-Reformers, was to give up the quest for human knowledge and accept truths in religion on faith alone as God reveals them to us. Montaigne's fideism may have been less than sincere, but a stronger form of sceptical fideism was offered by his follower Father

Pierre Charron, by François La Mothe Le Vayer, tutor of the Dauphin, and the strongest form, of course, by Blaise Pascal.[20] For Pascal, scepticism eroded all rational bases for any kind of knowledge, and faith overcame scepticism. Religion was not based on evidence or argument, but on listening to God, and on pure faith.[21] Pierre Bayle offered a Protestant version of this kind of religious Pyrrhonism, a view much like that later expressed by Kierkegaard.[22]

A renewed interest in revealed and inspired knowledge, particularly the interest in prophesy and millenarianism discussed earlier in this essay is also connected with this religious Pyrrhonism. One of the greatest theoreticians of and interpreters of prophetic knowledge was the highly learned and very pious Joseph Mede of Christ's College, Cambridge. Mede had entered the university in 1603 and tells us that he happened to see a copy of Sextus Empiricus's works open on a student's desk. He perused the work and soon fell into a sceptical crisis, in which nothing he thought he knew was supportable. He then studied all the kinds of knowledge offered at Cambridge and found them wanting. He finally emerged from his *crise pyrrhonienne* when he found certainty in the truth of scriptural prophecies. He wrote the *Clavis apocalyptica* as his answer to scepticism, and as the basis of a new understanding, founded upon the knowledge emerging from the fulfilling of prophecies. Mede was the teacher of many of the Cambridge Platonists, including Henry More and Ralph Cudworth.[23]

A correspondent of Mede's, the irenical Scottish millenarian, John Dury, imbibed Mede's outlook. In 1634–5 Dury met Descartes in Holland and learned that the latter was seeking for absolute certainty in mathematics. Dury told Descartes that he had gone through the same process until he found the basis for certainty in the understanding of Scripture prophecies.[24] At the time, the view that knowledge is based on prophecy was seen by Dury at least as an alternative to Descartes's mathematical vision. In fact, Dury wrote his own discourse on method in answer to that of Descartes.[25]

2. Probabilism

In philosophy, sceptical argument often led to a relaxation of the standards for certainty in some thinkers, the view that we must not insist on certain knowledge, but that we must make do with probability. This, too, is reflected in religious thought of the seventeenth century.

Some of those weary of the struggle with intolerant religious factions sought in theory and action to show that one ought to settle for less than complete certainty in religion, and that this would make for a more harmonious (and tolerant) world. This kind of view is usually traced back to Erasmus and Sebastian

Castellio in the sixteenth century. Its first main advocate in the seventeenth century was Hugo Grotius, who was a victim of the dogmatic Calvinists who gained control at the Synod of Dort. In the controversy over the doctrine of predestination, Grotius was a leading moderate Calvinist, an Arminian. As a result, to avoid being arrested, and even executed (as some of his fellow Arminian leaders were), he fled, hidden in a trunk, to Paris. In Paris he formulated his probabilistic theology. Appealing to Aristotle's maxim that one should not demand more proof than the case admits of, Grotius granted that we cannot gain absolute certainty in religion, but argued that there is enough evidence to satisfy a reasonable person. His much republished *De veritate religionis christianae* offered an argument he thought would be convincing to ordinary people. (The book was written for Dutch sailors to contemplate as they sailed to Asia and America.) The argument consisted mostly of an appeal to the evidence of design observable in all aspects of the world. Christianity was held the most reasonable explanation of the nature of the Designer. In Grotius's annotations on the Scriptures he granted that most of the disputed questions about biblical texts could not be resolved with certainty, but it did not matter.[26]

Grotius's probabilism had great influence on the group of moderate followers of Archbishop Laud in the Great Tew circle, the people who gathered around Lord Falkland. This group included Thomas Hobbes and Lord Clarendon, as well as the person who was to be become its most important theologian, William Chillingworth, Laud's godson.[27] Chillingworth was seduced by the sceptical arguments presented to him by a Jesuit who came to England in disguise to argue with bright university students. He then went to the Continent where he became a Catholic. Not long thereafter, like Pierre Bayle after him, he convinced himself by similar arguments that the Catholic view was also dubious. He returned to England and Falkland's circle, but did not rejoin the Church of England, because he was not certain that its thirty-nine articles were true. He devoted himself to composing his masterpiece, *Religion of Protestants* (1638), in which he contended that there was no way of gaining absolute certainty in science, philosophy, or religion. Following on the sort of case Descartes had just presented, he granted that one could not really answer all of the objections, *but,* and this is an important *but,* one is able to function and deal with enough questions in order to live and to function and to feel sufficiently secure in one's religious beliefs. If one had to await complete demonstration before daring to eat, walk, work, or worship, one would not do anything. However, if one looks at how problems are in fact dealt with by people who have not sought complete evidence, one sees that the mailman delivers the mail without knowing with certainty that the external world exists or that other people exist. Ordinary people in ordinary situations function according to the sort of proof the cases admit of. Judges decide cases though there are always possible doubts about their decisions. They decide the cases 'beyond all reasonable doubt', which is all that can really be expected. So, too, in religion all one can do is look at the evidence, the questions, and act as best one can, without waiting eternally for complete and sufficient evidence that what one believes is true.[28]

Chillingworth's formulation of the limited certitude that is achievable became the prevailing approach of the Anglican leaders after the Restoration. Bishops Stillingfleet, Tillotson, Burnet, and Wilkins all offered versions of this view which has been identified as the 'philosophy' of the Latitudinarians, those who tried to build a broad consensus of belief about a few central principles to replace the narrow factionalism of the Puritan period.[29] (Even the broad consensus, of course, excluded all sorts of people.) It was only after the Glorious Revolution that the consensus included, even informally, Catholics, Quakers, nonconformists, and Jews. (It should be noted that equality as citizens was only granted to Catholics and Jews in England in the nineteenth century.)

Bishop John Wilkins and the philosopher-preacher Joseph Glanvill presented another developed theory of limited certitude in philosophy, science, and religion. Glanvill was greatly influenced by the Cambridge Platonist, Henry More, with whom he did research on spirits and witches.[30] Wilkins had been a member of the Hartlib-Boyle spiritual brotherhood in the 1640s. He married Cromwell's sister and became Warden of Wadham College at Oxford. In his rooms there a group met which included a number of founder-members of the future Royal Society, interested in advancing natural philosophy through organised experimental research. At the Restoration, Wilkins changed alliances and became the son-in-law of the Archbishop of Canterbury; he also became Bishop of Chester, and a leading figure in the then-new Royal Society. Wilkins and Glanvill both argued that it is not possible to attain absolute or infallible certainty, even in mathematics: the most fully demonstrated propositions could always be false, given the possibility of something like Descartes's deceiving deity or demon. If even our best-grounded views could possibly be false, we have to settle for that certainty which exists when we have no reason to believe otherwise. This is certainty beyond all *reasonable* doubt. That is sufficient to ground our beliefs in religion and science. Such certitude, as Glanvill pointed out, rests on our reliance on our faculties. If our faculties deceive, whatever we take to be most certain could still be false. Hence, our reliance on our faculties is an act of faith, and our reliance on our faith an act of reason which recognises the greatest certainty we can have about the matter.[31]

This limited certainty was taken to constitute the basis for reasonable belief, a belief that a reasonable person could be expected to have. Bishop Gilbert Burnet pointed out that we cannot be absolutely sure that we have the correct text of Scripture, but we can be reasonably sure, and that is enough.[32] And Bishop Stillingfleet, who was later Locke's opponent, contended it was beyond reasonable doubt that the Bible was not a fraud and deception. The sort of ongoing conspiracy that would be required to keep such a fraud from being discovered was beyond any evidential data that we possessed or could possess.[33] The theory of limited certainty and mitigated scepticism worked out by the Anglican theologians became the theory of the Royal Society, and of the English law courts as well.[34]

Because of their appeal to reasonableness, the Latitudinarians were accused of Socinianism. This view, derived from Faustus Sozzini, began as a kind of biblical literalism, insisting that if one read the Bible without any preconceptions, there was no evidence that Jesus was a divine being. If reasonableness were used as the criterion of establishing the meaning of texts, scriptural and otherwise, one would come to the Unitarian view. Socinianism came by the late seventeenth century to stand for the view that reasonableness (in some sense of the term) was the arbiter of religious controversies and the criterion for establishing religious truth.[35] The Anglican appeal to reasonableness looked to opponents to be a kind of Socinianism, and reading Bishop Burnet's argument that there is no reasonable basis in the Bible for the doctrine of the Trinity, one indeed suspects that some of the Latitudinarians were close to being Socinians.[36]

Reasonableness as the measure of religion became in various forms the liberal Christianity of the Dutch Remonstrants Jean Le Clerc and Philip van Limborch, and their close friend, John Locke. It became the basis for deism in the hands of John Toland, who applied Locke's criteria for reasonable empirical knowledge to religion and thereby found reasons for questioning the truth of Christianity.[37] It became a tool of radical criticism of biblical interpretation in the hands of Dr. Louis Meyer and his friend, Spinoza, who applied canons of rational evaluation in mathematics and science to evaluation of biblical texts.[38] The appeal to reasonableness as the measure of religion became the entry-wedge to rejection of religion in the Age of Reason.

3. Mysticism, quietism, and Hassidism

The distrust of reason central to the sceptical tradition is also implicated in other religious movements of the seventeenth century.

Although the seventeenth century has been called the Age of the Scientific Revolution, it is also an age of mystical revolution in Catholicism, Protestantism, and Judaism. Along with the endless arguments between the Western religious groups as to which was *the* true religion, an intense kind of religious activity emerged on which to base religious adherence. In Spain first, the Spanish Inquisition's attempt to force a formal acceptance of a rigidly defined Catholicism, was met by the emergence of the intense mysticism of Santa Teresa of Avila, San Juan de la Cruz, and Saint Ignatius Loyola (all of whom were originally hindered by the Inquisition). Their religious mysticism became the living core of the Counter-Reformation and attracted a broad spectrum of adherents.[39] As explained by Juan de la Cruz, the way to the mystic life was a thoroughgoing negation of the worldly and intellectual life.[40] Spanish mysticism became the basis for the views and practices of the French Oratorians, the group that encouraged Descartes on his search for truth from his meeting with Cardinal Bérulle in 1628 and then all through his career.[41] Bérulle gave Descartes his mission to find a new basis for certainty, and Descartes kept seeking approval of the Oratorians for each of his publications. His theory can be viewed as a rational, scientific way of explaining their cosmos, a divinely dominated world, in which God constantly creates, conserves, and orders the world according to His All Powerful Will.[42]

Among the Protestants, a great mystical movement developed from the views of the German, Jacob Boehme, and the revival of some of the mediaeval mystics. Boehme, a cobbler, was always identified on the title pages of his books as 'the God taught philosopher' who knew the real essences of things. In the 1640s and 1650s his books were published in England, Holland, and Germany and became all-important in the intellectual communities in Protestant Europe.[43] The millenarians found in Boehme a theosophy that grounded their historical vision of what was going on.[44] Leading thinkers including some of the Cambridge Platonists and the Dutch Collegiants took Boehme's prolix writings most seriously,[45] although Henry More dared to say that Boehme was not a real prophet and had no special insight into metaphysical questions.[46] (More, when he read Spinoza's *Opera posthuma,* dismissed this great pantheistic metaphysical system as just Boehmism all over again.)[47]

From the Jewish side, a new kind of mystical theosophy was emerging in the dynamic interpretation of the mediaeval mystical tradition of the kabbalah. The kabbalah was being seen as both a way of gaining insight into the universe and as a picture of how God's dynamical actions in the universe went on, justifying intense expectation of the imminent coming of the Messiah.[48] Postel had translated the main mediaeval kabbalistic work, the *Zohar,* into Latin.[49] A new interpretation of kabbalistic doctrine was developed by Isaac Luria in Safed, a hill-top town in Palestine long associated with mysticism, and taught secretly to a dozen or so disciples. This view began to become known in Christian Europe in the early seventeenth century. One of Luria's disciples started giving lectures in Dubrovnik.[50] From him the theory became known to Abraham Cohen Herrera[51] and Joseph del Medigo.[52] The latter was actually at one time Galileo's assistant, then taught in Amsterdam and finally in Poland. Herrera was raised in Florence and Venice. His father was the business agent of the Duke of Tuscany. Young Herrera was given a deep education in Renaissance and ancient Platonism and in Arabic, Christian, and Jewish mediaeval philosophy. Through a series of mishaps, he was captured in the Earl of Essex's raid on Cadiz, imprisoned in England for four years, and then became one of the founders of the Jewish community in Amsterdam.[53] He wrote the most philosophical explanation of the Lurianic kabbalah, as well as texts in logic. His works were in Spanish. The major one, *Puerta del cielo,* appeared in a Hebrew abridgement in 1655, and in Latin in 1678.[54] It became the way Christian Europeans knew of the Lurianic kabbalistic doctrines, and the way they interpreted them, as a mystic form of Neoplatonism. Herrera was read by Leibniz, Newton, Locke, and on up to Schelling.[55] There is some evidence that Spinoza read Herrera early in his career.[56] Some readers could not distinguish the view in Spinoza's *Ethica,* Book I, and the first chapters of Herrera and saw Spinoza as a Neoplatonic kabbalist who disguised his views in Cartesian jargon.[57] They saw Spinoza's view that everything necessarily follows from the nature of the one substance, God, as the same as Herrera's emanation theory.[58] And, lastly, the theory of space of Newton and Henry More, conceiving of space as the sensorium of God, may have owed something to the Latin explanations of the kabbalah.[59]

If mysticism provided such rich food and impetus to new theorising, it also provided a most forceful form of scepticism. The movement called 'quietism' swept the Catholic world and turned up in Protestantism as pietism and in Judaism as Hassidism. The Catholic version of Miguel Molinos stressed the need to go beyond suspense of judgement, to the negation of all judgement in order to reach the spiritual life. One is to empty one's mind and await direction from God on all matters. Molinos stated his view in his *Guia Epiritual (Spiritual Guide)* as a string of quotations from Santa Teresa and San Juan de la Cruz.[60] His view had tremendous appeal in Italy and was endorsed by leading church figures. His opponents, however, saw that his view denied any value to church activities, to confession, to the church itself, or even to Mary or Jesus, since God Himself was the only source of one's ideas or beliefs if one had quieted the emotions and reason. Molinos was accused of justifying fornication between a priest and a nun, contending that this could be moral if God directed the souls of each. His Jesuit opponents had him arrested, and 20,000 letters to him from ladies were found, including some by his closest disciple, Queen Christina of Sweden. Molinos was ultimately condemned, in the same room as Galileo, but unlike Galileo, Molinos spent the rest of his life rotting away incarcerated.[61]

His views as expressed in his *Guia Epiritual* were translated and published all over Europe, in Catholic and Protestant countries, and have had continuing influence. A somewhat similar view was the most forceful Protestant version of quietism set forth by Jean de Labadie. Labadie began life as a Jesuit, became a Jansenist (the group Pascal and Arnauld belonged to), then became a Calvinist, teaching philosophy in Geneva, where he was the teacher and inspirer of the founder of German pietism, Jacob Spener. Labadie next moved on to Holland where he and the renowned Dutch scholar, Anna Maria van Schurman, reputed by many to be the most learned woman of the seventeenth century, developed a Christianity without a church, beyond all denominations and creeds, with no ceremonies, no special sabbath days, just spiritual harmony. They set up spiritual communes in Germany and Holland; the first American ones are offshoots of theirs.[62]

The philosophical form of quietism was expounded most completely by Pierre Poiret in Holland,[63] and by the Chevalier Andrew-Michael Ramsay, Hume's original patron.[64] For Poiret, one must doubt all principles, all logic. One must place reason and judgement on the dunghill, he declared. Then God would reveal true principles.[65] Poiret attacked the rational philosophies of his time, principally Cartesianism and Spinozism, as based on human presumption that human reason could find the truth. When one turned over one's mind to God, then one could overcome scepticism and accept the core of Cartesianism by faith and revelation, rather than by reason.[66]

Ramsay, a Scottish convert to Catholicism (who converted in order to overcome Pyrrhonism) was the teacher of the exiled Prince Charles Stuart (Bonnie Prince Charlie) and the leader of the French Free Masons.[67] He developed a mystical quietism, which involved some of the basic features that later appeared in David Hume's scepticism about human knowledge. He advised and patronised Hume at the beginning of his philosophising. Hume stayed with Ramsay when he went to France in 1734 to write *A Treatise of Human Nature,* and there are passages in Hume that come right out of Ramsay.[68] They finally parted company when Hume refused to adopt Ramsay's mystical solution to scepticism. Ramsay had some influence on John Wesley and the early Methodists, who cite him, and on the American philosopher-theologian, Jonathan Edwards, who also referred to him. Some of his ideas come up in writings connected with the eighteenth-century American revivalist movement, the Great Awakening.

Kabbalistic mysticism as presented by Herrera and del Medigo provided a dynamic kind of Neoplatonism as a metaphysics for the new science. Quietism provided a super-scepticism as a basis for God-taught philosophy and science. Both views were seriously considered by leading seventeenth-century thinkers, such as Malebranche and Leibniz, and some of their ideas were incorporated into the philosophical discussions of the time.[69]

IV. RELIGION UNDERMINED

An important feature of the philosophy of the seventeenth century is its increasing secularisation. This, too, is connected with important intellectual developments in seventeenth-century religion, the interest in Judaism and polytheism, the development of biblical criticism. These lead directly into the rise of libertinism in the century.

1. Judaism and polytheism

Much of the interest in Judaism in the seventeenth century is closely connected with the millenarianism discussed earlier in this essay. For Comenius, Dury, and Hartlib, among many others, the crucial penultimate event before the onset of the Millennium was prophesied to be the conversion of the Jews to Christianity.[70] Attempts to force Jewish conversion had backfired in Spain and Portugal by spawning a fake Christianity in the converts, who remained Jews at heart and were more anti-Christian than ever. Mede and others had indicated that the conversion would probably take place in 1655–6.[71] The spiritual brotherhood saw that they could not *cause* the conversion of the Jews, but they could and should prepare for it. Dury and Hartlib contended that it was necessary to 'make Christianity less offensive to the Jews' and to make Christians aware of what Jews really believed. They tried to found a College of Judaic Studies in London in 1640–1, which would teach Christians about Judaism and Jews about Christianity. The College would translate the Jewish classics into European languages, and translate Christian ones into Hebrew. The staff was supposed to be one rabbi, Menasseh ben Israel of Amsterdam, and two Christian Hebraists, Christian Ravius of Berlin and Adam Boreel in Amsterdam.[72]

Possibly as a continuation of this unfulfilled plan, Boreel, the leader of the Dutch Collegiants, a non-denominational spiritual group that later took Spinoza into their fellowship, started a project with another Dutch rabbi, Judah Leon, to edit the *Mishna* in a modern Hebrew edition with vowel points added. This would be followed by translating this early rabbinical compendium into Latin and

Spanish. The point of this venture, which consumed several years and a great deal of money, was to make it possible for Christians to learn what Jews really believed, so they could interact with them, and to make it possible for Jews to learn their own religion 'objectively', so that they could see that it was fulfilled in Christianity.[73] Dury, Hartlib, Boreel, and other philo-Semites, thought that Christians mainly knew of Judaism from negative comments in the New Testament, and even more negative comments by anti-Semites. It was thought they should learn both what actual living Jews believed, and what was put forth in the post-biblical Jewish classics. Jews should also learn what 'pure' Judaism is, in contrast to the jumble of superstitions they had learned from their rabbis. Then the relation between Judaism and Christianity would become clear to the Jews.

Similarly, a later project, the publication in Latin of many Lurianic kabbalistic tracts, including that of Herrera, by Knorr von Rosenroth and Van Helmont, was intended as a way of convincing Jews that the real message of the kabbalah was that Jesus is the Messiah.[74] Their book, the *Kabbala denudata,* served as a source for Christian Europe well into the nineteenth century. Many were convinced that the Jews had some secret knowledge that was vital for understanding the world. Henry More actually rejected this in a letter that appears in the middle of the *Kabbala denudata,*[75] and in 1742 the first modern historian of philosophy, Jacob Brucker, so classified philosophy that 'Jewish Philosophy' as well as Cambridge Platonism, fell beyond the pale, and were excluded from the serious forms of philosophy from then on.[76] For Brucker, Jewish philosophy and various forms of Neoplatonism were religious and theosophical outlooks, not philosophical views.

Another, more activist approach was to bring the Jews back to England, from whence they had been expelled in 1290, so that they could see the pure, uncorrupted Christianity of Puritan England, and would then react accordingly.[77] In 1650, rabbi Menasseh ben Israel of Amsterdam published his *Esperanza de Israel,* setting forth the Jewish Messianic expectations soon to be realised as the prophecies accepted by the Jews were being fulfilled. (This work was written because of questions asked of him by some English millenarians, including his friend, John Dury.) For the Jews, the crucial prophecy was the return of the Lost Tribes of Israel. The 'discovery' by Jewish explorers and Christian missionaries that the Indians or some group of them were practising Judaism triggered off an explosion of literature about the significance of the supposed Jewish Indians in world history.[78]

Menasseh gave a restrained version, but he clearly expected that the time of the end was near. Dury arranged for an English translation and publication of Menasseh's work, with a dedication to the English Parliament, and with an essay on the conversion of the Jews by the translator at the end. Dury and others then got Cromwell's government to invite Menasseh to England to negotiate on behalf of world Jewry on the terms for the re-admission of the Jews to England.[79]

This episode is usually portrayed as a bizarre curiosity undertaken at Menasseh's initiative. He has been portrayed as full of his own self-importance, trying to advance himself through his contacts with millenarian Christians.[80] The facts as they are now becoming clearer show that Menasseh was reluctant to go to England. His congregation opposed his voyage since they thought the Dutch authorities would not approve. On the English side, a strong group of millenarian ministers urged the visit, and a leading British diplomatic team tried to induce the Amsterdam rabbi to come.[81] He only decided to make the voyage after a strange visit to Belgium, where he met with Queen Christina of Sweden who had recently abdicated her throne, and with Isaac La Peyrère, the secretary of the Prince of Condé, and the author of *Du rappel des Juifs* and *Prae-Adamitae*.[82] Recent findings indicate that Condé, Cromwell, and Christina were negotiating to create a theological-political world state, involving overthrowing the Catholic king of France, among other things.[83] La Peyrère had been proclaiming that the Jewish Messiah would soon arrive and would join with the king of France (the prince of Condé), and with the Jews to liberate the Holy Land, to rebuild the Temple, and to set up a world government of the Messiah and his regent the king of France.[84]

Menasseh returned from Belgium and rushed to tell the Dutch millenarians that the coming of the Messiah was imminent (the first time he had said this). He helped write *Bonum nunciam Israeli,* an extreme millenarian work by the Czech Lutheran mystic Paul Felgenhauer. Giving some of the evidence for this, Menasseh revealed who else *knew* the Messiah is coming, and named four Christian millenarians (one, Jacob Boehme's chief disciple) and La Peyrère.[85] He then wrote his most Messianic work, *La piedra gloriosa,* an interpretation of part of the Book of Daniel with four magnificent illustrations by Rembrandt.[86] Menasseh then packed his bags and left for England, and wrote to various synagogues in Germany and Italy telling them of his voyage, and announcing that he was going as the agent for the whole Jewish world, and that he would take care of any problems they wished.[87]

In England Cromwell appointed a committee to deal with Menasseh. It was top-heavy with important millenarian clergymen and government officials and included the Cambridge Platonist Ralph Cudworth. Menasseh was wined and dined by the spiritual brotherhood in England. Lady Ranelegh, Robert Boyle's sister, had dinner parties for him. Henry Oldenburg met him, as did Henry More. Cudworth tried to find out from him why the Jews did not convert and was sold a strongly anti-Christian manuscript. When the negotiations got nowhere, Menasseh visited Oxford and Cambridge and met the erudite scholars there and examined the collections of Hebrew books. He finally was completely discouraged, and after his son died, left, and died himself on the way home.[88]

It is not known why the negotiations broke down, but the millenarians kept up their hopes of converting the Jews. During the last half of the seventeenth century, one development after another was taken seriously by millenarians from Cudworth and More and Oldenburg and Boyle to Isaac Newton. There are indications that so-called reasonable thinkers like Spinoza, Locke, and Leibniz were well aware of the frenetic activities of those interpreting scriptural prophecies, and that they were in constant interaction with the millenarians and Messianists.[89] Spinoza was greatly helped after he was expelled from the Jewish community by leading Dutch millenarians.[90] His own concern with prophecy may not just be a way of rejecting his Jewish training, but may be related to the activities of some Dutch millenarians hoping to recreate the ancient Hebrew Republic, a theocracy, in The Netherlands.[91] Similar efforts went on in England during the Cromwell Protectorate.[92] Locke discussed prophetic interpretation with Newton. Leibniz knew and consulted such millenarians as Van Helmont and Knorr von Rosenroth.[93] Important interpretations of prophecies, especially those in the books of Daniel and Revelation, were written by Henry More, Isaac Newton, and Pierre Jurieu, Bayle's nemesis, among others.[94] There were both Catholic and Protestant millenarians who were leading intellectuals of the time, whose views formed a vital part of the ferment of ideas throughout the seventeenth century.

An important interest in Judaism was, thus, connected with Christian Messianic thought. But in addition, many theologians held that Judaism had an important rôle in explaining Christianity. Consequently, there were many editions and translations of the Jewish classics, as well as commentaries on them from the late fifteenth century onward. Perhaps the most interesting cases for historians of philosophy are the rôles of Maimonides, Herrera, and the Lurianic kabbalah in seventeenth-century thought. Maimonides's *Moreh Nebuchim* (Guide for the perplexed) was translated into Latin and was very widely read. I suspect it became an acceptable substitute for Saint Thomas Aquinas's writings, since it tried to reconcile science and religion, and was written by a non-Catholic. It was cited by Grotius, More, Cudworth, Stillingfleet, Leibniz, Bayle, Malebranche, Newton, and many others.[95] It was a major source of information about mediaeval Arabic philosophy, and was, perhaps, one source of the doctrine of occasionalism among the Cartesians.[96]

But Jewish materials also provided a vital challenge to Christianity. Because of the more tolerant conditions in Amsterdam, Jewish objections to Christianity could be stated without causing the death or imprisonment of the speaker. Debates took place there, and many anti-Christian treatises were written and circulated in manuscript. Isaac Troki's *Chissuk Emuna* (Fortification of the faith), Elijah Montalto's attack on the Christian interpretation of Isaiah 53, the treatises of Saul Levi Mortera and Isaac Orobio de Castro against the Christian interpretation of Jewish history, and many others were copied and studied by Jewish intellectuals. These Jewish critiques, usually written in Spanish or Portuguese, were based on current historical and philological data and were put together in tight argumentative form. Most of the authors were Iberians who had studied in Christian schools in Spain, Portugal, and Italy. Some taught there, or in France. The authors were so-called New Christians, forced converts to Catholicism, or descendants of the same. They fled to Holland usually because (like Spinoza's parents) they were accused of being fake Christians, Marranos, who secretly practised Judaism, and were the object of persecution by the Inquisition.[97] The anti-Christian material written by these Marranos in Holland became part of the Enlightenment challenge to Christianity when it became available in the early eighteenth century.[98] Baron d'Holbach published a version of one of these works, Isaac Orobio de Castro's *Israel vengé*.[99]

These relations between Christians and Jews also led to various attempts to reconcile Judaism and Christianity, to make them compatible versions of how God operates in the world. A view was offered by La Peyrère, Menasseh ben Israel, and John Dury that the New Testament might possibly describe what happened in the first century, while the Jewish expectation describes what will happen in the seventeenth century. Menasseh, in the only work he published when he was in England, quotes this theory of La Peyrère's.[100] Versions of it reappeared a decade later when Sabbatai Zevi announced that he was the long-awaited Jewish Messiah. Some millenarian Christians accepted him and said that Menasseh had told them that there had been a Messiah from the house of David, and there will be one from the house of Joseph.[101] La Peyrère had advanced a two-Messiah theory to justify his peculiar form of Messianism (asserting that the Jewish Messiah was about to appear and would be allied to the king of France and the Jews who would rebuild Jerusalem). His friend, the great biblical critic and scholar, Father Richard Simon, told him this would destroy Christianity, but he seemed to be unperturbed.[102]

Another way of reconciling Judaism and Christianity was put forth by an amazing figure, Moses Germanus. He was born Johann Peter Spaeth, a Catholic in Germany, and was trained by the Jesuits when he became a disciple of the pietist, Jacob Spener. He then became Knorr von Rosenroth's assistant, working on the *Kabbala denudata*. (He was apparently known to Leibniz at that point.)[103] He became involved with fringe Protestants, Mennonites, Quakers, and Socinians and was about to revert to Catholicism when he had a revelation about the true meaning of Isaiah 53, the passage about the suffering servant. He 'saw' that it did not refer to Jesus, but rather to the Jewish people. He became a convert to Judaism, moved to Holland, and became a rabbi.[104] He became involved in one of the first controversies about how to interpret Spinoza's philosophy.[105] In some of his writings he offered the view that Jesus was a fine, moral Jewish rabbi, and that Judaism and Christianity were the same moral teachings. His demythologising of the rôle of Jesus, and his reduction of biblical religion to ethics was taken over by some German Enlightenment writers as a way of absorbing the religious tradition in a secular world-view.[106]

But the exposure to Judaism also led to attempts to go beyond both religions. A kind of universalism was developed, especially by Quakers such as Samuel Fisher. God's Word was knowable, he asserted, by all people at all times and places. If Abraham and the Patriarchs could know about God without having the Scripture, why could not the American Indians do the same? Why could not the csame light be found in America, Asia, and Africa, as well as Europe?[107] Fisher was active in the Quaker mission in Amsterdam in 1657 and apparently knew Spinoza shortly after the latter's excommunication.[108] Spinoza's view that God's message, the moral law, is knowable by all mankind by reason, looks not unlike the Quaker view that it is knowledge by Spirit that is accessible to everyone.[109]

Various thinkers offered forms of Jewish Christianity and Christian Judaism. The former accepted Jesus as a great, or as the greatest moral teacher (Spinoza), while the latter reduced Christianity to a simple extension of Judaism, removing all the practices and creeds offensive to Jews (this was La Peyrère's suggestion in *Du rappel des Juifs* for a Jewish Christian church). There were important intellectual Christians who lived a life quite similar to that of the Amsterdam Jews. Some of them accepted the Jewish Sabbath, Jewish dietary laws, and Hebrew as the language of divine communication. This led in some cases to a Christianity without a church, and finally to a Judeo-Christian moral outlook, rather than a religion.[110] The Collegiants, the group that took in Spinoza after his excommunication, were Chrétiens sans église. They formed a spiritual community with no practices or creeds.[111] (The same was true of the Labadie-Van Schurman group.)[112] For some it was easy to go from unaffiliated Christianity and Judaism to a religious humanism, or to a secular humanism.

Similar developments emerged out of the realisation that polytheism had not only been rampant in ancient times, but was so in the present era.[113] In view of the varieties of religious experience and expression, how is one to justify Judeo-Christianity as *the* true religion? One theory which tried to account for the known facts was advanced by Gerard Vossius, in his *De theologia gentili*. . . . This theory was taken over by Ralph Cudworth, Isaac Newton, and in a radically different way by the English deists from Herbert of Cherbury onward.[114]

Vossius was a leading Dutch humanist and one of the most important Arminians at the time of the Synod of Dordrecht. His close friend, Hugo Grotius, had to flee from Holland, and Vossius lost his professorship at the University of Leiden. Vossius wrote inordinately about ancient literature and philosophy.[115] The *De theologia gentili* . . . was published in 1641 as a three-volume complement to his son's edition of Moses Maimonides's tractate, *De idolatria liber.*[116] The elder Vossius offered the view that all religions are partial statements of a basic or Ur-religion, mixed with natural myths and human politics. All of this, he claimed, ultimately derives from the Mosaic revelation. By careful examination, one can trace back the characters and events in various polytheisms to those in the Mosaic account. Greek polytheism and atheism can be traced back from Democritus to Moschus, who was a corrupted version of the Moses figure. Thus the original revelation – the Mosaic one (which includes a pre-figuring of the Christian Trinitarianism) – is in all religions; they are just corrupted or perverted forms.[117]

Ralph Cudworth, Regius Professor of Hebrew at Cambridge, in his *True Intellectual System,* 1678, took over Vossius's picture with some modifications. Cudworth, for instance, made anti-Trinitarianism a dangerous pagan development that was halted by Athanasius.[118] Isaac Newton, in his unpublished writings and in the *Chronology of Ancient Kingdoms Amended,* tried to justify Vossius's theory by a new chronology that proved that Judaism was the oldest religion in the world and that the Bible is the oldest book.[119] Unlike Cudworth, Newton claimed that anti-Trinitarianism was a basic part of the original religion, and that Athanasius and others conspired to corrupt and destroy the original religion. Newton was a leading theoretician of anti-Trinitarianism, or Arianism, and saw all developments in Christian history from the Council of Nicea (A.D. 325) onward as the grand iniquity of the church, which was soon to be overcome.[120] Even in Newton's day, it was not safe, even for the world's leading scientist, to say this in public. Yet the view appears many times in his unpublished papers (most of which are still unpublished), but never in print.[121] His disciple, and successor as Lucasian Professor of Mathematics at Cambridge, William Whiston, publicly aired his anti-Trinitarian views on the steps of St. Paul's Cathedral, and was promptly dismissed from his university post, in disgrace for the rest of his long life.[122]

Herbert of Cherbury, the so-called father of deism, corresponded with Vossius, and got the idea of a universal natural religion from the latter's work. The implications of this, sharply drawn out by the deists Charles Blount, John Toland, and Matthew Tindal, were that Judaism and Christianity were *just* forms of the one natural religion that all mankind started with. All religions were put on the same level. All were taken to have a natural rational moral view as a core, along with unneeded trappings, priesthood, church institutions, and practices, owing to various political and psychological factors. A conspiracy of priests and princes kept mankind subjugated by fear and force.[123] Blount wedded the naturalist implications of Vossius's explanation of polytheism to the social, political, and psychological explanation of how religions developed, offered by Hobbes and Spinoza.[124] (Blount was the first to translate Spinoza into English. He first published just Spinoza's chapter about miracles from the *Tractatus,* and in 1683 a full translation of the *Tractatus* appeared.[125] He also tried to alert Hobbes, just before Hobbes died, to the important insights about the nature of religion now available from the study of polytheism.)[126] English and French deists used the information about polytheism as a way of naturalising all religion instead as a way of defending Judeo-Christianity. Hume's *Natural History of Religion* represents a final step in making polytheism the natural religion, and non-biblical monotheism the reflective view of the wise, and agnosticism the most rational view.[127]

2. *Biblical criticism*

Among the schoolmen, the Bible was an unquestioned authority on philosophical questions. Not so in general for the seventeenth century, in good part because of developments in biblical criticism. The accuracy of the text has been questioned from ancient times to the present. The acceptance of the text as having special significance and containing special knowledge is usually based on an acceptance of the first five books of the Old Testament as having been written by Moses to record what God had revealed to him. The Bible itself tells that the original holograph copy was destroyed, and the text had to be reconstructed by Ezra. Ezra's text went through many misfortunes, and finally, in post-biblical times, a council of rabbis established the canon of what is the Bible, the book.[128]

A Spanish rabbi of the late eleventh century, Abraham Ibn Ezra, discussed the point that in Deuteronomy, supposedly all written by Moses, the death of Moses is described as well as some events after his death. Ibn Ezra noted there were forty verses that post-dated Moses. He did not question the truth of these verses but indicated that they had a special status.[129] The commentaries of Ibn Ezra were among the earliest works printed, and they were studied by Jewish and Christian exegetes.[130] Hobbes and La Peyrère seem to be the first to make a fuss about his point. Hobbes in *Leviathan* said he accepted the Bible on the authority of the Church of England, but that Moses could not have been author of the whole Pentateuch because of the verses about his death.[131] La Peyrère used the evidence to introduce a multiple authorship theory. And Spinoza then made the problem of the Mosaic authorship the opening wedge for questioning the accuracy and authenticity of the entire text.[132] Spinoza, along with the Quaker Samuel Fisher questioned the reliability of the text that has come down to us through all of the vicissitudes of human history.[133] Spinoza insisted the work only made sense contextually, as a collection of writings by ancient Hebrews, without any super-natural status. The evidence adduced by Spinoza was used and extended by the French biblical scholar, Richard Simon, who knew far more than Spinoza did about the history of the manuscripts and the variants in them. Simon said he agreed with Spinoza's method but not with his conclusion. He agreed that all known manuscripts are man-made, and the results of historical circumstances. But Father Simon insisted the Bible was divinely inspired; it is just unfortunate that none of the extant copies is. So, Simon suggested an endless research program to try to get back to the inspired copy. In so doing, he indicated the epistemological problems involved in trying to establish a historical fact.[134]

Simon's *Critical History of the Old Testament* raised all sorts of doubts among thinkers at the end of the century, and his work in all likelihood helped feed the growing questioning of the status of Scripture.[135] Isaac Newton studied Simon's work and agreed that the present texts of both the Old and New Testaments are a mess. However, Newton insisted, God preserved the accuracy of the crucial prophetic texts, Daniel and Revelation, and so the condition of the rest did not matter.[136] Bishop Burnet, not a millenarian or a prophetic interpreter, agreed about the mess, but insisted, as Spinoza did, that the essential moral message was still there, so the condition of the rest did not matter.[137]

One special problem in biblical interpretation concerned the literal interpreta-tion of the story of Adam. Reports from explorers wandering in America, Asia, Africa, and the South Pacific suggested the possibility that all of mankind could not be descended from Adam and Eve, and that the biblical account could not square with the presently known varieties of mankind and their dispersion over the planet.[138] The presentation of the pre-Adamite theory by Isaac La Peyrère in his *Prae Adamitae* attempted to resolve the difficulties. La Peyrère's book was written in Paris around 1641 (when the author became the secretary of the prince of Condé), but only published in Amsterdam in 1655 when Queen Christina offered to pay for its printing.[139] The author was there at the time, and his presence was known to Menasseh ben Israel and to Felgenhauer. The book was dedicated to all of the Synagogues in the world and was probably known right away in the Jewish community at the time. (Menasseh wrote a refutation in 1655–6, which has disappeared.)[140] The States of Holland banned the work in 1656, and it was quickly banned and burned throughout Europe. The author was arrested in Belgium and was persuaded to convert to Catholicism (he had been a Calvinist, probably of Jewish ancestry) and to apologise personally to the pope.[141] His work directly influenced young Spinoza, who developed some of his biblical criticism from La Peyrère's book.[142]

La Peyrère's polygenetic view haunted seventeenth-century attempts to understand the nature of man in terms compatible with the Bible. Many of the brightest intellectuals in Europe from Grotius onward tried to refute La Peyrère and to explain the diversity of mankind, and their present locations in monogenetic terms within the time frame of the biblical history, that is, starting at 4004 B.C. It was only with the rise of anthropology in the eighteenth century that 'scientific' polygenetic explanations began to appear, as well as monogenetic explanations employing a much larger time frame.[143] La Peyrère's pre-Adamite theory (contrary to the author's benign universalism) was developed from the seventeenth century onward as a basis for racism, and a justification for the enslavement of Africans in America and the mistreatment of the native Indians.[144]

The discussions of pre-Adamism definitely undermined some people's acceptance of the Bible as the true and complete history of the human race. La Peyrère's theory was known long before publication to people in Mersenne's and Condé's circles in Paris, including Gassendi, La Mothe Le Vayer, Gabriel Naudé, and many others.[145] Only Grotius reacted hostilely and negatively, and wrote a refutation twelve years before the publication of the work, contending that the Indians in America were descendants of the Viking expeditions, the Vikings were Adamites, hence no problem.[146] La Peyrère showed his manuscript to people everywhere he went, and it only caused a stir when it came out in print in five editions in one year.[147] The young Spinoza and some of his associates seem to have taken it up and used pre-Adamism in their biblical criticism.[148] Later in the century the view was offered in *Letters Writ by a Turkish Spy*. The spy reports that his brother had been to India and had learned that Indian history far ante-dated biblical history.[149] The same evidence was offered in Charles Blount's *Oracles of Reason* and in Thomas Burnet's *Theory of the Earth*.[150] It became a popular view of deistically inclined people at the end of the century, and a view used to criticise acceptance of the Bible as history.[151]

3. Atheism and libertinism

It has been claimed that it was a logical step from the first questioning of evidence for religion and the existence of God to the denial of supernatural religion and the avowal of atheism.[152] On the other hand, as it has been pointed out, although atheism is just the denial of theism it was not a view that anyone publicly held until the latter part of the eighteenth century.[153] There are claims that there were secret atheists from the Renaissance onward, but what has been offered as evidence are views that are heterodox, but not necessarily atheistic.[154] So, there has been a myth of Italian and French atheists, but nothing indicates that this was a reality in the seventeenth century.[155] There were probings and questionings which, though not logically implying the denial of Judaism and Christianity, did in historical fact lead to it.

There is a series of unpublished works starting with Giordano Bruno's *Spaccio de la bestia triofante* and Jean Bodin's *Colloquium heptaplomes,* dating from the last decade of the sixteenth century, to the as yet not clearly dated *De tribus impostoribus,* and the separate and different *Les trois imposteurs,* which circulated widely among European intellectuals and libertine aristocrats. Bruno's work, which was first published in the eighteenth century by John Toland, raises nasty questions such as why God wants us to believe the biblical story when the evidence that the world is much older and that people come from various sources is all around us.[156] Bodin's work, only published in the mid nineteenth century, is a dialogue between various Christians, a Jew, a Moslem, and a natural philosopher, discussing what is the true religion. What is amazing about Bodin's dialogue is not only that the Christians lose, but the Jew wins![157] The two different (three impostor's) texts raise questions about the biblical text, and the French version contends the three impostors were Moses, Jesus, and Mohammed, who each created religions for personal gain.[158]

Was it possible, as related in *Les trois imposteurs,* that religions are just man-made? Hobbes and Spinoza had provided the basis for explaining how religions came to be, and continued to be, because of certain psychological and sociological factors.[159] If we can see that some religions are man-made, why not all? Enlightenment thinkers were willing to start from the question and offer reasons for doubting the special status of any religion, and finally to come to see religion as a debilitating force in the human world, to be replaced by the religion of reason.

Who read these works? Bruno's work is in manuscript in a large number of European libraries, including the library of the Duke of Brunswick in Wolfenbüttel, where Leibniz was the librarian. Also in Wolfenbüttel, there is a copy of Bodin's dialogues prepared for publication, but not published, by Leibniz, Jacob Thomassius, and Herman Conring.[160] We know from correspondence that Henry Oldenburg, Boyle's assistant, and later secretary of the Royal Society, and Spinoza's most significant foreign friend, made a copy of Bodin's manuscript in Paris.[161] He regarded the work as horrendous and was sure it would never be published. So he made a copy for John Milton, who apparently sent his copy to John Dury. Oldenburg asked Adam Boreel of the Dutch Collegiants to write a refutation of it to save Christianity.[162] Although no printed copy or manuscript of *Les trois imposteurs* is known before the very end of the seventeenth century, the impostor theme is discussed all through the century. Queen Christina offered an enormous sum for a copy but did not obtain one.[163] Oldenburg apparently heard the thesis of the work at Oxford.[164] It echoes various discussions in Spinoza's circle, and the work in final form borrows heavily from both Hobbes and Spinoza.[165] The distribution of copies all over Europe (and some in America) suggests a wide readership.[166] These works, and others like them, stated views that in all probability could not be published because of censorship (even in Holland). No one has been identified who lost his or her belief in Judaism or Christianity from reading these works.

V. CONCLUSION

We have considered some of the different religious frameworks in which intellectual life went on in the seventeenth century. All of the heroes of modern philosophy were involved in, or influenced by, the issues raised, and some were involved in the movements described. It has proved rewarding to examine scientific developments in terms of the lively religious issues; it has also been rewarding to examine political developments in these terms. Perhaps, if we recognised that our philosophical heroes (who were often scientists and politicians as well) lived in historical time and space, in some part religious time and religious space, we could better understand why they wrote on various topics, and maybe also why they developed certain kinds of views. We now tend to judge them using post-Enlightenment standards, assuming that reasonable men do not care about these religious issues. Whether this is true or not, it is important to remember that European thinkers only attained this post-Enlightenment point of view because these religious issues were fought over by theologians, philosophers, scientists, and politicians.

NOTES

1 See Popkin 1983.
2 Hobbes, *Lev.* xxx; Spinoza, *Tract. th.-pol.* i and ii.
3 See Hill 1971, 1975; van der Wall 1987; Williamson 1979, 1989.
4 See Webster 1986; Popkin 1986a.
5 On this, see Webster 1986.
6 See Trevor-Roper 1967, pp. 237–93; Dury 1650.
7 On Comenius and Harvard, see Turnbull 1947, pp. 368–70.
8 Popkin 1986a, pp. 36–7; de Vleeschauer 1937; Thijssen-Schoute 1954, pp. 615–18. A translation of Comenius's account of the meeting appears in Young 1971, p. 50.
9 See Scholem 1971, 1973.
10 See, e.g., Charles Leslie, *A Short and Easy Method with the Jews,* in Leslie 1721, vol. 1, p. 52. See also, Popkin 1990g, p. 9.
11 Popkin 1987d, pp. xxv–xlv. The letters in *The Turkish Spy* of the Spy to Nathan, the Sultan's Jewish agent in Vienna, in Marana 1753, volumes 4 and 5, present this attempt. The history of *The Turkish Spy* is quite curious. Volumes 1 and 2 were written by J. P. Marana, and published first in Italian and French, respectively. Volumes 3 to 8 were published (and presumably written) in English, after Marana's death by an author or authors currently unknown.
12 Popkin 1989a, chap. 1.
13 On Veron, see Popkin 1989a, chap. 4, pp. 70–8.
14 Popkin 1989a, chap. 4, pp. 74–7.
15 See Popkin 1989a, chap. 1, pp. 15–17, and 1963, pp. 1321–45.
16 Cf. Labrousse 1963–4, vol. 1, chaps. 3 and 4.
17 La Placette 1696; Turrettini 1692; Sergeant 1665.
18 This appears in the manuscript by Abraham Gomes Silveyra, written against Isaac Jacquelot. The manuscript is in the collection of Ets Haim in Amsterdam, HS EH 49 A 16. See also his *El juez de las controversias,* HS EH 48 B 17.
19 Popkin 1989a, 1960.
20 Popkin 1989a, 1988a.
21 Pascal, *Pens.* 131, 835.
22 Pierre Bayle, *Dictionaire historique et critique,* art. Pyrrhon, remarks B and C, and Eclaircissement sur les Pyrrhoniens. See also, Popkin 1972.
23 On Mede, see Popkin 1986a, pp. 23–4; Firth 1979.
24 The text of the Descartes–Dury encounter appears in de Waard 1953. See also Popkin 1986a, p. 26.
25 See Turnbull 1947, pp. 168–9. Truncated published versions of the method appear in the letter to Lord Forbes and in Dury's 'An Epistolical discourse from Mr. John Durie to Mr. Sam. Hartlib, concerning this Exposition of the Revelation, Nov. 28, 1650,' in Mede 1651. Manuscript versions also exist in the Hartlib papers, Sheffield, England, as well as in collections in the Royal Archives in Stockholm and in the Staats-archiv in Zurich.
26 See Trevor-Roper 1987a, chaps. 2 and 4.
27 See Trevor-Roper 1987a, chap. 4; Van Leeuwen 1963; chap. 2, pp. 15–31; Griffin 1992, chap. 7.
28 Cf. Van Leeuwen 1963; and Waldman 1959.
29 Van Leeuwen 1963; Carroll 1975; and Shapiro 1983.

30 On Wilkins, see Van Leeuven 1963; and Shapiro 1969. On Glanvill, see Popkin, introduction to the photoreproduction edition of Glanvill 1676 (New York: Johnson Reprint Co., 1970); Cope 1956; and Talmor 1981. See also Griffin 1992.
31 Popkin, introduction to Glanvill 1676, pp. xxi–xxv; Popkin 1959a, esp. pp. 13–14.
32 See Burnet 1699, regarding article 6, pp. 85–8.
33 Stillingfleet 1662.
34 See Van Leeuwen 1963; Shapiro 1983; Waldman 1959.
35 On Socinianism, see Williams 1962.
36 Burnet 1699, comments on article one, p. 40.
37 See Le Clerc 1709, 1724; van Limborch 1686; Locke 1695; Toland 1696. This is what alarmed Bishop Stillingfleet about Locke's views. See Popkin 1971.
38 Meyer 1666 (French translation Meyer 1988). Spinoza, *Tract. th.-pol.* vii–viii.
39 On Spanish mysticism, see Peers 1927–30; Castro 1954.
40 See John of the Cross 1974.
41 Gouhier 1954b.
42 Gouhier 1972, p. 72; Popkin 1989a, pp. 175–6.
43 On Boehme, see Koyré 1929; Jones 1954.
44 Webster 1982, 1986.
45 See Colie 1957; Kolakowski 1987.
46 See Henry More, *Philosophiae teutonicae censura sive epistola ad amicum quae responsum complectitur ad quaestiones quinque de philosopho J.B. [Jacob Boehme] illusque philophiae,* in More 1679a, vol. 1, p. 536.
47 More's letter to Lady Conway, *Ad. V. C. epistola altera, quae brevem tratatus theologico-politici confutationem complectitur* and *Demonstrationis duarum praepositionum, viz. ad substantium quatenus substantia est, necessariam existentiam pertinere &, unicam in mundo substantiam esse quae praecipuae apud Spinozium atheismi sunt columnae, brevis solidaque confutatio,* in More 1679a, vol. 1, pp. 563–614. See Colie 1957, chap. 5.
48 On Jewish mysticism, see Scholem 1961, 1978; Idel 1988.
49 See Postel 1969, 1971; Kuntz 1981.
50 This was Rabbi Israel Sarug. On the Lurianic kabbalistic theory, see Idel 1988.
51 On Herrera, see Kenneth Krabbenhoft's introduction to Cohen de Herrera 1987.
52 On Del Medigo, see Barzilay 1974.
53 On his capture in England, see Popkin 1989c.
54 An abridgement of the original Spanish has recently been published by Krabbenhaft; see Cohen de Herrera 1987.
55 See Krabbenhaft's introduction to Cohen de Herrera 1987; Gershom Scholem's introduction to the German edition, Cohen de Herrera 1974; Popkin 1992b.
56 See Wolfson 1934, vol. 1, p. 245.
57 Popkin 1992b. Readers, such as J. G. Wachter and Jacques Basnage, saw Spinoza's theory of the relation of substance and modifications like Herrera's Neoplatonic emanation theory.
58 This reading appears in Jacques Basnage's long discussion of Spinoza in his *Histoire des Juifs,* and J. G. Wachter's *Spinoza im Judentums.* It was also apparently Peter Spaeth's reading of Spinoza, Wachter reports. All of this occasioned a lengthy discussion about Spinozism before Spinoza in Jewish thought. See Brucker 1742, vol. 2, pp. 983–1067.
59 See Copenhaver 1980.
60 On Molinos's theory, see the article on him by Pacho 1980, and the articles 'Molinos' and 'Quietism' in the *New Catholic Encyclopedia* (Connolly 1967–89a and b).

61 On Molinos's persecution, see Valente 1974; and the introduction to Molinos 1909. On his relations with Queen Christina, see Stolpe 1966, chap. 8; Akerman 1991.

62 On Labadie, see Saxby 1987; Kolakowski 1987, chap. 8.

63 On Poiret, see Kolakowski, 1987, chap. 10.

64 On Ramsay, see Walker 1972.

65 Poiret 1713, vol. 1, chap. 10, 'Of Reason and Its Ideas', pp. 333–61, and vol. 5, chap. 4, 'Of Faith, as It Respects the Understanding', pp. 93–108.

66 See Poiret 1685, 1707. Also see Kolakowski 1987, pp. 684–8.

67 On Ramsay's biography and intellectual development, see Henderson 1952; Cherel 1918, p. 19; Popkin 1980a, pp. 135–7.

68 E.g., at the beginning of Hume's *Treatise of Human Nature,* Bk. I, pt. 3, sec. 11, Hume advanced Ramsey's distinction between demonstrative knowledge, proofs, and probabilities, which appears in Andrew Michael Ramsey, *Les voyages de Cyrus.* In Hume's *Natural History of Religion,* there is a two-page footnote taken from a later work of Ramsey's. On the relations of Ramsey and Hume, see Popkin 1980a.

69 See, e.g., Foucher de Careil 1861.

70 Popkin 1986a, p. 37; Hill 1988, pp. 12–36. For a general treatment of these themes, see Popkin 1980c.

71 Popkin 1986a, p. 37; Hill 1988, pp. 14–15. See also the pamphlet by Dury or Hartlib, *Englands Thankfulness, or an Humble Remembrance presented to the Committee for Religion in the High Court of Parliament* (London, 1642), in Webster 1970.

72 Dury 1649. See Popkin 1984a.

73 See Popkin 1988b.

74 On this project, see Coudert 1975.

75 See More 1677a.

76 Brucker 1742–4.

77 Katz 1982.

78 Katz 1982; Popkin 1986b, 1989b.

79 See the new edition of the 1650 English translation of Menasseh ben Israel's *Esperanza de Israel, The Hope of Israel,* edited by Méchoulan and Nahon (Menasseh ben Israel 1987); and Popkin 1987a.

80 See, for instance, Roth 1945, chap. 8. For a different view, see Méchoulan 1989.

81 See Katz 1982, esp. chap. 6; van der Wall 1989.

82 See Popkin 1974, 1984b.

83 Susanna Akerman and I are preparing a study on this. She has presented some of the evidence for this in Akerman 1990, pp. 142–60. In Popkin, forthcoming, I have sketched out some of this.

84 This is the thesis of his *Du rappel des Juifs.* See Popkin 1987b, esp. chap. 5.

85 Felgenhauer 1655, pp. 89–90.

86 On Rembrandt's relations with Menasseh, see Benesch 1969, pp. 23–6.

87 Katz 1982, chap. 6; Popkin 1984b, pp. 50–60.

88 Katz 1982, pp. 228–43; Méchoulan 1987, pp. 59–60; van den Berg 1989.

89 For instance, see the letter of Henry Oldenburg to Spinoza concerning reports about the Jewish Messianic claimant, Sabbatai Zevi, and the later reports to Oldenburg about this in his *Correspondence.* See Oldenburg to Spinoza, 8 December 1665, Oldenburg 1965–86, vol. 1, pp. 636–7, and subsequent letters to Oldenburg from Serrarius and others regarding Sabbatai Zevi. There are many unpublished notes in the Locke papers on biblical prophecy. The items are in the Lovelace Collection of papers of John Locke in the Bodleian Library, Ms. Locke C.27. Especially interesting in this group of papers

God

on various religious topics is a table written by Sir Isaac Newton in 1691 for Locke illustrating the fulfilment of the prophecy of the seven seals and trumpets and its interpretation according to the Revelation of Saint John, fols. 88–9. Locke and Isaac Newton met together once to compare their readings of the prophecies in the Book of Revelation. They each made notes in the biblical text, which exists in the Locke papers at Oxford. See Westfall 1980, p. 491. Leibniz was interested in the work being done by Christian Knorr von Rosenroth and J. B. Van Helmont on the kabbalah and on prophecy. He went to Sulzbach to visit them. On this visit, see the paper by Allison Coudert in Popkin and Weiner 1994.

90 See Popkin 1985a.

91 See, for instance, the seventeenth-century work by the Leiden professor Petrus Cunaeus, much reprinted, Cunaeus 1617. This work was republished up to the end of the seventeenth century. It also appeared in English translation.

92 See Capp 1972; Katz 1982, esp. chap. 3.

93 Allison Coudert has found evidence that some fundamental ideas of Leibniz seem to derive from those of Van Helmont and von Rosenroth. Leibniz visited them for a sizeable length of time at Sulzbach to discuss their views. See Coudert 1995.

94 Newton 1733; More 1680, 1681; Jurieu 1687.

95 See Popkin 1990e.

96 See Naify 1975 on Arabic occasionalism and Cartesianism. Malebranche cited Maimonides as his source in the *Eclaircissements* to the *Recherche*. See Mal. *OC* III 249 (Malebranche 1980a, p. 683).

97 See Popkin 1992a.

98 Popkin 1992a, and 1987c, which discusses how these manuscripts became available to the general European audience.

99 Orobio de Castro 1770. Orobio knew John Locke, and wrote the only Jewish answer of the time to Spinoza. On him, see Kaplan 1989.

100 See Menasseh ben Israel 1656, p. 18. See also Popkin 1987b, pp. 98–105; Popkin 1984c, 1989d. La Peyrère developed this thesis in *Du rappel des Juifs* (La Peyrère 1643). In unpublished letters now in the Staats-Archiv in Zurich about interpreting Sabbatai Zevi's appearance, Dury offered the view that there could be a messiah for the Gentiles and another for the Jews. On this, see Popkin 1989e.

101 See McKeon 1976; van der Wall 1987, chap. 10; Popkin 1989e.

102 Popkin 1987b, chap. 1, pp. 18–21. Some correspondence of Simon to La Peyrère exists as well as a short biography the former wrote of the latter. These appear in Simon 1702, vol. 2, pp. 1–28, vol. 4, pp. 36–45.

103 He is mentioned by Leibniz in sec. 9 of the 'Discours preliminaire' of the *Essais de theodicée,* where he is identified as a Swabian who became a Jew 'et dogmatisant sous le nom de Moses Germanus, s'étant attaché aux dogmes de Spinoza, a cru que Spinoza renouvelle l'ancienne Cabale des Hebreux'.

104 On his career, see Broydé 1905; Michael 1971. See also Popkin 1992b.

105 See Wachter 1699. See also Popkin 1992b.

106 His views influenced the forerunners of Higher Criticism of the Bible in Germany, Reimarus, and Edelman.

107 Fisher, *The Rustic Alarm to the Rabbies,* in Fisher 1679, p. 696. 'Is the Light in America any more insufficient to leads its Followers to God then the Light in *Europe, Asia, Africa . . .*'

108 Popkin 1984d.

109 Popkin 1984d, 1987e; Katz 1988, pp. 156–61.

110 See Katz 1988, which deals with various such groups and individuals in England and New England. In Popkin 1992c, I deal with some other interesting cases.
111 See Kolakowski 1987, esp. chap. 3.
112 See Saxby 1987, chaps. 9 and 10.
113 See Rossi 1984.
114 See Popkin 1990b, 1990c.
115 On Gerard Vossius, see Rademaker 1981.
116 D. Vossius 1641; J. G. Vossius 1641.
117 See Popkin 1990b.
118 See Cudworth 1678, chap. 4; Popkin 1990b; and Popkin's memorial lecture for the 300th anniversary of Ralph Cudworth's death, in Popkin 1990d.
119 Manuel 1963; Popkin 1988c.
120 Newton's writings on the subject have still not been published. They appear in many of his manuscripts, especially those against Saint Athanasius, and the Grand Iniquity of the Church. See Westfall 1980; Popkin 1988c, pp. 83–5.
121 The papers are to be found in manuscripts in the Yahuda Collection in the National Library of Israel in Jerusalem, the Keynes Collection, King's College, Cambridge, the Babson Library in Gloucester, Mass., the Bodmer Library in Geneva, and the William Andrews Clark Library at UCLA.
122 See Force 1985.
123 See *Anima Mundi* and *Great Is Diana of the Ephesians,* in Blount 1695.
124 Popkin 1990b.
125 [Benedictus de Spinoza], *Miracles no Violation of the laws of Nature,* 1683. The *Tractatus* appeared by 1689. No translator has been identified. The same translation was reissued in 1739, and a copy of it was in Benjamin Franklin's library.
126 See Blount's letter to Hobbes in Blount's *Oracles of Reason,* in Blount 1693.
127 See Popkin 1990c. Two recent doctoral dissertations, by A. Karsh (Columbia) and R. Harrison (Queensland), place Hume's *Natural History of Religion* in the tradition of discussions of polytheism.
128 This is reported in the Talmud and in Josephus's *History of the Jews.* See Ackroyd and Evans 1970.
129 See his commentary on Deuteronomy, often reprinted, and included in the notes of the Bomberg Hebrew Bible of the sixteenth century.
130 See Goshen-Gottstein 1989, p. 34.
131 *Lev.* xxxiii. See also Popkin 1987b, chap. 4.
132 La Peyrère 1655, lib. 4, cap. 1; Spinoza, *Tract. th.-pol.* vii–viii.
133 Popkin 1985b. Christopher Hill called Fisher the most radical biblical critic of the time.
134 Simon 1680, esp. the introductory essay.
135 See Hazard 1935.
136 Popkin 1990f.
137 Burnet 1699, article 6; Spinoza, *Tract. th.-pol.* xii and xiii.
138 See Popkin 1976.
139 Popkin 1987b. An English edition of *Prae Adamitae* was published in London in 1656 as *Men before Adam.*
140 On Menasseh and La Peyrère, see Popkin 1974, 1984b, and 1987b, chap. 8.
141 See Popkin 1987b, pp. 15–19.
142 Popkin 1987b, chap. 7, and 1989d.
143 See Popkin 1987b, chaps. 9 and 10.

144 Popkin 1987b, chap. 10, and 1980b, 1978.
145 Popkin 1987b, chaps. 3, 4, and 7.
146 Grotius 1643.
147 Popkin 1987b, chap. 7.
148 Popkin 1987b, chap. 7, pp. 84–7.
149 Popkin 1987b, chap. 9, pp. 116–17; Marana 1753, vol. 3, pp. 250–5.
150 Blount, *Oracles of Reason*, in Blount 1693: Part 1, Vindication of Dr. Burnet's Archeologia; Part 2, 7th and 8th chapters of same; Part 3, Of Moses' description of the original state of same; and Part 4, Dr. Burnet's appendix of the Brachmin's religion.
151 See Popkin 1987b, chaps. 7–9.
152 Buckley 1987.
153 Berman 1988.
154 See Kristeller 1968.
155 See Betts 1984; and Kors 1990.
156 The Italian text of the *Spaccio de la bestia triofante* is found in Bruno 1957, and translated in Bruno 1964.
157 The Latin text is found in Bodin 1857, and in English translation in Bodin 1975.
158 The French text was published in Piere Rétat, *Traité des trois imposteurs* 1973. A critical edition of the original 1719 printing is now available, edited by Silvia Berti, *Tratto dei tre impostori,* 1984. The Latin *De tribus impostoribus* is available in an edition put out by the Berlin Academy, *De tribus impostoribus* 1960. There is a new book on the history of the *De tribus impostoribus,* Niewöhner 1989. Much new research concerning the origin, sources and distribution of the French text is at present in progress. See, e.g., Berti, Charles-Daubert, and Popkin 1996.
159 Hobbes, *Lev.* xii; Spinoza, *Tract. th.-pol.,* chaps. 1–5, and *Eth.,* Bk. I, appx.
160 This manuscript is entitled Johannis Bodinus, *Colloquium heptaplomeres,* Herzog August Bibliothek, Wolfenbüttel, Handschrift Extrav. 89.1. Handschrift Extrav. 220.2 has variants and corrections in the hands of Conring, Thomasius, Leibniz and others. On this, see Popkin 1988d.
161 See Popkin 1986c; Oldenburg to Hartlib, 13 and 25 August 1659, Oldenburg 1965–86, vol. 1, pp. 302, 306–7.
162 See Popkin 1988d; Oldenburg to Hartlib, 25 August 1659, Oldenburg 1965–86, vol. 1, pp. 306–7; Hartlib to Worthington, 30 January 1659/60, in Worthington 1846, pp. 166–8.
163 See Stolpe 1966, p. 130.
164 Oldenburg to Boreel, April 1656, Oldenburg 1965–86, vol. 1, pp. 89–92.
165 See Popkin 1990a.
166 See Wade 1938, esp. chap. 2; Borkowski 1904; and Benitez 1988. Additional manuscripts are being turned up each year. There are, for instance, eight now located in the collection of the Hebrew Union College in Jerusalem.

IV

BODY AND THE PHYSICAL WORLD

THE SCHOLASTIC BACKGROUND

ROGER ARIEW AND ALAN GABBEY

Today the study of the physical world and its contents is principally the concern of the physicist, chemist, engineer, or biologist, rather than that of the philosopher, even the philosopher of science. In keeping with this disciplinary demarcation, non-historical discussions of the nature of body or of the constituents of the physical world make infrequent appearances in volumes or journals devoted to contemporary philosophy. By contrast, the disciplinary demarcations of the early modern period were such that investigations and speculations on 'body and the physical world' were legitimate concerns not just of those one would now describe as 'scientists', but of most of the philosophical community, who shared a much broader conception of the scope of 'philosophy' than is common among philosophers today.

I. PERIPATETIC NATURAL PHILOSOPHY

The Peripatetic tradition was the intellectual framework within which most seventeenth-century philosophers were educated and within which many of them pursued their philosophical careers (see Chapter 1). Peripateticism, in whatever propaedeutic form, was the earliest contact they had as individuals with serious philosophical and scientific concerns. However unsatisfying it became for some of them, at least it comprised a rigorously organised body of doctrine that included a systematic interpretation of the diversities of nature.[1] It showed the thoughtful student of nature that an intelligible and comprehensive account of natural phenomena was a *prima facie* possibility. At the same time, and perhaps inevitably, Peripatetic natural philosophy was the principal object of criticism for many of those who participated in the philosophical and scientific revolutions of the period. Once they began to find in it doctrinal debility, associated for many with the declining fortunes of natural magic (see Chapter 16), the more adventurous minds, encouraged in some cases by the diversity of alternative approaches to the study of nature that emerged during the Renaissance, perceived a challenge to produce something more in tune with new philosophical and critical sensibilities and more in keeping with the multiplying discoveries of the new science.

These remarks should not be taken to imply that Peripateticism constituted a doctrinal monolith, as is sometimes assumed. There was great diversity within the Peripatetic tradition; no homogeneous set of doctrines or agreed technical vocabulary was taught throughout the schools; indeed, some Peripatetic philosophers showed great inventiveness and flexibility in re-interpreting Aristotle to accommodate elements of the new philosophy or the findings of the new science.[2] Most seventeenth-century thinkers were aware of the doctrinal and terminological diversities, but they did not always appreciate them and often acted, usually for their own polemical purposes, as though such diversities did not matter.[3]

The institutional primacy of Peripateticism does not imply its preemption of the historical contexts out of which emerged the novel worlds of seventeenth-century natural philosophy. Less institutionally anchored, but of a correspondingly challenging cultural presence, were other forms of natural philosophy, such as Greek atomism in Renaissance dress (see Chapter 18), or the various Renaissance 'philosophies of nature'. The nature philosophers, irritated with Aristotelian interpretations of nature, believed that nature was infinitely more complex than the Aristotelians thought and should therefore be explored afresh with new resources, both conceptual and experimental, and a new cosmological vision. The universe of the nature philosophers was one of Neoplatonic or Hermetic inspiration, with its World Soul, its ensouled planets and stars, its occult sympathies and antipathies, a world in which networks of astrological influence linked the microcosm, the human world, to the macrocosm, the universe at large.[4] The ideas and doctrines of the new philosophers of nature, such as Giovanni Pico della Mirandola, Ficino, Pomponazzi, Cardano, Paracelsus, Telesio, or Bruno, did have an impact on seventeenth-century philosophy and science (see Chapters 2 and 16), but it was the Peripatetic philosophy, not the teachings of the *novatores,* that was the institutional cradle of the new philosophies. To understand where the new philosophies arrived at, it is important to see something of where they came from.

In the Peripatetic tradition, philosophy was typically understood to comprise two broad divisions: speculative philosophy and practical philosophy, which usually subdivides into active or moral philosophy (ethics, home economics, and politics) and the mechanical arts, themselves open to further disciplinary division. Some writers included logic as a branch of philosophy, though it was more commonly seen as an art.[5] As an art, magic was a part of practical philosophy, though of dubious status for many. There were two major divisions of magic: natural magic, and demonic or illicit magic. In natural magic, natural powers (usually occult, but not exclusively) were employed for human benefit, often to produce marvellous effects to win the admiration of others. In black magic, incantations and other procedures were employed to conjure demons or spirits for darker purposes (see at length Chapter 16).[6]

Speculative philosophy divides into metaphysics (or first philosophy), the mathematical sciences, and natural philosophy. Natural philosophy is the science of 'natural body in so far as it is natural'. In other words, natural philosophy is the science of the causes of change and rest in the natural world, the artificial domain being the concern of the mechanical arts. There are two branches of natural philosophy: general and particular. The former deals with the general *per se* principles (*principia*) and accidents of natural bodies, on which all natural science depends. These principles constitute one important sense of 'nature' (*natura*) and are either intrinsic or extrinsic. Principles intrinsic in, and partly constitutive of, bodies are either active or passive, the active principles being the forms (*formae*), or formal causes, from which originate actions and change, the passive principle being the prime matter (*materia prima*), or material cause, which has the capacity to receive and retain the changes conferred. Extrinsic principles are the causes *per se* of change, the efficient and final causes; and the causes *per accidens,* fortune and chance.

The other branch (also called 'special physics') deals with the particular principles of bodies that are simple or mixed (chemically and mechanically), animate or inanimate, and includes notably the doctrine of elements and of qualities, both manifest and occult. All individual bodies are composed of varying combinations of the traditional four elements, earth, air, fire, and water, each of which is the elemental principle deriving from combinations of prime matter with appropriate pairs of the four primary qualities, dry, cold, hot, moist. An influential alternative doctrine of the elements that arose in the sixteenth century was that of Paracelsus (1493–1541), who nominated just three elemental principles: salt (the principle of mass), sulphur (the principle of organisation), and mercury (the principle of activity). Paracelsus's theory was a development of a two-element theory (sulphur and mercury) that first appeared in the writings of Jabir ibn Hayyan (eighth century) and was introduced to the West by Albertus Magnus in his *De mineralibus.*[7]

Natural philosophy, therefore, is the science of natural things, dealing with the capacities of natural bodies to act and be acted on, and with their associated actions, qualities, and properties. The terms *philosophia naturalis, physica,* and *physiologia* were used as near-equivalent labels, except that *physiologia,* the all-encompassing *logos* of *physis,* often enjoyed a more specialised extension in late Renaissance writers. For example, Peucer numbers simiotic medicine, oneiropoly, physiognomy, metoposcopy, chiroscopy, and chiromancy among 'the physiological sciences', while he lists 'the objects of physiology' as 'all kinds of material and formal qualities in plants, animals, minerals, with their properties, effects, sympathies and antipathies'. In his incomplete treatise on physics of 1636–7, *physiologia* was Gassendi's preferred term for the study of nature.[8]

The basic conception of natural philosophy as the search for the causes of change, however interpreted by individual philosophers or schools, was shared by everyone, of whatever philosophical stamp, and did not change significantly during the early modern period. Scientific dictionaries of the early eighteenth century, for example, continued to define the discipline as the science of natural bodies, of their powers, natures, operations, and interactions.[9] This continuity is what one should expect, quite apart from any Peripatetic influences. Natural bodies do in fact exhibit a multiplicity of powers, qualities, and properties, if these words are used in their everyday senses. Bodies do act on each other, and on human beings, to produce changes the natural philosopher wants to explain. This holds good for Peripatetics as much as for Stoics or Atomists, for Gassendists or Hobbesians as much as for Cartesians, for Leibnizians as much as for Newtonians. Their differences were not about the phenomena *per se,* observational accuracy or plausibility apart, but on how to make sense of them through conceptual frameworks that promised intelligible causal explanations grounded in viable doctrines of body and spirit.

Again, throughout the seventeenth century there was general agreement within and beyond the confines of Peripateticism on the range of topics understood to fall within the domain of natural philosophy. Taking as representative the subject headings of Johannes Magirus's *Physiologia Peripatetica,*[10] we find that it deals with the general principles of natural things, place, vacuum, motion, time, the infinite; the planets, the fixed stars, eclipses; the elements, primary, secondary and occult qualities, mixed bodies; meteors and comets, tides, winds, the motion of the earth; metals, minerals, plants, spirits, animals, man, embryology, zoophytes; the soul, the senses, dreams, the intellect, the will. A similar agenda for natural philosophy was assumed, with differing emphases and topical interests, both in the Peripatetic manuals and by the new natural philosophers.

In 1629 Descartes declared his intention 'to explain all the phenomena of nature, that is to say, the whole of physics'.[11] He did not fulfil that intention, notwithstanding the wide range of topics addressed in *Le Monde, L'Homme,* and the *Principia philosophiae,* but the Letter-Preface to the French edition (1647) of the *Principia* shows that at that date he still envisaged a physics of Peripatetic scope. After a general description of *Les Principes* as published, he continued:

I ought in the future to explain in the same way the nature of each of the other more particular bodies to be found on earth, namely minerals, plants, animals, and principally man; then finally, to deal in an exact way with medicine, ethics and mechanics. That is what I would have to do to let people have a complete body of philosophy.[12]

In 1642 Gassendi explained to his patron Louis Emmanuel de Valois, comte d'Alais, that his Epicurean physiology, then in progress, would deal with the whole universe of things and with the *vis* or *principium agendi* in things taken both universally and individually.[13] Leibniz's *Elementa physicae,* drafted in the early 1680s, planned to deal with 'body and its qualities, both the intelligible ones which we conceive distinctly and the sensible ones which we perceive confusedly', and it listed as topics for study space and its geometrical properties, the vacuum, infinity and the continuum, the motion and collision of bodies, forces and powers, resistance, machines, vessels, pendular motion, centres of gravity, strength of materials, elasticity, magnetism, meteors, crystals, optical and chemical phenomena.[14] Newton, too, shared this conception of the scope of natural philosophy, which for him included most importantly alchemy.[15]

Evidently, in the early modern period 'natural philosophy', often abbreviated simply as 'philosophy', included many areas of inquiry that are more typically the concern of the historian of science.[16] Whenever these terms appear in a seventeenth-century text, one must therefore be aware of their resonances and connotations for a seventeenth-century reader. John Donne's famous lines beginning 'And new philosophy calls all in doubt'[17] do not allude to the latest innovations in logic, metaphysics, or epistemology, but to the Copernican upheavals in astronomy and cosmology and to the Renaissance revivals of ancient atomism. When Descartes explained in the Letter-Preface that 'the whole of philosophy is like a tree', he saw metaphysics as its roots, but general physics (natural philosophy) as its trunk, with medicine and mechanics accompanying moral philosophy on the branches as the principal fruits of philosophy.[18]

II. HYLEMORPHISM

The doctrine of hylemorphism (*hyle,* matter, *morphe,* form or shape) was central to Peripatetic philosophy. In *Physica* I Aristotle taught that there are three principles of natural things: prime matter, form, and privation. 'There is a sense in which the principles are two and a sense in which they are three', says Aristotle, and Aquinas echoes: 'There are two *per se* principles of the being and becoming of natural things, namely form and matter, and one *per accidens* principle, namely

privation.'[19] So individual substances are composites of two *per se* intrinsic principles: prime matter (*materia prima*) and substantial form (*forma substantialis*), with
privation (*privatio*) as the principle or cause *per accidens* of generation. Prime matter
is not 'matter' as the term would be used of marble or modelling clay. It is
(following Aquinas for the moment) potentiality (*potentia*), that is, the potentiality
to become a substance, just as by analogy an unformed piece of modelling clay has
the potentiality to become moulded into the shape of a leaf, or a chunk of marble
to be sculpted into a statue. The substantial form is a determinative active principle
informing and conferring essence on matter, defining the resulting substance, and
locating it in its class or species. Thus the substantial form of copper informs
passive prime matter to produce the substance copper. Furthermore, the substantial form yields the sensible and insensible qualities (*qualitates*) possessed by the
substance in question and is the immediate cause of the phenomena that are
characteristic of it. Thus a copper pot feels hard because it possesses the sensible
quality of hardness, and it falls to earth because of the insensible quality of
heaviness; the copper pot looks rosy-pink because it possesses the sensible quality
of rosy-pinkness.

Since form must necessarily be absent before the generation of substance via
the addition of form to matter, privation, the contrary of substantial form, makes
possible the generation of substance as its cause *per accidens*. If the form were
present, the substance would already exist, and if another form were present, there
would already be a different substance precluding the direct generation of the first
substance. *Privatio* seems to fade as a major issue in late Peripateticism, perhaps
because its definition (the absence of form *F* in a subject fitted to receive *F*) makes
it merely a logical requirement of the generation of substance. Magirus explains
how Aristotle came to the idea of privation as a principle of natural things and
rehearses the arguments for and against this *tertium principium*. He defends *privatio*
on the grounds that it is not quite a *non-ens* or a pure negation, which could not
be the cause of anything, but is a principle of generation rather than a principle of
things *per se*.[20]

Hylemorphism shares one important feature with mechanical philosophies
(and, indeed, with modern physical theories). This is the (often implicit) belief,
shared by all, though conceptualised in different ways, (1) that something persists
during change in the natural world; (2) that, to avoid causal regress or *a se* causality
(reserved for God), the persisting 'something', taken to be passive, is causally
distinct from the observed change; and therefore (3) that natural change is the
work of an active 'something else' that is distinct from the persisting passive
'something'. For Peripatetics the 'something' is prime matter in some sense; for

mechanists it is body in some form (atoms, *res extensa*). For Peripatetics the 'something else' is substantial form (attended by privation); for mechanists it is forces and local motions. These considerations show that the scholastic doctrine of hylemorphism, though dismissed as ineffectual by the 'new philosophers' of the seventeenth century, shared with their natural philosophies a 'deep structure' that is a constant feature of all systematised attempts to conceptualise and explain natural change.[21]

The hylemorphic doctrine spawned many problems, some of which were to have their counterparts in the mechanical philosophy.[22] One was the problem of individuation (see Chapter 9): how does this piece of marble differ from that, this pool of milk from that? Albertus Magnus and Aquinas had argued that the principle of individuation is not the substantial form nor the matter prior to receiving form, but the matter actualised as 'designated matter' (*materia signata*), which becomes the individuating principle of quantity and spatial relations.[23] Another question was whether matter can exist without form and form without matter. All seventeenth-century scholastics seem to have agreed that at least one form can subsist without matter, namely the rational soul,[24] but they disagreed about whether matter can exist without any form, indeed, about whether the concept of prime matter is even intelligible. According to Aquinas (whose position was represented earlier), prime matter is pure potency (*potentia*), or has only potential being, so prime matter is not brought into being without form; it cannot subsist without it, and when it is combined with it, it is no longer prime matter *simpliciter*.[25] But Scotus and Ockham disagreed; they held matter to be a positive entity really different from form that can subsist in its own right distinct from form, and Ockham claimed that matter is a quantified entity with dimensions.[26] In Scotus's case the motivation for his position seems to have been the wish to preserve God's absolute omnipotence as much as possible. Scotus claimed that God can create matter without any form, whether accidental or substantial: 'Every absolute thing that God produces among creatures by the intermediary of a second cause, he can create without this second cause, which is not part of the effect. Now, the form that confers existence on matter is a second cause and is not part of the essence of matter insofar as it is matter. Hence God can create the matter without the form.'[27] Toletus knew both positions. In his *Commentaria* on the *Physica* (Lib. I, Quaest. XIII), he asks whether prime matter is a substance and details both Scotus's affirmative and Aquinas's negative reply. Toletus shares Aquinas's view, his own doctrine being that prime matter is imperfect in itself. Then he asks whether matter can exist without form, and he refers to Aquinas's argument that that would be impossible (since it implies a contradiction), and to

Scotus's doctrine (though without references) that it is possible, should God will it. Again he favours Aquinas's position, that there cannot be matter in act without form, and against Scotus he again argues that matter is imperfect in itself.[28]

Eustachius a Sancto Paulo's teaching differed from that of Toletus. There is no problem about form existing without matter: 'If divine virtue separated form from matter, form, with the exception of rational soul, could not cohere by itself without divine virtue sustaining it.' The problem arises with respect to matter existing without form. Eustachius supports a variant of Scotus's doctrine, though, as usual, without citing sources or mentioning Scotus by name (or mentioning Aquinas's doctrine): 'Although matter cannot be produced or annihilated by any natural agent, God can create or annihilate it . . . God can strip naked all forms, substantial and accidental, from matter, or create it naked, without form, *ex nihilo*, and allow it to subsist by its own power in such a state.'[29] Abra de Raconis agreed; quoting both Aquinas and Scotus, he says that matter is an incomplete substance but maintains that God can create matter without substantial form.[30]

Scipion Dupleix throws into relief the disagreement between Thomists and Scotists:

Thus matter deserves the name of substance because it subsists by itself and is not in any subject. This reply is based on the Philosopher's doctrine, but it does not satisfy everyone, particularly Saint Thomas Aquinas and his followers, who hold that such matter is not in nature, and cannot be in it, and even that this is so repugnant to nature that God himself cannot make it subsist thus stripped of all form. But this opinion is too bold, too mistaken, and it has been rejected by Scotus the Subtle [Doctor] and by several others.[31]

Thus it would be difficult to locate a common doctrine among the schoolmen on this important topic. All of them talked about matter, form, and privation, but their interpretations of these terms ranged from genuine hylemorphism, as in the case of Aquinas, to a kind of dualist position, following Scotus, whose *forma corporeitatis* (originally due to Avicenna) actualised all matter independently of its reception of substantial form.[32] In the 'new philosophy' these problems became transformed into issues concerning the relation between quantity and body, the possibility of quantity without body, that is, the vacuum, and the intelligibility of the substratum said to underlie dimensioned body and its qualities.

III. NATURAL BODY

As pointed out earlier, natural body is the concern of natural philosophy, 'artificial bodies' the concern of the mechanical arts. Since every artifact or machine is composed exclusively of natural bodies of whatever kind, however, *natural* body was the primary interest of the schoolmen *qua* speculative philosophers. There had long been different views among them as to the precise identification of 'natural body'. Magirus, for example, rehearsed different views on the question among earlier interpreters of Aristotle. For Aquinas (explained Magirus), 'mobile being' (*ens mobile*) is the subject of physics, whereas Albertus Magnus had claimed that it is 'mobile body' (*corpus mobile*). For the Scotists the subject of physics is 'natural substance' (*substantia naturalis*). Then the moderns (*recentiores*), whose view Magirus shares and among whom he seems to include the Paduan Aristotelian Jacopo Zabarella, say that the common subject of the whole of natural science is *corpus mobile* taken generally, comprising both celestial and terrestrial body and in so far as it is natural, that is, in so far as it possesses *per se* the principles of motion and rest.[33] Abra de Raconis covers the same ground as Magirus (without citing authorities), arguing that the proper object of natural philosophy is 'natural body' (*corpus naturale*), and discusses the other candidates: *ens naturale, ens mobile, substantia naturalis, substantia mobilis,* and *corpus mobile.* But *corpus mobile* is the same thing as *corpus naturale,* he reasons, and the other four are ineligible, because, for example, they are *per se* the subjects of the affections or properties with which natural philosophy deals only in so far as they are composites of matter and form, in which case they are identical to natural bodies, and the affections in question – quantity, place, time, motion – are those that pertain *per se* to natural body.[34]

As for spirits, Magirus claimed that they, including God, being instances of pure act and immaterial form, do not have a 'nature' in that they are not subject to motion and rest and cannot therefore be the subject of physics. In particular, 'since God is above nature [*supra naturam*], He cannot be part of the subject of physics.'[35] The atomist Johann Sperling excluded the doctrine of angels from physics, and Johann Heinrich Alsted argued that divine action is neither physical nor metaphysical motion, but *motus hyperphysicus.*[36] Much later in the century, Isaac Newton was to take a broader view. Recognising a wide variety of natural phenomena not amenable to mechanical explanation, he inferred the existence of active and passive principles acting as God's spiritual intermediaries in the physical world. Accordingly, natural philosophy was a discipline of wide extension: 'To discourse of [God] from the appearance of things, does certainly belong to Natural Philosophy.'[37]

It is important for the present discussion that Peripatetic writers like Abra de Raconis and Magirus considered the object of physics to be natural/mobile body, since that affords a direct link to the modern conception of physics as the foundational science of body and its affects. The ground for the mechanical philosophy was prepared not only by reborn Greek atomism, but also to an appreciable extent by the Peripatetic tradition in which its protagonists were educated, yet against which they are conventionally seen to have instigated whole-sale rebellion. The late Peripatetic simplification of the object of physics was something that the mechanists were to take over and extend. The *recentiores* who appeared on the scene after Magirus – such as Descartes (born the year Magirus died), Gassendi, Hobbes, and other mechanist philosophers – shared these views, though collectively they differed from the Peripatetics on the nature of *corpus* itself and on the principles of motion and rest in bodies *per se,* and differed from the Peripatetics and among themselves on the rôle and nature of spirit.

Another relevant aspect of the later scholastics' conception of natural body is that though it is essentially a composite of form and matter, three-dimensionality is an inalienable property or, as Toletus expressed it, a *proper accident* that derives from the essence.[38] Alsted writes:

Quantity is the first property of natural body, by which it is extended, that is, has one part beyond another. Accompanying it are a certain rarity or density, shape, and situation [*situs*].

Rule V. Quantity is an affection [*affectio*] inseparable from natural body. The reason for this rule is that quantity does not differ in reality from the matter of natural body. . . . So just as matter cannot be separated from body because it constitutes its essence, so neither can quantity. Whence it is a plain contradiction to say that there can exist a body that lacks quantity.[39]

And *corpus* 'is what has a length [*lineatum*], and is wide and broad: or, a figure capable [*capax*] of three dimensions. It is also called a solid, *sereno* [Greek].'[40] In his philosophical dictionary of 1619, Chasteigner de la Rochepozay, Bishop of Poitiers, described the traditional three kinds of *corpus:* (1) logical or metaphysical body, which is a genus of the category of substance; (2) mathematical body, or body viewed with respect to measure, which is three dimensions in the category of quantity; (3) physical body, or body viewed with respect to matter, which is either part of a composite, or is the whole itself. However, one senses a significant confluence of the traditional and the new (i.e., the Cartesian) in the 1658 edition of the dictionary prepared by François Samuel Desmarets, Descartes's friend and supporter. Desmarets's note on de la Rochepozay's description of *corpus* reads:

The opposition between physical and mathematical body concerns more our ways of conceiving, than the thing itself, because we consider body mathematically as measurable, physically as extended and having parts beyond parts. Otherwise every physical and natural body ought to be a *quantum* making up three dimensions in length, breadth and depth. In fact the formal ground [*ratio*] of corporeity is sited in that quantitative extension, which we cannot separate or abstract from body without contradiction.[41]

IV. IMPENETRABILITY AND THE VOID

The tri-dimensionality of physical body was a basic idea shared also by all proponents of the mechanical philosophy. Furthermore, they shared the Peripatetics' view that physical body requires impenetrability as the necessary concomitant of its mere extendedness in three dimensions. Goclenius spoke for everyone when he wrote: 'The penetration of dimensions of body is against nature, that is, nature abhors penetration, it conflicts with the customary order of nature.'[42] If the interpenetration of physical bodies were possible, it was generally agreed, there would be no resistance between bodies in mutual contact, any number of bodies could congregate in the same place at the same time, and 'the customary order of nature' would quickly become total disorder. However, there was no general agreement, among either the scholastics or the mechanist philosophers, on how to explain the forces that ensure, as a matter of physical fact, that no penetration of dimensions ever takes place.

Scholastic discussions of corporeal interpenetration (such as whether it can happen naturally and whether God can make it happen)[43] were occasioned largely by Aristotle's arguments against the void, in which the impenetrability of dimensioned body played an important rôle. These arguments can be separated into two general kinds (*Physica* IV.6–9). First, there are arguments concluding that the void is impossible if it is thought to be a place with nothing in it, or a place deprived of body, distinct from the bodies that occupy it. If it were three-dimensional, it would be a body, and could not therefore receive another body: 'If void is a sort of place deprived of body, when there is a void where will a body placed in it move to? It certainly cannot move into the whole of the void.'[44] Instead of accepting the arguments that motion requires either void or the unacceptable interpenetration of bodies, Aristotle turns the argument against his opponents, arguing that void itself would require the interpenetration of bodies.

The second kind of argument against the void was derived from Aristotle's laws of motion. A body moving by violence (see Section VI) moves in proportion to the force exerted on it and in inverse proportion to the resistance of the medium through which it moves. Since a void would provide no resistance, the body in a would-be void 'would move with a speed beyond any ratio'[45] – which cannot happen.

Scholastics generally tried to soften Aristotle's arguments against the void, not to proclaim its existence, but to accept its possibility in the sense that God, should He wish, *could* create a void.[46] Towards that end, there were numerous discussions of

Aristotle's argument against the void based on the impossibility of local motion in the void. Many of these discussions were prompted by an internal criticism of Aristotle's position, probably due to Philoponus, but known through Averroes's rejection of it. The criticism is that in Aristotle's system the heavens have a determined speed of rotation but are not slowed down by the resistance of any medium. If one applied Aristotle's reasoning about the impossibility of motion in the void to the heavens, then the heavens would have to rotate with a speed beyond any ratio. Rejecting Aristotle's reasoning might lead one to conceive a notion of mass as internal resistance to motion, thus invalidating the conclusion that a body in the void would move with a speed beyond any ratio. Duhem argues that that was Aquinas's view, but that he was often misrepresented by subsequent thinkers.[47]

There was not much disagreement among seventeenth-century scholastics about the existence of the void and motion within it. Toletus, concurring with Aquinas, understood him to hold against Aristotle that motion in the void would not be instantaneous. Eustachius agreed, calling motion in the void extremely probable, and he clarified his notion of imaginary space above the heavens by asserting that it is not a vacuum properly speaking. Dupleix also denied Aristotle's argument against the impossibility of motion in the void; he asserted that the speed of motion is due not just to the resistance of the medium, but also to the weight and shape of the mobile.[48] Théophraste Bouju seems to have been the only exception to the general agreement, arguing that 'nothing can move in the void; . . . if space were void, there would be no resistance and motion would be instantaneous.'[49] But Bouju rejoined the common view with respect to the supernatural possibility of the void. Although it is impossible for a wholly void internal place or space, being a quantity, to be without body, 'as much as a quantity is an accident which requires a body in which to inhere, without which it cannot exist', yet 'God by his absolute power can give subsistence to quantity, as he does, in the Holy Eucharist, to the species of bread and wine which remain after transsubstantiation.'[50]

V. PLACE AND TIME

In *Physica* IV Aristotle defines proper *place* as the boundary of the containing body in contact with the (moveable) contained body; but straightaway he modifies this definition by asserting that place is the innermost *motionless* boundary of what contains (*Physica* IV.1–5). Thus the place of a boat on a river is not the flowing water, but the whole river, because the river as a whole is motionless whereas with respect to the boat the water acts not *qua* container but *qua* vehicle.[51] The tension between Aristotle's two definitions gives rise to questions about whether place is mobile, and whether the ultimate sphere has a place. It seems the ultimate sphere does not have a place, since there is no body outside it to contain it; yet it needs to have a place, since it rotates, and local motion involves change of place. Recognising the difficulties, Aristotle distinguished between place *per se* and place *per accidens.* Place *per se* belongs properly to bodies capable of locomotion or growth. Place *per accidens* belongs indirectly to things through other things conjoined with them in an intermediate way. In this sense the ultimate sphere is in a place, 'for all its parts are; for on the orb, one part contains another.'[52]

According to Aquinas's modification of Aristotle's account of the place of the ultimate sphere, the parts of the ultimate sphere are not actually in place, but the ultimate sphere is in a place accidentally because of its parts, which are themselves potentially in place.[53] Aquinas also rejected Averroes's solution to the same problem, that the ultimate sphere is lodged because of its centre, which is fixed. On the subject of the immobility of place, Aquinas produced an interesting view.[54] The technical vocabulary developed to interpret Aquinas's view is a distinction between *material* and *formal* place, where formal place is the *ratio* of place, in Aquinas's vocabulary. As material place, place is then moveable accidentally, and is immoveable *per se* as formal place, defined as the place of a body with respect to the universe as a whole. Thus the ship is formally immobile (with respect to the universe as a whole) when the water flows around it.

Modifying Aquinas's account, Scotus and the Scotists rejected the distinction between material and formal place, arguing instead that place is a relation of the containing body with respect to the contained body. Place is then a relative attribute of these bodies. They also used 'the where' (*ubi*) to refer sometimes to inner place, to denote the symmetric relation of the contained body with respect to the containing body. Since the relation changes with any change of either the contained body or the containing body, the place of a body does not remain the same when the matter around it renews itself, even though the body might remain immobile with respect to the universe as a whole. When a body is in a changing medium, the body is in one place at one instant and in another at another instant. With respect to local motion, the two places are distinct but *equivalent places.*[55] On the question of the ultimate sphere, Scotus denied the solutions of both Averroes and Aquinas, claiming that heaven can rotate even though no body contains it and even if it contained no body; it can rotate even if it were formed out of a single homogeneous sphere; Scotus even denied that the Empyrean heaven could have lodged the ultimate sphere. But he did not provide any positive account of the place of the ultimate sphere.[56]

Late sixteenth- and seventeenth-century scholastic discussions of these questions followed the expected patterns of Thomist Jesuits and Scotist non-Jesuits.
Toletus, for example, took Aquinas's side against Scotus on both questions.[57] So
did Théophraste Bouju, who also retained some Averroist elements in his doctrine. Bouju asserted that place is moveable *per se* in what he called *lieu de situation*
and *per accidens* in what he called *lieu environnant:*

> The earth . . . is in a *lieu environnant* and can also be said to be in a *lieu de situation* with
> respect to the poles of the world. But it cannot change place with respect to its totality;
> thus it is immobile in that respect and mobile only with respect to some parts that can be
> separated from the totality and moved into others. The firmament is also in a *lieu de situation*
> with respect to the earth, but it cannot change except with respect to its parts and not in
> its totality, in the fashion of the earth.[58]

Eustachius a Sancto Paulo and Abra de Raconis, on the other hand, used Scotus's
vocabulary: place and *ubi* are relations between the containing and contained
bodies, and places are the same *by equivalence.*[59] Eustachius develops briefly some
interesting views about the place of the ultimate sphere. The place of the outer-
most sphere is internal place or space, and external but imaginary place.[60] This
seems to be a seventeenth-century development of the Scotist view, since Abra de
Raconis advances a similar doctrine. He discusses two kinds of place: external
place is the surface of the concave ambient body, internal place is the space
occupied by the body. The ultimate heaven is in place internally, or occupies a
space of three dimensions.[61]

As is often the case, it is Scipion Dupleix who provides the greatest contrast of
opinions. The opinion he wants to advance, and which is approved by Philoponus
and Averroes, is that place is immobile in itself, even though bodies change
place. He asserts that Aquinas disagrees with that view (probably because of the
moveability of material place) and that Aquinas advances another, which he rejects
completely. Dupleix's gloss on the doctrine of formal place is that one can imagine
a distance from each place to certain parts of the world, with respect to which a
given place, though changeable, is said to be immobile.[62] He is surprised that this
opinion is received in several schools of philosophy, but then there are 'so many
weak though opinionated brains' who will follow their leader right or wrong.
When air blows round a house, the place of the house changes accidentally
(*accidentairement*). The house is in the same place *by equivalence.* As for the place of
the universe, Dupleix also rejects Aquinas's opinion as completely mistaken.[63] He
holds that the heavens do not change place or move locally, since they merely
rotate within their own circumference.

There are hidden within these debates between Thomists and Scotists questions about the relativity of motion, but by contrast with the contributions of earlier figures such as Aquinas, Buridan, and Oresme and of the seventeenth-century 'new philosophers' (see Chapter 20), contemporary scholastic representations of these debates do not make much progress on the issue. As with the scholastic challenge to Aristotle's conception of place, the Augustinian challenge to his conception of time contains some questions about the relativity of time, but again, not much progress is made by attempts within seventeenth-century school doctrines to resolve the difficulties.

For Aristotle, time is the number of motion; that is, time is the enumeration of motion (*Physica* IV.10–14). There cannot be any time without there being some change. The link between time and motion is extremely close, given that we measure motion by time and time by motion. Consequently, there are as many times as there are motions, and these times are all able to serve as the definition of time. However, choosing a motion to measure time is not an indifferent choice: the measure must be of the same kind as the object it serves to measure, but it must also play the rôle of principle with respect to the latter. Although Aristotle thinks that time has no reality independent of the motion it measures, he does not think that time has no reality independent of the measurer of the motion. Time is independent of soul:

Whether if soul did not exist time would exist or not, is a question that may fairly be asked; for if there cannot be some one to count there cannot be anything that can be counted, so that evidently there cannot be number; for number is either what has been, or what can be, counted. But if nothing but soul, or in soul reason, is qualified to count, there would not be time unless there were soul, but only that of which time is an attribute, i.e., if *movement* can exist without soul, and the before and after are attributes of movement, and time is these *qua* innumerable.[64]

The questions raised by the scholastics dealt with the subjectivity of time and its intimate connexion with motion. Scotus rejected many elements of Aristotle's doctrine; inspired by Augustine's theory of time, he argued that even if all motion were to stop, time would still exist and would measure the universal rest.[65] That doctrine seems not to survive in Toletus or Eustachius. The seventeenth-century scholastic view seems to be that time began with the motion of the heavens and will end with it. Toletus argues a Thomistic line that if there is no motion, there is no generation or time, and Eustachius argues that time is divisible into real time and imaginary time, where imaginary time is what we imagine precedes the creation of the world.[66] Dupleix refers favourably to Augustine's account of time and talks of time measuring both motion and rest, but it is unclear what that amounts to, since he does not specifically mention universal rest.[67]

VI. LOCAL MOTION

For Aristotle, motion was a general concept. It meant change from one state to another and included alteration (change with respect to quality), augmentation, and diminution (change with respect to quantity), local motion (change from place to place), and sometimes (though improperly)[68] generation and corruption (change from one kind of substance to another) (*Physica* III, 201a10). All of these different kinds of motion were later united under the single definition, often to be mocked later by seventeenth-century philosophers: 'motion is the act of an entity in potentiality, insofar as it is in potentiality', or in the Latin formula frequently found in the Scholastic textbooks, 'motus est actus entis in potentia prout in potentia est.'

As for local motion, Aristotle had chosen it as the primary one of his three categories of motion. Augmentation without a preceding alteration is impossible, he argued, and alteration is impossible without the something that alters being now nearer now further away from the thing altered, which in turn is impossible without motion with respect to place. Furthermore, augmentation and diminution entail change of magnitude with respect to place, and local motion is the only kind of motion that does not change the body's qualities or essential nature. Again, local motion is the motion produced by things that move themselves, and the self-mover is the first principle and source of all that is moved (*Physica* VIII.7). The atomists of antiquity also provided a fundamental rôle for local motion, which is inherent in the atoms and is thereby the source of all activity and change. This feature of atomist physics was assimilated by the Stoics into their theory of elemental change.[69]

Naturally, Aristotle's arguments for the primacy of local motion were common features of Peripatetic *summae* and commentaries on Aristotle. As Magirus put it, 'local motion is the primary kind, because the others cannot exist without it, as Aristotle teaches.'[70] Toletus follows Aristotle's threefold division: motion with respect to quantity (*augmentatio* and *diminutio*), with respect to quality (*alteratio*), and with respect to *ubi* (*motus localis, latio*). But note his remark on the third kind of motion:

Now motion with respect to 'the where' does not have a name, either general or special, but it may be called 'carriage' [*latio*], although [strictly speaking] the term applies only to things that move [*moventur*] naturally and do not have the faculty for initiating or terminating motion, for these are properly said to be carried [*ferri*]. But the term may now be applied to any motion according to place.[71]

Taking our cue from Toletus, 'carriage' being only tentatively provisional, we leave *latio* without an English equivalent in the following passage from Keckermann, who is marginally more helpful by equating it with the Greek for 'locomotion':

> There are four species of passive motion: 1, *latio* or *phora*; 2, alteration; 3, augmentation; 4, diminution. *Latio* is a passive motion of a body by which it moves from place to place, and is either natural, or violent, or a mixture of both. Natural *latio* occurs when the body moves from place to place by an internal cause and by a certain native propensity.[72]

The Coimbran commentators devoted a *quaestio* on 'whether *latio* inheres in the mobile, or in a circumadjacent body'. Their conclusion was that it inheres in the mobile itself, and they note that *latio* is 'when a thing is transported from one part of space [*spatium*] into another'.[73] Although *latio* cannot be defined, as it seems, except in terms that already employ or imply the *definiendum*, that never prevented anyone, Peripatetic or new philosopher, from using the notion in a fruitful way (see Chapter 20).

This *quaestio* is an instance of the important general worry about the ontological status of local motion. Does it exist as an entity independently of the thing moved? Does it differ from the circumadjacent place through which the motion takes place, or from the *terminus* attained at each instant? The realist position, represented principally by the Thomists and Scotists, was that motion is an instance of *fluxus formae,* a successive acquisition of forms, a real accident, and that it has its own cause. In particular, Paul of Venice claimed that motion is not a ratio between distances (in unit time) or between times (taken to move unit distances), because 'a ratio is only a relative accident, whereas motion is an absolute accident.'[74]

On the other hand, the nominalist position, represented principally by the Ockhamists, was that motion has no existence independent of the mobile, that it is an instance of *forma fluens,* nothing more than the termini successively attained by the mobile.[75] Ockham argued that the cause that keeps a projectile moving is neither the hand that has thrown it, nor the air, nor a power (*virtus*) in the projectile, but simply the mobile itself and of itself. Since motion is not a new effect, it does not need a cause:

> The mover is wholly indistinct from the moved. If you say that a new effect has some cause, but local motion is a new effect [therefore etc.], I reply that local motion is not a new

effect, whether absolute or relational [*respectivus*], and I do so while denying 'the where' [*ubi*], because local motion is nothing other than the mobile coexisting with diverse parts of space in such a way that it coexists with no single part long enough for contraries to be true of it. . . . For it would be extraordinary if my hand, by touching a stone through local motion, caused some power [*virtus*] in the stone.[76]

In addition to the inevitable divisions within each of the nominalist and realist positions, there were ambivalent and perhaps reconciliatory positions between the two extremes. John Major (1467/9–1550) and his followers appreciated both positions, arguing that there is truth on both sides, and suggesting in particular that the differences between them are principally terminological. In his *Super octo libros physicorum Aristotelis quaestiones* (1555), Domingo de Soto (1495–1560), who studied at Paris under Major, avoided the 'sinful' excesses of the realists and nominalists, arguing that there is no real distinction between motion and mobile, but that there is a modal distinction, or a distinction of reason. Yet motion is not thereby just an *ens rationis:* it has its own cause, because it is still the case that 'everything that moves is moved by something else.'[77]

As noted in section IV, 'Impenetrability and the Void', one of Aristotle's arguments against the void depended on the law that the speed of a 'violent' motion varies directly as the force exerted on the mobile and inversely as the resistance acting against the motion. The distinction between natural and violent motion, and that between natural and non-natural place, were especially significant because they operated at the heart of Aristotelian cosmology and at the same time were among the target doctrines that were overthrown by the new philosophy. In the Aristotelian tradition, the natural tendency of a heavy body to fall, and of a light body to rise, were interpreted as the striving of the preponderant element in each body to reach its natural place. Earth and water both strive (earth more so than water) to reach the centre of the universe, that is, of the earth: fire and air both strive (fire more so than air) to reach the sphere of the moon. If a preponderant element is moved further away from its natural place and released, it returns, striving to be once more as close as possible to its natural place. In each case the actualisation of the natural striving is the body's 'natural motion.' It is rectilinear, it is slower at the beginning of the motion, and it accelerates the closer it approaches the body's natural place. When the preponderant element is moved in a direction opposite to its natural tendency, the resultant motion is forced, or 'violent'. Prior to the seventeenth century there was some debate as to whether natural and violent motions could co-exist in the same mobile. Some denied the possibility, others accepted it, admitting 'mixed motions' to explain (for example) the trajectory of a stone thrown between two points on the ground. As for the celestial spheres, composed of the fifth element (*quintessence*), their natural motions are uniform, circular, and unmixed.

Accompanying the distinction between natural and violent motion was the distinction between their causes. It was axiomatic that 'everything that moves is moved by something else' (omne quod movetur ab alio movetur), but this causal principle requires careful interpretation in individual cases: neither the identity of the 'something else', nor the question of its separateness from the mobile, is always a straightforward matter. The 'something else' that causes natural motion is intrinsic to the mobile, and was identified variously as an 'intrinsic form', an 'innate' or 'native propensity' or, where the mobile is animate, as a soul. But the uniform natural motions of the celestial spheres, which seem to be self-moving, and the composite nature of animals, which are self-moving, called for a qualification of the basic causal principle. As Keckermann, for example, explains, the heavens move by themselves, according to some, or by angels or intelligences, according to others, but with animals there is no room for doubt:

> When a man walks from place to place, he indeed moves by himself as long as one part [of his body] pushes another. When a bird flies, its body is moved by the wings, which are a part of the bird. In sum, every animate body is moved by its soul as an internal principle of motion, and since the soul is not something separate from the animated body, it must not be said that everything that moves is moved by other things completely separate from it, but the axiom should be formulated disjunctively: everything that moves is moved either by some part of itself, or by another external and separate body.

The general theorem for passive motion is that 'everything that moves is moved either by another thing, or by itself considered according to its power acting against a part of itself.'[78]

Violent motions, on the other hand, arise from some *extrinsic* motor or principle of motion operating through contact with the mobile and contrary to its natural inclination.[79] But those violent motions in which the motor is no longer in contact with the mobile created a puzzle. For example, why do thrown stones and other projectiles continue to move after they have left the projector? One notorious solution from antiquity was the *antiperistasis* ('mutual replacement') argument, first reported by Aristotle: on leaving the hand of the thrower the stone pushes the air in front, which in turn moves other air round to the back of the stone, to prevent the formation of a vacuum, which in turn pushes the stone from behind. Aristotle seems to have rejected this argument, preferring to identify the air itself behind the stone as the direct transmitter of the hand's original force.[80] These arguments met with decisive objections during late antiquity and the

mediaeval period, to be replaced first by John Philoponus's doctrine of an impressed incorporeal kinetic force, then by the closely related idea in Islamic writers
(notably Avicenna) of an inclination (*mail*) transmitted from projector to projectile,
and finally by the view most widely accepted after the fourteenth century, the
impetus theory, whose principal advocate was Jean Buridan. According to the
impetus theory, the projector impresses on the mobile a power or force, which
now as an internal cause maintains the motion until (according to some) the
impetus naturally dies away, or until (according to Buridan) the impetus, as a
naturally permanent force, meets with an opposing resistance. In the case of the
celestial spheres, where there is no resistance, Buridan claimed that the impetus
imparted to them at the Creation ensures their perpetual motion.[81]

VII. INFINITY AND CONTINUITY

Aristotle's doctrine on infinity (*Physica* III.4–8) concerns the two infinites, infinite
by addition and infinite by division. But when we say that 'something is infinite',
the 'is' in that sentence means either what potentially is or what actually is, so
there are four possibilities: potential infinite by division and addition, and actual
infinite by division and addition. Aristotle denies actual infinities, thereby denying
both the actual infinitely large and the actual infinitely small, and affirms the
potential infinite by division in magnitude and number, while denying the potential infinite by addition in magnitude (except in the case where one is adding a
part determined by a ratio, instead of keeping the parts equal).

For Aristotle, however, what is potential will be actual. This seems to license
the inference from the existence of the potential infinite to the actual infinite.
Using Aristotle's example, when we speak of the potential existence of a statue,
we mean that there will be an actual statue. It is not so with the infinite. There
will not be an actual infinite. There are then at least two senses of 'potential',
according to Aristotle. One sense, which the potential infinite shares with the
Olympic games and things whose being is not like that of substance, consists in a
process of coming to be and passing away, a process which is finite at every stage,
but always different. The Olympic games are potential both in the sense that their
being consists in a process, and in the sense that they *may* occur. It is only in the
latter sense that when a state is potential, there will be an actual state. That is how
Aristotle can affirm potential infinities such as the infinite in time, in the generations of man, in the division of magnitudes, and in numbers, while denying the
actual infinite. But when Aristotle denies the potential infinite in magnitude by
the addition of equal parts, he does so by asserting that 'there is no infinite in the

direction of increase. For the size which it can potentially be it can actually be. Hence, since no sensible magnitude is infinite, it is impossible to exceed every assigned magnitude; for if it were possible, there would be something bigger than the heavens.'[82] Thus Aristotle's physical world is finite and cannot grow, but in that world magnitude is continuous (or indefinitely divisible), and time and generation are unending (or extendable indefinitely).

The standard scholastic terminology for dealing with the problems of infinity was imported from logic. Logicians distinguished between *categorematic* terms and *syncategorematic* terms: categorematic terms have a signification by themselves, and syncategorematic (cosignificative) terms do not. Examples of the first kind are substantival names and verbs, and examples of the second kind are adjectives, adverbs, conjunctions, and prepositions (every, whole, both, of every sort, no, nothing, neither, but, alone, only, is, not, necessarily, contingently, if, unless, but that, infinitely many). The distinction is applied to infinity to yield both a categorematic and syncategorematic infinite. 'The phrase "infinitely many" is both syncategorematic and categorematic, for it can indicate an infinite plurality belonging to its substance either absolutely or in respect to its predicate.'[83] One can then define the two kinds of infinite separately; the syncategorematic infinite may be defined as 'for any number or magnitude there is a greater' and categorematic infinite as 'greater than any number or magnitude, no matter how great'.[84] With the distinction one can solve logical puzzles, since it may be true that something is infinite, taken syncategorematically, and false that something is infinite, taken categorematically.[85] It also enables one to ask separately whether there are syncategorematic and categorematic infinites in nature, without worrying about potentialities. Naturally, various scholastics took differing views with respect to the existence of various infinities and often disagreed with Aristotle's doctrines. It is not difficult to see why this should be so, given that portions of Aristotle's doctrine about infinity are clearly in conflict with the conception of an absolutely omnipotent God who is a creator. The standard doctrine (or correction of Aristotle) was the denial of the categorematic infinite (in number and magnitude) and acceptance of the syncategorematic infinite (in number and magnitude). Of course, there were some thinkers, notably Gregory of Rimini and Albert of Saxony, who argued that God could create a categorematic infinite in nature.

The seventeenth-century school doctrines simply conflated syncategorematic infinite with potential infinite and categorematic infinite with actual infinite but denied the inference from syncategorematic infinite to categorematic infinite.[86] There followed a denial of infinity in act. However, seventeenth-century scholastics were also careful to state that others argued that God could create a categorematic infinite.[87] Toletus ably treats such topics as the categorematic infinite, division into proportional parts, and whether a body can be actually infinite, but he affirms a generally conservative position. On the other hand, he does refer his readers to Albert of Saxony's more daring position.[88] Roughly the same can be said about the Coimbrans and Abra de Raconis, except that de Raconis gives accurate references to William of Ockham and Gregory of Rimini.[89] According to Brockliss, there was a schoolman, du Chevreul, professor at Paris in the 1620s and 1630s, who taught that Aquinas was wrong to deny that God could create an infinite body.[90]

Eustachius a Sancto Paulo's doctrine seems to differ significantly from the standard view, so it is worth detailing. Eustachius apparently thinks of syncategorematic infinite as a species of infinite in act. Inquiring into the ways in which something is infinite, Eustachius divides the infinite into infinite in actuality and potential infinite. He then divides it into categorematic actual infinite and syncategorematic actual infinite, depending upon whether all the parts of a given infinite are actually separated. Infinites whose parts are not all in actuality are of three kinds: infinite in succession, addition, and subtraction.[91]

Eustachius does think that the continuum is divisible into infinite parts. But in the final analysis his doctrinal deviations from the standard view are more cosmetic than real. He argues that the continuum is not divisible by equal magnitudes, but by equal proportional parts (or by parts whose magnitudes diminish by halves). Thus it is infinitely divisible successively, and not simultaneously. The continuum is divisible to infinity not in such a way that there can exist simultaneously actually separated infinite parts, but in a way that one can progress in the division:

If you object that it follows that if one has to posit an actual infinity in nature, it would follow that either one can divide a continuum into infinite parts or those parts in the continuum would not be actually infinite, we reply, *infinity in act* can be conceived in two ways: one, properly speaking, in which all the parts are actually separated and distinct from one another, which is called categorematic infinite; the other in truth improperly speaking, whose parts are not actually separated from one another, but are said to be communicating with one another, in which the smaller are contained in the larger, which is called syncategorematic infinite. Thus a continuum can be divided to infinity and it does not follow that we have to hold an actual infinity, properly speaking, but only an infinite in act in the second way, improperly speaking. From this it is to be understood that all parts of the continuum are actually in the continuum, not however actually infinite categorematically and properly, but syncategorematically and improperly.[92]

Eustachius is clearly playing verbal games with 'actual infinity' and 'syncategorematic infinite'. He does not really hold that syncategorematic infinites are, properly speaking, actual infinites. In fact, he reaffirms that 'only actual categore-matic infinite is truly and properly infinite. . . . Thus actual syncategorematic infinite is not properly an infinite in actuality . . . it is to be called potential infinite.'[93] And he rejoins the standard doctrine. He even is careful to look as if he is upholding God's absolute omnipotence when denying Him the power to create a categorematic infinite: 'There is no actual categorematic infinite, not because it is repugnant to God's power, but because nature cannot suffer it.'[94]

The intent of this chapter was to convey important aspects of late scholastic doctrines on a range of topics that collectively form the broad context of the arguments and debates examined in the chapters that follow. However much later philosophers distanced themselves from these doctrines, the dominance of Peripatetic philosophy in the schools ensured that it continued to be common currency for much of the century. This is the background against which one should try to understand the notable achievements in natural philosophy in the early modern period.

NOTES

1 This point is well made with reference to Newton, the archetypal hero of the Scientific Revolution, in Westfall 1980, p. 85.

2 Schmitt 1983a, 1983b; Mercer 1993.

3 Descartes, e.g., used the traditional terminology when he thought it appropriate, yet he did not always pay serious attention to the minutiae of terminological analysis, or the known differences among various school doctrines, which he saw as symptomatic of their collective philosophical effeteness: 'As for the philosophy of the School, I hold that it is not at all difficult to refute, because of the diversities in their opinions. For one can easily overturn all the foundations on which they agree among themselves; and that accomplished, all their disputes on particular matters appear silly.' Descartes to Mersenne, 11 November 1640, AT III 231–2. See also Morin to Descartes, 22 February 1638, AT I 541; Descartes to Morin, 13 July 1638, AT II 201–2. Descartes's awareness of the many doctrinal discords among his predecessors was one reason for his intention to start afresh. 'Maxims and opinions, such as those of the Philosophers, cannot be taught directly, from the fact that they are given as assertions. Plato says one thing, Aristotle another, Epicurus yet another. Telesio, Campanella, Bruno, Basso, Vanini – each of the innovators [*Novatores*] says something different from the others. Of all these people, which of them can teach not just me but anyone who loves wisdom?' Descartes to Beeckman, 17 October 1630, AT I 158. Cf. Gabbey 1970.

4 Ingegno 1988; Copenhaver 1988a; Copenhaver and Schmitt 1992, pp. 285–328.

5 For Toletus's division into *speculative, practical,* and *factive* philosophy, on which the above division is based, see Wallace 1988b, pp. 209–13. For the disciplinary divisions and sub-divisions common in Germany, see Freedman 1985, pp. 65–105. On the three-way division of moral philosophy, see Kraye 1988, pp. 303–6.

6 Clulee 1988, pp. 64–7; Copenhaver 1988a. For the Coimbrans' account of the two

kinds of magic, see Gilson 1979, art. 262. On the complexities of magical theory and of its relations to religion, see Walker 1958.

7 Debus 1977, pp. 8, 12, 78–84. Newman 1991, pp. i–iv, 134–8, 204–8; 1993. There is some dispute over the origin of the two-element theory: Hooykaas 1949; Debus 1965, p. 45, n. 35.

8 Peucer 1584, livre 13, pp. 512–13, 544–5. Rochot 1944, p. 89. On *philosophia naturalis,* see Gilson 1979, pp. 228–32; Wallace 1988b, pp. 209–13. No single term conveys the many senses of *logos:* in addition to Liddell and Scott 1968, see Peters 1967, pp. 110–12, and Dod 1982, p. 67. As for *physiologia,* Cicero refers to 'naturae ratio, quam physiologiam Graeci appellant', meaning 'inquiries into natural causes and phenomena' as understood by Aristotle, Epicurus, and others: *De divinatione* I.41.90; II.16.37; see also *De natura deorum* I.8.

9 See, e.g., Harris 1708–10, vol. 1, articles on 'Natural Philosophy', 'Physicks', and 'Physiology'.

10 First edition Frankfurt 1597, with at least thirteen editions during the seventeenth century. The edition consulted was Magirus 1642.

11 Descartes to Mersenne, 13 November 1629, AT I 70.

12 AT IXB 17.

13 Rochot 1944, p. 89.

14 Leibniz 1982–91, vol. 3, pp. 649–53 (Leibniz 1969, pp. 277–80).

15 Dobbs 1975, 1982, and 1991; also Gabbey 1990a, pp. 244–6.

16 The same is true of the Renaissance: see Wallace 1988b, pp. 213–14.

17 John Donne, *An Anatomy of the World: The First Anniversary* (1612), line 205.

18 AT IXB 14.

19 *Physica* I (190b 28–30). *De Physico Auditu sive Physicorum Aristotelis* I, lectio 13, Thomas Aquinas 1953, I, lectio 13 (Thomas Aquinas 1963, p. 53). See also *De principiis naturae ad Fratrem Silvestrum,* Thomas Aquinas 1965, p. 10.

20 Magirus 1642, pp. 11, 19–20.

21 Cf. Weisheipl 1965a, pp. 147–9; the editor's Introduction to McMullin 1965, pp. 1–23.

22 For a list of twenty problems on prime matter, listed originally in Mas 1599, see Wallace 1988b, p. 214, n. 39.

23 Weisheipl 1965a, pp. 151–3.

24 Support for this position comes from *De Anima* III.5, concerning the active intellect.

25 *Summa th.* I q7 a2 and q66 a1. See Wippel 1982, pp. 407–10.

26 *Opus Oxoniense,* II, dist. 12, q. 1. Adams 1987, pp. 639–47.

27 *Opus Oxoniense,* II, dist. 12, q. 2: Duns Scotus 1639, vol. 6, pt. 2, p. 682.

28 Toletus 1589, fol. 34v, fol. 35r. Théophraste Bouju also follows the Thomist line on the reality of prime matter. See Bouju 1614 , vol. 1, pp. 315–16 (chap. 6: 'Que la premiere matiere est pure puissance passive, et comment'); pp. 319–20 (chap. 11: 'Comment la premiere matiere est moyenne entre l'estant et le non estant'); p. 322 (chap. 15: 'Comment la forme donne l'estre au composé); pp. 326–7 (chap. 23: 'Que la nature et forme naturelle ne se trouvent jamais separees naturellement l'une de l'autre'); pp. 329–30 (chap. 26: 'Refutation d'une pretendue puisance objective en la premiere matiere, et de l'acte objectif qui lui respond'); pp. 330–1 (chap. 27: 'Rejection de l'acte entitatif ou objectif, que quelques uns ont estimé estre en la premiere matiere'); p. 331 (chap. 28: 'Refutation de l'opinion que la premiere matiere peu estre naturellement sans la forme').

29 Eustachius 1629, pp. 16–17, 22–3 (*Physica,* Lib. I, disp. 2, q. 4, 9).

30 *Tractatus de Principiis*, membrum quartum, 'Utrum materia sit pura potentia metaphysica': Abra de Raconis 1651, pp. 35, 38, 39.
31 Dupleix 1990, p. 131. It is interesting to note that Dupleix argues against St. Thomas's doctrine of prime matter partly because the sacrament of the Eucharist requires the reality of prime matter (p. 132). This is the complement of a question posed against Cartesians and Atomists later in the century – whether the sacrament of the Eucharist requires real qualities. Some Thomists got around the accusation by accepting the reality of matter as a miracle. See, e.g., Ceriziers 1643, chap. 3, which argues that there can be no form without matter and no matter without form naturally, but adds (pp. 51–2): 'However, one must not deny that God can conserve matter without any form, since these are two distinct things which do not depend on one another any more than accident does on substance, which can be seen separated from substance in the Eucharist.' The solution seems unstable, so that by 1665 there is even a Jesuit opposing the Thomists on prime matter: Pierre Gaultruche, who taught at La Flèche, Caen, and Paris, and who publicly rejected many other Thomist doctrines. Gaultruche 1665, vol. 2, *Physica Universalis*, p. 27. See Armogathe 1977.
32 The Thomist doctrine of matter was still held by some during the late seventeenth century. The views of Scotists such as Frassen seem to have won the day (Frassen 1686, pp. 36–41), with some Thomists and Jesuits holding a middle position (Barbay 1676, pp. 64–72; Vincent 1658–71, vol. 2, pp. 74–7). Yet we find the Dominican Antoine Goudin writing in 1668: 'It seems that matter cannot exist without form even by means of God's absolute power. That is what Saint Thomas states . . . God himself cannot make it that something exist and not exist. He cannot make something that implies a contradiction and, consequently, he cannot make matter be without form' (Goudin 1864, art. 4, p. 131).
33 Magirus 1642, pp. 1, 3–4. Zabarella 1586, cap. 2. Burgersdijck also nominates 'natural or mobile body' as the subject of physics, referring for support to Pereira and Zabarella, and to the Coimbrans and Toletus as dissenting voices. Burgersdijck 1654, p. 4. For a useful synopsis of the categorisations of philosophical sects in German textbook authors of the time (though not Magirus), see Freedman 1985, pp. 131–6.
34 *Tertia pars philosophiae, seu physica*, 'Arbor physicae praefatiuncula', *Praeludium* 2, *sect.* 2, Abra de Raconis 1633, pp. 28–32. Burgersdijck, too, states that the subject of physics is 'rectissimè . . . corpus naturale sive mobile'. Burgersdijck 1654, p. 4.
35 Magirus 1642, p. 8.
36 Sperling 1664, p. 25; Alsted 1623, pp. 150–1.
37 Newton 1934, p. 546. Cf. Gabbey 1990a, pp. 261–2.
38 Toletus 1589, fol. 123v, col. 1.
39 Alsted 1649, vol. 2, pp. 106–7 (*Physica*, pars I, cap. 10, 'De quantitate corporis naturalis').
40 Alsted 1626, p. 3275.
41 Chasteigner de la Rochepozay 1619, p. 21; 1658, p. 55 (Desmarets's note). François Samuel Desmarets (Maresius) was professor of theology at the University of Groningen from 1642 to 1673. He supported Descartes in the Voetius affair and in 1670 published *De abusu philosophiae cartesianae in rebus theologicis et fidei* (Groningen). See Nauta 1935; Dibon 1950, pp. 287–8; Verbeek 1992a, *passim*.
42 Goclenius 1613, p. 469.
43 See Eustachius 1629, p. 59 (*Physica, tractatus* II, q. III: 'An duo corpora in eodem loco et idem corpus in duobus locis esse possit'); and Dupleix 1990, pp. 259–62 and 267–9.

44 *Physica* IV.8 (214b 18–20).
45 *Physica* IV.8 (215b 24).
46 Although the attacks on Aristotle's views about the void preceded Etienne Tempier's Condemnations of 1277, it is clear that the attacks gained theological inspiration from the Condemnations. The two relevant condemned propositions were: no. 66, 'That God could not move the heaven in a straight line, the reason being that He would then leave a vacuum', and no. 190, 'That he who generates the world in its totality posits a vacuum, because place necessarily precedes that which is generated in it; and so before the generation of the world there would have been a place with nothing in it, which is a vacuum.' Clearly, these condemnations also have implications for the previous questions about the place of the universe and the relativity of motion. The numbering above is that of the edition of the Latin text in Mandonnet 1908–11, vol. 2, pp. 175–91, at pp. 181, 189, and the trans. is by E. L. Fortin and P. D. O'Neill, in Lerner and Mahdi 1972, pp. 335–54, at pp. 343, 352.
47 Duhem 1985, chaps. 9–10. For Duhem's account of Aquinas's concept of mass, see ibid., pp. 371–87. See also Grant 1981, chap. 3.
48 Toletus 1589, fol. 129r–30r (*Commentaria . . . in octo libros de Physica auscultatione,* IV, q. IX: 'An si esset vacuum, motus esset in non tempore'). Apparently, some Thomists may have thought motion in the void instantaneous. Gaultruche rejects what he thinks of as a Thomist doctrine about the impossibility of motion in the void: Gaultruche 1665, vol. 2, p. 361. Eustachius 1629, pp. 59–60, 61 (*Physica,* tract. III, 2a disp., q. 5 ['An motus in vacuo fieri possit'], q. 4 ['An detur vacuum']). For other interpretations of imaginary place or space, see Grant 1981, chaps. 6–7; Dupleix 1990, pp. 273–4. Interestingly, Ceriziers shared Dupleix's view, though implying that it was also Aristotle's: 'But how likely is it to state that it would be impossible for a man to move the tip of his finger in the void . . . we have reason to believe that the Philosopher denied motion in the void against the ancients only because they did not posit any other cause for its duration than the resistance of the medium' (Ceriziers 1643, pp. 104–6).
49 Bouju 1614, vol. 1, pp. 465–8 (chap. 14: 'Qu'il n'y a point de vide').
50 Bouju 1614, vol. 1, pp. 468–9 (chap. 15: 'Comment le lieu environnant peut et ne peut estre vide, par la puissance absolue de Dieu').
51 *Physica* IV.4 (212a 10–20).
52 *Physica* IV.5 (212b 12–14); cf. 212b 8–10.
53 Thomas Aquinas 1953, IV, lectio 7; 1963; and 1954. See also Duhem 1985, chaps. 4–6. Averroes's view clearly requires the immobility of the earth at the centre of the universe. Aquinas's view does not seem to require the immobility of the earth, but does require the immobility of the universe as a whole, an opinion that was condemned in 1277. See note 46.
54 Thomas Aquinas 1953, IV, lectio 8; 1963; and 1954.
55 *Quaestiones in librum II Sententiarum,* dist. II, q. VI, Duns Scotus 1639. See also Duhem 1985, chaps. 4–6.
56 *Quaestiones Quodlibetales,* q. 12, Duns Scotus 1639.
57 Thomas Aquinas 1953, IV, q. V ('An locus sit immobilis'), and q. VII ('An ultima sphaera sit in loco'). Toletus 1589, fol. 120r–1r, 121v–2v. There is an abbreviated version of the doctrine in Du Moulin 1644, chap. 9, 'Du Lieu et du Vide': 'Particular place (*lieu particulier*) is the inner surface of the body that immediately contacts the contained body. Thus the inner surface of a barrel is the place of the wine with which it is filled. This place is mobile. But there is an immobile place, namely, the one considered with respect to the universe.'

58 Bouju 1614, vol. 1, pp. 458–9 (chap. 7: 'Comment le ciel et la terre sont en lieu, et peuvent estre dits se mouvoir de mouvement de lieu'); see also p. 460 (chap. 9: 'Que le lieu naturel est immobile').

59 Eustachius 1629, pp. 56–8 (*Physica*, tract. III, disp. 2, q. 1 'Quid sit locus'). Abra de Raconis 1651, pp. 205–6 (IV, tract. II, sec. 3).

60 Eustachius 1629, pp. 58–9 (*Physica*, tract. III, disp. 2, q. 2, 'Quotuplex sit locus'). For more on imaginary place, see Grant 1981, chaps. 6–7. Imaginary space is rejected in Ceriziers's *Métaphysique:* 'the word imaginary is understood as an infinite void one claims to be above the heavens, in which one places the all-perfect being, for fear that he would be confined by the vast and large vaults of the Empyrean heaven. Those who hold this opinion base themselves on the Scriptures and reason: on the Scriptures which assure that God is above the heavens; on reason which cannot suffer any limit to infinite essence. But who does not see that this great void is a being of the imagination, that is to say, a chimera? For either these spaces are something or they are nothing; if they are something real, one is wrong to call them imaginary. If they are nothing, why does one say that God is in nothing?' (Ceriziers 1643, pp. 86–90). Ceriziers's opposition to any God-filled imaginary space is an interesting counterpoint to his (ambiguous) acceptance of the relativity of the reference for motion (Ceriziers 1643, p. 91).

61 Abra de Raconis 1651, pp. 204–5 (IV, tract. II, sec. 1–2). The distinction between external and internal place (or space) can also be found in Toletus and the Coimbrans; but they do not use the distinction to resolve the two standard problems about the mobility of place and the place of the universe. For more on internal and external place, see Grant 1981, chap. 2. The fact that Toletus distinguishes between internal and external place has allowed some commentators to argue that Toletus is the source for Descartes's two kinds of place. One commentator even provides parallel texts as support; see Echarri 1950. But that methodology cannot be conclusive, since there may be even greater parallelism between Descartes's text and other texts.

62 A similar account of *external* or *physical* place is retailed 'ex Conimbricensibus' in Chasteigner de la Rochepozay 1619, p. 51.

63 On the place of the heavens as a whole, Dupleix says of Thomas's opinion: 'Mais c'est abuser et mescompter.' Dupleix 1990, p. 257. By mid-century, even the Jesuit Gaultruche was rejecting the Thomist doctrine of place, including the doctrine that the universe cannot move as a whole (Gaultruche 1655, vol. 2, p. 331). As with matter and form, the debate on the concept of place was not completely settled within the scholastic tradition by the end of the seventeenth century. Vincent 1660, vol. 2, pp. 847–925; Goudin 1864, vol. 2, pp. 504–6; Barbay 1676, pp. 261–72; Frassen 1686, p. 357.

64 Aristotle, *Physica* IV.14 (223a 14–21).

65 Duns Scotus 1639, *Quaestiones Quodlibetales*, q. XI. See also Duhem 1985, chaps. 7–8.

66 Toletus 1589, IIII, q. XII: 'An tempus sit numerus motus secundum prius, & posterius', fol. 142v–3v. Eustachius 1629, pp. 63–4 (*Physica*, tract III, q. II: 'Quomodo distinguatur tempus a motu').

67 Dupleix 1990, pp. 299–303.

68 Aristotle viewed generation and corruption as 'mutations', not as motions strictly speaking (*Physica* V, 224a21–226b15). This view was shared by many writers in the Peripatetic tradition.

69 Hahm 1985, pp. 50–1.

70 Magirus 1642, lib. I, cap. 5, p. 34.

71 Toletus, *Physica* (1573), lib. 5, cap. 2, text. 18: Gilson 1979, sec. 292, p. 189.

72 'Porrò etiam passivi motus specius sunt quatuor: 1. latio sive *phora:* 2. alteratio: 3. accretio: denique 4. diminutio. / Latio est motus passivus corporis, quo de loco in locum movetur. / Latio est vel naturalis; vel violentia; vel denique mixta. / Naturalis latio est, quando corpus de loco in locum movetur ex causa interna & nativa quaedam propensione. / Theorema de latione naturali est. / Latio naturalis ab initio est tardior, in fine autem velocior.' *Systema physicum septem libris adornatum, et anno Christi MDCVII publice propositum in Gymnasio Dantiscano,* Keckermann 1614, col. 1399.

73 *Commentarii . . . in octo libros physicorum Aristotelis Stagiritae,* lib. III, cap. III, q. 2, arts. 1 and 2, Collegium Conimbricense 1625, pp. 252–4, 253.

74 Paul of Venice, *Espositio . . . super octo libros phisicorum Aristotelis,* lib. 3, comment. 18, dub. 2, as quoted in Wallace 1981, p. 68.

75 For the translation of an important fourteenth-century nominalist defence of the claim that motion is not distinct from the mobile, see Clagett 1959, pp. 615–25. The text, attributed (unconvincingly) by some to Marsilius of Inghen (c. 1330–96), appeared as *Quaestio 7* on Bk. III of the *Physica* in Duns Scotus 1639, vol. 2, pp. 188–94. On the *fluxus formae/forma fluens* distinction, which derived from Averroes via Albertus Magnus, see further Murdoch and Sylla 1978, p. 215.

76 William of Ockham, *Quaestiones in librum secundum Sententiarum, Reportatio,* q. 26, William of Ockham 1990, pp. 140–1, our trans. Perhaps a gloss on 'long enough for contraries to be true of it' is in order: Ockham means that if the moving body were to remain in the same place for longer than an instant, then it would be both in rest and in motion at the same time. On Ockham's account of motion, see further Murdoch and Sylla 1978, pp. 215–17.

77 Wallace 1981, pp. 66–8 (the nominalist and realist positions), 68–71 (John Major and his school), 71–3 (Celaya and Soto).

78 'Theorema generale de motu passivo est: Omne quod movetur vel ab altero movetur, vel à seipso secundum diversam sui partem & virtutem spectato. . . . Quando enim homo progreditur de loco in locum, sane movetur à seipso, dum una pars alteram impellit. Quando avis volat, corpus aviculae movetur ab alis, quae alae sunt pars aviculae. In summa, *omne corpus animatum movetur à sua anima tanquam interno principio motus,* quae anima cum non sit separatum quid a corpore animato, ideò dici non debet; omne id quod movetur, movetur ab alios à se planè separato: sed disiunctivè formandum est axioma: Omne quod movetur, movetur vel à parte aliqua sui, vel ab alio corpore externo & separato.' Keckermann 1614, col. 1399. On the famous causal principle 'omne quod movetur ab alio movetur', see Weisheipl 1965b.

79 For a useful account of Peripatetic doctrines of motion see the anonymous fourteenth-century introduction to Bradwardine 1505, fol. 9r–10r, translation and original text in Clagett 1959, pp. 445–53, 454–62.

80 *Physica* IV.8 (215a 14–17); VIII.10 (266b 25–267a 20).

81 Maier 1955, 1968, *passim;* Clagett 1959, pp. 505–40; Murdoch and Sylla 1978, pp. 210–13. See also Wallace 1981, pp. 110–11, 320–3.

82 *Physica* III.7 (207b 16–21).

83 William of Sherwood 1968, p. 41.

84 See, e.g., Gregory of Rimini 1522, II, fol. 35, col. b, also Duhem 1985, chaps. 1–3.

85 E.g., 'I would agree with this [syncategorematic] proposition: along all the parts, a spiral line is drawn; and I would not agree with this [categorematic] proposition: a spiral line is drawn along all the parts.' Buridan 1509, fol. 59, col. c.

86 Goclenius states: 'Syncategorematice: Potentia, mentali abstractione, ut Zabarella loqui-

tur. Ab infinito in potentia, ad infinitum actu nulla est consecutio. Categorematice: Actu. Haec immensitas non potest communicari ulli creaturae.' Goclenius 1613, p. 237.

87 The Condemnation of 1277 influenced the discussions of the possibility of syncategore-matic and categorematic infinites in nature. Among the condemned propositions was the claim 'that the first cause cannot make more than one world': Mandonnet 1908–11, vol. 2, p. 178, prop. 27; Lerner and Mahdi 1972, p. 340. This proposition challenged directly the Aristotelian doctrines of the singularity of the universe and the impossibility of the potential infinitely large in magnitude. It also suggested that one should be careful when denying the actual infinitely large.

88 *Physica*, III, q. v–vii. Toletus 1589, fol. 100, col. a - fol. 103, col. d, and at fol. 103, col. a ('Alber. Saxo. hoc lib. q. 9').

89 *Physica*, Collegium Conimbricense 1592, vol. 1, col. 509–40, especially col. 524. 'Prior est Ochami in 2. qu. 8 & quodlibeto 2. q. 5 Greg. Ariminensis in 1. dist. 43. q. 4 & aliorum per divinam potentiam infinitum actu categorematicum posse creari' (Abra de Raconis 1651, pars III, p. 194).

90 Brockliss 1987, p. 338. Ceriziers held that God can create an actual infinity: 'What one refuses to nature must not be refused to its author. Can he not create everything he can create at this moment – for example, all the men he can produce? If he can do so, their multitude would be either finite or infinite; to say that it is finite would be to limit God's power; to grant it infinite is to agree with my opinion. . . . Those who want to tie down our Samson say that he cannot make at once everything he can do successively, because then his power would have been spent. But other than that he could conserve, annihilate, and then reproduce everything he had already made, I do not see that it is worse to say that he can no longer do anything when he has done everything, than to say that there remains nothing left for him to know, when he has known everything . . . one must not attribute the properties of finite quantity to infinite quantity' (Ceriziers 1643, chap. 7, 'Que dieu peut produire l'infiny', pp. 126–8).

91 Eustachius 1629, p. 54 (*Physica*, tract. III, q. 5, 'Quid et quotuplex sit infinitum').

92 Eustachius 1629, p. 53 (*Physica*, tract. III, q. 4, 'An continuum sit divisible in infinitum').

93 Eustachius 1629, p. 54 (*Physica*, tract. III, q. 5).

94 Eustachius 1629, p. 56 (*Physica*, tract. III, q. 7, 'An detur aut falsum dari possit infinitum').

16

THE OCCULTIST TRADITION
AND ITS CRITICS

BRIAN COPENHAVER

I. THE SOURCES AND STATUS OF
THE OCCULT PHILOSOPHY IN
THE EARLY SEVENTEENTH CENTURY

One of the first members of Rome's Accademia dei Lincei, established in 1603 to advance the understanding of natural philosophy, was Giambattista Della Porta, Galileo's colleague in the renowned Roman society and his rival in the development of the telescope. Four decades before, Della Porta had founded his own Accademia dei Secreti della Natura, only to see it fail when the Inquisition called him up on charges of sorcery. He died in 1615, long after publishing his *Magia naturalis libri IV* in Naples in 1558; a much enlarged edition followed in 1589, commanding enough interest through the seventeenth century to support many Latin and vernacular printings. Readers of the English version (London, 1658) learned in the first chapter that 'Magick is taken amongst all men for Wisdom, and the perfect knowledge of natural things: and those are called Magicians, whom . . . the Greeks call Philosophers.' This overture to a treatise on magic was commonplace in its own time and had been familiar since antiquity, but when Della Porta called magicians philosophers, he struck a note that jars modern ears.[1]

'There are two sorts of Magick,' he explained; 'the one is infamous . . . because it hath to do with soul spirits and . . . Inchantments . . . and this is called Sorcery. . . . The other Magick is natural. . . . The most noble Philosophers . . . call this knowledge the very . . . perfection of natural Sciences.' In other words, the good natural magic that Della Porta traced to Pythagoras, Plato, Aristotle, and other philosophical worthies was not the evil demonic magic that 'all learned and good men detest'. Moreover, as Giovanni Pico and Cornelius Agrippa had put it, this good natural magic was 'the highest point of natural philosophy'. Since magic is 'a practical part of Natural Philosophy', argued Della Porta, 'therefore it behoveth a Magician . . . to be an exact and very perfect Philosopher.'[2] In calling magic *practical,* Della Porta expressed his pragmatic intentions accurately; the twenty books of the expanded *Magia naturalis* are mostly a collection of techniques and recipes, quite unlike the refined speculations of Marsilio Ficino, the architect of magical theory in the Renaissance. Most of Della Porta's first book, however, is a summary of Ficino's philosophy of magic; he begins with a theory of *magia naturalis* as a department of *philosophia naturalis,* as those terms had been understood since Ficino's time and as some still understood them in Leibniz's day. Practical interest in astrology, alchemy, and other departments of the occultist tradition ran strong throughout the early modern period among serious thinkers in many disciplines, but after Francis Bacon philosophers paid less attention to occult technology than to the theoretical underpinnings of magic.[3]

For seventeenth-century philosophers the theory of natural magic was part of a larger puzzle that had occupied Western European thinkers since antiquity: the intellectual and moral status of 'occultism', taken here to include magic, astrology, alchemy, demonology, divination, kabbalah, witchcraft, spiritualism, and kindred beliefs. Since late antiquity, various forms of occultism, but especially natural magic, found support in authoritative philosophical sources, both pagan and Christian. Philosophy's fickle response to the charms of magic was especially ardent at two moments – once in the age of Plotinus, Porphyry, Iamblichus, Proclus, Synesius, and the lesser Neoplatonists, and again in the time of Ficino, Pomponazzi, Agrippa, and Della Porta. Ficino's theory, announced in 1489 in his *De vita libri tres* and then vulgarised by Agrippa and Della Porta, influenced a multitude of sixteenth-century thinkers – physicians and philosophers especially – who joined in a complex debate still unsettled when the century ended.[4]

A hundred years after the enlarged edition of Della Porta's *Magia naturalis,* the science whose mathematical principles Isaac Newton established was still known to him and his readers as 'natural philosophy'. But by the time Newton quarrelled with Leibniz about occult qualities, many advocates of the new learning had come to scorn the natural magic that was fashionable in the Renaissance. For sixteenth-century thinkers of every stripe, natural magic had been a prominent topic in natural philosophy. But by the eighteenth century it was an embarrassment; what had been *philosophia* in the Renaissance passed the bounds of good sense and good taste for *philosophes* of the Enlightenment. The advance guard of the scientific revolution had abandoned magic even earlier: the twentieth century had to exhume Newton's alchemy because the eighteenth century buried it. Once a source of power and prestige, magic became a scandal. This is why Leibniz could torment Newton with a leading term of art in the theory of natural magic: the phrase 'occult quality'.[5]

These same words, used by Leibniz and Newton to trade abuse, were well known in the Peripatetic natural philosophy of which natural magic had been a part. Arguments about occult qualities and substantial forms in the theory of natural magic echoed a larger controversy about Aristotelian thought. Neither can be understood without the other. But students of the mechanical and corpuscular paradigms that displaced Aristotelianism, falsely assuming that the Peripatetic system was no use to the magicians who depended on Neoplatonism, have not always noticed the effect of Aristotle's demise on the decay of magic, or the reverse. Della Porta's readers knew better. They saw his many references to the Neoplatonists whom Ficino had restored, but they also read his chapters on the Peripatetic doctrine of matter and form, substance and quality as fundamentals in the theory of magic. It was this theory – the metaphysics, physics, and magic of hylemorphism – that preoccupied seventeenth-century philosophers who argued about natural magic. When magic lost its intellectual authority, the loss involved a larger crisis of confidence in the principles of Aristotelian philosophy. If magic flourished in the sixteenth century after Ficino accommodated his revived Neo-platonism to Peripatetic teaching on forms and qualities, it withered away in the seventeenth century after Descartes and others ignored the Neoplatonists and repudiated Aristotle.[6]

Yet some varieties of occultism in the early seventeenth century were hostile to Aristotelianism. The mysterious Rosicrucians who agitated Paris in 1623 were known from pamphlets that praised Paracelsus for rejecting Aristotle and Galen. A pamphlet war on alchemical medicine broke out in France in the first quarter of the new century. In August of 1624 these disputes attracted a large Parisian crowd to hear a public defence of fourteen theses – opposed to Paracelsus as well as Aristotle – presented by the chemist Estienne de Clave and his associates.[7] Marin Mersenne recognised what was at stake in an alchemical assault on Aristotelian matter, form, and quality: not only the immateriality of the soul and the reality of the eucharist but also the foundations of magic as understood in scholastic philosophy. If the professors of theology had come to depend on Aristotle, so had the students of natural magic, who, from the time of Avicenna and Aquinas, also put their arguments in Peripatetic terms. But since the fifteenth century the Philosopher's prerogative had been tested on several fronts: by ancient Platonists, Epicureans, Stoics, and Sceptics newly resurrected; and by audacious innovators like Paracelsus, Fracastoro, Cardano, Telesio, Patrizi, Bruno, Campanella, Bacon, and Basso.[8]

Sebastian Basso, Nicholas Hill, Daniel Sennert, and other atomists issued a strong challenge to Aristotelian matter-theory, but even this revived Epicureanism could be tinged with alchemy or indebted to Neoplatonist occultism or influenced by Stoic conceptions of *spiritus* (*pneuma*) or committed to a disguised hylemorphism and its apparatus of occult qualities.[9] Official reaction to magical novelties could be severe, sometimes fatal. In 1615 Giulio Cesare Vanini reasserted Pietro Pomponazzi's astrological naturalism, long feared as a threat to Roman Catholic teaching on angels, demons, and miracles; Vanini went to the stake in Toulouse in 1619, recalling the horror of Bruno's burning in Rome in 1600. In that year a vision inspired the shoemaker Jacob Boehme to write the mystical books that caused Hegel to say that 'through him . . . Philosophy first appeared in Germany'; he died of natural causes in 1624, begrudged the last rites by his pastors.[10] Around the same time, Mersenne was writing *Quaestiones in Genesim* (Paris, 1623); Gabriel Naudé was making his name against the Rosicrucians; and Pierre Gassendi was preparing his *Exercitationes paradoxicae adversus Aristoteleos* (Grenoble, 1624). Between 1616 and 1621 Robert Fludd published his vast theosophical volumes; Tommaso Campanella's most famous work on magic saw its first edition in 1620; and in 1622 appeared the first of thirteen editions of Franco Burgersdijck's popular manual on natural philosophy. Burgersdijck, Campanella, and Fludd showed their century three ways to befriend occultism. Like Burgersdijck and other school philosophers, one could propagate the traditional Aristotelianism that sustained belief in magic; or one could replace the Peripatetic basis of magic with a new system intended to be intelligible as philosophy, which was Campanella's aim; or, like Fludd, one could detach occultism both from philosophy's Aristotelian past and from its Cartesian future.[11]

II. BURGERSDIJCK, CAMPANELLA, AND FLUDD

1. Burgersdijck

In their final and decayed state, the principles of the Peripatetic theory of magic are visible in the work of Franco Burgersdijck. He wrote no books on occultism, but he taught its philosophical elements in the usual manner of late scholasticism, thus leaving a record of school philosophy in the service of magic. Near the beginning of one of his popular textbooks, *Idea philosophiae naturalis* (Leiden, 1622), the Protestant Burgersdijck cited Francisco Suárez, Benito Pereira, and their fellow Jesuits, the Coimbra commentators, to introduce the hylemorphic fundamentals. Like many scholastics before him, he explained that 'there are substantial forms of natural bodies [that] do not exist in matter before generation . . . but are educed from the potency of matter.' Another feature of natural bodies, he added, is quality . . . manifest or occult: the former affects the senses in itself; the latter is perceived only from effects, and sympathies and antipathies are to be referred to it. . . . The heavens act on lower beings, and do so through motion, light and occult qualities. . . . In the eduction of substantial form, the heavens assist as efficient cause, remote but primary; the proximate and instrumental cause is elementary heat.

Burgersdijck taught the physics and metaphysics that had long made astrology and natural magic departments of natural philosophy. His Calvinist students in Leiden learned that the most basic process of nature, the generation and corruption of the composite material object, occurs by celestial agency and through occult as well as manifest causes.[12] Burgersdijck's outline would have been familiar to Catholic scholars at Coimbra. Their Jesuit masters maintained that 'because substantial form cannot be an immediate principle of action, nature had to procure some instrument of action for it to use, and this is quality.'[13]

These guardians of Aristotelian orthodoxy also repudiated 'the calumny of recent philosophers who call occult properties an asylum of ignorance. . . . For not only authorities on medicine but also philosophers are compelled to explain many effects by them, . . . nor can effects always be referred . . . to the four primary qualities', hot, cold, wet, and dry. Moreover, according to the Coimbra commentary on Aristotle's *Physics,* magical action need not be demonic: 'By an artifice of natural magic that joins occult powers of natural causes to one another, many things are done without demonic intervention and excite wonderment because they seem to be caused beyond the capacity of nature, yet in truth they have a physical basis.'[14] Father Suárez, champion of the Counter-Reformation, agreed that certain phenomena were 'most occult [and] must be traced to some power of a higher order, . . . a wondrous and occult power . . . assisted perhaps by some special and connatural celestial influence'. Suárez distinguished natural magic based on occult qualities from superstitious magic involving evil spirits. Although curiosity about magic might lead to superstition, natural magic was not in itself wrong. In fact, as Della Porta had also claimed, *magia* might be seen as equivalent to *philosophia naturalis* if limited to 'unusual effects that people find amazing because they are rare and have occult causes' – effects that do not 'exceed the power of natural causes' because they come from 'applying active things to passives with a precise understanding of their powers'.[15]

For Suárez the understanding of nature began with Aristotle, and the Coimbra commentators on the *Physics* assigned the key concept of substantial form a clear Peripatetic pedigree. Although Aristotle never actually used the term *eidos ousiôdes,* he laid the groundwork for this important Peripatetic principle. Later, Galen and his medical heirs connected the topic of substance with the notion of occult

qualities. Galen preferred to explain medical phenomena from the manifest qualities (hot, cold, dry, wet) of the four elements (fire, earth, air, water), but when
reliably reported effects – such as the healing power of an amulet – could not be
explained in this way, he referred them to *idiotêtes arrêtoi* or 'undescribable properties', the *qualitates occultae* of mediaeval Latin medicine and philosophy. Galen had
empirical reasons for thinking that a peony amulet relieved epilepsy and that
rhubarb was purgative, but he could not fully account for the observed powers of
these simples from their manifest properties. Instead, he derived them from the
plant as a whole, claiming that they worked *kath holên tên ousian,* 'according to the
whole substance'. From the point of view of later hylemorphic metaphysics, the
Galenic whole substance of a thing resembled a Peripatetic substantial form.[16]

Two dichotomies basic to Aristotle's philosophy (see Chapter 15) are substance/
accident and form/matter. In the Thomist interpretation, the matter of a natural
composite object individuates it, makes it this peony plant rather than that one; its
form makes it an object of a given kind or species, peony rather than rhubarb. In
the hylemorphic union, matter (*hulê*) and form (*morphê*) join to make an autonomous composite, a substance, this particular member of the peony kind existing
of its own. But the colours on the plant's leaves have no independent existence;
they are accidents or accidental forms, and they can change without affecting the
plant's species or substance. Most accidental forms are either primary manifest
qualities of the elements (like heat and cold) or secondary elementary qualities
(like gravity and levity); they are perceptible in themselves, but substantial form
remains hidden. Just as Galen linked his 'undescribable properties' with the whole
substance, Peripatetic philosophers made imperceptible substantial form the cause
of qualities (such as peony's anti-epileptic property) called *occultae* or 'hidden',
which cause manifest effects (such as relief of epileptic symptoms).[17] The senses
have direct access to moisture or dryness in the peony, so these qualities are also
manifest; they are intelligible because they fit the pattern of four elements and
their properties. But *as an object of perception* the plant's curative quality remains
occult because only the effects of that quality are sensible. The same quality is
occult *as an object of analysis* because it lies outside the Peripatetic scheme of
manifest qualities. Neither perceptual nor analytic occultness entails unintelligibility, however: for the perceiving subject, an occult quality is simply insensible; for
the inquiring subject, the burden of its intelligibility shifts from physics to metaphysics, that is, to the framework of substantial form.[18]

To explain changes in quality and substance, the Peripatetics extended Aristotle's theory of generation and corruption. If a pharmacist burned a peony amulet,
the plant would change substantially to ash and qualitatively to something dry and

powdery. If there was a new substantial form of ash, where did it come from? Where did the old form of peony go? And what about the water manifestly present in the fresh plant but not in the dry powder? Did the form of the vanished element also have to be accounted for? Mediaeval and Renaissance debate on these questions was indecisive. Some philosophers and physicians traced new substantial forms to the heavens and sought a celestial source for their associated occult qualities as well. As in Burgersdijck's *Idea philosophiae,* a common formulation of this astrological process was that substantial forms are 'educed from the potency of matter' when 'the heavens assist as efficient cause'. Thus, according to the Coimbra commentators, 'the power of the magnet and certain similar hidden properties of other bodies . . . arise not from primary qualities but are impressed by heavenly bodies', which act on terrestrial objects not only by heat and light but also through 'other powers called influences that produce other qualities'.[19]

2. Campanella

In 1635, when Burgersdijck died, Tommaso Campanella's *Medicinalium iuxta propria principia libri septem* was printed in Lyon, though Campanella had begun it long before. In this work and others written during a quarter-century of imprisonment, the dissident Campanella faced the same problems that had driven Burgersdijck and other school philosophers to the 'asylum' of occult properties. For centuries philosophers and physicians had been puzzled by veridical phenomena – the attractive force of the magnet, the stunning effect of the electric ray, the purgative power of rhubarb – unexplained by the elements and their manifest qualities. Campanella distinguished the active and passive 'qualities of simple medicines . . . heat and cold, . . . wetness and dryness' from the 'occult powers of drugs'. The latter, he explained,

are not in drugs in a bodily way from the elements . . . nor from a demon or a star but in the forms and qualities of things, the instruments and vessels of the primalities (*primalitates*). . . . Objects are composed not only of body and heat reduced to a particular form, nor only of bodily elements, but also of the bodiless – power, wisdom and love. Therefore, actions that give rise to amazement are to be attributed to these causes [to] the similarity . . . of the aforesaid primalities reduced to a particular grade by their embodiment.[20]

Except for the odd term 'primalities', Campanella's account may sound like the usual Peripatetic defense of occult qualities. Like Burgersdijck, he speaks of occult powers in terms of forms and qualities. Yet his theory of magic marked a deep break with normative doctrine, an original effort to reform the philosophy of magic.

Campanella's first book was *Philosophia sensibus demonstrata* (Naples, 1591), a huge anti-Peripatetic tirade defending the naturalism of Bernardino Telesio. What Campanella took from Telesio was simple: heat and cold as active principles competing to possess matter as passive substrate. Campanella chose to build a new system on the humble facts of hot and cold matter, given in daily experience, rather than compose another variation on Peripatetic themes. Among the verbal fictions that he exploded were scholastic matter, form, and quality: 'The top Peripatetics', he roared, 'what emptyheaded buffoons! Prime matter is supposed to be nothing really and privation nothing, and yet form gets drawn from the potency of prime matter, which is nothing and does not exist. . . . How great is the ignorance of these people.' Assailing Peripatetic metaphysics at its foundations, he insisted that the senses know form directly and that matter is just bodily mass, the body or matter that we touch every day. He equated form with 'temperament, . . . the final state (*abito*) of the mixture . . . , as when water becomes air . . . the final rarity or heat that constitutes it as air is called the form of air', and he described temperament as the structure of matter, a sturdier construct than the flimsy forms of the schools and a concrete basis for a new analysis of occult qualities.[21]

These new ideas first appeared in book two of *Philosophia sensibus demonstrata,* 'On the heavens and the universe', where Campanella argued that of his two active forces only heat is really present in the heavens:

Having established this, we say that the force proper to heat concurs in the constitution of a thing, whatever it may be. . . . Since there are so many different stars in the heavens, furnished with much different forces and heats, it happens that each thing has by nature a consimilar constitutive heat . . . consimilar, I mean, to the heat of a particular star [so that] each thing in the universe can have its own star in heaven corresponding to its constitutive heat and leading to procreation and growth, as Hermes, Enoch and Mercurius said, [who] saw such effects and, not knowing how to investigate their causes, attributed them to occult influences and the souls of the stars.

The young Campanella believed in astrological causes, but he did not think of them as occult. Instead, he used manifest celestial forces, heat and cold, to displace the occult powers which had long been part of the hylemorphic metaphysics that he also abandoned. Telesio had wanted physics freed from metaphysics, but Campanella was not hostile to metaphysics, as he proved in his *Universalis philosophiae seu metaphysicarum rerum . . . libri 18,* begun as early as 1590 but not published until 1638, in Paris. He claimed that Telesio depended too much on heat and cold as natural causes of bodies, contending that these physical powers were instruments of a 'diviner cause' reaching down from God to the primalities, their influences (*influxus*), and the world-soul.[22] Campanella's new theories were in print by 1617. In 1620 his chief work on magic, *De sensu rerum et magia,* appeared in Frankfurt, naming as its subject 'occult philosophy, showing the cosmos to be a living, conscious statue of God' and describing the world's 'parts and particles [as] having sensation . . . enough for their conservation'. The pansensism of this provocative book is loosely compatible with Telesio's physics. Since the strife between heat and cold begins all natural action, a hot object must somehow sense the enmity of cold; otherwise, the impulse of each force to inform all passive matter would go unchecked; the combat would end, and with it the world of generation and corruption.[23] Campanella's physics becomes metaphysical only when he connects the world with its trinitarian Creator. He puts the primalities – Power, Wisdom, and Love – within all things as the ground of their being, thus adding a divine metaphysical wisdom to the physical sense in Telesio's nature.[24]

Campanella used the term 'occult' to describe various forces and phenomena, but rather than revert to hylemorphic occultism, he worked out a new philosophy of magic. In his cosmos the primalities and influences are literally *in* the nature of things. The three great *influxus,* called Necessity, Fate, and Harmony, seem to correspond: to properties of an object arising *necessarily* from its physical structure; to *determinate* relations of such properties with those of other objects; and to *harmonious* effects of such relations on the good of the whole. Flowing from the primalities, the influences also mirror the triune God, whose ideas they reflect towards objects with the help of angels. Angels, ideas, influences, primalities, and God are the metaphysical chain from which physical objects depend, but the forms of objects – products of heat and cold acting as physical instruments of these metaphysical agents – are structures as material in Campanella's mature metaphysics as in his youthful Telesian manifesto. However, the *Universalis philosophia* admits occult causality excluded in *Philosophia sensibus demonstrata,* where an occult quality is just a mistake made by astrologers who misunderstand the physical power of heat.[25] Campanella distinguished three types of cause: material, active, and metaphysical. The first requires contact between bodies; the second needs communication of physical force; the third transcends physics and comes from 'the power of the primalities, which to the physicians seemed occult'. The three kinds of causation may be mixed, but sometimes the primalities predominate, especially in cases of sympathy and antipathy. The magnet attracts iron rather than other metals 'because iron is more like it and connected in its temperament and in the primality of this attraction, for it is clear that in their similarity active powers and bodily things are signs of conformity of primalities'. In one sense, then, metaphysical similitude of primalities enhances a likeness that also has a physical basis and manifestation. But in another sense, the distinction between physics and metaphysics vanishes in the parade of participations through which the primality is always present, even in the lowest order of causality. No cause of a natural effect stands entirely apart from the physical or from the metaphysical order. As in the production of forms, the primalities have a rôle in the kind of causation that traditional medicine and philosophy had labelled 'occult', but, even when linked with the primalities, neither forms nor occult qualities seem to have become purely metaphysical for Campanella.[26]

In fact, we may ask whether Campanella ever allowed occult qualities as his contemporaries knew them. He certainly dispensed with traditional hylemorphic qualities. The main mechanisms of magic in *De sensu* are not occult qualities but the world-soul, heat, spirit, similarity, sympathy, and antipathy. Campanella believed that his primalities and active forces had explained what others called 'occult' so that they could evade the task of explanation. But he remained interested in the problems that normally fell under the rubric 'occult'. His books are heavy with them – magnet, rhubarb, heliotrope, torpedo, remora, the lion that fears the cock – and usually he attacks these ancient puzzles with a physical armory of hot spirits, similitudes, and *consensus*. In his earliest work, Campanella had treated magical phenomena as misunderstood effects of heat, light, spirit, and other physical causes. Even after he formulated a metaphysics, he seldom admitted causes that he was willing to call occult, but when he did admit them, he required them to be other than physical: that is, they act beyond the capacities of matter, of heat and cold, of material and active causation; their power is metaphysical, from the primalities. In the final analysis, he acknowledged metaphysical causation, and sometimes he called it 'occult', but his brand of occultism was still a world apart from the routine allegiance to occult qualities in the philosophy of the schools.[27]

3. Fludd

A world farther apart from the teachings of the schools was the idiosyncratic pictorial theosophy of Robert Fludd, whose enormous and unfinished *Utriusque cosmi historia* appeared in Oppenheim and Frankfurt between 1617 and 1621. Fludd's earlier career of study at Oxford and travel on the continent took an uncommon turn only when Paracelsianism coloured his decision to take up medicine and set him at odds with the London medical establishment, which recognised the new chemical therapies but shunned alchemy's grander pretensions as a general system of theology and philosophy. Following the lead of Oswald Croll's influential *Basilica chymica* (Frankfurt, 1609) and earlier works, Fludd made himself, with Michael Maier, the leading spokesman for a universal chemical philosophy. His first works, appearing in 1616–17, replied to attacks on the Rosicrucians by another chemist, Andreas Libavius, who had also criticised Croll from a Peripatetic point of view. In these pamphlets Fludd rejected Aristotelian school philosophy as superficial and urged a Rosicrucian reform of education that would reveal the inner secrets of God and cosmos to the initiate. Then he opened his arcana (which were not especially original) in the ponderous but magnificently illustrated *Utriusque cosmi historia,* aiming to raise alchemy above the material clutter of ferments and alembics to God's cosmic laboratory and seeking to present theological chemistry as a new kabbalah, a key to the riddles that the creator had spoken at the creation.[28]

Like Paracelsus and many of his followers, Fludd saw alchemy as a divine mission. He approached traditional problems in divinity through his alchemical kabbalah, a far cry from the genuine Zoharic and Lurianic secrets that Knorr von Rosenroth would unveil to Latin-reading Christians later in the century. Having repudiated Aristotle, Fludd took his natural philosophy from the Bible, especially Genesis and John's Gospel, but he read scripture through the eyes of Hermes Trismegistus, Plato, the Neoplatonists, Ficino, and Francesco Giorgi, honoring the Rosicrucians as the last in his doxography of ancient theologians. Fludd saw creation itself as an alchemical separation of light, darkness, and water. He traced the effects of divine light and spirit through three increasingly material levels of the cosmos – empyrean, ethereal, and elemental – making the Sun God's seat in the elemental world, the point of equilibrium between dark matter and light spirit, between the *voluntas* and *noluntas* of a dualist godhead. God acts in the cosmos through a retinue of ministers: the Biblical angel Michael, the kabbalist power Metatron, the World Soul, the Messiah, Nature, and Art, whom Fludd depicted as Nature's ape, chained to her (as she was bound to God) and perched atop the earthly globe. Fludd was extravagant not in his originality but in his heterodoxy; he made himself vulnerable as dualist, pantheist, vitalist, even polytheist, idolatrous, and blasphemous. Yet he did not free himself entirely from the common world-view of his day, rejecting Copernicus and maintaining a traditional stance on various features of Galenic medicine.[29]

He was most inventive – and most perplexing to critics like Johann Kepler – in setting out the harmonies and proportions of the cosmos, his infamous pyramids and monochords, not as representations of perceptible, measurable structures but as direct presentations, creative (literally) works of art, aping nature as nature aped God – which to Fludd was a higher duty than mere analysis. 'What Kepler expressed in many words and lengthy speech', he contended, 'I have explained briefly, in hieroglyphic figures of great significance, not because I am fond of pictures . . . but in order to unite many things in few and, like the chemists, . . . to recover the essence extracted while discarding the feculent matter.' Fludd's picturing was an alchemical kabbalah meant to distill meaning. He sought to make sense of natural objects not by naming qualities (like the scholastics) or calculating quantities (like Kepler and Mersenne), but by weaving a tapestry of symbols that tied the meaning of each partial object to a cosmic whole bound together by God's perfect meaningfulness. Real knowledge of the cosmos is a mythopoeic kabbalah – knowing the names of God through a mystic alchemy that identifies the metal gold, for example, as a real, non-arbitrary symbol of divine wisdom; such knowledge comes from God, the alchemist who marks the universe with symbolic signatures of his work. Fludd has sometimes been credited for his openness to observation and experiment, especially for his interest in barometric and thermometric instruments. But even his famous weather-glass was a symbolic device, meant to mimic rather than explain the cosmic process of contraction and expansion and the primeval enmity between light and dark. Kepler accused Fludd of being a theosophist rather than a natural philosopher, and Kepler was right. As a voice in the seventeenth-century debate about magic and philosophy, he tells more about the future of theosophy than about the past of natural magic, speaking more effectively to the Swedenborgs and Madame Blavatskys than for the Ficinos and Campanellas. Johannes Baptista Van Helmont, an heir of the older occult philosophy, dismissed him as 'a poor physician and a still poorer alchemist, talkative, loud, thinly learned, inconsistent, . . . a fluctuating Fludd'. Gassendi had theological objections: 'When Fludd explains his alchemy, he always intrudes on Holy Scripture.' Despite Van Helmont's quip, Fludd's stature is evident in the eminence of his critics, who included not only Gassendi and Kepler but also Mersenne.[30]

III. FROM MERSENNE TO DESCARTES

1. Mersenne

Marin Mersenne studied with the Jesuits at La Flèche, entered an order of friars founded by a noted thaumaturge, and ended as amanuensis of the mechanical philosophy. He launched his crusade against occultism sometime before 1620, when he began to assemble his huge Genesis commentary of 1623. Its 1900 folio columns have much to say about biblical exegesis, about musical humanism, but above all about the magical arts. Mersenne aimed his book at 'atheists and deists', and among the subverters of religion he counted Fludd and many others who argued for magic: Pomponazzi, Paracelsus, Agrippa, Giorgi, Vanini, and Campanella, to name a few.[31] Mersenne roused the opposition to occultism that would overwhelm both traditionalists like Burgersdijck and innovators like Fludd and Campanella. Neither the memory of his victory nor the oblivion of the vanquished should blind one to the import of the struggle, whose casualties were more than academic reputations. The charges that sent Vanini to the flames in 1619 now seem contradictory: he was condemned as a sorcerer but also attacked as an unbelieving naturalist, both the results of what he took from Pomponazzi. The gentle Mersenne remarked that Vanini 'must have had his head completely filled and choked with smoke . . . when he supposed that [physical vapors] are the cause of ghosts and apparitions. . . . No wonder . . . he was killed at Toulouse.' Vanini was also on the mind of Père François Garasse when he published *La Doctrine curieuse des beaux esprits de ce temps* (Paris, 1623), but the Jesuit's *bête noire* was Théophile de Viau, whose poems (one a favourite of Descartes) expressed a pantheist mysticism that reminded people of Vanini and Bruno. Claude Pithoys, a Minim like Mersenne, revealed a different attitude in *La descouverture des faux possedez* (Chalons, 1621), a lively little book opposing quick belief in demonic possession. Although this dangerous and bitterly disputed issue had entangled French religious politics for decades, Pithoys registered his astonishment 'that people let themselves be tricked so easily'. But his incredulity was rare, alien to zealots like Garasse and undeveloped in aspiring rationalists like the young Mersenne.[32]

Soon after the Genesis commentary Mersenne published two apologetic treatises, *L'Impieté des deistes* (Paris, 1624) and *La Verité des sciences* (Paris, 1625). More readable than the bulky *Quaestiones,* these vernacular polemics were still hostile to the Italian philosophers of nature, especially Bruno, whom Mersenne saw as a fountainhead of pernicious libertinism and impious occultism, both grave threats to religion. In *L'Impieté* he claimed that French free-thinkers had been seduced by Bruno, 'an atheist burned in Italy, [who] maintains that all things are, if not animals, at least animated and sharing a life-spirit which he detects in dead roots, . . . in precious stones that produce . . . rare effects, in necromancers who want to work many miracles'. Similar charges against Bruno and harsh assaults on all the varieties of occultism had filled the pages of the *Quaestiones,* but the philosophical basis of Mersenne's opposition to magic, arising originally from his piety, became clearer in the French works of 1624–5.[33] At first Mersenne remained loyal to Aristotle, praising him as 'an eagle in philosophy' and scorning the 'spring chickens' who opposed him. The Peripatetics provided a stable, orderly philosophy of nature that guaranteed the integrity of a corresponding supernature. They defined a natural order against which Christ's miracles stood out as extraordinary, while the panpsychism of the Italian naturalists obscured the difference between God's miracles and sports of nature. The Christian Philosopher who speaks in *La Verité* had a theological stake in a clear distinction between bodily matter and spiritual form. He branded his alchemical interlocutor as 'sensual', lauding Aristotle as 'an intellectual and rational philosopher . . . who has left behind all the senses to penetrate to . . . the essence of things, which is invisible and insensible'. Yet in the same work Mersenne permitted his sceptical voice to doubt inward impalpable forms, and whispers of his disenchantment were audible even earlier in *L'Impieté*; there, he belittled Bruno's world-soul by comparing it to specific forms, finding 'no more satisfaction in the one than in the other for [explaining] effects whose cause is hidden within things'. Such hints were indecisive, however, for when Mersenne rejected the world-soul as incompatible with eucharistic transubstantiation, he also insisted on preserving substantial forms to account for the sacramental mystery: 'One must follow . . . philosophers who teach that each individual is composed of matter and substantial form [because] it is more difficult to explain . . . our faith' on the alternative principles proposed by Aristotle's rivals.[34]

Mersenne's breach with Aristotle remained incomplete for another decade, until he had learned enough from Descartes, Gassendi, Galileo, and others to reach the clearly mechanist and anti-occultist conclusions expressed in the *Questions théologiques* and their four companion treatises (Paris, 1634). Although he had been uneasy about occult qualities even in the Genesis commentary, his early suspicions were philosophically immature, no freer of the hylemorphism that sustained occultism than the older critique that he admired in Thomas Erastus, a sixteenth-century physician whose attack on occultism was unusually vigorous for its time. By the 1630s Mersenne's questions became sharper. Recognising that 'one usually calls those powers occult whose effects are perceived without knowing the reason', he demanded to know 'what occult powers are and where they come from', concluding that the hidden reason behind them lay in material structure, whether atomic or chemical. 'These qualities are occult only to the ignorant', he proclaimed, 'for learned people . . . do not use these terms, showing that what one calls occult is evident to them; and if there are qualities that they do not know, they freely admit their ignorance', unlike those who rely on the vacuous vocabulary of sympathies and antipathies 'to cover their defects'. To use such language was to 'confess freely that they know nothing. . . . Sympathy vanishes with ignorance.'[35]

Mersenne believed that the use of occult qualities deferred basic questions of physics to a region of terminology and ontology beyond the reach of explanation.

His insight was not new (witness the slogan 'asylum of ignorance' in earlier polemics on occult qualities), yet he reached it not only by joining the long march away from hylemorphism but also by a newer route: a phenomenalist physics absolved of metaphysical obligations, a moderate scepticism that preserved the new mechanist science as an operational goal while it abandoned the ideal of a demonstrative science of nature. Human perception stops at the bark and surface of bodies, which is why the ancients were unable to provide deeper knowledge of corporeal quality. Sceptical epistemology, pragmatic method, and voluntarist theology converge in the view that certainty about internal essence is God's privilege, leaving humans to find useful, contingent information in what is superficially accessible to their weaker faculties. Since only surfaces and quantities are knowable, occult qualities are worse than invisible; they are fictions unmentionable in scientific discourse, casualties of mitigated scepticism.[36]

Mersenne's *Harmonie universelle* (Paris, 1637) has been called his discourse on method and the first fruit of the new mechanical philosophy. Seeing these heady words, one notes with surprise that in the same period Mersenne sent queries to Peiresc about the evil eye, the healing power of words and such mainstays of occultist literature as Lull, Cardano, and the *Picatrix*. Mersenne appreciated the cost of such inquiries. 'People spend most of their life and labor on curiosities', he decided, 'and so they use them less for what is needful.' Yet curiosity had its value: while maintaining due scepticism about occult phenomena, 'a Christian philosopher can . . . do experiments to disabuse the simple . . . and destroy fake observations . . . with true experiments.' Still, 'if one were to examine all that Croll and the other chemists and naturalists have written, . . . not four out of a hundred [claims] would be found true.'[37] In theory Mersenne knew why Montaigne had warned against explaining causes before confirming facts, but in practice his hunger for information was insatiable. In 1633, for example, he passed on to Peiresc a story about

a monastery . . . in Aleppo [whose monks] are good at singing, . . . and one of them knows music quite well. . . . If you . . . strike up a friendship with him, we would have the singular pleasure of conferring together about several pretty problems, for they tell me that he . . . works at chemistry . . . and even that he knows magic, what kind I know not. In any event, we should see if the Orient produces any better minds than our Occident.

Peiresc knew his friend's limitations. When 'poor good Father Mersenne' reported a case of sight penetrating flesh and walls, Peiresc shook his head, yet he pursued the problem and preferred Mersenne's credulity to the 'incredulity of others who neglect everything and want only to mock'. This was the verdict of a learned naturalist whose science had shaken off its metaphysical ills but was not yet healed of an incontinent curiosity, a fever that gripped Mersenne even more tightly.[38] Between 1634 and 1637 Mersenne traded letters with the physician Christophe de Villiers, who wrote him mainly about the demonic possessions at Loudun but also about Nostradamus, kabbalah, astrology, and alchemy, as Johannes Van Helmont had written him a few years before about Paracelsus, antipathies, signatures, and the *spiritus mummialis*. Whether acquiring Van Helmont's weapon-salve, or testing zoological specimens to check claims about sympathy, or recording an eye-witness report of 'a gentleman . . . who thickens the air so much that he can walk on it . . . through a deep understanding of philosophy', Mersenne reveled in an empiricism as reminiscent of Della Porta or Bacon as of Harvey or Galileo. He was a grandchild of the Renaissance. His humanist education prepared him to accept scepticism and admire mathematics, but it also taught him the magical charms of classical learning.[39]

2. Gassendi

Like Mersenne, Gassendi first learned to dislike the school philosophers and to listen to the sceptics as a student of the humanities, but the stultifying erudition that he acquired was deeper than Mersenne's, better grounded in history and philology and a richer seed-bed for philosophy. He began his career with the anonymous *Exercitationes paradoxicae adversus Aristoteleos* (Grenoble, 1624), but he soon put away this anti-Peripatetic polemic and turned to the immense labour of Epicurean doxography and commentary that occupied him for the next twenty years, leaving less than a decade for the last phase of his work, the original *Syntagma* of logic, physics, and ethics that filled the first two volumes of his posthumous *Opera omnia* (Lyon, 1658). He wrote smaller treatises on physical and astronomical topics, his logic was well regarded, and his atomism was abbreviated and popularised by others, but none of this could equal the fame that came to him as Mister Flesh, author of the fifth set of *Objectiones* to Descartes's *Meditationes*.[40] Gassendi also earned his place in history as a philosophical critic of magic, going further than Mersenne in proposing physical and metaphysical alternatives to the magical hylemorphism discredited epistemologically by them both.

Gassendi and Mersenne were both priests, and both were moderate sceptics who believed that human perception reaches 'only to the outer bark, . . . not to the inward nature'. The lesson that Gassendi took from his epistemological humility was constructive: human lust for divine secrets must finally be thwarted, but a search frustrated in the end can still be an orderly way of collecting data.[41] 'Nothing can be known from the objects of nature beyond their history,' he wrote.

As for those who make many observations, . . . I do not mind calling them . . . experts on nature. . . . But I shall never force myself to speak this way of those who supposedly see things from the inside, as if they knew the true and proximate causes of marvellous effects. For me . . . there is nothing that is not a magnet or a remora, so the least little animal or plant . . . is a thunderclap.

Gassendi exploits the magnet-remora pairing as a topos in the literature on magic; the lodestone and the ship-holder were prominent items in the catalogue of magical objects whose unexplained effects had long justified appeal to occult qualities and forms.[42] But he brought down the curtain on the old metaphysical magic show, ridiculing the Peripatetic principles of

matter, form and privation. . . . Use them, I beg you, to show me the essence of just one object, even the tiniest in nature, and the true root and cause of all the effects and properties seen in it. I won't challenge you with anything as grand as the magnet or remora. . . . I'll take the little beast that often infests you, the flea. . . . You say that matter and form are in the flea. . . . What might this matter be, . . . and what is this form, . . . by what power does the flea sting you? . . . What a fine philosophy! . . . One word makes everything perfectly clear, once we've learned that everything has matter and form.

Thus Gassendi mocked the old occult philosophy, turning objects prized as magical into objects of ridicule.[43]

Except where his faith forbade it, he also abandoned hylemorphism, substituting material structures and mechanical causes for immaterial forms and qualities – including occult qualities. He defined quality as 'the mode of arrangement of a substance, a state and condition in which material principles are joined together', and he devoted a large portion of the section on physics in his *Syntagma* to a corpuscularian account of quality. Its final chapter, 'On the qualities called occult', judges the magnet, the remora, the electric ray, and other odd phenomena not by ruling them out of court but by forcing them within the jurisdiction of mechanics.[44] First, he turns the usual distinction between manifest and occult qualities on its head: 'There is no faculty or quality that is not occult', he insists, 'when one asks its cause and presses the question deeply. . . . And however much some causes, being not altogether remote, may be brought somewhat nearer, it is still the case that the nearby ones . . . always escape detection.' Having displayed his sceptical credentials, he then asserts that 'nothing acts on an object at a distance, an object not present in itself or through an intermediate or transmitted instrument . . . that must be corporeal.' Contact may occur invisibly among the smallest bodies which our senses are too dull to detect. The common sight of hooks and strings binding things together or of goads and poles pushing them apart may have its unseen analogue in 'tiny hooks, strings, goads and poles . . . which, even though invisible and impalpable, are not undescribable'. The porosity of most bodies, permitting them to emit and receive 'insensible effluxions', promotes the hidden work of such *organula*. On this basis, Gassendi explained the properties of amber and other mystifying objects, applying his microscopic speculations to some, dropping others from the docket of occult problems. Marine currents, not the remora, stopped ships, but the narcotic ray was more recalcitrant and still required an emission of unseen corpuscles to dull its victim's *spiritus*. Aware that such explanations were conjectural, Gassendi insisted (like Lucretius) only that there be *some* microscopic bodies at work, 'some tiny invisible instruments . . . to do the job of pulling or pushing'.[45]

The irreducibles in Gassendi's mechanics were not atoms and the void but a material and an efficient principle; the latter (in the order of second causes) he considered corporeal and therefore clearer to the mind than the disembodied agents of Platonists, Pythagoreans, and Peripatetics. His dislike of Platonism broke sharply with the Renaissance ancient theology that traced Plato's thought to the primordial wisdom of Hermes Trismegistus and used the Hermetic genealogy to sanctify occultism. 'There have been two ways of doing philosophy', wrote Gassendi, 'one dim, the other lucid.' In the latter group he put atomists, Stoics and sceptics, in the former Orpheus, Pythagoras, Plato, and also Aristotle, who 'expressed himself so obscurely . . . that he was compared to the cuttlefish . . . that hides behind its ink, as he hid behind his prose'. Given Aristotle's importance to the *philosophia occulta* as Gassendi saw it, he naturally associated the Stagirite with other philosophers often tarred as occultists. He disliked all fables, riddles, dogmas, and ambiguities, detecting them not only in Italian naturalists who claimed the Platonic heritage but also in their Peripatetic competitors.[46] All were at fault for mixing matter with spirit. Gassendi contrasted their muddlement with the clarity of his own views, sometimes treating tales of prodigies as beneath his consideration, more often taking the trouble to discredit magic, astrology, and demonology. Like Mersenne, he wanted his nature safe for the supernatural, an arena in which 'almighty God can use . . . phenomena to show whatever he likes', while ordinarily letting 'nature manage its own processes and preserve its order, once in his great wisdom he has established an order in nature'.[47] His lengthiest complaint against a disordered nature was directed against Fludd and written in 1630 at Mersenne's request after Fludd had attacked the Minim in 1629. A critical issue was that Fludd's pictorial fancies, like Aristotle's forms, confused the tangible with the intangible: 'Fludd weaves his geometrical lines however he likes, allotting the cube to the thickest part of matter, the square to the middle sort, the base to the thinnest. . . . Is there any result he cannot get by pulling and squeezing everything

all about just as he wants?' 'You pursue an open and empirical (*sensibilis*) philosophy', he told Mersenne, 'while he philosophizes as if he always wants to skulk
away, exuding the ink under which to escape the hook.'[48]

Mersenne may not have been happy with the cuttlefish allusion, which smeared
Aristotelians and Rosicrucians with the same ink. As for Gassendi, he had long
since abandoned Peripatetic authority. His Epicurean conversion left traces of
occultism, however. Whether his atomism was substantive science or a sceptic's
manoeuvre, it implied a problematic dynamism. One of the issues on which he
corrected Epicurus was the atom's motility, which he attributed to God's creative
act rather than to the atom itself. But once created, the atom is its own perpetual
motion machine; its gravity is 'a natural and internal faculty or power whereby to
stir and move itself on its own, . . . an inherent, innate, inborn and inalienable
propensity to motion, an intrinsic impetus and propulsion'.[49] A possible source of
this new matter-theory was the *Paradoxes ou traittez philosophiques des pierres* (Paris,
1635) of the condemned alchemist Estienne de Clave. He and other alchemists
may have helped Gassendi animate his Lucretian *semina rerum,* molecular seeds
assisted by a *spiritus elaborator* in endowing various substances with odd properties.
Although he saw his motile molecules as replacing astrological causes of generation
and corruption, they scarcely qualify as inert mechanical agents. He attributed
mineral formation to 'the seminal power in an active sort of substance aware of its
own effects, as only a spirit can be', and he located 'something analogous to
sensation' and 'a sort of soul' in the iron attracted by a magnet. If this was
pansensism or animism, one must recall what Gassendi meant by *anima.* Except in
man, soul was only a *flos materiae,* matter's rarest bloom but material nonetheless.
He was constitutionally uneasy about immaterial entities in natural philosophy,
even though his original antagonism to a Platonist world-soul diminished in the
Syntagma.[50]

When Pierre de Cazrée baited Gassendi on the topic of magnetism in 1642,
the Jesuit saved his sharpest jabs for

those invisible little hooks and grapples. . . . Magnet and iron rush to a mutual embrace not
because they are drawn by these fictive grapples and invisible chains, . . . but because they
are set in motion . . . spontaneously. . . . Why are you afraid . . . for a magnetic quality . . .
to be felt by the iron? . . . If generation and corruption are seen as nothing more than the
local motions . . . of atoms . . . , it's all over for substantial forms. . . . What will become of
the sacred mysteries of our religion?

Gassendi claimed not to understand how magnet and iron could join spontaneously. The magnetic embrace was the problem, not the solution; spontaneous

action was 'an unworkmanlike answer that we use for everything whose causes we don't know'. He defended his invisible barbs and chains as 'various degrees of instrumental causes' and declared their exploration to be the goal of physics. Enticed by the prospect of microscopy, Gassendi proposed to improve natural philosophy by pursuing analogies that ran from the visible world to the invisible. But when he invented souls and spirits as well as strings and hooks, he eroded the concreteness that made his metaphors clear. The strength and the weakness of his physics were revealed by Hélène Metzger, who called it 'the mechanics of joiners or carpenters' that simply transposed the shapes of simple tools to the atomic level.[51] Gassendi's artifice was crude and, for the moment, no improvement empirically on the physics of qualities, yet strong enough to shake the foundations of the occult philosophy.

3. Naudé

Besides Mersenne and Peiresc, Gassendi's friends included the group known as *libertins érudits* – Gabriel Naudé, Elie Diodati, François La Mothe Le Vayer, and several others, a small circle proud to be *déniaisés,* sceptical sophisticates ready to discard the follies of simpler folk. The libertines inherited the eclectic wealth of Renaissance thought, from Pomponazzi's stiff Latin heterodoxies to the supple questions of Montaigne's French essays. Despite the link between natural magic and naturalist philosophy in Pomponazzi and others whom they idolised, they wanted to strip occultism of its Renaissance glories. But magic had confronted scepticism long before the doubting libertines, in Agrippa's *De vanitate* and in later defences of demonology against the sceptical critique of sense knowledge. The disbelief of the medical profession had recently become infamous in Michel Marescot's epigrammatic diagnosis of the spirits who possessed Marthe Brossier, a scandal that ended in 1604: 'much pretense, many natural problems, none demonic'. Critics of astrology wielded weapons forged by another sceptical physician, Sextus Empiricus, thus resisting the naturalist Aristotelians since Pomponazzi who used astrology and occult qualities – both understood as within the natural order – to combat demonology.[52]

Naudé learned medicine as well as philosophy, acquiring Peripatetic along with sceptical instincts first as a student in Paris, then as a follower of the secular Aristotelians of Padua. His Italian education gave Naudé experience not only of a country that seemed to be populated by free-thinkers but also of a natural philosophy in which natural magic was a main fixture. Wide reading in Renaissance authors prepared him well to criticise this hybrid of rationalism and occultism, but his first blast against the occultists, the *Instruction à la France sur la verité de l'histoire des Freres de la Roze-Croix* (Paris, 1623), is a work of rhetoric and erudition rather than philosophy. His pamphlet is a well-informed but badly organised polemic, proving little more than that people are easily tricked. But Naudé also explained the Rosicrucian scare historically: the religious turbulence of the Reformation stirred up hurricanes of confused conviction, and Rosicrucianism was a squall that blew in their wake.[53] History was central in his next and better book, the *Apologie pour tous les grands personnages qui ont esté faussement soupçonnez de magie* (Paris, 1625), which treats cases of ancient, mediaeval, and Renaissance celebrities slandered as magicians. To get to the truth, Naudé proposed rules of evidence and methods of research; his first law was to assume everything false until inquiry confirms it. People are too trusting; witnesses forget or lie; error piles up when tradition repeats mistakes and complicates them. Naudé was a bibliophile, so he knew how print multiplies false authority, especially the bad credit of 'historians and demonographers' who propagated credulity about magic. His remedy was to put texts to the question, asking who wrote them, when, and in what context. Using such methods, one learned that the famous were often accused of magic because their success caused jealousy, because sloppy authors reproduced bad testimony, and because people who read dishonest books believed them out of malevolence and gullibility.[54]

Naudé admitted that Cornelius Agrippa had written some magical volumes, while noting that 'the avarice of booksellers' and not Agrippa had produced the pseudonymous fourth book that had been added to *De occulta philosophia libri tres*. Cardinals, popes, and kings had honoured Agrippa, yet his memory was ruined by historians who could not or would not recall his efforts to rescue a poor woman from accusations of witchcraft. As for Paracelsus, it was strange and obscure language that tarnished his fame, terminology so bizarre that 'one could not tell whether he was talking about a turd or a pill. . . . No doubt he used his magic to . . . disguise his teaching and not betray the emptiness of his art, which he judged to be the more admired the less it was understood.' The story was that Paracelsus kept the philosopher's stone or a demon in the pommel of his sword: more likely it was laudanum. He may have been a heretic, but he was no magus. To absolve him of sorcery, Naudé offered a deceptive but durable distinction that was to survive in modern anthropology: 'I believe . . . he should not be suspected of magic, seeing that magic does not consist in speculation and theory . . . but in the work of the Circle and invocations.'[55]

In other words, what Naudé found wrong in magic was ritual meant to have practical effects on human or spiritual persons; mere theory meant to explain the world of nature was harmless. In keeping with this distinction, he divided magic into its various categories, of which he permitted only the natural and the divine. He conceded that most of his subjects had studied natural magic, and he covered them with its classic definition: 'joining passive effects to active powers and bringing elementary things from here below nearer to the actions of stars and heavenly bodies'. On Bacon's authority, Naudé argued that natural magic belonged to natural philosophy and was 'nothing more than practical physics, as physics is a contemplative magic', a formula that might have pleased Ficino. As history his *Apologie* was acute, and as polemic it was effective, but recognising natural magic could only slow the disenchantment of natural philosophy. Stiffer resistance to occultism came in his later, less accessible works, written after his friend Gassendi had begun to oppose magic in earnest by 1629. As alert historical critics, Naudé and the learned libertines prepared the way for Bayle, Fontenelle, and Tartarotti. Except as a master of the French vernacular and a beneficiary of Montaigne's scepticism, Naudé had less in common with a clearer but quieter critic of scholastic occultism in natural philosophy – René Descartes.[56]

4. Descartes

Descartes was not the first to expel magic from the new philosophy. Galileo had as little use for occultism. His *Assayer* rejected the physics of qualities, and his limited concept of inertial motion chased the ghosts from nature's machine. But unlike Galileo, Descartes had large philosophical ambitions. He left the old castle of scholasticism for a palace of his own making, where corridors of reason led from a basement of method and metaphysics to a penthouse of morals, mechanics, and medicine. The humanist architecture of erudition and rhetoric, where Naudé found his plans for sceptical history, was no part of this design. In order to rebuild philosophy's house, Descartes turned away from the antique monuments of humanism, ignoring the Renaissance of history and philology. Naudé, Gassendi, and Mersenne all despised occultism, but they clothed their contempt in an erudite discourse, whose core lexicon was classicism. Conspicuous among the ruins restored by the humanists were ancient signposts to the truth and significance of magic, astrology, divination, and demonology. In the Renaissance landscape of antiquity, Hermes, Plato, Pliny, and Plotinus were seen telling the tales that Naudé doubted. The old sages haunted history's terrain, but Descartes averted his eyes.[57]

As he turned away from occultism, Descartes had as few regrets for modern authors as for ancient *auctores*. Because of its title, he knew he could skip Jacques Gaffarel's *Curiositez inouyes sur la sculpture talismanique des Persans, horoscope des Patriarches, et lecture des estoiles* (Paris, 1629), but he looked inside Athanasius Kircher's *De arte magnetica* (Rome, 1641) before calling the learned Jesuit 'more charlatan than scholar'. He admitted, fifteen years after reading it, that he had seen Campanella's *De sensu* in 1623, noting that he had found 'little solidity' in it. Around the same time, Mersenne suggested that he look at material by Campanella printed after Naudé and his circle had brought the contentious friar to Paris, but Descartes declined. By this time there was no room for the visionary Campanella in his philosophical dreams.[58] In earlier days he had not yet blocked every channel between himself and the occultist tradition. In the pansophic spirit of his time, he had glanced at the works of Ramon Lull in 1619 before warning Isaac Beeckman away from them. Travelling in Holland and Germany, he naturally heard of the Rosicrucians and wanted to meet one of them, but the young thinker's wish left little trace on the work of the mature philosopher – though Rosicrucian allegories may have entered his famous dreams of 10 November 1619. In a notebook of that period he mentioned the Rosicrucians, counting them in the reckless company of those 'who promise to produce wondrous novelties in all the sciences'. On the next anniversary of his dreams, he left a bold note of his own: 'I have begun to understand the basis of a wondrous [*mirabilis*) discovery.' Then he added a few remarks that sound more like Campanella than Beeckman: 'The active force in things is one: love, charity, harmony' and 'every corporeal form acts through harmony.' From that point on, the rest of the manuscript is mainly geometry, algebra, and mechanics.[59]

In his *Discours de la méthode* (Leiden, 1637) Descartes recorded his youthful passage through the compartments of knowledge, including 'even those full of superstition and falsehood, in order to know their true value and guard against being deceived by them'. Although his list recalls the vain learning that deluded Marlowe's Faustus, Descartes's departure from the traditional curriculum had different results. He claimed to have put no trust in 'the false sciences [knowing] their worth well enough not . . . to be deceived by the promises of an alchemist, . . . the predictions of an astrologer [or] the tricks of a magician'. Some phenomena often seen as magical – magnetism, birthmarks, optical illusions – held his attention, but the usual occult problems are mainly ignored in his published work. When they came up in his letters it was usually because of Mersenne. Still, his theory of particulate matter included vapours and spirits which, like other derivatives of the Stoic *pneuma,* linked the new mechanist physics to Ficino's magic of *spiritus.* Unlike Ficino, Descartes was not a magus or a physician, but he was always curious about medicine and capable of treating the psychology of healing as other than mechanical, as when he alluded to the Socratic *daimôn* in telling Princess Elisabeth that inward joy has some secret power to make fortune more favourable. He allowed himself few such sentiments. When Mersenne sneered at alchemy,

Descartes smirked with him, adding that 'such illusions aren't worth a moment's thought from a decent person.' As for astrology: 'It makes people die who without it might not have been sick. [Of] astrology, chiromancy and other such nonsense [*niaiseries*] . . . I can have no good opinion.'[60]

From the time he composed his posthumously published *Regulae ad directionem ingenii* (1620–8?), Descartes saw the occult sciences as arsenals of bad method. He asked why 'so many people should investigate . . . the virtues of plants, the motions of the stars, the transmutations of metals . . . while hardly anyone gives a thought to good sense'. His fifth rule illustrates the proper order of inquiry with the contrary example of astrology, which treats 'difficult problems in a very disorderly manner. [Astrologers] do not . . . make any accurate observations of celestial motions, yet they expect to be able to delineate the effects of these motions.' The eighth rule calls it 'foolish . . . to argue about the secrets [*arcana*] of nature, the influence of the heavens on these lower regions, the prediction of future events . . . without ever inquiring whether human reason is adequate for discovering matters such as these'. Rule nine, like Gassendi's remarks on the flea, claims that for a clear and distinct intuition of truth one must 'concentrate . . . upon the most insignificant and easiest of matters', and Descartes amplified this precept with examples familiar to the occultist tradition:

The sciences, however abstruse [*occultae*], are to be deduced only from matters which are easy and highly accessible, and not from those which are grand and obscure. . . . To inquire whether a natural power can travel instantaneously to a distant place, . . . I shall not immediately turn my attention to the magnetic force, or the influence of the stars. . . . I shall, rather, reflect upon the local motions of bodies . . . readily perceivable. . . . I shall not have recourse to the remedies of the physicians, . . . nor shall I prattle on about the moon's warming things by its light and cooling them by means of some occult quality. Rather, I shall observe a pair of scales . . . and similar examples.

As anti-type of the clear speech needed for proper inquiry, rule twelve describes scholastic discourse as 'magic words which have a hidden meaning [*vis occulta*] beyond the grasp of the human mind'. 'In the vast majority of issues about which the learned dispute', according to rule thirteen, 'the problem is . . . one of words.'[61] This principle still applied in 1646 when Descartes rebuked chemists for speaking 'in terms outside common usage as a pretense of knowing what they do not know'. The danger was that 'those who brag of having secrets – in chemistry or judicial astrology, for example – never fail . . . to find some curious folk to buy their swindles at high cost.'[62] Whatever he found esoteric, obscure, or vacuous Descartes wished to eliminate from his new philosophy, whose clear and distinct ideas were to end the reign of the occult.

The same high standard of clarity that ruled his own thinking was to regulate divine conduct as well. An undeceiving deity should work only clear and distinct wonders: 'Why would God do a miracle unless he wanted it known as a miracle?' Descartes steered clear of the miraculous when he could, either by openly refusing the question or by fencing it in with method, as in the 'new world' of the posthumous *Le Monde* (1630–33?), where 'God will never perform any miracle . . . , and . . . the intelligences . . . will not disrupt . . . the ordinary course of nature.'[63] The world that Descartes lived in was a messier place and a nursery of wonderment, as he learned in the feud with Gijsbertus Voetius that began in 1639. Magic, occult qualities, and substantial forms were some of the many threads in the fabric of this tedious dispute. Voetius linked Cartesianism with atomism and scepticism, denounced it as incompatible with scripture, and condemned it for rejecting Christian doctrine on the soul, the incarnation, demonic possession and miracles. After sorting out his theological hesitations, Descartes called Voetius wrongheaded to depict occult qualities and forms as a *docta ignorantia* restraining the pansophic lust to reduce everything to geometry and mechanics. 'Obviously, one can account for no natural action through these substantial forms', he replied, 'since their proponents admit that they are occult and do not understand them. . . . From the mere fact that they do not know the nature of some quality, they conclude that it is occult or inscrutable for all mankind.'[64]

These 'scholastic wars' sputtered on for years, as Voetius vented his rage by calling Descartes a crypto-atheist and implicating him with Vanini, the Jesuits, Paracelsians, and Rosicrucians. One slander that stunned Descartes was Voetius's charge that his algebraic geometry was a kind of magic. He could 'only ask whether [Voetius] rightly understands this philosophy that he condemns, a man so stupid . . . that he wishes to bring it under suspicion of magic because it has to do with shapes'. If Voetius were right, then 'a key, a sword, a wheel and all other objects whose effects depend on shape are . . . tools of magic'.[65] This rejoinder missed one likely point of Voetius's accusation, whose background was a famous controversy about the magical effects of pictorial shapes carved on natural objects, that is, astrological talismans. Aquinas had proposed a hylemorphic account of efficacious astrological figures, calling them 'quasi-specific forms'. Debate continued through the Renaissance with Ficino, Campanella and others until Fludd taunted Mersenne with the problem. Voetius, who feared the danger to Christian school philosophy, saw quantitative mechanics as eroding the qualitative physics of the schools, and he cunningly linked this decay to a curriculum corrupted by magic.

When one attributes efficacy and movement to quantity and shape, though they are usually attributed to forms and their active qualities, one must realize that as a consequence the young may sometimes unwisely admit that magical axiom hitherto rejected by all Christian theology and philosophy: that there is some efficacy in quantity and figure, which in itself or along with other things behaves as an active principle of change.

This was the metaphysical and the professional fuel for Voetius's rage at the new mathematics as an arrogant pansophic kabbalah. He took offense at the Cartesian conviction of having found in algebra 'not only an encyclopedia and compendium of human wisdom, but also a kind of cornucopia in which all the treasures of every possible science and discipline lie hidden'.[66]

Much of Descartes's fight with the Peripatetics, whom he wished not to attack frontally, was about substantial forms. His liveliest arguments against forms dealt with soul and mind, central issues for occultism because of the link between animism or vitalism and magic. To purge the mind of separable forms, Descartes devised a contact model of sensation without phantasms, the ineffable entities deployed by the scholastics at the 'mysterious limit' between mind and its material objects. Separable forms and real accidents 'were aligned with substance like little souls in bodies', thus blurring the distinction between matter and mind. To treat properties of matter as real separable qualities was to make them autonomous substances and thereby to confuse 'the power whereby the soul acts on the body with that whereby one body acts on another'. To resolve the confusion, Descartes moved beyond *res cogitans* and *res extensa* to a third notion of the union of mind and body in the human composite, whose soul is 'the only substantial form'.[67] Giving the human soul this unique status exposed the inverse error of treating natural objects as hylemorphic composites and showed how the physics of qualities bred a magical animism when people projected their inward apprehension of the body/soul junction onto other bodies. Descartes diagnosed hylemorphism as a psychosomatic disease:

Although I called [gravity] a 'quality', . . . I was . . . thinking that it was a substance. . . . I still did not attribute to it the extension . . . of a body [and] saw that the gravity, while remaining coextensive with the heavy body, could exercise all its force in any one part . . . , exactly the way in which I now understand the mind to be coextensive with the body. . . . What makes it especially clear that my idea of gravity was taken largely from the idea I had of the mind is the fact that I thought that gravity carried bodies towards the centre of the earth as if it had some knowledge of the centre.

Descartes showed how easy it was to slip souls or even minds into bodies under the guise of qualities and forms, thus scouting the terrain that Leibniz would occupy when he attacked Newton for injecting forces into bodies 'like little demons or imps'.[68]

His own species aside, Descartes wanted a world cleanly divided between the mental and the material, with no room for magical qualities or hylemorphic hybrids. He once considered compiling a natural history of qualities, but eventually he decided that it was 'these qualities themselves [that] need explanation'. Qualities are not real things but modes of things or mental responses to them. Replacing the physics of qualities, the new science of mechanics would solve even such hard cases as magnetism and heat. After the long account of the magnet in the *Principia,* Descartes took only a few lines to add that 'shape, size, position and motion' cover 'all the other remarkable effects . . . usually attributed to occult qualities', concluding that 'there are no powers . . . so mysterious, and no marvels attributed to sympathetic and antipathetic influences . . . so astonishing that they cannot be explained in this way.' Matter in motion accounts for all these 'rare and marvellous effects' – amber's attractive power, feats of imagination, and telepathy, even the murdered corpse that bleeds when the killer comes near. Mersenne had written reams against occult qualities; Gassendi and others enlarged the pile of words; but Descartes closed the question with a snub.[69]

IV. FROM DIGBY TO LOCKE

1. Digby

Among the first English thinkers influenced by Descartes were the credulous virtuoso Kenelm Digby and the methodical mechanist Thomas Hobbes. Both were in France in the mid-1630s, and both sympathised with recent innovations in French philosophy. Digby's *Two Treatises* appeared in Paris in 1644, but he had already explained one of its purposes in his *Observations upon Religio Medici* (London, 1643), hastily composed towards the end of that year after he read a manuscript of Thomas Browne's famous book. He agreed with Browne that 'there are not impossibilities enough in religion for an active faith', yet 'a totall survey of the whole science of bodyes' was needed to establish the soul's immortality. He promised to provide such a study to 'shew . . . all the motions of nature, and unto them . . . fit intelligibly the termes used by her secretaries, whereby all wilde fantasticke qualities and moods (introduced for refuges of ignorance) are banished'. Digby criticised Browne for conceding too much to astrologers, diviners, and magicians, though he had his own reasons for believing in ghosts. 'Neither do I deny there are witches', he added; 'I only reserve my assent, till I meete with stronger motives.' The motives too weak for Digby foreshadowed the remarkable influence of talk about witches and ghosts on English philosophy and theology for the rest of the century. Confessing that 'our physicians experience hath the advantage of my philosophy in knowing there are witches', Digby nonetheless admitted 'no temptation to doubt of the deity nor . . . spirits. I do not see such a necessary conjunction betweene them.'[70] The conjunction binding theism to spiritualism and sorcery led Henry More and others to conclusions contrary to Digby's.

The first and larger of Digby's *Two Treatises* is a study of body as prelude to the understanding of soul. Digby claimed that 'a body is a body by quantity.' Then he defined quantity as divisibility and divisibility as local motion, so that 'all operations among bodies are either locall motion or such as follow out of locall motion [among] the least sort of natural bodies.' Major casualties of Digby's mechanism – despite professions of loyalty to Aristotle – were the 'uselesse cobwebbes and prodigious chymeras' of Peripatetic philosophy, particularly the doctrine of qualities understood as 'reall entities . . . distinct from the bodies they accompany'. Gravity and levity, for example, are not things in themselves but bodily states caused by external impulse. No matter how abstruse the effect of heat or light or magnetism, 'no body can worke upon another remote from it, without working first upon the body that lyeth between', and usually this happens 'by the emission of little partes out of one body into another . . . passing through the interjacent bodies which . . . furnish them, as it were, with channels and pipes'. Digby believed that such emissions 'may yield a reason for those magicall operations, which some attribute to the Divels assistance'. Fearing that it would 'in a manner renounce all humane fayth', he hesitated to discard all the testimony for magical effects. Instead, he proposed 'to make these operations of nature not incredible' by explaining them mechanically.[71]

His leading example of an allegedly occult phenomenon reducible to 'down right material qualities' was the powder of sympathy, a relative of the weapon salve publicised by Fludd and others before him. In 1658 Digby published the original (Paris) edition of his *Discours . . . touchant la guerison des playes par la poudre de sympathie,* which eventually saw twenty-nine editions in five languages. Expanding his earlier discussion of the powder in the *Two Treatises,* he told how he had learned of it three decades before from a monk returned from Asia; how witnesses as trustworthy as King James and Chancellor Bacon certified its power; how the secret eventually leaked and spread; and how its ingredients might be obtained and compounded. When experience showed that the powder, mixed with blood from a wound, could promote healing even when physically removed from the patient, Digby reasoned that 'light transporting the atomes of the vitriol [in the powder] and of the blood, and dilating them to a great extent in the aire, the wound . . . doth attract them, and thereby is immediately solac'd, . . . healed by the spirits of the vitriol, which is of a balsamicall virtue.' He preferred invisible particles to the usual 'effect of charme or magick', calling it 'a poor kind of pusillanimity and faintnesse of heart, or rather a grosse ignorance . . . to confine all the actions of nature to the grossenesse of our senses'.[72]

2. Hobbes

Although he looked beyond sense data to unseen mechanisms, Digby was an experimentalist and thus friendlier than Hobbes to the Baconian strain of pragmatic, collective empiricism that was to blossom in the Royal Society of Boyle's day. Closer in spirit to Descartes than to Bacon, Hobbes trusted method and reason more than experience. He aimed at a systematic philosophy, and he attempted a metaphysics, but from his early writings through *Leviathan* (London, 1651) and *De corpore* (London, 1655) what preoccupied him was motion and its relation to sensation. Ruling out action at a distance and reducing the world to bodies in motion, Hobbes could have based his mechanics on transmitted particulate emissions like Digby's; instead, like Descartes, he focused on the medium through which bodies interact – perhaps because emissions recalled the *species* applied by Aristotelians to such difficult cases as magnetism. The *Little Treatise* once attributed to Hobbes treats such *species* as vehicles of sympathetic 'conveniency and disconveniency by which the agents . . . attrude and repell'. A key to Hobbes's own views on transmission through the medium was the concept of *conatus* (endeavour), the infinitesimal motion of unobservable bodies that helped him account even for human psychology in mechanical terms.[73] Less sensitive but still difficult was the phenomenon of iron's motion towards a magnet without contact, in apparent conflict with the principle that 'whatsoever is moved, is moved by some contiguous and moved body.' Hobbes reasoned that

> the first endeavour which iron hath towards the loadstone is caused by the motion of that air . . . contiguous to the iron . . . generated by the motion of the next air, and so on . . . till . . . we find . . . some motion . . . in the loadstone itself, which motion . . . is invisible. It is therefore certain that the attractive power of the loadstone is nothing else but some motion of the smallest particles thereof. . . . As for those that say anything may be moved . . . by itself, by species, . . . by substantial forms, . . . by antipathy, sympathy, occult quality, and other empty words of schoolmen, their saying so is to no purpose.

Hobbes was quick to uncover the scholastic subterfuge: 'They put for cause of natural events their own ignorance . . . disguised in other words, . . . as when they attribute many effects to occult qualities; that is, qualities not known to them.'[74]

Hobbes wanted to cure philosophy of abstraction, even imagining a language with no verb 'to be' and wondering what would then happen to such terms as 'essence'. He traced metaphysical trouble to such vacuities and claimed that he studied words so that 'separated essences' would no longer terrify people and

fright them from obeying the laws of their country with empty names. . . . For it is upon this ground that when a man is dead and buried, they say his soul . . . can walk separated from his body. . . . Upon the same ground they say that the figure and colour and taste of a piece of bread has a being there, where they say there is no bread. And upon the same ground . . . a great many other . . . errors [are] brought into the Church from the entities and essences of Aristotle.

From Peripatetic abuse of the copula Hobbes derived such seditious errors as fear of ghosts and reverence for the host.[75] Behind his original critique of language lay an even more threatening metaphysics. Identifying substance with body permitted him to claim that the term 'spirit', even as used in Scripture, could refer only to something embodied – however lightly embodied – or else to a mistake of perception. Angels and demons may exist, but they must have 'subtle bodies, . . . endued with dimensions', and he could find no biblical evidence for their incorporeality. Hobbes also reinterpreted the biblical stories of Moses and the Egyptian wizards, long-standing proof-texts for magic. Arguing that words can affect only those who understand them by signifying passion or intention and causing emotion, he concluded that the 'arts of magic and incantation' in the Bible must have been either ordinary verbal suggestions or else conscious deceptions. The alternative was to give some other meaning to the scriptural text, 'and yet there is no place of Scripture that telleth us what an enchantment is.' As for contemporary belief in magic, Hobbes claimed to know no one who 'ever saw any such wonderous work . . . that a man endued but with a mediocrity of reason would think supernatural'.[76] His hostility to occultism was thorough and clear, but its exposition in his larger critique of religion made his rejection of magic and traditional demonology less useful to contemporaries than otherwise it might have been. Like Lucretius, Hobbes derived the religious instinct from fear and ignorance, especially from confusions about souls, dreams, and visual images. By setting these outrageous views alongside less radical criticisms of 'the opinion that rude people have of fairies, ghosts and goblins, and of the power of witches', he bound the failing cause of occultism to the future of a religion that for most Europeans was still no illusion.[77]

3. More

That some thinkers linked a rational Christianity with residues of the occultist tradition is evident in the group of English philosophers called the Cambridge Platonists – especially but not uniquely so in Henry More. As a young man, More sought refuge from determinism and scepticism in various millenarian, Arminian, and Platonist beliefs. Even after he found certainty in 'the Spirit Divine', he remained tolerant, eclectic, and always suspicious of 'enthusiasm', a false sense of inspiration such as he saw in the magus and alchemist, Thomas Vaughan. Vaughan dedicated his *Anthroposophia theomagica* (London, 1650) to the Rosicrucians, proclaiming his kinship to the occultists of the previous century and professing his hatred of Aristotle. More answered Vaughan, launching an exchange of polemics in which More contended that religion based on enthusiasm decays easily into atheism. In *Enthusiasmus triumphatus* (London and Cambridge, 1656), he attributed the 'misconceit of being inspired' to a diseased imagination that he detected in 'many of your chymists and several theosophists'.[78]

This early hostility to occultism, which may seem misplaced in the Cambridge that rediscovered Ficino, was in keeping with More's first, warm embrace of the philosophy whose English name he was to coin, Cartesianism. But closer reading of More's early reaction to Descartes reveals important disagreements between the two, particularly More's insistence that some natural effects have no mechanical explanation and hence show the need for a spiritual substance active in nature. Having turned away from Aristotle for religious reasons, More embraced Descartes as a non-Aristotelian proponent of theism and the soul's immortality. Even though his writing became overtly theological only around 1660, his deepest motives were always religious, as is apparent from two earlier works, *An Antidote against Atheism* (London, 1653) and *Conjectura Cabbalistica* (London, 1653). In the former book, when he blamed Descartes for the atheist perils of the mechanical philosophy, More expressed the spiritual panic provoked by Hobbes. But in the *Conjectura* he interpreted Cartesian physics positively as the latest version of a sacred tradition (or kabbalah) of atomism first revealed by Moses in Genesis. That More felt free to select from Descartes what he needed for purposes never dreamt of in Egmond or Paris is clear from a remark in one of his treatises against Vaughan, *The Second Lash of Alazonomastix* (Cambridge, 1651):

Divine Spirit and Life . . . is worth not only all the Magick that thou Pretendest to, but . . . Des-Cartes Philosophy to boot, . . . a fine, neat, subtil thing [that] bears no greater Proportion to that Principle . . . than the dry Bones of a Snake . . . to the Royal Clothing of Solomon. But other Natural Philosophies . . . are even less.

Later, More's alienation from Descartes increased. When he learned genuine Lurianic kabbalah from Knorr von Rosenroth and tried to apply it to his theory of divinised space, he crowned Descartes 'Prince of the Nullibists' who denied God any place in the cosmos.[79]

The word 'Cartesianism' first appeared in 1662 to disparage the 'mechanical surmises' of its eponym. If Descartes and Gassendi hoped to make the material world autonomous, More and the Cambridge Platonists feared that they might enlarge the 'very hideous chasme or gaping breach in the order of things' opened by the naturalist Aristotelians. They filled the gap with a soul housed not only in the body but also in aerial and aetherial vehicles that joined matter to spirit magically. Likewise, a spiritual God could act on His material creation through a medium, a spirit of nature or hylarchic principle, 'a substance incorporeal, but without sense and animadversion, pervading the whole matter of the universe, and exercising a plastical power therein, . . . raising such phaenomena in the world . . . as cannot be resolved into mere mechanical powers'.[80] More applied his spirit of nature to long-standing problems, such as 'the phaenomenon of gravity, wherein . . . both [Descartes] and Mr. Hobbs are quite out of the story'. Recalling that Plotinus called nature 'the grand magus', More also claimed that 'the unity of the soul of the universe . . . and . . . the continuity of subtile matter' accounted for 'not onely the sympathy of parts in one particular subject, but of different and distant subjects, . . . such as is betwixt the party wounded and the knife . . . besmeared with the weapon-salve, . . . which certainly is not purely mechanical but magical'. Although he cited Digby on the powder of sympathy, he denied that 'any agency of emissary atoms' could explain the cures that he reported.[81]

That More saw the defects of mechanics in the topics of gravity and sympathy – and that he considered these problems cognate – shows his dependence on Neoplatonism as much as his distance from Descartes. Even when he used such characteristically Cartesian notions as the ontological argument or innate ideas, he put them in strange company. To prove God's existence and confute the atheists, he told tales of ghosts, witches, demoniacs, apparitions, even the Pied Piper of Hamlin, anything to aid his quest for 'such effects discovered in the world as are not deemed natural, but extraordinary and miraculous [and] cannot be resolved into any natural causes, . . . but are so miraculous that they do imply the presence of some free subtile understanding Essence distinct from the brute matter and ordinary power of nature'. More filled his works with such stories gathered not only from the demonographers whom Naudé had scorned but also from his own experience and that of contemporaries. He developed criteria to sort fact from fable – rules of evidence and testimony – and he applied them in case after case,

as when he proved to himself the 'unexceptionable truth and authentickness' of
reports of a haunted house in Burgundy from 'the observation . . . not by one
solitary person, but by many together, nor by a person of suspected integrity, but
of singular gravity, . . . the experience not made once or twice, but . . . every
day for a quarter of a year'.[82] More's inquest into the supernatural was not
undiscriminating. While authenticating ghost stories as proofs of a spiritual God,
he criticised astrology for related reasons: attempts to trace extraordinary effects to
physical causes in the heavens were evasions, contrived by materialist Aristotelians,
'of the truth . . . concerning apparitions'. His spiritualist researches made his
theological convictions invincible. 'I am as well assured in my own judgement of
the existence of spirits', he boasted, 'as that I have met with men in Westminster-
Hall or seen beasts in Smithfield.'[83]

4. Glanvill

The certainty that More found in haunted houses was not new or eccentric in
English natural philosophy. John Dee had recorded his talks with angels in the
previous century, and in More's day the hunt for spirits interested not only Ralph
Cudworth and the Cambridge Platonists but also Robert Boyle of the Royal
Society. One avid pursuer of poltergeists was the sceptical Joseph Glanvill, author
not only of *The Vanity of Dogmatizing* (London, 1661) but also of *Lux orientalis*
(London, 1662), *Some Philosophical Considerations Touching Witches and Witchcraft*
(London, 1666), and *Plus Ultra, or the Progress and Advancement of Knowledge since
the Days of Aristotle* (London, 1668) – a remarkable quartet. In *Plus Ultra* Glanvill
defended the Royal Society and the new science, which Thomas White had
attacked in 1663 along with what he took to be Glanvill's free-thinking abandonment of authority in *The Vanity of Dogmatizing*. When Meric Casaubon answered
Plus Ultra in 1669, he accused Glanvill of speaking 'the common language of all
extravagant chymists [who in] professing Christianity would raise admiration by
broaching unheard of mysteries'. Casaubon, who saw proofs of spirits everywhere,
linked Glanvill with Fludd because both put Aristotle away when they took up
the Bible. To conservatives like Casaubon, Glanvill's sin was enthusiasm, one of
the most adaptable slurs of the age. He and other prophets of the new learning
were elitist mystics as well as amoral materialists; they abandoned tradition for 'an
universitie consisting of chimists, Behemists and enthusiasts'. Glanvill, however,
saw himself as warring against his own version of enthusiasm, struggling for a
rationalism that would resolve passions and dogmas in a broad-minded empiricism.
He found the old certainties powerless against the impious novelties of Hobbes,
but he believed that a programme of experiment directed towards probable truth

and based on suspension of judgement could reveal enough about matter to secure the realm of spirit. Since Glanvill's nature is the province of second causes, it must be diabolical rather than divine spirit that often reveals itself in this world; so he urged the Royal Society to back a research programme on witches, the devil's agents.[84]

Glanvill aimed to establish the facts about witches and ghosts through case histories and testimony. He began his spiritual sleuthing in 1663 with the drumming demon of Tedworth. He inspected the afflicted house, heard the notorious knocking, spoke with the spirit and wrote an account of it still read in the next century. Assisted by More, Boyle, and others, his researches culminated in the *Sadducismus triumphatus* (London, 1681), edited posthumously by More. When critics wanted to replace supernatural causes with natural mechanisms, Glanvill applied the tools of the mitigated sceptic: reporting the data and admitting ignorance of causes, he turned the phenomenalism of Mersenne and Gassendi to queer purposes. His scepticism was partly theological. Adam's sin had epistemic as well as moral consequences. Before the Fall, his 'sight could inform him whether the loadstone doth attract by atomical effluviums. . . . The mysterious influence of the moon . . . was no question in his philosophy, no more than a clocks motion is in ours. . . . Sympathies and antipathies were . . . no occult qualities.' But in postlapsarian times, the Peripatetic philosophy made fallen humanity 'conclude many things within the list of impossibilities which yet are easie feasables, . . . leaping from the effect to the remotest cause' and accepting the 'impostures of charms and amulets and other insignificant ceremonials'. Too many phenomena 'are noted in the book of vulgar opinion with *digitus dei* or *daemonis,* though they owe no other dependence to the first then what is common to the whole syntax of beings, nor . . . to the second then what is given it by . . . unqualifi'd judges'. Doctrinaire scholastics too lazy to penetrate nature's 'more mysterious reserves' are too satisfied that 'qualities . . . occult to Aristotle must be so to us.' Not only gravity but heat, cold, and other qualities called manifest are empty names as occult as all the rest. Only the effects of manifest qualities are rightly named. Since their causes are 'confessedly occult', it is evident that 'the Peripatetick philosophy resolves all things into occult qualities, and the dogmatists are the only scepticks.'[85]

Glanvill found the old philosophy 'inept for new discoveries'. He described nature as driven by 'the most subtil and hidden instruments, which it may be have nothing obvious which resembles them'. Simple observation cannot penetrate 'the more hidden frame' within. Discarding Aristotelian elements and qualities, Glanvill put his hope in Cartesian and other innovations that might yield pragmatic as well as philosophical rewards. His leading example of such hopes was a magnetic

mechanism for 'conference at distance by impregnated needles . . . without . . .
daemoniack correspondence', a crude anticipation of the telegraph derived from
a programme of 'magical history . . . enlarged by riper inspections'. He also
envisioned 'sympathised hands' producing 'a new kind of chiromancy' and mentioned Digby's atoms as a basis for sympathetic cures. As to the true mechanism of
Digby's powder, Glanvill confessed that 'it is out of my way here to enquire
whether the *anima mundi* be not a better account then any mechanical solutions.
The former is more desperate, the latter hath more of ingenuity. . . . It is enough
for me that *de facto* there is such an entercourse, . . . and I need not be solicitous
of the cause.' After telling the tale of the scholar-gypsy who could 'bind the
thoughts of another . . . by the power of advanc'd imagination', he was again
ambivalent about spiritual or mechanical causation, proposing 'the hypothesis of a
mundane soul lately reviv'd by that incomparable Platonist and Cartesian, Dr. H.
More', as well as 'a mechanical account [of] a motion of certain filaments of the
brain'. Having traced his sceptical history from the lost perspicuity of Eden
through the obscurity of the Peripatetics to the clarity of Descartes, Glanvill could
not yet dispense with what Ralph Cudworth called the 'one vital unitive principle
in the universe, . . . a certain vital energy . . . fatally sympathetical and magical'.[86]

5. *Boyle*

One of the correspondents who gave Glanvill evidence of mediating spirits was
'the illustrious Mr. Boyle', who founded 'the mechanick philosophy [and] made
. . . substantial forms and real qualities . . . needless and precarious beings'. Both
Boyle and Glanvill wanted to rescue chemistry from 'delusory . . . Rosie-crucian
vapours, magical charms and superstitious suggestions' and to make it 'an instrument to know the depths and efficacies of nature'. Boyle was even more influential
than Glanvill as a spokesman for experimental method and mechanical explanation. He replaced traditional and alchemical elements with particles unqualified
except by size, shape, and motion or rest, and he made motion the ultimate
determinant of his minimal bodies, which are unobservable in principle. His
corpuscular theory covered cases of action at a distance, approaching the problem
of invisible agents through a mechanism established in *The Sceptical Chymist*
(London, 1661) – 'the effluviums of amber, jet and other electricall concretes,
[which] by their effects . . . seem to fall under . . . our sight, yet do . . . not as
electrical immediately affect any of our senses'. Such properties emerge not
directly from sensation but indirectly from our contemplating the sense effects of
a structure (the effluvium) of imperceptible particles. School philosophy referred
the same phenomena to occult virtues, but Boyle's effluvia were concrete material

entities intelligible by analogy with visible vapors and steams. Despite their opacity to observation and their kinship with magical *spiritus,* Boyle's effluvia were in the spirit of corpuscular philosophy and – if only because his reasoning about them avoided the circular arguments of his predecessors – an improvement on occult qualities. Although many admired his explanations and experiments, Leibniz and others complained that Boyle did not push his mechanics far enough. His essays on gems and drugs, two strongholds of occultism, were 'infected with the plague of credulity'. He tried to bring these most notoriously occult phenomena – including even cures by amulet – within the scope of the new science. But his critics were more disappointed by his willingness to certify occult effects than convinced by his efforts to trace their causes to material effluvia.[87]

Boyle, Glanvill, and other virtuosi followed the exploits of the healer Valentine Greatrakes, whose early success came in touching for the 'King's Evil', or scrofula. His visit to England in 1666 failed to cure Lady Conway's migraines but put the Irish stroker at the centre of stormy debate about the cessation of miracles and the causes of wondrous effects. Boyle, who attended dozens of stroking sessions, entered the controversy to answer a pamphlet that emphasised a physical agency for Greatrakes's cures. Boyle accepted the cures as valid and natural but disputed their cause; he also worried that people might think that even scriptural miracles had natural causes. Greatrakes covered himself supernaturally, attributing his healing effluvia to a special providence, an option with obvious attractions for Henry More, for whom a series of benign Protestant healing miracles was a better bet than either haunted houses or Boyle's particles.[88] It may seem odd that a founder of modern chemistry concerned himself with the spiritualism of More, Glanvill, and Greatrakes. Yet one should recall not only the famous lectures that bore Boyle's name, endowed to combat atheist materialism, but also his wish to reform astrology rather than reject it altogether, as well as his dealings with the swindler Georges Pierre. Pierre plied him with alchemical secrets and tried to lure him into a 'Sacred Kabbalistic Society of Philosophers'. He claimed to see Boyle as the new Hermes, an honourable title for someone who near the end of his life wanted 'to leave a kind of Hermetic legacy . . . and to deliver candidly . . . some processes chemical and medicinal that are . . . kin to the noblest Hermetic secrets'. In light of Newton's long alchemical quest, it is no surprise that the sceptical chemist himself shared the same esoteric habits, though it might disappoint some to learn that Boyle worked to have Parliament repeal the mediaeval statute against transmutation of base into noble metals.[89]

Despite disingenuous criticism from Newton, who in this area was as much rival as judge, Boyle persisted in his alchemical experiments, which account for his wish to see the old law off the books. Boyle's pursuit of transmutation was an obvious avenue for the new science. As an experimenter he thought he had achieved transmutation by reducing water to a solid, and as a corpuscularian he could explain it – indeed, must expect it – as a rearrangement of particles. Above all, as scourge of the school philosophers, he did not account for transmutation by any transfer of scholastic real qualities. He learned enough from Bacon, Galileo, Descartes, and Gassendi to make him a foe of Peripatetic obscurity, and his research in medical chemistry convinced him that the spagyrists were just as confused. Boyle argued that nothing as complex as Peripatetic fire or spagyric sulfur could be an element of explanation or ontology since further reduction of such properties as heat or combustibility was obviously required. His most famous work was *The Sceptical Chymist* of 1661, but *Origine of Formes and Qualities* (Oxford, 1666) was richer theoretically. Occult qualities were a leading object of Boyle's inquiries. He preferred corpuscles to forms and qualities not because he could see them but because he trusted them as material and picturable. Homely metaphors based on keys, locks, clocks, pins, and mills helped him demystify the origin of qualities, even though his analysis ended in the imperceptible. From experiment and from analogy between the seen and the unseen, he postulated objects that he could not sense, aiming for a corpuscular solution to the problem of occult qualities, even the most intractable. Obsession with substance had led chemists and scholastics to forget structure, as if one could show how the workings of a clock keep time by telling whether its gears and springs are brass or steel. By demoting form to a set of material properties, and by reducing species to a convention of human use, Boyle robbed specific forms of their reality and their magic. Like plastic powers or world-souls, substantial forms explain nothing, leaving 'the curious enquirer as much to seek . . . as men commonly are for the particular causes of . . . witchcraft, though they be told that it is some devil that does them all'.[90]

6. Locke

So strong was Boyle's influence on John Locke that one might characterise Locke's matter-theory as a refinement of Boyle's, in contrast to Locke's more original critique of substance, species, and the various confusions that obscured the use of these terms in school philosophy. Locke abolished forms and species through an analysis of naming, knowing, and classification that exceeded the physical ambitions of Boyle's programme. His views on quality, however, remained close to Boyle's. Beginning with a fundamental distinction between *ideas* as percepts or concepts and *qualities* as powers in objects to produce ideas in us, he distinguished further among three kinds of quality. Real primary qualities such as 'solidity, extension, figure and mobility' are so basic that all bodies must possess them. They produce ideas in us that actually resemble their causes. Not so with secondary qualities, which 'are nothing in the objects themselves but powers to produce various sensations in us by their primary qualities'. Qualities of the third kind act like secondary qualities, except that they cause sensations in us indirectly by first changing the texture of some other object. All phenomena intelligible to us, even those long treated as occult, reduce to primary qualities or their textures, though the debility of human knowledge has kept nature's mechanism a secret.[91]

Before the *Essay concerning Human Understanding* (London, 1690) made him famous, Locke spent much of his time in the study and practice of medicine. Until he read Thomas Sydenham's *Methodus curandi febres* (London, 1666), it was iatrochemistry that chiefly occupied him, and it was Boyle especially who guided him in the new science of matter. His relations with Boyle peaked in 1666, when the *Origine of Formes and Qualities* appeared along with Sydenham's *Methodus,* a year before Locke left Oxford for London to serve as Lord Ashley's physician. Sydenham introduced Locke to a phenomenalist medicine that discarded natural philosophy as a basis for clinical practice, replacing speculation about the causes of disease with natural-historical observation of the course of illness. Their collaboration may have influenced early drafts of the *Essay.* While travelling in France after 1675, Locke maintained the medical journals that he had begun as early as 1652. His wish to compile a great body of clinical data reflects his respect for Baconian natural history as well as his partnership with the sceptical Sydenham. The notes, recipes, and experimental records that fill Locke's commonplace books also show how his culture acquainted him with medical magic.[92]

During his Oxford period, Locke's iatrochemical reading – like Boyle's – included authors prominent in the recent history of occultism: Fernel, Cardano, Paracelsus, Campanella, Sennert, and the elder Van Helmont. In the mid-1660s he read the alchemical works of Basil Valentine, and although his ardour for chemistry cooled as Sydenham's influence grew, his duties as Boyle's literary executor in the early 1690s relit the Hermetic flame, leading to a correspondence about transmutation in which Newton tried to dampen Locke's interest, as he did earlier with Boyle himself. Scattered comments in Locke's journals about alchemy and other varieties of occultism do not show that he believed in amulets, ghosts, or astrological botany. But they are evidence that these topics were still part of the conversation among scientific revolutionaries. Locke registered clinical data against Digby's use of mole's blood to cure epilepsy, but his account of a patient's mole-like behaviour ('in a fit he would run his nose against the ground like a mole') sounds like sympathetic magic. A recipe of 1686 says: 'Split a standing young oak, passe child between the divided parts. Binde the tree togeather agen and as the tree closes and heales up again soe will the burstnesse close in the child.' Locke cited a colleague's contempt for the bezoar and dismissed the snake-stone as 'for the most part if not wholy factitious and of noe such virtue for extracting of poison as is reported', but he also recorded his intention to experiment on bezoar 'which is truly orientall and not counterfeit' and wrote out a long description of 'the vertues of the wound wood'. Locke's journals remind one that the natural-historical impulse in early modern thought owes as much to magic as to science, as much to Della Porta as to Bacon.[93] Reflections of the *Essay*'s crisp abstractions in subsequent Anglo-American philosophy should not eclipse the murkier pages of the journals, which reveal other continuities linking their author to an older world where magic still lurked in natural philosophy. Boyle lived his professional life in that world, while Locke – like Newton – turned his public face away from it.

As a physician, Locke knew the medical lore in which poisonous, purgative, narcotic, and other effects of drugs were referred to occult qualities that also explained why peony root hung about the neck cured epilepsy or why a lapis lazuli amulet relieved quartan fever. In principle if not in fact, these and all other properties of objects are to be explained mechanically. 'The color and taste of opium', he argued, 'as well as its soporific and anodyne virtues, [are] mere powers, depending on . . . primary qualities.' Since Galen's day, the powers of such drugs had proved refractory to post-Aristotelian physics, but Locke applied the simple notion of fitness between parts, using Boyle's locks and keys to open the door to a demystified theory of matter. 'Did we know the mechanical affections of the particles of rhubarb, hemlock, opium and a man, as a watchmaker does those of a watch', claimed Locke, 'we should be able to tell beforehand that rhubarb will purge, hemlock kill, and opium make a man sleep.' Physicians had made such predictions for millennia, but, without a convincing theory to explain their clinical experience of opium, hemlock, or rhubarb, they could only reify the want of an explanation in purgative, poisonous, or narcotic qualities. Locke found these qualities in no way occult; they are 'no more difficult to know than it is to a smith to understand why the turning of one key will open a lock, and not the turning of another'.[94]

Nonetheless, the clinical scepticism that he had learned from Sydenham made Locke cautious, less hopeful than Robert Hooke or Henry Power that microscopes might actually reveal nature's secret workings. Gravity was another topic that made him hesitate. The first version of the *Essay* declared that bodies can affect one another only by contact, a position muted in later editions, after Newton's *Principia* (London, 1687) changed Locke's mind. Still insisting that contact was the only corporeal interaction conceivable to him, he allowed that he had been

convinced by . . . Mr. Newton's incomparable book, that it is too bold a presumption to limit God's power . . . by my narrow conceptions. The gravitation of matter towards matter, by ways inconceivable to me, is not only a demonstration that God can . . . put into bodies powers . . . above what can be derived from our idea of body, or can be explained by what we know of matter, but also an unquestionable and everywhere visible instance, that he has done so.

When Locke and Boyle argued from bodies visibly in motion to analogous but invisible motions of microscopic matter, their theories were more credible than the doctrine of occult qualities because they depended on atomic motions, which, unlike occult qualities, were intelligible precisely in their likeness to gross mechanical phenomena. When Locke attributed powers to body that were professedly inconceivable and beyond physical explanation, he seems to have abandoned any claim to superior intelligibility for the mechanical philosophy as applied to the problem of gravity, long considered an occult quality and now, in its Newtonian guise, to be condemned again as occult by Leibniz.[95]

V. NEWTON AND LEIBNIZ

1. Newton

Although the first notice of the *Principia* in the *Acta eruditorum* of 1688 voiced no complaint about Newtonian gravity, the idea of attractive force quickly became controversial for Leibniz and other ministers of the new commonwealth of science, convinced as they were that mechanical causes explain all physical action. Even though attacks on gravity as a retreat to occult qualities reached their full pitch only two decades after his revolutionary book appeared, Newton knew from the start that his concept of force acting over distance would seem a startling defection from the mechanist camp. As if to anticipate the critics, the first sentence of the first edition of the *Principia* declared Newton's allegiance to a mathematical reform of mechanics based on the work of 'the moderns, rejecting substantial forms and occult qualities'.[96] Exquisite qualifications and careful disguises of his ontology of force followed regularly thereafter. When Richard Bentley prepared the Boyle lectures of 1692 for publication, Newton asked Bentley not to ascribe to him 'gravity as essential and inherent to matter' because it would imply an

Epicurean abandonment of God's cosmic dominion. Newton also had reason to worry about the magical connotations of the term 'innate gravity'. Twenty years later, he bristled when Leibniz compared him to Roberval, who had not only made gravity resident in bodies but even acknowledged it as an occult quality. A graver insult was the charge in the *Acta eruditorum* that Newtonians had betrayed the mechanics of Boyle for the mystifications of Fludd. Such outrages strained the public debate between Newton and Leibniz only after 1708, but the gulf between them was fixed from the early 1690s.[97]

Newton wrote in 1712 that three accounts of the cause of gravity were acceptable to him and – contrary to Leibniz – that none was a retreat to occult qualities. Gravity might be 'a power whose cause is unknown to us, or . . . a power seated in the frame of nature by the will of God, or . . . a power seated in a substance in wch bodies move & flote without resistance & . . . acts by other laws than those that are mechanical'. This last proposal was for a non-mechanical aether related to the many others – material, spiritual, dense, subtle, phlegmatic, elastic, electric, alchemical – that Newton never fully renounced nor embraced. But he showed little interest in mechanical aethers from the time just before he finished the *Principia* until the period leading up to the first Latin *Optice* (London, 1706), when he returned to them because his heterodox gravity seemed too vulnerable.[98] A second option, making God the cause of gravity, was compatible with a scientific programme meant to yield knowledge of God, 'to discourse of whom . . . does certainly belong to Natural Philosophy'. Newton's voluntarist theology, in which an omnipresent deity continually energises creation, ill suits the omnipotent hero of enlightened science deceptively immortalised in Pope's couplets. The Newton who ended the *Principia* with a paean to the 'Lord God *pantokratôr* [who] constitutes duration and space' had been touched by the spiritualist cosmologies of More and Cudworth. Like the Platonists who taught in his university, the young Newton believed that Cartesian mechanism was 'a path to atheism', and he followed More and Cudworth in trying to reconstitute a pious physics from the remains of ancient wisdom – gentile and Jewish, Stoic and Philonic – reaching back not only to a pre-Socratic Mosaic atomism but also to theologies of space transmitted from the rabbis of late antiquity to the kabbalists of mediaeval and Renaissance Europe. Physically as well as theologically, the fundamental tone that Newton heard in the pipes of Pan was the utter dependence of passive matter on an active spiritual God. What better locus for a universal force of attraction than the seat of the omnipresent Almighty?[99]

Even before Leibniz accused him of basing his physics on a continuing miracle, Newton often settled on a third approach to the cause of gravity – which was not to explain it at all. He admitted the search for causes as a methodological imperative, but he often let a hesitant phenomenalism cover his efforts, as when a draft of the General Scholium to the *Principia* echoes the anti-magical scepticism of Mersenne and Gassendi as well as Locke's closer influence: 'We do not know the substances of things. . . . We gather only their properties from the phenomena, and from the properties [we infer] what the substances may be. . . . By no sense . . . do we know the innermost substances.' A sceptical prudence also guided Newton's most important public statement on occult qualities, a passage towards the end of Query 31 of the *Opticks* that best defines the differences between him and Leibniz on this contentious issue. Referring to the Peripatetic context of the doctrine and to the related question of specific forms, Newton wished to show that a quantified phenomenalist account of gravity – limited to experimental facts and mathematical calculations without reference to any cause, whether divine or spiritual or mechanical – was not an appeal to occult qualities but the expression of a physical law. To explain the phenomena of falling bodies, Newton referred to a causal principle, gravity, characterised as a manifest (not occult) force with an unknown cause. Conceding that this cause of gravity is occult in the sense of being unknown (though not necessarily unknowable), he denied that gravity itself is occult. Gravity is manifest, no less manifest to Newton than *caliditas* to Suárez. But Newton maintained that the scholastic analogue of his gravity, the occult quality *gravitas,* differs from his gravity in being itself an occult cause. Furthermore, the schoolmen derived their *gravitas* from an imperceptible metaphysical abstraction, the specific form. For Newton and the scholastics both, two levels of causality account for phenomena of descent, but for Newton the more proximate cause is the manifest force that he called gravity. Only gravity's more distant cause is occult for Newton, while for the Peripatetic the proximate cause is also occult, and the remote cause is metaphysical, an insensible specific form. On other occasions, Newton looked to theology rather than metaphysics for the cause of gravity, finding it in a living God who touches the world everywhere.[100]

The mature Newton was never content with a mechanical account of gravity. Always a corpuscularian, he had already distanced himself as a young man from mechanism in the Cartesian or Leibnizian sense. Like Henry More, he feared the mechanical philosophy as a danger to religion, and he saw a thoroughly mechanist physics as doomed to end in begged questions, like Gassendi's 'hooked atoms'. By the late 1670s, he was ready to break the first commandment of the mechanical philosophy, the law of contact action, and to replace it with a new physical covenant based on 'some principle acting at a distance'. He had made this non-mechanical force the ground of most natural phenomena by the time he wrote the *Principia*. Alchemy contributed as much as astrophysics to this remarkable breach with the prevailing ordinances of natural philosophy, but some of his motives lay within the domain of conventional physics. At the macroscopic level, orbital dynamics left no room for a resistant mechanical aether, and no mechanical explanation of cohesion worked in the microscopic realm. Rejecting fancifully shaped atoms as well as bodies 'glued together by rest, . . . an occult Quality', Newton preferred to 'infer from their Cohesion that their Particles attract one another by some Force'. He asserted an analogy reaching from visible to invisible bodies, the assumption that 'if Nature be simple and pretty conformable to herself, causes will operate in the same kind of way in all phenomena, so that the motions of smaller bodies depend upon certain smaller forces just as the motions of larger bodies are ruled by the greater force of gravity.' Newton drew the broadest conclusions from his 'analogy of nature', speculating that 'almost all the phenomena of nature will depend on the forces of particles, . . . although the names of attractive and repulsive forces will displease many.' He made the hitherto magical notion of action at a distance a scientific law by demonstrating it experimentally and measuring it mathematically, thus appealing to two of the prime canons of the quantitative physics that he invented.[101]

Newton's immense authority as patriarch of science makes it easy not only to misread some of his views on the ontology of force but also to evade the hard facts about their alchemical pedigree. When Newton agreed with Bentley that it was 'unconceivable that inanimate brute matter should (without ye mediation of something else wch is not material) operate upon & affect other matter wthout mutual contact', Bentley certainly saw the theological point of the parentheses. Newton, of course, believed that the mediating agency was divine and that divinity was spiritual, active, and vital, in the closest communion with creation. One source of his theological physics was the *prisca cosmologia* reconstructed by More, Cudworth, and others, but a more immediate source was alchemy, taken less from the respectable Boyle than from other adepts in the Hermetic art – Eirenaeus Philalethes, Michael Sendivogius, and older authorities. Until recently, these arcane researches of the prophet of modern physics were hidden from his admirers, and even today their relation to his 'scientific' accomplishments is in dispute. Indisputable, however, are the following facts: that Newton devoted enormous labour to alchemy, having written over a million words about it; that his Hermetic labours covered more than a quarter-century before 1693, with over half the alchemical papers compiled after the *Principia* was published; and that he gave his best to the art, respecting its esoteric conventions but also bringing to it his experimental, quantitative, and methodical genius. Neither a juvenile indiscretion nor a senile aberration, alchemy occupied most of Newton's energies during his best years, before and after the *Principia*. Before losing interest in alchemy in the mid-1690s, Newton corresponded with Locke in 1692 about the secrets in Boyle's papers – in particular, the recipe 'for ye sake of wch Mr B procured ye repeal of ye Act of Parl. against Multipliers' – and in 1693 he wrote his culminating essay in alchemy, titled 'Praxis', which described the substances 'fit for magicall uses' that led him (as he thought) to achieve the 'multiplication' of gold, the main goal of the alchemical work.[102]

'Praxis' was only one of Newton's original alchemical treatises, some of which bear on his central physical ideas. Shortly before 1670 he wrote 'The Vegetation of Metals', which uses an alchemical model for active principles embedded in the matrix of a conventional aether and capable of 'a more subtile secret & noble way of working', thus foreshadowing the 'secret principle of unsociableness' that activated the otherwise mechanical aether in the 'Hypothesis of Light' of 1675. Later, in 1692, came *De natura acidorum*, which described 'particles of acids . . . endowed with a great attractive force . . . in [which] force their activity consists'. In this late work, active alchemical principles are evolving into the attractive forces of Newton's physics. Throughout his alchemical career, he referred to a number of substances and processes that suggest a Hermetic basis for physical ideas. His hunt for the 'green lion', an ore of antimony, produced a purified crystalline metal, called the 'star regulus' of antimony and believed to have attractive powers. A variant of the same process yielded the 'regulus of Mars', which Newton treated as a model for inter-particulate forces. Another rare substance was the alchemical 'net', which led him to think about 'retiform particles' in matter that would 'offer unrestricted passage . . . to magnetic effluvia and . . . light'. Perhaps the most important message for Newton in alchemy's cryptic language was its constant reference to spiritual, vital, organic, and indeed sexual properties of matter, properties alien to the post-Newtonian science of matter but crucial to Newton himself, who needed such sources of energy to activate an otherwise passive world of 'mere mechanical causes'.[103]

When Newton wrote to Oldenburg in 1676 about an experiment of Boyle's on the 'incalescence of gold', he doubted the procedure but advised that it ought 'not to be communicated wthout immense dammage to ye world if there should be any verity in ye Hermetick writers'. Despite the disclaimer, and given Newton's lonely years of labour in alchemy as well as his connexions with the alchemical underground of his day, it seems clear that this complex genius – who saw only 'cheats and impostures' in a Cambridge haunted house where More would have seen the hand of God – had more tolerance for occultism than some would like in a champion of science. The quest for secrets – what Bachelard called 'cette valorization intuitive de l'intérieur' or the 'substantialist obstacle' to scientific thought – was the engine of alchemy, whose arcana Newton found hidden in physical phenomena. After giving Boyle an account of inter-particulate repulsions and attractions from pressure changes in the aether, he added a long passage on various alchemical substances as instances of 'a certain secret principle in nature by wch liquors are sociable to some things & unsociable to others'. In context, it is hard not to link this secret sociability with occult sympathies and antipathies, a topic familiar to the young Newton of the *Quaestiones,* where gravity and levity are items in a typically scholastic catalogue of qualities.[104] The older Newton took gravity out of this setting, where physics and magic were parts of the same natural philosophy, but his concept of inter-particulate forces left him open to charges of having restored the discredited magic of occult qualities.

2. Leibniz

Newton and his followers refuted these accusations on many occasions. Leibniz understood their replies but did not accept them, not only because of his priority dispute with Newton but also because his continuously evolving metaphysics and dynamics conflicted with the Newtonian system. The *Nouveaux Essais* were not published until 1765, so Newton and Locke were spared one of Leibniz's more savage retorts, composed several years before the public feud erupted. Holding that 'everything which is in accord with the natural order can be . . . understood by some creature', Leibniz took the further step of equating physical with me-chanical intelligibility, thus forbidding any non-mechanical physical explanations unless they are also miraculous. 'This distinction between what is natural and explicable and what is miraculous and inexplicable removes all the difficulties', he claimed.

To reject it would be to uphold something worse than occult qualities, and thereby to renounce philosophy and reason [in] an irrational system which maintains not only that there are qualities which we do not understand – of which there are only too many – but . . . some which could not be comprehended by the greatest intellect if God gave it every possible opportunity.

Leibniz was sure that his distinction was indispensable to 'any rational philosophy'. A philosophy without it would be either 'fanatical, like Fludd's *Mosaicall Philosophy* which saves all phenomena by ascribing them . . . miraculously to God, or barbarous, like that of . . . philosophers and physicians . . . who . . . fabricat[e] faculties or occult qualities, . . . like little demons or imps [to] perform whatever is wanted'. Had Newton known that Leibniz associated with gold-makers, had he thought that Leibniz may have taken philosophical inspiration from alchemy, or had he realised that Leibniz's youthful interest in the Lullian art grew into a 'universal characteristic' with roots in Renaissance occultism, Newton might have seen the magic-baiting as hypocritical.[105]

The mature monadic philosophy might likewise have puzzled him. Beneath Leibniz's unflinchingly mechanist and anti-Newtonian physics lay a dynamic, vitalist metaphysics with strong links to the *philosophia occulta*. Principles taught by Ficino and Agrippa were invoked by Leibniz. Organic sympathies sustain the harmonies of his cosmos, a world of immaterial substances that behave like souls and minds. Called monads in the mature system, these substances derive from the scholastic substantial forms that underlay the traditional philosophy of magic. Leibniz built his universe not of material particles but of these indivisible 'atoms of substance, . . . real unities . . . which are the sources of action and the absolute first principles. . . . One could call them metaphysical points. They have something vital and a kind of perception.' Borrowing a Greek term that had been in the air since John Dee and Giordano Bruno, and which he might have found closer to hand in Lady Conway or the younger Van Helmont, Leibniz began to use the word 'monad' for these immaterial atoms in the 1690s. Having no parts or shapes to mark them, monads are indistinguishable 'except by . . . internal qualities and actions, and these can only be . . . perceptions . . . and . . . appetitions'. Monads are changeless except as they tend from one perception to another; this tendency is what Leibniz calls appetition. At creation God fixes the sequence of states through which each monad passes, so that it has no real causal relation with anything but the Creator. This is the basis for an abstract notion of monadic perception, a variety of expression, such that 'one thing expresses another . . . when there is a constant and regular relation between what can be said about one and about the other.' Only metaphysical properties are real. We observe mechanical properties in bodies veridically, but only in the sense that we see rainbows, which as rainbows have no substance, no centre of unity or action. 'In themselves material things are merely well-regulated phenomena', and the only real entities are immaterial substances. Having made matter a mere phenomenon, however, Leibniz seems to have reduced impact to a spectral dance of unreal bodies or, worse, a shadow play at two removes, since corporeal substances, acting out the script of final causes, do not really address one another. On the other hand, the world is a pleroma of sympathetic animation. Its real component is living substance and its phenomenal element is matter: 'There is nothing fallow, sterile or dead in the universe.' Every substance is to some degree life and mind, and every mind perceives the activity of the whole, though more or less confusedly, as one hears the roaring of the sea.[106]

Long before he committed Newton's force to the asylum of occult qualities, Leibniz had picked his own route to a metaphysics of force based on a revival of substantial forms. In some places his path ran against the mechanical traffic in post-Cartesian philosophy, and he chose it in full awareness of the likely reaction: that is, that his restoration of forms (like Newton's use of force) would be seen as treason against the Cartesian revolution and that his ensoulment of substance would tie him not just to Aristotle and the schoolmen but to disreputable figures of the Renaissance. Leibniz took pains to distance himself from the magical enthusiasms of the previous century and the 'inscrutable and implausible hypotheses' of his own, but unlike Descartes, he never repudiated erudition or history. His memory of the history of philosophy was rich, but it was also critical. In his early letter to Thomasius (1669), he pictured 'the mantle of philosophy' as having been ripped apart not only by atomists and mechanists but also by the less modish *novatores* who had challenged authority by promoting new kinds of occultism. By contrast, in a revealing passage of the *Nouveaux Essais,* Theophilus (Leibniz) tells Philalethes (Locke) that he has 'been impressed by a new system [that tells] how to make sense of those who put life and perception into everything – e.g., of Cardano, Campanella, and (better than them) of the late Platonist Countess of Conway, and our friend the late M. Franciscus Mercurius Van Helmont (though otherwise full of meaningless paradoxes) together with . . . the late Mr Henry More [who also] went wrong'. Despite their misconceptions, Leibniz respected the Renaissance nature-philosophers and Platonists for their vitalist ontology, propagated in the seventeenth century by Campanella, More, Cudworth, Ann Conway, Damaris Masham, and the younger Van Helmont. His comments on their doctrines – the world-soul, the hylarchic principle, metempsychosis – ranged from criticism to derision. Yet in an eirenic spirit he also embraced 'the vitalism of the kabbalists and hermetic philosophers who put a kind of feeling into everything', along with Platonic and Pythagorean harmonies, 'the Stoic connectedness' and 'the forms and entelechies of Aristotle and the Scholastics'. In his own system Leibniz saw 'all of these . . . united as if in a single perspective center. . . . Our greatest failure has been the sectarian spirit.'[107]

Doctrinal concord was a suitable wish for a thinker who believed in metaphysical harmonies. In the first published statement of his mature metaphysics, the 'Systeme nouveau de la nature et de la communication des substances . . .' which appeared in the *Journal des sçavans* in 1695, Leibniz unveiled the notion of pre-established harmony that he had long been considering. One of its ancestors was the Stoic and Neoplatonic concept of sympathy revived in Renaissance theories of magic. 'God has originally created . . . every . . . real unity', he explained, 'in such a way that . . . there will be a perfect accord between all these substances which produces the same effect that would be noticed if they all communicated . . . by a transmission of species or qualities.' Leibniz's harmony substituted concomitance for all causes but the divine. Both the monads and the matter embodying them undergo changes – motion among bodies, perception among monads – and every created substance accommodates the changes of every other in a harmonious order. Phenomena change symmetrically with substances because God made them to do so, like 'two clocks . . . in perfect agreement', and the phenomenal changes that we perceive as effects of efficient causes are really shadows of a higher order of final causes. When one body seems to influence another, the real action transcends them both, residing in the divine disposition of immaterial substances as the sole vehicles of active force. In this special context, Leibniz declares that 'all the bodies of the universe are in sympathy', each expressing all others from its own point of view. To the metaphysical concert of perceptions corresponds a physical concord of motions. 'Every motion in this plenum has some effect upon distant bodies . . . to any distance whatever. As a result, every body responds to everything which happens in the universe.' A symphony of minute perceptions accounts 'for that marvellous pre-established harmony . . . amongst all the monads . . . which takes the place of an untenable influence of one on another'. Forces of life and mind make the world coherent. 'To exist is nothing other than to be harmonious', wrote Leibniz, adding that 'the mark of existence is organized sensations.'[108]

This was the metaphysical platform from which Leibniz hoped to expose Newton's infidelity to the mechanical philosophy, a strange, intricate, and elegant construct made all the more remote from typical physical concerns by Leibniz's willingness to 'deny the action of one corporeal substance upon another'. If Newton's physics demanded action at a distance, Leibniz's metaphysics required an equally odd relationship among bodies. The young Leibniz offered an oblique compliment to Campanella's *De sensu* for recognising that bodies possessed of little formal souls should also be equipped with sense. The older Leibniz could also sound remarkably like the pansensist Campanella, having found 'reason to think that there is an infinity of souls . . . possessing something analogous to perception and appetite, and that all of them are . . . substantial forms of bodies'. But there is no confusing Leibniz's system with the occult philosophies that it resembles. Although similar attributes of power, perception, and appetite had made nature magical for Campanella, Leibniz found a way to keep his living cosmos disenchanted. He revived substantial forms, likened them to souls, and endowed them with organic force, but he defined these points of vital power in strictly metaphysical terms. Monadic powers of life and sense operate on a plane removed from the everyday sense of the organic that had grounded the occultist world-view. Each monad expresses and perceives every other, yet 'monads have no windows through which anything could enter or depart'. Leibniz specified that 'these forms change nothing in the phenomena and must not be used to explain particular effects.' In order for substantial forms to have a rôle in natural magic – as when Newton described form as the source of scholastic occult qualities – they had to bear some causal relation to discrete physical phenomena. But it was just this causal knot that Leibniz cut, thereby loosing hylemorphism from its bondage to natural magic. Deaf to any external direction after the original creative act, Leibniz's chorus of living monads was of little practical use to the magus, despite its kinship with ancient and early modern theories of natural magic. Mechanics ruled rigorously in Leibniz's world. Even after he decided against Cartesian extension, he maintained the necessity – indeed, the uniqueness – of mechanical explanation in physics, including the physics of organic and invisible bodies. Despite his immaterialism and animism, despite his talk of sympathies acting at a distance, Leibniz could claim that his dynamics was loyal to the mechanist paradigm if – at least in principle – he could explain the motions of bodies, once created, by contact action.[109]

VI. THE END OF THE OCCULT PHILOSOPHY

Before the seventeenth century, many important philosophers from Plotinus and Proclus through Albertus and Aquinas to Ficino and Pomponazzi had been deeply engaged in the philosophical analysis of magic, but after the seventeenth century the engagement ended. Since late antiquity, many discussions about physics, metaphysics, psychology, ethics, and other departments of philosophy had influenced, and were influenced by, the efforts of some thinkers to find good reasons to believe in magic and of others to deny those reasons. Though he doubtless intended it as a comment on the new immaterialist philosophy that he published a year or two later, George Berkeley left a telegraphic entry in his notebooks of 1707–8 that can also stand as epitaph to the philosophical debates on magic of the preceding era: 'Anima mundi. Substantial Forms. Omniscient radical Heat. Plastic vertue. Hylarchic principle. All these vanish.' With such exceptions as Berkeley's own *Siris,* occultism vanished from the canonical history of philosophy after

Leibniz. Moreover, magic's erasure from the philosophical agenda of the Enlightenment was so complete as to conceal its significance in earlier periods. Just as Fontenelle found Newton's early curiosity about astrology too embarrassing to mention in his obituary, so later historians of philosophy seldom bothered to ask whether the elders of their profession were interested in topics so contemptible.[110]

Hence it may be surprising to learn that Leibniz gave the occult philosophy a last hour of respectability, though the moment was troubled and fleeting. His sympathetic harmonies and living monads expressed a nostalgia for the magical cosmos of the Renaissance, but to no great effect. His system left its mark on science by way of Boscovich and on philosophy by way of Wolff and Kant, but it did nothing to rescue the occult philosophy from disgrace – not that he would have wished such a deliverance. Reading Leibniz today, when occultism has long since lost its intellectual authority, should make us wary of a Whig history in which philosophy and science inevitably and unerringly part ways with magic.[111] The divorce still had to be settled in the seventeenth century, when the strong language in which Descartes heaped scorn on the schoolmen and Leibniz hurled fury at Newton alerts us to the power and scope of the disagreement. When Leibniz castigated Newton's gravity by calling it 'occult', his words were potent enough to unsettle the mighty physicist in his days of glory. The adjectives that Leibniz spat at Newton's spokesman, Samuel Clarke, in 1716 carried even more venom: 'inexplicable, unintelligible, precarious, groundless and unexampled, . . . a chimerical thing, a scholastic occult quality'.[112] Newton had the last word only in outliving Leibniz. Neither broke free of the occultist tradition, whose last major episode on the stage of philosophy's history they acted together.

NOTES

1 Della Porta 1658, p. 1; Diogenes Laertius, *Lives and Opinions of Famous Philosophers* I, proem, 1–6.
2 Della Porta 1658, pp. 1–3; Copenhaver 1988a, pp. 264–8.
3 Della Porta 1658, pp. 7–20; Rossi 1968, pp. 1–35; Copenhaver 1988a, pp. 274–85, 291, 296–300; Copenhaver 1988b; note 56 in this chapter. For Bacon, see the last section of Copenhaver 1988a.
4 Although the English noun 'occultism' belongs to the nineteenth century, early modern usage of the adjectives 'occult' or 'occultus' covered the range of theory and practice given in this paragraph, as is evident from the contents of the influential work that Henry Cornelius Agrippa titled *De occulta philosophia,* whose first complete edition appeared in Cologne, 1533. See also Ficino 1989; Nauert 1965, pp. 222–91; Zambelli 1960, 1976; Zanier 1975, 1977; Pine 1986, pp. 4, 13, 34–7, 104–5, 235–367; Copenhaver 1984, 1988a, 1988b, 1990.

5 Enlightenment responses to occultism have not been explored as extensively as those of earlier periods, but for two very different reactions, see Darnton, 1970; Parinetto 1974. For Newton and Leibniz, see notes 96–7, 100, 105, 112.

6 Della Porta 1658, pp. 4–8; Zanier 1975, pp. 1–16; Zambelli 1978; Schmitt 1983a, pp. 93–101; Copenhaver 1984; 1988a, pp. 271–4, 280–7. Although anti-occultism in the seventeenth century is often hard to distinguish from anti-Aristotelianism, this chapter focuses on the former. Beginning with Thorndike 1923–58, the secondary literature on occultism in the early modern period became extensive and controversial, most of all after the publication of Thorndike's last volume. See especially Garin 1937, 1954, 1983; Walker 1958, 1972; Kristeller 1960; Yates 1964, 1968, 1975; Nauert 1965; McGuire and Rattansi 1966; Hesse 1970; Thomas 1971; Zambelli 1973a, 1973b, 1991; Dobbs 1975, 1991; Debus 1977; Rhighini Bonelli and Shea 1975; Westman and McGuire, 1977; Schmitt 1978; Copenhaver 1978, 1990, 1992c, pp. xxxii–lix; Vickers 1979, 1984, 1991, 1992; Webster 1982; Hutchison 1982; Müller-Jahncke 1985; Henry 1986b; Clulee 1988; Ficino 1989.

7 Mersenne 1932–88, vol. 1, pp. 154–5, 166–7, vol. 2, p. 590; Arnold 1970, pp. 43, 56, 63–8, 73–89, 115–40, 189–91; Hannaway 1975, pp. 79–80, 92–3, 97; Yates 1975, pp. 71–80, 91–8, 126–50, 279–80, 286; cf. Webster 1982, pp. 60–1; Debus 1977, vol. 1, pp. 159–68, 262–5; Debus 1991, pp. 46–101; Shea 1991, pp. 95–8; note 53 in this chapter.

8 Mersenne 1625, pp. 79–8; Naudé 1625, p. 331; Busson 1933; Lenoble 1971, pp. 150–2, 208–11; Lasswitz 1890, vol. 1, 339, 482–7; Metzger 1969, pp. 57–9, 121–6; note 50. For Renaissance anti-Aristotelianism, see Chapter 2.

9 Basso 1621, pp. 150, 245–69, 343–4; Lasswitz 1890, vol. 1, pp. 333–9, 436–54, 455–81; Gregory 1964, pp. 43–53, 56–62; Gregory 1966, pp. 44–60; Pagel 1984, pp. 87–91.

10 Mersenne 1624, vol. 1, pp. 236–7; Spink 1960, pp. 28–41; Namer 1980; Weeks 1991, pp. 1–5, 35–78, 130–8, 209–19; Hegel 1995, vol. 3, p. 188; Copenhaver 1992b, pp. 161–2.

11 Busson 1933, pp. 28–31; Pintard 1943, pp. 31, 62–3; Spink 1960, pp. 5–12. For Naudé in this context, see Copenhaver 1992b, pp. 161–2.

12 Burgersdijck 1631, pp. 8–9, 16, 32–3, 51; 1632, sig. K4^v. For Burgersdijck's more original views, see the posthumous *Institutionum metaphysicarum libri duo* (Leiden, 1640), pp. 161–2; Ruestow 1973, pp. 4, 12–17, 21–2; Dibon 1954, pp. 90–6, 100, 113–16, 123–5; see also AT V 125.

13 *Collegium Conimbricense* 1603, pp. 210–14; *Collegium Conimbricense* 1606b, p. 378; *Collegium Conimbricense* 1609a, pp. 276, 382, 412.

14 *Collegium Conimbricense* 1609b, pp. 311–17.

15 Suárez *Op. omn.* 13, p. 558; *Op. omn.* 25, p. 665; Eustachius 1648, pp. 170, 184, 215; notes 1–3 in this chapter.

16 *Collegium Conimbricense* 1609a, p. 225; Aristotle *Phys.* 190^{a}l3–91^{a}22, 193^{a}lo–93^{b}21; *Gen. et Corr.* 335^{a}24–36^{a}13; *De anima* 412^{a}l–13^{a}lo; *Metaph.* 1029^{b}l2–30^{b}l3, 1069^{b}31–4; Galen *Loc. aff.* 5.6; *Meth. med.* 13.6; *Simpl. med.* 4.9; 5.1,7,18; 6.1; 10.2.1,21; 11.12.23, 13.48; 12.1.34; *Comp. med. s. loc.* 8.8; *Comp. med. p. gen.* 1.16; [*Aff. ren.*]; Röhr 1923, pp. 96–9, 107–12; Copenhaver 1984, pp. 525–8.

17 Copenhaver 1984, pp. 539–49.

18 Although Röhr 1923 remains the best guide to the classical sources of the doctrine of occult qualities, Hutchison 1982 and 1991 are important articles on the seventeenth-century phase of the debate. Hutchison's work has stimulated other inquiries, such as Millen 1985, and has also influenced discussions of related topics, such as Schaffer 1985; Henry 1986b; Clarke 1989; Wilson 1990. See also Bianchi 1982; Hutchison 1983;

Richardson 1985; Wear 1985. In Hutchison 1982 and the subsequent literature, a key claim is that insensibility and unintelligibility are the essential determinants of occultness, which is contrary to the view expressed here.

19 Burgersdijck 1631, pp. 9, 51; *Collegium Conimbricense* 1603, p. 213; *Collegium Conimbricense* 1606b, p. 378; *Collegium Conimbricense* 1609b, p. 314; Copenhaver 1984, pp. 542–6; note 12 in this chapter.

20 Campanella 1635, pp. 231–6, 240–2; Firpo 1940, pp. 107–9.

21 Campanella 1638a, I.ii.iv.5–7, pp. 133–45; Campanella 1974, pp. xxx–xxxiii, 64–78, 112–19, 134–8, 146–52, 246, 310–11, 422, 446; Blanchet, 1920b, pp. 167–76, 270; Firpo 1940, pp. 31–2; Di Napoli 1947, pp. 109–113, 332, 337–40; Corsano 1961, p. 169; Femiano 1968, pp. 104–7, 111–22, 307, 315–18; Franco 1969, pp. 115–26; Copenhaver 1988a, pp. 291–5. For a fuller view of Campanella, see also Copenhaver and Schmitt 1992, pp. 309–28, summarised here in part.

22 Campanella 1638a, I.ii.iv.5, p. 141; Campanella 1925, pp. 19–21; Campanella 1939, pp. 58, 185–95, 200–13; Campanella 1974, pp. xxx–xxxi, xliii, 223–9, 447; Blanchet 1920b, pp. 142–4, 310–13; Firpo 1940, pp. 119–22; Di Napoli 1947, pp. 115, 235–43; Corsano 1961, pp. 32–3; Corsano 1965, pp. 316–17; Franco 1969, pp. 122–34; Femiano 1969, p. 157; Copenhaver and Schmitt 1992, pp. 319–20.

23 Campanella 1617, pp. 28–32; Campanella 1925, pp. xxxi–15; Firpo 1940, pp. 27, 67–70; Di Napoli 1947, p. 356; Corsano 1961, pp. 85–7.; Badaloni 1965, pp. 46, 62–8; Milano 1969, pp. 164–5; Copenhaver and Schmitt 1992, p. 320.

24 Campanella 1925, pp. 19–21, 131–3, 146–51; Campanella 1939, pp. 185–7; Di Napoli 1947, p. 237; Femiano 1968, p. 411; Copenhaver and Schmitt 1992, pp. 320–1.

25 Campanella 1638a, I.ii.iv.5, pp. 138–41, II.ix.i, pp. 176–7; Campanella 1925, pp. xxxi, 9, 131–3, 221, 254; Campanella 1939, pp. 244, 250; Campanella 1974, pp. 228, 334; Copenhaver and Schmitt 1992, pp. 321–2.

26 Campanella 1638a, I.ii.v.4, 7, pp. 155–6, 197; Campanella 1925, pp. 20, 131–2; Amerio 1972, pp. 160–1.

27 Campanella 1635, pp. 240–2; Campanella 1638a, I.ii.iv.7, 12–13, pp. 143, 150–1, III.xv.–viii–ix.5, pp. 189–93; Campanella 1925, pp. 23–7, 68, 212, 218–19, 230, 250–3, 284–5, 323, 329; Campanella 1957, 166–74, 192–4; Copenhaver 1990, pp. 270–5.

28 Craven 1902, pp. 16–49, 78; Cafiero 1964–65, I, pp. 394–5; Ammann 1967, p. 198; Hannaway 1975, pp. 92–116; Debus 1977, vol. 1, pp. 205–24; Godwin 1979, pp. 5–8, 14, 93–4; for a recent study of Fludd, see now Huffman 1988, pp. 10–18.

29 Fludd 1659, pp. 171–83; Cafiero 1964–65, I, pp. 372–8, 382, 398; Yates 1964, pp. 403–7; Debus 1977, vol. 1, pp. 117–26, 225–40, 291; Godwin 1979, pp. 13–15, 20–8, 31, 76; Scholem 1974, pp. 120, 187, 200–1, 240, 395, 416–19; on Knorr and kabbalah, see also Chapter 14 in this book.

30 Cafiero 1964–65, I, pp. 378–86, 395–8, 408–9, II, 6–9, citing Fludd 1621, p. 5; Fludd 1629, pp. 75–7; Fludd 1633; Mersenne 1932–88, vol. 2, pp. 132–41, 448–35, 584, vol. 4, p. 350; Gassendi 1658, vol. 3, pp. 211–68; Ammann 1967, pp. 204, 210–12; Debus 1977, vol. 1, pp. 239, 253–60, 265–76; Debus 1987, 109–43, 374–93; Godwin 1979, pp. 12, 17–18, 429, 54–5, 69, 93; Westman 1984, pp. 177–207; Bianchi 1987, pp. 87–123; Brundell 1987, pp. 110–12; Huffman 1988, pp. 50–69, 100–105; Copenhaver 1990, pp. 281–6; note 48 in this chapter.

31 Mersenne 1623, cols. 130, 285–8, 489, 739–40, 937–46, 1164, 1743–4, 1750.

32 Mersenne 1623, cols. 285–8, 489; Mersenne 1932–88, vol. 1, pp. 42, 148–9; Charbonnel 1919, pp. 302–83; Busson 1933, 28–31, 479–80; Lenoble 1971, pp. 67–76; Spink 1960, pp. 5–47; Whitmore 1972, pp. xiv–xix, xxvi–xxxiii, 8–11; Mandrou 1980, pp. 121–52;

Walker 1981, pp. 1–17; Shea 1991, pp. 124–5; Copenhaver 1992b, pp. 161–2; notes 34, 39 in this chapter.

33 Mersenne 1624, vol. 1, pp. 211, 220–1, 229–38, vol. 2, pp. 292–9, 326–42, 360–2; Mersenne 1625, p. 109; Yates 1964, pp. 348–59.

34 Mersenne 1623, cols. 539–74; Mersenne 1624, vol. 1, pp. 212, 220–1, 225–32, vol. 2, pp. 369, 372, 377–8, 450–5; Mersenne 1625, pp. 27–8, 108–113, 125–6; Mersenne 1932–88, vol. 1, p. 147; Busson 1933, pp. 339–41; Lenoble 1971, pp. 9–10, 109–12, 150–2, 157–8, 166, 200–201, 208–17, 222, 373–6; Popkin 1979, p. 135; cf. Dear 1988, p. 42.

35 Mersenne 1623, cols. 541, 548–54, 1359–63, 1437–52, 1493–6, 1807; Mersenne 1634, pp. 109–11; Mersenne 1636–7, vol. 2, p. 26; Mersenne 1932–88, vol. 4, pp. 227, 240; Lenoble 1971, pp. 38–9, 49–51, 83–4, 119–20, 133, 336–52, 370–8; Dear 1988, p. 4.

36 Mersenne 1624, vol. 2, pp. 373–4; Mersenne 1634, pp. aii–iiii, 11; Lenoble 1971, pp. 48, 218–21, 252–3, 310–25, 352–6, 385–8, 390–1, 415, 420, 438; Popkin 1979, pp. 129–40; Dear 1988, pp. 3–4, 7, 15–22, 27–42, 77–8, 171, 179–85, 200, 210–22, 225–6; note 14 in this chapter.

37 Mersenne 1634, pp. 5, 88, 91; Mersenne 1932–88, vol. 4, pp. 253, 258, 328, vol. 5, p. 204, vol. 6, pp. 40–1, 217; Lenoble 1971, pp. 92–5, 336–7, 370–1.

38 Mersenne 1932–88, vol. 3, p. 394, vol. 6, pp. 47, 68; Montaigne 1967, p. 413; Lenoble 1971, pp. 67–72.

39 Mersenne 1932–88, vol. 2, pp. 497–8, 514, 520–1, 530–40; vol. 3, pp. 13, 39, 54, 62–5, 78–9, 82, 98, 111, 117, 143, 153, 180–4, 462–3; vol. 4, pp. 53, 125, 190–8, 371–4; vol. 5, pp. 83–8, 120–3, 189–91, 196, 232, 541–6, 560; vol. 6, pp. 137–9. Also Lenoble 1971, pp. 4, 12, 16–23, 72–6, 80–1, 310–13, 447; Mandrou 1980, pp. 257–9; Pagel 1982, p. 13; Ross 1985, pp. 106–7; Dear 1988, pp. 7, 15–22, 28–42, 45–6, 53–5, 107, 224; Debus 1991, pp. 71–4, 106–11.

40 Rochot 1944, pp. vii, 3–9, 44–5; Gregory 1961, pp. 48–52; Bloch 1971, pp. xxvi–xxx, 31–2, 75, 148, 155–6, 160; Jones 1981, p. 11–95, 281; Brundell 1987, pp. 15–19, 21–3, 27.

41 Gassendi 1658, vol. 2, pp. 456, 463, vol. 3, pp. 99, 205; Gassendi 1959, pp. 494–5; Gassendi 1972, p. 199; Gregory 1961, pp. 52, 152–9; Popkin 1979, pp. 99–104; Jones 1981, pp. 107–9, 135–7; Brundell 1987, pp. 19, 99–101, 133–4.

42 Gassendi 1658, vol. 3, p. 653; Gregory 1961, pp. 66–7; Copenhaver 1990, pp. 275–80; 1991, p. 374.

43 Gassendi 1658, vol. 3, p. 203; Gassendi 1959, pp. 489–91; Bloch 1971, pp. 166–71; Copenhaver 1991, p. 375.

44 Gassendi 1658, vol. 1, pp. 372, 449–57; Rochot 1944, pp. 107–8, 143–4, 198; Gregory 1961, pp. 153–4, 190, 228–9; Bloch 1971, pp. 164–5, 243; Brundell 1987, pp. 122–5.

45 Gassendi 1658, vol. 1, pp. 449–50, 454–5; Bloch 1971, p. 210; Copenhaver 1991, pp. 391–2.

46 Gassendi 1658, vol. 1, pp. 14–17; Gregory 1961, pp. 61–3, 230; Schmitt 1965; Walker 1972, pp. 1–21; Jones 1981, pp. 282–6; Brundell 1987, pp. 108–10, 113, 117–28, 134–5.

47 Gassendi 1658, vol. 3, pp. 659–60; Gregory 1961, pp. 53–5, 58–9, 63, 158, 189–91; Bloch 1971, pp. 157, 205; Jones 1981, pp. 286–9; Brundell 1987, pp. 71, 113.

48 Gassendi 1658, vol. 3, pp. 213, 246; Mersenne 1932–88, vol. 2, p. 149, 181–201; Gregory 1961, pp. 53–62; Cafiero 1964–5, I, pp. 385–6, II, pp. 6–9; Brundell 1987, pp. 110–12; note 30 in this chapter.

49 Gassendi 1658, vol. 1, p. 273; Rochot 1944, p. 185; Schmitt 1965; Bloch 1971, pp. 162–

3, 205–13, 228–32, 447–57; Popkin 1979, pp. 104, 141–6; Jones 1981, pp. 292–3; Brundell 1987, pp. 26–7, 50–9, 71, 82, 100–101, 104–7, 137–43.

50 Gassendi 1658, vol. 2, pp. 114, 132; Brundell 1987, pp. 126–33; for the connexion with de Clave, see especially Bloch 1971, pp. 233–69, 371–6, 447–57.

51 Gassendi 1658, vol. 3, p. 633, vol. 6, p. 450; Rochot 1944, pp. 118–19; Metzger 1969, pp. 286–7, 432–3, 449–68; Brundell 1987, pp. 101, 132–4; Copenhaver 1991, p. 391. On the microscope as a new way of seeing what is occult, see Wilson 1990.

52 Naudé 1649, pp. 310–11; Charbonnel 1919, pp. 280, 383–5; Busson 1933, pp. 165–9, 224–44, 316–39, 361–3; Pintard 1943, pp. 80, 174–5, 187–90, 223, 273, 370–1, 437–40; Spink 1960, pp. 7–14; Popkin 1979, pp. 23–6, 82–3, 87–90; Mandrou 1980, pp. 126–33, 138–43, 163–91; Walker 1981, pp. 33–4; note 8 in this chapter. For more extensive treatments of Naudé, see Copenhaver 1992a, 1992b, summarised here in part.

53 Naudé 1623, p. 88; 1701, pp. 6–7, 38, 115–17; Rice 1939, pp. 10–14, 52–62; Pintard 1943, pp. 157–64, 170, 257, 263, 367, 442–3, 451–4, 467–8, 482–9; Copenhaver 1992a, pp. 394–5; 1992b, pp. 162–6; note 7 in this chapter.

54 Naudé 1625, pp. aiiii–vi, 634–49; Busson 1933, p. 367; Rice 1939, pp. 63–71; Pintard 1943, pp. 445–57; Copenhaver 1992b, pp. 166–7.

55 Naudé 1625, pp. vi, 24–45, 389–413; Copenhaver 1992b, p. 167; note 4 in this chapter.

56 Naudé 1625, pp. 42–4; Pintard 1943, pp. 444–5, 463; see also La Mothe le Vayer 1662, vol. 1, pp. 145, 164; Popkin 1979, pp. 90–7; Durkheim 1968, p. 58; Mauss 1972, p. 22; Copenhaver 1988a, pp. 297–9; 1992b, p. 167; note 3 in this chapter.

57 AT II 380, AT X 204; Galilei 1957, pp. 240–1, 265–79; Galilei 1967, pp. 95, 110–11, 232–7, 399–410, 421, 462; Gouhier 1958, pp. 46, 68, 142–9; Gouhier 1962, pp. 71–5, 95–104; Copenhaver 1978, pp. 97–171; Copenhaver 1988a; Drake 1981, pp. 387–93; Cohen 1985, pp. 117–19. On erudition and magic in Descartes and Naudé, see the more detailed treatment in Copenhaver 1992a and 1992b, summarised here in part.

58 AT I 25, 31; AT II 436, 659–60; AT III 522; AT IV 718; AT V 547; Gilson 1967a, pp. 259–68; Gouhier 1962, pp. 63–6; Ross 1985, pp. 100–101; Copenhaver 1992b, pp. 175–6; Copenhaver and Schmitt 1992, pp. 325–8.

59 AT II 629; AT VI 11, 17; AT X 63–5, 156–7, 164–9, 173–88, 193–200, 214, 216, 218; Baillet 1946, pp. 36–41, 50–1; Gouhier 1958, pp. 26–8, 38–55, 110–11, 115–16, 134–41, 151; Arnold 1960, pp. 266–84; Arnold 1970, pp. 139–63; Copenhaver 1992b, p. 176. On the Rosicrucians and Descartes's dreams, see especially Shea 1991, pp. 44–5, 93–120, published several years after this section was drafted, and cf. Cole 1992, esp. pp. 214–26; Gaukroger 1995, pp. 15–20, 384–405.

60 AT I 21, 153, 351; AT II 284–5, 351–2, 498, 573; AT III 8, 15, 20, 42, 49–50, 85, 120–2, 124, 130–1, 146, 163, 177, 598–9, 669, 673; AT IV 72–3, 189–91, 218–19, 529–30, 579–80; AT V 65–6, 338; AT VI 3–11, vol. 8-2, p. 353; AT IXB 392; AT X 90, 504; AT XI 518, 606; Marlowe, *Doctor Faustus* I.i.1–60; Scott 1952, pp. 167–74; Ross 1985, p. 97; Copenhaver 1992b, p. 177; Gaukroger 1995, pp. 59, 129, 191.

61 AT X 360, 379–80, 398–403, 426, 433–5, 439, 442–3.

62 AT IV 569–70; AT V 327; notes 35, 46, 48, 55, 75, 85–6 in this chapter.

63 AT II 557–8; AT III 214; note 85 in this chapter.

64 AT II 73–4, 363–8; AT III 211–12, 367, 371–2, 420–1, 460–4, 487–517; AT VI 239, 249; Gaukroger 1995, pp. 352–61.

65 AT III 523–4, 528, 535, 558–9, 598–9; AT IV 77–8, 85–9; AT V 125–8; AT VII 586, 596; AT VIIIB 15–16, 22–33, 142, 150–2, 174, 179; Descartes 1959; Lindeboom 1979, pp. 22–7; Ruestow 1973, pp. 34–65; Dibon 1954, pp. 194–219; Ross 1985, p. 103; Shea

1991, pp. 333–8. Roman Catholic teaching on the eucharist provoked Protestant charges of magic. Philosophically, the argument involved the topics of qualities and substantial forms, which considerations of space forbid examining further here; on this and related topics in Cartesian thought, see: Rosenfield 1968; Balz 1951; Bohatec 1912; Thomas 1971, pp. 29–36, 46–57, 273–5; Armogathe 1977; Gouhier 1978; Watson 1982; Clarke 1989; note 75 in this chapter.

66 AT VIIIB 151–2; cf. AT I 21; Thomas Aquinas, *Summa contra gentiles* 3.105; Mersenne 1623, col. 1151; Mersenne 1932–88, vol. 2, pp. 443–5; Hobbes *Eng. Works,* vol. 3, p. 671; Copenhaver 1984, pp. 531–46; 1988a, pp. 282–3, 295.

67 AT I 323–4; AT II 199–200, 222–4, 363–8, 544, 635; AT III 19, 211–12, 420–1, 424–5, 430–1, 493, 503, 505, 508, 545, 648–9, 667–8 ; AT IV 700 ; AT V 222–3, 291–2; AT VI 85, 113–14, 130, 135 ; AT VII 247–54, 433–7, 587; AT VIIIA 322–5; Gilson 1967a, pp. 18–27, 143–53, 158–9, 163–73, 189, 247–8 (Gilson uses the phrase '*limite mystérieuse*' on p. 23); Gouhier 1978, pp. 153–6; Schaffer 1985, pp. 126–7; Garber 1992a, pp. 94–116.

68 AT VII 440–3; Gilson 1967a, pp. 168–74, 247–8; Gouhier 1962, p. 362; note 105 in this chapter.

69 AT I 109, 228; AT II 440; AT III 648–9; AT V 291–2; AT VI 113–14, 130; AT VII 440–3; AT VIIIA 24–31, 314–15, 318, 322–3; AT VIIIB 348–9, 366; AT IXB 308–9; AT XI 25–36; Copenhaver 1992b, pp. 177–8; note 57 in this chapter.

70 Digby 1644a, p. 275; 1644b, pp. 11, 14–16, 31–2, 36–7, 46–8; Petersson 1956, pp. 86, 98, 107–9, 115, 120–8, 165–75; Peters 1956, pp. 21–8; Redwood 1976, pp. 134–5; Schaffer 1985, pp. 118–19.

71 Digby 1644a, pp. 2–4, 7, 35–8, 81, 138–9, 163–5; Petersson 1956, pp. 181–93.

72 Digby 1644a, pp. 164–5, 184, 332; Digby 1658, pp. 1–16, 19–34, 65, 146–7, 151; Petersson 1956, pp. 262–74, 326. On Digby's natural philosophy and alchemy, see especially Dobbs 1971, 1973, and 1974.

73 Digby 1644a, pp. 182–5; Hobbes *Eng. Works,* vol. 1, pp. 65–6, vol. 3, p. 664; *De corpore* I.vi.5–6, II.ix.7, IV.xxv.1–2, xxx.15; *Lev.* i; Petersson 1956, p. 108; Foucault 1966, pp. 33–4; Peters 1967, pp. 15–18, 22–6, 45–51, 75–7, 83–9; Shapin and Shaffer 1985, pp. 110–54; Sorell 1986, pp. 4–7, 51–2, 59–60, 69–77; on particulate *species* and sympathy in the *Little Treatise,* see Brandt 1928, pp. 14–17, 30–1, 42–4, 62–9, 100–105, 294–7.

74 Hobbes, *De corpore* IV.xxvi.7, xxx.15; *Lev.* xlvi; just before this last passage, Hobbes criticises Peripatetic uses of 'endeavour' in a circular or teleological sense.

75 Hobbes, *De corpore* I.iii.4; *Lev.* xlvi; Peters 1967, pp. l20–8; Spragens 1973, pp. 86–7; Martinich 1992, pp. 237–9, 322–4, 328–9; cf. Sorell 1986, pp. 37–41; note 65 in this chapter.

76 Hobbes, *Lev.* v, xii, xxxiv, xxxvii, xlv; Peters 1967, pp. 88–9, 233–9; Martinich 1992, pp. 237, 247–55.

77 Hobbes, *Lev.* ii, vi, xii, xlv; Peters 1967, pp. 225–33. Martinich 1992, pp. 19–67, 333–7, describes Hobbes as a broadly orthodox Calvinist whose novelties in natural philosophy, theology, and biblical interpretation made it possible for Arminian and Aristotelian enemies to depict him as an atheist and an anarchist.

78 More, *Enthusiasmus triumphatus* I–II, VI, XLIII–XLIX; Vaughan 1984, pp. 47–9, 235, 363; Cudworth 1678, pp. 700–715; Hoyles 1971, pp. 3–7, 13–17, 93; Burnham 1974, pp. 39–49; Cristofolini 1974, pp. 31–2, 51–2; Redwood 1976, pp. 50, 272; Brann 1979–80, pp. 105–12; Heyd 1981, pp. 259, 264, 272–4; Popkin 1986a pp. 21–7.

79 Richard Ward, who published More's biography in 1710, cited this passage from the

Second Lash to show that More's 'transported Admiration of Des–Cartes' was always constrained by his theology; Ward 1911, pp. 102–4. See also Cassirer 1953, p. 43; Cope 1956, p. 92; Lichtenstein 1962, pp. 49–53; Hoyles 1971, pp. 5, 14–15, 19–20, 38–40; Copenhaver 1980, pp. 515–29; Gabbey 1982, pp. 175, 187, 190–205, 214, 219–23, 238, 242; Funkenstein 1986, pp. 77–80.

80 More, *Immortality* pref. 6, I.x.2, II.xiv.7–8, III.i.1–4, xii.l; Cassirer 1953, pp. 139–45; Boylan 1980, p. 395; Gabbey 1982, pp. 234–6; Walker 1986, pp. 35–45, 59–73.

81 More, *Antidote* II.ii.7; *Immortality* pref. 11, II.x.7, xv.8, III.xii.2–6, xiii.6–7; Plotinus, *Ennead* 4.4.40.5–9, 44.29–30; Boylan 1980, p. 397; Copenhaver 1986, pp. 362–3; 1988b, pp. 86–8.

82 More, *Antidote* III.i–xvi (esp. i, iii.8–9, vi.2), app. xii–xiii; *Immortality* pref. 11–13, I.x.2, II.xvi, III.ii.7; Cassirer 1953, pp. 129–3; Hoyles 1971, pp. 26–7; Brann 1979–80, pp. 113–14, 121–2; Gabbey 1982, pp. 202–3; Schaffer 1985, pp. 121–5.

83 More, *Antidote* III.vii.14–viii.l, xv.8; *Immortality* I.xiii; Curry 1989, pp. 49–50.

84 Cudworth 1678, p. 835; Casaubon 1669, pp. 20–2, 7–9, 16–23, 38, 97, 105–19, in Spiller 1980;; Cope 1956, pp. 2–6, 9–31, 38, 56–65, 92–102, 129–40; Webster 1982, pp. 92–100; Clulee 1988, pp. 203–30; see also Clark 1984, pp. 351–74. 'Behemist' refers to followers of Jacob Boehme, whose influence was strong in England at mid-century; note 10 in this chapter.

85 Glanvill 1668, pp. 110–28; 1970, pp. 6–7, 11–14, 114–16, 150–6, 169–72; Cope 1956, pp. 11–15, 19, 38, 56–65, 92–102; Webster 1982, pp. 93–7; note 63 in this chapter.

86 Glanvill 1970, pp. 178–81, 195–212; Cudworth 1678, pp. 160–5; Gysi 1962, pp. 21–3; Henry 1986b, p. 359 ; Walker 1986, pp. 47–57.

87 Glanvill 1668, pp. 10–12, 57, 100–102; Boyle 1911, pp. 104–5; 1772, vol. 3, pp. 68–71, 134, 517, 529, 539–44, 560, 659–62, 669, 678, 688, 701–2; Boas Hall 1965, pp. 79–80, 251; Boas Hall 1981, p. 489; More 1944, pp. 279–83; Boas Hall 1958, pp. 102–7; Maddison 1969, pp. 192–3; Schaffer 1985, pp. 132–3; Alexander 1985, p. 64.

88 Bloch (1989), pp. 203–23; Maddison 1969, pp. 123–7; Thomas 1971, pp. 198–211; Steneck 1982, pp. 173–5; Walker 1984b, pp. 343–4, 350–4; 1986, pp. 75–98.

89 Boas Hall 1965, pp. 67–70; quotations are from documents printed in More 1944, pp. 225–30; and Maddison 1969, pp. 166–76. Cf. Dobbs 1975, p. 68; Capp 1979, pp. 180–9; Redwood, 1976, p. 103; Curry 1989, pp. 57–64; notes 102–4 in this chapter.

90 Boyle 1911, pp. 104–5, 177–9, 182; Boyle 1772, vol. 3, pp. 1–2, 4–25, 27–9, 32, 35, 38–9, 46–7, 69–71, 113–18, 121, 128–31, 136, 278; Boyle 1979, pp. xxxi, 14–33, 120, 129, 134, 139–40, 144–5; Boas Hall 1965, pp. 11–13, 17–28, 38, 46, 53, 59–74, 111–13, 178, 233–4; Boas Hall 1981, pp. 435–40, 460–4, 483; More 1944, pp. 214–23, 231–5, 244, 250–3, 263–4, 280; Boas Hall 1958, pp. 95–7, 102–3; Maddison 1969, pp. 103, 119–20, 190–2; Webster 1975, pp. 57–67; Dobbs 1975, pp. 62–80, 198–204; Pagel 1984, pp. 148–55; Alexander 1985, pp. 18, 39, 48, 55–9, 61–84; notes 94, 104 in this chapter.

91 Locke, *Ess.* II.viii.2, 7–10, 15, 17, 22–3; Yolton 1970, pp. 20–5; Yolton 1985, pp. 112–14; Alexander 1985, pp. 5–9, 87–8, 115–22, 131–4, 139.

92 Dewhurst 1963, pp. 3–4, 21–3, 26–8, 33–9, 44; Yolton 1970, pp. 4–6, 35, 42; Duchesneau 1973, pp. 2–10, 32–41, 46–53, 93–6.

93 Dewhurst 1963, pp. 4–10, 19, 31, 48–9, 88, 128–9, 159, 170, 188–9, 208, 241, 250–1, 262–4, 272–6, 279, 283–5; notes 92, 111 in this chapter.

94 Locke, *Ess.* II.xxiii.8–9; IV.iii.25; Yost 1990, pp. 261–2, 267; Alexander 1985, pp. 150–1, 162, 168–174.

95 Locke, *Ess.* II.viii.11–13, xxiii.11–12, xxxi.6; III.vi.9; IV.iii.25–6; Locke 1976–92, vol.

2, p. 785; Locke 1823, vol. 4, pp. 467–8; Yolton 1970, pp. 11, 21–2, 45–7, 51–2, 64–5; Duchesneau 1973, pp. 83–7; Alexander 1985, pp. 124–5, 164; Rogers 1990, pp. 374–5; Wilson 1990, pp. 95–104; Yost 1990, pp. 260–70. Cf. Jolley 1984, pp. 54–73.

96 Newton 1959–77, vol. 4, pp. 266–7, vol. 5, p. 392; Newton 1972, vol. 1, p. 15 (Newton 1934, p. xvii); Koyré 1968a, pp. 13–14, 56–9, 118, 139–42; Hesse 1978, pp. 122–5; Boas Hall 1978, p. 97; Westfall 1980, pp. 462–4, 472, 508, 645, 730, 744, 793; Hall 1980, pp. 149, 151, 157, 164; note 105 in this chapter.

97 Newton 1959–77, vol. 3, pp. 240, 244, 249, 253–4, 286–7, vol. 5, pp. 115–16; Newton 1972, vol. 2, p. 555 (Newton 1934, p. 400); Pascal 1904–14, vol. 1, pp. 177–8, 184; Huygens 1888–1950, vol. 19, pp. 628–30; Roberval 1644, pp. 1–3, 7, 16; Koyré 1968a, pp. 59–60, 139; McMullin 1978a, pp. 58, 79; Hall 1980, pp. 145, 149, 161–3; Westfall 1980, pp. 464–5, 472, 505, 508, 730; Westfall 1984, p. 325; note 105 in this chapter.

98 Newton 1952, pp. 347–54, 364–5; Newton 1959–77, vol. 1, pp. 175–6, 360–9, vol. 2, pp. 290, 295, 439, 447, vol. 5, pp. 299–300, 363–7; Newton 1962, p. 208; Newton 1972, vol. 2, p. 764 (Newton 1934, p. 547); Newton 1983, pp. 275–85, 363–5; McGuire 1967, pp. 84–5; 1968, pp. 155, 175–81, 185–7; 1977, pp. 109–11; Hawes 1968, pp. 121–30; Snow 1975, pp. 147–50, 157–8; Dobbs 1975, pp. 204–10; 1982, pp. 525–6; 1988, p. 55; Boas Hall 1978, p. 97; Westfall 1980, pp. 91, 94, 306–8, 372, 377, 390, 641–4, 747–8, 793–4; Walker 1984a, pp. 243–4.

99 Newton 1959–77, vol. 2, p. 415, vol. 3, p. 240, vol. 5, pp. 300, 397; 1952, pp. 369–70, 403–5; Newton 1962, pp. 109, 142–3, 213, 216, 223, 359, 363; Newton 1972, vol. 2, pp. 759–65 (Newton 1934, pp. 543–7); McGuire and Rattansi 1966, pp. 109, 112, 118, 124, 134–5; McGuire 1968, pp. 154, 161–4, 184–5, 193, 196; McGuire 1977, pp. 95–105, 128–9; Dobbs 1975, pp. 102–8; Dobbs 1982, pp. 516–18, 526–8; Dobbs 1988, pp. 59–74; McMullin 1978a, pp. 29–30, 54; Copenhaver 1980, pp. 540–8; Westfall 1980, pp. 55–6, 89, 97, 301–4, 318–21, 348–51, 415, 441, 505, 509–11, 647–8, 748–9; Westfall 1984, p. 331; Henry 1986b, pp. 336–8, 351–5.

100 Newton 1952, pp. 369, 376, 394, 401–2; Newton 1959–77, vol. 2, p. 288, vol. 5, p. 299, vol. 5, pp. 63–5; Newton 1962, pp. 106–11, 140–5, 304, 307, 322, 327–8, 331, 334, 340–1, 345, 350, 353, 356, 360–1; Newton 1972, vol. 1, pp. 15–16, vol. 2, pp. 764–65 (Newton 1934, pp. xvii, 546–7); Koyré 1968a, pp. 56, 146; McGuire 1968, pp. 194–7, 206; Parkinson 1969, pp. 93–4; McMullin 1978a, p. 57, 65–9; Westfall 1980, pp. 390, 422, 462–5, 505, 645–6, 730–1, 748–9, 773, 779; Westfall 1984, p. 324; Hall 1980, p. 230; Henry 1986b, pp. 339–40, 358.

101 Newton 1959–77, vol. 3, pp. 249, 253–4, vol. 5, pp. 363, 366, vol. 6, pp. 116–17; Newton 1952, pp. 339, 369–71, 376, 388–9, 394, 397–401; Newton 1962, pp. 89–90, 109, 142–3, 217, 223, 303–4, 306–7, 321, 327–8, 331–3, 341, 345, 350–1, 353–4, 356, 360; Newton 1972, vol. 1, pp. 19–20, vol. 2, pp. 550–4, 759–65 (Newton 1934, pp. xx, 398–9, 543–7); McGuire 1970, pp. 5, 11–13, 29, 37–40; Snow 1975, pp. 166–7; McMullin 1978a, pp. 20, 50–1, 58–9, 102–3; Westfall 1980, pp. 301–3, 372–3, 377, 381, 388–90, 407, 415, 420, 454, 462, 469, 505–6, 521–2, 641–3, 647, 779; Westfall 1984, p. 324; Dobbs 1988, p. 55.

102 Newton 1959–77, vol. 2, p. 2, vol. 3, pp. 193, 195, 215–19, 249, 253–4, vol. 7, p. 393; Keynes 1947; Dobbs 1975, pp. 6–20, 49–53, 66–8, 89–90, 121–60, 175–82, 191–5, 199, 210–13; this work revolutionised modern views of Newton's alchemy, and see now also Dobbs 1991. See also Boas Hall 1975, pp. 239–46; McGuire 1977, pp. 124–5; Whiteside 1977; Westfall 1980, pp. 281–6, 289–95, 299–301, 309, 357–61, 365–9, 407, 488–93, 524–33, 537–40; Westfall 1984, pp. 315, 318–21, 325–6, 330; Cohen 1980, p. 10; Gjertsen 1986, p. 13; Henry 1988, p. 143; for Gassendi's influence on

Locke and, possibly, Newton, see now Lennon 1993, pp. 149–63, 279; notes 87–90, 92–3 in this chapter.

103 Newton 1959–77, vol. 1, p. 368, vol. 3, pp. 205, 209; Newton 1962, pp. 223, 328, 341; Newton 1972, vol. 2, p. 760 (Newton 1934, p. 544); Dobbs 1975, pp. 146–55, 160–3, 230, 249–50; Dobbs 1982, pp. 515–16, 521–4; Dobbs 1988, pp. 58–9; McMullin 1978a, pp. 43–7, 75–8; Westfall 1980, pp. 293–6, 299–300, 303–7, 363, 366, 375, 389, 509, 527–30, 645; Westfall 1984, pp. 319, 322–3, 326, 328–31; note 104 in this chapter.

104 Newton 1959–77, vol. 2, pp. 2, 292; Newton 1962, pp. 321–47; Newton 1983, pp. 359–67, 376–7, 396–7; Bachelard 1967, pp. 97–102; Dobbs 1975, p. 186; Westfall 1980, pp. 307, 373, 389, 502, 530; note 103 in this chapter.

105 Newton 1959–77, vol. 3, pp. 286–7, vol. 5, pp. 115–16, 299, 393, 397, vol. 6, pp. 252–3, 285, 460, vol. 7, pp. 161–4; Newton 1962, pp. 303, 305, 327, 341, 350, 353, 356, 360; 1934, vol. 1, pp. xxvi–xxvii; Leibniz and Clarke 1956, pp. 118–19; Ger. III 580, 620 (Leibniz 1969, pp. 663, 657); Ger. IV 58–9, 143, 520–1 (Leibniz 1969, pp. 82, 124, 494–5); Ger. VI 586–7 (Leibniz 1969, p. 623); Ger. VII 293–5, 418–19 (Leibniz 1969, pp. 230–31, 716–17); Ger. Math. II 19–20 (Leibniz 1969, p. 249); Ger. Math. VI 242 (Leibniz 1969, p. 441); LAkad VI.I 268 (Leibniz 1969, p. 88); *Nouv.* ess. pref., II.vii.6–13, II.xxi.47, IV.iii.6 (LAkad VI.VI 61–8, 130–1, 196, 379, 382); *Théod.* disc. prelim., sec. 19; Koyré 1968a, pp. 59–60, 139, 141–6; Ross 1974, pp. 222–48; Ross 1978, pp. 167–74; Ross 1982, pp. 40–5; Coudert 1978, pp. 106–14; Weimann 1978, pp. 155–65; Westfall 1980, pp. 472, 648, 730, 749–50, 772–3, 779; Hall 1980, pp. 145, 149, 157, 161–4, 221, 224; Hübener 1983, pp. 103–12; Aiton 1985, pp. 18, 74, 92; note 68, 96–7 in this chapter.

106 *Disc. mét.* sec. 22; *PNG,* secs. 1–4; *Mon.,* secs. 8–19, 56–75; Leibniz 1903, pp. 521–2 (Leibniz 1969, pp. 269–70); Leibniz 1982–91, vol. 3, pp. 638–43 (Leibniz 1969, pp. 287–9); Ger. II 111–12, 118, 504 (Leibniz 1969, pp. 338–9, 343, 614); Ger. IV 469–70, 478–82, 499, 510–11 (Leibniz 1969, pp. 433, 454–6, 460, 503–4); Ger. VI 539, 586–7 (Leibniz 1969, pp. 586, 623); LAkad VI.III 472–7, 509–10, 513–17 (Leibniz 1969, pp. 157–60, 161–2, 160–1); *Nouv.* ess. pref., I.i.1, II.xxvii.14 (LAkad VI.VI 53–6, 72–3, 240); Martin 1964, pp. 139–42, 166–8; Michel 1973, pp. 141–9; Broad 1975, pp. 85, 87, 90–2, 94–7, 135–6; Becco 1978, pp. 119–41; Merchant 1979, pp. 255–69; Rescher 1979, pp. 70–1, 76–7; Butts 1980, pp. 47–62; Mittelstrass 1981, p. 156; Mates 1986, pp. 37–9, 199, 204–5; Aiton 1985, p. 201; Clulee 1988, pp. 77–96.

107 *Disc. mét.* secs. 9–12; Leibniz 1768, vol. 2.1, pp. 222–25 (Leibniz 1969, pp. 592–4); Leibniz 1982–91, vol. 3, pp. 640–1 (Leibniz 1969, p. 288); Ger. I 15–17, 25–7 (Leibniz 1969, pp. 93–5, 100–102); Ger. II 116–17 (Leibniz 1969, p. 342); Ger. III 427, 611–13, 618–21, 580–1 (Leibniz 1969, pp. 631–2, 655–6, 656–7, 663); Ger. IV 390–1, 468–9, 479–80, 504–5, 522–3 (Leibniz 1969, pp. 409, 432, 454–5, 499, 496); Ger. VI 529–31, 540–4 (Leibniz 1969, pp. 554–5, 587–9); Ger. Math. VI 242 (Leibniz 1969, p. 441); LAkad VI.I 487–8 (Leibniz 1969, pp. 260–1); *Nouv.* ess. I.i.1, II.xxvii.14, III.x.15 (LAkad VI.VI 71–2, 240, 344); *Théod.* disc. prelim., secs. 9–11, pt. I secs. 19, 112, 372; Politella 1938, pp. 120–1; Loemker 1955, p. 43; Iltis 1973, pp. 348–52; Broad 1975, pp. 3, 49–56, 67–9, 75–86; Allen 1983, pp. 4, 8–9; Ross 1983, pp. 126–34; Aiton 1985, pp. 196–9, 276–7; Mates 1986, p. 191; notes 57–8 in this chapter.

108 *Disc. mét.* secs. 9, 14, 22; *PNG,* secs. 3–4, 12–18; *Mon.,* secs. 50–70; Leibniz 1903, pp. 519–20 (Leibniz 1969, pp. 268–9); Leibniz 1982–91, vol. 3, pp. 640–43 (Leibniz 1969, pp. 288–9); Ger. II 111–12, 118, 126–7 (Leibniz 1969, pp. 338–9, 343, 347–8); Ger. IV 483–7, 498–500, 510–11, 520–1 (Leibniz 1969, pp. 457–9, 459–60, 503–4, 494); Ger. VI 539–40 (Leibniz 1969, pp. 586–7); LAkad VI.III 472–7, 509–10, 513–17 (Leibniz

1969, pp. 157–60, 161–2, 160–1); *Nouv. ess.* pref. (LAkad VI.VI 53–6); Broad 1975, pp. 87, 99–101, 135–6; Rescher 1979, pp. 65–6; Mates 1986, pp. 205–6.

109 *Disc. mét.* secs. 10–13, 33–4; *PNG,* sec. 3; *Mon.,* secs. 56–64, 79–81; Leibniz 1903, pp. 518–23 (Leibniz 1969, pp. 268–71); Leibniz 1982–91, vol. 3, pp. 638–41 (Leibniz 1969, pp. 287–8); Ger. I 15–27 (Leibniz 1969, pp. 94–102, 189); Ger. II 111–12, 116–17, 126–7, 504 (Leibniz 1969, pp. 338–9, 342–3, 347–8, 614); Ger. IV 106, 228, 469–70, 481–7, 498–500, 510–11 (Leibniz 1969, pp. 110–12, 139, 433, 456–9, 459–60, 503–4); Ger. VI 540–1 (Leibniz 1969, p. 587); Ger. VII 265 (Leibniz 1969, p. 173); Ger. Math. III 551–3 (Leibniz 1969, pp. 511–13); Ger. Math. VI 234–5 (Leibniz 1969, pp. 435–6); LAkad II.I 541–2 (Leibniz 1969, pp. 275–6); LAkad VI.I 508–10 (Leibniz 1969, pp. 115–17); LAkad VI.III 472–5 (Leibniz 1969, pp. 157–8; *Nouv. ess.* III.vi.24 (LAkad VI.VI 317–18); Gueroult 1967, p. 173; Martin 1964, pp. 128, 139–42, 166–8; Broad 1975, pp. 54, 65, 69, 85, 90–2, 99–101; Rescher 1979, pp. 65–6, 76–7, 80; Mates 1986, pp. 192, 204–6; Allen 1983, pp. 15, 19; Aiton 1985, pp. 18, 74, 92, 193–4; notes 23, 27, 68, 100 in this chapter.

110 Berkeley 1948–57, vol. 1, pp. 3–5, 76, vol. 5, pp. 3–23, 90–1, 126–51; Newton 1958, pp. 433–6, 444–74.

111 However, I disagree with the views expressed in Millen 1985, p. 215: 'By the end of the seventeenth century, occult qualities not only had been incorporated into modern science; they had become the foundation'; see also Hutchison, 1982; note 18 in this chapter.

112 Ger. VII 418–19 (Leibniz and Clarke 1956, p. 94); cf. Schaffer 1985, pp. 135–9.

17

DOCTRINES OF EXPLANATION IN LATE SCHOLASTICISM AND IN THE MECHANICAL PHILOSOPHY

STEVEN NADLER

I. EXPLANATION AND CAUSE

A natural phenomenon is said to consist of the properties (physical, chemical, etc.), states, or behaviours of a body or system of bodies. Whereas a descriptive account of a phenomenon relates *what* these properties are, an explanation tells *why* they are as they are, or *how* the phenomenon in question came about. Humankind's concern with 'why' and its importance for scientific understanding goes back at least as far as Aristotle. In the *Posterior Analytics,* Aristotle distinguishes between 'knowing the fact [*to hoti*]' and 'knowing the reason why [*to dioti*]'[1] and identifies true scientific understanding with 'knowing both that the cause on account of which [*ten aitian di' hen*] the object is its cause, and that it is not possible for this to be otherwise'.[2] Mediaeval Aristotelians referred to this kind of knowledge (*scientia*) as *demonstratio propter quid.*

Explanation, so understood, has historically and conceptually been linked with the notion of causation. To explain is to explain *causally,* and the kind of account sought in scientific understanding is usually a causal narrative. The content of the explanation of a phenomenon should provide, at the very least, an aetiology which both identifies the cause(s) of the phenomenon and, ideally, makes clear how that cause is productive of the phenomenon. Again, Aristotle is the earliest systematic source for this view. In the *Physics,* he insists that 'knowledge is the object of our inquiry, and people do not think they know a thing until they have grasped the "why" [*to dia ti*] of it, which is to grasp its primary cause [*ten prote aitia*].'[3]

The notion that explanation provides knowledge of the cause of a phenomenon is a common feature of Aristotelian systems and the mechanical philosophies of the seventeenth century. For Aristotle, Saint Thomas, later scholastics, and the proponents of the new science, the relationship between *explanans* and *explanandum,* whatever else it may be (logical, necessary, functional, divinely ordained), must above all be *causal.* Given the several species of causation recognised by many of these thinkers, as well as the historical variations and philosophical complexities in the general notion of 'cause', there is, however, little agreement between them as to what may count as an acceptable *explanans.* As the understanding of what qualifies as a 'cause' evolved between Aristotelianism and mechanism and became somewhat more restrictive, the constraints on 'explanation' were modified. What was acceptable as a causal explanation of a phenomenon for certain mediaeval and later scholastics was, by the canons of the mechanical philosophy, vacuous and trivial.

II. PERIPATETIC EXPLANATION

Before turning to the doctrine of explanation operative among seventeenth-century scholastics, it is helpful to examine the more orthodox Aristotelian account from which it derives. The following discussion is more a generalised and highly distilled synopsis than a precise description of any one thinker's views, least of all Aristotle's. Some elements in it are explicitly found in Aristotle; others come directly from Saint Thomas; still other features are more common within the Peripatetic tradition, both before and after Thomas. For the purposes of this discussion, the question as to how much Aristotle's own views are represented or distorted by his mediaeval and early modern followers can be set aside.

For the Aristotelian, the proper objects of scientific inquiry are the states, properties, and behaviours of, as well as the changes in and between, substances. Every substance (taken in its primary sense to mean a concrete existing individual – a rock, a tree, a person) is a compound entity consisting of matter and form. The matter not only gives the substance its materiality, but also thereby individuates it numerically (but not qualitatively) with respect to other substances. It is the particular, discrete substratum underlying all properties. The form, on the other hand, is what gives the substance its own peculiar identity, particularly as a being of such and such a kind. The form is responsible for all the properties and qualities by which a thing is what it is. Shape, size, texture, solidity, motion, colour, and other non-relational properties all belong to a substance in virtue of its form.[4]

Forms are substantial or accidental according to whether the properties they ground and generate are essential or accidental to the substance. The substantial form of a human being, for example, will impose on the particular matter it informs just those properties essential to being a human – animality and rationality. The substantial form thus makes the substance belong to its species. The other properties belonging to an individual and differentiating it from other members of its species result from any number of accidental forms informing the same matter[5] (or, as Aristotle suggests at one point, informing or qualifying the substantial form itself).[6] Hair and eye colour, skin pigmentation, height, and other accidental qualities belonging to a human body all flow from the particular accidental forms which serve to complete the substance and make of it a particular individual. Thus, Thomas claims that

substantial form gives a thing existence, so that it presupposes mere capacity to exist. Whereas accidental form does not give existence as such, but causes a thing to exist with such and such features or size or to exist in some manner or other, so that it presupposes something actually existing already . . . accidental form exists to complete its subject.[7]

The Aristotelian hylemorphic doctrine of substance and its properties engenders its own general theory of explanation. Any account as to why a substance has such and such properties or powers or behaves in such and such a way will necessarily involve specifying certain determinate forms constituting that substance and informing its matter. Those forms are *causally* responsible for the substance's being such as it is, for all its observable qualities and capacities. More particularly, the *explanans* will take the form of identifying in detail both (1) the essence of the substance as embodied in its substantial form and (2) those accidental forms responsible for its non-essential properties.[8] Thus, Aristotle insists that 'what we seek is the cause, that is the form, by reason of which the matter is some definite thing.'[9] He fails to state, however, just how a form *causes* or brings about what it does.

Aristotelians considered explanation of this kind particularly important in any account of alteration or change in a substance, or in any discussion of the dynamical behaviour of bodies. They explained change by means of the privation of some form and the acquisition of another. In substantial or essential change, whereby a thing of one kind is transformed into a thing of another kind (e.g., water into air), the material substratum loses one substantial form and gains another. In cases of accidental change, the substance, while remaining what it is essentially, undergoes some alteration in one or more of its accidental properties (e.g., its colour). This, too, is explained in terms of the loss and gain of (accidental) forms.[10]

In Aristotelian physics, and the dynamics of bodies in motion and at rest, a similar explanatory model is at work, although it is somewhat different in its details from the metaphysics of substance. Aristotle identifies four fundamental elements or primary bodies, out of which all physical bodies are composed: fire, air, water, and earth. Each of these four elements is itself made up of two of four primary qualities: heat, cold, dryness, and moisture.[11] The two qualities of a primary body inform its material substratum. And, like forms, these first qualities, through their combination and mixture in various proportions in the primary bodies and, hence, in macroscopic physical bodies, are ultimately responsible for the observable behaviour of bodies. The properties of ordinary fire (its capacity to dry or to burn other bodies), for example, are explained by the preponderance in it of the element fire and thus of that element's primary qualities: heat and dryness.

Hence, in any general Peripatetic schema, reference to the possession of the relevant form (substantial or accidental) or quality (elementary or otherwise) by the natural body in question is thought to constitute an adequate aetiological account of the properties, states, and powers of that body. Change and causal interaction are likewise explained by means of the loss, gain, and communication from one substance to another of certain forms or qualities.

III. LATER SCHOLASTICISM

Although several distinct mediaeval philosophical traditions were influential in the revival of scholasticism in the late sixteenth and early seventeenth centuries, the overwhelming tendency was towards Aristotelianism, particularly of the Thomistic variety.[12] Although one should be cautious about identifying scholasticism with Aristotelianism,[13] the categories and conceptual apparatus of the Peripatetic system deeply inform later scholastic metaphysics, logic, and physical science. In fact, the general doctrine of explanation of natural phenomena adopted by such thinkers as Suárez, Eustacius a Sancto Paulo, and the Jesuit authors of the Coimbrian Commentaries is simply a development of the schema just outlined.

In late scholasticism one still finds, above all, an unwavering commitment to the Aristotelian doctrine of substance. Every concrete individual thing is composed of passive matter, with all its innate potentialities, and actualising form. Together, matter and substantial form constitute a *unum per se,* with the substance acquiring its essential and peculiar characteristics (*functiones*) – reasoning in humankind, neighing in horses, heating in fire, and so on – from its substantial form.[14] In fact, the substantial form is the ultimate (although not necessarily the *immediate*) source of *all* the properties and powers of a natural body, essential and accidental. Thus, any account as to why (*cur*) these accidents rather than some others are in this parcel of matter will consist, at least in part, in specifying the form inhering in that material substratum.[15]

Later scholastics also continued to maintain the doctrine of four elements and their corresponding analysis into 'first qualities'. They were explicit, however, in adding to Aristotle's four primary sensible qualities (heat, coldness, moisture, dryness) two primary motive qualities (*qualitates motrices*): heaviness (*gravitas*) and lightness (*levitas*).[16] Moreover, they accorded increased importance to such qualities in explanations of natural phenomena and expanded their number beyond the original primary ones.[17] All were transformed into what became known as 'real qualities' and 'virtues' (or, sometimes, 'accidental forms'). Eventually, every sensible (and insensible) property and behaviour of a body was explained in terms of the body's possession of the relevant form or quality. These *qualitates reales,* characterised simply in terms of the observable property or capacity to be explained, belong to and derive from (*consequi*) the substantial form of that body but are separable from it and transferable to another body. In general, a distinction is maintained between the substantial form responsible for the unity and essential properties or general 'species characteristics' of the object and the real qualities immediately responsible for its particular non-essential or accidental individualising properties (although this is not always the case, since the substantial form is itself often considered simply a collection of real qualities, namely, just those real qualities necessary and sufficient for a thing to belong to such and such a species).[18] Real qualities, accorded an active power (*vis agendi*), are considered the efficient causes of their respective sensible and insensible effects. Thus, the real quality 'heat' (*calor*) begets (*generare*) sensible warmth or the power of warming in a body; the quality 'dryness' (*siccitas*) begets sensible dryness in a body; 'redness' begets a sensible red tincture, and so on.[19] Explanation consists in specifying both the form or essence of the body and the various real qualities informing it. The qualities responsible for the observable properties to be explained were themselves unanalysable and irreducible. The ultimate and only possible explanation of observable property *x* in a body *b* is the intrinsic presence in *b* of the real quality or form *x*-ness. Explanations of this sort were considered complete and satisfactory, 'the final answer to all queries'.[20]

This model of explanation is easily illustrated by three important cases of natural *explananda* – colour, gravity, and magnetism. Why, for example, is a swan white, wine red, and gold yellow? A swan is white (*albus*) because of the presence in it of whiteness (*albedo*); and wine and gold have their respective visible colours because of the presence therein of the requisite real qualities.[21] True colour, then, unlike merely apparent colour, is neither a property of light or some other medium, nor an effect in the sense organ or mind of the perceiver, but a certain *qualitas* really inhering in a body and causing it to appear in such and such a way.[22]

As for the phenomenon of gravity, heavy bodies fall and light bodies (e.g., fire) naturally rise upwards because of the innate presence in the former of heaviness and in the latter of lightness. The quality or 'motive virtue' (*virtus motrix seu potentia*) *gravitas* serves as the primary efficient cause of the motion of a heavy body towards the centre of the world.[23] In the view of the Coimbrian commentators, 'Since heavy and light things . . . tend toward their natural places, there must be some means [*instrumentum*] present in them . . . by the power [*vi*] of which they are moved. This can be nothing other than their substantial form and the heaviness and lightness which derives from it.'[24] In the case of magnetism, the lodestone has its capacity to attract iron because it possesses the attractive quality or magnetic virtue, often explicitly referred to as an 'occult' quality.[25]

IV. MECHANISTIC EXPLANATION

By the mid to late seventeenth century, explanations in terms of scholastic forms and qualities had become the object of both literary satire and philosophic critique. Molière's candidate, in *Le malade imaginaire* (1673), when asked why opium puts one to sleep, responds, 'because there is a dormitive virtue in it, the nature of which is to dull the senses'. The chorus of examiners enthusiastically welcomes him into 'our learned body'.[26]

In a more rigorous vein, philosophers and scientists accused the partisans of Peripatetic natural philosophy of offering trivial, vague, and empty explanations. Descartes, for example, insists that the 'qualities or forms which certain philosophers suppose to inhere in things' do not at all make clear how the phenomenon to be explained is produced.[27]

They have all put forward as principles things of which they did not possess perfect knowledge. For example, there is not one of them, so far as I know, who has not supposed there to be weight in terrestrial bodies. Yet although experience shows us very clearly that the bodies we call 'heavy' descend towards the center of the earth, we do not for all that have any knowledge of the nature of what is called 'gravity', that is to say, the cause or principle which makes bodies descend in this way.[28]

It may be true, but it is certainly not at all helpful to claim that a body is heavy and falls to the centre of the earth because it possesses the quality 'heaviness'. The principle which is offered as an *explanans* itself stands in need of explanation, particularly with respect to its operation.[29]

For Boyle, the neo-Aristotelian reliance on substantial forms and real qualities produces 'unsatisfactory and barren' accounts of natural phenomena. Explanations wherein the *explanans* is simply characterised in terms of the *explanandum* (e.g., the *white* colour of a swan is explained by the presence in it of *white*ness), while they may tell us *what* is responsible for the observed phenomenon, do not tell us 'by what means and after what manner' the phenomenon comes about.[30] More-over, an *explanans* so specified is circular and trivial, since it merely repeats the property being explained.

> The Schools [have] made it thought needless or hopeless for men to employ their industry in searching into the nature of particular qualities and their effects. As, if (for instance) it be demanded how snow comes to dazzle the eyes, they will answer that it is by a *quality* of whiteness that is in it, which makes all very white bodies produce the same effect; and if you ask what this whiteness is, they will tell you no more in substance than that it is a *real entity,* which denominates the parcel of matter to which it is joined *white.*[31]

For those working within the emerging mechanistic modes of thought, then, the most striking limitation of Peripatetic natural philosophy was that it was incapable of providing what they took to be properly explanatory schemes for dealing with natural phenomena. One way of seeing the situation from their point of view is to look at typical Peripatetic schemata listing corporeal qualities, such as the two *tabulae* outlining the 'methodum totius philosophiae naturalis' that Clemens Timpler placed at the beginning of his *Physica, seu philosophia naturalis* (1605), one of the more widely used philosophical textbooks of the seventeenth century.[32] The sub-division listing the concerns of 'physiology strictly understood' divides into (1) internal and external principles of natural body and (2) two classes of physical affections of natural body. The former divide further into nine kinds of principle: primary and secondary material internal, generic and specific formal internal, physical and hyperphysical final external, and primary and secondary (universal and particular) efficient external. The affections divide further into quantity, quality, relation, and motion, which in turn break down into two kinds of quantity (magnitude and time); six insensible active and passive physical qualities and fifty-four sensible qualities (corresponding to the five senses); six sensible and insensible physical relations; seven genera of motion, and four species of active and passive motion, namely, generation, corruption, accidental motion, and mutation. Under further taxonomic dissection, the four species of motion yield eleven kinds of generation, seven kinds of corruption, five kinds of mutation, and seven kinds of accidental motion, two of the latter being alteration, of which there are thirty-three varieties, and local motion, of which there are twenty-eight varieties. Such taxonomic schemata offer an impressive armoury of categories for *describing* the unending and bewildering variety of natural phenomena. But for the protagonists of the new philosophy (who need only the three or four explanatory elements provided by body and its small number of simply conceived attributes and modes), they are absurdly complex and, more to the point, are useless as tools for *explaining* the phenomena of the natural world.

Thus, part of the motivation for the mechanical philosophy in the seventeenth century was the desire for clear and helpful explanations – that is, explanations which answer in a simple and non-trivial way the causal question regarding the production of a phenomenon by telling how and why the phenomenon happened as it did, and why it did not happen otherwise. For Descartes, Boyle, Gassendi, Mersenne, and others, only an explanation framed in terms of matter and motion alone could be truly perspicuous and informative. The mechanistic programme was premised on the claim that all natural phenomena, no matter how complex, all the sensible and insensible properties and behaviours of bodies, can be causally explained in terms of the arrangement and motion (or rest) of minute, insensible particles of matter (corpuscles), each of which is characterised exclusively by certain fundamental and irreducible properties – shape, size, and impenetrability.[33] Colour, figure, odour, viscosity, texture, gravity, magnetism, combustion, hardness, and other effects could all be understood as the result of the movement and position of individual corpuscles or relatively stable collections of corpuscles. Atomists such as Gassendi believed in ultimate particles which are, in fact and in principle, indivisible, as well as in a void in which they move. Descartes, on the other hand, insisted on both a plenum and the indefinite divisibility (at least in principle) of any parcel of matter. Despite such differences in the details of their respective physics, however, all proponents of the new philosophy shared a basic general commitment to this reductive explanatory model.

Such a mode of explanation is an example of a kind that has recently been termed 'structural'. Structural explanations account for the properties or behaviour of a complex entity 'by alluding to the structure of that entity', where 'structure' refers to 'a set of constituent entities or processes and the relationship between them'. The resulting explanation is causal, since the structure alluded to is considered the cause of the properties or behaviour being explained.[34] Mechanical explanations are 'structural' in so far as the phenomenon is causally explained by linking it (through laws of nature) to a structure of insensible particles, to an arrangement of minute bodies related to each other by position and motion, rather than to some single entity or to a number of entities considered individually.[35]

Because, however, the structures employed in mechanical explanations are inaccessible to observation, given the minute and insensible size of their constituent entities, any account of the mechanical cause of a phenomenon must necessarily be more or less hypothetical. The *de facto* unobservability of the causal mechanism itself and the in-principle unobservability of its causal efficacy mean that the best one can do is postulate its existence and composition, demonstrate its initial plausibility, and then show why it is preferable to (i.e., more likely than) any other possible explanation. As the Cartesian Bernard Lamy suggests, 'It must be admitted that in a great number of things, even with the help of microscopes . . . we still cannot penetrate what Nature has hidden from us. We cannot see what is inside. What can a physicist do, then, except conjecture?'[36] Seventeenth-century mechanists generally recognised the hypothetical nature of their proffered explanations, although in many cases this tended *not* to diminish their confidence in the absolute certainty of their conclusions.

Two assumptions about the physical world underlie mechanical explanation. First, it is assumed that nature is completely homogeneous in material: in Boyle's words, 'there is one catholic or universal matter common to all bodies', whether at the microscopic or macroscopic level.[37] The insensible particles are not materially different from the larger bodies which they compose (in fact, this must necessarily be the case, since the larger bodies are nothing more than collections of collections of particles). Second, nature is uniform in its operations. The same operations characterise, and the same laws govern, both the unobservable behaviour of the minutest particles of matter and the observable behaviour of complex bodies.

This ontological and nomological uniformity allowed mechanists to employ models from the macroscopic world to represent the microscopic, insensible structures and operations constituting their explanations. At a general level, Boyle's favourite example of a perceptually accessible relationship between observed behaviour and mechanistic explanation was the clock. The causal link between the movement of its hands (*explanandum*) and the arrangement and motion of its inner parts (*explanans*) is an analogue for the mechanical way nature works at every stratum.[38] Lamy elevated this analogy into a principle to guide any scientific research program: 'In order to have the right to imagine that one understands things, one must be able to explain them just as one would explain a watch which one opens so that one sees the movement and shape of its parts. . . . Everything which appears in a body is just like the case of the watch which hides the mechanism [*la machine*]. One must, therefore, open this box.'[39] At a more specific level, Descartes employed the motive behaviour of tennis balls as a model for the way in which the rotations and trajectories of the particles constituting a light ray (which is nothing more than the trajectory of the pression from a luminous body through a material medium) can be modified.[40] Such representation, or even reproduction, of invisible explanatory structure and causal connexion at the observable level allowed for greater perspicuity in explanation, since appeal was generally made to familiar and well-understood notions and mechanisms. As Descartes suggests,

No one who uses his reason will, I think, deny the advantage of using what happens in large bodies, as perceived by our senses, as a model for our ideas about what happens in tiny bodies which elude our senses merely because of their small size. This is much better than explaining matters by inventing all sorts of strange objects which have no resemblance to what is perceived by the senses [such as 'prime matter', 'substantial forms' and the whole range of qualities that people habitually introduce, all of which are harder to understand than the things they are supposed to explain].[41]

This model-approach, it was felt, allowed for greater predictive power and more fruitful conjectures regarding imperceptible causes. Although, as was noted earlier, any account of the insensible mechanism underlying a phenomenon must involve hypothesising to some degree, the task can be facilitated by our experience of machines and other artifacts 'whose operations are performed by mechanisms which are large enough to be perceived easily by the senses', since, Descartes insists, 'mechanics is a division or special case of physics, and all the explanations belonging to the former also belong to the latter.'[42]

V. DESCARTES

The *Principia Philosophiae* (1644) was intended to supplant the Aristotelian system as a comprehensive account of 'the entire visible world'. As Descartes claims, rather optimistically, there is 'no phenomenon of nature' which he has not explained in his treatise by the principles enumerated, namely, the various sizes, shapes, and motions which are found in all bodies.[43]

According to Descartes, a satisfactory explanation must, first of all, be couched in terms which are 'utterly evident [*evidentissime*]' and free from any obscurity. The concepts it employs must be simpler and better understood than the phenomenon to be explained; the entities and operations it posits must be 'clearly and distinctly' conceived. Second, the *explanans* must specify the cause (*causa*) of the phenomenon. Unlike the scholastics he criticises, however, Descartes recognises only efficient causation as relevant to scientific understanding. Final causes and all teleological considerations are banished from natural philosophy, and explanations ought to make no reference to ends and purposes in nature. 'It is not the final but the efficient causes of created things that we must inquire into. When dealing with natural things we will never derive any explanations from the purposes which God or nature may have had in view when creating them <and we shall entirely

banish from our philosophy the search for final causes>.'[44] Causation among physical substances – observable (and unobservable) effects produced by bodies or figured particles of various sizes in motion in accordance with certain laws – is efficient, transient causation.[45] In this schema, there are only material agents imparting motion to, or hindering the motion of, other matter by impact alone. Descartes occasionally describes one body causing motion in another in terms of the 'transference' or communication of the motion from the former to the latter when collision occurs.[46] But, as he elsewhere concedes, if motion is a mode of a substance, then literal transference is ruled out, since a mode cannot pass from one substance to another.[47]

Finally, the *explanans* must agree with experience and allow the *explanandum* to be 'deduced' from it. This does not mean that the effect must be derivable from the cause in a logically strict sense, but there must at least be an evident 'necessary connection' between the two. That is, it must be clear precisely how the effect follows from the cause, and why it should be this effect rather than some other. This is a demand for the kind of intelligibility Descartes felt Aristotelian explanations lacked.

Now we understand very well how the different size, shape and motion of the particles of one body can produce various local motions in another body. But there is no way of understanding how these same attributes (size, shape and motion) can produce something else whose nature is quite different from their own – like the substantial forms and real qualities which many philosophers suppose to inhere in things; and we cannot understand how these qualities or forms could have the power subsequently to produce local motions in other bodies.[48]

Only explanations of the mechanical variety, Descartes believed, are capable of fulfilling the above criteria. For Descartes, there is, strictly speaking, only one material substance, continuously and indefinitely extended throughout the universe and leaving no room for a vacuum. This universal matter (pure extension) is divided up into an indefinite number of parts of various sizes, shapes, and arrangements by means of motions of differing directions and velocities. Physical bodies just are parcels of matter in motion, collections and configurations of such parts.[49] Hence, all the real and apparent properties of a body (its shape, size, solidity, color, taste, texture, etc.), as well as all of its capacities and operations (solubility, flexibility, digestibility, etc.), are explained by means of the size, shape, position or configuration, and motion of its constituent material particles. Only such explanations can display 'in a clear and evident manner' how and why such and such properties and powers belong to a body, or how and why such and such a phenomenon has occurred. 'All the variety in matter, all the diversity of its forms, depends on motion. . . . All the properties which we clearly perceive in [matter] are reducible to its divisibility and consequent mobility in respect of its parts, and its resulting capacity to be affected in all the ways which we perceive as being derivable from the movement of the parts.'[50] There is no phenomenon of nature, no matter how *mirabile* or *admirandum* which cannot be explained in this way, without the help of occult qualities, mysterious powers or virtues, or sympathetic influences operating at a distance.

Let us return to our three test cases: colour, gravity, and magnetism. Where the Peripatetic explained the white colour of a swan by the presence in it of a certain real quality, whiteness, Descartes's account of colour relies solely on the relationship between the rotational and linear velocities of the minute particles (*globulos*) composing the second element ('light rays' are simply the trajectory or 'tendency' of the impulse communicated from a luminous body through this very subtle material element) as they strike the eyes. 'Red', for example, consists in nothing but a stronger tendency in the particles to rotate than to move in a straight line. An object is red (or, more accurately, *appears* red) when it is disposed to deflect and modify the motions of those particles so that when they strike the eye their rotational speed is faster than their rectilinear motion.[51]

Heaviness and the force of gravity are explained by means of the action of the particles composing the celestial matter that surrounds the earth. The globules of this matter, as they drive the earth around on its centre, always move upwards and away from the centre of the earth. In doing so, they force the particles of the terrestrial matter, which have less of a propensity to move away from the earth, downwards. Thus, the gravity of any terrestrial body is simply that body's being pushed down by the ascending celestial matter immediately displacing it.[52]

Finally, a magnet points northward and attracts iron not because of any occult attractive virtue, but because of the mechanical operation of minute particles constantly circulating through the interior and exterior realms of the earth. Each particle is threaded or 'grooved' in one of two directions. Depending on its threading, it circulates in either a north to south or south to north direction. The pores of the magnet (and of iron) are peculiarly suited for receiving these grooved particles and facilitating their circulation, unlike other terrestrial bodies which hinder their movement. Since the particles most easily pass through that pole of the magnet whose pores are suited to their threading and direction of circulation, they force by impact a magnet which is not already lying on a north-south axis to be so positioned. A magnet and a piece of iron approach each other because, as the grooved particles which pass through them emerge, they expel the air between the two bodies. The expelled air then forces the bodies closer together until they are in contact.[53]

VI. HYPOTHESES AND CERTAINTY

Later Cartesians, like Descartes himself,[54] exhibited an acute awareness of the unavoidability of proceeding hypothetically in mechanistic physical science. The unobservable mechanisms and operations offered to explain a phenomenon can be no better than hypotheses framed on the basis of observations (an hypothesis must 'agree with experience') and in conformity with 'first principles' (whereby prior metaphysical commitments set constraints as to what kinds of entities and processes can be admitted in explanations) and the general laws of nature. Lamy's concession in this regard has already been mentioned. Likewise, the physicists Jacques Rohault and Pierre-Sylvain Régis were clearly aware of the limitations imposed on mechanistic science by its explanatory principles. Thus, Régis claims:

> The properties of a mathematical body are easily deduced from its nature, since it is very simple and very easy to understand. . . . One can also very easily explain the effects of machines; because their parts are gross and tangible, one can easily perceive the relations they have among themselves, and thus predict the effect they must produce when acting together. But it is not at all the same with a physical body. Since its parts are insensible, one cannot perceive their order or arrangement, and the most one could do would be to guess at it from the effects.[55]

Now, one would expect that a recognition that the method of mechanistic science is hypothetical would be accompanied by an acknowledgement that its results – that is, its conclusions regarding imperceptible causes – must be something less than absolutely certain, and that the best one can do is present a highly probable account (in relation to competing theories). This expectation is encouraged by the significant developments in probability theory during the seventeenth century, which meant that Cartesians had available a language in which they could express the merely relative certainty of their hypotheses.[56]

One finds some degree of epistemic restraint among Cartesians. Thus, early in the *Traité de physique,* Rohault states, 'We must content ourselves for the most part to find out how things may be; without pretending to come to a certain knowledge and determination of what they really are; for there may possibly be different causes capable of producing the same effect.'[57] Régis, too, admits that 'one cannot be entirely certain of what [physics] teaches . . . it would be as unreasonable to demand demonstrations in physics, as it would be to be content with probabilities in mathematics. Just as the latter must not admit anything but what is certain and demonstrated, so the former is obliged to accept everything which is probable.'[58]

On the other hand, these physicists also continued to insist that their explanations were 'true', 'certain', and 'demonstrated'. In the paragraph immediately following the one quoted above, Rohault goes on to suggest a number of criteria by which a probable hypothesis can be confirmed as true.

> Now as he who undertakes to decipher a letter, finds out an alphabet so much the more probable, as it answers to the words with the fewest suppositions; so may we affirm of that conjecture concerning the nature of any thing, that it is the more probable, by how much the more simple it is, by how much the fewer properties were had in view, and by how much the more properties, different from each other, can be explained by it. . . . And indeed there may be so many, and so very different properties in the same thing, that we shall find it very difficult to believe, that they can be explained in two different ways. In which case, our conjecture is not only to be look upon as highly probable, but we have reason to believe it to be *the very truth*.[59]

Régis, in the midst of his concessions that 'nothing demonstrative belongs to speculative physics', nonetheless suggests that there is really only 'one single system' that can explain natural phenomena (where a 'system' is a set [*un amas*] of interdependent hypotheses which can be connected with first truths by a necessary connexion). Hypotheses so systematised will constitute the *truth* (*le veritable système de la Physique*).[60] The system Régis has in mind is, of course, the Cartesian one.

This apparent inconsistency among Cartesians regarding the epistemic status of their explanations probably results from a fundamental tension inherent in the Cartesian mechanistic programme. On the one hand, these natural philosophers inherited from their mentor a commitment to a certain ideal of science, whereby its claims are certain and demonstrable (although it is not clear that even Descartes thought that this ideal was thoroughly realised in his practice).[61] On the other hand, the ontology and methodology of the mechanical philosophy require hypothetical reasoning. It has also been suggested that Cartesians claimed absolute certainty for their theories, in spite of their hypothetical nature, in order to avoid the accusation from critics that they were simply offering 'mere' (i.e., arbitrary and *ad hoc*) conjectures regarding imperceptible causes.[62]

VII. BOYLE

In his theoretical writings on the mechanical philosophy, Boyle makes several demands of a successful explanation, a number of them similar to those made by Descartes. First, the concepts employed in the explanation must be intelligible and clear, free from the kind of 'obscurity, ambiguity and darkness' which plagued Peripatetic doctrines. It must be evident both what the entities are which it refers to and how they operate. This condition is satisfied, according to Boyle, by the corpuscular theory:

> Men do so easily understand one another's meaning, when they talk of *local motion, rest, bigness, shape, order, situation,* and *contexture* of material substances, and these principles do afford such clear accounts of those things that are rightly deduced from them only, that even those Peripatetics or chemists that maintain other principles acquiesce in the explications made by these, when they can be had, and seek not any further – though perhaps the effect be so admirable as would make it pass for that of a hidden form or occult quality.[63]

Moreover, the explanatory principles must be 'primary' and 'simple'. Sometimes Boyle appears to take these terms in an absolute sense, whereby the elements in the *explanans* must not themselves be further resolvable into components, nor reducible to or explicable in terms of some more fundamental principles. This would be peculiarly true of matter and motion.[64] Elsewhere, however, he clearly has in mind a primacy and simplicity relative to the *explanandum:* 'to explicate a phenomenon [is] to deduce it from something else in nature more known to us than the thing to be explained by it.'[65] So understood, the condition is satisfied by more complex notions, such as 'texture', that is, the overall structure or arrangement of corpuscles in a body, which is itself understood in terms of the shape and relative positions of the constituent particles.

It follows from the definition just quoted, of course, that the explanation must be couched in terms other than those which describe the phenomenon to be explained. It will not do, Boyle insists, to explain white coloration by means of 'whiteness', nor warmth by means of some calorific quality. Explanations of this variety make no progress in advancing our understanding of the phenomenon, since they merely repeat the property or behaviour under consideration in a hypostasised form.

Most important, a satisfactory explanation must tell us not just what the agent is that is bringing about the effect, but also the manner in which the effect is wrought. The *explanans* should make clear precisely *how* the phenomenon in question is produced, and why it happened one way rather than another.

> An inquisitive person . . . seeks not so much to know what is the *general* agent that produces a phenomenon, as *by what means* and *after what manner,* the phenomenon is produced. . . . The chief thing that inquisitive naturalists should look after in the explicating of difficult phenomena is not so much what the *agent* is or does, as what changes are made in the *patient* to bring it to exhibit the phenomena that are proposed, and by what means, and after what manner, those changes are effected.[66]

Only with this kind of understanding do we have a full causal account of a phenomenon, one which allows us to 'deduce' it from 'something else in nature more known to us'. Again, 'deduction' here need not have its narrow, logical meaning. Rather, the explanation as a whole should simply exhibit, in a non-trivial and perspicuous way, the necessary connexion(s) between the cause and the phenomenon, including all the intermediate structures or events linking the two.[67]

Given these criteria, Boyle argues, a properly causal explanation will be framed entirely in terms of the local motion, impact, and arrangement of minute particles of matter having particular shapes and sizes. All qualities, powers, events, and operations are 'explicated' as the effects of 'the catholic affections of matter, and [are] deducible from the size, shape, motion or rest, order and resulting texture of the insensible parts of bodies'.[68] Alteration and change, for example, are explained not by the loss and acquisition of some substantial form or real qualities, but by the rearrangement of the internal structure of a body's material parts. Heat results not from some *qualitas caloris,* but from the extreme agitation of the corpuscles of a body. In this regard, the world and its phenomena are no different from the behaviour of any other machine.

In explicating *particular phenomena,* [the naturalist] considers only the *size, shape, motion* (or *want of it), texture,* and the resulting qualities and attributes, of the small particles of matter . . . the phenomena [the world] exhibits are to be accounted for by the *number, bigness, proportion, shape, motion,* (or *endeavor), rest, coaptation,* and other mechanical affections, of the springs, wheels, pillars, and other parts it is made up of; and those effects of such a watch that cannot this way be explicated must, for aught I yet know, be confessed not to be sufficiently understood.[69]

Causation for Boyle is primarily mechanical efficient causation (although he elsewhere insists on the importance of final causes). All effects and changes follow immediately from the motion and collision of matter. There is no action at a distance, no forces or powers which can exert their influence over empty space. And while Boyle often emphasises the importance of 'texture' in explaining a body's properties and powers, he is quite clear that motion is the chief causal agent (outside of God) in natural and artificial phenomena, 'the principal amongst secondary causes, and the grand agent of all that happens in nature'.[70] While the requisite internal structure may be a necessary condition for the production of any effect (just as a key must have the proper shape to be able to open a lock, and the internal mechanism of a clock must be ordered correctly with all the right parts), nothing at all can happen until motion is applied.

VIII. THE DEBATE OVER FINAL CAUSES

Aristotelian and scholastic science stressed the importance of final causes in the explanation of natural phenomena, viewing nature as teleological and acknowledging a purposiveness in the production of physical entities and events.[71] Aristotle himself insists that nature, as a cause, always operates for a purpose: 'All natural things are for the sake of something . . . action for an end is present in things which come to be and are by nature.'[72] In many instances, especially those of natural (and artificial) generation and maturation, specifying the form is tantamount to identifying the final cause, since the complete substance, as the actualisation by form of certain potentialities in matter, is the end of the process. In this case, the form itself is 'that for the sake of which'.

As already pointed out, Descartes banishes final causes from physics. Teleological explanation has no rôle whatsoever to play in the investigation of natural phenomena.[73] Finite causation (that is, causation apart from God's universal causal activity) is efficient and material, the communication of motion by impact of one body on another.

In this attitude towards final causes, Descartes was followed, albeit in a more extreme form, by Spinoza. Spinoza's concept of *Natura naturata* entails that all effects, all phenomena and events, follow with absolute necessity from the divine nature (*Natura naturans*). There is nothing in the physical world which, as a modification of one of God's infinite attributes (extension), does not come about and produce its effects without being determined to exist and to act in such and such a manner by some other modification of that attribute, which itself is determined by some prior modification, and so on. Such is the nature of mechanical (efficient) causation in Spinoza. The series is necessary, and things could not have been produced or ordered in any other way.[74] It follows from this, Spinoza argues, that 'Nature has no end set before it, and that all final causes are nothing but human fictions . . . all things proceed by a certain eternal necessity of nature, and with the greatest perfection.'[75] Nothing occurs 'for the sake of anything else'. If one seeks to understand why some thing happened as it did, one must look not to some future end to be achieved, nor to some overall plan governing the series of events ('As God exists for the sake of no end, God also acts for the sake of no end').[76] Rather, the cause is only to be found in some prior event(s) which themselves are necessary and sufficient to bring about the effect being investigated. 'This doctrine concerning the end turns nature completely upside down. For what is really a cause, it considers an effect, and what is an effect it considers as a cause. What is by nature prior it makes posterior.'[77]

Not all partisans of mechanistic explanation, however, share this antipathy to final causes. Boyle, in particular, took Descartes to task 'for rejecting final causes altogether'. It is quite clear, Boyle insists, that in the investigation of animate and even certain inanimate creatures, a full understanding of their structures and operations requires a consideration of the ends for which they are suited, as established by the Author of nature. An explanation as to why the eye has the mechanical structure it has must refer to the purpose for which it was created, namely, sight and, more generally, the convenience and well-being of the organism.

There are some things in nature so curiously contrived, and so exquisitely fitted for certain operations and uses, that it seems little less than blindness in him, that acknowledges, with the Cartesians, a most wise author of things, not to conclude . . . that they were designed for this use. . . . When, upon the anatomical dissection, and the optical consideration, of a human eye, we see it is as exquisitely fitted to be an organ of sight, as the best artificer in the world could have framed a little engine, purposely and mainly designed for the use of seeing; it is very harsh and incongruous to say, that an artificer, who is too intelligent either to do things by chance, or to make a curious piece of workmanship, without knowing what uses it is fit for, should not design it for a use, to which it is most fit.[78]

This regard to final causes is useful in the study not just of the parts of animals and plants, but even of the general design and structure of the visible universe – particularly the sun and other celestial bodies. A complete explanation will employ both mechanical reasons in a 'physical account of [the] making of those things', and teleological or functional considerations which are essential to 'explicate the fabric and operations' of the object, much as in an account of the workings of a clock it would be insufficient to employ only mechanical causes (the positions and motions of its parts) without referring to the use of the machine intended by its maker.[79]

Leibniz, too, emphasises the importance and 'utility' of final causes in the investigation of natural phenomena. A true understanding of 'the mechanical structure of bodies, the general economy of the world, and the constitution of the laws of nature' is to be sought not in chance or 'material necessity', but in the ends proposed by God, the intelligent author of all things, who, acting with infinite wisdom and perfection, always chooses the best and most perfect product.

It is unreasonable to introduce a sovereign intelligence as the orderer of all things, and then, instead of making use of his wisdom, to employ only the properties of matter in explaining phenomena. This is as if an historian should try to explain the conquest of some important place by a great prince, by saying that it occurred because the small particles of gunpowder, set free by the contact of a spark, escaped with a velocity capable of pushing a hard and heavy body against the walls of the place, while the little particles which composed the bronze of the cannon were so firmly interlaced that this velocity did not force them apart; instead of showing how the foresight of the conqueror led him to choose suitable time and means, and how his power overcame all obstacles.[80]

Certainly, the material principles of any event are important, and essential to a scientific explanation of the phenomenon. And if one is seeking only 'the immediate and particular efficient causes' of natural things, there is no need to consider final causes at all. Thus, one can understand the workings of the human body in purely mechanical terms and through the material causes of its various properties and capacities. Although in the context of such a limited project any phenomenon can be explained by mechanical causes alone, ultimately the fabric and operation of these causes, particularly the laws governing them, are to be 'derived from higher reasons'.[81]

The operation of a body cannot be understood adequately unless we know what its parts contribute; hence we cannot hope for the explanation of any corporeal phenomenon without taking up the arrangement of its parts. But from this it does not at all follow that nothing can be understood as true in bodies save what happens materially and mechanically.[82]

In addition to the mechanical relations of parts among themselves and to the whole, one must also take into account (albeit at a level of explanation higher than that of physics) the 'metaphysical considerations' which provide the foundation for the laws of nature. God decreed the laws governing mechanical operations (by actualising one world over all other possible worlds) on the basis of their simplicity and fecundity and their contribution (along with the richness of their effects) to the overall optimality of the universe. 'Those who are wise know that every effect has a final cause as well as an efficient cause [and that mechanical] laws themselves are finally resolved into metaphysical reasons and these metaphysical reasons arise from the divine will or wisdom.'[83]

IX. PROBLEMS IN MECHANISTIC EXPLANATION

Even before Leibniz and Newton forced a reconsideration of its fundamental ontology and explanatory schema, the mechanical philosophy was plagued by apparent deficiencies and faced opposition on both philosophical and scientific (and even theological) grounds. One critical issue concerns the limits of mechanical explanation and the identification of those phenomena which cannot be explained mechanically. Descartes, in his claim that 'there is no phenomenon of nature' which he has failed to explicate in accordance with his principles, includes not just the properties and operations of physical bodies among themselves, but also their effects in the human mind – in particular, sensations.

> The nature of our mind is such that the mere occurrence of certain motions in the body can stimulate it to have all manner of thoughts which have no likeness to the movements in question. . . . The sensation of pain is excited in us merely by the local motion of some parts of our body in contact with another body; so we may conclude that the nature of our mind is such that it can be subject to all the other sensations merely as a result of other local motions.[84]

There is a problem, however, in any attempt at a mechanical causal explanation of mental events. As explained earlier, any such explanation must be framed entirely in terms of matter and motion, with local contact serving as the *sine qua non* of interaction. Since the mind is immaterial and unextended, it cannot come into local contact with an extended material body. This would seem to rule out any kind of causal interaction of a *mechanical* nature between mind and body (although it does not necessarily rule out interaction of some other variety). Princess Elisabeth of Bohemia recognised this *a priori* limit to mechanical explanation when she asked Descartes to clarify how the soul and body can affect each other, since contact (*l'attouchement*) and extension are excluded from the Cartesian notion of an immaterial thinking substance.[85]

Gassendi insists that if Descartes's explanations of mental phenomena in terms of their material causes are to be complete and satisfactory, he must show 'how contact can occur without a body'.[86] He thus questions the legitimacy of extending mechanistic explanation beyond the physical realm and into the arena of interaction between an incorporeal soul and a material body. Moreover, even bracketing this *general* question of causal interaction, since there are no discoverable similarities whatsoever between any particular corporeal motions and the sensations which they produce (a clear example here is the motion of a feather and the feeling of a tickle), no necessary connexions can be found between the former and the latter. How, then, can a clear and intelligible explanation be made in mechanical terms as to why this particular structure and motion is followed by this particular feeling and not some other? Simply discovering the corporeal modifications which invariably precede the sensation does not causally explain why on this occasion we should feel this sensation rather than another.[87] Clearly, Gassendi and others felt, here is a domain in which mechanistic explanation breaks down, in spite of Descartes's attempts to explain everything (motivated, perhaps, by his desire to replace the Peripatetic philosophy as a complete and comprehensive system).

When faced with this apparently unbridgeable gap between mental *explanandum* and mechanistic *explanans,* Descartes had recourse to 'nature' or 'God', and thus left himself open to precisely the same charges of triviality and question-begging which he leveled against Scholastic explanations.[88] A certain material texture causes one to feel pleasure when touching it because the motions it communicates through the body to the brain (the 'seat of the soul') are such that they are determined 'by nature' to give rise to such and such a feeling in the mind. A body appears red to us because its corpuscular structure is such that it causes motions in the particles of the medium which, when they strike the retinal nerve and pass to the brain, naturally (i.e., as instituted by God) occasion the perception of red. There is still room here for specifying elaborate corpuscular structures and presenting detailed mechanical operations. But, in the end, an explanatory lacuna remains, to be filled in non-mechanistically.

I maintain that when God unites a rational soul to this machine [the human body], he will place its principal seat in the brain, and will make its nature such that the soul will have different sensations corresponding to the different ways in which the entrances to the pores in the internal surface of the brain are opened by means of the nerves. Suppose, firstly, that the tiny fibers which make up the marrow of the nerves are pulled with such force that they are broken and separated from the part of the body to which they are joined, with the result that the structure of the whole machine becomes somehow less perfect. Being pulled in this way, the fibers cause a movement in the brain which gives occasion for the soul . . . to have the sensation of pain.[89]

Fibers so moved 'cause' pain because that is their nature, as established by God. Explanations of this sort clearly lack the kind of perspicuity and intelligibility demanded by proponents of the mechanical philosophy, and recall the Scholastic 'dormitive virtue' type of explanation satirised by Molière.

A second line of criticism came from those who felt that mechanistic principles fail to explain even those natural phenomena that involve bodies alone. Henry More, for example, was sceptical about the success and comprehensiveness of mechanistic explanation boasted of by Descartes. For More, the limits of mechanicism are particularly represented by a whole class of physical phenomena which appear to be inexplicable in terms of the 'mere Mechanical powers of matter and motion'. What is needed in such cases is some immanent, active 'immaterial principle' to guide and check the motion of matter. This principle, which More calls the 'Spirit of Nature', is defined as 'a substance incorporeal, but without Sense and Animadversion, pervading the whole Matter of the Universe, and exercising a Plastical power therein according to the sundry predispositions and occasions in the parts it works upon, raising such Phaenomena in the world, by directing the parts of the Matter and their Motion, as cannot be resolved into mere Mechanical powers'.[90] Indeed, were the principles of the mechanical philosophy (devoid as they are of any such incorporeal agent) true, the phenomena would be different from what they are, and bodies would behave in ways entirely contrary to experience. For example, More agrees with Descartes that the 'immediate corporeal cause' of the descent of heavy bodies is the action of the 'Aethereal matter'. But he argues that 'there must be some immaterial cause . . . that must direct the motions of the Aetherean particles to act upon these grosser Bodies to drive them towards the Earth.' Otherwise, the extreme agitation of the particles of this matter, which takes them in every which direction, would keep a body suspended in equilibrium by colliding with it on every side.[91] Similarly, while Descartes has explained 'with admirable artifice' the immediate material causes of the attractive powers of the lodestone by means of his particles and pores, 'the efformation of the particles is above the reach of the mere Mechanical powers in Matter, as also the exquisite direction of their motion.'[92] More's 'immaterial cause' clearly does not operate in a mechanical fashion (that is, by impact). Rather, it is needed to supplement the mechanistic elements in the account, which otherwise would have serious explanatory lacunae, no matter how much we knew of the mechanisms underlying the phenomenon in question.

Leibniz, too, felt that some kind of 'active immaterial principle' was needed to supplement the Cartesian ontology underlying mechanistic explanation. He rejected, however, More's contention that mechanism alone was unable to account for the phenomena (at least at the level of physics) and ridiculed More's use of an 'Archaeus (unintelligible to me) or hylarchic principle. . . . All corporeal phenomena are indeed to be explained by mechanical efficient causes.'[93] Leibniz saw his contribution to the mechanical philosophy as consisting in providing a metaphysical framework for its explanations; in particular, in discovering some metaphysical principle to ground the laws governing mechanical operations. 'The particular events of nature I confess can be explained mechanically, but only after having recognised or presupposed the principles of mechanics. These can be established *a priori* only through metaphysical speculation.'[94]

If, as Descartes asserted, bodies consisted in extension alone, then the laws of nature and the phenomena, Leibniz argues, would be entirely different from what they in fact are.

If there were nothing in bodies but extended mass and nothing in motion but change of place and if everything should and could be deduced solely from these definitions by geometrical necessity, it would follow . . . that upon contact, the smallest body would impart its own speed to the largest body without losing any of this speed; and we would have to accept a number of such rules which are completely contrary to the formation of a system.[95]

Leibniz's conclusion is that there must be something more to bodies than mere extension, some 'vital principle superior to material notions'[96] to explain why bodies behave as they do and provide some real basis in bodies for the dynamical properties they have (e.g., to distinguish a moving body from a body at rest). This quality immanent in bodies is called 'force' by Leibniz, and is irreducible to properties of extension.

This force is something different from size, shape, and motion, and one can therefore judge that not everything conceived in body consists solely in extension and in its modifications, as our moderns have persuaded themselves. Thus, we are once again obliged to reestablish some beings or forces which they have banished. And it becomes more and more apparent that, although all the particular phenomena of nature can be explained mathematically or mechanically by those who understand them, nevertheless the general principles of corporeal nature and of mechanics itself are more metaphysical than geometrical, and belong to some indivisible forms or natures as the causes of appearances, rather than to corporeal mass or extension.[97]

This immaterial force or 'soul' which resides in bodies, since it is a purely metaphysical concept, plays no rôle in physics proper, and has no place in the mechanistic explanation of specific phenomena.[98] To be sure, the phenomena would not be what they are without it. The dynamical behaviour of bodies – inertia, impenetrability, elasticity, momentum – causally depends on force, and it is in this sense that force grounds the laws of nature. Primitive active force, for example, is the ultimate cause of a body's motion; hence, it serves as a metaphysical foundation in the phenomena for the laws of motion.[99] Nonetheless, 'whenever we deal with the immediate and specific efficient causes of natural things [as the physicist does], we should take no account of souls or entelechies.'[100]

   Leibniz sees his introduction of force into bodies as a kind of rehabilitation of the substantial forms of the Scholastics.

I perceived that the sole consideration of extended mass was not enough but that it was necessary, in addition, to use the concept of force, which is fully intelligible, although it falls within the sphere of metaphysics. . . . It was thus necessary to restore and, as it were, to rehabilitate the substantial forms which are in such disrepute today, but in a way which makes them intelligible and separates their proper use from their previous abuse.[101]

Although the belief in substantial forms or soul-like forces 'has some basis' and utility, 'if they are used appropriately and in their proper place', the Scholastics went too far and thought they could be used to account immediately for the properties of bodies and to explain particular phenomena.[102] As Leibniz insists in his critical remarks on More, mechanical explanation is not inconsistent with a belief in 'incorporeal beings' and, consequently, with final causes.[103] In fact, mechanism is misguided and metaphysically ungrounded without them.

Besides the kinds of problems in physics picked out by More and Leibniz, the mechanical philosophy faced rather critical difficulties in biology. For example, it was unclear how a mechanical explanation could be provided for the origin of life in conception. How could lifeless particles of matter in motion give rise to a living being such as an embryo? That there must be something more to a living creature besides being a mere material machine, however complex, is suggested by Bernard de Fontenelle: 'You say that animals are machines just as much as watches? However, if you put a dog-machine and bitch-machine beside each other, a third little machine may result. But two watches may be next to each other all their lives, without ever producing a third watch.'[104] Malebranche, a non-orthodox partisan of mechanism, acknowledges the difficulty:

We will never understand how laws of motion can construct bodies composed of an infinity of organs. We have enough trouble conceiving that these laws can little by little make them grow. . . . That [the union of two sexes] should be the cause of the organization of the parts of an animal . . . is certainly something we shall never understand. [Descartes's] unfinished work can help us understand how the laws of motion suffice to make the parts of an animal grow little by little. But that these laws can form them and bind them all together is what no one will ever prove.[105]

He offers, instead, a theory of preformation, whereby living creatures (plants, animals, humans) preexist in a miniature form in seeds and were all produced by God at creation.[106]

X. OCCASIONAL CAUSATION

Recent studies make it clear that, contrary to the traditional textbook mythology,[107] seventeenth-century occasionalism was not formulated as an *ad hoc* solution to a mind–body problem peculiarly faced by Cartesian dualism. In fact, the textual evidence reveals that the major occasionalists of the period – Malebranche, Cordemoy, Geulincx, and de la Forge – did not even think that there was some particular conceptual problematic about mind–body causal interaction that, because of a commitment to dualism, was different in nature from some other problematic about body–body interaction.[108] Occasionalism was a full-bodied theory of causal relations generally, physical as well as psycho-physical, and was intended in part to provide a metaphysical foundation for explanations in Cartesian mechanistic natural philosophy.

Occasionalists subscribed to the Cartesian version of the dualistic ontology which grounds the mechanistic account of the physical world. Matter consists in pure extension, and bodies are devoid of any admixture of spiritual or immaterial elements (such as the substantial forms of the Scholastics). However, on just this basis, they found the notion of mechanical, transient causation incoherent. Material substances cannot be genuine causes. Cartesian bodies (parcels of extension) are inert, passive, and inactive entities, and therefore could not be the source of either their own motions or the motions of other bodies. What the occasionalists sought, then, was a metaphysical framework in which mechanical explanation could be saved by being ultimately grounded in something higher than mere extension: a framework in which motion is given a true causal foundation in an active power or force, which in turn is identified with the will of God. They thus insisted that any complete explanation of a natural phenomenon must refer not just to its material antecedent conditions (matter and motion), but, more importantly, to the only being which can truly be called a 'cause' – God.

For Malebranche, if one thing, *x,* is to count as the cause of another thing, *y,* there must be a necessary connexion between the existence of *x* and the existence of *y* (where '*x*' and '*y*' can stand for substances, states of substances, or relations). 'A true cause as I understand it is one such that the mind perceives a necessary connection [*liaison nécessaire*] between it and its effects.'[109] On the basis of this criterion (where the kind of necessity required is apparently logical), Malebranche argues that a physical body *cannot* be the true efficient cause of some other physical event. For, he insists, there is never any necessary connexion between one physical event or state of affairs and another, such that it would be a contradiction to deny that the one follows the other. The relevant necessity is found only between the will of an omnipotent and infinitely perfect being and its effects – such is the nature of omnipotence. Thus, it is 'inconceivable' that the motion of a body could be the real cause of the motion of another body.[110]

Moreover, it is clear, Malebranche insists, that no body has the power to move itself;[111] and since it cannot set itself in motion, it cannot *keep* itself in motion (since the same action is responsible for both). Thus, a body does not have in itself any moving force. Furthermore, a body could not move another body without communicating moving force to it; but how could it communicate something which it does not have?

In another argument to the same effect, Malebranche insists that if one attends to the clear and distinct conception of body, one finds that no body, large or small, could have any efficacy or power (*puissance*) to move either itself or another body. The concept of body just is the idea of pure extension and represents it as having only one property: the entirely passive faculty of receiving various figures and movements. It certainly does not represent body as having any active power, whereby it can initiate change and be the efficient cause of any effects. In fact, such a power or force is perceived to be *incompatible* with the notion of pure extension, since it cannot be reduced to or explained in terms of shape, divisibility, and relations of distance, the only modifications of which extension is capable.[112]

Finally, according to Cartesian metaphysics (which Malebranche accepts with slight deviations) the moving force of a body would be simply a modification belonging to it, and modifications cannot be transferred or communicated from one substance to another: 'If moving force belonged to bodies, it would be a mode of their substance, and it is a contradiction that modes go from substance to substance.'[113] Thus, if for one body to cause motion in another were to mean that the former communicates its moving force to the latter (and Descartes, as Malebranche reads him, occasionally suggests as much),[114] then clearly no body can be the cause of another body's motion. On the other hand, if a body were to cause motion in a second body not by communicating its own moving force, but by creating it in the second body *ex nihilo,* this would be to admit in bodies a power to create, which is likewise inconsistent with our clear and distinct idea of extension.

Gérauld de Cordemoy's main argument against any transient causation among bodies proceeds from the 'axiom' that nothing has 'from itself [*de soi*]' that which it might lose while remaining what it is. Thus, since any body can lose its movement without thereby ceasing to be a body (the essence of body consisting in extension alone), no body is the source of its own movement. Nor, then, is any body the first cause of the motion of bodies generally, since such a first cause would have to have motion from itself. And because an action can only be continued by the agent which initiated it, since no body initially caused motion in bodies, bodies cannot be that which subsequently continue to move other bodies.[115]

The occasionalist conclusion drawn by Malebranche and Cordemoy is that an explanation of any natural effect which refers only to matter and motion – that is, which specifies only the shapes and sizes of material particles moving with given directions and velocities in accordance with certain laws – will ultimately fail to account fully for the phenomenon, since physical bodies have no causal efficacy. In fact, there is and can be only one true cause of any phenomenon, namely, the infinitely powerful will of God. God alone has a power to act, and there is a necessary connexion only between God's will and its effects. All events in the natural world, all motions, collisions, separations, changes, and other effects in bodies have God as their direct and immediate author. Thus, any metaphysically complete explanation of a phenomenon must refer at least to the divine volition which is its efficient cause (although, as we shall see, in physics one need not take explanation to this high a level).

The most powerful argument for this claim, employed by Malebranche and Louis de la Forge, appeals to God's rôle as creator and sustainer (i.e., re-creator) of the universe. The argument is intended to show that it is an 'absolute contradiction' that anything besides God should move a body. God's activity is required not only to create the world but also to maintain it in existence. To insist otherwise is to mistake the kind of dependence creatures have upon God. And from God's point of view, there is no essential difference between the divine activity as creator and the divine activity as sustainer. 'If the world subsists, it is because God continues to will that the world exist. On the part of God, the conservation of creatures is simply their continued creation.'[116] Now, when God conserves/re-creates a body, he must re-create it in some particular place and in some relation of distance to other bodies. If God conserves it in the same relative place from moment to moment, it remains at rest. If God conserves it successively in different places, it is in motion. As Malebranche puts it, the motion of a body is only its being transported by a divine act (or, more accurately, by a series of divine acts).[117] But this means that God is and can be the *only* cause of motion. The divine power is both necessary and sufficient to bring about the effect, and leaves no room or rôle for truly efficacious finite causes.

This is not to say that mechanical considerations have no rôle to play in explanation. When God acts on bodies, his activity is not arbitrary and *ad hoc*. Rather, in the ordinary (non-miraculous) course of nature God always acts in accordance with general physical laws. Such laws (framed as 'if *x,* then *y*' conditionals) specify how bodies in motion (given their various directions and velocities) behave upon impact with stationary or other moving bodies. Thus, when God moves a body which has collided with another (which collision is itself brought about by God), He is simply carrying out the dictates of some law. The collision of the two bodies (e.g., billiard balls) is the *occasional* cause, which determines the real cause (God) to move the struck body (the second ball) in such and such a way, as commanded by the law. Thus, a complete explanation will refer not just to the true efficient cause of the phenomenon (in all cases, God), but also to the motions, structures, and mechanical operations which occasion the operation of that cause, as well as to the law which links those material conditions with the effect wrought by God on that occasion.

In fact, Malebranche insists that in ordinary physical inquiry, all that is really sought are the mechanical secondary 'causes' which occasion the effect being investigated; and that scientific explanation need not go so far as to include the will of God.

> I grant that recourse to God as the universal cause should not be had when the explanation of particular effects is sought. For we would be ridiculous were we to say, for example, that it is God who dries the roads or who freezes the water of rivers. We should say that the air dries the earth because it stirs and raises with it the water that soaks the earth, and that the air or subtle matter freezes the river because in this season it ceases to communicate enough motion to the parts of which the water is composed to make it fluid.[118]

When offering an explanation of a specific phenomenon, it is true but vacuous to claim that its cause is the will of God – God is the cause of *every* phenomenon. Rather, one should specify just those occasional (secondary) causes whose structures and motions are to be nomologically conjoined with the *explanandum* as a mechanical operation. Thus, explanation takes place on two levels. At the level of physics proper, explanation employs 'the natural and particular cause of the effect in question',[119] and can proceed mechanistically: 'It could be said that this body is the physical or natural cause of the motion which it communicates, since it acts in accordance with natural laws.'[120] But one must remember that the behaviour of such secondary causes are but the expression of God's universal and lawlike causal activity. Thus, at a higher level of explanation, the phenomena and the laws of physics are given a metaphysical ground in God's efficacious will.

It should be noted that occasionalists saw themselves as simply drawing out consequences of Descartes's own theory of causation in the physical world. (In fact, Descartes was justifiably perceived by some of his occasionalist disciples as an occasionalist himself.)[121] Descartes's account of motion and mechanical causation clearly has a metaphysical dimension which, although it may not play a rôle in the explanation of particular phenomena (this will be purely mechanical), provides, like occasionalism, a grander schema within which the operation of finite causes is to be understood.

First, the argument from continuous creation employed by Malebranche and other occasionalists has its roots in Descartes's doctrine of divine sustenance. This doctrine asserts that God does not merely create a world which then has the power to exist on its own, independently of God. Rather, God is also the direct, efficient cause of the continued existence of the world, including bodies with all their modes. And God so sustains the world by means of a continuous action which is 'identical with the original act of creation', since ultimately the distinction between preservation and creation is 'only a conceptual one'.[122]

Second, Descartes's God is also 'the universal and primary cause . . . of all the motions in the world'.[123] It is God who is causally responsible for the ways bodies in motion characteristically behave. God moves bodies; and when they collide God modifies their motions in determinate ways, as described by the laws of nature. For example, God distributes motion among bodies such that its total quantity is preserved – hence, the conservation law. Without God imparting motion to bodies, they would remain at rest: 'If matter is left to itself and receives no impulse from anywhere it will remain entirely at rest. But it receives an impulse from God, who preserves the same amount of motion or translation in it as he placed in it at the beginning.'[124] (The actual distribution of motion at any one time, in so far as the natural scientist is concerned with it, is a function of the laws, 'the secondary and particular causes of the various motions we see in particular bodies'.)[125]

Descartes often speaks of bodies (and minds) as real causes of each others' modifications. Yet it is difficult to avoid the conclusion that, ultimately, with respect to body–body 'interaction', Descartes's position is an occasionalist one: God is the only genuine cause of the motion of inanimate bodies.[126]

Leibniz, like the occasionalists, denies that real body–body interaction is possible. The state of a physical substance cannot be the true cause of the state of another physical substance. But rather than causally attributing the changes in and operations of bodies directly to God, as occasionalists do,[127] Leibniz insists that each and every body is itself the source of its own sequence of modifications (although God *is* responsible for preserving substances by 'producing them continually by a kind of emanation').[128] Thus, as with respect to force, for Leibniz bodies are genuinely active individuals (here lies the source of his dispute with occasionalism);[129] but they are not genuinely *interactive*. Whatever state a body is in at any particular moment follows immediately and only from its own previous state, together with some immanent law of order or succession (which law 'constitutes the individuality of each particular substance').[130] 'In my opinion it is in the nature of created substance to change continually following a certain order which leads it spontaneously . . . through all the states it encounters.'[131]

These conclusions regarding causation are apparently entailed, for Leibniz, by metaphysical considerations regarding the nature of substance (as a being having a complete individual concept) and logical considerations regarding the nature of truth (in particular, the *inesse* principle).

Each substance is a world by itself, independent of anything else except God. . . . In a way, then, we might say, although it seems strange, that a particular substance never acts upon another particular substance, nor is it acted upon by it. That which happens to each one is only the consequence of its complete idea or concept, since this idea already involves all the predicates and expresses the whole world.[132]

In His infinite wisdom, God has so created and harmoniously coordinated substances that their sequences of states correspond to each other. Thus, there results a grand 'concomitance', the unitary system of the physical world in which the phenomena are in agreement. 'So there will be a perfect accord between all these substances which produces the same effect that would be noticed if they all communicated with each other.'[133] The motions and changes in bodies are reciprocal and have the appearance of being causally related. Effects can thus be explained in accordance with mechanical laws. This means that the project of explanation in physics proper remains unchanged, although the true metaphysical foundation for the behaviour of bodies and the character of the laws of nature is revealed.[134]

XI. NEWTON AND FORCES

Newton's philosophy of nature represented a fundamental revision of mechanism in at least two crucial respects. First, he was ultimately committed to the existence of forces in nature which, while they may play an essential rôle in the behaviour of material bodies, are not necessarily to be explained in mechanistic terms. Second, in contrast with the optimistic program of earlier mechanists, who saw their task as one of discovering the hidden mechanisms of observed phenomena, Newton insisted on abstaining from dealing with questions that did not appear to be tractable from observation and experiment and (at least in his remarks on method, if not in his actual practice) on a restraint from postulating 'hypothetical' entities and processes which were not derived immediately from phenomena.

In his early years, Newton was a mechanist, of the atomistic variety. His 'An Hypothesis Explaining the Properties of Light' (1675), for example, offered an explanation of various optical effects and other phenomena (including heaviness) by means of an extremely rarefied but material aether, composed of tiny particles and extended throughout all of space. By 1686, however, when he was composing the *Philosophiae Naturalis Principia Mathematica,* the mechanical operations of this aether with respect to heaviness are replaced by a force working at all levels of nature, from the most minute particles of bodies to the planets and other celestial bodies. Thus, in addition to their extension, hardness, impenetrability, and mobility, 'all bodies whatsoever are endowed with a principle of mutual gravitation'; all matter attracts all other matter with one universal force of attraction.[135] In the first Latin edition of the *Opticks* (1706), one sees the number and kinds of forces multiplied. They now include both gravity and 'some other attractive and repelling powers' (with some of the latter operating only at short range among minute particles) and are accompanied by the suggestion that such forces operate at a distance.

Have not the small particles of bodies certain powers, virtues, or forces by which they act at a distance, not only upon the rays of light for reflecting, refracting, and inflecting them, but also upon one another for producing a great part of the phenomena of nature? For it is well known that bodies act upon one another by the attractions of gravity, magnetism, and electricity; and that these instances show the tenor and course of nature, and make it not improbable but that there may be more attractive powers than these.[136]

The impression here is that these forces are *not* mechanically explicable. In fact, Newton is quite explicit in expressing his dissatisfaction with the two standard mechanistic explanations for the cohesion of bodies (namely, those offered by Democritean atomists and Descartes, respectively):

The parts of all homogeneal hard bodies which fully touch one another stick together very strongly. And for explaining how this may be, some have invented hooked atoms, which is begging the question; and others tell us that bodies are glued together by rest, that is, by an occult quality, or rather by nothing; and others that they stick together by conspiring motions, that is, by relative rest amongst themselves. I had rather infer from their cohesion that their particles attract one another by some force, which in immediate contact is exceedingly strong, at small distances performs the chemical operations above mentioned, and reaches not far from the particles with any sensible effect.[137]

Now Newton constantly insists that his goal is *not* to provide some 'physical' or metaphysical account of the operation of these forces, *not* to investigate the causes thereof and their manner of action, whether at a distance or by contact alone; but rather simply to discover their laws and properties and describe them in precise mathematical terms.[138] Nonetheless, the merest suggestion of action at a distance – that is, of an agent exerting causal power where it is not present, hence in some way other than by impact – was anathema to mechanists.

Newton, however, vehemently denies that his inclusion of forces among the principal concepts of physics involves action at a distance: 'That gravity should be innate, inherent, and essential to matter, so that one body may act upon another at a distance through a *vacuum*, without the mediation of anything else . . . is to me so great an absurdity that I believe no man who has in philosophical matters a competent faculty of thinking can ever fall into it.'[139]

In order to placate mechanist critics, who saw Newton as reviving occult powers and action at a distance (an impression fostered by the absence of any denial of action at a distance in the *Principia* itself),[140] he revived in the second English edition of the *Opticks* (1717) the mechanical explanation of gravity by means of the aether.[141] This failed to convince mechanists, however, since the particles of the aether appear to have their own repellent force which exerts itself at a distance.

On the whole, Newton's considered position – a kind of agnosticism – regarding the relationship between the forces he investigated and mechanism must be, to the mechanist's eye, somewhat troubling. He certainly does not intend to assert positively that gravity and other forces act at a distance and thus *cannot* be explained mechanistically.[142] But neither does he want to commit himself to the claim that their explanation, whatever it may turn out to be, *must* at least be a mechanical one. Rather, in the absence of sufficient empirical evidence one way or the other, he favours a suspension of judgement regarding the nature (mechanical or otherwise) of the underlying causes of these forces. Whether or not gravity, for example, has a mechanical explanation can only be discovered through experiment and observation. This is not a question that can be answered *a priori* (although this was the approach, Newton believes, taken by Descartes and others, who on metaphysical grounds insisted that the explanation of any physical phenomenon will be found solely in the motion and impact of minute particles of matter). And Newton just does not see that experiment and observation yet provide a certain answer to this second-order problem. Thus, he simply leaves it an open question as to what *kind* of thing the cause of gravity (and other forces) is. It may be something that operates mechanically; but, then again, it may not. 'Hitherto I have not been able to discover the cause of those properties of gravity from phenomena, and I frame no hypotheses; for whatever is not deduced from the phenomena is to be called a hypothesis, and hypotheses, whether metaphysical or physical, whether of occult qualities or mechanical, have no place in experimental philosophy.'[143] In Query 31 of the *Opticks,* he claims that 'what I call "attraction" may be performed by impulse, or by some other means unknown to me . . . perhaps electrical attraction may reach to such small distances even without being excited by friction.'[144] In a letter to Bentley, he concedes that 'gravity must be caused by an agent acting constantly according to certain laws, but whether this agent be material or immaterial I have left to consideration of my readers.'[145]

Thus, Newton, in his unwillingness to exclude the possibility that his forces have a non-mechanical explanation, has already violated the fundamental tenet of the orthodox mechanical philosophy. For any phenomenon, the mechanist claims, there will be a purely mechanical explanation, even though we may not as yet be able to discover what it is. Newton refuses to assert this dogmatically, and allows that for all we know there may be powers in nature not reducible to or explicable in terms of matter, motion, and impact. To be sure, it might be the case that all phenomena *can* be so explained; but there is no warrant for positing this until it is borne out by observation and experiment. In contrast with Descartes, Boyle, Leibniz, and others, Newton did not believe that mechanism was necessarily the only possible mode of explanation.[146]

This reluctance to engage in speculation regarding the underlying, imperceptible causes of gravity and other forces is a reflection of Newton's general methodological maxim, likewise a departure from the mechanical philosophy, that one ought not to pursue in physical theory questions which take one so far from the phenomena and what is certain.

The mechanists saw their task as inquiring (in a necessarily hypothetical manner) into the hidden mechanisms causally generating observed phenomena. For Newton, on the other hand, while the force of gravity was clearly a concept necessary for understanding the behaviour of physical bodies and was describable in mathematical terms, to postulate its origin or cause in some mechanical or other agent without directly 'deducing' the nature of this agent from the phenomena (the possibility of which, as we have just seen, Newton is sceptical about) would be to 'feign hypotheses'. Thus, gravity and other attractive forces, as far as Newton was concerned, are only 'general laws of nature . . . their truth appearing to us by phenomena, though their causes be not yet discovered'.[147] Similarly, in his *New Theory of Light and Colors* (1671–2), Newton was satisfied to establish the heterogeneity of white light, without offering any 'conjectures' about the ultimate nature of light.[148]

Rather than 'imagining' mechanical models to explain some effect, the scientist should concentrate on obtaining certainties directly from experimental results. 'Particular propositions' are to be 'inferred' from the phenomena (such conclusions are derived from the data in accordance with the four rules of reasoning presented in Book III of the *Principia*). These propositions are then 'rendered general' by induction and converted into laws.[149] An 'hypothesis', on the other hand, is a 'proposition as is not a phenomenon nor deduced from any phenomenon, but assumed or supposed – without any experimental proof',[150] and whose content so transcends experience that its truth cannot be demonstrated.[151] This was the status Newton accorded mechanism as a whole, since it was not clear to him that such a universal doctrine could be derived from the phenomena alone, independently of any *a priori* metaphysical commitments.[152] It also described, for

Newton, the multitude of particular hidden mechanisms put forth by Cartesians and others in their explanations. Thus, although the relationship between the degree of refrangibility of a light ray and colour is demonstrated from experiences, the claim that light is of a corpuscular nature belongs to the realm of hypotheses (at least until such a claim is itself deduced from and justified by some experiments).[153]

With Newton, then, both the fundamental (even *a priori*) assumption of the mechanical philosophy that *all* effects in nature will have some purely mechanistic explanation and the mechanists' methodological commitment to hypothetical reasoning are exchanged for ontologically opaque forces and the deduction of laws from phenomena. By the mid eighteenth century, both in England and on the continent, Newtonianism had fairly well eclipsed mechanism as the dominant model of explanation and scientific inquiry.[154]

NOTES

1 *Post. An.* I.13, 78a22.
2 *Post. An.* I.2, 71b9–11.
3 *Physics* II.3, 194b17–19. See Wallace 1972–4, pp. 1–7.
4 See Aristotle, *Metaphysics* VII and VIII; Saint Thomas, *De ente et essentia*, secs. 17–22.
5 Saint Thomas, *De ente et essentia*, secs. 17–18.
6 *Metaphysics* VII, 1029a23.
7 *Summa th.* I q77 a6. See also q76 a4.
8 See Ayers 1981a, pp. 250–3; Boas Hall 1952, pp. 414–17.
9 *Metaphysics* VII, 1041b8.
10 See Aristotle, *Physics* I.7; *De gen. et cor.* I. Saint Thomas, *Summa th.* I q76 a4.
11 *De gen. et cor.* II.
12 See Trentman 1982.
13 See Schmitt 1981, pp. 161–2.
14 *Collegium Conimbricense* 1602, Bk. I, chap. 9, qstn. ix. The Jesuits at the University of Coimbra (Portugal) published a number of commentaries on the Aristotelian texts in the late sixteenth and early seventeenth centuries. They were standard textbooks in Jesuit education at the time (Descartes studied from them at La Flèche).
15 'Talium accidentum originem ad formam substantialem, uti ad ipsorum fontem referendam esse', *Collegium Conimbricense* 1602 I.9.ix.
16 See Eustachius a Sancto Paulo, *Summa philosophica quadripartita* III, pt. 1, tract. ii, q. 4–6, Eustachius 1648, III, pp. 120–5.
17 See Boas Hall 1958, p.77.
18 *Collegium Conimbricense* 1602 I.9.x–xi.
19 *Collegium Conimbricense* 1602 I.7.xix; Suárez, *Disp. met.* XVI.1.3–4.
20 Boas Hall 1952, p. 415. See also Alexander 1985, pp. 40–1.
21 See Suárez, *Disp. met.* XVI.1.4.
22 See Eustachius, *Summa*, III, part 3 tract iii, qu. 6. Eustachius also suggests that colour might simply result from the four primary qualities being mixed and arranged in a

certain way. This hypothesis is also offered by the Coimbrian fathers, *Collegium Conimbricense* 1598 II.7.ii.

23 *Collegium Conimbricense* 1602 VIII.4.i.2: 'Gravia et levia, quoties naturalia loca petunt, moventur a generante ut a principe causa effectrice sui motus.'

24 *Collegium Conimbricense* 1602 VIII.4.i.3.

25 Madeira Arrais, *Novae philosophiae et medicinae de qualitatibus occultis* (1650), pp. 1–19. Arrais was trained at the University of Coimbra. See Heilbron 1982, pp. 16–17.

26 Act III, troisième intermède, lines 58–66: 'A quoi respondeo/Quia est in eo/virtus dormitiva/cujus est natura/sensus assoupire.'

27 *Princ.* IV 198.

28 *Princ.*, Preface to the French edition, AT IXB 8.

29 See *Le Monde,* AT XI 25–6.

30 *Of the Excellency and Grounds of the Corpuscular or Mechanical Hypothesis,* in Boyle 1979, p. 144; *The Origin of Forms and Qualities according to the Corpuscularian Philosophy,* in Boyle 1979, pp. 16–17, 67–8.

31 *Origin of Forms and Qualities,* Boyle 1979, p. 16. See Alexander 1985, chap. 2, for a discussion of Boyle's critique of the Peripatetic philosophy.

32 On Timpler, see Freedman 1982; Schmitt 1988, p. 803.

33 See Gabbey 1985, pp. 9–15; Dijksterhuis 1961, pp. 414–15; Boas Hall 1952. Descartes only includes impenetrability as an irreducible property of body when prodded by Henry More. He initially denies that impenetrability is an 'essential differentia' like extension in a letter to More, 5 February 1649 (AT V 269). But then see the letter to More of 15 April 1649 (AT V 341–2).

34 See McMullin 1978b.

35 See Gabbey 1985, p. 10.

36 *Entretiens sur les sciences* (1683), in Lamy 1966, p. 259. See Clarke 1989, chaps. 5 and 6.

37 *Origin of Forms and Qualities,* Boyle 1979, p. 18. See also Descartes, *Princ.* III 46: 'Constat omnium mundi corporum unam & eandem esse materiam.'

38 See *Origin of Forms and Qualities,* Boyle 1979, pp. 19–20.

39 *Entretiens sur les sciences,* Lamy 1966, pp. 256–8.

40 *La dioptrique,* Discours II.

41 *Princ.* IV 201; the bracketed clause was added in the French edition. It has been suggested that in their use of macroscopic models to explain microscopic structures, mechanists often ended up with accounts as circular as those of the Peripatetics – the mechanist is, ultimately, explaining the observable behaviour of a machine (any physical body) by means of some smaller machine (the microscopic mechanism) whose operation can only be understood in terms of the behaviour of a macro-level machine; see Gabbey 1990c.

42 *Princ.* IV 203.

43 *Princ.* IV 199.

44 *Princ.* I 28; bracketed clause added in French edition. There are good reasons, however, for questioning the 'purity' of Descartes's strictures against teleological considerations in physics. For example, one finds Descartes insisting to Clerselier that his seven rules of impact in the *Princ.* (II 46–52) all follow from the principle that when two bodies with 'incompatible modes' meet, the change in these modes (namely, the speed of the body or its directional determination, or both) will always be 'the least possible' that is necessary to make them compatible (Descartes to Clerselier, 17 February 1645, AT V 185). In the *Princ.* itself (II 48), considerations of parsimony appear in Descartes's argument for the third rule.

45 Although Descartes ultimately appears committed to an occasionalist picture of body–body 'interaction'; see the discussion in Section X.

46 See *Princ.* II 42: 'The motion [God] preserves is not something permanently fixed in given pieces of matter, but something which is mutually transferred [*transeuntem*] when collisions occur.'

47 See Descartes to More, August 1649, AT V 404–5.

48 *Princ.* IV 198.

49 *Princ.* III 46; *Le Monde,* chaps. 5 and 6.

50 *Princ.* II 23; see also IV 187.

51 *La description du corps humain* IV, AT XI 255–6; *La dioptrique,* Discourses I and V; *Les météores,* Discourse VIII. See Sabra 1981, chaps. 2 and 3.

52 *Princ.* IV 20–7. Earlier in life, Descartes had accepted the scholastic account of gravity, 'as if it were some sort of real quality, which inhered in solid bodies'; see Resp. VI, AT VII, 441–2.

53 *Princ.* IV 133–83.

54 See, e.g., *Disc.* VI, AT VI 64–5.

55 Régis 1691a, vol. 1, p. 274. See also Rohault, *Traité de physique,* Part II, chap. 1, in Rohault 1723, vol. 2, p. 4.

56 See Hacking 1975a; Clarke 1989.

57 *Traité de physique* I.3, Rohault 1723, vol. 1, p. 14. I am indebted to Clarke (1989) in my discussion here.

58 Régis 1691a, vol. 1, p. 275.

59 *Traité de physique* I.14. Rohault is here repeating what Descartes has to say about the certainty of his conclusions, in an almost identical passage, in *Princ.* IV 205.

60 Régis 1691a, vol. 1, pp. 275–8. See Clarke 1989, pp. 212–17; and Watson 1964. For more on this issue, see Mouy 1934, chaps. 4 and 6.

61 See *Princ.* IV 205–6.

62 Clarke 1989, chap. 7. This suggestion seems to have particular credibility with respect to Régis, who stresses the distinction between his system of *vrayes hypotheses,* on the one hand, and *les hypotheses arbitraires,* on the other; see Régis 1691a, vol. 1, pp. 276–8.

63 *Excellency of the Mechanical Hypothesis,* Boyle 1979, p. 140.

64 *Excellency of the Mechanical Hypothesis,* Boyle 1979, pp. 140–1.

65 *Origin of Forms and Qualities,* Boyle 1979, p. 67.

66 *Excellency of the Mechanical Hypothesis,* Boyle 1979, p. 145. See also *The Sceptical Chymist,* in Boyle 1772, vol. 1, p. 557.

67 See also the *Notes on a Good and an Excellent Hypothesis,* in Boyle 1979, p. 119.

68 *Origin of Forms and Qualities,* Boyle 1979, pp. 36–7.

69 *Origin of Forms and Qualities,* Boyle 1979, p. 71.

70 *Origin of Forms and Qualities,* Boyle 1979, p. 19.

71 See Aristotle, *Physics* II.3, 194b16–35; *Metaphysics* V.2, 1013a25–35. The contrast here, of course, is with the ancient atomism of Leucippus and Democritus, wherein nature operates by a kind of blind necessity.

72 *Physics* II.8. Saint Thomas gives priority to final causes and accords them greater explanatory power than the other three species of causation which, in various ways, are subordinate to it. See *De principiis naturae,* IV.25; *Commentarium in Aristotelis Posteriorum Analyticorum,* I.16. Also Serene 1982, pp. 506–7; Wallace 1972–4, pp. 73–80.

73 But see note 44.

74 *Eth.* I, props. 28–33.

75 *Eth.* I, Appendix.
76 Here Spinoza departs from Descartes, who at least is willing to recognise that God does act with certain ends in mind, even if the knowledge of these ends is beyond our finite understanding.
77 *Eth.* I, Appendix.
78 'A Disquisition about the Final Causes of Natural Things' (1688), in Boyle 1744, vol. 4, p. 579.
79 'A Disquisition about the Final Causes of Natural Things', Boyle 1744, vol. 4, p. 520.
80 *Disc. mét.* (1686), sec. 19. See also sec. 20.
81 See *Spec. dyn.* (1695), pt. I.
82 'On the Elements of Natural Science' (1682–4), in Leibniz 1969, p. 289. (The Latin original is not currently available.)
83 'On the Elements of Natural Science', p. 288. There is a second sense in which metaphysical considerations ground the laws of nature, as I discuss later in the chapter with respect to Leibniz's conception of 'force'.
84 *Princ.* IV 197.
85 Elisabeth to Descartes, 16 May 1643 (AT III 661). In response to Elisabeth, Descartes insists that the principles of explanation and understanding that are proper to the material realm – namely, the principles of mechanicism – should not be used to try to explicate operations in the realm of mind–body interaction; see Descartes to Elisabeth, 21 May 1643, AT III 665–6. Why, then, in the *Princ.* does he include sensation among those phenomena which can be explained 'by the laws of mechanics alone'?
86 Obj. V, AT VII 344.
87 See Dijksterhuis 1961, pp. 426–7. But see Gabbey 1985, pp. 15–17, for a partial defence of the Cartesian mechanical account of sensation.
88 See Fromondus (Froidment) to Plempius (Plemp), for Descartes, 13 September 1637 (AT I 408).
89 *L'homme,* AT XI 143–4.
90 *The Immortality of the Soul* (1662), More 1980, Bk. III, chap. 12, sec. i. Later, More takes a more extreme position and insists, 'I am abundantly assured that there is no purely Mechanicall Phaenomenon in the whole Universe.' See *Divine Dialogues* (1668), 'The Publisher to the Reader'. Also Henry 1986b, p. 356.
91 *The Immortality of the Soul,* More 1980 III.13.i.
92 *The Immortality of the Soul,* More 1980 III.12.vi. For a discussion of More's critique of mechanism, see Gabbey 1990b.
93 *Spec. dyn.,* Ger. Math. VI 242.
94 Leibniz to Arnauld, 30 April 1687 (Ger. II 98).
95 *Disc. mét.,* sec. 21.
96 *Spec. dyn.,* Ger. Math. VI 242.
97 *Disc. mét.,* sec. 18.
98 *Disc. mét.,* sec. 10; 'On the Elements of Natural Science', in Leibniz 1969, p. 289.
99 For a discussion of Leibniz's concept of force, and its rôle in his dynamics, see Garber 1985.
100 *Spec. dyn.,* Ger. Math. VI 242.
101 *Syst. nouv.,* Ger. IV 478–9.
102 *Disc. mét.,* secs. 10–11.
103 *Spec. dyn.,* Ger. Math. VI 242.
104 See Letter XI in Fontenelle 1825, vol. 1, p. 323.

105 *Entretiens sur la métaphysique,* Dialogue XI, sec. 8.
106 See *Rech.,* I.6. Also Clarke 1989, pp. 179–82.
107 See Copleston 1958, vol. 4, pp. 176–8. For a corrective view, see Lennon 1974a; Loeb 1981.
108 See Nadler forthcoming.
109 *Rech.,* VI.2.3.
110 *Rech.,* VI.2.3.
111 *Rech.,* VI.2.3.
112 *Entretiens sur la métaphysique* VII.1–2; *Rech.,* Eclaircissement 15.
113 *Réponse à une Dissertation de Mr. Arnauld contre un Eclaircissement du Traité de la Nature et de la Grace* (1685), VII.6, in Mal. *OC* VII 515–16.
114 See note 46.
115 *Le discernement du corps et de l'âme* (1666; in later editions, *Six Discours sur La Distinction & l'Union du Corps & de l'Ame*), Discours IV. For discussions of Cordemoy's occasionalism, see Balz 1951; Battail 1973.
116 Malebranche, *Ent. mét.* VII.7.
117 *Ent. mét.* VII.11. See also de la Forge, *Traité de l'esprit de l'homme* (1666), chap. 16. For a discussion of de la Forge and occasionalism, see Clair 1976.
118 *Rech.,* Eclaircissement 15, in Mal. *OC* III 213.
119 Eclaircissement 15, Mal. *OC* III 213.
120 *Méditations Chrétiennes,* in Mal. *OC* X 54. See also Cordemoy, *Le discernement du corps et de l'âme,* Discours IV: 'When it is claimed that bodies move bodies, it ought to be understood as meaning that . . . their impact is an occasion for the mind which moved the first to move the second. But, since we are not always concerned with this first cause of motion . . . we are satisfied, when we want to say why a certain body which was at rest began to move, to explain how it was impacted upon by another body, which was moving; thus citing the occasion as the cause' (Cordemoy 1968, p. 139). See Clarke 1989, p. 116.
121 See *Traité de l'esprit de l'homme,* chap. 16, in de la Forge 1974, p. 242ff. For a study of the ways in which later occasionalists drew their doctrine(s) out of Descartes, see Prost 1907.
122 See *Princ.* I 21, II 39, 42; *Med.* III; *Le Monde,* AT XI 44–6; *Resp.* V, AT VII 369.
123 *Princ.* II 36. In the *Princ.,* Descartes argues as though this aspect of God's rôle in the physical world is entailed by the doctrine of divine sustenance. Garber (1987a) argues that these two activities should be distinguished.
124 Descartes to More, August 1649, AT V 404.
125 *Princ.* II 37.
126 See Garber 1987a.
127 Leibniz felt that occasionalism called for a 'perpetual supervisor', and accused Malebranche of introducing 'continuous miracles' into the course of nature; see *Syst. nouv.,* secs. 12–13 (Ger. IV 483–4).
128 *Disc. mét.,* sec. 14.
129 See *De ipsa natura,* sec. 9.
130 See 'Eclaircissement des difficultés. . .', Ger. IV 518.
131 'Eclaircissement des difficultés. . .', Ger. IV 518. See also *Spec. dyn.:* 'Every passion of a body is spontaneous or arises from an internal force, though upon an external occasion' (Ger. Math. VI 251).
132 *Disc. mét.,* sec. 14.
133 *Syst. nouv.,* Ger. IV 484.

134 'However metaphysical these considerations may seem, they are also of remarkable service to physics in establishing the laws of motion' (*Syst. nouv., Ger. IV 486).

135 *Philosophiae Naturalis Principia Mathematica* (henceforth abbreviated to *Principia*), Bk. III, Rule 3, Newton 1972, vol. 2, p. 554 (Newton 1934, p. 399). Newton insists, however, that gravity is not an essential property of bodies, as the other properties are; see his letter to Richard Bentley, 17 January 1692/3, Newton 1779–85, vol. 4, p. 437.

136 *Opticks,* Query 31 (Newton 1952, p. 375).

137 *Opticks,* Query 31 (Newton 1952, p. 388–9).

138 *Opticks,* Query 31 (Newton 1952, p. 376); *Principia,* Bk. III, General Scholium (Newton 1934, p. 547).

139 Letter to Bentley, 25 February 1692/3, Newton 1779–85, vol. 4, p. 438.

140 See Koyré 1968a, Appendix B.

141 See *Opticks,* Queries 18–22; also, an earlier letter to Boyle, 28 February 1678/9, Newton 1779–85, vol. 4, pp. 385–94.

142 In the General Scholium in Part III of the *Principia,* he at least appears to exclude a mechanistic explanation of gravity when he asserts that the 'cause' of the power of gravity 'operates not according to the quantity of the surfaces of the particles upon which it acts (as mechanical causes do), but according to the quantity of solid matter which they contain.' See Newton 1972, vol. 2, p. 764 (Newton 1934, p. 546).

143 *Principia,* Bk. III, General Scholium, Newton 1972, vol. 2, p. 764 (Newton 1934, p. 547).

144 Newton 1952, p. 376.

145 25 February 1692/3, Newton 1779–85, vol. 4, p. 438.

146 See Larmore 1987b.

147 *Opticks,* Query 31 (Newton 1952, p. 401).

148 'But to determine more absolutely what light is, after what manner refracted, and by what modes or actions it produces in our minds the phantasms of colors, is not so easy. And I shall not mingle conjectures with certainties' (Newton 1779–85, vol. 4, p. 305). The mechanist Huygens insists that Newton's account of colours is incomplete without an explanation of the ultimate (i.e., mechanical) nature of light: 'I have seen how M. Newton attempts to defend his new opinion concerning colours. It seems to me that the most important objection one could make against him, in the form of a Quaere, is whether there may be more than two sorts of color. As for me, I think that an hypothesis that should explain mechanically and by the nature of motion the colors yellow and blue, would be sufficient for all the rest. . . . Neither do I see why M. Newton is not content with the two colors, yellow and blue, for it will be much easier to find an hypothesis by motion, which will explicate these two differences, than for so many diversities as there are of other colors. And until he has found this hypothesis, he has not taught us what the nature and difference of colors consists in' (letter to Oldenberg, 14 January 1673, in Huygens 1888–1950, vol. 7, pp. 242–3). See also his letter to Leibniz, 29 May 1694, vol. 10, p. 612.

149 *Principia,* Bk. III, General Scholium, Newton 1972, vol. 2, p. 764 (Newton 1934, p. 547). In a letter to Cotes (March 1713), Newton states that the laws of nature are '[principles] deduced from phenomena and made general by induction, which is the highest evidence that a proposition can have in this philosophy' (Newton 1959–77, vol. 5, p. 397).

150 Letter to Cotes, March 1713 (Newton 1959–77, vol. 5, p. 397).

151 See Koyré 1968a, chap. 2, for a discussion of Newton on hypotheses.

152 See Larmore 1987b.

153 Newton's reserve on these matters may have been influenced by Locke's agnosticism regarding unobservable causes and our knowledge of real essences. See *Ess.* IV.iii. For a study of Locke's influence on Newton, see Rogers 1978.

154 For studies of Newton's influence in France, see Brunet 1931; Cohen 1964b; and Hall 1975a.

18

NEW DOCTRINES OF BODY AND ITS POWERS, PLACE, AND SPACE

DANIEL GARBER, JOHN HENRY, LYNN JOY, AND ALAN GABBEY

Philosophy at the beginning of the seventeenth century was in many ways continuous with the philosophy of the sixteenth century. Aristotle and Aristotelianism continued to be taught in the schools, and thrived there. Furthermore, Renaissance naturalism, Neoplatonic thought, and the occult tradition continued to exert influence (see Chapters 15 and 16). However, quite striking in the late years of the sixteenth century and the first years of the seventeenth is a new interest in another non-Aristotelian tradition, that of atomism, and, more generally, in what were later to be called mechanist views of the world. Mechanists tended to see the world as a great machine, on an analogy with a clock, for example, and tried to explain the manifest properties of things in terms of the size, shape, and motion of the insensible particles that were taken to compose them.[1] With those new natural philosophies came new conceptions of body and the contents of the physical world. Although the so-called new philosophers agreed that the form and matter of their teachers must go, they disagreed about what these were to be replaced by, what the physical world was to contain, what the nature of body was, whether bodies were active or passive, the nature of the place or space in which they are found, among many other questions. The views of the new philosophers can best be understood by examining first their view of the physical world in the early part of the century; second the view of the physical world held by three of the important mechanist system-builders in mid-century, Gassendi, Descartes, and Hobbes; and third later views on body and the physical world, including reactions to earlier mechanist conceptions of body, and attempts to escape the bounds of the new mechanist orthodoxy.

John Henry is mostly responsible for the sections on British philosophers; Lynn Joy is mostly responsible for the sections on Continental atomists; Daniel Garber is mostly responsible for the sections on Spinoza and Leibniz, and with the collaboration of Alan Gabbey, the section on Descartes. Garber is responsible for editing the chapter as a whole.

I. ATOMISTS AND OTHERS:
EARLY SEVENTEENTH-CENTURY CONCEPTIONS OF BODY

The late Renaissance advocates of atomism who challenged the hegemony of Aristotle's metaphysics and physics constituted a remarkably heterogeneous group. Their rôles as opponents or, in some cases, reinterpreters of Aristotle are apt to be misread as the activities of a coherent atomist movement. Late Renaissance atomist thinkers drew on a wide variety of intellectual sources. However, these thinkers by no means constituted a single philosophical movement, nor were their criticisms of the dominant Aristotelian tradition in philosophy organised in such a way as to provide a unified alternative.[2]

1. Aristotelian atomism: Sennert and others

One important type of atomist speculation emerged from efforts to revise the interpretation of Aristotle. Late Renaissance philosophers who developed compromises between Aristotelianism and a limited notion of atoms found precedents for such compromises in the interpretative disputes that had focused on certain problematic passages in the *Physica* and *De generatione et corruptione*. One key passage was that in which Aristotle appeared to be acknowledging the existence of physical *minima,* that is, the smallest units of a substance such as flesh, from which it was impossible to extract any further units of that substance.[3] Flesh, the passage seemed to imply, was a substance whose form could instantiate itself in matter only if the resulting piece of flesh were of a requisite size. Such a thesis, if Aristotle had in fact maintained it, would have contradicted his well-established principles (1) that all continuous magnitudes are, at least potentially, infinitely divisible, and (2) that generation and corruption do not occur through the association and dissociation of indivisibles. The thesis further offered an opportunity for reinterpreting Aristotle's views about substantial forms in a way that would affirm that there are minimal parts of forms. This could then be used to revise greatly the Aristotelians' accounts of the intension and remission of forms.

Possibilities such as these were noted by some Aristotelians affiliated with the University of Padua. Marcantonio Zimara (c. 1475–1532), for example, remarked in his *Solutiones contradictionum in dictis Aristotelis, et Averrois super libros physicorum* (Venice, 1562) that considerable attention was being given by his fellow Aristotelians to Averroes's reading of the passage in the *Physica* (187b 25–188a1) concerning the division of a substance.[4] Disagreements had arisen among Zimara's contemporaries as to whether Averroes had inferred from the passage that there must be *minima,* parts of the forms of the four elements, and whether Averroes had held that Aristotle would have allowed both the generation and alteration of the elements to occur through the action of minimal parts.[5]

Although Zimara worried about the provenance of this concept of *minima naturalia* in Averroes's commentaries, later Aristotelians like Daniel Sennert had fewer qualms about attributing the concept to Aristotle himself. In such works as *De chymicorum cum Aristotelicis et Galenicis consensu ac dissensu liber I* (Wittenberg, 1619) and *Hypomnemata physica* (Frankfurt, 1636), Sennert, a professor of medicine at Wittenberg, attempted to unite in a single corpuscular philosophy the principles of Aristotle, Galen, and Paracelsus.[6] Hence not only did he ally himself with the subgroup of Aristotelians who had accommodated themselves to limited corpuscular notions, but he also independently developed a controversial interpretation of Galen to suit his project. Galen had strongly opposed Democritus's and Epicurus's accounts of the composition of various organs of the human body from small, unalterable corpuscles and their consequent explanations of the generation and destruction of substances in terms of the association and dissociation of these corpuscles.[7] Sennert nonetheless attributed to Galen a corpuscular theory of the elements, defending this novel reading of his texts because he believed it would enable him to reconcile Aristotelian physics, Galenic medicine, and Paracelsian chemistry. He saw no obstacle to asserting that the four elements of both Aristotle and Galen are analysable into minimal particles, from which can be composed various mixtures which then become new substances.[8] Sennert held that the forms of the elements within the minimal particles remain intact and persist in the mixtures, but he also specified that a separate, supervening form is present in each new substance. This supervening form organises and dominates the aggregation of particles to which it belongs, and its reception by the mixture is prepared for by a mutual interaction among the minimal particles when they combine.

Because of this last issue, Sennert drew a sharp distinction between his own definition of *minima naturalia* and those offered by other Aristotelians. Thus he criticised Jacopo Zabarella (1533–89), professor of philosophy at Padua, who had not shared his conviction that the mixture assumes a new form distinct from the forms of the minimal particles themselves. Moreover, Sennert voiced the same objection against contemporary anti-Aristotelians, especially Basso, whose description of mixtures resembled Zabarella's.[9] In the case of the ancient Greek atomists, however, Sennert was surprisingly conciliatory. He acknowledged that Democritus had erred in maintaining that substances are generated simply through the commingling of atoms, and hence that mixtures of atoms possess no additional supervening forms. Yet he was reluctant to condemn Democritus for these views or for the view that atoms themselves possess neither substantial nor elemental forms. Indeed, Sennert found it difficult to believe that Democritus's atoms could have differed so radically from his own *minima naturalia*. He never responded critically to the fact that Democritean atoms were minimal particles of a uniform matter, and that any differentiation among them depended solely on their sizes and figures, not on elemental qualities such as hotness or dryness. And though he was interested in Democritus's atomism, Sennert seems to have been uninterested in the questions concerning space and vacuum that were often connected with the atomist tradition.

Sennert's influence on later atomists is difficult to judge. Jean Chrysostom Magnen, the French physician who taught at the University of Pavia, cited Sennert's *Hypomnemata physica* twice (at least) in his defence of atomism, *Democritus reviviscens* (Pavia, 1646), once when describing how atoms of one substance diffuse themselves through the pores of another substance, and again when referring generally to the work of the chemists.[10] Magnen himself argued that atoms must exist because, among other reasons, a continuum or continuous magnitude cannot be composed of an infinity of parts. Atoms, the fundamental units of all bodies, possess three, not four distinct elemental forms (fire, water, and earth) and hence are the indivisible parts of the three elements. Despite the references to Sennert, therefore, his views departed significantly from Sennert's. Magnen's atomist philosophy even departed from several well-known principles of Democritus, the philosopher whose beliefs he was seeking to revive. For instance, he denied the existence of the void, which had been central to Democritus's account of the physical world. Perhaps the most notable thing that he and Sennert shared was a willingness to characterise themselves as followers of Democritus while adopting corpuscular principles seriously at odds with the known principles of Democritean atomism. Even taking into account the fragmentary nature of the writings of Democritus available to Sennert and Magnen, it seems puzzling to the modern reader that both philosophers would ignore or subvert Democritean positions already well established in the second-hand summaries given in the widely read works of Aristotle, Cicero, and Sextus Empiricus.[11]

2. Basso and van Goorle

Aristotle's texts may have inspired such corpuscular speculations, but by far the more prevalent types of atomism during the late sixteenth and early seventeenth centuries originated in a variety of efforts to refute Aristotle's physics and metaphysics. The physician Sebastian Basso based his conception of atoms, in his *Philosophiae naturalis adversus Aristotelem libri XII* (Geneva, 1621), on a sceptical attack on the definitions of continuity and continuous magnitudes which had been fundamental to Aristotle's demonstration that ordinary bodies, conceived as continuous magnitudes, cannot be composed of atoms. Basso also carefully distinguished his sort of atomism from the contemporary Aristotelian theories of *minima naturalia.* In both these efforts, he tried to enhance the credibility of his views by relating them to the concepts of indivisibles of Plato and Democritus. He claimed that these concepts were compatible with each other and that they could both be made compatible with yet a third theory, Empedocles' theory of the elements.[12] This consensus, which Basso tried to construct among three ancient philosophical rivals of Aristotle, helped him to justify his own dissent from Aristotelian physics. Still, it would be wrong to conclude that Basso was a convert to a genuinely Democritean-Epicurean natural philosophy. He cited Democritus as a precedent for his own views, yet he also denied the existence of Democritus's void, preferring to equate it with the Stoic concept of an ether. Furthermore, although Basso strongly opposed those Aristotelians who held that the *minima naturalia* in a mixture assume a new supervening form replacing or predominating over the elemental forms originally possessed by the *minima,* he attributed to his atoms at least some of the qualities associated with elemental forms.[13] Thus he retained a theory of the elements that would have been superfluous to a genuinely Democritean concept of atoms, which ruled out atomic qualities other than size and shape.

Basso, trained as a physician, employed even the authority of Hippocrates to defend his atomism. Linking Democritus to Hippocrates on somewhat slender grounds, Basso suggested that modern doctors who followed Hippocratic teachings would profit from studying the principles of Democritus.[14] Basso's linking of Hippocrates and the ancient atomists may have stemmed from what is now widely believed to be a spurious story told by several ancient medical writers who described Hippocrates as Democritus's student in philosophy.[15]

Many other atomists independently arrived at objections similar to Basso's against Aristotle's argument that since bodies are continuous magnitudes, they must be infinitely divisible and thus cannot be composed of atoms. The Dutch atomist David van Goorle, for example, attacked Aristotle's anti-atomist arguments as part of his more general rejection of the Aristotelian definition of nature. In his posthumously published *Idea physicae* (Utrecht, 1651), van Goorle stated that Aristotle had incorrectly identified nature with the principle and causes of motion and rest. Van Goorle preferred a definition of nature in which the natural world is an aggregation of beings, some animate and others inanimate. He saw no reason to retain the view that natural substances are unions of forms and matter; all bodies are composed of atoms, a conclusion he reached by denying that a continuous magnitude must be infinitely divisible. What seemed to him to follow from the infinite divisibility of continuous magnitudes was the composition of a finite continuous body from an infinite number of parts. Unaware that an infinite converging series can be both finite in magnitude and infinite in the number of its parts, van Goorle thought such a conclusion absurd. Thus he chose to endorse what he regarded as the only viable alternative conclusion, namely, that a finite continuous body is composed of indivisibles, or atoms. Bodies are simply aggregations of atoms, and as such are mixtures whose component parts are united not by a substantial form, but only by mutual contact. Van Goorle declined, however, to give up the concept of elements entirely, and while he pared down the number of elements to two (water and earth), he still considered it useful to explain the composition of bodies from these two elements. He also conceded that the three Paracelsian alchemical principles - salt, sulphur, and mercury - were somehow instrumental in the generation of certain kinds of bodies, such as metals and stones, in the earth.[16] Van Goorle believed that before creation, there was a void, and that even after creation, there is void beyond the limits of the world. Like Gassendi after him, van Goorle argued that space is neither substance nor accident, though, at the same time, he argued that it is not a 'real being'.[17]

3. Harriot, Warner, and Hill

So far we have been emphasising the importance of atomism on the continent. But atomism and other non- and anti-Aristotelian strains of thought were important in England as well. Innovations in the concepts of body, space, and force in English thought can first be seen in the development of eclectic systems of natural philosophy predating the introduction of the mechanical philosophy. Historians have tended to categorise these systems as atomistic, but they owe a great deal to Renaissance Neoplatonism. This historiographical bias derives partly from the distortion of hindsight and partly from the somewhat exaggerated attention paid to the atomistic speculations of Thomas Harriot. Harriot was a brilliant mathematician and natural philosopher, but his literary remains do not fulfil the expectations inspired by his reputation. Better historical sources for innovatory natural philosophy in late Renaissance English thought can be found in the papers attributed to a close associate of Harriot's, Walter Warner, and in Nicholas Hill's *Philosophia Epicurea* (Paris, 1601). Harriot has been regarded as the leader of this trio, but the system of philosophy expounded in Warner's papers goes far beyond anything we know of Harriot's philosophising, and there is no real evidence that Hill was part of Harriot's circle, or that they were in any way acquainted with one another.[18]

Harriot's most protracted discussion of atomism concerned problems associated with infinite divisibility.[19] Like Galileo, Harriot apparently wanted to combine mathematical demands for infinite divisibility with physical atomism. Unfortunately, his manuscript papers do not reveal how or even whether he managed to reconcile mathematical indivisibles (infinitely small dimensionless points) with Epicurean physical atoms endowed with size, shape, and weight. It is clear that he believed in both halves of the ancient atomist formula, 'atoms and the void', but again, it is impossible to say what his arguments for the void might have been.[20]

The Neoplatonic antecedents of Hill's and Warner's philosophy are evident from the fact that they eschewed the Aristotelian categories and based their systems on four principles or, as Hill called them, four 'tetrarchs'. They considered space, time, and matter to be definitive prerequisites for any physical ontology. The fourth principle was the active principle, responsible for all change. For Warner this is simply *vis,* force or power: for Hill it is God, a constant source of energy and formative power at work in the universe.[21] In both systems, time and space are infinite, co-essential and co-eternal with God, although Warner feels it necessary to acknowledge that time is 'more prime' than space, 'not tempore [!] yet natura' because space exists through time but time does not exist in space. With the exceptions of time and space, therefore, 'The state of being or existence of a thing is the continuation of the being thereof in time and space'. Space, which Warner, echoing Plato, calls the 'universall vessel or receptacle of things', is described as continuous, eternal, immoveable, homogeneal, absolutely penetrable, and without solidity or resistance.[22] Similarly, Hill describes space as 'indifferently receptive, mixable, [penetrable], not subject to form. Unlocatable, unbounded, to be understood conjointly with every physical being. Inherent in nothing, bordering on nothing, underlying nothing'.[23]

The active principles of Warner and Hill have marked Neoplatonic characteristics, which is particularly evident when they are compared with light, the most prominent Neoplatonic cosmogonic principle. According to Hill, 'primary incorporeal light' (*lux*) is 'a universal, primary, corporeal substantial form', the impression of the deity in nature, and as such is the driving force behind all physical operations.[24] For Warner, the active principle of the universe is *vis radiativa* or 'vertue radiative' and 'may be called light whether sensible or insensible'.[25] In Hill's system light informs all things, while for Warner the *vis radiativa* is 'the squarer and cutter of atomi'.[26] Strange though these notions may seem in these contexts, they are entirely typical of the Neoplatonic tradition usually referred to as 'light metaphysics'.[27]

The atomistic antecedents of these two philosophies really become apparent only when their authors discuss their respective material principles. Here the dominant argument is the Lucretian insistence that motion and change are conceivable only in atomist terms: 'If it [matter] were absolutely and wholly continuall', Warner writes, 'there could be no motion or alteration of the parts inter se.' Matter must therefore be 'in partes discreet and discontinuall for the necessary salving of appearances.'[28] Warner, on the one hand, refers to these discrete parts as 'atomi' but he does not hold them to be categorically indivisible. Hill's atoms, on the other hand, are indivisible and indissoluble, and they betray their Platonist origins in having the shapes of the regular solids, whereas the shapes Warner envisages are not specified except for being 'plain figured', 'rotundity' of atoms being dismissed as unworkable.[29] In spite of such differences of detail, both men hold to the fundamental belief of atomism: in Warner's words, 'The matter of all and everything is one, the difference [between things] is numero, forma, magnitudine, situ, distantia'.[30]

The eclectic natures of these two systems of natural philosophy are reminiscent of contemporary, or slightly older, systems developed elsewhere. In particular, it is easy to see the influence of the three leading Italian 'nature philosophers', Telesio, Bruno, and Patrizi. They, too, combined Neoplatonism with atomism to produce systems in which space and time are absolute realities without which no physical existence is possible, and in which a passive matter principle is sculpted and moved by an active principle which is light or some supposed analogue of it, such as heat or fire. The influence of Bruno on Hill is especially obvious, while Warner seems to owe more to Patrizi.[31]

There is little evidence to substantiate early stories that Warner practised alchemy together with Thomas Harriot and their common patron, the 'Wizard Earl', Henry Percy, Ninth Earl of Northumberland. Yet Warner's knowledge of the subject cannot be doubted, and there are strong indications that he and Hill drew upon developments in contemporary (al)chemical theorising. In Warner's lengthy discussion of the effects of fire, we learn that combustible liquids, like oils, are immediately resolved 'into fumosity wch is nothing but discontinuation vel resolutio continuitatis eius in minima speciei'. Solid combustibles, by contrast, like resins and waxes, must first be resolved into liquid.[32] Similarly, in an examination of 'vital heat' – the power by which animals maintain their bodily heat – Warner reveals knowledge of Paracelsian concepts when he wonders whether 'mere agitation' is sufficient to heat up all liquids or only those which 'containe in their substance some nitrous or sulfureous or nitrosulfureous or mercuriall or saline spirit'.[33]

Hill makes several references to alchemical processes, such as the transmutation of metals and extraction of the Elixir, and even defends the empiricism of alchemical adepts on the grounds that their work is all for the benefit of mankind.[34] Moreover, he suggests that atoms do not remain separate and independent but come together by some preordained divine virtue to form 'seeds' or 'spermatic forms' capable of imposing their form and arrangement on other atoms to generate similar bodies. This notion owes much to the Stoic belief in a divine *logos spermatikos,* but it was also a common feature of mediaeval and Renaissance alchemical traditions.[35]

The papers attributed to Warner were written sometime during the first three decades of the seventeenth century, so it is possible that they owe something to Hill's earlier speculations. It is not necessary, however, to assume a direct influence between them. Subsequent developments indicate that atomist and Neoplatonic natural philosophies and Paracelsian and other chemical speculations were constant and pervasive influences on seventeenth-century English thinkers.

4. Geometrical atomism

Not every late-sixteenth- or early-seventeenth-century atomist devoted himself to the reinterpretation or refutation of Aristotle, and not every atomist found precedents for his ideas in the ancient philosophical rivals of Aristotle. Among those who profited from consulting a quite different group of ancients in developing their own indivisibilist notions were the mathematicians who formulated the new geometry of indivisibles.

Galileo is well known for his distinction in *Il Saggiatore* (Rome, 1623) between the real, geometrical qualities of bodies and their smaller parts and the sensible qualities that they cause, a distinction that is quite clearly derived from the ancient atomist tradition.[36] But more interesting in this context is an attempt to derive a kind of atomism from mathematical considerations, an argument most prominent in Galileo's *Discorsi e dimostrazioni matematiche intorno à due nuove scienze* (Leiden, 1638). The argument he uses begins with a consideration of the so-called *rota Aristotelis.* Consider a circle with an inscribed concentric circle, two wheels of different sizes turning on the same axis, for example. The two concentric circles will go the same distance if rolled together through the same angle along parallel tangents. But how can this happen, given that their diameters are of different lengths, and that each would therefore roll independently along its tangent through a distance proportional to its diameter? Galileo begins by considering the case not of two concentric circles, but of two regular polygons rotating on the same axis. If we imagine them rotating with the larger resting on a flat surface, the motion described by the smaller polygon will follow the arc of a circle, and thus

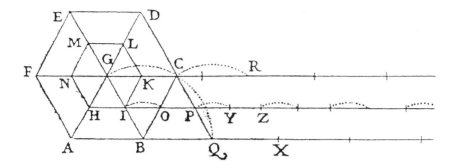

Figure 18.1 (from Galilei 1890–1901, vol. 8, p. 68)

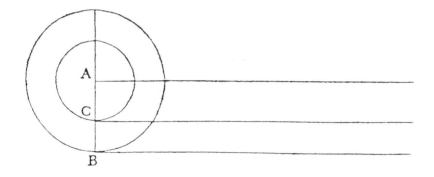

Figure 18.2 (from Galilei 1890–1901, vol. 8, p. 68)

will appear to skip over portions of the line parallel to the path followed by the outer polygon. And so, the path followed by the smaller polygon would be shorter than the path followed by the larger one (see Figures 18.1 and 18.2). But as we increase the number of sides in each polygon, the polygons approach circles. Very roughly, Galileo argues that the apparently continuous paths the circles follow are made up of an infinity of non-extended parts separated by an infinity of voids and that the inner, smaller wheel skips over some of these voids, enabling it to cover the same distance as the larger wheel in the same time, despite its smaller diameter. In this way, purely mathematical considerations lead us to a kind of mathematical atomism. Galileo then extends this mathematical analysis to bodies and uses it to solve certain problems connected with cohesion, rarefaction, and condensation.[37]

Such an account, though congenial to the sort of mathematical physics that Galileo was trying to articulate, was difficult to apply to the problems that more chemically minded thinkers worried about and so had little significant influence among natural philosophers of a more chemical bent.

But Galileo's thought was influential elsewhere. Galileo's mathematically in-spired atomism was pressed farther in the direction of pure mathematics by his students Bonaventura Cavalieri and Evangelista Torricelli. Though no seventeenth-century mathematician had access to their Greek predecessor's explic-itly indivisibilist work known as *The Method,* Cavalieri and Torricelli undertook the study of Archimedes' works, particularly his *De quadratura paraboles,* in which certain classic geometrical problems had been solved through the method of exhaustion. But even without the benefit of *The Method,* they devised their own indivisibilist techniques for solving many of the same problems that had fascinated Archimedes.[38] These techniques were used in works such as Cavalieri's *Geometria indivisibilibus continuorum nova quadem ratione promota* (Bologna, 1635) and Torri-celli's *De dimensione parabolae, solidique hyperbolici problemata duo* (Florence, 1644). What made their indivisibilist techniques impressive was that they yielded results consistent with those obtained through more conventional Euclidean proofs, proofs which presupposed the infinite divisibility of all continuous magnitudes, such as lines, surfaces, and volumes. The production of results consistent with Euclid's from the contrary assumption, that continuous magnitudes are composed of indivisibles, was indeed striking. Cavalieri, for example, assumed the existence of an indefinite number of similarly situated indivisible 'lines' which he conceived as composing or generating similar plane figures with different areas, for example, similar triangles of different sizes. He then showed that the ratio of their areas equals the ratio of their respective sets of indivisible lines.[39] Starting from proposi-tions like this, Cavalieri further derived theorems such as the one stating that the sum of the lines of a parallelogram is double the sum of the lines of the two triangles formed by the diagonal. Also important in this area was Gilles Personne de Roberval, whose *Traité des indivisibles* (written c. 1636, published Paris, 1693) showed great expertise in manipulating the basic indivisibilist techniques in the discovery of further important results in pure geometry.

5. Bacon and Gilbert

Atomism was an important alternative to the philosophy of Aristotle and his followers. But not all new philosophers of the early seventeenth century were atomists. Examples of alternative new philosophies include the thought of Francis Bacon, would-be programmatic reformer of natural philosophy, and that of William Gilbert (1540–1603), pioneer of the experimental method and founder of 'magnetic philosophy'.

Bacon was clearly sympathetic to atomism, but his own theory of matter owed far more to Paracelsian ideas. He held that matter exists in two states: dense, heavy, cold, and inert tangible matter; and tenuous, weightless, invisible, and incessantly active pneumatic matter or spirit. There are many kinds of 'pneumaticals' or 'spirits' attached to, or imprisoned within, tangible matter. It is the combination of inert tangible matter and active pneumatic matter which accounts for the properties, behaviour, and interactions of both animate and inanimate bodies. In addition there are four pure, or unattached, spirits: air, ether, terrestrial fire, and sidereal fire. The Paracelsian antecedents of this theory are evident in Bacon's grouping of air and ether together with water and mercury in what he calls the 'mercury quaternion', and of the two fires together with sulphur and oil in the 'sulphur quaternion'. He rejected the third of the Paracelsian *tria prima,* salt, as an absurd contrivance and insisted that salts were merely intermediaries, being compounds of mercury and sulphur.[40] The two quaternions represent the cosmological principles of Bacon's philosophy, while all other bodies are held to be intermediates compounded from the two sets of opposed principles. Although the result may differ in its details from Paracelsianism, it is no less a chemical cosmology than that of Paracelsus.

Bacon's interest in atomism, which was minor and fleeting, seems to have stemmed from a belief that it was useful for putting across the view that many physical phenomena could not be explained by recourse only to manifest processes accessible to the senses, but must be explained by the interactions of invisible and non-isolable substances.[41] Bacon's chemical preoccupations prevented him from supposing infinite divisibility, but he tended to reject atomism nevertheless. The doctrine of atoms implied the false hypotheses of a vacuum and the unchangeableness of matter. There are indications, however, that some of his physical explanations assumed that matter is particulate in structure. 'Heat is a motion', he argued, 'expansive, restrained, and acting in its strife upon the smaller particles of bodies.'[42]

Although atomistic or corpuscularian speculations played a small rôle in Bacon's thinking, they proved to be more influential than his idiosyncratic adaptation of Paracelsian ideas. Bacon's two most protracted, and favourable, discussions of atomism, *Cogitationes de rerum natura* (1604?) and *De principiis atque originibus* (c. 1610–19), were published posthumously in Amsterdam by Isaac Gruter in 1653.[43] Significantly, the same collection contained the only systematic discussion of Bacon's (al)chemical cosmology, the *Thema coeli* of 1612. Given that corpuscularian and atomist approaches to natural philosophy were then in vogue, and that

Paracelsianism was becoming increasingly associated with some of the more extreme radical and subversive movements of the Interregnum (1649–60), it is not surprising that the much admired Bacon should henceforth be seen as a corpuscularian, rather than a Paracelsian, philosopher.[44]

Gilbert was even less concerned with atomism than Bacon. He discussed only briefly the atomist account of electrical attractions and immediately dismissed it. His own theory of matter was a uniquely modified four-element theory, drawing upon both Paracelsian and Neoplatonic influences[45] in which 'earth', instead of being dead and inert, was animated with magnetic virtue. Because of their magnetic activity, iron and the lodestone are closest in nature to pure elemental earth, which remains inaccessible deep below the surface of our globe.[46] Gilbert was led to this view by his concern to provide a physics supporting the Copernican theory of a moving earth. He used the rotatory self-orientating property of lodestones to show that 'the whole earth is fitted, and by its own forces adapted for a diurnal circular motion.'[47]

Extending these ideas to a more general cosmology, Gilbert suggested that each of the heavenly bodies is surrounded by its own 'orb of virtue' so that earthy bodies seek to be reunited with the earth, lunar bodies with the moon, and so forth. These spheres of influence limit the material effluvia surrounding each heavenly body. To emphasise this point Gilbert insisted that the space between the 'effluvia materialia' of each of the planets and stars is a vacuum. Nevertheless, the moon is still within the earth's orb of virtue (which explains the moon's geocentric orbit, and the smaller effect of its weaker virtue on the tides), and the earth and other planets are within the Sun's orb of virtue.[48] Gilbert's easy acceptance of void space beyond the earth did not prevent him from denying the contingency of void space within the region of the *effluvia terrena materialia*. Gilbert's effluvia, unlike those of Robert Boyle and other corpuscularian philosophers, were continuous entities that guaranteed a plenum.

Gilbert's elemental theory was to have no significant influence, but his concept of 'orbs of virtue' surrounding bodies played a rôle in the development of concepts of force in England. By shifting the emphasis in Gilbert's work from notions of magnetic 'souls' to locutions about 'a magnetic strength or energy [*vigor*]', or 'the agent force [*vis agens*]',[49] a small but influential group of natural philosophers – John Wilkins, Christopher Wren, Robert Hooke, and William Petty – introduced into the mechanical philosophy the occult concept of action at a distance. In his inaugural lecture as professor of astronomy at Gresham College in 1657, Wren praised Gilbert for giving 'an exact account . . . of the secret, and more obscure Motion of Attraction and Magnetical Direction in the Earth'.[50] By 1674 Robert

Hooke was using the idea of an orb of attractive virtue around the Sun extending at least to the orbit of Saturn, and suggesting that a planet's exact orbit can be explained in terms of a tangential motion diverted from its rectilinear path by a single attractive force pulling the planet towards the Sun. In the hands of Newton this idea was to lead to the principle of universal gravitation.[51] Petty's *New Hypothesis of Springing or Elastique Motions* (London, 1674) rested on the supposition that each atom or corpuscle is a spherical magnet, and by employing the self-moving and orientating properties of magnets and their attractive and repulsive forces, was intended to account not just for elasticity but for all other physical phenomena such as hardness, fluidity, heat, moisture, and fermentation. In the Cartesian and Hobbesian systems, magnetism had to be explained in purely mechanical terms. In the *Principia philosophiae* (IV 133, IV 137–8), for example, Descartes elaborated a theory of screw-threaded particles continually driven out of each pole of a magnet and circulating back to the opposite pole (or interacting with other poles). He accounted for repulsion and attraction by supposing that there are right- and left-handed threads on the particles and in the pores of the magnet in which they do or do not fit. While Descartes tried (somewhat desperately?) to avoid recourse to any occult powers, Petty simply embraced magnetism as a fact and extended it to the particulate level. This was no balk to the progress of natural knowledge, because 'all the Motions I fancy in my Atoms', Petty wrote, 'may be presented in gross Tangible Bodies, and consequently may be made intelligible and examinable'. In other words, magnets can be manipulated experimentally and their behaviour catalogued in detail with a view to understanding the interaction of the putative atomic magnets.[52]

6. Digby

The earliest systematic attempt to develop a corpuscular philosophy to be published in English is to be found in Sir Kenelm Digby's *Two Treatises* (1644). Digby's intention here was to establish the *natural* immortality of the soul (a theological point which divided Anglicans and other Protestants from Roman Catholics).[53] The preliminary discussion of materialist phenomena required a treatise to itself, the first of the *Two Treatises,* and grew to twice the length of the treatise on the immaterial soul. The matter theory of the treatise on body was clearly inspired by the work of Descartes and Hobbes, both known to Digby, but his own predominant interest in alchemy and his Catholic commitment to Aristotelianism meant that his matter theory owed a great deal to Aristotelian atomists like Daniel Sennert.

Digby entered enthusiastically into the anti-scholastic rhetoric of his day but his religious beliefs led him to develop his mechanical philosophy as a representation of Aristotelian natural philosophy, properly understood. Digby was devoted to Thomas White, an English secular priest who was one of the leaders of the Roman Catholic community in England and a major figure in efforts to return England to Catholicism, although these very efforts led him increasingly to be seen by his own church as a heresiarch.[54] White and Digby, in debate with Anglicans, made extensive use of Roman Catholic claims to authority on the basis of tradition. The Roman church, they claimed, was the only church with a continuous tradition back to the Apostles and to Christ himself, and the continuity of this tradition guaranteed its reliability.[55] Given the close association between Roman Catholicism and Aristotelianism, it seemed to follow, for White and Digby, that their natural philosophy should be shown to be in accordance with Aristotelian doctrines: 'Whosoever followeth his principles in the maine, cannot be led into error.'[56]

Accordingly, Digby implicitly denies the concept of 'space' as a three-dimensional receptacle for all material beings. The 'natural and true' notion 'of being in a place' is the same for everyone, and a body is 'environed and enclosed by some one, or several others that are immediate unto it'.[57] The possibility of extended vacuum is dismissed simply because 'Aristotle in his fourth booke of Physics, hath demonstrated that there can be no motion in vacuity.' The supposition of interstitial vacua between atoms or corpuscles is rejected on the grounds that fluid bodies, for example, being rarer than solid ones, would 'be of themselves standing like nettes or cobwebbes: wheareas contrariwise, we see theire natures are to runne together and to fill up every creeke and corner'.[58]

Similarly, Digby draws upon standard Aristotelian arguments to reject atomism. Quantity, which he equates with extension, cannot be composed of indivisibles, 'neither finite nor infinite ones'.[59] He uses his notion of 'quantity', together with his Aristotelian definitions of rarity, density, and gravity,[60] to vindicate Aristotelian matter theory. The density or cohesion of a body can be overcome by gravity causing it to break down and form a sphere around the centre of gravity. Such behaviour gives rise to our notion of 'moistness' because it is the way fluids behave. Dry bodies have 'a greater proportion of density in respect of their gravity'. Gravity must be combined with rarity in the same way to give rise to other manifestations of wetness and dryness. A body so rare that gravity has no effect on it will be dry. But such extremely rare, dry bodies will give rise to our notion of heat because they will be able to penetrate into the porousness of bodies and separate its parts, 'which is the notion whereby Aristotle hath expressed the nature of heat'. A dense, moist (fluid) body, by contrast, will compress other bodies, making them stick strongly together. Experience teaches us that these effects follow from cold. In conclusion, then, extremely rare bodies are dry and very hot (fire), weighty rare bodies are moist and 'meanely hot' (air), fluid dense bodies are wet and very cold (water), while extremely dense bodies are dry and 'meanely cold' (earth).[61]

Having confirmed the four qualities and the four elements of Aristotle in this way, Digby goes on to discuss the operations and activities of the elements. Here he develops a mechanistic system of philosophy, comparable with those of Descartes and Hobbes. Change takes place as particles of fire, for example, penetrate the pores of a body, breaking it down and separating its parts, which then fly off to interact with other parts of matter by contact. It is not long before Digby is describing phenomena in terms of the interaction of atoms: 'by which word *Atome* no body will imagine we intend to express a perfect indivisible, but onely the least sort of natural bodies'.[62] The gravitational attraction of a body in the air, for example, is explained by the continual downward pressure of a stream of earthy particles. As successive impacts accelerate the falling body, its motion causes the much smaller impelling particles to overcome their natural (Aristotelian) tendency to fall more slowly than a heavier object by causing them to close in behind it very suddenly, 'to hinder vacuity of space'.[63] But what causes the continual descent of the earthy particles? They are displaced by an ascending stream of particles, which, although less dense, are forcibly driven upwards. As sunlight strikes the ground, the energetic particles of light combine with earth particles and bounce off the surface, taking the earth particles with them.[64] The newly formed combined particle of earth and light is less dense than the earth particle taken singly. Eventually, high above the ground, the two particles separate, the light continuing its energetic course, while the denser earth particle, being displaced in the plenum by combined light-earth particles following behind, circulates downwards to avoid formation of a vacuum.

The only feature of this account which fails to meet strictly mechanical precepts is the unexplained incessant activity of light. Fire, which appears in even more rarefied form as light, is held to be so 'fierce' that its nature 'will not let it lye still and rest'. They are both held to have 'spheres of activity' within which they 'enlarge their place, and consequently come out and fly abroad'. Light 'extendeth it selfe into a great sphere' by 'extreme multiplication and rarefaction', and as it proceeds, 'of necessity, it giveth motion to all circumstant bodies'. The Sun, moreover, is described as 'a constant and perpetuall cause' whose influence gives fire 'its universal action'.[65]

Digby's *Two Treatises* was widely read and, at least with respect to details and specific examples, could be said to have been influential. However, its self-professed Aristotelianism and its obvious religious purpose prevented Digby's system from being adopted as a whole. Digby's co-religionist and mentor, Thomas White, wrote a number of treatises which promoted Digby's system, either explicitly or implicitly,[66] but his influence was even more seriously curtailed by his reputation among English Protestants as a devout Roman Catholic, and among Catholics as a proscribed heresiarch.[67]

II. BODY AND THE PHYSICAL WORLD IN GASSENDI, DESCARTES, AND HOBBES

The figures discussed in the first section of this essay show the wide variety of positions on body found among the new philosophers in the early part of the century. But in mid-century, in the 1640s and 1650s, three figures emerged whose views in a way set the agenda for the rest of the century with respect to this issue, as with others. The mechanist philosophical systems of Gassendi, Descartes, and, to a lesser extent, Hobbes defined the issues that later thinkers had to deal with.

1. Gassendi and the revival of Epicurean atomism

Considering the multiplicity of types of atomism which emerged during the late Renaissance, it may seem surprising that by the second half of the seventeenth century atomism was increasingly identified primarily with its most radical ancient form, the philosophy of Epicurus.[68] The tradition of Epicurean atomism exerted a dominant influence on corpuscular discussions because its proponents were extremely skillful in knowing how to construct a full-fledged philosophical tradition and how to use it to address modern as well as ancient problems.

A case in point is the full-scale revival of Epicurean atomism undertaken by Pierre Gassendi. Gassendi, a Catholic priest who was dean of the cathedral of Digne and a professor of mathematics in the Collège Royal in Paris, achieved prominence both as an observational astronomer and as the principal rehabilitator of the logic, physics, and ethics of Epicurus. He published the first exhaustive Latin commentary on the Greek texts of Epicurus in his *Animadversiones in decimum librum Diogenis Laertii* (Lyon, 1649) and afterwards transformed this commentary into his own lengthy atomist treatise, the *Syntagma philosophicum* (Lyon, 1658), published posthumously. Gassendi conceived of his historical reconstruction of Epicurus's principles as providing a much-needed corrective to the erroneous interpretations which had been given them by modern proponents of other corpuscular philosophies and by certain Hellenistic critics of Epicurus, especially

Cicero, Plutarch, and Sextus Empiricus.[69] The modern thinkers whose views he sharply distinguished from Epicurean atomism proper included Paracelsus, Bruno, Fludd, Severinus, Telesio, Patrizi, Campanella, Digby, Cavalieri, and Torricelli.[70]

However, errors committed by these modern authors seemed to Gassendi to be far less serious than those of the Hellenistic critics of Epicurus. One measure of the negative influence of the second-hand accounts of Epicureanism given by Cicero, Plutarch, and Sextus Empiricus was the fact that not even the publication of numerous editions of *De rerum natura,* Lucretius's well-known defence of Epicurean atomism, had rectified the contemporary misunderstandings of Epicurus's actual views. There appeared in Europe no less than thirty-eight printed editions of *De rerum natura* between 1473 and 1626.[71] But they had not, in Gassendi's estimation, led to an accurate understanding of the atomist philosophy expounded by Lucretius.[72]

Gassendi aimed to dispel these popular prejudices against Epicurus and his exponent, Lucretius, by means of a two-pronged attack. On the one hand, he reconciled Epicurean atomism with the fundamental doctrines of the Christian religion; on the other, he showed that the Hellenistic critics of Epicurus had misinformed their modern readers about the true meaning of atomism. His reconciliation of Epicurean atomism with the Christian religion took the form of a revision of several important atomist principles that directly contradicted Christian beliefs, such as the principle that atoms are eternal and uncreated beings.[73] Gassendi also worked to rehabilitate Epicurus's reputation as a libertine who had advocated an ethics based on pleasure and his reputation as a materialist who had denied the immortality of the soul.[74] In his *De vita et moribus Epicuri libri octo* (Lyon, 1647), he confronted what he thought were the inaccurate characterisations of Epicureanism given by Cicero, Plutarch, and Sextus Empiricus.[75] Furthermore, unlike previous humanist interpreters such as Lorenzo Valla, Francesco Filelfo, Cristoforo Landino, and Cosma Raimondi, who had focused on Epicurean ethics,[76] Gassendi broadened the discussion and redefined Epicureanism as a natural philosophy whose atomist physics could rescue modern sceptics (followers of Cicero and Sextus Empiricus) as well as modern Aristotelians from their untenable views concerning knowledge of the natural world.

Gassendi used his account of Epicurus's views to indicate why atomism constituted a natural philosophy that was preferable to any based on Aristotle's concepts of substance and motion. In contrast to Aristotle's explanation of substances as unions of form and matter, he emphasised Democritus's and Epicurus's treatment of all natural bodies as aggregations of indivisible units of matter. These aggregations require no substantial forms to determine their qualities. The atoms themselves possess only a few essential qualities: size and shape, according to Democritus; size, shape, and weight (which causes atomic motions), according to Epicurus.[77] The further property of impenetrability, or solidity, was inferred by Epicurus from the definition of the atom as an indivisible containing neither internal parts nor void spaces by which it can be penetrated and divided. Gassendi himself adopted Epicurus's rather than Democritus's enumeration of the qualities possessed by the atoms. He also defended Epicurus's argument for the existence of the void and employed it in attacking Aristotle's analysis of motion through a plenum. Epicurus had argued that if there were no void, the motions of atoms and composite bodies could not occur. Gassendi now applied this reasoning to two sorts of cases. He endorsed it first in the case of the motions of the planets through the infinite, 'extramundane' void space in which all stars and planets are located. Second, he endorsed it in the case of the motions of atoms, for instance, the motions of air atoms during the compression and rarefaction of air, which involve, he argued, the movement of air atoms into and out of the tiny void spaces that normally exist between them. When air is compressed, the air atoms are forced to occupy in greater numbers these interstitial void spaces, which previously remained unfilled in a given volume of air. Finally, Gassendi maintained with Epicurus that all atoms possess constant rectilinear motion unless they are deflected by collisions with other atoms or unless they are captured in an aggregation of atoms constituting a composite body. He then showed how the three sorts of natural motion recognised in substances by Aristotle (qualitative and quantitative change, and local motion) can all be better explained in terms of the local motions of atoms.[78]

Especially interesting is Gassendi's treatment of the activity of atoms. Gassendi agreed with Epicurus that the source of activity is within the world, that it is atoms themselves that are genuine causes of motion in the world. He wrote:

It seems that we must say . . . that the first moving cause in physical things is atoms; while they move through themselves and through the force which is continually received from the Author from the beginning [*ab initio usque*], they give motion to all things. And therefore, these atoms are the origin, principal, and cause of all motions which are in nature.[79]

The author in question here is of course God, whom Gassendi believed to be the primary cause of everything. Like Epicurus, Gassendi maintained that atoms are, in a sense, active and self-moving. But he also emphasised that this activity is itself bestowed upon them by God and maintained by divine concurrence.[80]

Gassendi's atomist definition of body served him in his efforts to refute the contemporary sceptics' claim that knowledge of bodies is impossible. Several seventeenth-century followers of the Pyrrhonian sceptic Sextus Empiricus (fl. A.D. 100–200) advanced this claim in part because they believed that Sextus had long ago proven that all conceptions of body that affirm the composition of bodies from indivisibles of any kind must be incoherent. One of the ways in which Sextus Empiricus had demonstrated this incoherence was to argue that any body composed of an odd number of indivisibles cannot be bisected. Because he held that this conclusion is absurd, he denied the truth of the premise that the body is composed of indivisibles. Gassendi was well aware of this and other puzzles which Sextus had generated in order to discredit the atomists' conception of body. In works such as his *Against the Physicists* (commonly cited as *Adversus Dogmaticos,* Books iii–iv, or *Adversus Mathematicos,* Books ix–x) Sextus had used these puzzles to raise doubts about whether physics as a whole could be a viable form of knowledge.[81] What alarmed Gassendi, as he compared Sextus's account of Greek atomism with the actual texts of Epicurus, was the extent to which the sceptic had misinterpreted the Epicurean concept of atoms. Sextus had thought it possible to treat this concept as if it were interchangeable with the mathematical concept of indivisibles, which had been a subject of dispute among Euclidean geometers. In the *Syntagma philosophicum,* Gassendi warned that Sextus had, as a result, ignored Epicurus's principal arguments for the existence of atoms: (1) that the existence of composite bodies which undergo changes of various kinds is self-evident, and (2) that composite bodies cannot undergo changes unless they are composed of atoms capable of persisting as a substratum of these changes.[82] Therefore Sextus had not successfully refuted Epicurus's atomist conception of body, and the Pyrrhonian sceptics' claim that knowledge of bodies is impossible could not be sustained.

Having both redefined the concept of body and quelled the modern sceptics' doubts about whether the knowledge of bodies is even possible, Gassendi completed his Epicurean project by explaining the relationship between material bodies and various incorporeal entities. For his world also encompassed an assortment of immaterial beings, including angels, space, time, and the rational souls of humans.

Especially noteworthy, and influential for later philosophers, is his treatment of space and place. Gassendi, like Epicurus, admitted that there could be empty space. Space and place are therefore incorporeal in so far as they can exist without body, but real nonetheless. He wrote:

Place [*locus*] and time must be considered real things, or actual entities, for although they are not the same sort of things as substance and accident are commonly considered, they still actually exist and do not depend upon the mind like a chimera since space endures steadfastly and time flows on whether the mind thinks of them or not.[83]

It is important to Gassendi here that we not try to fit space or place (or time) into the scholastic metaphysics of substance and accident; they are neither substance nor accident but are, in a sense, *sui generis.*[84]

In the *Syntagma,* at least, though perhaps not in some of his earlier writings, Gassendi also recognised as real certain incorporeal substances, such as angels and the incorporeal rational souls of humans.[85] Essential to his atomism was the caveat that although the modes of existence of material things are determined by their atomic constitutions, other modes of being are possible for several kinds of incorporeal natures. Because Gassendi did not rule out these incorporeal beings, he had little difficulty in reconciling the basic tenets of Catholic Christianity with his modified brand of Epicurean metaphysics. As God is the creator and first cause of the world composed of atoms, His Providence therein is fully compatible with the laws of atomic motions which govern natural phenomena.[86] Moreover, neither the existence of immortal, rational human souls nor the existence of angels, according to Gassendi, impugns the atomic constitutions of material bodies.

Why did Gassendi think himself justified in making such wholesale adjustments both to Epicurus's metaphysics and to Christian doctrine? Here the rôle of traditions in the formulation of late Renaissance philosophy must be fully appreciated. As a late Renaissance philosopher, Gassendi viewed the progress of human knowledge as consisting in the identification and development of certain superior traditions. Epicurean atomism and Catholic Christianity were, in his judgement, the two pre-eminent traditions which any rational person of the time would have chosen to join. Their superiority to all other traditions was what he laboriously tried to establish in his history of philosophy, the *Syntagma philosophicum,* and it was this superiority that recommended them to him and constituted for him their rational justification. That he would need further to justify the modifications he made in the two traditions, when integrating them into a single, coherent metaphysical framework, did not crucially concern him. Traditions are never foolproof, he believed, and they are always open to modification by future thinkers because of the unavoidable imperfections of human knowledge. Even the most reliable knowledge, obtained through the theories and empirical investigations of the best traditions, is only an approximation to the truth.[87]

2. Descartes

Descartes begins his *Discours de la méthode,* his first published writing, with a flamboyant rejection of the past. After a catalogue of all that he claimed to have studied in school, Descartes declared that he rejected all learning: 'As soon as I was old enough to emerge from the control of my teachers, I entirely abandoned the study of letters.'[88] But even though Descartes's philosophical programme called for the rejection of all learning, his writings show the traces of other traditions in natural philosophy, such as atomism, or of Peripateticism, the intellectual framework of his education. He had understandable polemical reasons to discount scholastic physics in particular, but tradition was not to be denied so easily. It would be a mistake to categorise the appearance of the Cartesian conception of body and its properties as the replacement of one natural philosophy, or of one set of natural philosophies, by another incommensurable with them in all important respects.

Many influences attended the evolution of Descartes's natural philosophy. At La Flèche he benefitted from the eclecticism of Jesuit instruction. While the *Ratio studiorum* followed at La Flèche emphasised scholastic Aristotelianism, as interpreted by Saint Thomas, it did not confine itself to scholastic commentaries and manuals but introduced the students to the Platonic, Pythagorean, Stoic, Augustinian, and Hermetic traditions;[89] and Descartes's personal reading ranged well beyond the prescribed texts and outside the provisions of the *Ratio studiorum.* If we are to take at face value his recollections in the *Discours de la méthode,* he read everything he could find that dealt with 'the rarest and most recondite sciences',[90] and the independent evidence of his earliest extant writings (c. 1620) and later correspondence suggests that by 1630 at the latest his reading had included (though it is uncertain how seriously), '*novatores*' such as Cardano, Telesio, Campanella, Bruno, Vanini, and the atomists Epicurus and Basso.[91] Descartes's corpuscularianism did not arise *ab ovo* with the first outlines of his mechanical ideas in *Le monde.*

Descartes's views on the connexion between body and extension could not help but have been influenced by what he read in the school textbooks common to the period. Generally speaking, scholastic writers understood 'body' in three senses: mathematical body (three-dimensional extension), metaphysical or logical body (of the genus substance, with body as difference), and physical body (the form–matter composite). Furthermore, quantity is the primary property or affection of natural body, and is inseparable from it, because it is through quantity that body is extended, and because, as Alsted put it, 'in reality quantity does not differ from the matter of natural body.'[92]

There are many resonances of scholastic teachings in Descartes's writings on body. In Regula XIV of the *Regulae ad directionem ingenii* he dismisses the distinction between extension and quantity, though extension is more easily perceived by the imagination than is quantity; and extension *per se* is not distinct from the extended thing, nor is the tri-dimensional distinguishable from body other than through an act of intellectual abstraction; whether dimensions have a basis in reality is a question for the physicists, and the proposition 'Body possesses extension', *à parte rei,* is equivalent to the proposition 'That which is extended is extended.'[93] Descartes's familiar equation of corporeal extension and essence, a cornerstone of his system that was evidently well in place by the late 1620s, comes across as a radical transformation of the Peripatetic canon of the inseparability of body and quantity, though of course it was a transformation that was to call into question virtually the entirety of the Peripatetic system of natural philosophy. Writing to Mersenne in 1640 on Villiers's philosophy of Universal Salt, Descartes makes the revealing comment: 'I find that in his whole reasoning on salt he proves only that terrestrial bodies are made from each other, but not that air or earth are made from salt rather than salt from air or earth. So he ought to conclude only that salt, as much as all other bodies, are only of the same matter; which agrees with school philosophy, and with mine, except that in the schools they do not explain this matter very well, making it a *pura potentia,* adding to it substantial forms and real qualities, which are only chimeras.'[94] This passage implies that Descartes saw his *materia,* his *res extensa,* and the schools' *materia prima* – more correctly the Thomists' *pura potentia* (see Chapter 15) – as two widely differing descriptions of the same substratum, the scholastic description being misconceived and inadequate. This is not the same as saying that the Peripatetic doctrine of corporeal body is wholly wrong, that it is mistaken in every respect. Neither does it imply that Cartesian *res extensa* can be intelligibly parsed into a distinctly conceived *res* characterised as being *extensa.*

In addition to the influences from within the schools, there were influences from without. Isaac Beeckman was a particularly decisive personal influence. When he met Beeckman, Descartes encountered, possibly for the first time, a kind of natural philosophy markedly different from that he had been exposed to in the formal curriculum at La Flèche. Beeckman's program in natural philosophy included notably atomism (from which Descartes later dissociated his *Principia philosophiae*), the rejection of substantial forms, and the unity of the sciences, particularly the ideal of uniting mathematics with physics.[95] There was nothing new about the themes *per se* of the chain of knowledge and the unity of the sciences: these themes were advocated by Renaissance encyclopaedists and scholastics such as Antonio de Bernardis (1503–65) and Francisco Suárez.[96] There was nothing new in Beeckman's advocacy of atomism, one of the far-reaching aspects of the Renaissance re-discovery of the philosophies of antiquity.[97] Yet Beeckman's conjunction of these ideas with the ideal of mathematisation made a deep impression on the young Descartes, who had begun to think along similar lines.[98]

Note, however, that Beeckman's *mathematico-physica* is not identical to the mathematisation of nature that Descartes advocated (though not in those terms) in his later writings. Beeckman's ideal was a sophisticated form of practical mathematics, the general application of mathematics to physical problems, whereas Descartes's programme involved replacing Peripatetic conceptions of corporeal substance by the geometrical conception of body, and the development of the implications of that irreducibly simple conception for natural philosophy. Mersenne also provides an instructive contrast with Descartes in this context. They first met, probably in Paris, on Descartes's return from Italy in May 1625, when he began to frequent the group of *savants* of which Mersenne was the centre and animator.[99] Because he denied the possibility of knowing the essence of body, Mersenne's mathematisation of nature involved the mathematisation of phenomena alone. But Descartes's mathematisation was precisely of the essence of body itself and its modes, that is, extension moving (or at rest) according to the laws of nature. In this sense Descartes's mathematisation of nature was more profound and thoroughgoing than that of Beeckman or of Mersenne.[100]

Although there are suggestions of it earlier, most notably in the early but unfinished *Regulae ad directionem ingenii,*[101] it is in *Le monde* that Descartes first clearly introduces his celebrated account of the nature of body. Descartes beguilingly introduces his three-dimensional matter by inviting the reader to dismiss as characteristic of it the traditional Peripatetic forms and qualities: neither the forms of Earth, Fire, and Air (no mention of Water), or of wood, a stone, or a metal, nor the qualities of hot or cold, dryness or wetness, levity or gravity, or of having a certain taste, smell, sound, colour, or light, and so on. Nor should the reader think that Descartes's matter is the prime matter of the Peripatetics, 'which has been so well stripped of all Forms and Qualities that there remains nothing that can be clearly conceived'. Rather, urges Descartes, 'let us conceive it as a real perfectly solid body that fills uniformly all the lengths, widths and depths of the immense space in the middle of which we have fixed our thoughts, so that each of its parts always occupies a part of this space so proportioned to its size that it cannot fill a larger part, nor squeeze itself into a smaller, nor allow, while it remains there, another part to find room there.'[102] As a consequence, Descartes does not allow any empty space into his world; all is full, and full with body.[103]

Le monde was not published during Descartes's lifetime, but was withheld when Galileo was condemned. The doctrine of body he introduced there was not presented at all in the *Discours de la méthode* and *Essais* that he did publish in 1637, and only barely mentioned in the *Meditationes* of 1641.[104] Furthermore, the doctrine was not presented there with full argument; Descartes feigns that God creates the world under examination in the imaginary spaces, beyond this world, and simply stipulates what this new world will be like. The fullest and most carefully set out version of Descartes's views on body and the related views on space is found in the *Principia philosophiae* of 1644. Descartes begins part II of the *Principia* with an account of body. After rehearsing the argument for the existence of material things, he argues that 'the nature of body consists not in weight, hardness, colour, or the like, but simply in extension.' The argument he uses there involves a kind of thought experiment; we can conceive of body without hardness, weight, colour, and the like, but we cannot conceive of it without extension. Therefore, he concludes, body is essentially extended and nothing else.[105] Descartes next draws out some of the consequences this doctrine has for empty space. Using an argument similar to the one he used to establish the nature of body, he argues that space and body are to be identified with one another: when we realise that all properties of bodies can be eliminated but extension, we must conclude that the idea of body is the same as the idea of a three-dimensional extension, that is, space.[106] Indeed, Descartes argues, 'it is a contradiction to suppose there is such a thing as a vacuum, i.e., that in which there is nothing whatsoever.'[107] He writes:

It is no less contradictory for us to conceive of a mountain without a valley than it is for us to think of the concavity apart from the extension contained within, or the extension apart from the substance which is extended; for . . . nothingness cannot possess any extension. Hence, if someone asks what would happen if God were to take away every single body contained in a vessel, without allowing any other body to take the place of what had been removed, the answer must be that the sides of the vessel would, in that case, have to be in contact. For when there is nothing between two bodies, they must necessarily touch each other.[108]

In this way, Descartes sides with the scholastics and against the atomists in denying the possibility of a vacuum. From this he draws some important conclusions for his physics. Though the argument is somewhat obscure, he argues first since we can imagine space beyond any possible boundary, it must really exist, and since space is body, body must therefore extend indefinitely.[109] Furthermore, since the nature of body as such is extension, there can be no distinction between the terrestrial and the celestial, as there is in Aristotelian natural philosophy.[110] Perhaps most important, since all there is in body is extension, everything in the purely physical world can be explained purely in terms of size, shape, and motion. Unlike Aristotle and his followers, Descartes says there are no elements, each with its own natural tendency to behaviour, tendencies to be hot or cold, to rise or fall; there is precisely one kind of stuff in the material world, extended substance, and all differences between things are to be explained in terms of its modes.[111]

Descartes's natural philosophy obviously shares much with that of the atomist Gassendi. Like Gassendi, Descartes eschews explanation in terms of the forms and qualities of the Aristotelian scholastics in favour of the explanation of the properties of bodies in terms of the size, shape, and motion of the smaller parts that make them up.[112] But there are important differences as well, as Descartes was keen to emphasise. As mentioned earlier, unlike the atomists, Descartes denied the possibility of empty space. But most important, Descartes denied the existence of atoms, smallest particles that are not themselves divisible into smaller parts.[113] For Descartes, all body, every portion of extended substance, is divisible into smaller parts. In fact, Descartes argues, there are certain situations in which bodies are actually divided into parts indefinitely small, so that for any part, of any size, one can always find a particle smaller still.[114] In general, though, the real difference between Descartes and the atomists is somewhat obscure. For Descartes, the indefinite divisibility of matter derives ultimately from divine power; because God is omnipotent, he can always divide a portion of matter into smaller parts, however small it might be.[115] But surely no Christian atomist would deny that. Gassendi, for example, characterises an atom as being such that 'there is no force in nature that can divide it', a formulation that would seem to leave open the possibility that a supernatural force, God, could split it.[116]

Descartes's view of body was enormously influential later in the seventeenth century and had numerous followers. However, it was not without serious problems, one of which concerned the individuation of bodies (see Chapter 9). In the *Principia,* Descartes defines an individual body in terms of motion, as 'whatever is transferred at a given time'. At the same time, he defines motion as the 'transfer of one piece of matter, or one body' from the vicinity of one group of bodies to that of another, giving rise to a circularity that, while apparently trivial, was one of the criticisms often cited by his contemporaries.[117]

A second noteworthy problem concerns the notion of impenetrability. As pointed out earlier, Gassendi, in the tradition of Epicurus, included impenetrability as one of the basic properties of atoms. But in defining body in terms of extension alone, Descartes was apparently unable to account for their impenetrability. Interestingly enough, the issue hardly comes up in Descartes's writings before it is raised by Henry More, in a series of letters written in 1648 and 1649.

There More is attempting to convince Descartes of his view, that incorporeal substance, like body, is extended, and that there can be empty space. He argues that impenetrability is distinct from extension, so there can be extension without impenetrability (empty space, spirit), and extension with impenetrability (body), and that these are different.[118] Descartes responds with an account of how extension, by itself, entails impenetrability:

> We cannot even understand one part of an extended thing penetrating another part equal to it without understanding by that very fact half of that extension eliminated or annihilated. But what is annihilated does not penetrate another thing. And thus, in my judgment, it is demonstrated that impenetrability pertains to the essence of extension. . . . Therefore, impenetrability must be admitted in every space.[119]

Descartes's view is that the real penetration of one body by another is simply inconceivable. Since body is defined by extension, he argues, then two bodies cannot occupy the same dimensions at the same time. So, if we imagine body A to penetrate body B, what is really happening is that a portion of body A has been annihilated, that portion corresponding to the supposed overlap between the two bodies. And that which is annihilated, does not penetrate. This is Descartes's version of the scholastic commonplace that two bodies cannot occupy the same place at the same time (see Chapter 15). In the words of Micraelius, 'There is no penetration of dimensions. And if a body must penetrate [another], quantity must necessarily give way to quantity. But quantity does not receive quantity into itself, seeing that it has been occupying the whole of [its] place.'[120]

Finally there is the issue of force and activity in bodies. By defining body in terms of extension alone, Descartes would seem to eliminate all activity from bodies. But bodies do move, and Descartes must account for that. Furthermore, terms like 'force' and 'endeavour' do also appear in Descartes's account of body and its laws.[121] But how can that be? Descartes explains his use of the term 'force' in his law of impact in the *Principia* as follows:

> The force each body has to act on another or to resist the action of another consists in this one thing, that each and every thing tends, insofar as it can [*quantum in se est*], to remain in the same state which it is, in accordance with the law posited earlier. Hence . . . that which is at rest has some force for remaining at rest . . . ; [and] that which moves has some force for persevering in its motion.[122]

The 'law posited earlier' to which Descartes refers here is what he calls his first law of nature, that 'each and every thing, insofar as it can, always perseveres in the same state.'[123] Now, this is a law that, Descartes writes, derives from the immutability of God, the same immutability that grounds Descartes's basic law of the conservation of motion. According to that law, God creates bodies in motion, and, because of His immutability, maintains in bodies the same motion He put there when He first created them. God, then, Descartes argues, is both the first and continuing cause of motion in the world. This, then, is the ground of the force that Descartes appeals to in his laws of motion: to talk about there being a force for motion to continue, or a force that keeps a body in rest, Descartes claims, is just to talk about how it is that God in His immutability causes and maintains motion in the world. And with this, we have a solution to the problem of the activity of bodies as well. On Descartes's view, extended bodies are not themselves active; all activity comes from outside bodies, from God in the typical case of inanimate bodies, or from minds, in the case of human beings or (more rarely), bodies animated by angels. In response to a question that More raised, Descartes wrote, 'I consider *matter left to itself and receiving no impulse from anything else* as plainly at rest. But it is impelled by God, conserving the same amount of motion or transference in it as he put there from the first.'[124] In an earlier passage from the same reply, Descartes says it perhaps more clearly still: 'The force moving [a body] can be that of God conserving as much transference in matter as he placed in it at the first moment of creation or also that of a created substance, like our mind, or something else to which [God] gave the power of moving a body.'[125] In this way Descartes can render consistent his claim that bodies are by their nature extended, while accounting for the evident activity in the world: activity, for Descartes, comes from without.

This view should be contrasted with that of Gassendi. For Gassendi, as for Descartes (and as for every properly Christian philosopher) all activity, as all being, ultimately derives from God, and must be sustained by God. But there is a radical difference in how that activity is manifested in the world. For Gassendi, bodies, atoms, are genuinely active, it would seem; God, in creating them, endowed them with genuine self-motion, which He sustains. Not so for Descartes. Descartes's God created bodies inert; what activity there is in the world derives from the action of beings that are not bodies, from God or from finite incorporeal substances, like our minds. This opposition is fundamental to later seventeenth-century thought about body. Many will follow Descartes in holding that body is by its nature inert, and its motion and activity must come from without; such are the occasionalists of the Cartesian school, as well as philosophers like Henry More, who saw the mechanical philosophy as an argument for the existence of incorporeal substance.[126] On the other side are those, Newton and Leibniz most visibly, but probably also Spinoza, who argued for a world of bodies in themselves active.

3. Hobbes

In a sense, Descartes and Gassendi set the agenda for the rest of the century; their conceptions of body constitute the main alternatives between which adherents of the new mechanical philosophy argued. But there is a third important figure at mid-century as well. Although Thomas Hobbes is better known today for his political thought, to his contemporaries he was equally well known for his uncompromising adherence to the mechanical philosophy. Because of his materialistic views on mind and heterodox theology, as well as his politics, Hobbes did not exert the direct and explicit influence on later thinkers that Descartes and Gassendi did. Despite that fact, he deserves to be considered in their company.

The mechanical philosophy of Hobbes, like that of Descartes and Gassendi, relied exclusively on the motions and contact actions of bodies for its explanations of all change. The only force allowed by Hobbes was the contact force of impact, produced and measured by the speeds and magnitudes of colliding particles; in this sense, motion and force are identified with one another.[127] Hobbes invoked no principles of movement or activity in his system except for the initial impetus given to the whole by God at the Creation. Hobbes's system thus seemed open to the atheistic interpretation that God is not required at all, that the world system may be supposed to be eternal and uncreated. This interpretation, together with Hobbes's political and moral views, his clear statements about the church, clergy and anthropomorphic 'spirits' as nothing more than means of social control, and his extreme materialism, ensured that Hobbes was regarded with great suspicion by devout thinkers both in England and on the continent. Even so, it is abundantly clear that he was regarded as an intellectual force to be reckoned with, and his works were influential at the very least in a negative sense – stimulating many critiques and opposed positions.[128]

At the outset of the discussion of 'The First grounds of Philosophy', in Part II of *De corpore* (London, 1655), the principal exposition of his natural philosophy, Hobbes makes the Ockhamist move[129] of asking what would remain for someone left alone after the annihilation of all other things.[130] The answer, according to Hobbes, is the memory and imagination of magnitudes, motions, sounds, colours, and other sense-impressions. 'All which things', he goes on, 'though they be nothing but ideas and phantasms, happening internally to him that imagineth; yet they will appear as if they were external, and not at all depending on any power of the mind' (II.7.1). Our hypothetical survivor, by remembering that something, before the annihilation, had an existence outside the mind, has *ipso facto* a conception of space. The Platonic idea of space as a receptacle for containing bodies, which Hobbes insists is what 'all men' mean when they talk of space, is then defined as 'the phantasm of a thing existing without the mind simply; that is to say, that phantasm, in which we consider no other accident, but only that it appears without us' (II.7.2). This is what Hobbes calls imaginary space.

'Real space' is introduced to accommodate body, which Hobbes defines as 'that, which having no dependence on our thought, is coincident or coextended with some part of space' (II.8.1). So although our sense-impressions lead us only to an imaginary concept of space, we can infer on rational grounds that extension is an essential prerequisite for all material existence: 'No body can be conceived to be without extension, or without figure' (II.8.3).[131] Real space, therefore, is the extension or magnitude of a body. But Hobbes is careful to distinguish between this view and the Cartesian notion of extension: 'Coextension [of a body with space] is not the coextended body' (II.8.2). Furthermore, responding directly to Descartes's arguments against the void, he dismisses as absurd the notion that 'two bodies must therefore necessarily touch one another, because no other body is between them': 'If there intercede any imagined space which may receive another body, then those bodies are not contiguous'. Vacuum can exist, therefore, but only in imaginary space (II.8.9). In this way, Hobbes, unlike Descartes, distinguishes between space and body. But despite the distinction in theory, which would seem to place him against the Aristotelians, Hobbes rejected as invalid all arguments in support of void space and required the universe to be a plenum. His own 'unanswerable' argument in *De corpore* against the vacuum, however, merely repeats the age-old descriptions of the operation of the clepsydra, or (in his case) a gardener's watering can from which water will not flow if air cannot enter to replace it (IV.26.2).

Hobbes's conception of body was essentially corpuscularian; as in Descartes and Gassendi, the sensible qualities of bodies are to be explained in terms of their make-up by smaller bodies with characteristic sizes, shapes, and motions. One of his 'Six suppositions for the salving of the phenomena' in *De corpore* was that 'in the body of the air there are certain other bodies intermingled, which are not fluid; but withal that they are so small, that they are not perceptible by sense' (IV.26.5). For Hobbes, then, extension, figure, and motion or rest (one or other of which must also pertain to every body) are the primary qualities, or, to use his terminology, accidents of body. An accident is 'the manner of our conception of body', or 'that faculty of any body by which it works in us a conception of itself' (II.8.2). All other qualities are 'certain motions either of the mind of the perceiver, or of the bodies themselves which are perceived' (II.8.3). Like Descartes he takes this to entail that every such extended thing is divisible, however small it might be, and that, consequently, there are no atoms, no perfectly hard and indivisible bodies (II.7.13; II.8.8). In this way, though his personal sympathies were closer to Gassendi than to Descartes, his natural philosophy seems closer to Descartes than to Gassendi's Epicurean atomism.[132]

Hobbes's view on the activity of matter seems to undergo something of an evolution in the course of his philosophical development. The text known as the 'Short Tract on First Principles' (untitled by Hobbes, written c. 1630–1)[133] is generally agreed to be his first attempt to develop a system of natural philosophy. In the 'Short Tract' it is possible to see traces of a more 'animistic' conception of natural phenomena than appears in the mature work. The 'Short Tract' relies partly upon the heuristic convenience of a putative 'agent that hath active power inherent in it self'. This agent is clearly modelled on luminous bodies, supposedly capable of acting upon other bodies by their spontaneous and continual emission of light. Roger Bacon's *De multiplicatione specierum,* a renowned work in the tradition of light metaphysics that Hobbes is known to have had access to and in which he is known to have expressed an interest, seems to have been a major influence on the 'Short Tract'.[134] Even in his protracted response (c. 1642–3) to Thomas White's *De mundo* (Paris, 1642), Hobbes invokes the power of the Sun as the driving force for many physical phenomena, including the rotation of the Earth. The fact that the Sun is a luminous body entails that it must have a continuous dilatory and contracting motion – light now being regarded by Hobbes as an expanding motion in the surrounding aether caused by the outward pulse of the dilating Sun. Significantly, he refers to this motion of the Sun as its 'systole and diastole'.[135] Another probable influence in this connexion is Francis Bacon's speculative philosophy, with which Hobbes was acquainted, and in which visible 'species' operating in a material medium play an important rôle.[136]

By the time he was ready to publish *De corpore* in 1655, Hobbes had excised from his system such unexplained, taken-for-granted active principles. The driving force of the Sun now came from its 'simple circular motion'. Hobbes supposed the Sun's motion to be analogous to that of a sieve; that is to say, the Sun's centre makes small circular revolutions, so that successive points on the Sun's surface push outwards against the surrounding medium and send out a pulse of light. The only difference between this and the earlier diastolic movement of the Sun is that the pulse of light is sent off in different directions at slightly differing times, rather than simultaneously. The crucial point about this new theory, however, was Hobbes's claim that this kind of 'simple circular motion' is perpetual. Once God has set up this 'cribrating' ('sieve-like') movement it will continue indefinitely. Here Hobbes was adapting the concept of perpetual circular motion developed by

Galileo in his *Dialogo sopra i due Massimi Sistemi del Mondo* (Leiden, 1632) to account for the motion of the Earth, Moon, and other planets. Among Hobbes's 'Six suppositions for the salving of the phenomena of nature' in *De corpore* was the claim 'that in the sun and the rest of the planets there is and always has been a simple circular motion' (IV.26.5). Moreover, drawing upon his earlier claim that 'such things as are moved with simple circular motion, beget simple circular motion' (III.21.10), Hobbes went on to invoke simple circular motion in his explanations of many physical phenomena. To take an everyday example from the *Seven Philosophical Problems,* to those who are 'much distempered with drinking wine', nearby objects seem 'to go and come in a kind of circling motion'. This is because particles of wine have a 'good degree' of simple circular motion, and when 'heated in the veins' they transfer their motion to the brain.[137]

III. MECHANISM AND BEYOND IN THE LATE CENTURY

Gassendi, Descartes, and to a lesser extent Hobbes set the questions that the later seventeenth century had to deal with. However, there were many and diverse responses to the mechanist systems that they presented and the different conceptions of body and space that they espoused.

One interesting response was backward looking. It attempted to reconcile the new mechanist philosophy with the older Aristotelian philosophy of the schools. In the second half of the seventeenth century there were numerous books with titles like Jean-Baptiste Du Hamel's *De consensu veteris et novae philosophiae* (Paris, 1663), Jacques Du Roure's *La physique expliquée suivant le sentiment des anciens et nouveaux philosophes; & principalement Descartes* (Paris, 1653), Johannes de Raey's *Clavis philosophiae naturalis sive Introductio ad contemplationem naturae Aristotelico-Cartesiana* (Leiden, 1654), and René Le Bossu's *Parallèle des principes de la physique d'Aristote & celle de René Des Cartes* (Paris, 1674). These works and others by like-minded authors tried to show either that everything the moderns did could be found in Aristotle and his followers, or that, at least, what the new philosophers were doing was fully consistent with the traditional learning. In particular, there were valiant attempts to show that the new conceptions of body and space were consistent with Aristotelian analyses of the physical world in terms of substance, matter, and form.[138]

There were other interesting responses as well. For some, the master, be he Descartes or Gassendi, set out the true path, and all that was left was to elaborate and defend the system already found in outline in the *Principia philosophiae* or the *Syntagma philosophicum.* But not everyone was happy with discipleship. There were also those who responded to the tensions within and between the different schools of mechanism by attempting to articulate new mechanist conceptions of body and the physical world within the bounds of the mechanical philosophy. And finally there were those who stepped outside of the boundaries of mechanism altogether.

1. Cartesianism and Gassendism

Descartes's view of the physical world had numerous followers, thinkers who followed Descartes in holding that the world is constituted by a plenum of bodies characterised by the attribute of extension, holding that there is no distinction between space and body, and thus that there cannot be a vacuum in the world, a space that does not contain body. The members of the Cartesian school also generally followed Descartes in denying the possibility of genuine atoms, and held that extended substance, as such, was indefinitely divisible. Closely connected with this is the doctrine of occasionalism, the view that God is the only genuine cause in the world, and that He and He alone is responsible for the activity and motion in the world. Although the roots of the doctrine are somewhat complex, and transcend questions concerning the notion of body, and although it is not absolutely clear that Descartes himself was an occasionalist, members of the Cartesian school found the view quite congenial.[139] In so far as the notion of extension would seem altogether to exclude activity, God would be an obvious cause to which to look as a source of motion in the world. Although there were debates within the Cartesian school about various aspects of his system, these basic aspects of his view of body, space, and vacuum were shared by such followers as Regius, Clauberg, Clerselier, de La Forge, Rohault, Régis, and Malebranche, among many others.[140]

Despite the general agreement among members of the school, one interesting heretic is worth noting, the Cartesian atomist, Gérauld de Cordemoy. Cordemoy, a card-carrying member of the Parisian Cartesian circle of the 1660s, set his views out in his popular and often reprinted book, *Le discernement du corps et de l'âme en six discours* (Paris, 1666). Like other Cartesians, Cordemoy believed that there are only two sorts of substance, extended bodies and thinking non-extended minds, and like most, he argued for the necessity of an external cause for the motion of inert bodies, in particular, God.[141] Cordemoy also offered occasionalist accounts of mind–body union and distinction that are very much in line with those that other Cartesians of the period offered.[142] But Cordemoy's account of body, matter, and space are quite different from those that other Cartesians offered. Basic to Cordemoy's view is a distinction between 'body' and 'matter'. A body is defined as an 'extended substance', very much in the spirit of Descartes. But very much against that spirit is a conclusion that he draws from that definition. While his reasoning is not altogether clear, Cordemoy infers that since a body is a substance, it is thereby indivisible. Matter, on the other hand, is a collection of such indivisible bodies, and is not a substance, but merely an aggregate. So while body is indivisible, matter is not; it is only because people have confused body and substance with the notion of matter that they have thought that bodies are divisible.[143] Again, contrary to Descartes and his followers, Cordemoy also recognised the possibility (and actuality) of the vacuum. Unlike the Cartesians, Cordemoy simply saw no problems with saying that two bodies can be situated in such a way that other bodies *could* be placed between them, without there *actually* being bodies that come between.[144] Needless to say, Cordemoy's more orthodox Cartesian colleagues were not sympathetic to this curious twisting of the Cartesian tradition.[145]

There were also those who followed the Gassendist line, arguing in favour of indivisible atoms and the void. The most visible disciple was François Bernier, whose seven-volume *Abrégé de la philosophie de Gassendi* (Lyon, 1678) made Gassendi's massive and very learned *Syntagma* accessible to a wider audience, including, of course, his accounts of atoms and the void. Also important for the diffusion of Gassendist ideas in Britain was Walter Charleton's *Physiologia Epicuro-Gassendo-Charletoniana* (London, 1654), which included many passages translated and paraphrased from Gassendi's *Animadversiones in decimum librum Diogenis Laertii* (Lyon, 1649), the translation and commentary on Epicurus that constitutes a kind of early draft of the later *Syntagma*. Other important Gassendists include Pierre Petit, Giles de Launay, Jean Chapelain, Antoine Menjot, Samuel Sorbière, and, perhaps, Marin Cureau de La Chambre, among others.[146]

The battle between the Cartesian and the Gassendist versions of the mechanical philosophy and their different conceptions of body and space was one of the important intellectual events of the second half of the seventeenth century. Not everyone, even among the mechanists, chose to participate; some, like Robert Boyle, for example, chose to sit on the side-lines. As 'the restorer' in England of the mechanical philosophy, as his contemporaries described him, Boyle's program was to show the superfluity of substantial forms and real qualities and to replace the vacuous explanations characteristic of Peripateticism (the 'quality of whiteness' in snow explains why it dazzles the eyes) by explanations employing the 'two grand and most catholic principles of bodies, matter and motion', matter being composed of corpuscles, with motion 'the grand agent of all that happens in nature'; and he was an important link in the pre-Locke development of the distinction between primary and secondary qualities. Yet Boyle dismissed as mere metaphysics the debate between the Cartesians and the atomists about whether matter is infinitely divisible, which, he thought, was irrelevant to his concerns as an experimentalist,[147] and he had little to say *de motu*. Similarly, Boyle and Hooke refused to become embroiled in discussions about the possibility of a vacuum. They referred to the state of affairs inside their evacuated air-pump as the *vacuum Boylianum,* but they were always careful to insist on defining this vacuum merely instrumentally.[148]

Despite the determined agnosticism of some, Gassendi seemed to have the edge in Britain, where his atomism seemed to be more widely influential than Cartesian mechanism. Walter Charleton, in voluntary exile in Paris during the Civil War period, was a friend of Thomas Hobbes and was well acquainted with Cartesian natural philosophy. But even though he knew Descartes's thought, and held it in high esteem, he generally sided with Gassendi against Descartes. The fact that he adopted Gassendi's version of the new philosophy presumably derives from what he took to be Gassendi's superior knowledge of, and respect for, contemporary developments in (al)chemical theorising. Indeed, it seems safe to assume that the appeal of Gassendi's philosophy in Britain derived from the fact that it was more amenable to the traditions of English 'sooty empirics' than to the rationalist mechanical philosophy of Descartes.[149] It is hardly surprising that the two foremost exponents of the new philosophy in England, Robert Boyle and Isaac Newton, should later show the same intellectual commitment to chemistry (they were both involved with (al)chemical experimentation) and to Neoplatonism.[150]

But on the Continent, it was Descartes's mechanism that seemed to flourish. Gassendi directed himself primarily against the schoolmen, and against the eclectic and incoherent atomisms of the earlier part of the century. But Gassendi's philosophy of atoms encountered its most formidable opponent from an unexpected source, the corpuscular philosophy of René Descartes, which had little to do with the multiple atomisms of the late Renaissance. Prominent followers of Gassendi did realise, eventually, that Cartesianism had become the greatest barrier to Gassendism. Samuel Sorbière, secretary of Montmor's academy in Paris and translator of Hobbes, and Jean Chapelain, the powerful literary critic who was instrumental in selecting the fifteen original members of the Académie Royale des Sciences, were among the Gassendists who came to view the Cartesians as their most important rivals.[151] Descartes's explicit call for the complete rejection of learning and tradition had persuaded many Cartesians that they, at least, now possessed a permanent foundation for philosophy that no mere tradition could hope to supply. Even the tradition of Christian Epicureanism which Gassendi had established failed to offer such a guarantee. In the ensuing competition between Gassendists and Cartesians, not only would the future of atomism be affected, but the relevance of history and tradition to philosophical inquiry would also be decided. As a result of the conflict, Gassendi's great achievement of re-creating the Epicurean atomist tradition became increasingly obscured as Descartes convinced his readers that they could justify their belief in his corpuscular physics without the bother of having to learn the history of philosophy; Descartes washed his hands of history and simply declared in effect that corpuscular physics henceforth began with himself.

2. Correcting mechanism: More and Cudworth

One of the most interesting reactions to the developments earlier in the century was that of the Cambridge Platonists, particularly Henry More and Ralph Cudworth, who attempted to combine mechanism with a variety of Platonism.

More and Cudworth were committed by their own brand of rationalist theology to a categorical disjunction between matter and spirit. If matter was passive, its opposite, spirit, had to be immaterial and active. For More and Cudworth all activity, even the fall of a heavy body, had to be caused and carried out by a supervising immaterial principle, separate from and external to matter. Known variously as *hylarchic spirit,* or the 'Spirit of Nature', this architectonic and supervising principle owed something to contemporary ideas about a 'plastic principle' in Nature. But whereas for some natural philosophers this principle, like the Stoic *logos spermatikos,* was usually conceived in materialist terms as a principle at once subtly material and active (like the Gassendist animal soul), More and Cudworth vigorously denied its corporeality. Being theologians, their main philosophical concern was to establish beyond doubt God's existence. The only way to succeed in this, they believed, was to show that the physical world cannot operate without the existence of an immaterial supervising principle, whereupon it would be comparatively easy to establish the existence of immaterial souls, and finally God.[152]

More was a leading figure in the early popularisation of Descartes's natural philosophy in England, but it is clear that from the outset he used Cartesianism principally as a means of promoting his own rather different ideas.[153] More set aside Descartes's philosophical objections to atomism, for example, insisting that while every particle is indefinitely divisible in thought and actually so divisible by God, as Descartes claimed, it can still be in reality indivisible by any created power. This argument served two purposes. First, it enabled More to insist that the Cartesian philosophy was 'in a manner the same with that of Democritus', which in turn provided him with further grounds for arguing that the new philosophy, like that of Democritus, derived ultimately from divine wisdom known to Moses.[154] Second, More's adoption of atomism automatically provided him with a number of arguments, found in ancient and modern atomists alike, for the real existence of void space. Indeed, much of his philosophical output was devoted to the establishment of space as a perfect exemplar of incorporeal being, a somewhat surprising aspect of these efforts being his insistence that everything must be extended, including immaterial souls, angels, even God. As he humorously put it in the *Divine Dialogues* (London, 1668), space is 'so imaginary that it cannot possibly be dis-imagined by human understanding'.[155]

Unlike Patrizi, Gassendi, Hill, Warner, and some others, More did not exclude space from the Aristotelian categories of substance and accident but insisted that there cannot be a real attribute without some real subject to support it. Accordingly, the dimensions of space become one of the attributes of immaterial substance, and matter partakes of extension by virtue of subsisting in spirit. For More, unlike for Descartes, extension is not an attribute of body alone. More held that both corporeal and incorporeal substance are extended; what differentiates the two is impenetrability, which is present in corporeal substance, and lacking in incorporeal substance. Furthermore, when dealing with empty space, the spirit in which body resides, More came to decide, is God. Even in his first letter to Descartes (December 1648), More had insisted that God's omnipresence entails His extension and occupation of 'all the spaces' of the world, and furthermore that God's infinite immensity implied that space is also infinite. By the time of his *Enchiridion metaphysicum* (London, 1671), More had explicitly identified space with the immensity of God. This can be seen, he believed, by comparing 'about twenty titles which the metaphysicians attribute to God' with the attributes of his concept of space: 'One, Simple, Immobile, Eternal, Complete, Independent, Existing in itself, Subsisting by itself, Incorruptible, Necessary, Immense, Uncreated, Uncircumscribed, Incomprehensible, Omnipresent, Incorporeal, All-penetrating, All-embracing, Being by its essence, Actual Being, Pure Act' (8.8). It should be noted that More did not believe that extension necessarily entails divisibility. An extended God could no more be divided than one area of infinite space could be physically separated from the surrounding space. This was as absurd, More said, as cutting off part of the Sun's rays with 'a pair of Scissors made of pellucid Crystall'.[156]

Although in *Enchiridion metaphysicum* he spoke of space as 'not only something real but even something Divine' (8.8), he did not fully identify space with God. Space, after all, shows none of the attributes of life and activity which belong to

God. Furthermore, although all physical phenomena could be said to take place within the space of God's immensity, More did not wish to develop a proto-pantheist philosophy. To maintain a measure of transcendence for God, and to protect the notion of free will, More invoked individual souls, and the universal Spirit of Nature as the active principles required to drive the otherwise purely mechanical world. The Spirit of Nature is 'the Vicarious Power of God upon this great *Automaton, the* World',[157] 'the great *Quartermaster-General* of Divine Providence':

A substance incorporeal, but without Sense and Animadversion, pervading the whole Matter of the Universe, and exercising a Plastical power therein according to the sundry predispositions and occasions in the parts it works upon, raising such *Phaenomena* in the World, by directing the parts of the Matter and their Motion, as cannot be resolved into mere Mechanical powers.[158]

Ralph Cudworth took a similar line towards concepts of space and matter. Seeking to promote a variety of mechanical philosophy purged of all atheistic implications, Cudworth referred to a 'most ancient and genuine' form of atomism 'that was religious, called Moschical (or if you will Mosaical) and Pythagorical'.[159] Cudworth's desire to identify a mysterious Phoenician philosopher, Moschus, the supposed originator of this genuine religious atomism, with Moses remained unfulfilled, but he was not above the use of innuendo and rhetorical implication.[160]

One of the major hostages to atheism, implicit in all supposedly corrupt versions of atomism, was the suggestion that there might be principles of activity inherent in matter. This is what Cudworth called 'hylozoism'. According to that doctrine, 'all Body, as such, and therefore every smallest Atom of it, [has] *Life* Essentially belonging to it'.[161] Both More and Cudworth were anxious to deny this notion. Here again, it can be seen that More commended Cartesianism (at least before 1660) because of what he believed it could not do, rather than what it could do; Descartes's strict distinction between inert extended substance and active incorporeal substance would seem to exclude any kind of hylozoism. A thorough study of Descartes's philosophy, he wrote, would show 'the just extent of the Mechanical powers of Matter, how farre they will reach, and where they fall short. Which will be the best assistance to Religion that Reason and the Knowledge of Nature can afford'.[162] Clearly, the superaddition of other, more occult, active powers to matter itself, such as gravity, fermentation, and the 'spring' or autodiffusive power of air implied by certain experiments conducted with Boyle's newly invented air-pump, jeopardised More's enterprise. Once it was allowed that some activities could be enacted by matter itself, the way was clear to deny any need for a spiritual realm. More and Cudworth were not swayed by the natural philosophers' claim that superadded active principles in matter presupposed a supreme being, presumably because they knew of or (perhaps it is more accurate to say) thought they could discern contemporary developments among various heretical sects, in which matter was supposed to be inherently, or essentially, active. The groups they had in mind were the Paracelsians, the followers of Hendrik Niclaes (c. 1502–80), founder of the so-called Family of Love (Familists) but also popular with Ranters, Quakers, and Seekers, the numerous diverse followers of Jacob Boehme (1575–1624), and in later years Spinozists and certain natural philosophers, such as Francis Glisson, the author of a *Tractatus de natura substantiae energetica, seu de vita naturae* (London, 1672). Whether or not More and Cudworth were right to see these different groups as hylozoic, there is no clear indication that other leading natural philosophers were nearly as perturbed by these same religious or philosophical developments.[163] While there were certainly many, most notably the Cartesian occasionalists on the Continent, who agreed with More and Cudworth in distinguishing radically between inert matter and active spirit, there were also a number who emphasised the internal activity of body.

3. Stretching mechanism: Spinoza

More and Cudworth, on one hand, wanted to supplement mechanism by adding incorporeal substances of many sorts so as to explain things that, they thought, mechanism itself could not explain. Spinoza, on the other hand, wanted to eliminate the explanatory appeal to incorporeal things in the physical world, without eliminating those things themselves. The result was a world of bodies exactly parallel to a world of thought, but a world in which everything that goes on among bodies can be explained entirely in terms of extension and its modes, while everything that goes on in the world of thought can be explained entirely in terms of thinking things. Put more technically, Spinoza recognised just one substance, God or Nature. But, Spinoza argued, this substance has an infinity of attributes. From this one infinite substance follow with necessity all possible modes; these finite modes are the finite things of the world. These modes must be comprehended through substance, and since substance itself can be comprehended through different attributes, so each mode must be comprehensible through different attributes. While God has an infinity of attributes, Spinoza acknowledged that we are only acquainted with two, thought and extension. In this way, Spinoza's God is both a thinking thing and an extended thing. But in so far as each mode is itself comprehensible through both thought and extension, each finite thing is both a thinking thing and an extended thing. Take a human being, for example. I am a single finite mode of substance. As an extended thing, I am a body in the physical world, an extended thing made up of parts, which are made up of parts smaller still, a complex thing with a complex organisation. As a thinking thing, I am, for Spinoza, the idea of that body, and, by virtue of that fact, the mind of that body. But I am both mind and body, and both are modal expressions of the same thing.[164]

This, in outline, is Spinoza's metaphysics. But the question immediately at hand is the status of the physical world on Spinoza's view. The fullest discussion of this question is found in what is a sort of digression in part II of the *Ethica,* a series of axioms, lemmata, and definitions that immediately follow proposition 13. In the immediately preceding propositions, Spinoza had established that the mind is the idea of the body. Since every body would seem to have an idea, it would seem to follow that every body would have a mind in some sense, something that Spinoza accepts. But in so far as the human body differs from other bodies, the human mind will differ from other minds. This is the immediate occasion for the digression. But even though pure physics is not Spinoza's main preoccupation here, the text does give us a good idea of his conception of the physical world.

Leaving aside the larger metaphysical framework in which Spinoza places it, the world that he presents in the *Ethica* is broadly Cartesian. Spinoza's bodies are not substances; only God is. But they are finite modes under the attribute of extension, extended things, things that are distinguished from one another in terms of size, shape, and motion alone. Spinoza's discussion in the *Ethica* is structured around a distinction he draws between the 'simplest bodies' and the complex bodies that they go to make up. The simplest bodies are uniform and uncomposed though extended things that are individuated purely by motion and rest. Complex bodies are made up of smaller parts, ultimately the 'simplest bodies' on the picture developed in the *Ethica*. Indeed, the world as a whole, understood under the attribute of extension, is such a complex body, what he calls the '*facies totius universae*' in an important letter. The picture is reductionist; everything in the physical world is explicable in terms of the size, shape, and motion of these 'simplest bodies' that ultimately compose things. Though the issue is not altogether clear, Spinoza seems to have regarded these 'simplest bodies' as being themselves divisible. Furthermore, while his reasons may have been different from those that Descartes offered, like Descartes he rejected the atomist claim that vacua are possible.[165]

But one place where Spinoza seems to depart from Descartes is on the question of activity. For Descartes, extended bodies are inert and move by virtue of the activity of incorporeal substance, God in the general case, and finite minds in the special case of human bodies. For Descartes's followers this is connected with the doctrine of occasionalism; God is the only genuine cause of activity and change in the world. But this, of course, will not do for Spinoza. Finite minds are, in a sense, identical with bodies, he argues, the same mode of substance comprehended under two different attributes, and there can be no causal influence from mind to body. Furthermore, Spinoza's God is immanent; everything that is, is in God. And so, there is no external God to which he can appeal. But even though it is clear that occasionalism is not open to Spinoza, it is not altogether clear what exactly is. The issue comes up not in the *Ethica* itself, but in a series of letters written at the very end of Spinoza's life, and in the context of a somewhat different question.

Several times in the mid-1670s Walter von Tschirnhaus confessed that he found it 'exceedingly difficult to conceive how the existence of bodies having motion and figure can be proved *a priori,* since there is nothing of this kind in Extension when we consider it absolutely'. To this Spinoza replied with the observation that 'from extension as Descartes conceives it, that is, as a quiescent mass, it is not only, as you say, difficult to prove the existence of bodies, but absolutely impossible. For matter at rest will continue at rest as much as possible and will not be set in motion except by some stronger external cause. For this reason I did not hesitate to say once that Descartes's principles of natural things are useless, not to say absurd.'[166] The question of the individuation of body naturally involves the question of the cause of motion because for Spinoza, as for Descartes, individual bodies are individuated by motion and rest. But since this reply was not altogether to the point, Tschirnhaus asked Spinoza again how he would deduce 'the variety of things' from extension, reminding him that Descartes had to fall back on the motion created in extension by God. Spinoza's reply simply affirmed the impossibility of deducing corporeal variety *a priori* from extension alone, and 'that therefore matter is badly defined by Descartes as Extension, but that it must necessarily be defined by an attribute which expresses eternal and infinite essence. But perhaps, if life lasts', he continues disappointingly, 'I will discuss this question with you some other time more clearly. For so far I have not been able to write anything about these things in proper order.'[167] The 'other time' did not arrive, since this letter of 15 July 1676 was the last Spinoza wrote to Tschirnhaus, and, perhaps, the penultimate letter he wrote to anyone. While it is somewhat difficult to say exactly what Spinoza had in mind here, it does seem that he is criticising Descartes for thinking of body in terms of extension alone; it is because of that that Descartes must appeal outside of body itself to find a cause for the activity of bodies. This, as Spinoza well knew, was the grounds of Descartes's derivation of the laws of motion, which followed for Descartes from the immutability of God as a cause of motion in the world. But for Spinoza, God is *natura naturans,* the active aspect of nature inherent *in* nature, the source of all activity in nature that is itself infused through nature.[168] Perhaps Spinoza's idea here is that in conceiving bodies not through extension considered as a common notion, abstracted from the bodies of our experience,[169] but from extension considered as an attribute of God, we conceive bodies as in themselves active, having an inherent activity that does not depend on a transcendent God acting on bodies from without. Perhaps this is what he meant when he suggested that matter 'must necessarily be defined by an attribute which expresses eternal and infinite essence'. If so, then Spinoza is here separating himself from the dualist tradition of Descartes, the Cartesians, and the Cambridge Platonists, all of whom radically separated inert matter from active spirit, and allies himself with those who see bodies as having a kind of internal activity. In this, he would seem to agree with the next figure whom we shall discuss, Leibniz.

4. Stretching mechanism: Leibniz

Earlier in this chapter we discussed attempts in the seventeenth century to marry the hylemorphism of the Aristotelian tradition with the new mechanical philosophy. This tendency remained strong through the century. One can point to many figures, both mechanists and Aristotelians, who were eager to argue that the two apparently contradictory points of view were really reconcilable. There were many good reasons for reconciliation, ranging from the prestige that the new philosophy offered to the adherents of the old, and the safety the name of Aristotle offered to the adherents of the new, to the general belief, inherited from the Renaissance, that at the deepest level all philosophies agree.[170] It is in this context that we must view Leibniz's programme for physics and the conceptions of body, space, and substance that went with it.

Leibniz outlined his philosophical development and his synthetic conception of philosophy in an important letter to Nicolas Remond, written in January 1714, near the end of his life. Leibniz told Remond that he had always tried 'to uncover and reunite the truth buried and scattered through the opinions of the different sects of philosophers'. He continued: 'I have found that most sects are correct in the better part of what they put forward, though not so much in what they deny. . . . I flatter myself in having penetrated the two kingdoms and in having seen that . . . everything in the phenomena of nature happens both mechanically and at the same time metaphysically.'[171] Leibniz's attempt to reconcile the two competing systems of thought began quite early in his career. He was converted from his early school-boy preference for the traditional philosophy (certainly encouraged by the very conservative Protestant universities he attended)[172] to the new mechanism quite early, at age fifteen, if we are to believe what he wrote to Remond. But by the time he was twenty-two, he had joined the ranks of those who were trying to combine the old with the new. In an important letter to his former teacher Jakob Thomasius from April 1669, later printed largely unchanged in the preface to an edition of writings by the Humanist Mario Nizolio that he published in 1670, Leibniz reinterpreted Aristotle in mechanist terms, establishing, as he thought, that however his later followers may have distorted his thought, the Philosopher was really a mechanist too.[173] Leibniz's strategy for reconciling the old and the new was not very sophisticated; he simply claimed that there is not a 'principle of Aristotle which cannot be explained by magnitude, figure, and motion'.[174] The bulk of the letter, then, was occupied with making good on this claim, showing that notions like matter, form, and physical change can be given interpretations in terms of the basic notions of the mechanical philosophy, and, moreover, that such interpretations are what Aristotle himself had in mind. Only the distortions of later schoolmen have prevented us from seeing the true, mechanist Aristotle, something that he and others of his contemporaries are uncovering.

The sort of crude reconciliation of Aristotle and the mechanists, or better, the reduction of the former to the latter that Leibniz envisioned here is obviously tied to the sort of strict mechanism that he seems to have held in his early years.[175] But a crucial step in Leibniz's development seems to have taken place a few years after the letter to Thomasius, in Paris. There, on a visit between 1672 and 1676, Leibniz had the opportunity to study with Christiaan Huygens, and in the course of this study, he reported to Remond in 1714, he came to see difficulties with the mechanist programme to which he had become converted:

When I sought the ultimate reasons for mechanism and the very laws of motion, I was completely surprised to see that it would be impossible to find them in mathematics, and that one must return to metaphysics. This led me back to entelechies, and from the material to the formal, and made me finally understand, after many corrections and advances in my thought, that monads or simple substances are the only true substances, and that material things are only phenomena, though well founded and well interconnected.[176]

In this we find the kernel of Leibniz's mature view. The particular version of mechanism he held in his youth is abandoned for a genuine blend of mechanism and Aristotelianism, a highly original position that represents one of his most distinctive contributions to seventeenth-century philosophy.

Leibniz's mature position began to emerge in the late 1670s, and became a

matter of public record in such important documents as the *Brevis Demonstratio*
published in 1686, and in the letters he wrote to Antoine Arnauld between
1686 and 1690.[177] But his conception of the physical world, his distinctive and
idiosyncratic version of mechanism pervade his writings, both public and private,
for the rest of his career. There are some important differences of detail from text
to text and time to time; one could hardly expect Leibniz not to rethink matters
large and small over the course of forty years, from the first introduction of the
programme to his death in 1716. But the general programme remained remarkably
consistent.

Leibniz's views on the physical world are very complex and difficult to summarise. A good place to begin is with his frequent critiques of what he took to be
the mechanist ontology. Leibniz offered many arguments for rejecting the standard
mechanist conceptions of body in terms of size, shape, and, perhaps, impenetrability. Some are directed against the specifically Cartesian version of that doctrine, in
accordance with which body is constituted by extension and extension alone.
Leibniz argues, for example, that one cannot have bare extension that is not the
extension of some quality; extension is a relative concept, he claims, and is
comprehensible only with respect to some quality or other that is extended, 'as
for example, malleability or specific gravity or yellowness is in gold, whiteness is
in milk, and resistance or impenetrability is generally in body'.[178] Other arguments
are more general, and are directed against those who are willing to add other
qualities, like impenetrability, to extension to constitute body. One important
argument is what might be called the aggregate argument; this argument focuses
on the fact that for many (though not all) mechanists, body is infinitely or (to use
Descartes's phrase) indefinitely divisible.[179] In writing to Arnauld in the late 1680s,
Leibniz announced one of his fundamental commitments: 'I hold this identical
proposition, differentiated only by emphasis, to be an axiom, namely, that what is
not truely one being is not truly one being either.'[180] So, Leibniz concluded, the
ultimate existents in his world must be things that are genuinely one, genuine
unities. But the bodies of the mechanical philosophy are not such unities, in so far
as they are always divisible.[181] And so, Leibniz continued, 'We must then necessarily come down either to mathematical points, of which some authors constitute
extension, or to the atoms of Epicurus or Cordemoy (which things you reject
along with me), or else we must admit that we do not find any reality in bodies;
or finally we must recognize some substances that have a true unity.'[182] That is, for
extended bodies to be real, they must ultimately be composed of things that are
genuine unities, something that cannot be found in extension or bulk alone. It is

evident from this passage that Leibniz did not consider atoms to be unities of an appropriate sort to ground the mechanical philosophy either; as extended bodies, they, too, are aggregates, and thus not genuine unities.[183]

The arguments examined so far all concern the notion of extension. Other arguments Leibniz presents concern the inertness of bodies on the Cartesian view. In his 'De Ipsa Natura' of 1698, he begins with the premise that 'the very substance of things consists in a force for acting and being acted upon'. And so, if God had not given his creatures the ability to be the genuine sources of their own activity, as the mechanists claim they are not, then 'God would be the very nature or substance of all things, the sort of doctrine of ill repute which a recent writer, subtle indeed, though profane, either introduced to the world or revived.'[184] In that same work of 1698 Leibniz argued that since the mechanists conceived body as uniform and homogeneous, those, like Descartes, who deny the vacuum are faced with a world without change; the 'perpetual substitution of indistinguishables' leads Leibniz to the conclusion that in such a world, 'there would be no way of distinguishing different momentary states from one another.'[185] His conclusion, again, is that there must be something more to body than mere extension.

Many arguments were also directed against other aspects of other mechanist ontologies. It was standard among mechanist philosophers to hold that while bodies might not really be red, or sweet, or odiferous, they did really have the modes of extension that pertain to them, in particular, shape and motion. But Leibniz denied both claims. Writing to Simon Foucher in 1687, Leibniz noted: 'I also prove that extension, shape, and motion contain something imaginary and only apparent. . . . For in motion taken by itself, one cannot determine to which subject it pertains, and I think that it can be demonstrated that there is no exact shape in bodies.'[186] The point about motion is that when we consider motion only in terms of the changing relations a body holds with respect to other bodies, 'not even an angel could determine with mathematical rigor which of the . . . bodies . . . is at rest, and which is the center of motion for the others.'[187] Indeed, Leibniz held that not only is motion considered in itself as mere change of place completely relative, but even that there is no experiment we can perform to determine what is really in motion and what is really at rest. And so Leibniz even rejected Newton's celebrated bucket experiment in this context and argued that we are free to assign motion to Newton's twirling bucket, or to set the bucket at rest and twirl the universe around it.[188] The point about shape is that when we look more closely at any supposedly determinate shape, Leibniz argued, we see that the apparently smooth lines are actually irregular, and made up of smaller straight lines, which in turn are made up of still smaller lines, and so on down to infinity, thus robbing the body of any definite shape whatsoever.[189]

Leibniz also argued against conceptions of space found, for example, in Gassendi, Henry More, and Newton, in accordance with which space is something real, something that exists independently of the bodies that fill it. Against this view Leibniz argued :

> I hold space to be something merely relative. . . . I hold it to be an order of coexistences, as time is an order of successions. For space denotes, in terms of possibility, an order of things which exist at the same time, considered as existing together. . . . Space is nothing else but . . . order or relation, and is nothing at all without bodies but the possibility of placing them.[190]

And so, Leibniz insisted to Clarke that since space is just the structure of relations that holds between bodies existing at a given time, it makes no sense to imagine God as having created the world five inches to the left, or reversed from right to left; indeed, the fact that there could be no reason for God to choose one or another of these states constitutes a proof that there is no real difference between them.[191] An interesting consequence of Leibniz's account of space is that in contrast with Descartes's view, a vacuum, a space without body is possible, though in the best of all possible worlds, an empty space would violate God's wisdom.[192]

So far the chapter has focused on Leibniz's reaction against the views of others. But out of those negative arguments emerges a positive view of what the world is like. On this view, the world is made up of genuine individuals that are the source of their own activity. These active individuals, what Leibniz called individual or singular substances in his earlier writings and after circa 1698 called monads, are the basic building blocks of his world.[193] In Leibniz's view, these two characterisations are closely linked. For something to be active, the source of its own activity, it must be a genuine individual; Leibniz often quoted the scholastic phrase '*actiones sunt suppositorum*' to express this view, appealing to the scholastic notion of a suppositum, a general term for the subject of a predication.[194] It is in this way that he introduced one of the most interesting and often commented upon discussions of individual substances, the account in terms of the complete individual concept he offers in Section 8 of his *Discours de métaphysique* of 1686.[195] But Leibniz also argued the converse, that for something to be a genuine individual, it must be genuinely active; a world of things without activity is a world in which things are not really things at all, but only modes of God. Important to Leibniz here, of course, is the claim that activity is actually in the world, that the basic building blocks of the world are the sources of their own activity, and that they are not merely moved around by God. In this way Leibniz explicitly rejects the radical distinction between inert matter and active spirit characteristic of the Cartesians, and the occasionalism that goes with it.[196]

Leibniz's active individuals, his monads, might be seen to come out of a Neoplatonic tradition, where the emphasis in metaphysics is clearly on the notion of unity.[197] But this is not the connexion that Leibniz himself generally made. Rather, Leibniz turned to the schoolmen and their conception of substance in terms of matter and form to explain his views. This comes out with especial clarity in the letters to Arnauld. There Leibniz made liberal use of what I have called the aggregate argument to explain to Arnauld why extended substance is not enough to ground the world. What he substituted for the Cartesian body is an Aristotelian substance, a unity of matter and substantial form, or, better, a collection of such substances. The bodies of everyday experience and the mechanical philosophy emerge on this view as aggregates of such active individuals, looking something like a pile of stones, or, better, a flock of sheep or a pool of wriggling fish, to use comparisons Leibniz often used. On this view, bodies (inanimate bodies at least) are phenomenal in so far as it is we who put the pieces (individual substances or monads) together to form a thing. As Leibniz explained it to Arnauld:

> Our mind notices or conceives some true substances which have certain modes; these modes involve relations to other substances, so the mind takes the occasion to join them together in thought and make one name account for all these things together. This is useful for reasoning, but we must not allow ourselves to be misled into making substances or true beings of them. [198]

It is important to recognise that Leibniz seems to have held more than one conception of these substances that ground bodies in his writings. In the Arnauld letters the model is the human being, an incorporeal soul that unites a complex, extended body: 'Man . . . is an entity endowed with a genuine unity conferred on him by his soul, notwithstanding the fact that the mass of his body is divided into organs, vessels, humors, spirits.'[199] More generally, Leibniz wrote to Arnauld:

> I accord substantial forms to all corporeal substances that are more than mechanically united. . . . Every part of matter is actually divided into other parts as different as the two diamonds of which I spoke, and since it continues endlessly in this way, one will never arrive at a thing of which it may be said: 'here really is an entity' except when one finds animate machines whose soul or substantial form creates substantial unity independent of the external unity of contiguity. And if there are none, it follows that apart from man there is apparently nothing substantial in the visible world.[200]

Leibniz's view in the letters to Arnauld was that such substances are everywhere in nature: 'The whole of matter must be full of substances animate, or at least, living.'[201] The world he presented there is a world of Aristotelian substances, form and matter united to form something like organisms, complex substances which in turn contain smaller substances, and so on without end. The bodies that physics treats would then be aggregates of such organic substances.

This strain in Leibniz's thought is quite prominent throughout the 1680s and 1690s (though it is not entirely clear that it was the only strain of thought even then). But, of course, it is not the only view Leibniz held. Leibniz also tended to think of these individual substances on analogy with Cartesian souls or minds, and thus saw the basic building blocks of the world in more mentalistic terms. This tendency can certainly be found in the 1680s and 1690s but is especially pronounced in the writings after 1704 or so, and seems to be the dominant view in the late summary of his metaphysics that has come to be known as the 'Monadology'. In these writings, Leibniz still presents an animate world, where everything is ultimately made up of living creatures with both bodies and souls, contained within one another to infinity. However, Leibniz only rarely referred to these living creatures as genuine substances and quite clearly no longer saw them as the basic building blocks; the basic building blocks here are the mindlike monads. But even here, the Aristotelianism was very much in evidence. Form and matter are here understood not as the soul and body of an organism, but as two aspects of the simple, mindlike substance that is what he calls a monad. Form, then, corresponds to the active aspect of the monad, and matter corresponds to the passive.[202] On this view of the ultimate make-up of things the inanimate bodies physics would be, in a sense, doubly phenomenal. First of all, they consist of an infinity of living things, rudimentary organisms. But these organisms are, in turn, phenomenal, aggregates of genuine substances, monads and are not themselves fully real. The view is a difficult one. But Leibniz's position seems to be that if all these are monads, simple substances understood on the model of souls, then extended things wouldn't really be real, in a sense, but merely the confused appearances of simple substances which, strictly speaking, exist outside of space and time. He writes to Des Bosses, for example:

Aggregates themselves are nothing but phenomena, since things other than the monads making them up are added by perception alone, by virtue of the very fact that they are perceived at the same time. . . . If nothing substantial existed beside monads, that is, if composites were mere phenomena, then extension itself would be nothing but a phenomenon resulting from simultaneous and mutually ordered appearances.[203]

Elsewhere in the same correspondence Leibniz compares bodies in a world of monads to rainbows or images in a mirror.[204] The point there seems to be that just as the rainbow or mirror image is the confused perception of a reality quite different than it appears, either a collection of raindrops or a smooth reflective surface, extended bodies are the confused perception of a reality quite different in nature, a world of non-extended simple substances.[205] On this view, in a sense, it is we who impose extension and its modes onto a world of a very different nature.

Leibniz presented his view as a kind of return to scholasticism.[206] But he saw important advances in his version. Unlike the others holding this view, Leibniz thought that he had a clear account of what form and matter are: the key is force. Leibniz's notions of force are supposed to clarify the concepts of matter and form that constitute the substance of the schools. Leibniz held that what the scholastics called 'soul or substantial form' is just what he calls primitive active force, and 'that which is called primary matter in the schools, if correctly interpreted' is just primitive passive force.[207] This has important consequences for the proper understanding of the scholastic doctrine, according to Leibniz. The form and matter of the schools are somewhat obscure; forms are understood simply as the cause of characteristic behaviour of individuals, and the matter is understood as that which remains constant in substantial change, as a thing changes from one kind of substance to another. But if form and matter are to be understood in terms of force, then Leibniz can appeal to the relatively intelligible concept of local motion to explicate them. For Leibniz's forces are connected directly to local motion, either actual motion, its endeavour, or resistance to motion, and so the previously mysterious and occult notions of matter and form can be conceived as the causes or grounds in body of motion and resistance. Furthermore, Leibniz held that force always obeys the same laws. And since form and matter are just active and passive primitive force, it follows that all bodies must satisfy the same laws, the laws of motion and impact. In this way Leibniz can argue that though he recognises the substantial forms of the schools, he does not use them as the schools did, to explain particular phenomena, such as why fire rises and stones fall. Form and matter, active and passive primitive force is in body, and must be there in order to ground the laws bodies obey. But explanation in physics must derive from the universal laws that govern all bodies, and not directly from form.[208]

Leibniz thus abandoned the simple mechanist ontology of material substance, homogeneous extended stuff, in favour of a world of active individual substances, interpreted as composites of substantial form and matter, primitive active and primitive passive force. But in adopting a self-consciously scholastic ontology, he did not thereby abandon the world of the mechanical philosophy. Leibniz wanted to agree with both the mechanists and the scholastics, and so he transformed the scholastic view, using it not as a competitor to mechanism, but in order to ground mechanism. The world is ultimately composed of matter and form, that is, force. But the passive force in bodies manifests itself as extension, and the active force as motion, and the extended bodies in motion that thus result all satisfy the same basic laws of nature, expressible in terms of the familiar notions of size, shape, and motion. In this way Leibniz's scholastic world of individual substances or monads gives rise to a mechanist world of extended bodies in motion. Although extension and motion are not metaphysically basic in Leibniz's world, and although these notions must admit of a more basic account in terms of the notions of force, primitive force grounds a world that can, at a certain level, be described entirely in terms of size, shape, extension, motion, and the laws governing motion. This is the final resting place of Leibniz's philosophy of body, as he reported it to Remond in 1714.

5. *Mechanism and beyond: Newton and Locke*

Perhaps the most striking representative of the anti-Cartesian current in English natural philosophy is Isaac Newton. In contrast to the distinctly outlined, alchemy-free Cartesian universe of simple mechanical forces exerted by *res extensae* in motion and rest, the Newtonian universe is much more complex, much more open to the possibility of other sorts of force in nature. In Query 31 of the second English edition (London, 1717–18) of his *Opticks* Newton writes: 'The *Vis inertiae* is a passive Principle by which Bodies persist in their Motion or Rest, receive Motion in proportion to the Force impressing it, and resist as much as they are resisted. By this Principle alone there never could have been any Motion in the World.' Newton goes on to surmise that

God in the Beginning form'd Matter in solid, massy, hard, impenetrable, moveable Particles, of such Sizes and Figures, and with such other Properties, and in such Proportion to Space, as most conduced to the End for which he form'd them. . . . It seems to me farther, that these Particles have not only a *Vis inertiae,* accompanied with such passive Laws of Motion as naturally result from that Force, but also that they are moved by certain active Principles, such as is that of Gravity, and that which causes Fermentation, and the Cohesion of Bodies.[209]   .

At this time 'fermentation' referred to a wide range of chemical and other exothermic activities. Newton himself saw it as the cause of the 'perpetual Motion and Heat' of the heart and blood, the internal heat of the Earth, volcanic activity, the 'burning and shining' of bodies, and the activity of the Sun. Although he did not explicitly say so, he might well have considered that fermentation plays a rôle in the response of gunpowder to a match. The notion of active principles enabled Newton to speak readily of forces of attraction and repulsion. In the Preface to *Principia mathematica* (London, 1687) he writes, 'I am induced by many reasons to suspect that [the phenomena of Nature] may all depend upon certain forces by which the particles of bodies, by some causes hitherto unknown, are either mutually impelled toward one another and cohere in regular figures, or are repelled and recede from one another.'[210] Furthermore, like Walter Warner, Newton could draw upon Neoplatonic and (al)chemical traditions, according to which light is the principle of activity in bodies. So his secret alchemical speculations in 1669 that bodies may be concreted out of aether and a more active spirit which is 'ye body of light',[211] can appear again, modified but recognisable, in Query 30 of the 1717 edition of the *Opticks:* 'Are not gross Bodies and Light convertible into one another, and may not Bodies receive much of their Activity from the Particles of Light which enter their Composition?'[212]

Also important are Newton's conceptions of space. Newton's earliest discussion of space appears in the manuscript 'De gravitatione et aequipondio fluidorum'. Like Gassendi, whose theories were known to him through Charleton's *Physiologia* (London 1654), Newton begins by stating that space 'has its own manner of existence which fits neither substances nor accidents'.[213] Infinite in extent, space is a three-dimensional receptacle for all other beings: 'No being exists or can exist which is not related to space in some way'. This applies equally to 'created minds', which must be 'somewhere', and to God, who is everywhere. This being so, space must be co-eternal with God, and Newton declares that it is in fact 'an emanent effect of an eternal and immutable being' – a fairly common notion in the Neoplatonic tradition,[214] although it would seem from this that space is an attribute of God, and therefore an accident after all.

In the first edition of his *Philosophiae naturalis principia mathematica* (London, 1687), Newton was careful to avoid theology, and the concept of space he describes there – the absolute, infinite frame within which his physics is enacted – owes more to Lucretius, Gassendi, Charleton, and the demands of an exercise in geometrical physics, than to the more theologically inclined Cambridge Platonists. However, in the first Latin (London, 1706) and second English edition (London, 1717–18) of the *Opticks,* he returned to the theological dimension of space, insisting that God is literally omnipresent in the world. But Newton's motivation here was not to clarify or justify his concept of space *per se* (which he now took for granted), but to account for physical causation. 'Does it not appear from Phaenomena', he asks in Query 28, 'that there is a Being incorporeal, living, intelligent, omnipresent, who in infinite Space, as it were in his Sensory, sees the things themselves intimately, and thoroughly perceives them, and comprehends them?'[215] The aetiological point of this is revealed in Query 31, where God 'is more able by his Will to move the Bodies within his boundless uniform Sensorium, and thereby to form and reform the Parts of the Universe, than we are by our Will to move the Parts of our own Bodies'.[216] Similarly, in the second edition of the *Principia* (Cambridge, 1713), Newton writes that God 'is not duration or space, but he endures and is present. He endures forever and is everywhere present; and by existing always and everywhere, he constitutes duration and space'.[217]

It is quite common in the literature to see this feature of Newton's position as deriving from the thought of Henry More, who, in a sense, identified God with space, as discussed above. But what similarities there are may derive as much from the common background in Neoplatonic thought as they do from any influence of More on Newton; and while there are some obvious similarities, there are also important differences worth emphasising.[218] It is important to note, for example, that Newton never regarded space as a type of 'spirit' and, unlike More, he did not develop his concept of space to help to establish the existence of incorporeal substance in general and God in particular. Although Newton's talk of space as God's sensorium has sometimes been seen as a statement of belief in the *direct* intervention of God in the universe, for the most part (though not always) Newton suggested that change is brought about by the intermediating active principles discussed earlier, such as the attractive force of gravity, which are superadded to matter by God. There is no real similarity, however, between Newton's active principles and More's mediating 'Spirit of Nature'. In the 'General Scholium', for example, Newton explicitly says that God 'governs all things, not as the soul of the world, but as Lord over all; and on account of his dominion he is wont to be called *Lord God pantokrator*, or *Universal Ruler*; for *God* is a relative word, and has a respect to servants; and *Deity* is the dominion of God not over his own body, as those who fancy God to be the soul of the world, but over servants'.[219] The point, presumably, is that God's creatures, His 'servants', are themselves active agents.

The difference between More and Newton on this fundamental issue can also be seen by comparing their speculations on the nature of matter. In 'De gravitatione' Newton elaborates on the notion of God's ability to change the universe by His will in the same way that we can move our bodies. God can simply make a portion of space impenetrable by 'the sole action of thinking and willing'. He continues: 'If he should exercise this power, and cause some space projecting above the Earth, like a mountain or any other body, to be impervious to bodies and thus stop or reflect light and all impinging things, it seems impossible that we should not consider this space to be truly body from the evidence of our senses.'[220] Newton and More shared the belief that matter is characterised by impenetrability rather than by extension, which also pertains to space and to God, and, in More's case at least, to other immaterial spirits. But there the similarity ends. For More the impenetrability of matter is an aspect of its inertness: for Newton it is the result of an active force of repulsion. For More spirit is the only active principle at work in nature, it penetrates and is penetrable, whereas matter, the contrary of spirit in More's system, must be impenetrable and inactive, virtually by definition. For Newton, however, matter is itself dynamic. Although God could produce this impenetrable space by an act of will, Newton was not an occasionalist. He drew here upon the old voluntarist distinction between the absolute and the ordinary powers of God. Having created bodies by making parts of space impenetrable, and by making this impenetrability transferrable 'hither and thither according to certain laws', God can choose to suspend his absolute power and not interfere further in the system of nature, but merely maintain the laws of nature by His ordinary power.[221]

It is also important to distinguish Newton and More on the question of force. When More wrote that the fall of a stone or other heavy body 'is enormously contrary to the Laws of Mechanicks',[222] he spoke uncontroversially as far as English natural philosophers were concerned. His insistence that gravity must be caused by something 'immaterial and incorporeal' has been seen, unjustifiably, as the inspiration for Newton's 1693 comments on gravity to the then up-and-coming Anglican divine, Richard Bentley. Asked by Bentley for help in showing how Newtonian philosophy could be used to combat atheism, Newton famously took exception to the implication in Bentley's letters that gravity was essential to matter. 'Pray do not ascribe that notion to me', Newton wrote, 'for the cause of gravity is what I do not pretend to know', and in his next letter he explained:

It is inconceivable, that inanimate brute Matter should, without the Mediation of something else which is not material, operate upon and effect other Matter without mutual Contact, as it must be, if Gravitation, in the Sense of *Epicurus,* be essential and inherent in it. . . . That gravity should be innate, inherent, and essential to Matter, so that one Body may act upon another at a Distance thro' a *Vacuum,* without the Mediation of anything else, by and through which their Action and Force may be conveyed from one to another, is to me so great an Absurdity, that I believe no Man who has in philosophical Matters a competent Faculty of thinking, can ever fall into it. Gravity must be caused by an Agent acting constantly according to certain Laws, but whether this Agent be material or immaterial I have left to the Consideration of my Readers.[223]

Newton is *not* saying that gravitational attraction cannot operate between two bodies at a distance, separated by empty space. He is merely saying that if it does so operate (and he thinks it does), then that power must have been superadded to matter by an immaterial agent. The issue is confused somewhat by Newton's shift in focus from God, the explicitly immaterial agent required to endow matter with gravity, to the secondary agent which actually performs these ubiquitous, everyday attractions between all the particles of the universe. Significantly, he at least allows, in a way that More would never have countenanced, that this secondary cause or agent might be material.[224]

But even if gravity requires a Creator, the problem of its ordinary agency, the way in which it operates, remained open. For this Newton turned not to More's immaterial hylarchic spirit for inspiration,[225] but to something quite different. In one place, for example, he wrote that 'the gravitating attraction of the earth' may be caused 'by the continual condensation' of an aetherial spirit:

For, if such an aetherial spirit may be condensed in fermenting or burning bodies, or otherwise coagulated in the pores of the earth and water into some kind of humid active matter, for the continual uses of nature, adhering to the sides of those pores, after the manner that vapours condense on the sides of a vessel; the vast body of the earth, which may be every where to the very centre in perpetual working, may continually condense so much of this spirit, as to cause it from above to descend with great celerity for a supply.[226]

This version of the 'Cartesian aether', so to speak, appeared in a somewhat more mechanist form in a letter of 1679 to Boyle and in eight Queries added to the 1717–18 English edition of the *Opticks*.[227] It may have been something like this that Newton had in mind when he intimated to Bentley that the agent responsible for gravity might possibly be material,[228] but aether theories seem to have won less favour with Newton than the view that there are *immaterial* forces of attraction and repulsion (again, possibly on the inspiration of alchemical notions) continually operating across the distances between particles of matter. Indeed, the evidence suggests that Newton reverted to aether theories in the *Opticks* only as a sop to continental critics who disliked what they saw as occult forces in the *Principia*. Even then, Newton's aethers (at least after 1679) were not strictly mechanical, being composed of vanishingly small particles held at a distance from one another by strong repulsive forces.[229]

This appeal to non-mechanical active principles led many readers to question Newton's allegiance to the mechanical philosophy, as well they should, and, like Leibniz, to accuse Newton of reviving the substantial forms and occult qualities of the scholastic tradition.[230] In a real sense Newton's conception of the physical world does go beyond the narrow mechanism of the orthodox Cartesians or Gassendists. But it is unfair to accuse him of reviving the obscurities of earlier scholastic natural philosophy. The emphasis in England among the 'new' philosophers was not so much that their philosophy was 'mechanical', or that it was 'corpuscularian' or 'atomist', but that it was *experimental,* as noted earlier in connexion with Boyle and Hooke. This mood is conveyed by Sprat, the first official historian of the Royal Society, whose motto 'Nullius in verba' in itself proclaimed a commitment to unremitting experimentalism. In his *History of the Royal Society* (London, 1667), Sprat runs a critical eye over three sorts of 'new philosophers', the first two of which are the 'modern dogmatists' (which include the Cartesians), and those who renounce Aristotle to restore the ancient philosophies of Epicurus and Democritus. Both are found wanting, which leaves the third sort, valiantly struggling against the vicissitudes of the experimental life: 'Those who have not onely disagreed from the Ancients, but have also propos'd to themselves the right course of slow, and sure Experimenting: and have prosecuted it as far, as the shortness of their own Lives, or the multiplicity of their other affairs, or the narrowness of their Fortunes, have given them leave.'[231] Although the *operations* of occult qualities in matter could not be explained in terms of easily intelligible causes, the qualities themselves could be shown to exist through experiment and could be analysed in some detail, making possible precise predictions about many aspects of physical behaviour, such as the directions and speeds of planets, or the displacement of one metal from a solution by the addition of another with a greater 'affinity' for the solvent.[232]

Newton was able to draw upon this English tradition to refute Leibniz's charge that he had re-introduced 'scholastic occult qualities' into natural philosophy, after Descartes had so successfully ejected them. Gravity and the other active principles he discussed in Query 31 of the *Opticks* were presented not as 'occult Qualities, supposed to result from the specifick Forms of Things, but as general Laws of Nature, by which the things themselves are form'd; their Truth appearing to us by Phaenomena, though their Causes be not yet discover'd. For these are manifest Qualities, and their causes only are occult.'[233] In the *Principia* Newton summed it up like this: 'In this philosophy particular propositions are inferred from the phenomena and afterward rendered general by induction. . . . And to us it is enough that gravity does really exist and act according to the laws which we have explained, and abundantly serves to account for all the motions of the celestial bodies and of our sea.'[234] This underwrote Newton's famous statement that he 'feigns no hypotheses', and this approach was held to take natural philosophy as far as it was safe to proceed,[235] though, as noted earlier, he was not always allowed to leave it there. Just as he was persuaded by insistent criticism to introduce his 'aether Queries' into the second English edition of the *Opticks,* so sometimes he felt obliged to go beyond his positivist attitude towards gravitational attraction. Here, he invoked not an intermediary spirit of Nature in the manner of More, but the direct intervention of God who is able 'by his Will to move the Bodies within his boundless uniform Sensorium'.

John Locke, Newton's distinguished countryman, came eventually to appreciate and endorse Newton's conception of the physical world, and its departures from strict mechanism. Like Newton, and those in the atomist tradition, Locke distinguished between body and space and allowed that there could be vacuum, space empty of body. And like Gassendi and his followers, Locke argued that space stands outside the traditional Aristotelian categories of substance and accident. Though he did not think that we could penetrate to the real essences of bodies, that which makes gold gold, or lead lead, he did seem to think that what characterises body as body is just its primary qualities, its '*Solidity, Extension, Figure,* and *Mobility*', qualities 'such as are utterly inseparable from the Body, in what estate soever it be; such as in all the alterations and changes it suffers, all the force can be used upon it, it constantly keeps; and such as Sense constantly finds in every particle of Matter, which has bulk enough to be perceived, and the Mind finds inseparable from every particle of Matter'.[236] Furthermore, he claimed in the early editions of the *Essay,* '*Bodies operate* upon one another . . . manifestly *by impulse,* and nothing else. It being impossible to conceive, that Body should operate on what it does not touch . . . or when it does touch, operate any other way than by Motion.'[237]

Locke's controversy with Edward Stillingfleet, Bishop of Worcester, showed that he was slow to recognise the positivist tendencies within English natural philosophy and the consequences thinkers like Newton drew from it on the nature of body and the way bodies act on one another, possibly as a result of his periods of self-imposed exile on the continent. He admitted to Stillingfleet:

It is true, I say, 'that bodies operate by impulse, and nothing else' [*Essay* II.viii.11]. And so I thought when I writ it, and can yet conceive no other way of their operation. But I am since convinced by the judicious Mr. Newton's incomparable book [*Principia*], that it is too bold a presumption to limit God's power, in this point, by my narrow conceptions. The gravitation of matter towards matter, by ways inconceivable to me, is not only a demonstration that God can, if he pleases, put into bodies powers and ways of operation above what can be derived from our idea of body, or can be explained by what we know of matter, but also an unquestionable and every where visible instance that he has done so. And therefore in the next edition of my book [i.e., the fourth edition of 1700] I shall take care to have that passage rectified.[238]

In the event, Locke fought shy of going deeply into the matter. He changed this paragraph from a consideration of 'how Bodies operate one upon another' to thoughts about 'how Bodies produce Ideas in us' – which he felt safe in claiming was 'by impulse'.[239]

Locke's reluctance to enter into an analysis of the concept of gravitational attraction is also seen in his brief, posthumously published *Elements of Natural Philosophy*. While he conceded that 'all bodies have a tendency, attraction, or gravitation toward one another', he was careful to add the qualification, 'as far as human observation reaches'. The claim that two separated bodies 'will put one another into motion by the force of attraction' has to be taken as 'a principle in natural philosophy' because it is 'made evident to us by experience'.[240] Locke probably held out some hope that a mechanical explanation of this action at a distance would be forthcoming, thus enabling him to maintain his commitment in the *Essay* to the reductionist thesis that all physical phenomena derive from the arrangement, motions, and impacts of insensible particles of matter.

According to the *Elements,* matter 'is an extended solid substance; which, being comprehended under distinct surfaces, makes so many particular distinct bodies'.[241] Bodies are endowed with the so-called primary qualities of solidity, extension, shape, and motion or rest. Many physical phenomena are explained in terms of combinations of numerous invisibly small particles or corpuscles whose primary qualities affect our senses, thereby causing tastes, colours, smells, and other secondary qualities, which are therefore not illusory, but real. Indeed, the secondary qualities provide clues about the primary qualities. The pricking sensation of an acid on the skin or tongue, for example, implies that its invisible particles are needle-shaped. Locke's ideas, as expounded in the *Essay,* are entirely typical of contemporary theorising in mechanical philosophy, and the influence of Gassendi and Boyle is particularly evident,[242] but his attitude to force reveals that he is far less typical of the English experimental philosophy with its greater empirical and positivist leanings. It seems that it was only when he came to write his letters to Stillingfleet and the *Elements of Natural Philosophy* that he realised that bodies might be said to operate in ways other than 'by impulse'.

But when Locke did come to appreciate these other options, he immediately allied himself with the leading English natural philosophers, including Charleton, John Wilkins, Glisson, Petty, Robert Hooke, Boyle, Thomas Willis, Nehemiah Grew, and Newton, virtually all of whom used the concept of non-mechanical active principles superadded to passive matter as a proof both of God's existence and of the omnipotence of His arbitrary will. Indeed, Locke extended it even further still, conjecturing that God could superadd not only activity, but even perception and thought to bare matter: 'For I see no contradiction in it', he wrote, 'that the first eternal thinking Being should, if he pleased, give to certain Systems of created senseless matter, put together as he thinks fit, some degrees of sense, perception, and thought' (*Essay* IV.iii.6). God's omnipotence is constrained only by what is logically impossible. He cannot make a body without solidity, since solidity is part of the essence of matter; to make a body without solidity is to make immaterial matter. Certainly, God can change body into immaterial substance, but He cannot meaningfully arrange for body not to be body. The power of thinking, however, cannot be said to be a property that is incompatible with our concept of matter, since 'we know not wherein thinking consists, nor to what sort of substances the Almighty has been pleased to give that power, which cannot be in any created being but merely by the good pleasure and bounty of the Creator.'[243] This idea and other philosophical issues raised by the new natural philosophy of the seventeenth century continued to generate philosophical debate throughout the eighteenth century.[244]

NOTES

1 For general accounts of the mechanical philosophy, see, e.g., Dijksterhuis 1961; Westfall 1971a. For an interesting attempt to relate the new mechanical philosophy to the older Aristotelian philosophy, see Hutchison 1982.

2 The diversity of sources and aims among late Renaissance atomists has prompted modern scholars, ranging from Lasswitz to Hooykaas, van Melsen, Dijksterhuis, Kargon, and more recently Meinel, to compile comprehensive prosopographies of the numerous atomist authors. These scholars have also established historical typologies of the different kinds of arguments – metaphysical, mathematical, optical, chemical, or otherwise – which were employed by the atomists. Beyond this, however, no consensus has been reached concerning the relative importance of individual atomists, nor have the historical relations among them been exhaustively studied. See, e.g., Lasswitz 1890; Hooykaas 1947; van Melsen 1960; Dijksterhuis 1961; Kargon 1966; Meinel 1988b; Clucas 1994.

3 *Physica* 187b 25–188a 1. Cf. *De gen. et cor.* 316a 23–317a 16. For the later history of the *minima naturalia* theory in the Renaissance and seventeenth century, see especially Emerton 1984, chaps. 3–4.

4 Zimara 1562, fol. 472v–3r. On Zimara's career, see Schmitt 1983a, pp. 98–9, 101–2.

5 Averroes 1562–74, vol. 4, fol. 24r–5v, 266r–7r.

6 For summaries of Sennert's views, see Gregory 1966; Kangro 1975.

7 Galen 1979, I.xii.27–30; I.xiv.51–2; II.vi.97–101.

8 Sennert 1619, pp. 999–1000. As Emerton 1984, pp. 106ff. emphasises, the *minima naturalia* theory was generally accepted as the only viable theory of mixture, even by those whose sympathies were for more classical atomistic views well into the seventeenth century.

9 On Zabarella and Basso, see Sennert 1637, pp. 195–6.

10 Magnen 1646, pp. 110, 168.
11 For the doctrines of Magnen, see Magnen 1646, pp. 70–1, 96, 104–6, 223, 226. For the summaries of Democritus's doctrines, see *Physica* 187a 1–3, 188a 22, 194a 20, 203a 20, 251b 16; *De gen. et cor.* 315a 30–316a 10. Cicero, *De finibus,* I.vi.17–21. Sextus Empiricus, *Outlines of Phrrhonism,* I.xxx.213–4. Sextus Empiricus, *Against the Physicists,* I.19–24.
12 Basso 1649, pp. 366–8, 425–6. On Basso's work, see Gregory 1964; Guareschi 1916; Partington 1961–70, vol. 2, pp. 387–8; Nielsen 1988.
13 Basso 1649, pp. 339, 75–6. On Basso's views on the ether and the vacuum, see Nielsen 1988, pp. 318–20. On Basso's use of the *minima naturalia* theory in connexion with mixtures, see Emerton 1984, pp. 107–8.
14 Basso 1649, Letter to the Reader, pp. [xxx–xxxi].
15 W. D. Smith 1979, pp. 215–22. On the possible influence of Democritus on Hippocrates, see especially the contrasting interpretations of Smith 1979 and Lonie in Hippocrates 1981, pp. 62–71.
16 Van Goorle 1651, pp. 2–4, 23–4, 41–2, 51. On van Goorle's brief career, see Jaeger 1921, p. 210; Partington 1961–70, vol. 2, pp. 386–7.
17 See Grant 1981, p. 392.
18 Shirley 1983; Trevor-Roper 1987b. Warner's papers are in the British Library, Add. MSS 4394–6, 6754–6, and in Sion College, London, MS ARC. L40.2/E10.
19 British Library, Add. MS 6782b, fol. 362r–74v; Add. MS 6785b, fol. 436–7.
20 Jacquot 1952; Kargon 1966; Henry 1982a.
21 British Library, Add. MS 4394, fol. 389v; Hill 1601, arts. 352, 363, 368, 370, 376. (Hill's *Philosophia Epicurea* consists in a straight run of 509 numbered articles, without any other division, and without any discernible topical order.)
22 British Library, Add. MS 4394, fol. 400r–v; Add. MS 4395, fol. 204v.
23 Hill 1601, art. 359, p. 65. Hill's terminology does not make for easy translation. The original text of art. 359 reads: 'Indifferenter receptivum, immiscibile impenetrabile [*sic: read* penetrabile], non formabile. Illocabile, incomprehensum, cointelligendum omni enti physico. Non inhaerens, non adiacens, non substantians.'
24 Hill 1601, art. 284. Also arts. 165, 245, 246, 299, 300, 304, 334.
25 British Library, Add. MS 4394, fol. 129v, 212r, 386r; Sion College, MS ARC. L40.2/E10, fol. 88v.
26 British Library, Add. MS 4394, fol. 397r.
27 Crombie 1953, pp. 104–10, 128–31; Lindberg 1976, pp. 94–102, 107–19; McEvoy 1982, pp. 149–88; Lindberg 1986.
28 British Library, Add. MS 4394, fol. 383r–v.
29 Hill 1601, arts. 332, 391, 410, 436, 473; British Library, Add. MS 4394, fol. 397r.
30 Sion College, MS ARC. L40.2/E10, fol. 88v.
31 For Bruno's influence on Hill see Massa 1977; Kargon 1966; Jacquot 1974; Trevor-Roper 1987b. Warner's discussions of time, space, matter, and *vis* are remarkably close to those in Patrizi 1591, to which Warner had access: see de Fonblanque 1887, vol. 2, pp. 626–30.
32 British Library, Add. MS 4395, fol. 50r.
33 British Library, Add. MS 4394, fol. 149r.
34 Hill 1601, arts. 63, 263, 280, 309, 310, 365, 394.
35 Hill 1601, arts. 2–5, 19, 112, 169, 504. Cf. Hahm 1977, pp. 60–2, 75–6; Multhauf 1966, pp. 53–5, 63–5, 73–6, 85–7.
36 See Galilei 1890–1909, vol. 6, pp. 347–50 (Galilei 1957, pp. 273ff.).
37 For the original statement of the problem, see the pseudo-Aristotelian *Mechanica,* q. 24.

For the mathematical argument, see Galilei 1890–1909, vol. 8, pp. 68–72; for the extension to body, see ibid., pp. 72–3, 92–3. On Galileo's atomism, see Shea 1970, A. M. Smith 1976; H. E. Le Grand 1978.

38 See Torricelli 1644, pp. 120–1, and a letter of 1621 from Cavalieri to Galileo quoted in Drake 1978, pp. 282–3. The tenth-century manuscript of Archimedes' *Method* was only rediscovered by J. L. Heiberg in 1899.

39 Pedersen 1980, pp. 32–7.

40 Rees 1975, 1977b.

41 Rees 1980.

42 Bacon 1857–74, vol. 4, pp. 126, 154.

43 Bacon 1857–74, vol. 3, pp. 3–9; Kargon 1966, pp. 43–4.

44 Rattansi 1963; Rees 1977a.

45 Freudenthal 1983, pp. 27–30; Kelly 1965, pp. 103–4.

46 Gilbert 1600, pp. 21–4 (Gilbert 1958, pp. 38–43); Freudenthal 1983, p. 24.

47 Gilbert 1600, p. 223 (Gilbert 1958, p. 332). Gilbert's experiments had led him to conclude that the earth is a giant lodestone.

48 Gilbert 1651, pp. 59, 68, 186–92, 195–6, 202; Gilbert 1600, p. 224 (Gilbert 1958, p. 333); Kelly 1965, pp. 32–3, 34–5, 37, 39.

49 Gilbert 1600, pp. 65, 217 (Gilbert 1958, pp. 105, 322).

50 Wren 1750, p. 204.

51 Westfall 1971a, pp. 209–11, 268–72; Westfall 1980, pp. 382–9; J. A. Bennett 1975, 1981, 1989.

52 Petty 1674, pp. 134, 133. See further Henry 1986b, pp. 350–1. On the magnetical philosophy in the later seventeenth century in England, see J. A. Bennett 1981.

53 See, e.g., Digby 1644a, dedicatory letter ('To my sonne Kenelme Digby'), preface, p. 144, pp. 340ff., etc. For a discussion of the second treatise, on the soul, see Chapter 23 in this book.

54 Bradley 1966; Southgate 1981; Henry 1982a.

55 White 1651; Digby 1638.

56 Digby 1644a, p. 46.

57 Digby 1644a, p. 6.

58 Digby 1644a, pp. 19–20, 21.

59 That is to say, an infinite number of indivisibles. Digby 1644a, p. 12.

60 Gravity is a species of quantity, and 'a body is rare whose quantity is more, and substance less, and dense where substance is more and quantity less'. Digby 1644a, pp. 26, 23.

61 Digby 1644a, pp. 29, 30.

62 Digby 1644a, p. 38.

63 Digby 1644a, p. 88.

64 Here Digby differs from Aristotle by holding light to be material and corpuscular: Digby 1644a, pp. 39–44.

65 Digby 1644a, pp. 37, 38 (see also pp. 62, 137), 79, 76, 143 (see also p. 91). Note the similarity between Digby's account of light and Roger Bacon's light metaphysics, as expounded in his *De multiplicatione specierum*.

66 White 1646, 1656, 1657.

67 Bradley 1966; Southgate 1981; Henry 1982a.

68 Robert Boyle, for instance, stated that the two major mechanical philosophies which he endeavoured to surpass were Epicurean atomism and the corpuscular philosophy of the Cartesians. See Boyle 1666, pp. 455A–B, 461B; Boyle 1674, p. 450A.

69 On the relationship between Gassendi's historical writings and his atomist philosophy, see Joy 1987, pp. 41–80, 130–94.
70 Gassendi 1658, vol. 1, pp. 244A–7B, 263B–6A.
71 Gordon 1962, pp. 29–30.
72 Gassendi's view was shared by John Evelyn, the English atomist who brought out a translation into the vernacular of Book I in 1656. Evelyn remarked, even at this late date, that his fellow countrymen had still not apprehended the significance of the poem because many of them had refused to take seriously the work of an author such as Lucretius, who 'prevaricates on Providence, the Immortality of the Soul, [and] the spontaneous coalition of Principles' (Evelyn 1656, Preface, quoted in Mayo 1934, p. 47). Evelyn cited Gassendi as another author who had observed that Lucretius's impieties had kept Christian readers from seriously studying the poem.
73 Gassendi 1658, vol. 1, pp. 280A–2B, 311A–19B, 335B.
74 The disapproval voiced by English writers of the impieties of Epicurus and Lucretius are described in Harrison 1934, pp. 9–51. However, it has also been argued by Røstvig that the reluctance of English readers to accept Epicurean ethical and physical principles lessened dramatically after the Restoration. See Røstvig 1962–71, vol. 1, pp. 227–310.
75 Gassendi 1647, pp. 226A–8B; Cicero, *De finibus* I.20; Plutarch 1967; Sextus Empiricus, *Against the Professors,* I.1.
76 On these fifteenth-century treatments of Epicurean ethics, see Jones 1981, pp. 216–22; Kraye 1988, pp. 380–2.
77 Gassendi 1658, vol. 1, pp. 231A, 247B–50A, 266A–79B. See also Epicurus, *Letter to Herodotus,* secs. 54, 61. On the conflicting reports of Democritus's views of the qualities of atoms, see Kirk, Raven, and Schofield 1983, pp. 413–16, 421–3.
78 Gassendi 1658, vol. 1, pp. 185A–216B, 273B–9B.
79 Gassendi 1658, vol. 1, p. 337A.
80 Gassendi 1658, vol. 1, pp. 279B. 280A, 337B. On the necessity of divine concurrence, see especially p. 323B. See further Bloch 1971, pp. 350–62. The position he takes in the *Syntagma* seems different from the position that he took somewhat earlier in his critique of Descartes's *Meditationes*; see AT VII 300–302, though it is not clear whether Gassendi means in Obj. V to be presenting his own views, or simply pressing Descartes's arguments as hard as he can. As we shall explain when discussing Descartes's position, although Gassendi shares with Descartes the necessity of divine concurrence, he differs from Descartes in holding that the things God maintains in existence are themselves genuinely active, and not inert, moved around by God.
81 Sextus Empiricus, *Against the Physicists,* I. 281–4, 367–439, II. 142–68. Sextus Empiricus *Against the Professors,* III. 19–82. The seventeenth-century sceptics who followed Sextus included Gassendi's friends Gabriel Naudé and François de la Mothe le Vayer. See Naudé 1627, p. 167; La Mothe le Vayer 1669b, pp. 85, 101–8.
82 For Gassendi's criticisms of Sextus Empiricus, see Joy 1987, pp. 144–58.
83 Gassendi 1658, vol. 1, p. 182A.
84 Gassendi 1658. For a general discussion of Gassendi's account of space and time, see Bloch 1971 and Grant 1981, pp. 206–15.
85 Gassendi 1658, vol. 2, p. 256A–B. Again, although this is so for the *Syntagma,* Gassendi seems to have taken a more materialistic position in earlier writings. See Chapter 23.
86 Gassendi 1658, vol. 1, pp. 322B–3B.
87 Gassendi 1649, pp. 133, 203, 220; 1658, vol. 1, pp. 82A, 269A–70A.
88 AT VI 9.

89 For the *Ratio studiorum*, see Pachtler 1887–94; Fitzpatrick 1933; Lukács 1986. On the history of La Flèche, see Rochemonteix 1899. On education in seventeenth-century France, see de Dainville 1978; Brockliss 1987. Of particular interest here may be Jean François, one of Descartes's mathematics teachers at La Flèche. François taught mathematics at La Flèche from 1612 to 1616. See Gilson's commentary on the *Discours*, Descartes 1967, pp. 126–9; Rodis-Lewis 1971, vol. 1, pp. 20–21; vol. 2, pp. 431–2, notes 24, 25; Garber 1992a, p. 311, note 18. See particularly François's *Traité de la quantité considerée absolument et en elle mesme* (1655), which appeared five years after Descartes's death. François argues that all quantity can be represented in some way and can be divided into four kinds: arithmetical, theological, geometrical, and physical. Each being necessarily possesses extension and duration, and 'each of our senses has for common object the quantity of the object itself' (François 1655, p. 49). Also important in Descartes's early development at La Flèche would have been the influential ideas of the great Jesuit mathematician Christopher Clavius, who contributed an essay to the *Ratio studiorum* arguing that physics cannot be properly understood without recourse to mathematical disciplines. See Ariew 1990, p. 298; Garber 1992a, pp. 7–8, and 311, note 21; Lattis 1994, pp. 32–8.

90 Descartes 1967, pp. 5, 110 (the *Ratio* regulations). The 'rarest and most recondite sciences' included alchemy, astrology, and magic, which Descartes would probably have been warned about by his mathematics teacher, Jean François, who published an anti-astrological treatise in 1660. See Gilson's note: Descartes 1967, pp. 120–1.

91 Rodis-Lewis 1971, pp. 66, 458–9.

92 Alsted 1649, vol. 2, pp. 106–7 (*Encyclopedia, Physica*, pt. I, Cap. X). See further Chapter 15. Although Alsted presents views representative of the period, and although his earliest writings appeared while Descartes was at school (see Alsted 1610 and 1614), his major writings did not appear until much later, and there is no particular reason to believe that Descartes would have read him at La Flèche.

93 AT X 441–9.

94 Descartes to Mersenne, 28 October 1640; AT III 211–12.

95 Van Berkel 1983a, also 1983b.

96 Rossi 1960, pp. 51–61, 153–61. Cf. Sirven 1930, pp. 127–8, 158–68.

97 See the earlier discussion in this chapter and Meinel 1988a, pp. 70–2.

98 See esp. Beeckman 1939–53, vol. 1, p. 244 (23 November–26 December 1618).

99 Rodis-Lewis 1971, pp. 80–1, 465 (note 47).

100 Lenoble 1971, pp. 346–9, 354–6.

101 See Regula 14, AT X 444–7, and the discussion in Garber 1992a, p. 327 n. 1.

102 *Le monde*, chap. VI, AT XI 33.

103 *Le monde*, chap. IV, AT XI 16ff.

104 For Descartes's cagey remarks on body in the writings of 1637, see AT VI 42–3, 239. In the *Meditationes*, the question is broached in the course of the proof of the existence of the external world of bodies, AT VII 80. Despite Descartes's care in the *Meditationes*, Antoine Arnauld, one of the small group to which Descartes sent the *Meditationes* for comment picked up on the view, and drew out the obvious problems for the doctrine of transubstantiation. See AT VII 217–8.

105 *Princ.* II 4. For a fuller account of the different arguments Descartes uses to establish his account of body, see Garber 1992a, chap. 3.

106 *Princ.* II 11. We should note here a distinction Descartes draws between internal and external place. Internal place is just the same as the space a body occupies; see *Princ.* II

10. External place refers rather to the position of a body with respect to other bodies, and can be identified with place in the Aristotelian sense, the surface of the surrounding body; see *Princ.* II 15. This is a distinction familiar to the scholastic literature, and Descartes's use of it here is one of the clearest fruits of readings he did in the scholastic philosophy in late 1640 and 1641, though we should not discount late recollections of lessons taught at La Flèche. See Garber 1992a, pp. 24–5, 134–6, 342 n. 61.

107 *Princ.* II 16.

108 *Princ.* II 18. This striking argument is a variant on scholastic arguments. On this, see Garber 1992a, chap. 5, esp. pp. 132–4; Grant 1981, pp. 335–6, nn. 33–4.

109 *Princ.* II 21. On the distinction between the indefinite and the infinite in Descartes, see Ariew 1987.

110 *Princ.* II 22.

111 *Princ.* II 23, 64. Descartes does recognise differences between three different kinds of bodies that correspond, in a way, to three of the four Aristotelian elements, what he calls elements of the first, second, and third kind, namely, fire, air, and earth (water as an element is curiously omitted); see *Le monde,* chap. 5 ('On the number of elements, and their qualities'), and *Princ.* III *passim.* However, Descartes is quite clear that his elements differ from one another only in their sizes, shapes, and motions, and that all are composed of the same material substance whose essence is extension.

112 See Gilson 1967a, pp. 143–84; Garber 1992a, chap. 4.

113 *Princ.* II 20, IV 202.

114 *Princ.* II 34.

115 *Princ.* II 20.

116 See, e.g., Gassendi 1658, vol. 1, p. 256B. For Gassendi's discussion of Descartes's view, and his distinction between Descartes's natural philosophy and atomism, see Gassendi 1658, vol. 1, pp. 257B–8A. In addition to the points discussed here, Descartes notes that he differs from the atomist tradition in so far as he, Descartes, denies that his corpuscles are by their nature heavy; heaviness (gravity) for Descartes is explained in terms of the interaction between a body in the vicinity of the earth, and the vortex that swirls around it. Descartes also points out that the atomists promise more than they deliver in terms of actually explaining things in terms of their atoms, whereas he, Descartes, offers real explanations. See *Princ.* IV 202. For a general discussion of the relation of Descartes to the atomist tradition, see Garber 1992a, chap. 5.

117 For a fuller discussion of this, see Chapter 9 in this book and Garber 1992a, pp. 175–81.

118 See, e.g., AT V 238–40, 301–2, 378–9.

119 AT V 342. Impenetrability had been discussed earlier in Descartes's writings, but only in passing; see AT VII 442.

120 Micraelius 1653, col. 331. For a fuller account of the issue of impenetrability in Descartes, see Gabbey 1980a, pp. 299–300, n. 27; Garber 1992a, pp. 144–8.

121 See, e.g., *Princ.* II 40–3; *Princ.* III 56–7.

122 *Princ.* II 43.

123 *Princ.* II 37.

124 AT V 404. The portion in italics is a quotation from More's earlier question; see AT V 316, 381.

125 AT V 403–4. This passage is somewhat controversial, and some commentators see Descartes as endorsing the claim that bodies have causal efficacy. For a discussion of

this issue, see Garber 1992a, pp. 302–3. For a fuller discussion of the very complex issue of force and activity in Descartes's natural philosophy, see Garber 1992a, chap. 9; Hatfield 1979; Gabbey 1980a; and Prendergast 1975.

126 For a fuller discussion of occasionalism, see Chapter 17. It should be emphasised that even though Descartes was obviously the inspiration for the occasionalism of his followers, it is not entirely clear that he himself was an occasionalist. See Garber 1993a.

127 *De corpore* (1655) II.8.18; II.9.7, in *Eng Works,* vol. 1. All subsequent quotations from *De corpore* are taken from this edition.

128 Mintz 1962; Shapin and Schaffer 1985; Rogers 1988.

129 See Grant 1981, pp. 208, 390–1 (n. 169); Funkenstein 1986, pp. 64, 185–6.

130 This is what Richard Tuck has recently called a post-sceptical science; see Tuck 1988.

131 On the distinction between real and imaginary space in Hobbes, see Schuhmann 1992.

132 On Hobbes's affinities with the philosophy of Gassendi, his personal sympathies with Gassendi, and his hostility to Descartes, see Brandt 1928, pp. 178ff. On the relations between Descartes and Hobbes, particularly on questions in natural philosophy, see Tuck 1988; Zarka 1988.

133 British Library, Harley MS 6796, fol. 297–308, published by Jean Bernhardt with French translation in Hobbes 1988. It should be noted that the evidence for its being by Hobbes is merely circumstantial; see Tuck 1988. Bernhardt argues, however, that the manuscript is an autograph, and that Hobbes is indeed the author; see Bernhardt in Hobbes 1988, pp. 8–9.

134 Pacchi 1965; Gargani 1971, pp. 97–123; Roger Bacon 1983. The claim that Hobbes knew Roger Bacon is based on the assumption that Hobbes is the author of certain MS booklists, an assumption recently called into question by Noel Malcolm, who attributes them to Robert Payne. See Hobbes 1994, vol. 2, p. 874.

135 Hobbes 1973, p. 162 (Hobbes 1976, p. 101).

136 Bernhardt in Hobbes 1988, p. 167. On Bacon's 'other' (i.e., speculative) philosophy in general, see Rees 1975, 1977a, 1977b, 1980, and Rees's Commentary in Bacon 1984.

137 Chap. 4, 'Problems of Heat and Light'. *Eng. Works,* vol. 7, p. 29. The *Problemata physica* appeared in London, 1662, and the English translation (quoted here) as *Seven Philosophical Problems . . .* in London, 1682.

138 For more detailed discussions of this response to the new philosophy, see, e.g., Mercer 1989, pp. 37–55, and 1993; Lennon 1993, pp. 52–62.

139 For a general discussion of occasionalism, see Chapter 17. For a discussion of the question as to whether or not Descartes himself was an occasionalist, see Garber 1993a.

140 On occasionalism, see de Lattre 1967; Weier 1981; Nadler 1993b, forthcoming. For a general account of the diffusion of Cartesian natural philosophy, see Mouy 1934.

141 See particularly *Le discernement,* disc. IV, in Cordemoy 1968, pp. 134ff.

142 See *Le discernement,* disc. V and VI, Cordemoy 1968, pp. 145ff.

143 See Cordemoy 1968, pp. 95–102.

144 See Cordemoy 1968, pp. 103–4. On Cordemoy's Cartesian atomism, see Prost 1907, chap. 3; Battail 1973, chap. 4.

145 The main Cartesian critic of Cordemoy was Dom Robert Desgabets. For accounts of his views and the views of other Cartesians, see Prost 1907, chap. 8; Battail 1973, pp. 111ff.

146 For a more detailed discussion of the Gassendist school, see Lennon 1993, chap. 2.

147 Boyle 1744, vol. 1, pp. 355–6.

148 See, e.g., Boyle 1744, vol. 3, p. 509; Shapin 1984.

149 Gassendi 1658, vol. 3, p. 102; Bloch 1971, pp. 236–74.

150 It is one of the main theses of Lennon 1993 that Locke should be read as a member of the Gassendist camp, and as opposing the enthusiasm of the Cartesians. See esp. chap. 3.

151 Sorbière witnessed with disapproval several acrimonious disputes between the Cartesians and their critics during his tenure as secretary of Montmor's academy. See Brown 1934, pp. 85–8; Taton 1965, pp. 21–7. Chapelain similarly noted his disapproval of the dogmatic opinions of the Cartesians in his correspondence with François Bernier, Carrel de Sainte-Garde, and Gerardus Joannes Vossius. See Collas 1912, pp. 153–4; Taton 1965, pp. 29–31. For a general account of the battles between Cartesians and Gassendists, see Lennon 1993, chap. 1.

152 For further discussion of this, see Chapter 23.

153 Gabbey 1982.

154 More 1662a, 'An Appendix to the Defence of The Philosophick Cabbala', p. 104; Sailor 1964.

155 More 1713, p. 54.

156 *An Antidote against atheisme* (More 1653), p. 16; also 3d ed. in More 1662a.

157 More 1653, p. 46; also in More 1662a.

158 More 1662d, pp. 203, 193. On the explanatory limitations More saw in the mechanical philosophy, see Gabbey 1990b.

159 Cudworth 1678, p. 74.

160 Sailor 1964; Walker 1972.

161 Cudworth 1678, p. 105.

162 More 1662d, Preface, p. 13.

163 Colie 1963; McGuire 1972; Henry 1987; Crocker 1990; Hutton 1990; Henry 1990. Cf. Jacob 1977, pp. 159–64, 175–6. A possible exception is Robert Boyle, whose *A Free Enquiry into the Vulgarly Receiv'd Notion of Nature* (London, 1685/6) has been interpreted in this light, but it is as much an attack on More and Cudworth's so-called hylarchic principle as it is upon hylozoism.

164 The view is developed most fully in *Eth.* I and II. For accounts of Spinoza's metaphysics particularly sensitive to the historical context, see Gueroult 1968–74; Curley 1988; Donagan 1988. Spinoza's account of mind is discussed in Chapter 23 in this book.

165 For Spinoza's account of divisibility and the vacuum, see *Eth.* I prop. 15 schol., esp. Geb. II 59. Spinoza implies there that a line is divisible to infinity, suggesting that bodies are too, but there is no statement of it there. Atoms are also discussed in Spinoza's commentary on Descartes's *Principia,* where he appears to agree with Descartes. In *Eth.* I prop. 15 schol., Spinoza also asserts there that there is no vacuum, implying that although this view does not follow from the Cartesian vase argument discussed above, it does follow from the fact that extended substance (i.e., God comprehended under the attribute of extension) is not made up of independent parts. Spinoza makes reference to the '*facies totius universae*' in a letter to Schuller, 29 July 1675, Geb. IV 278 (Spinoza 1928, p. 308).

166 Tschirnhaus to Spinoza, 2 May 1676, and Spinoza to Tschirnhaus, 5 May 1676, Geb. IV 331, 332 (Spinoza 1928, pp. 361, 363). See also Tschirnhaus to Spinoza, 5 January 1675, Geb. IV 268 (Spinoza 1928, p. 298). See also Gabbey 1996, note 42. It is not clear what exactly Spinoza is referring to when he mentions having once demonstrated the inadequacy of Descartes's 'principles of natural things'. There is no detailed refutation of Descartes's natural philosophy in the texts that survive. Perhaps he is referring to a discussion he had with Tschirnhaus on some prior occasion.

167 Tschirnhaus to Spinoza, 23 June 1676, and Spinoza to Tschirnhaus, 15 July 1676, Geb IV 333–4, 334–5 (Spinoza 1928, pp. 363, 365).

168 See *Eth.* I, prop. 26, 27, 29 schol.

169 See *Eth.* II, prop. 40, schol. I.

170 On attempts to reconcile the new mechanical philosophy with scholastic thought, see especially Mercer 1989, chap. 2. Equally interesting are seventeenth-century attempts at associating Cartesian thought with Augustinianism: see Gouhier 1978.

171 Leibniz to Remond, 10 January 1714, Ger. III 607 (Leibniz 1969, p. 655).

172 On the teaching of philosophy in seventeenth-century Germany and on Leibniz's philosophical education, see Lewalter 1967; Moll 1978; Petersen 1921; Beck 1969, chap. 7.

173 Leibniz to J. Thomasius, 20/30 April 1669, LAkad II.I 14–24 (Leibniz 1969, pp. 93–103). For the version reprinted in the introduction to Nizolio, see LAkad VI.II 433–4. Though the differences between the two versions are small, they are significant. See Garber 1982; Mercer 1989, chap. 2.

174 LAkad II.I 16 (Leibniz 1969, p. 95).

175 For accounts of Leibniz's early thought, which was not as simplistic as he later sometimes makes it out to be, see, e.g., Hannequin 1908; Kabitz 1909. For a later and oversimplified account of the early thought, see Leibniz's remarks in the 'Specimen Dynamicum' of 1695, Leibniz 1982b, pp. 18–24 (Leibniz 1989, pp. 123–5).

176 Ger. III 606 (Leibniz 1969, p. 655).

177 On the transition from the early physics to the mature writings, see Belaval 1964; Fichant 1974, 1978; and Fichant's notes and commentary in Leibniz 1994. The 'Brevis Demonstratio' is found in Ger. Math. VI 117–19, together with a later manuscript appendix on pp. 119–23 (Leibniz 1969, pp. 296–301). The correspondence with Arnauld is found with related documents in Ger. II 11–138 (Leibniz 1967). Other writings centrally concerned with the foundations of Leibniz's account of physics and the notion of body include: (1) the *Dynamica de potentia et legibus naturae corporeae*, written during Leibniz's trip to Italy in 1689–90 with the intention of publication, but unpublished during his lifetime, Ger. Math. VI 281–514; (2) a summary of the main philosophical points of the *Dynamica*, the 'Specimen Dynamicum,' published in the *Acta Eruditorum* in 1695, Leibniz 1982b (Leibniz 1989, pp. 118–38); (3) an essay, the 'De Ipsa Natura', published in the *Acta Eruditorum* in 1698, Ger. IV 504–16 (Leibniz 1989, pp. 155–67); (4) an essay criticising the Cartesian conception of body dated May 1702, Ger. IV 393–400 (Leibniz 1989, pp. 250–6); and (5) at the end of Leibniz's life, the correspondence with Clarke, a stand-in for Isaac Newton, with whom Leibniz had quarrelled bitterly (Leibniz and Clarke 1956; Leibniz and Clarke 1957). Of course, in addition there are many other relevant notes and letters, as well as more technical work on physics.

178 Ger. IV 393–4 (Leibniz 1989, p. 251). See also 'Extrait d'une lettre de M. D. L. . . .'(1693), Ger. IV 467; Leibniz to Malebranche, late January or early February 1693, Robinet 1955, p. 301; Leibniz to de Volder, 24 March/3 April 1699, Ger. II 169–70 (Leibniz 1989, pp. 171–2); 'Conversation of Philarète and Ariste' (1715), Robinet 1955, p. 443 (Leibniz 1989, p. 261); etc.

179 For theological reasons, Descartes held that matter is not infinitely divided, strictly speaking, but only indefinitely divided; see, e.g., *Princ.* I 26. However, it should be pointed out that whatever Descartes's terminology, he did hold that in at least some circumstances, it is actually divided into smaller parts in such a way that every part, no matter how small, is composed of smaller parts still. See *Princ.* II 34.

180 Leibniz to Arnauld, 30 April 1687, Ger. II 97 (Leibniz 1967, p. 121).

181 Of course, this argument is not directed against those who hold that there are atoms, naturally indivisible smallest parts of bodies.

182 Ger. II 96 (Leibniz 1967, pp. 120–1).

183 Leibniz offered a variety of other arguments against atomism. For example, there cannot be perfectly hard atoms made of the same stuff, because otherwise the principle if the identity of indiscernables would be violated; see 'De Ipsa Natura' (1698), §13, Ger. IV 514 (Leibniz 1989, p. 164). Elsewhere he argues from the Principle of Sufficient Reason that there cannot be atoms because there is no reason to stop the divisibility of matter at one place rather than another; see Leibniz to Caroline, 12 May 1716; Leibniz and Clarke 1957, p. 77 (Leibniz and Clarke 1956, p. 44). Leibniz's most frequent argument is that if there were perfectly hard bodies, as atoms are supposed to be (and must be, since they have no parts to move with respect to one another), then in collision they would have to change their speeds instantaneously, without passing through all intervening speeds. See, e.g., the 'Dynamica' (1690), Ger. Math. VI 491, and the 'Specimen Dynamicum', Leibniz 1982b, pp. 44–6 (Leibniz 1989, pp. 131–2).

184 Ger. IV 508–9 (Leibniz 1989, pp. 159–60). The reference here is obviously to Spinoza.

185 Ger. IV 513 (Leibniz 1989, p. 164). In addition to these arguments from activity, there are some rather more technical ones in Leibniz's writings. In the 'Specimen Dynamicum' of 1695 he argued that if bodies are inert, as the Cartesians hold, and if the laws of motion are to be explained from the nature of bodies alone, then since there is no ground for resistance (or any other sort of activity) in such bodies, the laws of impact will just reduce to the laws of the composition of velocities, from which Leibniz draws absurd consequences. See Leibniz 1982b, pp. 18–24 (Leibniz 1989, pp. 123–5). A further argument followed from his celebrated principle of the conservation of *vis viva*. In a letter to Bayle, Leibniz explained his new law of the conservation of force, as measured by mv^2. Leibniz often emphasised that his new law preserves the ability a body has to do work. Leibniz writes: 'I have shown that force ought not to be estimated by the product of speed and size, but by the future effect. However, it seems that force or power is something real at present, while the future effect is not. From which it follows that we must admit in bodies something different from size and speed, at least unless one wants to refuse bodies all power of acting' (Leibniz to Bayle, undated, Ger. III 48). Leibniz argues that neither size nor speed (nor their product), what the Cartesians allow to be in body, can represent in a body at a time t the ability that that body has at some future time to do work. But since the body really does have that ability at time t, there must be something else it has at that time by virtue of which it has that future ability, something that goes beyond its geometrical properties. See the discussion of this argument in Gueroult 1967, pp. 46–9.

186 Leibniz to Foucher June 1687(?), Ger. I 392.

187 Leibniz 1903, p. 590 (Leibniz 1989, p. 91). This is taken from an unnamed piece in which Leibniz attempts to show the advantages his views on motion have for the issue of Copernicanism. On Leibniz's attempts to use his doctrine of the equivalence of hypotheses in connexion with the issue of Copernicanism and the church, see Bertoloni Meli 1988.

188 For a general assessment of Leibniz's relations to Newton in physics and cosmology, see Bertoloni Meli 1993, which contains some recently discovered manuscripts that give Leibniz's first thoughts on Newton's *Principia*. For other of Leibniz's comments on Newton on motion, see, e.g., Leibniz to Huygens, 12/22 June 1694, Ger. Math. II 184–5 (Leibniz 1989, p. 308); there are also comments in the 'Specimen Dynamicum',

Leibniz (1982b) pp. 22–4, 58, 74 (Leibniz 1989, pp. 125, 136). There is not space here to examine in detail Leibniz's arguments for the general claim that there is no way to tell what is in motion and what is at rest. For a discussion of Leibniz's complex position and the various tangled arguments he offered for it, see Stein 1977, pp. 3–6, with notes and appendices, and Bernstein 1984. See also the discussion in Chapter 20.

189 For a good discussion of this argument, see Sleigh 1990a, pp. 112–4.

190 Leibniz to Clarke, 25 February 1716, Leibniz and Clarke 1957, p. 53 (Leibniz and Clarke 1956, pp. 25–6).

191 See, e.g., Leibniz to Clarke, 25 February 1716, Leibniz and Clarke 1957, p. 54 (Leibniz and Clarke 1956, pp. 26–7); Leibniz to Clarke, 2 June 1716, Leibniz and Clarke 1957, pp. 86–9 (Leibniz and Clarke 1956, p. 38).

192 See, e.g., Leibniz to Johann Bernoulli, 13/23 January 1699, Ger. Math. III 565 (Leibniz 1989, pp. 170–1). The same argument also comes up a number of times in the Leibniz–Clarke correspondence: Leibniz to Clarke, end of November 1715, Leibniz and Clarke 1957, p. 36 (Leibniz and Clarke 1956, p. 16); Leibniz to Caroline, 12 May 1716, Leibniz and Clarke 1957, pp. 76–7 (Leibniz and Clarke 1956, pp. 43–5).

193 The term 'monad' appears in Leibniz's philosophical vocabulary as early as 1696; see Leibniz to Fardella, 3/13 September 1696, Leibniz 1857, p. 326. There Leibniz defines the monad as 'a real unity'. The first use found in print is in the 'De Ipsa Natura' of 1698; see Ger. IV 511, 512 (Leibniz 1989, pp. 162, 163). Although one may be able to find the term used earlier, it is only in the late 1690s that it becomes an important technical term for Leibniz. On the earlier history of the notion of a monad, a term used by a variety of thinkers, including Neoplatonists and Pythagoreans, from the ancients to the seventeenth century, see Heimsoeth 1960, pp. 77–83. For a variety of pre-Leibnizian passages, see, e.g., Eisler 1910, vol. 2, p. 815.

194 Leibniz himself defines a suppositum as a 'substantial individual' in a 1668 fragment on transubstantiation; see LAkad VI.I, p. 511 (Leibniz 1969, p. 117).

195 In section 8 of the *Discours de métaphysique,* Leibniz establishes that individual substances are such as to admit of a complete individual concept, 'a notion so complete that it is sufficient to allow us to deduce from it all the predicates of the subject to which this notion is attributed'. In showing that individual substances have complete individual concepts, Leibniz takes himself to have established that they are the active sources of all of their properties. As Leibniz paraphrases the conclusion of the argument in section 14, 'each substance is like a world apart, independent of all other things, except for God; thus all our phenomena, that is, all the things that can ever happen to us, are only consequences of our being.' Leibniz also thinks that it follows from the same argument that individual substances must be genuine individuals. He writes to Arnauld in his letter of 28 November/8 December 1686: 'A substantial unity requires a thoroughly indivisible and naturally indestructible being, since its notion includes everything that will happen to it, something which can be found neither in shape nor in motion' (Ger. II 76 [Leibniz 1967, p. 94]). Though this argument plays a central rôle in the *Discours de métaphysique* and a few other texts, it is interesting that it seems to drop out of Leibniz's bag of tricks before long and, indeed, never manages to make it into any of his published writings.

196 On Leibniz's rejection of occasionalism, see Sleigh 1990b; Rutherford 1993.

197 On the importance of the notion of unity in Neoplatonic thought, see, e.g., Heimsoeth 1960, pp. 77–83. On the more general question of Leibniz's relation to Platonistic thought, see Brunner 1951, chap. 1. Despite Leibniz's obvious debt to the Platonic tradition, there is very little in the way of secondary material on the question.

198 Leibniz to Arnauld, 30 April 1687, Ger. II 101 (Leibniz 1967, p. 126).
199 Leibniz to Arnauld, 9 October 1687, Ger. II 120 (Leibniz 1967, p. 154).
200 Leibniz to Arnauld, 28 November/8 December 1686, Ger. II 77 (Leibniz 1967, p. 95). The diamonds to which he refers here are the diamond of the Grand Duke and the diamond of the Grand Mogul, physically distant from one another, but united by virtue of being given a single name. See also Leibniz to Johann Bernoulli, 20/30 September 1698: 'What I call a complete monad or singular substance [substantia singularis] is not so much the soul [anima] as it is the animal itself, or something analogous to it, endowed with a soul or form and an organic body' (Ger. Math. III 542 [Leibniz 1989, p. 168]). Note also Leibniz's remarks on Fardella, in which he suggests that the soul taken apart from the body with which it forms a corporeal substance is not itself a genuine substance. See Leibniz on Fardella, March 1690, Leibniz 1857, p. 322 (Leibniz 1989, p. 105). This conception of Leibniz's metaphysics is developed at some length in Garber 1985. For another view, see Adams 1994, pt. III.
201 Leibniz to Arnauld, 9 October 1687, Ger. II, p. 126 (Leibniz 1967, p. 161).
202 See, e.g., Leibniz to de Volder, 20 June 1703, Ger. II 252 (Leibniz 1989, p. 177); Leibniz to Remond, 11 February 1715, Ger. III 636 (Leibniz 1969, p. 659); 'De modo distinquendi phaenomena realia ab imaginariis' (1683–6), Ger. VII 322 (Leibniz 1969, p. 365); etc.
203 Leibniz to Des Bosses, 29 May 1716, Ger. II 517 (Leibniz 1989, p. 203).
204 Leibniz to Des Bosses, 5 February 1712, Ger. II 435–6 (Leibniz 1989, p. 199).
205 See also Leibniz to de Volder, 30 June 1704, G II 268 (Leibniz 1989, pp. 178–9); Leibniz to de Volder, 1704 or 1705, G II 275 (Leibniz 1989, p. 181); "Antibarbarus Physicus" (1710–16?) G VII 344 (Leibniz 1989, p. 319–20). For a fuller development of this conception of body in Leibniz, see Adams 1983, 1994 (part III); Rutherford 1995 (part III); Catherine Wilson 1989, esp. sec. 30. It should be noted that in the correspondence with Des Bosses, Leibniz was experimenting with the view on which some monads were bound together by virtue of a 'substantial chain [*vinculum substantiale*]' which somehow bound them together into a genuine corporeal substance. On this view, the metaphysical status of bodies and extension would seem to have been different, Leibniz suggests. For a discussion of this view, see also Boehm 1962.
206 See, e.g., his remarks in *Disc. mét.*, secs. 10–11.
207 Leibniz 1982b, pp. 6–8 (Leibniz 1989, pp. 119–20). For a fuller discussion of Leibniz's complex notions of force, see Gueroult 1967; Garber 1995.
208 See, e.g., *Disc. mét.*, secs. 10–11, and the fuller discussion in Garber 1985, pp. 92–9. Leibniz's laws of motion are expressed in a series of conservation principles, all ultimately grounded in his metaphysical principle of the equality of cause and effect, in accordance with which there must be as much power or force (ability to do work) in the effect as there is in the cause. The conservation of mv^2 or living force (*vis viva*) is given in many places, including *Disc. mét.*, sec. 17. For a variety of derivations, both *à priori* and *à posteriori,* see the preliminary specimen to the *Dynamica,* Ger. Math. VI 287–92 (Leibniz 1989, pp. 106–11). For a more general discussion of a variety of Leibniz's conservation principles see his 'Essay de dynamique . . .', Ger. Math. VI 215–31. See also the discussion in Garber 1995, sec. 4.3.
209 Newton 1952, pp. 397, 400–401.
210 Newton 1962, p. xviii.
211 Burndy MS 16, fol. 4r.
212 Newton 1952, p. 374. See Rattansi 1972; Westfall 1972, 1984.

213 Newton 1962, p. 132. The dating of 'De gravitatione' divides scholarly opinion: traditionally it is thought to have been written about 1668, but gaining ground is the view that it dates from the early 1680s; see Dobbs 1991. Its principal importance in Newton's intellectual history is that it contains a detailed critique of Descartes's concepts of place, space, and motion; the vortex theory; and other features of his natural philosophy.

214 Newton 1962, pp. 136–7.

215 Newton 1952, p. 370.

216 Newton 1952, p. 403.

217 Newton 1934, p. 545.

218 More was only one of several influences on Newton; Newton had his own very powerful (even obsessive) commitments not only to a particular natural philosophy but also, as his extensive theological manuscripts reveal, to an idiosyncratic theology. These preoccupations, together with the general background of seventeenth-century philosophy and theology, enable us to make plausible reconstructions of the development of Newton's thinking in which More plays only a small part. On this see Burtt 1932; Koyré 1957; McGuire 1977. Cf. Westfall 1971b, pp. 326–7, and 1980, pp. 301–4; McGuire 1978a; Copenhaver 1980; Grant 1981, pp. 238–47; McGuire in Newton 1983; Hall 1990, pp. 202–23; Henry 1993.

219 Newton 1934, p. 544.

220 Newton 1962, p. 139.

221 Newton 1962, p. 139. See also Oakley 1961, 1984; McGuire 1968, 1972; Hooykaas 1972; Klaaren 1977; Funkenstein 1986, pp. 124–52.

222 More 1662d, p. 12. See further Gabbey 1990b.

223 Newton to Bentley, 17 January, 25 February 1692/93. Newton 1959–77, vol. 3, pp. 240, 253–4.

224 Confirmation of this reading can be inferred from Bentley's own use of the argument in his Boyle Lecture of 7 November 1692. See 'A Confutation of Atheism from the Origin and Frame of the World', Newton 1978, p. 341. Robert Boyle provided in his will for the establishment of an annual series of lectures to defend Protestant Christianity against atheism and materialism. On the use of this familiar sort of argument against the atheistic implications of the mechanical philosophy, see, e.g., McGuire 1968; Henry 1986b; Gabbey 1990b. On atheism in this context, see Hunter 1981, pp. 162–87. On Newton, action at a distance and gravity as an inherent property of body, see Henry 1994.

225 As shown in McGuire 1977, pp. 106–7. McGuire notes that Newton explicitly repudiated More's hylarchic spirit and Cudworth's plastic nature in Newton 1714/15, p. 223.

226 'Hypothesis explaining the Properties of Light' (1675), Newton 1978, p. 181.

227 Boyle 1744, vol. 1, pp. 70–3. Newton 1978, pp. 250–3. Newton 1952, pp. 347–54.

228 Cohen 1980, p. 117.

229 Newton's struggles with the aether hypothesis are a complicated story. See Westfall 1971b, *passim,* and 1984; Dobbs 1975, *passim;* McGuire 1977; McMullin 1978a, *passim;* Cohen 1980, *passim.*

230 See, e.g., Leibniz's strong condemnation of Newton and his followers in his 'Antibarbarus physicus', Ger. VII 337–44 (Leibniz 1989, pp. 312–20).

231 Sprat 1667, p. 35.

232 Multhauf 1966, pp. 299–310; Meinel 1988a, pp. 96–8.

233 Newton 1952, p. 401.

234 Newton 1934, p. 547.

235 McGuire 1970; Cohen 1971, 1980.

236 *Ess.* II.viii.9. For Locke's view of space, see *Ess.* II.xiii; for Locke's views on real and nominal essences, see *Ess.* III.iii and III.vi.

237 *Ess.* II.viii.11. This is the text, with minor variations, for editions 1 (1690), 2 (1694), and 3 (1695).

238 Locke to Stillingfleet, 4 May 1698 (Third Letter). Locke 1823, vol. 4, pp. 467–8.

239 Locke 1975, pp. 135–6.

240 Locke 1823, vol. 3, pp. 304, 306. The *Elements* appeared in *A Collection of Several Pieces of Mr. John Locke* (London, 1720).

241 Locke 1823, vol. 3, p. 303.

242 Aaron 1971; Alexander 1985; Lennon 1993.

243 *Ess.* IV.iii.6. This view is discussed in more detail in chapter 23.

244 Thackray 1970; Schofield 1970; M. Wilson 1979; Ayers 1981b; Yolton 1983; Alexander 1985, pp. 227–35.

19

KNOWLEDGE OF THE EXISTENCE OF BODY

CHARLES McCRACKEN

Can we know whether or not there is a material world? Before Descartes, this question was rarely asked. A few thinkers in antiquity were reported to have expressed sweeping doubts about the existence of things. For instance, Sextus Empiricus tells us that Gorgias of Leontini defended the threefold claim that nothing exists; that even if something existed, we could not understand it; and that even if we could understand it, we could not communicate that understanding to anyone else. Zeno of Elea is alleged, by Seneca, to have asserted that nothing exists. And Metrodorus of Chios, according to Cicero, thought we cannot know whether anything exists.[1] But expressions of such world-annihilating doubt were rare, their interpretation is debatable, and they provoked no sustained debate about whether we can know that bodies exist. It was far more common for the ancient sceptics to argue that we cannot get beyond the *appearances* of bodies, to discover their true nature, than to raise doubts about their existence. Thus Sextus, in a well-known passage, said we must grant that honey *appears* sweet to us, but we cannot determine whether honey in itself *is* sweet; but Sextus did not suggest that, apart from the appearance, there may be no honey at all.[2]

A few mediaeval thinkers do seem to have voiced doubts about the existence of the bodies our senses perceive. al-Ghazālī, for example, held that we cannot be certain that, at death, we will not find this life to have been a dream and the things we seem to have perceived in it but 'empty imaginings'.[3] And Nicolaus of Autrecourt said that if it is granted that God can cause our sense perceptions, then we cannot be sure that bodies exist, for we cannot be sure that God Himself is not causing our perceptions.[4] But al-Ghazālī and Nicolaus were exceptional in raising this possibility, and the question of the existence of the material world seems never to have become one of the *quaestiones disputatae* in the mediaeval schools. The Renaissance saw a great revival of scepticism, but like their precursors in antiquity, Renaissance sceptics were more apt to deny that we can know the nature of bodies than to raise doubts about their existence. Montaigne, for example, argued that we cannot know what bodies really are, but, like Sextus, he did not voice a doubt about whether there really *are* any.[5]

It was Descartes's *Meditationes* that focused the attention of philosophers on the question, 'Can we know there is a material world?' How can we be sure, asked Descartes, that our sensations are caused by the action of bodies on our own body and not in some other way – by some powerful god or demon, say, who produces in our minds all our sensations, though no bodies (not even our own) exist? Persuaded that this question must be answered if physics is to be given a secure foundation, Descartes set out what he took to be a proof that bodies exist. At first, even Descartes's severest critics showed little interest in this proof, or indeed in his project of proving that bodies exist. In time, however, the merits of his proof came to be much discussed, especially among the Cartesians themselves, and a number of philosophers were led to inquire whether, or how, we can be certain that bodies exist, some even concluding that, without the aid of divine revelation, we cannot be certain they do – a view that in turn prepared the way for those in the eighteenth century who denied the existence of material substances. Thus, though the topic provoked little interest before Descartes, it came to be a widely debated one in the course of the seventeenth century.

I. DESCARTES'S PROOF THAT BODIES EXIST

Eager to lay an unshakable foundation for knowledge, and in the process to refute the sceptic, Descartes proposed to adopt the sceptic's own method: to doubt everything, unless something was found that could not be doubted.[6] In his first published work, the *Discours de la méthode* (1637), Descartes spoke of his doubt as encompassing all his former beliefs; but he did not raise the possibility that the bodies he seemed to perceive might be an illusion wrought in his mind by an evil demon (nor did he offer an explicit proof that bodies exist). Instead, he based his doubts on grounds the sceptics had long made familiar – the unreliability of the senses and the puzzle of how to tell waking from dreaming.[7] But in the *Meditationes* (1641) he sought a wider ground for doubt than the sceptical tradition afforded. To be sure, he again retailed some well-worn sceptical reasons for doubting the senses: that they sometimes deceive us, that the delusions of the mad seem as real to them as our perceptions do to us, that in dreams we seem to see things that do not exist.[8] But these grounds seemed to him too narrow to sustain a general doubt about the existence of the whole material world. For though our senses may mislead us about the remote or the minute, they do not mislead us about things nearby and familiar; though madmen may take themselves to be robed in purple when they are naked, it would be a sign of madness in us if we began to wonder whether we, too, were mad; and though we cannot be sure whether we are now awake or dreaming, we cannot doubt that we are *sometimes* awake, for the things we dream we see are only distortions and recombinations of things we see when awake.[9]

At the outset of inquiry, however, argued Descartes, I cannot preclude the possibility that *all* my sensations come from some source other than bodies – a possibility he made concrete by the hypothesis of a powerful demon who takes pleasure in producing in my mind all the sensations that persuade me there is a world of bodies when, in fact, no bodies exist. The hypothesis, conceded Descartes, is unlikely in the highest degree. (It may, nonetheless, have struck some readers of the time more forcefully than it does us, for belief in demonic beings who may beguile and mislead mankind was still widespread – indeed, only shortly before the *Meditationes* appeared, France had been rocked by the trial of Père Grandier, who was charged with having loosed a host of demons on the convent at Loudun.)[10] But unlikely as the hypothesis of an evil demon is, Descartes held that until we can be certain that our senses are not wholly deceptive (or, more strictly, that the judgements we make, in consequence of our sense perceptions, are not altogether false), we cannot be sure that the bodies our senses seem to disclose to us really exist. As he began his inquiry, therefore, Descartes could not suppose there are bodies, for he had not yet excluded the possibility that what seem to be bodies 'are merely the delusions of dreams which he [the evil demon] has devised to ensnare my judgement'.[11]

Only in the last of his *Meditationes* – after he had persuaded himself of the existence both of himself, as a thinking being, and of God, an all-perfect being – did Descartes think he could prove that we are not victims of some cosmic deception, and that our conviction that bodies exist is justified. There he argued, first, that it is *possible* that bodies exist, for we can form a clear and distinct idea of three-dimensional objects, and we cannot doubt that God can create anything we can clearly and distinctly conceive the nature of.[12] Second, it is *probable* that bodies exist, and that our mind is united to a particular body, for this hypothesis provides the most likely explanation of the fact that, though our pure intellect can form a perfectly clear and distinct idea of a chiliagon or of far more complex figures, our imagination can form only very confused and indistinct *images* of such things. The pure intellect belongs to the very nature of the mind, and so can draw clear geometrical concepts from the mind's innate store of ideas. But the imagination does *not* belong to the mind essentially, for the mind would not cease to be if it ceased to have the power of forming pictorial images; rather, its power to form such images may be supposed a consequence of the mind's union with the body – a supposition that will explain the imagination's limitations as an effect of that faculty's dependence on a certain corporeal organ (namely, the brain). Thus the hypothesis that there are bodies and that our mind is united to one particular body explains the striking disparity between the great scope of our pure intellect (which can grasp the concept of what is mathematically infinite) and the great limitation of our imagination (which can form clear images only of very simple figures). But since other explanations of this disparity are possible, the evidence it affords for the existence of bodies is only probable.[13]

It is from our *sensations* that we can come to know with *certainty* that there are bodies. We know that we have sensations, and we know further that they *seem to us* to be caused by bodies, and that they *must* be caused by something. Now we do not ourselves cause our sensations – that is clear, for we receive them whether we want to or not. Their cause, then, must be something, corporeal or incorporeal, that is independent of us. If their cause is *incorporeal,* it must be either that God Himself produces in us sensations that appear to come from bodies, or that God allows some other incorporeal agent to produce such sensations in us. But we can rule out the possibility that either God or some other incorporeal being produces our sensations.

For God has given me no faculty at all for recognizing any such source for these ideas; on the contrary, he has given me a great propensity to believe that they are produced by corporeal things. So I do not see how God could be understood to be anything but a deceiver if the ideas were transmitted from a source other than corporeal things.[14]

Since it would be contrary to God's perfect nature to deceive us, or so to constitute us that we were naturally inclined to believe what is false, we can be sure that bodies do exist.

Two conditions are here specified which together, thought Descartes, show that God would be a deceiver if our sensations were not produced by bodies: first, that God has so constituted us that we have a natural inclination to believe that our sensations are conveyed to us by bodies; second, that God has given us no means by which to discover this belief to be false. Since God is the author of our nature, whatever we are naturally inclined to believe must always contain some measure of truth. Descartes granted that our nature, considered as a union of mind and body, sometimes misleads us.[15] Thus sufferers from dropsy have a natural inclination to believe that their bodies need drink when their throats feel parched. But though this belief arises from 'a true error of nature' (*verus error naturae*), God has given us the means to discover that it is false, and so God cannot here be charged with deceiving us. More generally, since God is no deceiver, there cannot be 'any falsity in my opinions which cannot be corrected by some other faculty supplied by God'.[16] Since God has given me no faculty to correct my natural inclination to believe that sensations come from bodies, I can conclude with certainty that bodies exist.

Sensation thus plays, for Descartes, an indispensable rôle in the proof that bodies exist, for where our pure intellect's clear and distinct idea of extension reveals only the *possibility* that extended things exist, and our imagination's limited power to form images of such things shows their existence *probable,* our sensations (considered in the light of our natural – God-given – tendency to believe that bodies produce them in us and our certainty that God is no deceiver) give us *certainty* that a corporeal world exists. This should not, however, lead us to suppose, with the empiricists, that our whole concept of body is derived from our senses, nor again that bodies have exactly those properties that our senses seem to disclose in them. For though sensation is essential to our knowledge that bodies *exist,* we can come to know the *nature* of bodies, and their possible modes, only if we turn away from the senses and consult our innate geometrical idea of extension. When we do, we discover that many of the qualities that an uncritical reliance on our senses had led us to suppose present in bodies – colour, odour, taste, warmth, and so forth – do not belong to bodies *per se* (though such 'sensible qualities' *are* signs of various minute figures and motions that *do* belong to bodies), but reflect instead how our composite psycho-physical nature influences how bodies appear to us.[17] For Descartes, thus, physics, as a fully developed science of corporeal extension, depends *both* on our sensations, which disclose the existence of bodies, *and* on our clear and distinct innate idea of extension, from which we learn the nature of bodies and can form exact geometrical and mechanical concepts of the modes (i.e., the figures and motions) bodies admit of.

II. DOUBTS AMONG THE CARTESIANS ABOUT DESCARTES'S PROOF

Descartes's first critics – the philosophers and theologians whose objections to the *Meditationes* were printed (with Descartes's replies) in its first edition – showed little interest in this project of proving that a material world exists. They said little of this proof other than to suggest that God *may,* on occasion, deceive us for our own good – as doctors sometimes do their patients, or parents their children; and here what interested his critics was not chiefly Descartes's proof of a material world but rather the question of whether it would be inconsistent with the divine nature for God to deceive us, an issue over which the opinion of the schoolmen had been divided.[18] This lack of interest in the proof of bodies is not surprising, for these early critics of Descartes often fixed their attention on his treatment of topics long debated in the schools – the proofs of God's existence, of the immateriality of the soul, of its separability from the body, and so forth. Even Gassendi, who was so impressed by his reading of Sextus that in *Syntagma Philosophicum* he summarised and replied to arguments of classical scepticism, summarily dismissed Descartes's whole inquiry into the existence of bodies, saying it could not be supposed Descartes had any real doubt about their existence.[19]

One of the first attempts to refute Descartes's proof of a material world was made by his erstwhile follower, Henricus Regius, a professor at Utrecht. Regius's enthusiasm for the novelties of Cartesian physics had alarmed the University Senate and led it, in 1642, to condemn the Cartesian philosophy. But in time it became clear that, although Regius accepted much in Descartes's physics, he rejected some of the metaphysical theses that Descartes believed were the indispensable foundation of his physics. In 1647 Regius published a broadsheet attacking those metaphysical theses.[20] Among them was the proof that bodies exist. We cannot be certain, argued Regius, that what we perceive are bodies, for 'the mind can be affected by imaginary things just as much as by real things', by which he seems to have meant that there is no qualitative difference in the appearance things present to us whether we perceive them by sense or only dream or hallucinate that we perceive them. We can be certain that bodies exist, he said, not from any proof that reason can give, but because the Scripture assures us that God created heaven and earth.[21]

Regius developed this theme more fully in *Philosophia Naturalis* (1654), where he argued that in science we cannot hope to arrive at conclusions that are more than probable – not even about the existence of bodies. To Descartes's proof of a material world, he made two replies. First, God may have good reason to deceive us, perhaps for our own sake, or to punish us for our sins. And second, God would *not,* in any case, be deceiving us if, though no bodies existed, He produced sensations in our minds that seemed to have bodies as their probable cause. God would deceive us, to be sure, if He then so constituted us that we were irresistibly constrained to believe that our sensations came from bodies. But such is not the case. We are free to limit our judgement to this conclusion: certain appearances are now present to our minds and it is likely that bodies are their cause. Were this our judgement (and were there no bodies), we would no more be deceived by God than was a cautious thinker in antiquity who, noting the Sun's daily transit from east to west, judged that the Sun appears to move and that a likely explanation of this is that the Sun revolves around the earth. We would, of course, be deceived if we believed it *certain* that there were bodies when in fact none really existed; but the fault then would not be God's but ours, for assenting without reservation to something doubtful. Indeed, said Regius, we should consider that nothing would seem more in accord with our complete dependence on God than for our sensations to come from him, not from bodies. In the end, we can be sure there are bodies, he said, not because of what reason can discover but because of what the opening chapters of Genesis reveal to us.[22]

Similar views were held by Gérauld de Cordemoy, who, though an atomist, embraced much of Descartes's philosophy. Many people, said Cordemoy, think it certain that bodies exist, for they suppose we see and touch them, but they think only faith assures us we have a soul. But the situation, he argued, is the reverse. It is the soul we cannot doubt the existence of, for in our every thought we are aware of that in us which thinks; but only faith can assure us beyond doubt that bodies exist. By our senses we *seem* to perceive bodies, but in dreams we also seem to perceive bodies, though we do not. Like Regius, Cordemoy holds that how bodies appear to our senses is qualitatively indistinguishable from how they appear in our dreams; and so from the evidence of sense – our *only* evidence of bodies – we cannot conclude with certainty that bodies exist. (Cordemoy made no reply to Descartes's argument from God's veracity, nor to Descartes's claim that waking experience differs markedly from dreaming in that memory never connects our dreams with each other or with the rest of our lives, as it does our waking experiences.)[23] Cordemoy concluded that, though reason and revelation alike assure us that the *soul* exists, we can be sure bodies exist only because Scripture reveals that God the Father made heaven and earth and God the Son took flesh and dwelt among us.[24]

Nicolas Malebranche was deeply influenced by Descartes, but he subjected Descartes's proof that matter exists to searching scrutiny and reached the same conclusion Regius and Cordemoy had: only from divine revelation can we be certain that bodies exist. Malebranche was the foremost (but not the first) defender of occasionalism, a doctrine that seemed to lend a certain plausibility to the notion that there might be no material substances. Occasionalists taught that God alone is the true cause of everything that happens in the universe. If a brick strikes a window, it is God, not the brick, that causes the window to break. So too, if something impinges on one of my sense organs, it is God who causes a change in that organ, as well as in my nervous system and brain, and God, too, who produces the correlated sensation in my mind. Thus, where Descartes held that 'if God were himself immediately producing in our mind the idea of such extended matter, . . . there would be no way of avoiding the conclusion that he should be regarded as a deceiver',[25] Malebranche held that it *is* God who produces sensations in our minds *on the occasion* of some event (also caused by God) occurring in our brain. The details of Malebranche's theory of perception are complex: suffice to say that what we perceive, he held, is not material extension, but rather the uncreated idea of extension in God, and we distinguish one part of this 'intelligible extension' from another by means of colour, warmth, smell, taste, and so forth, though these 'sensible qualities' are really just sensations produced in our minds by God.

Now Malebranche saw that this doctrine makes the existence of matter problematic. If what we perceive are not bodies but intelligible things in God, and if we distinguish one part of this intelligible world from another by sensations that God produces in our minds, why should we think there *are* any bodies? Malebranche's own answer to this was that the sensations God produces in the mind are occasioned by changes in our body; but he himself, in his controversy with Antoine Arnauld, remarked that it would be quite possible for God to produce the same sensations in our minds even if there were no bodies, and that 'one might even say – to confound M. Arnauld – that God does nothing useless, and it is useless to create bodies, since they cannot act on the mind, and since, strictly speaking, what the mind perceives is not bodies but . . . something representative of them, which God causes, or can cause, in our minds even if there are no bodies.'[26] Bayle and Berkeley would later use a similar argument to show that the occasionalists themselves should have abandoned belief in material substance.

Malebranche himself, however, was persuaded that Descartes had given powerful reasons to believe in the existence of bodies. 'Descartes', he declared, 'has found the strongest proofs that can be given by unaided reason for the existence of bodies.'[27] But they are not, thought Malebranche, demonstrative proofs; they lead to a conclusion that is highly probable but not certain. We have, he agreed, a natural inclination to believe that bodies occasion our sensations, and it is probable that what God inclines us by nature to believe is true. But God might have some good reason for inclining us to believe something false. For example, if we touch fire, our nature inclines us to believe that the warmth we feel is in the fire; this belief, Malebranche holds, is false but useful, for because of it we quickly get our hand out of the fire. Now God is not here a deceiver, for He does not force us to believe that warmth is in the fire – we can suspend our judgement, concluding, on reflection, that the heat we feel is a sensation, not a quality in the fire.[28] So, too, there might be some good reason why God inclines us to believe that our sensations come from bodies, even if there are no bodies; such a false belief might even be a punishment for our sins – but it is not one God forces us to assent to.[29]

Arnauld responded that if we suppose that, to punish us, God may incline us to believe what is false, we may equally suppose that, to punish us, He may make what is false appear to us to be clearly and distinctly true – in which case there is nothing we can be certain of.[30] But Malebranche thought the cases were not comparable. God gives us the power to suspend our assent to 'natural judgements' that may be false; He thus enables us to escape error. By contrast, we are *irresistibly* constrained to judge that what we clearly and distinctly perceive to be the case *is* the case; hence, were such things false, God would lie to us. That bodies exist, held Malebranche, is something we are inclined by nature to believe but are not compelled, by clear and distinct perception, to assent to:

It is by a free act, and hence one subject to error, that we assent [to this belief], and not because we are irresistibly constrained to; we believe it because we freely will to do so, and not because we have for it the kind of evidence by which belief is forced on us as it is by a mathematical demonstration.

Hence, if we wish to avoid error, we should withhold our complete assent from the proposition that there is a corporeal world:

For in matters of philosophy, we should not believe something until the evidence forces us to. We should make as much use of our freedom as we can. Our judgements should not reach farther than our perceptions. So, when we see bodies, let us judge only that we do see them and that these bodies, sensible or intelligible, do, in fact, exist; but why should we judge positively that there is an external material world resembling that intelligible world we perceive?[31]

Or rather, this is what we should conclude if the opening chapters of the Bible did not assure us that God created the corporeal world. Descartes's defenders hastened to point out a circularity in this repeated attempt to ground, in the Bible, our certainty that bodies exist. For what, asked the noted Cartesian, Pierre-Sylvain Régis, *is* the Bible but a *book,* and what is a book but a *body?* Unless, then, we believe that bodies exist, we will not believe that the Bible exists; and unless we believe that the Bible exists, we have nothing to reveal to us that God created bodies.[32] Malebranche had tried to evade this objection by arguing that we can at least be certain that something *appears* to us to be the Bible, and that by that *appearance* of Scripture we are taught that God created bodies; since we can be sure that what God reveals to us, even in an appearance, is true, we can be sure that bodies exist.[33] This drew from Arnauld the retort that unless one first believed that prophets and apostles had lived, taught, and wrought miracles, one would have as good reason for believing the 'appearance' of the Koran to be God's revelation as for believing the 'appearance' of the Bible to be – to which Malebranche replied that faith led him to accept the Bible, not the Koran, as divine revelation.[34]

Some occasionalists went further than Malebranche in rejecting the Cartesian proof of bodies. Thus, Pierre Lanion and Michelangelo Fardella, while granting that Descartes had shown it *possible* that bodies exist, did not think he had shown it to be even particularly likely that they do. If Descartes had shown how bodies could cause our sensations, and if we could conceive no other way by which they might arise in the mind, argued Lanion, then the existence of bodies would be shown very probable. In fact, however, he said, we cannot conceive how bodies can produce effects in the mind, but we can easily conceive that God can do so – indeed, as a convinced occasionalist, Lanion held that God *does* cause all of our sensations. And since God produces effects by the simplest means, it would seem *unlikely* that He would take 'the long detour he would have to take were he to create extended things in order to make me see things'.[35] To those who said God would have no reason to produce sensations in our mind except to inform us of states of our body, Lanion answered that God might give us sensations so that we could more perfectly express our love for Him by freely transcending our concupiscent desires. And like Malebranche, Lanion held that our assent to belief in bodies is voluntary, so if bodies did not exist, we – not God – would be responsible for our error in judging that they did. But Lanion, too, granted that the testimony of Scripture assures us there are bodies; unaided reason, however, can affirm only that, as the concept of extension involves no contradiction, it is *possible* that bodies exist.[36]

The view of the Italian occasionalist Michelangelo Fardella was similar. Descartes, he said, has shown that colour, warmth, smell, and taste exist only in the mind; may that not be true too of extension, figure, and motion? Though all these are properties of the appearances present to our mind, nothing compels us to believe they are properties of anything other than appearances. Like Lanion, Fardella held that it would seem more consonant with the simplicity of God's ways were He to produce sensations in the mind *without* creating an unperceivable world of bodies as their correlate. And, going farther than others, Fardella denied that even Scripture makes the existence of bodies certain; for though the Bible speaks of bodies, we must not suppose it uses terms in the exact way of the metaphysician, for its aim is not the solution of metaphysical puzzles but the salvation of souls. Its talk of 'bodies', therefore, may reflect its use of popular idiom rather than its vindication of some philosophical doctrine. Fardella did not go so far as to deny that matter exists, but these views brought him closer than the earlier occasionalists to immaterialism.[37]

The English Platonist John Norris, deeply influenced by Malebranche, embraced Malebranche's view that reason shows it highly probable, but not certain, that bodies exist. But, like Fardella, Norris denied that divine revelation makes it certain they exist. For we know God's revelation only from the Bible; and we know there is a Bible only because we perceive it by sense. But, he held, from our senses we never get more than probable evidence for the existence of anything (save our sensations themselves). We have, therefore, only probable evidence that the Bible exists, and so only probable evidence that it *is* divine revelation. In consequence, neither reason nor revelation can make it more than probable that there are bodies.[38]

We see then by what degrees these heterodox Cartesians retreated from Descartes's confidence[39] that the existence of a material world can be proven with certainty: Regius and Malebranche thought reason, unaided by Scripture, can show it only probable that there is such a world; Lanion and Fardella thought reason can show it possible, but not even very probable; to which Fardella and Norris added that even Scripture does not guarantee beyond a doubt that bodies exist.[40]

III. THE POST-CARTESIAN SCEPTICS

Descartes boasted that he was 'the first philosopher ever to overturn the doubt of the sceptics'.[41] The sceptics, in turn, busied themselves with the work of overturning Descartes. Attacks on Cartesianism poured from the pens of sceptical writers like Simon Foucher, Pierre-Daniel Huet, and Jean Du Hamel. Among other things, they attacked Descartes's purported proof of a material world. Before Descartes, I have said, the efforts of sceptical philosophers aimed not so much at calling into doubt the existence of bodies as showing that we cannot know their nature. But after Descartes raised doubts about the existence of the material world and then sought, by argument, to allay those doubts, many sceptics tried to show that Descartes's own principles doomed his project. We can know there are bodies only if something – some *idea* – represents them to our minds. But, argued the sceptics, one thing can represent another only if there is some resemblance between them; a portrait can represent its subject only if it bears that subject some likeness. Now how, asked the sceptics, can an idea resemble, and so represent, a body? For Descartes, an idea is a mode of thought (*façon de penser*), and thought is wholly unlike extension; no idea, therefore, can make body known to mind.[42] Pierre-Sylvain Régis responded that not all representation involves resemblance. Words, for example, as Descartes himself remarked, represent things they do not resemble; so, too, said Régis, a sensation, for example, warmth, can represent a property in a body without resembling it. Further, the sceptics err in supposing all mental representation to be a kind of *picturing;* to have a clear idea of a thing is to know its nature and properties, but that need not entail having a mental image of it, as Descartes himself noted in the case of our clear geometrical idea of a chiliagon.[43]

To Simon Foucher, however, the problem went beyond how an idea can represent something that is supposed external to, and unlike, thought. Extension and figure, he argued, *are* ideas, just as are light and colour (which the Cartesians themselves grant do not exist apart from the mind that perceives them); hence, 'extension and figures are not less in our souls than are light and colours.'[44] Further, a thing's colour cannot be in one place (in mind) and its extension and figure in another (in matter), for colour always extends over some area, its boundary being identical with shape. So if colour exists only in the mind, as Descartes holds, the same must be true of extension and figure.[45] The conclusion seemed clear: on Descartes's principles, the world our ideas make known to us cannot exist outside our minds, and any world there may be outside our minds cannot be made known to us by our ideas.

The culmination of the seventeenth-century sceptics' attack on our putative knowledge of the existence of bodies came in Pierre Bayle's *Dictionnaire historique et critique* (1697). In the articles 'Pyrrho' and 'Zeno of Elea', Bayle used almost every argument that had been advanced against Descartes's proof of a material world: that extension and figure are as much ideas as colour, smell, taste, warmth, and so we have no more reason to believe that the former exist outside the mind than that the latter do (Foucher); that God can give us the same sensations, whether there are bodies or not, and so sensations are no proof of bodies (Malebranche); that God does not compel us to believe that bodies exist, and so does not deceive us if they do not exist (Regius, Malebranche, Lanion); that, on Descartes's own view, our senses are misleading about the sensible qualities of bodies and even about their true size, shape, and motion, and so they may also mislead us about their existence (Foucher, Malebranche, Fardella); that God produces effects in the simplest ways, and it would seem simpler for Him directly to cause our sensations than for Him to create a world of bodies as their cause (Lanion, Fardella).[46] To these arguments Bayle added another that proved influential: the extension, size, shape, and motion bodies appear to us to have are as relative to the condition of the perceiver as are their colour, smell, taste, warmth; hence, if relativity to the perceiver affords a reason to deny that colour and other properties exist outside the mind, the same must, by parity of reasoning, be true of extension.[47]

But what settles the matter definitively, argued Bayle, is that our concept of an extended thing is a concept of something inherently impossible. If extended things exist, they must be composed at bottom of either (1) indivisible *unextended* parts, (2) indivisible *extended* parts, or (3) infinitely divisible parts. But (1) is not possible, for no adding together of unextended parts can produce an extended thing. Nor is (2) possible, for any extended part, however small, will be divisible into a left and a right side, which, since they are in different places, will be different bodies, for the same body cannot be in two places at once. As for (3), Bayle thought it clear that 'an infinite number of parts of extension, each of which is itself extended and distinct from all the others . . . cannot be contained in a space one hundred million times smaller than the hundred-thousandth part of a grain of barley.'[48] In support of the last claim Bayle cited various paradoxes that, he held, the doctrine of infinite divisibility leads to. For example, were extension infinitely divisible, one body would never be immediately contiguous to another (for any part of one body would always be separated from any part of another body by infinitely many intervening parts), and yet the superficial parts of one body would actually *penetrate* those of adjacent bodies (for experience shows that bodies do touch each other, and two things could not merely touch at their extremities, that is, at their last parts – for if extension were infinitely divisible, no part of a body would lie at its extremity or be its 'last part'; so in touching each other, two bodies would actually penetrate one another). Thus were bodies infinitely divisible, it would follow that they penetrate each other without being contiguous – which is absurd.

Again, were extension infinitely divisible, the side of a square would have just as many parts as its diagonal (for lines connecting every point on one side of the square with the parallel points on the opposite side would pass through corresponding points on the diagonal, and there would be no point on the diagonal that was not intersected by one of these lines). Hence the diagonal and the side of a square would be composed of an equal number of aliquot parts and so would be equal in length – which is absurd. Further, were extension divisible *ad infinitum*, nothing could ever begin to move. For object A begins to move across area B only if the first part of A passes over B, then the second part of A passes over B, then the third part, and so forth; but if extension is infinitely divisible, no part of A would be its 'first part', or its 'second', and so on, and so it would be impossible for an object to begin to move – which is absurd. By such paradoxes Bayle sought to prove that extension cannot be infinitely divisible.[49]

Since extended things would exist only were one of the three aforementioned alternatives possible, and since none *are* possible, said Bayle, we should draw the same conclusion about three-dimensional things that mathematicians draw about two-dimensional ones: 'They can exist only in our mind; they can exist only *ideally*.'[50] Or rather, Bayle piously declared, such is what reason would be forced to conclude, were it not overruled by Scripture, which reveals that God has created bodies.[51] It is debatable how much in earnest Bayle was about what he claimed reason led him to doubt or faith led him to believe; but in any case he saw fit, at the end of the seventeenth century, to produce, in these articles, a virtual anthology of objections made by sceptics and heterodox Cartesians to the attempt to prove that extended substances exist. As there is good evidence that both Berkeley and Hume read one or both of these articles, Bayle was probably the medium whereby some of these objections got transmitted to the leading eighteenth-century critics of the idea of material substance.[52]

IV. SPINOZA AND LEIBNIZ

According to Descartes, extension is a substance (a thing that exists in itself), but it is also, he held, a contingent thing, dependent on God for its creation and conservation.[53] It was this contingency that made its existence problematic, for God was free not to create extended things if He so chose. As Malebranche put it:

> It is not possible [apart from divine revelation] to know with complete assurance whether or not God is truly the creator of a material and sensible world. For . . . there is no necessary relation between God and such a world. It was possible for him not to create it, and if he has created it, it is because he has willed to do so, and freely willed to do so.[54]

Spinoza, by contrast, held that extension *necessarily* exists – it is not possible for it *not to be;* once this truth is grasped, the doubts of the sceptics and Cartesians about its existence cannot arise.

Spinoza's reason for asserting the necessary existence of extension is that God necessarily exists and extension is necessarily an attribute of God. God is, by definition, a being having infinitely many attributes (Spinoza takes this to entail that God has every possible attribute), and each of these attributes is itself infinite.[55] Now attributes, according to Spinoza, are things that can be conceived through themselves rather than through something else.[56] Extension is just such a thing. For although we cannot conceive, say, motion or shape without conceiving something else, namely, extension, we need conceive no other thing in order to conceive extension itself. Further, extension is infinite, for the only thing that can limit any part of extension is more extension. Extension, then, is an infinite attribute. Since every infinite attribute belongs necessarily to the divine nature, infinite extension must be among God's attributes.[57] Put otherwise, it belongs to

God's essence to be infinitely extended. Since Spinoza believed he could prove that God's existence is necessary, and that His existence and essence are the same thing,[58] whatever belongs to God's essence cannot fail to exist. Extension belongs to the essence of God; so extension necessarily exists.

Thus far only *extension* has been spoken of. What about *bodies?* Spinoza claimed to prove not only that God has infinitely many attributes but, further, that each of His attributes itself comprises infinitely many modes.[59] Now in the case of extension, he held, these modes or modifications *are* bodies;[60] so in proving the existence of extension, he took himself to have proved that bodies exist. He concluded:

> To prove that there is a body in Nature can be no difficult task for us, now that we already know *that* God is, and *what* God is, whom we have defined as a being of infinite attributes, each of which is infinite and perfect. And since extension is an attribute which we have shown to be infinite in its kind, it must therefore also necessarily be an attribute of that infinite being. And as we have also demonstrated that this infinite being exists, it follows at once that this attribute also exists.[61]

Thus, though Spinoza and Descartes both believed the existence of bodies demonstrable, their proofs differ significantly: Descartes, believing the existence of extension contingent on the will of God, gave a proof that appealed to divine veracity and contained an *a posteriori* premise, namely, that we have a strong natural inclination to believe that our sensations come from bodies; Spinoza proposed a purely *a priori* deduction of the existence of bodies drawn directly from God's existence and nature. Not, to be sure, that Spinoza undertook to prove, directly from God's nature, the existence of some *particular* finite body; from the divine nature, he claimed only to deduce that there *are* infinitely many bodies. But an examination of the nature of the human mind and its objects, he held, will assure us of the existence, in particular, of our own bodies (and those bodies that act immediately on our own); for, rightly understood, the mind and the body are not two different things, but the same thing considered under two different divine attributes (thought and extension). When this is grasped, we know the existence of our bodies as surely as we do that of our minds.[62]

Leibniz, on the other hand, agreed in this matter with the heterodox Cartesians: we cannot prove beyond all doubt the existence of the bodies we seem to perceive by sense. 'I agree with you', he wrote to Malebranche, 'that it would be hard to prove that there is extension outside of us in the sense in which this is usually understood.'[63] Like al-Ghazālī, Leibniz thought we could not completely exclude the possibility that this life is a long, highly coherent dream:

For if some invisible power were to take pleasure in giving us dreams that are well tied into our preceding life and in conformity with each other, could we distinguish them from reality before we had awakened? Now, what prevents the course of our life from being one long well-ordered dream, about which we could be undeceived in a moment?[64]

Would God deceive us, were this life a long dream? No more in that case, thought Leibniz, than He does now in allowing us to dream for an hour. For a dream of an hour takes up an incomparably greater proportion of a life of seventy years than a dream of seventy years would take up in the everlasting life of our immortal soul:

Since we are destined for eternity, and this whole life, even if it were to contain many thousands of years, would be like a point with respect to eternity, how trifling a thing is this small dream, to be interposed upon such fullness of truth, to which its relation is less than that of a dream to a lifetime.[65]

Leibniz also echoed the objections of the heterodox Cartesians to Descartes's appeal to divine veracity: God does not *compel* us to believe that bodies exist – we voluntarily judge that they do; God does not deceive us in allowing colours to seem to be outside the mind although (as Descartes admits) they really are not, and the same might be true of extension; God might even allow us to be deceived as a punishment for sin, or for some other reason unknown to us.[66] He concluded: 'Thus by no argument can it be demonstrated absolutely that bodies exist, nor is there anything to prevent certain well-ordered dreams from being the objects of our mind, which we judge to be true and which, because of their accord with each other, are equivalent to truth so far as practice is concerned.'[67]

But if it cannot be demonstrated with perfect ('metaphysical') certainty that the bodies we perceive exist, the probability that they do is so great that it amounts to a practical ('moral') certainty. There are, Leibniz held, many criteria by which we distinguish the real from the imaginary: the vividness of our perceptions; the congruence of the testimony of our several senses; the agreement of what we perceive with what others report they perceive; above all, our power to predict our future perceptions from our past ones.[68] As all these criteria of what is real are satisfied by our normal sense experience, the probability is very great that the bodies we perceive by sense exist. It might be objected that all these criteria could also be satisfied if life were a highly coherent dream; but Leibniz held that 'even if this whole life were said to be a dream, and the visible world only a phantasm, I should call this dream or this phantasm real enough if we were never deceived by it when we make good use of reason.'[69] For although, against Descartes, Leibniz denied that the existence of bodies can be proved beyond doubt, he, like Locke, held that it can make no practical difference to our expectations, deliberations, and choices whether this life be supposed real or only a highly coherent dream.[70]

It amounts thus to a practical certainty that the extended things we perceive are real. Such things are not, however, as Descartes believed, *extended substances,* for nothing, thought Leibniz, can have the unity and simplicity of a true substance merely in consequence of being extended.

> Extension, motion, and bodies themselves, insofar as they consist in extension and motion alone, are not substances but true phenomena, like rainbows and parhelia. For figures do not exist in reality and if only their extension is considered, bodies are not one substance but many. For the substance of bodies there is required something which lacks extension; otherwise there would be no principle to account for the reality of the phenomena or for true unity.[71]

The extended, figured, moving bodies perceived by our senses are well-founded or true *phenomena,* that is, they are how aggregations of monads (or simple unextended substances) appear to us. Some of these aggregations of monads – for example, those that appear to us as the organic bodies of plants, animals, and human beings – are themselves corporeal substances, each unified by a single dominant monad that is its 'soul' or 'substantial form'. But such corporeal substances are not extended; rather, they are a composite of unextended monads that form the 'body' of a compound substance, united by a dominant monad that constitutes its 'soul' (as for inorganic bodies – for example, a brick or rock – they are not even an appearance of true composite substances, but merely the appearance of accidental aggregations of monads that lack a unifying soul or substantial form). But if the bodies we perceive by our senses are phenomena, they are nonetheless real (in contrast to bodies we merely dream of or imagine), for they are *phenomena bene fundata* – that is, they are how aggregations of monads appear to us.

V. LOCKE

Locke had little patience with speculations about whether what we perceive might be a mere dream world. To one who, like Descartes, is unsure whether he is sitting before his fire or only dreaming he is, Locke says he should try putting his hand in the fire – and 'he may perhaps be wakened into a certainty greater than he could wish, that it is something more than bare Imagination.'[72] But while Locke had no sympathy with protestations of doubt about matters nobody really has doubts about, he was eager to discover the extent of human knowledge, including our knowledge of what exists; hence it was necessary for him, too, to address the question of how we know that bodies exist. We each can have, he held, intuitive knowledge that we ourselves exist and demonstrative knowledge that God does.[73] When it comes to bodies, however, he, like the heterodox Cartesians, held that we do not have demonstrative knowledge that they exist;[74] but he rejected the view that the best we can attain is only *highly probable belief* in their existence. Rather, there is, in addition to intuition and demonstration, a third degree of knowledge, 'which going beyond bare probability, and yet not reaching perfectly to either of the foregoing degrees of certainty, passes under the name Knowledge'.[75] This third degree, *sensitive knowledge,* is that we get 'of the existence of particular external Objects, by that perception and Consciousness we have of the actual entrance [into our minds] of *Ideas* from them'.[76]

As I look at the book I hold in my hand, my senses make known to me an object and I cannot doubt that it exists independently of my mind, for I am 'invincibly conscious' how great a difference there is between these ideas that come into my mind, by way of my senses, from some external object, and the ideas produced by my mind itself when I merely imagine something; thus, 'when our Senses do actually convey into our Understandings any *Idea,* we cannot but be satisfied, that there doth something at that time really exist without us, which doth affect our Senses, and by them give notice of it self to our apprehensive Faculties, and actually produce that *Idea,* which we then perceive.'[77] Some, in a disputatious mood, may pretend to doubt the existence of the things our senses disclose to us, but 'I think no body can, in earnest, be so sceptical, as to be uncertain of the Existence of those Things which he sees and feels.'[78] For the senses themselves immediately assure us of the existence of these things.

This direct testimony of sense is corroborated by other considerations: that we cannot, by mere act of will, arouse sensations in our minds (if we could, the blind would see and the deaf hear); that when, by a voluntary act, we open our eyes, we involuntarily perceive what is before them; that such ideas as we may raise voluntarily in our minds, by recalling something, are never as vivid as those that come from our senses; that when we call up in memory an idea of, say, extreme heat, it does not produce pain in us as it did when it came to us by sense: all considerations that show the ideas we get by sense to come not from the mind itself but from things external to it.[79] This is also shown by the way our several senses agree with one another, and with the reports of other observers, about what they perceive.[80] Finally, though sensitive knowledge is less perfect than the intuitive certainty we each have of our own existence, or even the demonstrative knowledge we have of God's existence, it 'is not only as great as our frame can attain to, but as our Condition needs'. God gave us our senses that we might preserve our lives, pursuing what benefits us, avoiding what harms us, and they fulfil this end when the assurance they give 'of the Existence of Things without us is sufficient to direct us in the attaining the Good and avoiding the Evil, which is the important concernment we have of being made acquainted with them'.[81]

But our knowledge of bodies is very narrow in scope. The bodies I perceive I know to exist while I am perceiving them; but when I turn away, I cannot be sure they still exist, though I may have reason to believe it highly probable that they do (a probability that diminishes as the time I last saw them grows more remote). And though I am certain those bodies *existed* that I now remember having perceived in the past, I can have but probable evidence that they exist still.[82] Since we *know*, Locke holds, only what we are certain of, our knowledge of what exists in the material world is limited to that little stretch of it we now perceive or now remember having perceived. (I think Locke supposed we can be certain that *there are* bodies other than those we actually perceive or have perceived; but we have only probable belief about the existence of any *particular* body save those bodies in fact perceived by us. But he is not explicit about this.) Far the greater part of our acquaintance with bodies, therefore, cannot go beyond probable opinion. Which shows 'how foolish and vain a thing it is, for a Man of narrow Knowledge, who having Reason given him to judge of the different evidence and probability of Things, and to be sway'd accordingly; how vain, I say, it is to expect Demonstration and Certainty in things not capable of it.'[83]

VI. AFTER LOCKE

Thus a question that was of little interest to Descartes's first critics – how or whether we can be certain that a material world exists – came to be a much debated one as the century wore on. That debate would grow keener in the next century, when thinkers appeared who denied that there are any material substances. Few in the seventeenth century went that far, though Leibniz, as noted earlier, denied that extended things are substances;[84] and late in the century, Jean Brunet, a French physician, argued that it is logically impossible to attribute existence to something without *thinking* of it, from which he concluded that, although thought can be distinguished from things, we cannot conceive that things exist apart from thought.[85] But immaterialists were rare in the seventeenth century (though an older form of immaterialism found expression in the writings of the Platonist F. M. Van Helmont, who rejected the doctrine that God created matter *ex nihilo;* matter, said Van Helmont, is not a positive thing – so not a creation of God's at all – but a privation of being, the last dark stage in the falling away of spirit from the perfect unity of the Godhead; Anne Conway held similar views).[86] Fully articulated systems of immaterialism did not appear, however, until early in the eighteenth century, in the works of Arthur Collier and George Berkeley. Collier, deeply influenced by Malebranche and Norris, advanced nine arguments against the existence of matter in *Clavis Universalis* (1713); but his views attracted little attention.[87] It was, of course, Berkeley who made famous the doctrine that matter does not exist. Though Berkeley's doctrine belongs to the eighteenth century, something may here be said of its relation to the seventeenth-century views examined in this chapter.

The notebooks in which the young Berkeley worked out his philosophy show him well versed in Locke's *Essay* and Malebranche's *Recherche,* and acquainted, too, with Bayle's views about the existence of matter.[88] Almost certainly, study of these thinkers suggested this line of thought to Berkeley early on: the passive nature of our sense-experience makes us aware that there is an external cause of our sensations (Locke had stressed this in his discussion of our knowledge of bodies); this external cause of our sensations is God Himself (a doctrine Male-branche had argued for at length); but if God causes our sensations, we have no need to suppose there are any material substances (an argument developed by Bayle in 'Zeno of Elea'). Such reasoning made Berkeley an immaterialist well before he had framed his most characteristic arguments against matter (arguments that turn on what it *means* to say that a sensible thing exists).

And Berkeley found in these writers other weapons he could use in his assault on matter, among them the following: (1) Bayle's argument that the reason given by the 'new philosophers' to prove that secondary qualities (colour, smell, taste, warmth, and so forth) depend on the minds that perceive them – namely, because how they appear changes with changes in the perceiver's condition – can be used to prove the same thing about the primary qualities (extension, figure, motion, and so forth).[89] (2) Malebranche's contention that neither sense nor reason can prove that matter exists (the senses cannot, for they disclose only sensations; and reason cannot, for it can infer the existence of a thing from our idea of it only by discovering some necessary connexion between the thing and the idea, but there *is* no necessary connexion between our ideas and bodies, as is shown by dreams in which we have ideas of bodies that do not even exist).[90] (3) Malebranche's related claim that our sense-experience can never prove bodies, since God can cause in our souls all the sensations we now have, whether bodies exist or not.[91] (4) Locke's contention that when philosophers resort to an unknowable substratum to explain what supports the qualities we perceive, they instruct us as little as did the Hindu who said that the earth is supported by an elephant supported by a tortoise supported by he knew not what.[92]

Such arguments were not, in the end, central to Berkeley's attempt to prove that matter does not exist; still, he found a use for them all in defending his views, and almost certainly they played a rôle in the growth of his immaterialist convictions. But Berkeley wrought an important change in how the question about the existence of bodies is to be construed. Most of the thinkers of the preceding century treated 'material substance' and 'body' as synonyms: to reject one was to reject the other. Not so Berkeley. By 'bodies' he understood the things we perceive by sense. We cannot doubt *their* existence, for we see and feel them. 'I am certain of that which Malebranche seems to doubt of, viz., the existence of bodies.'[93] But bodies are really collections of ideas, and so cannot exist unperceived. By 'material substance', however, he understood an unperceivable (and unperceiving) thing, and it was this he denied the existence of. For Berkeley, therefore, in contrast to most of his seventeenth-century predecessors (with Leibniz as a noteworthy exception), it was quite possible to deny that there are any material substances and yet affirm that bodies exist; this consideration was pivotal to his conviction that his philosophy was not in conflict with common sense.

When later eighteenth-century thinkers discussed how we can know that bodies exist, the seventeenth-century roots of the question remained clearly visible. Bayle's influence can be discerned in Hume's discussion of the matter;[94] Kant's 'Refutation of Idealism' took Descartes and Berkeley as its stalking horses;[95] and Reid, in order to expose and weed out scepticism's roots, felt it necessary to trace in detail the seventeenth-century theories about how we know there is an external world.[96] Thus the question of the existence of bodies, first come to prominence in the seventeenth century, persisted long after that century closed.

NOTES

1 Sextus Empiricus, *Adversus dogmaticos,* I, 65–87; Seneca, *Ad Lucilium epistulae morales,* epistle lxxxviii, 44; Cicero, *Academica,* chap. 23.

2 *Outlines of Pyrrhonism,* Bk. I, chap. 10. Whether *any* pre-seventeenth-century thinkers doubted the existence of the material world is a disputed question. Cf. Burnyeat 1982; Groarke 1984.

3 al-Ghazālī 1953, pp. 74–5.

4 Nicolaus of Autrecourt 1964, pp. 510–11.

5 Montaigne 1962a, vol. 1, pp. 673–7.

6 On the relation of Cartesian doubt to classical scepticism, see Gouhier 1962, pp. 31–40; Gilson 1925, pp. 267–9; Curley 1978, pp. 68–9; Popkin 1979, chap. 9.

7 Descartes told Silhon that he hesitated to present his initial doubt in its most radical

form in a work written in the vernacular lest he betray 'weaker minds' into scepticism. See AT I 353–4.

8 The argument from sense deception was a set piece in sceptical writers; the delusions of the mad and the difficulty of telling waking from dreaming were given as grounds for doubting the senses by Cicero and Sextus. Cicero, *Academica,* chaps. 27–8; Sextus Empiricus, *Adversus dogmaticos,* I, 61–4, 401–8.

9 AT VII 18–20.

10 Popkin 1979, pp. 180–1.

11 AT VII 22. Translations are from Descartes 1984–91, vol. 2. Since these translations are keyed to the pagination in AT, no separate references to the translations will be given.

12 AT VII 71.

13 AT VII 72–3.

14 AT VII 79–80.

15 AT VII 88–9.

16 AT VII 80.

17 AT VII 80–3. In *Princ.* II 1, Descartes gives the argument for the existence of bodies in a shorter form that does not stress our natural inclination to believe that sensations come from bodies or our lack of a faculty to discover that they do not; this is not perhaps surprising, for the *Princ.* follows the 'synthetic' order of exposition, the *Meds.* the 'analytic', and it is in the latter that Descartes gives most fully the justification for his fundamental metaphysical doctrines, which is why he says that in order to understand aright the metaphysical parts of the *Princ.,* one should first read the *Meds.*; see AT IXB 16. For a detailed analysis of Descartes's proof of the existence of body, see Gueroult, 1984, vol. 2, chaps. ix–xii, and esp. chap. xiv.

18 AT VII 125–6, 195, 415–16. On scholastic views about the possibility of God's deceiving us, see Gregory 1974; Normore 1982, pp. 373–8.

19 AT VII 332; cf. pp. 257–8, 345. See also Gassendi 1962, pp. 39–45.

20 Descartes responded with *Notae in Programma quoddam,* published in Amsterdam in 1648, and often appended, after 1660, to Latin editions of the *Objectiones et Responsiones* to the *Meditationes.*

21 AT VIIIB 344.

22 Regius 1654, pp. 347–51.

23 AT VIIIB 356–7; cf. AT VII 89–90.

24 Cordemoy 1968, pp. 151–5.

25 AT VIIIA 40–1.

26 Mal. *OC* VI 184.

27 Mal. *OC* III 60.

28 Malebranche, *Rech.* I.7 and I.14.

29 Mal. *OC* VI 185.

30 Arnauld 1775–83, vol. 38, pp. 653–4.

31 Mal. *OC* III 60–4. For his full argument, see *Rech.* VI.2.6, and Eclaircissement VI.

32 Régis 1690, vol. 1, p. 75. For a defence of Malebranche against this charge of circularity, see Vidgrain 1923, pp. 141–54.

33 Mal. *OC* III 64–5.

34 Arnauld 1775–83, vol. 38, pp. 359–60; Mal. *OC* VI 186; cf. Mal. *OC* XII 142–3.

35 Lanion 1678, pp. 63–5.

36 Lanion 1678, pp. 40–67. Lanion's *Méditations* were reprinted in Bayle 1684.

37 Fardella 1691, vol. 1, appx. 2, pp. 486–528. On Fardella, see Werner 1883. Berkeley

mentions Fardella early in his notebooks (Berkeley 1948–57, vol. 1, p. 15), but Fardella's work was rare and Berkeley probably knew his views only from Bayle's *Dictionary*.

38 Norris 1701–4, vol. 1, pp. 189–90, 208–10, 217–23. On Norris on the existence of matter, see McCracken 1983, pp. 166–70.

39 Even Descartes, it should be noted, said that the proof of the existence of bodies is not as strong as the proofs that God and our own minds exist. AT VII 15–16.

40 Some orthodox Cartesians, on the other hand, offered new proofs (or revised versions of Descartes's proof) that bodies exist. See Arnauld's eight proofs of an external world (all but two of which are arguments for the existence not of bodies but of other minds) in Arnauld 1775–83, vol. 38, pp. 354–8, and Régis's attempt to give a purely *a priori* proof that makes no appeal to divine veracity or to our natural inclination to believe that our sensations come from bodies, Régis 1690, vol. 1, pp. 74–8.

41 AT VII 550.

42 An early form of the argument appeared in Gassendi's objections to Descartes (AT VII 337–8 and 387). Later versions of the argument can be found in Foucher 1675, pp. 50–2; Huet 1689, chap. 2; Du Hamel 1692, pp. 27–30.

43 Régis 1692, pp. 8–11. Cf. AT XI 3–5, and AT VII 72–3. See also Foucher 1675, pp. 56–60.

44 Foucher 1675, pp. 78–80.

45 Foucher 1679, p. 46. The argument anticipates Berkeley's denial that we can abstract colour from extension, *Principles of Human Knowledge*, Intro., sec. 10. See also Popkin 1980d, the title essay; and Watson 1987, esp. pt. 2.

46 Bayle 1730, vol. 3, s.v. 'Pyrrhon', rem. B, p. 732, and vol. 4, s.v. 'Zénon d'Elée', rem. H, p. 534.

47 Bayle 1730, vol. 4, rem. G, p. 541.

48 Bayle 1730, vol. 4, rem. G, p. 540.

49 Bayle 1730, vol. 4, rem. G, pp. 540–1. Paradoxes about infinite divisibility continued to play an important rôle in eighteenth-century discussions of extended things. They were central to Arthur Collier's denial of matter's existence (Collier, 1713, pt. 2, chaps. 3–4), and Berkeley thought one benefit of immaterialism was that it did away with such paradoxes (*Principles of Human Knowledge*, secs. 123–34). Bayle's formulation of them influenced Hume's treatment of space (*Treatise of Human Nature*, bk. I, pt. 2, secs. 1–2), and Kant said it was because of such antinomies that he first undertook that critique of pure reason from which he concluded that space, time, and matter belong to appearances rather than to things in themselves (see Kant's letter to Christian Garve of 21 September 1798; cf. *Kritik der reinen Vernunft*, B454–71 and B545–55).

50 Bayle 1730, vol. 4, rem. G, p. 540.

51 Bayle 1730, vol. 4, rem. H, pp. 543–4.

52 On Bayle's relation to Berkeley and Hume, see Popkin 1980d, pp. 149–59, 297–318; Ayers 1984, pp. 306–14.

53 AT VIIIA 10, 24–5.

54 Mal. *OC* III 64.

55 *Eth.* I dfn. 6 and expl.

56 *Eth.* I prop. 10.

57 *Eth.* II prop. 2.

58 *Eth.* I props. 11 and 20.

59 *Eth.* I prop. 16.

60 *Eth.* II ax. 1.

61 *Korte Ver.*, pt. II, chap. XIX, Geb. I 90.

62 On the identity of mind and body, see *Eth.* II props. 7, 13, and 21 schol. On the existence of particular bodies, see *Eth.* II props. 11–19.

63 Ger. I 330 (Leibniz 1969, p. 210). Translations are from Leibniz 1969.

64 Ger. I 372–3 (Leibniz 1969, pp. 153–4). The appeal to the possibility that this life is a long, coherent dream is repeated in various places, e.g., Ger. IV 366–7; VI 502; VII 320–1 (Leibniz 1969, pp. 391–2; 549; 364–5); *Nouv. ess.* IV.ii.14, at end.

65 Ger. VII 320–1 (Leibniz 1969, pp. 364–5).

66 Ger. I. 373; IV 366–7 (Leibniz 1969, pp. 154, 391–2); *Nouv. ess.* III.iv.2.

67 Ger. VII 320–1 (Leibniz 1969, p. 364).

68 Ger. VII 319–20 (Leibniz 1969, pp. 363–4).

69 Ger. VII 320 (Leibniz 1969, p. 364).

70 Cf. *Nouv. ess.* IV.ii.14 and *Ess.* IV.ii.14.

71 Leibniz 1903, p. 523 (Leibniz 1969, p. 270). Leibniz gave various accounts of body in his works (see especially his letters to A. Arnauld, B. de Volder, and B. des Bosses), and the exact interpretation of his view is disputed (the letters to the Jesuit, des Bosses, present a particular problem of interpretation, for there he modified his theory of body to show how it could be made compatible with the dogma of transubstantiation). For various interpretations of his theory of body, see Broad 1975, pp. 88–92; Garber 1985, pp. 27–130; Mates 1986, pp. 204–6; Adams 1994, chap. 10; Brown 1984, chap. 10; Jolley 1986; Sleigh 1990a, chap. 5; C. Wilson 1989, pp. 190–6; M. Wilson 1987; Rutherford 1995, chap. 10.

72 *Ess.* IV.xi.8.

73 *Ess.* IV.ix–x.

74 *Ess.* IV.iii.21.

75 *Ess.* IV.ii.14. In *Regulae ad directionem ingenii* III, Descartes had said that only by intuition and demonstration can we know things. AT X 368–70.

76 *Ess.* IV.ii.14.

77 *Ess.* IV.xi.9.

78 *Ess.* IV.xi.3.

79 *Ess.* IV.xi.4–6.

80 *Ess.* IV.xi.7.

81 *Ess.* IV.xi.8.

82 *Ess.* IV.xi.9–11.

83 *Ess.* IV.xi.10.

84 Leibniz lived long enough to read Berkeley's *Principles of Human Knowledge;* he found much right, he said, in Berkeley's views, though Berkeley expressed them in an unnecessarily paradoxical way. See Robinet 1983, pp. 217–23.

85 Brunet 1686, pp. 209–11, and esp. the 'Additions et corrections' at the end of the volume. Brunet (he appears as 'Claude Brunet' in the Bibliothèque Nationale's catalogue) also wrote *Projet d'une nouvelle métaphysique* (Paris, 1703), but no copy is now known to exist. See Robinson 1913, pp. 15–30.

86 Van Helmont 1677, printed in Knorr von Rosenroth 1677, pp. 293–312. (Van Helmont 1682 is a translation of this work.) This view was opposed by another noted Platonist, Henry More, in More 1677a (also in Knorr von Rosenroth 1677). Cf. Conway 1982, chaps. 6–9. See Coudert 1975.

87 Collier 1713. On Collier's relation to Malebranche and Norris, see McCracken 1983, pp. 191–204; on his relation to Berkeley, see Johnston 1923, appx. 1; on his relation to Kant, see Lovejoy 1908, and de Vleeschauwer 1938.

88 The views of Descartes, Malebranche, Fardella, Bayle, and Locke about the existence of

bodies are discussed by Berkeley in the following places in his notebooks (*Philosophical Commentaries*, in Berkeley 1948–57, vol. 1): entries 79, 80, 89, 265, 288, 358, 424, 424a, 477, 477a, 563, 686, 686a, 790, 800, 801, 818.

89 Bayle 1730, vol. 4, s.v. 'Zénon d'Elée', rem. G, p. 541; the argument appears very early in Berkeley's notebooks, as well as in his chief defences of immaterialism, Berkeley 1948–57, vol. 1, p. 10 (entry 20); vol. 2, pp. 46–7 and 188–91.

90 Mal. *OC* I 42–3; Mal. *OC* III 55–6, 60–4. Berkeley uses the argument in *Principles of Human Knowledge*, sec. 18. On the relation of Berkeley's immaterialism to Malebranche, see Luce 1934; McCracken 1983, chap. 6.

91 Mal. *OC* I 413–14; Mal. *OC* III 58–9. Berkeley uses the argument in *Principles of Human Knowledge*, sec. 20 (cf. also *Philosophical Commentaries*, entry 476).

92 *Ess.* II.xiii.19 (cf. I.iv.18; II.xxiii.2). Berkeley commented on this passage early in his notebooks (entry 89); its traces can be discerned in the attack on an unknowable material substratum in *Principles of Human Knowledge*, secs. 16–17.

93 Berkeley 1948–57, vol. 1, p. 84 (entry 686a). He hit on this view early, though not its final form; cf. entries 79–80 and 563.

94 *A Treatise of Human Nature*, I.iv.2.

95 *Kritik der reinen Vernunft*, B274–8.

96 *Essays on the Intellectual Powers of Man*, II, secs. 7–15.

20

NEW DOCTRINES OF MOTION

ALAN GABBEY

I. INTRODUCTION

As noted in Chapter 15, Aristotle and the Peripatetics held that local motion is primary with respect to all other kinds of motion or change. Proponents of the new natural philosophies of the seventeenth century, including neo-atomists and those of Stoic inspiration,[1] would have accepted this view and, indeed, would not have spurned the way it was presented by some of the later Peripatetics. They would not have been out of sympathy with the Aristotelian Keckermann, whose teaching on this issue in the Danzig Gymnasium in 1607 was not far removed from the new understanding of the rôle of local motion: 'According to the order of nature, local motion is the first among motions, partly because it is common to the totality of all natural bodies, partly also because the other motions arise from it as from a cause [*tanquam à causa*].'[2] Nor would they have been seriously at odds with Chasteigner de la Rochepozay: 'All other motions are included in local motion as in a cause [*ut in causa*], on account of [its being] the primary motion, because it is the cause of every corporeal motion, and without it there cannot be any other motion.'[3] Yet it is not clear whether the causality in these texts is real or analogical or, if real (assuming it to be efficient), whether proximate, partial, or productive efficient causality is intended.[4] The causal rôle reserved for local motion by some early seventeenth-century scholastics is still not the special rôle reserved for it by the proponents of the mechanical philosophy. The primacy of local motion that consists in its being the *sine qua non* of all other categories of Peripatetic motion is not what the mechanists had in mind. For Aristotle, on the one hand, alteration – that is, change of quality – requires local motion to ensure the necessary changes in distance between the thing altered and the source of the alteration (see Chapter 15). For the mechanists, on the other hand, local motion is the key to intelligible explanations of the qualities themselves, whether in alteration or not. More generally, in the mechanical philosophy the primacy of local motion consisted in its being the explanatory *sine qua non* of *all* physical phenomena, assumed to be the effects of bodies in motion and in various dispositions, exerting forces according to laws of nature (see Chapters 17 and 18). Doctrinal differences *de motu* between the scholastic tradition and the varieties of 'new philosophy' in the seventeenth century turned not on the question of whether local motion (hereafter usually 'motion') is the primary kind of physical change but on the more testing issue of the appropriate interpretation of that primary status. Correspondingly, practitioners of the new philosophy, in contrast to their scholastic predecessors and contemporaries, insisted on the importance of discovering new properties of motion and of finding nomological relations between motions and their causes. The efficient *causes* of corporeal phenomena were to be found in the motions (and rest) of bodies and the associated forces, in their corporeal characteristics and mutual dispositions, and in the laws or rules of motion believed to be applicable in the situation under investigation. Changes in the natural world might be *described* as 'motions' in the broad Peripatetic sense, but other-than-local motions do not provide causal explanations of anything, other than explaining *obscurum per obscurius* (see Chapter 17).

This enhanced status of motion within new conceptual frameworks had far-reaching effects in early modern natural philosophy. Since *local* motion was the only category of motion that had genuine explanatory work to do in the new scheme of things, its treatment differed in notable respects from what had been typical of the Peripatetic tradition. Many of the 'new philosophers' cultivated the view that motion is essentially a *simple* category, so that little need be said about its nature, the 'change-of-place' definition being assumed without much reflection. A smaller number of them had new and important things to say about motion *qua* motion, believing that the common definition harboured difficulties that had to be resolved before solid achievements in natural philosophy could be assured. Whatever their individual accounts of motion *per se,* the new philosophers shared a number of positions and concerns that were characteristic of their philosophies of motion. There was general agreement on the redundancy of the traditional distinction between natural and violent motion (see Chapter 15, Section VI, 'Local Motion') in favour of the principle that all motions, whatever their Peripatetic categorisations, are the natural effects of motive forces, and conversely, that all forces, whatever their origin, act *secundum naturam* to cause motions and rest.[5] In keeping with this re-alignment of the force–motion relationship, there was increasing interest in finding quantitative relations between motions and their forces, whether originating from gravity or from bodies in motion and at rest. Another question of general concern was whether motions, or rather the forces that are their ontological ground, are conserved or lost in corporeal interactions, and whether they are conserved in the universe as a whole. Over-arching these issues was the quest for general laws of motion, of which it was expected, or at any rate hoped, that quantitative exchanges of motion would be so many empirical instantiations.

II. THE NATURE OF MOTION

One of the characteristic issues in earlier discussions on motion was whether motion exists as a real entity in some sense independently of the mobile, as a successive acquisition of forms (*fluxus formae*), or whether it has no such independent existence, being merely a *forma fluens* represented by the successive places occupied by the mobile (Chapter 15). This opposition between realist and nominalist doctrines of motion is reflected in the innovative analyses of motion of the seventeenth century, though it is not always easy, or indeed appropriate, to interpret them in quite the same terms that were current in earlier centuries. Some thinkers were nominalists (though not using that denomination), or can be assumed to have been effectively nominalists, in the sense that they had little interest in debating the quiddity of motion *per se,* and used causal notions such as forces, powers, or *impetus* as working tools without having much to say about their ontological standing. Others were nominalists as to motion itself but took a realist position on the ontology of force as its cause.

Galileo's work on the properties of motion and their mathematical expression was the most important of the early-seventeenth-century investigations of the subject, yet little in his writings elucidates the *quaestiones* about the nature of motion that were standard fare in the Peripatetic manuals. By 1607 Galileo was declaring what was to become a recurring theme in the Second Day of the *Dialogo . . . sopra i due massimi sistemi del mondo, tolemaico, e copernicano* (Florence, 1632): 'Motion is nothing other than the change of one thing with respect to another.'[6] And in 1619 he made the intriguing claim: 'If I had all the time and space I need to explain my view, I would go so far as to say that motion, inasmuch as it is simple, cannot make a moving body hot or cold or alter it in any other way except to change its place; hence it produces nothing that would not have occurred had the body remained at rest.'[7] The opening of the Third Day of his *Discorsi . . . intorno à due nuove scienze* (Leiden, 1638) reads: 'We bring forward a brand new science concerning a very old subject. There is perhaps nothing in nature older than Motion, about which volumes neither few nor small have been written by philosophers; yet I find many essentials [*symptomata*] of it that are worth knowing which have not even been remarked, let alone demonstrated.'[8] Significantly, the first definition of the Third Day is not of motion *per se,* but of *uniform* motion, an essential prerequisite for the subsequent theorems on uniform and naturally accelerated motion (see Chapter 22). Galileo was less interested in mulling over the definitions and causes of motion than in employing new ideas about its properties to solve particular problems in physics, most famously the problem of free fall under gravity. In this light, it is not surprising that his concept of force (both motive and static) is rarely clear, nor was it employed with consistency.[9] In his early years, for example in a dialogue on motion written about 1590 during his time as professor of mathematics at Pisa, Galileo took a realist view of the cause of motion, advocating an *impetus* theory in which the *impetus,* unlike that of Buridan (see Chapter 15), was self-dissipating. At the same time, he was sceptical about the nature of the force or impetus impressed on a body in violent motion: 'What that force is is hidden from our knowledge.'[10] In his mature years, his interest shifted from motive and accelerative forces to a proto-positivist concern with only the mathematically expressed properties of uniform and accelerated motions. In the Third Day of the *Discorsi* (1638), Salviati's (i.e., Galileo's) policy is clear:

> The present does not seem to me to be an opportune time to enter into the investigation of the cause of the acceleration of natural motion, concerning which various philosophers have produced various opinions. . . . Such fantasies, and others like them, would have to be examined and resolved, with little gain. For the present, it suffices our Author that we understand him to want us to investigate and demonstrate some attributes [*passiones*] of a motion so accelerated (whatever be the cause of its acceleration) that the momenta of its speed go increasing, after its departure from rest, in that simple ratio with which the continuation of time increases, which is the same as to say that in equal times, equal additions of speed are made.[11]

The atomist Isaac Beeckman followed a straightforwardly nominalist line on the cause of motion. On the nature of motion itself there is nothing in his *Journal* more elaborate than the assumption that motion is simply change of position in an empty atomist space. At the same time, there are many entries on its properties, especially those relating to the collision of hard bodies, where Beeckman uses the terms *vis* (force) and *impetus.* Yet he was economical with these ontological counters, at least in his collision theory.[12] One can see why from the following revealing application of the principle of sufficient reason:

> A stone thrown in a vacuum therefore moves perpetually; but air obstructs it, and continually strikes it, so causing its motion to diminish. Indeed what the Philosophers say about a force [*vis*] being implanted in the stone is seen to be groundless. Who can conceive what this force is, or how it keeps the stone in motion, or in what part of the stone it is seated? Rather it is easier to conceive that in a vacuum a moved body will never come to rest,

because it encounters no cause that would change it: nothing changes without there being some cause of change.[13]

The *Tractatus physicus de motu locali* (Lyon, 1646) of the Jesuit philosopher Honoré Fabri shows that he falls into the realist camp as to the cause of motion. The first book of the *Tractatus* consists in an analysis not of motion, but of *impetus,* because Fabri thinks it more important to study the *cause* of motion. Right at the outset of the treatise he explains that he is beginning

with *impetus* itself, on the knowledge of which indeed the whole business depends. Since *impetus* is the immediate cause of motion, as we will demonstrate at length below; and because a thing cannot be known unless its cause be known; there can be no doubt that the treatment of *impetus* must come first, so that the properties [*affectio*] of motion itself may then be demonstrated through their cause. Indeed I might make bold to say that not just motion itself, but also the whole of physics, depends on a knowledge of *impetus* alone.[14]

Fabri's perception of this ontological order, and therefore of the order of composition of his treatise, is in keeping with his comment on his Definition I, which is of local motion as a 'continuous flux' by which a body is transferred from place to place. Nonetheless, Fabri refers the reader to metaphysics for an explanation of the definition, since, he remarks, it would not be much use in the present context.[15]

Hobbes stands in contrast to virtually everyone who wrote about motion in the seventeenth century. In his *De corpore* (London, 1655) he defines motion as 'a continual relinquishing of one place, and acquiring of another', the former place being the *terminus a quo,* the latter the *terminus ad quem,* and place being a part of space, which he conceives rather obscurely as 'the phantasm of a thing existing without the mind simply'.[16] From this point on, however, Hobbes describes everything other than body ('that which having no dependance upon our thought, is coincident or co-extended with some part of space') in terms of motion alone, and his account of the cause of motion is wholly nominalist. His concept of 'endeavour' (*conatus*) is 'motion made in less space and time than can be given; that is, less than can be determined or assigned by exposition or number; that is, motion made through the length of a point, and in an instant or point of time', where 'point' is to be understood not as indivisible, but as undivided, just as the instant is undivided, not indivisible time. As for *impetus,* he defines it as 'the quickness or velocity of the body moved, but considered in the several points of that time in which it is moved. In which sense *impetus* is nothing else but the quantity or velocity of endeavour.'[17] Thus all causes of motion, all force, all power, have evaporated from Hobbes's universe, leaving only body continually relinquishing (or not, in the case of rest) one place for another. It would be difficult to find in the seventeenth century a more nominalist understanding of motion and its causes than that of Hobbes's natural philosophy (see Chapter 18).

Given the background represented by these diverse figures, Descartes's case stands out as especially significant. His treatment of the nature of motion was complex, and it changed between his early work and the *Principia Philosophiae* (Amsterdam, 1644). During the late 1620s, the period in which he composed the *Regulae* and the early drafts of *Le Monde,* Descartes shared the Peripatetic view of the primacy of local motion, than which 'nothing in the whole genus [of motion in the broad sense] can be more evident to the senses',[18] and which is therefore the starting point in the exploration of natural powers. Yet he took motion to be simple 'change of place', and he explicitly discounted the Aristotelian concept of place (see Chapter 15), though it is unclear what his own concept of place was at this period:

> Who does not perceive all of whatever it is according to which we change when we change place, and who is there who conceives the same thing when he is told, 'place is the surface of the surrounding body'? For that surface can change, though I might be immobile, not changing place; or on the contrary, it can move together with me so that although it surrounds me, nonetheless I am no longer in the same place.

So it is foolish to explain motion by reference to something allegedly more simple, a fault that Descartes found in the traditional Aristotelian definition of motion as applied to local motion:

> But as for those who say that motion, something perfectly well known to everyone, is 'the actuality of a being in potentiality, in so far as it is in potentiality', do they not seem to utter magic words with an occult meaning beyond the reach of the human mind? Who understands these words? Who does not know what motion is? And who would not agree that these people might as well have tried to find a knot in a bulrush?[19]

In *Le Monde* Descartes described local motion as that 'by which bodies pass from one place [*lieu*] into another, successively occupying all the spaces [*espaces*] in between', and rest as 'a quality [*qualité*] to be attributed to matter while it remains in one place, as motion is a quality attributed to it while it changes place'. And in October 1639, five years before the *Principia Philosophiae,* Descartes was telling Mersenne that 'someone walking in a room understands what motion is better than someone who says that it is *the actuality of a thing in potentiality insofar as it is in potentiality.*'[20]

This early impatience with Peripatetic accounts of motion had yielded to a different attitude by the time Descartes came to write *Principia Philosophiae* (1644).

Now writing with a didactic purpose, he offers two definitions of motion, one being motion in 'the ordinary sense', the other 'from the truth of the matter'. Motion 'as ordinarily understood' (*ut vulgò sumitur*) is simply 'the action [*actio*] by which a body passes [*migro*] from one place to another', because 'we ordinarily think there is action in every motion, and a discontinuance [*cessatio*] of action in rest.' Ordinarily, we would say that a man seated on deck a moving ship is at rest, because he feels no action within himself, which would be the case were he to walk about the deck. Yet we and the voyager see that both he and the ship are moving with respect to dry land, so he is both moving and not moving in different senses at the same time (*Princ.* II 24). However, if we want to go beyond ordinary usage to the truth of the matter (*ex rei veritate*) to settle on a *determinate* nature for motion, we can say that 'it is the transference [*translatio*] of one part of matter, or of one body, from the adjoining neighborhood of the bodies in immediate contact with it and considered as being at rest, to the neighborhood of others'[21] (*Princ.* II 25). I will call this kind of motion 'true motion', since a principal concern of *Principia* II 24–25 is to provide criteria for a real distinction between the contrary modes of motion and rest (*Princ.* II 44). True motion is reciprocal (as explained in *Princ.* II 29), which means that there is a distinction of reason between the motion of a body and the posited rest of its contiguous neighbourhood; but since there cannot be both separation and non-separation of the same contiguous surfaces at the same time, there is *for the same body* a true modal distinction between true motion and true rest.[22]

It is evident from elsewhere in *Principia* II 25 that Descartes intends his contrasting descriptions of ordinary and true motion to be a warning that the source or cause of motion must not be confused with motion *per se*. The passage also affirms Descartes's nominalist position that motion has no existence other than being a mode wholly dependent on the mobile:

I say [true motion] is the *transference,* not the force, or if you like the action, that transfers, to show that the former is always in the mobile, not in the mover, because these two things are not normally distinguished with sufficient accuracy. And it is only a mode of the mobile, not some subsistent thing, just as shape is a mode of a thing that has shape and rest a mode of a thing at rest.[23]

Although the *actio* of *Principia* II 24 seems to be simply a near-synonym of motive force, Descartes's intended primary sense of the term is probably the traditional understanding of *actio* as the source of motion, in contrast to *passio:* 'Motion is said to be an action [*actio*] according as it is the act [*actus*] of the agent as proceeding from it, but it is said to be a passion [*passio*] according as it is an act of the patient as it is in it.'[24] This sense of the term allows for Descartes's explicit identification of *actio* as force above and in *Principia* II 26 ('no more action is required for motion than for rest'). It is also in keeping with the rôle of *actio* in the 1638 dispute with Jean-Baptiste Morin on the theory of light in *La Dioptrique* and *Les Météores*. Descartes had hypothesised that light is 'a certain motion, or very quick and nimble action [*action*]', or 'the action or inclination to move' of the Cartesian subtle matter.[25] But an action or an inclination to move cannot also be a motion, Morin argued, since these differ as do power and act. Descartes replied that there is no contradiction in saying in one place that light is a motion or action, and saying elsewhere that it is simply an action. The term 'action' has a general sense that includes both power or inclination to move and motion itself: 'when one says that someone is always in action, that means that he is always moving [*se remuer*]', and more significantly, 'the motion is the action by which the particles of this [subtle] matter change place.'[26] So in 1638 Descartes was making scientific use of the ordinary sense of motion he was to exclude from 'the truth of the matter' in the *Principia* of 1644. This is not to flag a contradiction, or even a change of mind. It is rather that the Morin exchanges prefigure the problematic rôles ordinary and (therefore) true motion will play in the physics of the *Principia Philosophiae*.

It is important to note that the definitions of ordinary and true motion precede that point in Part II of the *Principia* where Descartes turns his attention to causal considerations. *Principia* II 36 begins, 'Having thus treated the nature of motion, it is appropriate to consider its cause, which is two-fold', the primary cause being God's creative and conserving power, the secondary cause, or rather causes, being the individuated expressions of the primary cause through the laws of nature and the forces of motion and rest that produce particular physical effects, for example the seven rules of collision set out in *Principia* II 46–52.[27]

Several difficulties attend this topical transition from nature and definition to cause and force. Forces are already involved in the true–ordinary motion distinction, and force must be required to create true motion and rest, just as much as it is required (in equal measure)[28] to create ordinary motion and rest. But Descartes does not explain how true motion and rest relate to the forces at work in his laws of nature and the seven rules of collision, nor is it clear how the true–ordinary motion distinction is meant to clarify the laws and the rules, or whether the laws and rules hold for true or ordinary motion (and rest), or for both (see section on 'Relativity of motion' below). A fortiori, it is not clear how or whether the distinction is meant to apply throughout Descartes's natural philosophy as a whole. The most notorious example of this difficulty is Descartes's claim (*Princ.* III 26–9) that the earth and the planets are not in true motion, because, being embedded in the planetary vortex, there is no separation of contiguous surfaces. Indeed, the earth is not in ordinary motion either, because there is no fixed point among the fixed stars that would make such motion determinate, and there is no reason to believe the stars motionless rather than the earth. So the earth is motionless on both counts, yet its vortex carries it round the sun. . . . It is still not a settled question whether Descartes introduced the dual motion distinction to escape anti-Copernican censure, which has been the traditional view, or whether his apparent denial of Copernican motion to the earth was a politically convenient by-product of a theory of motion devised for other purposes.[29]

A further difficulty is that it is not clear in what sense Descartes's true motion is a change of 'place'. Earlier in *Principia* II, he had presented his version of the distinction, found in Toletus and the Coimbrans, between 'internal place or space', a body's three-dimensional extension, and 'external place', which Descartes interprets as the two-dimensional separating boundary common to the body and to those contiguously surrounding it.[30] Descartes implies his approval of external place in this sense (as opposed to Aristotelian place, the innermost surface of the surrounding bodies), yet he claims, via the same man-on-the-deck argument (*Princ.* II 13), that there are no really permanent places in the universe, except those we determine by thought, and further argues (*Princ.* II 15) that a body does not change place if its external place (in his sense) remains fixed with respect to *other* external bodies assumed to be at rest. This is in keeping with Descartes's explicit denial that *translatio* is transference from 'place' to 'place' (*Princ.* II 28), but he does not say what kind of place is constituted by 'the adjoining neighborhood of the bodies in immediate contact' with a body in true motion or at rest (*Princ.* II 25). Oddly, the answer seems to be Aristotelian place, which Descartes's version of external place was intended to supplant.

A related difficulty that concerns less the distinctions of *Principia* II 24–5 than the causal and nomological considerations beginning at *Principia* II 36 is the question of force in Descartes's physics. It is clear that Descartes, in common with others such as Gassendi, More, Newton, or Leibniz (though not Hobbes), took the view that God is in some sense the ultimate creative source of all bodily force, power, and activity. The central problem in Descartes's case is that although his ontology of force is clearly realist, what is not clear is its precise ontological status. It is not a substance, but it might qualify as a mode, to the extent that it is causally associated with motions or states of rest. Whether it is an attribute of body, like extension, depends on whether extension is the sole principal attribute of body already posited as an existing thing, or on whether force, too, is a principal

attribute of body because as the expression of God's sustaining power it is a
necessary condition of a body's duration in existence, whatever its modal state,
which existence and duration are explicitly identified by Descartes as attributes.
The question is very difficult, partly because Descartes gave no formal account of
corporeal force and power, and partly because force and power seem to fall outside
the Cartesian categories of substance, attribute, and mode.[31]

As for *translatio,* Descartes's careful choice of term for his motion *ex rei veritate,*
it calls to mind the Peripatetics' use of *latio* (adding sometimes the Greek equivalent *phora*) as an equivalent term for *motus localis.*[32] Also, it echoes the title of
Gassendi's *De motu impresso a motore translato epistolae duae . . .* (Paris, 1642), that is
(literally), 'Two letters concerning the motion impressed by a transferred motor'.
Newton too used *translatio* for local *motion* in his *Principia Mathematica* (London,
1687), though it is difficult to say if this is a pointed re-usage of Descartes's term.
In the *De gravitatione et aequipondium fluidorum,* written probably in the early 1680s,
Newton remarks: 'I have defined motion as change of place, because motion,
transition, translation, migration and so forth seem to be synonymous words. If
you prefer, let motion be transition or translation of a body from place to place.'[33]
Newton was clearly a nominalist as far as motion itself was concerned and, unlike
Huygens,[34] a full-blooded realist on the question of force.

More important for Newton than terminology was the concern to devise a
coherent account of motion with which he could counter that in Part II of
Descartes's *Principia Philosophiae,* and at the same time provide the appropriate
setting for his own system. *De gravitatione* contains a lengthy rebuttal of Descartes's
true–ordinary motion distinction, in the form of ten or eleven ingenious arguments. Two of them will suffice by way of illustration. Descartes says that the
earth and the planets do not move, properly speaking, yet he explains their
respective positions in terms of an equilibrium between their centrifugal tendencies and the inward pressure of the vortex carrying them around the sun (*Princ.* III
140). Does this centrifugal tendency arise from the true rest of the earth and
planets, or from their ordinary motion? Again, if the places of a moving body are
defined with respect to surrounding bodies, it will be impossible to say where the
body was at the beginning of its motion or at any subsequent time, because the
surrounding bodies may have moved meanwhile with respect to yet other bodies.
Where was Jupiter a year ago? There is no Cartesian answer to that question. It
follows that in Descartes's world a moving body has no determinate path, and
therefore no determinate speed. 'So it is necessary that the determination of
places, and hence of local motion, be referred to some motionless thing, such as
extension alone or space in so far as it is seen to be truly distinct from bodies.'[35]

The required 'motionless thing' was the absolute space that Newton presented in his *Philosophiae naturalis principia mathematica* (1687). At the beginning of the Scholium following the Definitions preceding Book I, he writes: 'So far it has seemed right to explain the lesser known terms and the sense in which they are to be understood in what follows. I am not defining time, space, place, and motion, as being well known to everyone.' Nonetheless, he continues, 'it is to be noted that the ordinary person conceives these quantities [*quantitas*] only in relation to sensible objects. And thence arise certain prejudices, for whose removal it is convenient to distinguish these quantities into absolute and relative, true and apparent, mathematical and common.' So Newton (apparently innocent of the dangers of tautology) proceeds to explain that 'absolute, true and mathematical time' (also called duration), in itself and by its own nature, 'flows equably without relation to anything external'; relative time is a sensible and external measure of duration 'by means of motion'. Absolute space 'by its own nature, without relation to anything external, remains always similar and immovable'; relative space is 'some moveable dimension or measure' of absolute space. Place is 'a part of space which a body occupies, and, according to the space, is absolute or relative'. Finally, 'absolute motion is the transference [*translatio*] of a body from absolute place into absolute place, relative motion from relative place into relative place.'[36] As explained in section IV ('Relativity of Motion'), Newton proceeds to demonstrate the real existence of absolute space and absolute motion and rest through an empirical example whose interpretation involves the fundamental principle that only absolute (that is real) motions and rest are caused and altered by forces. The reality of corporeal forces ensures the reality of their effects.

Absolute space, time, and motion constituted a framework that enabled Newton to pursue his program in mathematised natural philosophy. Lucretius and Gassendi were important influences (see Chapter 18), but so was Descartes, in the sense that Newton's natural philosophy took shape in the light of serious criticisms of the doctrines *de motu* in the *Principia Philosophiae,* of which *De gravitatione* contains the most extended examples. Newton could now handle motions and their corresponding forces, in mathematised form, secure in the belief that he was dealing with real causal relationships subject to empirical control. The foundational centrepiece of this programme in the mathematical principles of natural philosophy was the famous three laws of motion, coupled with the *vis inertiae* which Newton claimed to be a property of every physical body (see Chapters 21, 18). There are considerable difficulties with these foundations, not in the application of the definitions and the three laws in the rest of *Principia Mathematica,* but rather in philosophical questions relating to absolute space and the concept of inertial force. Newton had difficulty with the ontological status of space: not a substance, nor an accident in an ordinary sense, it seemed to be an emanent effect of God, or perhaps one of His attributes.[37] As for a body's *vis inertia*, it reacts equipollently against any force (*vis impressa*) only when that force tries to change the body's state, yet for that very reason it lurks within the body, *in potentia* in some sense, preserving its present state and in preparation so to speak for an intervention from an impressed force from without.[38]

Leibniz, too, underlined the difficulties in Descartes's doctrine of motion, in his unpublished *Animadversiones in partem generalem Principiorum Cartesianorum* (1692). If motion is nothing other than the reciprocal change of contiguous surfaces (*Princ.* II 25), then it will be impossible to say if anything is really moving, and there will be no reason to attribute motion to one thing rather than to another. The upshot will be that 'there is no real motion.' To be able to say that something is moving, we need not just change of place, 'but also that there be within itself a cause of the change, a force, an action'.[39] Of course, Leibniz's emphasis on force (in various forms) as the key to understanding corporeal substance predated the *Animadversiones* by a decade. As is explained in detail in Chapter 18,[40] Leibniz's increasing opposition to Descartes's extensional conception of body, which began in the mid-1670s, led to the views that extension is a purely phenomenal aspect of bodies, that 'the very substance of things consists in a force of acting and of being acted upon', that 'strictly speaking, motion (and likewise time) never really exists, since the whole never exists, inasmuch as it lacks co-existent parts', and that

if we consider only what motion comprises precisely and formally, that is, change of place, motion is not something entirely real, and when several bodies change position among themselves, it is not possible to determine, merely from a consideration of these changes, to which body we should attribute motion or rest. . . . But the force or proximate cause of these changes is something more real, and there is sufficient basis to attribute it to one body more than to another. Also, it is only in this way that we can know to which body the motion belongs more.[41]

Leibniz's unequivocal realism regarding the forces that ontologically ground physical body contrasts strikingly with his equally unequivocal nominalism regarding motion (see section IV).

III. THE STRAIGHT AND THE CURVED

Not only did Aristotle nominate local motion as the primary motion, he nominated circular or rotational motion as the primary kind of local motion. Each local motion is either circular, or rectilinear, or a mixture of the two, and circular motion is primary to all others, because it is simpler and more complete. Rectilinear motion cannot be infinite in Aristotle's cosmos, so as finite it is either composite (should the mobile retrace its path), or incomplete and perishable; that is, it has *termini ab quo* and *ad quem,* and for the same reason it cannot be eternal. But circular motion is single and complete, because there are no determinate *termini ab quo* or *ad quem,* and it can be eternal, because it can be continuous. Finally, circular motion can be uniform, unlike rectilinear motion, which always increases in speed the further the mobile gets from the position of rest.[42]

This discrimination between circular and rectilinear motion became a standard element in Peripatetic teaching and was a staple item in the scholastic physics manuals. In presenting and developing Aristotle's argument, Keckermann, to take an interesting example, uses the distinction that had been drawn in some versions of the *impetus* theory between the *impetus* with which a motion begins and that with which the motion terminates. His Theorem II on circular motion reads:

> In circular motion, just as there is no express terminus *à quo* and *ad quem,* so also there is no designated *impetus* [*designatus impetus*], or if you like there is none of that designated minimum that is in motion as a moment [*momentum*] is in time.
>
> We have said before that in every motion there is something indivisible that corresponds to moment and point, which indivisible we have called *Impetus.* So where there is a distinct and separate terminus *à quo* and *ad quem,* there is a distinct *impetus* from which the motion begins and in which the motion ends. For example, when a stone moves downwards, the *impetus* with which the stone begins to move is distinct from the *impetus* with which the same stone ceases to move. But in circular motion those *impetus* cannot be distinguished from each other, since the termini cannot be distinguished.[43]

So circular motion is eternal, as Aristotle said. It will be noted that Keckermann's indivisibilist impetus resembles Hobbes's divisibilist *conatus,* without it leading him to any suggestion of innate rectilinearity in motion, whatever its geometric form.

However, re-interpretations of ordinary experience, including notably the obvious fact that projectiles typically move in non-circular curves, the gradual dissolution post-Copernicus of the Ptolemaic-Aristotelian universe, and a critical look at motion in a vacuum, raised doubts about the comparative status of rectilinear and circular motions. The behaviour of stones in slings, or bodies placed on the circumference of rapidly rotating wheels, suggested that bodies in motion have a primary natural tendency to move in straight lines. There is a striking example in the *Diversarum speculationum mathematicarum, et physicarum liber* (Turin, 1585) of Giovanni Battista Benedetti (1530–90), one of the major sixteenth-century contributions to mechanics and 'mathematical physics'. Chapter

17 gives the 'true explanation' of Question 12 of pseudo-Aristotle's *Mechanica:* 'Why does a missile travel further from the sling than from the hand?' Continuously repeated swings of the sling increase the *impetus* of the projectile, explains Benedetti, which in turn increases the tension the hand feels in the string, and increases the 'certain natural tendency [by which the projectile would] seek to proceed in a straight line', that is, along the tangent at each point of its circular motion.[44]

There had always been the question of how a body would move in the imaginary spaces, but the increasing presence of atomistic ideas in the sixteenth century shifted the question to the domain of the real: what is the natural motion of a body moving in a vacuum? For most Peripatetics the question made no sense, but for many others the answer was that the natural motion of a body in a vacuum would be rectilinear and uniform. Yet this did not mean that circular motion immediately took second place to rectilinear motion. Galileo's circular 'inertia'[45] applied in the case of a body moving in a circle with neither violent nor natural motion in the traditional senses, but with a kind of in-between motion that would endure perpetually in the absence of impediments (for example, a body moving on a smooth horizontal plane round the earth).[46] For Beeckman, for whom circular motion was as natural to bodies as rectilinear motion, there were two 'inertial' principles: perpetual motion in a circle and perpetual motion in a straight line (in the absence of impediments in both cases).[47] In his *De motu impresso a motore translato epistolae duae* (1642) Gassendi stated clearly, and for the first time in print, that a body moving in a vacuum will continue its motion perpetually with a constant speed and in a straight line, but it is odd that he used as illustration of this claim the example of a ball rolling on a horizontal plane (as did Galileo), and (again like Galileo) analysed the matter in terms of the violent–natural motion distinction.[48] It cannot be claimed that Galileo, Beeckman, or Gassendi understood the significance or meaning of the 'inertial' principle as stated in differing forms and applied (in differing ways) by Descartes, Huygens, Leibniz, and Newton.

The fundamental difference between the two sets of 'inertial' principles can be summed up in the idea of the over-riding primacy of only uniform rectilinear motion, and rest, as the innate and impediment-free natural states of all physical bodies, whatever their location or behaviour within a world that others might describe in terms of the natural–violent distinction. Furthermore, for Descartes, Huygens, Leibniz, and Newton this idea is understood and presented as a first-order explanatory principle of natural philosophy from which all other motions must be derived, not simply another observation, however recognisedly important, made about the observed or imagined behaviour of bodies. The 'inertial' principle in this sense was first stated ambiguously by Descartes in *Le Monde* (1629-1632, though not published until 1664) and in *Principia Philosophiae* (1644), with Newton's reformulation of Descartes's insight, as the First Law of Motion of the *Principia Mathematica*, being now the most influential canonical expression of this fundamental property of physical body: 'Every body perseveres in its state of resting or moving uniformly in a straight line, except insofar as it is compelled by impressed forces to change that state.'[49] The 'inertial' principle was originally a simple inference from a limited range of everyday experiences (as in Benedetti's analysis of the sling), but in the hands of Descartes and his successors it became a fundamental explanatory principle of universal extension, whatever its derivation and justification in individual cases.[50] In particular, it enabled Newton and Leibniz (though not Descartes) to deal in a mathematically sophisticated way with not just motion in a circle, but with curved motion, notably the Keplerian motions of the planets and the motion of projectiles in resisting media. But that step required more sophisticated mathematical techniques than were available to Descartes or his immediate contemporaries.[51]

One term used by Descartes in the explanation of his second law of nature merits special mention. Following the first law, that 'each single thing, insofar as it is simple and undivided, and by its own nature, remains as far as possible [*quantum in se est*] in always the same state, and never suffers change except through external causes', Descartes complements it with 'the next law of nature', 'that each single particle of matter, considered individually, never tends to continue moving along any deviating lines, but only along straight lines – although many particles are often compelled to deviate, because of collisions with others'.[52] In his commentary on the second law, notably that it derives from the immutability and simplicity of the operation by which God conserves motion in bodies, Descartes explains:

For he [God] conserves it precisely as it is only at the very moment of time at which he is conserving it, it being of no relevance how it might have been a short time previously. And although no motion takes place in an instant, it is still evident that in each single instant which can be designated during the motion of anything that moves, it is determined [*determinatum*] to continue its motion in some direction along a straight line, never along any curved line.[53]

The notion of *determinatio* ('determination') at work here has been usually misunderstood by Descartes scholars to mean the 'direction' of a body's motion. Even so, it is not easy to pin down what Descartes himself took it to mean, since he never provided a clear and precise definition of the term. The question is too complicated to address here, but it seems safe to characterise *determinatio,* as employed by Descartes in his natural philosophy, as 'the directional mode of motive force'.[54] One reason the concept is important in Descartes's thought is that his doctrine of divine creation and conservation, in which God maintains His ucreation in existence by lending it, so to speak, its *esse*, carries with it the need to link in some way the divine conserving power to its multiple and diverse appearances in the world. If there is to be diversity in the divinely maintained corporeal world, there must be principles of diversification. For Descartes these principles are the speeds of bodies, conceived as 'scalar' quantities (as we would now call them), and their *determinationes*, which we will not stray in conceiving as adumbrations of what later became known as 'vectorial' quantities. We are re-minded that for Aquinas *determinatio* (in a different though related sense) was the first principle of plurality.[55]

IV. RELATIVITY OF MOTION

Given that motion is change with respect to the body's 'surroundings', it is natural to wonder if those surroundings can be said to move with respect to the body. The origins of this question, which go back to antiquity, are unlikely to have been purely theoretical.[56] It would have occurred to any thoughtful person in smooth vehicular motion on land (rare in antiquity, one assumes), or in a boat leaving harbour on a calm sea (common at any time). Recall the line from Virgil's *Aeneid* (III, 72): 'We sail out of harbor, the lands and cities recede.' In his *Adversus Physicos,* Sextus Empiricus had asked if motion exists, and cited the example of a man on a ship carrying a vertical rod from the prow to stern at the same speed as the ship moves before the wind. He is in motion on the deck of the ship, yet with respect to the shore he is at rest. This apparent contradiction enabled Sextus to conclude that one must suspend judgement on whether motion is anything at all, an argument reminiscent of later nominalist denials that local motion has any exis-tence independent of the body moved.[57] In the thirteenth century Witelo and Aquinas, and Oresme and Buridan, in the fourteenth, argued that local motion is detectable through the senses only in so far as bodies are seen to be in different respective mutual dispositions. However, Oresme and Buridan argued further that of two observers each on the deck of his own ship, each will think himself at rest with respect to the other, irrespective of whether (from a third-party point of view) both ships are at rest or both are in the same (uniform) motion, or either of them is in (uniform) motion while the other is at rest. The context of these arguments was the traditional issue of the earth's rotation, so Oresme and Buridan went on to argue that *from a purely observational standpoint* it is all the same whether one says that the celestial sphere rotates diurnally about the motionless earth, or that the earth rotates diurnally on its polar axis at the centre of the now immobile celestial sphere. In his *De revolutionibus orbium coelestium* of 1543 (Book I, Chapters 5, 8) Copernicus used similar arguments to support his claim that astronomy would be better served by the theses that the earth and the five planets revolve around the sun, and that the earth rotates diurnally with respect to the celestial sphere. These theses accounted for the sun's apparent annual motion, the apparent motions of the planets, and the apparent diurnal motion of the celestial sphere, just as had the Ptolemaic-Aristotelian theses that the sun, planets, and celestial sphere revolve or rotate, in their different ways, about the motionless earth.[58]

One important feature of this relativity principle, *qua* principle, is that it was understood solely in terms of the observed phenomena (e.g., the archetypical boat example). Questions about the possible interplay of forces in a given instance of relative motion seem not to have been asked before Galileo's famous discussion in the Second Day of his *Dialogo* (1632). To illustrate the undetectability of the earth's motion via experiments conducted on the earth, and thereby the ineffectiveness of the traditional physical arguments against its Copernican motion, Galileo takes the boat example, but develops it in a crucially significant way. He asks Sagredo to go on board a large ship, but to confine himself in a cabin below-decks with a friend, a few butterflies, and some goldfish in a bowl, and to have to hand a bottle dripping water into a receptacle. When the boat is at rest the animals and the water droplets behave in the usual way, and 'in throwing something to your friend, you need throw it no more strongly in one direction than another, the distances being equal; jumping with your feet together, you pass equal spaces in every direction.' What will appear to happen to all these motions (the butterflies, the goldfish, the dripping water, the throwing and the jumping) when the boat is in uniform motion? Nothing whatsoever:

You will discover not the least change in all the effects named, nor could you tell from any of them whether the ship was moving or standing still. In jumping, you will pass on the floor the same spaces as before, nor will you make larger jumps toward the stern than toward the prow even though the ship is moving quite rapidly, despite the fact that during the time that you are in the air the floor under you will be going in a direction opposite to your jump. In throwing something to your companion, you will need no more force to get it to him, whether he is in the direction of the bow or the stern, with yourself situated opposite.[59]

This brilliant use of an everyday observation demonstrates Galileo's twin insights that the forces between interacting moving bodies remain invariant whether their frame of reference is in uniform motion or at rest, and if it is in uniform motion, that they all share that motion unless impeded by some cause external to the reference frame. However, Galileo did not match his insight with an attempted explanation of the invariance (which is a direct consequence of the inertial principle and Newton's third law of equal and opposite action and reaction). Galileo's 'inertial principle' is not at all the same as the 'inertial principles' of Descartes or Newton, since for Galileo the boat experiment works for both rectilinear and circular uniform motion, that is, on the surface of the ocean.[60]

A relativity principle is often attributed to Descartes. Such an attribution is misleading, if it implies a principle that mirrored the Galilean or inspired the Huygenian relativity principle. As noted earlier, Descartes's 'ordinary' motion is associated with action or force, and rest with the absence of action, so a man sitting on the deck of a ship leaving harbour will ordinarily think himself at rest; yet he will think the contrary if he looks shorewards. Defining motion 'according to the truth of the matter' obviates the troublesome consequences of the normal association with action, because the mutual separation *per se* of contiguous bodies does not depend on the perceived presence or absence of forces. True motion is reciprocal, and it is relative in the sense that if pairs of contiguous bodies are in proper motion, each of them moves relative to the other taken to be at rest. But this means that one cannot speak of reciprocity of true motion between *non-*contiguous bodies, which leaves Descartes's doctrine of motion 'according to the truth of the matter' powerless to deal in general with problems *de motu* for whose solution one would naturally turn to the Galilean relativity principle or to principles that are causally equivalent to it. In particular, reciprocal transference cannot apply to colliding bodies, since they touch each other only on impact, at which instant there is no mutual separation of surfaces. Furthermore, Descartes's true motion, and therefore reciprocal transference, and the relative motion observed by the man in the ship, are purely phenomenal. Like everyone else who had ever boarded a ship, Descartes would have noticed phenomena similar to those described in the Second Day of the *Dialogo* (above), but he seems not to have realised their significance: there is no sign in his writings of the *invariance* of interacting forces that distinguishes Galileo's analysis. Descartes seems not to have noticed that the interplay of forces within a physical system is quite independent of whether or not the system is in uniform motion. This is not to credit Galileo with a proto-Newtonian understanding of force–motion relations, nor is it even to deny it to Descartes in some of his thinking.[61] But it does highlight the absence in Descartes's writings of a Galilean insight that was to become a key point of empirical reference in the consolidation of the Newtonian doctrine of motion.

By contrast, Christiaan Huygens did not overlook the importance of Galilean invariance, which he applied to great effect in his collision theory. Right from his first researches on collision (1652–4), Huygens knew that the Galilean relativity principle must be applicable in the solution of collision problems. He began with the concept of a 'force of collision' (*vis collisionis*), which is the sum of the motive forces of the colliding bodies, and which he identified with the interacting forces in Galileo's boat example. As he soon realised, however, his *vis collisionis* cannot be equated in general with Galileo's interacting forces. While the equation holds for equal bodies, irrespective of the relativistic speed chosen for each body, for eunequal bodies each chosen relativistic speed yields a different *vis collisionis,* which renders the concept useless for the solution of collision problems (and which explains why Huygens never referred to it again after these early researches).[62] But further reflection showed Huygens that he could ignore the interacting forces in a collision, because the Galilean relativity principle means that these forces (whatever their values) remain the same for a collision on a moving boat (say) as on the same boat at rest. Consequently, the *effects* produced by these forces – that is, the motions as viewed by someone in the boat and by someone on land – transform geometrically into each other in a way that ensures consistency in whatever *causal* accounts of the motions the respective observers might present. Galileo's principle ensures that a collision on the moving boat observed from land is the same state of affairs, causally speaking, as the collision observed when the boat is at rest.[63] Huygens could therefore use moving-boat hypotheses as transformational devices in his mature collision theory. In general terms, the data of a (direct) collision within one reference frame transform into the different data of another collision when the reference frame and its contents are set in uniform motion with respect to a second reference frame. If either collision problem is already solved, the solution to the other transformed problem follows readily on choosing an appropriate relative speed between the two reference frames.[64]

Given the Galilean–Huygenian relativity principle, the confused doctrine of motion in Descartes's *Principia Philosophiae,* and the contemporary debates about the reality of the Copernican motion of the earth (and of the sun's Copernican rest), there arises the question of whether there is such a thing as 'real motion', and whether there are criteria for detecting it. Descartes's flawed distinction between true and ordinary motion, and their confused relations to force, constituted an important catalyst in the emergence of Newton's concepts of absolute space, time, and motion. For Newton it was fundamental that 'absolute and relative rest and motion are distinguished from each other by their properties, causes, and effects.' This means that there is a causal correspondence between forces, which are real, and absolute motion and rest, which are equally real.

Accordingly, 'true and absolute motion cannot be determined by the transference from the adjoining neighborhood of bodies which are considered as being at rest. For the external bodies ought not only to be considered as being at rest, but ought also to be really at rest.'[65] Circular motion is of crucial significance: 'The effects that distinguish absolute from relative motions are the forces of receding from an axis of circular motion.' There is therefore empirical proof of the existence of absolute space and motion. Hang a bucket of water from a long cord, twist the cord so that upon release the bucket starts its accelerating spin. At the beginning of the rotation, the surface of the water is flat and the bucket moves quickly with respect to the water (Cartesian true motion), but gradually the water, through friction, gains on the bucket until it is spinning at the same speed (Cartesian true rest). At that point, however, the water will have climbed up the inside of the bucket to form a concave surface, a real effect whose cause must be real. This cause is clearly not Cartesian 'true rest', but is the liquid's endeavour to recede from the axis of rotation. There is therefore a real force acting on the water, and since the behaviour of the whole apparatus does not depend on any other bodies in the universe, the bucket and the water are in absolute motion with respect to absolute space. Real motion does exist, and one criterion for detecting it is the effects of centrifugal force arising from circular motion.

Prior to the appearance of Newton's *Principia,* Huygens, too, believed that the centrifugal force of a body in circular motion provides a criterion for detecting true motion, as he admitted to Leibniz in August 1694.[66] As the author of *De vi centrifuga* (1659), which contained the first derivation of the formula for centrifugal force, he had been well placed to appreciate the relevance of circular motion to the question, yet his position was not fully thought out, since he seems not to have realised that it required some accommodation with his Cartesian rejection of space as something independent of bodies.[67] However, after reading Newton's Scholium, Huygens changed his mind, and he began a series of manuscript notes in which he tackled the question of absolute motion and struggled with the problem of how to describe circular motion, complete with centrifugal force, in relativistic terms. It seems ironic that Huygens should begin to argue against the 'circular-motion criterion' for real motion just at the time Newton had set out strong arguments pointing the other way. But Huygens saw that the doctrines *de motu* in the *Principia,* however well they supported relativistic methods in the solution of particular problems involving both linear and curvilinear motions, were indissociable from an absolute space, which Huygens firmly rejected as a meaningless notion.

One of the basic difficulties was that relativistic equivalence, which Huygens had applied so successfully to linear motions, seems not to hold in the case of circular motions. If small weights are suspended freely from the rim of a rotating wheel, centrifugal forces will cause them to hang obliquely away from the centre of motion, as an observer at rest outside the system can easily see; but this will not happen if the wheel and weights are at rest and the observer revolves round them with the same speed in the opposite direction.[68] Yet Huygens insisted again and again throughout his notes on relativity that there is no such thing as true motion or rest, that *all* motions, *all* states of rest, are relative, and that there is relative motion when the distances between bodies change, relative rest when the distances remain constant. Well, not quite. If a number of bodies lying on a table are linked to each other by (taut) cords, they and the table are at relative rest, yet the whole lot might be moving – with circular motion about the appropriate centre! In which case there must be *some* sense in which there is relative motion. Huygens's way out of the dilemma was to suggest, as he put it in one of the notes written probably post-*Principia,* that circular motion 'is relative motion in parallel straight lines, the direction being changed continually and the distance [between the parts of the rotating body] being maintained through the bond [connecting them together]'.[69] Or to paraphrase the example given elsewhere in the post-*Principia* notes, imagine two equal bodies A and B moving with equal speeds towards each other along parallel lines. They are in relative motion. Then suppose that when the distance AB is least, that is at the moment they 'pass each other', they are simultaneously caught on (say) two hooks linked by a taut cord. The bodies will begin rotating about the point halfway between them. So at any subsequent instant the bodies will remain at the same distance from each other, yet will be in instantaneous relative motion along two directionally opposite and parallel tangents. Before hook-up, A and B were in relative motion along parallel lines: after hook-up, they are still in relative motion along parallel lines, except that the lines themselves now continually change direction because of the new physical constraint, which maintains A and B, still moving 'inertially', at the same distance and provides the physical condition for the appearance of the centrifugal force that maintains the tautness in the cord.[70] It is unfortunate that Huygens (who died in 1695) did not engage the difficult mathematical task of showing how his relativistic account of circular motion might dispose of Newton's bucket argument for absolute space.

As for the contrast between Leibniz's realism regarding forces and his nominalism regarding motion, that opposition was the principal ground on which he could proclaim the complete *observational* relativity of all motions whatever, whether circular or not (*pace* Newton), while at the same time claiming that in each body there is some measure of *real* motion, that is, some measure of (Leibnizian) force.[71] In his earlier days Leibniz had entertained an absolutist conception of space and motion, which he later revised on examining the notions of place advanced by Aristotle and Descartes,[72] and he had been struck by the circular-motion criterion for true motion that Huygens explained to him during their meetings in Paris (1673–6), something he noticed later in Newton's *Principia*.[73] But before then he had already concluded that 'circular motion has no advantage in this',[74] and in his mature thought, the Leibniz–Clarke correspondence being the most famous piece of documentary evidence, there is no absolute space or time, and therefore no absolute motion in bodies. Furthermore, Leibniz claimed that all motions whatever are either rectilinear or compounded of rectilinear motions, a claim which produced the significant mathematical result that since rectilinear motions are relative, all motions must be relative, including even circular and curved motions. In part II of the *Specimen dynamicum* (1695) Leibniz explains:

> Since only force and the nisus [effort] arising from it exist at any moment (for motion never really exists, as we discussed above), and since every nisus tends in a straight line, it follows that *all motion is either rectilinear or composed of rectilinear motions*. From this it not only follows that what moves in a curved path always tries to proceed in a straight line tangent to it, but also – something utterly unexpected – that the *true notion of solidity* derives from this. . . . For if we assume something we call solid is rotating around its center, its parts will try to fly off on the tangent. . . . But since this mutual separation disturbs the motion of the surrounding bodies, they are repelled back . . . as if the parts themselves contained a centripetal force. Thus the rotation arises from the composition of the rectilinear nisus for receding on the tangent and the centripetal conatus among the parts.[75]

Whatever one makes of this account of solidity (which implies, absurdly, that only rotating bodies can be solid), it is clear that for Leibniz, Newton's bucket experiment does not prove what Newton claimed.[76] In return, it is not at all clear how, for a body observationally in relative motion or rest, its real Leibnizian motion, that is its inherent Leibnizian force, is to be measured or even empirically detected.

V. NEW PROBLEM DOMAINS

One striking outcome of the new currents of thought described at the beginning of this chapter was a growing awareness of the existence of, and of the importance of solving, problems that had not been part of the regular Peripatetic programme in natural philosophy.[77] These new problems included the investigation of the mathematical properties of motion, the search for its laws and their mathematical formulation, and the innumerable challenges presented by bodies moving according to those laws under whatever forces (notably gravity), whether the bodies be celestial or terrestrial, in mutual collision, or moving in rigid or fluid conglomeration. It is significant that none of the manual writers in the Peripatetic tradition ventured into the new problem domains created by Harriot, Benedetti, Galileo, Beeckman, Mersenne, Descartes, Roberval, Baliani, Gassendi, Borelli, Fabri, Marci von Kronland, Huygens, Wallis, Wren, Leibniz, or Newton. (Conversely, it is equally significant that only a few of *these* figures continued to ask and answer the old question 'Quid sit motus?')

The importance of the new problem domains can be gauged by noting their foundational status in the advance of the mathematical sciences during the Scientific Revolution. Mediaeval attempts to bridge the gap between the mathematical and the physically real had been brought to fruition through investigations of the fall of bodies, the one important species of natural motion whose mathematisation, at the hands of Galileo in particular, demonstrated the legitimacy of the mixed discipline of 'mathematical physics' and set it off on new paths of discovery. The mathematical description of the motion of the simple pendulum, again initially at the hands of Galileo, was a natural extension of the theory of free fall, and with the problems of the compound pendulum (centres of percussion and of oscillation), first posed by Mersenne, began the systematised study of rigid body motion, in which the pioneering names include Descartes, Roberval, Huygens, and supremely in the eighteenth century, Leonhard Euler. The problem of circular motion was the problem of 'naturalising' in a mathematical way what the Peripatetics were content to accept as just another example of violent motion (e.g., a stone in a sling), or as the natural motion of the celestial regions alone. For many, post-Copernicus, the motions of the planets about the sun, and the motion of a stone in a sling, whatever the physical causation involved in each case, instantiated similar motion–force relations and required therefore similar kinds of mathematical analysis.

Of particular importance was the problem of collision, which created enormous interest throughout the seventeenth century (see further Chapter 21), and which seems to have been first addressed within the 'Northumberland circle' in England, where atomism was the predominant natural philosophy (Chapter 18). Thomas Harriot (1560—1621), the most gifted of the group, devised a systematic collision theory (c. 1619) consisting in a complicated set of descriptive rules of great interest, though of lesser value on the question of the mathematical relations between motions and the forces causing them.[78] Given the aims of the emerging mechanical philosophy, it became of fundamental importance to discover how to quantify (and geometrise) the motions exchanged during the collision of 'simple' bodies (however understood) of given sizes and speeds. This concern derived also in an important measure from the Renaissance revival of Greek atomism, though it should not be overlooked that in pseudo-Aristotle's *Mechanica* can be found the cardinal principle of early collision theory that the same force moves bodies with speeds inversely as their sizes.[79] Another principle, of anthropomorphic stamp, that informs all seventeenth-century accounts of collision is the idea that when body meets body there is a 'contest' of forces in which larger forces are the winners, smaller forces the losers.

These principles were employed, in one form or another, by all seventeenth-century writers on collision theory. Beeckman, a formative influence on the young Descartes, provided ingenious solutions to a range of hard-body collision problems that he began to tackle in 1618. His basic principle was the mutual annihilation of equal and opposite forces (*impetus,* measured by speed times *corporeitas*) and the addition of forces of bodies colliding in the same direction. That is, forces of collision add *algebraically,* the resultant forces undergoing a uniform redistribution per corporeal unit.[80] A similar principle is at work in the systematic collision theory devised by Marcus Marci von Kronland in his *De proportione motus* (1639), the most notable treatise on the subject prior to Descartes's *Principia Philosophiae,* and where the main concern was to establish mathematical relations between motion and its cause, *impulsus* (weight times speed). Marci's theory is not entirely coherent, largely because he tried to extend the hard-body principle to collisions between elastic bodies.[81]

The notoriety of Descartes's seven rules of collision (*Princ.* II 46–52) has arisen not merely from the fact that they have only a nodding acquaintance with the empirical world. It is also that their empirical infirmity was the first sign ('selon l'ordre des raisons') that the foundations of Descartes's physics were not as solid as the confident tone of his programme in natural philosophy led his readers to expect (see further Chapter 21). Yet it was the very weaknesses of Descartes's collision theory, set against the general background of his massively influential philosophical system, that inspired or provoked others to find new ways of tackling the collision problem or of conceptualising force–motion relations. Huygens provided the first coherent, and empirically sustainable, response to the Cartesian rules of collision, and at the same time the first general theory of elastic-body collision, in his unpublished *De motu corporum ex percussione* of 1653–6.[82] Contributing to his success in this area were his ingenious employment of the Galilean principle of relativity, of Galileo's law of free fall and of 'Torricelli's Principle' (the centre of gravity of a number of bodies moving freely under gravity cannot rise higher than where it was at the beginning of the motion). Two major results of

Huygens's collision theory were the principles of the conservation of motion in the same direction and of the conservation of the product 'bodily size times speed squared'. Huygens missed the wider significance of these findings, but they did not escape Leibniz.[83]

As for Newton the mathematical physicist, his central concern was not collision theory, but the general problem of how motions quantitatively express forces as their causes, and in particular how to apply these quantitative relations, cast in nomological form, to solve problems both celestial and terrestrial. Nevertheless, the revolutionary explanatory power of the famous three laws of motion had the effect of making collision theory a by-product of a grander doctrine *de motu*. Others who participated in the widespread attempts to capture the laws of collision in mathematical form were Giovanni Alfonso Borelli, Claude-François de Chales, Honoré Fabri, Leibniz, Malebranche, Edmé Mariotte, Ignace Pardies, John Wallis, and Christopher Wren.[84]

The advancement of mechanical or atomistic ideas did not necessarily entail a special interest or competence in the technical business of mathematising motions. In his *Philosophia Epicurea* (Paris, 1601), Nicholas Hill, described puzzlingly by John Aubrey as 'a great mathematician and philosopher', advances an atomistic philosophy, but he does not pursue the implications of the mechanical philosopher's claim that all is explicable in terms of matter and motion. That claim was often a slogan, easy to declaim and argue for in general terms, but much less easy to bring to fruition in the form of an explanatory account of phenomena governed by mathematically expressed laws.

NOTES

1 Barker and Goldstein 1984, pp. 156–7; Barker 1985, 1991.
2 'Motus localis secundum naturae ordinem primus est inter motus: tum quia communis est in universum omnibus corporibus naturalibus: tum etiam, quod reliqui motus ab hoc tanquam à causa oriantur.' *Systema physicum*, Bk. I, cap. 9, 'De actione sive operatione corporum naturalium', 'Theoremata generalia de motu locali', theor. I. Keckermann 1614, vol. 1, cols. 1392–3. The heading of the physics section reads: 'Systema physicum septem libris adornatum, et anno Christi MDCVII Publice propositum in Gymnasio Dantiscano . . .', cols. 1357 et seq.
3 'In motu locali includuntur omnes alii motus ut in causa, propter primum motum, quia est causa omnis motus corporalis, & sine illo nullus alius motus potest esse.' Chasteigner de la Rochepozay 1619, 'Supellex axiomatum', p. 58.
4 On these and other species of efficient cause in scholastic thought, see the excerpt from part III of Eustachius a Sancto Paulo's *Summa philosophica* quoted in Gilson 1979, pp. 40–1.
5 Descartes's remark typifies the general mood: 'I assume no difference between violent

and natural motions, for what does it matter whether a stone is pushed by a man or by subtle matter?' Descartes to Mersenne, 11 March 1640. AT III 39. Here 'subtle matter' refers to the 'second element' in Descartes's physics. For Descartes's three elements, material particles distinguished only by shape, size, and motion, see *Princ.* III 52.

6   Clavelin 1974, p. 218.

7   *Discorso delle comete* (Florence, 1619), p. 55, quoted in Clavelin 1974, p. 217.

8   Galilei 1890–1909, vol. 8, p. 190 (Galilei 1974, p. 147). It seems preferable to read Galileo's *symptomata* as 'properties', or possibly 'effects', rather than 'essentials'.

9   Westfall 1971b, pp. 1–47 (*passim*), 526–8 (Appendix A: 'Galileo's Usage of Force'). Clavelin 1974, pp. 215–21.

10 Drake and Drabkin 1969, pp. 329–87 (texts), 338 (quotation). Clavelin 1974, pp. 126–33.

11 Galilei 1890–1909, vol. 8, p. 202 (Galilei 1974, p. 158–9).

12 The same holds for another notable author of a theory of collision, Johannes Marcus Marci von Kronland. Nowhere in his *De proportione motus* (Prague, 1639) does he examine the nature of motion, and he is content to define impulse as 'a locomotive virtue or quality, which moves [*movet*] only in time, and through a finite space'. Marci von Kronland 1639, Prop. I (the book is unpaginated).

13 Beeckman 1939–53, vol. 1, pp. 24–5 (July 1613–April 1614).

14 'Liber primus de impetu', introductory paragraph. Fabri 1646a, p. 1.

15 Fabri 1646a, p. 1. On Fabri see Lukens 1979 and Caruso 1987.

16 *De corpore*, II.7.2; II.8.10, Hobbes 1839a, vol. 1, pp. 94, 109.

17 *De corpore*, III.15.2, Hobbes 1839a, vol. 1, pp. 206–7.

18 'Nihil in toto hoc genere magis sensibile esse potest . . .', *Reg.* IX, AT X 402.

19 *Reg.* XII, AT X 426. There is a striking similarity between this passage and the terms in which Gassendi a few years earlier had expressed his impatience with the same definition of motion: 'Great God! Is there any stomach strong enough to digest that? The explanation of a rather familiar thing was requested, but this is so complicated that nothing is clear any more. What man, pray, no matter how unschooled, does not conjure up some intelligible idea of motion the minute he hears the word?' (*Exercitationum paradoxicarum adversus Aristoteleos libri septem* [1624], Bk. II, exerc. V, art. 4: trans. Brush in Gassendi 1972, p. 74.)

20 *Le Monde*, chap. VII, AT XI 40. Descartes to Mersenne, 16 October 1639. AT II 597 (translation from Garber 1992a, p. 159). See further Garber 1992a, pp. 157–9.

21 *Princ.* II 24, 25, AT VIIIA 53, italics in original AT edition. 'Transference' reflects directly the verbal root (*transfero*) of *translatio,* and at the same time avoids the additional figurative baggage attaching to the alternatives 'transfer' or 'translation'.

22 See Descartes's notes on his *Principia Philosophiae*: AT XI 656–7. For a full discussion of this question, see Garber 1992a, pp. 167–72. *Princ.* II 25 is headed 'What motion is, properly understood' ('Quid sit motus propriè sumptus'); in *Princ.* III 28, where it is argued that the earth does not move *propriè loquendo,* Descartes parenthesises 'if we may speak properly [*propriè*] and according to the truth of the matter' in his reprise of *Princ.* II 25; and in *Princ.* II 29 he talks of place being determined *juxta philosophicum sensum,* which implies that true motion is equivalently motion 'in the philosophical sense'. Still, it seems preferable to emphasise Descartes's *translatio* as being motion 'according to the truth of the matter', for the reasons just given in the text. Note that for the Coimbran commentators it was a *quaestio* whether '*latio* [carriage] inheres in the mobile, or in a circumadjacent body.' Descartes shared their view that it inheres (though only modally, for him) in the mobile itself. See Chapter 15.

23 *Princ.* II 25, AT VIIIA 53–4, italics in original AT edition. Garber suggests that Descartes should not be understood to mean that motion is 'an intrinsic and strictly nonrelational property of an individual body', but rather, that because of the reciprocity of *translatio* motion is a mode 'of the system composed of the body taken together with its contiguous neighborhood': Garber 1992a, pp. 172–3.

24 'Motus dicitur actio secundum quod est actus agentis ut ab hoc, dicitur autem passio secundum quod est actus patientis ut in hoc.' Chasteigner de la Rochepozay 1619, Supellex axiomatum, p. 57. See also Thomas Aquinas on *actio* as the source of motion: *Summa Theologiae,* pt. I, q. 41, resp. ad obj. 2. Deferrari *et al.* 1948, p. 13. For Goclenius motion is an *actio* improperly speaking, in that it is an incomplete entelechy: Goclenius 1613, p. 42.

25 *La Dioptrique,* Discours I, AT VI 84, 89.

26 Descartes to Morin, 13 July and 12 December 1638, AT II 203, 363–4.

27 *Princ.* II 36, AT VIIIA 61.

28 'No more action is required for motion than for rest': art. 26, AT VIIIA 54–5.

29 For further discussion, see Garber 1992a, pp. 181–8. For the traditional view, which seems to have begun with Henry More, see More 1662a, Preface General, p. xi; Blackwell 1966, p. 227; Aiton 1972, p. 41; Koyré 1978, pp. 261, 265.

30 *Princ.* II 10–15, AT VIIIA 45–9. See also Chapter 15, and Garber 1992a, pp. 134–6.

31 See further Chapter 18; Prendergast 1975; Hatfield 1979; Gabbey 1980a, pp. 234–9; Gueroult 1980; Garber 1992a, chap. 9 (*passim*); Gaukroger 1995, pp. 376–7. On existence and duration as attributes, see *Princ.* I 56.

32 Note, e.g., Toletus's use of *latio* in his commentary on the *Physics:* Toletus 1573, lib. V, cap. 2, text. 18, quoted in Gilson 1979, p. 189. Also Collegium Conimbricense 1625, pp. 252–4; Eustachius a Sancto Paulo 1609, para. III, p. 111, quoted in Gilson 1979, p. 190; Goclenius 1613, p. 1139; Chasteigner de la Rochepozay 1619, p. 60; Alsted 1626, p. 1803; Magirus 1642, p. 34.

33 'Definivi . . . motum esse loci mutationem, propterea quod motus, transitio, translatio, migratio &c videntur esse voces synonymae. Sin malueris esto motus transitio vel translatio corporis de loco in locum.' Newton 1962, pp. 91, 122 (translation).

34 I mean this in the sense that Huygens, without denying the existence of forces, managed his mathematical physics in such a way that he did not need them, either as *explicanda* or as parameters in his problem solving (see section IV, 'Relativity of Motion'). There is certainly no hint in his writings of any interest in what we might call the metaphysics of force.

35 'Necesse est itaque ut locorum determinatio adeoque motus localis ad ens aliquod immobile referatur quale est sola extensio vel spatium quatenus ut quid a corporibus revera distinctum spectatur.' Newton 1962, pp. 98 (Latin), 131 (translation, modified).

36 Newton 1972, vol. 1, pp. 46–7. Cf. also Newton 1934, pp. 6–7.

37 These issues are addressed in more detail in Chapters 18, 14. See McGuire 1978a; Grant 1981, pp. 238–47.

38 The issue is complicated. See Cohen 1964a; McMullin 1978a, pp. 36–42; Nicholas 1978; Gabbey 1980a, pp. 272–86.

39 Ger. IV 369 (Leibniz 1969, p. 393).

40 For general analyses of Leibniz's doctrine of force, see Gueroult 1967; Iltis 1971, 1974; Gale 1973; Westfall 1971b, chap. 6; Garber 1985, 1995; Duchesneau 1994; Mercer, forthcoming, chap. 7.

41 The three quotations, successively: *De ipsa natura sive de vi insita actionibusque creaturarum, pro Dynamicis suis confirmandis illustrandisque* (1698), sec. 8, Ger. IV 508; *Specimen dynam-*

icum (1695), Ger. Math. VI 234 (Leibniz 1989, p. 118); *Disc. mét.*, sec. 18, Ger. IV 444 (Leibniz 1989, p. 51, translation slightly modified).

42 *Physica* VIII, chap. 8, 261b 28, and chap. 9, 265a 15–265b 15.

43 'In motu circulari ut non est expressus terminus à quo & ad quem, ita etiam non est designatus impetus, sive designatum illud minimum, quod ita est in motu, ut in tempore momentum. Ante diximus in omni motu esse aliquid indivisibile, quod correspondeat momento & puncto, quod indivisibile appellavimus Impetum. Ubi ergo est loco distinctus ac separatus terminus à quo & ad quem, ibi distinctus est impetus à quo incipit motus, & in quem desinit motus: exempli gratia, cum lapis movetur deorsum, distinctus est impetus lapidis quo incipiebat moveri, ab impetu lapidis eiusdem, quo desinit moveri. Sed in motu circulari isti impetus ita discerni non possunt: cum termini discerni non possint.' *Systema physicum*, Bk. I, cap. 9, 'De actione sive operatione corporum naturalium', 'Theoremata de motu circulari', theor. II. Keckermann 1614, vol. 1, col. 1394.

44 Benedetti 1585, pp. 160–1, translated in Drake and Drabkin 1969, pp. 188–9. *Mechanica,* q. 12. On Benedetti, see also Koyré 1959; Clagett 1959, pp. 663–5. Note that for Benedetti and most of his contemporaries 'pseudo-Aristotle' was not pseudo at all, but the real thing. This fact is crucial for a proper appreciation of Aristotle's overall influence in the Renaissance and seventeenth century. Cf. Rose and Drake 1971, p. 72. De Gandt 1986a, p. 393. Copenhaver and Schmitt 1992, pp. 66–8.

45 The scare-quotes round 'inertia'/'inertial' remind us that it is anachronistic to ascribe a 'principle of *inertia*' to anyone prior to Newton. Even Newton labelled his version of the principle simply the first of his 'Axiomata sive leges motus' (Newton 1972, vol. 1, p. 54), though for good reasons it is not misleading to call his First Law 'the' principle of inertia. See further Gabbey 1980a, pp. 288–9.

46 See the discussion in Wallace 1981, pp. 271, 283–4, 313–14.

47 E.g., 'In a vacuum, whatever is once moved always moves, whether in a straight line, or in a circle, as much about its own centre, such as the diurnal motion of the earth, [as about another centre, such as its] annual [motion].' *Journal,* 23 November–26 December 1618. Beeckman 1939–53, vol. 1, p. 253. See Rochot 1952; Berkel 1983b, pp. 187–93.

48 Gassendi 1658, vol. 3, p. 495; vol. 1, pp. 343, 354–5 (*Syntagma philosophicum*). Compare the interpretations of Westfall 1971b, pp. 99–104; and Bloch 1971, pp. 220–32.

49 'Corpus omne perseverare in statu suo quiescendi vel movendi uniformiter in directum, nisi quatenus a viribus impressis cogitur statum illum mutare.' Newton 1972, vol. 1, p. 54. For an analysis and comparison of the two formulations of the principle, see Herivel 1965, pp. 42–53; Gabbey 1980a, pp. 290–7. On Descartes's laws of nature in general, see the detailed analyses in Garber 1992a, chaps. 7 and 8.

50 Nadler 1990 claims that Descartes's laws of nature derive their *confirmation* from observation and experiment.

51 For excellent recent accounts of these topics see Bertoloni Meli 1993, *passim,* especially pp. 56–91, 172–90; Blay 1992, *passim.*

52 *Princ.* II 37, AT VIIIA 62–5. On the phrase 'quantum in se est', see Cohen 1964a.

53 *Princ.* II 39, AT VIIIA 63–4.

54 See the analyses in Gabbey 1980a, pp. 248–61, and in Garber 1992a, pp. 188–93.

55 *Quaestiones quodlibetales* Q. 7, Art. 3.

56 For a recent general account of the early development of relativist ideas (up to the Newtonian age) see Barbour 1989.

57 Sextus Empiricus 1935, pp. 238, 239.

58 Clagett 1959, pp. 585–6, 594–5, 601–2 (Buridan and Oresme); Munitz 1957, 157–8, 161–4 (Copernicus, who quotes the line from the *Aeneid*).

59 Galilei 1890–1909, vol. 7, p. 213 (Galilei 1967, pp. 187).

60 See Clavelin 1974, pp. 245–7.

61 Cf. Gabbey 1980a, pp. 268–72.

62 In Newtonian terms, for bodies of equal mass the action and the reaction each equal the product 'mass times relative speed of approach', which is Huygens's *vis collisionis*. For bodies of unequal mass M, m the action and reaction are given by the product 'relative speed of approach times $2Mm/(M + m)$', but the *vis collisionis* can have any value between 'M times relative speed of approach' and 'm times relative speed of approach', depending on whether m or M is taken to be at rest or on whether both of them are taken to move with respective speeds whose algebraic difference is the same relative speed of approach.

63 See further Gabbey 1980b, pp. 168–70, 175–85; Vilain 1993, pp. 110–210; Mormino 1990, 1993, *passim*.

64 For an English translation of Huygens's *De motu corporum ex percussione*, see Huygens 1977 (trans. Richard J. Blackwell), and for analyses of various aspects of Huygens's collision theory, see Costabel 1956, 1957; Westfall 1971b, pp. 148–58; Vilain 1993, pp. 110–78.

65 'Distinguuntur autem quies & motus absoluti & relativi ab invicem per proprietates suas & causas & effectus . . . motus verus & absolutus definiri nequit per translationem e vicinia corporum, quae tanquam quiescentia spectantur. Debent enim corpora externa non solum tanquam quiescentia spectari, sed etiam vere quiescere.' *Principia mathematica,* Scholium following Definitions preceding Book I: Newton 1972, vol. 1, p. 49. Note that Newton is quoting almost verbatim from Descartes's *Princ.* II 25: '[Motum] dicere possumus esse *translationem unius partis materiae, sive unius corporis, ex viciniâ eorum corporum, quae illud immediatè contingunt & tanquam quiescentia spectantur, in viciniam aliorum.*' AT VIIIA 53 (italics in original AT edition).

66 Huygens to Leibniz, 24 August 1694, Ger. Math. II 192, Huygens 1888–1950, vol. 10, p. 670. He also made the admission in one of his post-*Principia* notes on relativity and absolute motion: 'For a long time I believed that in circular motion there exists a criterion of true motion.' ('Me in circulari motu diu credidisse *criterion* [Greek] existere veri motus.') Huygens 1888–1950, vol. 16, p. 226.

67 *De vi centrifuga:* Huygens 1888–1950, vol. 16, pp. 255–301. Although completed by October 1659, the full treatise did not appear until 1703, in the *Opera postuma.* Thirteen of its theorems (minus the proofs) were published in 1673 with the *Horologium oscillatorium.* On the inconsistency of Huygens's earlier position, see Bernstein 1984.

68 'Pièces et fragments concernant la question de l'existence et de la perceptibilité du "mouvement absolu" ' (editors' title), Fragment I (date uncertain), Huygens 1888–1950, vol. 16, p. 220.

69 Huygens 1888–1950, vol. 16, p. 226.

70 Quotation: 'Motus circulationis est motus relativus in rectis parallelis, mutata continuè directione, et manente distantia propter vinculum.' Huygens 1888–1950, vol. 16, p. 226. The same idea appears in another series of notes on relativity, dating probably from the 1690s: op. cit., vol. 21, pp. 507–8. The bodies-in-parallel-lines example appears several times in different forms: ibid., vol. 16, pp. 219–20, 222, 223–5, 227–9, 232–3. For differing analyses of the example and the other notes, see Stein 1977; Bernstein 1984, pp. 89–92; Vilain 1993, pp. 261–91. Note that although the motions of A and B before

'hook-up' are individually uniform (with respect to some other body taken to be at rest), their *relative* motion is not, but decelerates continually until it reaches a constant value with which each body begins hooked revolution. Huygens was fully aware of this, of course, but his analysis is incomplete: Huygens 1888–1950, vol. 16, pp. 219, 232.

71 See in particular the 1694 correspondence with Huygens: Ger. Math. II 179–99, *passim* (Leibniz 1969, pp. 413–20 [selections], Leibniz 1989, pp. 308–9 [selections]).

72 Gueroult 1967, pp. 26 (ex *Phoranomus, seu de potentia et legibus naturae,* 1689), 24–6; Bertoloni Meli 1988.

73 Leibniz to Huygens, 4/14 September 1694, Ger. Math. II 199 (Leibniz 1969, p. 419, Leibniz 1989, p. 308).

74 Leibniz to Huygens, 4/14 September 1694, Ger. Math. II 199 (Leibniz 1969, p. 419, Leibniz 1989, p. 308).

75 Ger. Math. VI 252–3 (Leibniz 1989, pp. 135–6). On Leibniz's attempts to persuade the Church, on relativistic grounds, to lift the ban on Copernicanism, see Bertoloni Meli 1988.

76 See further the important Bertoloni Meli 1993, pp. 76–8, 99–100, which examines new manuscript notes that contain Leibniz's earliest reactions to Newton's *Principia.* See also Stein 1977, pp. 3–6; and Bernstein 1984, pp. 92–102 (on the relations between Huygens' and Leibniz's ideas on relativity and absolute space and motion).

77 Cf. Murdoch and Sylla 1978, pp. 213, 222.

78 Jacquot 1974; Kalmar 1977.

79 Pseudo-Aristotle, *Mechanica,* query 24. On the importance of the *Mechanica* in the Renaissance and seventeenth century, see Rose and Drake 1971; De Gandt 1986a.

80 Beeckman 1939–53, vol. 1, pp. 265–6 (1618); vol. 2, pp. 45–6 (1620); vol. 3, p. 129 (1629). Also Gabbey 1973; Berkel 1983b, pp. 209–14. Berkel 1983b is the definitive account of Beeckman's life and work.

81 Marci von Kronland 1639; Westfall 1971b, pp. 117–25; Sørensen 1976. The extent of Marci's influence is not clear, though Huygens knew his work on collision theory (and on optics). It is important to note that seventeenth-century collision theory was greatly complicated by the fact that bodies in the real world show differing degrees of hardness and elasticity, which could not be treated mathematically other than *ex suppositione.* Beeckman's and Wallis's hard bodies are perfectly non-elastic, and therefore *behave* in the same way as soft bodies. On the other hand, the hard bodies of Descartes's collision theory behave like perfectly elastic bodies, as do those of Huygens's *De motu corporum ex percussione,* except that Huygens was shrewd enough to side-step the difficulties with his Hypothesis 2: '*Whatever may be the reason why hard bodies rebound from mutual contact when they strike each other,* we suppose that when two equal bodies with equal speeds collide directly from opposite directions, each rebounds with the same speed with which it came.' Huygens 1888–1950, vol. 16, pp. 32–3, italics added. On the cosmological implications of the Beeckmanian annihilation of equal motions, see Gabbey 1973, and 1985, pp. 38–41.

82 The treatise was not published in its entirety until 1703, in the *Opuscula postuma.* Huygens presented his collision theory to the Académie des Sciences in January 1668, and some theorems and their demonstrations were read to the Royal Society in January 1669. Seven of the theorems, minus the demonstrations, appeared in the *Journal des Sçavans* for 18 March 1669, and a month later (in a Latin version) in the *Philosophical Transactions.* On the difficult question of elasticity, see note 81.

83 On Huygens, see Westfall 1971b, chaps. 4, 5; Costabel 1956, 1957; Bos 1972; Gabbey 1980b. On Leibniz, see Westfall 1971b, chap. 6; Garber 1995, pp. 309–25; Fichant 1974,

1978, 1992 and his presentation of Leibniz 1994; Duchesneau 1994. On the Fellows of the Royal Society and the problem of collision, see A. R. Hall 1966. More generally, see Maclean 1959; Dugas 1957, 1958.

84 On Pardies, de Chales, Borelli, Mariotte, Wallis, Wren, and Newton, see Westfall 1971b, chaps. 5, 7. On Newton, see Herivel 1965. On Fabri, see Lukens 1979, Caruso 1987. On Malebranche, see Costabel's and Robinet's notes on Malebranche, 'Des lois du mouvement (1675–1712)', Mal. *OC* XVII (1) 1–236. On Mariotte, see Costabel 1986; Fichant 1993.

21

LAWS OF NATURE

J. R. MILTON

That complex sequence of events which we have come to refer to as the scientific revolution brought about radical changes not merely in the content of the explanations accepted but also in the forms of explanation considered appropriate. The idea that one of the main aims – perhaps *the* main aim – of a natural philosopher should be the discovery of the laws governing the natural world emerged clearly for the first time during the seventeenth century.[1] The Greeks had made little use of any concept of a law of nature.[2] The phrase itself occurs infrequently indeed in the original texts (though more often in some translations), and when it can be found, its manner of use often seems to suggest that the whole idea was recognised as being odd and somewhat paradoxical.[3] Given the extremely wide acceptance in the post-sophistic period of a fundamental antithesis between *nomos* (law, or convention) and *phusis* (nature), the marginal character of any idea of a law of nature is easy to understand. Even in later centuries, however, when the force of the *nomos–phusis* antithesis had greatly weakened and the idea of a moral law of nature had become familiar and widely accepted, there was still no parallel acceptance of any idea of nature as a system governed by, and explicable in terms of, physical laws. The theory of scientific explanation set out by Aristotle and accepted by such scientists as Ptolemy and Galen had no room for any such concept. Aristotelian explanations – or, rather, explanatory ideals – were essentialist in that they took as their fundamental premises definitions setting out the essences of things. There was no way in which anything analogous to Newtonian laws of motion could be inserted into such explanations, and neither Aristotle nor any of his successors made the slightest attempt to do so.

The idea of nature as a system governed by laws, and the idea that one of the main aims of a scientist (or natural philosopher) should be the discovery of these laws, is therefore historically quite specific. They are not ideas, like that of time, which can be traced back in one form or another as far as our sources permit; still less are they Kantian categories which govern any possible thought about the subject. Though they first emerge as centrally important to scientific thinking in the seventeenth century, they inevitably have an earlier history; and without some attention to this, their later development cannot properly be understood.

I. SOME BACKGROUND

By the beginning of the seventeenth century the idea of a moral law of nature already had a long and complex history. Its ultimate origins go back to the Greek Stoics, for whom the good life was one lived in accordance with nature. By the end of the thirteenth century a complex theory had been developed, blending the original Stoic ideas with others from Roman law and from the Bible; perhaps the most thoroughly worked out and certainly the most widely influential version of this can be found in Thomas Aquinas's *Summa theologiae*.[4] This way of thinking about morality continued as perhaps the dominant intellectual tradition within moral philosophy until after the end of the seventeenth century and is therefore described in more detail elsewhere in this volume.[5] Our concern here is only with the possible influence of the natural law tradition on ideals of explanation within natural philosophy.

Within the natural law tradition there was always a problem about whether the law of nature extended to irrational creatures, which by their nature could literally neither understand nor obey any law by which they might be supposed to be governed. Aquinas and Suárez held that it did not.[6] They did not, of course, reject the Old Testament picture of God issuing laws to the sea or to the elements,[7] but they insisted that such language was metaphorical and not to be taken literally.

The opposite view can be found just before the beginning of our period in Book I of Richard Hooker's *Laws of Ecclesiastical Polity* (1593). Hooker's general definition of a law certainly seems to leave room for laws governing the behaviour of irrational agents: 'That which doth assigne unto each thing the kinde, that which doth moderate the force and power, that which doth appoint the forme and measure of working, the same we tearme a *Lawe*'[8] That such an interpretation is indeed correct is made clear a few pages farther on: 'Whereas therefore things naturall which are not in the number of voluntarie agents, (for of such only we now speake, and of no other) do so necessarily observe their certaine lawse, that as long as they keepe those formes which give them their being, they cannot possiblie be apt or inclinable to do otherwise than they do.'[9] That the word 'form' in this passage is to be taken in a technical Aristotelian sense, is made clear by the footnote which Hooker appended: 'Forme in other creatures is a thing proportionable unto the soule in living creatures. Sensible it is not, nor otherwise discernible, then only by effects. According to the diversitie of inward formes, things of the world are distinguished into their kindes.' It is clear that for Hooker explanations in terms of forms and explanations in terms of laws were not alternatives, but correspond to different levels of description. It would be possible to develop from Hooker's account a theory of science in which laws describe observable regularities which themselves arise from occult forms. This was not the course that the natural sciences were to follow during the century after Hooker's death for many reasons, but above all because almost all the exponents of the new philosophy saw laws of nature and substantial forms as mutually exclusive alternatives, and were determined to discredit and eliminate the latter.

There are other ways in which Hooker's theory of natural law differs from the view that was later to become dominant. In Hooker's theory the physical and the moral merge into one another in such a way that any separation seems artificial. Natural agents not only obey a law which 'directeth them in the meanes whereby they tende to their owne perfection', but also another law 'which toucheth them as they are sociable parts united into one bodie; a lawe which bindeth them each to serve unto others good, and all to preferre the good of the whole before whatsoever their owne particular'. An example of this is a heavy body which moves upwards against its natural tendency, 'even as if it did heare itself commanded to let go the good it privately wisheth, and to relieve the present distresse of nature in common'.[10]

This kind of intimate blend of the moral with the physical would have seemed entirely natural to Hooker's readers. It can be found in the seventeenth century in such apparently dissimilar authors as Lord Herbert of Cherbury[11] and Thomas Sydenham,[12] and at the end of the eighteenth century in Edmund Burke.[13] As an intellectual and cultural phenomenon it deserves attention in its own right, but its relevance to the natural sciences remained very small. The whole tradition, going right back to Cicero, is marked by a preference for (sometimes magnificent) rhetoric rather than for the cold prose of philosophical analysis. Given the purpose of the tradition this is understandable: the reference to the laws of non-human nature was always made in order to recommend or discountenance some mode of human behaviour, never to throw any light on the workings of nature itself. The content of the non-moral laws could therefore be left utterly vague; indeed, any precise specification might serve only to weaken the analogy.

With hindsight it can be seen that the old theory of natural law had an inherent character that made it difficult to modify the theory for use in the natural sciences. Its origins and moral orientation ensured that the concepts of law which it engendered would tend to be either too general or too particular to be of any real use in constructing scientific explanations. The law of nature itself was always too general; it could be appealed to, but it defied precise formulation, and hence use. When it did come to be applied, however, it was natural to apply it to individuals either directly or as members of the appropriate species. Completely individualised laws, as many in number as the individual substances to which they correspond, would necessarily lack the kind of generality required for scientific explanation. Laws governing species, on the other hand, would be general in the wrong kind of way: there are no scientific laws that apply to men *qua* men, or sheep *qua* sheep. A theory of this kind would be quite as heuristically sterile as the old theory of substantial forms – the only change would be a purely superficial one from occult forms to laws which would be equally occult because they could never be formulated.

The natural law theories of Hooker and Suárez were concerned above all with morality. Their application to the world of inanimate nature was problematic precisely because it was peripheral to the purposes of the main theory. There was, however, another less conspicuous intellectual tradition in which the terminology of laws had become established. Roger Bacon had used the word *lex* for rules of various kinds on quite a number of occasions in his treatment of optical problems in the *Opus Maius* and elsewhere, and in this he was followed by later writers on optics up to, and including, Kepler.[14] A similar pattern of usage can be found in writers on astronomy from Regiomontanus onwards. It has been suggested that the modern idea of a law of nature emerges directly from these traditions – indeed, that all the essential elements of the modern idea had been formulated before the middle of the sixteenth century.[15] Without seeking to deny the importance of either tradition, one might well doubt whether one of the main explanatory innovations of the scientific revolution was already completed and ready for use even before Copernicus had published *De Revolutionibus*. New methodological and explanatory concepts are never fully articulated in advance of their concrete applications.

The evidence available from the sixteenth-century writers shows that the word *lex* and its cognates were widely (though not particularly frequently) used in connexion with the natural world. It is one thing to recognise this, but quite another to suppose that a well-defined notion of a scientific law was already in existence. Most of the remarks made about laws were extremely vague, and there was not even an approximate consensus as to what kinds of laws there were. Moreover, the laws that were mentioned were given no clearly defined explanatory role. George Joachim Rheticus, for example, praised Copernicus for having discovered 'the laws of astronomy' (*leges astronomiae*),[16] but there are no laws as we understand them in *De Revolutionibus.* Copernicus certainly used the word *lex* on several occasions, but even quite an attentive reader might fail to notice this.[17] No one could overlook the laws of motion in Newton's *Principia.* The obvious explanation for this is that Newton's laws are part of the central explanatory core of the *Principia,* and the equivalent of this in *De Revolutionibus* is the Hipparchan geometrical apparatus of epicycles and eccentrics. *De Revolutionibus* could very easily be rewritten so as to exclude any mention of laws, and the basic content of Copernicus's theory would be quite unchanged. The *Principia* could not.

By the beginning of the seventeenth century the idea of nature being governed by laws had become widely acceptable. Francis Bacon quotes James I as saying that 'Kings ruled by their laws as God did by the laws of nature, and ought as rarely to use their supreme prerogative as God doth his power of working miracles.'[18] Such a remark would hardly have been made if any of James's audience had been likely to find it obscure; the occurrence of the same analogy a few years later in John Donne's *Essayes in Divinity*[19] suggests that it was on the way to becoming a commonplace. That neither James nor any of his hearers could have stated any of the laws by which God governed the world was quite immaterial to the point he was concerned to make.

It was, however, one thing for a notion to become part of the general currency of ordinary non-technical discourse, quite another for it to be given a precise rôle in scientific explanation. The fundamental reason why no clear well-defined notion of a law of nature had emerged by the end of the sixteenth century is that there was no room for any such idea within the inherited and still intellectually dominant systems of Aristotelian physics and epicyclic astronomy, whether geocentric or heliocentric. The terminology of laws of nature was available and was clearly metaphysically acceptable, as its wide diffusion bears witness: the old Greek antithesis of *nomos* and *phusis* was no longer effective, and the idea of a divine lawgiver had become well established. What was still lacking was a new kind of natural philosophy, which could serve as a satisfactory replacement for scholastic Aristotelianism.

The idea of discarding the natural philosophy of the schools and replacing it with a new kind of natural science, based on different principles and using a different method, was widely shared during the latter part of the sixteenth and the first part of the seventeenth centuries. That scholastic physics with its apparatus of substantial forms and real qualities had to be discredited and abandoned was hardly in dispute. It was about the positive character of the new science that disagreement arose.

II. BACON

In Francis Bacon's writings several conceptions of the law or laws of nature may be distinguished. In some places he referred to one single summary or positive law of nature, which is enacted by God for the whole of creation, and which may for ever lie beyond human comprehension.[20] In other places he referred to 'laws' in the plural, or to this or that particular law – as, for example, the law that matter cannot be separated from matter, [21] or that the total quantity of matter in the world is always the same.[22]

Both of these conceptions, of a single law of nature and of a plurality of particular laws, can be found in earlier writers, but some other things which Bacon said have no obvious parallel, either among his predecessors, contemporaries, or successors. The *Novum Organum* (1620), for example, makes reference to 'fundamental and universal laws which constitute forms' [*leges fundamentales et communes, quae constituunt formas*] and 'the form or law which governs heat, redness and death'.[23] It is difficult to think of any close parallel to this kind of language. Bacon's general remarks about the law or laws of nature are broadly traditional and would have been recognised as such by his contemporaries; his apparent identification of laws and forms has continued to puzzle successive generations of readers.[24]

From some of Bacon's remarks it might appear that forms and laws are the same, and that Bacon retained the old term simply because it was more familiar:

For when I speak of forms, I mean nothing other than those laws and determinations of pure act [*actus puri*] which govern and constitute any simple nature, such as heat, light, or weight, in every kind of matter and subject that is susceptible of them. Therefore the form of heat or the form of light is the same thing as the law of heat or the law of light.[25]

In other words, where Bacon wrote 'form', read 'law'. If, however, we make this substitution, there are many other passages which are transformed from something obscure to something simply unintelligible, such as *Novum Organum* II 24: 'For since every body contains in itself many forms of natures united together in a concrete state, the result is that they severally crush, depress, break, and enthrall one another, and thus the individual forms are obscured.' If we replace 'form' by 'law', the whole passage instantly becomes nonsensical. Such a consequence is quite unavoidable: whatever its specific content, if a law is conceived as a rule which agents must (literally or metaphorically) obey, then explanations in terms of laws cannot but have a quite different structure from explanations in terms of forms.

Despite much effort, no one has ever succeeded in subsuming everything that Bacon said about laws and forms into a single coherent account, and one may reasonably suspect that the enterprise is impossible. Instead historians should try to understand why it is that his theory is so radically incoherent. One explanation is that Bacon's natural philosophy is a system in transition. The old theory of substantial forms had been at least officially abandoned; the intention was to replace it by a theory of natural laws, but the precise character of the explanations involved remained obscure even to Bacon himself. The outcome was an incoherent blend of a decried but only partially abandoned theory, with its dimly foreseen and imperfectly sketched replacement.

The *Novum Organum* was widely read, both in England and abroad, but Bacon's views on laws and forms were too confused to influence anybody. If the idea of a law of nature was to do any real work, it had to be given a much more definite character and a specific explanatory rôle. It was that other reformer of the sciences, René Descartes, who made the decisive innovation, by formulating and bequeathing to his successors the vision of a science of moving bodies in which laws of nature, conceived quite specifically as laws of motion, were the most fundamental principles of explanation. It is his rôle in bringing the idea of a law of nature from the margin of natural philosophy to its centre that makes Descartes the most important single figure in the entire history of that idea.

III. DESCARTES, HUYGENS, AND LEIBNIZ

The earliest general account of Descartes's physics can be found in *Le Monde,* a work he completed in 1633 and then suppressed after receiving news of Galileo's condemnation; it remained unpublished until 1664. Descartes's aim was to replace the old Aristotelian physics by a completely new system. In order to expound this in the most effective way, he made use of a remarkable device: instead of attempting to explain the workings of our world, he would describe the construction of an entirely new world, brought into being by God somewhere in the extramundane space, far away from our own world. The point of this manoeuvre is, as the last chapter of *Le Monde* makes clear, that the new world should appear to its hypothetical inhabitants exactly like the old world that we ourselves inhabit; the ultimate implication, never stated but quite unmistakable, is that the laws which govern the new world are the same as those which govern our own.

The great recommendation of this approach for Descartes was that (like the method of doubt) it enabled him to make, as he hoped, a completely fresh start. In the *Meditationes,* our knowledge of the external world is assembled anew from the immediate data of consciousness; in *Le Monde,* we see, from the viewpoint of the Creator, another new world being constructed as diverse motions are imposed on the parts of a uniform, homogeneous matter. In this respect, Descartes's approach was utterly different from that previously chosen by Galileo. Galileo, following Archimedes, had taken as his starting point the world that we find ourselves living in, one already characterised by phenomena such as weight, and had set out to provide a mathematical description of motions we observe, or rather of the idealised counterparts to which they are a close approximation. Descartes, on the other hand, began with God and God's action in creating the world and maintaining it in existence. The most fundamental physical principles are the rules governing the local motion of every portion of matter. It is because these rules are directly imposed by God that it is appropriate to describe them as laws of nature.

In Chapter 7 of *Le Monde* Descartes sets out three fundamental laws:

1. Each individual part of matter always continues to exist in the same state until another body compels it to change.
2. When one body pushes another, it cannot give the other any motion which does not at the same time lose from itself, nor can it take away any motion from the other body without its own being increased by the same amount.
3. When a body moves, even when its motion takes place most of the time along a curved line . . . each of its individual parts nevertheless tends always to continue its motion along a straight line.

All three laws are ostensibly grounded on the same metaphysical principle: that God is immutable and simple in His operations, and that this must consequently be true also of the action by which He maintains the world in existence. Taken literally, the most natural deduction from this principle might seem to be that the universe is itself an unchanging Parmenidean whole. This was obviously unacceptable, and Descartes's view was that God's immutability manifests itself in the way He conserves the same quantity of motion in existence. This conservation law and the law of inertia were to be the two cardinal principles of Cartesian mechanics.

It was in the *Principia Philosophiae* (1644) that Descartes first made public the physical theory of *Le Monde,* in a somewhat altered and much augmented form. The three laws of nature appear in a different order but otherwise substantially unchanged, except in one respect. The new third law, formerly the second, now states that 'a body, on coming in contact with a stronger one loses none of its motion; but on coming into contact with a weaker one, it loses as much as it transfers to the weaker body.'[26] The stronger body is not necessarily the larger one: it is the one which has more force, understood as the product of the magnitude of the body and its speed.

One major difference between *Le Monde* and the *Principia Philosophiae* is that in the latter Descartes included, perhaps as an afterthought,[27] a set of rules for determining the motion of colliding bodies. These rules (so described because they are derivative rather than fundamental principles) are needed because in Cartesian physics the only way in which one body can act on another is by impact: if we can work out a set of rules which enable us to calculate the motions of bodies after impact from their motions before, then we understand the basic interaction which determines all the changes which take place in the material world.

The basic principle underlying all Descartes's collision rules is that the quantity of motion is the same before and after the collision. All the rules conform with this requirement. It is however by itself insufficient to determine fully the motions of the bodies after collision. If we consider the only case which Descartes attempted to treat in a quantitative manner – two bodies impacting directly, so that all motions take place along one straight line – we have the equation

$$Au_A + Bu_B = Av_A + Bv_B$$

where A and B are the magnitudes of the two bodies, u_A and u_B their speeds before impact, and v_A and v_B their speeds afterwards. We have therefore one equation with two unknowns (v_A and v_B).

For later writers like Leibniz, the solution was to look for an equally general second equation linking v_A and v_B with other known quantities. Descartes did not attempt to do this. Instead, he made use of the third law with its distinction between weaker and stronger bodies to divide the general problem into a series of special cases which were then individually solved. The set of rules which resulted were not formally inconsistent – their domains of application were carefully distinguished – but they could hardly be described as forming a coherent system.

It quickly became apparent that Descartes's collision rules were exceedingly vulnerable to criticism, both theoretical and empirical. Descartes was certainly aware of the latter difficulty and attempted to block it by pointing out that the rules apply only to pairs of bodies wholly isolated from their surroundings. Since according to Descartes's own principles no such isolated bodies can ever exist in nature, any apparent experimental falsifications of the collision rules are irrelevant.[28]

The isolated bodies whose motions are described by Descartes's collision rules are therefore theoretical abstractions, incapable of separate existence, but useful as a theoretical tool for explaining the behaviour of the more complex systems which actually do exist. Descartes did at least provide a qualitative sketch of how such bodies would move, but he understandably made no attempt to derive any quantitative results. The result of this was that the collision rules were effectively immune from any kind of empirical test, either direct or indirect. Unsurprisingly, therefore, few of Descartes's successors outside the ranks of the most committed Cartesians were inclined to follow him on this issue. Mathematicians such as Huygens, Brouncker, and Wren applied the collision rules directly to macroscopic bodies and were quite ready to compare Descartes's prediction with results gained from experiment.

One of the first and arguably the most profound of all Descartes's critics was Christiaan Huygens. As early as 1652, Huygens had come to the conclusion that most of Descartes's collision rules were false, and during the course of the next four years he worked out a detailed and rigorously organised theory to replace them. The full work, *De motu corporum ex percussione*,[29] remained unpublished until 1703, but Huygens communicated some of his results to other mathematicians, notably to Brouncker and Wren during a visit to London in 1661, and a list of theorems without proofs were published in 1669 in both the *Philosophical Transactions* of the Royal Society and the *Journal des sçavans.*[30]

The merits of *De motu corporum* are undeniable; if nothing else had survived from Huygens's pen, it alone would establish him as one of the greatest mathematical physicists of the seventeenth century. It raised the discussion to an entirely new level: by its side Descartes's *Principia* appears arbitrary and incoherent, a mere *roman de la nature,* as Huygens himself disdainfully described it.[31] Huygens's treatise does have some limitations, however, and paradoxically these arise from the same source as many of its chief virtues: its rigour. A full axiomatic treatment of a subject can serve to expose its basic intellectual structure with peculiar clarity, but in other circumstances it can conceal it from any but the most careful reader. Huygens never stopped to explain or justify his choice of terminology, but it can hardly be without significance that whereas he was quite prepared to use the terminology of laws of nature elsewhere,[32] he made no use of it in the formal apparatus of *De motu corporum*. The premises from which he deduced the eleven theorems that made up this work are described neither as laws nor as axioms, but more neutrally as hypotheses.[33] Only two look really fundamental – the law of inertia and the principle of relativity, which states that the outcome of any collision depends only on the velocities of the bodies relative to one another; the others have the appearance of possible theorems waiting to be proved from still more fundamental axioms. It is significant that although Huygens showed that two quantities (*vis viva* and linear momentum) are conserved, he seems to have regarded neither result as being in any way fundamental. For Descartes, Malebranche, and Leibniz, conservation laws were peculiarly important because they are a manifestation of the constancy of God's action in governing the world and maintaining it in being. Their disagreements were about which quantities were conserved, and not whether such laws are fundamental. Huygens, more sceptical about theology and less inclined to metaphysics, preferred to treat conservation rules as theorems, derived from simpler though less metaphysically suggestive premises.

As far as results are concerned, Huygens established the main elements of the theory of colliding bodies as it is accepted today; all that remained was to extend it to oblique collisions of all kinds. Unfortunately, his work was less immediately influential than it could have been. In part this was because he failed to publish a full-scale treatise on the subject. A mere list of theorems derived by unspecified means from unstated axioms was no substitute. There was nothing evidently self-authenticating about Huygens's theorems, and many investigators who were determined to replace Descartes's rules by something better paid them little attention.

One thinker who did study Huygens's work carefully was Leibniz, though he did not start by doing so. His first work on the discipline that he was himself to name 'dynamics' was the *Hypothesis physica nova* of 1671, a rather unpromising work written under the influence of Hobbes's *De corpore*.[34] It was not until he came to Paris in 1672 and met Huygens that the significance of the latter's work became apparent to him. Thereafter, Leibniz's work on dynamics can best be understood as an attempt to develop and extend Huygenian dynamics, and to place it on proper (that is Leibnizian) metaphysical foundations.

Leibniz commenced his onslaught on the still dominant Cartesian school with a short paper in the *Acta eruditorum* for March 1686, entitled *Brevis demonstratio memorabilis erroris Cartesii*. His argument was that Descartes had been correct in supposing that the total quantity of motive force in the world must be conserved, but mistaken in identifying this with the quantity of motion: the true measure of force is not mv but mv^2, the quantity he was later to call *vis viva*. Huygens had already shown that this was conserved in straight-line collisions, but he seems to have attached little importance to the result. Leibniz saw the conservation of *vis viva* as one of the fundamental laws of nature, derivable directly from the metaphysical axiom that an effect is equal in force to its cause. It was because it was a conservation principle that it merited the status of a law.

For the remainder of his life, Leibniz attached particular importance to the law of conservation of *vis viva,* but he was well aware that it could never be the sole foundation for a science of dynamics. Descartes's dynamics had been founded on a single conservation law, and as a result he had been forced to account for the motions of colliding bodies by using a large number of mutually incoherent rules, each applicable only to a specific range of situations. Leibniz believed firmly in the continuity of nature and saw that this required the use of equations of unrestricted generality. He was well aware that the law of conservation of *vis viva* was by itself insufficient to determine the motions of colliding bodies. As early as 1687 he introduced a second principle: conservation of the quantity of motion in a particular direction. Later still, in the *Essai de dynamique,*[35] he was to set out three conservation principles governing the collision of elastic bodies: the linear equation, which states the conservation of relative velocity; the plane equation, which states the conservation of progress or directed quantity of motion (linear momentum); and the solid equation, which states the conservation of *vis viva.* As Leibniz remarked, these equations are not independent, in that from any two the third may be derived. They are nevertheless by no means of equal status: in Leibniz's view, neither relative velocity nor progress has the absolute character possessed by *vis viva.* Relative velocities are by definition relative, and the magnitude we ascribe to the progress of any body is affected by the orientation we choose for the axes of co-ordinates.

IV. NEWTON

Leibniz differed from Huygens in seeing conservation laws as being peculiarly important, but both men regarded impact as the fundamental mode of physical interaction. Newton disagreed with Leibniz on both issues. He was not, of course, completely uninterested in the mechanics of colliding bodies. His investigations appear in several of his early manuscripts, notably the Waste Book of c.1665 and the paper on 'The Lawes of Motion', probably written before 1669.[36] A general formula for determining the motions of colliding bodies appears among Newton's lectures on algebra for 1675.[37] In the *Principia* (1687), however, he dealt with the whole subject quite briefly in the corollaries to the laws of motion. This placing is significant: the real centre of Newtonian mechanics lay elsewhere.

Newton paid relatively little attention to the theory of collisions because he was preoccupied with a different set of problems, most notably those of bodies moving with continuously changing velocities along curvilinear paths. These were the problems that would have to be solved if any genuinely mathematical science of celestial mechanics were to be established. The Cartesians and their successors had made no attempt to discuss them in anything other than a purely qualitative way. What mattered to them was that an intelligible mechanism should be specifiable, and about this they had no doubts: the curved orbits of celestial bodies were to be explained by the combined impact on the moving body of countless imperceptible corpuscles. By the time he came to start writing the *Principia,* Newton was much less confident about this, but in any case the question seemed to him of remote importance. The task of mechanics, as he saw it, was to establish laws of motion describing the effects of forces on the motions of bodies, to deduce from the motions of bodies in particular situations the mathematical laws governing the forces acting on these bodies, and on the basis of those laws to predict what the motions of bodies would be in other circumstances. Problems about how exactly the forces acted could be settled later.

Newton's mechanics differs, therefore, from the systems developed by Huygens, Leibniz, and others working in the Cartesian tradition in that it contains laws of two quite different types: laws of force, which describe the forces acting between bodies; and laws of motion, which describe the motions which the forces bring about.[38] Newton's use of the latter term is too familiar to require documentation. He saw the laws of motion as the foundation of his whole system and indicated their importance by setting them out at the beginning of the *Principia* as Axioms or Laws of Motion.[39]

There are on the other hand no laws of force included among Newton's axioms. This was not because Newton rejected the word 'law' in this connexion. The only law of force for which he was able to give a mathematical description was the inverse-square law of gravitation, and it was essential to the whole strategy of the *Principia* that this should be deduced as a theorem, and not listed as an assumption. As both the *Principia* and Newton's other writings show, he was quite ready both to talk in general terms about 'the law of gravity'[40] and to prove specific theorems about the dynamical consequences of laws describing different kinds of centripetal forces.[41]

V. CONCLUDING REMARKS

By the close of the seventeenth century, the idea that the main objective of natural philosophy lay in the discovery of the laws of nature had triumphed. There was as yet no general agreement as to the correct formulation of those laws, but a consensus had been reached in several areas, and there was every reason to suppose that this trend would continue. This was not something that could be said of the metaphysical and epistemological problems generated by the new explanatory paradigm.

Among these philosophical problems three (all closely related) seem of particular importance:

1. In what way, if any, should the laws of nature be regarded as necessary?
2. What part does God play in ordaining laws and governing the world?
3. Is it possible for the laws of nature to be discovered otherwise than through observation and experiment?

1. In the *Theodicy* (1710), Leibniz, looking back on the debate of the preceding three-quarters of a century, saw three distinct positions as exhausting the choice available to philosophers concerned about the necessity or contingency of the laws of nature. The first, held quite unambiguously by Spinoza, was that the laws are absolutely necessary, their necessity being of exactly the same kind as that possessed by the axioms and theorems of geometry. The second view, attributed explicitly to Bayle, is that the laws of nature are wholly arbitrary and depend simply on God's free choice.[42] The third view, held by Leibniz himself, is that the laws of nature are logically contingent but morally necessary. God's will is determined by His own goodness to create only the best of all the possible worlds which present themselves to His intellect.

Leibniz was extremely proud of his own theory: in his eyes its great merit was that it provided the only middle way between the unattractive extremes of Spinozan necessitarianism and the kind of voluntarism that represented God as a purely arbitrary agent. It is, however, far from clear that Leibniz's critics really supposed God to be arbitrary in this way. Certainly his most tenacious opponents on this point – the English Newtonians – never held the view that God's choice was wholly unmotivated by moral considerations of any kind. Any such view would immediately and fatally undermine that favourite recourse of eighteenth-century theology, the Argument from Design. God's wisdom and goodness could hardly be manifested by a world arbitrarily chosen, even if it were to happen by chance that the world thus selected should appear to invite such an interpretation. In his exchange of letters with Leibniz (1715–16), Samuel Clarke, the spokesman of the English Newtonians, was concerned to assert only that God might in some cases be confronted with two equally good alternatives and could then arbitrarily choose either; there is no suggestion that God might deliberately prefer a worse possibility to a better, or be indifferent as to which He should choose.[43]

It is worth noting that Leibniz, rightly, did not ascribe the view that the laws of nature are purely arbitrary to Descartes, even though it would have been easy to do this. Descartes had held such strongly voluntaristic views about God's ability to alter the truth or falsity of propositions in both mathematics and ethics that it might seem natural to suppose that he would also have held the view that God could ordain any laws of nature, without restriction.[44] After all, voluntarism with respect to physical laws became far more common during the seventeenth century than either of the other two varieties; indeed, in England it acquired something of the status of an orthodoxy.[45] One can, however, understand why Descartes avoided this apparently tempting line of thought. If God could choose any laws whatever, then there would seem to be no way in which anyone could work out by metaphysical reasoning what the laws of nature must be. Physics would have to be a purely *a posteriori,* experimental enquiry, within which the kind of *a priori* arguments deployed in Part II of the *Principia Philosophiae* would have no place. Some kind of quasi-Cartesian philosophy on these lines can easily be imagined, but it would never have had much appeal for Descartes himself. He had been forced to use hypothetico-deductive arguments for the details of his physics, but these had at least been employed within a system whose basic principles had been established by *a priori* proofs. It is difficult to see how a purely hypothetical physics could ever possess the kind of certainty that always remained one of Descartes's chief desiderata.[46]

Descartes chose to ground his derivation of the laws of nature on the intrinsic character of the one being not subject to God's arbitrary power, namely, God Himself. In this respect, his position is very similar to that later adopted by Spinoza, as Spinoza's derivation of the Cartesian laws of motion in his geometrical reconstruction of the *Principia Philosophiae* makes quite clear. None of Spinoza's axioms has any appearance of being in any way the subject of divine choice, and all of them appear at least Cartesian in spirit.[47] Descartes and Spinoza did, of course, have very different conceptions of the being they both referred to as God, but Spinoza could with some plausibility have argued that nothing of Descartes's voluntaristic (and, in his view, anthropomorphic) conception is contained in the metaphysical axioms from which the laws of motion are actually derived.

The universal necessitarianism implied by Spinoza's own view that things could not have been produced by God in any other manner or order than that in which they were produced[48] found few adherents. It must have seemed to many, as it did to Newton, that such a conclusion can hardly be reconciled with the immense variety of things evident in the world.[49] A more restricted kind of necessitarianism could, however, avoid such objections. If the laws of motion alone are necessary, then it would seem that God still has a choice between an infinity of possible worlds, each corresponding to a different set of initial conditions. Descartes notoriously denied this and held that a world exactly similar to ours would eventually come into existence, whatever the original distribution of matter might have been.[50] This was one of the parts of Descartes's philosophy that caused greatest scandal: if such a view were true, then the order of the world could hardly be regarded as a manifestation of divine wisdom and providence. Malebranche maintained, on the contrary, that such complex structures as the bodies of animals and plants could only reproduce themselves for generation after generation because each organism contained within itself (in smaller and smaller size) the embryonic forms of all its progeny. This kind of mechanistic preformationism clearly required that at the creation God should have created matter in structures of quite stupefying complexity and endowed every minute portion of matter with such a motion that no further particular divine interventions would be required.[51]

The view that there are an indefinitely large number of possible worlds, each characterised by a particular set of initial conditions, is clearly compatible with a necessitarian conception of the laws of motion, though it in no way requires it. A restricted necessitarianism of this kind had a wider appeal than the universal necessitarianism of Spinoza. Malebranche himself came to doubt whether the laws of motion were in any way necessary, but despite the criticisms of both Leibniz and the Newtonians, various forms of necessitarianism flourished in the eighteenth century; notable advocates included Johann Bernoulli, D'Alembert, and (in his early writings) Kant.[52] There is, however, one major difference between this kind of necessitarianism and the Cartesian or Spinozan kinds. In the earlier theories the necessity of the laws was ultimately theological, being founded on divine immutability; in the later theories it was geometrical. Descartes's voluntaristic philosophy of mathematics would have undermined this latter kind of necessitarianism, inherently more congenial to the more anti-metaphysical scientists of the Enlightenment, but it can legitimately be seen as one part of the Cartesian inheritance.

2. On the question of the relationship between God and the world, there again appear to be three broadly distinct views. What was undoubtedly the most widely held view was that God, having once created the world, has subsequently left it to run by itself, except for more or less frequent direct interventions in the form of miracles. Spinoza, who described and excoriated this way of thinking in Chapter 6 of the *Tractatus Theologico-Politicus,* saw it as the common position of the philosophically unenlightened masses; perhaps for this reason it is difficult, despite its indisputable popularity, to find an exposition of it of any degree of philosophical sophistication.

In opposition to what, following Spinoza, might be called the vulgar view, there are two positions. One is that God acts continuously to maintain the world in existence and regulate the changes which occur within it. This was the normal view among theologians; it follows directly from the standard scholastic principle that creation and conservation are ultimately the same.[53] The other position, submerged rather than absent in the seventeenth century, is the deistic view that God, though initially responsible for bringing the world into being, has since then left it entirely alone, without miraculous intervention of any kind.

The second and third of these views are apparently utterly opposed to each other, but in practice it can on occasion be quite difficult to determine where someone's ultimate allegiances really lie. Descartes, for example, ostensibly held the second view, but as critics such as Pascal saw, it was all too easy to eliminate God altogether from His mechanistic cosmogony.[54] The formal metaphysics of Spinoza's position resembles that of the scholastics, but its consequences are those of the Enlightenment deists. On the one hand, God is the cause of both the existence and essence of every finite thing and determines how it comes into existence; on the other, nothing exists outside nature, either to intervene or to maintain it in existence.[55]

The differences between the three views are made particularly clear if we consider the question of miracles. The implications of the first view are straightforward enough: miracles occur whenever God intervenes in the processes of nature so as to produce states of affairs that would not otherwise have occurred, and which in some cases could never come about by natural means alone. The problem with this criterion for those who held the second or the third view is that it would appear to make either everything miraculous or else nothing. Spinoza was prepared to accept the latter conclusion (in substance, though not verbally), but few of his contemporaries were prepared to follow him.[56] For those who wished to retain some place for the supernatural, a re-examination of the concept of a miracle was clearly necessary.

The older conception of a miracle, established by the scholastics and maintained in the seventeenth century by Leibniz, was that God performs a miracle by endowing an agent with powers that do not follow from its nature, or of removing from it capacities that do so follow.[57] Such an analysis clearly embodied a broadly Aristotelian theory of substances and their natures and was objectionable to several seventeenth-century philosophers on precisely that account. For Malebranche, the natures presupposed by this theory simply do not exist:[58] everything is produced by the direct action of God. This does not mean that any distinction between the miraculous and the non-miraculous disappears. The difference lies in the manner of God's action. Natural events are those which are produced when God acts in accordance with general volitions or laws; supernatural events are those produced by particular volitions.[59]

The difference between these two conceptions of the miraculous became one of the central issues in the Leibniz–Clarke correspondence, as a result of Leibniz's claim that Newton's theory of gravity involved a perpetual miracle. Clarke's general views about God's relation to the world were very close to those of Malebranche.[60] God acts continuously on every part of matter either immediately or through the mediation of created intelligent beings. The difference between the miraculous and the non-miraculous is therefore essentially one of frequency.[61] If God were to start producing what we had hitherto thought of as miracles on a regular basis, then there would no longer be anything miraculous about them. The laws of nature are simply those rules, whatever their content, by which God usually acts.

For Leibniz, however, there has to be an 'internal real difference' between the miraculous and the natural.[62] 'We ought to make an infinite difference between the operation of God, which goes beyond the extent of natural powers; and the operations of things that follow the law which God has given them, and which he has enabled them to follow by their natural powers, though not without his assistance.'[63] This idea of each thing following a law prescribed to it by God can be found elsewhere in Leibniz's writings. In his last letter to Arnauld (23 March 1690), he maintained that bodies are not substances properly speaking, but aggregates of substances, and each of the true substances is an indivisible entity which contains in its nature 'the law of the continuation of the series of its operations'. The doctrine of the pre-established harmony holds that 'every simple substance has perception, and that its individuality consists in the perpetual law [*loy*] that brings about the sequence of perceptions that are assigned to it.'[64] These internal laws (as Leibniz calls them) constitute the individuality of each particular substance.[65]

This individualised conception of law has in many ways more in common with the conception implicit in Hooker than with the Cartesian idea of a law of motion. Leibniz was of course quite ready to formulate laws of the Cartesian kind in his dynamics, but within his system the collisions of extended bodies in an infinite material plenum had only a secondary, phenomenal kind of reality. The ultimate entities were the unextended, non-interacting monads; explanations at this level could not be made in terms of Cartesian-type laws of motion. Leibniz could have confined explanations in terms of laws to the phenomenal world and used more traditional essentialist terminology for the monads; it is a sign of the intellectual dominance of the ideal of explanation by laws that he chose not to do so.

3. The methods required for the discovery of the laws of nature evidently depend on the views held about their necessity. If they are necessary in the way

that the theorems of geometry have usually been supposed to be, then presumably they also can be shown to be true by some kind of *a priori* proof. This in no way rules out any recourse to experiment; this might have a valuable heuristic rôle, just as it can in pure mathematics. Even Archimedes had freely used empirical methods to discover his theorems about centres of gravity before he constructed his proofs, but it was only the latter that generated knowledge as opposed to conjecture.

The epistemological implications of a theory like Leibniz's are less straightforward. The view that God has chosen the best of all the infinite number of possible worlds carries with it no requirement that we should ourselves be capable of calculating the total perfection either of our world or of any of the rejected alternatives; indeed, it might appear to be only a reasonable gesture of intellectual humility to admit we do not. On such a view the doctrine that we live in the best of all possible worlds might provide some ultimate metaphysical reassurance, but it would have no relevance for the practice of natural philosophy.

Leibniz was, however, quite unwilling to accept any line of thought that would detach physics from metaphysics. He made, of course, no attempt to give an example of one of God's calculations: one of his own doctrines was that all such calculations involve an infinite analysis that no finite mind could ever complete. He was nevertheless very reluctant to give up arguments from perfection in physics. The newly developed calculus of variations seemed to provide a technique for this, and in the *Tentamen Anagogicum* he attempted to show how the use of maximisation and minimisation principles in optics followed from the general principle of perfection. Just as any part of the curve of the quickest descent is itself the curve of quickest descent between its own end-points, so 'the smallest parts of the universe are ruled in accordance with the order of greatest perfection; otherwise the whole would not be so ruled.'[66] The analogy is problematic, and the conclusion is difficult to reconcile with one of the cardinal principles of Leibniz's theodicy, that the evident imperfections of one part of the universe are outweighed by greater perfections existing elsewhere.

If the laws governing the world depend on God's free choice, and if the reasons for this choice cannot be grasped by finite minds, then any attempt at an *a priori* derivation of the laws of nature has to be abandoned. The only path to knowledge lies through empirical investigation. This was a conclusion eagerly proclaimed by empirically minded thinkers in England; it was also accepted, rather more wearily, by a disappointed rationalist. Malebranche, looking back in old age on a series of unsuccessful attempts to deduce the laws of nature from metaphysical principles, was forced to admit the decisive rôle of experience:

It is certain that in this case one cannot discover the truth except by experience. For since we can neither grasp the designs of the creator nor understand all the relations which he has to his attributes, whether to conserve or not to conserve a constant absolute quantity of movement seems to depend on a purely arbitrary decision by God, about which we cannot become certain except by a species of revelation, such as is given by experience.[67]

Malebranche was careful not to say that God's decision really is arbitrary, merely that to us it unavoidably appears so, but the outcome was the same. For such intellects as ours, experience must be the ultimate arbiter.

With the advantage of hindsight it becomes possible to see why nothing closely resembling the modern post-Cartesian idea of a law of nature emerged in the ancient world. Despite the immense variety of theories worked out during more than a millennium of philosophical speculation, no one arrived at a position at all similar to the characteristic seventeenth-century blend of a voluntarist theology and a mechanistic, corpuscularian physics. Indeed, those philosophers who came closest to the later ideas in one area were furthest removed in the other. The Demiurge of Plato's *Timaeus* is perhaps the nearest approach in Greek philosophy to the omnipotent creator of Christian theology, but Plato detested the mechanistic atomism of Democritus. Conversely, one of the cardinal principles of Epicureanism was the absence not merely of a creator, but of any kind of divine government of, or even interest in, the workings of our world.

By the end of the sixteenth century the idea of God ordaining laws of nature had become sufficiently familiar to require no special explanation or defence. It remained, however, very general and unspecific and was therefore of little scientific use. It was Descartes who more than anyone else created the modern idea of a law of nature, by conceiving the laws of nature specifically as laws of motion,[68] and by making these laws the ultimate explanatory principles of his physics. The actual laws proposed by Descartes proved unsatisfactory, though the general principle of inertia embodied in his first two laws has become the cornerstone of all subsequent dynamics. By contrast, the forms of explanation which he introduced are with us still.

NOTES

1 There is no satisfactory general history of the idea of a law of nature. For a variety of different approaches, see Zilsel 1942; Needham 1951; Oakley 1961; Milton 1981a; Ruby 1986.
2 Grant 1952; Koester 1968.
3 Aristotle, *De caelo,* 268a14; Plato, *Gorgias,* 483E.

4 See *Summa th.* II.I q90–4.

5 See Chapters 35 and 36.

6 See Thomas Aquinas, *Summa th.* II.I q91 a2 ad3, a6; Suárez, *De legibus* I.i.2.

7 'Quando ponebat pluviis legem', Job xxviii.26, Vulgate; 'certa lege et gyro vallabat abyssos', Prov. viii.27; 'legem ponebat aquis, ne transirent fines suos', Prov. viii.29.

8 Hooker, *Laws of Ecclesiastical Polity,* I.ii.1.

9 Hooker, *Laws of Ecclesiastical Polity,* I.iii.4.

10 Hooker, *Laws of Ecclesiastical Polity,* I.iii.5.

11 'Quidni enim ex decreto naturali immota quaedam legis suae principia tum in Astris, tum in cordibus hominum descripserit summus Deus.' Herbert of Cherbury 1663, p. 49, quoted by Walker 1972, p. 180.

12 Dewhurst 1966, pp. 146, 154, 157. Cf. Locke 1954, p. 109.

13 Burke 1989, p. 147.

14 Ruby 1986, pp. 343–52.

15 'By 1540, then, except for the association of scientific laws with the names of their discoverers which, to my knowledge, occurs first with Ramus in 1567, all the familiar modern scientific uses of "law" were in place.' Ruby 1986, p. 357.

16 Ruby 1986, p. 357.

17 See, e.g., *De revolutionibus,* IV.1; V.22, 25; VI.proem.,1.

18 Bacon 1857–74, vol. 3, p. 429.

19 '*Nature* is the *common-law* by which God governs us, and *Miracle* is his *Prerogative.*' Donne 1952, p. 81.

20 Bacon 1857–74, vol. 3, pp. 220, 265, vol.5, p. 463.

21 Bacon 1857–74, vol.5, p. 496.

22 Bacon, *Nov. org.* II 4.

23 Bacon, *Nov. org.* II 5, II 17.

24 See Pérez-Ramos 1988, chaps. 6–11.

25 Bacon, *Nov. org.* II 17.

26 *Princ.* II 40.

27 Gabbey 1980a, p. 262.

28 See *Princ.* II 53.

29 Huygens 1888–1950, vol. 16, pp. 30–91.

30 Huygens 1888–1950, vol. 16, pp. 172, 179–81.

31 Huygens 1888–1950, vol. 10, p. 403. Huygens is echoing here Descartes's own advice concerning how to read his *Principia*; cf. AT IXB 11–12.

32 E.g., Huygens 1888–1950, vol. 16, pp. 33, 181, 202–4.

33 Huygens used the same terminology in his other main work on mechanics, *De Horologium Oscillatorium* (1673), Huygens 1888–1950, vol. 18, p. 125.

34 Hobbes himself made no use of any notion of a law in his mechanics. In his view, the theorems of such a science should be deduced solely from definitions. Hobbes, *Eng. Works,* vol. 1, pp. xi, 81–2, 206–12.

35 Ger. Math. VI 227.

36 Herivel 1965, pp. 133–5, 168–79, 211–15.

37 Newton 1967–81, vol.5, pp. 148–50.

38 Strictly speaking, the third law is a general constraint on the forms of possible laws of force rather than a law of motion. One of its main functions was to allow the first two laws to be used in situations such as impact where no mathematical description of the law of force was available.

39 The successive changes in Newton's categorisation of his fundamental principles during

the period he was writing the *Principia* can be found in Newton 1967–81, vol. 6, pp. 2, 76, 96–8, 192–3; cf. Cohen 1971, pp. 62–6.

40 In the draft preface to the *Principia,* Newton referred to 'leges et mensuras gravitatis et aliarum virium', Newton 1962, p. 305. Cf. *Principia,* I, props. lxi, lxvii, lxviii; III, props. iv, v.

41 *Principia,* I, props. vii–xiii, xxxix, xlii; II, prop. xviii.

42 *Théod.,* pt. I, secs. 340, 344.

43 Clarke to Leibniz, Third Letter, secs. 7, 8.

44 On Descartes's voluntarism, see Chapter 12.

45 Boyle 1772, vol. 4, p. 161; vol. 5, pp. 139–40, 414. Locke, *Ess.* IV.iii.29.

46 For a discussion of hypotheses and probabilistic reasoning in Descartes and other seventeenth-century natural philosophers, see Chapters 7 and 31.

47 See Geb. I 183–5.

48 See *Eth.* I prop. 33.

49 *Principia,* General Scholium, Newton 1972, vol. 2, p. 763 (Newton 1934, p. 546).

50 *Princ.* III 47.

51 Malebranche's preformationist embryological theories are most fully described in *Ent. mét.,* x–xi.

52 Tonelli 1959; Hankins 1967.

53 'Conservatio rerum a Deo non est per aliquam novam actionem sed per continuationem actionis qua dat esse.' *Summa th.* I q104 a1 ad4.

54 *Pens.,* 1001.

55 *Eth.* I props. 14, 24–5.

56 *Tract. th.-pol.* vi.

57 *Summa th.* II.I q113 a10. McRae 1985, Rutherford 1993.

58 Malebranche, *OC* III 90, 145, 222–4 (Malebranche 1980a, pp. 589–90, 622–3, 667–8).

59 *Ent. mét.,* viii.3, xi.9.

60 Clarke 1738, vol. 2, p. 697.

61 Clarke to Leibniz, Fourth Letter, sec. 43; Fifth Letter, secs. 107–9.

62 Leibniz to Clarke, Fifth Letter, sec. 110.

63 Leibniz to Clarke, Fifth Letter, sec. 112.

64 *Théod.,* pt. I, sec. 291.

65 Ger. IV 518, 507 (Leibniz 1969, pp. 493, 500).

66 Ger. VII 272–3 (Leibniz 1969, p. 478).

67 Mal. OC XVII-1 55.

68 The term 'law of motion' is associated above all with Newton, but it can be found in many earlier writers, e.g., Charleton 1654, p. 271; More 1662c, pp. 36, 46; Oldenburg 1965–86, vol. 5, pp. 103, 117, 125, 167, 193, 358, 554, 556.

22

THE MATHEMATICAL REALM OF NATURE

MICHAEL MAHONEY

I. MATHEMATICS, MECHANICS, AND METAPHYSICS

At the beginning of what we now call the scientific revolution, Nicholas Copernicus (1473–1543) displayed on the title page of *De revolutionibus* (1543) Plato's ban against the mathematically incompetent: 'Let no one enter who is ignorant of geometry.' He repeated the notice in the preface, cautioning that 'mathematics is written for mathematicians.' Although Isaac Newton posted no such warning at the front of the *Principia* a century and a half later, he did insist repeatedly that the first two books of the work treated motion in purely mathematical terms, without physical, metaphysical, or ontological commitment.[1] Only in the third book did he expressly draw the links between the mathematical and physical realms. There he posited a universal force of gravity for which he could offer no physical explanation but which, as a mathematical construct, was the linchpin of his system of the world. 'It is enough', he insisted in the *General Scholium* added in 1710, 'that [gravity] in fact exists.' No less than the *De revolutionibus*, the *Principia* was written by a mathematician for mathematicians.

Behind that common feature of the two works lies perhaps the foremost change wrought on natural philosophy by the scientific revolution.[2] For although astronomy had always been deemed a mathematical science, few in the early sixteenth century would have envisioned a reduction of physics – that is, of nature as motion and change – to mathematics. Fewer still would have imagined the analysis of machines as the medium of reduction, and perhaps none would have accorded ontological force to mathematical structure. Yet, by 1670 John Wallis treated mechanics and the science of motion as synonymous, positing at the start of his *Mechanica, sive de motu* that 'we understand [mechanics] as the part of geometry that treats of motion and inquires by geometrical arguments and apodictically by what force any motion is carried out.' Newton echoed the definition in the preface to his *Principia,* concluding that 'rational mechanics will be the accurately proposed and demonstrated science of the motions that result from any forces and of the forces that are required for any motions.'[3] As his account of gravity shows, the mathematisation of nature and the mechanisation of nature ultimately went hand in hand, each supporting the other in its claim to provide a truly intelligible account of the physical world.

Converging in the concepts and techniques of infinitesimal analysis, rational mechanics became a branch of mathematics, and mathematics opened itself to mechanical ideas. The convergence occurred by an indirect route. The symbolic algebra and the theory of equations from which infinitesimal analysis took inspiration and form were aimed initially at abstracting mathematics from the concrete world and had the effect of freeing it to create imaginary and counterfactual structures irrespective of their real or even possible instantiation. The new analysis pointed mathematics away from physical ontology by shifting attention from objects and their properties to the structure of combinatorial relations among objects, some of which existed only by virtue of the relations, namely as ideal objects needed to complete the structure. Yet, at the same time, mathematics increasingly turned to the physical world for its problems and for guidance in solving them. Almost paradoxically, mathematics enhanced its explanatory power over nature by moving conceptually beyond the intuitive limits of the physical world.

The changing language of mechanics reflected the shift in mathematical thinking. In 1623 Galileo proclaimed that 'philosophy is written in this most grand book . . . (I am speaking of the universe) [which] is written in the language of mathematics, and its characters are triangles, circles, and other geometrical figures.'[4] In the 1660s and 1670s Huygens and Newton maintained Galileo's focus on those shapes, while treating them in the new analytical style. But the universal mechanics of Newton's *Principia* had its full effect only after mathematicians on the continent, beginning with Pierre Varignon, recast its geometrical style into the symbolic algebra of Gottfried Wilhelm Leibniz's calculus. As Bernard de Fontenelle insisted in retrospect, 'It was by the geometry of infinitesimals that M. Varignon reduced varying motions to the same rule as uniform [motions], and it does not seem that he could have succeeded by any other method.'[5]

In particular, the new calculus (whether Newtonian or Leibnizian) enabled philosophers to comprehend nature in terms that lay beyond the resources of traditional mathematics. While Galileo spoke of triangles and circles, Willebrord Snel and René Descartes determined that the refractive properties of lenses lie in ratios of sines. Galileo could express his law of falling bodies in the simple terms of a ratio of squares, but the pendulum he used to determine that law lay beyond the reach of traditional geometry. Christiaan Huygens found that even its approximate, tautochronic behaviour, and that of a growing family of simple harmonic oscillators shown to be at work in the world, required the resources of trigonometic relations embodied in the cycloid, itself defined in terms of the arc-length of a circle. The measure of angular position dictated by Johann Kepler's first two laws could not be expressed in finite algebraic form.[6] The world of mathematical mechanics at the turn of the eighteenth century was filled with new curves – cycloid, tractrix, isochrone, caustics, logarithmic spiral, sail curve, and the like – that eluded the grasp of finite algebra and required what Leibniz called the 'hidden geometry' of infinitesimal analysis or the 'new calculus of transcendents', which 'is properly that part of general mathematics that treats of the infinite, and that is why one has such need for it in applying mathematics to physics'.[7]

Philosophical concerns followed, rather than led, this dual process of mathematisation and mechanisation. During the sixteenth and early seventeenth centuries, panegyrics on mathematics emphasised its certainty and its utility. They were distinct qualities, the former resting on Euclid's *Elements* as the prime exemplar of an Aristotelian demonstrative science and the second on a range of applications from the so-called mixed or middle sciences of astronomy, optics, music, and mechanics to areas of practical concern, including commerce, surveying, architecture, and the construction of stage scenery. Over the course of the seventeenth century, mathematics became increasingly useful, in terms both of enhanced problem-solving power and of the transformation of the mixed sciences into natural philosophy itself. Accomplishing that, however, involved new forms of mathematical reasoning that cast its certainty in doubt, or at least called for new criteria of certainty, among them effective practice and intuitive understanding based on experience of the physical world. Thus, mathematical explanations of nature and mathematical reasoning itself were interwoven in a new fabric of natural philosophy. Each depended on the other for conceptual support, which was rooted in the technical practice of the new, combined subject. For closer examination, one can separate the weave into two threads of development: the new science of mechanics and the new algebraic analysis.

II. THE MATHEMATISATION OF NATURE

The idea of treating a mathematical object as a representation of a physical phenomenon had its origin in Greek philosophy. Plato, who may have got the idea from the Pythagoreans with whom he studied, expounded it in the *Timaeus*, first by modeling the daily and annual motions of the sun by means of two spheres turning uniformly on different axes and then by sketching a theory of matter based on the division and combination of two kinds of triangle.[8] In both cases the representation was meant to be analytic in the sense that the properties of the mathematical object match those of the phenomenon being represented and that the deductive relationships among the mathematical properties correspond in some way to the causal relationships among the physical properties. The precise nature of the correspondence between the physical world and its mathematical representation became a standing question. Is the physical world inherently mathematical, as the Pythagoreans maintained? If so, is the lack of fit between model and empirical data a fault of the model, or is matter inherently inexact, as Plato insisted? Is all of nature mathematical, or just portions of it, as Aristotle argued, making it the job of physics to identify the subjects that are essentially mathematical, such as optics, astronomy, and mechanics? How do mathematical models explain physical phenomena? Is a model merely hypothetical, 'saving the phenomena' without commitment to the reality of its mathematical elements, or does mathematical coherence carry ontological and metaphysical weight? In short, does mathematics follow physics or guide it?

Debates in the fourteenth century over the reality of epicycles and corresponding arguments in the sixteenth century over the real or hypothetical nature of Copernicus's new system show that these questions were current before the extension of the domain of mathematics during the seventeenth century. The dispute between Cartesians and Newtonians over action at a distance and the nature of force shows that the questions remained afterward, though perhaps in more sophisticated form. During the period, one finds mathematicians and philosophers of equal calibre on both sides of the issues, which persist down to the present.

These issues took a decisive turn in the seventeenth century, not so much from new metaphysical insights as from the proliferation of successful examples of the application of mathematics to natural philosophy on the model of machines.[9] It is a matter of emphases rather than alternatives, but one will understand Galileo Galilei's new sciences best by looking not at Plato's Academy, nor even at the Accademia dei Lincei, but at the Arsenal of Venice. That is where Galileo placed his interlocutors, and the opening words of the *Discorsi* straightforwardly announce the new relation of theory and practice embodied in the mechanical philosophy: what engineers know is worthy of the philosopher's attention.[10]

1. From machines to mechanics

Nature was mathematised in the seventeenth century by means of its extensive mechanisation, which by the end of the century extended, at least programmatically, to the living world of plants and animals. The mathematical models were abstract machines, which in turn were models of the physical world and its components. Kepler spoke in 1605 of the 'celestial machine',

not on the model of a divine, animate being, but on the model of a clock – if you think a clock to be animate, you attribute glory to the work of the craftsman. In [that machine] almost all the variety of motions [stems] from one most simple, physical magnetic force, just as in the clock all motions stem from a most simple weight. And I mean to call this form of reasoning 'physics [done] with numbers and geometry . . .'.[11]

Kepler's vision found its realisation in Newton's *Principia,* where universal gravitation played the rôle of the central weight, and the laws of motion converted its force into the motions of the wheels as described by Kepler. In Query 31, added to the *Opticks* in 1713, Newton imagined similar forces of attraction and repulsion governing chemical and physiological processes, thus making nature 'very conformable unto her Self'.

Separating the vision from its realisation was the development of a science of mechanics capable of describing mathematically the motion of bodies under constraint, although only in hindsight can the task be phrased so clearly and purposefully. That machines could be the subject of scientific (i.e., demonstrative) knowledge, that they consisted essentially of bodies moving under constraint, and that the constraints and the motions could be related mathematically were in themselves ideas that gradually took shape over the sixteenth and seventeenth centuries in response to a variety of social and conceptual influences. As Alan Gabbey has insisted, Newton's system lies on one line of development in mechanics, Huygens's mechanics of rigid and elastic bodies on another.[12] Nonetheless, they share the common view that the essential workings of any mechanical system can be captured in an abstract mathematical model and hence that mechanics is the job of a mathematician. That view they took in common from Galileo, and with him ultimately from Archimedes.

2. Galileo and the new science of motion

New to European society in the late Renaissance was the engineer, who emerged from the anonymity of guild practice to take charge of the design and execution of large structures and of the machines necessary to build them. With the new social rôle came a new literature to give his know-how cultural standing: manuals of engineering, 'theaters of machines', editions and translations of classical works on machines, accounts of great feats such as Domenico Fontana's *Del modo tenuto nel trasportare l'obelisco Vaticano* (Rome, 1589), and compendia based on classical

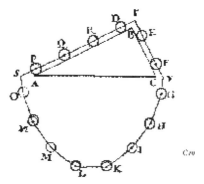

Figure 22.1

models, such as Georgius Agricola's *De re metallica* (Basel, 1556). Out of this effort to codify practice emerged what might be called 'maxims of engineering experience'. Phrased in various ways, they came down to such rules as:

1. You cannot build a perpetual-motion machine.[13]
2. You cannot get more out of a machine than you put into it.
3. What holds an object at rest is just about enough to get it moving.
4. Things, whether solid or liquid, do not go uphill by themselves.
5. When you press on water or some other liquid, it pushes out equally in all directions.

Beginning in the 1580s with the work of Simon Stevin and Galileo Galilei, engineers aspiring to natural philosophy transformed these maxims into the principles of mechanics by translating them into mathematical form. Often, that translation involved devising an abstract mathematical model of the physical mechanism that embodied the maxim.

To analyse the inclined plane, for example, Stevin took a triangle (see Figure 22.1), around which he imagined a 'wreath of spheres' (*clootcrans*), consisting of equal weights connected by a weightless, flexible cord. Once placed in position, the wreath will not move one way or the other of its own accord; if it did so, it would retain the same configuration and hence 'the spheres would by themselves carry out a perpetual motion, which is impossible (*valsch*).'[14] By symmetry, the portion below the triangle pulls equally in both directions, and hence may be removed without disturbing the equilibrium. Clearly, then, the portions on the two sides counterbalance one another, and their weights are as the number of spheres, which in turn are as the lengths of the sides. Since the sides have a common height, the weights are as the sines of the base angles, which is the law of the inclined plane.

The sciences in Galileo's *Discorsi e dimostrazioni matematiche intorno a due nuove scienze* (Discourses and mathematical demonstrations about two new sciences concerning mechanics and local motions) (Leiden, 1638) were singly new in different ways, as the different languages and typefaces of the original publication suggest. What was new about the first, the strength of materials, was calling it a 'science' at all. The vernacular and italic font seem to reflect the artisanal roots of the question, Why did big machines not always perform as well as smaller ones of the same design?[15] The second, *scientia de motu locali,* had a philosophical pedigree apposite to both the Latin in which it was couched and the roman font in which it was set. But it had the new form of a thorough-going mathematical theory built on empirical grounds, a prime example of the union of *sensata experienza* and *necessarie dimostrazioni*.[16]

That they were two sciences rather than one reflected not only their diverse origins but a compromise born of Galileo's unsuccessful efforts to relate force to motion mathematically. Initially following the lead of Archimedes and of the author of the *Mechanica,* ascribed at the time to Aristotle, Galileo sought models in machines and mathematised the machines by abstraction. That is, he translated physical devices into mathematical configurations by abstracting their geometrical structure from the physical material of which they were constructed. For statics, the approach worked well, facilitating a shift of focus from one machine to another; for example, from the effective moment of a body on a bent-arm balance to its positional weight on an inclined plane perpendicular to the arm (yielding as a by-product the law of the inclined plane), and from there to the pendulum as the body sliding along a sequence of inclined planes tangent to the arc of its swing.[17] By combining such abstractions, Galileo arrived at the distinction between gravific and positional weight. Since the latter is zero on a horizontal plane, where the body is indifferent to motion, he concluded that weight accounts not for motion itself, but for change of motion: in free fall, weight produces acceleration.[18]

The Archimedean approach worked less well in exploring how weight changes motion. Studies with the inclined plane and pendulum showed that bodies gain force as they move faster and that the force they gain in free fall from rest is just enough to raise them to their initial height. Although Galileo knew the relation between length of fall and final velocity, he also knew that it was independent of the body's size, while its *momento,* or *impeto,* depended on the size of the body as well as its speed, and he could not find a way to disaggregate them. He did point the way, however. An unpublished Fifth Day of the *Discorsi* dealt with the force of impact, and in others' hands the pendulum proved to be the instrument for measuring and modeling that phenomenon. For the moment, he could separate kinematics from dynamics. Experiments with the pendulum showed that the acceleration is the same for all bodies, and on an inclined plane the constant positional weight should produce uniform acceleration, or what the mediaeval science of motion referred to as 'uniformly difform motion'. Building what he could on the principle that a constant force produces constant acceleration, he left open the question of variable forces and the resulting motions.

Galileo linked the science of motion to two classes of mathematical problems. The laws of accelerated motion associated the distance traversed by a moving body with the area under the graph of the relation between velocity and time and thus tied kinematics to the quadrature of curves. The analysis of projectile motion in terms of uniform horizontal and accelerated vertical components connected trajectories with curves defined in terms of their axes and ordinates. In the latter case, Galileo could take advantage of Apollonius's *Conics* to relate the components of motion to the *symptomata,* or defining properties, of the parabola and then to work from properties of that curve to the kinematic relations of projectile motion. But he did not undertake to develop the mathematics itself or to explore other, more general connexions between curves and the motion of bodies along them. That came with the work of Roberval and others on the generation of curves by compound motion (see Section III). By contrast, Galileo played a central rôle in the development of the first class of problems, both directly and through his followers. The nature and extent of the influence of the mediaeval science of motion on his analysis of accelerated motion remains a matter of debate, but it is clear that he knew of Federigo Commandino's (1509–75) work on Archimedes' method of quadrature and later of Bonaventura Cavalieri's method of indivisibles: an appendix to the *Discorsi* contains several theorems on centres of gravity of solids using similar methods.[19]

The concept of 'uniformly difform motion' had a picture associated with it. In the doctrine of the configurations of qualities, also known as the latitudes of forms, uniformly difform qualities took the shape of a triangle. In moving from statics to kinematics, Galileo appears initially to have identified that triangle of motion with the abstract figure of the inclined plane on which the motion took place. The effect was to link velocity acquired in acceleration to the distance along the plane, which is proportional to the vertical distance of free fall. For a short time in 1604 Galileo believed that from such a definition of uniform acceleration it followed that the distance traversed varies as the square of the time, a proposition he had already established through experiments with inclined planes.

Closer examination of the mathematics of the diagram of motion revealed the problem with the definition and the flaw in his deduction. It also confronted him with the problem of reasoning with infinite aggregates. The mediaeval doctrine referred to configurations of *qualities,* or latitudes of *forms:* that is, the extensive representation and measure of intensive properties. The paradigm was a body exhibiting different degrees or intensities of hotness at different points. In a similar sense, the degree of speed measured the intensity of a body's motion, either at different parts of the body in the case of rotation about a fixed point or at different times in the case of motion over a distance. The measure of the velocity as intensity of motion at each point or at each instant was derived from its total effect, or 'total speed', over the course of the motion. If the motion was uniform, any degree was representative of the whole; if difform, one sought a particular degree that was representative in the sense that, if the body were to move uniformly at that degree, it would have the same total speed as it did in its difform motion. The famous 'mean speed theorem' expressed the rule in the case of uniformly difform motion: the total speed would be the same if the body were to move uniformly at half the final speed.

That theorem originated among the 'calculators' at Merton College, Oxford, in the fourteenth century and was justified by appeal to the intuitive notion that every defect on one side of the mean is counterbalanced by a corresponding excess on the other.[20] In the geometric form devised by Nicole Oresme (1320?–82), the measure of total motion became the area of the figure determined by lines, or latitudes, representing the degrees of speed in one dimension and a baseline, or longitude, representing the body or the time in the other.[21] Just how the individual degrees of speed were related to the total speed – that is, how the latitudes were related to the area – did not arise as a question. In the case of two uniform motions over a common interval, it was evident that the areas were to one another as the latitudes, but the heterogeneity of the terms of the proportion precluded taking the cross-product of latitude and longitude to form the area.

Moreover, in the mediaeval doctrine the meaning of 'total speed' remained vague, as did the meaning of 'motion' when referring to an end result rather than a process. What, for example, was the 'motion' of a body rotated about one of its points, once the motion was completed? In general, both terms were taken to refer to the distance traversed, evidently on the premise that a body moved from

A to *B* has somehow 'acquired' the distance *AB,* and that the whole effect of the different intensities at which it acquired that distance is the distance itself.

However well Galileo understood the mediaeval doctrine, it seems clear that he had it in mind when he attacked the problem of the kinematics of falling bodies and that he fell afoul of the doctrine's vagaries. Having identified motion along an inclined plane with the triangle of uniformly difform motion, with the distance traversed from rest as longitude and the speed acquired as latitude, he tried to move to the conclusion that the distance acquired is proportional to the square of the time. To bring time into the picture, he appealed to the mean speed theorem. But, as he soon recognised, only a paralogism could avoid the instantaneous motion that followed from applying the theorem to that configuration of motion. For if $v \, \alpha \, S,$ then by the configuration the total distance will be proportional to the final speed and by the mean speed theorem will be proportional to half the final speed. But that can obtain only if the motion occurs in an instant.

In addition to redefining uniform acceleration as the acquisition of equal increments of speed over equal intervals of time, Galileo drew two conclusions from his mistake. First, the graph of motion is a mathematical representation rather than an abstraction from the physical world, and one must distinguish between the two in drawing diagrams. Hence, in the revised version of his theorems on accelerated motion, the triangle of speeds and times appeared alongside a line representing the trajectory of motion (see Figure 22.2). Second, a properly mathematical science of motion would require confronting directly the relation between speed as an instantaneous intensional quality and distance as an extensional measure of motion over time, which is also an extended magnitude.[22] Through the mediation of the geometrical configuration, that problem was embedded in the larger questions of mathematical atomism, the paradoxes of the infinite, and the nature of continuous magnitude. These questions crop up in various forms throughout the *Discorsi,* and Galileo passed them on to his disciples and their students, foremost among them Cavalieri and Evangelista Torricelli.

Galileo was too well trained in scholastic philosophy not to appreciate both the power and the pitfalls of reasoning with infinites. The concept of one–one correspondence that shows that there are as many square numbers as there are numbers also resolves Zeno's paradox and the relation of motion to rest: whatever the fraction of the distance to be traversed, there is a corresponding fraction of the time in which it is traversed; as a body slows down, to every speed, however small,

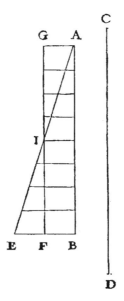

Figure 22.2

there corresponds an equally small interval of time through which motion at that speed takes place. But, as Galileo pointed out to Cavalieri, the concept as embodied, say, in the method of indivisibles (see Section IV.2) had its paradoxes. One could use it, for example, to argue that a point is equal to a line. Draw (Figure 22.3) semicircle *AFB* about centre *C*, rectangle *ADEB* around the semicircle, and triangle *CDE* on base *DE,* and then imagine the configuration rotated about axis *CF* to generate a hemisphere, a cylinder, and a cone, respectively. Removing the hemisphere reduces the cylinder to a 'bowl'. Galileo then asserts that any plane *GN* parallel to base *DE* will cut the bowl and the cone in equal cross-sections – that is, the 'band' of which *GI* and *ON* are opposite parts is equal to the disk *HL* – and that the portions of the bowl and cone cut off by the plane are equal to one another.[23] The paradox arises at the upper limits of the configuration, where the equality of cross-sections would seem to lead to the conclusion that the point *C* is equal to the circle *AB*. As Cavalieri argued in response, the paradox is more semantic than logical: neither the point as the last of the circles nor the circle as

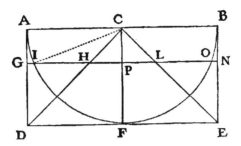

Figure 22.3

the last of the bands constitutes an area, or, rather, each has zero area, and hence the two are equal only in that sense.[24]

Semantic or logical, the paradox pointed to potential problems. Galileo demonstrated only the first part of the proposition, referring for the full demonstration to Book II, Proposition 12 of Luca Valerio's *De centro gravitatis solidorum* (Rome, 1604). Nonetheless, the accompanying discussion suggested that the equality of volumes followed from the one–one correspondence of cross-sections, and Galileo went on to speculate about how one might conceive of finite quantities as composed of an infinite number of indivisibles; in this case of the bowl and the cone consisting respectively of all the corresponding cross-sections. The paradox reflected a danger lurking behind the use of one–one correspondences over open infinite sets to apply a shared property to a limiting value not belonging to the set, for example, to apply to a circle a property shared by all inscribed polygons. That, too, formed a continuing strategy of the new mathematics of change. It got Galileo into trouble in reasoning from motion along chords in a circle to motion along the subtending arcs, and Newton exercised appropriate caution in shaping the theorem in the *Principia* on the centripetal force constraining uniform motion in a circle.

In the demonstration of the mean speed theorem in Theorem 1 on uniform acceleration in the Third Day, Galileo moved from speculation to assertion. Taking *AB* as the time of motion from rest at *C,* and *BE* as the final velocity, he drew *AE* and claimed that 'all the lines drawn parallel to *BE* from each of the points of line *AB* will represent the increasing degrees of speed after instant *A*.' Having constructed parallelogram *AGFB* on *FB* = *BE*/2, he argued that the triangle and the

parallelogram would be equal, because 'if the parallels of triangle *AEB* are extended to *IGF,* we will have the aggregate of all the parallels contained in the
quadrilateral equal [*aequalem*] to the aggregate of those contained in the triangle
AEB, for those in triangle *IEF* are equal [*paria*] to those contained in triangle
GIA, and those in trapezium *AIFB* are common.' Each of the parallels then
became a 'moment of speed' [*momentum velocitatis*], and the respective aggregates
of moments became the distances covered. The demonstration did not proceed by
ratios of distances and speeds with time held constant, but by summation of
indivisible distances traversed at instantaneous speeds over instants of time.[25]

   Although the argument appeared to rest on the principle of correspondence,
logical difficulties lurked in the equating of the indivisibles of triangle *IEF* with
those in triangle *GIA.* For there was no rule of correspondence that tied the
cross-sections to a common base. Arguing that lines *GI* and *IF* contained the
same number of points with corresponding cross-sections led to an immediate
counterexample. Consider rectangle *ABCD* (Figure 22.4) and on the diagonal *AC*
construct rectangle *AEFC* with *AE = AB.* Now, drawing 'all the parallels' to *AC*
establishes a one–one correspondence between all the points on *AD* and all those
on *AC.* Using those points to draw 'all the parallels' to *AE* should establish a one–
one correspondence of equality between the two aggregates of parallels, whence
rectangle *ABCD* is equal to rectangle *AEFC.* But that clearly is not the case.

   It was a mathematical rather than a physical puzzle, and Galileo left it for his
pupils. The solution lay in the notion of indivisibles varying in thickness according
to the bases on which they stood. Fully articulated in the technique of transmutation of areas based on infinitesimals (see Section IV.2), it came back to bear on
mechanics in the work of Huygens, who followed Galileo's mathematical lead in
dealing with questions posed by Descartes's physics.

3. Descartes: Mathematics and the cosmology of light

In a sense, Descartes picked up where Galileo had left off, having arrived there
independently along a shorter path. Although interested in practical devices,
Descartes was more a philosopher than an engineer like Galileo. Taking Kepler
more seriously and persuaded that a physical account of the laws of optics,
especially refraction, would open up larger questions of cosmology, he could not
avoid dynamics. His radical scepticism allowed the physical reality only of matter
and motion, and the latter could be defined only relatively. Both experience and
reason told him that bodies continue to move at the same speed in the same
direction, and hence along a straight line, unless other bodies push them in new

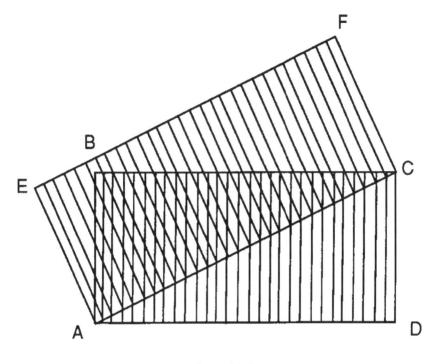

Figure 22.4

directions at new speeds. Thus impact became the central dynamical phenomenon of Cartesian physics.

In applying mathematics to physical questions, Descartes had his greatest success in optics. Since he strove in his later writings to make his results look methodical, one must reconstruct his heuristic path. Evidence suggests that his independent determination of the sine law of refraction in the mid-1620s emerged from measurements made with a refractometer (Figure 22.5), which he generalised by applying the 'image rule' traditionally used to account for magnification of refracted images.[26] By abstracting the refractometer to a circle and then adjusting the radius of the lower half by means of the image rule applied to a single pair of incident and refracted rays, he arrived at a mathematical configuration that allowed the construction of any other pair. The conjectured original configuration, which

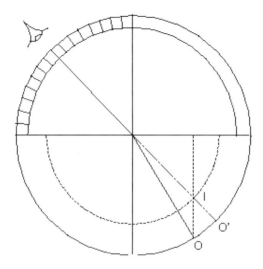

Figure 22.5

in essence incorporated the sine rule into a geometrical calculating device, presupposed no particular mechanism for the phenomenon and implied no derivation of the law.

In the years immediately following, Descartes combined his optical research with his work in mechanics to construct a derivation of the laws of reflection and refraction. Believing on both empirical and metaphysical grounds that light is a force (a tendency to move) transmitted instantaneously by a medium and proportional in magnitude to its density, he likened the behaviour of light rays at an optical interface to the static forces counterbalancing one another at a point at rest: equal forces cancel one another along the same line; unequal forces counteract one another at a compensating angle. To make that model more accessible to general experience, Descartes translated it into kinematical terms, likening a pulse of light to a tennis ball and equating force with velocity. To this model he added the notion of impact, assumed to affect only the component of motion normal to the surface. The analogy to tennis worked best for reflection: should a body moving at a given speed strike an unyielding surface at a given angle (Figure 22.6), it would be reflected at an equal angle, retaining its speed. In the case of refraction, one must imagine the ball breaking through the surface, thus losing some of its speed along the normal and being deflected from it. However, the real model

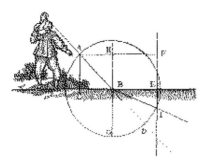

Figure 22.6

behind the analogy required that, on entering a denser medium, the ball be deflected towards the normal, and hence that the ball gain speed by an extra stroke along the normal on impact. By such seemingly *ad hoc* adjustments, the final version of Descartes's argument as published in *La dioptrique* (Leiden, 1637) posed conceptual difficulties that have been the subject of extensive commentary, but they have little to do with mathematics. In the shift from abstract instrument to support for a derivation, the diagram ceased to be constructive or operational. It simply exemplified kinematical relations based on dynamical principles that could not be located in the mathematical configuration.

As Book II of the *Géométrie* shows, Descartes could apply the laws of optics mathematically to derive the reflective and refractive properties of curved lenses, and in that sense his theory of optics was fully mathematical. Yet, the laws themselves did not follow mathematically from the mechanical cosmology meant to explain them. In describing that cosmology in *Le monde, ou Traité de la lumière* (1633, Paris, 1664), and later in his *Principles of Philosophy* (Amsterdam, 1644), Descartes spoke of forces and the motions that arose from them, but he could not relate them to one another mathematically. He could not convert his analysis of centrifugal force into a mathematical relationship between velocity and radius, and his principle of conservation of quantity of motion, measured by the product of magnitude and speed, did not suffice to characterise the interaction of two unequal bodies striking one another. Indeed, as Huygens would show, if conceived in absolute rather than relative (that is, vectorial) terms, it could not account for two equal bodies striking at unequal speeds.

4. Huygens and the pendulum: From instrument to relation

Huygens lacked Descartes's philosophical sophistication, but his continuing engagement with physical mechanisms, especially the pendulum and the mechanical clock, enabled him to make the mathematical connexions Descartes had missed. Pursuing the full implications of relativity of motion (see Chapter 20) and modifying the law of conservation of motion to include the relative direction of bodies, Huygens established laws of impact consonant both qualitatively and quantitatively with experiments carried out with pendulums. Using infinitesimal quantities to trace change of motion at a point, he identified centrifugal acceleration with the acceleration of free fall and determined a measure of the former. Taking advantage of new techniques of quadrature and rectification via transmutation of areas (see Section IV.2), which he himself enhanced, he derived the approximately constant period of a simple pendulum for very small oscillations and, by analysing the nature of the approximation, found that the measure is exact for any system in which the force moving the body is proportional to the displacement from equilibrium, in particular for a pendulum tracing a cycloidal[27] path and for a spring obeying Hooke's Law. The same body of mathematical techniques underlay his derivation of the centre of oscillation of a compound pendulum.[28]

As the touchstone of Huygens's mechanics, the pendulum embodies the main pattern of development of mathematical physics in the seventeenth century. What began as a physical system became an experimental apparatus and then an abstract model ultimately expressed in mathematical terms and thus divorced from its original physical configuration.[29] Huygens's use of the pendulum as a means of experimenting with and analysing the impact of bodies rested on its abstraction from a single object to a system. The isochrony of two pendulums of the same length swinging over small arcs from the centre provided a means of measuring the initial and final speeds of impact of two bodies by means of their initial and final heights. More important, swinging two impacting pendulums from a common suspension suggested a crucial generalisation of a principle of mechanics first enunciated by Torricelli but surely drawn from engineering practice: two heavy bodies joined together cannot move on their own unless their common centre of gravity descends.[30] In applying the principle, Huygens dissolved the physical link between the bodies. Two pendulums starting from initial heights have a common centre of gravity. As they descend to the point of impact, so, too, does the centre of gravity; as they rise again after impact, so, too, does the centre. If no motion is lost on impact, the bodies will continue indefinitely to bounce back and forth against one another. But they can do that only if the centre of gravity rises to its original height each time, that is, only if it acts in the manner of a pendulum. Since the time of rise and fall is the same, it follows that the speed of approach is equal to the speed of separation, and from Galileo's law relating height of fall to the speed acquired it follows that 'if two bodies collide with each other, that which results from multiplying the magnitudes of each by the square of their velocities, added together, is found to be equal before and after collision; if, that is, the ratios of both the magnitudes and the velocities are posited in numbers or lines.'[31] The proposition became a staple of Huygens's mechanics, as he took advantage of the techniques of infinitesimal analysis to apply it to continuous as well as discrete systems. Yet the central parameter, mv^2, remained a mathematical construct for which he hypostatised no physical correlate. Only in the hands of Leibniz did it become *vis viva,* the 'live force' of a moving body.

To free the laws of collision from the experimental apparatus, Huygens took the centre of gravity as fixed and placed the bodies in two moving frames of reference. In the version intended for publication, these were presented in terms of a man in a boat moving past a colleague on the shore, handing the pendulums over at the moment of impact. Hence the central rôle of the centre of gravity receded behind the concept of relativity of motion, as gravity itself disappeared from the mathematical space in which the bodies moved and collided in accord with abstract relationships. Gravity re-entered the space as a mathematical relationship in Huygens's derivation of the centre of oscillation of a solid bar in Chapter IV of his *Horologium oscillatorium* (Paris, 1673). Dividing the bar into an arbitrarily large number of equally weighted segments, he imagined it to swing rigidly from its initial position, and, as it passes through the vertical, to dissolve into its individual components, each of which then rises vertically to a height determined by the velocity it acquired over the downswing. The velocity of each depends on the centre of oscillation of the bar, which is located by setting the heights of the centres of gravity of the constrained and the unconstrained systems equal to one another. Equating the 'actual descent' and 'potential ascent' of bodies in motion proved to have broad application, perhaps most impressively in Daniel Bernoulli's (1700–82) *Hydrodynamica* (Strassburg, 1738). Its effectiveness as a physical principle ultimately depended on the mathematical resources available to carry out the quadratures and cubatures (i.e., integrations) involved.

As experimental apparatus, the pendulum only approximated the essential property that gave it power as an analytical model, namely, a period independent of amplitude, or, anachronistically, simple harmonic oscillation. Huygens's discovery that a cycloidal pendulum is exactly tautochronic relocated the property from the pendulum to the cycloid, that is, from a physical system to a mathematical curve. In the process, it stimulated the development of the theory of evolutes, the basis for the later theory of curvature. Further analysis showed that motion along the cycloid is tautochronic because the tangential component of the force on a body sliding along its concave surface is proportional to the distance along the curve from the vertex at the bottom. Thus, the property was again relocated from the cycloid as a particular mathematical curve to any curve or system in which the motive force is proportional to the displacement from equilibrium, and Huygens's later notebooks abound with such systems, motivated by the search for a robust sea-going clock. Although Huygens himself did not embrace Leibniz's calculus, the generality embodied in the equation $ddS = -kSdt^2$ is fully consonant with the level of abstraction reached in those investigations. In turn, the plethora of mechanisms instantiating the abstract relationship lent intuitive support to the concepts underlying its mathematical expression.

5. *Newton: Pendulums and moons*

Huygens's success in analysing centrifugal force and in determining the dynamical basis of tautochronic oscillation did not lead him to a general treatment of forces and the resultant motions. Tautochronic oscillation was a special case, and Huygens found no means of giving to what he called *incitation* and defined as 'the force that acts on a body to move it when it is at rest or to increase or decrease its speed when it is in motion' a mathematical form that would allow its application to other situations. By 1674, when Huygens set down this definition, Newton had already worked out just such a mathematical formulation, thinking along the same lines as Huygens but focussing on a different problem, namely, the motion of bodies acted on by a centripetal force.[32] The trick lay in accounting for both change of speed and change of direction, and an early analysis of uniform circular motion appears to have provided the model. Modifying his diagram and argument slightly to bring out the underlying reasoning (Figure 22.7), consider a body moving at speed v along the sides of a polygon inscribed in a circle and reflected by the circle at each vertex. If the body were not reflected, it would continue at the same speed in the same direction by the first of Descartes's laws of motion. However, the body is reflected onto the succeeding side, and the change of motion is the distance between the next point of impact and where the body would have been had it continued unreflected. Denoting that distance as Δv and the distance along the side as v (in uniform motion, distance is proportional to speed), one has from similar triangles $\Delta v/v = v/R$, where R is the radius; that is, $\Delta v = v^2/R$. Nothing in this relation depends on the number of sides or frequency of impact. It holds for any number of sides of a given polygon, and it applies to all

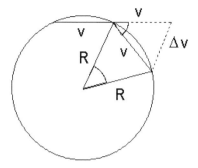

Figure 22.7

inscribed polygons of however many sides. Hence (by an assumed principle of continuity), it holds for all corresponding arcs of the circle that is the limiting figure.[33]

Proposition I,1 of the *Principia* uses the same mathematics to prove that a body moving under any central force will describe a plane orbit at a speed such that the line connecting it to the centre of force sweeps out equal areas in equal times. Again, Newton begins (Figure 22.8) with a finite, rectilinear motion from point *A* over some interval of time at speed *v*. At point B, he imagines the body pushed instantaneously towards the centre *S*, changing the body's direction towards C. Had the body not been pushed, it would have proceeded over an equal interval of time to *c*, where *Bc* = *AB*, and hence the line *cC*, drawn parallel to *BS*, represents the change of motion. The measure of that change is not of immediate concern; rather, the fact that *cC* is parallel to *BS* makes triangles *SBC* and *SBc* equal, and *AB* = *Bc* means that triangle *SBc* = triangle *SAB*. Again Newton argues that the mathematical relations hold independently of the number and frequency of the impulses towards the centre and therefore hold of the curve that limits the rectilinear cases. The crucial steps in the derivation are the mathematical expressions of the first two laws or axioms of motion with which Newton opened the *Principia:* the law of inertia and the law of force: 'Change of motion is proportional to the impressed motive force and takes place along the straight line in which that force is impressed.'

To get a measure of the force in the case of a curvilinear orbit requires several geometrical results that relocate its representation from a hypothetical interval *cC* to some combination of the finite parameters of the orbit, and the bulk of the first

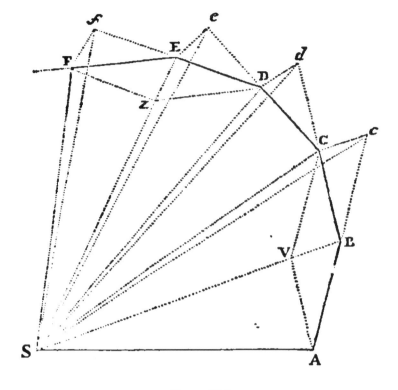

Figure 22.8

ten sections of Book I is addressed to evaluating that combination for a variety of known shapes, foremost among them the ellipse (Δ v α $'/R^2$, where R is the distance from the body to the attracting focus), and extending it to the case of an infinitely distant centre of force so as to encompass Galileo's laws of motion for bodies close to the surface of the earth.[34] It is by that extension that the pendulum's swing becomes a limiting case of the moon's orbit, and the heavens are tied to the earth in a common mathematical structure, which, Newton asserts, reflects their common physical structure.

While the main argument of the *Principia* amounts to showing that Kepler's laws of planetary motion entail an inverse-square force, Newton also laid the groundwork for working in the other direction, namely, finding the orbit, given a force law and initial position and momentum. Here the effectiveness of the mechanics depends on one's skill and repertoire as a mathematician, since, as

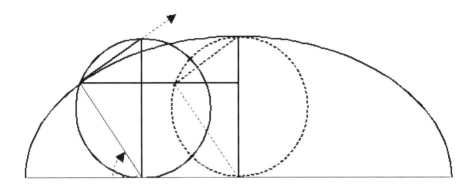

Figure 22.9

Propositions 39–41 demonstrate, the problem ultimately comes down to the quadrature of curves, for which there is no general algorithm. In the 'inverse problem of forces', however, lay the promise of Newton's mathematical mechanics in its application to any system of bodies attracting or repelling one another, whether they be planets acting under gravity or small particles of bodies exhibiting chemical or electrical properties. 'And thus Nature will be very conformable to her self', he mused in a 'Query' added to his *Opticks* in 1713, 'and very simple, performing all the great Motions of the heavenly Bodies by the Attraction of Gravity which intercedes those Bodies, and almost all the small ones of their Particles by some other attractive and repelling Powers which intercede the particles.'[35] Nature's mathematical structure was all-embracing, and Newton's approach to analysing it held sway through the eighteenth century.[36]

III. MECHANICAL MATHEMATICS

Despite popular legend, Newton did not create fluxions to accommodate problems involving motion. To the contrary, as the first essay of what would become his technique of fluxions shows, he began with motion, and in that he followed a line of thought rooted in the classical sources but given new vitality by the developments in mechanics just described. Until the creation of the calculus, however, the analysis of curves generated by motion was mathematically suspect. For example, Descartes readily determined (Figure 22.9) the tangent to the cycloid at any point by considering its mode of generation. As the circle rolls along the

plane, the direction of the fixed point on its circumference is perpendicular to the
chord linking the point to the point in contact with the plane, for it is momen-
tarily rotating about that point at the end of the chord.[37] But the perpendicular to
that chord is simply the chord from the moving point to the vertex of the circle.
That is, from the point on the cycloid draw a parallel to the plane. Where it
intersects the generating circle about the centre of the cycloid, draw a chord to
the vertex. A line through the given point parallel to that chord is tangent to the
cycloid.

Yet, Descartes would not admit the cycloid among the curves he considered
geometrical, because it could not be described in terms of an algebraic relation
among rectilinear segments. Requiring circular motion for its description, it
formed a 'mechanical' curve and hence required mechanical means of constructing its tangent. However neat and clever the means, he thought them a
curiosity, not mathematics.[38] Others among his contemporaries were less particular. In *Observations sur la composition des mouvements et sur le moyen de trouver les
tangentes des lignes courbes,* Gilles Personne de Roberval showed how to express the
defining properties of curves both old and recent in terms of the compound
motion of points describing them, from which the tangent then followed as the
resultant.[39] Roberval based his techniques on an extension of the parallelogram of
motions from uniform to non-uniform motion, taking as axiomatic that 'the
direction of the motion of a point describing a curve is the tangent of the curve
at each position of that point.' His work was thus of a piece with Galileo's
determination of the parabolic trajectory and with Descartes's analysis of circular
motion into normal and tangential components, as Roberval's basic terms –
mouvement uniforme, mouvement irrégulier ou difforme, puissance, impression, and so
forth – make clear. Expounded by Isaac Barrow in his *Lectiones geometricae* in the
mid-1660s, the technique was the basis of Newton's first version of the theory of
fluxions in 'To resolve problems by motion' in 1666, and it underlay the analyses
of curves in the *Principia.* The various expositions differed largely in the specific
means used to express the defining properties of curves in terms of compound
motions and to resolve the motions into directional components at the point of
tangency.

With the method of fluxions Newton recast the analysis of curves by motion
into wholly algebraic terms, set usually in a Cartesian framework.[40] If p is the rate
of 'flow' of a point in the x-direction and q is the corresponding rate of flow in
the y-direction, then q/p determines the direction of the tangent. The rule for
finding p and q for an algebraic equation $f(x,y) = 0$ remained the same in all
versions: multiply each term by p/x times the power of x in the term and,

similarly, by q/y times the power of y in the term, and add the results. Behind the rule lay the notion of the momentary increase (or decrease) of x and y, whereby over a 'moment' o each grows by an infinitely small amount proportional to its velocity at that point. That is, over a 'moment' non-uniform motion may be treated as uniform, whence $p:q = po:qo$. Here, the kinematical model hooked into the algebraic method of maxima and minima and of tangents created by Fermat and expounded as a 'rule' by a series of writers (section IV.1).[41]

As used by Newton here, the notion of 'moment' was suggestively ambiguous, connoting both an instant of time and the force by which a mechanical system is held in equilibrium or with which it first begins to act. It tied the method of fluxions to the determination of the centres of gravity of curvilinear figures, a problem of increasing interest to mathematicians and mechanicians from the time of its introduction through the works of Archimedes in the sixteenth century. In this literature, plane and solid figures acquired a uniformly distributed 'weight', by which portions of them could be balanced against one another with reference to their distance from a point. If one imagined an area sliced into very small sections, then each of them constituted a 'moment' of the area with respect to its centre of gravity. Generalised to denote the rate by which the area grows when generated by a moving ordinate, the 'moment' of the area $A(x)$ under $y = f(x)$ becomes the fluxion of A, which Newton showed is simply y itself.[42] In that relation of area to moment lies the inverse relation of fluxion to fluent, that is, the fundamental relation of the calculus. Leibniz arrived at similar results through an 'analysis of quadrature by means of centres of gravity' at roughly the same stage in his path to the calculus.[43]

One need not look hard to find other examples of mechanical thinking in seventeenth-century mathematics. Balances, levers, centres of gravity, velocities, moments, and forces informed creative mathematics while mathematics became the means to express and understand them. In particular, machines stimulated mathematicians' interest in mechanical systems and the curves traced by the motion of their parts. The cycloid was only the first of a host of curves introduced into mathematics from nature construed mechanically; it was soon joined by tractrix and the catenary (respectively, the shapes of a flexible cord dragging a weight along a plane and of one hanging freely), by the curve of descent at a uniform vertical rate and that of a sail under a constant wind, and by families of caustics generated by optics. The new science of mechanics legitimated these curves as mathematical objects and spurred the development of mathematical methods for analysing, transforming, and ultimately constructing them. Although often couched in geometrical terms, these methods increasingly derived from the

Body and the physical world

conceptual resources of a new way of talking about mathematics, namely symbolic algebra.

IV. ALGEBRA AND THE ART OF ANALYSIS

Leibniz's calculus and Newton's fluxions arose out of a line of mathematical thought reaching back to François Viète (1540–1603) and passing through Descartes and Pierre de Fermat. It may be termed the 'analytic programme', and it was aimed at the development of a systematic body of techniques for solving any mathematical problem, or at least classifying it according to the nature of its solution, if it could not be solved explicitly. In particular, the analytic programme sought a means of expressing curves in a form that captured all their essential properties and that could be analysed and transformed to reveal those properties. The properties of particular interest over the period included the tangent and normal to a curve at any point, the area under it, the length of its arc, and its curvature. As these properties of curves acquired significance within a geometrical mechanics, the new analytical methods of determining them became identified with mechanics, which in turn was then couched directly in the language of those methods.

The analytic programme rested on the idea of algebra as the symbolic art of analysis. In retrospect one can see adumbrations of the idea in sixteenth-century discussions of a 'universal mathematics', for which the classical reference was Aristotle's *Metaphysica,* which spoke of a body of concepts and propositions common to all the distinct branches of mathematics, and hence superordinate to them.[44] As specified by Viète, however, the art of analysis was specifically rooted in

a certain way of seeking truth in mathematics, which Plato is said to have been the first to invent, and which was called 'analysis' by Theon and defined by him as 'the assumption of what is sought as if admitted [and the passage] by consequences to an admitted truth. Conversely, synthesis [is] the assumption of what is admitted [and the passage] by consequences to the goal and comprehension of what is sought.[45]

Viète took his definitions from the classical discussion at the beginning of Book 7 of Pappus of Alexandria's *Mathematical Collection,* where it served as introduction to a compendium of treatises providing tools for the working geometer and thus constituting what Pappus called 'the field of analysis' (Gr. *ho topos analyomenos*). As Pappus described the method, one proceeds analytically by assuming that a proposed theorem is true, or a problem is solved, and then chasing out the consequences of that assumption until one arrives at a theorem known to be true, or a problem known to be solved. Synthesis turns the process around by starting with what is known and proceeding deductively to a proof of the theorem or a construction of the problem. Synthesis is necessary because the advantages of analysis as a method of discovery come at the price of logical rigour: $A \Rightarrow B$ may suggest a way of proving A by means of B, but one cannot simply reverse the implication.[46]

Viète sought to capture the heuristic power of analysis in a general form common to arithmetic, geometry, and the other branches of mathematics.[47] The practical art of algebra, applied traditionally to numbers, provided the basis. To solve a problem, one expressed it in the form of an equation linking the known number with the unknown, denoted by a symbol. Manipulating the unknown as if it were known, the rules of algebra specified how to reduce the equation so that the unknown stood alone on one side, equated to a known number on the other. Moreover, most of the reductions involve substitution of equivalent forms and hence run logically in both directions. Viète extended the basis through a re-formed algebra in which the letters of the alphabet represent general quantities, 'the species or forms of things', characterised only by their being subject to the four operations of addition, subtraction, multiplication, and division, suitably defined. Multiple application of those operations results in composite quantities represented by expressions and equations. Taking advantage of a symbolic convention that distinguishes between unknowns denoted by vowels and parameters denoted by consonants, the art of analysis reveals the structures [*constitutiones*] of those equations and hence the relations among them that provide the means of reducing a problem to a form for which a solution is known.

By focusing on structures, the new symbolic algebra directed attention away from the properties of mathematical objects to the relationships among the objects and from techniques of solution to analysis of solvability. Thus, while including in the analytic art the canonical procedures for the numerical resolution of equations and for the geometrical constructions corresponding to them, Viète focused attention (in *De aequationum recognitione et emendatione tractatus duo* [Paris, 1615]) on the transformations by which given equations were reduced to the canonical forms to which those procedures could be applied. Although he did not introduce the term 'theory of equations', Viète laid out the foundations of the subject and made it the core of his 'art'.[48]

In establishing a new style of mathematics, Viète also set down an agenda for investigation. He called for the recovery of the content of the ancient corpus of analysis reported in varying detail by Pappus and for the discovery of the analysis that lay hidden under the synthetic form of the great works of Apollonius, Archimedes, and others. The algebra Viète had inherited from its Arabic authors extended only to the solution of linear, quadratic, and some cubic equations in one unknown.[49] Those same authors had pointed out the relation of their numerical procedures to theorems in Books II and VI of Euclid's *Elements,* thus suggesting to Renaissance mathematicians the idea of an algebra underlying Greek geometry – as Viète put it in his *Apollonius Gallus* (Paris, 1600), 'the (wholly geometrical) algebra that Theon, Apollonius, Pappus and other ancients handed on'. Apollonius's *Conics* in turn related the defining properties (*symptomata*) of the conic sections to Euclid's technique of the application of areas; indeed, that was the source of the names 'parabola', 'hyperbola', and 'ellipse'. But these and other curves served algebra only as a means of constructing solutions to determinate equations, and algebra in turn offered aid in solving section problems in geometry. Although Pappus's corpus included indeterminate problems for which curves constituted solutions, traditional mathematics offered models neither for the algebraic treatment of loci nor for the geometrical expression of indeterminate equations.

1. Curves and the theory of equations

Working independently of one another, Fermat and Descartes first devised those models and then extended the techniques of the analytic art to the structural properties of curves. Although Descartes claimed not to have read Viète's work until after composing the *Géométrie* in the early 1630s, Descartes's thinking developed along remarkably similar lines beginning in the late 1610s. He, too, sought to recover a hidden art of analysis from the classical Greek texts and from the 'barbarous' notation of Arabic and cossist algebraists.[50] He too proposed a new alphabetic symbolism aimed at expressing the combinatory relationships common to all quantities, whatever their specific form. However, he went beyond Viète by reformulating the concept of magnitude to reflect the focus on structural analysis. To maintain subtraction as the inverse of addition, Descartes accepted negative quantities, though he referred to them as *fausses.* Rejecting the classical view that, in the absence of a common measure, the product of two line segments could only be the rectangle formed by the factors and hence incomparable with either of them, Descartes argued that for algebraic purposes one can choose a common measure at will. Multiplication then takes the form of a proportion, $1{:}a = b{:}ab$, all the terms of which are homogeneous and comparable.[51] If 1, a and b are lines (Figure 22.10), then so too is ab, and the proportion is represented by a pair of similar triangles. By the same means, quotients, powers, and roots can also be represented by simple line segments in parallel with numbers.

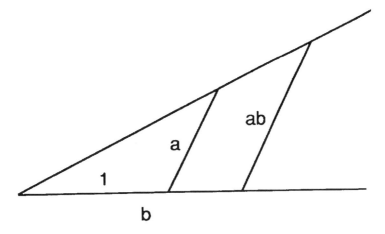

Figure 22.10

Two major developments flowed from this approach. First, Descartes could express a general polynomial of the form $x^n + a_1x^{n-1} + a_2x^{n-2} + \ldots + a_n = 0$, where n was a definite number and the a_i either numbers or algebraic expressions. Arguing by induction in Book III that every polynomial of degree n could only result from the multiplication of n binomial factors $x - \alpha_i$, the constant terms of which are the zeros of the polynomial, Descartes derived what are now called the elementary symmetric functions expressing the relationship between the roots of an equation and its coefficients. He also called into existence a new species of quantity necessary to maintain the generality of his analysis, namely the α_i he called *imaginaires* because they could not be reached by any operations on ordinary quantities and yet could be combined with them and with each other to yield real values. For example, expressed in the form $(x - 1)(x - \alpha)(x - \beta) = 0$, the equation $x^3 - 1 = 0$ has, in addition to the real root 1, two imaginary roots, α and β, the sum of which is -1 and the product, 1.[52] Enhancing the power of his method by the addition of ideal elements was a bold strategy to which Leibniz would later appeal in defence of infinitesimals.

The second development followed from the removal of dimensionality from the degree of an equation. Since all the relations inherent in an equation in one unknown can be expressed as segments of a single line, those of an equation in two unknowns require two lines which, placed at an angle to one another, define a plane. The equation determines the relations among corresponding segments of the two lines and is represented by a curve in the plane. Since the equation captures the metric structure of the curve, the determination of its properties, including the tangent and normal to any point, became a matter of algebraic analysis, as indeed Descartes noted by way of introduction to his method for drawing the normal to a curve.

Simply by knowing the relation that all the points of a curve have to those of a straight line, in the manner I have explained, it is easy to find also the relation they have to all other given points and lines, and consequently to know the diameters, axes, centers, and other lines or points to which each curve will have some more specific or simpler relation than to others, and thus to imagine various means of describing them and from among those [means] to choose the simpler ones. . . . That is why I shall believe I have set out here all that is required for the elements of curves when I shall have given generally the means of drawing straight lines that fall at right angles [to the curve] at any of its points one might choose. And I dare to say that this is the most useful and more general problem, not only that I know but that I have ever wanted to know in geometry.[53]

Thus, by this construction, Descartes extended Viète's analytic programme to the classical treatises on loci, foremost among them Apollonius's *Conics.*

Aiming the *Géométrie* at a specific problem and ultimately at an application to optics, Descartes offered few details of the new system. But Fermat had arrived at the same system and had laid out its fundamentals in his *Ad locos planos et solidos isagoge* (*Introduction to plane and solid loci* [*ca.* 1635]).[54] He posited that equations in two unknowns correspond to curves in the plane determined by two lines of reference: a fixed main axis with a point on it as origin, and a variable ordinate translated parallelly at a fixed angle to the axis. The axial system stemmed from Apollonius's *Conics,* and Fermat argued for the general proposition by showing how the conic sections, including circle and straight line, accounted for all possible cases of the general quadratic equation in two unknowns, and conversely. The demonstration had two components: linking the defining parameters of the individual curves to their canonical equations, for example, the centre and radius of the circle to the equation $x^2 + y^2 = r^2$, and reducing equations to one of the canonical forms by steps that correspond to translation, change of scale, and rotation of the axial system.

The *Ad locos planos et solidos isagoge* essentially reduced the contents of Books I–IV of the *Conics* to algebraic form, showing how the various structural properties of the conics corresponded to relations among the parameters of their equations. Although Book V was not extant at the time, Fermat and his contemporaries knew it involved the determination of tangents and normals to the conic sections, elements central to their optical properties as reflectors and refractors. Eliciting those elements from the equations led both Fermat and Descartes to another extension of Viète's new analysis. For Fermat, the crucial hint came from Pappus of Alexandria, who insisted on the uniqueness of extreme values. Consider the equation $bx - x^2 = M$. In general, it has two roots, say u and v. By a technique taken from Viète, $bu - u^2 = M = bv - v^2$, or $b(u - v) = u^2 - v^2 = (u + v)(u - v)$, or $b = u + v$. That, argued Fermat, is a general relationship linking the roots of the equation to one of its parameters.[55] In the case where M is the maximum or minimum value of the expression $bx - x^2$, the equation will have a single, repeated root, that is, $u = v = b/2$ (whence $M = b^2/4$). If one represents the two roots in terms of their difference, that is, u and $u + e$, then Fermat's analysis takes a familiar algorithmic form: $b(u + e) - (u + e)^2 = bu - u^2$, whence $be - 2ue - e^2 = 0$, or $b - 2u - e = 0$. That is the general relationship for all pairs of roots $u + e$ and u. In the case of a repeated root, $e = 0$, whence $b = 2u$, and so forth.[56]

To understand the conceptual origins of the calculus, it is essential to recognise that Fermat's difference e is a counterfactual, rather than an infinitesimal, quantity. That is, Fermat treated an equation with a repeated root *as if* the two roots were unequal, used the theory of equations to derive a relation that is generally true of all such unequal pairs, and then extended the relation to equal roots. The assumption of inequality covered the division by a quantity that in fact is 0. For the method of maxima and minima, at least, he made no appeal to limits or infinitesimals to justify that extension. That is, e carried no connotation of ranging over only very small values, as it later acquired when interpreted as an infinitesimal. Descartes followed a similar line of reasoning in his method of normals in Book III of the *Géométrie*. It was in keeping with the reasoning that lay behind his assumption of imaginary roots to maintain the full generality of his theory of equations.

Counterfactual reasoning also shaped Fermat's method of tangents, which he claimed to have derived from the method of extreme values, although the derivations he offered seem contrived after the fact. Given a point B on a curve (Figure 22.11), assume the tangent to have been drawn, intersecting the axis at E. Let OI be drawn parallel to BC at a distance e from it, intersecting the curve at O'. Except when OI coincides with BC, O and O' will be different points. Assume, however, that they coincide. Then, on the one hand, the subtangent EC is to BC as EI, that is, $(EC - e)$, is to OI. On the other hand, OI, that is, $O'I$, together with DI, that is, $(DC - e)$, satisfies the conditions of the curve. Expressing the first relation in terms of the second and carrying through the sequence of operations for the method of maxima and minima leads to a determinate expression for the subtangent in terms of the given ordinate and abscissa.

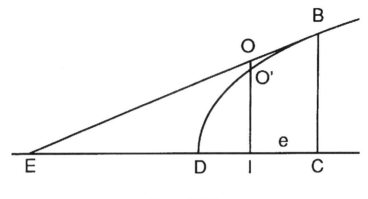

Figure 22.11

2. From counterfactuals to infinitesimals

Fermat and Descartes thought of their methods of determining tangents and extreme values in terms of special cases of general algebraic relations. They viewed the increments essential for deriving those relations as counterfactual quantities, which took the value 0 not by being negligibly small nor by convergence on a limit, but by instantiation of the special case.[57] It was a matter of the manipulation of symbolic forms without reference to the particular meaning of their constituent terms.[58] The structure of quadratic equations dictates that they have two roots, even when they appear to have only one. Using symbols for the roots preserves the structural distinction between them, even when they have the same value.

That view avoided infinitesimals only by excluding two classes of problems: curves defined with reference to other curves and the quadrature of curvilinear figures (that is, finding their areas or volumes). The first class included the 'special curves' cited by Pappus and other Greek sources, but it expanded rapidly with the addition of curves representing physical phenomena, such as the cycloid, the locus of a point on the circumference of a circle rolled along a line. Since most of the curves could not be represented by an algebraic expression, they were not open to algebraic analysis, including the method of tangents, without assuming that over small intervals their curvilinear elements could be treated as if they were rectilinear. That is how mathematicians, including Fermat, began to treat the curves and were thus drawn by specific instances into the realm of infinitesimal quantities and evanescent differences. Neither they nor their successors over the next half-century felt entirely comfortable there, and algebraic reduction of relations among infinitesimals to finite terms was one of the ways they sought to get out again.

The second class of problems had classical origins, notably in the works of Archimedes, who, following Eudoxus's 'method of exhaustion', proved his results by containing a curve between two rectilinear figures differing from one another by an arbitrarily small amount. Archimedes hinted at a more direct, heuristic form of the technique, and the spread of his works in the sixteenth century combined with the revival of atomism to shape the method of indivisibles, or infinitesimals. Although traditionally associated with Cavalieri, various forms of the technique emerged in several places at about the same time.[59]

Cavalieri stated as a principle that if two figures are bounded by the same parallel lines or planes, and the cross-sections generated by any line or plane parallel to the boundaries are equal, then the figures are equal. In that form, the method offered a means of comparing the figures, not calculating the area of either one. While 'all the lines' of one figure might be equal to all those of another, or indeed might be a multiple of all those of another, one could not add up the lines to constitute an area. However, imagining the cross-sections as slices of indefinitely narrow width, Torricelli tied Cavalieri's indivisibles to infinite series, and thus the areas to the sums of those series. In France, Fermat and Roberval independently took a similar approach, differing from one another in the range and variety of series they could handle.[60] By the mid-1640s, when Torricelli communicated his and Cavalieri's results to the French, Fermat had already established the general quadrature of curves of the form $y^m = px^n$ and $x^n y^m = p$, the so-called higher parabolas and hyperbolas. The achievement lay in determining the sum $\sum_{i=1}^{N} i^k$ for any k, integer or fraction, and success on that front derived more from number theory and the theory of equations than from any new concept of the infinite or infinitesimal.

When coupled with the method of tangents, however, the notion of infinitesimal slices of an area or volume did suggest a means of comparing areas on an element-by-element basis, rather than in the aggregate as Cavalieri's method required. The result was a technique of transformation or, as it came to be called, transmutation of areas, which became then the basis of the integral calculus. The Torricelli–Roberval correspondence offers one of the earliest examples, which the two authors treat in slightly different ways.

Let ADB be a curve (Figure 22.12). From each point of the curve, draw a line segment parallel to the axis and equal to the length of the subtangent to that point, thus generating another curve $AO'Z'$, or COZ, depending on the direction

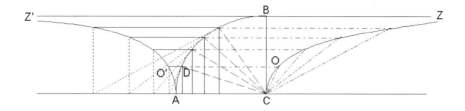

Figure 22.12

in which the segments are drawn. In the first case, Torricelli shows that the area between *ADB* and *AO'Z'* is equal to that under ADB; in the second, Roberval establishes that the area between *ADB* and *COZ* is equal to twice that under ADB. Both arguments rest on the division of the two areas into corresponding infinitesimal segments, which bear to one another a relation that holds only in the limiting case and, short of that, rests on the assumption that a very small arc of a curve coincides with the tangent. The length of the tangent then mediates between the two segments. In Roberval's case, it becomes the common base of a triangular segment of ADB and a rhomboidal segment of *ABZC,* both contained between the same parallel lines. In Torricelli's case, it establishes that the bases of corresponding rectangular slices of the two areas are inversely as their heights, whence the slices are equal.

If, now, one shifts focus from the generated curve to an ordinate of the original curve, it is evident that the tangent maps any division of the axis of a curve into a corresponding division of its final ordinate. Consider, that is, the parabola $y^2 = px$ (Figure 22.13), and imagine the area under it sliced into infinitesimal rectangles by parallel ordinates y erected on axis x over the interval $[0,a]$. If for brevity's sake the rectangles are designated by the ordinates, the area under the curve corresponds to 'all the y over a'.[61] But one can also erect a set of segments x on axis y over the interval $[0,b]$. In that case the area under the curve with respect to the y-axis will be 'all the x over b'. The area under the curve with respect to the x-axis is then rectangle ab - (all x over b). Hence,

all y over $x = ab$ - all x over y.

That relation becomes productive by taking account of the differing widths, albeit infinitesimal, of the segments drawn one way and the other. From some point P on the curve, draw the corresponding slices, PQ and $PR,$ the bases of which

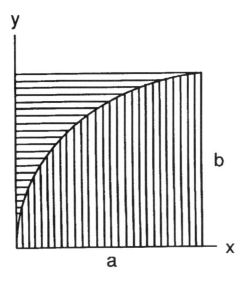

Figure 22.13

correspond to one another through the medium of their common infinitesimal element P of the parabola. Construct (Figure 22.14) the tangent PT intersecting the x-axis at T. Then, on the premise that P coincides with the tangent, P is to infinitesimal Q as $PT:QT$ and to infinitesimal R as $PT:PQ$; that is, $R:Q = PQ:QT$, or $PQ \times Q = QT \times R$ for each pair of corresponding slices Q and R. In the case of the parabola, $QT = 2OQ$. Hence all PQ over OQ is equal to twice all OQ over OR ($= PQ$); or, in the symbolic terms Leibniz will soon establish,

$$\int ^{ydx} = \int ^{subtangent \times dy} = \int ^{2xdy}.$$

Used to reduce unknown figures to known ones, the transmutation of areas took various forms in mid-century. Fermat attached it to his analytic geometry, and hence to the analytic programme, by adapting it for application directly to the equations of curves and algebraically transforming, for example, the curve $b^3 = x^2y + b^2y$ into $b^2 = u^2 + v^2$ by means of the auxiliary curves $by = u^2$ and $bv = xu$ to show that its quadrature involves the quadrature of the circle.[62] By contrast, Barrow and James Gregory retained its geometrical formulation while expanding the means of transformation to include the normal and the subtangent.[63] It is precisely in this work that historians have perceived anticipations of the calculus

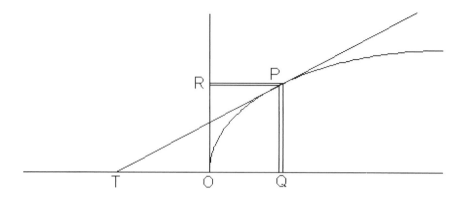

Figure 22.14

and sought the source of Newton's and Leibniz's inspiration. Yet, none of the writers on transmutation of areas tied the way in which tangents and normals were being used there to the method of determining them. In their minds, the problem of drawing the tangent to a curve apparently remained separate from the problem of measuring the area under it. The credit for linking them remains with Newton and Leibniz.

Barrow's *Lectiones geometricae* suggests by contrast the nature of their insight. Although Barrow embraced the new notion of symbolic magnitude as a relation, he ultimately distrusted the abstractive power of algebra, refusing in particular to accept the notion of ratio as quantity. Although he was willing to extend the concept of relation to include equations, he did not see the method of tangents as an operation on an equation yielding another, derived equation and therefore a relation of the same sort. Barrow viewed Fermat's algorithm as a means of determining the finite ratio of the unknown subtangent to the known ordinate by means of the ratio of infinitesimal increments of elements of the curve, usually but not always the abscissa and the ordinate. The elimination of the infinitesimals in the limiting case fixed a value for the latter ratio and hence a value for the subtangent, understood always as a line segment on the axis, rather than as a variable bearing a relationship to another variable expressed by an equation. Barrow inherited from classical geometry the notion of the quadratrix of a curve, namely a curve of which the ordinate is proportional to the area of the base curve on the same abscissa, and his treatment of these 'squaring curves' has invited credit from historians for adumbrating the calculus. But Barrow never thought about

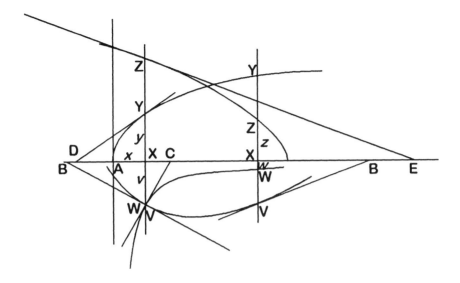

Figure 22.15

reversing the relationship between the curves, seeing the base curve as proportional to the tangent of the quadratrix.[64]

Leibniz first presented his differential calculus in 1684 as 'a new method for
maxima and minima, and also for tangents, which stops at neither fractions nor
irrational quantities, and a singular type of calculus for these', thus suggesting that
he was simply improving earlier methods rather than offering something quite
new.[65] Yet, he began where Barrow had left off:

> Let *AX* be an axis [Figure 22.15] and let there be several curves, such as *VV, WW, YY, ZZ,*
> of which the ordinates, perpendicular to the axis, are *VX, WX, YX, ZX,* which shall be
> called respectively *v, w, y, z*; and *AX* itself, the abscissa on the axis, shall be called *x*. Let the
> tangents be *VB, WC, YD, ZE,* meeting the axis at points *B, C, D, E,* respectively. Now let
> some straight line taken at will (*pro arbitrio*) be called *dx,* and let the straight line which is
> to *dx* as *v* (or *w,* or *y,* or *z*) is to *XB* (or *XC,* or *XD,* or *XE*) be called *dv* (or *dw,* or *dy,* or
> *dz*) or the difference of these *v* (or of these *w,* or *y,* or *z*).

Speaking of *dx* as a line of arbitrary length misled some readers, who, like the
Marquis de l'Hôpital, saw at first merely a change in notation from Fermat's and
Barrow's *a* and *e*. They missed the significance of Leibniz's notation, which in

labelling the differences by a common prefix marked them as the result of an operation (he would later refer to it as 'a certain modification') on quantities, presenting the rules – indeed, he used the term *algorithm* – that governed its application to their sums, differences, products, quotients, powers, and roots; that is, to the ordinary operations by which equations are constructed. Thus, he defined, rather than derived, the differential of a product dxy as $xdy + ydx$ without raising the question of its relation to the form $xdy + ydx + dxdy$, which results from defining dxy as $(x + dx)(y + dy) - xy$ in line with the general notion of difference introduced at the start of the article.

The method of tangents, too, was a matter of definition: $dy{:}dx = y{:}subtangent$. The definition formed two bridges. While tying back to the earlier method, it also thrust forward into the new realm. The reason why the new method 'did not stop' lay in the special properties of differentials, for 'to find the tangent is to draw a straight line which joins two points of the curve which have an infinitesimally small distance [between them], or [to draw] the extended side of the infinitangular polygon that for us is equivalent to the curve.'[66] That is, in differentiating the curve's equation to determine the relation of dx and dy, one also transformed the curve into the infinite number of rectilinear sides ds that joined the end points of the differentials. The relationship $ds^2 = dx^2 + dy^2$ meant that at the level of differentials all of the curves were algebraic because, in a sense, all of the lines were straight.

Thus, infinitesimal analysis served to open the 'hidden geometry' of transcendental curves, which Descartes had labelled 'mechanical' and excluded from mathematics proper.[67] In Leibniz's calculus, differential equations enjoyed the same status as algebraic equations in representing curves and their properties, and a suitable theory of differential equations would provide means of eliciting from them the same kind of structural information as did the theory of ordinary equations. 'It is true, as you very well note', Leibniz wrote to Huygens in 1691, 'that what is best and most convenient in my new calculus is that it offer truths by a species of analysis and with no effort of imagination, which often succeeds only by luck, and it gives us all the advantages over Archimedes that Viète and Descartes have given us over Apollonius.'[68] The d denoted a symbolic operation that provided a path from the finite to the infinite and back. The algorithm of the differential calculus linked the realms of the algebraic and the transcendental symbolically, while the method of tangents tied them together metrically. Expressed symbolically, differentials played the same rôle in infinitesimal analysis that imaginary quantities did in ordinary analysis; as Leibniz explained to Varignon in 1702:

If someone will not admit infinite or infinitely small lines as metaphysically rigorous or as real things, he can use them surely as ideal notions which shorten reasoning, similarly to what one calls 'imaginary roots' in common analysis (as for example $\sqrt{-2}$), which, for all that they are called 'imaginary', are no less useful, and even necessary, for expressing real magnitudes analytically.[69]

Speaking of 'well founded fictions', Leibniz continued the theme of counterfactual reasoning on which Fermat had originally based his method of maxima and minima. Pressed later on how to move from fiction to reality, Leibniz tried to show in some detail that, although differentials are infinitely smaller than finite quantities and hence have no ratio to them, the ratios of infinitesimals to one another are determinate and equal to ratios between finites; the relation $dy/dx = y/subtangent$ was the touchstone. The ratios establish a correspondence between the two realms, much as combinations such as $\sqrt{1+\sqrt{-3}} + \sqrt{1-\sqrt{-3}} = \sqrt{6}$ link imaginary to real roots.[70]

In Leibniz's mind, ideal elements simply gave mathematicians purchase on real processes. There is no last term of an infinite series, but one can imagine the form of that term as it grows smaller and appeal to the 'law of continuity' to preserve that form as the term reaches the limit, just as by that law 'it is permitted to consider rest as an infinitely small motion (i.e. as equivalent to its contradictory in a sense) and coincidence as an infinitely small distance, and equality as the last of the inequalities, and so on.' For that matter, continuity itself could be considered an ideal object, for nothing in nature corresponded to it. Yet,

in recompense, the real does not cease to be governed by the ideal and the abstract, and it happens that the rules of the finite succeed in the infinite, as if there were atoms (i.e. assignable elements of nature), even though there is no matter actually divided without end; and conversely the infinite succeeds in the finite, as if there were metaphysical infinitesimals, even though one does not need them and the division of matter never reaches infinitely small pieces.

'That is how everything is governed by reason,' he concluded, 'otherwise there would be neither knowledge nor reason, and that would not conform to the nature of the sovereign principle.'[71]

3. Proof, truth, and utility

Mathematics extended its utility in part by incorporating into theory what had up to then been treated as craft practice. Pressure to do so came in part from the practitioners, as they sought new status for their craft. Persuaded that the 'barbarous' art of algebra, inherited from the Arabs, contained traces of the method of analysis the Greek geometers used to find solutions to problems and proofs of theorems and then masked in their demonstrations, Viète created a new symbolism and elevated algebra to the 'art of analysis'. Descartes followed suit, redefining 'geometry' as the class of problems subject to algebraic expression and treatment, and subsequent developments in the methods of series and infinitesimals extended that class. By the end of the century, 'analysis' covered most of mathematics beyond the elementary subjects. Each step moved analysis farther away from what Greek mathematicians took to be its inseparable counterpart, synthesis: the rigorous demonstration from first principles or from theorems already derived from first principles. In working by hypothesis from the unknown to the known, analysis had heuristic power but lacked demonstrative force. In the absence of proof that each of the steps of an analysis could be inverted, analysis could not compel assent.

The mathematicians who created and used the new analysis were fully aware of its weakness and they offered two related responses. First, they argued that any analysis could be reversed to form a synthetic demonstration, albeit not always directly. At worst, the result determined analytically formed the starting point of a double *reductio ad absurdum,* the steps of which would also follow from the analysis. Fermat often recognised the need for a synthetic demonstration, even if he then waived it as 'easy' or 'not worth the effort' to carry out in detail. In this, he leaned towards the second response to critics of analysis, expressed perhaps most clearly by Descartes in his responses to the second set of objections to the *Meditationes.* Analysis, he argued, made clear to the attentive reader how the result had been achieved and hence conveyed intuitive understanding even if it did not constitute conclusive proof.

Descartes's identification of geometry with algebraic polynomials kept derivations close enough to demonstrations for practitioners to believe that the inversion from analysis to synthesis was straightforward. Rather than posing questions of interpretation, imaginary roots by their very impossibility indicated the absence of a solution to a problem. Descartes and Fermat could persuade themselves that their respective methods for drawing tangents rested on finite algebraic foundations, and, indeed, the pseudo-equalities used to find the tangent served as the inequalities needed to demonstrate its unique contact with the curve at the given point. But attention soon shifted to the extension of the method of tangents to non-algebraic curves, requiring assumptions about the negligibility of differences between, say, arcs and their chords over infinitesimal intervals, and it was less obvious how to invert those assumptions in a synthetic demonstration.

Similarly, methods of quadrature and rectification also rested on assumptions about differences over small intervals, in particular when they can be neglected.

Once dropped during analysis, they could not readily be recalled during synthesis. But, just as Archimedes inspired the methods of analysis, he also provided the model of synthesis in the form of double *reductio ad absurdum,* examples of which abounded in his works. Again, the apparently close relation between the pseudo-equalities or limit-sums of infinitesimal analysis and the inequalities on which the reductions rested lent intuitive confidence that proof was a matter of detail. 'I have set out these lemmas beforehand', wrote Newton in a scholium to Book I, Section I, of the *Principia,* dealing with the 'method of first and last ratios, with the aid of which what follows is demonstrated',

so that I may avoid the tedium of carrying out involved demonstrations *ad absurdum,* in the manner of the ancient geometers. For demonstrations are rendered more concise by the method of indivisibles. But since the hypothesis of indivisibles is harder, and for that reason that method is deemed less geometrical, I wanted to reduce the demonstrations of the following matters to the last sums and ratios of evanescent quantities, and to the first [sums and ratios] of nascent [quantities], and for that reason to set out beforehand demonstrations of those limits with all possible brevity.[72]

Newton intended the lemmas to define his meaning even if he subsequently spoke in terms of ratios and sums of indivisibles or took curved 'linelets' for straight lines. Through the lemmas, the language of indivisibles translated into that of limits, which could be used 'more securely' as 'demonstrated principles'.

Leibniz used similar terms in asserting safe passage between the realms of the infinitesimal and the finite. The fact that later generations found the passage more hazardous than he, Newton, and their immediate followers portrayed it is less important historically than the fact that they were aware of the difficulties of fitting their concepts and techniques to the reigning standards of rigour as set by Aristotle and Euclid and were attempting to resolve those difficulties by showing that the paths of the calculus, or at least the results reached by them, could be retraced in classical steps and by introducing new canons of intelligibility and criteria of effectiveness as warrants of the soundness of their methods.[73] That dual strategy had been laid down over the century and was evidently persuasive to the audience the practitioners of the new methods were addressing. That is worth bearing in mind, lest nineteenth- and twentieth-century concerns with formal rigour be projected back onto the seventeenth century, investing the original concepts of the calculus retrospectively with meanings they did not have for their creators and consequently overlooking the meanings they did have.

Those meanings depended in significant part on shared practice.[74] Barrow's *Lectiones mathematicae* show how much mathematicians' understanding of the philosophical issues depended on their knowledge of mathematics itself. At several points he found it difficult, even impossible, to explain to an unskilled undergraduate audience a concept such as 'possible congruence' which underlay Cavalieri's technique for determining that one curved figure was equal in length or area to another. One could not understand the concept without using it. As Bacon had insisted of scientific knowledge as a whole, so too in mathematics truth and utility were 'one and the same thing'.[75] Intuitive confidence in the new mathematical techniques derived from knowing that they worked, and that knowledge came from knowing how to make them work.

Conversely, philosophical discussions of mathematics that were not rooted in practical experience had little bearing on the developments that would prove of philosophical importance. Barrow dismissed Andreas Tacquet's critique of Cavalieri's method because Tacquet showed he did not know how to apply it to simple problems. Thomas Hobbes's criticism of mathematicians suffered the same fate. In 1695 Bernhard van Nieuwentijdt wrote in the *Acta eruditorum* of his perplexity over second differentials, and Leibniz tried to explain. But by then Jakob and Johann Bernoulli had shown the vast range of problems – some old, some new – that second differences opened to analysis, thus placing them beyond debate among practitioners. Fontenelle spoke for the majority of the Académie des Sciences when he emphasised the new canons of intelligibility by which they measured Leibniz's calculus:

Although the mathematical infinite is well understood, its principles quite unshakeable, its arguments fully coherent, most of its investigations a bit advanced, it does not cease still to cast us into the abyss of a profound darkness, or at the very least into realms where the daylight is extremely weak. . . . [A] bizarre thing has happened in higher mathematics [*haute géométrie*]: certainty has undermined clarity. One always holds onto the thread of the calculus, the infallible guide; no matter where one arrives, one had to arrive, whatever shadows one finds there. Moreover, glory has always attached to great discoveries, to the solution of difficult problems, and not to the elucidation of ideas.[76]

The new mathematics belonged to those who knew how to do it.

This 'proof-of-the-pudding' approach to what by 1700 was viewed as the twofold field of ordinary and infinitesimal analysis drew support and inspiration from the application of mathematics to mechanical problems. The centre of gravity was only one of several foci of mechanical action locatable only by determining the areas and volumes of curved figures. Conversely, by concentrating varying degrees of change in one point, such centres of action suggested a strategy for capturing change mathematically by reduction to a mean value. Although mechanics did not create the problems of drawing tangents to curves and measuring their areas, it did offer intuitive support for the means of solving those problems. The notion of speed made sense of change over an interval, and acceleration gave meaning to a change of change. Viewing speed as an intensional quality made extensional by imagining it counterfactually to be held for a period of time or by summing up its effect over a finite interval gave substance to the notion of 'indivisibles' and of their transition into infinitesimals. As Barrow summed it up in his *Lectiones geometricae*:

To every instant of time, or to every indefinitely small particle of time; (I say 'instant' or 'indefinite particle' because, just as it matters nothing at all whether we understand a line to be composed of innumerable points or of indefinitely small linelets [*lineolae*], so it is all the same whether we suppose time to be composed of instants or of innumerable minute timelets [*tempusculis*]; at least for the sake of brevity we shall not fear to use instants in place of times however small, or points in place of the linelets representing timelets); to each moment of time, I say, there corresponds some degree of velocity which the moving body should be thought to have then; to that degree corresponds some length of space traversed (for here we consider the moving body as a point and thus the space only as length).[77]

Thus the intuition of motion, of its continuity, of the speed of motion at a given moment, and of the reducibility of variations of that speed to some mean measure provided a touchstone for the new techniques of analysis, whether algebraic or geometric in style.

What did algebra have to do with mechanics in the seventeenth century? The common factor was analysis, understood as resolution or reduction into constituents. Algebra was called analysis initially because it embodied Pappus's description of the process of moving from a problem to its solution. But Viète put a new twist on it by introducing the notion of the structure of equations (*constitutio aequationum*) and making algebra, or the analytic art, the body of techniques by which that structure is analysed into its basic parts or transformed into equivalent structures. Descartes and Fermat built from there, applying the art to curves and adding techniques for drawing from the structure of equations of curves the properties of their tangents and areas. Those new techniques involved infinitely small quantities and considerations of limiting values, setting the basis for the calculus as devised by Newton and Leibniz. But underlying the new quantities and techniques for calculating with them lay the original themes of the analytic art: a method of heuristic that proceeds by resolution into parts. Infinitesimals allowed the art to analyse motion and the continuum.

It may sound like a truism, but mechanics was linked to analysis through the notion of a machine. What counteracts the truism is the identification of mechanics as the science of motion, canonised by the title of Wallis's treatise; nothing in

the concept of a science of motion entails resolution into parts. Machines, however, are quintessentially analytic: one understands their working by taking them
apart and seeing how the parts go together. Machines are nothing more or less
than the sum of their parts. Mechanising the world meant making it a machine,
that is, conceptualising it as a structure resolvable into constituents which, understood individually, combine to explain the action of the whole. Francis Bacon was
talking mechanistically when he said:

> But to resolve nature into abstractions is less to our purpose than to dissect her into parts;
> as did the school of Democritus, which went further into nature than the rest. Matter
> rather than forms should be the object of our attention, its configurations and changes of
> configuration, and simple action, and law of action or motion; for forms are figments of
> the human mind, unless you will call those laws of motion forms.[78]

Whether or not Bacon expected those laws to be expressed mathematically,
Descartes certainly did. The 'laws of nature' by which God created and conserves
the world are statements about parts of matter in motion according to quantitative
relations.

> I could set out here many additional rules for determining in detail when and how and by
> how much the motion of each body can be diverted and increased or decreased by colliding
> with others, something that comprises summarily all the effects of nature. But I shall be
> content with showing you that, besides the three laws that I have explained, I wish to
> suppose no others but those that most certainly follow from the eternal truths on which
> mathematicians are wont to support their most certain and evident demonstrations; the
> truths, I say, according to which God Himself has taught us He disposed all things in
> number, weight, and measure.[79]

Understanding an 'effect of nature', then, comes down to analysing it into its
constituent parts of matter and expressing the effect in terms of their interaction
by the laws of motion.

That view of nature as analytic in the same sense as a machine does not in itself
entail an algebraic description. Clearly, as most of the literature of seventeenth-
century mechanics shows, one can understand both the parts and their motions in
geometrical terms. Yet, as the mechanics probed deeper, the many dimensions of
bodies in motion – their position, velocity, acceleration, momentum, force –
strained the capacity of geometrical configurations to accommodate them opera-
tionally rather than just illustratively. Couching the parameters of motion in
algebraic terms made explicit their structure and the structure of the relations
between them, and it made those structures accessible to manipulation. As a
calculus of motion, analytic mechanics thus made motion a form of machine to

be taken apart and reassembled. In that calculus, created at the turn of the eighteenth century, the new mechanics and the new mathematics met to form a new metaphysics.

4. Analytic mechanics: Mathematics, motion, and metaphysics

Galileo and Descartes both wrestled with the continuum and its implications for a mathematical account of nature. They knew from Aristotle the logical inconsistencies that attend any geometry based on atomism or actual infinities.[80] In the former, all magnitudes are commensurable; in the latter, all magnitudes are equal. Potentially infinite divisibility sustained the continuity necessary for incommensurability and ordering, as Eudoxus showed in his theory of proportions and the method of exhaustion based on it. As mathematicians, Galileo and Descartes were wary of infinites and infinitesimals, on the one hand, and indivisibles, on the other. Both notions courted mathematical incoherence. Acceptable perhaps as shortcuts and temporary expedients for problem solving, they constituted problems in themselves, to be controlled if not resolved by formal demonstration of the results reached by them. Mathematicians throughout the century shared this view, even as they developed the new methods of infinitesimals and infinite series. They differed over what constituted proper grounding of those methods, not on the need for grounding. Without an unambiguous correspondence between the domain of the infinitesimal and that of the finite, mathematicians could talk only by analogy. However different in form, Newton's lemmas concerning first and last ratios and Leibniz's principle of continuity based that correspondence on the possibility of a definite ratio among indefinite magnitudes.

Equally persuasive to Galileo, Descartes, and their successors was the notion that at some level of fineness the physical world must consist of atoms.[81] To make sense mechanically, matter at some point has to resist division and push back. Whatever the differences in their metaphysics, mechanicians shared the intuitive model of small balls bouncing against one another, whether suspended on strings or rolling along the ground. In that model their interaction was also discontinuous: they met at certain speeds and separated at new speeds, and the change had to be instantaneous; as atoms, they had no substructure to explain the lag required by deceleration and acceleration. Hence, whatever problems discontinuous matter posed for mathematical description, the mechanical model of impressed forces ran headlong into the continuity of time and motion.

Galileo emphasised that continuity as a means of incorporating rest into the state of motion, so that a body might pass through all degrees of motion to zero and then acquire speed again, without ever stopping. Descartes's insistence on the relativity of motion entailed the same continuity, even if his laws of impact violated it, as both Huygens and Leibniz pointed out. It posed a problem for Newton in giving his laws of motion mathematically effective form. In Definition VIII he posited the motive quantity of centripetal force as 'its measure proportional to the [quantity of] motion it generates in a given time', that is, to the rate of change of momentum over time. In the second of the laws of motion that served as axioms for the theorems to follow, he asserted that 'the change of [quantity of] motion is proportional to the motive force impressed and takes place along the straight line in which that force is impressed.' Time had disappeared from the process. The difference between the two statements has raised the much-debated question of whether Newton was thinking of continuous force or discrete impulse.

Phrasing the question as an alternative, however, overlooks the interdependence of mathematics and metaphysics in Newton's system. When Newton applied the axiom in Theorem I, he was reasoning on the basis of the orbit as a geometrical object. Drawn in two-dimensional space, the configuration allowed the representation of velocity and time only indirectly by means of lines and areas proportional to them. To show change in velocity, therefore, he needed first to show velocity as a finite segment traversed over an interval of time. Time itself remained off the diagram at the start, divided into a succession of equal intervals, while the orbit began as a concatenation of straight lines each proportional to the distance traversed uniformly during each interval at the current velocity, and thus to the velocity. Change in velocity could be represented only by comparing the path traversed during the next interval at the new velocity and the path that would have been traversed had the body continued during that interval at the old velocity. Hence the force was applied at the end of each interval and it was measured at the end of the next interval by a line segment parallel to the radius drawn to the previous endpoint and bounded by the two paths. In short, the mathematics required that the force act impulsively at discrete intervals. Newton could approach continuity, both of orbit and of applied force, only by shortening the intervals and increasing their number. In assuming that relations that remain unchanged however small the intervals of time between impulses are preserved when time flows as a continuum and the force is continuously impressed, the demonstration of Proposition 1, Theorem 1 echoes Leibniz's principle of continuity.

Newton himself evidently believed that his limit argument reconciled the mathematics of discrete impulses to the metaphysics of continuous forces.

Whether consciously or not, he assumed that the variation in the direction of the force acting continuously over a small interval can be ignored. To phrase the second law in terms of rate of change would have required a different body of mathematical tools, which enabled one to articulate the nature and implications of that assumption. In recasting the geometrical analysis of the *Principia* into the infinitesimal analysis of Leibniz's calculus, Varignon showed what such tools might look like.

In 1700 Varignon sketched a general theory of motion determined by central forces and in a series of memoirs rendered into the language of the calculus the mechanical substance of Book I, Sections 2–10, of the *Principia*. His first memoir, 'Manière générale de déterminer les forces, les vitesses, les espaces, & les temps, une seule de ces quatre choses étant donnée dans toutes sortes de mouvement rectilignes variés à discrétion', aimed at capturing Newton's theorems on rectilinear centripetal motion in two 'general rules', from which all else followed by the techniques of ordinary and infinitesimal analysis. His modification of the configuration of Proposition 39 of the *Principia* reveals both the different form of mathematics Varignon was working with and the different ends to which he was applying it.

All the rectilinear angles in the adjoined figure [Figure 22.16] being right, let *TD, VB, FM, VK, FN, FO* be any six curves, of which the first three express through their common abscissa *AH* the distance traversed by some body moved arbitrarily along *AC*. Moreover, let the time taken to traverse it be expressed by the corresponding ordinate *HT* of the curve *TC*, the speed of that body at each point *H* by the two corresponding ordinates *VH* and *VG* of the curves *VB* and *VK*. The force towards *C* at each point *H*, independent of [the body's] speed (I shall henceforth call it *central force* owing to its tendency towards point *C* as center) will be expressed similarly by the corresponding ordinates *FH, FG, FE* of the curves *FM, FN, FO*.

The axis *AC*, with the centre of force at *C*, stemmed from Newton. The six curves were inspired by Leibniz. They represent graphically the various combinations of functional dependency among the parameters of motion: the 'curve of times' *TD* represents time as a function of distance; the 'curves of speed' *VB* and *VX*, the velocity as functions of distance and time, respectively; and the 'curves of force' *FM, FN,* and *FO*, the force as functions of distance, time, and velocity, respectively. To translate those designations into defining mathematical relations, Varignon turned to algebraic symbolism. At any point *H* on *AC* set the distance $AH = x$, the time $HT = AG = t$, the speed $(HV = AE = GV) = v$, and the central force $HF = EF = GF = y$. 'Whence', Varignon concluded from the perspective of the calculus, 'one will have *dx* for the distance traversed as if with a uniform

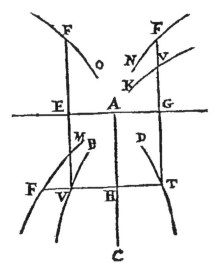

Figure 22.16

speed (*comme d'une vitesse uniforme*) *v* at each instant, *dv* for the increase in speed
that occurs there, *ddx* for the distance traversed by virtue of that increase in speed,
and *dt* for that instant.' The first of the two general rules simply expressed
symbolically the basic assumption of uniform motion over infinitesimal intervals.
Since 'speed consists only of a ratio of the distance traversed by a uniform motion
to the time taken to traverse it', $v = dx/dt$, whence, by the rules of differentiation,[82] $dv = ddx/dt$.

The second rule took account of the change of speed and of the increment of
distance that results from it: 'Moreover, since the distances traversed by a body
moved by a constant and continually applied force, such as one ordinarily thinks
of weight, are in the compound ratio of that force and of the squares of the times
taken to traverse them, $ddx = y\, dt^2$, or $y = ddx/dt^2 = dv/dt$.' The rule appears to
have stemmed in the first instance from the *Principia*. The first half of the measure
expresses the second law, and the second half translates into the language of the
calculus Lemma 10, which in turn sets out a principle also found in Huygens's
analysis of centrifugal force. Varignon's version of the rule literally brings a new
dimension to it, however, by capturing through the second differential *dds* that the
effect is a second-order variation of the motion of a body.

Those two rules, $v = dx/dt$, and $y = dv/dt$, sufficed, Varignon maintained, to give a full account of forced motion along straight lines. For, given any one of the six curves set out above, one can use the rules to carry out the transformations necessary to produce the other five. That central proposition reduces the mechanics in question to a matter of mathematics, and for the remainder of the memoir Varignon pursued an essentially mathematical point, echoing in the style and direction of his discussion two articles published by Leibniz in 1694.[83] The solution of the differential equation $v(x) = dx/dt$ yields the curve DT determined by $HT = t(x)$, and, if $VB = v(x)$, then $v'(x)dx = dv = ydt$ will produce $y(x,t)$, which can take two forms, depending on how the curve DT is expressed. Either $FG = y(x(t),t)$ or $FH = y(x,t(x))$. The other curves emerge by similar transformations. As Varignon noted at the outset, the general claim rests on the dual assumption of complete solvability in the two realms of analysis: the resolution of any algebraic equation – that is, getting $x(t)$ from $t(x)$ – and the integration of any differential equation. The limits of the mechanics in question were those of the calculus.

Varignon pushed further towards those limits in later memoirs. In particular, he directed his analyses towards expressions which presupposed no differential as constant, that is, no variable as independent. Depending on that choice, the expression took on several different forms. Put another way, the expression determined a family of differential equations, each transformable into the others by a change of variable. In articulating Leibniz's calculus, Johann Bernoulli had shown how that set of transformations led to the solution of various integrals and differential equations. By linking it now to the mechanics of central forces, Varignon meant to extend its power even further, first by using it to free his mechanics from dependence on any particular choice of coordinates and second to bring mechanics to bear on mathematical problems.

The details of his argument are of less concern here than the direction in which it took mechanics as the prime expression of nature understood mathematically. Generalising the expression of mechanical relations to the point of rendering them independent of the choice of independent variable brought to a culmination the trend away from diagrams and towards symbolic expressions that began with Galileo's analysis of acceleration. Varignon's analyses proceeded by manipulation of symbols according to the rules of finite and infinitesimal algebra supplemented by those of kinematics and dynamics expressed symbolically, and the resulting combinations of variables took their meaning from those operations. Varignon, at least, had pointed mechanics towards Euler and Lagrange.

While vastly extending the effective range of mechanics, the symbolic approach brought into sharper focus the question of the relationship between the structure of the mathematical model and the structure of the physical system it is meant to represent and thereby to explain. Put most succinctly, what do the intermediate steps linking two mathematical statements about a physical system have to do with the processes that tie the two physical configurations together? Huygens had felt no need to posit the existence of something in nature corresponding to the measure mv^2, even though he used its conservation as a primary tool for analysing dynamical problems. By contrast, Newton confronted the dilemma of a real force which he could not explain mechanically but which he needed mathematically, and he chose the mathematical horn. An old problem, of which the mediaeval debate over the reality of epicycles is one form, it assumed new importance with the use of mathematics to analyse the nature of motion and its relation to force. The widening empire of mathematical physics over the next two hundred years would carry the question into new realms of nature.

NOTES

1 For example, at the end of the definitions of Book I: 'I use the words "attraction", "impulse", or "tendency" of anything towards the center interchangeably with one another, considering these forces not physically but only mathematically. Whence the reader should beware lest he think that by such words I am anywhere defining a species or mode of action or a physical cause or explanation, or that I am actually and physically attributing forces to centers (which are mathematical points), if perhaps I should say either that centers attract or that centers have forces.' Newton, 1687, pp. 4–5.

2 So it appeared to Joseph Needham viewing the origins of modern science from the perspective of his study of Chinese science; see Needham 1959, sec. 19(k).

3 'Sed [*mechanicen*] eam Geometriae partem intelligimus, quae *Motum* tractat: atque Geometricis rationibus, & [*apodeiktikos*], inquirit, quâ vi quisque motus peragatur.' Wallis 1670, p. 1. Cf. Newton 1687, Praef. ad lect.: '*Quo sensu* Mechanica rationalis *erit Scientia Motuum qui ex viribus quibuscunque resultant, & virium quae ad motus quoscunque requiruntur, accurate proposita ac demonstrata.*' On the varied and changing meanings of 'mechanics' in the sixteenth and seventeenth centuries, see Gabbey 1992.

4 Galilei 1969, vol. 1, p. 281.

5 Fontenelle 1725, p. 87.

6 Newton 1687, Bk. I, sec. VI, Lemma XXVIII: 'There is no oval figure, of which the area cut off by any straight line can be found generally by means of equations finite in the number of terms and dimensions.'

7 See Leibniz 1686, 1694a. Cf. Bos 1988.

8 Vlastos 1975.

9 Hatfield 1990.

10 'It seems to me that the everyday practice of the famous Arsenal of you gentlemen of Venice, in particular in that part called "mechanics", opens to speculative minds a wide field for philosophizing.' Galilei 1638, p. 1. Cf. Robert Boyle's brief argument 'That the Goods of Mankind may be much Increased by the Naturalist's Insight into Trades', resting on the propositions that 'the phaenomena afforded by the trades are (most of

them) a part of the history of nature, and therefore may both challenge the naturalist's curiosity, and to [!] add to his knowledge,' and that '[the phaenomena of trades] show us nature in motion, and that too, when she is (as it were) put out of her course, by the strength or skill of man, which I have formerly noted to be the most instructive condition, wherein we can behold her' (Boyle 1772, vol. 3, pp. 442–3; as published in Boyle 1965, pp. 163–5).

11 Kepler to Herwart von Hohenberg, 10 February 1605, in Kepler 1937– , vol. 15, p. 146.

12 Gabbey 1990d. For a more extensive survey of the changing meaning of 'mechanics' in the seventeenth century, see Gabbey 1992.

13 For a survey and analysis of various notions of perpetual motion and their relation to the principles of mechanics in the seventeenth century, see Gabbey 1985.

14 Stevin 1586, Bk. I, prop. 19, pp. 175–9. One may question the cogency of Stevins's reasoning here, to wit, whether the perpetual motion he describes is in fact impossible in the abstract. But the point at hand concerns his translation of its practical impossibility into a mathematical argument.

15 The frontispiece of Fontana's treatise on moving the obelisk graphically illustrates the problem of scaling, as many of the competing proposals portrayed there are clearly unfeasible when scaled to the full-sized obelisk.

16 Letter to Castelli, 21 December 1613; in Galilei 1969, vol. 1, p. 177.

17 See, for example, chap. [14] of his *De motu* [*antiquiora*] (*ca.* 1590) in Galilei 1960b, p. 64.

18 On Galileo's early work in mechanics, see Clavelin 1974, chap. 3.

19 On the relation of Galileo's new science of motion to mediaeval sources as mediated by the sixteenth-century scholastic curriculum, see Wallace 1984, esp. chap. 4.

20 On the 'mean speed theorem' and mediaeval kinematics in general, see Clagett 1959, esp. pt. II.

21 For an overview, see Clagett 1968.

22 Molland 1982.

23 Galilei 1638, p. 28.

24 Cavalieri to Galileo, 2 October 1634, in Galilei 1890–1909, vol. 16, pp. 136–7; 19 December 1634, ibid., pp. 175–6.

25 On the general question of the concept of *momentum* in Galileo's thought, see Galluzzi 1979.

26 Schuster 1977, pp. 299–352.

27 A *cycloid* is the path traced by a fixed point on the circumference of a circle as the circle rolls along a straight line; see sec. IV.2 in this chapter.

28 For a general account of Huygens's mechanics, see Gabbey 1980b; for its rôle in his work on clocks and the determination of longitude, see Mahoney 1980.

29 Galileo had first called attention to the pendulum as a system that would continue to oscillate uniformly, falling and then rising to the same height, were it not for external damping forces. He established that the period is independent of the weight of the bob and asserted that it is also independent of the amplitude. Although Galileo saw the pendulum as a time-keeping device and suggested attaching it to the escapement of a clock, he himself used it primarily as a means of experimenting with falling bodies, and thus to argue the speed of fall is independent of weight and that a body in falling acquires enough *momento* or *impeto* to raise it to its original height. See Bedini 1991.

30 Torricelli, *De motu gravium naturaliter descendentium et projectorum,* in Torricelli 1919–44, vol. 2, p.105. E. J. Dijksterhuis first brought out the relation between Torricelli and Huygens; see Dijksterhuis 1961, pp. 370–2.

31 Huygens 1659, prop. XI.

32 Note, e.g., the similarity between Huygens's remark in 1675 that 'the quantity of incitation at each instant of motion is measured by the force required to prevent the body from starting to move at the place where it is and in the direction it is headed' (Huygens 1888–1950, vol. 18, p. 496), and Newton's definition of an impressed force as 'the action carried out on a body to change its state either of motion or of moving uniformly in a straight line' (Newton 1687, Bk.I, def. 4). Cf. Gabbey 1980b, pp. 176–7.

33 Herivel 1965, pp. 129–30, from Newton's *Waste Book* in a section dating from 1664. Newton recalled this earlier derivation in a scholium to Proposition I,4 of the *Principia,* where he emphasised the total force exerted by successive impacts. Over a given period of time, he reasoned, that force is proportional to the velocity and to the number of reflections. For a polygon of any given number of sides, the velocity will be as the distance travelled, and the number of reflections will be as that distance divided by the length of a side, which in turn is proportional to the radius. Hence the total force will be as the square of the distance divided by the radius, 'and thus, if the polygon with infinitely diminished sides coincides with the circle, as the square of the arc described in the given time divided by the radius'. Again the transition from inscribed polygons to the circle as limit rests on a property that is seemingly independent of the number or size of the sides.

34 For greater detail and further references, see Mahoney 1993.

35 Newton 1952, p. 396.

36 See Heilbron 1993.

37 Descartes to Mersenne, 28 August 1638, AT II 309.

38 AT II 313: 'One should also note that curves described by rolling circles (*roulettes*) are entirely mechanical lines and count among those I have rejected from my *Geometry*; that is why it is no wonder that their tangents are not found by the rules I have set out there.'

39 Roberval 1693, pp. 1–89.

40 'To resolve problems by motion', <October, 1666>, in Newton 1967–81, vol. 1, pp. 400–48.

41 As a simple example, let $y^2 = x^3$. Adding moments, $(y + qo)^2 = (x + po)^3$, or $y^2 + 2yqo + q^2o^2 = x^3 + 3x^2po + 3xp^2o^2 + p^3o^3$. Deleting the equal terms and dividing the others by o yields $2yq + q^2o = 3x^2p + 3xp^2o + p^3o^2$. Since o is infinitely small, so too are all terms containing it, whence $2yq = 3x^2p$, or $y^2(2q/y) = x^3(3p/x)$, as the rule states.

42 Newton, 'De analysi per aequationes numero terminorum infinitas', in Newton 1967, vol. II, pp. 206–47; cf. the fully developed (but long unpublished) tract 'On the Methods of Series and Fluxions' (1671), in Newton 1967–81, vol. 3, pp. 32–353. Despite claims made during the priority dispute with Leibniz, Newton did not replace p and q with the now familiar dot notation, or 'pricked letters' $\dot{x}$ and $\dot{y}$ until 1691 (Newton 1967–81, vol. 3, p. 72, n. 86).

43 Leibniz 1855, vol. I, appx. II; summarised in English with translated excerpts in Leibniz 1920, 65ff.

44 For a discussion of the Aristotelian passages (*Metaphysica* VI, 1,1026ᵃ23–7, and XI, 7, 1064ᵇ8–9) and their subsequent interpretation, see Sasaki 1988, chap. 6. More generally, see Crapulli 1969.

45 *In artem analyticen isagoge,* in Viète 1646, p. 1: 'Est veritatis inquirendae via quaedam in Mathematicis, quam Plato primus invenisse dicitur, à Theone nominata Analysis, & ab eodem definita, Adsumptio quaesiti tanquam concessi per consequentia ad verum

concessum. Ut contrà Synthesis, Adsumptio concessi per consequentia ad quaesiti finem & comprehensionem.'

46 The precise meaning of Pappus's description of analysis and synthesis is a matter of dispute. See Mahoney 1968; Hintikka and Remes 1974; and, most generally, Knorr 1993.

47 Mahoney 1994, chap. 2; Morse 1981.

48 The constituents of his *Opus restitutae mathematicae analyseos, seu algebra nova,* all composed in the 1570s and 1580s, were published separately over the course of several decades and brought together for the first time in Viète 1646. They include *In artem analyticem isagoge* (Tours, 1591), *Ad logisticen speciosam notae priores* (Paris, 1631), *Zeteticorum libri quinque* (Tours, 1593), *De aequationum recognitione et emendatione tractatus duo* (Paris, 1615), *De numerosa potestatum ad exegesin resolutione* (Paris, 1600), *Effectionum geometricarum canonica recensio* (Tours, 1592), *Supplementum geometriae* (Tours, 1593), *Theoremata ad sectiones angulares* (Paris, 1615), and *Variorum de rebus mathematicis responsorum liber VIII* (Tours, 1593). For the complex history of Viète's works, see Van Egmond 1985, and, more extensively, Grisard 1976.

49 To these, Tartaglia, Cardano, and Ferrari had added general solutions of the cubic and quartic equation. On the Arabic background and its influence on European developments, see Rashed 1984.

50 See, for example, Reg. IV of the *Regulae ad directionem ingenii,* AT X 377: 'Finally, there have been some most ingenious men who have tried in this century to revive the same [true mathematics]; for it seems to be nothing other than that art which they call by the barbarous name of "algebra", if only it could be disentangled from the multiple numbers and inexplicable figures that overwhelm it, so that it would no longer lack the clarity and simplicity that we suppose should obtain in a true mathematics.'

51 In the sense that, given any two terms of the progression, the smaller can be added to itself a sufficient number of times to exceed the greater. Adding a line to itself however many times will not produce an area. See his *Géométrie* (Leiden, 1637, as part of the *Discours de la méthode* and *Essais*; repr. separately with English trans. in Descartes 1954), pp. 297–8.

52 Descartes 1954, Bk. III, p. 380: 'Au reste tant les vrayes racines que les fausses ne sont pas tousiours reelles; mais quelquefois seulement imaginaires; c'est à dire qu'on peut bien tousiours en imaginer autant que iay dit en chasque Equation; mais qu'il n'y a quelquefois aucune quantité, qui corresponde a celles qu'on imagine. Comme encore qu'on en puisse imaginer trois en celle cy, $x^3 - 6xx + 13x - 10 = 0$, il n'y en a toutefois qu'une reelle, qui est 2, & pour les deux autres, quoy qu'on les augmente, ou diminue, ou multipie en la façon que ie viens d'expliquer, on ne sçauroit les rendres autres qu'imaginaires.' Just over a century later, Euler commented on the analytic value of imaginaries: 'We must finally drop our concern that the doctrine of impossible numbers might be viewed as useless fantasy. This concern is unfounded. The doctrine of impossible numbers is in fact of the greatest importance, since problems often arise in which one cannot know immediately whether they demand something possible or impossible. Whenever their solution leads to such impossible numbers, one has a sure sign that the problem demands something impossible' (Euler 1959 [1770], pt. I, sec. 1, para. 151).

53 Descartes 1954, Book II, p. 342.

54 For a detailed study of the development of Fermat's mathematics, see Mahoney 1994. With the exception of one treatise published anonymously in 1660, Fermat's works circulated only in manuscript copies during his lifetime. His son, Samuel, gathered a

collection of them, which he issued as Fermat 1679. The main source today is Fermat 1891–1922.

55 It is, of course, one of the elementary symmetric functions of the equation. Viète's theory of equations brought out some, but not all, of these relations. Descartes focused on them as the links between an equation written as a polynomial and as a product of the linear binomials containing its roots.

56 Fermat first announced his method in an essay, 'Methodus ad disquirendam maximam et minimam et de tangentibus linearum curvarum', sent to Mersenne in 1636 but based on results achieved in 1629. The essay gave no hint of its origins, which Fermat revealed only in the course of a dispute with Descartes in 1638. For details, see Mahoney 1994, chap. 4.

57 Viewing the origins of the calculus through Bishop Berkeley's lenses obscures the lines of thought that avoided infinites and infinitesimals altogether or that sought to keep them in a separate domain from finite quantities, linked only by common relationships.

58 Grosholz 1991 offers a sustained critique of this approach both to mathematics and to physics.

59 Cavalieri 1653. See Andersen 1985.

60 Fermat refined his methods of quadrature in the late 1630s and early 1640s, making them known largely through his correspondence with Roberval; see Mahoney 1994, chap. 5. Roberval's methods similarly were known only to his network of correspondents and perhaps also to his students at the Collège Royal de France (Collège de France after the Revolution) until the publication of his *Traité des indivisibles* in Roberval 1693. For Roberval's correspondence with Torricelli in the mid-1640s, on which the discussion to follow is based, see Torricelli 1919–44, vol. 3, *passim*.

61 This is how the language of Cavalieri's method of indivisibles became attached to a method of infinitesimals conceptually different from it, thus creating the historical misunderstanding that the techniques of quadrature from which the integral calculus emerged stemmed from Cavalieri.

62 Fermat, *De aequationum localium transmutatione et emendatione ad multimodam curvilineorum inter se vel cum rectilineis comparationem . . .*, [late 1650s], Fermat 1891–1922, vol. 1, pp. 255–85; see Mahoney 1994, chap. 5, sec. IV.

63 Barrow 1670; Gregory 1668; Mahoney 1990.

64 On Barrow, see Mahoney 1990.

65 Leibniz 1684; in Ger. Math. V 220–6.

66 Leibniz 1684, p. 223.

67 Leibniz 1686; Ger. Math. V 226–33.

68 Leibniz to Huygens, 21 September 1691, Huygens 1888–1950, vol. 10, p. 157.

69 Leibniz to Varignon, 2 February 1702, Ger. Math. IV 92. 'To tell the truth', he added a few months later (ibid., 110), 'I am not altogether persuaded myself that our infinites and infinitesimals should be considered other than as ideal objects or as well founded fictions.' Cf. Leibniz to Johann Bernoulli, 29 July 1698, Ger. Math. III 524: 'Inter nos autem haec addo, quod et jam olim in dicto Tractatu inedito adscripsi, dubitari posse an lineae rectae infinitae longitudine et tamen terminatae revera dentur. Interim sufficere pro Calculo, ut fingantur, uti imaginariae radices in Algebra.'

70 See Bos 1974.

71 Leibniz to Varignon, 2 February 1702, Ger. Math. IV 93–4.

72 Newton 1687, p. 35. Cf. De Gandt 1986b.

73 On the first strategy, see Jesseph 1989.

74 Cf. Breger 1990.

75 Bacon, *Nov. org.* I 124; in Bacon 1960, *ipsissimae res* is rendered 'the very same things'.
76 Fontenelle 1727, Préface, [biv^r].
77 Barrow 1670, pp. 167–8.
78 Bacon, *Nov. org.* I 51.
79 Descartes, *Le monde,* chap. 7, AT XI 47 (Descartes 1970b, p. 75). The final clause is quoted from the Bible, *Sapientia* (*Wisdom*), VIII, 21.
80 The discussion in the *Discorsi* of the paradoxes of the infinite may have made them understandable to a wider, popular audience, but it did not go beyond what Aristotle had said.
81 Even if, to preserve the continuity of space identified with matter, Descartes was not prepared to accept any minimal size of the particles of matter but rather posited potentially infinite subdivision; see, for example, *Princ. phil.* II 34.
82 Varignon takes dt as constant, i.e., $ddt = 0$. Doing so in Leibnizian calculus is equivalent in the modern form to choosing t as the independent variable, i.e., as the variable with respect to which one is differentiating. The Leibnizian version allows a greater flexibility in analysing differential relations, as Bernoulli had shown in his lectures on the method of integrals and as Varignon emphasised in his later memoirs. On the mathematical point, see Bos 1974.
83 Leibniz 1694b, 1694a.

V
SPIRIT

23

SOUL AND MIND: LIFE AND THOUGHT IN THE SEVENTEENTH CENTURY

DANIEL GARBER

Philosophers certainly worried about the problems of mind and soul – what differentiates humans from dogs, dogs from trees, and trees from stones – long before 1600. But in this essay I shall try to emphasise the seventeenth-century contribution to the question – in particular, the way in which the new mechanical philosophy suggested both new problems and new solutions to old problems connected with life and thought. Following some historical background, we shall discuss various views concerning the soul and the existence and nature of the incorporeal substance that most seventeenth-century thinkers posited. The essay will end with a brief discussion of some of the reactions to the mainstream accounts of mind and soul.

I. BACKGROUND

It is impossible to give an adequate view of the historical setting of seventeenth-century accounts of mind and soul in a few pages. But a brief sketch can at least serve to indicate something of the background against which seventeenth-century philosophers worked in formulating their conceptions of soul, mind, and the like.

The history of the concept of the soul in the years that immediately preceded the seventeenth century is extremely complex. In addition to the Aristotelianism that continued to dominate the schools, there were significantly different traditions of thought on the question, including Platonic, Hermetic, and Paracelsian views, not to mention the views within the medical tradition; the full history of the question, integrating all these perspectives, has yet to be written. Elements of these traditions will find their way into the accounts of seventeenth-century figures provided later in this chapter. For the moment, the important details to note concern the Aristotelian view of the soul and mind, which was the common one in the environment in which seventeenth-century writers worked. Innovations and unorthodoxies of sixteenth-century writers were by no means ignored, but they had not succeeded in supplanting the orthodox Aristotelian viewpoint. Early seventeenth-century writers found themselves in much the same situation as their immediate predecessors: in general they attempted to offer alternatives to a generally accepted way of thinking about soul and mind, grounded in Aristotle and Saint Thomas Aquinas and laid out in an expanding series of commentaries, treatises, and textbooks.

The picture reflected in the Aristotelian literature of the sixteenth century is quite consistent. Apart from some subtle differences, the various writers all saw the central problem as that of accounting for life. What is it, they asked, that differentiates a living thing, a tree, a rabbit, or a human being from its dead counterpart? The general response was that the soul is what accounts for all the properties that differentiate the quick from the dead. On the Aristotelian view, all bodies are composed of form and matter; the matter is common to all bodies and remains constant in change, while the form explains why a given body has the particular properties it has at a given time.[1] In the special case of living bodies, the soul was taken to be that form. Aristotelians believed souls could possess three groups of faculties, which in turn defined three kinds of soul. Lowest were the vegetative faculties, those responsible for nutrition, growth, and reproduction. All souls (which is to say, all living things) were thought to have at least these faculties, whereas (the souls of) plants were thought to have only these faculties. The next higher group of faculties were those associated with sensation and self motion. The former were all connected with the external senses (vision, hearing, etc.), but through the so-called common sense (which combined the deliverance of particular senses), also gave rise to memory and imagination. The so-called motive faculties included those that produce the emotions and those that result in the physical motion of a living thing. The souls of all animals, both humans and lower animals, were said to have such faculties in addition to the vegetative faculties. Although lower animals have only the vegetative sensitive and motive faculties, humans, it was thought, have something more: intellective faculties that differentiate them from all other animals. These faculties include will and intellect, both the so-called active intellect and the passive intellect. These faculties, it was said, made humans capable of grasping genuine universals and also of reflecting on themselves and their own mental operations. In general, it was held that organisms have only one soul: the soul that has only vegetative faculties was called a vegetative soul, the soul with vegetative and sensitive faculties was called a sensitive soul, and the soul with vegetative, sensitive, and intellective faculties was called a rational soul. The rational soul, unique to humans, was called *mind* (*mens*) in the strict sense.[2]

There were, to be sure, many disputes and disagreements among those who counted themselves in the Aristotelian camp. A notable one concerned whether each human soul has its own distinct intellect, active or potential, or whether there is a single intellect common to all.[3] Another important question concerned immortality. In a sense, the traditional Christian doctrines of immortality sit awkwardly within an Aristotelian philosophy, where the soul is the form of the living body; when the living body ceases to be alive, there is no obvious rôle left for the principle of life to play, no apparent way for the soul to continue in its existence. One of the problems for thirteenth-century Aristotelianism was how to graft a Christian conception of immortality onto the Aristotelian conception of the soul.[4] The principal arguments Saint Thomas gave in his *Summa theologiae* are representative of what became the standard arguments for later Aristotelians. Thomas argued: 'The intellectual principle, which is called mind or intellect, has an operation in itself which it does not share with the body. But nothing can operate in itself except what persists in itself. . . . It therefore follows that the human soul, which is called intellect or mind, is something incorporeal and subsisting.'[5] The specific operation Thomas calls attention to here is the ability of the intellect to know the natures of all bodies, something it could not do if it were itself a body, with a particular corporeal nature that could interfere with the apprehension of other corporeal natures. Furthermore, although Thomas rejected claims that we have knowledge of Plato's ideas, he also argued that the immateriality of the intellective soul can be established from its ability to comprehend the intelligible forms of bodies, forms abstracted from matter.[6]

This question was by no means uncontroversial. Despite the decree of the Fifth Lateran Council in 1513 that the immortality of the individual human soul is capable of philosophical demonstration, Pietro Pomponazzi argued in his *De immortalitate animae* in 1516 that even the human soul requires matter and cannot exist without it, at least as far as we can establish by reason. Pomponazzi did grant that we can know that the soul is immortal through faith and revelation. But his other remarks created enormous controversy and showed the continuing trouble raised by the question of the immortality of the human soul within the context of a Christian Aristotelianism.[7]

Much of the debate over soul and mind in the seventeenth century can be seen as a direct continuation of the earlier discussions. The basic problems remained the same: to make sense of life in general and what is special to human beings in particular in the context of a variety of philosophical and theological commitments. But the new context, especially the growing dominance of mechanistic views of nature in the seventeenth century, was transforming the questions.[8] The rising popularity of innatist accounts of the intellect among some (the Cartesians, for example) who denied that the contents of the intellect derive in any way from the senses, and mechanist accounts of thought among others (Hobbes and perhaps Gassendi, for example) who denied the existence of the intellect altogether make much earlier discussion about abstraction, universals, and the relation of the intellect to the senses irrelevant. Similarly, as the concept of the intellect changed, the heated debates about Averroism and the existence of a single active or passive intellect for all become less important, though arguably it continues in the systems of Spinoza and Malebranche. More important for present purposes, though, is a significant transformation that took place in the question of the separability and immortality of the soul. It is dangerous to speak glibly of the rejection of substantial forms in the seventeenth century; many even among the mechanists held on to the Aristotelian language, if not the conception; indeed, Aristotelian language, suitably reinterpreted, was sometimes used to *attack* Aristotelian conceptions.[9] But in a mechanist world in which all the properties of inanimate bodies are to be explained in terms of size, shape, and motion in a material substance taken to be the same everywhere, the problem of separability is somewhat different from what it is for the Aristotelian. For the Aristotelian, the problem is one of the detachability of a constituent of body, its form, which together with its matter constitutes the body as such; the question is whether in some bodies, those of humans, for example, the substantial form is capable of existence independent of matter in a way in which it is not in other bodies. But for the mechanist, whose conception of body does not include form, it is not a question of the detachability of some *constituent* of body; it is a question of what (if anything) we must *add* to body, a question of establishing the limits of what can be explained in terms of body alone, and what must be posited over and above body. Ralph Cudworth argued that this point of view (which he attributed directly to the ancient atomist philosophy then being revived) makes the questions of incorporeal substance and the separability of the soul intelligible in a way that they never could be within the context of the Aristotelian philosophy. Writing in his *True Intellectual System of the World* (London, 1678), he noted:

He that will undertake to prove that there is something else in the World besides Body, must first determine what Body is, for otherwise he will go about to prove that there is something besides *He-knows-not-what*. But now if all Body be made to consist of two Substantial Principles, whereof one is *Matter* devoid of all *Form*, . . . the other, *Form* . . . devoid of all *Matter* . . . ; I say, in this way of Philosophizing, the Notions of Body and Spirit, Corporeal and Incorporeal, are so confounded, that it is Impossible to prove any thing at all concerning them. . . . But the ancient Atomical Philosophy, setling a distinct

Notion of Body, that it is . . . *a Thing Impenetrably extended,* which hath nothing belonging to it, but Magnitude, Figure, Site, Rest, and Motion, without any Self-moving Power; takes away all Confusion; shews clearly how far Body can go, where Incorporeal Substance begins; as also that there must of necessity be such a Thing in the World.[10]

Things are, perhaps, not quite as simple as Cudworth takes them to be. Platonic conceptions of the distinction between body and soul had so penetrated the Christian tradition that many professed Aristotelians felt perfectly comfortable talking about 'how far Body can go, [and] where Incorporeal Substance begins'; indeed, after the Fifth Lateran Council of 1513 it was the official position of the Catholic church that the immortality of an individual soul separated from its body was philosophically demonstrable.[11] At the same time, many seventeenth-century mechanists agreed with Cudworth that the elimination of substantial form and prime matter in favour of a mechanist world of material substance, atoms or whatever was a major advance in understanding soul and mind.

In the seventeenth century the question of the soul becomes the question of incorporeal substance; the history of the soul in the seventeenth century is by and large about the ways in which philosophers either make use of or reject incorporeal substance in accounting for life and other features of the physical world. This question is the central concern in the remainder of the chapter. In dealing with this question, one must distinguish a number of issues. The first is the existence or non-existence of incorporeal substance and the different grounds – physical, metaphysical, theological, and moral – on which the question was settled. Most philosophers in the mainstream opted for some sort of incorporeal something. Thus the second issue is their various conceptions of the nature of non-bodily substance: whether incorporeal substances are simple or complex, indivisible or divisible, whether they are extended or non-extended, and the senses in which they can properly be said to occupy a place. Incorporeal substances, it is important to note, play a number of rôles in seventeenth-century thought. For some, they are the direct successors of the Aristotelian souls and account for the phenomenon of life, which encompasses nutrition, sensation, locomotion, and rational thought. For others, the function of incorporeal substances is broader or narrower; for some they explain the order of the inanimate world, whereas for others, they explain only what is uniquely human, namely, rational thought, speech, and the like. The third issue of concern is the wide variety of incorporeal substances that various thinkers recognised, from angels and human souls, to animal souls, spirits of nature, and monads. Although incorporeal substance almost inevitably comes up in connexion with human beings, for many thinkers, the human soul is but one of many kinds of incorporeal substance in the world.

A multitude of writers touched on these questions in the period. At least two large classes of writers will be ignored here – those writing in generally theological contexts, sermons, tracts, and the like, and those writing in the medical tradition – in order to concentrate on what I understand to be the mainstream philosophical tradition.[12] The figures and schools in this tradition divide up in a number of ways. First, there seems to be a clear change somewhere around mid-century. Although the divide is not absolute, the thinkers of the first half of the century can be seen as setting the problems and positions for and against which those writing in the second half reacted. The positions are what have come to be called dualism and materialism, and the main figures behind them are Descartes and Hobbes. We shall begin, then, by exploring their views and the historical context in which they arose. We shall then examine some of the reactions to these positions, especially attempts to reconcile the apparently opposing views of the dualists and the materialists.

II. DESCARTES

Descartes, of course, was one of the key figures in the new mechanical philosophy, the attempt to explain physical phenomena in terms of size, shape, and motion. This mechanist revolution extended to biological phenomena as well; just as thinkers sought mechanical explanations for colour, magnetism, and heaviness, they also sought to fit human flesh and blood into the world of corpuscles and offer mechanical explanations of a wide variety of biological phenomena.[13] This programme, in direct opposition to the Aristotelian account of life in terms of soul, was clearly stated in Descartes's writings. In the *Traité de l'homme* (1633), for example, Descartes claims to have given mechanistic explanations for, among other things:

> the digestion of food, the beating of the heart and arteries, the nourishment and growth of the members, respiration, waking and sleeping, the reception by the external sense organs of light, sounds, smells, tastes, heat, and all other such qualities, the imprinting of the ideas of these qualities in the organ of common sense and imagination, the retention or imprint of these ideas in the memory, the internal movements of the appetites and passions, and finally, the external movements of all the members.[14]

But this was one of his ambitions. The *Traité de la lumière* (1633) and the *Principia philosophiae* (1644) attempted to derive the present state of the physical world, sun and planets, magnets and mountains, from an initial chaos, using only the laws of motion. It is clear that Descartes intended to extend this to all living things, showing not only that (human beings aside) they consist of matter alone, but how the complex arrangement of parts that constituted plants and animals could have arisen from matter alone.[15]

Descartes's biology was a direct extension of a strategy central to many formulations of the new mechanical philosophy, the elimination of substantial forms and the replacement of explanations based on innate natures or principles of activity with explanations based on size, shape, and motion. But mechanism had its limits for Descartes. Although he wanted to explain the living functions associated with nutrition, sensation, and locomotion in mechanist terms, he did not claim that everything is body and everything is explicable in this way; for Descartes, our every thought testifies to the existence of something over and above body, a mind or soul that is the proper seat of this thought.[16]

In a sense, the existence of mind or soul follows out of the celebrated *cogito* argument. As developed in Meditatio II, for example, Descartes argues from the experience of thought directly to a something that has that thought, a thinker, a thinking thing. Descartes means here to contrast his view with that of the Aristotelians and demonstrate that contrary to their view, the existence of our mind can be known before we know the external world of body, and independently of our knowledge of body.[17] But although the *cogito* argument establishes the existence of a thinking thing and establishes it before we know of body, it does not establish that the thinking thing in question is not corporeal; Descartes makes quite clear in Meditatio II that the thinking thing established by the argument might well be a thinking *body*.[18] The mind or soul is shown to be incorporeal only when it is shown to be a substance that is really distinct from body.

This central doctrine receives its most careful development in the *Meditationes* of 1641. There, in Meditatio VI Descartes begins: 'Since I know that everything I clearly and distinctly understand can be produced by God just as I understand it to be, it is enough that I can clearly and distinctly understand one thing without another for me to be certain that one is different from the other.'[19] Now, Descartes holds, the ideas in question, the idea of a thinking thing and the idea of an extended thing are certainly ideas that I can clearly and distinctly understand apart from one another. And so, God can create an extended thing without thereby creating a thinking thing, and *vice versa*. This suffices for us to say that mind or soul and body are distinct substances.[20] Because the soul is separate from the body, Descartes argues, it does not necessarily perish when the body dies. Furthermore, in so far as it is not made up of parts, it cannot lose its identity through their rearrangement. In this sense the human mind can be said to be naturally immortal.[21]

Descartes's main argument is an interesting one, particularly for what it is not. It is not a simple and straightforward argument from the limits of mechanism; Descartes does not here point to one or another phenomenon and simply claim that obviously there is no possible mechanical explanation available, as a number of his contemporaries did, as we shall see. Nor does it seem to be an argument in the scholastic tradition either; it is certainly not the standard sort of argument found in Saint Thomas Aquinas, for example, the argument that goes from the assumption that the intellect has a non-corporeal operation to the self-subsistence of the human soul. Although one might be able to reconfigure Descartes's argument into one or another of these forms, he himself does not do so; it is not the operation of thought or the inability to explain it in corporeal terms that convinces him of the real distinction between mind and body, but the very idea we have of a thinking thing, a substance whose principle attribute is thought. Though, as we shall see, Descartes does make use of such strategies in discussing the problem of animal souls, the main argument of Meditatio VI seems to be something different.

Descartes's conception of the soul was a significant departure from the Aristotelian tradition in which he was educated. Descartes's soul has no connexion whatsoever with the vital functions that are so central to the Aristotelian conception of the soul; in that sense Descartes can be said to have rejected the notion of the soul altogether, retaining only those aspects of the Aristotelian soul that pertain to human beings alone.[22] Or, to put the point another way, for Descartes there is nothing to the soul over and above the mind: 'I consider that mind is not a part of the soul, but the thinking soul in its entirety.'[23] Even though Descartes persisted in calling the soul the substantial form of the human body – indeed, the only such form that he recognises in his mechanical world – the rejection of all vital functions from the soul makes the Cartesian form quite distant from anything that Aristotle or his scholastic followers imagined in this connexion when calling the soul the form of the living body.[24]

The Cartesian conception of the soul contrasts in an obvious way with the standard Aristotelian conception of the soul as a principle of life. But it also contrasts with the Aristotelian conception of the human soul or mind as essentially rational or intellective. The human soul, the only soul that Descartes recognised, angels aside, is, to be sure, rational and has a pure intellect. But it is *thought* that is its essence, and not reason or intellect. Descartes considered this conception of the soul to be original with him; in the *Notae in programma* (Amsterdam, 1648), he wrote: 'I am the first who considered thought as the principal attribute of incorporeal substance.'[25] Descartes often interpreted this quite broadly to include a wide variety of thoughts. For example, in Meditatio II he wrote: 'A thinking thing. What is that? Namely a thing that doubts, understands, affirms, denies, wills [*volens*], rejects [*nolens*], and also imagines and senses.'[26] He often asserted, at least in his mature writings, that these thoughts divide into two main sorts, perceptions and volitions, and that the soul can be said to have two faculties, a faculty of perception, which includes the bare contemplation of the ideas of sensation, imagination, and pure intellection, and a faculty of judgement, which deals both with practical decision making and the assertion of truth. But Descartes often suggested that sensation and imagination have a somewhat more complex status than this picture might at first suggest. Although sensations and imaginations of a sort are thoughts that pertain to souls, minds, thinking substances, they do so *only* when the soul is joined to a body.[27] Souls separated from bodies have no sensations or imaginations;[28] indeed, some passages suggest that sensations and imaginations are properly thought of as pertaining to the *union* of mind and body, and to neither considered by itself.[29] Taken by itself, that is, taken apart from the body to which it is attached, the soul has only the ideas of pure intellect, ideas that constitute a pure, non-imaginary and non-sensual contemplation of a concept.[30] Though the Cartesian soul is principally a thinking thing, one can certainly see in it more than a hint of the intellective soul of the Aristotelians.[31]

Note that in distinguishing between the mind or soul and body, Descartes means to exclude all extension, properly speaking, from the mind. Descartes concedes that we often do think of the mind or soul as extended, indeed extended throughout the whole body.[32] He furthermore grants that there is a sense in which it is proper to speak of it as extended; in so far as incorporeal substances like God, angels, and the human mind have the ability to cause changes in extended substances, they have a kind of extension, an *extensio potentiae*.[33] But in so far as the mind or soul can be (clearly and distinctly) conceived as the subject of thought alone, existing entirely without extended substance, God can so create it. And thus, for Descartes, incorporeal substance, properly understood, lacks *all* extension and its modes, even *place*.

It is from our immediate experience of ourselves as thinking things that we know that we have a soul whose essence is thought and which is distinct from the body, for Descartes. But matters are quite different when we are dealing with other creatures. For animals (and, presumably, for other human beings) all we have to go on is external behaviour.[34] Descartes's considered view is that while the essence of the soul is thought, the *only* kind of thinking soul there is is one that has reason and pure intellect as well. And so, Descartes denies animals not only vital souls, principles of life, but thinking souls as well.[35] To establish this conclusion, Descartes uses a kind of argument reminiscent of the arguments the schoolmen used in similar contexts; though the immediate experience of thought testifies to the existence of our own souls, Descartes turns to reason to settle the question in others. Now, it is only in pure intellection, the exercise of reason without the aid of sensation, imagination, without the influence of the passions, that 'the mind can operate independently of the brain.'[36] And so, Descartes reasons, it is only rational behaviour – behaviour that shows the thing in question is capable of such abstract and non-bodily reasoning – that can show us something has an incorporeal soul as we do. Descartes recognises two ways in which rationality is displayed in our behaviour, two ways in which we can distinguish between human beings, who have incorporeal souls, and beasts which, he claims, lack such souls: the ability to use language, and the ability to respond appropriately to a large variety of unforseen circumstances.[37] Since animals display neither of these two signs of rationality, and since he argues that all of the behaviour that we do observe in them can be explained mechanistically, Descartes argues that we have no grounds on which to attribute souls to them, that is, incorporeal substances capable of acting without a body. And since he assumes *only* rational behaviour requires a non-mechanistic cause, Descartes infers that *all* of their overt behaviour is explicable in purely mechanical terms, through the size, shape, and motion of the parts that make them up.[38] In depriving animals of incorporeal souls, Descartes claims that they lack *all* thought (*cogitatio, pensée*) of the sort that we have.[39] In particular, they lack sensation, feeling, and even volition in the sense in which we have them.[40] Lacking both an Aristotelian principle of life and a Cartesian principle of thought, they are mere machines for Descartes.

But it is important to note that this argument does not establish its conclusion with certainty, as Descartes eventually came to see. Writing to More on 5 February 1649 he noted: 'However, although I take it as having been demonstrated that it cannot be proved that there is thought [*cogitatio*] in the brutes, I don't think that it can be demonstrated from that that they have no thought, since the human mind does not reach into their hearts.'[41] He goes on to suggest that his view, the view that animals have no souls, the view that their behaviour is explicable in purely mechanical terms, is simply the view that is 'most probable'.[42] Descartes's caution here is quite proper. In so far as animals appear to lack reason, the ability for abstract thought, the one ability whose manifestation *requires* us to attribute incorporeal souls to other humans, we lack one convincing argument for attributing souls to animals. But rationality is not the only manifestation of an incorporeal soul. *We* know that *we* have souls not because we reason but because each of us experiences thought, something that, Descartes argues, pertains to a substance distinct from the substance that constitutes the subject of the modes of extension.[43] Though they do not reason, Descartes in the end grants More that it is at least conceivable that animals experience thoughts in something like the way we do. Though we may never be able to 'reach into their hearts' and decide one way or another, it is a possibility that cannot altogether be excluded. This admission seems to show once more the tension between Descartes's main conception of the soul as a thinking thing, a uniquely Cartesian conception of the soul that underlies and motivates the main argument for the distinction between mind and body in the *Meditationes,* and the more Aristotelian conception of the human soul in terms of intellect and rationality that grounds the standard scholastic arguments for the separability of the human soul from its body, and seems to ground his argument for denying animals souls.[44]

Descartes was an important mechanist adherent of the view that there is incorporeal substance, and his view was widely influential in the later century. As shown in Chapter 25, later Cartesians differed considerably on a number of issues connected with the interaction between mind and body and the nature of the union between mind and body. Nevertheless, there was remarkable agreement among Descartes's later followers over the basic questions, the nature of the human soul as a thinking thing, the rejection of the Aristotelian conception of soul as principle of life, and the distinction of the soul from the extended body.[45] But Descartes and his school were not the only seventeenth-century mechanists to hold such views. Some of the distinctive features of the Cartesian position can be brought out by briefly examining the views of two of Descartes's contemporaries who also argued for the existence of an incorporeal human soul, Kenelm Digby and Pierre Gassendi.

III. INCORPOREAL SUBSTANCE IN DIGBY AND GASSENDI

The question of the soul is the main focus of Digby's principal work, the *Two Treatises . . . ,* first published in Paris in 1644 and reprinted in numerous later editions. The two treatises of the title are, first, a treatise on 'the nature of bodies', and second, a treatise on 'the nature of mans soule', in which Digby investigates 'the way of discovery of the immortality of reasonable soules'. In the first treatise, Digby, like Descartes before him, attempted to show how a wide variety of physical phenomena, including biological phenomena like the origin of plants and animals and the functioning of sensation, can be 'reduced to locall motion, and to materiall application of one body unto another'.[46] But Digby makes it clear that his system of physics is intended mainly as a prelude to his account of the soul, intended to forestall the objection that anything he claims is done by an incorporeal soul is *really* the work of an occult corporeal cause.[47] In a sense, for Digby, we must study mechanist physics in order to know the *limits* of mechanist explanation: 'Our intention in this discourse, concerning the natures and motions of bodies, ayming no further then att the discovery of what is or may be done by corporeall Agents; thereby to determine what is the worke of immateriall and spirituall substances.'[48] While Digby offers a jumble of various arguments for the existence of an incorporeal soul, the main strategy is rather straightforward. Digby catalogues the main 'operations' of the human soul – simple apprehension, knowing (judgement), discoursing (method), and action. Under each of these categories falls a series of arguments for the existence of an incorporeal substance; each of these operations, Digby claims, has features that preclude it from being performed by a body. From this he concludes that there must be something in us other than our bodies.[49] While Digby claims not to know the real nature of the soul he discovers in this way,[50] his conception is really quite close to the Cartesian conception of the soul. As with Descartes, the soul is unextended and without place, properly speaking; indeed, it is even outside of time.[51] And as with Descartes, the human soul seems to be a thinking thing from which all vital functions have been removed and placed in bare matter.[52] For Digby, as for Descartes, it is our very ability to have ideas, internal representations of external things, abstracted from their particularities that leads him to posit an incorporeal mind.[53] Furthermore, also like Descartes, Digby argues that animals are incapable of such internal representations; they are like machines and can be entirely comprehended through their bodies.[54]

In many ways, Digby's views are very close to those of Descartes, and he may be regarded as one of the first to be influenced by him on these questions. But the differences are also important. Descartes and Digby share much in their conception of the soul. But Descartes's principal argument for the distinction between soul and body proceeds in a somewhat different way. For Descartes, the distinction follows from the very ideas we have of the soul and the body and God's power to create separately what we conceive as separate. Digby, on the other hand, depends mainly on arguments from the limits on the behaviour of mechanical systems. In this way, Digby's whole approach to the question is also more than a little suggestive of the standard Aristotelian argument for the separability and substantiality of the human soul, the argument that the intellective soul in humans 'has an operation in itself which it does not share with the body'. Although the conceptions of body are radically different, and although the operations Digby appeals to may be somewhat different, in both cases the argument proceeds from a claim about faculties humans have that cannot be performed by a body to the claim that it must be something non-bodily that is the seat of the faculty. In a sense, Digby's main arguments for the existence of an incorporeal soul in man can be regarded as simply the older arguments, adapted to the new mechanist context.

Pierre Gassendi was another contemporary of Descartes's, who, like Descartes, defended the existence of incorporeal substance, though in a form different from that posited by either Descartes or Digby. Much of Gassendi's work was concerned with his revival of Epicurus and Epicureanism, and it is no real surprise that his first published writings that touch on the soul, the *Objectiones Quintas* to Descartes's *Meditationes* (Paris, 1641), and the expansion of these *Objectiones,* the *Disquisitio metaphysica* (Amsterdam, 1644), suggest an Epicurean view of the soul as material, a view discussed later in this chapter. But, as Gassendi's drafts show, his views apparently changed immediately after the completion of the *Disquisitio*.[55] There is much debate over whether Gassendi really changed his view, whether his later view is to be taken as sincere, and why his later writings are so different from his earlier.[56] But in his edition-cum-commentary on Epicurus, the *Animadversiones in decimum librum Diogenis Laertii* (Lyon, 1649), and in the posthumously published *Syntagma philosophicum* (Lyon, 1658), Gassendi presents and defends a doctrine of incorporeal substance.

In his final work, the *Syntagma,* Gassendi divides his discussion of the soul into three parts on the Aristotelian model, treating first the vegetative soul of plants, the sensitive soul of animals, and finally, the rational soul of humans. In the course of this discussion, Gassendi, like Descartes, carefully distinguished the question of *life* from the question of *rational thought*.[57] Unlike Descartes, however, Gassendi posited a material soul as the source of vital functions in both animals and humans, an *anima,* a particularly subtle collection of atoms spread through the living body, what he sometimes calls the most noble part, or flower of matter (*flos materiae*), and which he considers a variety of fire.[58] But even though he posits a vital soul, since this soul is material, Gassendi would agree with Descartes and Digby that all vital functions are explicable mechanically.

For the orthodox Epicurean, this material soul, the *anima,* is all there is in living creatures. But in his mature writings, at least, Gassendi departed from the strict Epicurean view, and also recognised a rational soul, an *animus* that is incorporeal. The arguments he offered for this view are, he admitted, only probable, and it has been argued that it was his Christian faith that ultimately induced him to introduce an incorporeal soul into the Epicurean world of atoms and the void.[59] Be that as it may, Gassendi offers four main arguments for the immateriality of the rational soul or mind. Gassendi argues from the ability the mind has to apprehend purely intellectual notions that are not images, from its ability to reflect on itself, from its ability to form universals, and from its ability to comprehend both corporeal and incorporeal substance; all of these abilities indicate, for Gassendi, that humans must have an incorporeal intellect.[60] In sum, there is quite simply a certain disproportion between the properties one attributes to matter and the operations of the intellect; Gassendi simply cannot see how matter, however disposed, could do what the intellect obviously does do, an argument, again, reminiscent of the Thomistic argument. From the fact that the human soul is incorporeal, Gassendi takes it to follow directly that the human soul is naturally immortal, since that which is incorporeal lacks parts, and that which lacks parts cannot naturally be destroyed.[61]

Although both Descartes and Gassendi admit incorporeal souls in humans, there are important differences as well. Strictly speaking, for Gassendi the human soul is bipartite, consisting of a non-rational and material vital soul, an *anima*, united with a rational and incorporeal *animus*.[62] But even with respect to the incorporeal part of the soul alone, there are important differences with Descartes. Descartes's mind includes *all* thought; whereas sensation and imagination require a body, sensations and mental images, in the sense we have them, are in the mind. Not so for Gassendi. For him, sensation and imagination are strictly a function of the lower, material soul. The incorporeal part of the soul functions only in connexion with those thoughts and operations that go beyond sensation and imagination; it is the seat of the intellective functions alone. Despite the independence that the incorporeal soul appears to have, however, it cannot function without these lower faculties, Gassendi argues; as in the Aristotelian tradition, the intellect is ultimately dependent upon the faculties of sensation for the objects on which it works, and thus the rational soul has a kind of inclination to join itself to body that Cartesian souls lack.[63] Although his views are much like those of Descartes and his followers, Gassendi is in many ways more connected to his past, both to his scholastic roots and to the Epicurean branches he attempted to graft to those roots; in many ways, Gassendi's conception of the human soul is like that of the schoolmen, an incorporeal rational soul of the Aristotelian sort, joined with the vegetative and sensitive soul interpreted in accordance with Epicurean atomism.

Descartes was perhaps the most visible and influential advocate of the view that there are incorporeal minds or souls over and above the material substance of the mechanical philosophy. But it is important to remember that he was not the only such advocate, and that there were important divergences among adherents. Later we shall see some further variations on this theme. But first I would like to turn to a different theme, that of materialism.

IV. MATERIALISM: GASSENDI AND HOBBES

The doctrine that has come to be called materialism, the doctrine that asserts, roughly, that the human being is body alone and denies that there is anything in the world that is incorporeal, has a long history that stretches back to antiquity.[64] The question of materialism comes up in a number of contexts in the seventeenth century. The Protestant Reformation in the sixteenth century introduced a number of sects that argued for various materialistic accounts of the soul for various reasons. These thinkers appealed to evidence that ranged from strict biblical authority to direct religious experience to argue against more traditional Christian doctrines of an immortal and incorporeal soul.[65] These religious thinkers were complemented by anti-theological writers, 'libertines', and opponents of religious orthodoxy who, in a literature in part open, in part clandestine, asserted the mortality of a material soul as part of a general attack against religion.[66] Although it is important to be aware of this background, the present chapter concentrates on the development of materialism in a more narrowly philosophical context among some contemporaries of Descartes writing in the first part of the century.

One of these was Pierre Gassendi. Gassendi was discussed earlier in connexion with his mature views as expressed in the *Animadversiones* (Lyon, 1649) and *Syntagma philosophicum* (Lyon, 1658), in which he defends a version of the doctrine of incorporeal substance. But in his somewhat earlier *Objectiones* to Descartes's *Meditationes* (Paris, 1641) and in the *Disquisitio metaphysica* (Amsterdam, 1644) that grew out of the *Objectiones,* he presented a somewhat different view much closer to that of Epicurus.[67]

Gassendi's basic claim throughout his work is that Descartes's arguments do not establish the existence of an incorporeal soul in humans. In order to do so, Gassendi argues, Descartes must locate some operation (*operatio*) that we perform independently of our bodies, some operation that goes beyond what the beasts can do.[68] The obvious candidate here is intellection, which Descartes attempts to distinguish from the corporeal faculties of sensation and imagination.[69] But Gassendi will not grant Descartes the point; intellection, Gassendi here argues, is just the comparison of images and thus involves the imagination.[70] Furthermore, Gassendi argues, Descartes does not establish that matter is incapable of thought and that mind without body can think, nor does he show how a non-extended thing can be diffused in an extended thing or how a non-moving thing can cause motion.[71] Gassendi insists that for all of what Descartes claims, he has not established the *nature* of the substance that thinks.[72] Throughout, Gassendi opposes Descartes's account with an Epicurean account of the soul as the 'flower, or the most refined and pure and active part' of matter, which will later appear as the vital soul in his mature writings.[73] The suggestion throughout is that reason leads us to the view that thought is simply a function of the organisation of matter.[74]

But it is perhaps too strong to say that Gassendi is a materialist here. Although Gassendi consistently denies that Descartes has established the existence of an incorporeal soul or enlightened us about its nature, there is no suggestion that the notion of an incorporeal soul is incoherent, however incomprehensible it might be to us on the basis of experience and reason. Though reason may lead us to materialism, faith leads us to an incorporeal and immortal soul, Gassendi admits.[75]

For Gassendi, among others, materialism is a view that reason leaves open, but revelation appears to exclude. But the first part of the seventeenth century experienced another strain in materialist thought, a strain best represented by Thomas Hobbes.

Hobbes, like Gassendi in his *Objectiones* to Descartes and his *Disquisitio,* recognised no faculty of pure intellection distinct from sensation and imagination.[76] Since sensation and imagination are nothing 'but divers motions; (for motion, produceth nothing but motion)',[77] Hobbes argued, there is no need to posit an incorporeal soul over and above the material body. Responding to the distinction Descartes draws between imagination and intellection, he suggested that reasoning is simply the manipulation of names, from which he draws the conclusion that 'reasoning will depend upon names, names upon the imagination, and imagination (as I think) will depend upon the motion of corporeal organs, and thus mind will be nothing but motion in certain parts of an organic body.'[78] But Hobbes goes beyond this. Since he believed that all of our notions come to us through the senses, 'a man can have no thought, representing any thing, not subject to sense. No man therefore can conceive any thing, but he must conceive it in some place; and indued with some determinate magnitude; and which may be divided into parts.'[79] At the very least, this means that the sorts of incorporeal souls posited by Descartes and the Christian tradition from which he drew are not possible objects of knowledge, a view that Hobbes seems to take in *De corpore.*[80] But more radically, Hobbes holds that the very notion of an incorporeal substance is incoherent and self-contradictory. In *Leviathan* Hobbes wrote:

The Word *Body,* in the most generall acceptation, signifieth that which filleth, or occupyeth some certain room, or imagined place. . . . The same also, because Bodies are subject to change . . . is called *Substance,* that is to say, *Subject,* to various accidents. . . . And according to this acceptation of the word, *Substance,* and *Body,* signifie the same thing; and therefore *Substance incorporeall* are words, which when they are joined together, destroy one another, as if a man should say, an *Incorporeall Body.*[81]

Therefore the immaterial soul that Descartes and others of Hobbes's contemporaries attempted to introduce into the mechanical world is also incomprehensible. The pretended notion of an incorporeal substance, along with popular notions of ghosts and apparitions, and the scholastic notion of a substantial form or separated essence derive, for Hobbes, from a misuse of language, from treating terms such as life (or thought), the names of faculties, or acts of a living (human) body, as if they named things, a soul or a mind.[82] In this way, Hobbes links Descartes to his scholastic forebears and tars them with the same brush.[83]

Hobbes, unlike Gassendi, wants to assert not only that materialism is the position to which reason leads, but that it is also *true*; for Hobbes, revelation does not intercede on behalf of the incorporeal soul. This is not to say that revelation is irrelevant; Hobbes is quite keen to show that his denial of incorporeal substance and soul, heterodox as it may seem, is quite consistent with biblical revelation. He writes, 'Scripture acknowledges spirits, yet doth it nowhere say, that they are incorporeal, meaning thereby, without dimension and quality; nor, I think, is that word incorporeal at all in the Bible.'[84] Hobbes's claim is supported in *Leviathan* with copious biblical quotation and citation, intended to establish that even such Christian doctrines as resurrection and eternal life are, in their biblical sources, perfectly consistent with his philosophy.[85] In this respect, Hobbes seems reminiscent of the so-called Christian mortalist tradition in theology, so active in England during the Civil War years in which Hobbes formulated his ideas and wrote his most important statements of his views on body and mind.[86]

The debate over soul, mind, and immaterial substance started earlier in the century continued, of course. But by mid-century the basic issues were set, and much later seventeenth-century thought on the question can be traced directly to one or another of the sources we have discussed, particularly to Descartes and to Hobbes. Both positions had their direct followers. The later Cartesians followed their master's lead, and though they may have departed from orthodoxy in their conception of the union between soul and body and the way in which they interact, as noted in Chapter 25, they unanimously repeated with enthusiasm Descartes's arguments for the existence of a thinking soul, a non-extended incorporeal substance distinct from body. Others followed Hobbes into a thoroughgoing materialism,[87] though Hobbes's direct influence consisted more in providing a position against which to argue than a position to adopt.

V. HENRY MORE

One of the most interesting positions on the soul in the latter part of the seventeenth century was held by members of the so-called Cambridge Platonists, a group of religious thinkers centred around Cambridge University and active from the 1640s to the 1670s or so. Especially important here are the views of Henry More. More's interest in the question of the soul is evident in his theological poems from the early and mid-1640s, which in part constitute poetical refutations of the Epicurean poet, Lucretius.[88] But his mature philosophical doctrine of the soul is best developed in his correspondence with Descartes (1648–9), *An Antidote against Atheism* (London, 1653), *The Immortality of the Soul* (London, 1659), and in his late *Enchiridion Metaphysicum* (London, 1671). More's account of the soul and immaterial substance in these works draws on the ancient and Renaissance Platonic sources that characterise the Cambridge Platonists, but also shows a keen awareness of the systems of Descartes and Hobbes, the intellectual currents which dominated European learned discourse.

More directed his doctrine quite specifically against mechanists, such as Hobbes, who would deny the existence of an incorporeal and immortal soul.[89] In his fight against Hobbesian materialism, he squarely allied himself with Descartes until at least the mid-1660s; in the preface to his 1662 *Collection of Several Philosophical Writings* he described his philosophy as an 'interweaving Platonisme and Cartesianisme'.[90] It is not surprising that More saw in Descartes an ally against the more thoroughgoing mechanism of a Hobbes; like Descartes, More was committed both to a broadly mechanical world view and to the existence of immaterial substance.

But there are important differences to note as well. Though the arguments he used are in general more traditional than those Descartes employed, he, like Descartes, argued for an immortal soul in humans.[91] However, More recognised many more kinds of incorporeal substance than Descartes did. Like Digby, More found the new mechanical philosophy extremely useful for the establishment of incorporeal substance in so far as it clearly determines what body is and sets clear limits on the mechanical explicability of things in the world; he believed that the physics of 'that admirable Master of Mechanicks Des-Cartes' should be required reading for that reason.[92] But he argued that much of what others like Descartes and Digby think is mechanically explicable is not. For one thing, More thought that life is not mechanistically explicable, and unlike Descartes, saw the soul as an incorporeal principle of life, both in us and in animals, presumably.[93] But most interesting is his claim that we must appeal to an incorporeal substance (what he calls the 'spirit of nature') to explain what 'remands down a stone toward the Center of the Earth, . . . keeps the Waters from swilling out of the Moon, curbs the matter of the Sun into roundness of figure', and determines the shapes of plants and animals as well.[94] More characterised his spirit of nature as 'a substance incorporeal, but without Sense and Animadversion, pervading the whole Matter of the Universe, and exercising a Plastical power therein . . . , raising such Phaeno- mena in the world, by directing the parts of Matter and their Motion, as cannot be resolved into mere Mechanic powers'.[95] This spirit of nature, which Descartes rudely rejected when More casually mentioned it in a letter,[96] is 'the lowest Substantial Activity from the all-wise God, containing in it certain general Modes and Lawes of Nature for the good of the Universe',[97] the ultimate explanation of a variety of phenomena, including gravity and magnetism, thought to be explicable mechanically by the likes of Descartes.

More differed from Descartes over what incorporeal substances do in the world. But he also differed significantly from Descartes over what these substances are like. More agreed with Hobbes that 'there is no real Entity but what is in some sense extended.'[98] But from this he concluded not that there is no incorpo- real substance, but that 'spirit is in some sort extended.'[99] Matter, More said, is extended substance that is impenetrable and divisible. Spirit is 'a substance indis- cerpible, that can move it self, that can penetrate, contract, and dilate it self, and can also penetrate, move, and alter the Matter'.[100] Though it is extended, More argued, spiritual substance can 'invincibly hold its parts together, so that they cannot be disunited nor dissevered'.[101] Using the analogy of light, More likened the soul to a luminescent centre with rays proceeding outward; it is extended, but we cannot clip the individual rays out. This is, indeed, his model for the human soul, a vital centre or primary substance, that exists in a small but extended region of space, that 'can send forth out of itself so large a sphere of Secondary Substance . . . that it is able to activate grand portions of Matter'.[102] More held this view, which has its origin in the Neoplatonic tradition, from the time of his correspon- dence with Descartes. But it is mainly in his later works the *Divine Dialogues* (London, 1665) and the *Enchiridion metaphysicum* (London, 1671) that he empha- sised his extreme disagreement with Descartes on this issue, calling Descartes the *Nullibistarum princeps,* 'the Prince of the Nowhere Men', and arguing for the incoherence of the notion of a non-extended incorporeal substance that exists nowhere.[103] Though the notion of *unextended* substance is incomprehensible, that of *incorporeal* substance is not.[104]

More attempted to steer a middle course between the two main alternatives; with Hobbes he recognised the unintelligibility of the Cartesian notion of unextended substance, but with Descartes, he recognised limitations on the mechanical philosophy, and the necessity to appeal to immaterial substance. Others followed him in this enterprise, most notably Ralph Cudworth but also, perhaps, Locke and Newton.[105]

Much of the debate about incorporeal substance and the soul in the seventeenth century concerns the question of the extent of mechanism; Hobbes holds that all phenomena in nature can be explained mechanically, whereas others, like Descartes, Digby, and More exclude greater or lesser domains for the activity of incorporeal substances of various sorts and natures. But in the brilliant systems of Spinoza and Leibniz we face an altogether different sort of strategy. Both, in a sense, attempt to combine the uncompromising mechanism of Hobbesian materialism with the spirituality of a dualist position like that of Descartes.

VI. SPINOZA

Spinoza's account of mind is one of the central foci of his monumental *Ethica* (1677), on which he worked for many of his later years. In that work, the account of mind follows directly from the account of God in *Ethica* I and, in turn, grounds the moral psychology and the account of immortality and true happiness that is the ultimate aim of the book. Spinoza was often considered a materialist, and on the basis of his account of mind, as well as other of his doctrines, he was often linked with Hobbes.[106] Spinoza's view on mind and the human being does have certain affinities with that of Hobbes. But his position is considerably more complex than that.

The story for Spinoza begins with God. Spinoza's God is a substance, something that 'is in itself and is conceived through itself', something that is in conception and in actuality independent of all else.[107] This God has an infinity of attributes, of which we know two and only two, thought and extension.[108] Each of these attributes is 'what the intellect perceives of a substance as constituting its essence'.[109] Unlike Descartes, for whom distinct attributes entail distinct substances, Spinoza insists that 'it is far from absurd to attribute many attributes to one substance; indeed nothing in nature is clearer than that each being must be conceived under some attribute, and the more reality, or being it has, the more it has attributes.'[110] This view of God, *one* thing that can be understood and understood completely through either thought or extension, is the basis of Spinoza's account of mind. Spinoza argues that God, the substance with an infinity of attributes, necessarily exists, and that 'except God, no substance can be or be conceived'.[111] Finite things emerge in Spinoza's metaphysics as modes, 'that which is in another through which it is also conceived'.[112] It is not clear whether Spinoza understood modes as properties or accidents that inhere in substance as their subject (as, for example, Descartes did) or as genuine things which depend causally upon substance (God) but do not literally inhere in it.[113] For our purposes, though, it does not matter how this interpretative issue is settled. What is important is that just as there is only one God understood through His different attributes, there is just one world of modes, understood through the different attributes of God: 'The thinking substance and the extended substance are one and the same substance, which is now comprehended under this attribute, now under that. So also a mode of extension and the idea of that mode [i.e., the corresponding mode of thought] are one and the same thing, but expressed in two ways.'[114] Corresponding to every mode of extension, to every body is a mode of thought, an idea, which two modes are identical in a sense, though comprehended through different attributes.[115] Spinoza argues that the human mind is the mode of thought that corresponds to the human body, the idea of the body.[116] And so, Spinoza claims, 'the Mind and the Body are one and the same thing, which is conceived now under the attribute of Thought, now under the attribute of Extension.'[117]

Spinoza's conception of mind is apparently quite different from Descartes's.[118] Spinoza's mind, unlike Descartes's is not a substance. But more important, unlike Descartes's, it is a complex entity, made up of proper parts: 'The idea that constitutes the formal being [*esse*] of the human Mind is not simple, but composed of a great many ideas.'[119] Just as the human body contains a complex of interrelated parts, the mind contains parts, ideas corresponding to each of the parts of the body.[120] This is in radical contrast to the Cartesian soul, which is a single, indivisible substance. Furthermore, for Spinoza, every mode of extension can be comprehended through the attribute of thought, since as a mode of God, it must be comprehensible through each of His modes. Consequently, corresponding to every mode of extension there is an idea, and thus every extended thing has a mind, in a sense: 'The things we have shown are completely general and do not pertain more to man than to other Individuals, all of which, though in different degrees, are nevertheless animate.'[121] What differentiates other minds from ours is just their complexity, the complexity of the ideas that make them up, varying as the complexity of the bodies to which they correspond. This, of course, is quite different from Descartes, for whom the only minds in nature are human minds. And finally, since Spinoza's view is that mind is the idea of an actual body, having a mind requires having a body, whereas for Descartes, the mind can exist apart from the body.[122]

This last feature of Spinoza's suggests the position of Hobbes. Although Hobbes is barely mentioned in Spinoza's writings, his direct influence on Spinoza's account of mind and human being can scarcely be doubted. For Spinoza, each attribute of substance is distinct,[123] and he therefore argues: 'The modes of each attribute have God for their cause only insofar as he is considered under the attribute of which they are modes, and not insofar as he is considered under any other attribute.'[124] As a consequence, 'The body cannot determine the Mind to thinking, and the Mind cannot determine the Body to motion, to rest or to anything else (if there is anything else).'[125] And so, for Spinoza, as for Hobbes, one can give a purely mechanistic account of everything that a human being does, from digestion and locomotion, to building, painting, and the construction of temples.[126]

Spinoza, like Hobbes, subscribes to a universal mechanism and rejects the view that we must appeal beyond body to mind to explain what goes on in the world of body.[127] At the same time, it is important to acknowledge the Cartesian elements in Spinoza's account of mind. The Cartesian influence is evident in the very choice of divine attributes Spinoza chooses to recognise: thought and extension, the two attributes that characterise Descartes's created world, attributes whose metaphysical importance Descartes saw himself as the first to recognise. Spinoza's mind is in this sense like Descartes's, a thinking thing, which is completely unconnected to the vital functions that characterise the Aristotelian hierarchy of souls.[128] And while Spinoza's mind is a complex of interrelated parts, it is not extended. Indeed, it is radically distinct from extension, even more so than Descartes's is. For Spinoza, the mind is not the cause of motion in the world of bodies, but then the body is not the cause of sensation or imagination in the mind either; just as everything corporeal has a corporeal cause, so everything mental has a cause in the world of modes of thought. Mind and body, in Descartes's sense, are not distinct, separate substances that can exist apart from one another. But, in another sense, they are quite distinct. And although there is a sense in which everything is explicable mechanically, thought is not eliminated or reduced to motion, as it seems to be in Hobbes.

In Spinoza, the question of mind is *not* a question of the limits of mechanism, as it is for so many others in the seventeenth century; he is not concerned to argue for (or against) the existence of mind distinct from body on the basis of what body alone can or cannot do. His interest is in reconciling a conception of thought, distinct from extension, with a universal mechanism, in reconciling his Cartesian intuitions with his Hobbesian tendencies. His solution is to identify the mind with the body without reducing the one to the other.

VII. LEIBNIZ

Leibniz had a great deal to say about minds and bodies. But his view can best be understood only in the wider context of his thought about body and the mechanical philosophy.

One of the great reforms of the new philosophy of the seventeenth century was the general elimination of substantial forms from the physical world. Instead of Aristotelian substances, unions of matter and form, many mechanists posited material substance, a stuff characterised and individuated not by substantial form but by shape, size, and motion, whose real attributes included their geometrical properties, impenetrability, usually, and, in the case of the atomists, indivisibility at the most basic level.[129] Although there may have been a brief period in which he accepted such an account,[130] in general Leibniz objected to such a conception of the ultimate make-up of the world, and he did so from his earliest years. In the 'Confessio Naturae contra Atheistas' (1669), for example, Leibniz appealed to the fact that the space a body fills, the motion it has, and the coherence it has, are inexplicable from the nature of body in order to show that 'bodies are not self-sufficient and that they cannot subsist without an incorporeal principle', which he there identifies with God.[131] In 1671, he claimed that 'every body is a momentary mind', a mind without memory.[132] In the difficult Paris Notes of 1676, Leibniz held that 'solidity or unity of body comes from the mind, and that there are as many minds as vortices, as many vortices as there are solid bodies'.[133]

This general theme, that the entire world of bodies, both animate and superficially inanimate, rests on a foundation of something non-bodily is one that followed Leibniz through the rest of his career. In his mature writings, those from the 1680s on, we find a number of arguments intended to establish that there is something in bodies over and above the material substance of the mechanical philosophy.

One argument proceeds from the idea of unity. Leibniz held that the only true beings are genuine individuals. As he wrote to Arnauld: 'I hold as axiomatic the identical proposition which varies only in emphasis: that what is not truly *one* entity is not truly one *entity* either. . . . [The] plural presupposes the singular, and where there is no entity, still less will there be many entities.'[134] From this, Leibniz concluded that Cartesian extended stuff cannot be all there is in the world, and that there must be some genuine unities from which the extended and infinitely divisible bodies physics treats are composed or result, 'formal atoms' that are 'conceived in imitation of the idea we have of souls', as he put it in the *Système nouveaux* (1695).[135] A second sort of argument departs from the observation that the extended bodies of the mechanical philosophy are completely inert. Left to themselves, the only law they would obey would be the law of the composition of velocities, since, being inert, they would offer no resistance to the acquisition of new motion. But if so, Leibniz argued, then the smallest body in motion could set the largest body at rest into motion, without losing any of its own speed, a result that conflicts with both common experience and with metaphysics, in so far as it would lead directly to perpetual motion. And so, Leibniz concluded in the *Specimen Dynamicum* (1695): 'A certain superior and, so to speak, formal principle must be added to that of material mass. . . . Whether we call this principle form, entelechy, or force does not matter.'[136]

A different sort of argument derives from Leibniz's celebrated predicate-in-notion principle, the principle that in every true predication, the concept of the predicate is included in the concept of the subject. In section 8 of *Discours de métaphysique* (1686), among other places, Leibniz used this principle to argue that every individual substance has a complete individual concept that contains everything that was true, is true, and will be true of that individual. Each individual substance, Leibniz concluded, contains marks and traces of all of its past, present, and future properties. This, as he wrote to Arnauld, requires that there be something over and above body in the world: 'Substantial unity requires a complete, indivisible and naturally indestructible entity, since its concept embraces everything that is to happen to it, which can be found neither in shape nor in motion . . . but which can be found in a soul or substantial form, on the model of what is called *me*.'[137] Leibniz's argument seems to be that since there will, at any time, be truths and falsities about a given substance, and since at any time we can talk about what *this* substance is and what *this same* substance was, there must be some single thing that persists that makes the individual the individual it is and serves as the subject of its properties. This cannot be body, Leibniz argues, which divides and dissipates. He concludes, for there to be individual substances with complete individual concepts, there must be something over and above the mechanists' bodies.

With these (and other) arguments, Leibniz attempted to establish that there must be something over and above the extended bodies of the mechanical philosophy, something he characterised in terms of soul, entelechy (an Aristotelian concept closely connected to soul), form, or force. But just what that is, and how it is related to body (indeed, just what *body* comes to for Leibniz) is not altogether clear, nor is it entirely clear that there is a single answer that can unambiguously be attributed to Leibniz. In the correspondence with Arnauld from 1686 to 1688, his view seems to be that the unities that constitute the real entities in the physical world are corporeal substances conceived on analogy with human beings, non-extended and indivisible souls or forms, that serve to unite extended bodies and together constitute living things. Each animal body is, in turn, composed of smaller living things, souls uniting bodies, in a sequence that goes on indefinitely. Although one cannot be absolutely sure, there is some reason to believe that Leibniz recognised two distinct principles, the soul or form, and the matter it unites.[138] A slightly different view is suggested in the *Specimen dynamicum* (1695), where he characterised the ultimate individuals in terms of what he calls primitive active and primitive passive force. Primitive active force, which he associated with soul or substantial form, is the ground of derivative active force, which includes both the living force found in bodies actually moving, and the dead force found in stretched springs and taut bows. Primitive passive force, associated with matter, is the ground of derivative passive force, which includes impenetrability and resistance. These two primitive forces come together to make up corporeal substances, the individuals that ground the reality of the world.[139] And finally there is the view put forward in the *Monadologie* (1714), as well as in many other works. Here, incorporeal substance seems to have replaced material substance altogether; the only things in the world are monads, conceived on broad analogy with our own souls. The physical world, on this view, is organised into living things, as in the Arnauld letters, but these living things are not considered to be genuine substances, genuine individuals that ground the physical world. Rather, bodies are usually conceived as aggregates of monads, confusedly perceived together, and organisms are regarded as organised collections of monads.[140]

Forms, entelechies, or monads, as Leibniz came to call them in the late 1690s, have properties similar to those found in Cartesian souls. They are non-extended, simple, and immortal and contain two faculties, what Leibniz called perception and appetition, the faculty for having perceptions and the faculty for changing them, which correspond to the faculties of understanding and volition, respectively, in the Cartesian soul. Furthermore, our comprehension of these substances derives from the immediate experience we have of our own souls, Leibniz held.[141] At the same time, there are some important differences. Unlike Descartes's souls, Leibniz's have no genuine *causal* links to anything but God; all causal links are merely apparent, a matter of pre-established harmonies between what goes on in different substances. In this, though, Leibniz is not unlike the occasionalists of the later Cartesian tradition (see Chapter 25). Furthermore, Leibniz recognised an infinite gradation of consciousness in his monads, from perceptions that are completely unconscious to those that are fully conscious. In this way Leibniz can distinguish an infinite variety of souls, from God, aware of everything, to human souls, and down to what he calls 'bare' monads, all confusion and no consciousness at all. Indeed, Leibniz held that there are some souls or other everywhere in nature, in the smallest bit of matter. And finally, though Leibniz seems to have conceived body differently at different times, he seems always to have held that souls are always connected to some body or other and never exist alone in nature. Even in death, Leibniz held that we hang onto a body, though generally a body much smaller and perhaps less complex than the body we have in normal life.[142]

As complex and unorthodox as Leibniz's views may seem, there is a sense in which they are quite simple and quite traditional. Leibniz often saw himself as a reconciler of a number of disparate traditions.[143] First, he was attempting to reconcile the Aristotelian metaphysics of matter and substantial form with the mechanist teachings. As normally viewed in the seventeenth century, the mechanist programme for explaining the behaviour of body in terms of size, shape, and motion was in explicit opposition to the explanation of phenomena in terms of substantial form, the tiny souls (as Descartes characterised them) attached to body that explain the characteristic behaviour of different sorts of things. Leibniz often represented himself as reviving this view. In the *Discours de métaphysique,* Leibniz wrote that 'the belief in substantial forms has some basis, but that these forms do not change anything in the phenomena and must not be used to explain particular effects.'[144] Leibniz held that upon further analysis of the notions of body and substance, we must admit incorporeal substances of a sort that he associated with the forms taught by the scholastics. But unlike the scholastics, he says these are not to be used to explain particular phenomena, such as why fire rises and stones fall; all particular phenomena are to be explained mechanically. Everything happens mechanically, but to understand the bodies of the mechanical philosophy and the laws they satisfy, we must admit something like souls.[145] The form or soul enters here not to disrupt a perfect mechanism or to explain what cannot be explained mechanically, as it does in Descartes or Digby or the Cambridge Platonists, but to *ground* mechanism. And from this comes a way of reconciling the Cartesian view with that of Hobbes. Leibniz wrote in a response to Bayle in 1702:

The body is made in such a way that the soul never makes any resolutions to which the movements of the body do not correspond. . . . In a word, so far as the details of phenomena are concerned, everything takes place in the body as if the evil doctrine of those who believe, with Epicurus and Hobbes, that the soul is material were true, or as if man himself were only a body or an automaton. . . . But in addition to the general principles which establish the monads of which compound things are merely the results, internal experience refutes the Epicurean doctrine. This experience is the consciousness within us of this Ego which perceives the things occurring in the body. And since this perception cannot be explained by figures and movements, it establishes the other half of my hypothesis and makes us recognize an indivisible substance in ourselves. . . . According to this second half of my hypothesis, therefore, everything occurs in the soul as if there were no body, just as everything occurs in the body as if there were no soul. . . . [T]his shows that our view combines what is good in the hypothesis of both Epicurus and Plato, of both the greatest materialists and the greatest idealists.[146]

This is one statement of Leibniz's celebrated hypothesis of pre-established harmony, a doctrine discussed in greater detail in Chapter 25. The movement of the arm follows upon the volition to raise the arm. But it is a direct causal consequence only of the states of the substances that make up the arm; it is, Leibniz claims, explicable in a purely mechanical way, as is everything in the body. And in this sense Hobbes is correct, and reconciled with Descartes.

VIII. LOCKE

The preceding pages have shown attempts to reconcile Cartesian and Hobbesian views about mind, soul, and incorporeal substance. Locke, in his influential *Essay concerning Human Understanding* (London, 1690), does not so much reconcile the differences as reject the question altogether. Locke's position is considered at greater length in Chapter 24. Briefly, though, Locke argued that our idea of the substratum that is the seat of the qualities and powers by which we distinguish and define spirit is only the idea of a something-I-know-not-what that supports those qualities and powers, an idea exactly the same as the idea I have of the substratum that underlies the qualities and powers by which we know body.[147] Although Locke acknowledged that it is most probable that the human mind is immaterial[148] and although he liberally added 'immaterial' to numerous occurrences of the word 'spirit' after the third edition of 1695,[149] his considered position seemed to be that

we shall never be able to know, whether any mere material Being thinks, or no; it being impossible for us, by the mere contemplation of our own *Ideas,* without revelation, to discover, whether Omnipotency has not given to some Systems of Matter fitly disposed, a power to perceive and think, or else joined and fixed to Matter so disposed, a thinking immaterial Substance.[150]

Since it is probable that our souls are immaterial, and since we know that there will be an afterlife, whether or not we have immaterial souls, ''tis not of such mighty necessity to determine one way or t'other, as some over zealous for, or against the Immateriality of the Soul, have been forward to make the World believe'.[151] Locke simply rejected the question that had so vexed earlier philosophers: 'He who will give himself leave to consider freely, and look into the dark and intricate part of each Hypothesis, will scarce find his Reason able to determine him fixedly for, or against the Soul's Materiality.'[152]

Though Locke rejected what most had taken to be the fundamental question, he attempted to set out what we can know about our minds in particular and spirit in general without knowing the nature of its substratum. The idea of spirit, for Locke, is composed of the ideas of two operations: '*Thinking, and Will,* or a power of putting Body into motion by Thought, and, which is consequent to it, Liberty'.[153] These are taken to inhere in a substratum of unknown nature. In addition, the idea of spirit contains the ideas of existence, duration, and mobility, which it shares with the general idea we have of body.[154] From the fact that spirit has mobility, Locke infers that it has place, if not extension.[155] Though the soul is a thinking thing for Locke, unlike Descartes, he does not infer from that that the soul always thinks.[156] While we know our own minds best, Locke thinks that through revelation and analogy we know of the existence of spirits below and above us.[157] Though Locke rejected the central question of earlier seventeenth-century writers on mind and soul, there is much he seems to have learned. Like Descartes, he seems to have rejected the vital functions of the Aristotelian soul in favour of thought and will, and like Henry More, he seems to have recognised a variety of spirits[158] and seems to have placed them in space. Though we cannot know the true nature of spiritual substance, says Locke, we can know a great deal about spirit. Indeed, we can know spirit just as well as we can know body.[159]

IX. CONCLUSION

The story does not end in any neat way in 1700, of course; many of the views discussed in this chapter have their influence in later figures, and new views and arguments continue to surface. But if the seventeenth-century discussion of mind, soul, and incorporeal substance does not offer closure on the issue, it does represent a place for beginning a new discussion. In so far as it is fair to say that the mechanical philosophy advanced by the new philosophers of the seventeenth century inaugurates modern natural philosophy and science, it is also fair to say that the discussion of mind and soul in the seventeenth-century context represents the beginning of the modern discussion on mind and soul. Vitalism and dualism, still serious options in the seventeenth century, may have eventually given way to various forms of materialism with regard to questions of life and thought, but it is still the seventeenth century that set the questions, what body, suitably organised, can and cannot do, and what we may or may not have to add to inanimate body in order to comprehend the phenomena of life and thought.

NOTES

1 See the discussion of hylemorphism in Chapter 15.

2 For a general account of the conception of mind in late mediaeval and Renaissance thought, see Park and Kessler 1988; Park 1988; and Kessler 1988. For a bibliography of the literature on psychology in the Renaissance, see Schüling 1967.

3 This is one of the problems of Averroism. On this, see Kuksewicz 1982a, 1982b; Mahoney 1982. For some further disputes over lesser issues, see Park 1988, pp. 473–84.

4 See Pegis 1934.

5 *Summa th.* I q75 a2c; see also q50 a1,a2; q75 a3; q76 a1; q78 a1. The argument has its roots in a brief passage from Aristotle, *De Anima* III.4, 429a24ff.

6 *Summa th.* I q88 a1c, q75 a5, q84 a1c.

7 See Kessler 1988, pp. 500–507, and Chapter 2 in this book.

8 On the new mechanistic view of nature, see Chapters 17–21.

9 On the relations between the mechanists and the more conservative Aristotelians, see especially Mercer 1990, 1993, and forthcoming.

10 Cudworth 1678, p. 49; see also Digby 1644a, preface p. [3].

11 See Kessler 1988, pp. 494–5, 500.

12 For a study of some aspects of the medical and theological traditions as they relate to this question in seventeenth-century England, see Henry 1989a. Henry emphasises that there was a real divide between the medical and the philosophical traditions; see pp. 92–3. For a bibliography that includes medical items of relevance here, see Diethelm 1971; Schüling 1967. Some aspects of the theological question of the soul are discussed in Burns 1972.

13 On this, see Westfall 1971a, chap. 5; T. S. Hall 1969.

14 AT XI 201–2.

15 The idea is sketched out in the beginning of *Disc.* part V, AT VI 43–6. It is, of course, tempting to see in this view an anticipation of Darwin and modern theories of evolution. It must be remembered, though, that Descartes had no real detailed suggestion about mechanisms. Furthermore, the idea is hardly original with Descartes; see, e.g., Lucretius, *De rerum natura* V 416ff.

16 For reasons to be discussed later in this section, Descartes does not distinguish between mind and soul.

17 On this, see especially Carriero 1986.

18 AT VII 27.

19 AT VII 78.

20 For a more extended treatment of this argument, see Garber 1992a, chap. 3. In addition to this argument, Descartes employs at least two others. First, in *Disc.* part IV, Descartes argues for the real distinction between mind and body from the fact that I could doubt the existence of the world of bodies without doubting my own existence; see AT VI 32. This argument also comes up in *Princ.* I 8. However, in the preface to the *Meditationes* Descartes appears to deny that this is intended as an argument; see AT VII

7–8. And second, in Med. VI, Descartes argues for the distinction from the fact that while bodies are divisible, minds are not. See AT VII 85–6. The related question of the union of mind and body is taken up in Chapter 25.

21 See *Disc.* V, AT VI 59–60 and the synopsis of the *Meditationes,* AT VII 13–14. Although it is naturally immortal, God could, of course, choose to destroy it when the body is destroyed; see Resp. II, AT VII 153–4. Descartes's account of memory raised some problems for his account of immortality. Initially, he held that memory resides in the body (brain) alone, so that when the body dies, all memory is lost. This raises obvious problems for a Christian conception of personal identity; without memory, it would seem difficult to distinguish one mind from another. This caused Descartes to introduce a notion of non-corporeal memory. On Descartes's account of memory, see Chapter 26.

22 See AT VII 263.

23 AT VII 356; see also Descartes to Regius, May 1641, AT III 371.

24 See Gilson 1967a, pp. 245–55.

25 AT VIIIB 348.

26 AT VII 28.

27 See Descartes to Gibieuf, 19 January 1642, AT III 479.

28 See Descartes to More, August 1649, AT V 402.

29 See, e.g., the French version of *Princ.* I 48. The union of mind and body in Descartes is taken up in greater detail in Chapter 25.

30 AT VII 72, 358; cf. with Thomas's position, as discussed in sec. I.

31 The centrality of reason and intellect in Descartes's conception of the soul is emphasised in Wilson 1978, chap. 6.

32 See, e.g., the account of the 'vulgar' conception of mind in Med. II, and the remarks in Descartes to Mersenne, 21 April 1641, AT III 362.

33 Descartes to More, 15 April 1649, AT V 342. See also Descartes to Elisabeth, 28 June 1643, AT III 694; Descartes to More, 5 February 1649, AT V 269; Descartes to More, 15 April 1649, AT V 343; cf. Thomas, *Summa th.* I q52 a1.

34 See AT VII 358.

35 See, e.g., AT VII 426; Descartes to [the Marquess of Newcastle], 23 November 1646, AT IV 573–6; Descartes to More, 5 February 1649, AT V 276–9.

36 AT VII 358; see also Descartes to More, August 1649, AT V 402.

37 AT VI 57–8. See also AT VII 230; Descartes to [the Marquess of Newcastle], 23 November 1646, AT IV 574; Descartes to More, 5 February 1649, AT V 278.

38 See AT VII 230–1, 426; Descartes to Reneri for Pollot, April 1638, AT II 39–41; Descartes to Mersenne, 30 July 1640, AT III 121; Descartes to [the Marquess of Newcastle], 23 November 1646, AT IV 575–6; Descartes to More, 5 February 1649, AT V 277–8; AT XI 519–20. Descartes considers rational behaviour a 'certain sign' of a soul (Descartes to More, 5 February 1649, AT V 278), and claims that it is '*moralement impossible*' that rational behaviour could derive from a purely mechanical source (*Disc.* part V, AT VI 57). Elsewhere, Descartes suggests that animals have corporeal souls, which can be identified with their blood; see Descartes to Plempius for Fromondus, 3 October 1637, AT I 414–6; Descartes to [Mesland], 2 May 1644, AT IV 64–5.

39 AT VII 426; Descartes to [the Marquess of Newcastle], 23 November 1646, AT IV 573–6; Descartes to More, 5 February 1649, AT V 276–9; *Pass. âme* sec. 50.

40 See AT VII 426; Descartes to [the Marquess of Newcastle], 23 November 1646, AT IV 573–6; Descartes to More, 5 February 1649, AT V 276–9; Descartes to Mersenne, 30

July 1640, AT III 121; AT IX 519–20; Descartes to Mersenne, 11 June 1640, AT III 85; Descartes to Reneri for Pollot, April 1638, AT II 39; Descartes to Regius, May 1640, AT III 372; *Pass. âme* sec. 50. It should be noted that there is an extended sense in which Descartes grants that animals have sensation and passions, but he emphasises that such sensations and passions are not thoughts, as ours are. See *Traité de l'homme, passim,* AT VII 436–7, Descartes to [the Marquess of Newcastle], 23 November 1646, AT IV 574.

41 AT V 276–7.

42 AT V 277.

43 See AT VII 358.

44 Descartes's brief discussions of this question gave rise to a lively debate later in the century. For a general account of Descartes's thought on animal souls and the discussion of the question later in the century, see Rosenfield 1968.

45 See, e.g., Clerselier 1667b, p. 641; de La Forge 1974, pp. 107ff., 214ff.; Clauberg 1664a, pp. 323–5; Cordemoy 1968, pp. 152ff.

46 Digby 1644a, p. 306; more generally see chaps. 23ff.

47 See the introduction to the second treatise, Digby 1644a, p. 350.

48 Digby 1644a, p. 144.

49 Other arguments include argument from the absurdity of 'spiritual accidents' in matter, which is divisible, and an argument from our ability to conceive of ourselves independently of matter, which he attributes to Descartes and Avicenna; see Digby 1644a, pp. 415–16.

50 See Digby 1644a, Pref. p.[1].

51 See Digby 1644a, Pref. pp. 412, 424.

52 See Digby 1644a, pp. 416–17, 422. In the first of these two passages, Digby explicitly cites Descartes's use of doubt in *Disc.* IV and *Med.* II to eliminate everything corporeal, without thereby eliminating the soul. Digby takes this to show that the soul is incorporeal.

53 See Digby 1644a, Bk. II, chap. 5.

54 See Digby 1644a, Bk. I, chaps. 23, 36–8.

55 See Bloch 1971, pp. 375, 397.

56 See especially Osler 1985a; Bloch 1971; Tack 1974, chap. 8.

57 On the soul of plants, see Gassendi 1658, vol. 2, pp. 144ff. and 253a–b; Bernier 1678, vol. 5, pp. 341ff., 467–8. The animal sensitive soul is treated in Gassendi 1658, vol. 2, pp. 250ff.; Bernier 1678, vol. 5, pp. 454ff. The human soul as a whole is treated in Gassendi 1658, vol. 2, pp. 255ff.; Bernier 1678, vol. 5, pp. 480ff., and the rational soul or mind is treated in Gassendi 1658, vol. 2, pp. 425ff.; Bernier 1678, vol. 6, pp. 342ff. The immortality of the soul is discussed in Gassendi 1658, vol. 2, pp. 620ff.; Bernier 1678, vol. 6, pp. 367ff. (Bernier 1678 is a selective translation and paraphrase into French of the *Syntagma* that generally follows Gassendi's line on these issues. It is much more accessible than the *Syntagma* itself, and so I will cite corresponding passages.) Gassendi distinguishes between the *anima,* which is the organic soul, responsible for the vital functions, and the *animus,* the intellectual soul. See Gassendi 1658, vol. 2, p. 237b; Bernier 1678, vol. 5, p. 441; Osler 1985a, p. 167.

58 The material *anima* in animals is discussed in Gassendi 1658, vol. 2, pp. 250b–1a; Bernier 1678, vol. 5, p. 456; the material part of the soul in humans is discussed in Gassendi 1658, vol. 2, pp. 256a–b; Bernier 1678, vol. 5, pp. 480–1. See also Bloch 1971, p. 168; Osler 1985a, pp. 168–9; Canguilhem 1955, chap. 4.

59 See Bloch 1971, pp. 398, 405–6. Gassendi often appeals to the requirements of the true faith in his discussion of the soul; see, e.g., Gassendi 1658, vol. 2, pp. 237b, 627a; Bernier 1678, vol. 5, p. 440.

60 The argument from the distinction between intellect and imagination or phantasy is given in Gassendi 1658, vol. 2, p. 440b; Bernier 1678, vol. 6, p. 342. Although this would appear to be inconsistent with Gassendi's critique of Descartes in the *Objectiones* and the *Disquisitio,* where Gassendi appears to deny that there are ideas of the intellect, as opposed to ideas of imagination (AT VII 329ff.), Bloch 1971, pp. 408–9 argues that the two positions are quite consistent. The argument from our ability to understand ourselves is given in Gassendi 1658, vol. 2, p. 441a; Bernier 1678, vol. 6, p. 345. The argument from our ability to comprehend universals is given in Gassendi 1658, vol. 2, pp. 441a–b; Bernier 1678, vol. 6, pp. 346–7. It should be noted here that like Aristotle, although Gassendi distinguishes between the imagination and the intellect, and holds that the mind can grasp universals, all the contents of the mind or rational soul ultimately derive from the senses. See Gassendi 1658, vol. 1, pp. 92aff.; Bernier 1678, vol. 3, pp. 10ff. However, he also holds that the phantasy is just the starting-place from which the intellect elevates itself. See Gassendi 1658, vol. 2, pp. 441a, 442b; Bernier 1678, vol. 6, pp. 344–5, 350. The argument from our ability to comprehend both corporeal and incorporeal substances is given in Gassendi 1658, vol. 2, pp. 441a–2b; Bernier 1678, vol. 6, pp. 349ff.; Bloch 1971, pp. 404–5. This argument is especially reminiscent of Saint Thomas; see *Summa th.* I a75 a2c. In addition to these arguments, Gassendi briefly suggests that the incorporeality of the mind can be established from will, the fact that it seeks non-sensual goods, and from its freedom; see Gassendi 1658, vol. 2, p. 440b, Bernier 1678, vol. 6, p. 352.

61 Gassendi 1658, vol. 2, p. 628a; Bernier 1678, vol. 6, pp. 367ff. This is the main physical argument Gassendi offers for the immortality of the soul. In addition, he offers a number of 'moral' arguments for immortality, including an argument from common consent, an argument from the universal desire for immortality, and an argument from divine justice, from the fact that evil people are not always punished in this life. See Gassendi 1658, vol. 2, pp. 629bff.; Bernier 1678, vol. 6, pp. 368ff.

62 Gassendi 1658, vol. 2, pp. 256a–b; Bernier 1678, vol. 5, pp. 480–1. See Bloch 1971, pp. 368 n. 63, 408–11; Tack 1974, p. 200 n. 317. The unity of the soul in Gassendi is discussed in Chapter 25.

63 See Gassendi 1658, vol. 2, pp. 443b–4a; Bernier 1678, vol. 6, pp. 361–3.

64 For a brief account of the history of materialism, see Bloch 1985.

65 See Burns 1972.

66 On the so-called 'libertins érudites', see especially Pintard 1943; Spink 1960. For a recent survey of work on this group, with a very helpful bibliography of recent (and not so recent) literature, see Charles-Daubert 1985. The work of clandestine literature most widely discussed among recent commentators is the anonymous *Theophrastus Redivivus,* now available in a modern edition, *Theophrastus Redivivus* 1981–2. However, it is not clear how widely read or influential it was in the seventeenth century; see Kors 1990, pp. 219–25. For another anonymous materialist tract of the period, see *L'âme matérielle* 1969.

67 When discussing these views of Gassendi's, it is important to remember that they appear as part of a critique of Descartes and may not represent his own views; it is one thing to say that the soul is material, and quite another to say that Descartes has not established through his arguments that it is not. See AT VII 257; Gassendi 1658, vol. 3, p. 273b.

68 AT VII 269; Gassendi 1658, vol. 3, p. 303b.

69 See, e.g., AT VII 30–1, 72–3.

70 AT VII 266–7, 269, 329–31; Gassendi 1658, vol. 3, p. 325b. See Bloch 1971, pp. 369–70. This is an apparent difference between his view in the early 1640s and the view he presents in his later works.

71 AT VII 262–3; AT VII 338–40, 343–4; AT VII 260, 261. See also Bloch 1971, p. 372 n. 85.

72 See AT VII 266, 275, 338. Cf. Gassendi's comments on Descartes's piece of wax, AT VII 271–2.

73 AT VII 265; see also AT VII 260–1, 336–7, 342.

74 See, e.g., AT VII 262–3. See also Bloch 1971, pp. 369, 373.

75 AT VII 257; Gassendi 1658, vol. 3, pp. 368b–9a. An interestingly similar case is made by Descartes's erstwhile disciple, Henricus Regius. Regius held, as did Descartes, that the human soul is a substance whose essence is thought, and that it is distinct from extended substance that constitutes body; see AT VIIIB 342 and Regius 1646, p. 245. But, Regius held, this is something we know not by reason, but by revelation. In the *Fundamenta Physices,* Regius trots out a series of scriptural quotations to establish what reason cannot, that mind is an incorporeal substance, distinct from body. See Regius 1646, p. 246; cf. AT VIIIB 343, #4. In the broadsheet summary of his views on the mind, he goes farther and suggests that 'so far as the nature of things is concerned, . . . mind could be either a substance or a certain mode of corporeal substance' (AT VIIIB 342, #2). Regius's idea is not that thought might be in some sense reducible to extension and motion, as Hobbes will be seen to hold, or that thought is a feature of the organisation of matter, as Gassendi suggested in his critique of Descartes; Regius seems clear that the two attributes in question, thought and extension, are 'different' (*diversa*) and that 'the one is not included in the concept of the other' (Regius 1646, p. 343). His point is that nothing excludes that possibility that thought is an attribute of extended substance. Regius's view is weaker than Gassendi's; for Regius, reason only leaves open the possibility of materialism, and does not lead us to adopt it. For Regius, reason also leaves open the possibility that there is an incorporeal soul, a notion that he finds as fully comprehensible as does Descartes.

76 *Lev.* i, ii.

77 *Lev.* i, Hobbes 1968, p. 86.

78 AT VII 178. See also *Lev.* iv and the nominalist account of reasoning in part I of *De corpora,* Hobbes 1981. While this would appear to reduce thought to the mechanical motion of the parts of the brain, Barnouw 1980 argues for a more complex reading of Hobbes's view here.

79 *Lev.* iii, Hobbes 1968, p. 99.

80 *De corpore,* part I, chap. 1, sec. 8.

81 *Lev.* xxxiv, Hobbes 1968, pp. 428–9. See also *Lev.* iv, Hobbes 1968, p. 108; *Lev.* xlvi, Hobbes 1968, pp. 689, 691. See also *Human Nature: or the Fundamental Elements of Policy,* chap. 11, sec. 6.

82 AT VII 172–3, 177; *Lev.* iv, v, Hobbes 1968, pp. 108, 114–15; *De corpore,* part I, chap. 5.

83 See AT VII 177, where Hobbes explicitly links Descartes's view on mind to that of the schoolmen. The philosophy of the schools is explicitly attacked in *Lev.* xlvi; though Descartes is not mentioned by name here, his views on the soul clearly fit into the scope of Hobbes's attack.

84 *Human Nature . . . ,* chap. 11, sec. 5.

85 See *Lev.* xxxiv.

86 See Overton 1644 and Burns 1972, esp. chap. 4. See also the discussion in Chapter 2.
87 Most notable here is Anthony Collins. For an account of some aspects of British materialism later in the century, see Attfield 1977; Yolton 1983.
88 See D. C. Allen 1964, pp. 171–7.
89 See, e.g., *The Immortality of the Soul,* More 1662d, pp. 65–6.
90 More 1662a, Preface general, p. vi. For an illuminating account of More's relation to Cartesianism, see Gabbey 1982.
91 More used arguments from the comprehension of non-sensory notions, from the existence of a common sense, from the passivity of matter, from the necessity of a non-material cause of motion, and from the need for an explanation of spontaneous action. See, e.g., *Antidote Against Atheism* I.xi; *Immortality of the Soul* I.xi, II.iff.; *Enchiridion metaphysicum,* chaps. 6, 25. In addition, More employed arguments from the reality of ghosts and witches, which he considered one of the best evidences for the existence of incorporeal spirits. See *Immortality of the Soul* I.xiii, *Enchiridion metaphysicum,* chap. 26. More also edited (and augmented) his friend Joseph Glanvill's long defence of the reality of witchcraft, *Saducismus Triumphatus, or Full and Plain Evidence Concerning Witches and Apparitions,* Glanvill 1689.
92 *The Immortality of the Soul,* More 1662d, pp. 12, 13.
93 *The Immortality of the Soul,* More 1662d, pp. 35, 102–3. The question of animal souls is quite prominent in More's correspondence with Descartes.
94 More 1662a, Preface general, p. xv; see also *The Immortality of the Soul* I xii, More 1662d, pp. 12–13, *Enchiridion metaphysicum,* chaps. 11–24.
95 *The Immortality of the Soul,* More 1662d, p. 193.
96 See Gabbey 1982, pp. 211–12.
97 More 1662a, Preface general, p. xvi.
98 More 1662a, Preface general, p. xii.
99 More 1662a, Preface general, p. xii.
100 *The Immortality of the Soul,* More 1662d, p. 25.
101 *The Immortality of the Soul,* More 1662d, p. 25.
102 *The Immortality of the Soul,* More 1662d, p. 26.
103 *Enchiridion metaphysicum,* chap. 27; see Gabbey 1982, pp. 236ff. for discussion of More's rejection of Descartes in his later writings.
104 *The Immortality of the Soul,* I.ix–x; II.i–ii.
105 Cudworth's massive *True Intellectual System* (Cudworth 1678) has as one of its main tasks the refutation of Hobbesian materialism. But unlike More, Cudworth remains agnostic on the question of whether souls are extended; see Cudworth 1678, pp. v, 833–4. Though he grants that souls can be extended, he disagrees with both More and Hobbes and holds that the Cartesian notion of an unextended incorporeal substance is coherent: 'It is not our part here, to oppose *Theists,* but *Atheists:* wherefore we shall leave these *Two Sorts* of *Incorporealists* to dispute it out friendly amongst themselves' (Cudworth 1678, p. 833). Another of the Cambridge Platonists worthy of mention here is John Smith, whose *Discourse Demonstrating the Immortality of the Soul,* probably written in the mid-1640s, was published after his death in his *Select Discourses* (1660). Smith, appealing to rational argument, and buttressed with numerous quotations from Plato and later Neoplatonists like Plotinus and Proclus, attempts to establish that 'the soul of man is not corporeal', that it is 'something really distinct from its body, and of an indivisible nature' (chap. 3). He takes the Epicurean doctrine of a corporeal and mortal soul to be simply absurd, suggesting at one point that if its advocates were right, then even the grass could 'by the help of Motion, spring up into so many

Rational Souls and prove as wise as any Epicurean'. (Quoted in Allen 1964, p. 169.) Though charmingly written, it is fundamentally a piece of religious pleading; the arguments are conventional, and outside of its immateriality and indivisibility Smith has little of philosophical interest to say about the nature of the soul. The echo of More's critique of the Cartesian 'nowhere men' may be discerned in Locke's insistence that the soul has a genuine place in exactly the same sense that bodies do, and is genuinely capable of motion. See *Ess.* II.xxiii.19–21. It should be remembered, though, that for Locke, while the soul is probably immaterial, we cannot know that for certain, and so the soul might be material; see Chapter 24.

106 See, e.g., Leibniz's essay from the late 1670s, 'Il y a deux sectes de Naturalistes', Ger. VII 333–6 (Leibniz 1989, pp. 281–4). The two sects of naturalists in question are the Hobbesists and the Spinozists.

107 *Eth.* I dfn. 3.

108 *Eth.* I dfn. 6, *Eth.* II props. 1, 2.

109 *Eth.* I dfn. 4.

110 *Eth.* I prop. 10 schol.

111 *Eth.* I prop. 11, prop. 14.

112 *Eth.* I dfn. 5; prop. 14 corr. 2.

113 For the view that Spinoza's modes are to be understood as properties or accidents that inhere in substance, see, e.g., Bennett 1984, pp. 92–6; for the view that modes are genuine things, see, e.g., Curley 1969, pp. 4–28, 36–8, 74–7, and Curley 1988, pp. 31–6.

114 *Eth.* II prop. 7 schol.

115 See *Eth.* II ax. 3.

116 *Eth.* II props. 11, 13.

117 *Eth.* III prop. 2 schol.

118 In his introduction to Spinoza's commentary on Descartes's *Principia philosophiae*, Lodewijk Meyer calls special attention to the fact that Spinoza's own view of mind differs considerably from the Cartesian view Spinoza sets out in that work; see Geb. I 131–2. Similarly, in his first letter to Oldenberg, September 1661, Spinoza singles out Descartes's doctrine on the nature of the mind as one of the principal differences he has with Descartes; see Geb. IV 8.

119 *Eth.* II prop. 15.

120 There is something of an ambiguity in Spinoza's account here. It is not entirely clear whether Spinoza intends that the mind is the idea of the entire body, or whether it is the idea of some important part of it, like the brain or some special part of the brain.

121 *Eth.* II prop. 13 schol. This does not necessarily entail that every arbitrary hunk of extension has a mind. In the def. in the short digression on physics following *Eth.* II prop. 13, Spinoza defines a complex body or individual as a stable configuration of bodies in motion and rest with respect to one another; see Geb. II 99–100. His intention may be that only bodies so defined correspond to ideas and thus have minds. But that is by no means clear.

122 It should be noted that despite the apparent identification of the mind and the body, Spinoza does hold that there is a sense in which the human mind exists eternally, indeed, more or less so depending on the proportion of adequate ideas, knowledge of the second and third kind that it contains. See *Eth.* V prop. 21ff. Reconciling this with Spinoza's apparently more materialistic tendencies is one of the central interpretive problems in Spinoza's philosophy. For some attempts to interpret this doctrine, see, e.g., Donagan 1973, Hardin 1978, and Harris 1975.

123 *Eth.* I prop. 10.
124 *Eth.* II prop. 6.
125 *Eth.* III prop. 2.
126 See *Eth.* III prop. 2 schol.
127 See *Eth.* V pref.
128 See Spinoza's discussion of the notion of life in *Cogitata metaphysica,* part II, chap. 6, Geb. I 259–60.
129 See Chapters 15 and 18.
130 See *Syst. nouv.,* Ger. IV 478 (Leibniz 1989, p. 139); Leibniz to Nicholas Remond, 10 January 1714, Ger. III 606 (Leibniz 1969, pp. 654–5). Leibniz reports to Remond that he turned away from substantial forms and towards the moderns at the age of fifteen, in 1661. No documents survive from that earliest intellectual period.
131 LAkad VI.I 490 (Leibniz 1969, p. 110). See also the contemporary fragment on transubstantiation, LAkad VI.I 509 (Leibniz 1969, p. 116).
132 *Theoria motus abstracti,* praedemonstrabilia, sec. 17, LAkad VI.II 266 (Leibniz 1969, p. 141); Leibniz to Arnauld, early November 1671, LAkad II.I 173 (Leibniz 1969, p. 149). For discussions of Leibniz's theory of mind at this time, see Hannequin 1908, esp. part 2, and Mercer forthcoming.
133 Note dated 15 April 1676, LAkad VI.III 509–10 (Leibniz 1969, p. 162).
134 Leibniz to Arnauld, 30 April 1687, Ger. II 97 (Leibniz 1989, p. 86).
135 Ger. IV 478–9 (Leibniz 1989, p. 139).
136 Ger. Math. VI 241–2 (Leibniz 1989, p. 125). For other developments of the same argument, see *Disc. mét.* sec. 21; Ger. IV 464–7; Ger. VII 280–3 (Leibniz 1989, pp. 245–50).
137 Leibniz to Arnauld, 28 November/8 December 1686, Ger. II 76 (Leibniz 1989, p. 79).
138 For a more detailed development of this view, see Garber 1985, pp. 29–62.
139 See Garber 1985, pp. 75–99.
140 See the account of body in Leibniz in Chapter 18. See also Adams 1983; Rutherford forthcoming.
141 Leibniz to de Volder, 1699(?), Ger. II 194 (Leibniz 1969, p. 522).
142 See, e.g., Leibniz to Arnauld, 30 April 1687, Ger. II 99–100 (Leibniz 1989, pp. 87–8); *Nouv. ess.* II.xxvii.7; *PNG* secs. 3–6; *Mon.* secs. 14, 18–21, 66–76.
143 See Leibniz to Nicholas Remond, 10 January 1714, Ger. III 606–7 (Leibniz 1969, pp. 654–5).
144 *Disc. mét.,* sec. 10.
145 See, e.g., *Disc. mét.,* secs. 10, 18; Leibniz to Arnauld, 28 November/8 December 1686, Ger. II 78 (Leibniz 1989, p. 80); 'De prima philosophiae emendatione', Ger. IV 469–70 (Leibniz 1969, p. 433); *Syst. nouv.,* Ger. IV 478 (Leibniz 1989, p. 139); 'Antibarbarus physicus', Ger. VII 343–4 (Leibniz 1989, p. 319).
146 'Reponse aux reflexions . . . de M. Bayle', Ger. IV 559–60 (Leibniz 1969, pp. 577–8).
147 *Ess.* IV.iii.6; *First Letter to [Edward Stillingfleet] the Bishop of Worcester,* Locke 1823, vol 4, pp. 32ff. Locke's view bears important affinities to those of Gassendi and Malebranche; see Chapter 24.
148 *Ess.* II.xxvii.25; *Ess.* IV.iii.6, Locke 1975, p. 541; *First Letter to [Edward Stillingfleet] the Bishop of Worcester,* Locke 1823, vol. 4, pp. 33, 37.
149 This is most evident in *Ess.* II.xxiii. There I count eleven places where Locke adds the word 'immaterial' in the fourth edition to make it clear that he thinks that the human spirit is immaterial. (There is one new occurrence in §§16, 21, 26, and 31; two in §§22 and 32; and three in §15.) There is only one instance of the word appearing in

earlier editions of that chapter. In II.xxiii.31, Locke refers to 'an immaterial knowing substance' from the first edition on. Although there may be a number of reasons for these changes, I find it hard to believe that they were not at least in part in response to the sorts of criticisms that Stillingfleet levelled against Locke's orthodoxy on the issue of the soul. On this, see Ayers 1991, vol. II, pp. 42–7.

150 *Ess.* IV.iii.6, Locke 1975, pp. 540–1.

151 *Ess.* IV.iii.6, Locke 1975, p. 542. What Locke is alluding to here is the view of the Christian mortalists; cf. the discussion of Hobbes in Section IV in this chapter.

152 When Locke considers materialism, it does not seem to be the Hobbesian position, exactly, that all thought is just motion, but a somewhat different position. Locke seems to hold that mental predicates are genuinely different from corporeal predicates, but that the *substratum* of thought, etc., may be the same as the *substratum* of shape, etc. Locke's position here seems similar to that of Henricus Regius; see note 75.

153 *Ess.* II.xxiii.18; see also *Ess.* II.xxi.73, II.xxiii.5.

154 *Ess.* II.xxiii.18.

155 *Ess.* II.xxiii.19–21.

156 *Ess.* II.i.9f. Descartes asserts that the soul must always think as a consequence of the fact that the essence of mind is thought; see, e.g., Resp. V, AT VII 356–7; Descartes to Hyperaspites, August 1641, AT III 423; Descartes to Arnauld, 4 June 1648, AT V 193.

157 *Ess.* IV.iii.27; IV.xvi.12.

158 Though, apparently, not animal souls. See *Third Letter to [Edward Stillingfleet] the Bishop of Worcester,* Locke 1823, vol. 4, pp. 462–3. I would like to thank Michael Ayers for this observation.

159 *Ess.* II.xxiii.5, 15ff. For an account of later reactions to Locke's views on mind, see Yolton 1983.

24

KNOWLEDGE OF THE SOUL

CHARLES McCRACKEN

As Chapter 23 showed, a number of seventeenth-century philosophers grappled with the question, What is the soul? But they also pursued some related questions: How much can we know about the soul, and how do we gain that knowledge? In particular, do we know – and if we do, *how* do we know – that the soul exists? If it exists, what can we know of its nature? And where does our knowledge of the soul stand in relation to the rest of our knowledge? The scholastic doctrine that there is nothing in the intellect – not even its knowledge of itself – that does not come by way of the senses (*nihil est in intellectu quod non fuerit in sensu*) continued to play an important rôle in seventeenth-century thought, for it was accepted by the latter-day schoolmen, who continued to be a dominant influence in the universities, as well as by some anti-scholastic philosophers, such as Hobbes and Gassendi, although it was rejected by Descartes and many other influential thinkers.

Accordingly, this chapter begins with an account of Saint Thomas Aquinas's views about our knowledge of the soul, for his doctrines provide the theoretical basis for the claim that even our knowledge of the soul must begin with our senses. Descartes's theory of self-knowledge is then traced in some detail, for his doctrine, which departed radically from the Thomistic theory, provided a new framework within which much of the discussion of the topic was carried on during the rest of the century. Next an account is given of the views of several thinkers – Malebranche, the Cambridge Platonists, and Leibniz – who agreed with Descartes that we can know the soul to be an immaterial substance but who differed from him about the precise nature of the soul and the scope of our knowledge of it. The chapter concludes by looking at Spinoza, Hobbes, Gassendi, and Locke – thinkers who disagreed with Descartes about many matters, including our knowledge of the soul, though Descartes's views had considerable influence on Spinoza and Locke and had to be taken into account even by Hobbes and Gassendi, two of Descartes's earliest critics and most resolute foes.

I. THE THOMISTIC THEORY OF
KNOWLEDGE OF THE SOUL

Two of Saint Thomas Aquinas's central doctrines about the soul's knowledge of itself stood in sharp opposition to the theory Descartes was to propound. One was Aquinas's denial that the human intellect can be the *first* object of its own knowledge; the other, his denial that the intellect has direct or intuitive knowledge of its own nature. He proposed the following proof that the intellect cannot be the first object of its knowledge. Like the senses, what the intellect can first know of an object is its actual state, not its mere potentialities. The eye cannot *see* a thing's potential colour, only its actual colour (though once we actually see a thing, we may learn from experience that what is now actually black is potentially red – would be red, say, were it heated). In the same way, what the intellect first knows about a thing is its actual, not its potential, state. Because this is true of its knowledge of *anything,* including itself, the intellect must be in some determinate, actual state before it can discover any truth about itself. But until it begins to know or apprehend something, it is merely a potential understanding (and so is called a 'possible intellect'); it is the acquisition of knowledge that 'reduces the intellect from potency to act'.

How then does the human intellect come to know or apprehend anything? We have, Aquinas held, no innate ideas, so it must be by apprehending something distinct from itself that the intellect's potential for knowledge is first actualised. And since he rejected the Platonic doctrine that the human soul can apprehend some purely intelligible world, Aquinas concluded that human beings (in contrast to pure intellectual substances like the angels) can never pass from potential to actual knowledge until some corporeal object acts on their sense organs.[1] When those organs are stimulated by an object, a sensible image ('phantasm') arises in the mind, and though this phantasm is not in itself intelligible, the mind possesses an active power (the 'agent intellect') that can abstract a universal from a particular sensible image. It is this universal that makes intelligible to us the objects perceived by our senses. The first objects of our knowledge, therefore, are corporeal things that stimulate our sense organs. It is in knowing them that the intellect passes from potency to act; only then can it reflect on *itself* and inquire into its own nature. Hence it is clear, Aquinas concluded, that the human intellect cannot be the first object of its own knowledge.

Further, even once the human intellect is 'in act', it cannot (in this life, at any rate) directly reflect on itself and intuit its own nature. If the soul could intuit itself directly – if it were transparent to itself – there would be no controversy about its nature; what it is would be apparent to all who focused their attention on it, as the truth of a first principle is evident to all who contemplate it. That this is not the case is clear, since some philosophers have believed the soul to be an organ of the body; others have thought it an element, like fire; still others, a harmony among bodily parts, or a number, or something else.[2] Instead of directly beholding itself, according to Aquinas, the intellect can discover both *that* it is and *what* it is only by reflecting on its own cognitive acts. For it *does* have reflexive awareness of those acts, and from that it can inquire what kind of powers it must have in order to perform those acts, and what kind of nature it must have in order to exercise those powers. 'Thus the process by which we know the soul must start from external things from which the intellect draws the intelligible concepts in which it perceives itself; so we must proceed from objects to acts, from acts to powers, from powers to essence.'[3]

Aquinas's account of the cognitive act, whereby the intellect comes to know an object, and from which it may infer its own nature, is complex and its details need not be examined here. What is of central importance is the doctrine that the intellect comes to know the nature of an object by means of a universal that it abstracts from a particular sensible image. Like Aristotle, Aquinas holds that this universal is really the *same* species or form (in Aristotle's sense of *form*) that determines the nature of the object known. The form, that is, that constitutes the nature of the object is united, in a purely intelligible way, to the intellect; thus, in a sense, the intellect *becomes* – albeit in a purely formal or non-material way – the object it comes to know: 'Sense receives the species of all things sensible, and the intellect, of all things intelligible, so that the soul of man is, in a way, all things by sense and intellect.'[4] It is in this formal identity of the intellect and its object (the 'adequation' of the intellect and the thing) that the intellect's knowledge of that object consists. This means that the intellect must have the power of receiving into itself the form, without the matter, of an object. And from this consideration, Aquinas thought, we can infer that the intellect cannot be a material thing, or a composite of form and matter. For when matter receives the form of, say, a stone, it *becomes* stone; were the intellect, therefore, material, in whole or in part, it would itself become stone when, by abstracting the form from the sensible image, it receives in itself the form of a stone. That this does not happen shows the intellect immaterial. From its immateriality, we may in turn infer its immortality. For a thing ceases to be through the separation either of its form from its matter or of its material parts from one another; since the soul is neither material nor a composite of form and matter, it is naturally immortal.[5] Thus, 'from a study of the nature of the species abstracted from sensible things we discover the nature of the soul in which such a species is received, just as matter is known from form'.[6]

It is a mistake, however, according to Aquinas, to conclude that the human soul is a separate spiritual substance, like an angel, that has, independently of the body, a nature complete in itself. Were that the case – were the soul related to the body as a pilot to his ship, as Plato believed – then a human being, having both soul and body, would really be an accidental being, the product of an external and inessential union of two independent beings. In that case it would not be a human being, Socrates, who knows or acts, but a separate spiritual substance that uses Socrates as its instrument. But that is to suppose that the soul is related to the body rather in the way a man is related to his clothes, and experience shows us, Aquinas thinks, that our relation to our body is far more intimate and intrinsic than that: we know, for example, that states of our body play an essential rôle in our having sensations or feeling emotions such as anger or fear.[7] Now if the soul is neither a complete, separate spiritual substance nor a material thing, nor a composite of form and matter, the remaining possibility, Aquinas held, is the Aristotelian doctrine that the soul is the substantial form of a living substance, the body its matter.[8] As the form of a living substance, the soul has many functions – some merely organic, such as those involved in growth and nutrition; others that involve sensory awareness; still others that are purely cognitive, such as the abstraction of universals from particular sensible images. Now it must not be supposed, Aquinas held, that there are in us distinct forms corresponding to each of these functions, as if a vegetative soul, a sensitive soul, and a rational soul were each united to the same body. Were that the case, then three beings, not one, would somehow share the same body, each performing a different function. Instead, one and the same subject grows, is nourished, senses, and reasons.[9] Aquinas concluded that the human soul is one immaterial form that gives life, sentience, and knowledge to a human being.

Thus we see why Aquinas believed that the human soul cannot be the first object of its own knowledge, and why he held that, in this life, we cannot directly inspect our soul to determine its nature but must infer its nature from the kinds of cognitive acts it performs in coming to know an object. Since those acts involve abstracting a universal from a sensible image, Aquinas concluded that the knowledge we have of our own souls is not different in kind from the knowledge we have of other things, and so Aristotle was right to hold that 'the possible intellect understands itself in the same way that it does other things'.[10] Even the soul's knowledge of itself is thus no exception to the principle that there is nothing in the intellect that does not come by way of the senses.[11]

II. DESCARTES

A very different theory of mind, and of our knowledge of it, was proposed by Descartes. As Chapter 23 has shown, Descartes ascribed only cognitive and volitional functions to the mind, for he believed a purely physical and mechanical explanation could be given of the organic, vital, and even sensory functions that were assigned to the soul by the Aristotelians. We have, then, for Descartes, not a life-infusing soul that regulates the growth and vital functions of our body, but a mind whose sole function is to think – whose very essence is *thought*. To discover the existence of such a mind, and to grasp its essence as *res cogitans,* a thinking thing, we need pursue no tortuous path of inference, as the schoolmen supposed. That in us that thinks is, as it were, transparent to itself and so is certain of its own existence, even when it is uncertain about everything else. That we cannot doubt the existence of the mind, as a thinking thing, even if we doubt all else, shows – again contrary to the teaching of the schools – that the mind is the first object of knowledge.

In an early work, the *Regulae ad directionem ingenii* (c. 1628), Descartes specified two mental operations on which our knowledge depends: 'intuition', or our recognition of something as so manifestly true that, as soon as we consider it, we assent to it; and 'deduction', or our power to move along a chain of inferences, perceiving by intuition that each link follows necessarily from the one before, whereby we pass from truths evident in themselves to others that are not self-evident but are necessary consequences of ones that are. In that work he gave, as examples of intuition, my knowledge that I think and that I exist (Rule 3). In his mature works he spoke usually not of what we 'intuit' but of what we can clearly and distinctly perceive, but he continued to hold that our mind is something whose existence is so manifest to us – is so clearly and distinctly perceived by us – that we cannot doubt it.[12] For even if a powerful demon uses all his craft to deceive me, I cannot doubt that I am now having certain thoughts – doubting, imagining, sensing, remembering (or at least *seeming* to sense and remember) something. And it is evident I cannot doubt, imagine, sense, remember (or even seem to sense or remember) unless I am a thinking (i.e., a conscious) being, for all these are but ways ('modes') of thinking. Thus I know intuitively that I think. But clearly I cannot think unless I am. Even the most powerful deceiver can deceive me only if I exist. Thus, 'this proposition, *I am, I exist,* is necessarily true whenever it is put forward by me or conceived in my mind.'[13] Descartes did not here say that it is a necessary truth that he exists; he supposed his existence contingent – he might not have been. But since it is impossible for him to think unless he exists, it *is* a necessary truth that he exists at any time he thinks 'I am' (or, indeed, anything at all). Thus, though he might be deceived about the existence of *other* contingent things (including his own body), he cannot be mistaken about the existence of what in him thinks, that is, his mind; the mind is, therefore, the first object of our knowledge and *Cogito ergo sum* the first truth we can be certain of.[14]

Some critics objected that the *Cogito* cannot be the first truth we can know with certainty, for it is really an enthymeme, and so its conclusion ('I am') cannot be known unless we first know the implicit major premise ('Whatever thinks, is'). But Descartes replied that one who recognises the truth of the *Cogito* 'does not deduce existence from thought by means of a syllogism, but recognizes it as something self-evident by a simple intuition of the mind'.[15] We do not, he said, *first* discover general truths, *then* recognise their particular instances. Instead, in seeing something necessary in a particular case, we come to recognise some general truth – for example, we *first* recognise the whole to be equal to the sum of its parts by seeing its necessity in a particular case and thereby grasp the necessity of the general principle. So, too, it is only because I see that *I* cannot think unless *I* am, that I recognise the general truth that *whatever* thinks, exists.[16] To this, Gassendi objected that *thinking* is not the only activity from which I can conclude that I am; for there can be *no* activity without an agent, so 'I walk, therefore I am' is as evidently true as 'I think, therefore I am.'[17] But, replied Descartes, I may be *mistaken* that I am now walking (for I may be dreaming), but I cannot be mistaken that I am now thinking. More generally, from no activity that depends on the body can I be sure I exist, for a powerful demon might make me think I had a body even if I were a disembodied spirit; but even a powerful deceiver cannot make me *think* I am thinking – unless I *am* thinking. Only from thinking, then, can I be sure that I am – that is, that my mind (what thinks in me) exists.[18]

Others objected that the *Cogito* cannot be the first thing we know, for we cannot even understand *Cogito ergo sum* unless we already know what *thought* and *existence* are. Descartes granted this; indeed, so indispensable are concepts like knowledge, certainty, truth, existence, and thought to all our thinking, he said, that if we lacked them we could neither acquire them from experience or by dint of investigation nor derive them from more primitive concepts. These fundamental concepts must, therefore, be innate – not in the sense that we reflect on them before anything else, but because they are implicitly involved in, and presupposed by, all our thinking; the schoolmen therefore erred in believing that there is nothing in the mind that does not come from the senses.[19] But although we must possess these concepts in order to think at all, the first thing whose *existence* can be known with certainty is the mind itself.[20] In that sense, the mind is the first object of our knowledge.

But what is this mind or thinking thing? Gassendi told Descartes that he had, at most, shown *that* the mind exists, not *what* it is. Descartes replied that we could not know *that* a thing existed if we were wholly in the dark about *what* it is.[21] Coming to know the most fundamental truths – those underlying all others – never involves, Descartes believed, acquiring an idea where formerly we had none; rather, it is to pass from perceiving something in a confused way to perceiving it clearly and distinctly (rather as Plato took learning to be the awakening of the mind to a truth it already possesses but has not hitherto recognised). In this way, included in our first intuition *that* we are, is some perception of *what* we are, though careful reflection is needed if we are to perceive our nature clearly and distinctly. Descartes therefore asked himself, what precisely is this thing – the 'I' – of whose existence I am certain? This, he thought, is, in effect, to ask what it is that I find inseparable from myself. What is it that I cannot conceive that I, who am sure that I am, can exist without? It is not my body or any of its states, for I can conceive myself to think, and so to be, even if I have no body but am only deceived by a powerful demon into believing I have one. By contrast, I cannot separate *thinking* or consciousness from the thing I am sure exists, for it is the fact that I think that assures me that I am. Nor need I conceive any other thing in order to conceive myself to be – only that I think. Thus what is inseparable from the *I* that I am certain exists is thought itself.

The nature of the *I* or mind, then, is *thought:* the mind is a thing that thinks. Might this thinking thing be corporeal? In Meditatio II, where he gave his proof that the mind exists and is a thinking thing, Descartes declined to answer this question, for he did not yet know what bodies are or whether they exist.[22] He returned to it in Meditatio VI, where he argued that, as we clearly recognise thought to be the only thing inseparable from our mind, we can form a clear and distinct idea of our mind quite independently of forming any idea of that extended thing that is our body. Now God surely has the power to bring about, if He chooses to, any state of affairs we can clearly and distinctly conceive. Hence, since I can clearly recognise that my mind will exist, so long as I continue to think, whether I have a body or not, it must be in God's power to cause my mind to exist without my body, or, for that matter, my body without my mind. But if it is possible for two things to exist without each other, they must be distinct from each other. So mind and body are distinct things.[23]

This argument provoked stormy protests. Leibniz said he was 'amazed that so able a man could have based so much on so flimsy a sophism'. All Descartes has shown is that he can doubt that his body exists, though he is certain his mind exists, which he could do even if the mind were corporeal, so long as he were ignorant of that fact.[24] Arnauld nicely illustrated the objection: someone ignorant of the Pythagorean theorem might be certain a given triangle is right-angled but be in doubt about whether the square on its hypotenuse is equal to the squares on its other sides; but he would be mistaken if he concluded from this that *therefore* it must not belong to the nature of a right-angled triangle for the square on its hypotenuse to equal the squares on its other two sides.[25] The analogy, Descartes replied, is flawed. For he had argued that if we can form a clear and distinct idea of A, without conceiving of B, *and* a clear and distinct idea of B, without conceiving of A, then A and B are distinct. One might have, as in Arnauld's example, a clear idea of what a right-angled triangle is, yet not know the Pythagorean theorem; but one could not clearly and distinctly conceive a triangle of which it was true that the square on its hypotenuse is equal to the squares on its other sides without conceiving it to be right-angled. But, he held, we *can* form a clear and distinct idea of a thinking thing without conceiving it to be extended, *and* of an extended thing without conceiving it to be thinking, and so a thinking thing must be unextended.[26]

The bone of contention here was Descartes's confidence that we can *clearly and distinctly* conceive a thinking thing without conceiving anything else. Underpinning this confidence was his theory of substance. Properties can exist, he held, only if there is something they are the properties of – for example, *sphericity* cannot exist, only things that are spherical.[27] If we consider whatever we can predicate of some particular thing, we always find that there is one predicate (the 'principal attribute') of which *all* the others (the 'modes') are but particular determinations. Now there is an asymmetrical relation between the principal attribute and any particular mode: the former can exist without the latter, but the latter cannot exist without the former. For example, if we consider what can be predicated of a body, we see it can have a certain size, shape, motion, location, and so forth only if it is extended – for these are but particular determinations of extension; but it can be extended without having the particular size, shape, motion, location, and so forth that it now has. Extension is thus the principal attribute of one kind of substance, namely, body.[28] Now the distinction between a substance and its principal attribute is only a conceptual, not a real, distinction. If, for example, being extended in three dimensions is the principal attribute of a body, then there is no real distinction between a body and its extension, for were the body to cease to be extended, it would cease to be, *simpliciter.* Hence, in clearly conceiving the principal attribute of a thing, we are really conceiving the thing – the substance – itself.[29]

Now whatever we can predicate of a mind (sensing, imagining, doubting, desiring, etc.) is always some particular determination of thought or consciousness. Hence, none of these states can exist unless the thing that has them is thinking or conscious; but a thing can be thinking without being in any one of these particular states. Further, as long as the mind thinks, it exists; but if it ceases to think, it ceases to be. *Thought,* then, is the principal attribute of the mind. Since a thing and its principal attribute are the same, thought or consciousness is a thing or substance. Not, to be sure, that it exists as an impersonal or abstract *cogitatur* – 'it thinks' or 'thought occurs'. For I am always aware that it is *I*, the conscious subject, who think. Even a madman who thinks he is Caesar cannot be mistaken that he is now the subject of certain thoughts, however delusional they may be. The mind, concluded Descartes, is a thinking thing and nothing more.[30]

Thus, rejecting the scholastic doctrines that all knowledge depends on the senses, and that the human mind can have no direct intuition of itself, Descartes concluded the mind knows *that* it is immediately and without inference, and that implicit in this intuition of the mind's existence is the idea of its nature as a *res cogitans,* though only by reflecting on our knowledge *that* we are do we bring to perfect clarity our knowledge of *what* we are. Further, Descartes held that the *Cogito* expresses a primary truth, not just because we can be certain of it before anything else, but because enfolded, as it were, in it are the other fundamental truths of metaphysics: for in his awareness of himself, as a thing that doubts, Descartes realised that he is a finite being, something he could recognise, he held, only if something had already produced in him the idea of an *infinite* being; from that, in turn, he deduced God's existence and perfection; and from that, that God would not deceive him about the existence of bodies or any other thing he clearly and distinctly perceived; this gave a foundation to natural science, by proving that there *is* a natural world and by disclosing the criterion by which something can be recognised as true, namely, that we perceive it clearly and distinctly to be the case. Thus the *Cogito* contained, Descartes thought, the germ of his whole philosophy.[31] It was a philosophy that provoked attack from many quarters – from latter-day schoolmen such as Bourdin, sceptics such as Huet, materialists such as Hobbes, and many others. But it also had many admirers, and defences of Descartes's theory of our knowledge of the mind can be found in the works of many philosophers who, though now largely forgotten, were well known in the seventeenth century, among them Johannes Clauberg, Louis de La Forge, Gérauld de Cordemoy, Pierre-Sylvain Régis, and François Lamy.[32]

III. MALEBRANCHE

One of the thinkers most deeply influenced by Descartes was Malebranche, and yet Malebranche's philosophy was in many ways un-Cartesian and in some ways anti-Cartesian. His account of our knowledge of the soul shows both his debt to Descartes and his independence of him. Descartes held that what we can most clearly and distinctly conceive are ideas that are innate to our minds. But Malebranche rejected this doctrine. For, he argued, we can in principle form clear and distinct ideas of, for example, infinitely many different figures, or even infinitely many different triangles; yet our minds, being finite, cannot *contain* infinitely many ideas, so cannot have been *created* with an infinite fund of such ideas. On the other hand, the schoolmen's belief that all the ideas present to the intellect come to it from the senses must also be wrong, for we cannot suppose that sense-experience could endow the mind with an infinite collection of ideas, even if the mind could contain such a collection. The most plausible explanation, he held, of our ability to think of infinitely many things is that our minds are immediately united to God, who contains within Himself infinitely many ideas, and that God discloses to us any of His ideas that He chooses to.[33]

But if Malebranche disagreed with both the Cartesians and the schoolmen about the source of our ideas, he sided with Descartes, against the schoolmen, in holding that the first thing we can know with certainty is that our minds exist; and he further agreed with Descartes that the mind is not the life-infusing soul of the schoolmen, but rather a thing that thinks. He denied, however, that we have any clear idea of what *thought* is and so denied that we can have any clear idea of the mind's nature. He wrote, in *Recherche de la vérité* (1674–5):

Of all our knowledge, the first is of the existence of our soul; all our thoughts are incontestable demonstrations of this, since there is nothing more obvious than that what actually thinks, is actually something. But if it is easy to know the existence of our soul, it is not so easy to know its essence and nature.[34]

To speak strictly, we have no *idea* of the soul, according to Malebranche. By an 'idea', Malebranche meant what represents something in a clear and distinct way to the mind. The only ideas we clearly and distinctly perceive are such of God's archetypal ideas of things as God has chosen to disclose to our minds. We know, for instance, in a clear and distinct way what *extension* is because we actually perceive 'intelligible extension', that is, God's idea of extended things.[35] But while God discloses to us infinitely many ideas, He has not chosen to disclose to us *all* His archetypal ideas, and, in particular, He has not revealed to us His idea of the human mind itself (though He must, of course, have such an idea – for He is the mind's creator and must have an idea of whatever He creates). Perhaps, conjectured Malebranche, if God had made known to us the nature of mind with the same clarity with which He makes known the nature of body, the union of our mind and body would be weakened, for we would perceive clearly what radically different things they are.

Because we lack an idea of the mind, all we can know about our nature is what we experience of ourselves through our self-awareness or inner feeling (*conscience ou sentiment intérieur*). This suffices to make known to us

> that our soul is something of importance. But what we know of it might be almost nothing compared to what it is in itself. . . . To know the soul perfectly, then, it is not enough to know only what we know through inner sensation – since the consciousness we have of ourselves perhaps shows us only the least part of our being.[36]

He found evidence for the claim that we have no idea of the mind in the chasm separating the kind of knowledge we have of extension from that we have of thought. We need but consider our *a priori* idea of what extension is to see that circles, squares, triangles, and the like are among its possible modes. But we have no comparable idea of what thought is from which to deduce that a sensation of warmth, an emotion of hatred, a feeling of pain are among *its* possible modes. Once we *feel* or *sense* these things within us, we recognise them to be modes of thought, for we see that we could not feel or sense them unless we were conscious. But 'we have no clear idea of thought as we do of extension, for thought is known only through inner sensation or consciousness.'[37] Had we a clear idea of what thought is, we could discover from it, by *a priori* reasoning, the properties of sensations, emotions, imaginings, and so forth, just as a geometer, from a clear idea of extension, can discover *a priori* the properties of plane and solid figures. That we cannot do this shows how limited our knowledge of the mind is.

The noted Cartesian, Pierre-Sylvain Régis, responded that we can no more deduce, from our idea of extension, that a human body will have a liver or a kidney than we can deduce, from our idea of thought, that a human mind will feel a sensation of warmth or an emotion of fear. Yet Malebranche does not count the former as evidence that we lack a clear idea of body; so he should not take the latter for evidence that we lack a clear idea of mind.[38] Malebranche replied that the Cartesians themselves believed that we have, in geometry and mechanics, *a priori* sciences of body *because* we have a clear idea of extension, and yet they were unable to produce any comparable 'geometry of the mind', though they claimed that we have an equally clear idea of thought.

Malebranche found further evidence of the obscurity of our understanding of the mind in the way the Cartesians themselves defended the doctrine that 'sensible qualities' (colour, sound, smell, taste, warmth, etc.) are sensations in the mind, not properties of bodies. They defend it, he said, by trying to *exclude* these qualities from our idea of body (by arguing that the modes of body are all just so many determinations of size, shape, or motion, and then trying to show that sensible qualities are none of these, so cannot be in the body). Had we as clear an idea of the mind's nature as we have of the body's, we could prove *directly* from our idea of *thought itself* that sensible qualities are among its modes and would not have to resort to an indirect proof. Furthermore, the mind, according to Descartes, differs more from the body than does, say, a square from a circle (for these latter, though different, are both extended). Why, then, is it that everybody easily recognises that a square and a circle are different things, while many people, including some profound philosophers, fail to recognise that the mind and body are different things? This can only be, he held, because we have no clear idea (strictly, no idea at all) of the mind's nature.[39]

But though we lack clear knowledge of what the mind *is,* we can determine, he held, by an indirect proof, that it is *not* corporeal. The body's modes can be reduced to figures and motions, both of which are directly measurable, which is why the physical world can be represented mathematically. But, he argued, we can form no mathematically exact idea of things like sensations, emotions, or desires. Consider, he said, the difference in how the physicist deals with a thing's *size* and its *sound* (when by 'sound' we mean a sensible or phenomenal quality). Its size can be measured directly; but its sound is measurable only because we associate it with something to which a mathematical value can be directly assigned – for example, the length of the string that, when plucked, produces the sound. If I can make an exact comparison between two sounds produced by a plucking of strings, it is because I can compare the physical properties of the strings – 'because I know that there are twice as many vibrations in an equal amount of time, or something like this. It is because the disturbances in the air, the vibrations of the string, and the string itself are things that can be compared through clear ideas, and because we know distinctly the relations that can obtain between the string and its parts as well as between the rates of different vibrations. But the sounds cannot be compared in themselves, in so far as they are sensible qualities and modifications of the soul.'[40]

So, too, he held, sensations of colour, warmth, taste, smell, pleasure, pain, and so forth cannot be measured directly but, if at all, only because we identify them with the measurable figures or motions of the bodies that cause or occasion them.

Were the mind corporeal, such mental modes as sensations, emotions, desires would be directly measurable, like any of the modes of body. Since they are not, we have indirect proof that the thing of which these are modes is not an extended substance; and yet they must be modes of *some* substance, and so – whatever the mind is – it is some kind of unextended substance. Thus for Malebranche our knowledge of the mind is far more limited than Descartes took it to be, for although Descartes was right to hold that the existence of the mind is a first truth, and that we can prove the mind to be an unextended thing, he erred in believing us to have a clear positive idea of its nature.[41]

IV. THE CAMBRIDGE PLATONISTS

Like the Cartesians, the Cambridge Platonists rejected the view that all our ideas come to us from an external source. The human soul, said Ralph Cudworth, has 'an Innate Cognoscitive power . . . of Raising Intelligible Ideas and Conceptions of Things from within it self'. He concluded:

Knowledge is not a Passion from any thing without the Mind, but an Active Exertion of the Inward Strength, Vigour and Power of the Mind; . . . and the Intelligible Forms by which Things are Understood or Known are not Stamps or Impressions passively printed upon the Soul from without, but Ideas vitally protended or actively exerted from within it self.[42]

The belief that all our ideas come from the senses makes inexplicable the knowledge we have of our own souls. For our senses cannot actually *perceive* cognitive power (nor, indeed, *any* active power), so it cannot be from sense that we get ideas of cognitive power or other active powers. Rather, such ideas are innate and are disclosed to us by our self-awareness:

Were Existence to be allowed to nothing, that doth not fall under Corporeal Sense, then must we deny the Existence of Soul and Mind, in ourselves and others, because we can neither Feel nor See any such thing. Whereas we are certain of the Existence of our own Souls, partly from an inward Consciousness of our own Cogitations, and partly from the Principle of Reason, that Nothing cannot Act.[43]

But if the Platonists at Cambridge agreed with the Cartesians that knowledge of the mind comes from the mind's inward awareness of its thoughts, they rejected the Cartesian doctrine that the *essence* of the mind is thought; rather, *activity* is the essential property of spirit. Matter, they said, is an inert, dead, inactive thing; spirit is what acts. Many others in the seventeenth century agreed that matter is inert, spirit active. Malebranche, for example, invoked this doctrine to defend occasionalism (the theory that there are no secondary causes), arguing that, because bodies are inert, no body can initiate or continue motion in itself, or transmit it to another body, from which he concluded that a spiritual substance (God) must be the true cause of all motion in the world.[44] Although Malebranche held that the only active being is spirit, he did not take activity to be the *essence* of spirit, in part because he held that finite spirits are sometimes passive, in part because he supposed that a being can act only because it has a will, and it can have a will only if it is a thing that thinks.[45] So, though he denied that we have a clear idea of the mind's essence, Malebranche, like the Cartesians, took *thought* to be a more fundamental characteristic of spirit than is *action*.

The Cambridge Platonists, by contrast, held that activity is the essential property of spirit; they held, in fact, that some spirits neither *think* nor *will,* but all spirits *act.* Cudworth therefore rejected 'the Narrow Principles of some late Philosophers' – namely, the Cartesians – who make 'the first General Heads of all Entity to be *Extension* and *Cogitation,* or Extended Being and Cogitative [Being]'. Instead, Cudworth proposed that the chief division of being is into 'Resisting or Antitypous Extension' and 'Internal Energy and Self-activity', the former being matter, the latter spirit; and that spirit in turn 'be subdivided into such as either acts with express Consciousness and Synaesthesis, or such as is without it'.[46] Henry More, too, rejected Descartes's division of beings into the thinking and the extended, agreeing with Cudworth that, while all spirits act, they do not all think, and holding, further, that *both* bodies *and* spirits are extended. Bodies, More said, are divisible and impenetrable extended things, devoid of motion, life, and perception; spirits are indivisible and penetrable extended things, endowed with motion and life.[47] On More's view, two bodies cannot occupy the same place, since bodies are impenetrable; but the human soul, though extended, is *penetrable* and so can occupy the same place as the human body: if it could not, the soul could not act on the body. Hence it is no puzzle that corporeal and incorporeal substances can be 'united', for they can occupy the same space at the same time.[48]

Against Hobbes's claim that the very expression 'incorporeal substance' is contradictory, More declared that the concepts of body (corporeal substance) and spirit (incorporeal substance) are *equally intelligible,* for the inseparable properties of spirits (penetrability, indivisibility, and activity) and of bodies (impenetrability, divisibility, and passivity) are correlative, and our understanding of each involves our understanding of the other.[49] More and Cudworth were, thus, dualists, like Descartes, but theirs was a dualism of active and passive substances, rather than of thinking and extended substances. Anne Conway, More's 'heroine pupil', espoused a kabbalistic Platonism that rejected dualism – 'the grand Cartesian Errour' of supposing 'Body and Spirit to be contrary Things, and inconvertible one into another' – but she, too, distinguished spirit and body as active and passive:

In every visible Creature there is a Body and a Spirit, or *Principium magis Activum, et magis Passivum,* or, *more Active and more Passive Principle,* which may fitly be termed Male and Female, by reason of that Analogy a Husband hath with his Wife. For . . . all Generations and Productions whatsoever they be, require an Union, and conformable Operation of those Two Principles, to wit, Spirit and Body.[50]

Since all activity is the work of spirit, the Cambridge thinkers agreed with the Aristotelians that it is the soul that gives life and self-motion to organisms. Accordingly, they rejected the Cartesian belief that natural phenomena can be given a wholly mechanical explanation, and concluded that where there is activity in nature, there spirits are at work, though many spirits work 'easily, cleverly, and silently', with no awareness of themselves or the ends they pursue – as when plants send forth shoots, fish return to the place of their spawning, embryos take form in the womb. They thus filled the universe with spirits, some capable of sensing, some of thinking, some of both, some of neither; included among them are the 'seminal forms' of plants, the sensitive souls of animals, the rational souls of men, the 'aerial and aethereal spirits' of angels.[51] And below them all is a universal but unconscious 'Plastick Nature' (Cudworth) or 'Spirit of Nature' (More), a universal spirit that, while devoid of sense or consciousness ('animadversion'), is the cause of all that activity in inanimate nature that cannot be explained mechanically.[52] And ruling over the whole universe of spirits and bodies is the infinite and eternal spirit who created and knows all things. The world of spirits thus forms, for Cudworth and More, an immense chain, reaching up from the wholly unconscious spirit of nature to the all-knowing spirit of God.

Once we are clear about *what* spirit is, we find abundant evidence that spirits exist. Each of us human beings has an immediate inner awareness, not derived from our senses, of ourselves as active beings who perceive, imagine, remember, judge, and will (even sensation, said Cudworth, involves activity – were it just a passive reception of corporeal images, mirrors would be sentient).[53] So by 'animadversion' or self-reflection we each know ourselves to have souls. And we can infer, from our observation of other human bodies, that they are animated by *rational souls* – that they have souls is clear from their spontaneous movement, and that their souls are rational is clear from their intelligent discourse: 'The Existence of other Individual Souls is manifest to us, from their Effects upon their Respective Bodies, their Motions, Actions, and Discourse.'[54] Further, we can infer the existence of non-human spirits from what we observe in nature – from the growth of plants, from the spontaneous movement and instinctual behaviour of animals, even from the attractive power of the lodestone.[55] To this, More added that reports of preternatural phenomena, witchcraft, and ghostly apparitions give further evidence that spirits exist.[56]

Thus the Platonists at Cambridge, like the Cartesians, taught dualism of body and spirit, and held that our knowledge of spirit cannot be traced back merely to what we learn or infer from our sense experience but involves an immediate awareness of our own minds. But theirs was a dualism that denied that thought is essential to spirits or (in More's case at least) that extension is unique to bodies; and so their account of our knowledge of spirits relied not just on our narrow reflection on ourselves as thinking beings, as did Descartes's, but on our observation of all the living, active beings in nature. The influence of this insistence that activity is essential to spirit can later be discerned both in Locke's speculation that 'Pure Spirit, viz. God, is only active; pure matter is only passive; those beings that are both active and passive, we may judge to partake of both', and in Berkeley's ontological dualism of passive ideas and active spirits.[57]

V. LEIBNIZ

Leibniz agreed with the Cartesians and the Platonists that the mind has within itself a source of knowledge that is independent of what it learns from experience. Always conciliatory towards those he opposed, he liked to urge that the schoolmen's maxim merely needed 'modification' to 'there is nothing in the intellect that does not come from the senses *except the intellect itself.*'[58] But this was not a *minor* modification, for Leibniz held that our most fundamental metaphysical concepts come from the mind's self-awareness. He agreed with Descartes that the mind can have immediate knowledge of its own existence, though he denied that it is the only thing of whose existence we have immediate knowledge. 'First truths' – things known immediately, without inference – are, said Leibniz, of two kinds: (1) those we know because 'nothing comes between the subject and the predicate' (in contrast to a truth deduced syllogistically, where a middle term must connect subject and predicate), and (2) those we know because 'nothing comes between the understanding and its object' (in contrast to things known by means of a representative idea). The first kind are those truths of reason (propositions true of all possible worlds) that are instances of the law of identity; the second, those truths of fact (propositions true of the actual world) that are known because an object is directly present to the mind.[59] First truths *of fact* 'can conveniently be reduced to these two: "I think" and "Various things are thought by me." Whence it follows not only that I am, but that I am affected in various ways.'[60] From one of the first truths of fact ('I think'), I know immediately that I am, for *I am* (*je suis*) is contained in *I am thinking* (*je suis pensant*).[61] From the other ('Various things are thought by me'), I know that something other than me exists, for it is evident, Leibniz thought, that a thing will continue in the state it is in unless it is acted on by something else, and so changes in my thoughts disclose something (other than me) that causes them. Hence Descartes was right to insist, against the schoolmen, that 'I exist' is a first truth, but he failed to see that 'Something exists in addition to me' is a first truth, too.[62] To this Leibniz added that, although *God's* knowledge that I exist is *a priori* (for He knows He has decreed that the best possible world exists, and from His mere concept of that world He knows every individual it contains), *my* knowledge that I exist is *a posteriori,* for it comes from 'immediate experience'.[63] Thus 'I am' is, for me, a first *a posteriori* truth of fact.

When it comes to our knowledge of our mind's *nature,* Leibniz thought we must avoid two extremes. One is Descartes's conviction that we can have a perception of the mind's nature that is both clear *and* distinct; the other is Locke's doctrine that its nature is completely hidden from us. This second doctrine is the farther from the truth, and so the more dangerous error; and in opposition to it, Leibniz urged that self-reflection ('apperception') does give us a clear, though not a distinct, idea of what mind is. By self-reflection I am made aware of my identity through change. If *I* did not endure through the succession of my thoughts, I could not, from the fact that *I think,* conclude that *I am,* for 'I' would not refer to the same subject in these successive judgements. The reply to the sceptic who doubts that we *are* the same through successive thoughts is that he can understand his own *doubt* only because *he* remains the same thinker through the interval it takes him to think it.[64] By reflection we experience not just the mind's identity through time, but also its unity at any given time, for we can perceive several things in the same moment only because they are held together in one unitary consciousness – a unity, Leibniz believed, too fundamental to be itself the product of a union of parts. Now what is identical through change and has a simple, non-composite unity is a substance (monad), and so through self-reflection the mind experiences itself as a substance.

It is, in fact, from self-reflection, Leibniz thought, that we *get* the concepts of substance and property, identity and difference, unity and plurality, action and passion, cause and effect – indeed *all* the categories of metaphysics. They cannot be gotten from the senses, which reveal only a kaleidoscopic succession of quali-ties. The mind may, in a sense, be said to 'discover' these categories by its reflection on itself, but it could not discover them in itself if it did not already contain them innately; reflection really only focuses our attention on ideas that we have used all along in our thinking without being aware of doing so.[65] Those, therefore, who suppose the mind to be a *tabula rasa* until the senses act on it are wrong, and Descartes was right in believing that our knowledge of the mind is, in a sense, the foundation of all the rest of our knowledge; for without these fundamental categories, we would have no knowledge, and we get these categories from reflection on our own mind.

From what self-reflection has disclosed to us we can infer the mind's incorporeality. For what is corporeal is extended, and what is extended cannot be a simple, unitary thing, since every part of extension, however minute, contains a repetition of parts. Descartes was thus also right that the mind is an unextended substance (though he erred in supposing that there are also *extended substances,* for no extended thing has the simple unity that substances have). And he was right in holding that the soul must always think or perceive, for nothing is ever perfectly inactive (no body, for example, is ever at absolute rest), and the mind's activity ('appetition') consists in passing from one perception to another; so the mind can never be without some perception. But as some motions in bodies are too small for us to be aware of them, so some perceptions (e.g., those we have in sleep) are too minute to be noticed by us.[66]

Thus from self-reflection, and what we can infer from it, we get a *clear idea* of what the mind is: a simple, unitary, unextended substance that always thinks or perceives and is always actively in movement from one perception to another. So Locke erred profoundly in believing the mind a 'something I know not what'. But Descartes went too far when he claimed that we have not only a clear but also a *distinct* idea of the mind's nature. We perceive a thing clearly when we can distinguish it from other things, but we perceive it distinctly only when we know all those characteristics that make it what it is. A prospector has a *clear* idea of what gold is if he can distinguish it from what is not gold, but he may lack distinct ideas of the elements gold is composed of. So it is with our perception of thought: we can distinguish it from other things, but we are ignorant of all those minute perceptions that make it what it is.[67] For a mind does not contain, as the Cartesians seem to suppose, just one thought, but a great succession of thoughts:

I do not at all approve of the doctrine of attributes which people are formulating today; as if one simple absolute predicate, which they call an attribute, constituted a substance. . . . Certainly thought and extension, which are commonly proposed as examples, are far from being such attributes. . . . The mind coincides with the thinker indeed (though not formally) but not with the thinking. For it is a property of the subject to involve future and past thoughts in addition to present ones.[68]

To speak strictly, thought is not the *essence* or principal attribute of the mind, but rather an essential *activity* of the mind, with one thought arising as another passes away. A thing's *essence,* by contrast, is something that persists through all the changes in its states.

Thought is not the essence of the soul, for a thought is an act, and since one thought succeeds another, that which remains during this change must necessarily be the essence of the soul, since it remains always the same. The essence of substances consists in the primitive force of action, or in the law of the sequence of changes, as the nature of the series consists in the [law that orders the] numbers.[69]

The mind's essence – that which endures through its changing thoughts and perceptions – is a *law* or *force* that determines the order in which thoughts and perceptions arise in the mind (Leibniz used 'law' or 'force' interchangeably, much as people speak of gravity as a 'law' or 'force'): 'All individual things are successions or are subject to succession. . . . For me nothing is permanent in things except the law itself which involves a continuous succession and which corresponds, in individual things, to that law which determines the whole world.'[70] Contrary to appearances, our perceptions are not really caused by – though they are correlated with – external objects; rather, God creates a mind with all its perceptions already contained in it in a virtual way – rather as a statue is 'already contained' in the veins of a block of marble – and God endows the mind with a law or force that determines the order in which those perceptions will rise from the soul's hidden depths into its express consciousness.[71]

It is this *law* that *persists* through changes in our consciousness, so *it* really constitutes our nature. Now in no two minds is that law the same – if it were, those minds' perceptions would be identical, which Leibniz denies can be the case ('the Identity of Indiscernibles'). For this reason, we may say of *all* minds (indeed of all substances) what Aquinas said of the angels: each one is a species unto itself, each possessing an *individual* nature.[72] If we could know the 'law' that orders our perceptions, then from any one of our perceptions we could deduce all those that will follow after it, just as a mathematician who knows the principle that orders a series of numbers can deduce, from any given number, what its successors will be.[73] But the discovery of such a thing in the case of our minds altogether exceeds our powers. Only God, who established the law that determines the order of succession in my perceptions, has an idea of my individual nature that is *both* clear *and* distinct;[74] I can have a *clear* idea of my mind's nature as an unextended, perceiving substance, but, ignorant of the law that determines the order in which my perceptions occur, I cannot have a *distinct* idea of my mind's individual nature, for it is constituted by that ordering law.[75]

Malebranche, the Cambridge Platonists, and Leibniz thus agreed with Descartes that the mind is an incorporeal substance and, like him, believed the mind to have some direct access to itself, so rejected the scholastic doctrine that all knowledge – including knowledge of the mind – depends on the senses, though they also rejected important features of the Cartesian account of our knowledge of mind. The thinkers examined in the rest of this chapter, however, held far more un-Cartesian or anti-Cartesian views about our knowledge of the mind.

VI. SPINOZA

Spinoza distinguished three kinds of knowledge. The first depends on our memory or imagination, or what we learn from the testimony of others; the second depends on reasoning from an effect to its cause or from premises to a conclusion. The body and its sense organs are involved in gaining these kinds of knowledge. But the third kind of knowledge, 'intuitive science' (*scientia intuitiva*), does not depend on the senses but on the mind's power to find in itself an adequate idea of God's nature.[76] 'The human mind', said Spinoza, 'is a part of the infinite intellect of God.'[77] Because of this, 'it is as necessary that the mind's clear and distinct ideas are true as that God's ideas are.'[78] In particular, because it is a part of God's mind, our mind contains within itself an 'adequate idea' – an idea that bears in itself the mark of its truth – of certain of God's attributes. This adequate idea is the basis of the most perfect knowledge we can attain.[79] Spinoza thus agreed with Descartes that what we know most clearly and distinctly comes not from the senses but from the mind itself, but where Descartes took our knowledge of our own mind, as a thinking thing, to be the starting point of all inquiry, Spinoza held that God's nature is first, not just in the order of being, but also in the order of knowing and so is the foundation of what we can most clearly know to be the case.[80] It is not surprising, therefore, that where Descartes's *Meditationes* began with the human mind (Meditatio II) and moved to God (Meditatio III), Spinoza's *Ethica* begins with God (*Ethica* I) and moves to the human mind (*Ethica* II), for the surest knowledge 'advances from an adequate idea of the formal essence of certain attributes of God to the adequate knowledge of the essence of things'.[81]

Note that it is the *essence* of things, including the human mind, that Spinoza here said we could come to know adequately from a consideration of God's attributes, for he did not undertake to deduce the *existence* of the human mind, or indeed of *any* specific finite thing, from God's nature alone. He held, to be sure, that every finite thing is a *necessary consequence* of God's nature (in opposition to those who think God free to create finite beings or not, as He chooses), but he did not think any finite thing an *immediate consequence* of God's nature.[82] Instead, each finite thing depends on earlier members of an infinite series of causes and effects and, though the whole infinite series is an immediate consequence of God's nature, no finite member of it is (since it is an *infinite* series, it has no first member, so no paradox arises from holding that the whole series depends immediately on God although no member of it does).[83] Now were it possible for us to know all the members of this infinite causal chain, seeing clearly how they come necessarily from God and how one finite thing gives rise to another, we could deduce the existence of specific finite things from God's nature. But such knowledge exceeds the reach of finite minds.[84] It is not surprising, therefore, that in the *Ethica* no attempt is made to deduce the existence of the *human* mind from the divine nature, though Spinoza did think he could prove, in a general way and without determining their specific nature, that *finite* minds or souls exist (and, indeed, that there are infinitely many of them). The existence of the *human* mind, however, is assumed, in the *Ethica,* by the axioms of Part Two. (In the 'Prolegomena' to his first published work, *Renati Des Cartes principiorum philosophiae pars I & II* [1663], Spinoza seemed to endorse Descartes's view that we cannot doubt that we exist, for 'from the very possibility that we are deceived, we can at once infer, with certainty, our own existence.')[85]

It was the nature, not the existence, of the human mind that Spinoza sought to discover from a consideration of God's nature, and even here he does not seem to have supposed that our mind's nature can be fully determined by *a priori* deductions from God's nature; instead, both *a priori* and *a posteriori* elements play a rôle in his inquiry into the nature of the human mind. But we can begin that inquiry only by discovering *a priori* some of the consequences of God's nature. God is a substance consisting of infinitely many attributes, and each of these attributes comprises infinitely many modes.[86] One of these attributes is thought; and, like the other divine attributes, thought contains infinitely many finite modes.[87] These modes are, in fact, the ideas or knowledge God has of all the infinitely many modes that belong to each of His infinitely many attributes. Taken collectively, these ideas comprise one infinite idea (one infinite mode) in God, by which God knows, eternally and perfectly, all things. But when these ideas are considered individually, as finite modes of thought, Spinoza takes them to be finite souls or minds: 'Each thing is expressed in infinitely many modes in the infinite intellect of God, yet the infinitely many ideas by which it is expressed cannot constitute

one single mind of an individual [finite] thing, but an infinity of minds.'[88] Thus
understood, every finite mind is actually an *idea,* for corresponding to every finite
mode of each of God's attributes there will be a finite mind or soul that constitutes
the *idea* – that is, the knowledge God has – of that mode. In this way, Spinoza
took himself to be able to prove *a priori* the existence of *finite* souls, even if he did
not give an *a priori* proof of the existence of specifically human souls. Further, he
believed he had thereby determined *a priori* what, in general, a soul – *any* soul,
not just the human soul – is:

> The essence of the soul consists only in the being of an Idea, or objective essence, in the
> thinking attribute [of God], arising from the essence of an object which in fact exists in
> Nature. I say *of an object that really exists,* etc., without further particulars, in order to include
> here not only the modes of extension, but also the modes of all the infinite attributes,
> which have a soul just as much as those of extension do.[89]

Each 'idea' (i.e., *soul*) perfectly reflects the 'object' (i.e., the *mode*) that it is an
idea of; so Spinoza concludes that 'ideas differ among themselves, as the objects
themselves do, and that one is more excellent than the other, and contains more
reality, just as the object of the one is more excellent than the object of the other
and contains more reality.'[90] Thus, though all things are animate or have souls,
many of these souls will be ideas of relatively simple modes, and so will be souls
(*animae*) that lack the complexity, penetration, and excellence of the human mind
(*mens*). Further, each soul and its object – that is, each idea in God of some mode
and the mode of which it is an idea – are really the same thing, comprehended
under two different attributes: the soul under God's attribute of thought, the
object under whichever of God's attributes it is a mode of.[91]

Thus we can determine *a priori* that a *human* mind will be the idea, in God, of
some finite mode of *one* of God's attributes. But which attribute? Since our idea
of God is of a being having *infinitely* many attributes, we cannot, it seems, from
our idea of God alone, determine to *which* of these attributes those modes must
belong that human minds are ideas of. Hence it is not surprising that Spinoza's
attempt to determine the specific nature of the *human* mind relies on some axioms
that express *a posteriori* truths about ourselves – truths that experience makes
known to us. Among them are these: we each have a certain felt awareness of the
states of, and changes in, a certain mode of *extension,* namely, a body each of us
identifies as 'my body'; and we have no awareness or perception of *any* finite
things *except* bodies and modes of thought.[92] From these axioms, together with
what he believed he had established *a priori* about finite minds, Spinoza concluded
that each human mind is the idea, in God, of a particular *body* – the one each of

us calls our own. Since a mind (an idea) and its object (an *ideatum*) are the same thing, conceived under two of God's attributes, the human mind and the human body are the same thing, conceived under the attributes of thought and extension.[93] Each human mind has unity because its object, the body, has unity.[94] To this it may be added that our own body is the *first* but not the *only* finite object we are aware of, for through our awareness of our own body, we come to perceive other bodies, in so far as they cause changes in our own body.[95] Further, the human mind has a reflexive awareness of itself (is an *idea reflexiva* or an *idea ideae*), for in knowing its body it also *knows* that it knows it, and thereby it knows *itself*; the mind's reflexive awareness of itself is thus dependent on its awareness of its own body, a view markedly unlike Descartes's.[96]

It is now possible to give a general characterisation of Spinoza's view of our knowledge of the nature of the human mind: that knowledge is in part *a priori,* for from our idea of God's nature we determine that *any* soul or mind is an idea, in God, of some mode under one or another of His infinitely many attributes; but it is in part *a posteriori,* derived from our felt awareness of our own bodies, whereby we determine that *our* minds – *human* minds – are ideas of certain modes of God's attribute of *extension,* namely, those modes that are the particular human bodies each of us calls 'my own'. From these sources together we can then know that the human mind and body 'are one and the same thing, which is conceived now under the attribute of Thought, now under the attribute of Extension'.[97]

VII. HOBBES

Hobbes's materialist theory of mind was the antithesis of Descartes's doctrine of mind as an unextended substance. Unsurprisingly, there was equally sharp opposition between the Hobbesian and the Cartesian accounts of how we come to know the mind. Where Descartes believed in innate ideas, Hobbes opened the *Leviathan* (1651) with a version of the scholastic principle that there is nothing in the intellect that does not come from the senses: 'There is no conception in a man's mind, which hath not at first, totally, or by parts, been begotten upon the organs of sense.'[98] Our notion of our own selves is no exception to this rule. If we had to discover, by *thought* alone, that we exist, we would be plunged into infinite regress – for we should require another thought by which to think that we are thinking, and another by which to think that thought, and so on. But that, Hobbes told Descartes, is impossible:

I do not infer that I am thinking by means of another thought. For although someone may think that he *was* thinking (for this thought is simply an act of remembering), it is quite impossible for him to think that he *is* thinking, or to know that he is knowing. For then an infinite chain of questions would arise: 'How do you know that you know that you know . . . ?'[99]

And – again agreeing with the schoolmen – Hobbes argued that *thought* is not a *thing* but an activity, and as such requires some objects that it can be directed toward; those objects are ideas that first come to us from our senses, for we have no other source of ideas. It is to the senses, therefore, that we must look for the source of our notion of the self. What do I mean by *my self?* I mean either my body or my soul. If by *my self* I mean *my body,* then I know myself by my own senses, especially sight. If by *my self* I mean *my soul,* I know that only by inference from what I perceive by sense. For we perceive that human bodies, including our own, move themselves, and so 'we rationally infer that there is something within the human body which gives it the animal motion by means of which it has sensations and moves; and we call this "something" a soul, without having an idea of it.'[100]

Hobbes thus held that Descartes was quite mistaken to suppose the soul the first object of knowledge, and to believe that we can have immediate ('intuitive') knowledge that it exists; rather, we infer from what we perceive by sense that we have a soul. He used 'soul' here in a broader and more traditional way than Descartes had, for by it he meant not only that in us which thinks and perceives but also that which animates us and causes our spontaneous movement. For Hobbes, organic processes, self-movement, perception, and thought are all functions of the corporeal human organism. Jumping is an activity of that organism, and so is thinking. There must, to be sure, be something in the organism that causes it to jump or to think. But we need no more suppose that the thing that causes us to think is an incorporeal 'thinking substance' than we need suppose that what causes us to jump is an incorporeal 'jumping substance'. To speak of 'mind' or 'soul' is really just to give a *name* to the processes within a living thing that cause it to jump or to think, and there is no reason not to suppose that those processes are 'motions occurring in various parts of an organic body'.[101] (Thus when he told Descartes that we have no 'idea' of the soul, Hobbes did not mean that the soul is an unknowable something, but rather that our senses provide us with no *image* of it; it is instead something theoretical that our observation of organisms leads us to infer the existence of.)[102]

This view of the mind reflects Hobbes's most general convictions about human knowledge. Since all our ideas come from our senses, and what the senses perceive are bodies, our whole idea of substance is of something corporeal; hence, the very expression 'incorporeal substance' is self-contradictory.[103] Now the changes our senses discover in bodies are, at bottom, changes in their figure, motion, or location; and the only cause we can conceive of such changes is *motion*. 'For the variety of all figures arises out of the variety of those motions by which they are made; and motion cannot be understood to have any other cause besides motion.'[104] Thus, understanding how things – including human beings – change is the same as understanding how they move or are moved. Hobbes concluded that sensations, thoughts, emotions, and volitions are really just complex motions inside our bodies. He did not pretend that we can come to know with any great exactitude precisely what internal motions constitute our soul. For though he thought that from the definitions of such general terms as 'body', 'motion', 'space', 'time', 'cause', 'effect', 'quantity', and 'figure', truths can be deduced *a priori* about motion in general (that only motion can cause change in a body, that a motion once begun will continue until impeded by something, that there can be no action at a distance, etc.), he held that when we want to explain particular internal motions of complex bodies, the best we can do is construct an account of these motions that is consistent with the general truths about motion. But such an account cannot pretend to be perfectly exact, 'for there is no effect which the power of God cannot produce by many several ways'.[105]

In the case of our sensations, for example, though we can be confident they are motions in our bodies, nobody knows precisely *which* motions in the palate, say, cause us to taste different flavours. To be as definite as some atomists have been about the shape and motion of the atoms that cause sweet and bitter tastes, said Hobbes, 'would be to revolt from philosophy to divination'.[106] What we *can* be sure of is that our sensations are some kind of 'reactive motions' produced in our brains – the end product of motions set up in our sense organs by external bodies and continued from the sense organ through the body to the brain; that imagination, in turn, is a continuation of that motion in the brain, even after its external causes no longer act on the sense organ; that emotions are motions continued from the sense organs or the brain to the heart, where they enhance or inhibit vital processes, and so forth.[107]

What is notable here is that Hobbes takes our knowledge of both the existence and the nature of the mind to be of a piece with our knowledge of the rest of nature and to *depend on* our knowledge of bodies in general and the motions that govern them.[108] Hence, though his materialist theory of soul was opposed to the notion of soul as the incorporeal form of the body of the Aristotelian schoolmen, he agreed with them that we cannot know either the soul's existence or its nature *before* we know anything else. To the contrary, our knowledge of the soul presupposes many other things: ideas we get from our senses, names we give to those ideas, definitions we frame for those names, deductions of general truths about motion that we make *a priori* from those definitions, and explanations we construct *a posteriori* that, consistently with those general truths about motion, seek to account for the particular effects we perceive in bodies, including our own. In fact, however, Hobbes made little attempt to show just how, from our senses alone, we can get ideas of such mental acts as perceiving, imagining, remembering, judging, doubting, or believing (despite a celebrated injunction at the beginning of *Leviathan* that he who would understand another should look into himself and consider what he does when he believes or hopes or fears something, Hobbes proposed no source of ideas of mental acts comparable to Locke's notion of 'reflection' or introspection). But he was emphatic that we come to know the soul in the same way we come to know anything else in nature.

VIII. GASSENDI

Like Hobbes, Gassendi held that there is nothing in the mind that does not come from the senses and concluded that we can have positive ideas only of corporeal things.[109] So when we try to form a positive idea of any being, even of God, an angel, or our own selves, we must clothe it in corporeal form.[110] Since I can form no positive conception of myself save as a corporeal being, my own existence is obvious to me, for I can perceive myself by my own senses. Hence he heaped ridicule on Descartes's project of *proving* his own existence:

Here no doubt was a truth hidden in darkness worse than that of the lands of the Cimmerii, so unfamiliar and doubtful to you that if somebody had before now asked you, 'Descartes, do you exist?', you would not have had a thing to say in reply to a question so surprising, unheard of, unfathomable, and before answering it you would have needed to think about it . . . for a few months, or at least a few weeks![111]

Anybody *really* in doubt about his own existence, suggested Gassendi, does not need an argument but a cure for madness.[112] *That* we are is obvious; the philosopher's puzzle is only about *what* we are. In his *Objectiones* to Descartes (1641), Gassendi argued that Descartes had failed to show that anything in our nature is incorporeal. Every mental power that Descartes attributed to an unextended human mind – sensing, imagining, thinking, willing – can also be attributed, though perhaps in less developed form, to animals, which are, as Descartes himself granted, wholly corporeal. Animals even reason in simple ways (thus a dog, seeing the familiar dish in his master's hand, infers that he is about to be fed and runs to his master) and use a simple language to signal each other.[113] Gassendi did not assert, in his *Objectiones,* that the mind *is* corporeal, but rather that Descartes had failed to prove that it is *not* corporeal. In fact, said Gassendi, the substance of things remains hidden from us – it is their accidents we perceive. Whether we're talking about the substance of wax or of the human soul, 'our conception of this substance is merely a confused perception of something unknown.'[114] His *Objectiones* to Descartes, therefore, leave the reader with the impression that Gassendi believed the substance of the mind unknowable, but that, for all we can determine, it may be a corporeal thing.

In his chief work, *Syntagma Philosophicum* (1658), he still defended the doctrine that we can form no positive idea of what the human soul is, but there he advanced many reasons to believe that – whatever it is – it is probably *not* a corporeal thing. Here his view differed markedly from Hobbes's contention that the very expression 'incorporeal substance' is contradictory. For, said Gassendi, though it is true that all our positive ideas come from our senses, and so true that we can form no positive idea of any incorporeal thing, we must be able to understand the meaning of the judgement, 'X is incorporeal', for it is only the negation of a judgement – 'X is corporeal' – that we understand perfectly well.[115] So the belief that there may be some incorporeal beings is not unintelligible to us. Now many of our mental acts can be performed by a wholly corporeal agent, for whether we sense something, or remember what we sensed, or infer from some present sensation another that will follow, we deal always with particular corporeal *images* that are first impressed on our sense organs by other bodies, then transmitted to and stored in some corporeal organ within us, from which they can be called up again. Hence nothing incorporeal need be supposed to account for these mental acts; from which Gassendi concluded that both animals and men possess a corporeal soul.[116] But from other considerations, he argued, we can infer that we, unlike other animals, *also* possess an *incorporeal* soul. We have no direct knowledge of such a soul, nor can we form any positive idea of it; but we can infer its existence from certain things we know about our thinking, among them that, though our thought always begins with corporeal images received from sense, it is not limited to those images (thus astronomers can form an idea of the sun as many times bigger than anything they have ever actually seen); that the mind has a reflexive awareness of itself and so 'acts on itself', something no corporeal thing can do; that we can abstract universals from our perception of particulars, whereas the corporeal soul can (literally) take into itself only particular corporeal images; and that we can comprehend the negative judgement 'Some thing is not corporeal' – a judgement that would be unintelligible to the corporeal soul.[117]

From these considerations, he inferred that human beings have *two* souls – one corporeal, one incorporeal – and that the corporeal soul 'mediates' between the body and the incorporeal soul.[118] (Gassendi may have thought he thus resolved a problem he had raised about Descartes's theory – namely, how there could be any causal interaction between the corporeal body and the incorporeal mind.[119] But it seems the problem now merely recurs in a new version: how can there be causal interaction between the corporeal soul and the incorporeal soul?) The human soul is, thus, for Gassendi a purely theoretical entity, and the knowledge we get of it is mainly negative: we conclude what it is *not,* namely, a corporeal thing, but not what it *is.* Gassendi's two-soul theory did not enjoy the vogue Descartes's concept of mind did, but it was defended by several seventeenth-century thinkers, among them Samuel Sorbière and François Bernier.[120] Marin Cureau de la Chambre also held that we have both an animal soul and a human soul, the former corporeal, the latter incorporeal, though (like Henry More) he held that even the incorporeal soul is extended.[121]

IX. LOCKE

The empiricism of Locke was broader than that of Hobbes and Gassendi, who held that *all* ideas come from the senses. Locke held that there are *two* 'fountains of knowledge': the senses and the mind's power to reflect on its own operations.[122] The maxim that there is nothing in the intellect that does not come from the senses is true of us in infancy, for the mind is a blank page until the senses write upon it; but as we mature, 'the Understanding turns inwards upon it self, reflects on its own Operations, and makes them the object of its own Contemplation.'[123] Thereby we get 'another set of Ideas, which could not be had from things without: and such are Perception, Thinking, Doubting, Believing, Reasoning, Knowing, Willing, and all the different actings of our own Minds'.[124] From our reflective awareness of these mental acts comes our knowledge that we exist. That knowledge is immediate, for it involves no inference, though it is knowledge we acquire only when the mind matures enough to 'turn inward upon itself'.

Experience then convinces us, that we have an intuitive Knowledge of our own Existence, and an internal infallible Perception that we are. In every Act of Sensation, Reasoning, or Thinking, we are conscious to our selves of our own Being; and, in this matter, come not short of the highest degree of Certainty.[125]

We have *intuitive knowledge,* according to Locke, when 'the Mind is at no pains of proving or examining, but perceives the Truth, as the Eye doth light, only by being directed toward it.'[126] And so he agreed with Descartes that we have a non-inferential, intuitive knowledge of our own existence: 'If I doubt of all other

Things, that very doubt makes me perceive my own Existence, and will not suffer me to doubt that. . . . Or if I know I doubt, I have as certain a Perception of the Existence of the thing doubting, as of that Thought, which I call *doubt*.'[127] Indeed, the *only* thing I can know intuitively to exist is myself (though I can have demonstrative knowledge of God's existence and 'sensitive knowledge' of the existence of bodies); for though we can have intuitive knowledge of many truths, they are not truths about what *exists,* but only about 'the Essences of Things, which being only abstract Ideas . . . give us no knowledge of Real Existence at all.'[128]

But if Locke agreed with Descartes that we have intuitive knowledge of our existence as thinking beings, he denied that we can know the *nature* of the thing in us that thinks. The nature of *any* substance, material or spiritual, is hidden from us. For all our ideas come from sensation or reflection, and sensations make known to us such properties of bodies as solidity and motion, but not the substratum to which those properties belong, while reflection discloses mental acts like perceiving, thinking, and willing, but not the thing that performs them.

The substance of Spirit is unknown to us; and so is the substance of Body, equally unknown to us: Two primary Qualities, or Properties of Body, viz. solid coherent parts, and impulse, we have distinct clear Ideas of: So likewise we know, and have distinct clear Ideas of two primary Qualities, or Properties of Spirit, viz. Thinking and a power of Action.[129]

But the subject of those qualities is, for us, only 'a something we know not what'. We infer, to be sure, that *something* has the qualities perceived by sense, and *something* performs the operations that reflection discloses, for we cannot suppose either qualities or operations to exist in themselves. And since certain qualities are presented together to our senses (e.g., the redness, roundness, sweetness of an apple), we conclude that they must belong to one substance; similarly, since certain mental operations occur together (the same subject sees the apple, judges it good, and desires it), we conclude that there must be one subject that performs those operations. But the only idea we can form of these substances is the abstract one of a *being* or *thing* to which those properties belong.[130]

Mindful, perhaps, of Hobbes's contention that 'spiritual substance' is a contradiction in terms, Locke insisted repeatedly that our idea of spiritual substance is no less clear (really, no more *unclear*) than our idea of material substance.

We have as clear a Notion of the Substance of Spirit, as we have of Body; the one being supposed to be (without knowing what it is) the Substratum to those simple Ideas we have from without; and the other supposed (with a like ignorance of what it is) to be the Substratum to those Operations, which we experiment in our selves within.[131]

Indeed, if we consider the paradoxes about the infinite divisibility of matter, we find that our idea of material substance is fraught with 'consequences that carry greater difficulty, and more apparent absurdity, than any thing [that] can follow from the Notion of an immaterial knowing substance'.[132] Although we have no idea of the nature of these substances, we cannot doubt that they exist. 'Sensation convinces us, that there are solid extended Substances; and Reflection, that there are thinking ones: Experience assures us of the Existence of such Beings; and that the one hath a power to move Body by impulse, the other by thought; this we cannot doubt of.'[133]

Locke believed he could prove that, at the very least, *one* thinking substance – God – cannot be corporeal. 'Matter *qua* matter', he held, cannot think, since – whatever its underlying substratum may be – it is something solid, extended, figured, and movable, and no combination of these can produce thought. Thus in his proof of the existence of God, Locke argued that no single particle of matter can think, nor can all particles of matter taken together, nor can any particular configuration of particles.[134] One might as well try to make an extended thing out of unextended parts as a thinking thing out of unthinking parts. Now we know that thinking, intelligent beings exist – for reflection shows that we ourselves think and cognise; and 'it is as impossible to conceive, that ever bare incogitative Matter should produce a thinking intelligent Being, as that nothing should of it self produce Matter.'[135] Since we, thinking intelligent beings, are contingent and so must be caused to be, we can be certain that that cause is an *incorporeal* thinking being (namely, God). We can know, therefore, that at least one incorporeal thinking substance exists. Locke sometimes spoke (especially in the *Essay*'s chapter on our idea of substance) as if the human mind, too, were an immaterial substance; and, indeed, he thought it likely that it is. But he did not think we could prove that it is. For though 'matter as matter' cannot think, it must be granted that the omnipotent God can, if he chooses, give 'to some Systems of Matter fitly disposed, a power to perceive and think'.[136] The human mind may, therefore, be not an immaterial substance, but only 'a faculty of thought' that God has added to the human body. It may be hard, Locke granted, to conceive how matter might be endowed with such a faculty, but no harder than to conceive how an immaterial thinking substance should be united to a material extended one, as Descartes supposed is the case.

Several of his critics, most notably Bishop Stillingfleet, accused Locke of inconsistency here. If no configuration of bits of matter can think, how could a material substance have a faculty of thought?[137] Locke replied that God can, and does, add to matter faculties not inherent in it. In itself, matter is inert. But God adds *motion* to it. In itself, matter is inanimate. But in plants and animals God adds *life* to it. So, too, in itself matter is unthinking, but it must be supposed in God's power to add a faculty of *thinking* to it.[138] Thus, he concluded, our knowledge of our nature, as thinking beings, is very limited. That we think, perceive, will (and so *exist*), we are intuitively certain of; but whether that in us which thinks is a spiritual substance, or a power of thinking that God has added to matter, we cannot know. In this he showed himself more sceptical than either Malebranche or Gassendi, who, while denying that we have a positive idea of what the mind is, gave arguments to try to show it incorporeal. Locke, too, in his controversy with Bishop Stillingfleet, said repeatedly that our minds are probably incorporeal, but his reasons for holding this seem to have been mainly theological; unlike Gassendi, he did not offer arguments to try to prove this the most likely of the alternatives he thought possible (unless we count as argument his 'conjecture' that pure spirit is active, pure matter passive, and beings that are both active and passive are a union of spirit and matter).[139] He sometimes spoke, in fact, as if the alternatives – mind as an immaterial substance or as a faculty in matter to think – were equally plausible; as if he, too, might say, as Hume would a half-century later of *his* unsuccessful efforts to get clear about the nature of the mind, 'I must plead the privilege of a sceptic, and confess, that this difficulty is too hard for my understanding.'[140]

X. CONCLUSION

Rejecting the Aristotelian-Thomistic doctrine that we know the soul only by inference, many seventeenth-century thinkers followed Descartes in holding that we can have some immediate, intuitive knowledge of the mind, although some, like Malebranche and Locke, limited this to the *existence* of the mind or that in us which thinks. Others, like Hobbes and Gassendi, agreed with the Aristotelians that all our ideas come to us by way of the senses, and so held that we get knowledge of the mind only by inference from what we perceive by sense. As to how much we can know about the mind, opinion ranged from Descartes's confident conviction that we can have a clear and distinct idea of its nature, through Leibniz's belief that we can know it clearly but not distinctly, to the view of thinkers like Malebranche, Gassendi, and Locke that we can have no positive idea of the mind. Those who thought that we *can* know what the mind is, proposed quite diverse theories of it, ranging from the Cartesian doctrine of mind as immaterial substance to Hobbes's view that the soul is a complex pattern of corporeal motions. Several thinkers, including Leibniz and the Cambridge Platonists, shared, at least in some measure, Descartes's belief that knowledge of our own mind plays an important rôle in our knowledge of other things, and even Locke held that our knowledge of our mind's existence, contingency, and passivity in perception plays a part in our knowledge that God and other things exist. Others, however, rejected the view that knowledge of our mind is the foundation for our knowledge of other things. Spinoza gave that distinction to our knowledge of God's nature, and Hobbes and Gassendi located the study of the human soul in the larger context of the study of nature – Hobbes making our knowledge of human nature dependent on our understanding of motion, and Gassendi, in *Syntagma Philosophicum,* treating the study of the soul as a part of biology.

But Descartes's conviction that inquiry must begin with the examination of the mind itself, a conviction new in the seventeenth century, was long to prevail, though it often took the form of an epistemological inquiry about the competence of the mind to know, rather than an ontological one about the mind's existence and nature. Belief that the starting point of inquiry should be the examination of the mind came to be almost second nature to philosophy in the modern period. If, of late, a different view has gained wider currency – the view that the mind that thinks and knows is a natural phenomenon that should be studied in the same way as other natural phenomena – that view has had to struggle against a persisting conviction that both mind and knowledge must be examined in a way different from other things, a conviction inherited from the seventeenth century. And even those eager to 'naturalise' the study of the thing that thinks and knows have, wittingly or not, roots in doctrines of seventeenth-century thinkers like Hobbes and Gassendi. That century's debates about knowledge of the mind thus cast a long shadow – one that still falls over our thinking about the subject who thinks.

NOTES

1 Thomas Aquinas, *Summa th.* I q84 a3–4.
2 Thomas Aquinas, *Summa contra gentiles,* Bk. III, pt. 1, chap. 46(4–5).
3 Thomas Aquinas, *In II De Anima,* lec. 6, no. 308.
4 *Summa th.* I q80 a1.
5 *Summa contra gentiles,* Bk. II, chaps. 49–50.
6 Thomas Aquinas, *De veritate,* q10 a8 (9').
7 *Summa contra gentiles,* Bk. II, chap. 57.
8 *Summa contra gentiles,* Bk. II, chaps. 68–72.
9 *Summa contra gentiles,* Bk. II, chap. 58.
10 *Summa contra gentiles,* Bk. III, pt. 1, chap. 46(7).

11 Aquinas deals most fully with the question of how we know the soul in *Summa th.* I q87 a1–4; *Summa contra gentiles,* Bk. III, pt. i, chap. 46; and *De veritate* q10 a8. See also Gilson 1956, pp. 220–2; Gardeil 1956, vol. 3, pp. 176–91.

12 *Disc.,* pt. 4; Med. II; *Princ.* I 7.

13 AT VII 25. Translations are from Descartes 1984–91; since these translations are keyed to the pagination in AT, no separate references to the translations will be given.

14 *Cogito ergo sum* is prefigured by Saint Augustine's reply to the sceptics: If I am deceived, I am. *De civitate Dei* XI.26; cf. *De trinitate* X.10.14. Unlike Aquinas, Augustine held that, although we know corporeal things through the senses, we know incorporeal things, including the soul, through our awareness of the soul itself. See *De trinitate* IX. 3. Descartes's older contemporary, Tommaso Campanella, also argued that to defeat scepticism we should begin with the mind's knowledge of itself. Campanella 1638a (completed in 1611), pt. I, pp. 30–2, 73–4. On precursors of Descartes's *Cogito,* see Blanchet 1920a and Gilson 1925, pp. 295–8.

15 AT VII 140. On *Cogito ergo sum* an enthymeme, see Gassendi 1962, p. 85; and Hintikka 1962.

16 AT VII 140–1, and AT IXA 205–6.

17 AT VII 258–9.

18 AT VII 352; cf. AT II 37–8.

19 AT VII 413 and 422. See also AT IXA 206, AT V 147. Descartes said the same of basic principles of reasoning like the law of contradiction. For basic concepts and principles ('simple natures' or 'common notions') that we grasp by 'a kind of natural light', see AT III 665–6, AT VIIIA 9–10, 22–4, AT X 419–20. This objection to Descartes was also made in Regius 1661, p. 399.

20 *Princ.* I 10.

21 AT VII 359; cf. pp. 129 and 275–6.

22 AT VII 27–8.

23 AT VII 78.

24 Ger. IV 357 (Leibniz 1969, p. 385).

25 AT VII 201–3; cf. pp. 100 and 122–3.

26 AT VII 224–5; cf. pp. 120–1 and 132–3.

27 *Princ.* I 11.

28 *Princ.* I 53, 61.

29 *Princ.* I 62.

30 *Princ.* I 63.

31 On Descartes's theory of mind, see Alquié 1950, chap. 9; Beyssade 1979, chap. 5; Gouhier 1962, chaps. 12–14; Gueroult 1984, chaps. 3–4 and 15; B. Williams 1978, chaps. 3–4; Wilson 1978, chap. 2; Cottingham 1986, chap. 5; Carriero 1986; Markie 1992.

32 See Clauberg 1656, pp. 35–44; La Forge 1666, pp. 6–10, 20–6, 37–43; Cordemoy 1666, pp. 140–1, 146–51; Régis 1690, vol. 1, pp. 68–70, 96–8, 164–5; Lamy 1694–8, vol. 2, pp. 372–83.

33 Mal. *OC* I 429–31.

34 Mal. *OC* II 369 (Malebranche 1980a, p. 480). Translations are from Malebranche 1980a.

35 *Rech.* III.2.6, Mal. *OC* I 437–47 (Malebranche 1980a, pp. 230–5). Malebranche agreed with Descartes that *sensations* are modes of the mind, but he drew a sharp distinction between *sensations* and *ideas;* see Mal. *OC* I 445.

36 Mal. *OC* I 451 (Malebranche 1980a, p. 238).

37 Mal. *OC* I 381–2 (Malebranche 1980a, p. 198).

38 Régis 1690, vol. I, p. 165.
39 Mal. *OC* III 170–1 (Malebranche 1980a, pp. 637–8).
40 Mal. *OC* III 168–9 (Malebranche 1980a, p. 636).
41 For Malebranche's detailed account of our knowledge of the mind, see *Rech.* Bk. III.2.7, sec. 4; *Eclaircissement XI*; and *Méditations chrétiennes,* IX, in Mal. *OC* I 451–3, Mal. *OC* III 163–71, and Mal. *OC* X 102–6. On Malebranche's theory of mind, see Gueroult 1955–9, vol. I, chaps. 2 and 8; Robinet 1965, pp. 344–56; Rodis-Lewis 1963, chaps. 8–9.
42 Cudworth 1731, pp. 127, 131.
43 Cudworth 1678, p. 637. In Cudworth 1731, Bk. IV, chaps. 1–2, the thesis is defended that basic metaphysical concepts come not from sense but are innate. Henry More defended the same view; cf. More 1662c, Bk. I, chaps. 5–7.
44 Mal. *OC* II 312–13. The same doctrine can be found in Cordemoy 1666, pp. 93–7. On the doctrine of matter's passivity in the seventeenth and eighteenth centuries, see Yolton 1983.
45 Mal. *OC* I, pp. 381–3.
46 Cudworth 1678, p. 159.
47 More 1662c, I.iv.3; 1662d, Bk. I, chap. 3; 1668, I.30; 1671, chap. 28, secs. 1–4. Cudworth did not embrace More's doctrine of extended spirit, but he gave it a sympathetic hearing. See Cudworth 1678, pp. 833–4.
48 More 1671, chap. 27, sec. 5.
49 More, 1662d, Bk. I, chap. 3; cf. chaps. 5 and 7. Divisibility, according to More, characterises only 'integral or compound matter', for he embraced atomism and so rejected the Cartesian doctrine of matter's infinite divisibility. More 1662d, preface, sec. 3.
50 Conway 1982, pp. 188–9, 221–2.
51 More 1662d, Bk. I, chap. 8.
52 More 1662d, Bk. III, chaps. 12–13; Cudworth 1678, pp. 154–5, 178–81.
53 Cudworth 1731, Bk. IV, chap. 1; Cudworth 1678, pp. 845–6; More 1662d, Bk. II, chap. 2.
54 Cudworth 1678, p. 637.
55 More 1671, chap. 24.
56 More 1662c, Bk. III; 1662d, Bk. I, chap. 13.
57 *Ess.* II.xxiii.28; Berkeley, *Principles of Human Knowledge,* sec. 89.
58 Leibniz, *Nouv. ess.* II.i.2; II.vii.1 (this work was completed in 1704, but not published until 1765). Cf. Ger. VI 499–503, 532 (Leibniz 1969, pp. 547–9). Translations are from Leibniz 1969.
59 Leibniz, *Nouv. ess.* IV.ix.2.
60 Ger. IV 357 (Leibniz 1969, p. 385).
61 *Nouv. ess.* IV.vii.7.
62 Ger. I 370–2 (Leibniz 1969, pp. 152–3).
63 Leibniz 1903, pp. 518–23 (Leibniz 1969, pp. 267–70); cf. *Nouv. ess.* IV.vii.7.
64 *Nouv. ess.* II.xxvii.13.
65 *Nouv. ess.,* Preface and I.i.23.
66 *Nouv. ess.,* Preface and II.i.
67 Ger. II 121; IV, 365 (art. 54); IV 422–6 (Leibniz 1969, pp. 344, 390 [art. 54], 291–4); *Nouv. ess.* II.xxix.
68 Ger. II 249 (Leibniz 1969, p. 528).
69 From Leibniz's notes on Simon Foucher's *Réponse à la Critique de la Critique de la*

Recherche de la vérité, printed in Rabbe 1867, appx. p. xlii (Leibniz 1969, p. 155); cf. *Nouv. ess.* II.xix.4.

70 Ger. II 263–4 (Leibniz 1969, pp. 534–5).

71 Ger. II 56–8 (Leibniz 1969, pp. 337–8).

72 Ger. IV 433–4, sec. 9, and Leibniz 1903, pp. 519–20 (Leibniz 1969, p. 308, sec. 9, and p. 268).

73 Ger. II 263–4 (Leibniz 1969, pp. 534–5).

74 Ger. II 47–59, 134–8 (Leibniz 1969, pp. 331–8, 359–61); *Nouv. ess.* III.iii.6.

75 On Leibniz's theory of mind, see Broad 1975, chap. 5; Loemker 1972, chap. 10; Jolley 1984, chap. 6; Mates 1986, pp. 206–8; McRae 1976, pp. 30–5.

76 Geb. II 10–7 (Spinoza 1985, pp. 12–6) and *Eth.* II props. 40–3.

77 *Eth.* II prop. 11 cor. Translations in the text are from Spinoza 1985.

78 *Eth.* II prop. 43 schol.

79 *Eth.* II props. 25, 43, 45–7.

80 *Eth.* II prop. 10 schol. 2.

81 *Eth.* I prop. 40 schol.

82 *Eth.* I prop. 28 dem. and schol.

83 This is Spinoza's difficult doctrine of infinite modes, which we must here pass over. Cf. *Eth.* I props. 21–3; letters 63–4; and *Korte Ver.,* pt. I, chaps. 8–9. On this doctrine, see Wolfson 1934, chap. 11; Gueroult 1968–74, vol. 1, p. 342; Curley 1969, pp. 55–74.

84 Geb. II 36–7 (Spinoza 1985, pp. 41–2).

85 Geb. I 147 (Spinoza 1985, pp. 236–7).

86 *Eth.* I dfn. 6 and prop. 16.

87 *Eth.* II prop. 1.

88 Geb. IV 280 (letter of 18 August 1675).

89 Geb. I, p. 119 (Spinoza 1985, p. 154).

90 *Eth.* II prop. 13 schol.

91 *Eth.* II prop. 7.

92 *Eth.* II ax. 4–5.

93 *Eth.* II props. 11, 13, and prop. 21 schol.

94 For his complex theory of the unity of the body, see *Eth.* II prop. 13, lemmas 1–7, and prop. 15.

95 *Eth.* II prop. 26.

96 *Eth.* II props. 20–1.

97 *Eth.* III prop. 2 schol. On Spinoza's theory of mind, see Collins 1984, chap. 3; Gueroult 1968–74, vol. 2; Roth 1954, Bk. 2, chap. 3; Wolfson 1934, chap. 13; Allison 1987, chap. 4; Curley 1988, chap. 2; Donagan 1988, chap. 7; M. Wilson 1980.

98 *Lev.* i.

99 From Hobbes's 2nd objection to Descartes, AT VII 173.

100 From Hobbes's 7th objection to Descartes, AT VII 183.

101 AT VII 178; cf. pp. 172–3.

102 Cf. Hobbes's 4th, 5th, 8th, and 9th objections to Descartes.

103 *Human Nature* (1650), chap. 11, sec. 4; Hobbes 1968, pp. 108, 113, 429. Even God and the angels are corporeal, though of a matter too subtle to be perceived by us. *Human Nature,* chap. 11; *Lev.* xxxiv.

104 *Eng. Works,* vol. 1, p. 69.

105 *Eng. Works,* vol. 7, p. 3. Cf. *De corpore* (1655), chap. 25, sec. 1.

106 *Eng. Works,* vol. 1, p. 507.

107 The full account is given in many places: *De corpore,* chap. 25; *Lev.* i–vi; *Human Nature,* chaps. 2–7; 'A Short Tract on First Principles', in Hobbes 1928, pp. 156–66. Hobbes speaks sometimes as if these mental events were *identical to* motions in the brain and heart, sometimes as if they were mere epiphenomena *caused by* those motions. On Hobbes's theory of mind, see Laird 1934, chap. 4; Peters 1956, chaps. 3–4.

108 Hobbes set forth a comprehensive doctrine of motion that sought to explain change at every level, from inanimate bodies to the body politic. He first sketched it in 'A Short Tract on First Principles' (see Hobbes 1928, appx. I). He treated of body in general in *De corpore* (1655); of the human body in *Human Nature* (1650), *Leviathan* (1651), pt. I, and *De homine* (1658); of the body politic in *De cive* (1642), *De corpore politico* (1650), and *Lev.,* pt. II.

109 Gassendi 1658, vol. 1, p. 92, canons 2–3.

110 Gassendi 1962, pp. 529–33.

111 Gassendi 1962, pp. 81–3.

112 Gassendi 1962, p. 75.

113 AT VII 268–71; and Gassendi 1658, vol. 2, p. 410–12.

114 AT VII 275; cf. AT VII, pp. 271–3, 286–7, and Gassendi 1962, pp. 175–9.

115 Gassendi 1658, vol. 2, pp. 442, 451.

116 Gassendi 1658, vol. 2, pp. 250–2, 403–5, 409–13. Much in Gassendi's account of perception came from Epicurus.

117 Gassendi 1658, vol. 2, pp. 440–2, 451–2. Gassendi did not take the mind's reflexive awareness of itself to be an exception to the principle that all our positive ideas come from the senses, presumably because the mind gets no positive idea of itself from its power to reflect on its own acts.

118 Gassendi 1658, vol. 2, p. 258. On Gassendi's theory of soul, see Bloch 1971, pp. 362–76 and Osler 1994, pp. 59–77.

119 AT VII 343–5.

120 Sorbière 1660, pp. 83–8, 248–9. Bernier 1678 made Gassendi's views known to a wider audience than did Gassendi's own huge, dense Latin tomes.

121 On animal and human souls, see Cureau de la Chambre 1647, pp. 142–3, 241–54, 258–60; on the human soul as incorporeal but extended, see Cureau de la Chambre 1664, pp. 337–56. On Cureau de la Chambre, see Balz 1951, chap. 3.

122 *Ess.* II.i.2.

123 *Ess.* II.i.6–8; II.i.8; cf. II.i.23–4.

124 *Ess.* II.i.4.

125 *Ess.* IV.ix.3.

126 *Ess.* IV.ii.1–3,7,14.

127 *Ess.* IV.ix.3.

128 *Ess.* IV.ix.1–2; cf. IV.vii.7.

129 *Ess.* II.xxiii.30.

130 *Ess.* II.xxiii.1–5.

131 *Ess.* II.xxiii.5; cf. secs. 22–7.

132 *Ess.* II.xxiii.31.

133 *Ess.* II.xxiii.29; cf. sec. 15.

134 *Ess.* IV.x.14–16.

135 *Ess.* IV.x.10.

136 *Ess.* IV.iii.6. On Locke's theory of mind, see Aaron 1971, pp. 142–53; Ayers 1991, vol. 2, chap. 4; Bennett 1994; Lennon 1993, pp. 314–33; Woolhouse 1983, chap. 17.

137 Stillingfleet 1697b, pp. 77–9. The objection was also made by Gerdil 1747 and Flemyng 1751.
138 Locke 1699, pp. 396–404, 410–11. See Ayers 1981b; Jolley 1984, chap. 4; Wilson 1979; and Yolton 1983, chap. 1.
139 *Ess.* II.xxiii.28.
140 Hume 1978, p. 636.

25

MIND–BODY PROBLEMS

DANIEL GARBER AND MARGARET WILSON

Most seventeenth-century thinkers regarded mind and body as distinct entities, though a few philosophers, such as Hobbes, did embrace versions of radical materialism.[1] But dualism, as this chapter shows, inherently presents certain fundamental problems. We shall first discuss two distinct but closely related issues: (1) the nature of the 'union' between mind and body in a given human individual and (2) the question of whether mind and body can and do interact causally – and, if not, what may truly be said about the relation between a given state of mind (such as a pain or an intention) and a state of body (such as a pinprick or arm movement) normally taken to be its cause or effect. Descartes's position on these two problems is of particular interest in that he established the framework of argument – for both followers and opponents – throughout the seventeenth century. Then in Section II we shall turn to later dualists' responses. Finally, in Section III we shall address important questions for dualism connected with the new mechanist world-view. The most crucial from this perspective is perhaps the following: What is the relation between human volitions, conceived as irreducibly non-physical states, and the universal laws of motion which lie at the heart of the new science? If volitions are genuinely effective, must they result in unacceptable disruption of the uniform working of such laws?

I. DESCARTES ON MIND–BODY UNION AND INTERACTION

The Cartesian 'real distinction' between mind and body in human beings raised questions both about the nature of the interaction between the two types of entity and about the nature of their 'union' in a single human being. Descartes – from his earliest to his latest works – assumed that mental states cause physical states, and vice versa. On the one hand, much human behaviour is caused or produced

Section I is mostly the work of Margaret Wilson; Section III is mostly the work of Daniel Garber; Section II was written jointly.

by the volitions of the rational soul, acting on the body. On the other hand, sensory and imaginative states of the mind have brain states as causes.[2] Descartes sometimes suggests that this two-way interaction is virtually a datum of ordinary experience.[3] Elsewhere, he argues on more theoretical grounds. In the *Meditationes* and in the *Principia Philosophiae,* for example, Descartes argues for the existence of the external world on the grounds that God would be a deceiver if our sensations were not caused by external bodies;[4] and in the *Discourse de la méthode,* he maintains that human use of language and other 'rational' behaviour obviously require a non-mechanical, immaterial cause.[5] These types of causal interaction involve issues closely intertwined with Descartes's views about the mind–body union.

Central to Descartes's position on both interaction and mind–body union is the claim that he (as a mind) is not merely 'present in my body as a sailor is present in a ship'.[6] The experience of such sensations as pain, hunger, and thirst show, he says, that the mind is 'very closely joined and, as it were, intermingled' with the body; these sensations arise 'from the union and so to speak intermixture of the mind with the body'. Thus, when my body is harmed, I feel pain, rather than perceiving the damage 'by way of the intellect'. At one point, Descartes says that an angel in a human body would 'simply perceive the motions caused by external objects', rather than having 'confused perceptions' such as pain, which characterise 'a mind really united to' a body.[7] Similarly, he clearly implies that mind–body causation, as manifested when one effectively wills the motions of one's limbs, is not sufficient to establish 'union'; the experiences of sensation (and other 'passions'), he insists, show that our relation to our body is not one of mere causal manipulation, but something much more intimate.[8] Descartes uses other terms to make what is apparently the same point when he indicates that the mind is *substantially* united to the body, or that 'the whole mind is united to the whole body.'[9] Similarly, he talks about the mind being united to the body as a substantial form is united to matter.[10] These remarks (among others) have suggested to some that Descartes holds that the mind and body united constitute a genuine substance, different from both the thinking and the extended substance that constitute it.[11]

One might suppose that Descartes, in making such comments, was simply pandering to orthodoxy, attempting to package his own doctrine in a way acceptable to the theologians. This interpretation appears to derive support from a seemingly unguarded remark Descartes made in a letter to his then-disciple Henricus Regius, who, he feared, was getting into political trouble with the Faculty of Theology at the University of Utrecht for understating the nature of the mind–body union:

Whenever the occasion arises, in public and in private, you should give out that you believe that a human being is a true *ens per se,* and not an *ens per accidens,* and that the mind and the body are united in a real and substantial manner. You must say that they are united not by position or disposition, as you say in your last paper – for this is too open to objection, and in my opinion quite untrue – but by a true mode of union, as everyone agrees, though nobody explains what this means and so you need not do so either.[12]

One might suppose that Descartes here is just giving Regius a line to take in public to keep his disciple out of trouble, and his own name out of controversy. But this passage is hardly decisive evidence for that claim. On the other hand, it does strongly suggest that Descartes did not think that he could explain this 'true mode of union' any better than anyone else, even if he felt that he was equally entitled to affirm it.[13]

One of the very few places where Descartes attempts an extended account of his views on interaction and union is found in some letters he exchanged with the Princess Elisabeth of Bohemia in 1643.[14] Elisabeth initiated this correspondence with a question about interaction: how could the mind, an unextended entity, possibly impress motion on the body? She observes that the 'determination of motion' seems to depend on physical contact (*l'attouchement*) and on shape. But shape requires extension, which Descartes has 'entirely excluded' from his concept of the soul; and Elisabeth supposes that physical contact is incompatible with the notion of an incorporeal thing.[15] Descartes's response focuses on the notion of mind–body union. He indicates that the notion of the mind's (or soul's) union with the body is a 'primitive' notion: it stands side by side with our primitive notions of the essential properties of mind and matter, respectively, plus a few additional primitives such as 'being' which apply to everything we can conceive. He maintains that our notion of the body's power to affect the mind and our notion of the mind's power to move the body both 'depend on' this simple notion of union. Human knowledge consists in carefully distinguishing these notions from each other; we must further recognise that it is the nature of a primitive notion not to be susceptible to further analysis or clarification. A particularly common source of error, he continues, lies in our tendency to try to explain something in terms of the wrong primitive notions: for instance, to try to understand the action of mind on body in terms appropriate only to interaction between bodies (as he hints that Elisabeth had been doing).[16]

These explanations only bewildered Elisabeth.[17] And indeed, Descartes's appeal to a third 'primitive notion' does not explain anything at all; it seems to reduce to the claim that we simply have an innate notion of mind–body interaction and union that makes these phenomena intelligible to us without any further difficulty.

Furthermore, it is not clear in what sense exactly Descartes considered the notion of union to be primitive: it is difficult to see how the notion of the union of mind and body could be intelligible to anyone who did not have, first, the notions of mind and body. Interestingly, the doctrine of the three primitive notions advanced in this celebrated and often cited discussion of interaction seems not to appear in Descartes's writings before these letters, nor does it seem to appear in the writings that follow.[18] Perhaps Descartes took Elisabeth's bewilderment to heart.

Descartes's difficulties in providing a clear account of the union and interaction of mind and body do not prevent him from being anatomically specific about the 'principal site' at which mind and body connect. The pineal gland, he holds, is particularly well suited to serve this function by virtue of its central location in the brain, its mobility, and the fact that there is only one such gland. Because there is only one pineal gland and because it is at the centre of the brain, it can serve as the common sense, the locus in which the data of the different sense organs come together. Because of its mobility, it is well suited to convey to the mind the motions of the parts of the body, and to the body, the volitions of the mind.[19] But, at the same time, Descartes insists that the mind is joined to the whole of the body. In the *Passions de l'âme,* Descartes writes that 'we recognize that the soul is really joined to the whole body, and we cannot properly say that it exists in any one part of the body to the exclusion of the others.'[20] Although this appears to conflict with the claim that the mind is principally joined to the pineal gland, it is possible to reconcile the two statements. Descartes writes, again in the *Passions de l'âme:*

For the body is a unity which is in a sense indivisible because of the arrangement of its organs, these being so related to one another that the removal of any one of them renders the whole body defective. . . . The soul has its principal seat in the small gland located in the middle of the brain. From there it radiates through the rest of the body by means of the animal spirits, the nerves, and even the blood.[21]

The soul is attached most directly to the pineal gland. But because of the intricate organisation of the human body, and because of the special place that the pineal gland occupies in that body, the soul's attachment to the pineal gland connects it to the body as a whole; were it attached directly to a finger, say, it would not be united to the whole of the body. In this sense Descartes can say, somewhat metaphorically, perhaps, that the soul 'radiates through the rest of the body'. The soul is not literally present in the finger, but because of the organisation of the body, it can sense a pin prick, and can, in turn, cause the finger to move away from the cause of the pain.

Descartes's account of union and interaction was considered highly problematic both by his contemporaries and by later thinkers. Allegations that the supposed interaction between mind and body is impossible or inconceivable have constituted one of the most persistent objections to his system. Often critics explicitly rely on a restriction on causality known as the 'causal likeness principle', which requires that the cause be 'like' the effect. Their claim is that the unextended Cartesian mind and the unthinking Cartesian body are so unlike that the one could never cause any effect in the other, nor could one be united with the other. This objection was articulated particularly forcefully by Simon Foucher in the later seventeenth century.[22] It had considerable effect on how some of Descartes's followers articulated their positions. A closely related view, as discussed in the next section, formed the basis of Spinoza's denial of mind–body interaction. But in fact, Descartes almost never says that the cause must be 'like' the effect. Rather, he claims that the cause must have 'at least as much reality' as the effect, or 'contain the effect, formally or eminently'. ('Eminent' containment allows, precisely, that the cause does not have the same properties as the effect, as long as it has 'other, more excellent' ones.)[23] When challenged directly about the possibility of causal interaction between substances of different natures, he twice insists to his objectors that there is simply no problem.[24] Indeed, particularly when discussing sense experience, Descartes takes great pains to *stress* the dissimilarity between physical causes (motions and figures in the brain) and their mental effects (such as sensations of colour or taste). In the early *Le Monde* (1633), for example, Descartes emphasises that a sensation need be no more like its cause than a word is like its object.[25]

Problems with mind–body unity and interaction helped push some of Descartes's later followers to the doctrine of occasionalism. According to the occasionalists, God is the only genuine cause in the world; all other supposed causes are only occasional causes, occasions on which God acts to change one thing in response to the state of another. In particular, according to the occasionalists, mind and body do not interact directly; rather, God mediates between mind and body, causing appropriate sensations in the mind on the occasion of certain events in the brain, and causing motions in the body on the occasion of certain volitions in the mind.[26] It is still an open question whether – or to what extent – Descartes himself was an occasionalist, either in the general sense or with respect to mind–body interaction. It is often held that for Descartes, God is the only real cause of motion in the world of inanimate bodies, and that bodies cannot be the real cause of motion in the physical world, even in impact;[27] to this extent, Descartes may be considered an occasionalist of sorts. Now, sometimes Descartes actually speaks of brain states as the 'occasions' of the production of sensation or other mental states, using language suggestive of that used by later occasionalists to mark the indirect causal connexion between mental and corporeal states. In another passage,

found in the late *Notae in Programma* (1647), he actually says that all of a mind's
ideas, especially sensations, are innate, produced or summoned out of the mind
itself, suggesting that an event in the brain cannot be the genuine cause of an
event in the mind. Descartes writes:

> Nothing reaches our mind from external objects through the sense organs except certain
> corporeal motions. . . . But neither the motions themselves nor the figures arising from
> them are conceived by us exactly as they occur in the sense organs. . . . Hence it follows
> that the very ideas of the motions themselves and of the figures are innate in us. The ideas
> of pain, colours, sounds, and the like must be all the more innate if, on the occasion of
> certain corporeal motions, our mind is to be capable of representing them to itself, for
> there is no similarity between these ideas and the corporeal motions.[28]

Elsewhere he also uses language that suggests that the causal relation between
mind and body is somewhat indirect, particularly when dealing with the bodily
causes of sensation.[29] But it is not clear how to take such passages as these,
particularly in the light of Descartes's own clear assertions of mind–body interaction. In the passage from the *Notae,* for example, Descartes might just be concerned to emphasise, again, the radical dissimilarity between sensations and their
causes – without intending to deny that the sensations are elicited in us directly by
an event in the body. (We can say that a text must be 'innate' in the memory of a
computer without denying that the keystrokes that bring it to the screen are the
real cause of its being elicited from the memory.) Furthermore, though these
passages may suggest an indirect causal relation between mind and body, none of
them introduce God as a causal agent to mediate the connexion between the two.
And finally, although Descartes may be quite concerned with the specific cases of
mind and body, he seems almost completely uninterested in the more general
question that preoccupies almost all of the later occasionalist philosophers: namely,
whether or not finite substances as such can ever be genuine causes.[30]

   The evidence is not entirely decisive on this question. But there is no reason to
believe that Descartes worried about the general question of occasionalism in any
explicit or serious way, and there are insufficient grounds for thinking that he
believed in anything but a direct causal relation between mind and body.[31]

II. VIEWS OF THE MIND–BODY RELATION
AFTER DESCARTES

Many other seventeenth-century thinkers held to some variety of dualism or
other, some quite independently of Descartes. Among those who espoused non-

Cartesian varieties of dualism in the seventeenth century are Kenelm Digby, John Locke, Pierre Gassendi, and Henry More.

Digby never took the problems raised by dualism seriously; for Digby, it seems evident and unproblematic that the immaterial and immortal soul is joined to its body and capable of interacting with it.[32] Locke took these problems somewhat more seriously. Locke departs significantly from Descartes in so far as he admits the possibility that thought resides not in an immaterial substance joined to body, but directly in body itself.[33] Though he is very much concerned with the ontological status of mind and thought, he has nothing to say about the problem of the union of mind and body that so vexed Descartes and his followers. However, he repeatedly insists that there is a problem understanding how thought can cause bodily change and a state of the body can cause a sensation: 'How any thought should produce a motion in Body is as remote from the nature of our *Ideas,* as how any Body should produce any Thought in the Mind. That is so, if Experience did not convince us, the Consideration of the Things themselves would never be able, in the least, to discover to us.'[34] But it is important to realise that Locke acknowledges the problem only to claim that it is beyond our ability to solve. God, 'that All-wise Agent' 'has made them to be, and to operate as they do, in a way wholly above our weak Understandings to conceive'.[35] Although experience convinces us that mind and body do interact, Locke denies that we have the capacity to explain the interaction intellectually. In this case (as in many others involving causality), he is content to accept – indeed, stress – the inherent limitations of our knowledge.

Other dualists, such as Gassendi in his later writings, offered solutions that resemble Descartes's, despite the fact that he set himself against Descartes's system in so many ways. For the Gassendi of the *Syntagma,* the human soul is bipartite. The lower soul, that which is responsible for the vital functions and for sensation, is material and is composed of a collection of very fine atoms, what Gassendi calls the 'flower of matter' (*flos materiae*), spread through the living body. The higher soul or mind, which accounts for reason, is an immaterial substance, as the mind is for Descartes.[36] Gassendi, like Descartes, draws on scholastic terminology to describe how the soul and the body are united. For Gassendi, the higher immaterial soul is attached to the lower material soul as form is attached to matter, as act is connected with potency.[37] But unlike Descartes, Gassendi sees the subtle material soul, the *flos materiae,* as playing an essential rôle in uniting the mind to the body. For Descartes, as noted earlier, the soul is attached directly to the pineal gland, and through the pineal gland is capable of controlling the rest of the body. But, Gassendi argues, 'nature does not connect extremes except through intermediaries'; in particular, 'the rational part [of the soul] cannot be united with the body except through intermediate steps.' This is a function of the material soul, which is the least material of bodies, as it were, and but yet not itself incorporeal, like the rational soul.[38] This, of course, is not entirely satisfactory as it stands; though extremely subtle, the *flos materiae* is still material, and one might well ask how it can connect itself to the incorporeal rational part of the soul. To this Gassendi answers only that the human rational soul (unlike the angelic soul, a purely incorporeal substance) has a natural inclination to unite itself to the corporeal part of the soul.[39]

Henry More, like Descartes, believed in an incorporeal soul, a substance distinct from body. But unlike Descartes, he held that the soul as well as the body is extended, though only the body is impenetrable. More expressed the following view about the unity of the human mind and the body:

> That which ties the Soul and this or that Matter together, is an unresistible and unperceptible pleasure, if I may so call it, arising from the *congruity* of *Matter* to the *Plastick* faculty of the Soul: which *Congruity in the Matter* not failing, nor that in the Soul, the *Union* is at least as necessary as the continuation of eating and drinking, so long as Hunger and Thirst continues, and the Meat and Drink proves good.[40]

More also talks of a harmony between the soul and matter either fit to be organised or already 'shaped into the perfect form of an Animal', causing the vital faculties soul to want to unite with that matter, and drawing the sensitive and rational faculties with it.[41]

These figures, and others, indicate that as important as Descartes and Cartesianism were, it was not the only important trend in the later seventeenth century. At the same time, one should not underestimate the importance of Descartes's discussion of mind and body for later seventeenth-century thinkers, notably the many thinkers who explicitly identified themselves as Cartesians, followers of the master. They included more independent thinkers as well, such as Malebranche, Spinoza, and Leibniz, whose discussions of mind and body were in different ways shaped by Descartes's views and the problems that they raise. Few of Descartes's successors found the mind–body relation as unworrisome as he apparently did. In fact, philosophers after Descartes generally affirmed the impossibility of causal interaction between mind and body, while retaining other Cartesian dualist assumptions to a greater or lesser degree. These philosophers based their rejections of psycho-physical causation on different arguments, however. They also differed radically in their views about related issues, including the reality and scope of causal efficacy in the world generally, and the nature of the relation that does obtain between human minds and bodies.

1. Malebranche and later Cartesians

After Descartes's death there was widespread discussion about the causal powers of created entities – minds and bodies alike. Descartes's followers quickly came to the doctrine of occasionalism, the view that neither bodies nor minds have any real causal powers to affect one another, and that God is the only genuinely active cause in the world.[42] This, of course, had important consequences for the understanding of the relations between mind and body. A number of philosophers were involved, including Cordemoy, de la Forge, Clerselier, Clauberg, and Geulincx, among many others. The best-known and most important adherent of the occasionalist view of mind and body is, however, Nicolas Malebranche.[43]

Malebranche remains close to Descartes in his view of the basic forms of substantial existence: in his system, too, these include only God, or infinite mind, created human (and angelic) minds, and unthinking matter, of which the essence is extension, and which truly possesses only the quantifiable properties of figure and motion. But he differs radically from Descartes in his explicit position concerning the relations among individual bodies, between minds and bodies, and among minds and bodies and God. Like many later Cartesians, he denies virtually all causal efficacy to entities other than God.[44] Indeed, he goes beyond other adherents of the position in appearing to extend the thesis of occasionalism to the contents of the mind; for Malebranche, God provides us with an 'impression toward indeterminate and universal good', while the soul can only 'direct in various ways the inclination or impression that God gives it' towards particular goods.[45]

Although Malebranche is committed to the general denial of effective causality outside God's will, he devotes considerable space to specific consideration of the mind–body relation. He does acknowledge that our sense of volitional agency appears to conflict particularly vividly with the occasionalist theory, and he offers special arguments to show that this sense of direct agency is illusory.[46] But he also maintains that mind–body interaction is especially inconceivable, given the 'contrary' natures of the two entities.[47] Malebranche also adduces our ignorance of what transpires in our brains and the rest of our bodies in sensation and volitional action in support of the claim that what occurs in our minds is not really the effect or cause of what occurs in our bodies.[48]

Because there is no direct causal connexion between the world and us, Malebranche maintains, we know extended reality neither through ideas innate in our minds nor through ideas coming to us from external matter, but only through a union of our minds with God. This places him squarely within a Cartesian consensus. But he goes beyond other followers of Descartes in holding that God's rôle in our perception of bodies is not limited to causing sensations in our minds in response to the appropriate changes in our bodies. For Malebranche, all such perception requires, in addition to the sensations, apprehension of intelligible features of the extended world, as they exist in God's understanding; this is his celebrated doctrine that we see all things in God.[49]

Malebranche's view of God as an intermediary between us and the physical world has important consequences for his view of mind–body unity. Malebranche holds that the union of mind with God is 'immediate and direct', whereas the union of mind and body is merely derivative and secondary: 'Through the mind's clear vision we discover that we are united to God in a closer and more essential way than we are to our bodies.'[50] His position is that the mind–body union, correctly understood, consists exactly in God's producing sensations and the images of imagination in a given mind, upon the occurrence of certain changes in the body; and also producing certain changes in the body upon the occurrence of certain states (acts of will) in the corresponding mind. He writes:

> One need not imagine, as do most philosophers, that the mind becomes material when united with the body, and that the body becomes mind when it unites with the mind. . . . Each substance remains what it is, and as the soul is incapable of extension and movement, so the body is incapable of sensation and inclinations. The only alliance of mind and body known to us consists in a natural and mutual correspondence of the soul's thoughts with the brain traces, and of the soul's emotions with the movements of the animal spirits.[51]

In union as in interaction, Malebranche and the later Cartesians radically depart from the master. Like Descartes, some of these philosophers appeal to sensations and feelings to argue that the mind is genuinely united to the body, that we are not just pilots in our own bodily ships. Echoing Descartes, Cordemoy writes, 'Thus, if I sense pain, it is not because I have only a body or because I have only a soul, but because the one and the other are united.'[52] Although the words are close to Descartes's, the views are quite different. In so far as mind–body unity consists only in the correlation between the causes in the one and the effects in the other, a correlation grounded in God, there can be no genuine intermixture between mind and body; though united, in a sense, they are not a genuine unity, as Descartes tried to make them.

2. Spinoza

Like Malebranche and the Cartesians, Spinoza maintains that God is the universal cause. His interpretation of this doctrine differs significantly from theirs, however. Malebranche follows Descartes (and, of course, a long philosophical tradition) in regarding the physical world and human minds as substances separate from God. Spinoza, in contrast, holds that God is the only substance: all dependent things are 'in God'; they are, in fact, 'modes' or 'affections' of the 'attributes' that express God's infinite essence, or through which that essence is conceived. Although Spinoza maintains that God has infinitely many attributes, he holds that the only ones accessible to us are Thought and Extension, and his system centres on these two. But just as God can be conceived (and conceived completely) through any of His attributes, every finite thing created by God and dependent on Him can be conceived through any divine attribute, in particular, through Thought or Extension. Thus finite minds are said to be modes of the attribute of Thought, and finite bodies modes of the attribute of Extension. Indeed, the mind for Spinoza is just the idea of the body, the mode of Thought that corresponds to the mode of extension that is the body, or better, the very same finite thing, understood now under the attribute of Thought, now under the attribute of Extension. In extreme opposition to the Cartesian claim – endorsed by Malebranche – that only the human body, of all bodies in nature, has an associated mind, Spinoza maintains that *every* body does. He adds, though, that minds differ in excellence, in so far as their bodies differ in their capacity to receive a variety of stimuli from the environment and to react in complex ways.[53]

While Spinoza recognises thinking and extended things, as Descartes and his more immediate followers did, mind and body are, in an important sense, more radically distinct for him than they are even for the occasionalists. Spinoza realises that interactionist prejudices are widespread and strong; people are absolutely convinced, for instance, that 'at the mere bidding of the mind the body can now be set in motion, now brought to rest.'[54] But according to Spinoza, 'the body cannot determine the mind to think, nor can the mind determine the body to motion or rest.'[55] He bases this conclusion on the claim (an axiom in the *Ethica*) that 'knowledge (*cognitio*) of an effect depends on knowledge of the cause, and involves it.'[56] Spinoza infers from this that since attributes are conceptually distinct from each other, the modes of any given attribute can be conceived through that one attribute alone.[57] It follows, he thinks, that there can be no causal relations between modes of different attributes, and hence (since Thought and Extension are attributes) no mind–body causation. It should be stressed here that Spinoza is denying not only direct interaction, but even the sort of interaction that the occasionalists endorsed. *Everything* that goes on in mind can be explained in terms of the causal effect of finite modes of thought alone, and *everything* that goes on in body can be explained in terms of finite modes of extension alone; there is no need to appeal to bodies to explain mental states or minds to explain states of the body, with or without the help of the occasionalist's God. Spinoza particularly stresses that no mental intervention, direct or occasional, is required to explain any occurrence in the physical realm, including intelligent human behaviour of the highest order.[58] He also insists that there simply are no acts of 'free will', such as Descartes postulated: all mental states, like all physical states, have fully necessitating antecedents, modes of thought that necessitate any given state of the mind.[59] Whereas the heterogeneity of mind and body may not have disturbed Descartes, in Spinoza the radical difference between mind and body makes all causal interaction impossible.

But even though Spinoza denies mind–body interaction more radically even than the Cartesians, he conceives of the two as united even more closely than Descartes himself does. Although Spinoza's God has infinitely many attributes and can equally well be comprehended under any of His attributes, God is one. It is, in a sense, the same for the world of finite things. Spinoza writes, 'The thinking substance and the extended substance are one and the same substance, which is now comprehended under this attribute, now under that. So also a mode of extension and the idea of that mode are one and the same thing, but expressed in two ways.'[60] And so, on the one hand the body, and on the other its mind, for Spinoza the idea of that body, are, in a sense identical, the very same finite thing understood under different attributes; one cannot ask for a union closer or more inviolable than that. Because of this, there is a strict parallelism between what goes on in the one and what goes on in the other: 'The order and connection of ideas is the same as the order and connection of things.'[61] As a consequence, Spinoza holds that a mind has knowledge of, or 'perceives', everything that happens in its body, in so far as there will be in the mind ideas that correspond to all of the parts of that body.[62] And a given volition of the mind is simply the expression, under the attribute of thought, of the endeavour (*conatus*) a body has to persevere in its being.[63]

Spinoza gives every sign of believing that he has provided a clear and straightforward account of the mind–body relation, in place of untenable and obscurantist Cartesian teachings. His own position presents many difficulties, however. For one thing, because his explanation of the mind–body relation depends directly on the relation of modes and attributes to one another and to substance, it cannot fully be understood without a clear understanding of the latter relationship, one of the most difficult conceptions in Spinoza's thought.[64] Moreover, Spinoza gives us little or no help in coming to terms with some of the more problematic features of his theory of the mind–body relation in particular. For instance, he does not explain just how we are to understand the claim that the mind perceives 'everything that happens' in the body, or to reconcile that claim with our evident lack of awareness of a very great deal of what happens in our bodies. One thing that *is* clear is that Spinoza rejects the Cartesian dogma that all mental states are, by their very nature, accessible to consciousness. In this and some other respects his position on the mind–body relation is closer to Leibniz than to Descartes.

3. Leibniz

Leibniz's discussions of the mind–body relation are among the most detailed and complicated of the period: the subject is one of his favourites. Leibniz followed Descartes and Malebranche in regarding the human soul as an indivisible, immaterial thinking substance with perception and will. But according to his mature position, all reality is endowed with souls or soul-like substances, which he calls 'monads' in his later writings. Human and other animal souls have a mixture of conscious and unconscious perceptions; the human soul is, however, distinguished from the souls of subhuman animals by reason (which it shares with God – the chief monad – and angels). Souls of one sort or another are, then, spread throughout nature. But Leibniz gave a number of apparently different characterisations of the physical world of supposedly inanimate bodies and seems to have held a number of different views as to how souls are related to bodies. According to one characterisation, particularly prominent in the correspondence with Arnauld in the late 1680s, bodies are made up of tiny organisms, each of which has a soul. These tiny organisms are genuine (corporeal) substances, genuinely active unities whose soul is the form of the body. Elsewhere – in the *Specimen Dynamicum* (1695), for example – he portrays the physical world as composed of corporeal substance whose form and matter (soul and body) are characterised in terms of active and passive primitive force. Finally, in the view that dominates Leibniz's later years, bodies are resolved into aggregates of simple substances (monads), conceived on the model of a Cartesian soul.[65] At each stage of his thought, Leibniz conceived the world as filled with souls of various sorts; Leibniz, like Spinoza, was a kind of panpsychist.

Leibniz explained the relation between mind and body by means of what he came to call the hypothesis of pre-established harmony. (He was proud of having invented this position and regularly identified himself as the 'author of the system of pre-established harmony'. Though the doctrine has roots in Leibniz's earlier thought, it is first presented publicly in the *Système nouveau* of 1695, one of Leibniz's favourite publications.[66] The most striking presentation of the view in comparison with other conceptions of the mind–body relation appears in a response to criticisms of the *Système nouveau*. Leibniz writes:

Consider two clocks or watches in perfect agreement. Now this can happen in three ways: the first is that of a natural influence. . . . The second way to make two faulty clocks always agree would be to have them watched over by a competent workman, who would adjust them and get them to agree at every moment. The third way is to construct these two clocks from the start with so much skill and accuracy that one can be certain of their subsequent agreement. Now let us put the soul and the body in place of these two watches; their agreement or sympathy will also come about in one of these three ways. The way of influence is that of the common philosophy; but since we can conceive neither material particles nor immaterial qualities or species that can pass from one of these substances to the other, we must reject this opinion. The way of assistance is that of the system of occasional causes. But, I hold, that is to appeal to a *Deus ex machina* in a natural and ordinary matter, where, according to reason, God should intervene only in the sense that he concurs with all other natural things. Thus there remains only my hypothesis, that is, the way of pre-established harmony, through a prior divine artifice, which has formed each of these substances from the beginning in such a way that by following only its own laws, laws it received with its being, it nevertheless agrees with the other.[67]

This puts Leibniz's views into the historical context in which he saw them as fitting. Leibniz agrees wholeheartedly with Malebranche and the occasionalists that there can be no causal interaction between mind and body; indeed, he holds with them that there can be no causal interaction between *any* created substances. His reasons for holding this position are somewhat less evident, however. Often he seems to suggest that there could be causal interaction between substances only if there is 'influx' from one into the other, and that this notion is untenable and discredited.[68] At times, he argues that it is simply in the nature of a substance as such to contain the grounds of all of its properties, and so any sort of genuine causal interaction is superfluous.[69] At others, particularly in his later writings in which unextended monads seem to be the only substances he recognises, Leibniz argues that since 'monads have no windows', since they are simple and have no parts, they cannot be altered by any finite substance external to themselves.[70] Leibniz also has more specific reasons for denying the interaction between mind and body, claiming that action of mind on body would result in the violation of conservation laws in physics (see Section III).

Although Leibniz accepts the occasionalist critique of direct interactionism, he does not accept the positive doctrine. In particular, he insists that the occasionalist conception of divine causality involves the postulation of a continual miracle and must be rejected. In explaining this point to Arnauld, Leibniz holds that 'God performs a miracle when he does something that surpasses the forces he has given to creatures and conserves in them.'[71] And so, he reasons, the occasionalists make every voluntary motion of the body or adventitious idea in the mind a divine miracle, in so far as these are effects that bodies and souls cannot accomplish by their own power, according to the doctrine of occasionalism.[72]

In place of both direct interaction and occasionalism Leibniz seeks to establish his own conception of pre-established harmony: 'We must say that God has originally created the soul, and every other real unity, in such a way that every-thing in it must arise from its own nature by a perfect *spontaneity* with regard to itself, yet by a perfect *conformity* to things without.'[73] On Leibniz's view, then, what makes the events in minds and bodies correspond with one another is neither direct influence nor the immediate action of God, but a correspondence between states and events in the one and in the other, instituted from the beginning by an omniscient and omnipotent God.

But pre-established harmony has another implication for Leibniz. According to this doctrine, as he understands it, all of the 'perceptions' of the soul (a simple substance) arise from within the soul out of its own previous states, in accordance with an internal principle of activity which Leibniz likens to will, or (in the lowest monads) to something 'analogous to' appetition. Thus the changes in souls, according to Leibniz, are governed by teleological principles, 'laws of good and evil'. At the same time, he also vigorously maintains (like Spinoza and Hobbes) that in the world of bodies that results from his metaphysically basic substances, particular physical occurrences must always be explained by purely mechanical, physical causes. And by pre-established harmony, the two *always* correspond. Thus we can say not only that individual substances express one another's states ac-cording to a pre-established harmony, but also that a given mind and its body act in perfect harmony with each other, each according to its own laws (respectively teleological and mechanical). In a long exchange with Pierre Bayle, Leibniz insists particularly strongly on the point that even human bodies are, in all their behav-iour, mere automata, which would write, talk, and move just as they do now if (*per impossibile*) minds were altogether lacking in the world. In a comment on the 1702 edition of Bayle's *Dictionnaire,* Leibniz contrasts his position on the relation between human and animal bodies doubly with that of the Cartesians: 'According to me, they are all Automata, the bodies of men as well as those of Beasts, but all animated, the bodies of beasts as well as those of men.'[74] Or, as he put it later in the *Monadologie* (1714):

The soul follows its own laws and the body also follows its own; and they agree in virtue of the harmony pre-established between all substances, since they are all representations of a single universe. . . . Souls act according to the laws of final causes, through appetitions, ends, and means. Bodies act according to the laws of efficient causes or of motions. And these two kingdoms, that of efficient causes and that of final causes, are in harmony with each other. . . . According to this system, bodies act as if there were no souls (though this is impossible); and souls act as if there were no bodies; and both act as if each influenced the other.[75]

In explaining the relation between mind and body, Leibniz sometimes indicates that a given mind expresses its body (or the substances which ground the bodily appearance) more immediately and more distinctly than it expresses other bodies (or the substances which ground them): it expresses other bodies through its own.[76] This position, which has affinities with Spinoza's account of perception, is expounded in most detail in Leibniz's correspondence with Arnauld, just at the beginning of the period when his metaphysical system takes its mature form. Arnauld strongly questions the proposition that our soul generally expresses the state of our own body more distinctly than the states of distant bodies: if this were so, he suggests, our souls should be acquainted with an infinite number of bodily processes, such as digestion and nutrition, of which they have no knowledge.[77] Leibniz, in reply, indicates that his position does not require that we are distinctly aware of all bodily processes.[78] He stresses that 'conspicuous' changes in the body are more quickly noticed by the soul than any external changes.[79] In later writings he continues to indicate that the soul expresses other bodies through its expression of its own.[80]

Pre-established harmony provides an obvious solution to the problem of mind–body interaction, an alternative both to the direct interactionism that Descartes held and to the occasionalism of his followers. But the situation is somewhat less clear with respect to the unity of mind and body. Leibniz quite clearly intended the hypothesis of pre-established harmony to provide an account of the union of mind and body. In some notes from 1690 he writes, 'The union of soul and body in man consists in that most perfect agreement, in which the series of motions corresponds to the series of thoughts.'[81] Similarly, the *Système nouveau* of 1695, in which the view is first published, indicates in its full title that the essay will deal with the 'communication of substances and . . . the union of the soul and body'. In that essay Leibniz declares that it is the harmony between mind and body 'which alone brings about the union of soul and body'.[82] This claim was an important one for Leibniz. For in addition to unifying the body and soul in the human being, pre-established harmony was to explain – at least in the mid-1680s and 1690s – how souls and bodies were to be united throughout nature in forming corporeal substances, the unities that seem to ground the physical world.[83] Leibniz's view here is similar to that of the occasionalists, for whom mind–body unity consists simply in the correspondence God maintains between the one and the other.

But the sense in which pre-established harmony can unify the soul and the body turns out to be problematic, as Leibniz was made to see. The point was stressed by René-Joseph de Tournemine, who wrote, appealing to the two-clock formulation of Leibniz's doctrine: 'Thus correspondence, harmony, does not bring about either union or essential connection. Whatever resemblance one might suppose between two clocks, however justly their relations might be considered perfect, one can never say that the clocks are united just because the movements correspond with perfect symmetry.'[84] Leibniz has a problem here that the occasionalists do not have. For the occasionalists, mind and body are linked by God, who continually is relating what goes on in the one to what goes on in the other. This, one can argue, is a genuine bond between the two. But Leibniz's preestablished harmony allows the two to be linked only by bare correspondence; this, Tournemine claims, quite plausibly, is no link at all.

Leibniz's first response to Tournemine's objection is to dismiss the problem. In a letter he wrote to de Volder after seeing Tournemine's criticism, Leibniz argues that 'that metaphysical union, I know not what, that the schools add, over and above agreement, is not a phenomenon, and we do not have any notion of it or acquaintance with it. And so I could not have intended to explain it.'[85] In a published reply, Leibniz is a bit more sympathetic, comparing the mind–body unity with the mysteries of the faith; in so far as we have only obscure conceptions of them, we cannot offer genuine explanations.[86] But in his late correspondence with Des Bosses, Leibniz attacked the problem more directly, and experimented with various ways in which the soul (form) can be joined with the body (matter) so as to form a genuine unity, a genuine corporeal substance.[87]

Leibniz's position on the mind–body relation unsurprisingly encountered much resistance from his contemporaries.[88] Unlike occasionalism, pre-established harmony never became a generally accepted alternative to Descartes's interactionism, much to Leibniz's disappointment, no doubt.

III. MIND, BODY, AND THE LAWS OF NATURE

In discussing Leibniz, we noted that an important feature of his pre-established harmony was the fact that on that view, Leibniz thought that he could explain the apparent interaction between mind and body, the fact that a volition in the mind is followed by the wiggle of a finger, say, while at the same time everything that happens in the body can be given a mechanistic explanation in terms of size, shape, motion, and their laws. This raises a more general question about the relation of the mind to the world of the mechanical philosophy as treated more widely in the seventeenth century.

Important to the mechanist picture of the world was the idea of a law of nature; the behaviour of bodies, it was assumed, is governed by a nexus of quantitative laws expressible in terms of notions like size, mass, speed, and direction – laws that govern all bodies, at least all inanimate bodies.[89] It was not obvious, though, how human beings were to be fitted into the framework of physical law, that is, the extent to which human beings and their bodies are subject to the same laws that govern other bodies, and the extent to which our special status or our special endowments entitle us to exemptions from those laws. The general question of the place of the human being in nature and its relation to the world of inanimate bodies is an old question, one that can be raised in the context of virtually any philosophical system. But the question of whether human beings are governed by the same laws that govern inanimate nature is somewhat different, and although it may be a question that could have been raised earlier, it appears quite strikingly new when set against the background of late scholasticism, the dominant intellectual tradition against which the mechanical philosophy was proposed.

In the Aristotelian framework characteristic of late scholasticism, the world was divided into a number of kinds of substances, each with its own form, essence, or nature, and each with its characteristic behaviour derived from that form. As the Coimbrian Fathers wrote in their commentary on Aristotle's *Physics*, a book widely read in the schools in the early seventeenth century: 'Certain proper and particular behaviors [*functiones*] belong to individual natural things, as, for example, reasoning belongs to humans, neighing to horses, heating to fire, and so with other things. But behaviors of this sort cannot arise from matter, which as we showed above, has no force for bringing anything about. Therefore they arise from substantial form.'[90] The schoolmen were not entirely uninterested in either mathematical laws or in general laws that govern nature.[91] But it is fair to say that hylemorphism in metaphysics and the preference for explanations of the behaviour of a body in terms of its substantial form were central; what was of interest was not general law, but laws peculiar to specific kinds of entities. In this context, there was little in the way of general law into which a person might or might not fit. In this framework, the human being had its own characteristic behaviour, its own laws, derived from its own form, just like anything else in nature.

But one of the important moves in the mechanical philosophy was replacing this diversity with uniformity. Instead of a world of many substances, each with its own essence, the world of the mechanical philosophy was a world of material substances, all of which share the same *essence*.[92] For the mechanical philosopher, two bodies (at least inanimate bodies) differed not in their nature, but in their modes, in the particular shape, size, and motion that a body (or its parts) have. And so, it followed, since all bodies have the same essential nature, all bodies must have the same characteristic behaviour, behaviour expressed in the quantitative laws of motion and impact. It was only in the context of such a conception of the laws of nature that the question at hand could be raised; it was only when a world of distinct natures was replaced by a world of uniform nature with a single set of laws that philosophers could ask how human beings and their characteristic behaviour fit in.

For a materialist like Hobbes or a naturalist like Spinoza, there is no particular problem here. If there is nothing more to the human being than a body, as Hobbes argued, then the human being must satisfy the same laws that other bodies satisfy. And if human beings are modes of substance on a par with other modes, as Spinoza argued, then when we conceive of ourselves under the attribute of extension, we must satisfy the same laws that any other mode conceived under the attribute of extension would have to follow. But the problem would seem to be of some importance to those who saw humans as having an incorporeal soul, and thus being different from the rest of nature.

1. Leibniz's complaint and a Cartesian answer

Of all of the main figures of the seventeenth century, Leibniz was the one most explicitly concerned with the question at hand. His view comes out nicely in an argument directed against Descartes and his followers that Leibniz repeated often. Writing in the *Théodicée* in 1710, harping on a familiar theme of his, Leibniz set out Descartes's position as follows:

> M. Descartes wanted . . . to make a part of the action of the body depend on the mind. He thought he knew a rule of nature which, according to him, holds that the same quantity of motion is conserved in different bodies. He did not judge it possible that the influence of the mind could violate this law of bodies, but he believed, however, that the mind could have the power to change the direction of the motions which are in bodies.[93]

This brief account of Descartes's view requires some further explanation.

Basic to Descartes's account of the laws of nature was his conservation law, both in the early and suppressed *Le Monde* (1633) and in the final treatment in the *Principia Philosophiae* (1644).[94] According to that law, the total quantity of motion, as measured by the size (mass) of each body multiplied by its speed remains constant. It is important to remember, though, that Descartes's conservation law, unlike the principle of conservation of momentum (to use its modern name), which it superficially resembles, did *not* govern the direction in which a body is moving. So, if in a system of bodies one body changes its direction (if, e.g., it is reflected off a wall) then, as long as it maintains its original speed, there is no change in the total quantity of motion; no compensatory change in the direction of another body is required to satisfy Descartes's law, as would be the case in connexion with the conservation of momentum. Changes in direction were governed not by the conservation law, but by what is often called Descartes's law of inertia.[95] According to that law, a body in motion in a given direction will remain in motion in that direction unless it is interfered with by an external cause. And so although change of direction cannot be entirely arbitrary, changes in direction are by themselves irrelevant to the law of the conservation of motion.

This feature of Descartes's conservation law opened an obvious possibility with respect to his account of mind and body. Descartes clearly held that minds could cause events in the physical world by acts of free will. And it is also at least initially plausible to suppose, as Leibniz did, that Descartes wanted such interaction to take place without violating his conservation law. Now, if we suppose that mind acts on body by changing the *direction* with which some piece of matter is moving without changing its *speed,* then the two commitments could be reconciled, and mind could act on body without causing a violation in the laws that govern the rest of nature. Since speed would be unchanged, the quantity of motion would remain the same, and the conservation law would hold even for systems that included human beings. Furthermore, since the volition that would cause the change of direction is a cause external to the body in question, then the law of inertia would be unviolated as well. In this way, then, however different the Cartesian person might be from the surrounding bodies – a substantial union of mind and body in a world of extended substance – its body could be construed as falling under the same laws as the rest of the material world and causing no disruption in the world of the mechanical philosophy.

However, Leibniz is quick to point out that this position rests on a mistake and is undermined by the true laws of motion that he, Leibniz (among others), had discovered only after Descartes's death. In a passage immediately following the one quoted earlier. Leibniz writes:

[But] two important truths on this subject have been discovered since M. Descartes. The first is that the quantity of absolute force which, indeed, is conserved, is different from the quantity of motion, as I have demonstrated elsewhere. The second discovery is that the same direction is conserved among all of those bodies taken together which one supposes to act on one another, however they may collide. If this rule had been known to M. Descartes, he would have rendered the direction of bodies as independent of the mind as their force. And I believe that this would have led him directly to the hypothesis of pre-established harmony, where these same rules led me.[96]

The claim is that when Descartes's mistaken laws are replaced by the true ones, the position Leibniz attributed to him is no longer available. In particular, when the conservation of quantity of motion is replaced by the conservation of momentum, a law that constrains directionality as much as it does speed, then a change in direction through the activity of mind, a change that is allowable under the Cartesian laws of motion, is as much a violation of the laws of motion as a change in speed would be. In our world, Leibniz argues, Cartesian interactionism entails a violation of physical law, a conception of the human being as standing outside the laws of nature, whatever Descartes may have thought. This attack is directed not only at Descartes but also at his occasionalist followers: what is important to his attack is not the particular mechanism by which mind acts on body, but the very idea that mind can act on body in such a way as to disrupt the laws of nature. As Leibniz points out immediately after his attack on Descartes in the above passage, the system of occasional causes does no better than the 'common opinion' of direct interactionism at avoiding 'the derangement of natural law'.[97] The conclusion of this argument is, of course, Leibniz's own hypothesis of pre-established harmony, on which the appearance of interaction between mind and body is preserved without any disruption of natural law (see Section II.3).

2. Descartes on mind, body, and the laws of nature

Leibniz took it for granted that Descartes's laws of motion were intended to be universal and to apply to human beings in just the same way that they apply to everything else; his criticism of Descartes is cogent only if Descartes is committed to the universality of physical law. Many versions of the conservation law do, indeed, suggest that the law was intended to hold universally. For example, when introducing the conservation law in the *Principia,* Descartes wrote: 'God . . . in the beginning created matter along with motion and rest, and now, through his ordinary concourse alone, conserves just as much motion and rest in the whole of it as He put here at that time.'[98] It is hard to see how this statement could be true if minds were allowed to add and subtract motion from the world literally at will. But when Descartes was being especially careful, he seemed to have allowed that his conservation law may admit of some exceptions. For Descartes, the conservation law followed from the immutability of God. And so Descartes wrote just a few lines following the passage just quoted: 'Therefore, *except for changes [in quantity of motion] which evident experience or divine revelation render certain,* and which we perceive or believe to happen without any change in the Creator, we ought not to suppose that there are any other changes in his works, lest from that we can argue for an inconstancy in Him.'[99] Descartes clearly admitted that there *can* be violations of the conservation law, circumstances in which motion is added or taken away. The reference to divine revelation suggests that some such violations might arise from miracles. But Descartes also made reference to violations that 'evident experience . . . renders certain'. An obvious suggestion as to what Descartes had in mind is the ability that the human mind has to set the human body in motion, which, as he told Arnauld, 'is shown to us every day by the most certain and most evident experience'.[100] This natural reading is confirmed a few pages later in the *Principia,* where Descartes discussed his third law of motion, a law explicitly governed by the conservation law, in which he set out the general features of his account of impact. Descartes wrote, 'And all of the particular causes of the changes which happen to bodies are contained in this third law, at least insofar as they are corporeal; for we are not inquiring into whether or how human or angelic minds have the force [*vis*] to move bodies.'[101]

Furthermore, the change-of-direction account of mind–body interaction that Leibniz thinks is supposed to reconcile mind–body interaction with the universality of physical law is very difficult to find in Descartes's writings. Although there are hints and suggestions of this position,[102] there is nothing like a clear statement of the claim in Descartes's writings. In fact, there is one passage that suggests quite the contrary, that mind can cause changes in speed as well as direction. In an undated note, Descartes contrasted acceleration under a uniform force with the sort of acceleration that a heavy body in free fall has, an acceleration that on Descartes's account of gravity, must be non-uniform in so far as it is a consequence of the interaction of a body with the medium surrounding it. Descartes noted that a uniform accelerative force, whose properties he was then studying, 'is of course imparted [to a body] by mind, for there can be no such force otherwise'.[103] In so far as this force results in added speed, as Descartes assumed in the passage, mind can alter the speed of a body. Although the note is hard to date, it is almost certainly from the mid-1630s when Descartes's mature thought was reasonably well formulated. Though Descartes may have changed his position later in life, in the absence of any clear indications to the contrary there is reason to believe that the position Leibniz criticised may not have been the one Descartes held.[104]

But on what grounds could Descartes have exempted human beings from the laws of motion? Why does the fact that a body is united with a mind exempt it from the laws that it would otherwise have to obey? Although Descartes does not address this question directly, there are at least two lines he could have followed.

One line starts with a doctrine discussed in Section I:[105] Descartes conceived of the human being as a genuine union of mind and body, and in this sense something distinct from the mental and material substances that go to make it up. And so it would have been open to him to argue that in so far as the human being is different from body, it is not bound by the laws that bind bodies; like the Aristotelian substances after which it was, in a sense, modeled, it can be held to follow its own laws, deriving from the soul, its own substantial form. While this line is plausible, it has an evident problem. Surely some of the laws applicable to inanimate bodies are also applicable to bodies united to minds. A human body united to a mind must satisfy the laws of geometry; nor can it be in two places at once, or violate the strictures against vacua in Descartes's physics, among many others. If there are some laws that a human being can violate, it must somehow involve the nature of the laws themselves, as well as the nature of the creature.

This leads to another way of understanding why Descartes may have thought that humans are exempt from the conservation law.[106] The laws of motion for Descartes derived from God. In sustaining the world by continually re-creating it from moment to moment, God, in His immutability, created the world so as to preserve from one moment to the next the same quantity of motion.[107] But God is not the only cause of motion in the world. As Descartes wrote to Henry More in 1649:

> The translation which I call motion is a thing of no less entity than shape. Indeed it is a mode in a body. The force moving [a body] can be that of God himself conserving the same amount of translation in matter as he put in it in the first moment of creation, or also [it can be] that of a created substance, like our mind or that of some other thing to which He gave the force for moving a body.[108]

Now, when God causes motion, the motion he causes must observe the conservation law. But there is no reason at all to impose similar constraints on finite and imperfect causes of motion; they may add and subtract motion from the world, even if God cannot. If this is right, then for Descartes, animate bodies could stand, as it were, outside of the world of purely mechanical nature, and the conservation principle would seem to govern only purely mechanical systems in nature, systems in which God is the only cause of motion.[109] It is plausible to think that just as Descartes's *homme* was ontologically distinct from the mechanistic world, he was nomologically distinct as well.

Leibniz's argument attacked a particular way of reconciling mind–body interaction (voluntary motion) with the laws of motion within the framework of Descartes's physics and metaphysics. To the extent that Descartes may not actually have believed that the conservation law holds for humans, or that mind acts on the direction of motion alone, Leibniz's attack may not have been on the mark. But even if the position was not actually held by Descartes, it was not a straw man invented by Leibniz only for refuting. The change of direction account of mind–body interaction is found in a wide variety of texts written by Descartes's followers. It appears as early as 1646 in the writings of Henricus Regius, in the *Fundamenta Physices,* the Cartesian physics text that Descartes repudiated.[110] The same account of how the mind acts on the body appears again a little more than a decade later in a letter that Henry More wrote, where it is not endorsed but presented as a way that Descartes might be able to get himself out of the problem of the apparent violation of his conservation principle.[111] It appears in a 1660 letter from Claude Clerselier, Descartes's literary executor, to de la Forge.[112] After that, the change-of-direction account of mind–body interaction seems to have become a standard view among the Cartesians.[113] It is fair to surmise that even if Descartes may not have held such a position, it was a position associated with the Cartesian school, and, perhaps, part of the oral tradition of Cartesianism in the later seventeenth century.

3. Malebranche on mind, body, and the laws of nature

Descartes seems to have allowed human beings to add and subtract motion from the world. But some of the arguments that may have been open to Descartes were not open to the occasionalists writing later in the century, such as his disciple Malebranche, who perhaps more than Descartes himself was explicitly concerned with the question of fitting human beings and their voluntary motions into a nature governed by laws. Since on the occasionalist conception of the unity of mind and body, the human being is united only by God, through the divinely maintained correspondence between events in the mind and events in the body, and since the human being lacks the closer unity it seems to have for Descartes, an occasionalist could not appeal to the special nature of the human being to justify the way its body would appear to violate the laws of physics. And since occasionalists recognised only God as a genuine cause in nature, they could not allow minds to do anything in bodies that God would not do. For Descartes, activity was shared by God and His immaterial creatures, and a violation of the laws that govern the material world could be explained by the activity of finite creatures. But for the occasionalists, since God is the only active cause in the world, any disruptions would have to be laid at the feet of God Himself. As noted earlier, many occasionalists in the Cartesian school adopted the change-of-direction account of mind–body interaction and argued that there really were no disruptions of physical law, even in voluntary action. But Malebranche seems to have taken a different view.

On the one hand, Malebranche certainly recognised the apparent changes that we can produce in the world of bodies through acts of will. Malebranche's full position introduced many complexities that are not in Descartes; we do not, on his account, directly cause our bodily movements, nor can we demonstrate with absolute certainty that there is a world of bodies for us to move.[114] Nevertheless, he was certainly willing to grant that what we do has an effect on what goes on in the material world, if there is one and if it pleases God to mediate between our souls and the world. Furthermore, he was willing to admit that such voluntary action constitutes a genuine disruption in the laws of motion that otherwise govern body. Following Saint Augustine, Malebranche believed that since the soul is more perfect than the body to which it is joined, Adam must have been created with the ability to control his body absolutely (with God's help, of course), altering the laws it would follow were it left to its own devices. Were it not for the Fall we, too, would have this ability, and Malebranche argues that the limited control we do have over our bodies is a vestige of that original state.[115]

On the other hand, Malebranche's God is an orderly and parsimonious God. 'God always acts with order and in the simplest ways,' he wrote in the *Recherche de la vérité* in 1675.[116] At first casually announced, this conception of God became more and more central in Malebranche's thought, appearing conspicuously in the later *Eclaircissements* to the *Recherche,* in the *Traité de la nature et de la grace* (1680), and the *Entretiens sur la métaphysique* (1688). The order that governs God's activity would *seem* to favour laws that are universally applicable over laws that admit of exceptions. This, in turn, would seem to undermine the ability of the mind to act on the body, even with God's help; whether the mind is a real cause (as in Descartes) or an occasional cause of a motion (as in Malebranche), it is likely that its power over the body would be able to cause violations in any such universal laws. And if God is asked to cooperate in this business, He is being asked to disorder His own creation, it would seem.[117]

The apparent tension between the order that governs God's activity and the ability of mind to control body was resolved as Malebranche's system developed and as he worked out his notion of order in a more careful way. As the view developed, Malebranche came to hold that the order with which God created the world, that is, the order of the laws which God has taken it upon Himself to follow when performing His function as the sole active cause in nature, is an elaborate hierarchy. Although there were some complications, he came to recognise five discrete orders of divine law. As he characterised them in the *Entretiens sur la métaphysique* (1688), published fourteen years after the first edition of the *Recherche,* there are

1. General laws of the communication of motion. . . .
2. Laws of the union of soul and body, the modalities of which are reciprocally occasional causes of changes in each other. . . . It is by these laws that God unites me to his works.
3. Laws of the union of soul with God. . . .
4. General laws which give good and bad Angels power over bodies, substances inferior to their nature. . . .
5. Finally, the laws by which Jesus Christ received sovereign power in Heaven and on earth.[118]

Within this hierarchy, the laws of the higher order were in general intended to dominate those of lower orders in the sense that God would violate a law from a lower order if doing so were required for following a law of a higher order. And so, Malebranche held, laws of divine justice and angelic power dominate the laws of motion, and the latter must give way to the former when the blind following of the laws of motion would result in the violation of a higher law.[119] And similarly, on Malebranche's view, because the soul is more perfect than the body, we, too, can alter the laws of motion without violating the order God imposed on the world. The very raising of my arm would have to be a miracle standing outside the order of general law, if the only laws of nature we knew were those of the mechanical philosophy.[120] But order itself requires that the soul dominate the body.[121] That is, it is built into the very structure of the general laws that God has taken upon Himself to follow that He will suspend the laws of motion in favour of the laws of mind–body unity.[122] Such suspensions, Malebranche emphasised, are not changes or corrections; they are an integral part of the order itself.[123]

It would be misleading to suggest that Malebranche's conception of order and the hierarchy of law was primarily intended to deal with the problem of mind, body, and the laws of physics. Malebranche's motivation was complex, and if anything, his primary concerns were more theological than purely metaphysical on this issue. He was especially concerned to explain the presence of merely useless and genuinely evil things in the world, and why the just are not always rewarded while the unjust sometimes are.[124] Be this as it may, Malebranche's conception of law and order does in the end make coherent sense of the place of the human being in the order of nature. Human beings transcend the laws that govern body because God in His wisdom has granted them laws of behaviour that allow them to.

This account is different in significant ways from the one Descartes gave. For Descartes, it seems, human beings could cause violations of the laws of physics because of the kinds of things they are, because as causes of motion they are not bound by the laws that govern God as a cause of motion. For Malebranche, all laws ultimately derive from God's activity, so that the laws that govern mind–body interaction are laws that God had agreed to follow. When Malebranche talked of the ability the mind has to suspend, in its small way, the laws of motion, he was really talking about *God's* decision to suspend one set of laws and follow another in a specifiable circumstance.

Despite these differences, there is a kind of underlying similarity. As noted in Chapter 23, dualists like Descartes and Malebranche accommodated human beings into the mechanical world by positing something, an incorporeal soul, utterly unlike anything else in the world, and of use only in explaining what goes on in humans. In this way, human beings were, for mechanist dualists, in an important sense unlike the rest of the inhabitants of the natural world. But now with the special ontological status comes a special nomological status as well, at least for some dualists. Both Descartes and Malebranche fashioned conceptions of the laws of nature in general and the laws of physics in particular that placed the human being outside the scope of the laws that govern inanimate nature. In this way, Descartes and Malebranche join other thinkers, such as More and Cudworth, who believe that the mechanical philosophy tells only part of the story.[125]

NOTES

1 See Chapter 23 for a fuller development of this theme.
2 Descartes sometimes uses terms such as 'sense' and 'imagination' with reference to the cerebral states underlying the (conscious) mental ones: cf. *Traité de l'homme,* AT XI 77; Resp. VII, AT VII 436–7.
3 See Descartes to Elisabeth, 28 June 1643, AT III 691–2; Descartes to Arnauld, 29 July 1648, AT V 222.
4 See AT VII 79–80 and *Princ.* II 1. See the account of these arguments in Chapter 19 in this book.
5 AT VI 56–9. These arguments are discussed in more detail in Chapter 23.
6 AT VII 81, 227–8; see *Disc.* V, AT VI 59. On the historical background to this metaphor, see Gilson 1925, pp. 430–1.
7 Descartes to Regius, January 1642, AT III 493.
8 *Disc. VI,* AT VI 59; Med. VI, AT VII 80–1.
9 Descartes to Regius, January 1642, AT III 493, 509; *Pass. âme* 30–1.
10 See also the discussion in Chapter 23.

11 Although Descartes normally characterises sensations and passions as ('confused') modes of thought, occasionally he classifies them as modes of the mind–body union, as if the union really were a substance in its own right. See, e.g., *Princ.* I 48; Hoffman 1990, p. 318. Some have suggested further that Descartes saw the human being as a third kind of substance over and above mind and body. See, e.g., Laporte 1950, p. 183; Hoffman 1986; Broughton and Mattern 1978; Rodis-Lewis 1971, pp. 353, 543 n. 29. Cottingham 1986, pp. 127–32 suggests a kind of intermediate view. On that view, there are three kinds of attributes: mental, material, and sensory. Though there are substances associated with the first two kinds of attributes, he argues that Descartes did not associate the third with a distinct substance.

12 Descartes to Regius, January 1642, AT III 493. On the background to the question, see Verbeek 1992b.

13 In a number of places, Descartes compares his account of mind–body unity and interaction with the scholastic account of gravity, as he understands it. See Descartes to Elisabeth, 21 May 1643, AT III 667–8; Descartes to Hyperaspistes, August 1641, AT III 424; Descartes for Arnauld, 29 July 1648, AT V 222–3; and the letter to Clerselier published in the French version of the *Meds.* in place of Gassendi's Obj. V, AT IXA 213. His point seems to be that the idea we have of mind–body interaction is the fundamental notion in terms of which we understand how the so-called 'real quality' of heaviness acts on the heavy body in free fall. So, he argues, if we can understand how heavy bodies fall, as he assumed most of his scholastically educated audience would, then we should be able to understand how mind can act on body. On this analogy, see, e.g., Garber 1983a.

14 For Elisabeth's letters, dated 6/16 May, 10/20 June, and 1 July 1643, see AT III 660–2, 683–5, IV 1–3. Descartes's replies of 21 May and 28 June are at AT III 683–8 and 690–5.

15 AT III 661.

16 AT III 665–7.

17 See her letter of 10/20 June 1643, AT III 683–5.

18 In the Latin version of the *Princ.* (1644), e.g., Descartes seems to divide all ideas into only two classes, those that pertain to extended substance, and those that pertain to thinking substance; see *Princ.* I 48, 53, 63, 65, etc. However, it is almost certain that part I of the *Princ.* was drafted in 1641, before the correspondence; he reports being at work on it in December 1640 (AT III 276) and in February 1642 announces to Regius that the entire work will be out within the year (AT III 529). But even in the 1647 French version of the *Princ.* there is no prominent reference to the 'third primitive notion'. There may seem to be an echo of the discussion in the correspondence with Elisabeth in *Princ.* I 48, French version, where we find the claim that in addition to notions that pertain to mind and to body, 'there are also certain other things we experience in ourselves which ought not to be attributed to the mind alone nor to the body alone, but to the close union that there is between them' (*Princ.* I 48, French version). However, it is very difficult to determine whether this phrase is due to Descartes or to his translator.

19 See, e.g., the account in the *Traité de l'homme,* AT XI 174ff.; Descartes to Meyssonier, 29 January 1640, AT III 19–20; Descartes to Mersenne, 1 April 1640, AT III 48–9; *Pass. âme,* secs. 31–2.

20 *Pass. âme,* sec. 30.

21 *Pass. âme,* secs. 30, 34.

22 See Watson 1966, 1987.

23 On the notion of eminent causality, see especially O'Neill 1987. It is not obvious how

the notion of eminent causality applies to body–mind interaction since it is doubtful at best that Descartes would ascribe to body, or physical modes, 'more excellent' properties than those possessed by mind, or its ideas.

24 See the letter to Clerselier published in the French version of the *Meds.*, AT VII 213, and letter to Hyperaspistes, August 1641, AT III 424. On the other hand, see Descartes's remarks in the Conversation with Burman, AT V 163. Modern commentators have differed sharply on the question of whether Descartes himself considered mind–body interaction inconceivable, and whether or not the assumption of interaction involves an absurdity. For discussion and references, see Wilson 1991.

25 This is closely connected with Descartes's claim that a 'natural convention' grounds the systematic relations that obtain between brain states and their mental effects: it is readily conceivable that God could have set up quite different causal correlations than those He did establish. See *Le Monde,* chap. 1.

26 It should be emphasised that the doctrine of occasionalism was quite general, and that the motivation for the doctrine thus goes well beyond specific problems with mind–body interaction. For a more general discussion of occasionalism, see Chapter 17.

27 See the development Descartes gives of his laws of motion in chap. 7 of *Le Monde* and in *Princ.* II 36–52. There it is reasonably clear that it is the activity of God in sustaining motion from moment to moment that stands behind the laws bodies in motion obey. For more detailed accounts, see, e.g., Hatfield 1979; Gabbey 1980a; Gueroult 1980; Garber 1992a, chaps. 7–9. See also Chapter 21 in this book.

28 AT VIIIB 359.

29 The argument for the existence of bodies in Med. VI, e.g., concludes by asserting that there is an 'active faculty' in bodies responsible for causing sensations in us. In the version of this argument in the Latin edition of *Princ.,* II 1 asserts only that the idea 'comes from' things placed outside of us. The French version of that passage is weaker still, asserting only that an idea of sensation 'forms itself in us on the occasion of bodies from without'. For a subtle analysis of the language of indirect causation in Descartes and its historical antecedents, see Specht 1966.

30 For fuller discussions of Descartes and occasionalism, see Garber 1987a, 1993a.

31 For different views on occasionalism in Descartes, see, e.g., Prost 1907; Gouhier 1926a; Specht 1966; Battail 1973; Garber 1993a.

32 See, e.g., Digby 1644a, pp. 412, 441–2. For a fuller discussion of Digby's account of mind, see Chapter 23 in this book.

33 See the discussion of Locke's position in Chapters 23 and 24. Although Locke argues that we do not know whether the mind is immaterial or not, he does grant that it is probable that it is immaterial.

34 *Ess.* IV.iii.29.

35 *Ess.* IV.iii.29. See also *Ess.* I.xxiii.25, 28; IV.x.19.

36 See the fuller account of Gassendi's view on mind and soul in Chapter 23.

37 Gassendi 1658, vol. 1, p. 258a; Bernier 1678, vol. 5, p. 487.

38 Gassendi 1658, vol. 1, p. 258a; Bernier 1678, vol. 5, p. 488. Gassendi goes on to attribute similar views to Plato, Hermes Trismegistus, Plotinus, Themistius, and Philoponus. A similar view can also be found in Marin Cureau de la Chambre; see Darmon 1985, pp. 20–1, 142–3; Balz 1951, pp. 42–64.

39 Gassendi 1658, vol. 2, pp. 443b–4a; Bernier 1678, vol. 6, pp. 361–3.

40 *The Immortality of the Soul,* More 1662d, p. 121. The 'plastick faculty' of the soul is that by virtue of which the soul can organise matter into a living body; see ibid., pp. 101–2.

41 *The Immortality of the Soul,* More 1662d, pp. 120–1.

42 See the account of occasionalism in Chapter 17.

43 Malebranche's occasionalism is presented in his *Recherche de la vérité* (1674–5), and more succinctly in his later *Entretiens sur la métaphysique et sur la religion* (1688). For a discussion of Malebranche's arguments for occasionalism, see Chapter 17 in this book.

44 For a general account of the doctrine of occasionalism, see the discussion in Chapter 17.

45 *Rech.* I.1.2, Mal. *OC* I 48, 46 (Malebranche 1980a, pp. 5, 4). See also *Eclaircissement* II, Mal. *OC* III 39–41 (Malebranche 1980a, p. 449); and *Eclaircissement* XV, Mal. *OC* III 224–8 (Malebranche 1980a, pp. 668–71).

46 *Eclaircissement* XV, Mal. *OC* III 224–8 (Malebranche 1980a, pp. 668–71). At Mal. *OC* II 317 (Malebranche 1980a, p. 450) Malebranche asks us to suppose that 'God wills to produce the opposite of what some minds will, as might be thought in the case of demons or some other minds that deserve this punishment.' He says that in such cases the demon's willing to move to the left will be the natural cause of its moving to the right. 'Thus', he concludes 'all the volitions of minds are only occasional causes.'

47 At *Rech.* V.1, Mal. *OC* II 129 (Malebranche 1980a, p. 339), for instance, he writes: 'What relation can be conceived between the idea of an enemy's faults, or a passion of contempt or hatred, on the one hand, and the corporeal movement of the blood's parts striking against certain parts of the brain on the other?' He goes on to describe mind and matter as 'remote and . . . incompatible [*éloignées & . . . inalliables*]'. See also *Ent. mét.*, dialogue IV, secs. 6–8, Mal. *OC* XII 90–3 (Malebranche 1980b, pp. 85–7). Clerselier also regards the heterogeniety of mind and body as a motivation for turning to God; see Clerselier 1667b, p. 646. But other Cartesians seem unworried by this; see, e.g., Clauberg 1664a, p. 374; de La Forge 1974, p. 312. Sometimes (e.g., at *Ent. mét.*, dialogue IV, sec. 9, Mal. *OC* XII 96 [Malebranche 1980b pp. 89–90]) Malebranche also argues that body cannot have an effect on mind because it is less 'excellent' than mind, as well as being of a different nature. (For a similar argument, see Clauberg 1664a, p. 378, secs. 9–10.) In this passage, and many others, Malebranche also stresses the 'passivity' of body (on the Cartesian conception). Whether passivity constitutes an additional ground for denying causal efficacy, or is rather simply tantamount to the lack of causal efficacy, is a debatable question, however. The passivity of body is a central aspect of other Cartesian arguments for occasionalism, though; see, for example, Clerselier 1667b, pp. 641ff.; La Forge 1974, pp. 238ff.; Cordemoy 1968, pp. 134ff.

48 See *Rech.* VI.2.2, Mal. *OC* II 315 (Malebranche 1980a pp. 449–50); *Eclaircissement* VI, Mal. *OC* III 59 (Malebranche 1980a pp. 572); *Eclaircissement* XV, Mal. *OC* III 226 (Malebranche 1980a p. 669); *Ent. mét.*, dialogue VII, sec. 13, Mal. *OC* XII 167 (Malebranche 1980b p. 163). It should be noted that Descartes explicitly denies such a view in *Pass. âme* secs. 43–4. This view of Malebranche's is very close to Geulincx's principal argument for occasionalism; see his *Metaphysica Vera*, pars I quinta scientia, Geulincx 1891–3, vol. 2, p. 150, where he argues for occasionalism from the principle that 'quod nescis quomodo fiat, id non facis'. Geulincx, though, was relatively isolated, and stood outside the mainstream of later Cartesian thought, and it is not clear just what influence he had on Malebranche or anyone else.

49 For Malebranche's views on our knowledge of the external world, see Section IV.4 in this chapter; for Malebranche's doctrine that we see all things in God, see Chapter 30.

50 *Eclaircissement* VI, Mal. *OC* III 65–6, (Malebranche 1980a p. 575); *Rech.*, V.5, Mal. *OC* II 172 (Malebranche 1980a p. 366); see also the Preface to the *Rech.*, Mal. *OC* I 9–18 (Malebranche 1980a, pp. xix–xxiv); *Ent. mét.*, dialogue VII, sec. 13, Mal. *OC* XII 165 (Malebranche 1980b p. 163).

51 *Rech.* I.5.1, Mal. *OC* I 70–1 (Malebranche 1980a, p. 20); *Rech.* V.1, Mal. *OC* II 126–9 (Malebranche 1980a, pp. 337–9); *Eclaircissement* XV, Mal. *OC* III 226–7 (Malebranche 1980a, p. 670); *Ent. mét.,* dialogue IV, sec. 11, Mal. *OC* XII 96 (Malebranche 1980b, p. 91). Sometimes he refers to this union as a 'necessary or essential relation' (*Rech.* V.1, Mal. *OC* II 126 [Malebranche 1980a p. 337]); sometimes he indicates that 'strictly speaking' mind–body union is impossible (*Ent. mét.,* dialogue VII, sec. 1, Mal. *OC* XII 149 [Malebranche 1980b p. 147]). In the former case he means that the mind is *human* (i.e., pertains to the human animal) just so long as God maintains the appropriate psychophysical correlations with respect to it. In the latter case he is trying to get across the (perfectly compatible) point that our minds and bodies do not cause changes in each other. For similar views on mind–body unity, see Clauberg 1664a, pp. 335–6 secs. 787–90; de La Forge 1974, p. 210; Cordemoy 1968, p. 170.

52 Cordemoy 1968, p. 168; see also de La Forge 1974, p. 215; Clauberg 1664, p. 414. Sometimes Malebranche says things that may be interpreted as being similar; see, e.g., *Rech.* V.5, Mal. *OC* II 172 (Malebranche 1980a pp. 365–6). But generally Malebranche's view is a bit different. For Malebranche, sensation is what seems to bind us to our body only in a kind of psychological sense; it is because of the attractiveness of sensations that we turn our minds away from God and towards the bodies to which we are attached. See, e.g., *Rech.* I.12.1–3, and I.13.4, Mal. *OC* I 135–7, 146 (Malebranche 1980a pp. 56–7, 62). But it does not generally seem to be a special sign of the union between mind and body, as it is for Descartes. Indeed, Malebranche maintains that the soul will have sensations after it is separated from the body – though he says that they will be different from the ones it has in life, and even that they 'will surpass all sensation'. See *Rech.* III.1.1.2 and IV.2.4, Mal. *OC* I 385–6; vol. II, p. 25 (Malebranche 1980a, pp. 200, 274).

53 See *Eth.* II prop. 13 schol. See Chapter 23 for a fuller discussion of Spinoza's account of mind.

54 *Eth.* III prop. 2 schol.

55 *Eth.* III prop. 2.

56 *Eth.* I ax. 4.

57 See *Eth.* II prop. 6.

58 See *Eth.* III prop. 2 schol.

59 See *Eth.* I prop. 32.

60 *Eth.* II prop. 7 schol. The last phrase of this quotation might also be translated: 'expressed through two modes'. Note that although a given mode of thought and its corresponding mode of extension are different expressions of the same *finite thing,* it is not correct, for Spinoza, to say that the mode of thought is itself identical with the corresponding mode of extension, or that the two constitute the same 'mode of substance'.

61 *Eth.* II prop. 7.

62 See *Eth.* II prop. 12. This non-causal cognitive relation is at the heart of Spinoza's account of sense perception; the mind 'knows' external things through 'perceiving' the states that they cause in its body.

63 See *Eth.* III prop.6; *Eth.* III prop 9 schol.

64 For discussion of the interpretive problem, and a variety of proposed solutions, see Gueroult 1968–74, vol. I; Curley 1969; Mark 1977; Eisenberg 1990.

65 For a fuller development of Leibniz's metaphysical views on body and soul see Chapters 18 and 23.

66 The notion of general harmony is important to Leibniz at least as early as the so-called Paris notes of 1676 and may well go back further than that; see, LAkad VI.III 472

(Leibniz 1969, p. 157). See also Leibniz to Magnus Wedderkopf, May 1671, LAkad II.I 117 (Leibniz 1969, p. 146). The special doctrine of the harmony between the mind and the body is quite prominent in the *Disc. mét.* and correspondence with Arnauld in the mid-1680s, there called the 'hypothèse de concomitance'; see *Disc. mét.* sec. 33, and Leibniz to Arnauld 28 November/8 December 1686, Ger. II 74. The connexion between the general doctrine of harmony and Leibniz's special account of the relation between mind and body is made clear in Leibniz to Arnauld, 14 July 1686, Ger. II 57, and in the so-called First Truths paper, Leibniz 1903, p. 521 (Leibniz 1989, p. 33).

67 Postscript, Leibniz to Basnage de Beauval, 3/13 January 1696, Ger. IV 498–9 (Leibniz 1989, pp. 147–8). The image may have been suggested by a comment Foucher made, Ger. IV 488–9. The clock image occurs often in Leibniz's later expositions of his view.

68 See, for example, *Syst. nouv.,* Ger. IV 486 (Leibniz 1989, p. 145), and Postscript, Leibniz to Basnage de Beauval, 3/13 January 1696, Ger. IV 498–9 (Leibniz 1989, p. 148). On the theory of influx, see O'Neill 1993.

69 See, e.g., *Disc. mét.* sec. 14.

70 See, e.g., *Mon.* sec. 7.

71 Leibniz to Arnauld, 30 April 1687, Ger. II 93 (Leibniz 1989, p. 83).

72 See also *Syst. nouv.,* Ger. IV 483–4 (Leibniz 1989, p. 143); *Entretien de Philarète et d'Ariste,* Robinet 1955, p. 453 (Leibniz 1989, p. 265). On the general question of Leibniz's relation to occasionalism, see Rutherford 1993.

73 *Syst. nouv.,* Ger. IV 484 (Leibniz 1989, p. 143).

74 Ger. IV 53.

75 *Mon.,* secs. 78, 79, 81. See also Leibniz to Arnauld, 30 April 1687, Ger. II 94–5 (Leibniz 1989, p. 84); Leibniz's reading notes on J. G. Wachter's *Elucidarius cabalisticus,* Leibniz 1854, p. 60 (Leibniz 1989, p. 279); 'Anti-barbarus physicus', Ger. VII 344 (Leibniz 1989, p. 319); *Mon.,* sec. 79; Leibniz's Fifth Paper [to Clarke], sec. 124.

76 See especially *Disc. mét.,* sec. 33.

77 Arnauld to Leibniz, 4 March 1687, Ger. II 84.

78 Leibniz to Arnauld, 9 October 1687, Ger. II 112.

79 Leibniz to Arnauld, 30 April 1687, Ger. II 90–1; 9 October 1687, Ger. 112–14.

80 See, e.g., Leibniz to de Volder, 24 March/3 April 1699, Ger. II 171–2 (Leibniz 1989, pp. 173–4); *Mon.,* sec. 62.

81 Comments on Michel Angelo Fardella, March 1690, Leibniz 1857, p. 320 (Leibniz 1989, p. 104).

82 Ger. IV 484–5 (Leibniz 1989, p. 144).

83 See the discussion of Leibniz in Chapter 23. See also Garber 1985 for a fuller development of this view.

84 Tournemine 1703, pp. 869–70. Boehm 1962 especially emphasises the importance of Tournemine for understanding Leibniz's later thought.

85 Leibniz to de Volder, 19 January 1706, Ger. II 281 (Leibniz 1989, p. 184). In a passage from the first draft of the letter, Leibniz suggests that the supposed union Tournemine demands is a chimera of the mind, something that we impose onto nature and then 'struggle with . . . as with ghosts' (ibid.).

86 See 'Remarque . . . sur un endroit des *Mémoires de Trévoux*', Ger. VI 595–6 (Leibniz 1989, pp. 196–7).

87 The solution that Leibniz seems to favour in those letters involves the celebrated doctrine of the vinculum substantiale. It is a matter of great controversy just how committed Leibniz was to the doctrine. The term 'vinculum substantiale' first appears in Leibniz to Des Bosses, 5 February 1712, Ger. II 435 (Leibniz 1989, p. 198) and

appears regularly after that in their correspondence. On the vinculum substantiale, see Boehm 1962; Fremont 1981; Robinet 1986.

88 Two exchanges are particularly noteworthy in this connexion. (1) Leibniz had a short, but concentrated correspondence with Antoine Arnauld, mainly in 1686 and 1687 (Ger. II 10–138 and Leibniz forthcoming). Although it ranges over many aspects of Leibniz's thought, the issue of pre-established harmony comes up often. (2) Following the publication of Leibniz's *Syst. nouv.*, Pierre Bayle attacked Leibniz's thought in his *Dictionnaire historique et critique*, in the article 'Rorarius', focusing on the account of mind and body presented in that essay. Leibniz's responses from 1698 (to Bayle's first edition) and 1702 (to Bayle's second edition) can be found in Ger. IV 517–71 (partially translated in Leibniz 1969, pp. 492–7, 574–85).

89 See the discussion of the mechanical philosophy in Chapters 17–21.

90 *Commentarii in octo libros physicorum Aristotelis* 1,9,9,2, in Gilson 1979, p. 127. On the doctrine of hylemorphism, see Chapter 15.

91 The most visible instance of this is the mean speed theorem of the so-called Oxford Calculators. See Clagett 1959, pp. 199–329. Sylla 1982 argues, though, that the Oxford Calculators must be regarded more as logicians and less as natural philosophers in either a mediaeval or modern sense.

92 See the discussion in Chapter 18.

93 *Théod.*, pt. I, sec. 60. This seems to have been a favourite argument of Leibniz's. Similar passages can be found from the correspondence with Arnauld in the late 1680s (Ger. II 94) to the 1714 *Mon.*, sec. 80.

94 See Chapter 21 and Garber 1992a, chaps. 7–9.

95 See *Princ.* II 37–9. The principle also appears in chap. 7 of *Le Monde.* In Descartes's formulation, there are actually two separate laws, a law of the persistence of motion as such, and a law of the persistence of rectilinearity. Although we shall continue to call these laws of inertia, properly speaking, they ought to be called laws of persistence so as to avoid confusion with the superficially similar but substantively different Newtonian laws. See Gabbey 1980a; Garber 1992a, chap. 7.

96 *Théod.*, pt. I. sec. 61. Despite the fact that Descartes never did get the laws of motion right, he may have stumbled upon a version of pre-established harmony some years before Leibniz did. The evidence is a virtually unknown passage which appears to be Descartes's own marginal notes in the *Princ.* Descartes wrote that 'it is a strong conjecture to affirm anything which, if assumed, would make God understood as being greater or the world as being more perfect; as, for example, that the determination of our will to local motion always coincides with a corporeal cause determining motion' (AT XI 654). For a discussion of this, see Garber 1983b, pp. 132–3. Ironically enough, this note was preserved only in a copy that Leibniz had made for his personal use.

97 *Théod.*, pt. I, sec. 61. See also Leibniz to Arnauld, 30 April 1687, Ger. II 92–5.

98 *Princ.* II 36.

99 *Princ.* II 36, emphasis added.

100 Descartes to Arnauld, 29 July 1648, AT V 222.

101 *Princ.* II 40, emphasis added.

102 See Section I of Gabbey 1985. Gabbey cites a number of passages where Descartes says that the mind can '*determiner*' the behaviour of the body. But even though '*determiner*' and '*determination*' are the technical terms that Descartes uses in connexion with the directional component of motion in contexts where he is distinguishing speed from directionality (see Gabbey 1980a, pp. 247ff.), there is no indication that the terminol-

ogy is ever used in the technical sense in these passages. Furthermore, in none of the passages Gabbey cites does Descartes ever seem worried about reconciling mind–body interaction with his conservation law.

103 AT XI 629. For discussions of this document see Garber 1983b, pp. 114–15, 129–30; Gabbey 1985, pp. 17–19. Again, this note is only preserved in a copy Leibniz had made for his own use.

104 This reading of Descartes can be found in whole or in part in Hamelin 1911, pp. 372–3; Laporte 1950, pp. 245–8; Remnant 1979; Garber 1983b. Gabbey 1985, sec. I, argues that Descartes did change his mind in later years. Descartes was apparently thinking about these questions in his last years and intended to address them in the unwritten sequel to the *Principia*, *De homine*. At least one of the references to *De homine* (*Princ.* II 40) deals with the question of whether and how minds can move bodies. For an alternative point of view on this issue, see McLaughlin 1993.

105 This line is argued in Remnant 1979. See also Garber 1983b, pp. 117–19.

106 This line is developed in more detail in Garber 1983b.

107 On Descartes's derivation of the laws of motion, see Chapter 21 and Garber 1992a, chaps. 7–9.

108 Descartes to More, August 1649, AT V 403–4.

109 Descartes's doctrine of continual re-creation raises a potential problem with the idea that mind causes changes in the motion of bodies. Since God sustains the world by continually re-creating it, it is not clear that there is room for other causes, like mind, to act on bodies and move them in any real sense. For a discussion of this question, see Garber 1987a.

110 See Regius 1646, p. 298. See also pp. 248–9. The motivation for Regius's claim is not clear. Though he holds that mind can change only the directions in which the spirits move, he does not relate this to the question of the universality of the conservation principle.

111 See the *Epistola H. Mori ad V.C.*, p. 114 in *Henrici Mori Epistolae Quator ad Renatum Des-Cartes . . .*, More 1662b. Alan Gabbey dates the letter to 1658 in Gabbey 1982, p. 214. More knew Regius's views on the connexion between the body and the soul in the *Fundamenta* in a later edition of Regius's writings; he refers to it in the *Immortality of the Soul*, as printed in More 1662d, pp. 81, 82, 96, 101, 122. Indeed, on p. 101 he treats Regius as an authority of sorts on Descartes's thought, a loyal follower. It is quite possible that More got the account from Regius; More never exactly attributes the view to Descartes himself. It is interesting to note that in his last letter to Descartes More had asked whether the action of the mind on the body can change the quantity of motion in the world; see AT V 385. Unfortunately, Descartes never answered.

112 Clerselier 1667b, pp. 641–3. It is interesting here that Clerselier's worries are not particularly about the conservation principle. Rather, the claim appears as part of an argument for occasionalism, where it is used to establish that finite minds cannot be the real cause of motion in the world.

113 See, e.g., Clauberg 1664a, p. 378, sec. 7; de La Forge 1974, pp. 245–6; Cordemoy 1968, pp. 140–1, 151. In these writers it is quite clear that the change of direction account of mind–body interaction is motivated by a worry about the conservation principle. This view is also reflected in Spinoza's earliest metaphysical writings; see *Korte ver.* II.19, Geb. I 91.

114 For Malebranche's position on our knowledge of the external world, see Chapter 19.

115 See *Eclaircissement* VIII, Mal. *OC* III 74, 97–8 (Malebranche 1980a, pp. 581, 594); *Conversations crétiennes* II, Mal. *OC* IV 41–2; *TNG* II, 27 and II, 44, Mal. *OC* V 95,

105. See also the discussion in Rodis-Lewis 1963, pp. 235–6. For a statement of the parallel view in Augustine, see *De Civitate Dei* XIV, chaps. 15–18.

116 *Rech.* VI.2.4, Mal. *OC* II 325 (Malebranche 1980a, p. 455); see also *Rech.* III.2.6, Mal. *OC* I 438 (Malebranche 1980a, p. 230).

117 Cf., e.g., *Eclaircissement* XV, Mal. *OC* III 214–15; 218–20 (Malebranche 1980a, pp. 663, 665–6).

118 *Ent. mét.,* dialogue XIII, sec. 9, Mal. *OC* XII–XIII 319–20 (Malebranche 1980b, p. 321). Immediately following this list, Malebranche notes a few other laws, that by which hell's fire can torment demons, that by virtue of which baptismal water can purify, etc.

119 Cf. *TNG* I, 20, 21; Mal. *OC* V 33, 34; *TNG, Premier éclaircissement . . . ,* sec. V, Mal. *OC* V 149–50.

120 *TNG, Dernier éclaircissement . . . ,* Mal. *OC* V 198–9.

121 *TNG* II, 27, Mal. *OC* V 95.

122 Or, at least, he would for Adam. This law is corrupted by sin, it seems.

123 *TNG* I, 31, Mal. *OC* V 34.

124 Cf., e.g., Rodis-Lewis 1963, chap. XIII.

125 See also the account of More and Cudworth in Chapter 23.

26

PERSONAL IDENTITY

UDO THIEL

The problem of personal identity in the form in which it is so widely discussed today had its origin in the late seventeenth century, in John Locke's chapter 'Of Identity and Diversity' which he added to the second edition of his *Essay concerning Human Understanding* (1694). That chapter contains the most detailed and original contemporary treatment of the problem, challenging traditional views about both personality and identity. It was, indeed, revolutionary, and some aspects of it are still much discussed by philosophers.[1] Locke was not, however, the only seventeenth-century philosopher to consider the topic seriously and at length. Problems of personal identity and of identity in general were widely debated long before the seventeenth century, in relation not only to metaphysics, or what is now called 'philosophy of mind', but also to moral, legal, and, especially, theological questions. The problem of identity and individuation in general – that is, the problem of what constitutes the identity of any object – is discussed in Chapter 9 of the present book. That problem is the historical as well as the systematic basis for the question of what constitutes the identity of *persons*. But there have been various responses to this latter question, depending not only on views of identity but also on which concept of person is applied. Indeed, from the notion of person adopted by some philosophers a genuine problem about the *identity* of persons might not even arise.

Hence seventeenth-century notions of personal identity cannot be fully understood without some idea of which concept of person is being employed. The term 'person' has a complex etymology, the early aspects of which can be bypassed for the purposes of this discussion. What is important to note, however, is that throughout the seventeenth century 'person' most commonly referred to an individual human being: it was simply a term for the individual human self. But in some philosophical discussions 'person' referred to a particular aspect, quality, or function of the individual human being. Indeed, the Latin term 'persona' – a

I am grateful to Michael Ayers and Daniel Garber for helpful comments on an earlier version of this chapter. I thank Christian Jessen (Göttingen) for help in obtaining material that was hard to come by.

translation of the Greek *prosopon* (face) – originally signified the mask through which an actor communicated his *rôle* to the audience. 'Persona' was then used to denote this rôle or character itself, and its denotation was transferred from the rôle on the stage to the rôle or function that an individual human being fulfils in real life.[2] Cicero, for example, formulated a theory of four *personae,* or rôles, which apply to every human being.[3] And the distinction between individual human being and person implicit in this understanding of 'persona' as rôle or quality was not lost on the philosophers of the seventeenth century.[4] The meaning of 'persona' as rôle connects with the use of the term in moral and legal contexts: in Roman law *personae* were distinguished from *res* (things) as two distinct objects of law. 'Persona' simply referred to the individual human being in so far as he or she stands in a relationship to legal matters. In a later development, 'persona' was used to refer to all bearers of rights and duties, and as such the term applied to corporate bodies as well as to human individuals. The idea of the individual human being or person as a bearer of rights and duties is also central to the Christian tradition of natural law. It is therefore not surprising that many discussions of the problem of personal identity in the seventeenth century focused on moral and legal issues: a person is regarded as someone who has rights and obligations, to whom we attribute actions, and whom we hold responsible for those actions. This notion of person as responsible human agent is not necessarily tied to the old meaning of person as rôle. In fact, orthodox Christian and scholastic doctrine was to reject the Roman understanding of *persona* altogether and to replace it by a definition of person as an individual rational *substance.* This notion of person came onto the scene as a result of Christological and trinitarian debates in the early church: it has been shown that early mediaeval discussions of individuation and of the notion of person arose out of problems relating to the doctrine of the trinity.[5] Thus, Tertullian (160–220) is said to have coined the phrase 'una substantia tres personae' to explicate the trinity. Yet it seems unclear exactly what 'substantia' and 'persona' were supposed to mean. And even though the use of 'persona' for Father, Son, and Holy Spirit had been accepted in the Christian church since the Council of Alexandria in 362, Saint Augustine (354–430) was reluctant to use the term in the trinitarian context.[6] Augustine's book on the trinity is relevant to later discussions of personality, not because he employed the term 'persona', but because in his psychological arguments for the possibility of the trinity he argued that there are triads in the soul (for example, intelligence, memory, and will) which are consistent with the oneness of the soul. Augustine appealed to these triads as analogous to the divine trinity.[7]

The term 'persona' gained its classical definition around 500 when Boethius

(480–524) began using it to refer to an Aristotelian first substance whose essence consists in rationality. He defined person as 'the individual substance of a rational nature'. Applying this definition to the trinity, Boethius speaks of 'one essence, three substances and three persons of the Godhead'.[8] Boethius also applied 'persona' to individual human beings as consisting of 'soul and body, not [of] soul or body separately'.[9] What makes human beings persons, however, is, Boethius insisted, not their corporeity, but their rationality. Obviously, the old Roman notion of person as rôle is not present in Boethius. It is equally obvious, though, that Boethius's concept of person is not identical with the modern notion of a self-conscious subject. Boethius's 'ontological' view of person as a thing or individual substance, with its emphasis on rationality, was immensely influential. It prevailed not only in mediaeval scholastic thought but also in metaphysical disputes about the person throughout the seventeenth century. (This was true even of cases where no explicit reference to the problem of the trinity was made.)

The question of human personal identity is closely related to another theological issue that was much discussed in the seventeenth century, namely, the doctrine of life after death. Philosophers and theologians realised that for the idea of a future life to make sense one needs to assume (if not to argue) that after death we shall be the *same* persons that we are now: in other words, what is now sometimes referred to as the 'identity condition' needs to be satisfied.[10] This condition is important also for the reason that, according to Christian doctrine, we shall be judged and punished or rewarded by God for actions we performed in this life: the divine rewards or punishments can be said to be *just* only if the *same* person who acted in this life will be punished or rewarded for these acts in the next life. Thus, the problem of personal identity is closely linked to the two related questions of the immortality of the soul and the resurrection of the body. The issue of the identity condition raises the further question about what is required for the *same* person to exist in the future life. And on this question some philosophers argued that it is sufficient that the same human soul continues to exist, whereas others believed that in addition the very same body a person had on earth must be resurrected.

The problem of identity through time is central to those moral and legal issues concerning the person which are mentioned above. Obviously, the identity condition needs to be satisfied not only in relation to divine judgement but also in relation to the judgements of *human* courts of law. Thus, moral and legal problems led to more fundamental, metaphysical questions about what constitutes a person and its identity through time. But the 'right answers' to these metaphysical questions were often simply assumed, rather than argued for, when the context of the discussion was primarily moral and legal.

In general, most philosophers in the seventeenth century did not discuss the whole range of issues related to the problem of personal identity; some concentrated on theological topics, some focused on moral and legal points, and some gave priority to the metaphysical questions. Quite often the issue of personal identity was addressed merely as part of a larger theological or metaphysical argument. John Locke was the first to attempt to formulate a comprehensive theory of personal identity that could deal with all those various issues to which the problem of personal identity is related (with the exception of the trinity).

I. THE 'ONTOLOGICAL' VIEW OF THE SELF: SCHOLASTIC AND CARTESIAN CONCEPTIONS

As previously indicated, Boethius's definition of person as 'the individual substance of a rational nature', although sometimes slightly modified, became standard in scholastic thought. Aquinas, for example, makes explicit reference to Boethius in discussing the notion of person in the context of his own account of the trinity. Like Boethius, Aquinas also applies the term 'persona' to substances other than the divine ones, emphasising rationality as the main characteristic of persons: 'Among all other substances individual beings with a rational nature have a special name, and this is "person".' And because of their rationality, persons are substances which 'have control over their actions' and 'act of their own initiative'.[11] In applying 'persona' to human beings, Aquinas emphasises corporeity more strongly than Boethius did. According to Aquinas, 'persona' in relation to human nature refers to '*this* flesh, *these* bones, and *this* soul which are the sources [*principia*] of man's individuality; these are indeed part of what is meant by "a human person".'[12] For Aquinas, 'a human person' is synonymous with 'individual human being', where 'man' or 'human being' is understood as being composed of soul (form) *and* body (matter). The soul as the form of man is said to be the principle of life and intellectual operations, but not, on its own, to constitute the human person. Although Aquinas argues that, unlike other forms, human souls 'can exist apart' from matter, he insists that the soul alone does not make up the man or human person: 'We can neither define it [i.e., the soul] nor speak of it as a "person".'[13] In the late sixteenth century, the Spanish scholastic philosopher Francisco Suárez also adopted the Boethian notion of person. In the thirty-fourth disputation of his influential *Disputationes metaphysicae* (1597) Suárez cites the relevant passages from

both Boethius and Aquinas, and he defines person as a *suppositum,* or first substance, of an 'intellectual or rational nature'.[14]

    Scholastic views about what individuates persons vary with the *general* theory of
individuation the thinker adopted.[15] For Aquinas, all composite beings, including
human beings, are individuated by 'designated matter'. According to Suárez, it is
the whole 'entity' which brings about individuation of human beings, that is, 'this
matter and this form united to each other'.[16] However, Suárez argued that the
soul is the 'primary' principle of individuation because, despite bodily changes,
'the individual is said to be the same by reason of the same soul.'[17] Thus, although
the various scholastic philosophers disagree on the principle of individuation, they
all seem to adopt what is essentially a Boethian concept of *person.* It was through
influential scholastics such as Suárez that the Boethian definition of person made
its way into the metaphysical textbooks and dictionaries of the seventeenth century. In these textbooks 'persona' was mainly treated as a theological concept and
discussed in connexion with the immaterial kinds of being, God, angels, and souls
(as substantial forms). The Boethian definition was adopted by Catholic and
reformation philosophers alike. For example, the influential Christoph Scheibler,
who became known as the 'protestant Suárez', adopted the Boethian notion of
person in his *Metaphysica* (first published in 1617), where he points out the
importance of this notion to the problem of the trinity.[18] And in the middle of the
century Johann Micraelius still defines 'persona' as 'an individual, incommunicable
substance of an intellectual nature, which subsists independently'.[19] However,
there were dissenting voices, especially in the context of the anti-scholastic humanist movement in the fifteenth and sixteenth centuries. Lorenzo Valla (1405–
57) and, later, Miguel Serveto (1511–53) rejected the orthodox notion of person
as substance and attempted to rehabilitate the old Roman concept of person as
rôle or quality, which they also wanted to apply to the doctrine of the trinity.[20]
Whereas Valla survived the Inquisition, Serveto, having been attacked by Calvin
and charged in Geneva, died for his view of person. Melanchthon, another
humanist, defended the scholastic concept of person and publicly criticised
Serveto.[21] Clearly, scholastic doctrine about the notion of a person won the day,
and it continued to dominate metaphysical thought till about the middle of the
seventeenth century, by which time the Cartesians had developed a powerful rival
theory. Even in the late seventeenth and early eighteenth century, the Boethian
notion of person was alive and well, and it can be found in philosophers who
cannot be classed as simply neo-scholastics. Gerard de Vries, for instance, whose
textbooks were still used in the first half of the eighteenth century, defines
'persona' as a rational *suppositum*; and Stephanus Chauvin gives an account of the

Boethian definition of 'persona' in his *Lexicon philosophicum* which first appeared in 1692.[22] Valla's critique of Boethius's definition of person continued to be discussed until late in the seventeenth century. By and large, Valla's position was rejected, and for theological reasons. Christoph Scheibler, for example, criticises Valla's notion of person in considerable detail.[23] And as late as 1694 Richard Burthogge saw a need explicitly to defend Boethius's notion of person against Valla's critique.[24]

Although the Cartesians had developed a powerful rival theory of person, they did not disagree with the notion of person as individual rational substance, and it was certainly not their concern to re-introduce the old notion of person as rôle or quality. Nevertheless, their theory differs markedly from scholastic doctrine. Descartes does not use 'persona' or 'personne' as technical terms. In fact, like most of his followers, he rarely applies these terms when discussing the notion of the self which is so central to his metaphysics. And on the few occasions when he does use 'persona' or 'personne', it is to refer to the individual human being as consisting of soul and body.[25] According to Descartes, body and soul are rightly thought of as a single individual being, 'because to conceive the union between two things is to conceive them as one single thing'.[26] Neither body alone, nor soul alone, constitutes the human being or person: 'The union which joins a human body and soul to each other is not accidental to a human being, but essential, since a human being without it is not a human being.'[27] This account of 'man' appears to be very similar to the scholastic doctrine, and sometimes Descartes even makes use of the scholastic terminology when discussing the mind–body relationship.[28] However, Descartes's theory differs from the scholastic one in several respects. For Descartes, soul and body are not related to one another as form and matter, but as two independent substances. Although Aquinas, too, argued that the human soul is incorporeal, subsistent and indestructible, he still thought of it as form and not, as did Descartes, as a complete substance in itself. Also, Descartes places much less importance on the bodily part of man than do the scholastics. According to Descartes, the soul constitutes the essence of the self, whereas the body is something which the self merely 'has', to which it is 'very closely joined'.[29] Thus, Descartes implicitly distinguishes between the notion of human being or person which includes corporeity and the notion of the (essential) self, 'I', or soul as something which is not necessarily linked to a body. Whereas Aquinas insisted that the soul alone cannot be regarded as that which makes up the self, Descartes argues that the self is the same, with or without the body: 'This I [*ce moi*] – that is, the soul by which I am what I am – is entirely distinct from the body . . . ; and [the soul] would not fail to be whatever it is, even if the body did not exist.'[30] And the *soul,* that is, that 'by which I am what I am', is for Descartes a complete, simple, and immaterial substance.[31] Further, Descartes argues that *thought* is the 'principal property' of the soul: it is that which 'constitutes its nature and essence, and to which all its other properties are referred'.[32] The soul or mind (or self) is essentially a thinking thing, a *res cogitans.* Now, for Descartes, to say that thought is the essence of the soul is to say that the soul always thinks, not just that it has the *faculty* of thought: if the soul stopped thinking, it would cease to exist.[33] Descartes then defines thought in terms of *consciousness;* [34] and sees consciousness as an immediate relation to one's own thoughts. According to Descartes, 'to be conscious is both to think and to reflect on one's thought'.[35] Since the mind or soul always thinks, and since thought is always accompanied by consciousness, it follows that the soul is *always conscious:* for the duration of its existence, the self is continuously engaged in conscious activity. Our understanding of ourselves as thinking things is based on this consciousness which always accompanies thought. And this self-understanding is in turn the basis of our knowledge of ourselves as *individual* selves: 'From the mere fact that each of us understands himself to be a thinking thing and is capable, in thought, of excluding from himself every other substance, whether thinking or extended, it is certain that each of us, regarded in this way, is really distinct from every other thinking substance and from every corporeal substance.'[36]

   In the last analysis, then, consciousness understood as an immediate self-relation is the basis of our knowledge not only of the distinctness from the body of the soul, or self, as thinking thing, but also of the distinctness of the self from all other thinking things. However, it is of paramount importance to note that Descartes does *not* say that consciousness is what individuates the soul: all he claims is that we derive our *knowledge* of the individuality of our souls from the consciousness we have of our own thoughts. Descartes's argument implies that the individuality of the soul is given prior to consciousness of thoughts: he simply assumes the soul's individuality as given and fails to give an account of what brings about this individuality. Descartes does not argue that souls are individuated through their union with their bodies. Indeed, he could not have argued this, because on his theory, souls are complete individual substances by themselves *independently* of matter. Rather, the identity of the human body depends on the identity of the human soul.[37] It is because the self is equated with the unextended, immaterial part of man that a problem of personal identity through time does not arise. The real self is a simple, immaterial, 'pure' substance: its body and its 'accidents', that is, its thoughts, may change, but it does not thereby lose its identity: 'For even if all the accidents of the mind change, so that it has different objects of the understanding and different desires and sensations, it does not on that account become a different mind.'[38]

Many of Descartes's followers were dissatisfied with his account of the mind-body relationship and so developed alternative theories.[39] Nevertheless, they accepted Descartes's general dualistic picture of man, locating the real self in the soul understood as a *res cogitans* and an immaterial substance. Arnold Geulincx, for example, distinguishes between ethical and metaphysical considerations of the self: the self as human being, that is, as an embodied mind, is the object of ethics, while the true self, the self as mind or simple, immaterial, thinking substance, is the object of metaphysics.[40] Nicolas Malebranche argues that the knowledge we have of the self is imperfect, precisely because it is based on consciousness only ('sentiment intérieur ou conscience') and not on ideas mediated through God.[41] Yet, although knowledge based on consciousness is imperfect, it is certain and sufficient to yield the most important characteristics of the human soul, such as its liberty, spirituality, and immortality. Like other Cartesians, Malebranche did not address the question of personal identity through time in any detail.

The fact that scholastic doctrine of the person was not dead in the second half of the century is well illustrated by a debate that took place in England in the early 1690s between two theologians, William Sherlock and Robert South. The importance of this debate consists not only in the fact that it helps further to illuminate the difference between the scholastic and the Cartesian accounts of the person but also in the fact that it foreshadows arguments similar to those that were soon to be discussed in relation to Locke's new theory. Against the background of this debate, Locke's theory distinguishes itself from both Cartesian and scholastic theories. Sherlock and South are hardly known today, but their debate was much discussed by theologians and philosophers of the time (Richard Burthogge and Edward Stillingfleet, to name only two). The focus of the controversy was the doctrine of the trinity. South made it clear that he wished to defend the 'school-men's' account; Sherlock's position, by contrast, was labelled 'Cartesian' by con-temporaries, and rightly so.[42] The debate is not at all restricted to the notion of the divine person. Sherlock and South preface their arguments concerning the trinity with philosophical inquiries into the concept of the person in general, and into what constitutes the individuality of a human person. The old Boethian definition of person forms the background of the debate and is explicitly referred to by both Sherlock and South. Both hold the view that when applied to human beings, the term 'person' denotes the individual human being as a whole, consisting of soul and body. However, whereas South regards the body as an essential element of the person and argues that souls, when separated from their bodies, are not persons,[43] Sherlock maintains that the soul constitutes the person when united to a body and *is* the (same) person when separated from the body.[44] And the soul or person is, for Sherlock, 'a simple uncompounded thing, . . . which cannot consist of parts':[45] a person, human or divine, is essentially an individual spiritual substance. Thus, like Descartes, Sherlock distinguishes the notion of an individual human being or person as including corporeity from the notion of the essential self or soul as an incorporeal entity. Unlike Descartes, Sherlock also applies the term 'person' to this incorporeal spiritual entity, which may be confusing. When Sherlock comes to account for the *individuality* of persons, he does so in terms of *consciousness:* here, he seems to go further than Descartes, who argued that our *knowledge* of the soul's individuality is derived from consciousness. Sherlock seems to be saying that consciousness actually brings about the individuality of the person: 'Now this Self unity of the Spirit . . . can be nothing else but *Self-consciousness:* That it is conscious to its own Thoughts, Reasonings, Passions, which no other finite Spirit is conscious to but itself: This makes a finite Spirit numerically one, and separates it from all other Spirits.'[46] Sherlock, it seems, thinks that consciousness, understood as a unifier of thoughts and actions, individuates persons or finite spirits.[47]

South rejects this theory of personal identity, arguing instead that a person must have individuality prior to being conscious of thoughts and actions and that, therefore, consciousness cannot constitute this individuality.[48] In other words, South accuses Sherlock's theory of circularity; for according to South, Sherlock introduces as a principle of individuation that which in fact presupposes individuality. For South, consciousness presupposes an individual person because consciousness is an 'action' that 'issues from' the person: there must be a person before there can be acts (like those of consciousness) which originate in the person. Furthermore, South holds that consciousness presupposes other personal *acts* which are its objects. Since consciousness is a 'Reflex Act' on thoughts and feelings of the person, it 'must needs in Order of Nature be Posterior to the Act reflected upon by it. And therefore *Self-Consciousness,* which is by two degrees Posterior to Personality, cannot possibly be the *formal Reason* of it'.[49]

In setting out to defend his theory against South's charge, Sherlock in fact modifies it in order to escape South's criticism. He retreats to the view that consciousness is not, as he seemed to be saying, the *ratio essendi* of individual personality, but merely its *ratio cognoscendi.* Sherlock bases his position on a sceptical view about human knowledge of essence: all we know about spiritual substance is 'what we feel in our Selves';[50] therefore, 'self-feeling' or consciousness is the only means available to us for discovering our self-unity; and this is what it means to say that individuality of persons has its foundation in consciousness. Sherlock makes it clear that he does not wish to say that consciousness is the *real* ground of personal identity. He agrees with South's criticism in saying: 'There must be a Person, before there can be any *actual Self-consciousness*; that is to say, there must be a Self . . . before this Self can feel it Self, and by this Self-feeling distinguish Himself from all other Selfs.'[51] Yet, despite his scepticism about knowledge of essence, Sherlock thinks we can determine *a priori* what the *real* ground of personal identity is. He attempts to do this by employing the terminology of consciousness. However, it becomes clear that what he says is, again, a *modification* of his original position. Sherlock argues that 'the principle of Self-consciousness', rather than particular acts of consciousness, individuates the person.[52] And this 'principle' of consciousness is, of course, the *soul*: 'The Soul is the seat of Personality, the only Principle of Reason, Sensation, and a Conscious life.'[53]

South noticed that by moving from the 'acts' to the 'principle' of consciousness, in order to escape the charge of circularity, Sherlock thereby had altered the state of the debate.[54] More important, Sherlock, in attempting to explain the individuality of the person (soul) in terms of the 'principle of self-consciousness' (soul), quite obviously *fails* to account for the individuality of the person understood as immaterial substance, no less so than Descartes himself fails to account for the individuation of immaterial substances. Despite his un-Cartesian appeal to scepticism about essence, Sherlock's position on the self is close to the standard Cartesian one. The self is conceived of as an immaterial thinking substance, and its individuality is said to be *known* on the basis of consciousness; but what *constitutes* this individuality is left unexplained.

Given the trinitarian context of the debate, both Sherlock and South focus on the problem of individuation and do not address at any length the issue of identity through time. For Sherlock, just as for Descartes, no genuine problem of personal identity through time arises. The human body may change constantly, but since the essence of the self is located in the soul or immaterial thinking substance, these changes do not affect personal identity through time: 'Whatever change there be in the Body, the Person is the same still, which could not be, were the Body part of the Person, for then the change of the Body would be a partial Change of the Person too; and yet our Bodies are in a perpetual Flux, and change every day.'[55]

Despite the differences between scholastic and Cartesian theories of the person, as illustrated by the Sherlock–South debate, the two share the 'ontological' view of the self as thing or substance. For even though the Cartesians place a characteristically non-scholastic emphasis on consciousness and self-consciousness, they do not ascribe to consciousness a *constitutive* function for the self as person. This is true also of those seventeenth-century philosophers prior to Locke, such as the Cambridge Platonists and Spinoza, who cannot be classed as scholastics or Cartesians.

The Cambridge Platonists, for example, rejected both scholastic doctrine and a Cartesian-type dualism. Like Descartes, one of the leading thinkers of that school, Ralph Cudworth, distinguishes sharply between the corporeal and the incorporeal.[56] But, unlike Descartes, he holds that *all* life is incorporeal and that incorporeal life is not to be equated with thought and consciousness. Cudworth postulates a general plastic nature that is immaterial and acts according to divine wisdom and fulfills divine purposes, but that lacks knowledge of the reasons for its actions as well as consciousness of the fact that it performs the actions it does perform. Cudworth speaks of unconscious plastic natures, analogous to this general plastic nature of the universe, that are at work in each *individual* living being.[57] For Cudworth, as for Descartes, human souls are immaterial beings. Yet, by employing the notion of consciousness, Cudworth distinguishes two kinds of incorporeal life: a pure rational part of the soul which is conscious, and a 'plastic' power of the soul which is unconscious and is responsible for organic functions, reflex actions, habits, and dreams.[58] The notion of consciousness is, obviously, crucial to Cudworth's account. In applying this notion Cudworth makes explicit recourse not to the Cartesians, but to Neoplatonic sources, especially to Plotinus. It is clear from the text that Cudworth uses 'consciousness' as a translation of the Greek 'synaisthesis' and that he conceives consciousness as an immediate feeling of one's own thoughts and actions while one is performing them.[59] Unlike Descartes, Cudworth carefully distinguishes consciousness from self-knowledge, reflection, and other forms of relating to the self. Yet, like Descartes, he does not ascribe to consciousness a constitutive or individuating function. Consciousness is taken to be merely the basis of *knowledge* of the self which presupposes the latter's individuality: according to Cudworth, consciousness denotes a 'duplication' of the self. He says that a '*Duplication* . . . is included in the Nature of *synaisthesis, Con-Sense* and *Consciousness*.'[60] That is to say, consciousness is a relation to the self where the self is the subject (i.e., that which is conscious) as well as the object of consciousness.[61] Unlike Descartes, Cudworth makes frequent use of terms like 'person' and 'personality' for the human self, but then he equates 'person' and 'personality' with the soul and argues that 'Personalities' are 'unquestionably *Substantial Things* and *Really Distinct* from Matter'.[62] And like Descartes, he holds that the identity of persons understood as immaterial substances is secured by their immateriality.

Spinoza does not discuss the issue of human personal identity in any detail. Spinoza's account of 'man', although influenced by Descartes, differs from both scholastic and Cartesian doctrine. He holds that human beings consist of mind and body,[63] but this is said to be neither a union of form and matter nor a union of two distinct and independent substances. For Spinoza, human beings (like other individuals) are not, strictly speaking, *substances* at all. They are individual things (*res singulares*) existing *in* the one divine substance: the human self consists of body understood as a mode of the divine attribute of extension, and of mind understood as a mode of the divine attribute of thought.[64] The individuality of human beings is constituted, like that of other *res singulares,* by a limitation or negation of divine attributes. Spinoza seems to assume that, under normal circumstances, an individual person remains the same through time and partial change. He makes only few occasional remarks on the topic. Although Spinoza does not give a detailed account of *personal* identity, he does discuss the individuation of *bodies.*[65] The individuality of a body is brought about by its relations to, or connectedness with, other bodies in the one divine substance. The mind is understood as the 'idea of the body'; it consists in awareness of bodily events: 'The object of the idea constituting the human Mind is the Body.'[66] And since the mind is an idea (in God) of the body, the individuation and identity of the mind must run parallel to the individuation and identity of the body. Since the mind is nothing but the idea or knowledge of the body, the connexions between ideas correspond to connexions on the side of the body, that is, to the causes of the ideas.[67] Thus, Spinoza argues that imagination and memory are dependent on the body: 'The Mind can neither imagine anything, nor recollect past things, except while the Body endures.'[68] He suggests, further, that a human being loses his or her identity through loss of memory: Spinoza relates a story about a Spanish poet who, after having recovered from a disease, does not remember anything of his past life and who for that reason cannot be regarded as the same man as before the amnesia.[69] So, human personal (or mental) identity requires continuity of memory; and continuity of memory depends on continuity of the body. And since the mind or soul is 'only an Idea, knowledge etc. of a body', it follows that if the body is destroyed, the individual mind or person is destroyed too.[70] Nevertheless, Spinoza indicates that there is a sense in which the mind is eternal: the mind is eternal in so far as it is a mode or idea in the one divine substance.[71] As an individual being, however, the human mind is not eternal; there is no *personal* immortality. This is, obviously, a position which differs significantly from both Cartesian and scholastic conceptions of the self. Cartesians and scholastics alike argued for personal immortality, and they regarded the substantiality of the self as necessary to secure personal immortality (see the next section of this chapter). Spinoza's theory of the *oneness of substance* implies that the human *self* is not a substantial being; and this denial of the substantiality of the self undermines the basis of traditional theories of personal immortality. This is why Leibniz accuses Spinoza of Averroism, for Spinoza 'who recognizes only one single substance, is not far from the doctrine of a single universal spirit'.[72] Spinoza's denial of personal immortality may well be the reason that he does not discuss the issue of personal identity in any detail: since there is no personal immortality, personal *identity* through time does not constitute a pressing problem.

It has been suggested that, in remarking that personal identity cannot be retained through amnesia, Spinoza 'anticipates' Locke's theory according to which personal identity depends on consciousness.[73] It is doubtful, however, whether Spinoza's story about the Spanish poet really amounts to such an anticipation. It is true that both Spinoza and Locke link personal identity to consciousness in some way. Yet, Spinoza's story can be read as indicating merely that the poet has changed so much through his disease as to have lost his identity, and that as a *result* of this loss of identity he does not remember anything of his past life.[74] Locke argues that loss of consciousness *brings about* the loss of personal identity, because consciousness is what constitutes personal identity. There is a different, and perhaps more important, similarity between the two philosophers' accounts of the self: if Spinoza can be said to 'anticipate' Locke's revolutionary theory, this may be not because of Spinoza's occasional remark about amnesia, but because he does not conceive of human personality in terms of *substantiality*. The question of substantiality or non-substantiality of personality re-appears, although in a very different systematic context, in Locke's theory of personal identity.

The human self was approached from an entirely different perspective by Michel de Montaigne in the sixteenth century and, for example, Pascal and La Rochefoucauld in the seventeenth century.[75] They saw the person as an object, not of abstract metaphysical thought, but of psychological observation. They were somewhat sceptical about reason as a means of grasping the nature of the self and instead emphasised the constant changes that human beings undergo and the elusiveness of the self as an object of enquiry. For these authors, the emotional side of persons, rather than questions about their metaphysical make-up, is central. Pascal points out that whatever, metaphysically speaking, the essence of a person is, what matters is that we love a person because of his or her observable qualities:

What is the self? . . . if someone loves me for my judgement or my memory, do they love me? *me*, myself? No, for I could lose these qualities without losing my self. Where then is this self, if it is neither in the body nor the soul? And how can one love the body or the soul except for the sake of such qualities, which are not what makes up the self, since they are perishable? Would we love the substance of a person's soul, in the abstract, whatever qualities might be in it? That is not possible, and it would be wrong. Therefore we never love anyone, but only qualities.[76]

This focus on 'qualities' is reminiscent, of course, of the old Roman notion of person. However, Pascal does not elaborate on this point. And although his, and La Rochefoucauld's, psychological observations, presented in aphoristic style, amount to a description of what they take to be the nature of human persons – for example, that they have characteristics like vanity and weakness, that they are formed by outward influences and custom, and so on – neither Pascal nor La Rochefoucauld inquires systematically into the *concept* of person nor develops a *theory* about what it is to be a person and what would be required for a person to remain the same through time.

II. PERSONAL IDENTITY, MORAL RESPONSIBILITY, AND LIFE AFTER DEATH

Among those philosophers who rejected both scholastic and Cartesian metaphysics of man was Thomas Hobbes. Since he argues that 'every part of the Universe, is Body',[77] the Cartesian notion of an immaterial substance is, to Hobbes, a contradiction in terms.[78] According to Hobbes, man is simply a '*living Body*' who has the capacity to reason.[79] Hobbes also employs the term 'person' for the human self, but he distinguishes the notion of person from that of man. In fact, this concept of person leads to the issue of moral responsibility and its connexion with the problem of self-identity. However, although Hobbes devotes a whole chapter of his *Leviathan* to the topic 'Of Persons, Authors, and things Personated',[80] he does not set out to develop a theory of human personal identity. The main purpose of that chapter is, rather, to introduce the notion of 'artificial person' which Hobbes requires for his political theory. Nevertheless, what Hobbes has to say about 'person' in this context is, to some extent, also relevant to the notion of an individual human person. Hobbes's definition of person in general reads: 'A PERSON, is he *whose words or actions are considered, either as his own, or as representing the words or actions of an other man, or of any other thing to whom they are attributed, whether Truly or by Fiction*.'[81] In the first case, that is, when the 'words or actions' are ascribed to the individual who utters or performs them, the individual is a '*Naturall Person*'; in the second case, when the words and actions 'are considered as representing the words and actions of an other, then is he a *Feigned* or *Artificiall person*'.[82] Thus, whereas Hobbes defines 'man' in metaphysical terms as a 'reasonable' living body, he defines 'person' in terms of action ascription or ownership of actions. Hobbes explicitly introduces the notion of authorship in this context; he regards *natural* persons as persons who are considered to be the *authors* of those actions they perform. Hobbes does not discuss the conditions of action attribution in any detail here; but he does point out that the 'use of reason' is one of them. For he argues that human beings who do not have the 'use of reason' are not to be considered the *authors* of their actions, and this means that they are not (natural) persons: 'Likewise Children, Fooles, and Mad-men that have no use of Reason, may be Personated by Guardians, or Curators; but can be no Authors (during that time) of any action done by them, longer then (when they shall recover the use of Reason) they shall judge the same reasonable.'[83]

Even though Hobbes does not explicitly *draw* a distinction between 'man' and 'natural person', his statements clearly imply this distinction. For what he says is basically this: in most cases 'natural person' and 'man' may be applied to the same individual being; yet, even then, the two terms denote different aspects of the same being. Furthermore, there are cases in which we may apply the term 'man' but not 'natural person' (e.g., 'Mad-men'). When we consider an individual human being under the notion of *person,* we do not consider it with respect to its metaphysical make-up, but with regard to the actions attributed to that being, that is, under moral and legal aspects. Hobbes seems to take up the old legal usage of 'persona'. He reminds the reader of the history of the term 'persona' and appeals to Cicero's use of 'persona' as rôle. Yet he does not, in this context, address other issues that are relevant to the problem of moral responsibility such as that of the freedom of the will. Nor does he introduce the notion of person to his metaphysical discussion of identity in *De corpore,* where he distinguishes between the identity of man and the identity of body.[84]

Samuel Pufendorf, the German natural law theorist and critic of Hobbes, takes over the distinction between man and person, but, unlike Hobbes, he adopts a Cartesian dualistic view of man. Since his main concern is natural law, Pufendorf gives no detailed account of the metaphysics of man; he is more interested in the human self as a 'moral entity', to which he also refers as 'moral person' or 'natural person': 'Natural person' relates to the individual human being in so far as he owns actions and is held to be responsible for them.[85] Thus Pufendorf, too, links the notion of person to that of action attribution and, thereby, to moral responsibility. Like other natural law theorists before him, Pufendorf cites freedom and reason as the general conditions of action attribution. As in Hobbes, there is no discussion of personal identity through time. Given Pufendorf's Cartesian assumption that the real self is the immaterial soul, which is 'the great Principle and Spring of human Actions' whereas the body is merely 'a subordinate Instrument',[86] he would not encounter a *problem* of identity anyway. Thus, the assumed metaphysical constitution of the self is thought of as securing *a priori* the identity of the self relevant for the person and for moral responsibility, and therefore the issue of personal identity need not be addressed in its own right.

The notion of moral responsibility is, of course, part of the Christian doctrine of life after death which also continued to be much discussed in the seventeenth century. According to this doctrine, we shall receive in the future life God's judgement and reward or punishment for our actions in this life. And philosophers had to make their views about the human self at least compatible with this doctrine. Thus, the Cambridge Platonist Ralph Cudworth holds that 'Rational Souls' have 'both *Morality* and *Liberty* of *Will,* and [are] thereby . . . capable of *Rewards* and *Punishments,* and Consequently *Fit Objects* for the *Divine Justice* to display it self upon'.[87] Cudworth's appeal to rationality and freedom as grounds of action attribution obviously did not originate with him, since it can be found in traditional natural law thinking. Cudworth takes for granted that the 'identity condition' is satisfied: since God's rewards or punishments are, by definition, just, it is assumed that the person who will be rewarded or punished for actions in this life is the *same* person who committed those actions in this life. It is part of the doctrine of life after death that the human soul is immortal. And philosophers who adopted a Cartesian conception of man could regard the immortality of the soul and its identity into the next life as unproblematic: for them, both can be deduced from what was taken to be the *nature* of the soul, that is, from its immateriality and simplicity. The argument for the immortality of the soul from its immaterial nature was a common one in the seventeenth century. Seth Ward, for example, presented it in the form of a syllogism: 'Whatsoever substance is incorporeall it is immortall. But the souls of men are incorporeall substances, *Ergo* . . .'[88] And just as the Cartesian conception of the self as immaterial soul helped one avoid the problem of self-identity with respect to this life, so it did with regard to the future life. What was meant by 'immortality' was just the continued existence of the soul as an immaterial, 'pure' substance. However, for Descartes's own theory at least, the unresolved problem of individuation of immaterial substances reappears in this context: since the disembodied soul lacks sensation as well as the memory of any sensory experience, the question arises as to how genuine personal immortality is possible. What distinguishes one disembodied soul from another? Descartes's introduction of the problematic notion of a purely intellectual memory which survives the death of the body does not resolve the issue.[89] Materialist philosophers such as Hobbes, who preferred to speak of the 'Immortality of the Man', argued against this doctrine of 'natural immortality' and held that immortality depends on the grace of God.[90] But even anti-materialist critics of Hobbes, such as Ralph Cudworth, rejected the view that the immortality of the human soul can simply be deduced from its immaterial nature: to Cudworth, *all* life is essentially of an incorporeal nature, but is not thereby immortal. Whether the human soul lives after death depends on God's will; and our assurance of its immortality cannot be derived from syllogistic reasoning but requires faith.[91] Furthermore, since the existence of an immaterial substance does not necessarily include conscious experience, the notion of immortality must, for Cudworth, contain more than that of the continued existence of substance: to say we will receive God's rewards or punishments and to speak of a future state of *life,* we must believe that God will make the future state a state of consciousness. It is *consciousness* 'which makes a Being to be Present with it self, . . . to perceive it self to Do or Suffer, and to have a *Fruition* or *Enjoyment* of it self'.[92] Although Cudworth does not regard immateriality as sufficient for immortality, he insists, against the materialists, that it is *necessary:* it is necessary precisely because it is immateriality which secures the soul's unity and identity through time. Cudworth explicitly addresses the 'identity condition' when discussing the materialist challenge. If the soul were not immaterial, Cudworth argues, it could not even remain identical within this life. In fact, it could not be a simple substance at all; rather, it would consist of a '*Heap* of *Substances*'.[93] Since bodies consist of a large number of particles which change constantly, souls, if they were material, 'could not be Numerically the same throughout the whole space of their Lives. . . . Which Reason may be also extended further to prove the Soul to be no Body at all'.[94] Thus, if the soul's immateriality is denied, its identity through time is made impossible also, and so are just divine rewards or punishment and a meaningful notion of life after death.

These latter consequences of the materialist position are emphasised explicitly by another anti-materialist thinker towards the end of the century, Timothy Manlove. After having pointed out that the materialist position creates a problem of personal identity, Manlove says: 'If the [materialist] Hypothesis which I am writing against, be true, no man can rationally believe a Future State of Retribution. You have heard already how Individuation and Personality are overthrown by it, and by consequence there can be no just room for Rewards and Punishments hereafter, because the Person when he died had not the same Soul that he had a month before; and why should one Soul be *punished* for another's Crimes, and that other *go free* ?'[95] These arguments show that the metaphysical position adopted concerning the composition of the human self was thought to be, at least by the anti-materialists, of paramount importance for securing the identity required for the self as a moral and immortal being: only if the soul is an immaterial entity, so it was argued (or assumed), can there be moral accountability and life after death.

Platonist thinkers such as Henry More, who revived the doctrine of the *pre-existence* of our souls, also assumed that the identity of the self as immaterial substance transcends this present life. Critics of the doctrine of pre-existence – for example, Samuel Parker and Edward Warren – argued (among other things) that if there had been a previous life, there would be some trace of it in our memory now; since we have no memory whatsoever of a pre-existent state, it is unlikely that there was such a state.[96] But More rejects the implicit assumption that memory of the past is relevant to the continuous existence and identity of the soul and says that our memory is often deficient even with respect to this life; yet no one wants to say that because of this the soul does not remain the same throughout this life.[97]

But to return to the Christian doctrine of life after death, this doctrine, as mentioned at the outset of this chapter, holds that the human being as a whole will live. That is, it includes a belief not only in the immortality of the *soul* but also in the resurrection of the *body*. And here the question arose whether the identity condition needs to be satisfied in relation to the body as well, or only with regard to the soul. Does the body possessed on resurrection have to be the very same body one had in this life for there to be the same person in the future life? There are countless tracts, sermons, and pamphlets on this topic from the seventeenth century. Most authors answered the question in the affirmative, as Aquinas had done much earlier. For, so it was argued, if there is to be life after death, there will have to be the same human being as in this life, and this requires that there be the same body as well as the same soul. In a book which was much read and often reprinted in the seventeenth century, John Pearson points out that it is part of the *concept* of the resurrection that the *same* body will be restored to life which a person had here; for, 'if either the same body should be joyned to another soul, or the same soul united to another body, it would not be the resurrection of the same man.'[98] Furthermore, Pearson argues, since divine rewards or punishments relate to the body as well as to the soul, they could not be *just* rewards or punishments, if the resurrection-body were not the same as the pre-mortem body: 'That which shall receive the reward, and be lyable to the punishment, is not onely the soul but the body; it stands not therefore with the nature of a just retribution, that he which sinned in one body should be punished in another, he which pleased God in his own flesh should see God with other eyes.'[99]

The *disputes* about the identity of the resurrection-body concerned the conditions that need to be satisfied for there to be the same body at the resurrection as in this life. And here there were three main positions.[100] The first was that the resurrection-body has to consist of numerically the same particles as the pre-mortem body. This position was held by Sir Thomas Browne in *Religio medici*, for example, and by his critic Alexander Ross. Browne and Ross argue that we must ascribe to God the ability to re-unite the same atoms that made up a human body in this life. As Ross says, God 'can with as great facility re-unite these dispersed *atomes*, as he could at first create them'.[101] If the resurrection-body were not in this strict sense identical to the body in this life, then, Ross argues, there would be no resurrection at all, but rather a transmigration of the soul into a different body.[102] The second was that identity of the particles is *not* required for the body to be the same. Here, there were several positions as to which aspects or parts of the body are essential to its identity. Thus, there were Rabbinic theological speculations about the *luz* or 'resurrection-bone': the *luz* is a part of the human body which subsists and is not destroyed in death; it is a material substratum which guarantees the identity of the resurrection-body as a whole.[103] Some said, however, that the resurrection-body must be the same *organism* as in this life. This view was defended by Humphry Hody, and to some extent by Robert Boyle in *Some Physico-Theological Considerations about the Possibility of the Resurrection* (1675). Hody argues that only those particles of the pre-mortem body need to be re-united that are necessary to restore the same *organic body*, for the identity of the human body 'consists in a fit Construction and Organization of successively fleeting Particles of matter'.[104] Boyle, too, points out that 'there is no determinate bulk or size that is necessary to make a human body pass for the *same*.'[105] Even though Boyle argues for the possibility of the identity of the resurrection-body, he holds that sameness of the body in a 'strict and literal sense' is *not necessary* for the resurrection to be possible: it is sufficient that the individual soul remains the same. In other words, he accepts the third main view on this issue. On this view, all that is required for the resurrection-body to be the same is that it will be united to the same *soul* (understood either as 'form' or as a complete substance). Whether the body's material composition or structure will be the same is not regarded as relevant. This position conforms to Descartes's account of human bodily identity.[106] Although Boyle rejects the scholastic notions of 'form' and 'matter', he presents his view on the identity of the resurrection-man by making use of the old language: 'In regard that the *human soul* is the form of man – so that, whatever duly organised portion of matter it is united to, it therewith constitutes the same man – the import of the *resurrection* is fulfilled in this, that after death there shall be another state, wherein the soul shall no longer persevere in its separate condition.'[107]

Similar views were held before Boyle by Kenelm Digby, and after Boyle, by the Archbishop of Canterbury, John Tillotson.[108] Digby argues that the body, taken in separation from the soul, is never identical from one moment to the next; nevertheless, as Christians, 'wee must beleeve that we shall rise againe with the same body, that walked about, did eate, drinke, and live here on earth.'[109] Digby argues that whatever matter is joined to the same *soul* constitutes the same human body; therefore, the identity of the body at the resurrection is secured if *any* matter is united to the same soul:

If *God* should joyne the *Soule* of a lately dead man . . . unto a *Body* made of earth taken from some mountaine in *America*; it were most true and certaine that the body he should then live by, were the same Identicall body he lived with before his *Death* & late *Resurrection*. It is evident that *samenesse, thisnesse,* and *thatnesse,* belongeth not to matter by it selfe . . . but onely as it is distinguished and individuated by the Forme. Which, in our case, whensoever the same *Soule* doth, it must be understood alwaies to be the same matter and body.[110]

Although authors like Digby subscribe to the doctrine of the sameness of the resurrection-body, their position is really a thinly veiled version of the view that the identity of the body is *not* required for the restoration of the same self at the resurrection. This view appealed to those philosophers and theologians who followed Descartes at least in this: that they regarded the body not as an essential element of the person, and thought that the soul alone, whether embodied or disembodied, constitutes the same person. This was not to deny that the resurrection concerns the body; but it was argued that, since both human and divine courts judge only with respect to the same soul, the *identity* of the body is not required at the resurrection. As Arthur Bury, a defender of this view, wrote: 'If Human justice punish an old crime, though between the act and the discovery every particle of the body be chang'd, because the same soul makes him the same person; how can we doubt but Divine justice may at the resurrection do the same?'[111]

The position John Locke adopts on this issue is similar to that of those theologians who deny the identity of the resurrection-body. Yet he differs from them in that he does not regard the identity of the soul, as substance, as essential either. Locke interprets the doctrine of life after death against the background of his new theory of personal identity.

III. LOCKE'S THEORY AND SOME OF ITS CRITICS

Locke's chapter on identity was published in May 1694 as Chapter 27 of the second book of his *Essay* (second edition). Locke had written the chapter in mid-1693 at the suggestion of his Irish friend William Molyneux, but he had sketched views on the topic much earlier. The first journal note dealing explicitly with it dates from 1683, and some thoughts relevant to his later theory appear in a note on immortality of 1682 which reflects his reading of Cudworth's *True Intellectual System of the Universe*.[112] In the first edition of the *Essay* (1690) Locke makes some remarks on the topic when discussing the doctrine of the resurrection and the Cartesian doctrine that the soul always thinks.[113] Molyneux referred to these remarks when suggesting to Locke that he deal more extensively with the issue in the second edition. A passage in the first edition indicates that on Locke's view personal identity has to do with 'Consciousness of our Actions and Sensations, especially of Pleasure and Pain, and the concernment that accompanies it'.[114] In the second edition, Locke elaborates on this and presents a detailed theory of personal identity. Locke's theory is complex and intricate, and its interpretation is still a matter of debate.[115]

Locke was well aware of the traditional conceptions of personal identity discussed above. He rejected both the scholastic and the Cartesian accounts of the problem and broke with the traditional 'ontological' view of the person and of personal identity. Locke treats the special problem of personal identity in accordance with his general theory of identity: according to this theory, identity criteria are specified by the concept under which we consider that being whose identity is in question.[116] He argues that we need to be clear about the *concept* of *person* in order to be able to determine what constitutes the *identity* of persons: 'To find wherein *personal Identity* consists, we must consider what *Person* stands for.'[117] And to be clear about the concept of person, we have to distinguish it carefully from those of thinking substance or spirit, and of man or human being. Although these concepts are closely related and may be applied to the same individual being to whom we also apply 'person', they denote different aspects, respectively, under which we may consider the human self; and they need to be distinguished from one another for an account of identity, for each of these concepts carries with it different identity criteria: 'But yet when we will enquire, what makes the same *Spirit, Man,* or *Person,* we must fix the *Ideas* of *Spirit, Man,* or *Person,* in our Minds; and having resolved with our selves what we mean by them, it will not be hard to determine, in either of them, or the like, when it is the *same,* and when not.'[118]

Locke's position is that 'man' and 'person' denote different abstract ideas which may be applied to the self; this has the consequence that there are different possible answers to the question about the *identity* of the self, depending on which abstract idea we apply. Locke says: 'If it be possible for the same Man to have distinct incommunicable consciousness at different times, *it is past doubt the same Man would at different times make different Persons.*'[119] In other words, it is possible for *a* (at time *t*) to be identical with *b* (at time *t + n*) with respect to the notion of man, but not in regard to the notion of person, even though both notions may be applied to both *a* and *b*. This is what is now known as the *relativity thesis* about identity. Now, some commentators hold that Locke is *not* committed to the view that *identity* is relative.[120] Accordingly, it has been argued that in Locke 'man' and 'person' do not denote two different ideas under which we may consider the self, but two distinct *things* occupying the same place; for on this reading of Locke there is never a case where an individual *a* is both the same man and not the same person as an individual *b*. And so, Locke is said to be committed to a 'doctrine of double existence': at time *t* we do not have one self to which different ideas may be applied, but two entities: one man and one person.[121] The following passage, for example, seems to suggest that Locke adopts the 'doctrine of double existence'. When distinguishing his account of the self from the common sense view according to which 'man' and 'person' are synonymous terms, he says, 'I know that in the ordinary way of speaking, the same Person, and the same Man, stand for one and the same thing.'[122] This may be taken to imply that Locke's *own* view is that man and person are two *distinct things*. However, the passage need not be read that way. Rather, it may be interpreted as a statement about the use of the *terms* 'man' and 'person': these are said by Locke to denote distinct *ideas – abstract ideas –* which may be applied to the self.[123] The latter interpretation is confirmed by the moral and legal dimensions of Locke's theory, discussed in the following paragraphs, which show that Locke's concept of person (for which he also uses the term 'personality') comes close to the traditional notion of person as moral quality. In short, Locke regards soul or spirit, man, and person(ality) as different *abstract ideas* under which we may consider the self.

With respect to thinking substance or soul, Locke not only rejects the Cartesian view that the soul *always* thinks, but he also argues more generally, as Gassendi and others before him, that we have no certain knowledge at all about the real essence of the soul: we know that we have the faculty of thought, but our knowledge does not go beyond the evidence of inner experience here. We do not know whether the substance which thinks is an immaterial or a material being. Although Locke believes it is 'more probable' that the thinking substance is immaterial,[124] he regards it as possible that material substance has the power to think. Accordingly, Locke does not definitely make up his mind between a Cartesian dualist account of man and the view of man as an 'organiz'd living Body'.[125] He favours the non-dualist position only in so far as our (ordinary) *idea* of man is concerned. However, which account of man and of soul we choose is, to Locke, irrelevant to the problem of *personal* identity, for we have to distinguish the concept of person from both that of the soul and that of man in any case: to consider the self as person is to consider the self with regard to all those thoughts and actions of which it is *conscious*. Consciousness, Locke says, 'is inseparable from thinking, and . . . essential to it'.[126] And, by virtue of its presence in all acts of thinking, consciousness is said to serve as a *unifier* of thoughts and actions. They are 'appropriated to me now by this self-consciousness'.[127] The self as person is constituted by consciousness unifying thoughts and actions: 'That with which the *consciousness* of this present thinking thing can join it self, makes the same *Person*.'[128] This is why speculations about the soul's materiality or immateriality are irrelevant to an understanding of the self as person. Even if we knew for certain which account of thinking substance is correct, personal identity would still have to be determined in terms of consciousness. In the early manuscript note of 1683 Locke argues that even if the mind consisted of 'corporeal spirits', the identity of the person would not be constituted by 'their being the same', but by consciousness. And in the *Essay* Locke points out that ''tis evident the *personal Identity* would equally be determined by the consciousness, whether that consciousness were annexed to some individual immaterial Substance or no.'[129] Whereas Cartesians and Platonists alike hold that the identity of the person is secured by the soul's unchanging immaterial nature, Locke argues that 'whether we are the same thinking thing, *i.e.* the same substance or no' is a question which 'concerns not *personal Identity* at all'.[130]

Locke's position, then, can be described as follows: consciousness presupposes thinking substance (or man) as the agent who performs acts of consciousness and those thoughts and actions to which consciousness refers; consciousness does *not* bring about the identity of the self as soul or man. Although Cartesians and scholastics identify either the soul or the man with the person as a *res* whose individuality is constituted independently of, and prior to, consciousness, Locke argues that there are good reasons for carefully distinguishing the unity of the person from both that of the soul, as substance, and from that of life (man). For neither of the latter unities is co-extensive with that of consciousness; and 'person' or 'personality' is the term for this unity of conscious thoughts and actions. For the Cartesians at least, consciousness is a basis for the *discovery* of the individuality of the self (soul); but Locke ascribes to consciousness a *constitutive* function: the unity and identity of the self as person is not one that is constituted prior to acts of consciousness, but rather exists only by virtue of its being constituted by consciousness.[131]

According to Locke, consciousness relates to *past* thoughts and actions as well as to present ones; and it is through its reference to the past that consciousness constitutes the identity of the person *over time:* "'Tis plain consciousness . . . unites Existences, and Actions, very remote in time, into the same Person, as well as it does the Existence and Actions of the immediately preceding moment: So that whatever has the consciousness of present and past Actions, is the same Person to whom they both belong.'[132] In other words, I am at present the same person as I was in the past not because I am the same living body, nor because the same substance thinks in me, but only because my present conscious experience is connected with that of past conscious experience: they belong to one conscious life, and this means that they are part of one identical person. Now, Locke recognises the fact that there is 'no moment of our Lives wherein we have the whole train of all our past Actions before our Eyes in one view'. Our 'forgetfulness', Locke concedes, 'seems to make the difficulty':[133] for would one really be justified in saying, as one would have to on Locke's theory, that I am not the same person now as I was ten years ago, only because I do not remember what I did then? Does amnesia turn me into a different person? Locke argues that the difficulty arises only if we confuse the terms 'man' and 'person': if we stick firmly to the relevant conceptual distinctions, 'forgetfulness' does not pose a problem to his theory.

We must here take notice what the word *I* is applied to, which in this case is the Man only. And the same Man being presumed to be the same Person, *I* is easily here supposed to stand also for the same Person. But if it be possible for the same Man to have distinct incommunicable consciousness at different times, it is past doubt the same Man would at different times make different Persons.[134]

I am still the same human being as before the loss of memory, for my identity as 'man' does not require that I am conscious of my past, but I am *not* the same *person:* the self can be identical at different points of time with respect to the notion of man, while being non-identical with regard to the notion of person.

As already mentioned, the difference between the identity of the self as man and as person is crucial also to the moral and legal aspects of Locke's theory. Like others before him, Locke explicitly links the notion of person to that of moral and legal responsibility. 'Person', Locke emphasises, is a 'Forensick Term'.[135] He argues elsewhere in the *Essay* that human beings are free, that is, capable of determining their actions according to reason.[136] In the chapter on identity Locke indicates that 'person' can only be applied to such free, rational beings whom we hold responsible for their actions: the term 'belongs only to intelligent Agents capable of a Law, and Happiness and Misery'.[137] Locke also points out that the *identity* of the person is the foundation of 'all the Right and Justice of Reward and Punishment'.[138] This claim that the 'identity condition' needs to be satisfied for just rewards and punishment is not original to Locke. Within the framework of Cartesian doctrine, for example, the identity required for moral and legal responsibility was seen as guaranteed by the metaphysical composition of the self as an immaterial substance. But since Locke rejects Cartesian metaphysics, he cannot, as Descartes and his followers could, simply assume that the 'identity condition' is secured by the metaphysical make-up of the self. In Locke, the notion of self-identity required for moral and legal purposes takes on an entirely new meaning: morally and legally relevant action attribution requires *consciousness* in addition to freedom and reason. Thus, he links his practical considerations concerning the person to his theoretical or 'speculative' ones in terms of consciousness. For *Locke* to say that responsibility and just rewards or punishments are founded in self-identity is to say that it is required both that I was conscious of what I was doing when I performed the action and that I am now conscious of what I did then: we are liable to punishment for past crimes on account of our identity as persons (in Locke's sense), and not on account of our identity as thinking substances or human beings; for it is 'consciousness whereby [one] becomes concerned and accountable, owns and imputes to [oneself] past Actions'.[139]

If one wishes to place Locke's notion of person in relation to traditional ones, it is clear now that it comes closest to that of person as (moral) quality: 'person' or 'personality' denotes that aspect or quality of the self with respect to which I may be morally and legally judged. However, a number of commentators argue that 'person' in Locke denotes the idea of a rational substance.[140] In support of this interpretation, reference is sometimes made to a passage which does not appear in the chapter on identity, but in Book III of the *Essay* where Locke introduces the notion of 'moral man' as the idea of a '*corporeal rational Being*'.[141] This notion of 'moral man' is then used to suggest Locke's concept of moral person(ality) in the chapter on identity and is to be understood in essentially the same way as that of 'moral man', namely, as a rational substance.[142] It is not clear, however, why the 'moral man' passage should lead to such an understanding of Locke's notion of person. The point of the passage in Book III is to argue that the bodily shape of a being should not be a relevant consideration when deciding whether that being can be classed with 'man' in a moral sense (although bodily shape *is* relevant to the notion of man 'in a physical Sense'). We may class the being as a *moral man,* if it has rationality (and, that is, freedom).[143] Yet, rationality and freedom are necessary, but not sufficient conditions of *personhood:* the personality or that aspect of the self, in relation to which it may be morally and legally judged, is constituted through the *consciousness* of a rational substance. Thus, it is misleading to liken Locke's notion of person(ality) to that of 'moral man': that which is constituted by the consciousness of a rational substance is not itself a substance.

Locke's idea that 'punishment . . . [is] annexed to personality, and personality to consciousness'[144] means, of course, that actions of which I have no consciousness are not part of my personality and that, consequently, I cannot justly be held responsible for them: I do not have to accept authorship of actions which are not united to my personality through consciousness, and I cannot justly be punished for criminal acts which I do not ascribe to myself through consciousness. Appealing to the insanity defence, Locke holds that his theory, with its distinction between man and person, can explain and justify the practice of the law where the sane man is not punished for what he did when temporarily insane.[145] According to Locke, the sane man is not punished because he is not the same *person* as he was when insane; he is the same human being, but since he was 'besides himself', as Locke puts it, when he committed the crime, there is no link of consciousness, that is, no *personal* identity, and, consequently, no justification for punishment.[146] However, other cases which Locke discusses seem to suggest, as some of Locke's early critics noticed, that his theory is actually inconsistent with the practice of the law in his time. Locke raises the case of the drunkard. Since it is the practice of the law to punish the sober man for what he did when drunk, the man drunk and the man sober would have to be the same person on Locke's view; but since the man drunk committed the crime while being 'besides himself' and the sober man in any case may not remember what he did when drunk, Locke's theory does not *allow* that the man sober and the man drunk be regarded as the same person and that the former be punished for what the latter did. Locke attempts to reconcile his theory with legal practice by arguing that in the case of the drunkard human courts of law do not have to accept lack of consciousness as a plea, because they cannot know for certain whether the plea is genuine: 'They cannot distinguish certainly what is real, what counterfeit.'[147] And since I cannot *prove* my lack of consciousness, human courts will justly punish me if the fact that I committed the crime is proved against me, for example by an eyewitness. The courts are justified in simply assuming that my plea is not genuine and punishing me 'with a Justice suitable to their way of Knowledge'.[148]

Locke's friend William Molyneux and Thomas Becconsall challenged Locke on this point.[149] Molyneux argued that crimes committed by someone when drunk are punishable not for the reason Locke gives, but because drunkenness is itself a crime which is committed voluntarily and because one crime that brings about another crime cannot be used as an excuse for the latter. Now, it is certainly true that Molyneux's and Becconsall's arguments were more in line with English seventeenth-century legal thought than were Locke's: drunkenness was a punishable offence and it was not accepted as an excuse for a crime that resulted from it. The drunkard was thought of as *voluntarius daemon*; and, according to Coke, 'he hath . . . no priviledge thereby [i.e., by his drunkenness]; but what hurt or ill soever he doth his drunkenness doth aggravate it.'[150] Locke, however, in responding to the criticism, says that Molyneux's argument, 'how good soever', cannot be used by him: 'For what has this to do with consciousness? nay it is an argument against me, for if a man may be punish'd for any crime which he committed when drunk, whereof *he is allow'd not to be conscious,* it overturns my hypothesis.'[151] Locke conceded to Molyneux 'that drunkenness being a voluntary defect, want of consciousness ought not to be presum'd in favour of the drunkard';[152] but he still wanted to accommodate the drunkard case to his theory: the person, in this case, is *not* 'allow'd not to be conscious'. Rather, courts are justified in basing their judgement on the assumption that the person was conscious of what he did, because lack of consciousness cannot be proved in favour of the accused. Yet, even this defence concedes that just punishment or reward does not have to be based on the *actual* self-ascription of actions through consciousness. Indeed, consideration of the drunkard case gives rise to a more general problem for Locke's theory. Since personal identity is said to be the basis of judgements of human courts and since personal identity is said to be constituted only through inner consciousness, the question arises how human courts can *in principle* distinguish between genuine and pretended lack of consciousness: since a person's self-ascription of actions through consciousness is beyond the courts' knowledge, how can they ever 'distinguish certainly what is real, what counterfeit'? The only means available to them for identifying the individual are those that relate to the individual as human (i.e., bodily) being. In other words, they can judge only with regard to the identity of the self as human being, not as person. But if this is so, does Locke's claim that *personal* identity is the foundation of 'all the Right and Justice of Reward and Punishment' still make sense? To answer this, we have to take into account the theological aspect of Locke's theory.

Locke's talk of personal identity being the ground of just reward or punishment refers, in the last result, to the Last Judgement. And here the problem of the genuineness of self-ascription of actions through consciousness does not arise: Locke appeals to the belief that we shall have a purified consciousness free from all error: 'The Secrets of all Hearts shall be laid open', and 'No one shall be made to answer for what he knows nothing of.'[153] According to Locke, God will not only ensure that we shall not lack consciousness of actions we in fact committed consciously but also that we shall not wrongly ascribe actions to ourselves which we did not commit: divine justice and goodness 'will not by a fatal Error of theirs [i.e., God's creatures] transfer from one to another, that consciousness, which draws Reward or Punishment with it'.[154] Therefore, in relation to the Last Judgement, Locke can safely say: 'The Sentence shall be justified by the consciousness all Persons shall have, that they *themselves* in what Bodies soever they appear, or what Substances soever that consciousness adheres to, are the *same,* that committed those Actions, and deserve that Punishment for them.'[155] It is important to note that Locke's reference to the Last Judgement is an *essential* element of his theory: only by relating the question of moral responsibility and reward or punishment to the Last Judgement can Locke avoid all those problems which would arise from his position that consciousness-based personal identity alone is the foundation of just judgement. Thus, although it is correct to say that Locke's theory is 'revolutionary' in some respects – for example, in that he distinguishes personal identity from identity of substance – it is clear that, in other respects, it must be understood in the context of the traditional Christian doctrine of life after death. Locke also attempts to explain the way in which we at present relate to the future life and the divine judgement. He does so by linking the notion of consciousness to that of desire for happiness. For Locke, it is obvious that 'that which is conscious of Pleasure and Pain' desires that 'that *self,* that is conscious, should be happy.' He says that a 'concern for Happiness' is 'the unavoidable concomitant of consciousness'.[156] And it is through its link with this 'concern' that consciousness relates to the *future:* we are now motivated to act in such a way as to avoid future pain and to attain happiness; and when pursued rationally, the 'concern' relates to happiness in the *future life* after death.[157] For, according to Locke (and Christian doctrine), only the happiness of the future life is true happiness. Further, since our happiness or misery in the future life depends on God's judgement of our actions in this life, we are anxious to be able to ascribe actions to ourselves which please God, that is, actions which conform to the divine moral law, a law available to us through reason and revelation.

Having said that Locke's theory must be understood in the context of the traditional Christian doctrine of life after death, it must be pointed out that, at the same time, his conception of life after death is *based* on his new theory of the person and, thereby, differs considerably from some traditional views about the future life. Debates about the immortality of the soul, as noted earlier, revolved to a large extent around the question of the soul's nature, that is, around the question of whether the soul is a material or an immaterial substance: some theologians and philosophers argued that the 'identity condition' can be satisfied only if the soul is immaterial. Since Locke argues that questions about the essence of the soul are irrelevant to *personal* identity in this life, he regards them as irrelevant to personal *immortality* as well.[158] We are *assured* of our immortality, Locke says, through revelation.[159] And like Cudworth, he argues that by immortality 'is not meant a state of bare substantial existence and duration', but 'a state of sensibility'.[160] This means that immortality is a state in which we shall live as *persons,* as beings who are conscious of pleasure and pain. Locke argues that even if one has shown that the soul or mental substance is indestructible and continues to exist forever, one has not thereby shown that the *person* enjoys immortal *life.* The belief in immortality is, for Locke, the belief that God 'can and will restore us to the like state of Sensibility in another World, and make us capable there to receive the Retribution he has designed to Men, according to their doings in this Life'.[161] If the future state were not a state of consciousness or 'sensibility', there would be no distinction for us between reward and punishment, no distinction between heaven and hell.[162] Also, if the future life were merely 'a state of bare substantial existence and duration', we would not now be *concerned* for our future life and, consequently, not determine our actions accordingly. The identity condition which needs to be satisfied for a meaningful conception of a future life relates to the *person,* not to mental substance: it is required that present and future life form one unity of consciousness, that the consciousness of divine reward or punishment will be part of the same person who was constituted in this life by the consciousness of those actions which are the objects of divine judgement. Similarly, Locke re-interprets the doctrine of the resurrection of the body against the background of his theory of personal identity: since life after death means that the same *person* will be restored, he does not think it necessary that the resurrection-body be the very same as the pre-mortem body. Locke does not deny that we shall have a body, yet he argues that its *identity* is not essential; the crucial point for life after death is that our *personal* identity is retained: 'And thus we may be able without any difficulty to conceive, the same Person at the Resurrection, though in a Body not exactly in make or parts the same which he had here, the same consciousness going along with the Soul that inhabits it.'[163] Clearly, Locke is in agreement with thinkers such as Bury who held that bodily identity is not required by the doctrine of the resurrection. Yet he disagrees with Bury in arguing that the identity of the mental substance is not necessary either: all that is required, according to Locke, is that consciousness unites conscious experiences and actions of this life and thereby constitutes the same person who lived here.

Locke's distinction between substance and person even enables him to handle the doctrine of the pre-existence of souls. Unlike other critics of the doctrine, Locke does not appeal to the fact that we do not remember anything of our pre-existent life in order to *refute* the belief in pre-existence. To Locke, however, lack of consciousness of the past life means that the pre-existent state, assuming there was one, is completely irrelevant to the self as person in this life. If there had been a pre-existent state of our soul, our soul now and then would constitute different persons, because the two states do not form a unity of consciousness: 'So that personal Identity reaching no farther than consciousness reaches, a pre-existent Spirit not having continued so many Ages in a state of Silence, must needs make different Persons.'[164] A pre-existent state would only matter, Locke holds, if it were accessible to consciousness now; but this is not the case, as the proponents of the doctrine themselves seem to concede.

Locke's theory aroused controversy very soon after its first publication in 1694. Although some attempted to defend it,[165] most of Locke's contemporaries attacked it. Apart from the criticism by Molyneux and Beconsall, which relates to the moral and legal aspects of Locke's theory, there was also criticism based on metaphysical and theological arguments. Since Locke's theory does not commit him to either the materialist or the immaterialist account of the soul, it could, in principle, be accommodated to both accounts. Yet, as a matter of fact, although at least some materialists referred favourably to Locke's theory,[166] defenders of the immateriality of the soul tended to reject it, partly because it leaves open the very question of immateriality. The most prominent theological critic was Edward Stillingfleet, Bishop of Worcester, with whom Locke entered into a long controversy over the *Essay* as a whole. Like other critics of Locke, Stillingfleet believed that the identity of the body at the resurrection is an article of the Christian faith. He argued that Locke's interpretation of the doctrine of the resurrection and his theory of personal identity on which that interpretation is based are inconsistent with the Christian faith.[167] In reply, Locke tried to defend his position partly by restating some of his philosophical arguments, partly by producing textual evidence from the Bible in support of his view. Although he does not doubt 'that the dead shall be raised with bodies',[168] he points out to Stillingfleet that when Saint Paul 'speaks of the resurrection, he says, you, and not your bodies. l.Cor.vi.14'.[169] Those thinkers who, like Locke, denied the identity of the resurrection-body sometimes cited Locke's theory of personal identity in support of their theological position.[170] Philosophers criticising Locke's theory on *metaphysical* grounds did so mainly because they thought personal identity has to be tied to, or even equated with, identity of substance, and cannot be constituted solely by consciousness. This means they rejected, explicitly or implicitly, Locke's important distinction between man, mental substance, and person. According to Locke's Aristotelian critic John Sergeant, the person just *is* the individual man, and the individual man is a complete substance. But even though Sergeant says that he 'must forestall all his [i.e., Locke's] Subsequent Discourses by denying this Preliminary to them', [171] he produces further arguments against Locke. His main charge is the same as the one against the general theory of identity – that Locke's theory is circular.[172] He argues that a person (or man) must be an individual prior to becoming conscious. To Sergeant, consciousness refers to the self as the object in which acts of consciousness originate; therefore, the self must be an individual prior to the occurrence of acts of consciousness: 'Our Person, or Individual *Self* . . . is the *Object* of that *Consciousness; and Objects* must be *antecedent* and *presupposed* to the *Acts* which are employ'd about them, because the Objects are the *Cause* of those *Acts*.'[173] Obviously, this critique is successful only if one assumes the very thing that Locke explicitly challenged, namely, that the person is an object, a thing or substance to which consciousness relates as to an already individuated being. Had Locke adopted this position, Sergeant's criticism would indeed have struck home, just as South's critique of Sherlock had a few years earlier. Yet, unlike Sherlock, who in order to escape South's critique made it clear that he really holds a substance-view of the person, Locke can stick to his new conception of the person in terms of consciousness and be safe from the charge of circularity precisely because he insists on the distinction between man, mental substance, and person as three different ideas under which we may consider the self. Moreover, Sergeant misrepresents what Locke has to say about consciousness constituting personal identity when he claims that, for Locke, consciousness *of identity* constitutes identity.[174] Had Locke said this, his theory would have been quite obviously circular. But Locke does not hold that consciousness of sameness constitutes sameness; rather, he holds that consciousness of *thoughts and actions* constitutes the person and its identity over time. Locke did not reply to Sergeant; his marginal notes in his copy of Sergeant's book indicate, however, what his reply would have looked like: he would have appealed to his distinction between man and person. Locke can agree that the individuality of the self as 'man' must be presupposed for consciousness to occur; for he does not say that consciousness constitutes the identity of the self as man: I may have the individuality and identity of a human being independently of consciousness, but, Locke argues, I am not a person and have no personal identity without consciousness.[175] Even though the charge of circularity against Locke fails, it has been repeated many times since Sergeant up to the present day, most famously by Bishop Butler in the eighteenth century.[176]

IV. LEIBNIZ

Leibniz had worked out his own theory of self-identity and of identity in general well before he wrote the *Nouveaux essais sur l'entendement humain* (1704) against Locke and, indeed, even well before the first edition of Locke's *Essay* was published.[177] There are some similarities between Leibniz's and Locke's account of self-identity. For example, Leibniz, too, distinguishes between substantial and personal identity. However, the differences between Leibniz and Locke on this issue are, in the last analysis, more significant than the similarities. Although Leibniz emphasises in many places that on his view the self is never without a body,[178] it is clear that he regards the soul as the real self. And, for Leibniz, human souls are, like all monads, immaterial substances.[179] Unlike other monads, they have rationality and the ability to attain knowledge of moral truths and of their own essence. Their identity over time is, however, just like that of other substances, secured by their intrinsic nature or 'complete notion': Leibniz maintains that everything that is to happen to the self 'is already included virtually in his nature or notion, just as the properties of a circle are included in its definition'.[180] Thus, 'there is in the soul of Alexander for all time traces of everything that happened to him, and marks of everything that will happen to him.'[181] And this is what distinguishes his soul from all others and guarantees its identity through time. In the *Nouveaux essais* Leibniz explains this interrelation of 'marks' and 'traces' that constitutes identity in terms of his doctrine about 'minute perceptions', that is, unconscious states of the soul: 'These insensible perceptions also indicate and constitute the same individual, who is characterized by the vestiges or expressions which the perceptions preserve from the individual's former states, thereby connecting these with his present state.'[182] It follows that for Leibniz the identity of the self, as soul, does not require that we are conscious of those 'traces' or 'perceptions' and their interconnexion.[183] He consistently treats the problem of self-identity in the same way as he treats identity in general, distinguishing between the *a priori* ground of self-identity and the *a posteriori* criteria for discovering self-identity: the *a priori* ground of my identity lies 'in the complete concept of me which makes what is called myself, which is the basis of the connexion between all my different states and of which God had perfect knowledge from all eternity'.[184] Consciousness or 'my subjective experience' merely *convinces* me '*a posteriori* of this identity'.[185] The real identity, that of the soul, is constituted independently of consciousness. Consequently, Leibniz points out against Locke that consciousness of past states of the mind merely makes 'the real identity appear'.[186]

But then Leibniz does seem to ascribe to consciousness a constitutive function in a way; for he says that consciousness constitutes the identity of the self as *person*. And by 'person' he means the self as a *moral entity:* as persons we are members of the 'moral world or City of God, the most noble part of the universe'.[187] Not unlike Locke, so it seems, Leibniz bases moral or personal identity on consciousness; for he argues that human selves retain their personality or moral quality through a 'recollection, consciousness or power to know what they are, upon which depends the whole of their morality, penalties and punishments'.[188] Leibniz clearly distinguishes between the *metaphysical* identity of the self (as immaterial substance) and the *moral* identity of the self (as person) which is constituted by consciousness: 'The intelligent soul that knows what it is, and is capable of pronouncing this *me* which says so much, not only remains the same metaphysically . . . but it also remains morally the same and constitutes the same personality. For it is the memory and knowledge of this *me* that makes it liable to punishment and reward.'[189]

Also, Leibniz links the notion of consciousness-based personality to that of life after death. Like Cudworth and Locke, he argues against the view that the future life is merely a state of 'perpetual subsistence'.[190] The future life requires personal as well as substantial identity; that is, it requires that 'the soul possesses consciousness or is familiar in itself with what every man calls "my self"'. This renders it susceptible of moral qualities, and of reward and punishment, . . . [I]mmortality without memory would be useless.'[191] In the writings prior to the *Nouveaux essais* Leibniz holds that substantial identity is always and necessarily accompanied by personal identity, that is, that we always and necessarily retain a memory of our past actions.[192] He seems simply to assume that our memory will not fail us, because if it did, there would be no personal identity and no just divine judgement. Leibniz says that human souls or minds '*must* keep their personality and their moral qualities in order that the city of God lose no one', and it is '*necessary* that they be free from those upheavals in the universe which would make them totally unrecognizable to themselves, and would turn them, morally speaking, into another person'.[193] According to Leibniz, then, consciousness or inner experience constitutes personal identity *a posteriori*; but *that* consciousness does so and that it always *correctly* ascribes past actions to the self is a necessity. Leibniz does not seem to be disturbed by the common fact of forgetfulness and by cases of amnesia. Even in the preface to the *Nouveaux essais* he says of human souls that they 'are *destined* always to preserve the *persona* [*le personnage*] which they have been given in the city of God, and hence to retain their memories, so that they may be more susceptible of punishments and rewards'.[194] In the chapter on identity in the *Nouveaux essais,* however, Leibniz does take into account issues such as amnesia and incorrect memory. Yet, Leibniz argues, these issues do not affect what he calls immediate memory or consciousness, that is, consciousness of immediately preceding states: 'The consciousness or reflection which accompanies inner activity . . . cannot naturally deceive us.'[195] And he indicates that this immediate connexion between conscious states is all that is required for personal identity: 'To discover one's own moral identity unaided, it is sufficient that between one state and a neighbouring . . . one there be a mediating bond of consciousness.'[196] Just as substantial or 'real' identity is secured by the 'liaison' of minute perceptions, Leibniz seems to suggest, personal identity is preserved by the 'liaison' of immediate memories from one moment to the next. But what about forgetfulness concerning the distant past? Leibniz recognises that 'we can be deceived by a memory across an interval.'[197] Leibniz's discussion of the issue of amnesia shows that his theory differs markedly from Locke's account of personal identity. For here he argues that consciousness is *not* necessary for personal identity: the identity of the self as person can also be established by the testimony of others. Leibniz explicitly rejects Locke's idea that moral or personal identity is based *solely* on inner consciousness:

Thus, if an illness had interrupted the continuity of my bond of consciousness, so that I did not know how I had arrived at my present state even though I could remember things further back, the testimony of others could fill in the gap in my recollection. I could even be punished on this testimony if I had done some deliberate wrong during an interval which this illness had made me forget a short time later. And if I forgot my whole past, and needed to have myself taught all over again, even my name and how to read and write, I could still learn from others about my life during my preceding state; and, similarly, I would have retained my rights without having to be divided into two persons and made to inherit from myself. All this is enough to maintain the moral identity which makes the same person.[198]

These remarks are quite consistent, however, with Leibniz's statement in the same section, that consciousness does constitute moral or personal identity. For he does not say *tout court* that consciousness establishes personal identity; he says that consciousness does so 'when accompanied by truth', that is, when the self-ascription of actions through consciousness is a correct, truthful ascription of actions.[199] Leibniz realises, of course, that the testimony of others is not an absolutely reliable basis for action ascription either; there may be cases where others conspire to deceive me so that the external evidence turns out to be just as false as the internal evidence of consciousness might turn out to be. Leibniz finally resorts to God; for 'in relation to God, whose social bond with us is the cardinal point of morality, error cannot occur'.[200] But he rejects Locke's idea that the divine judgement is just because we shall have a purified consciousness which is free from error. Even human courts of law do not have to rely on the evidence of a person's consciousness and may refer to the evidence of eyewitnesses to establish the personal identity of the accused. The omniscient God does not have to rely on either individual consciousness or on the testimony of others; for the knowledge 'of that just Judge who is never deceived' is sufficient on its own.[201] The truth about action ascription lies in the intrinsic nature or 'complete notion' of the self as substance which is known to God.

Here lies the most fundamental difference between Leibniz and Locke: for Locke it is a real possibility that there be personal identity without substantial identity, or in Leibniz's terminology, 'that this apparent identity could be preserved in the absence of any real identity'.[202] To Leibniz, however, this is a mere logical possibility. It 'would be a miracle'[203]: it would 'disrupt the order of things for no reason, and would divorce what can become before our awareness from the truth – the truth which is preserved by insensible perceptions'.[204] According to the 'order of things', Leibniz argues, real identity must be presupposed by apparent identity. Thus, although he does not equate personal with substantial identity, he holds that the former depends on the latter. Whereas Locke argued for keeping personal and substantial identity separate, Leibniz maintained what was assumed by the Cartesians, namely, that the (personal) identity required for morality can be preserved only by the metaphysical identity of the self as immaterial soul.

V. THE EIGHTEENTH-CENTURY DEBATE

Locke's theory, not Leibniz's, dominated the disputes over personal identity in the eighteenth century. This is true especially, but not only, of British philosophy.[205] Leibniz's critique of Locke was not published until 1765, and by then Locke's theory had already had an immense impact on eighteenth-century thought. Its influence was not confined to philosophical disputes: summaries of Locke's theory appeared in some of the leading encyclopaedias of the time,[206] and it had a considerable impact on eighteenth-century literature, such as the works of Jonathan Swift and Laurence Sterne.[207] Nevertheless, most eighteenth-century thinkers who discussed the problem criticised and rejected Locke's theory. Some had theological motives for this and argued that Locke's theory is inconsistent with Christian doctrine which, they claimed, maintains the identity of the resurrection-body as an article of faith. Others, wishing to tie personal identity to substantial identity in some way or other, made metaphysical and logical objections. The charge of circularity against Locke was reiterated again and again, from Henry Lee (1702) to Joseph Butler (1736) and Thomas Reid (1785), to name only the better-known critics. As in Sergeant, who first brought forward this charge, the argument is based on an understanding of 'person' as substance. The most important eighteenth-century criticism was made by Berkeley in his *Alciphron* of 1732, later taken up by Thomas Reid (1785) in his famous 'gallant officer' story. The point of the criticism relates to the logic of identity: it is argued that Locke's theory is inconsistent with the transitivity of the identity relation. Reid's story is about a general who remembers his actions as an officer, but not what happened to him when he was a boy at school (where he was flogged 'for robbing an orchard'), although when an officer he did remember his boyhood experience. Now, on Locke's theory, the officer is the same person as the boy, and the general the same person as the officer, but the general is not the same person as the boy, because there is no link of consciousness here. However, Reid argues, it belongs to the logic of identity that if the boy and the officer and the officer and the general are the same person, respectively, then the general and the boy are the same person, too. But Locke's theory does not allow this, because 'the general's consciousness does not reach so far back as his flogging, therefore, according to Mr. Locke's doctrine, he is not the person who was flogged.'[208] For Reid (and Berkeley), Locke's theory which bases personal identity on consciousness must be rejected because identity is transitive, whereas consciousness is not. Many commentators have speculated how Locke could have responded to this criticism. Maybe Locke would have appealed to his distinction between man and person, arguing that general and boy are not the same person, but the same human being, and that the transitivity of identity is preserved in relation to the self as man. However, it could be argued against this that the transitivity of identity still holds even if we consider the self just under the concept of person. As a further reply it has been suggested, consistently with what Locke says, that Locke's theory of the person is not, in fact, a theory about an object's identity through time, but, rather, about personality being constituted at any one time through consciousness appropriating past actions, and that, therefore, the issue of transitivity does not affect Locke's theory.[209] This would mean that the notion of identity which Locke does use in the context of discussing personality differs from that of the standard logic even of his day.[210]

Berkeley's criticism of Locke's theory and his other references to the issue of personal identity are brief. Within his own immaterialist metaphysics, just as within Cartesian metaphysics, a real problem of personal identity through time does not arise. There were other eighteenth-century philosophers, of course, who developed independent and now well-known theories on the topic, among them, Shaftesbury and Hume; but even here, it is clear that Locke's theory provided the main background against which arguments were worked out. The most Lockean eighteenth-century account of personal identity is perhaps that of Edmund Law. Whereas most of Locke's critics explicitly or implicitly reject the distinction between man and person and interpret Locke's notion of 'person' in terms of substance, Law insists on the distinction between man and person, arguing that 'person' denotes a Lockean 'mode', rather than a substance. Law says that the term 'person' denotes 'some such quality or modification in man as denominates him a moral agent, or an accountable creature' and that when we apply the term to an individual human being 'we do not treat him absolutely, and in gross; but under a particular relation or precision.'[211] On this basis, Law explicitly defends Locke's theory against the charge of circularity.

In Germany, the influential Christian Wolff incorporated a largely Leibnizian account of the self in his metaphysical system, which dominated philosophy at German universities throughout the first half of the eighteenth century. It was not until the 1750s and 1760s that Locke's and other British theories made a serious impact on German thought and sparked analyses of human subjectivity which were less metaphysical in kind. These were taken up and transformed by Kant who, as recent research has shown, owed much more to Locke than the official pronouncements in his published works indicate.[212] With Kant, an entirely new tradition of the theory of the self began. Kant's main concern, it is true, is not with empirical personal identity. However, what Kant has to say about consciousness in general and the conceptual distinctions he draws in this connexion, especially between the self of the transcendental apperception, the self as noumenon, and the self as phaenomenon, are relevant to the topic. Kant's theory of self-identity is central to his philosophical system as a whole, and it proved to be a crucial element in the development of German Idealism in the late eighteenth and early nineteenth centuries.

NOTES

1 This is underscored by the fact that a 1993 review article on 'Recent Work on Personal Identity' has more references to 'Locke 1694' than to many of the contributions of the 1970s and 1980s which the article mainly discusses (see Baillie 1993). And in a chapter

entitled 'Neo-Lockean and Anti-Lockean Theories of Personal Identity in Analytic Philosophy', Michael Ayers points out, correctly, that 'for all the transformation of our motives, indeed, of our general philosophical theory . . . the debate on personal identity has hardly moved on since the innovations of the seventeenth and eighteenth centuries' (Ayers 1991, vol. 2, p. 281). The most prominent Neo-Lockean theory of personal identity is that of Derek Parfit who argues that personal identity is constituted through psychological, rather than material connexions (Parfit 1985, pp. 204–9). For a critique of Neo-Lockean theory see Ayers 1991, pp. 281–92. For a defence, see Rovane 1993.

2 On the history of the term 'persona', see Trendelenburg 1908; Rheinfelder 1928; Vogel 1963; Fuhrmann 1979; Greshake 1981; Mauss 1985; Teichman 1985.

3 *De Officiis* I. Compare Fuhrmann 1979, pp. 97–102, and Gill 1988.

4 See Hobbes, *Lev.* xvi (Hobbes 1968, pp. 217–18).

5 See Gracia 1984. See also Chapter 9 in this book.

6 *De Trinitate* V 9, 10; VII 4, 7–9.

7 *De Trinitate* X 11, 17–18. On Augustine, see Schmaus 1927; Lloyd 1972; O'Daly 1987, especially pp. 42, 57–8, 135–6, 148–51.

8 *Liber contra Eutychen et Nestorium,* in Boethius 1973, pp. 84–5 and 90–1. On Boethius, see Rheinfelder 1928, pp. 159–71, esp. pp. 169–71. See also Chadwick 1981, pp. 190–202.

9 *De Trinitate,* in Boethius 1973, pp. 10–11.

10 For an overview of seventeenth- and eighteenth-century views on immortality, see Mijuskovic 1974, pp. 19–57. For systematic discussions of the 'identity condition', see Williams 1973, pp. 91–2; Perrett 1987, pp. 93–6.

11 Thomas Aquinas, *Summa th.* I q29, a1.

12 Thomas Aquinas, *Summa th.* I q29 a4.

13 Thomas Aquinas, *Summa th.* I q29 a1.

14 *Disp. met.* XXXIV.1.13.

15 See Chapter 9.

16 *Disp. met.* V.6.15.

17 *Disp. met.* V.4.4. See also the discussion in Chapter 9 in this book.

18 See Scheibler 1636, 'Prooemium', and book 2, chap. 2, pp. 444–52.

19 Micraelius 1662, column 991. See also Scharf 1643, p. 251. On German seventeenth-century university metaphysics and the notion of person, see Wundt 1939, pp. 171, 220 ff.; Lewalter 1967, pp. 69 ff., 73.

20 Valla, *De linguae latinae elegantiae,* Book VI, chap. 34 (Valla 1688, pp. 519–21). Serveto 1531, pp. 29a and 36b; Serveto 1932, pp. 45 and 57.

21 For Serveto, see Rheinfelder 1928, pp. 167–9. For Melanchthon's critique of the notion of person as quality, see Trendelenburg 1908, pp. 13–14.

22 De Vries 1718, p. 58; Chauvin 1713, p. 485.

23 Scheibler 1636, pp. 444–6.

24 Burthogge 1694, pp. 277–80. See also Stillingfleet 1687, p. 25.

25 See, e.g., Descartes's letters to Elisabeth of 28 June 1643 (AT III 694) and of 15 September 1645 (AT IV 293). Compare also (Rodis-)Lewis 1950b, p. 237.

26 AT III 692.

27 AT III 508.

28 E.g., Descartes writes in a letter to Mesland that human bodies 'are numerically the same only because they are *informed* by the same soul' (AT IV 167; emphasis added).

29 Med. VI (AT VII 78).

30 *Disc.,* part IV (AT VI 33).

31 For a more detailed account of Descartes's notion of the soul, see Chapter 23 in this book.
32 *Princ.* I 53.
33 See Descartes's letter to Gibieuf, 19 January 1642 (AT III 478f).
34 *Princ.* I 9.
35 Descartes's 'Conversation with Burman' (AT V 149; CB, p. 7). In CB 'conscium esse' is translated as 'to be aware'.
36 *Princ.* I 60.
37 See Chapter 9.
38 'Synopsis' of the *Meditationes* (AT VII 14).
39 See Chapter 25.
40 See Geulincx 1891–3, vol. 3, p. 219.
41 *Rech.* III.2.7.
42 For a more detailed discussion of the Sherlock–South debate over the notion of person, see Thiel 1983, pp. 63–4, 107–16. For a different account of the debate see Wedeking 1990, pp. 165–72.
43 South 1693, p. 75; 1695, pp. 115–16.
44 Sherlock 1694, p. 47.
45 Sherlock 1694, p. 45.
46 Sherlock 1690, pp. 48–9.
47 In order to account for the unity of the three divine persons, Sherlock introduces the notion of 'mutual consciousness'. The divine persons have a mutual consciousness of one another, in addition to self-consciousness, 'and therefore are as essentially One, as a Mind or Spirit is One with itself' (Sherlock 1690, p. 68). For a similar account of the rôles of self-consciousness and mutual consciousness before Sherlock, see Turner 1685, pp. clii–cliii; also pp. cxxv–cxxvii.
48 South 1693, pp. 71, 94.
49 South 1693, p. 71. Similar arguments were brought forward against Sherlock by Richard Burthogge and Edward Stillingfleet. See Burthogge 1694, p. 273; Stillingfleet 1697a, pp. 71–2.
50 Sherlock 1694, p. 6.
51 Sherlock 1694, p. 39.
52 Sherlock 1694, p. 66.
53 Sherlock 1694, p. 60.
54 South 1695, p. 99.
55 Sherlock 1694, p. 51.
56 Cudworth 1678.
57 Cudworth 1678, pp. 167, 171.
58 Cudworth 1678, pp. 160–1.
59 Cudworth 1678, p. 159. Compare Plotinus, *Enneads* III.8.4; V.8.11/23.
60 Cudworth 1678, p. 159.
61 For a more detailed account of Cudworth's understanding of consciousness, see Thiel 1991, pp. 87–95. For a discussion of late seventeenth- and early eighteenth-century notions of consciousness, see Thiel 1994.
62 Cudworth 1678, p. 750.
63 *Eth.* II prop. 13 cor.
64 *Eth.* II prop. 21 schol.; II prop. 7 schol.
65 For Spinoza's account of the individuation of bodies and his argument for the oneness of substance, see Chapter 9.

66 *Eth.* II prop. 13.

67 *Eth.* II prop. 19 dem. In the early *Korte Verhandeling* (Short Treatise on God, Man, and his Well-Being) Spinoza states that change in our body 'which arises in us from the fact that other bodies act on ours, cannot occur without the soul's becoming aware of it, since it, too, changes constantly' (Geb. I 52n).

68 *Eth.* V prop. 21.

69 *Eth.* IV prop. 39 schol.

70 *Korte ver.* II, Geb. I 52n.

71 For Spinoza's views on the eternity of mind, see the concise account in Curley 1988, pp. 83–6.

72 *Ger.* VI 529–30 (Leibniz 1969, pp. 554–5).

73 Curley 1988, p. 86.

74 This is how Rice (1975, pp. 209–10) interprets the story.

75 For a detailed discussion of Pascal and La Rochefoucauld, see Krailsheimer 1962.

76 *Pens.* 688, as translated in Pascal 1966.

77 *Lev.* xlvi (Hobbes 1968, p. 689).

78 *Lev.* xxxiv (Hobbes 1968, pp. 428–9).

79 *Lev.* xlvi (Hobbes 1968, p. 691).

80 *Lev.* xvi (Hobbes 1968, pp. 217–22).

81 *Lev.* xvi (Hobbes 1968, p. 217).

82 *Lev.* xvi (Hobbes 1968, p. 217).

83 *Lev.* xvi (Hobbes 1968, p. 219).

84 See Chapter 9.

85 Pufendorf 1672, I.1.12–3; 1717, pp. 7–8.

86 Pufendorf 1672, II.4.1; 1717, p. 154.

87 Cudworth 1678, p. 869. Passmore argues that Cudworth is led to deny the Christian doctrine of *eternal* rewards and *eternal* punishments: 'For it is inconsistent with the nature of the human soul [according to Cudworth], which always contains within it the potentiality for good and evil, a potentiality which immortality could do nothing to remove' (Passmore 1951, pp. 77–8).

88 Ward 1652, p. 35.

89 Daniel Garber drew my attention to the importance of the notion of intellectual memory in this context. Descartes speaks of intellectual memory in several places. See, e.g., the letter to Huygens where Descartes says: 'We have, in my view, an intellectual memory which is certainly independent of the body' (AT III 798). For a detailed discussion of Descartes's notion of intellectual memory and the problem of immortality, see (Rodis-)Lewis 1950b, pp. 208–18.

90 *Lev.* xxxviii and xliv. For the view that immortality is not 'natural', but depends on the grace of God, see also Richard Overton's *Mans Mortallitie* of 1643–4. Overton says that 'all *hope* of future life and Being is in the Resurrection' (Overton 1644, p. 17).

91 Cudworth 1678, pp. 45 and 868–9.

92 Cudworth 1678, p. 159. See also p. 847: 'It is certain, that without *Consciousness* or *Understanding* nothing can be *Happy* (since it could not have any *Fruition* of itself).'

93 Cudworth 1678, p. 830. The argument that the materialist theory cannot account for the soul's unity and simplicity is not, of course, unique to Cudworth. See, e.g., Henry More, *An Antidote against Atheism*: 'This is to make the *several particles* of the *Brain* so many *individual persons*; a fitter object for Laughter then the least measure of Belief' (More 1662c, p. 34). Similarly, Richard Bentley argues that on the materialist hypothesis the human self cannot be a unitary entity: 'For every single Atom of our Bodies would

be a distinct Animal, endued with self-consciousness and personal Sensation of its own. And a great number of such living and thinking Particles could not possibly by their mutual contract and pressing and striking compose one greater individual Animal, with one Mind and Understanding, and a vital Consension of the whole Body' (Bentley 1699, p. 47). The Cambridge Platonist John Smith appeals to the 'knowledge which the soul retains in itself of things past, and in some sort prevision of things to come'; and he argues that only an immaterial soul 'can thus bind up past, present, and future time together' (Smith 1821, pp. 88–9).

94 Cudworth 1678, p. 46. See also p. 799: 'It is certain, that we have not all the same Numerical Matter, and neither more nor less, both in *Infancy* and in Old Age, though we be for all that the self Same Persons.'

95 Manlove 1697, p. 55.

96 Parker 1666a, p. 49; Warren 1667, p. 100.

97 More 1659, pp. 252–6.

98 Pearson 1659, p. 758.

99 Pearson 1659, p. 762.

100 For the problem of the identity of bodies, see also Chapter 9.

101 Ross 1645, pp. 98–9. See also Browne 1977, pp. 120–1.

102 Ross 1645, pp. 108–9.

103 Menasseh ben Israel 1636, pp. 198 ff. Cf. McMurrich 1913; Stewart 1961. There is a reference to the notion of *luz* in Leibniz's *Nouv. ess.* II.xxvii.6.

104 Hody 1694, p. 192.

105 Boyle 1979, p. 199.

106 See Descartes's letter to Mesland, 9 February 1645 (AT IV 162–70, esp. 166). The context of Descartes's discussion is not the problem of the resurrection, but the doctrine of transubstantiation. For an account of Descartes's view on human bodily identity, see Chapter 9 in this book. Cudworth, for example, rejects the notion of a strict identity of the pre-mortem body with the resurrection-body by emphasising that at the resurrection the body is purified and 'transformed into a spiritual and heavenly body' (Cudworth 1678, p. 799). Cudworth goes on to say: 'We conclude therefore, that the *Christian Mystery, of the Resurrection of Life,* consisteth not in the Souls being reunited to these Vile Rags of Mortality, these *Gross Bodies* of ours (such as now they are) but in having them *changed into the Likeness of Christ's Glorious Body,* and in *this Mortal's putting on Immortality'* (ibid.).

107 Boyle 1979, p. 206.

108 See Tillotson, *The Possibility of the Resurrection asserted and proved* (1682), in Tillotson 1728, vol. 3, pp. 248–55.

109 Digby 1644b, pp. 78–9.

110 Digby 1644b, pp. 85–7.

111 Bury 1690, p. 71.

112 See Locke 1683. Cf. Locke 1936, pp. 121–3, for the 1682 note on immortality.

113 *Ess.* I.iv.4–5; II.i.11–2. See also *Draft C* (Locke 1685) II.i.15–6.

114 *Ess.* II.i.11.

115 For a detailed discussion of Locke's theory in its historical context (and of the relevant secondary literature up to 1982), see Thiel 1983.

116 For a discussion of Locke's general theory of identity, see Chapter 9.

117 *Ess.* II. xxvii.9.

118 *Ess.* II. xxvii.15. See also *Ess.* II.xxvii.7: 'But to conceive, and judge of it [i.e., identity] aright, we must consider what *Idea* the Word it is applied to stands for: It being one

thing to be the same *Substance,* another the same *Man,* and a third the same *Person,* if *Person, Man,* and *Substance,* are three Names standing for three different *Ideas;* for such as is the *Idea* belonging to that Name, such must be the *Identity.*'

119 *Ess.* II.xxvii.20. Emphasis added. Locke's man–person distinction is still a focus in present-day debates over personal identity. See Wiggins 1980, pp. 29, 37, 161; Chappell 1989; Snowdon 1990; Thornton 1991; Ayers 1991, vol. 2, pp. 283–92; Baillie 1993, p. 197.

120 See Chapter 9.

121 This is how Chappell interprets Locke's distinction between man and person. See especially Chappell 1989, pp. 76–80. Chappell bases his interpretation on an analysis of two of Locke's examples: the 'prince-cobbler case' (*Ess.* II.xxvii.15), and the 'day-and-night-man case' (*Ess.* II.xxvii.23).

122 *Ess.* II.xxvii.15.

123 Chappell concedes that Locke 'is of course notorious for his use of thing-language to refer to ideas' (Chappell 1989, p. 72).

124 *Ess.* II.xxvii.25.

125 *Ess.* II.xxvii.8. Cf. *Ess.* II.i.11. See also *Ess.* II.xxvii.21.

126 *Ess.* II.xxvii.9.

127 *Ess.* II.xxvii.16.

128 *Ess.* II.xxvii.17.

129 *Ess.* II.xxvii.23.

130 *Ess.* II.xxvii.10.

131 For a more detailed account of the constitutive function that Locke ascribes to consciousness, see Thiel 1983, chap. 5. See also Thiel 1981, p. 184. Kenneth P. Winkler, too, emphasises the Lockean concern with what he calls the 'subjective constitution of the self'. At the same time, Winkler holds that, according to Locke, the person is a substance (Winkler 1991). Edwin McCann argues that consciousness is analogous to life: 'Consciousness makes for personal identity in just the way life makes for animal or vegetable identity' (McCann 1987, pp. 68–9). For a similar point, see Ayers 1991, vol. 2, pp. 261 and 323–4.

132 *Ess.* II.xxvii.16.

133 *Ess.* II.xxvii.10.

134 *Ess.* II.xxvii.20.

135 *Ess.* II.xxvii.26.

136 *Ess.* II.xxi.

137 *Ess.* II.xxvii.26.

138 *Ess.* II.xxvii.18.

139 *Ess.* II.xxvii.26.

140 See, e.g., Flew 1968; Mattern 1980a; Atherton 1983; Gallie 1987; Alston and Bennett 1988; Winkler 1991.

141 *Ess.* III.xi.16.

142 Mattern 1980a, pp. 25, 38–40; Winkler 1991, pp. 215–6.

143 As Locke says: 'For were there a Monkey, or any other Creature to be found, that had the use of Reason, to such a degree, as to be able to understand general Signs, and to deduce Consequences about general *Ideas,* he would no doubt be subject to Law, and, in that Sense be a *Man,* how much soever he differ'd in Shape from others of that Name' (*Ess.* III.xi.16).

144 *Ess.* II.xxvii.22.

145 For the history of the insanity defence, see Walker 1968.

146 See *Ess.* II.xxvii.20.
147 *Ess.* II.xxvii.22.
148 *Ess.* II.xxvii.22.
149 See Molyneux's letters in Locke 1976–92, vol. 4, pp. 767–8 (letter no. 1685), and vol. 5, pp. 20–2 (letter no. 1712). See Becconsall 1698, pp. 251–6.
150 Coke 1684, p. 247 (a) (Bk. 3, chap. 6, sec. 405).
151 Locke 1976–92, vol. 4, p. 785 (letter no. 1693). Emphasis added.
152 Locke 1976–92, vol. 5, p. 58 (letter no. 1744).
153 *Ess.* II.xxvii.22. Cf. 1. *Cor.* 14, 25.
154 *Ess.* II.xxvii.13.
155 *Ess.* II.xxvii.26.
156 *Ess.* II.xxvii.26.
157 See *Ess.* II.xxi.38, 60, and 70.
158 See *Ess.* IV.iii.6.
159 Locke 1823, vol. 4, p. 476.
160 Locke 1936, p. 121.
161 *Ess.* IV.iii.6.
162 Locke 1936, p. 122.
163 *Ess.* II.xxvii.15.
164 *Ess.* II.xxvii.14.
165 See, e.g., Bold 1705; Collins 1707, 1708.
166 E.g., Layton 1698.
167 Stillingfleet 1698, pp. 33–44.
168 Locke 1823, vol. 4, p. 334.
169 Locke 1823, vol. 4, p. 304.
170 E.g., Layton 1698, p. 126.
171 Sergeant 1697, p. 262.
172 For Sergeant's critique of Locke's general theory of identity, see Chapter 9.
173 Sergeant 1697, p. 267.
174 See Sergeant 1697, p. 265.
175 Locke's marginal replies to Sergeant's account of identity are reproduced in the 1984 reprint edition of Sergeant 1697, pp. 265 and 267. See also Thiel 1981, and 1983, pp. 49, 124–5.
176 See Butler 1736, first appendix. For present-day discussions of the charge of circularity against Locke and neo-Lockean theories of personal identity, see Flew 1968; Wiggins 1980, pp. 152–4; Parfit 1985, pp. 219–23.
177 For Leibniz's general theory of identity, see Chapter 9.
178 See, e.g., *Nouv. ess.*, Preface (Ger. V 50; Leibniz 1981, p. 58).
179 *Nouv. ess.* II.xxvii.14.
180 *Disc. mét.*, sec. 13. My translations from the *Disc. mét* are taken from Leibniz 1988.
181 *Disc. mét.*, sec. 8.
182 *Nouv. ess.*, Preface (Ger. V 48; Leibniz 1981, p. 55).
183 Cf. *Nouv. ess.* II.xxvii.14.
184 'Remarques sur la Lettre de M. Arnaud' (Ger. II 43; Leibniz 1967, p. 47).
185 'Remarques sur la Lettre de M. Arnaud' (Ger. II 43; Leibniz 1967, p. 46).
186 *Nouv. ess.* II.xxvii.14. One of Leibniz's objections to Locke's theory is based on his 'duplicate-world' thought-experiment (*Nouv. ess.* II.xxvii.23): suppose there is a world 'in another region of the universe' which is 'in no way sensibly different from this

sphere of earth on which we live, and inhabited by men each of whom differs sensibly in no way from his counterpart among us'. On Leibniz's general theory of identity (see Chapter 9), there must be a difference between originals and duplicates 'in their insensible constitutions', in addition to their numerical difference. Leibniz holds that if we accept Locke's theory we cannot distinguish between an original person and a duplicate-person, since the thought-experiment supposes that their states of consciousness are not distinguishable. Thus, Locke's theory would have the absurd consequence that original and duplicate are one and the same person.

187 *Disc. mét.*, sec. 36.
188 Letter to Arnauld, 9 October 1687 (Ger. II 125; Leibniz 1967, p. 160). This notion of person as moral quality is reminiscent of Valla's notion of *persona*. Leibniz explicitly refers to Valla's treatment of *persona* in Leibniz 1948, vol. 2, pp. 558–9.
189 *Disc. mét.*, sec. 34. See also *Nouv. ess.* II.xxvii.9. On the distinction between moral and metaphysical identity in Leibniz see also Scheffler 1976; M. Wilson 1976b.
190 *Disc. mét.*, sec. 34.
191 Letter to Arnauld, 4/14 July 1686 (Ger. II 57; Leibniz 1967, p. 64).
192 For a detailed discussion of the relationship between Leibniz's early and later writings on this issue, see Wilson 1976b.
193 Letter to Arnauld, 9 October 1687 (Ger. II 125; Leibniz 1967, p. 160). Emphasis added.
194 *Nouv. ess.*, Preface (Ger. V 51; Leibniz 1981, p.58). First emphasis added.
195 *Nouv. ess.* II.xxvii.13.
196 *Nouv. ess.* II.xxvii.9.
197 *Nouv. ess.* II.xxvii.13.
198 *Nouv. ess.* II.xxvii.9.
199 Vailati emphasises the importance of the phrase 'when accompanied by truth' in this context (Vailati 1985, pp. 41–3). Vailati argues against the charge of inconsistency against Leibniz, brought forward by Wilson 1976b, pp. 346–7; and Jolley 1984, pp. 136–9.
200 *Nouv. ess.* II.xxvii.9.
201 *Nouv. ess.* II.xxvii.22.
202 *Nouv. ess.* II.xxvii.9.
203 *Nouv. ess.* II.xxvii.23.
204 *Nouv. ess.* II.xxvii.18. For other accounts of the relationship between Leibniz's and Locke's theories of personal identity, see Curley 1982; Jolley 1984; C. Wilson 1989, pp. 232–49.
205 For a more detailed discussion of eighteenth-century British responses to Locke's theory, see Thiel 1983, pp. 175–98. For an account of Anglican responses to Locke's theory, see Tennant 1982.
206 See, e.g., Harris 1708–10; Chambers 1728.
207 The impact of Locke's theory of personal identity on eighteenth-century literature is discussed in MacLean 1962; Watt 1957; Tuveson 1955, 1960; Wertz 1975; Fox 1988.
208 Reid 1969, III. 6. For Berkeley's argument, see his *Alciphron,* in Berkeley 1948–57, vol. 3, pp. 296–9.
209 See, e.g., Mackie 1976, p. 183.
210 For other kinds of responses to the Berkeley/Reid objection, see Ayers 1991, vol. 2, pp. 271ff; Winkler 1991, pp. 207–8, 222. For a detailed discussion of Reid and Locke on personal identity, see Gallie 1989, chap. 8.

211 The quotations from Law 1769 are taken from the reprint in Locke 1823, vol. 3, pp. 165–84.

212 For Locke's influence on Kant's philosophy in general, see Brandt 1991; Winter 1986. For a brief comparison of Locke's and Kant's theories of the self, see Thiel 1983, pp. 198–201.

27

THE PASSIONS IN METAPHYSICS AND
THE THEORY OF ACTION

SUSAN JAMES

I. COLLOQUIAL UNDERSTANDINGS,
INHERITED TRADITIONS

The seventeenth century inherited a long and palimpsestic list of affections which served as a form of definition of the passions. No one could ignore the fact that among the principal examples were joy and distress in their many forms; hope, fear, and their variants; and desires in all their diversity. To enumerate these affections was thus one way of explaining what the category included, and interpretations of the category were in turn elaborated in the light of this canonical list. At the same time, discussions of what the passions are for, and of their part in human action, were articulated against a complex background of received assumptions. Some of these derived specifically from earlier philosophical traditions, while others were embedded in a wider range of practices such as medicine, pedagogy, and Christian meditation. Together, they formed an understanding of the passions which was sustained in relatively conventional treatments of the subject and was at the same time bound to inform any attempt at philosophical innovation.

Several threads of this loosely woven fabric stand out in discussions of the metaphysical and psychological aspects of the passions. Most striking, perhaps, is the shared presupposition that the passions are, in a broad sense, functional. Humans are endowed with instinctive drives or appetites for warmth, food, and so forth. But they also possess a less biologically basic set of dispositions which incline them to seek out states of affairs that are conducive to their well-being, and to avoid states that are detrimental to it. Passions such as desire, hatred, and fear were fundamentally portrayed as affects which move us to act in ways intended to improve our lot.

This view gave rise to two connected philosophical problems. First, what precise end do the passions serve? Is our passionate behaviour aimed, for example, at our physical survival, our happiness, our pleasure, or our well-being? The advantages and implications of these and similar hypotheses formed one focus of a debate which helped to shape several diverse interpretations of the nature of the passions. Second, what account can be given of the functional mechanism which directs us to a particular end, be it survival or happiness? Almost all answers to this question relied on the tenet that we are the workmanship of a benign God in order to explain the existence of any such dispositions in our nature; but seventeenth-century philosophers followed their predecessors in attempting to provide more detailed and circumstantial accounts of how passionate impulses interact with other mental and bodily capacities to promote our advantage and keep us from harm. As this chapter shows, some of the causal processes they posited were mechanical, whereas others appealed to connexions between our intentional states.

It was thus generally taken for granted that our passions drive us to respond to the external world, to manipulate the material objects we encounter in ways that go beyond our most basic needs, and to relate to other people. Without them, as many writers pointed out, we should be condemned to narrow and isolated lives.[1] However, the view that the passions are in these respects functional was counterbalanced by an equally deep-seated conviction that they are simultaneously dysfunctional – they are treacherous and wayward, and drive us to harm, frustration and misery. These dangers were held to stem from the fact that, although not blind, the passions are acutely myopic; in Thomas Wright's simile, they are like green spectacles.[2] While they incite us to pursue our advantage, they do not enable us to make fine discriminations between beneficial and harmful states of affairs and often dispose us to bring about ends which are actually detrimental to our well-being. They are consequently described as arbitrary, unpredictable, enslaving, uncontrollable, and even pathological.[3]

Theorists who wanted to elucidate the advantages of the passions could not ignore this pessimistic characterisation; it would have been merely wayward to dismiss the entrenched belief that our passionate impulses can bring us to every kind of privation and unhappiness. To resolve the conflict between function and dysfunction, some of them adopted the standard, Aristotelian view that our passions can be tamed and transformed into impulses which promote our well-being;[4] but a number of these philosophers felt the need to explain how, exactly, this Aristotelian goal can be achieved. Hobbes, Descartes, and Malebranche, for example, responded to the problem by mapping the various forces capable of acting on the passions and offering accounts of how they could be kept in check. At one level, this was a metaphysical undertaking, motivated by ontological issues about the nature of body and soul; but it also reflected a normative interest in the control of the passions which dominates the literature of this period.

Attempts to resolve the contradiction between the functional and dysfunctional aspects of the passions were carried on in the shadow of a traditional opposition between passion and reason. Whereas the passions were excessive, reason was moderate; whereas the passions were changeable, reason was as steady as the pole star; whereas the passions were weak, reason was powerful. This ancient trope continued to be subjected to close and polemical scrutiny and criticism, but nevertheless resonated through even the most novel and innovative seventeenth-century discussions and debates.[5] In particular, philosophical treatments of the subject made great play with the assumption that reason is active and the passions passive.

The pervasiveness of the second half of this antithesis is revealed, for example, by Edward Phillips's 1658 definition of a passion as a suffering,[6] as something that happens to one. Among philosophical writers, the same point is made particularly clearly by Spinoza, who defines a passion as an affection which occurs when someone is acted *on,* as opposed to acting.[7] The claim that people suffer or are acted on when they experience passions does not, however, imply that they are inert. On the contrary, the passions are regarded as violent and unruly so that, according to Descartes, they, more than other kinds of thought, agitate and disturb the soul.[8]

This conception of passions as things that happen to one is sustained by philosophers who analyse them as motions.[9] Motions, it is widely agreed, can be passive or active, as Locke emphasises in a description of the movements of physical bodies. 'When the ball obeys the stroke of a billiard stick', he tells us, 'it is not any action of the ball, but mere passion.'[10] The movement of the ball is a passion because it is caused by something else, in this case the impact of the billiard cue. So when physical bodies are moved by other things, their movements are passions, and they possess what Locke calls a passive power to be so moved. Contrasted with this is the active power of an object to move itself which we find in such mental capacities as 'the power to do or forbear, or to continue or end an action'.[11]

The idea that the passions are passive powers (dispositions to be moved by other things) works at several levels. In the first place, it accords with the understanding of the passions as beyond our control. Second, it captures the notion that many of our passions are prompted by our experience of other people and things; our loves, hates, desires, and so forth are characteristically responses to objects external to us and are thus passive motions in the sense of being caused by something else.[12] Third, the claim sustains an identification between passions and the motions of physical bodies. Passions, according to this view, are a species of motion, akin to the movements of billiard balls, and are at least partly susceptible to the same kinds of explanation.[13]

This last interpretation of the passivity of passion interlocks with a further set of connotations which divide passion from reason. Seventeenth-century philosophers both inherited and sustained the pivotal assumption that, whereas the ability to reason belongs to the mind, the passions are intimately connected with the body, both in that they are responses to sensory experiences and in that they have bodily manifestations such as the trembling and pallor that accompany fear.[14] Any analysis of the relation between passion and reason is thus at least in part an analysis of the relations between body and mind. However, the passions are not simply bodily states; they may have bodily causes and bodily effects, but they are themselves states of mind, and thus associated with cognition and activity. For many seventeenth-century authors, this tension within the very idea of a passion posed a pressing challenge – that of explaining how the passions can straddle the boundary between the mental and physical.

Although many of the philosophical problems addressed by seventeenth-century writers on the passions were shaped by a colloquial understanding of their subject-matter which extended far beyond the bounds of philosophy, they were also profoundly influenced by several specifically philosophical traditions. Unsurprisingly, the questions they asked and the terms in which they answered them are often derived from both ancient and scholastic philosophy, or from a rather heterodox mixture of the two.

Amongst the ancients, the Stoics, Plato, and Aristotle remained vital points of reference, though appeals to these classical authorities in early modern texts need to be interpreted in their own historical setting. While the names of the Greek philosophers were handed down unchanged, the doctrines with which they were associated underwent a series of complex adaptations, and the forms of Aristotelianism, Platonism, and Stoicism inherited by seventeenth-century writers thus bore the imprints of a series of superimposed traditions.[15] The classical legacy had in the first place been moulded to fit the contours of scholasticism, and although the schools were regularly decried for their arid classifying and syllogising, they continued to cast a shadow over their descendants. Furthermore, strenuous efforts had been made to reconcile classical philosophy with Christianity, and the resulting hybrids came to be generally recognised as the acceptable face of classicism. Finally, the humanist project of amalgamating the various schools into one superlative philosophy left an indelible mark on the philosophy of the seventeenth century. It accounts at least in part for the apparently indiscriminate way in which some authors appeal to Greek and Roman precedents, and also for the habit of deferring to classical sources which, though it was eschewed by some of the greatest philosophers of the period, remained widespread.[16]

Labels such as 'Stoic', 'Aristotelian', and 'schoolman' are thus by no means univocal; they are often employed merely to pick out one particular aspect of a view attributed to a school, and in many cases it would be misleading to impose a more precise meaning. However, some specific doctrines and debates drawn from the classical and scholastic traditions exercised an enormous influence on attempts to provide a more refined account of the workings of the passions and therefore deserve to be singled out.

Discussions of what the passions are and how they operate tended to be tacitly conducted against the background of two interconnected and long-standing debates within the Aristotelian tradition about the character of the soul. One of these concerned the so-called real distinction: is the soul really distinct from its various capacities such as its powers to reason, sense, and imagine? Aquinas had argued that the faculties of the soul are distinct from the soul itself, so the faculty of sight, for example, is separate from both the soul as a whole and its other faculties and has the eye as its particular seat.[17] This view had been challenged by advocates of the *via moderna,* who held that the soul and its faculties are identical, and that the capacities belonging to the organic soul are located in both the whole body and in each of its parts.[18] The power of sight is an integral part of the soul and is present in every part of the body. But the eye alone sees, because only the eye possesses a structure and shape suited to sight.

During the sixteenth century this view became widely accepted.[19] But the Thomist account of ontologically distinct faculties of the soul which operated from various parts of the body retained a strong hold,[20] so that many seventeenth-century philosophers still felt the need to criticise it. Among the objections they raised was the view that appeals to the faculties lack explanatory power. As Locke, among others, points out, if you want to understand how the mind works, it is supremely unhelpful to be told that there is a will which wills, sight which sees, reason which reasons, and so forth:

But the fault has been, that faculties have been spoken of, and represented, as so many distinctive agents. For it being asked, what it was that digested the meat in our stomachs? It was a ready, and very satisfactory answer, to say, That it was the *digestive faculty.* What was it that made anything come out of the body? The *expulsive faculty.* What moved? The *motive faculty:* and so on in the mind, the *intellectual faculty,* or the understanding, understood; and the *elective faculty,* or the will, willed and commanded which is in short to say, That the ability to digest, digested; and that the ability to move, moved; and the ability to understand, understood. . . . And in truth it would be very strange if it were otherwise.[21]

Moreover, as Locke also explains, once the faculties are separated, it becomes difficult to account for the fact that they communicate with one another.[22]

The judgement that talk about the faculties fails to explain anything thus provided one motive for developing a new, non-Aristotelian psychology. In addition, Descartes's insistence on the unity and immateriality of the soul went with a rejection of the scholastic conception of faculties as spread around the body.[23] If intentional processes were immaterial, they could not have bodily 'seats'. This meant that the passions could no longer be conceived as impulses of the material organic soul, any more than the conflict between passion and reason could be represented as a struggle between the organic and intellective souls. And once this landscape was abandoned, the need for a new analysis of the passions, consonant with Cartesian metaphysics, was soon felt.

A second seventeenth-century debate which remained deeply indebted to two classical traditions concerned the mechanisms which enabled reason to control the passions, and thus the rôle of the latter in action. On the one hand, it was widely held that the mind possesses the two capacities allocated in the Aristotelian tradition to the intellective soul – the capacity to reason or understand and the capacity to will.[24] These were the distinctively human abilities which men and women could use to moderate their irrational impulses, and many writers took it for granted that voluntary action resulted from the interplay between these capacities and the passions.

Set against this outlook was a more parsimonious analysis of action derived from Stoicism. For the Stoics, the passions, like the pronouncements of reason, were judgements. Passionate judgements were distinguished from rational ones, however, by the fact that they were excessive, in the sense of departing from the order of nature.[25] Rather than portraying reason and passion as two powers, pulling against one another, the Stoics presented the passions as a flawed kind of reasoning. In addition, they held that the process of overcoming one's passions was a matter of learning to reason correctly, thereby avoiding making mistakes. From the seventeenth-century point of view, the most striking feature of this analysis was the way it tied reasoning and acting so closely together that there remained no space for the will. The conflict between the resulting conception of the passions and Christian doctrine, together with the divergence between the two classical views, Aristotelian and Stoic, sustained a series of enduring philosophical debates.

As well as taking over many of the problems articulated within earlier philosophical traditions, theorists of the passions also inherited the habit of producing typologies – purportedly complete lists of the main passions and their variants, more or less systematically arranged.[26] One aim of these classifications, which are usually appended to philosophical treatments of the topic, was simply to lay out the emotions to which a theory was intended to apply. But a classification was also designed to strengthen the accompanying analysis by showing that the latter applied to the whole range of passions. In fact, seventeenth-century typologies rarely conform to this comparatively narrow goal and tend to be discursive and eclectic to the point of confusion. They do, however, lean heavily on a small number of forebears, whose views are either reproduced piecemeal or form the basis of amended lists.

Of the classical authorities, Aristotle provided several, not necessarily comprehensive, lists of passions, which he describes as affections which cause men to change their opinion in regard to their judgements and are accompanied by pain or pleasure.[27] In the *Rhetorica,* for example, he cites anger and mildness, love and hate, fear and confidence, shame and esteem, benevolence and non-benevolence, pity, indignation, envy and emulation.[28] Some seventeenth-century authors continue to use and build upon this list;[29] but others are drawn by their philosophical ambitions to more structured classifications.

This desire was in some ways better served by Cicero's influential view (in turn derived from the Greek Stoics) that there are only four fundamental passions – distress (*aegritudo*) and pleasure (*laetitia*), fear (*metus*) and desire (*libido*) – each of which has many sub-species.[30] The relations between these cardinal passions were variously interpreted in the seventeenth century, as they had been in antiquity. Some authors stuck to the Ciceronian view that each is a specific feeling with its own object.[31] *Laetitia* is a kind of delight at something believed to be a present good, *libido* a desire for a supposed good. *Metus* is a feeling of fear at what is believed to be a threatening evil, *aegritudo* is distress at a present thing held to be evil. Other theorists espoused versions of the view that gave priority to *libido* and *metus,* and interpreted *laetitia* and *aegritudo* as states of mind resulting from them. When we fail to get what we want or are confronted by things we fear, we experience *aegritudo*; when we attain the objects of our desires, or avoid the things we are afraid of, we experience *laetitia.* In this latter and more economical interpretation, the objects of our desires are characterised in a particular way, as bringing us delight or removing distress. Desire itself is thus seen as directed towards *laetitia* and away from *aegritudo,* as a disposition to seek out one state and avoid the other.[32]

Some seventeenth-century philosophers were attracted by the classical simplicity of Cicero's typology; but they also inherited a flamboyantly Christian re-
working of it – Augustine's Neoplatonic reinterpretation of the passions as species
of love. In *De civitate Dei,* Augustine adhered to Cicero's classification of four basic
passions, although he called two of them by different names. Joy remained *laetitia*
and fear *metus*; but the terms for desire (*libido*) and sorrow (*aegritudo*) seem to have
had physical and sexual connotations from which Augustine wanted to escape. He
therefore replaced *libido* with *cupiditas* and *aegritudo* with *tristitia*.[33] Having thus
purged them, he went on to analyse the passions as acts of will, and volitions as
species of love, thereby arriving at the view that 'a love which strains after the
possession of the loved object is desire; and the love which possesses and enjoys
that object is joy. The love that shuns what opposes it is fear, while the love that
feels that opposition when it happens is grief.'[34] All passions were thus gathered
under the unifying concept of love, an affection that Cicero had classified as just
one type of desire.

This interpretation exerted a considerable influence on seventeenth-century
thought and had a profound impact on discussions of the ethical significance of
the passions.[35] However, metaphysical and psychological treatments of the topic
were on the whole more responsive to the ornate typologies worked out by
scholastic writers. That of Thomas Aquinas, which identifies eleven basic passions,
continued to be used in the seventeenth century and provided the organising
categories for numerous treatises on the subject.[36] According to Thomas, the
passions are appetites of the sensible soul. We possess, first of all, a concupiscible
appetite which moves towards objects it perceives as good and away from those it
perceives as harmful, and to which belong three pairs of passions. When the
concupiscible appetite is drawn to the good, we feel love (*amor*), and when it is
repulsed by evil, we feel hatred (*odium*); when it is drawn to a good not possessed,
we feel desire (*desiderium*), and when it is repulsed by an evil not possessed, we feel
aversion (*fuga*); when it obtains an object of desire, we feel joy (*delectatio*), and
when it succumbs to an object of aversion, we feel sadness (*dolor*).[37]

The concupiscible appetite has a 'champion and defender' in the irascible
appetite,[38] which possesses the power to resist obstacles by inclining the soul
towards objects that are beneficial but hard to obtain, and away from objects that
are evil but difficult to resist. To speak anachronistically, it is a kind of Thomist
superego which gives rise to five further passions. When we fail to obtain
something we perceive as good, we may feel hope (*spes*) or despair (*desperatio*); in
relation to an unrealised evil, we may feel fear (*timor*) or daring (*audacia*); and in

the presence of a perceived evil, we feel anger (*ira*), the only passion that has no contrary.[39]

Central to this classification is a distinction between the straightforward attractions and repulsions of the concupiscible appetite and the more complex resistance put up by its irascible counterpart. To take a simple example, if I want to eat a greengage and foresee no difficulty in picking one from the tree in front of me, my desire is an impulse of my concupiscible appetite. But if greengages are out of season, my hope that I shall find one is an impulse of my irascible appetite. When, to make matters more complicated, I feel like eating a greengage but hope that I shall manage to resist the temptation, my irascible appetite works to stifle the impulse of my concupiscible appetite, and any accompanying sense of arduousness or difficulty stems, according to Aquinas, from the fact that my soul is both drawn to, and repulsed by, the greengage. The purported advantage of the two appetites is thus that they enable him to give an account of conflict between our passions.

Thomas draws attention to the fact that, whereas Cicero's classification of the passions turns on tense (*laetitia* and *aegritudo* are responses to the present state of affairs, whereas *libido* and *metus* relate to the future), his revolves around an agent's expectations.[40] Although these two sets of criteria overlap – for example, we hope for things that we are not sure of attaining, and this uncertainty typically attaches to things in the future – they are not the same. Daring is an impulse of the irascible appetite, for instance, not because it is directed to a future goal, but because it is directed to a goal that the agent regards as good but difficult to achieve.

These influential classifications, combined with an inherited sense of which aspects of the passions are straightforward and which problematic, formed a rich tradition that inspired, and sometimes burdened, philosophers of the seventeenth century. Working in its shadow, they went on to reinterpret the passions in the light of their own metaphysical and scientific positions.

II. WHAT THE PASSIONS ARE AND HOW THEY WORK

The belief that our passionate impulses are in some way beneficial, and not just a punishment imposed by God for Man's first disobedience, was widely held in the seventeenth century. Nevertheless, since it was no less widely acknowledged that the passions are frequently self-destructive urges, this belief stood in need of justification. What reason was there to hold that the passions work to our advantage? Many writers responded implicitly to this question when they defined particular passions in terms of the contribution they can make to our well-being; for example, desire disposes the soul to wish for the things it represents as agreeable, and hatred impels it to want to be separated from objects which are presented to it as harmful.[41] They also extended this kind of analysis to less obviously preservative emotions, such as love, interpreted as what we feel for objects that we regard as beneficial to us, or hope, understood as our feeling for an object which we believe would benefit us, but which we think we have little chance of acquiring.[42] Explanations of this sort undoubtedly set the tone of general discussion, but they are less convincing when applied to emotions which seem to increase rather than diminish our vulnerability, such as grief, envy, or despair. What, one may ask, is beneficial about these?

Christian philosophers were predisposed to believe that there must be a positive answer to this question; the very fact that God has given us passions implies that He must have had a reason for doing so consonant with His wisdom and benevolence.[43] Religious doctrine therefore provided general grounds for the conviction that the passions served some broadly beneficial end; but more detailed justifications for this conclusion depended on the precise interpretation of the end itself. Do the passions prompt us to increase our power, thereby reducing the risk of privation and death, as Hobbes held?[44] Are they, as Spinoza insisted, manifestations of our striving to persevere in our being?[45] Or do they, as Descartes believed, dispose our souls to want the things that nature deems useful to us?[46] Do they prompt us to attain things that are conducive to our happiness, as Locke suggested?[47] Or are they, as Malebranche claimed, impressions which incline us to love our bodies and all that is useful in their preservation?[48]

These interpretations have in common the idea that at least part of the point of the passions is to enhance our physical well-being. Hobbes's and Spinoza's conceptions of self-preservation certainly include, although they are not exhausted by, physical comfort; Descartes emphasises that the things nature deems useful to us are, amongst others, the things we need as embodied creatures; Locke points out that nothing destroys our happiness more quickly than physical pain; and Malebranche explicitly links the passions to the survival of our bodies. Yet it would be a mistake to make too much of this fact. These theorists regarded the whole range of our everyday desires and emotions as passions, so that, for example, the desire to spend the morning reading Aristotle, or a hatred of corruption, are just as much passions as are the desire for sexual satisfaction or the fear of physical injury. Although the passions are intimately connected to the body, they need not be directed towards our physical well-being.

This view obviously makes it more difficult to identify a single function that all the passions serve, a task which was further complicated by the existence of differing opinions about the terms in which such a function could be specified. For some philosophers it was not enough to say, in traditional vein, that the perception of certain types of objects causes us to feel fear, which in turn causes us to run away. Instead, they aimed to bring the latest scientific and medical discoveries to bear on our understanding of the passions and to provide a full physiological account of how the animal spirits pass from one part of the body to another, how they cause the emotion of fear in the mind, and how they cause the bodily movements which constitute flight.

The attempt to set a new explanatory standard was greeted with great enthusiasm in some quarters.[49] However, it also provoked a sceptical reaction among those who regarded it as unduly speculative. A number of philosophers who took this latter view continued the tradition of explaining our passions primarily in terms of intentional states, although their interpretations of such passions as love and hatred were by no means intended to mirror our everyday understanding of them. Despite their familiar names, these were theoretical terms to be analysed and defended in the light of prior metaphysical assumptions. Finally, a few philosophers turned self-consciously to experience, defending their approach as the one best suited to our limited powers of understanding. Locke's programme of investigating the knowledge we gain from ideas and appearances, rather than the constitutions of bodies, exemplifies this view, and leads him to an account of the passions which centres on a phenomenological analysis of pleasure and pain. The way to find out about our passions, he claims, is to attend carefully to our experience.[50]

While these three types of explanation co-existed, sometimes within a single work, each emphasised a different aspect of the passions. The second and third focused in different ways on our conscious experience of our emotions, while the first charted a series of unconscious physical events. Although seventeenth-century explanations of this latter type were allied to various interpretations of the relations between body and mind, the physical principles to which they appealed were drawn from the new science and varied little. In this area Descartes's work is exceptionally systematic and original.

Perhaps the most novel feature of Descartes's physiology, and one that unites it to his physics, is that it seeks to explain bodily phenomena entirely in terms of motion – the motions of the various parts of the body together with those of the animal spirits or fine parts of the blood.[51] The speed and force of all these movements depend on the temperature of the animal spirits, which move faster and more violently when they are hot. And the animal spirits gain their heat from the source of life itself, the invisible fires in the heart which are themselves matter in motion.[52] In appealing to this single mechanism, Descartes proposes an alternative to the Aristotelian sensible soul; but many of the individual processes he posits, though now accounted for solely in terms of motion, are taken from Galenic physiology.[53]

In analysing the kinds of motions that occur in our bodies, Descartes distinguishes those which depend on the body from those which depend on the immaterial soul. In the first class, he identifies many movements we can make without any contribution from the will, such as breathing, eating, walking, and indeed, 'any action which is common to us and the beasts'.[54] To take a particular example, if I perceive an external object such as a wild boar, an image of the boar is received by the eye. This causes the animal spirits to move along my optic nerve to my brain, where they disturb the animal spirits in my cerebral cavities. These particular movements of the animal spirits in the brain in turn cause the spirits to move down my nerves to particular muscles – say, to my leg muscles if the sight of the animal prompts me to run away.

This process, Descartes claims, can be entirely involuntary, as it is in animals and in some of our own responses.[55] It can occur 'in the same way as the movement of a watch is produced merely by the strength of its spring and the configuration of its wheels'.[56] In humans, however, automatic responses are comparatively rare, because our reactions to external objects are usually affected by thoughts of various kinds. Descartes divides these into two groups, volitions or actions of the soul which seem to depend on it alone, and perceptions or passions, most of which are caused by the body.[57] Of these, some represent external objects,[58] some inform us of the states of the body itself,[59] and some we feel to be in the soul. These last are passions in the narrow sense and Descartes defines them as the 'perceptions, sensations or emotions of the soul which we refer particularly to it, and which are caused, maintained and strengthened by some movement of the animal spirits'.[60]

How, though, is the soul able to experience emotions which are caused by movements of the body? Descartes's solution to this problem centres on his claim that although the soul is joined to the whole of the body, it exercises its functions in the pineal gland, located in the innermost part of the brain.[61] This gland can be moved by the animal spirits. So when, for example, we perceive a wild animal, a motion in the eye is transferred, by way of the animal spirits in the cavities of the brain, to the pineal gland.[62] The particular movement of the pineal gland causes the soul to have an idea of the wild animal; but this idea is not simply a representation of a physical object. Rather, it is an idea of the wild animal as a creature with certain properties which are grounds for passion.[63] So, for example, a person who encounters a boar for the first time will gain an idea of it as a strange and remarkable object and will simultaneously experience a passion which Descartes calls wonder – surprise at the unfamiliar. But anyone acquainted with boars will have an idea of it as dangerous and will thus experience the passion of anxiety.[64]

The fact that an object may excite different passions in different people, or in one person at different times, is due, Descartes claims, to the fact that our emotions vary with the temperament of the body, the strength of the soul, and our past behaviour.[65] But in a particular person at a particular time it is 'ordained by nature' that a given movement of the pineal gland will cause a specific passion in the mind.[66] The match between motions and passions is thus modified by experience and is subject to great individual variation; but there must nevertheless be some initial correlation to account for the fact that our passions are not random responses and to underpin the claim that they are beneficial to us. Descartes ascribes this correlation to nature, and thus ultimately to God; but he is not above speculating about its origins. He reflects:

For it seems to me that when our soul began to be joined to our body, its first passions must have arisen on some occasion when the blood, or some other juice entering the heart, was a more suitable fuel than usual for maintaining the heat which is the principle of life. This caused the soul to join itself willingly to that fuel, i.e. to love it; and at the same time the spirits flowed from the brain to the muscles capable of pressing or agitating the parts of the body from which the fuel had come to the heart, so as to make them send more of it. . . . That is why this same movement of the spirits has ever since accompanied the passion of love.[67]

Reflections such as this one reveal the extent to which, for theorists who are not content to refer simply to God's design, explanations of the functional character of the passions remain partial and obscure.

According to Descartes, therefore, our emotions about the objects we encounter are caused by physical movements in our bodies; they are spiritual side effects, as it were, of events which do not depend on the soul, and which, indeed, occur in animals without souls. Thus, processes which we describe as learning that wild boars are dangerous, or falling in love, are explicable as the side effects of such physical phenomena as the fact that whenever the animal spirits move in a certain way in response to a particular stimulus, they create a pathway which makes them more disposed to move in the same direction in future. At the same time, however, our passions are thoughts, of which we are conscious. Although Descartes describes them as perceptions and emphasises that they are passive in so far as they are independent of the will, we experience these perceptions as inductively grounded judgements. They are conceptions of external objects as having properties which make them harmful or beneficial to us, founded on and responsive to our experience.[68]

The fact that we are conscious of our passions, and have both memories and sensory perceptions of the situations in which they arise, provides the soul with a fund of thoughts or perceptions to which it can apply its power of understanding. Moreover, as discussed in Section IV, Descartes believed that the immaterial soul can affect the body by moving the pineal gland. His overall theory thus leaves the soul less at the mercy of bodily motions than the account so far given suggests; but it remains the case that the causes of our passions are physical events in our bodies, which are in turn usually responses to external objects.

While this interpretation of the physical workings of the passions was immensely influential,[69] Descartes's view that the body and mind can affect one another through the pineal gland excited general scepticism; as Henry More later remarked, it was 'a witty conceit though insufficiently grounded'.[70] Various other attempts were therefore made to explain the relation between motions and emotions, of which the most important within the Cartesian tradition was the occasionalism championed by Malebranche. Malebranche agreed with Descartes that the passions are emotions which affect the soul when the animal spirits move[71] but disagreed with his view that body and soul are causally connected. Although bodily motions are the occasional causes of passions, he argued, only God's will is the cause of their coincidence with the mind's perceptions. He consequently identified two processes, one physical, one spiritual, which always occur together when humans feel passion.

On the mental side, a passion starts with the mind's distinct or confused perception of the relation an object has to us and is followed by an impulse of the will, either towards the object or away from it. This in turn causes a sensation of the mind, for example, a feeling of love or hatred. Malebranche is at pains to emphasise that these three components of a passion are independent of the body, so much so that they would be capable of occurring in a disembodied soul. In mortals, however, they are accompanied by a movement of the blood and animal spirits which prepares the body to acquire a good or flee an evil. Such motions in turn coincide with sensible emotions in the soul (feelings of love, desire, etc. that are correlated with the disturbances of the animal spirits in the brain) which strengthen the sensations of the mind, and with sensations of delight which prompt us to give ourselves up to our passions.[72]

This separation of mental and physical elements, combined with a belief in

God's benevolence, allows Malebranche to give a distinctive account of the function of the passions as impressions given to us by God which incline us to love our bodies and all that is useful in their preservation.[73] By attaching the benefit to which we are driven by our emotions to the body alone, Malebranche is able to grant that passions such as envy or despair may be harmful to our souls. (Whereas Adam, before the Fall, was able to control his passions, we have lost the ability so that our bodily impulses tyrannise over our minds.)[74] However, it remains difficult for Malebranche to explain passions such as an excessive desire for food or drink. To say that these incline us to love our body, when they are actively harmful to it, seems to be stretching a point.

A further uneasiness in Malebranche's account stems from his claim that God maintains such a close union between soul and body that all inclinations of the soul are accompanied by movements of the animal spirits. For example, when we think about abstract objects such as numbers, or about things which are good or bad for the soul such as Heaven and Hell, the animal spirits move. And because these motions are in turn correlated with passions, our thoughts excite emotions in us. Thus, a mathematician working through a theorem may feel joyful, while a sinner meditating on Hell may feel terror and dread.[75] Once again, however, it is hard to see how passions like this last one can be directly construed as inclinations to look after the body. The fear in question accompanies a thought about the good of the soul, and on Malebranche's account should strengthen an inclination of the mind, regardless of the body.

These relatively local difficulties are manifestations of a more general problem faced by dualist philosophers – the problem of explaining the relation between body and mind. As was pointed out earlier, this quandary has a direct impact on two areas: on interpretations of the function served by the passions, and on attempts to explain how the passions can straddle the border between mental emotions and physical sensations. In dealing with the first, Descartes, and even more Malebranche, organise their analyses of the ends to which our passions drive us around the division between body and soul: for Descartes, they incline us to do what is beneficial for the soul; for Malebranche, they incline us to do what is beneficial to the body; and each philosopher sometimes makes use of the opposite view. In the second area, the physical and mental components of the passions are linked in explanations which themselves lie at opposite ends of a spectrum. Descartes defends the rôle played by the pineal gland on largely empirical grounds, to the detriment of his metaphysical claim that soul and body are distinct substances, whereas Malebranche offers a view of great metaphysical grandeur which suggests that a detailed understanding of the relation is beyond our grasp.[76]

One way to deal with these problems is, of course, to abandon dualism in favour of a theory of the passions which is not fashioned around two distinct substances. Perhaps the most draconian seventeenth-century advocate of such a solution was Thomas Hobbes, who incorporated an analysis of our passions into a thoroughgoing materialism according to which humans, like carriages or billiard balls, are simply extended bodies whose properties are to be explained in terms of motion. 'Neither in us', Hobbes insists, 'are there anything else but divers motions; (for motion produceth nothing but motion).'[77] There are, however, two kinds of motion found in humans: on the one hand, the vital motion in the heart which is responsible for many unconscious movements such as the pumping of the blood, and which can be helped or hindered; on the other hand, voluntary motions, 'as to go, to speak, to move any of our limbs in such a manner as is first fancied by our minds'.[78] As this passage indicates, our voluntary motions are preceded by fancies or thoughts, which are themselves motions in the brain and originate in sensory impressions. It is, however, the movements of the imagination which cause the voluntary movements of our bodies; as Hobbes puts it, 'The imagination is the first internal beginning of all voluntary motion.'[79]

Reverting to a psychological vocabulary for a moment, we can say that the voluntary motions of our bodies are caused by thoughts in the imagination. But these thoughts must be of a particular kind, representing objects and states of affairs as advantageous or detrimental. Hobbes expresses the point by saying that the thoughts which precede action are 'commonly called endeavour'. 'This endeavour', he goes on to explain, 'when it is towards something . . . is called appetite or desire . . . and when the endeavour is fromward something, it is generally called aversion.'[80] When a movement in the brain is transmitted to the heart where it hinders our vital motion, we experience pain; 'the motion in which consisteth pleasure or pain is also a solicitation to draw near to the thing that pleaseth or retire from the thing that displeaseth'; and we view the objects which cause pleasure or pain with love or hatred.[81]

In this account there is purportedly no problem about how our emotions are related to the physical events in our bodies; motions in the brain which we experience as feelings of love, aversion, and so forth simply cause and are caused by motions in other parts of our bodies which we experience as physical sensations. There is no need to postulate an 'automatic' bodily mechanism of the Cartesian variety which explains everything about the passions except our feelings. Nor is there any need to specify whether the passions are designed to benefit a material body or an immaterial soul, since there is no immaterial soul. Our passions, Hobbes argues, drive us to whatever we desire, and we desire whatever we believe will preserve us and bring us pleasure. But because the satisfaction of desire breeds further desires, this restless progress has no particular end point towards which our passions can be said to tend.[82]

It remains to ask what makes us feel particular desires and aversions. For Hobbes, as for Descartes, this depends on individual variations in our bodies and experience. Infants, he says, have few appetites; but the greater our experience, the better we become at making judgements about what is and is not harmful to us. The name for this skill is prudence, which is simply 'a presumption of the future contracted from the experience of time past'.[83] And the process of acquiring it is described both as cognitive – a matter of consciously classifying and assessing our own experiences – and mechanical – a matter of certain causal connexions between motions being reinforced by repetition.

The habit of shifting back and forth between mechanical and psychological descriptions, and between everyday explanations and self-consciously physical ones, is a feature common to all the theories so far discussed in this section. Their accounts of the bodily motions involved in the passions are, to be sure, informed by recent physiological discoveries (e.g., about the circulation of the blood), by long-established physiological beliefs (e.g., that the heat of the body originates in the heart), by anatomical observation (e.g., that all the parts of our brain and our sense organs are double, whereas the pineal gland is single), and by metaphysical assumptions. Nevertheless, these accounts often owe more to everyday experience of the passions and their symptoms than to anything else. Descartes's claim that the movements of the brain which cause fear also cause the animal spirits to flow to the leg muscles,[84] for example, is a translation into physical terms of the observation that people tend to run away from things that frighten them. A speculative physiology is here grounded on and driven by an informal psychological understanding of the passions, which in many cases does most of the explanatory work.

Theories as dissimilar as those of Descartes and Hobbes thus share a keen, though in practice rather unsteady, commitment to mechanistic explanation. But this superficial similarity can obscure the fact that Hobbes's view departs much more radically than that of his contemporary from the conventional oppositions in terms of which the passions were generally conceived. Descartes's passions have the cluster of traits that are habitually used to explicate the sense in which the passions are passive: they are caused by movements of the body and are thus connected to the animal part of human nature, they normally arise from external causes, and they are perceptions rather than actions of the soul. Hobbes, by contrast, undercuts the distinction between actions and passions. For this is nothing other than a distinction between motions which are self-caused and motions which are caused by something else. And since, in his view, there are no motions of the former sort, there are no actions in that sense of the term. For example, the abilities to do and forbear, sometimes cited as canonical cases of action, are, according to Hobbes, voluntary motions. And these, as has already been pointed out, are caused by the motions identified as desire and aversion, that is to say, by passions. As Hobbes insists, 'Although unstudied men do not conceive of any motion at all to be there, where the thing moved is invisible . . . yet that doth not hinder but that such motions are.'[85]

The contrasting work of Hobbes and Descartes reveals that partly speculative, mechanical analyses of the physical aspects of the passions could be incorporated into dualist or materialist frameworks. Equally, such speculation could be seen as a limitation of either. One philosopher who undoubtedly did regard it as a limitation and sought to avoid it was Spinoza, whose analysis of the passions in the *Ethica* is set in a metaphysical rather than physical context. The problems associated with the mechanical analysis of the passions can be overcome, Spinoza argues, once we are persuaded by purely philosophical argument that the psychological and physical aspects of the passions are two distinct sets of properties of a single substance. A passion psychologically described picks out an item which is in some sense identical with a passion physically described (though Spinoza believes that we in fact know very little about the physical aspects of our passions);[86] but the two are not causally connected, nor is one reducible to the other. A complete account of the passions can in principle be given in either physical or psychological terms.[87] This view sidesteps the Cartesian problem of allocating aspects of the passions to either the body or the soul; and it overcomes the overwhelming challenge, faced by Hobbes, of giving a physical account of our emotions.

Spinoza also offers an interpretation of the functional character of the passions which is in keeping with, if not strictly derived from, this monist view. Like everything else in the universe, he argues, humans are naturally disposed to strive to persevere in their being. Moreover, we refer to this striving or *conatus* in various ways. When we are talking about the striving of the mind alone, we call it will; the striving of the mind and body together we call appetite; and the conscious striving of mind and body we call desire.[88] The affect of desire (to which Spinoza gives pride of place) is thus our conscious awareness of a natural appetite to promote our preservation, an appetite which attaches to body and mind together. So our desires (and other passions) dispose us to preserve not just our bodies or minds, but the whole of ourselves, mental and physical.

III. DEFINITION AND CLASSIFICATION

As the foregoing discussion explains, competing interpretations of the functions served by the passions are closely allied to competing interpretations of the nature and relations of body and mind. At the same time, they are reflected in the classifications and definitions which remain a stock feature of treatises on the subject. The main pressure that prompted the more innovative among seventeenth-century philosophers to revise and elaborate the typologies they had inherited was their rejection of the Aristotelian conception of the soul. In abandoning the idea that the passions were appetites of the sensible soul, early modern philosophers also rejected the distinction between the concupiscible and irascible appetites around which Thomas Aquinas had organised his influential list of principal passions. The various accounts of the body and soul discussed in the previous section were therefore expressed in classificatory schemes which, although they did not separate concupiscible from irascible passions, were nevertheless deeply indebted to the various typologies handed down by tradition.

One way to avoid the perils of scholasticism in this area was to sidestep them by drawing on the insights of ancient philosophers other than Aristotle. Of those who adopted this approach, perhaps the most systematic was Spinoza, who took a modified version of the Ciceronian classification of the passions and embedded it firmly in his own metaphysical system. According to Spinoza, the essence of a thing is the power or striving by which it attempts to persevere in its being. Humans thus possess an active disposition to try as best they can to maintain themselves, and the pattern of their strivings is manifested in three primary affects or passions. The first – *cupiditas* or desire – encompasses, as noted earlier, all those strivings of which we are conscious,[89] while the remaining pair depend on the fact that our strivings may be more or less successful. When they succeed, we undergo a transition to a greater power which gives rise to the affect of *laetitia,* or joy. Correspondingly, when our power is diminished, we experience *tristitia,* or sadness.[90] Each of these affects or passions has many forms – for example, love, admiration, hope, and confidence are all kinds of *laetitia,* whereas hatred, envy, fear, and grief are among the varieties of *tristitia.* Although the members of each group manifest themselves as diverse emotions, they are united by the fact that they are all transitions to a greater or a lesser power.[91]

This analysis revolves around the central notion of our *conatus* or striving to persevere in our being. The classification of the passions that is integral to it is based on that of the *Tusculanae disputationes,* modified in two ways. First, Spinoza adopts the revised terms for Cicero's four fundamental passions suggested by

Augustine: instead of using *libido* and *metus, aegritudo* and *laetitia,* he amends *libido*
to *cupiditas* and *aegritudo* to *tristitia*.[92] Second, he takes the view, commonly held
in the seventeenth century and forcefully expressed by Descartes,[93] that because
desire can be directed to and from an object, it includes aversion. He therefore
reduces two of Cicero's affects (*libido* and *metus*) to one (*cupiditas*). Finally, he takes
over another widely accepted view – the claim that *cupiditas* is our primary driving
passion, while *tristitia* and *laetitia* are what we feel when our desires are thwarted
or satisfied. The result is a highly reductive classification of our emotions. However, because it is tightly connected to an over-arching account of human motivation, it offers a systematic way to analyse them, and lacks the air of arbitrary
compilation which mars so many of its competitors.

   Another way to deal with the shortcomings of the Aristotelian tradition was to
confront them head on, as Descartes did when he criticised the distinction
between the concupiscible and irascible appetites:

> As I have said already, I recognise no distinction of parts within the soul; so I think their
> distinction amounts merely to saying that the soul has two powers, one of desire the other
> of anger. But since the soul has in the same way the powers of wonder, love, hope and
> anxiety, and hence the power to receive in itself every other passion, or to perform the
> action to which the passions impel it, I do not see why they have chosen to refer them all
> to desire or anger. And besides, their enumeration does not include all the principal
> passions, as I believe mine does.[94]

Having swept Thomism aside, it remained only to reconstruct a fresh classification
of the passions in line with Descartes's account of their nature and function.

   Of the six primitive passions that Descartes identifies,[95] four overlap with those
Aquinas had allocated to the concupiscible appetite. Love (*l'amour*), hatred (*la
haine*), joy (*la joye*), and sadness (*la tristesse*) retain the dominant position they had
occupied in the scholastic schema. A fifth passion, desire (*le désir*), also keeps its
centrality, replacing the complementary pair of desire and aversion on the grounds
that one and the same movement gives rise to the pursuit of a good and the
avoidance of the opposite evil, as, for example, when we pursue riches and avoid
poverty.[96] So Descartes retains five of Aquinas's six concupiscible passions and
defines them in the functional manner one would expect. For example, 'love is an
emotion of the soul caused by a movement of the spirits, which impels the soul to
join itself willingly to objects that appear agreeable to it'.[97] A perfectly traditional
interpretation is here given a Cartesian gloss to which Descartes draws his readers'
attention: 'I say that these emotions are caused by the spirits not only in order to
distinguish love and hatred (which are passions and depend on the body) from

judgements which also bring the soul to join itself willingly to things that it regards as good, and to separate itself from those it regards as bad, but also to distinguish them from the emotion which these judgements produce in the soul.'[98]

Of the five passions of the irascible appetite, Descartes classifies four as sub-species of desire, thus producing a much simplified typology. Hope (*l'espérance*) is what we feel for a future good that we think we may attain, whereas despair (*le désespoir*) marks our conviction that we will not achieve it; and when we also believe that these outcomes depend on us, we experience terror (*l'espouvante*) or boldness (*la hardiesse*).[99] Our judgements about what is possible and about our own power thus do not breed distinct passions; they just modify our desires. In the same way, anger (*la colère*), the last of the irascible passions, becomes a form of sadness; it is what we feel about a present evil which is done by someone else and relates to us.[100] Here Descartes follows Aristotle's view that anger is provoked by any attempt to harm us or those close to us.[101]

So far, Descartes's reclassification seems relatively straightforward.[102] He reduces the number of passions by abandoning the distinction between the concupiscible and irascible appetites, and defines those that remain as functional intentional states caused by movements of the animal spirits. There is, however, a further feature of his account which is more puzzling – his definition of a sixth primitive passion, *l'admiration* or wonder. *L'admiration,* 'the first of all the passions',[103] is 'a sudden surprise of the soul' which we feel when we encounter an object that is in some way unexpected. It is caused by an impression of the brain which represents an object as unusual, and by a movement of the animal spirits which strengthens the impression and also keeps the sense organs fixed so that the impression is maintained. Alone of all the passions, it is not accompanied by any change in the heart or the blood, because, according to Descartes, when we wonder at an object we do not perceive it as good or evil. We simply perceive it as surprising, and the motions that constitute our perception are in the brain 'in which are located the organs of the senses used in gaining knowledge'.[104]

The fact that wonder does not provoke us to pursue or avoid anything makes it anomalous in Descartes's account, which is constructed around the idea that the passions dispose the soul to want things. In this section of the *Passions de l'âme* we find Descartes offering a somewhat modified account of what the passions are for; their utility consists, he says, 'in the fact that they strengthen and prolong thoughts in the soul which it is good for the soul to preserve and which otherwise might easily be erased from it'.[105] Immediately after this passage, he specifies that the function of wonder is to make us learn and remember things of which we were ignorant.[106] Presumably learning is good for the soul and wonder helps us to learn. Nevertheless, this shift of ground exemplifies two common difficulties: the problem of specifying exactly what the passions are for, discussed earlier in this section, and the problem of matching the definitions of particular passions with an over-arching interpretation of their use.

Another unusual feature of this classification is the fact that it treats wonder as a separate passion. In making it the first of all the passions, Descartes seems to suggest that humans are above all driven to learn about the world by sorting objects into the familiar and unfamiliar and then concentrating on the latter. This disposition is as strong as our impulse to seek out states of affairs that we regard as beneficial and avoid those that are harmful. So whereas the usual passions contain a mixture of cognitive and normative elements in that they are judgements grounded on training and experience about what is for our good, wonder is more purely cognitive; it inclines us to notice that something is the case.

It is instructive to compare this treatment with a comparable division in Hobbes's typology, which includes curiosity, 'the desire to know why and how' that distinguishes humans from other animals. It is, Hobbes says, 'a lust of the mind, that by a perseverance of delight in the continual and indefatigable genera-tion of knowledge, exceedeth the short vehemence of any carnall pleasure'.[107] This definition makes it easier to see why wonder and curiosity are classed as passions, but it also reveals a sharp difference between them. Hobbes follows tradition in defining curiosity as a species of desire which people experience when they think that it will benefit them to attain knowledge. It is on a par with the desire for riches (covetousness) and the desire to hurt another (revengefulness), to cite two of Hobbes's other examples, and is like all other passions in being directed at whatever an agent construes as their own advantage. So why does Descartes feel it necessary to distinguish wonder from desire? Perhaps because it is a way of retaining a version of the scholastic distinction between perception and appetite, between the cognitive capacity to see how things are and the normative capacity to relate this to a conception of the good.

The seventeenth-century classifications discussed here all attempt to define a relatively small set of primary passions. Even so, they inherit the long-standing problem of ensuring that their primary passions are really distinct. This difficulty is recognised by Hobbes, who resembles Spinoza in building his classification around the central notions of desire and aversion, which together make up what he calls endeavour.[108] But rather than complementing endeavour with further pairs of passions such as love and hatred, or joy and sadness, Hobbes argues that these are 'names for divers considerations of the same thing'.[109] Pleasure, appetite and love are all names for desire, 'save that by desire we always signifie the absence of the object; by love, most commonly the presence of the same',[110] just as pain, aversion and hatred are names for a single passion. There is thus only one motivating force in us – endeavour – which can be modified in various ways.[111]

By confronting the question of how particular passions are related to endeavour, Hobbes exposes a tension which runs through his own classification of the passions, and those of his contemporaries. All these typologies are informed by a drive to reduce and simplify, to impose some sort of order on the chaotic lists compiled by earlier generations of philosophers. At the same time, the wish to do justice to the vast diversity of our emotions and desires forces their authors to concede that there are infinitely many passions, and so a comprehensive classification is impossible. The problem then is to discover the factors which modify passions, converting desire into love or aversion into hatred. And it is at this point that the aspiration to systematise breaks down. No handful of modifiers yields an analysis of particular passions that is rich enough to capture the experience on which the compilers of classifications find themselves forced to rely.

IV. THE PLACE OF THE PASSIONS IN THE EXPLANATION OF ACTION

The benefits and dangers of the passions spring from the fact that they move us to action. If nothing intervened, we would do whatever our passions dictated, and their unruliness would ensure that our lives were turbulent and often unhappy. In fact, however, seventeenth-century philosophers believed that human action is determined by several factors, including the passions, the understanding, and the will. To explain our behaviour, it is necessary to work out how these interact.

Descartes approaches this task 'as a natural philosopher (*en physicien*), and not as a rhetorician or even a moral philosopher',[112] by dividing our thoughts into two groups – passions of the soul or perceptions, and actions of the soul or volitions. The passions in the narrow sense considered here are then a subset of the soul's perceptions, capable of interacting with different classes of perceptions such as sensations, and with volitions. Descartes believes that the relations between the will and the passions are indirect and cites as evidence the fact that one cannot simply will oneself to feel joyful or sad. However, he holds that the will does have the power to entertain thoughts that are known to cause certain emotions. For example, we can make ourselves respond bravely to danger by thinking about 'the reasons, objects, or precedents that persuade us that the danger is not great; that there is always more security in defence than in flight; that we shall gain glory and joy if we conquer, whereas we can expect nothing but shame and regret if we flee'.[113]

The fact that we cannot just will ourselves to feel brave is explained by the claim that our volitions cause movements of the pineal gland, which in turn move the animal spirits.[114] Particular thoughts are correlated by nature and habit with particular movements of the gland;[115] but the relevant correlations are not always, from a phenomenological point of view, transparent. For example, in the transactions between body and mind, certain movements of the animal spirits cause us to feel brave. But we cannot consciously reverse this process in the transactions between mind and body, and make ourselves act bravely by thinking about feeling brave.

We can, however, overcome this obstacle to some degree by experimenting on ourselves. Once we discover what thoughts are joined to the motions of the animal spirits which make us act bravely, or at least what thoughts inhibit the motions associated with fear, we can will ourselves to think those thoughts, in the knowledge that, by doing so, we will change our physical state.

In this account of our ability to modify our own patterns of motivation, Descartes pointedly offers a reinterpretation of one traditional view of the conflict between the passions and the will. This tension had habitually been conceived as a struggle between the intellectual and sensible souls; but Descartes presents it as a conflict between the soul and the body. It is to the body 'that we should attribute everything in us which can be observed to oppose our reason'. For the so-called conflict in the soul occurs when the pineal gland is pushed in one direction by the soul and in another by the animal spirits.[116]

It remains to ask how powerful the soul is in this struggle, and here Descartes seems to equivocate. He acknowledges that the soul is unable to overcome or ignore violent passions, any more than it can prevent itself from 'hearing thunder or feeling a fire that burns the hand';[117] yet he also asserts that 'even those who have the weakest souls could acquire mastery over all their passions if we employed sufficient ingenuity in training and guiding them'.[118] Although, as these passages suggest, absolute mastery may prove somewhat elusive, the crux of Descartes's view lies in the idea that, even if we cannot prevent ourselves from feeling powerful emotions such as terror or love, we can, first of all, learn to inhibit their effects. This can sometimes be done directly, as when we will ourselves not to run away from something that frightens us and this volition inhibits the flow of animal spirits to the legs. In addition, we can establish connexions between thoughts and bodily motions through habit, and can disjoin a thought from a particular emotion and connect it up to another one.[119] Sometimes these modifications are the result of practice. In other cases, however, they occur all at once. 'Thus, when we suddenly come upon something very foul in a dish we are eating with relish, our surprise may so change the disposition of our brain that we cannot afterwards look on any such food without repulsion.'[120]

This apparently stark analysis of the opposition between body and soul is softened by Descartes's adherence to a conventional conception of the relation between the understanding and the will – to the view that volitions are obedient to the judgements of the understanding. With some significant reservations, he also adheres to the deeply-entrenched belief that the will is the only active part of the mind. As he writes to Regius in May 1641, 'For strictly, understanding is the passivity of the mind and willing is its activity; but because we cannot will anything without understanding what we will, and we scarcely ever understand anything without at the same time willing something, we do not easily distinguish in this matter passivity from activity.'[121] When the animal spirits move the pineal gland, they cause the ideas in the soul that are our passions – ideas of fear, desire, love and so forth. These ideas, which are perceptions of objects as desirable or dangerous and are strictly speaking passive, in turn excite volitions, which incline us to do whatever our passions dictate. The conflict between body and soul thus has to be understood as a conflict between the volitions that accompany our ideas of our bodily states (our passions), and the volitions that accompany whatever other ideas are in our minds. The stronger of these will win out, and move us to action.[122]

What sort of ideas in the soul give rise to volitions strong enough to resist the volitions that accompany passions? In keeping with his guiding metaphor of motion, Descartes holds that an idea or judgement need not be true in order to successfully oppose a passion but need only be strongly held. The crucial factor is the strength of the volition accompanying a judgement, and this depends on the degree of conviction attaching to the latter. The firmer the judgement, the stronger the volition to which it gives rise and the greater its capacity to overwhelm the passions.[123]

Descartes's contemporaries were on the whole unimpressed by his view that the transactions between body and soul take place in the pineal gland; yet many were in agreement with large parts of his philosophy. Among the Cartesians, Malebranche agreed with Descartes that the passions are motions of the animal spirits in the body which cause in us feelings of fear, desire and so on. But he rejected the view that the body and soul interact in the pineal gland and was content to say that there must be some principal part of the brain at which the interaction occurs.[124] Moreover, bodily motions are not, in his view, the true causes of our intentional states; they are merely occasional causes, the real cause being God. By combining his occasionalism with an unqualified commitment to the traditional conception of the will as the only active capacity of the soul,[125] Malebranche developed a rival analysis of the rôle of the passions in the explanation of action, an analysis inextricably entwined with the Christian quest for salvation which is, in Malebranche's view, the object of all knowledge.[126]

Central to this account is an explanation of why it is that we so often follow our passions. A beneficent God has matched up particular motions of the animal spirits with ideas, which are perceived by the understanding. But because the understanding is entirely passive,[127] it can only present its ideas to the will, which inspects them to see whether they answer to its natural inclination to the good. Once satisfied by an idea, the will embraces it; otherwise, it continues its search.[128] In our fallen condition we do not realise that the only good capable of fully satisfying the will and bringing it to tranquillity and rest is the idea of God and instead endorse ideas which depart from the true good. One reason for this failing is that our wills are too easily satisfied – they turn too readily to apparent goods and too readily shun apparent evils. At the same time, we are led astray by a flaw in our understanding. Our perceptions of our bodily states are much stronger and more vivid than our perceptions of the inclinations of the soul; for example, our passions of grief and fear are habitually much stronger than our love of God. This has two significant consequences. First, it accounts for our confused idea that 'we' are identical with our bodies, and thus that what is good for our bodies is good for us. Our self-conception over-emphasises the importance of our passions.[129] Second, the understanding presents this self-conception to the will which, impressed by its strength and vividness, is then inclined to follow the courses of action that are presented as good for the body. The will is therefore liable to make mistakes; it judges wrongly that our passions are in line with our true good and goes along with them.

Turning to our power to combat the passions, Malebranche argues that these flawed dispositions can be countered in two distinct ways. First, we can try to love God and hope that, by the intercession of grace, we will be filled with a sacred love vivid enough to impress the will and fix its inclination steadily on the one true good. Grace, which has nothing to do with understanding, is in Malebranche's view the only really effective way to control the passions. There is, however, another way to keep them in check. If the understanding contains true ideas about human nature and the good for man, it will present them to the will which may then incline to them. The resulting volitions will prompt us to act in ways that are optimal for us; they are correlated with bodily motions that cause us to act in accordance with our true good, rather than with our passions – those motions which sustain the good of the body alone.[130]

Like Descartes, Malebranche allows that the acquisition of true ideas is far from easy but suggests that we can make some headway if we are aware of the need to avoid the sorts of errors just outlined, such as the disposition to confuse the good of the body with that of the soul. By self-consciously countering our intellectual limitations we can increase our knowledge; and God's benevolent design ensures that this process will be accompanied by the physical mastery of our passions.

Many seventeenth-century philosophers shared the view that we assess and modify our passions using a combination of the understanding and the will, and that our actions are to be explained as the outcome of this process. Other writers, however, regarded the claim that our passions can be modified by our volitions as erroneous and obfuscatory. Their dissatisfaction with this view was partly fuelled by the fact that a number of questions about the nature of the will were the topic of contentious debates which continued to engage philosophers and theologians and which spilled over into discussions of the passions. Malebranche, for example, testifies to their persistence when he reprimands those Thomist thinkers who hold that judgements are made both by the understanding (which assents to ideas) and by the will (which consents to them).[131] This view, he argues, has the unacceptable consequence of allocating the power of judging to both the understanding and the will, and obscuring the fact that the understanding is entirely passive.[132] Malebranche here takes a stand in a complex dispute about the rôle of the understanding in the explanation of action.

Among theorists who tried to by-pass these deadlocked negotiations, perhaps the most radical are Hobbes and Spinoza, who altogether deny that there are such things as volitions, distinct from judgements. Spinoza begins his discussion of this issue by alluding to the dangers of Faculty Psychology; there is no such thing as the 'will' or 'intellect', he warns, over and above our individual volitions and ideas.[133] Moreover, when we talk about the will, we simply mean 'the faculty by which the mind affirms or denies something true or something false and not the desire by which the Mind wants a thing or avoids it'.[134] So the question we must ask is whether our volitions – our affirmations and denials – are anything beyond our ideas themselves. For instance, when we affirm that the three angles of a triangle are equal to two right angles, do we just have the thought 'the three angles of a triangle are equal to two right angles', or do we perform a further act of affirmation or consent? Spinoza replies that we do not, and thus concludes that our volitions are simply our ideas. 'The will and the intellect', he says, 'are one and the same.'[135]

This repudiation of the will leads Spinoza to an explanation of action quite unlike those so far discussed. Clearly, actions can no longer be analysed as resulting from the interaction of passions with judgements and volitions. Instead, Spinoza regards them as the outcome of passions that are themselves confused or inadequate ideas about how to increase one's power. To desire to be friends with someone, for example, is to judge that this friendship will increase one's power to persevere in one's being; to hate someone is to judge that they are liable to reduce one's power; and so on. If we now ask how judgements, which are ideas, can move us to action, Spinoza replies that since ideas are identical with states of our bodies, changes in one are at the same time changes in the other: 'Both the decision of the mind and the appetite and determination of the body . . . are one and the same thing, which we call a decision when it is considered under, and explained through, the attribute of thought, and which we call a determination when it is considered under the attribute of extension and deduced from the laws of motion and rest.'[136] By means of this doctrine, he circumvents the need to posit a causal connexion between body and mind.

It remains to ask, however, whether this account condemns us to act on our passions, or whether it leaves us free to modify and overcome them. We cannot refuse to acknowledge them, since that would be to refuse to acknowledge our own judgements. Nor can we oppose them with volitions, since we have none. Spinoza's determinism binds him to the view that we only alter our ideas when we are caused to do so by other ideas, and thus to the conclusion that unless something brings about a change in our passions – causes us, for example, to give up a particular ambition – we will continue in them. In the ordinary course of events, our passions are modified by our experience; unhappy love affairs or political debacles may transform our desires and our patterns of action. But as long as the ideas on which we act remain inadequate, we remain passionate, and the only way to change this situation is to pursue understanding – to acquire correct or adequate ideas on which we will be bound to act.[137] Spinoza certainly suggests that this process is at least partly within our control and that we possess the means to increase our stock of adequate ideas.[138] However, because we can only pursue understanding if we are caused to do so, we remain to some extent at the mercy of circumstance.

According to this view, we are passionate when we are moved to action by inadequate ideas, and rational when our actions are the fruit of adequate ideas. The passions are not to be mechanically construed as one kind of force which combines with others to produce a resultant action. Instead, they are portrayed as motivating judgements that are defective in falling short of the truth, and as a mark of the finitude of our understanding.

This determinist interpretation of the rôle of the passions in the explanation of action diverges substantially from the Cartesian analysis considered earlier on. But the very extent of the metaphysical differences between the two views makes it easy to overlook the similarity of their practical implications. At first glance, the ability of the will to govern the passions suggests a higher degree of control over them than anything allowed for in the determinist story told by Spinoza. But on closer inspection, the chasm between the two accounts begins to narrow.[139]

According to Descartes, the will normally follows the understanding. Although it possesses what is called liberty of indifference – the insignificant ability to will the opposite of whatever the understanding dictates – its volitions in fact generally conform to the ideas that are strongest in the understanding at a particular time. The extent to which we can channel our wills into opposing our passions thus depends on our capacity for forming firm and determinate judgements, of which the firmest are clear and distinct ideas. But since, in most people, this capacity is poorly developed, it follows that our ability to modify and check our passions remains to a considerable extent only a potential one. Individuals do, of course, vary greatly; but as long as we are plagued by indecisiveness and lack of under-standing we will act on our passions.

In so far as it implies that the best way to control our passions is to improve our understanding, Descartes's position is not so very different from that of Spinoza. The will, as Descartes conceives it, can amplify the ideas in the under-standing but cannot otherwise add to them or change them, so that the onus of modifying the emotions rests with the intellect. His view diverges from the Spinozist one, however, over the question of exactly what kind of ideas are effective against the passions. While Spinoza insists that only true or adequate ideas can vanquish them, Descartes allows, as we have seen, that judgements which are firm but false can have the same effect.

Arguments about the respective rôles of passions and volitions in the explana-tion of action are grounded on the assumption that the two are distinct. Yet this presupposition, so central to the debates discussed so far, was itself scrutinised and called into doubt in the seventeenth century. We have already seen that philoso-phers of this period generally characterised volitions as movements or inclinations of the will by which it embraces, is drawn to, or attracted by certain ideas; and some of them added the proviso that the will inclines to ideas that it perceives as beneficial or good. Equally, they described desires as motions which draw or incline us to objects that we perceive as beneficial. In this, they acknowledged themselves to be the heirs of the Aristotelian doctrine that, whereas volitions are the appetites of the intellectual soul, desires are passions, or appetites of the sensible soul.

For scholastic writers, the distinction between these types of appetite was an integral part of the doctrine of the tripartite soul. The cognitive abilities of each soul must be complemented by an appetitive capacity to move or be moved, and the division between the intellectual and sensible souls was underscored by the fact that they possessed distinct appetites.[140] But for philosophers who claimed that the soul is unified, the rationale for maintaining the distinction between desires and volitions was less clear. If all thoughts are located in one soul, why does it need more than one kind of appetite to move it to action? Nevertheless, partly because it was so deeply embedded in Christian theology, and partly because it was one strand of the authoritative opposition between reason and passion, the traditional view retained a strong hold. Many seventeenth-century authors took it for granted that volitions are distinct from desires and continued to maintain that, although volitions are responses to perceptions of the understanding, desires are the effect of bodily motions; that volitions are directed to what is good for the soul, whereas desires concern what is good for the body; and so on.

One challenge to this distinction came from boldly un-Christian philosophers who simply jettisoned the will. Spinoza argued for its superfluousness by assimilating volitions to judgements. There was, however, another way to get rid of the will which also smacked of atheism and was adopted by Hobbes. Taking seriously the phenomenological similarity between volitions and desires, Hobbes identified them. When we deliberate about what to do, he reminds us, we more or less carefully and self-consciously consider the pros and cons of various courses of action and reach a decision. A volition is then simply the last appetite, on which we act. 'In deliberation, the last appetite or aversion, immediately adhering to the action, or to the omission thereof, is what we call the will; the act (not the faculty) of willing.'[141]

This reduction of volition to the passions of appetite and aversion, which in Hobbes's scheme together make up endeavour, contributes to his emptying out of the active/passive distinction around which theories of the passions were usually organised. The active will is reduced to the passive passions, in terms of which our actions must be explained. Like so much of Hobbes's philosophy, this doctrine proved too much for his contemporaries, but the relation between volitions and desires remained subject to debate. A quite different reinterpretation of it, which nevertheless seems to owe a good deal to Hobbes, was proposed by Locke, who incorporated it into a theory of action unlike any so far discussed.

According to Locke, the will does not incline to the good. If this were so, he remarks, 'I do not see how it could ever get loose from the infinite, eternal joys of heaven, once proposed and considered as possible.'[142] We can tell by reflecting on our own experience that the will is just the power to do or forbear, to continue or end an action,[143] and that volitions are just the thoughts with which the mind starts, continues, or terminates an action.[144] They are, however, to be distinguished from desires, for whereas the object of a volition is simply an action (I will to raise my hand or stop walking), the object of a desire goes beyond this (I desire to turn the page or look at a rare plant).

How, then, are desires and volitions related? Volitions, Locke claims, are prompted by what he calls uneasiness, defined as 'all pain of the body, of what sort soever, and disquiet of the mind'.[145] His aim here is partly to insist that the will is determined by all sorts of dissatisfaction, physical as well as mental, and not just by the idea of the good. But Locke also identifies uneasiness with one of the 'hinges on which our passions turn',[146] namely, pain. Our passions are directed towards pleasure and away from pain, towards pleasure and away from uneasiness. Thus sorrow is uneasiness of the mind upon the thought of a good lost, fear is uneasiness of the mind upon the thought of future evil, and so on. Most important, desire is a kind of uneasiness: 'The uneasiness a man finds in himself upon the absence of anything, whose present enjoyment carries the idea of delight with it, is what we call desire.'[147]

Locke emphasises that only uneasiness moves people to act.[148] But by identifying uneasiness with a range of passions he arrives at the startling conclusion that the will is almost invariably determined by some passion. Chief among these is desire 'for the will seldom orders any action, nor is there any voluntary action performed, without some desire accompanying it'.[149] Moreover, when we speak as though our wills were determined by other passions such as aversion, fear, or shame, this is because they are mixed with desire and therefore contain the element of uneasiness that moves the will.[150]

This conclusion has far-reaching implications for seventeenth-century theories of action. Locke shares with philosophers such as Descartes and Malebranche the view that the understanding alone cannot move us to act. We are moved, they all agree, by the will. This reply nevertheless raises the question of what moves the will, to which many philosophers give the traditional reply that the will moves itself. Because it is free, it must have the power to determine itself. Locke, however, proposes that the will is determined by uneasiness or desire, a suggestion that carries with it a major reinterpretation of the passions.

First of all, Locke's view implies that it is unduly limited to think of the will as opposing the passions, since nothing less than a passion determines the will. Desire and volition are not opposed but work together to cause our actions. Second, it is a mistake to think that the passions are passive and the will active. On the contrary, the passions are active forces which determine the will. In pressing this claim, Locke makes the historically decisive move of giving desire priority over the other passions in the explanation of action. Although many seventeenth-century philosophers held to the traditional view that we can act out of fear, love, anger, and so on – all of which, being passions, possess the power to move us – Locke claims that these passions are only efficacious when combined with desire or uneasiness. Third, it is an implication of this view that the dysfunctional aspects of the passions cannot be controlled by volitions. Our only resource is the passions that make us uneasy, because only these move us to act. And it is only by meditating on the consequences of our actions – particularly on our prospects in the afterlife – that we can hope to alter the states of affairs about which we feel uneasy and thus change our patterns of action.

Early modern philosophers grappled with an inherited conception of the passions as turbulent yet passive forces within us against which we have to exert the active aspects of our nature, a struggle which is itself a legacy of Adam's original sin. As they slowly abandoned the divisions within the soul that had made it natural to oppose passion to reason and desire to will, they faced a situation in which these oppositions had either to be re-established in theories organised around the idea of a unified soul or abandoned. During the seventeenth century, attempts to abandon them were far from inconceivable; both Hobbes and Spinoza proposed theories which effectively abolished the will. But they nevertheless proved unacceptable to the philosophical community in general, as the history of Hobbism and Spinozism attests. For the most part, then, theorists in this period were content to retain a fairly conventional understanding of the passions and ally it with their metaphysical beliefs about the structure of the mind and its relation to the body. In doing so, however, they began to articulate a novel set of positions which were in turn developed by their successors. Locke's theory of action is a case in point.

NOTES

1 See, e.g., Burton, *The Anatomy of Melancholy,* Burton 1989–94, vol. 1, p. 248: 'No mortal man is free from these perturbations; or if he be so, sure he is either a God or a

block'; Hobbes, *Lev.* viii, Hobbes 1968, p. 139: 'For as to have no desire is to be dead: so to have weak passions is dulnesse.'

2 Wright 1630, p. 49.

3 This negative conception of the passions is deeply entrenched in classical discussions. The view that they are actually diseases of the soul derives from the Stoic view that the passions are excessive impulses, contrary to reason. See, e.g., Stobaeus in Long and Sedley 1987, p. 410; Cicero, *Tusculanae disputationes* 3.7. See also Inwood 1985, pp. 127–8. It is fairly widely upheld in the seventeenth century. See, e.g., Charleton 1674, Prefatory Epistle. The more widespread view that the passions are unruly and unreliable is taken for granted in the early modern period and is held by all the authors discussed in this section. See, e.g., Hobbes, 'Passions unguided are for the most part meere madness', *Lev.* viii, Hobbes 1968, p. 142; Wright's comparison of the passions with sedition in the state, Wright 1630, p. 69. Spinoza's description of our passions as tossing us about like waves on the sea, *Eth.* III prop. 59 schol., is commonplace. See also Glanvill 1670, IV.18. Pascal dwells on this theme in his criticisms of imagination: *Pens.* 44.

4 Although subject to variation, this general view was widely held. See Section III of this chapter and Chapter 36.

5 For the broader significance of this distinction in seventeenth-century philosophy, see Lloyd 1984, chap. 3; Bordo 1987; Atherton 1993. For Pascal's claim that the imagination is stronger than reason, see Chapter 36.

6 See Phillips 1658.

7 Spinoza, *Eth.* III prop. 3. See also Cudworth, *A Treatise concerning Eternal and Immutable Morality,* Bk. III, chap. 1.

8 Descartes, *Pass. âme,* sec. 28.

9 This view is inherited from a pantheon of major authorities. See Aristotle, *De Anima* I.i; Cicero, *Tusculanae disputationes* III.x.24; Augustine, *De civitate Dei* 8.17; Thomas Aquinas, *Summa th.* I q81 a1–2.

10 Locke, *Ess.* II.xxi.4. For other discussions of this view, see Cudworth, *Treatise concerning True and Immutable Morality,* Bk. III, chap. 1; Cudworth 1845, vol. 3, p. 557. For a similar distinction, see Descartes, *Pass. âme* sec. 1, and also his letter to Regius, December 1641, AT III 455.

11 Locke, *Ess.* II.xxi.4.

12 The sense in which the objects of our passions are external to us is complicated, since it is evident that they are not always external in a physical sense. For example, one may remember saying something and then feel ashamed. See James 1993, pp. 313–14. However, early modern writers do regard the passions principally as responses to things that are physically external to us. This is evident, for example, in Descartes's standard classification of types of passion, *Pass. âme* sec. 20, and also in some definitions of particular passions. See, e.g., Hobbes's definitions of covetousness as desire of riches and ambition as desire for office and precedence. *Lev.* vi, Hobbes 1968, p. 123.

13 This is particularly evident in Hobbes's and Descartes's mechanical analyses of the passions. See Section II of this chapter.

14 For discussions of the physical manifestation of the passions, see Burton, *The Anatomy of Melancholy,* Burton 1989–94, *passim*; Cureau de la Chambre 1658, *passim*; Walkington 1639, *passim*. See Levi 1964, chap. 9. This subject was also important in aesthetics. See Le Brun 1696; Ross 1984.

15 See Copenhaver and Schmitt 1992, chaps. 2, 3, 4.

16 For debate about the status of classical authorities in this period, see Gaukroger 1991; Sorell 1993; Copenhaver and Schmitt 1992, chap. 5.

17 Thomas Aquinas, *Summa th.* I q77 a1. See also Park 1988; Kretzmann 1993, pp. 128–60.

18 The movement known as the *via moderna* was the last major school of scholastic philosophy, a self-conscious reaction against the *via antiqua* of the Thomists. Its most influential exponent was William of Ockham.

19 Park 1988, p. 479; Levi 1964, chap. 5.

20 Levi 1964, chap. 5.

21 Locke, *Ess.* II.xxi.20. For the same point see also Cudworth, *Treatise of Free Will,* Cudworth 1845, vol. 3, pp. 24–5; Arnauld, *Des vrayes et des fausses idées,* Arnauld 1775–83, vol. 38, p. 291. See also Clarke 1989, pp. 167–70.

22 Locke, *Ess.* II.xxi.20.

23 Descartes, *Pass. âme* sec. 47, and Med. VI, AT VII 85–6; Deprun 1988.

24 With the exceptions of Hobbes and Spinoza (see Section IV of this chapter), this view was held by all the authors discussed.

25 See Long and Sedley 1987, pp. 410–19.

26 See, e.g., Hobbes, *Lev.* vi; Hobbes 1968, pp. 118–30; Descartes, *Pass. âme,* pt. 2 (secs. 51–148); Spinoza, *Eth.* III. dfn. of the affects, Geb. II 190–204. See also More 1690, chap. 7, p. 43; Coëffeteau 1630, chap. 2, p. 17; Senault 1649, part II, pp. 193–510.

27 Aristotle, *Rhetorica,* II.i.8.

28 Aristotle, *Rhetorica* II.ii.2.– xi.7. See also *De Anima* I.i; Gastaldi 1987.

29 See, e.g., Hobbes, *Elements of Law,* pt. 1, chap. 9; Hobbes 1969, pp. 36–48.

30 Cicero, *Tusculanae disputationes,* III 24–5.

31 E.g., Wright 1630, pp. xlii, 23; Le Grand 1675, Discourse II, p. 77.

32 This interpretation derives from Stobaeus (see Long and Sedley 1987, p. 411). Seventeenth-century authors tended to condense his interpretation still further by combining *libido* and *metus* into one passion – desire – which is understood to include aversion. See Hobbes's analysis of endeavour, *Lev.* vi, Hobbes 1968, p. 119; Descartes, *Pass. âme* secs. 86 and 87; Spinoza, *Eth.* III props. 9, 11; Coëffeteau 1630, pp. 126–42.

33 Augustine, *De civitate Dei,* Bk. XIV, chap. 6. See O'Daly 1987, p. 46.

34 Augustine, *De civitate Dei,* Bk. XIV, chap. 7.

35 See Chapter 36.

36 Coëffeteau 1630, chap. 2, pp. 17–18; Camus 1614, pp. 96–7; La Mothe le Vayer 1662, vol. 1, p. 850 (*La Morale du Prince,* chap. 4); Cureau de la Chambre 1648, Advis nécessaire au lecteur; More 1690, chap. 4, p. 850.

37 Thomas Aquinas, *Summa th.*, II.1 q23 a2 and a4.

38 Thomas Aquinas, *Summa th.*, I q81 a2.

39 Thomas Aquinas, *Summa th.*, II.1 q23 a3.

40 Thomas Aquinas, *Summa th.*, II.1 q46 a4.

41 Descartes, *Pass. âme* secs. 79 and 86.

42 Descartes, *Pass. âme* secs. 79 and 58.

43 See for example Malebranche, *Rech.,* Preface.

44 Hobbes, *Lev.* viii, Hobbes 1968, p. 139.

45 Spinoza, *Eth.* III props. 9 and 11, dfn. of the affects II and III.

46 Descartes, *Pass. âme* sec. 52.

47 Locke, *Ess.* II.xx.3.

48 Malebranche, *Rech.* V.1, *OC* II 78.

49 E.g., by La Forge 1666.

50 Locke, *Ess.* II.xx.3.

51 Descartes, *Pass. âme* sec. 10.

52 Descartes, *Pass. âme* sec. 8.

53 See Lindeboom 1979; Carter 1983.
54 Descartes, *Pass. âme* sec. 16.
55 Descartes, *Pass. âme* sec. 13.
56 Descartes, *Pass. âme* sec. 16.
57 Descartes, *Pass. âme* sec. 17.
58 Descartes, *Pass. âme* sec. 23.
59 Descartes, *Pass. âme* sec. 24.
60 Descartes, *Pass. âme* sec. 27.
61 Descartes, *Pass. âme* secs. 31–4.
62 Descartes, *Pass. âme* sec. 35.
63 This view of perception as a kind of judgement is made still clearer by Malebranche, *Rech.,* I.2, *OC* I 49.
64 Wilson 1990.
65 Descartes, *Pass. âme* sec. 39.
66 Descartes, *Pass. âme* sec. 36.
67 Descartes, *Pass. âme* sec. 10.
68 See Rorty 1986c.
69 See Clarke 1989; Livet 1978.
70 More 1690, p. 38. See also Charleton 1674, Prefatory Epistle; Gabbey 1982; Henry 1986b.
71 Malebranche, *Rech.* V.1, *OC* II 78–9.
72 Malebranche, *Rech.* V.3, *OC* II 87–8.
73 Malebranche, *Rech.* V.1, *OC* II 78.
74 Malebranche, *Rech.* I.5, *OC* I 70–1.
75 Malebranche, *Rech.* V.2, *OC* II 86.
76 See, e.g., *Rech.* V.1, *OC* II 79.
77 Hobbes 1968, p. 86.
78 Hobbes 1968, p. 118.
79 Hobbes 1968, p. 118. See Pacchi 1987; Kassler 1991, pp. 553–78.
80 Hobbes 1968, p. 119.
81 Hobbes 1968, p. 119.
82 Hobbes 1968, pp. 129–30.
83 Hobbes 1968, p. 98.
84 Descartes, *Pass. âme* sec. 102.
85 Hobbes 1968, p. 118.
86 Spinoza, *Eth.* III prop. 2 schol.
87 For discussion of this parallelism, see Bennett 1984, chap. 6; Curley 1988, pp. 62–70; Della Rocca 1993.
88 Spinoza, *Eth.* III. prop. 9 schol.
89 Spinoza, *Eth.* III. prop. 9 schol.
90 Spinoza, *Eth.* III. prop. 11.
91 Spinoza, *Eth.* III. dfn. of the affects II and III (Geb. II 191).
92 See Section I of this chapter.
93 Descartes, *Pass. âme* sec. 87.
94 Descartes, *Pass. âme* sec. 68.
95 Descartes, *Pass. âme* sec. 69.
96 Descartes, *Pass. âme* sec. 87.
97 Descartes, *Pass. âme* sec. 79.
98 Descartes, *Pass. âme* sec. 79.

99 Descartes, *Pass. âme* secs. 58, 59.
100 Descartes, *Pass. âme* sec. 65.
101 Aristotle, *Rhetorica* II.ii.2.
102 See Levi 1964, pp. 273–84; Beyssade 1983; Taylor 1983.
103 Descartes, *Pass. âme* sec. 53.
104 Descartes, *Pass. âme* secs. 70, 71. Malebranche calls *l'admiration* an 'imperfect passion' (*une passion imparfaite*). *Rech* V.7, OC II 119.
105 Descartes, *Pass. âme* sec. 74.
106 Descartes, *Pass. âme* sec. 99.
107 Hobbes 1968, p. 124.
108 Hobbes 1968, p. 119.
109 Hobbes, *Elements of Law,* Hobbes 1969, p. 28.
110 Hobbes 1968, p. 121.
111 Hobbes 1968, p. 122.
112 Descartes, Prefatory letter to *Pass. âme.*
113 Descartes, *Pass. âme* sec. 45.
114 Descartes, *Pass. âme* sec. 41.
115 Descartes, *Pass. âme* sec. 44.
116 Descartes, *Pass. âme* sec. 47.
117 Descartes, *Pass. âme* sec. 46.
118 Descartes, *Pass. âme* sec. 50.
119 Descartes, *Pass. âme* sec. 50.
120 Descartes, *Pass. âme* sec. 50.
121 AT III 372. For Aquinas's view that the will is obedient to the intellect, see Gallagher 1991, pp. 582–4.
122 Meyer 1991, chap. 5.
123 Descartes, *Pass. âme* sec. 49.
124 Malebranche, *Rech.* II.I.1, OC I 194.
125 Malebranche, *Rech.* I.1, OC I 46.
126 Malebranche, *Rech.* Preface, OC I 16.
127 Malebranche, *Rech.* I.1, OC I 43.
128 Malebranche, *Rech.* IV.2, OC II 5–6.
129 Malebranche, *Rech.* V.5, OC II 109.
130 Malebranche, *Rech.* V.5, OC II 110.
131 Thomas Aquinas, *Summa th.* II.1 q15 a1. See Barad 1986; Levi 1964, pp. 32–6.
132 Malebranche, *Rech.* I.2 OC I 50–1.
133 Spinoza, *Eth.* II prop. 48 schol.
134 Spinoza, *Eth.* II prop. 48 schol.
135 Spinoza, *Eth.* II prop. 49 cor. 'Voluntas et intellectus unum et idem sunt.'
136 Spinoza, *Eth.* III prop. 2 schol. 2.
137 Spinoza, *Eth.* IV prop. 26.
138 This is implied by Spinoza's discussion of the way of life that wise men aim to sustain. *Eth.* IV props. 35–8.
139 See Cottingham 1988.
140 Thomas Aquinas, *Summa th.* I q80 a1 and a2; Levi 1964, pp. 32–5.
141 Hobbes 1968, p. 127.
142 Locke, *Ess.* II.xxi.38.
143 Locke, *Ess.* II.xxi.5.
144 Locke, *Ess.* II.xxi.30.

145 Locke, *Ess.* II.xxi.31.
146 Locke, *Ess.* II.xx.3.
147 Locke, *Ess.* II.xx.6. In the first edition of the *Essay* (1690), desire is only briefly referred to in II.xx.6. In the second edition of 1694, however, Locke adds a full discussion of desire in II.xxi.28–62.
148 Locke, *Ess.* II.xxi.36.
149 Locke, *Ess.* II.xxi.39.
150 Locke, *Ess.* II.xxi.39.